BEHAVIOR SCIENCE BIBLIOGRAPHIES

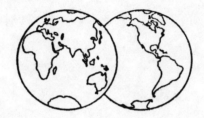

ETHNOGRAPHIC BIBLIOGRAPHY
OF NORTH AMERICA

3rd EDITION

GEORGE PETER MURDOCK

PUBLISHED BY

HUMAN RELATIONS AREA FILES

NEW HAVEN

1960

Library of Congress Catalog Number: 60-16689

© Copyright 1960

Human Relations Area Files, Inc.
New Haven, Conn.

CONTENTS

PREFACE   vii

KEY TO ABBREVIATIONS   xi

I   ARCTIC COAST   1
    1   Aleut   7
    2   Baffinland Eskimo   10
    3   Caribou Eskimo   11
    4   Copper Eskimo   11
    5   East Greenland Eskimo   12
    6   Iglulik Eskimo   15
    7   Labrador Eskimo   16
    8   Mackenzie Eskimo   19
    9   Netsilik Eskimo   20
   10   North Alaska Eskimo   20
   11   Polar Eskimo   23
   12   South Alaska Eskimo   25
   13   Southampton Eskimo   26
   14   West Alaska Eskimo   27
   15   West Greenland Eskimo   30
   16   Yuit   33

II MACKENZIE-YUKON   35
    1   Ahtena   37
    2   Beaver   37
    3   Carrier   38
    4   Chilcotin   39
    5   Chipewyan   39
    6   Coyukon   40
    7   Dogrib   41
    8   Han   41
    9   Hare   41
   10   Ingalik   42
   11   Kaska   42
   12   Kutchin   43
   13   Mountain   44
   14   Nabesna   44
   15   Sarsi   44
   16   Satudene   44
   17   Sekani   44
   18   Slave   45
   19   Tahltan   45
   20   Tanaina   46
   21   Tanana   46
   22   Tsetsaut   46
   23   Tutchone   47
   24   Yellowknife   47

III NORTHWEST COAST   49
    1   Bellabella   55
    2   Bellacoola   55
    3   Comox   56
    4   Cowichan   56

III NORTHWEST COAST (continued)
    5   Haida   57
    6   Klallam   59
    7   Kwakiutl   60
    8   Nootka   62
    9   Quileute   64
   10   Quinault   64
   11   Snuqualmi   65
   12   Tlingit   66
   13   Tsimshian   69
   14   Twana   70

IV OREGON SEABOARD   73
    1   Alsea   75
    2   Chastacosta   75
    3   Chehalis   75
    4   Chinook   76
    5   Coos   77
    6   Hupa   77
    7   Kalapuya   78
    8   Karok   79
    9   Kwalhiokwa   79
   10   Siuslaw   79
   11   Takelma   80
   12   Tillamook   80
   13   Tlatskanai   80
   14   Tolowa   80
   15   Wiyot   81
   16   Yurok   81

V   CALIFORNIA   83
    1   Achomawi   85
    2   Chimariko   86
    3   Costano   86
    4   Klamath   87
    5   Maidu   88
    6   Miwok   89
    7   Olamentke   90
    8   Pomo   90
    9   Salina   92
   10   Shasta   92
   11   Wailaki   93
   12   Wappo   93
   13   Wintun   94
   14   Yana   95
   15   Yokuts   95
   16   Yuki   96

VI PENINSULA   99
    1   Cahuilla   100
    2   Chumash   100
    3   Cochimi   102

VI   PENINSULA (continued)   IX   PLAINS (continued)
         4 Diegueno   102   6 Cheyenne   144
         5 Gabrielino   103   7 Comanche   146
         6 Kamia   103   8 Crow   148
         7 Kawaiisu   104   9 Gros Ventre   150
         8 Luiseno   104   10 Hidatsa   150
         9 Seri   105   11 Iowa   152
        10 Serrano   105   12 Kansa   152
        11 Tubatulabal   106   13 Kiowa   153
        12 Waicuri   106   14 Kiowa Apache   154
                                                            15 Mandan   154
VII BASIN   107   16 Missouri   156
         1 Bannock   108   17 Omaha   156
         2 Gosiute   109   18 Osage   158
         3 Mono   109   19 Oto   160
         4 Paiute   110   20 Pawnee   161
         5 Panamint   111   21 Ponca   163
         6 Paviotso   111   22 Quapaw   164
         7 Shoshoni   113   23 Santee   164
         8 Ute   113   24 Teton   167
         9 Washo   115   25 Wichita   172
        10 Wind River   116   26 Yankton   172

VIII PLATEAU   117   X   MIDWEST   175
         1 Cayuse   119   1 Fox   178
         2 Coeur d'Alene   119   2 Illinois   180
         3 Columbia   120   3 Kickapoo   181
         4 Flathead   120   4 Menomini   181
         5 Kalispel   121   5 Miami   183
         6 Klikitat   121   6 Potawatomi   183
         7 Kutenai   121   7 Sauk   185
         8 Lake   123   8 Shawnee   186
         9 Lillooet   123   9 Winnebago   187
        10 Molala   123
        11 Nez Perce   123   XI   EASTERN CANADA   191
        12 Nicola   124   1 Abnaki   194
        13 Okanagon   124   2 Algonkin   196
        14 Sanpoil   125   3 Beothuk   197
        15 Shuswap   125   4 Cree   198
        16 Spokan   125   5 Malecite   202
        17 Tenino   126   6 Micmac   204
        18 Thompson   126   7 Montagnais   206
        19 Umatilla   126   8 Ojibwa   209
        20 Wallawalla   127   9 Ottawa   217
        21 Wishram   127
        22 Yakima   127   XII NORTHEAST   221
                                                            1 Conestoga   224
IX   PLAINS   129   2 Delaware   226
         1 Arapaho   134   3 Erie   230
         2 Arikara   135   4 Huron   231
         3 Assiniboin   137   5 Iroquois   234
         4 Blackfoot   138   6 Mahican   246
         5 Caddo   142   7 Massachuset   248

XII	NORTHEAST (continued)	
	8 Metoac	250
	9 Mohegan	251
	10 Nanticoke	253
	11 Neutral	255
	12 Pennacook	255

XIII	SOUTHEAST	257
	1 Acolapissa	261
	2 Alabama	262
	3 Apalachee	262
	4 Biloxi	263
	5 Calusa	263
	6 Catawba	264
	7 Chakchiuma	266
	8 Cherokee	266
	9 Chickasaw	270
	10 Chitimacha	271
	11 Choctaw	271
	12 Creek	274
	13 Cusabo	277
	14 Hitchiti	277
	15 Huma	277
	16 Mobile	277
	17 Monacan	278
	18 Mosopelea	279
	19 Natchez	279
	20 Pamlico	281
	21 Powhatan	282
	22 Seminole	283
	23 Timucua	288
	24 Tunica	289
	25 Tuscarora	290
	26 Yamasee	290
	27 Yuchi	291

XIV	GULF	293
	1 Atakapa	293
	2 Coahuilteco	294
	3 Karankawa	294
	4 Tamaulipeco	295
	5 Tonkawa	295

XV	SOUTHWEST	297
	1 Acoma	306
	2 Cahita	308
	3 Chinipa	310
	4 Chiricahua	310
	5 Cocopa	311
	6 Concho	312
	7 Coyotero	312
	8 Guasave	314
	9 Halchidhoma	314

XV	SOUTHWEST (continued)	
	10 Havasupai	314
	11 Hopi	314
	12 Isleta	322
	13 Jemez	322
	14 Jicarilla	323
	15 Jumano	325
	16 Lipan	325
	17 Manso	326
	18 Maricopa	326
	19 Mescalero	326
	20 Mohave	327
	21 Navaho	329
	22 Nevome	342
	23 Opata	342
	24 Papago	343
	25 Pima	344
	26 Piro	346
	27 Queres	346
	28 Tano	348
	29 Taos	348
	30 Tarahumara	349
	31 Tewa	350
	32 Walapai	352
	33 Yavapai	353
	34 Yuma	353
	35 Zuni	354

APPENDIX: GENERAL NORTH AMERICA	359
ADDENDA	381
INDEX OF TRIBAL NAMES	391
TRIBAL MAP	395

Some thirty years ago the author began systematically to assemble bibliographical references on primitive and historical cultures with the object, partly of directing distributional and other studies in the classroom, partly of recommending library purchases, and partly of preparing for a projected study which later materialized as the Cross-Cultural Survey at the Institute of Human Relations.[1] By utilizing odd moments of time between appointments, useless for consistent research, to verify references in the Yale University Library, he was able to over a period of years to prepare a classified worldwide ethnographic bibliography of considerable size.

This bibliography proved exceedingly useful, to the author and to others, in directing dissertations, making classroom assignments, surveying the existing literature preparatory to field work, and providing ready access to the relevant sources for topical and regional studies of all kinds. A considerable demand was expressed that at least the portion on aboriginal North America be made generally available by publication. The present work in its several editions represents a response to that demand.

The principle of classification by tribal groups having been adopted as the most serviceable to modern anthropologists, the first task was to determine the groups to be used. As a compromise between the segregation of all tribes bearing traditional names, which would have increased the bulk and cost of the work by necessitating frequent repetition of the same references for adjacent peoples, and a classification into a few large areal groups, which would have reduced the usefulness of the volume, it was decided to adopt as a norm the nationally self-conscious tribes of regions with some measure of political development, e.g., those of the Plains. For regions with less extensive political integration, groups of approximately the same degree of linguistic and cultural homogeneity were formed by arbitrarily uniting a number of tribelets or local groups, usually under the name of one of them. Thus under Snuqualmi were lumped the Salishan Dwamish, Nisqualli, Puyallup, Samamish, Skagit, Snohomish, Snuqualmi, and Squaxon of Puget Sound; under Massachuset, the Algonkian Massachuset, Nauset, Nipmuc, and Wampanoag of southeastern New England; and under Wailaki the Athapaskan Kato, Lassik, Mattole,

Nongatl, Sinkyone, and Wailaki of Northwestern California. In this way, all of North America as far south as Tehuantepec was divided into 277 tribal groups, a manageable number.

The second task was to prepare a map showing the location of these groups. This was done in 1937 with the cooperation of the students in a graduate class in Systematic Ethnography. The map, which is appended to the present volume, shows, with approximate boundaries, the location of the various tribal groups as of the period of their first extensive contacts with Europeans.[2] It is thus not valid for any single period but represents a shifting date-line, which becomes later as one moves from south to north, from east to west, and from coast to interior. Since the locations of many tribes did not remain constant over three centuries, the shifting date-line made necessary a number of compromises in the fixing of boundaries. Careful mapping by a series of predecessors, notably Kroeber on California, Spier on the Plateau, Osgood on the Mackenzie-Yukon, and Sauer on Mexico, proved of invaluable assistance. Probably the least satisfactory area, because of severe early territorial dislocations, is the Midwest, despite aid generously given by the late Truman Michelson. It is gratifying to note the very high degree of correspondence between our map of North America and those prepared independently by Kroeber and by Driver, et al.[3]

In the selection of names for our 277 groups, established usage was followed in most instances. A few adjectival tribal names, e.g., Costanoan and Salinan, were changed to their nominal forms. Diacritical marks were eliminated. Where several well-known tribes were grouped together, the name of the most important or most familiar was usually given to the cluster. The only radical decision was with regard to names like Apache, Paiute, Shoshoni, and Sioux, which are ambiguous because applied, although commonly with qualifying adjectives, to several different tribal groups. Except in the case of the Eskimo, where it seemed impracticable, such names

---

1 See G. P. Murdock, "The Cross-Cultural Survey," American Sociological Review, V (1940), 361-70.

2 Only 276 groups are actually located. The Seminole of the Southeast, having originated subsequent to intensive white contact, do not appear on the map.

3 See A. L. Kroeber, "Cultural and Natural Areas of Native North America," University of California Publications in American Archaeology and Ethnology, XXXVIII (1939), Map 1A; H. E. Driver, et al., "Indian Tribes of North America," Memoirs of the International Journal of American Linguistics, IX (1953), end map.

were either eliminated entirely or confined to a single group. In a few instances this has resulted in a certain arbitrariness in naming. Thus the tradition-al Coast Miwok have been called Olamentke, the Eastern Dakota are termed Santee, the Owens Valley Paiute of Steward have been grouped with their west-ern congeners as Mono, the Western Apache are dubbed Coyotero, and the Western Shoshoni are named Panamint from their best known sub-group.

The preparation of the map prevented subsequent changes in our groupings, even when clearly advisable. Thus the Eyak, discovered by Birket-Smith and de Laguna, have been classed arbitrarily with the Ahtena (II-1) even though they deserve an independent classi-fication.

The map does not divide the tribal groups into culture areas, but this has been done for the presenta-tion of the bibliography. We have distinguished six-teen areas, adding Oregon Seaboard, Peninsula, Basin, Midwest, Eastern Canada, and Gulf to the ten pro-posed by Wissler.[4] The decision as to allocation has been close in several instances. Thus the Caddo might well have been placed in the Southeast instead of the Plains, the Klamath in the Plateau instead of in California, the Nanticoke in the Southeast rather than in the Northeast, the Sarsi in the Plains on the basis of culture instead of in the Mackenzie-Yukon on the basis of language, and the Seri in the Southwest rather than in the Peninsula. Mexico, an area em-bracing 24 tribal groups, though shown on the map, has not been included in the bibliography for the sole reason that pressure of other research has prevented the author from bringing this section of North Ameri-ca to a sufficient degree of completeness to justify publication at the present time. The bibliography therefore covers only 253 of the total of 277 tribal groups distinguished.

The work is organized by areas and within each area by tribal groups arranged in alphabetical order. Under the areal headings are included regional studies, geographical and historical sources, travel accounts, and other works presenting little specific original in-formation on individual tribes. Under the tribal head-ings are included works pertaining directly to the par-ticular group or its sub-groups. The order of arrange-ment of items under each heading is alphabetical by author's surname and thereunder by title. One excep-tion is to be noted: standard monographs covering

large segments of a tribal culture, or, in default thereof, other general works of considerable scope, are placed ahead of the alphabetical list of other sources. An appendix includes references to works on North America in general or on a number of areas; this list is very incomplete since no special effort was made to assemble such items.

To compress a classified bibliography on a whole continent into a single volume requires selectivity and compactness. The former has been achieved by including only such references as seemed likely to prove of value to an anthropologist desirous of dis-covering what is known about a particular culture. Works in which the tribe is barely mentioned or in which no new information of value is given have in general been excluded. Compactness has been sought through a standard system of abbreviating references. Space is saved by giving initials rather than full names of authors, by omitting unimportant informa-tion such as name of publisher, by using abbrevia-tions for journals, series, and collections which recur frequently,[5] by omitting subtitles except when neces-sary to indicate the content of a work, and by short-ening titles themselves wherever words or phrases could be deleted at the end of a title without loss of meaning or obscuring of content.

Pages have been indicated for all periodical items as a rough indication of quantity of material. For books, similarly, the number of volumes or of pages has been noted in most instances, although fre-quently the particular pages on which the most rele-vant information occurs are indicated instead. Dia-critical marks are omitted except for a few standard accents. Within a serial volume, the number is noted only when it is separately paginated. Where the indicated date of a volume differs from its actual published date, the former is usually given prefer-ence. A few inconsistencies have arisen as a result of changes in the procedure of notation over a period of years. In the earlier years of compilation, for in-stance, the number of pages of single books was not noted, and the date of actual publication was pre-ferred to the indicated date of a volume in a series. Since these inconsistencies did not seem serious, it was decided to ignore them rather than undertake the vast labor of checking back over all previous work.

---

4 C. Wissler, The American Indian (2d edit., New York, 1931), p. 219.

5 A key to abbreviations, which precedes the text, presents the full titles and places of publication of these serial works.

Approximately seventy per cent of the works cited have been personally examined by the author, and most of the rest have similarly been seen by his assistants in the course of amassing the references. Perhaps five per cent of the references, including all those that are incomplete, have not been personally assessed — most of them works listed in other bibliographical sources but not available in the Yale University Library.

Effort has been exerted to make the tribal bibliographies as complete as possible on all ethnographical subjects. Works on physical anthropology and linguistics, and on archeology where pertinent to a known historical culture, have been listed whenever obtained in the search for ethnographic items, but no extended canvass for them has been made and the coverage of these subjects, particularly in regard to earlier works, remains incomplete. Complete runs of most of the serials listed in the Key to Abbreviations have been searched for pertinent materials. No consistent search, however, has been made of United States Congressional documents and series, and references to these appear in the Bibliography only when they were obtained incidentally in the search for ethnographic materials. The Bibliography is restricted to published materials, and no reference is made to unpublished manuscripts, dissertations, etc. For such materials, researchers should consult the standard reference works. [6]

In general, fugitive materials and items appearing in popular journals have not been included in this Bibliography, except in cases where they seemed to be of some importance. The cut-off date of this third edition was originally intended to be December, 1958, and the Bibliography is reasonably complete as of that date. However, an effort was made to include materials in the major anthropological journals and important books which have appeared since that time. Coverage of materials appearing in 1959 and early 1960 is, therefore, very incomplete.

Mistakes are inevitable in a work such as this. The frequent recopying incidental to compilation introduces typographical errors which escape even careful proofreading. Important references are overlooked, lost, or misjudged and excluded, and errors of allocation occur in areas with which the author is not especially familiar. The present volume pretends to be only so accurate as reasonable care and effort can make it.

Fortunately there is a remedy for errors and omissions. In future editions, corrections can be made, newly published titles added, overlooked sources noted, the Mexican area included, the general North American appendix expanded, and the archeological, linguistic, and physical anthropological literature covered as exhaustively as the ethnographical. To accomplish really satisfactory revisions, the author must have the cooperation of his anthropological colleagues. He, therefore, requests that users of this work call his attention to errors and omissions in areas familiar to them.

The first edition of this Bibliography appeared in 1941 as Volume I of the Yale Anthropological Series. The second edition appeared in 1953 as a Behavior Science Bibliography published by the Human Relations Area Files. In terms of number of entries, the first edition had approximately 9,400 and the second edition about 12,700. The present edition contains more than 17,300 entries.

The author received valuable assistance from Donald Horton and Frederick W. Voget in the preparation of the first edition, and from Mrs. Allison Butler Matthews and John Musgrave in the preparation of the second edition. In regard to the present or third edition, he is indebted to many colleagues who have supplied new references, and especially to William C. Sturtevant of the Smithsonian Institution for generous advice and assistance. Its actual compilation is almost exclusively the product of the devoted effort of Timothy J. O'Leary.

Yale University   George Peter Murdock
June, 1960

---

[6] E.G., F.J. Dockstader, "The American Indian in Graduate Studies; A Bibliography of Theses and Dissertations," CMAI, XV (1957), and W.N. Fenton et al., American Indian and White Relations to 1830, Chapel Hill, 1957.

KEY TO ABBREVIATIONS

A	Anthropos. Mödling/Wien.	AH	Arizona Highways. Phoenix.
AA	American Anthropologist. Washington, New York, Lancaster, Menasha.	AHQ	Alabama Historical Quarterly. Montgomery.
AAA	Art and Archaeology. Baltimore, Washington.	AHR	Alberta Historical Review. Edmonton.
AAAG	Annals of the Association of American Geographers. Albany.	AI	America Indigena. México.
		AJB	American Journal of Botany. Brooklyn.
AAE	Archivio per l'Antropologia e l'Etnologia. Firenze.	AJP	American Journal of Philology. New York.
AAm	Acta Americana. México, etc.	AJPA	American Journal of Physical Anthropology. Washington.
AAn	American Antiquity. Menasha, Salt Lake City.	AJS	American Journal of Sociology. Chicago.
AAOJ	American Antiquarian (and Oriental Journal). Chicago.	AKAWB	Abhandlungen der Königlichen Akademie der Wissenschaften. Berlin.
AAR	Annual Archaeological Report, being Part of Appendix to the Report of the Minister of Education, Ontario. Toronto.	AlR	Alabama Review. University, Alabama.
		AMBG	Annals of the Missouri Botanical Garden. St. Louis.
ABC	Anthropology in British Columbia. Victoria.	AMGLS	American Museum of Natural History Guide Leaflet Series. New York.
ABCM	Anthropology in British Columbia Memoirs. Victoria.	AmI	The American Indian. New York.
ACFAS	Annales de l'Association Canadienne-Française pour l'Avancement des Sciences. Montreal, etc.	AMJ	American Museum Journal. New York.
		AN	American Naturalist. Salem.
ACISA	Acts of the International Congress of the Anthropological and Ethnological Sciences. Various places.	An	Anthropologica. Ottawa.
		Ane	Anthropologie. Paris.
ACM	Annals of the Carnegie Museum. Pittsburgh.	ANIET	Akademiia Nauk SSSR. Institut Etnografii. Trudy. Moscow.
AEUS	Archeology of Eastern United States. J. B. Griffin, ed. Chicago, 1952.	ANMAE	Akademiia Nauk SSSR. Muzei Antropologii i Etnografii. Sbornik. Moscow.
AFA	Archiv für Anthropologie. Braunschweig.	ANOH	Aarbøger for Nordisk Oldkyndighed og Historie. Kjøbenhavn.
AGSSP	American Geographical Society Special Publications. New York.	ANYAS	Annals of the New York Academy of Sciences. New York.

APAM   Anthropological Papers of the American Museum of Natural History. New York.

APMA   Anthropological Papers of the Museum of Anthropology of the University of Michigan. Ann Arbor.

APSS   Annals of the American Academy of Political and Social Science. Philadelphia.

APUU   Anthropological Papers of the University of Utah. Salt Lake City.

AQ   Anthropological Quarterly. Washington.

AR   Anthropological Records. Berkeley.

ARBAE   Annual Reports of the Bureau of American Ethnology. Washington.

ARCE   Annual Reports of the Chief of Engineers to the Secretary of War. Washington.

ARCGS   Annual Reports of the Canada Geological (and Natural History) Survey. Montreal.

ARCIA   Annual Reports of the Commissioner of Indian Affairs. Washington.

ARGGS   Annual Reports of the United States Geological and Geographical Survey of the Territories. Washington.

ArHQ   Arkansas Historical Quarterly. Fayetteville.

ARSI   Annual Reports of the Board of Regents of the Smithsonian Institution. Washington.

ARUNY   Annual Reports of the Regents of the (New York State Museum) University of the State of New York. Albany.

ARW   Archiv für Religionswissenschaft. Leipzig.

ASAIT   Acculturation in Seven American Indian Tribes, ed. R. Linton. New York, 1940.

ASC   Proceedings of the Alaskan Science Conference. Washington.

ASR   American Sociological Review. Menasha.

ASSF   Acta Societatis Scientiarum Fennicae. Helsingfors.

AWKR   Archiv für Wissenschaftliche Kunde von Russland. Berlin.

B   Beaver. Winnipeg.

BA   Baessler-Archiv. Berlin, Leipzig.

BAAS   Report of the First (etc.) Meeting of the British Association for the Advancement of Science. London, etc.

BAGS   Bulletin of the American Geographical Society. New York.

BAMNH   Bulletin of the American Museum of Natural History. New York.

BASC   Bulletin of the Archaeological Society of Connecticut. New Haven.

BASD   Bulletin of the Archaeological Society of Delaware. Wilmington.

BASNJ   Bulletin of the Archaeological Society of New Jersey. Trenton.

BBAE   Bulletins of the Bureau of American Ethnology. Washington.

BBSNS   Bulletin of the Buffalo Society of Natural Sciences. Buffalo.

BCDM   Bulletins (and Annual Reports) of the Canada Department of Mines, National Museum of Canada. Ottawa.

BCHQ   British Columbia Historical Quarterly. Vancouver.

BCIS   Bulletin of the Cranbrook Institute of Science. Detroit.

BCMR   British Columbia. Provincial Museum of Natural History and Anthropology. Report. Victoria.

BCNO   Les Bourgeois de la Compagnie du Nord-Ouest, ed. L.F.R. Masson. Quebec.

BEI   Bulletin of the Essex Institute. Salem.

BESAF   Bulletin of the Eastern States Archaeological Federation. Various places.

BFMUP   Bulletin of the Free Museum of Science and Arts, University of Pennsylvania. Philadelphia.

BGGST   Bulletin of the United States Geological and Geographical Survey of the Territories. Washington.

BGSP   Bulletin of the Geographical Society. Philadelphia.

BHLAL   Bulletin of the Hervas Laboratories of American Linguistics. St. Louis.

BHPSO   Bulletin of the Historical and Philosophical Society of Ohio. Cincinnati.

BKRR   Beiträge zur Kenntnis des Russischen Reiches (und Angränzenden Lander Asiens). St. Petersburg.

BLA   Bulletin of the Laboratory of Anthropology, General Series. Santa Fe.

BMAS   Bulletin of the Massachusetts Archaeological Society. Cambridge.

BMHS   Bulletin of the Missouri Historical Society. St. Louis.

BMNA   Bulletin of the Museum of Northern Arizona. Flagstaff.

BNMC   Bulletin of the National Museum of Canada. Ottawa.

BNYSAA   Bulletin of the New York State Archaeological Association. Albany.

BOAS   Bulletin of the Oklahoma Anthropological Society. Oklahoma City.

BPAS   Bulletin of the Philadelphia Anthropological Society. Philadelphia.

BPMCM   Bulletins of the Public Museum of the City of Milwaukee. Milwaukee.

BROMA   Bulletin of the Royal Ontario Museum of Archaeology. Toronto.

BSAFS   Bibliographical and Special Series of the American Folklore Society. Philadelphia.

BSAP   Bulletin de la Société d'Anthropologie. Paris.

BSAS   Bulletin of the Seattle Anthropological Society. Seattle.

BSG   Bulletin de la Société de Géographie. Paris.

BSGQ   Bulletin de la Société de Géographie. Quebec.

BSMGE   Boletin de la Sociedad Mexicana de Geografia y Estadistica. México.

BSRBG   Bulletin de la Société Royale Belge de Géographie. Bruxelles.

BSSA   Bulletin de la Société Suisse des Américanistes. Geneva.

BTAPS   Bulletin of the Texas Archeological [and Paleontological] Society. Abilene.

BUSNM   Bulletin of the United States National Museum. Washington.

CA   Canadian Art. Toronto.

CD   Cahiers des Dix. Montreal.

CFN   Canadian Field-Naturalist. Ottawa.

CGHS   Collections of the Georgia Historical Society. Savannah.

CGJ   Canadian Geographical Journal. Montreal; Ottawa.

CHR   Canadian Historical Review. Toronto.

CJ   Canadian Journal. Toronto.

CJEPS   Canadian Journal of Economics and Political Science. Toronto.

CKSHS   Collections of the Kansas State Historical Society. Topeka.

CMAI   Contributions from the Museum of the
        American Indian, Heye Foundation.
        New York.

CMHS   Collections of the Minnesota Historical
        Society. St. Paul.

CNAE   Contributions to North American Ethnology,
        Department of the Interior, United
        States Geographical and Geological Sur-
        vey of the Rocky Mountain Region.
        Washington.

CNG   Canadian Naturalist (and Geologist).
        Montreal.

CNYHS   Collections of the New York Historical So-
        ciety. New York.

CO   Chronicles of Oklahoma. Oklahoma City.

CPM   Comparative Psychology Monographs.
        Baltimore.

CPMHS   Collections (and Proceedings) of the Maine
        Historical Society. Portland.

CSAJ   Central States Archaeological Journal.
        Quincy, Illinois.

CSHSB   Cold Spring Harbor Symposia on Quantita-
        tive Biology. Cold Spring Harbor, N. Y.

CSHSW   (Annual Reports and) Collections of the
        State Historical Society of Wisconsin.
        Madison.

CUAS   Catholic University of America Anthropo-
        logical Series. Washington.

CUCA   Columbia University Contributions to Anthro-
        pology. New York.

D   Diogenes. Chicago.

DAMLS   Denver Art Museum Indian Leaflet Series.
        Denver.

DEFAS   Découvertes et Etablissements des Français
        dans l'Ouest et dans le Sud de l'Amérique
        Septentrionale, ed. P. Margry. Paris.

DJA   Davidson Journal of Anthropology.
        Seattle.

DR   Dalhousie Review. Halifax.

E   Ethnohistory. Bloomington.

EAMG   Estudios Antropologicas Publicados en
        Homenaje al Doctor Manual Gamio.
        México, 1956.

ECAS   Eastern Canadian Anthropological Series.
        Montreal.

ECTS   Early California Travel Series. Los
        Angeles.

EDCC   Economic Development and Cultural
        Change. Chicago.

Ee   L'Ethnographie. Paris.

EFWSI   Explorations and Field-Work of the
        Smithsonian Institution. Washington.

EG   Early Georgia. Athens.

EP   El Palacio. Santa Fe.

ERE   Encyclopaedia of Religion and Ethics, ed.
        J. Hastings. New York.

ES   Etnologiska Studier. Göteborg.

EWT   Early Western Travels, ed. R. G. Thwaites.
        Cleveland.

FA   Florida Anthropologist. Gainesville,
        Tallahassee.

FHS   Fergus Historical Series. Chicago.

FHSQ   Florida Historical (Society) Quarterly.
        Jacksonville.

FL   Folk-Lore. London.

FMAS   Field (Columbian) Museum (of Natural
        History) Anthropological Series.
        Chicago.

FMDAL   Field Museum of Natural History, Depart-
        ment of Anthropology, Leaflets. Chicago.

FMSW   Franciscan Missions of the Southwest. St. Michaels.

FTD   For the Dean. Essays in Anthropology in Honor of Byron Cummings. Tucson,1950.

FWRHS   The Far West and the Rockies Historical Series 1820-1875. A.H.Clark Co., Glendale.

GHQ   Georgia Historical Quarterly. Athens.

GJ   Geographical Journal. London.

GM   General Magazine (and Historical Chronicle), University of Pennsylvania. Philadelphia.

GR   Geographical Review. New York.

GSA   General Series in Anthropology. Menasha.

GT   Geografisk Tidsskrift. Kjøbenhavn.

H   Homo. Stuttgart.

HAHR   Hispanic American Historical Review. Baltimore; Durham.

HAIL   Handbook of American Indian Languages, ed. F. Boas. Washington, New York.

HB   Human Biology. Detroit.

HBRS   The Hudson's Bay Record Society. London.

HCL   Historical Collections of Louisiana (and Florida), ed. B.F.French. Philadelphia, New York.

HCPIT   Information respecting the History, Condition, and Prospects of the Indian Tribes of the United States, ed. H.R.Schoolcraft. Philadelphia.

HDAC   Homenaje al Doctor Alfonso Caso. 455 pp. México, 1951.

HF   Hoosier Folklore. Bloomington.

HM   Historical Magazine. Boston, New York, Morrisania.

HMM   Harper's (New) Monthly Magazine. New York.

HO   Human Organization. New York.

HPTC   Edward H. Spicer, ed., Human Problems in Technological Change. 301 pp. New York, 1952.

HSS   Works Issued by the Hakluyt Society, Second Series. London.

HSSCQ   Historical Society of Southern California Quarterly. Los Angeles.

IA   Ibero-Americana. Berkeley.

IAE   Internationales Archiv für Ethnographie. Leiden.

ICA   Proceedings of the International Congress of Americanists. Paris, etc.

IH   Indian Handcrafts. Lawrence, Kansas.

IJAL   International Journal of American Linguistics. New York.

IJHP   Iowa Journal of History and Politics. Iowa City.

ILC   Indian Life and Customs Pamphlets. Lawrence, Kansas.

ILR   Indian Life Readers. Office of Indian Affairs, Education Division. Washington, D.C.

ILSPSM   Indian Leaflets of the St. Paul Science Museum. St. Paul, Minnesota.

IN   Indian Notes, Museum of the American Indian, Heye Foundation. New York.

INM   Indian Notes and Monographs, Museum of the American Indian, Heye Foundation. New York.

ITUMV   The Indian Tribes of the Upper Mississippi Valley, ed. E.H.Blair. Cleveland.

IUPFS   Indiana University Publications. Folklore Series. Bloomington.

JAEA   Journal of American Ethnology and Ar-
        chaeology. Boston.

JAFL   Journal of American Folk-Lore. Boston,
        New York.

JAGS   Journal of the American Geographical So-
        ciety. New York.

JAI   Journal of the (Royal) Anthropological In-
        stitute of Great Britain and Ireland.
        London.

JAP   Journal of Applied Psychology. Worcester,
        Bloomington.

JEP   Journal of Experimental Psychology.
        Princeton.

JESL   Journal of the Ethnological Society.
        London.

JISHS   Journal of the Illinois State Historical So-
        ciety. Springfield.

JMH   Journal of Mississippi History. Jackson.

JMVL   Jahrbuch des Museums für Völkerkunde zu
        Leipzig. Leipzig.

JNH   Journal of Negro History. Lancaster;
        Washington.

JRGS   Journal of the Royal Geographical Society.
        London.

JSAP   Journal de la Société des Américanistes.
        Paris.

JSP   Journal of Social Psychology. Worcester.

JWAS   Journal of the Washington Academy of
        Sciences. Washington.

K   Kiva. Tucson.

KBDGA   Korrespondenz-Blatt der Deutschen Ge-
        sellschaft für Anthropologie, Ethnologie
        und Urgeschichte. Braunschweig.

KDVSS   Kongelige Danske Videnskabernes-Selskabs
        Skrivter. Kjøbenhavn.

KHQ   Kansas Historical Quarterly. Topeka.

LACMQ   Los Angeles County Museum. Museum
        Associates. Quarterly.

LEITA   Leaflets of the Exposition of Indian Tribal
        Arts. New York.

Lg   Language. Baltimore; Menasha.

LHQ   Louisiana Historical Quarterly. New
        Orleans.

LMAI   Leaflets of the Museum of the American
        Indian, Heye Foundation. New York.

LPTN   Les Litteratures Populaires de Toutes les
        Nations. Paris.

LS   Land of Sunshine. Los Angeles.

M   Masterkey. Los Angeles.

MA   Minnesota Archaeologist. St. Paul.

MAAA   Memoirs of the American Anthropological
        Association. Lancaster, Menasha.

MAES   Monographs of the American Ethnological
        Society. New York.

MAFLS   Memoirs of the American Folk-Lore So-
        ciety. Boston.

MAGW   Mitteilungen der Anthropologischen Ge-
        sellschaft. Wien.

MAH   Magazine of American History. New
        York, Mt. Vernon.

MAMNH   Memoirs of the American Museum of Na-
        tural History. New York.

MAPS   Memoirs of the American Philosophical
        Society. Philadelphia.

MBCDM   Museum Bulletins of the Canada Depart-
        ment of Mines, Geological Survey.
        Ottawa.

MBMIA   Museum Bulletin of the Museum of Indian
        Archaeology, University of Western
        Ontario. London.

MC   Les Missions Catholiques. Lyon.

MCDM   Memoirs of the Canada Department of
        Mines, Geological Survey. Ottawa.

MCM   Moravian Church Miscellany. Bethlehem,
        Pennsylvania.

MCN   Material Culture Notes, Denver Art Mu-
        seum. Denver.

MF   Mexican Folkways. México.

MG   Meddelelser om Grønland. Kjøbenhavn.

MH   Missionalia Hispanica. Madrid.

MHM   Michigan History [Magazine]. Lansing.

MHSC   Collections of the Massachusetts Historical
        Society. Cambridge.

MICA   Memoirs of the International Congress of
        Anthropology. Chicago.

MiH   Minnesota History. St. Paul.

MIJL   Memoirs of the International Journal of
        American Linguistics, or Indiana Uni-
        versity Publications in Anthropology and
        Linguistics. Bloomington.

MJ   Museum Journal, University of Pennsyl-
        vania. Philadelphia.

MKAW   Mededeelingen der Koninklijke Akademie
        van Wetenschappen, Afdeeling Letter-
        kunde. Amsterdam.

MLA   Memoirs of the Laboratory of Anthropology.
        Santa Fe.

MMH   Montana Magazine of History. Helena.

MMVH   Mittheilungen aus dem Museum für
        Völkerkunde Hamburg.

MNMNA   Museum Notes of the Museum of Northern
        Arizona. Flagstaff.

MNUSD   Museum Notes of the University of South
        Dakota Museum. Pierre.

MPR   Miscellanea Paul Rivet Octogenario
        Dicata. 2 vol., LXIV, 707; 903 pp.
        México, 1958.

MSAA   Memoirs of the Society for American
        Archaeology. Menasha, Salt Lake
        City.

MSASP   Montana State University. Anthropology
        and Sociology Papers. Missoula.

MVHR   Mississippi Valley Historical Review.
        Cedar Rapids; Lincoln.

MWF   Midwest Folklore. Bloomington.

NAV   Nouvelles Annales des Voyages. Paris.

NCHR   North Carolina Historical Review.
        Raleigh.

NDHQ   North Dakota Historical Quarterly.
        Bismarck.

NeH   Nebraska History [Magazine]. Lincoln.

NGM   National Geographic Magazine. Washing-
        ton, D.C.

NH   Natural History. New York.

NIAACH Betty Meggers, ed., New Interpretations
        of Aboriginal American Culture His-
        tory. 135 pp. Washington, 1955.

NIE   Noticiario Indigenista Español. Madrid.

NLAUN   Notebook of the Laboratory of Anthropol-
        ogy of the University of Nebraska.
        Lincoln.

NLPAC   News Letter of the Plains Archaeological
        Conference. Lincoln.

NLSAC   News Letter of the Southeastern Archaeo-
        logical Conference.

NMA   New Mexico Anthropologist. Albuquer-
        que.

NMFR   New Mexico Folklore Record. Albuquer-
        que.

NMHR   New Mexico Historical Review. Santa Fe.

NMQR   New Mexico Quarterly Review. Albuquer-
        que.

NOQ   Northwest Ohio Quarterly. Toledo.

NRS   Navajo Religion Series. Santa Fe.

NWHOM Newsletter of the William H. Over Museum. Pierre.

NYFQ   New York Folklore Quarterly. Ithaca.

NYHSQ New York Historical Society Quarterly. New York.

NYSMB New York State Museum Bulletin. Albany.

OAHQ   Ohio (State) Archaeological and Historical Quarterly (Publications). Columbus.

OCMA   Occasional Contributions from the Museum of Anthropology of the University of Michigan. Ann Arbor.

OFC   Our Forest Children. Owen Sound.

OHQ   Oregon Historical (Society) Quarterly. Eugene, etc.

OJS   Ohio Journal of Science. Columbus.

OM   Overland Monthly. San Francisco.

OMKMB Original Mittheilungen aus der Ethnologischen Abtheilung der Königlichen Museen. Berlin.

OW   Out West. Los Angeles.

OWS   Old West Series. Denver.

P   Plateau. Flagstaff.

PA   Pennsylvania Archaeologist. Milton.

PAA   Proceedings of the American Academy of Arts and Sciences. Boston.

PAAAS Proceedings of the American Association for the Advancement of Science. Philadelphia, etc.

PAAS   Proceedings of the American Antiquarian Society. Worcester.

PAC   Psychoanalysis and Culture, edited by G. B. Wilbur and W. Muensterberger. New York, 1951.

PAES   Publications of the American Ethnological Society. New York.

PAF   Publications of the Amerind Foundation. Dragoon.

PAHS   Publications of the Alabama Historical Society, Miscellaneous Collections. Montgomery.

PAIA   Papers of the Archaeological Institute of America, American Series. Boston.

PAJHS Proceedings of the American Jewish Historical Society. Baltimore.

PAMPM Publications in Anthropology of the Public Museum of the City of Milwaukee. Milwaukee.

PAPS   Proceedings of the American Philosophical Society. Philadelphia.

PASS   Publications of the American Sociological Society. Chicago.

PCAS   Proceedings of the California Academy of Sciences. San Francisco.

PCI   Proceedings of the Canadian Institute. Toronto.

PCNHS Proceedings and Collections of the Nebraska State Historical Society. Lincoln.

PCS   Publications of the Champlain Society. Toronto.

PDAS   Proceedings of the Davenport Academy of Sciences. Davenport.

PDS   Philological and Documentary Studies of the Middle American Research Institute. New Orleans.

PFAS   Publications of the Florida Anthropological Society. Gainesville.

PFLF   Publications of the Folk-Lore Foundation. Poughkeepsie.

PH   Pennsylvania History. Philadelphia.

PFSHS   Publications of the Florida State Historical Society. Deland.

PHAPF   Publications of the Frederick Webb Hodge Anniversary Publication Fund, Southwest Museum. Los Angeles.

PHR   United States Public Health Service. Public Health Reports. Washington.

PIAS   Proceedings of the Indiana Academy of Science. Greencastle.

PIPGH   Publicaciones del Instituto Panamericano de Geografica e Historia. México.

PKAS   Publications of the Kroeber Anthropological Society. Berkeley.

PIA   Plains Anthropologist. Lincoln.

PM   Primitive Man. Washington.

PMA   Papers of the Michigan Academy of Science, Arts and Letters. New York.

PME   Petermanns Mitteilungen, Ergänzungshefte. Gotha.

PMHB   Pennsylvania Magazine of History and Biography. Philadelphia.

PMHS   Publications of the Mississippi Historical Society. Oxford.

PMJP   Petermanns Mitteilungen aus Justus Perthes Geographischer Anstalt. Gotha.

PMP   Peabody Museum Papers (Archaeological and Ethnological Papers of the Peabody Museum, Harvard University). Cambridge.

PMVHA   Proceedings of the Mississippi Valley Historical Association. Cedar Rapids.

PNAS   Proceedings of the National Academy of Sciences. Washington.

PNJHS   Proceedings of the New Jersey Historical Society. Newark.

PNQ   Pacific Northwest Quarterly. Seattle.

PNSC   Personality in Nature, Society and Culture, edited by C. Kluckhohn and H. Murray, 2nd ed. New York, 1953.

PNSIS   Proceedings and Transactions of the Nova Scotian Institute of (Natural) Science. Halifax.

Po   Population. Paris.

PPAAI   Papers on the Physical Anthropology of the American Indian. New York. 1951.

PPAS   Publications of the Philadelphia Anthropological Society. Philadelphia.

PPC   Service, Elman R. A Profile of Primitive Culture. 488 pp. New York, 1958.

PPHC   Publications of the Pennsylvania Historical Commission. Harrisburg.

PPHR   Panhandle-Plains Historical Review. Canyon.

PPSC   Proceedings of the (Fifth) Pacific Science Congress. Toronto.

PQS   Publications of the Quivira Society. Los Angeles.

PRAS   Proceedings of the Rochester Academy of Science. Rochester.

PRCA   Publications of the Indiana University Research Center in Anthropology, Folklore, and Linguistics. Bloomington.

PRGS   Proceedings of the Royal Geographical Society. London.

PRMOPT Pitt-Rivers Museum Occasional Papers in Technology. Oxford.

PRS   Prehistory Research Series, Indiana Historical Society. Indianapolis.

PRSPF   Papers of the Robert S. Peabody Founda-
         tion for Archaeology. Andover.

PSHPMCM Popular Science Handbook of the Pub-
         lic Museum of the City of Milwaukee.
         Milwaukee.

PSHSW   Proceedings of the State Historical Society
         of Wisconsin. Madison.

PSM   Popular Science Monthly. New York.

PSMS   Publications of the Ethnographical Museum
         of Sweden, Stockholm Monograph Se-
         ries. Stockholm.

PSS   Psychoanalysis and the Social Sciences.
         New York.

PTFLS   Publications of the Texas Folk-Lore So-
         ciety. Austin.

PTRSC   Proceedings and Transactions of the Royal
         Society of Canada. Ottawa.

PUA   Proceedings of the Utah Academy of Sci-
         ences, Arts, and Letters. Provo.

PUSNM   Proceedings of the United States National
         Museum. Washington.

PWHGS   Proceedings and Collections of the Wyo-
         ming Historical and Geological Society.
         Wilkes-Barre.

PWVAS   Proceedings of the West Virginia Archaeo-
         logical Society. Morgantown.

QBASV   Quarterly Bulletin of the Archaeological
         Society of Virginia. Richmond; Char-
         lottesville.

QJSA   Quarterly Journal of Studies on Alcohol.
         New Haven.

RA   Revue d'Anthropologie. Paris.

RACHS   Records of the American Catholic Histori-
         cal Society of Philadelphia. Philadel-
         phia.

RBER   Reports of the Bureau of Ethnic Research.
         Tucson.

RCAE   Report of the Canadian Arctic Expedition.
         Ottawa.

RE   Revue d'Ethnographie. Paris.

REES   Revue des Etudes Ethnographiques et So-
         ciologiques. Paris.

RESRR   Reports of Explorations and Surveys to
         Ascertain the Most Practicable and Eco-
         nomical Route for a Railroad from the
         Mississippi River to the Pacific Ocean
         (33d Congress, 2d Session, H. R. Ex.
         Doc. 91). Washington.

RFTE   Report of the Fifth Thule Expedition.
         Copenhagen.

RHAF   Revue d'Histoire de l'Amérique Française.
         Montreal.

RIHSC   Rhode Island Historical Society Collec-
         tions. Providence.

RIT   Report on Indians Taxed and Indians not
         Taxed, United States Department of the
         Interior, Census Office, Eleventh Cen-
         sus. Washington.

RLPC   Revue de Linguistique et de Philologie
         Comparée. Paris.

RNYAS   Researches and Transactions of the New
         York State Archaeological Association.
         Rochester.

RP   Records of the Past. Washington.

RPCGS   Report of Progress of the Canadian Geo-
         logical Survey. Ottawa.

RPM   Reports of the Peabody Museum of Ameri-
         can Archaeology and Ethnology, Har-
         vard University. Cambridge.

RRNYSAA Research Records of the New York State
         Archaeological Federation. Albany.

RRRMAS   Records of Research of the Rochester Mu-
         seum of Science and Arts. Rochester.

RSCSV   Royal Society of Canada. Studia Varia.
         Ottawa; Montreal.

RSSCW   Research Studies of the State College of
        Washington. Pullman.

RUCAS   Records of the University of California
        Archaeological Survey. Berkeley.

RUSGS   Report upon United States Geographical
        Surveys West of the One Hundredth
        Meridian. Washington.

RUSNM   Reports of the United States National Mu-
        seum. Washington.

RVN   Recueil de Voyages au Nord. Amsterdam.

S   Samiksa, Journal of the Indian Psycho-
        Analytic Society. Calcutta.

SANAT   Eggan, F. (ed.) Social Anthropology of
        North American Tribes. 2nd ed. 589 pp.
        Chicago, 1955.

SCK   Smithsonian (Institution) Contributions to
        Knowledge. Washington.

SDHC   South Dakota Historical Collections.
        Aberdeen.

SE   Sovetskaiã Etnografiiã. Moscow.

SEMSM   Statens Etnografiska Museum (Riksmuseets
        Etnografiska Avdelning), Smärre Med-
        delanden. Stockholm.

SF   Social Forces. Chapel Hill.

SFMV   Studien und Forschungen zur Menschen-
        und Völkerkunde. Stuttgart.

SFQ   Southern Folklore Quarterly. Jacksonville.

SIS   Southern Indian Studies. Chapel Hill.

SJA   Southwestern Journal of Anthropology.
        Albuquerque.

SJG   Schmollers Jahrbuch für Gesetzgebung,
        Verwaltung und Volkswirtschaft im
        Deutschen Reich. Leipzig.

SKAW   Sitzungsberichte der Kaiserlichen Akade-
        mie der Wissenschaften, Philosophisch-
        Historische Klasse. Wien.

SKBGW   Sitzungsberichte der Königlichen Böhmis-
        chen Gesellschaft der Wissenschaften,
        Mathematisch-Naturwissenschaftliche
        Classe. Prag.

SLOP   Studies in Linguistics, Occasional Papers,
        Buffalo.

SM   Scientific Monthly. New York.

SMC   Smithsonian (Institution) Miscellaneous
        Collections. Washington.

SPBF   Special Publications of the Bollingen
        Foundation. New York.

SPISM   Scientific Papers of the Illinois State Mu-
        seum. Springfield.

SRGSC   Summary Reports of the Geological Sur-
        vey of Canada. Ottawa.

SS   Smoke Signals. Newark.

SSM   Social Science Monographs. Washington,
        D.C.

SW   Southern Workman. Hampton.

SWHQ   Southwestern Historical Quarterly. Austin.

SWL   Southwestern Lore, Colorado Archaeologi-
        cal Society. Gunnison.

SWML   Southwest Museum Leaflets. Los Angeles.

SWMMR   Southwestern Monuments Monthly Reports.
        Coolidge.

SWMP   Southwest Museum Papers. Los Angeles.

SZK   Studien zur Kulturkunde. Wiesbaden.

T   Tribus. Stuttgart.

TA   Tennessee Archaeologist. Knoxville.

TAES   Transactions of the American Ethnologi-
        cal Society. New York.

TAPS   Transactions of the American Philosophi-
        cal Society. Philadelphia.

TCAAS   Transactions (and Collections) of the
        American Antiquarian Society. Wor-
        cester.

TCC   Steward, J.H. Theory of Culture Change.
        244 pp. Urbana, 1955.

TCI   Transactions of the (Royal) Canadian In-
        stitute. Toronto.

TESL   Transactions of the Ethnological Society.
        London.

TFMSA   Transactions of the Free Museum of Sci-
        ence and Art, University of Pennsyl-
        vania. Philadelphia.

THLC   Transactions of the Historical and Literary
        Committee of the American Philosoph-
        ical Society. Philadelphia.

THQ   Tennessee Historical Quarterly. Nashville.

TJS   Texas Journal of Science. San Marcos.

TKAS   Transactions of the Kansas Academy of
        Science. Topeka.

TKSHS   Transactions of the Kansas State Historical
        Society. Topeka.

TLHSQ   Transactions of the Literary and Historical
        Society. Quebec.

TNYAS   Transactions of the New York Academy of
        Sciences. New York.

TRNHS   Transactions and Reports of the Nebraska
        State Historical Society. Lincoln.

TSHAQ   Texas State Historical Association Quarter-
        ly. Austin.

UAAP   Anthropological Papers of the University
        of Alaska. Fairbanks.

UASSB   University of Arizona Social Science Bul-
        letin. Tucson.

UCP   University of California Publications in
        American Archaeology and Ethnology.
        Berkeley.

UCPCS   University of California Publications in
        Culture and Society. Berkeley and Los
        Angeles.

UCPG   University of California Publications in
        Geography. Berkeley.

UCPH   University of California Publications in
        History. Berkeley.

UCPL   University of California Publications in
        Linguistics. Berkeley.

UCSSA   University of Colorado Studies. Series
        in Anthropology. Boulder.

UG   Die Ursprung der Göttesidee, by Wilhelm
        Schmidt. 14 volumes. Münster i. W.,
        1912-1956.

UHQ   Utah Historical Quarterly. Salt Lake City.

UNMB   University of New Mexico Bulletin, An-
        thropological Series. Albuquerque.

UNMBB   University of New Mexico Bulletin, Bi-
        ological Series. Albuquerque.

UNMPA   University of New Mexico Publications in
        Anthropology. Albuquerque.

UNMPB   University of New Mexico Publications in
        Biology. Albuquerque.

UOSA   University of Oregon Monographs. Studies
        in Anthropology. Eugene.

UPMAP   University of Pennsylvania Museum An-
        thropological Publications. Philadel-
        phia.

UPMB   University of Pennsylvania Museum Bul-
        letin. Philadelphia.

UWP   University of Wyoming Publications.
        Laramie.

UWPA   University of Washington Publications in
        Anthropology. Seattle.

VBGA   Verhandlungen der Berliner Gesellschaft
        für Anthropologie, Ethnologie und
        Urgeschichte. Berlin.

VFPA   Viking Fund Publications in Anthropology.
        New York.

VJS	Virginia Journal of Science. Charlottesville.	WVA	West Virginia Archaeologist. Moundsville.
VKAW	Verhandelingen der Koninklijke Akademie van Wetenschappen, Afdeeling Letterkunde. Amsterdam.	WVH	West Virginia History. Charleston.
		WVM	Wiener Völkerkundliche Mitteilungen. Vienna.
VM	Virginia Magazine of History and Biography. Richmond.	YPA	Yearbook of Physical Anthropology. New York.
VMKAW	Verslagen en Mededeelingen der Koninklijke Akademie van Wetenschappen, Afdeeling Letterkunde. Amsterdam.	YPMCM	Yearbook of the Public Museum of the City of Milwaukee. Milwaukee.
VN	Victoria Naturalist. Victoria, B.C.	YUPA	Yale University Publications in Anthropology. New Haven.
WA	Wisconsin Archeologist. Milwaukee.	ZDMG	Zeitschrift der Deutschen Morgenländischen Gesellschaft. Leipzig.
WeA	Western Anthropology. Missoula.	ZE	Zeitschrift für Ethnologie. Berlin.
WF	Western Folklore. Berkeley.	ZGE	Zeitschrift der Gesellschaft für Erdkunde. Berlin.
WHO	William H. Over Museum. Museum News. Pierre.	ZPAS	Zeitschrift für Phonetik und allgemeine Sprachwissenschaft. Berlin.
WHQ	Washington Historical Quarterly. Seattle.		
WPHM	Western Pennsylvania Historical Magazine. Pittsburgh.	ZVR	Zeitschrift für Vergleichende Rechtswissenschaft. Stuttgart.
WTHAY	West Texas Historical Association Yearbook. Abilene.	ZVS	Zeitschrift für Völkerpsychologie und Soziologie (Sociologus). Leipzig.

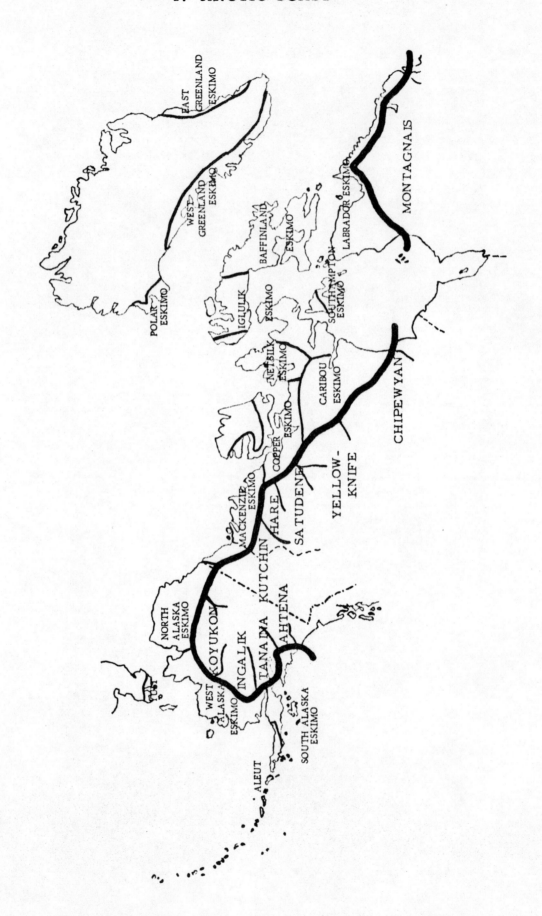

I. ARCTIC COAST

All the tribes of this area belong to the Eskimauan linguistic stock.

Ackerknecht, E.H. The Eskimo's Fight against Hunger and Cold. Ciba Symposia, X, 894-902. 1948.

--- Medicine and Disease among Eskimos. Ciba Symposia, X, 916-21. 1948.

Adamson, J.D. Poliomyelitis in the Arctic. Canadian Medical Association Journal, LXI, 339-48. 1949.

Allen, F.H. Summary of Blood Group Phenotypes in Some Aboriginal Americans. AJPA, n.s., XVII, 86. 1959.

Allison, A.C. et al. Urinary B-aminoisobutyric Acid Excretion in Eskimo and Indian Populations of Alaska. Nature, CLXXXIII, 118. 1959.

Anonymous. Canadian Eskimo Art. 40 pp. Ottawa, 1955.

Anonymous. Eskimo Art of the Canadian Eastern Arctic. 10 pp. Ann Arbor.

Anonymous. Eskimo Origins. Archaeology, XI, 217-8. 1958.

Aronson, J.D. The History of Disease among the Natives of Alaska. Alaska's Health, V, iii, 1-2; iv, 3-4; v, 5-6; vi, 4-5; vii, 3-4. 1947.

Arron, W.J. Aspects of the Epic in Eskimo Folklore. UAAP, V, 119-41. 1957.

Auer, J. Fingerprints in Eskimos of the Northwest Territories. AJPA, n.s., VIII, 485-88. 1950.

Baird, I. Summer School North of Sixty. CGJ, L, 18-23. 1955.

Bayliss, C.K. A Treasury of Eskimo Tales. 135 pp. New York, 1923.

Benveniste, E. The "Eskimo" Name. IJAL, XIX, 242-45. 1953.

Bergsøe, P. Where did the Eskimo get Their Copper? Nationalmuseets Skrifter, Etnografisk Raekke, I, 107-20. 1941.

Birket-Smith, K. Anthropological Observations on the Central Eskimos. RFTE, III, ii, 1-123. 1940.

--- Danish Activities in Eskimo Research Since 1940. ICA, XXVIII, 231-6. 1948.

--- Danish Activities in Eskimo Research 1949-1954. ICA, XXXI, ii, 1119-28. 1955.

--- Eskimo Cultures and Their Bearing upon the Prehistoric Cultures of North America and Eurasia. Early Man, ed. G.G. MacCurdy, pp. 293-302. Philadelphia, 1937.

--- Det eskimoiske slaegtskabssystem. GT, XXX, 96-111. 1927.

--- The Eskimos. 250 pp. New York, 1936.

--- Die Eskimos. Zürich, 1948.

--- Ethnographical Collections from the Northwest Passage. RFTE, VI, ii. 1945.

Birket-Smith, K. Five Hundred Eskimo Words. RFTE, III, iii, 5-64. 1928.

--- Folk Wanderings and Culture Drifts in Northern North America. JSAP, XXII, 1-32. 1930.

--- Moeurs et coutumes des Eskimos. New Edition. 292 pp. Paris, 1955.

--- Nye Fremskridt inden for Eskimoforskningen. Fra Nationalmuseets Arbejdsmark 1950, 81-100. København.

--- On the Origin of Eskimo Culture. ICA, XXIII, 470-6. 1930.

--- Preliminary Report of the Fifth Thule Expedition. ICA, XXI, ii, 190-205. 1924.

--- The Present Status of the Eskimo Problem. ICA, XXIX, iii, 8-21. 1952.

--- The Question of the Origin of Eskimo Culture. AA, n.s., XXXII, 608-24. 1930.

--- Recent Achievements in Eskimo Research. JAI, LXXVII, 145-57. 1951.

--- Spørgsmaalet om Eskimo-kulturens oprindelse. GT, XXXII, 222-39; XXXIII, 161-8. 1929-30.

--- Über die Herkunft der Eskimos und ihre Stellung in der zirkumpolaren Kulturentwicklung. A, XXV, 1-23. 1930.

Boas, F. The Eskimo. AAR, 1905, 107-16.

--- The Folk-Lore of the Eskimo. JAFL, XVII, 1-13. 1904.

--- Über die ehemalige Verbreitung der Eskimos. ZGE, XVIII, 118-36. 1883.

Bogoras, W.G. Elements in the Culture of the Circumpolar Zone. AA, n.s., XXXI, 579-601. 1929.

--- The Folklore of Northeastern Asia, as compared with that of Northwestern America. AA, n.s., IV, 577-683. 1902.

--- Le mythe de l'animal-dieux mourant et ressuscitant. ICA, XXII, ii, 35-52. 1928.

--- New Problems of Ethnographical Research in Polar Countries. ICA, XXI, i, 226-46. 1924.

--- Osnovnye tipy Fol'klora Severnoi Evrazi-i Severnoi Ameriki. Sovetskii Fol'klor, IV-V, 29-50. 1936.

Bolles, T.D. A Preliminary Catalogue of the Eskimo Collection in the U.S. National Museum. RUSNM, 1887, ii, 335-65.

Brown, G.M. Cold Acclimatization in Eskimo. Arctic, VII, 343-53. 1954.

Brown, R. The Origin of the Eskimo. Archaeological Review, I, 237-53. 1888.

Brown, R.N.R. Some Problems of Polar Geography. ARSI, 1928, 349-75.

Bruemmer, F. George Wetaltuk, Eskimo. CGJ, L, 157-9. 1955.

Bruet, E. L'Alaska. 451 pp. Paris, 1945.

Buliard, R.P. Inuk. 320 pp. London, 1956.

Bushnell, G.H.S. Some Old Western Eskimo Spear-throwers. Man, XLIX, 121. 1949.

Byhan, A. Die Polarvölker. 148 pp. Leipzig, 1909.

Cameron, J. Correlations between Cranial Capacity and Cranial Length, Breadth, and Height. AJPA, XI, 259-99. 1928.

Caswell, J.E. The Utilization of the Scientific Reports of the United States Arctic Expeditions 1850-1909. 304 pp. Stanford, 1951.

Chamberlain, A.F. The Eskimo Race and Language. PCI, ser. 3, VI, 261-337. 1887-88.

Choque, C. Comment Paul Vendit sa Fille Pour Une Longue-Vue. Eskimo, XXXI, 9, 12-13. 1954.

Clark, E.M. and Rhodes, A.J. Poliomyelitis in Canadian Eskimos. Canadian Journal of Medical Sciences, XXIX, 216-35, XXX, 390-402. 1951-1952.

Collins, H.B. Arctic Area. PIPGH, CLXX, 152 pp. 1954.

--- Eskimo Archaeology and Its Bearing on the Problem of Man's Antiquity in America. PAPS, LXXXVI, 220-35. 1943.

--- Eskimo Archaeology and Somatology. AA, n.s., XXXVI, 309-13. 1934.

--- The Origin and Antiquity of the Eskimo. ARSI, 1950, 423-67. 1951.

--- Outline of Eskimo Prehistory. SMC, C, 533-92. 1940.

Dadisman, A.J. Eastern Arctic Eskimo Land. PWVAS, XXVII, 91-4. 1956.

Danielo, E. Bapteme de Misère. Eskimo, XLII, 13-17. 1956.

--- Une Histoire de Sorcier. Eskimo, XXXVI, 3-6. 1955.

Debets, G.F. Antropologicheskie Issledovaniia v Kamchatskoi Oblasti. ANIET, XVII, n.s., 262 pp. 1951.

Erichsen, M. Désinences casuelles et personnelles en Eskimo. Acta Linguistica, IV, 67-88. 1944.

Estreicher, Z. Die Musik der Eskimos. A, XLV, 659-720. 1950.

Faustini, A. Gli Eschimesi. 204 pp. Torino, 1912.

Fellows, F.S. Mortality in the Native Races of the Territory of Alaska. PHR, XLIX. 289-98. 1934.

Findeisen, H. Der Adler als Kulturbringer. ZE, LXXXI, 70-82. 1956.

Freuchen, P. Out of the Stone Age. B, CCLXXXII, ii, 3-9. 1951.

Fritz, M.H. and Thygeson, P. Phlyctenular Keratoconjunctivitis among Alaskan Indians and Eskimos. PHR, LXVI, 934-39. 1951.

Gahs, A. Kopf-, Schädel- und Langknochenopfer bei Rentiervölkern. Festschrift P.W. Schmidt, pp. 231-68. Wien, 1928.

Garber, C.M. Eskimo Infanticide. SM, LXIV, 98-102. 1947.

Gates, R.R. Eskimo Blood Groups and Physiognomy. Man, XXXV, 33-34. 1935.

Gessain, R. L'Ajagaq, Bilboquet Eskimo. JSAP, n.s., XLI, 238-93. 1952.

--- Deux Journées d'un Chasseur Esquimau. Connaissance du Monde, II, 179-86. 1955.

--- Les Esquimaux Aiment à S'Amuser. Neuf, III, 66-71. 1951.

--- Les Esquimaux du Groenland à l'Alaska. 121 pp. Paris, 1947.

--- Figurine Androgyne Eskimo. JSAP, n.s., XLIII, 207-17. 1954.

--- Le Motif Vagina Dentata. ICA, XXXII, 583-6. 1958.

Giddings, J.L. Observations on the "Eskimo type" of Kinship and Social Structure. UAAP, I, 5-10. 1952.

Giffen, N.M. The Roles of Men and Women in Eskimo Culture. 114 pp. Chicago, 1930.

Gilbertson, A.N. Some Ethical Phases of Eskimo Culture. Journal of Religious Psychology, VI, 321-74; VII, 45-74. 1913-14.

Godsell, P.H. Is There Time to Save the Eskimo. NH, LXI, 56-62. 1952.

Goldstein, M.S. Caries and Attrition in the Molar Teeth of the Eskimo Mandible. AJPA, XVI, 421-31. 1932.

--- Congenital Absence and Impaction of the Third Molar in the Eskimo Mandible. AJPA, XVI, 381-8. 1932.

--- The Cusps in the Mandibular Molar Teeth of the Eskimo. AJPA, XVI, 215-36. 1931.

Grantham, E.N. Education Goes North. CGJ, XLII, 44-9. 1951.

Gsovski, V. Russian Administration of Alaska and the Status of the Alaskan Natives. 104 pp. Washington, 1950.

Haldeman, J.C. Problems of Alaskan Eskimos, Indians, Aleuts. PHR, LXVI, 912-17. 1951.

Hallock, C. The Eskimo and Their Written Language. AA, IX, 369-70. 1896.

Hammerich, L.L. The Cases of Eskimo. IJAL, XVII, 18-22. 1951.

--- The Origin of the Eskimo. ICA, XXXII, 640-4. 1958.

Hanna, R.E. and Washburn, S.L. The Determination of the Sex of Skeletons. HB, XXV, 21-7. 1953.

d'Harcourt, R. Arts de l'Amérique, 21-6. Paris, 1948.

Harrington, L. People Who Live in Snow Houses. Forest and Outdoors, XLV, iii, 24-25. 1949.

Harrington, M.R. A Hunter Outfit from the Central Eskimo. M, XXV, 66-8. 1951.

Harrington, R. Eskimos I Have Known. Geographical Magazine, XXVIII, 387-9. 1955.

Hassert, K. Die Völkerwanderung der Eskimos. Geographische Zeitschrift, I, 302-22. 1895.

Hatt, G. Arktiske skinddragter i Eurasien og Amerika. 255 pp. Kjøbenhavn, 1914.

--- Early Intrusion of Agriculture in the North Atlantic Subarctic Region. UAAP, II, 51-100. 1953.

--- Kyst- og indlandskultur i det arktiske. GT, XXIII, 284-90. 1916.

--- North American and Eurasian Culture Connections. PPSC, V, iv, 2755-65. 1934.

Haugaard, E. Five Eskimo Poems. American Scandinavian Review, XLIV, 163-7. 1956.

Heller, C.A. Alaska Nutrition Survey Report: Dietary Study. Alaska's Health, VI, x, 7-9. 1948.

--- Food and Dental Health. Alaska's Health, IV, xii, 4-5. 1946.

Henry, V. Grammaire Comparée de trois Langues Hyperboréennes. ICA, III, ii, 405-509. 1880.

Henshaw, H.W., and Swanton, J.R. Eskimo. BBAE, XXX, i, 433-7. 1907.

Hermant, P. Evolution economique et sociale de certaines peuplades de l'Amérique du Nord. BSRBG, XXVIII, 321-41. 1904.

Hirsch, D.I. Glottochronology and Eskimo and Eskimo-Aleut Prehistory. AA, LVI, 825-38. 1954.

Hoebel, E.A. Eskimo Infanticide and Polyandry. SM, LXIV, 535. 1947.

Hoffman, W.J. The Graphic Art of the Eskimos. RUSNM, 1895, 739-968.

Holcomb, R.C. Syphilis of the Skull among Aleuts and the Asian and North-American Eskimo about Bering and Arctic Seas. U.S. Naval Medical Bulletin, XXXVIII, 177-92. 1940.

Holtved, E. Blandt Sagnfortaellere i Grønland og Alaska. Det Grønlandske Selskabs Aarsskrift, 1950, 69-80. København.

--- Eskimo. I. Religionsgeschichtlich. Religion in Geschichte und Gegenwart, 690-1.

--- The Eskimo Legend of Navaranaq. Acta Artica, I, 1-42. 1943.

--- Eskimokunst. Alverdens Kunst, Vol. IV. 64 pp. 1942.

--- Remarks on Eskimo Semantics. ICA, XXXII, 617-23. 1958.

Hough, W. The Lamp of the Eskimo. RUSNM, 1896, 1025-57.

Hough, W. The Origin and Range of the Eskimo Lamp. AA, XI, 116-22. 1898.

Houston, J.A. The Creation of Anoutoaloak. B, CCLXXXVI, 50-53. Winter 1955-56.

--- Eskimo Handicrafts. 32 pp. Montreal, 1951.

--- In Search of Contemporary Eskimo Art. Canadian Art, IX, iii, 99-104. 1952.

Hrdlička, A. Catalogue of Human Crania in the United States National Museum Collections. PUSNM, XCI, 169-429. 1942.

Ivanov, S.V. Chukotsko-eskimosskaia Graviura na Kosti. SE, 1949, iv, 107-24. 1949.

--- O Znachenii Dvukh Unikal'nykh Zhenskikh Statuetok Amerikanskikh Eskimosoi. ANMAE, 1949, xi, 162-70. 1949.

Jacobsen, N.K. and Sveistrup, P.P. Erhvero og Kultur Langs Polarkredsen. 140 pp. Copenhagen, 1950.

Jenness, D. Ethnological Problems of Arctic America. AGSSP, VII, 167-75. 1928.

--- Indians of Canada. BCDM, LXV, 405-23. 1932.

--- Prehistoric Culture Waves from Asia to America. JWAS, XXX, 1-15. 1940.

--- Prehistoric Culture Waves from Asia to America. ARSI, 1940, 383-96.

--- The Problem of the Eskimo. The American Aborigines, ed. D. Jenness, pp. 373-96. Toronto, 1933.

Jochelson, W. The Ethnological Problems of Bering Sea. NH, XXVI, 90-5. 1926.

--- Past and Present Subterranean Dwellings of the Tribes of North Eastern Asia and North Western America. ICA, XV, ii, 115-23. 1906.

Jordan, D. Survey of Blood Grouping and Rh Factor in Eskimos of the Eastern Arctic. Canadian Medical Association Journal, LVI, 429-34. 1946.

Jørgensen, J.B. The Eskimo Skeleton. MG, CXLVI, ii, 158 pp. 1953.

Juel, E. Notes on Seal-hunting Ceremonialism in the Arctic. Ethnos, X, 143-64. 1945.

Keithahn, E.L. Igloo Tales. 142 pp. Lawrence, 1950.

Kidd, K.E. Trading into Hudson's Bay. B, CCLXXXVIII, iii, 12-17. 1957.

King, B. Eskimo Art of the Canadian Eastern Arctic. EP, LXI, 74-6. 1954.

King, R. On the Physical Characters of the Esquimaux. JESL, I, 45-59. 1848.

Knowles, F.H.S. The Glenoid Fossa in the Skull of the Eskimo. MBCDM, IX, iv, 1-25. 1915.

König, H. Gedanken zur Frage nach der Urheimat der Eskimo. ICA, XXI, 256-62. 1924.

--- Das Recht der Polarvölker. A, XXII, 689-746; XXIV, 87-143, 621-64. 1927-29.

König, H. Das Rechtsbruch und sein Ausgleich bei den Eskimo. A, XVIII-XIX, 484-515, 771-92; XX, 276-315. 1923-25.

Krenov, J. Legends from Alaska. JSAP, XL, n.s., 173-95. 1951.

Kroeber, A.L. Animal Tales of the Eskimo. JAFL, XII, 17-23. 1899.

Laguna, F. de. A Comparison of Eskimo and Palaeolithic Art. American Journal of Archaeology, XXXVI, 477-508; XXXVII, 77-107. 1932-33.

--- Eskimo Lamps and Pots. JAI, LXX, 53-76. 1940.

--- The Importance of the Eskimo in Northeastern Archaeology. PRSPF, III, 106-42. 1946.

Lantis, M. The Alaskan Whale Cult and Its Affinities. AA, n.s., XL, 438-64. 1938.

--- Eskimo Herdsmen. HPTC, 127-48. 1952.

--- Note on the Alaskan Whale Cult and Its Affinities. AA, n.s., XLII, 366-8. 1940.

--- Present Status of the Alaskan Eskimos. ASC, 1950, 38-51. 1952.

--- Problems of Human Ecology in the North American Arctic. Arctic, VII, 307-20. 1954.

--- The Reindeer Industry in Alaska. Arctic, III, 27-44, 1950.

--- The Religion of the Eskimos. In Ferm, V., ed., Forgotten Religions, 309-40. New York, 1950.

--- Security for Alaskan Eskimos. AmI, IV, 32-40. 1950.

Larsen, E.L. (ed.) The Eskimos, an American People. UAAP, V, 83-90. 1957.

Larsen, H.E. Grønlaenderne. In Birket-Smith, K., Grønlands Bogen, I, 205-52. 1950.

Larsen, H. Recent Developments in Eskimo Archaeology. CISA, IV, ii, 315-9. 1952.

Laufer, B. The Eskimo Screw as a Culture-Historical Problem. AA, n.s., XVII, 396-406. 1915.

Laughlin, W.S. The Alaska Gateway Viewed from the Aleutian Islands. PPAAI, 98-126. 1951.

--- The Aleut-Eskimo Community. UAAP, I, 24-48. 1952.

--- Blood Groups, Morphology, and Population Size of the Eskimos. CSHSB, XV, 165-73. 1950.

--- Contemporary Problems in the Anthropology of Southern Alaska. ASC, 1950, 66-84. 1952.

Laviolette, G. Notes on the Aborigines of the Prairie Provinces. An, II, 107-30. 1956.

Leechman, D. Aboriginal Paints and Dyes in Canada. PTRSC, ser. 3, XXVI, ii, 37-42. 1932.

--- Beauty's Only Skin Deep. B, CCLXXXII, ii, 38-40. 1951.

--- Eskimo Sculpture in Stone. CGJ, XLVIII, 126-7. 1954.

Leechman, D. Igloo and Tupik. B, CCLXXV, iii, 36-9. 1945.

Lergh, R.W. Dental Pathology of the Eskimo. Dental Cosmos, LXVII, 884-98. 1925.

Leroi-Gourhan, A. La Civilisation du Renne. 2nd ed. 178 pp. Paris, 1936.

--- Esquisse d'une Classification Craniologique des Eskimo. ICA, XXVIII, 19-42. 1948.

Lestrange, M. de. À Propos d'Empreintes d'Eskimo. ICA, XXVIII, 43-53. 1948.

Levin, M.G. K Antropologii Eskimosov. SE, 1947, VI-VII, 216-23. 1947.

--- Kraniologicheskie tipy Chukchei i Eskimosov. ANMAE, X, 293-302. 1949.

Lewis, H.W. and Wherrett, G.J. An X-Ray Survey of Eskimos. Canadian Medical Association Journal, LVII, 357-9. 1947.

Lot-Falck, E. Les masques eskimo et aléoutes de la collection Pinart. JSAP, XLVI, n.s., 5-44. 1957.

McMinimy, D.J. Preliminary Report on Tuberculosis Incidence in Alaska. Alaska's Health, V, x, 4-5. 1947.

MacNeish, R.S. A Speculative Framework of Northern North American Prehistory as of April 1959. An, n.s., I, 7-23. 1959.

Madsen, C. and Douglas, J.S. Arctic Trader. 283 pp. New York, 1957.

Maksimov, A. Eskimosy. Bol'shaia Sovetskaia Entsiklopediia, LXIV, 632-34. 1926-47.

Mallet, T. Glimpses of the Barren Lands. 146 pp. New York, 1930.

--- Plain Tales of the North. 136 pp. New York, 1926.

Marderner, J. Das Gemeinschaftsleben der Eskimo. MAGW, LXIX, 273-348. 1940.

Markham, C.H. On the Origin and Migrations of the Greenland Esquimaux. JRGS, XXXV, 87-99. 1865.

--- The Voyages and Works of John Davis the Navigator. 373 pp. London, 1880.

Markov, S. Letopis'Aliaski. 220 pp. Moscow, 1948.

Marsh, D.B. Life in a Snowhouse. NH, LX, 64-66. 1951.

Mary-Rousselière, G. Longévité Esquimaude. Eskimo, XLIII, 13-15. 1957.

Mason, O.T. Aboriginal American Harpoons. RUSNM, 1900, ii, 193-304.

--- Throwing-sticks in the National Museum. RUSNM, 1884, 279-89.

--- The Ulu or Woman's Knife of the Eskimo. RUSNM, 1890, ii, 411-16.

Mathiassen, T. Foreløbig beretning om femte Thuleekspedition. GT, XXX, 39-56, 72-88. 1927.

--- Notes on Knud Rasmussen's Archaeological Collections from the Western Eskimo. ICA, XXIII, 395-9. 1928.

Mathiassen, T. Preliminary Report of the Fifth Thule Expedition. ICA, XXI, 206-15. 1924.

--- The Present Stage of Eskimo Archaeology. Acta Archaeologica, II, 185-99. 1931.

--- The Question of the Origin of Eskimo Culture. AA, n.s., XXXII, 591-607. 1930.

--- Det vingede naalehus. GT, XXXII, 15-22. 1929.

Mauss, M., and Beuchat, M.H. Essai sur les variations saisonnières des sociétés Eskimos. L'Année Sociologique, IX, 39-130. 1906.

Meldgaard, J. Eskimo-Arkaeologien i Etnografiens Tjeneste. Menneskets Mangfoldighed, 25-39. København.

Morant, G.M. A Contribution to Eskimo Craniology. Biometrika, XXIX, 1-20. 1937.

Munn, H.T. Tales of the Eskimo. 196 pp. London, 1925.

Murdoch, J. Dr. Rink's "Eskimo Tribes." AA, I, 125-33. 1888.

--- On the Siberian Origin of Some Customs of the Western Eskimo. AA, I, 325-35. 1888.

--- Sinew-backed Bow of the Eskimo. SMC, XXXIV, ii, 168-71. 1893.

--- A Study of the Eskimo Bows in the U.S. National Museum. RUSNM, 1884, ii, 207-16.

Nippgen, J. Les resultats ethnographiques de l'Expedition Danoise dans l'Amérique arctique. Revue Anthropologique, XXXVI, 411-26. 1926.

Oetteking, B. Ein Beitrag zur Kraniologie der Eskimo. Abhandlungen und Berichte des Königlichen Zoologischen und Anthropologisch-Ethnographischen Museums zu Dresden, XII, iii. 1908.

Oswalt, W.H. The Saucer-Shaped Eskimo Lamp. UAAP, I, ii, 15-23. 1953.

Päivänsalo, P. Sosiologinen tutkimus eskimoiden lastenhoito ja kasvatustavoista. Suomen Mastavus-Sosiologisen Yhdistyksen julkaisuja, I, 1-158. 1947.

Pales, L. Les Perforations Posthumes Naturelles des Cranes Eskimo du Groenland. BSAP, Ser. 10, III, 229-37. 1952.

Paulson, I. The "Seat of Honor" in Aboriginal Dwellings in the Circumpolar Zone. ICA, XXIX, iii, 63-5. 1952.

Peck, E.J. Eskimo Grammar. 92 pp. Ottawa, 1919.

Pedersen, P.O. Anatomical Studies of the East Greenland Eskimo Dentition. ICA, XXIX, iii, 46-9. 1952.

--- Some Dental Aspects of Anthropology. Dental Record, July-August, 170-8. Copenhagen, 1952.

Petitot, E. Étude des Esquimaux. ICA, I, i, 329-39. 1875.

--- Origine Asiatique des Esquimaux. ICA, VIII, 296-7. 1892.

Pilling, J.C. Bibliography of the Eskimo Language. BBAE, I, 1-112. 1887.

Pinart, A. La chasse aux animaux marins et les pecheries chez les indigènes de la cote nord-ouest d'Amérique. 15 pp. Boulogne-sur-Mer. 1875.

Poncins, G. de M. Eskimos. 112 pp. New York, 1949.

Porsild, A.E. Edible Plants of the Arctic. Arctic, VI, 15-34. 1953.

--- Land Use in the Arctic. CGJ, XLVIII, 232-43, XLIX, 20-31. 1954.

Porsild, M.P. The Principle of the Screw in the Technique of the Eskimo. AA, n.s., XVII, 1-16. 1915.

Rabinowitch, I.M. Clinical and Other Observations on Canadian Eskimos in the Eastern Arctic. Canadian Medical Association Journal, XXXIV, 487-501. 1936.

Radin, P., and Gray, L.H. Eskimos. ERE, V, 391-5. 1912.

Rae, J. Correspondence with the Hudson's Bay Company on Arctic Exploration 1844-1855. HBRS, XVI, 509 pp. 1953.

Rainey, F. and Ralph, E. Radiocarbon Dating in the Arctic. AAn, XXIV, 365-74. 1959.

Rasmussen, K. Across Arctic America. New York, 1927.

--- Adjustment of the Eskimos to European Civilization. PPSC, V, iv, 2889-96. 1934.

--- Alaskan Eskimo Words. RFTE, III, iv, 1-83. 1941.

--- Du Groenland au Pacifique. Paris, 1929.

--- Eskimos and Stone-Age Peoples. GT, XXXII, 201-16. 1929.

--- Eskimos and Stone Age Peoples. PPSC, V, iv, 2767-72. 1934.

--- Tasks for Future Research in Eskimo Culture. AGSSP, VII, 177-87. 1928.

Rausch, R. On the Status of Some Arctic Mammals. Arctic, VI, 91-148. 1953.

Richardson, J. The Polar Regions. Edinburgh, 1861.

Riddell, F.A. Climate and the Aboriginal Occupation of the Pacific Coast of Alaska. PKAS, XI, 60-123. 1954.

Riedel, F. Die Polarvölker. 71 pp. Halle, 1902.

Rink, H. The Eskimo Dialects. JAI, XV, 239-45. 1886.

--- The Eskimo Tribes. MG, XI, 1-163. 1887.

--- The Migrations of the Eskimo. JAI, XVII, 68-74. 1887.

--- Om de eskimoiske dialekter. ANOH, XX, 219-60. 1885.

Rink, H. Om eskimoernes herkomst. ANOH, n.s.,
V, 185-208. 1890.

--- On a Safe Conclusion Concerning the Origin of
the Eskimo. JAI, XIX, 452-8. 1890.

Rink, S. The Girl and the Dogs — an Eskimo Folk-
Tale with Comments. AA, XI, 181-7, 209-15.
1898.

Ritter, A. A Doctor Among the Eskimos. Am I, VI,
i, 33-6. 1951.

Robertson, E.C. Family Allowances in the Canadian
Arctic. Polar Record, VI, xliii, 345-47. 1952.

Rodahl, K. Basal Metabolism of the Eskimo. Federation Proceedings, XI, 130. 1952.

--- The Body Surface Area of the Eskimo. Journal of
Applied Physiology, V, 242-46. 1952.

--- The Body Surface Area of Eskimos. AJPA, n.s.,
X, 419-26. 1952.

Roheim, G. Die Sedna Sage. Imago, X, 159-77.
1924.

Rousseau, J.J. L'Origine et l'Evolution du Mot
Esquimau. CD, XX, 179-98. 1955.

Rudenko, S.I. Drevniaia Kul'tura Beringova Moria i
Eskimosskaia Problema. 131 pp. Moscow, 1947.

Sargent, M. Folk and Primitive Music in Canada.
BNMC, CXXIII, 75-9. 1951.

Sauvageot, A. Caractère Ouraloide du Verbe Eskimo.
Bulletin de la Société Linguistique. XLIX, 107-21.
1953.

Schmitt, A. Die Alaska-Schrift. 200 pp. Marburg,
1951.

Schuster, C. A Survival of the Eurasiatic Animal
Style in Modern Alaskan Eskimo Art. ICA, XXIX,
iii, 35-45. 1952.

Sergeev, M.A. Skazni Narodov Severa. 685 pp.
Moscow, 1951.

Shapiro, H.L. The Alaskan Eskimo. APAM, XXXI,
347-84. 1931.

--- Some Observations on the Origin of the Eskimos.
PPSC, V, iv, 2723-32. 1933.

Simmons, H.G. Eskimaernas forna och nutida
utbredning samt deras vandringsvägar. Ymer, XXV,
173-92. 1905.

Soper, J.D. Eskimo Dogs of the Canadian Arctic.
CGJ, XX, 96-108. 1940.

Speck, F.G. Central Eskimo and Indian Dot Ornamentation. IN, II, 151-72. 1925.

Spencer, R.F. Eskimo Polyandry and Social Organization. ICA, XXXII, 539-44. 1958.

Steensby, H.P. An Anthropogeographical Study of the
Origin of Eskimo Culture. MG, LIII, 39-228. 1917.

--- Om eskimokulturens oprindelse. 219 pp.
København, 1905.

Stefansson, V. Clothes Make the Eskimo. NH, LXIV,
32-41. 1955.

--- The Eskimo and Civilization. AMJ, XII, 195-
204. 1912.

--- Eskimos. Encyclopaedia Britannica, 14th edit.,
VIII, 708-10. 1937.

--- Prehistoric and Present Commerce among the Arctic Coast Eskimo. MBCDM, VI, 1-29. 1914.

Steinert, W. Die Wirkung des Landschaftszwanges auf
die materielle Kultur des Eskimo. 58 pp. Hamburg,
1935.

Swadesh, M. Unaaliq and Proto Eskimo, IJAL, XVII,
66-70; XVIII, 25-34, 69-76, 166-71, 241-56.
1951-1952.

Swinton, G. Eskimo Carving Today. B, CCLXXXVIII,
iv, 40-7. 1958.

Taylor, W.E. Review and Assessment of the Dorset
Problem. An, n.s., I, 24-46. 1959.

Thalbitzer, W. The Cultic Deities of the Innuit. ICA,
XXII, ii, 367-93. 1926.

--- Eskimo. BBAE, XL, i, 967-1069. 1911.

--- Eskimo as a Linguistic Type. ICA, XXIII, 895-
904. 1928.

--- Eskimo Dialects and Wanderings. ICA, XIV, 107-
18. 1904.

--- Eskimo Language. Encyclopaedia Britannica, 14th
edit., VIII, 707-8. 1937.

--- The Eskimo Numerals. Journal de la Société
Finno-Ougrienne, XXV, ii, 1-25. 1908.

--- Eskimoiske stednavne fra Alaska og Grønland. GT,
XXXV, 137-55. 1932.

--- Der ethnographische Zusammenhang der Eskimo
Grönlands mit denen der Hudsonbai. BA, II, 32-44.
1912.

--- Is Eskimo a Primitive Language? Actes du Congrès
International de Linguiste, IV, 254-62. 1938.

--- Is there any Connection between the Eskimo Language and the Uralian? ICA, XXII, ii, 551-67.
1926.

--- Die kultischen Gottheiten der Eskimos. ARW,
XXVI, 364-430. 1928.

--- A Note on the Derivation of the Word "Eskimo"
(Inuit). AA, LII, 564, 1950.

--- A Phonetical Study of the Eskimo Language. MG,
XXXI, 1-406. 1904.

--- Possible Early Contacts between Eskimo and Old
World Languages. ICA, XXIX, iii, 50-54. 1952.

--- Uhlenbeck's Eskimo-Indoeuropean Hypothesis.
Travaux du Cercle Linguistique de Copenhague, I,
66-96. 1945.

Thibert, A. Dictionnaire Français-Esquimau — Esqui-
mau-Français. 200 pp. Ottawa, 1955.

Thibert, A. Dictionary English-Eskimo — Eskimo-English. 184 pp. Ottawa, 1954.

T.weedsmuir, J. Men and Beasts in the Canadian Arctic Islands. Geographical Magazine, XXVI, iv, 182-91. 1953.

Uhlenbeck, C.C. Eskimo en Oer-Indogermaansch. MKAW, LXXVII, A, vi, 179-96. 1935.

--- Ontwerp van eene vergelijkende vormleer der Eskimo-talen. VKAW, n.s., VIII, iii, 1-76. 1907.

--- Opmerkingen over het Eskimo-problem. Jaarboek der Koninklijke Akademie van Wetenschappen te Amsterdam, 1936, 1-14.

--- Oude aziatische Contacten van het Eskimo. MKAW, n.s., IV, 201-27. 1941.

--- Ur- und altindogermanische Anklänge im Wortschatz des Eskimo. A, XXXVII, 133-48. 1942.

--- Uralische Anklänge in den Eskimosprachen. ZDMG, LIX, 757-65. 1905.

--- Zu einzelnen Eskimowörtern. A, XLV, 177-82. 1950.

Ulving, T. Consonant Gradation in Eskimo. IJAL, XIX, 45-52. 1953.

--- Two Eskimo Etymologies. Studia Linguistica, VIII, 16-33, 1954.

Velde, F. L'Infanticide chez les Esquimaux. Eskimo, XXXIV, 6-8. 1954.

Vogeler, E. Lieder der Eskimos. 62 pp. Copenhagen, 1930.

Wachtmeister, A. Naming and Reincarnation among the Eskimos. Ethnos, XXI, 130-42. 1956.

Walton, W.G., ed. Eskimo-English Dictionary. 310 pp. Toronto, 1925.

Wardle, H.N. The Sedna Cycle, AA, n.s., II, 568-80. 1900.

Webster, J.H. Eskimos Glaze their Sled Runners. NH, LIX, 36-7. 1950.

--- Fishing Under the Ice. NH, LIX, 140-41. 1950.

Wells, R., and Kelly, J. English-Eskimo and Eskimo-English Vocabularies. U.S. Bureau of Education, Circular of Information, 1890, ii, 1-72.

Weyer, E.M. The Eskimos. New Haven, 1932.

White, G. Canadian Apartheid. Canadian Forum, XXXI, 102-03. Aug. 1951.

Williams, C.H.M. An Investigation Concerning the Dentition of the Eskimos of Canada's Eastern Arctic. Canadian Dental Association, Journal, VI, 169-72. 1940.

Wilson, C. The New North in Pictures. 223 pp. Toronto, 1947.

Wissler, C., ed. Notes concerning New Collections. APAM, II, 314-20. 1909.

1. ALEUT

Veniaminov, I. Zapiski ob ostrovax unalashkinskago otdela. 3 vols. St. Petersburg, 1840.

Alexander, F. A Medical Survey of the Aleutian Islands (1948). New England Journal of Medicine, CCXL, 1035-40. 1949.

Anderson, H.D., and Eells, W.C. Alaska Natives. 472 pp. Stanford, 1935.

Anonymous. Aleut. BBAE, XXX, i, 36-7. 1907.

Anonymous. Aleuty. Bol'shaia Sovetskaia Entsiklopediia, II, 96-97. 1950.

Bancroft, H.H. The Native Races of the Pacific States, I, 87-94. New York, 1875.

Bank, T.P. Aleut Vegetation and Aleut Culture. PMA, XXXVII, 13-30. 1951.

--- Birthplace of the Winds. 286 pp. New York, 1956.

--- Health and Medical Lore of the Aleuts. PMA, XXXVIII, 415-31. 1953.

Berg, L. On the Origin of the Aleut. PPSC, V, iv, 2773-5. 1934.

Bergsland, K. Aleut and Proto-Eskimo. ICA, XXXII, 624-31. 1958.

--- Aleut Demonstratives and the Aleut-Esquimo Relationship. IJAL, XVII, 167-79. 1951.

--- Aleut Dialects of Atka and Attu. TAPS, n.s., XLIX, iii, 128 pp. 1959.

Berreman, G.D. Effects of a Technological Change in an Aleutian Village. Arctic, VII, 102-7. 1952.

--- Inquiry into Community Integration in an Aleutian Village. AA, LVII, 49-59. 1955.

Bushnell, D.I. Drawings by John Webber of Natives of the Northwest Coast. SMC, LXXX, x, 1-12. 1928.

Buynitzky, S.N. English-Aleutian Dictionary. 13 pp. San Francisco, 1871.

Candela, P.B. Blood-Group Determinations upon the Bones of Thirty Aleutian Mummies. AJPA, XXIV, 361-83. 1939.

Chamberlain, A.F. Aleuts. ERE, I, 303-5. 1908.

Collins, H.B., Clark, A.H., and Walker, E.H. The Aleutian Islands. Smithsonian Institution War Background Series, XXI, 1-131. 1945.

Coxe, W. Account of the Russian Discoveries between Asia and America. 4th edit. London, 1804.

Czaplička, M.A. Aboriginal Siberia. 388 pp. Oxford, 1914.

Dall, W.H. Alaska and Its Resources, pp. 385-400. Boston, 1870.

--- Alaskan Mummies. AN, IX, 433-40. 1875.

--- Masks, Labrets and Certain Aboriginal Customs. ARBAE, III, 137-43. 1882.

Dall, W.H. On Succession in the Shell-Heaps of the Aleutian Islands. CNAE, I, 41-91. 1877.

--- On the Distribution and Nomenclature of the Native Tribes of Alaska. CNAE, I, 7-40. 1877.

--- On the Distribution of the Native Tribes of Alaska. PAAAS, XVIII, 263-73. 1869.

--- On the Remains of Later Pre-historic Man obtained from Caves in the Catherina Archipelago. SCK, XXII, vi, 1-35. 1878.

Eells, W.C. Mechanical, Physical, and Musical Ability of the Native Races of Alaska. JAP, XVII, 493-506. 1933.

--- Mental Ability of the Native Races of Alaska. JAP, XVII, 417-38. 1933.

Elliott, C.P. Salmon Fishing Grounds and Canneries. Compilation of Narratives of Explorations in Alaska, pp. 738-41. Washington, 1900.

Erman, A. Ethnographische Wahrnehmungen und Erfahrungen an den Küsten des Berings-Meeres. ZE, II, 295-327, 369-93; III, 149-75, 205-19. 1870-71.

Field, H. Contributions to the Anthropology of the Soviet Union. SMC, CX, xiii, 230-4. 1948.

Gapanovich, I.I. Rossiia v Severovostochnoi Azii. 2 vol. 402 pp. Peking, 1933-1934.

Garn, S.M. and Moorrees, C.F.A. Stature, Body-Build, and Tooth Emergence in Aleutian Aleut Children. YPA, VII, 45-54. 1953.

Gebhard, P., and Kent, K.P. Some Textile Specimens from the Aleutian Islands. AAn, VII, 171-8. 1941.

Geoghegan, R.H. The Aleut Language, ed. F.A.I. Martin. 169 pp. Washington, 1944.

Golder, F.A. Aleutian Stories. JAFL, XVIII, 215-22. 1905.

--- Eskimo and Aleut Stories. JAFL, XXII, 10-24. 1909.

--- The Songs and Stories of the Aleuts. JAFL, XX, 132-42. 1907.

Guggenheim, P. An Anthropological Campaign on Amchitka. SM, LXI, 21-32. 1945.

Haldeman, J.C. Problems of Alaskan Eskimos, Indians, Aleuts. PHR, LXVI, 912-17. 1951.

Hammerich, L.L. Russian Loan-Words in Alaska. ICA, XXX, 114-26. 1955.

--- The Russian Stratum in Alaskan Eskimo. Slavic Word, X, 401-28. 1954.

--- The Western Eskimo Dialects. ICA, XXXII, 632-9. 1958.

Heizer, R.F. Aconite Poison Whaling in Asia and America. BBAE, CXXXIII, 415-68. 1943.

Heizer, R.F. Archaeology of the Uyak Site, Kodiak Island, Alaska. AR, XVII, i, 205 pp. 1956.

--- A Pacific Eskimo Invention in Whale Hunting in Historic Times. AA, n.s., XLV, 120-2. 1943.

Hellwald, F. von. Das Volk der Aleuten. Ausland, LIV, 789-93. 1881.

Henry, V. Esquisse d'une grammaire raisonnée de la langue Aléoute. 73 pp. Paris, 1879.

--- Grammaire Comparée de trois Langues Hyperboréennes. ICA, III, ii, 405-509. 1880.

Hrdlicka, A. The Aleutian and Commander Islands and Their Inhabitants. 630 pp. Philadelphia, 1945.

--- Anthropological Explorations on the Aleutian and Commander Islands. EFWSI, 1937, 87-94.

--- Catalogue of Human Crania in the United States National Museum Collections. PUSNM, XCIV, 1-172. 1944.

--- Exploration in the Aleutian and the Commander Islands. EFWSI, 1938, 79-86.

--- Exploration of Mummy Caves in the Aleutian Islands. SM, LII, 5-23, 113-30. 1941.

--- Ritual Ablation of Front Teeth in Siberia and America. SMC, XCIX, iii, 1-32. 1940.

Ivanov, S.V. Aleut Hunting Headgear and Its Ornamentation. ICA, XXIII, 477-504. 1928.

--- Sidiachie Chelovecheskie Figurki. ANMAE, XII, 194-212. 1949.

Jacobi, A. Carl Heinrich Mercks Ethnographische Beobachtungen über die Völker des Beringsmeers. BA, XX, 113-37. 1937.

Jochelson, W. The Aleut Language and Its Relation to the Eskimo Dialects. ICA, XVIII, 96-104. 1912.

--- Archaeological Investigations in the Aleutian Islands. New York, 1925.

--- History, Ethnology and Anthropology of the Aleut. 91 pp. Washington, 1933.

--- Past and Present Subterranean Dwellings of the Tribes of North Eastern Asia and North Western America. ICA, XV, ii, 115-23. 1906.

--- People of the Foggy Seas. NH, XXVIII, 413-24. 1928.

--- Scientific Results of the Ethnological Section of the Riabouchinsky Expedition. ICA, XVIII, 334-43. 1912.

Kissell, M. An Aleutian Basket. AMJ, VII, 133-6. 1907.

Langsdorff, G.H. von. Voyages and Travels in Various Parts of the World, pp. 331-47. Carlisle, 1817.

Laughlin, W.S. The Aleut-Eskimo Community. UAAP, I, 24-48. 1952.

Laughlin, W.S. and Marsh, G.H. A New View of the History of the Aleutians. Arctic, IV, 75-88. 1951.

Lavrischeff, T.I. Two Aleut Tales. AA, n.s., XXX, 121-4. 1928.

Lazarev, A.P. Zapiski o Plavanii Voennogo Shliupa Blagonamerennogo. 475 pp. Moscow, 1950.

Lee, C.A. Aleutian Indian and English Dictionary. 23 pp. Seattle, 1896.

Leroi-Gourhan, A. Archéologie du Pacifique-nord. Travaux et Mémoires de l'Institut d'Ethnologie, XLVII. 1-542. 1946.

Lot-Falck, E. Les masques eskimo et aléoutes de la collection Pinart. JSAP, XLVI, n.s., 5-44. 1957.

Löwe, F. Wenjaminow über die aleutischen Inseln und deren Bewohner. AWKR, II, 459-95. 1842.

Lutké, F. Voyage autour du monde. 3 vols. Paris, 1835.

McCracken, H. God's Frozen Children. 291 pp. New York, 1930.

Marsh, G.H. A Comparative Study of Eskimo-Aleut Religion. UAAP, III, 21-36. 1954.

Marsh, G.H. and Laughlin, W.S. Human Anatomical Knowledge among the Aleutian Islanders. SJA, XII, 38-78. 1956.

Martin, F.I. The Hunting of the Silver Fleece. 328 pp. New York, 1946.

--- Three Years of Pribilof Progress. Am I, V, iii, 17-26. 1950.

--- Wanted, A Pribilof Bill of Rights. Am I, III, iv, 15-25. 1946.

Masterson, J.R., and Brower, H. Bering's Successors, 1745-1780. PNQ, XXXVIII, 35-83, 109-55. 1947.

May, A.G. Attu. NH, L, 132-7. 1942.

Moorrees, C.F.A. The Aleut Dentition. 206 pp. Cambridge, 1957.

Moorrees, C.F.A. et al. Torus Mandibularis. AJPA, X, 319-29. 1952.

Muir, J. The Cruise of the Corwin. Boston, 1917.

Petroff, I. The Limit of the Innuit Tribes on the Alaskan Coast. AN, XVI, 567-75. 1882.

--- The Population and Resources of Alaska. Compilation of Narratives of Explorations in Alaska, pp. 239-57. Washington, 1900.

--- Report on the Population, Industries and Resources of Alaska. U.S. Department of the Interior, Tenth Census, VIII, 146-60. 1881.

Pinart, A. Les Aléoutes et leur origine. Mémoires de la Société d'Ethnographie, XI, 155-65. 1872.

Preston, W.D. Some Methodological Suggestions based on Aleut Linguistic Material. IJAL, XIII, 171-4. 1947.

Quimby, G.I. Aleutian Islanders. FMDAL, XXXV, 1-48. 1944.

--- Periods of Prehistoric Art in the Aleutian Islands. AAn, XI, 76-9. 1945.

Quimby, G.I. Pottery from the Aleutian Islands. FMAS, XXXVI, 1-13. 1946.

--- Prehistoric Art of the Aleutian Islands. FMAS, XXXVI, 77-92. 1946.

--- The Sadiron Lamp of Kamchatka as a Clue to the Chronology of the Aleut. AAn, XI, 202-3. 1946.

--- Toggle Harpoon Heads from the Aleutian Islands. FMAS, XXXVI, 15-23. 1946.

Ransom, J.E. Aleut Linguistic Perspective. SJA, II, 48-55. 1946.

--- Aleut Natural-Food Economy. AA, n.s., XLVIII, 607-23. 1946.

--- Aleut Religious Beliefs: Veniaminov's Account. JAFL, LVIII, 346-9. 1945.

--- Aleut Semaphore Signals. AA, n.s., XLIII, 422-7. 1941.

--- Children's Games among the Aleut. JAFL, LIX, 196-8. 1946.

--- Derivation of the Word "Alaska." AA, n.s., XLII, 550-1. 1940.

--- Stories, Myths, and Superstitions of Fox Island Aleut Children. JAFL, LX, 62-72. 1947.

--- Writing as a Medium of Acculturation among the Aleut. SJA, I, 333-44. 1945.

Santos, A. Jesuitos en el Polo Norte. 546 pp. Madrid, 1943.

Scheffer, V.B. Use of Fur-Seal Carcasses by Natives of the Pribilof Islands. PNQ, XXXIX, 131-2. 1948.

Schott, W. Ueber die Sprachen des russischen Amerika nach Wenjaminow. AWKR, VII, 126-43. 1849.

Schwatka, F. Report of a Military Reconnaissance made in Alaska in 1883, pp. 111-8. Washington, 1900.

Shade, C.I. The Girls' Puberty Ceremony of Umnak, Aleutian Islands. AA, n.s., LIII, 145-8. 1951.

Sh[ternberg], L.I. Aleuty. Novyi Entsiklopedicheskii Slovar, II, 40-3. 1911-1916.

Spaulding, A.C. The Current Status of Aleutian Archaeology. MSAA, IX, 29-31. 1953.

Tarenetzky, A. Beiträge zur Skelet- und Schädelkunde der Aleuten, Konaegen, Kenai und Koljuschen. Mémoires de l'Académie Impériale des Sciences de St.-Pétersbourg, ser. 8. Classe Physico-Mathématique, IX, iv, 1-73. 1900.

Thalbitzer, W. The Aleutian Language compared with Greenlandic. IJAL, 40-57. 1921.

--- Et manuskript of Rasmus Rask om Aleuternes sprog. Oversigt over det Kongelige Danske Videnskabernes Selskabs Forhandlinger, 1916, 211-49.

Veniaminov, I. Charakterzüge der Aleuten. BKRR, I, 177-225. 1839.

--- Les Iles Aléoutes et leurs habitants. NAV, CXII, 66-82; CXXIV, 112-48. 1849.

Veniaminov, I. Introduction to the Study of the
Aleutian Language. 71 pp. Seattle, 1940.
--- Opyt grammatiki aleutsko-lisevskago Yazyka.
120 pp. St. Petersburg, 1846.
--- Zapiski ob Atkhinskikh Aleutakh i Koloskakh.
155 pp. St. Petersburg, 1840.
Wardle, H.N. Attu Treasure. UPMB, XI, 23-6. 1946.
Weyer, E.M. An Aleutian Burial. APAM, XXXI,
219-38. 1929.
--- Archaeological Material from the Village Site at
Hot Springs. APAM, XXXI, 239-79. 1930.
Winchell, M.E. Home by the Bering Sea. 226 pp.
Caldwell, 1951.
Yarmolinsky, A. Aleutian Manuscript Collection.
12 pp. New York, 1944.

2. BAFFINLAND ESKIMO

Exclusive of the Tununermiut of northwest Baffin-
land, grouped with the Iglulik Eskimo.

Boas, F. The Central Eskimo. ARBAE, VI, 390-669.
1888.
--- The Eskimo of Baffin Land and Hudson Bay.
BAMNH, XV, 1-570. 1901-07.

Abbes, H. Die Eskimos des Cumberlandgolfes. 60 pp.
No place or date given.
--- Die Eskimos des Cumberland-Sundes. Globus,
XLVI, 198-201, 213-18. 1884.
Anderson, G. A Whale is Killed. B, CLXXVII, 18-
21. 1947.
Anonymous. Starvation near Piling, Foxe Basin,
N.W.T. Arctic Circular, III, 31-2. 1950.
Bilby, J.W. Among Unknown Eskimo. 280 pp. Lon-
don, 1923.
Boas, F. Baffin-Land. PME, XVII, v, 1-100. 1885.
--- Cumberland Sound and Its Eskimos. PSM, XXVI,
768-79. 1885.
--- The Eskimo of Baffin Land. SMC, XXXIV, ii,
95-102. 1893.
--- Eskimo Tales and Songs. JAFL, VII, 45-50; X,
109-15. 1894, 1897.
--- An Eskimo Winter. American Indian Life, ed.
E.C. Parsons, pp. 363-78. New York, 1925.
--- Der Eskimo-Dialekt des Cumberland-Sundes.
MAGW, XXIV, 97-114. 1894.
--- Die religiösen Vorstellungen und einige Gebräuche
der zentralen Eskimos. PMJP, XXXIII, 302-16. 1887.
--- Religious Beliefs of the Central Eskimo. PSM,
LVII, 624-31. 1900.
--- Die Sagen der Baffin-Land Eskimos. VBGA,
1885, 161-6.

Boas, F. A Year among the Eskimo. JAGS, XIX,
383-402. 1887.
Boas, F. and Rink, H. Eskimo Tales and Songs. JAFL,
II, 123-31. 1889.
Flint, M.S. The Arctic, Land of Snowmen. 39 pp.
London, 1948.
Hall, C.F. Life with the Esquimaux. 2 vols. Lon-
don, 1864.
Harrington, R. The Cheerful Eskimo. B, CCLXXXII,
iv, 7-15. 1952.
Heinbecker, P., and Pauli, R.H. Blood Grouping of
Baffin Island Eskimos. Journal of Immunology, XV,
407-9. 1928.
Jenness, D. A New Eskimo Culture in Hudson Bay.
GR, XV, 428-37. 1925.
Kumlien, L. Fragmentary Notes on the Eskimo of
Cumberland Sound. BUSNM, XV, 11-46. 1879.
Markham, C.R., ed. The Voyages of William Baffin.
192 pp. London, 1881.
Marsh, D.B. An Eskimo girl builds a Snowhouse. NH,
LI, 46-7. 1943.
Meldgaard, J. Eskimoiske Stenalderkulturer i Arktisk
Canada. Polarboken, 1955, 113-27. Oslo.
Morgan, L.H. Systems of Consanguinity and Affinity.
SCK, XVII, 291-382. 1871.
Munn, H.T. The Economic Life of the Baffin Island
Eskimo. GJ, LIX, 269-73. 1922.
Nichols, P.A.C. Boat-building Eskimos. B,
CCLXXXV, i, 52-5. 1955.
Oetteking, B. A Contribution to the Physical Anthro-
pology of Baffin Land. AJPA, XV, 421-68. 1931.
Parry, W. Journal of a Voyage for the Discovery of a
North-West Passage, pp. 202-3, 276-88. London,
1821.
Rabinowitch, I.M., and Smith, F.C. Metabolic
Studies of Eskimos in the Canadian Eastern Arctic.
Journal of Nutrition, XII, 337-56. 1936.
Radwanski, P. Anthropological Structure of 101
Eskimo. An, I, 72-83. 1955.
Robinson, J.L. Eskimo Population in the Canadian
Eastern Arctic. CGJ, XXIX, 128-42. 1944.
Service, E.R. The Canadian Eskimo. PPC, 64-85.
1958.
Sewall, K.W. Blood, Taste, Digital Hair, and Color
of Eyes in Eastern Eskimo. AJPA, XXV, 93-9. 1939.
Speck, F.G. Eskimo Collection from Baffin Land and
Ellesmere Land. IN, I, 143-9. 1924.
Stefansson, V. Eskimos. Encyclopaedia Britannica,
14th ed., VIII, 708-10. 1929.
Stefansson, V., ed. The Three Voyages of Martin
Frobisher. 2 vols. London, 1938.

Stewart, S.J. White Whale Drive. B, CCLXX, ii, 23-5. 1940.

Washburne, H.C., and Blackmore, A. Land of the Good Shadows. 329 pp. New York, 1940.

Wells, J.R. The Origin of Immunity to Diphtheria in Central and Polar Eskimos. American Journal of Hygiene, XVIII, 629-73. 1933.

Wells, J.R. and Heinbecker, P. Further Studies on Immunity to Diphtheria among Central and Polar Eskimos. Proceedings of the Society for Experimental Biology and Medicine, XXIX, 1028-30. 1932.

Wilkinson, D. How I Became an Eskimo. Maclean's Magazine, LXVII, xxii, 28-30, 103-9. 1954.

--- Land of the Long Day. 261 pp. Toronto, 1955.

Wilson, C. White Whale Roundup. Forest and Outdoors, XLI, 187-88. 1945.

3. CARIBOU ESKIMO

Birket-Smith, K. The Caribou Eskimos. RFTE, V, 1-725. 1929.

Rasmussen, K. Observations on the Intellectual Culture of the Caribou Eskimos. RFTE, VII, ii, 1-114. 1930.

Anderson, G. Pagan Eskimos. B, CCLXXIV, ii, 38-40. 1943.

Banfield, A.W.F. The Barren-Ground Caribou. 58 pp. Ottawa, 1951.

Birket-Smith, K. Anthropological Observations on the Central Eskimos. RFTE, III, ii, 123 pp. 1940.

--- Geographical Notes on the Barren Ground. RFTE, I, iv, 1-129. 1933.

Boas, F. The Eskimo of Baffin Land and Hudson Bay. BAMNH, XV, 1-570. 1901-07.

Crile, G.W. and Quiring, D.P. Indian and Eskimo Metabolisms. Journal of Nutrition, XVIII, 361-8. 1939.

Gabus, J. La Construction des Iglous chez les Padleirmiut. Bulletin de la Société Neuchateloise de Géographie, XLVII, 43-51. 1940.

--- Iglous. 259 pp. Neuchatal, 1944.

--- Les mouvements migratoires chez les Esquimaux-caribous. A, XXXV, 221-38. 1940.

--- Préparation des peaux chez les Esquimaux-caribous. A, XXXV, 355-6. 1940.

Giddings, J.L., Jr. A Holiday with the Padlimiut. BPAS, VII, 3-5. 1953.

Gilder, W.H. Schwatka's Search. New York, 1881.

Hanbury, D.T. Sport and Travel in the Northland of Canada. New York, 1904.

Harrington, R. The Face of the Arctic. 369 pp. New York, 1952.

--- The Padleimiuts. CGJ, XLIV, 2-15. 1952.

Manning, T.H. Pipestems of the Caribou Eskimos. AA, n.s., L, 162-3. 1948.

Marsh, D.B. Canada's Caribou Eskimos. NGM, XLI, 87-104. 1947.

--- Life in a Snowhouse. NH, LX, 64-7. 1951.

--- Padlemiut Drum Dance. B, CCLXXVI, 20-1. 1945.

Mathiassen, T. Spørgsmaalet om Eskimokulturens oprindelse. GT, XXXII, 116-26; XXXIII, 65-74. 1929-30.

Michea, J.P. Some Eskimos of Chesterfield Inlet. CGJ, XLIII, 222-5. 1951.

Morgan, L.H. Systems of Consanguinity and Affinity. SCK, XVII, 291-382. 1871.

Mowat, F. People of the Deer. 352 pp. Boston, 1952.

Rasmussen, K. Iglulik and Caribou Eskimo Texts. RFTE, VII, iii, 1-160. 1930.

Sachot, J. Jusqu'au Dernier "Mangeur-decrui" 291 pp. Paris, 1944.

Scott, P.M. Wild Geese and Eskimos. 254 pp. New York, 1951.

Service, E.R. The Canadian Eskimo. PPC, 64-85. 1958.

Steenhoven, G. van den. Caribou Eskimo Legal Concepts. ICA, XXXII, 531-8. 1958.

Turquetil, A. Have the Eskimo the Concept of a Supreme Being? PM, IX, 33-8. 1936.

--- Le mariage chez les Esquimaux. Revue de l'Université d'Ottawa, Section Spéciale, IV, 125-37, 197-237. 1935.

--- Notes sur les Esquimaux de Baie Hudson. A, XXI, 419-34. 1926.

--- The Religion of the Central Eskimo. PM, II, 57-64. 1929.

Tyrrell, J.W. Across the Sub-Arctics of Canada. Toronto, 1897.

4. COPPER ESKIMO

Jenness, D. The Life of the Copper Eskimo. RCAE, XII, 1-277. 1922.

--- Material Culture of the Copper Eskimo. RCAE, XVI, 1-148. 1946.

Rasmussen, K. Intellectual Culture of the Copper Eskimos. RFTE, IX, 1-350. 1932.

Stefansson, V. The Stefansson-Anderson Arctic Expedition. APAM, XIV, 1-395. 1914.

Adam, C.I. The Bathurst Inlet Patrol. RCMP Quarterly, XVI, i, 12-25. 1950.

Anaveluk, E. Eskimo Week. B, CCLXXXV, ii, 42.
1954.

Beclard d'Harcourt, M. Le Système Pentaphone dans
les Chants des Copper-Eskimos. ICA, XXII, ii, 15-
22. 1928.

Buliard, R. Inuk. 331 pp. New York, 1951.

Cadzow, D.A. Eskimo Lamps and Cooking Vessels.
IN, I, 26-8. 1924.

--- Native Copper Objects of the Copper Eskimo.
INM, ser. 2, VIII, 1-22. 1920.

--- Unusual Eskimo Snow-Shovel. IN, I, 150-2.
1924.

Cameron, J. Osteology of the Western and Central
Eskimos. RCAE, XII, C, 1-79. 1923.

--- Researches in Craniometry. PTRSC, XX, v, 261-
7. 1926.

Chown, B. and Lewis, M. The Blood Group Genes of
the Copper Eskimo. AJPA, n.s., XVII, 13-18.
1959.

Coccola, R. de and King, P. Ayorama. 316 pp.
Toronto, 1955.

Collinson, R. Journal of H.M.S. Enterprise. London,
1889.

Finnie, R. Lure of the North. 227 pp. Philadelphia,
1940.

Godsell, P.H. Is There Time to Save the Eskimo?
NH, LXI, 56-62. 1952.

Hanbury, D.T. Sport and Travel in the Northland of
Canada. London, 1904.

Harrington, R. Coppermine Patrol. CGJ, XLI, 256-
69. 1950.

Hearne, S. A Journey from Fort Prince of Wales in
Hudson's Bay to the Northern Ocean. London, 1797.

Hewes, C.W. The Ainu Double Foreshaft Toggle Harpoon and Western North America. JWAS, XXXII,
93-104. 1942.

Jenness, D. The "Blond" Eskimos. AA, n.s., XXIII,
257-67. 1921.

--- Comparative Vocabulary of the Western Eskimo
Dialects. RCAE, XV, A, 1-134. 1928.

--- The Copper Eskimo. GR, IV, 81-91. 1917.

--- The Cultural Transformation of the Copper Eskimo. GR, XI, 541-50. 1921.

--- Eskimo String Figures. RCAE, XIII, B, 1-192.
1924.

--- Myths and Traditions from Northern Alaska, the
Mackenzie Delta and Coronation Gulf. RCAE,
XIII, A, 1-90. 1924.

--- The Origin of the Copper Eskimos and Their Copper Culture. GR, XIII, 540-51. 1923.

Jenness, D. The People of the Twilight. New York,
1928, 1959.

--- Physical Characteristics of the Copper Eskimos.
RCAE, XII, B, 1-84. 1923.

Joss, W.F. Sealing, New Style. B, CCLXXX, iv,
43-45. 1950.

Kidd, C.E. The Skull of a Copper Eskimo. Man,
XLVI, 1-2. 1946.

Marsh, D.B. The North Changes. B, CCLXXI, i,
46-50. 1940.

Merwin, B.W. The Copper Eskimo. MJ, VI, 163-8.
1915.

Richardson, J. Arctic Searching Expedition. 2 vols.
London, 1851.

Rickard, T.A. The Chalcolithic Eskimos. Man,
XXXVIII, 191-2. 1938.

Ritchie, S.G. The Dentition of the Western and Central Eskimos. RCAE, XII, Pt. C, 59-66. 1923.

Roberts, H.H., and Jenness, D. Songs of the Copper
Eskimos. RCAE, XIV, 1-506. 1925.

Seltzer, C.C. The Anthropometry of the Western
and Copper Eskimos. HB, V, 313-70. 1933.

Service, E.R. The Canadian Eskimo. PPC, 64-85.
1958.

Stefansson, V. The Friendly Arctic. New York, 1921.

--- My Life with the Eskimo. New York, 1913.

--- On Eskimo Work. SRGSC, 1912, 488-96.

Sullivan, L. The "Blond" Eskimo. AA, n.s., XXIV,
225-8. 1922.

Urquhart, J.A. Eskimos of the Canadian Western
Arctic. The New North-West, ed. C.A. Dawson,
pp. 271-82. 1947.

Velde, F.V.de. Les Règles du Portage des Phoques
Pris par la Chasse aux Aglus. An, III, 5-14. 1956.

Webster, J.H. Fishing Under the Ice. NH, LIX,
140-1. 1950.

Whittaker, C.E. Arctic Eskimo. 259 pp. London,
1927.

5. EAST GREENLAND ESKIMO

Holm, G. Ethnological Sketch of the Angmagsalik
Eskimo. MG, XXXIX, 1-147. 1911.

--- Ethnologisk skizze af Angmagsalikerne. MG,
X, 43-182. 1887.

Thalbitzer, W. The Ammassalik Eskimo. MG, XL,
113-564, 569-739; LIII, 435-81. 1917, 1921, 1941.

--- Ethnographical Collections from East Greenland.
MG, XXXIX, 319-755. 1912.

Victor, P.E. Contributions à L'ethnographie des Eskimo d'Angmagssalik. MG, CXXV, viii, 1-213. 1940.

Abel,W. Finger und Handlinienmuster ostgrönländis-
cher Eskimos. Wissenschaftliche Ergebnisse der
Deutsche-Grönland-Expedition, Vol. VI. 1933.

Amdrup, G. The Former Eskimo Settlements on the
East Coast of Greenland. MG, XXVIII, 285-328.
1909.

Bandi, H.G. and Meldgaard, J. Archaeological Investigations on Clavering Ø, Northeast Greenland.
MG, CXXVI, iv, 85 pp. 1952.

Bertelsen, A. Grønlandsk medicinsk statistik og
nosografi. MG, CXVII, iii, 1-234; iv, 1-246.
1940, 1943.

Birket-Smith, K. Etnografiske problemer i Grønland.
GT, XXV, 179-97. 1920.

--- The Greenland Bow. MG, LVI, 1-28. 1918.

--- The Greenlanders of the Present Day. Greenland,
II, 1-207. 1928.

Boas, F. The Relationships of the Eskimos of East
Greenland. Science, n.s., XXX, 535-6. 1909.

Clavering, D.C. Journal of a Voyage to Spitzbergen
and the East Coast of Greenland. Edinburgh New
Philosophical Journal, IX, 1-30. 1830.

Dumbrava, C. Une année au milieu des Esquimaux.
La Géographie, LI, 14-23. 1929.

Faure, J.L. Au Groënland avec Charcot. 249 pp.
Paris, 1933.

Fischer-Möller, K. Skeletons from Ancient Greenland
Graves. MG, CXIX, iv, 1-30. 1938.

Frederiksen, S. Stylistic Forms in Greenland Eskimo
Literature. 40 pp. Copenhagen, 1954.

Fürst, C.M., and Hansen, F.C.C. Crania groenlandica. 234 pp. Copenhagen, 1915.

Gessain, R. Statuettes eskimo composites à trois
personnages. JSAP, XLIV, n.s., 199-204. 1956.

--- La tache pigmentaire congénitale chez les Eskimo
d'Angmassalik. JSAP, n.s., XLII, 301-32. 1953.

Glob, P.V. Eskimo Settlements in Kempe Fjord and
King Oscar Fjord. MG, CII, ii, 1-97. 1935.

--- Eskimo Settlements in Northeast Greenland. MG,
CXLIV, vi, 1-40. 1946.

Graah, W.A. Narrative of an Expedition to the East
Coast of Greenland. London, 1837.

--- Undersøgelses-reise til østkysten af Grønland.
Kjøbenhavn, 1832.

Hansen, J. Dagbog om de hedenske östgrönländere.
Kjøbenhavn, 1900.

--- List of the Inhabitants of the East Coast of Greenland. MG, XXXIX, 181-202. 1911.

--- Liste over beboerne of Grønlands østkyst. MG, X,
183-206. 1888.

Hansen, S. Bidrag til Østgrønlaendernes anthropologi.
MG, X, 1-41. 1886.

--- Contributions to the Anthropology of the East Greenlanders. MG, XXXIX, 149-79. 1911.

Helms, P. Investigations into tuberculosis at Angmagssalik. MG, CLXI, i, 140 pp. 1957.

Henshaw, H.W. East Greenlanders. BBAE, XXX, i,
411-12. 1907.

Hoessly, H. Kraniologische Studien an einer
Schädelserie aus Ost-Grönland. Neue Denkschriften
der Schweizerischen Naturforschenden Gesellschaft,
LIII. 1916.

Holm, G. Konebaads-Expeditionen til Grønlands
Østkyst. GT, VIII, 79-98. 1886.

--- Legends and Tales from Angmagsalik. MG, XXIX,
225-305. 1912.

--- Sagn og fortaellinger fra Angmagsalik. MG, X,
235-334. 1888.

Holm, G., and Garde, V. Den Danske Konebaads-
expedition til Grönlands oestkyst. Kjöbenhavn, 1887.

Høygaard, A. Tuberculosis in Eskimos. Lancet,
CCXXXV, 758-9. 1938.

Hughes, C.C. Anomie, the Ammassalik, and the
Standardization of Error. SJA, XIV, 352-77. 1958.

Ingstad, H. East of the Great Glacier. 286 pp. New
York, 1937.

Johansen, A. Gitz. Characters of Greenland Mythology.
58 pp. Munksgaard, 1949.

Johansen, J.P. Den østgrønlandske angakoqkult og
dens Sorudsaetninger. GT, XLIII, 31-55. 1940.

Johnson, D.M. Observations on the Eskimo Remains on
the East Coast of Greenland. MG, XCII, vi, 1-69.
1933.

Jørgensen, J.B. The Eskimo Skeleton. MG, CXLVI,
ii, 154 pp. 1953.

Kruuse, C. Angmagsalikerne. GT, XVI, 211-17.
1902.

Larsen, H. Dødemandsbugten: an Eskimo Settlement
on Clavering Island. MG, CII, i, 1-185. 1934.

Laughlin, W.S. and Jørgenson, J.B. Isolate Variation
in Greenlandic Eskimo Crania. Acta Genetica et
Statistica Medica, VI, 3-12. 1956.

Leden, C. Über die Musik der Ostgrönländer. MG,
CLII, iv, 112 pp. 1954.

Le Méhauté, P.J. Un Hivernage au Groenland.
Archives de Médecine et Pharmacie Navales, CXXV,
5-39. 1935.

Le Méhauté, P.J. and Tcherniakofsky, P. Quelques
Considerations sur la Nosologie des Esquimaux du
Groenland Oriental. Presse Médicale, XLII, 491-92.
1934.

Lorm, A.J. Kunstzin der Eskimo's. 21 pp. 1945.

Markham, C.R. Papers on the Greenland Eskimos.
  Arctic Geography and Ethnology, pp. 163-229.
  London, 1875.

Mathiassen, T. The Archaeological Collection of the
  Cambridge East Greenland Expedition. MG, LXXIV,
  137-66. 1929.

--- Bidrag til Angmagssalik-Eskimoernes for-historie.
  GT, XXXV, 129-36. 1932.

--- The Eskimo Archeology of Greenland. ARSI,
  1936, 397-404.

--- Eskimo Migrations in Greenland. GR, XXV, 408-
  22. 1935.

--- The Former Eskimo Settlements on Frederik VI's
  Coast. MG, CIX, ii, 1-55. 1936.

--- The Prehistory of the Angmagssalik Eskimos. MG,
  XCII, 1-158. 1933.

--- The Sermermiut Excavations 1955. MG, CLXI,
  iii. 1958.

Meldgaard, J. Grønlaendere i tre tusinde Aar. Grønland, 1958, iv-v, 121-9, 170-8. 1958. København.

Mikkelsen, R. The Eskimo of East Greenland, Man,
  XXXVIII, 188-9. 1938.

--- The Eskimo of East Greenland. Scottish Geographical Magazine, LXIV, i, 16-24. 1948.

--- The Eskimos of East Greenland. CGJ, XLIII, 88-
  98. 1951.

--- Øst-Grønland. Grønlands Bogen, II, 251-68. 1950.

Mikkelsen, E., and Sueistrup, P.P. The East Greenlanders' Possibilities of Existence. MG, CXXXIV,
  ii, 1-244. 1944.

Mirsky, J. The Eskimo of Greenland. Cooperation
  and Competition among Primitive Peoples, ed. M.
  Mead, pp. 51-86. New York, 1937.

Murdoch, J. The East Greenlanders. AN, XXI, 133-
  8. 1887.

Nippgen, J. Le folklore des Eskimos. Revue d'Ethnographie et des Traditions Populaires, IV, 189-92.
  1923.

--- Les pretres payens du Groenland oriental. L'Ethnographie, n.s., III, 55-65. 1914.

Normann, C. En rejse langs Grønlands ostkyst i aaret
  1777. GT, II, 49-63. 1878.

Ostermann, H. Knud Rasmussen's Posthumous Notes
  on the Life and Doings of the East Greenlanders.
  MG, CIX, i, 1-212. 1938.

Paterson, T.T. Anthropogeographical Studies in
  Greenland. JAI, LXIX, 45-76. 1939.

Pedersen, A. Der Scoresbysund. 156 pp. Berlin, 1930.

Pedersen, P.O. Investigations into Dental Conditions
  of about 3,000 Ancient and Modern Greenlanders.
  Dental Record, LVIII, 191-8. 1938.

Pedersen, P.O. Anatomical Studies of the East
  Greenland Eskimo Dentition. ICA, XXIX, iii, 46-
  9. 1951.

--- The East Greenland Eskimo Dentition. MG, CXLII,
  iii, 1-244. 1949.

Pedersen, P.O., and Hinsch, E. Numerical Variations in Greenland Eskimo Dentition. Acta Odontologica Scandinavica, I, 93-134. 1939.

Peters, H. Anthropologie und Ethnographie. Wissenschaftliche Ergebnisse der Deutschen Grönland-Expedition Alfred Wegener, VI, 1-172. 1934.

Poulsen, K. Contributions to the Anthropology and
  Nosology of the East Greenlanders. MG, XXVIII,
  131-50. 1909.

Rasmussen, K. Eskimo Folk-Tales, ed. W. Worster.
  156 pp. London, 1921.

--- Myter og sagn fra Grønland, I, 1-382. Kjøbenhavn,
  1921.

--- South East Greenland. GT, XXXV, 169-97. 1932.

Richter, S. A Contribution to the Archaeology of
  North-East Greenland. Skrifter om Svalbard og
  Ishavet, LXIII, 1-149. Oslo, 1934.

Rink, H. Bemaerkninger til G. Holms samling of
  sagn og fortaellinger fra Angmagsalik. MG, X,
  335-45. 1887.

--- The East Greenland Dialect. MG, XXXIX, 203-
  23. 1911.

--- Notes to G. Holm's Collection of Legends and
  Tales from Angmagsalik. MG, XXXIX, 307-17.
  1912.

--- Østgrønlaenderne i deres forhold til Vestgrøn-
  laenderne og de ørrige Eskimostammer. GT, VIII,
  139-45. 1886.

--- Die Ostgrönlander. Deutsche Geographische
  Blätter, IX, iii, 228-39. 1886.

--- Den østgrønlandske dialekt. MG, X, 207-34. 1887.

Roberts, B. The Cambridge Expedition to Scoresby
  Sound. GJ, LXXXV, 234-51. 1935.

Roch, A. and Piderman, G. Quer durchs "Schweizer-
  land." 251 pp. Zürich, 1941.

Rosing, C. Østgrønlaendere (Tunuamiut). Det Grønlandske Selskabs Skrifter, XV. 1945.

Rosing, J. Den Østgrønlandske "Maskekultur." Grønland, 1957, vii. København.

--- Renjakt i det Gamle Grønland. Polarboken, 1956,
  99-112. Oslo.

Ryder, C.H. Om den tidligere eskimoiske bebyggelse
  af Scoresby Sund. MG, XVII, 281-343. 1895.

Schell, O. Die Ostgrönlander. Globus, XCIV, 85-8.
  1908.

Schultz-Lorentzen, C.W. Eskimoernes indvandring i
  Gronland. MG, XXVI, 289-330. 1904.

Schultz-Lorentzen, C.W. Intellectual Culture of the Greenlanders. Greenland, II, 209-70. 1928.

Skeller, E. Anthropological and Ophthalmological Studies on the Angmagssalik Eskimos. MG, CVII, iv, 231 pp. 1954.

Solberg, O. Beiträge zur Vorgeschichte der Osteskimo. Videnskabs-Selskabets Skrifter, Historisk-Filosofisk Klasse, 1907, ii, 1-92.

Sollas, W.J. On Some Eskimos' Bone Implements from the East Coast of Greenland. JAI, IX, 329-36. 1880.

Stolpe, H. Über die Forschungsergebnisse der schwedischen Grönland-Expedition. ICA, XIV, 101-5. 1904.

Tchernia, M.P. Considérations d'anthropologie physiologique sur les Esquimaux. BSAP, ser. 9, III, 44-55. 1942.

Thalbitzer, W. Cultic Games and Festivals in Greenland. ICA, XXI, ii, 236-55. 1924.

--- Eskimoiske digte fra Östgrönland. Kjöbenhavn, 1920.

--- Eskimokulturen ved Angmagssalik. GT, XIX, 56-69. 1907.

--- Ethnological Description of the Amdrup Collection from East Greenland. MG, XXVIII, 329-542. 1909.

--- Grønlandske sagn om Eskimoernes fortid. Stockholm, 1913.

--- The Heathen Priests of East Greenland. ICA, XVI, 447-64. 1908.

--- Leyendes et chants esquimaux du Groenland. 188 pp. Paris, 1929.

--- Les magiciens esquimaux, leurs conceptions du monde, de l'ame et de la vie. JSAP, n.s., XXII, 73-106. 1930.

--- Hos östgrönlaenderne i Grönlands sydfjorde. Ymer, XXXVII, 1-35. 1917.

Thalbitzer, W., and Thuren, H. Dans i Grønland. Fästskrift till F.H. Feilberg, pp. 77-97. Stockholm, 1911.

--- Melodies from East Greenland. MG, XL, 47-112. 1914.

Thomsen, T. The Angmagsalik Eskimo. MG, LIII, 379-434. 1917.

--- Eskimo Archaeology. Greenland, II, 271-329. 1928.

--- Implements and Artefacts of the North-East Greenlanders. MG, XLIV, 357-492. 1917.

Thostrup, C.B. Ethnographic Description of the Eskimo Settlements and Stone Remains in North-East Greenland. MG, XLIV, 177-355. 1917.

Thuren, H. On the Eskimo Music of Greenland. MG, XL, 1-45. 1911.

Vibaek, P. Contributions to the Study of the Eskimo Language in Greenland. MG, XXXIII, 9-60. 1907.

Victor, P.E. Apoutsiak. 32 pp. Paris, 1948.

--- Le bilþoquet chez les Eskimo d'Angmagssalik. JSAP, n.x., XXX, 299-331. 1938.

--- Les jeux de ficelle chez les Eskimo d'Angmagssalik. JSAP, n.s., XXIX, 387-95. 1937.

--- My Eskimo Life. 349 pp. London, 1938.

Wyss-Dunant, E. Sur les Hauts Plateaux Groenlandais. 207 pp. Paris, 1939.

6. IGLULIK ESKIMO

Including the Aivilingmiut, the Iglulingmiut, and the Tununermiut.

Boas, F. The Eskimo of Baffin Land and Hudson Bay. BAMNH, XV, 1-570. 1901-07.

Mathiassen, T. Material Culture of the Iglulik Eskimos. RFTE, VI, i, 1-242. 1928.

Rasmussen, K. Intellectual Culture of the Iglulik Eskimos. RFTE, VII, i, 1-304. 1929.

Bentham, R. and Jenness, D. Eskimo Remains in S.E. Ellesmere Island. PTRSC, ser. 3, XXXV, ii, 41-55. 1941.

Birket-Smith, K. Anthropological Observations on the Central Eskimos. RFTE, III, ii, 1-123. 1940.

Brown, M. et al. Parasitic Infections in the Eskimos at Igloolik, N.W.T. Canadian Journal of Public Health, XLI. 508-12. 1950.

Carpenter, E.S. Changes in the Sedna Myth among the Aivilik. UAAP, III, ii, 69-73. 1955.

--- Eskimo Poetry. Explorations, IV, 101-11. 1955.

--- Eternal Life. Explorations, II, 59-65. 1954.

--- Ivory Carvings of the Hudson Bay Eskimo. CA, XV, 212-5. 1958.

--- Space Concepts of the Aivilik Eskimos. Explorations, V, 131-45. 1955.

--- The Timeless Present in the Mythology of the Aivilik Eskimos. An, III, 1-4. 1956.

--- Witch-Fear among the Aivilik Eskimos. American Journal of Psychiatry, CX, 194-9. 1953.

Carpenter, E.S. et al. Eskimo. Explorations, IX, 64 pp. 1959.

Comer, G. Notes on the Natives of the Northwestern Shores of Hudson Bay. AA, n.s., XXIII, 243-4. 1921.

Dall, W.H. On Some Peculiarities of the Eskimo Dialect. PAAAS, XIX, 332-49. 1870.

Gilder, W.H. Schwatka's Search. New York, 1881.

Godsell, P.H. The Trail of Tamowenuk. Alberta
Folklore Quarterly, I, 74-8. 1945.

Hague, E. Eskimo Songs. JAFL, XXVIII, 96-8. 1915.

Hall, C.F. Narrative of the Second Arctic Expedition.
Washington, 1879.

Harrington, R. Walrus at Igloolik. B, CCLXXXIV,
Dec., 28-34. 1953.

Harrington, R. and E. Weyer. Walrus Hunt. NH,
LXV, i, 28-32. 1956.

Klutschak, H.W. Als Eskimo unter den Eskimos.
Wien, 1881.

Lyon, G.F. The Private Journal of Captain G. F.
Lyon of H.M.S. Hecla. London, 1824.

Manning, T.H. Eskimo Stone Houses in Foxe Basin.
Arctic, III, 108-112. 1950.

--- Notes on the Coastal District of the Eastern Barren
Grounds and Melville Peninsula from Igloolik to
Cape Fullerton. CGJ, XXVI, 84-105. 1943.

Mary-Rousselière, G. Ainsi Parlait la "Reine"
d'Iglulik. Eskimo, XXXVII, 7-12. 1955.

--- Dans le Folklore des Arviligjuarmiut. Eskimo,
XLII, 10-12. 1956.

--- Les "tunit" d'après les traditions d'Iglulik. Eskimo,
XXXV, 14-20. 1955.

---Trois Légendes d'Iglulik. Eskimo, 18-25. December, 1955.

Mathiassen, T. Archaeology of the Central Eskimos.
RFTE, IV, i-ii. 533 pp. 1927.

--- Traek af Iglulik-Eskimoernes materielle kultur.
GT, XXX, 72-88. 1927.

Okomaluk, W. Trois Légendes d'Iglulik. Eskimo,
December 1955, 18-23. 1955.

Papion, R. Le Hibou des Neiges Eskimo, XXXVI, 16-
17. 1955.

Parry, W.E. Journal of a Second Voyage for the Discovery of a North West Passage, pp. 492-569. London, 1824.

Rabinowitch, I.M., and Smith, F.C. Metabolic
Studies of Eskimos in the Canadian Eastern Arctic.
Journal of Nutrition, XII, 337-56. 1936.

Rae, J. On the Esquimaux. TESL, n.s., IV, 138-53.
1866.

Rasmussen, K. Iglulik and Caribou Eskimo Texts.
RFTE, VII, iii, 1-160. 1930.

Robinson, J.L. Eskimo Population in the Canadian
Eastern Arctic. CGJ, XXIX, 128-42. 1944.

Robitaille, B. L'Agglomération Esquimaude de
Resolute, Ile de Cornwallis. Cahiers de Géographie
de Québec, II, 206-7. 1957.

Service, E.R. The Canadian Eskimo. PPC, 64-85.
1958.

Speck, F.G. Eskimo Collection from Baffin Land and
Ellesmere Land. IN, I, 143-9. 1924.

Sutton, G.M. Eskimo Year. New York, 1934.

Velde, F. Religion et Morale chez les Esquimaux de
Pelly Bay. Eskimo, XXXIX, 6-8, 14-16. 1956.

Waterman, T.T. Hudson Bay Eskimo, ed. R.H. Lowie.
APAM, IV, 299-307. 1910.

7. LABRADOR ESKIMO

Hawkes, M.W. The Labrador Eskimo. MCDM, XCI,
1-165. 1916.

Turner, L.M. Ethnology of the Ungava District,
ARBAE, XI, 159-267. 1894.

Anonymous. Suhinimiut. BBAE, XXX, ii, 647. 1910.

Anonymous. Supplementary Materials on Location,
Numbers and Socio-Economic Conditions of Indians
and Eskimos. ECAS, I, 103-16. 1955.

Anonymous. Tuberculosis Survey: James and Hudson
Bays. Arctic Circular, IV, 45-7. 1951.

Appleton, V.B. Observations on Deficiency Diseases
in Labrador. American Journal of Public Health, XI,
617-21. 1921.

Balikci, A. Two Attempts at Community Organization
among the Eastern Hudson Bay Eskimos. An, n.s.,
I, 122-35. 1959.

Biays, P. Conditions et Genres de Vie au Labrador
Septentrionale. 33 pp. Quebec, 1955.

Bird, J.B. Archaeology of the Hopedale Area, Labrador. APAM, XXXIX, 121-86. 1945.

Boas, F. The Eskimo of Baffin Land and Hudson Bay.
BAMNH, XV, 1-570. 1901-07.

--- Two Eskimo Riddles from Labrador. JAFL, XXXIX,
486. 1926.

Bourquin, T. Grammatik der Eskimo-Sprache. London, 1891.

British and Foreign Bible Society, ed. Testamentetokak
hiobib aglangit salomoblo imgerusersoanga tikkilugit.
274 pp. Stolpen, 1871.

--- Testamentitak tamaedsa nalegapta piulijipta
Jesusib Kristusib apostelingitalo piniaringit
ajokertusingillo. 282 pp. London, 1876.

Bruemmer, F. George Wetaltuk-Eskimo. CGJ, L,
157-9. 1955.

Bruet, E. Le Labrador et le Nouveau-Quebec. 346 pp.
Paris, 1949.

Burgesse, J.A. Esquimaux in the Saguenay. PM, XXII,
23-32. 1949.

Cadzow, D.A. Archeological Work with the Putnam
Baffin Island Expedition. IN, V, 98-106. 1928.

Campbell, B.D. Where the High Winds Blow. 230 pp.
New York, 1946.

Cartwright, G. A Journal of Transactions and Events during a Residence of nearly Sixteen Years on the Coast of Labrador. 3 vols. London, 1792.

Chown, B. and Lewis, M. The Blood Group Genes of the Eskimos of the Ungava District of Canada. AJPA, n.s., XIV, 215-24. 1956.

Cloutier, F. Réflexions Médicales à propos des Esquimaux de l'Ungava. Laval·Medical, XIV, 532-38. 1949.

Cotter, J.L. The Eskimos of Eastmain. B, December, 1929.

Curtis, H. Fragments sur les Eskimaux. NAV, 1838, iv, 329-39.

Davenport, C.B. The Dietaries of Primitive Peoples. AA, n.s., XLVII, 60-82. 1945.

Davies, W.H.A. Notes on Esquimaux Bay (Hamilton Inlet). TLHSQ, IV, 70. 1843.

--- Notes on Ungava Bay and Its Vicinity. TLHSQ, IV, 119-37. 1854.

Desgoffe, C. Contact Culturel: le Cas des Esquimaux des Iles Belcher. An, I, 45-71. 1955.

Duckworth, W.L.H., and Pain, B.H. An Account of some Eskimo from Labrador. Proceedings of the Cambridge Philosophical Society, X, 286-91. 1900.

--- A Contribution to Eskimo Craniology. JAI, XXX, 125-40. 1900.

Dunbar, M.J. The Caribou of Northeastern Ungava. Annual Report of the Province of Quebec Association for the Protection of Fish and Game, XCI, 10-14. 1950.

--- Common Cause in the North, International Journal, I, 358-64. 1946.

--- The Ungava Bay Problem. Arctic, V, 4-16. 1952.

Erdmann, F. Eskimoisches Wörterbuch. Budissin, 1864.

Findlay, M. The Eskimo Population. ECAS, I, 97-100.

Flaherty, R.J. My Eskimo Friends. London, 1924.

Gathorne-Hardy, G.M. A Recent Journey to Northern Labrador. GJ, LIX, 153-69. 1922.

Gosling, W.G. Labrador. London, 1910.

Grenfell, W.T. Labrador. New York, 1909.

--- Medicine in the Sub-Arctic. College of Physicians of Philadelphia, Transactions, LII, 73-95. 1930.

Hanzsch, B. Beiträge zur Kenntnis des nordöstlichen Labradors. Mitteilungen des Vereins für Erdkunde zu Dresden, I, ix, 245-320. 1909.

--- Eskimo Stone Graves in North-Eastern Labrador. CFN, XLIV, 180-2. 1930.

Harp, E. An Archaeological Survey in the Strait of Belle Isle Area. AAn, XVI, 203-20. 1951

Harrington, R. Journey in Arctic Quebec. CGJ, XLI, 90-104. 1950.

--- People of the Snows. B, CCLXXX, iv, 16-21. 1950.

Hawkes, E.W. The Labrador Eskimo. MCDM, XCI, 143-50. 1916.

Hoebel, E.A. Law-ways of the Primitive Eskimos. Journal of Criminal Law and Criminology, XXXI, 663-83. 1941.

Honigmann, I. and J.J. Child Rearing Patterns among the Great Whale River Eskimo. UAAP, II, 31-50. 1953.

Honigmann, J.J. An Episode in the Administration of the Great Whale River Eskimo. HO.X. ii. 5-14. 1951.

Honigmann, J.J. Intercultural Relations at Great Whale River. AA, LIV, 510-22. 1952.

Honigmann, J.J. and I. Notes on Great Whale River Ethos. An, n.s., I, 106-21. 1959.

Honigmann, J.J. and Carrera, R.N. Cross-cultural Use of Machover's Figure Drawing Test. AA, LIX, 650-54. 1957.

Houston, J.A. Eskimo Sculptors. B, CCLXXXII, i, 34-9. 1951.

Hutton, M.W. Among the Eskimos of Labrador. Philadelphia, 1912.

--- By Eskimo Dog-Sled and Kayak. 219 pp. London, 1919.

--- An Eskimo Village. London, 1929.

Kleinschmidt, S. Grammatik der grönlandischen Sprache. 182 pp. Berlin, 1851.

Klimek, S. Przyczynek do kranjologji Indjan Amerykanskich. Bulletin de la Société des Naturalistes "Kopernik," ser. A, Mémoires, LIII, 809-29. 1928.

Kohlmeister, B., and Kmoch, G. Journal of a Voyage from Okkak on the Coast of Labrador to Ungava Bay. 83 pp. London, 1814.

König, H. Die Eskimo-Mundarten von Nord- und Nordost-Labrador. A, XXXII, 595-632. 1937.

Laguna, F. de. The Prehistory of Northern North America as seen from the Yukon. MSAA, III, 1-360. 1947.

La Trobe, C.I. Narrative of the Remarkable Preservation Experienced by the Brn. Samuel Liebisch and W. Turner. MCM, I, 297-304. 1850.

Leechman, D. Eskimo Summer. 247 pp. Toronto, 1945.

--- A New Type of Adze Head. AA, n.s., XLV, 153-5. 1943.

--- Two New Cape Dorset Sites. AAn, VIII, 363-75. 1943.

Lefebvre, G.R. Remarques Phonologiques pour une Orthographie du Dialecte Eskimau de l'Est de la Baie d'Hudson. An, II, 39-60. 1956.

Leitch, A. Village with a Mission. CGJ, XL, 102-
13. 1950.

Leith, C.H., and A.T. A Summer and Winter in
Hudson Bay. Madison, 1912.

Le Mehauté, P.J., and Tcherniskofsky, P. L'alimenta-
tion des Esquimaux. Bulletin de la Société Scientifique d'Hygiène Alimentaire, XXII, 8. 1934.

Low, A.P. Report on Explorations in the Labrador
Peninsula. ARCGS, n.s., VIII, 1-387. 1896.

M'Keevor, T. A Voyage to Hudson's Bay, pp. 27-45.
London, 1819.

McLean, J. Notes of a Twenty-Five Years' Service
in the Hudson's Bay Territory, ed. W.S.Wallace.
PCS, XIX, 1-402. 1932.

MacMillan, M. Far North with "Captain Mac."
NGM, C, 465-513. 1951.

Manning, T.H. Eskimo Stone House Ruins on the East
Side of Hudson Bay. AAn, XIII, 250-1. 1948.

--- Ruins of Eskimo Stone Houses on the East Side of
Hudson Bay. AAn, XI, 201-2. 1946.

Manning, T.H. and E.W. The Preparation of Skins
and Clothing in the Eastern Canadian Arctic. Polar
Record, XXVIII, 156-69. 1944.

Markham, C.R., ed. The Voyages of William Baffin.
192 pp. London, 1881.

Michea, J.P. Exploration in Ungava Peninsula.
BNMC, CXVIII, 54-8. 1950.

Miller, E.C. Aksunai. CGJ, LI, 256-63. 1955.

Mills, C.A. Eskimo Sexual Functions. Science,
LXXXIX, 11-12. 1939.

Oetteking, B. Ein Beitrag zur Kräniologie der Eskimo.
Abhandlungen und Berichte des Kgl. Zoologischen
und Anthropologisch-Ethnographischen Museums zu
Dresden, XII, iii, 1-58. 1908.

Packard, A.S. The Esquimaux of Labrador. Indian
Miscellany, ed. W.W.Beach, pp. 65-73. Albany,
1877.

--- The Labrador Coast. New York, 1891.

--- Notes on the Labrador Eskimo. AN, XIX, 471-81,
553-60. 1885.

Payne, F.F. A Few Notes upon the Eskimo of Cape
Prince of Wales. PAAAS, XXXVIII, 358-60. 1890.

--- Eskimo of Hudson's Strait. PCI, ser. 3, VI, 213-
30. 1899.

Pittard, E. Contribution à l'étude anthropologique des
Esquimaux du Labrador et de la Baie d'Hudson. Bul-
letin de la Société Neuchateloise de Géographie,
XIII, 158-76. 1901.

Postel, A.W. Dolls of the Netcetu'mint. Ethnos, II,
338-9. 1937.

Quimby, G.I. The Manitunik Eskimo Culture of East
Hudson's Bay. AAn, VI, 148-65. 1940.

Radwanski, P. Anthropological Structure of 101 Eskimo. An, I, 72-83. 1955.

Ribbach, C.A. Labrador. Tijdschrift van het
Aardrijkskundig Genootschap, I, 281-90. 1876.

Robinson, J.L. Eskimo Population in the Canadian
Eastern Arctic. CGJ, XXIX, 128-42. 1944.

Rousseau, J.J. Attroverso il Quebec Artico. Le Vie
del Mondo, XIV, 143-54. 1952.

--- Le Caribou et Le Renne dans la Québec Arctique
et Hémiarctique. Revue Canadienne de Géographie,
IV, 60-89. 1950.

Rousseau, J.J. Le Nom du Caribou chez les Montagnais-
Naskapi et les Esquimaux de l'Ungava. An, I, 212-
14. 1955.

--- Les Voyages du Pere Albanel au Lac Mistassini et
à la Baie James. RHAF, III, 556-86. 1950.

Russell, F., and Huxley, H.M. A Comparative Study
of the Physical Structure of the Labrador Eskimos and
the New England Indians. PAAAS, XLVIII, 365-79.
1899.

Schenk, A. Note sur deux cranes d'Esquimaux du
Labrador. Bulletin de la Société Neuchateloise de
Géographie, XI, 166-75. 1899.

Service, E.R. The Canadian Eskimo. PPC, 64-85.
1958.

Sewall, K.W. Blood, Taste, Digital Hair and Color
of Eyes in Eastern Eskimo. AJPA, XXV, 93-9. 1939.

Silvy, A. Relation par lettres de l'Amérique septentrionale, ed. C. de Rochemonteix, pp. 42-60. Paris,
1904.

Smith, H.I. Notes on Eskimo Traditions. JAFL, VII,
209-16. 1894.

Speck, F.G. Analysis of Eskimo and Indian Skin-
dressing Methods in Labrador. Ethnos, II, 345-53.
1937.

--- Collections from Labrador Eskimo. IN, I, 211-17.
1924.

--- Eskimo and Indian Backgrounds in Southern Labrador. GM, XXXVIII, 1-17, 143-63. 1935-36.

--- Eskimo Carved Ivories from Northern Labrador. IN,
IV, 309-14. 1927.

--- Eskimo Jacket Ornaments of Ivory. AAn, V, 225-
8. 1940.

--- Indian and Eskimo Backgrounds in Southern Labrador. GM, XXXVIII, 1-17, 143-63. 1935.

--- Inland Eskimo Bands of Labrador. Essays in Anthropology presented to A.L.Kroeber, pp. 313-30.
Berkeley, 1936.

--- Labrador Eskimo Mask and Clown. GM, XXXVII,
159-73. 1935.

--- Montagnais-Naskapi Bands and Early Eskimo Distribution in the Labrador Peninsula. AA, n.s.,
XXXIII, 557-600. 1931.

Stefansson, V. Eskimos. Encyclopaedia Britannica, 14th ed. VIII, 708-10. 1929.

Steinert, W. Die Wirkung des Landschaftzwanges auf die materielle Kultur des Eskimos. 58 pp. Hamburg, 1935.

Stewart, T.D. Anthropometric Observations on the Eskimos and Indians of Labrador. FMAS, XXXI, 1-163. 1939.

--- Change in Physical Type of the Eskimos of Labrador since the Eighteenth Century. AJPA, XXIII, 493-4. 1937.

Stewart, T.D. New Measurements on the Eskimos and Indians of Labrador. AJPA, XXI, 10. 1935.

Stupart, R.F. The Eskimo of Stupart Bay. PCI, ser. 3, IV, 95-114. 1887.

Suk, V. Congenital Pigment Spots in Eskimo Children. Anthropologie (Prague), VI, 1-34. 1928.

--- On the Occurrence of Syphilis and Tuberculosis amongst Eskimos and Mixed Breeds of the North Coast of Labrador. Publications de la Faculté des Sciences de l'Université Masaryk, LXXXIV, 1-18. 1927.

Tanner, V. Folk och kulturer pa Labrador. ASSF, XVII, Pt. ii. 1939.

--- Outline of the Geography, Life and Customs of Newfoundland-Labrador. Acta Geographica, VIII, i, pt. 2, 1-470. 1944.

--- Ruinerna pa Sculpin Island (Kanayoktok) i Nain's Skärgard. GT, XLIV, 129-55. 1941.

Turner, L.M. On the Indians and Eskimos of the Ungava District. PTRSC, V, ii, 99-119. 1887.

Turquetil, A. Notes sur les Esquimaux de Baie Hudson. A, XXI, 491-534. 1926.

Uhlenbeck, R.L. Eskimo Children. B, CCLXXI, 18-19. 1940.

Virchow, R. Eskimos von Labrador. VBGA, 1880, 253-74.

Waldmann, S. Les Esquimaux du nord du Labrador. Bulletin de la Société Neuchateloise de Géographie, XX, 430-41. 1910.

Wallace, D. The Long Labrador Trail. New York, 1907.

Washburne, H.C., and Anauta. Land of the Good Shadows. 329 pp. New York, 1940.

Waugh, L.M. Influences of Diet on the Development of the Jaws and Face of the American Eskimo. Journal of Dental Research, XIII, 149-51. 1933.

--- Nutrition and Health of the Labrador Eskimo, with Special Reference to the Mouth and Teeth. Journal of Dental Research, VIII, 428-9. 1928.

--- A Study of the Influences of Diet and of Racial Admixture on the Development of the Jaw and Face of the American Eskimo. Journal of Dental Research, XII, 426-9. 1932.

Wheeler, E.P. Journeys about Nain. GR, XX, 454-68. 1930.

--- List of Labrador Eskimo Place Names. BNMC, CXXXI, 109 pp. 1953.

Wintemberg, W.J. Eskimo Sites of the Dorset Culture in Newfoundland. AAn, V, 83-102, 309-33. 1939-40.

8. MACKENZIE ESKIMO

Ostermann, H., ed. The MacKenzie Eskimos, after K. Rasmussen's Posthumous Notes. RFTE, X, ii, 1-166. 1942.

Petitot, E.F.S. Monographie des Esquimaux Tchiglit du Mackenzie et de l'Anderson. Paris, 1876.

Boas, F. A. J. Stone's Measurements of Natives of the Northwest Territories. BAMNH, XIV, 53-68. 1901.

Bompas, W.C. Diocese of Mackenzie River. 108 pp. London, 1888.

Cameron, A.D. The New North. New York, 1910.

Cameron, J. Osteology of the Western and Central Eskimos. RCAE, XIII, C, 1-79. 1923.

Franklin, J. Narrative of a Second Expedition to the Shores of the Polar Sea. London, 1828.

Gates, R.R. Blood Groups of Canadian Indians and Eskimos. AJPA, XII, 475-85. 1929.

Godsell, P.H. Is There Time to Save the Eskimo? NH, LXI, 56-62. 1952.

Hourde, R.N. Sophisticated Eskimos. B, CCLXXXIII, 36-7. 1952.

Jenness, D. Comparative Vocabulary of the Western Eskimo Dialects. RCAE, XV, A, 1-134. 1928.

--- Eskimo String Figures. RCAE, XIII, B, 1-192. 1924.

--- Myths and Traditions from Northern Alaska, the Mackenzie Delta and Coronation Gulf. RCAE, XIII, A, 1-90. 1924.

McClure, R.J.L. The Discovery of the North-West Passage, ed. S.Osborn. London, 1856.

Mackenzie, A. Voyages from Montreal through the Continent of North America to the Frozen and Pacific Oceans. London, 1801.

Marsh, D.B. White Whales in the Arctic. CGJ, XLI, 34-40. 1950.

Mathiassen, T. Archaeological Collections from the Western Eskimos. RFTE, X, 1-98. 1930.

Nash, D.W. Arctic Farmer. Country Guide, LXVIII, 13, 34-5. 1949.

Osborne, D. Late Eskimo Archaeology in the Western Mackenzie Delta Area. AAn, XVIII, 30-9. 1952.

Petitot, E.F.S. Die Eskimos am Mackenzie und An-
    derson. Globus, XXXI, 103-5. 1877.
--- Les grands Esquimaux. Paris, 1887.
--- Quinze ans sous le cercle polaire, ii. Paris, 1889.
--- Traditions indiennes du Canada nord-ouest. Paris,
    1886.
--- Vocabulaire français-esquimaux. Paris, 1876.
Richardson, J. Arctic Searching Expedition. 2 vols.
    London, 1851.
Russell, F. Explorations in the Far North. Iowa City,
    1898.
Seltzer, C.C. The Anthropometry of the Western and
    Copper Eskimos. HB, V, 313-70. 1933.
Service, E.R. The Canadian Eskimo. PPC, 64-85.
    1958.
Simpson, T. Narrative of the Discoveries on the North
    Coast of America. 419 pp. London, 1843.
Stefansson, V. The Friendly Arctic. New York, 1921.
--- Hunters of the Great North. New York, 1922.
--- My Life with the Eskimo. New York, 1913.
--- Notes on the Theory and Treatment of Disease
    among the Mackenzie River Eskimo. JAFL, XXI,
    43-5. 1908.
--- Religious Beliefs of the Eskimo. HMM, CXXVII,
    869-78. 1913.
--- The Stefansson-Anderson Arctic Expedition.
    APAM, XIV, 1-395. 1914.
Taylor, P. Tales from the Delta. B, CCLXXXIV,
    June, 22-25. 1953.
Urquhart, J.A. Eskimos of the Canadian Western
    Arctic. The New North-West, ed. C.A.Dawson,
    pp. 271-82. 1947.
--- The Most Northerly Practice in Canada. Canadian
    Medical Association Journal, XXXIII, 193-6. 1935.

9. NETSILIK ESKIMO

Rasmussen, K. The Netsilik Eskimos. RFTE, VIII,
    1-542. 1931.

Amundsen, R. Nordvestpassagen. Christiania, 1908.
--- The North West Passage. 2 vols. London, 1908.
Birket-Smith, K. Anthropological Observations on the
    Central Eskimos. RFTE, III, ii, 1-123. 1940.
Boas, F. Über die Wohnsitze der Neitchillik Eskimos.
    ZGE, XVIII, 222-33. 1883.
Gilder, W.H. Schwatka's Search. New York, 1881.
Hall, C.F. Narrative of the Second Arctic Expedition.
    Washington, 1879.
Hanbury, D.T. Sport and Travel in the Northland of
    Canada. London, 1904.
Harrington, R. The Cheerful Eskimo. B, CCLXXXII,
    iv, 7-15. 1952.

--- Spring Break-up at Boothia. CGJ, XLVI, 150-62.
    1953.
Klutschak, H.W. Als Eskimo unter den Eskimos.
    Wien, 1881.
Learmonth, L.A. Interrupted Journey. B, CCLXXXII,
    ii, 20-25. 1951.
Petersen, C. Den sidste Franklin ekspedition. Kjøben-
    havn, 1860.
Poncins, G. de. Kabloona. 339 pp. New York, 1941.
Rae, J. Narrative of an Expedition to the Shores of the
    Arctic Sea. London, 1850.
Ross, J. Narrative of a Second Voyage in Search of a
    North-West Passage. London, 1835.
Schwatka, F. The Implements of the Igloo. Science,
    IV, 81-5. 1884.
--- The Netschilluk Innuits. Science, IV, 543-5. 1884.
Service, E.R. The Canadian Eskimo. PPC, 64-85.
    1958.
Urquhart, J.A. Eskimos of the Canadian Western Arc-
    tic. The New North-West, ed. C.A.Dawson, pp.
    271-82. 1947.

10. NORTH ALASKA ESKIMO

Murdoch, J. Ethnological Results of the Point Barrow
    Expedition. ARBAE, IX, 3-441. 1892.
Spencer, R.F. The North Alaska Eskimo. BBAE,
    CLXXI, 496 pp. 1959.

Anderson, H.D., and Eells, W.C. Alaska Natives.
    472 pp. Stanford, 1935.
Andrews, C.L. The Eskimo and His Reindeer in Alas-
    ka. 253 pp. Caldwell, 1939.
Boas, F. Property Marks of the Alaskan Eskimo. AA,
    n.s., I, 601-13. 1899.
Brevig, T.L. Apauruk in Alaska. 325 pp. Philadel-
    phia, 1944.
Burg, A. North Star Cruises Alaska's Wild West. NGM,
    CII, 57-86. 1952.
Cameron, J. Osteology of the Western and Central
    Eskimos. RCAE, XII, C, 1-79. 1923.
Collins, H.B. Archeological Investigations at Point
    Barrow. EFWSI, 1932, 45-8. 1933.
--- Caries and Crowding in the Teeth of the Living
    Alaska Eskimo. AJPA, XVI, 451-63. 1932.
Corcoran, P.A. et al. Blood Groups of Alaskan Eski-
    mos and Indians. AJPA, n.s., XVII, 187-94. 1959.
Cumming, J.R. Metaphysical Implications of the
    Folktales of the Eskimos of Alaska. UAAP, III, i,
    37-63. 1954.
Cummins, H. Dermatoglyphics in Eskimos from Point
    Barrow. AJPA, XX, 13-18. 1935.

Dale, G.A. Northwest Alaska and the Bering Sea Coast. I.T. Sanders, ed., Societies Around the World, I, 111-130. 1952.

Ford, J.A. Eskimo Burial Customs. EP, XXXIII, 198-9. 1932.

Giddings, J.L. The Arctic Woodland Culture of the Kobuk River. 154 pp. Philadelphia, 1952.

--- Dated Eskimo Ruins of an Inland Zone. AAn, X, 113-34. 1944.

--- Ethnographic Notes. Kobuk River Region. K, VI, 25-8. 1941.

--- Forest Eskimos. UPMB, XX, ii, 55 pp. 1956.

Gillham, C.E. Beyond the Clapping Mountains. 134 pp. New York, 1943.

Godsell, P.H. The Eskimo goes Modern, NH, XLV, 38-39, 56. 1940.

Hammerich, L.L. Russian Loan-Words in Alaska. ICA, XXX, 114-26. 1955.

--- The Russian Stratum in Alaskan Eskimo. Slavic Word, X, 401-28. 1954.

--- The Western Eskimo Dialects. ICA, XXXII, 632-9. 1958.

Harrington, M.R. The Huntley Eskimo Collection. M, XXIII, 165-73. 1949.

Hawkes, E.W. Skeletal Measurements and Observations of the Point Barrow Eskimo. AA, n.s., XVIII, 203-44. 1916.

Heller, C.A. The Alaskan Eskimo and the White Man's Diet. Journal of Home Economics, XLIV, 177-8. 1949.

Helmericks, C. and M. Our Summer with the Eskimos. 255 pp. London, 1952.

Holland, D. The Trophy is Still There. Elks Magazine, XXXI, vii, 6-7, 39-42. 1952.

Hooper, W.H. Ten Months among the Tents of the Tuski. London, 1853.

Hrdlicka, A. Anthropological Survey of Alaska. ARBAE, XLVI, 19-374. 1930.

--- Anthropological Work in Alaska. SMC, vii, 137-58. 1927.

--- Ritual Ablation of Front Teeth in Siberia and America. SMC, XCIX, iii, 1-32. 1940.

Ingstad, H. Nunamiut. 254 pp. London, 1954.

Irving, L. The Naming of Birds by Nunamiut Eskimo. Arctic, VI, 35-43. 1953.

--- On the Naming of Birds by Eskimos. UAAP, VI, 61-78. 1958.

Irving, W. Archaeology in the Brooks Range of Alaska. AAn, XVII, 52-53. 1951.

Jenness, D. Comparative Vocabulary of the Western Eskimo Dialects. RCAE, XV, A, 1-134. 1928.

--- Dawn in Arctic Alaska. 222 pp. Minneapolis, 1957.

Jenness, D. Eskimo Music in Northern Alaska. Musical Quarterly, VIII, 377-83. 1922.

--- Eskimo String Figures. RCAE, XIII, B, 1-192. 1924.

--- The Eskimos of Northern Alaska. GR, V, 89-101. 1918.

--- Myths and Traditions from Northern Alaska. RCAE, XIII, A, 1-91. 1924.

--- Stray Notes on the Eskimo of Arctic Alaska. UAAP, I, ii, 5-13. 1953.

Laguna, F. de. The Prehistory of Northern North America as seen from the Yukon. MSAA, III, 1-360. 1947.

Lantis, M. Alaskan Eskimo Ceremonialism. MAES, XI, 1-127. 1947.

Larsen, H. Archaeological Investigations in Alaska Since 1939. Polar Record, VI, 593-607. 1953.

--- The Ipiutak Culture. ICA, XXIX, iii, 22-34. 1951.

--- The Ipiutak Culture and its Position within the Eskimo Culture. ICA, XXVIII, 419-21. 1948.

--- Ipiutak Kulturen. Fra Nationalmuseets Arbejdsmark, 1948, 5-20. København.

--- The Material Culture of the Nunamiut. ICA, XXXII, 574-82. 1958.

--- The Position of Ipiutak in Eskimo Culture. AAn, XX, 74-9. 1954.

Larsen, H., and Rainey, F. Ipiutak and the Arctic Whale Hunting Culture. APAM, XLII, 1-276. 1948.

Laughlin, W.S. Blood Groups of the Anaktuvuk Eskimos, Alaska. UAAP, VI, 5-16. 1957.

--- Blood Groups of the Anaqtuavik Eskimos, Alaska. ICA, XXXII, 594. 1958.

Levine, V.E. Ascorbic Acid Content of the Blood of the Eskimo. Journal of Biological Chemistry, CXXXIII, lxi. 1940.

--- The Basal Metabolic Rate of the Eskimo. Journal of Biological Chemistry, CXXVIII, lix. 1939.

Levine, V.E. and Jorgensen, M.N. Urinary Chlorides and Blood Chlorides in the Eskimo. Journal of Biological Chemistry, CXL, lxxvii-lxxviii. 1941.

MacCurdy, G.G. An Example of Eskimo Art. AA, n.s., XXIII, 384-5. 1921.

Mason, J.A. Eskimo Pictorial Art. MJ, XVIII, 248-83. 1927.

--- Excavations of Eskimo Thule Sites at Point Barrow. ICA, XXIII, 383-94. 1930.

Mathiassen, T. Archaeological Collections from the Western Eskimos. RFTE, X, 1-98. 1930.

--- Notes on Knud Rasmussen's Archaeological Collections. ICA, XIII, 395-9. 1928.

Morden, I. We Liked the Eskimos. Alaska Sportsman, XVII, vii, 18-23, 35-36. 1951.

Morris, I.G. Arctic Trap Line. Alaska Sportsman, XVI, xii, 6-9, 25-26. 1950.

Murdoch, J. The Animals known to the Eskimos of Northwestern Alaska. AN, XXXII, 719-34. 1898.

Murdoch, J. Dress and Physique of the Point-Barrow Eskimos. PSM, XXXVIII, 222-9. 1890-91.

--- A Few Legendary Fragments from Point Barrow Eskimos. AN, XX, 593-9. 1886.

--- Fish and Fishing at Point Barrow, Arctic Alaska. American Fisheries Society, Transactions, XIII, 111-15. 1884.

--- Notes on the Counting and Measuring among the Eskimo of Point Barrow. AA, III, 37-43. 1890.

--- Notes on the Names of the Heavenly Bodies and the Points of the Compass among the Point Barrow Eskimo. AA, III, 136. 1890.

--- The Retrieving Harpoon. AN, XIX, 423-5. 1885.

--- Seal Catching at Point Barrow. SMC, XXXIV, ii, 102-8. 1893.

Ostermann, H. The Alaskan Eskimos. RFTE, X, iii, 291 pp. 1952.

Paul, J.R. et al. Antibodies to Three Different Antigenic Types of Poliomyelitis Virus in Sera from North Alaskan Eskimos. American Journal of Hygiene, LIV, 275-85. 1951.

--- Serological Epidemiology. Journal of Immunology, LXVI, 695-713. 1951.

Paul, J.R. and Riordan, J.T. Observations on Serological Epidemiology. American Journal of Hygiene, LII, 202-12. 1950.

Rainey, F.G. Culture Changes on the Arctic Coast. TNYAS, n.s., III. 122-6. 1941.

--- Eskimo Prehistory. APAM, XXXVII, 453-569. 1941.

--- The Ipiutak Culture at Point Hope Alaska. AA, n.s., XLIII, 364-75. 1941.

--- Mystery People of the Arctic. NH, XLVII, 148-55, 170-1. 1941.

--- Native Economy and Survival in Alaska. HO, i, 9-14. 1941.

--- A New Form of Culture on the Arctic Coast. PNAS, XXVII, 141-4. 1941.

--- The Whale Hunters of Tigara. APAM, XLI, 231-83. 1947.

Rausch, R.L. Notes on the Nunamuit Eskimo. Arctic, IV, 147-95. 1951.

Ray, P.H. Ethnographic Sketch of the Natives of Point Barrow. Report of the International Polar Expedition to Point Barrow, pp. 35-87. Washington, 1885.

Roberts, P.W. Employment of Eskimos by the Navy at Point Barrow, Alaska. ASC, III, 40-3. 1954.

Seltzer, C.C. The Anthropometry of the Western and Copper Eskimos. HB, V, 313-70. 1933.

Simpson, J. Observations on the Western Eskimo and the Country they inhabit. Arctic Geography and Ethnology, pp. 233-75. London, 1875.

Simpson, T. Narrative of the Discoveries on the North Coast of America. 419 pp. London, 1843.

Smith, M. Superstitions of the Eskimo. The White World, ed. R. Kersting, pp. 113-30. New York, 1902.

Solecki, R.S. Archeology and Ecology of the Arctic Slope of Alaska. ARSI, 1950, 469-95. 1951.

--- New Data on the Inland Eskimo of Northern Alaska. JWAS, XL, 137-57. 1950.

Spencer, M. The Child in the Contemporary Culture of the Barrow Eskimo. ASC, III, 130-2. 1954.

--- Forms of Cooperation in the Culture of the Barrow Eskimo. ASC, III, 128-30. 1954.

--- The Hunted and the Hunters. Pacific Discovery, VI, 22-7. 1953.

Spencer, R.F. and Carter, W.K. The Blind Man and the Loon. JAFL, LXVII, 65-72. 1954.

Stefansson, V.F. Eskimo Longevity in Northern Alaska. Science, CXXVII, 16-19. 1958.

--- My Life with the Eskimo. New York, 1913.

Stockton, C.H. The Arctic Cruise of the U.S.S. Thetis. NGM, II, 171-98. 1890.

Thompson, D.T. Two Eskimo Geographers. Journal of Geography, L, 342-47. 1951.

Totter, J.R. and Shukers, C.F. Nutrition Surveys of Eskimos. Alaska's Health, VI, x, 4-6. 1948.

Van Stone, J.W. An Eskimo Community and the Outside World. UAAP, VII, i, 27-38. 1958.

Walker, E.F. An Eskimo Harpoon-Thrower. M, XX, 193-4. 1946.

Watkins, J.A. The Alaskan Eskimo. American Journal of Public Health, IV, 643-48. 1914.

Waugh, L.M. A Study of the Nutrition and Teeth of the Eskimo of North Bering Sea and Arctic Alaska. Journal of Dental Research, X, 387-93. 1930.

Wells, R., and Kelly, J.W. English-Eskimo and Eskimo-English Vocabularies. Bureau of Education, Circular of Information, II, 1-72. Washington, 1890.

Wiggins, I.L. North of Anaktuvuk. Pacific Discovery, VI, 8-15. 1953.

Wilber, C.G. and Levine, V.E. Fat Metabolism in Alaskan Eskimos. Experimental Medicine and Surgery, VIII, 422-25. 1950.

Wilson, G.S. Barrow Day School Nutrition Program. Alaska's Health, VII, v, 1-3. 1949.

Wissler, C. Harpoons and Darts in the Stefansson Collection. APAM, XIV, 397-443. 1916.

11. POLAR ESKIMO

Also called Arctic Highlanders, Cape York Eskimo, Itanese, and Smith Sound Eskimo.

Kroeber, A.L. The Eskimo of Smith Sound. BAMNH, XII, 265-327. 1899.

Rasmussen, K. Nye mennesker. Kjøbenhavn, 1905.

--- The People of the Polar North. London, 1908.

--- Under nordenvindens svøbe. 202 pp. Kjøbenhavn, 1906.

Steensby, H.P. Contributions to the Ethnology and Anthropogeography of the Polar Eskimos. MG, XXXIV, 253-405. 1910.

Anonymous. Greenland's Harley Street. Geographical Magazine, XII, 36-41. 1940.

Astrup, E. Blandt nordpolens naboer. Christiania, 1895.

--- With Peary near the Pole. London, 1898.

Bessels, E. Die amerikanische Nordpol-Expedition, pp. 350-73. Leipzig, 1879.

--- Einige Worte über die Innuit (Eskimo) des Smith-Sundes. AFA, VIII, 107-22. 1873.

--- The Northernmost Inhabitants of the Earth. AN, XVIII, 861-82. 1884.

Birket-Smith, K. Etnografiske problemer i Grønland. GT, XXV, 179-97. 1920.

--- The Greenland Bow. MG, LVI, i, 1-28. 1918.

--- The Greenlanders of the Present Day. Greenland, II, 1-207. 1928.

Bryant, H.G. Notes on the most Northern Eskimos. Report of the Sixth International Geographical Congress, pp. 677-83. 1895.

Ekblaw, W.E. Distribution of Settlement among the Polar Eskimo. BMAS, VIII, 39-44. 1947.

--- Eskimo Dogs. NH, XXXVII, 173-84. 1936.

--- The Food Birds of the Smith Sound Eskimos. Wilson Bulletin, XXXI, 1-5. 1919.

--- The Material Response of the Polar Eskimo to Their Far Arctic Environment. AAAG, XVII, 147-98; XVIII, 1-24. 1927-28.

--- Significance of Movement among the Polar Eskimo. BMAS, X, 1-4. 1948.

Frederiksen, S. Stylistic Forms in Greenland Eskimo Literature. 40 pp. Copenhagen, 1954.

Freuchen, P. Arctic Adventure. 467 pp. New York, 1935.

--- Ivalu, the Eskimo Wife. 332 pp. New York, 1935.

--- Om plantekost hos Smith-Sund Eskimoerne. GT, XXIV, 306-10. 1918.

Fürst, C.M., and Hansen, F.C.C. Crania groenlandica. 234 pp. Copenhagen, 1915.

Haig-Thomas, D. Tracks in the Snow. 292 pp. London, 1939.

Hansen, P.M. Jagt og Fiskeri. Grønlands Bogen, II, 59-82. 1950.

Hayes, I.I. The Open Polar Sea. New York, 1867.

Heinbecker, P., and Pauli, R.H. Blood Grouping of the Polar Eskimo. Journal of Immunology, XIII, 279-83. 1927.

Holtved, E. Archaeological Investigations in the Thule District, III. Nugdlit and Comer's Midden. MG, CXLVI, iii. 1954.

--- Foreløbig beretning om den arkaeologisk-etnografiske expedition til Thule Distriktet. GT, XLI, 1-24. 1938.

--- Har Nordboerne Vaeret i Thule Distriktet? Fra Nationalmuseets Arbejdsmark 1945, 79-84. København.

--- Nugdlit, en Forhistorisk Boplads i Thule Distriktet. Grønland, 1954, iii, 89-94. København.

--- The Polar Eskimos: Language and Folklore. 2 vol. MG, CLII, i-ii, 520 pp. 1951.

--- Remarks on the Polar Eskimo Dialect. IJAL, XVIII, 20-24. 1952.

--- Thule District. Grønlands Bogen, II, 269-90. 1950.

Hovey, E.O. Child-Life among the Smith Sound Eskimo. AMJ, XVIII, 361-71. 1918.

Hrdlicka, A. Contribution to the Anthropology of Central and Smith Sound Eskimo. APAM, V, 177-280. 1910.

--- An Eskimo Brain. AA, n.s., III, 454-500. 1901.

Jørgensen, J.B. The Eskimo Skeleton. MG, CXLVI, ii, 154 pp. 1953.

Kane, E.K. Arctic Explorations. 2 vols. Philadelphia, 1856.

Knuth, E. Archaeology in the Farthest North. ICA, XXXII, 561-73. 1958.

--- Danmark Fjord. Fra Nationalmuseets Arbejdsmark, 1956, 71-8. København.

--- Det Mystiske X i Danmark Fjord. Naturens Verden. København, Feb. and Marts, 1958.

--- An Outline of the Archaeology of Peary Land. Arctic, V, 17-33. 1952.

--- The Paleo-Eskimo Cultures of Northeast Greenland. AAn, XIX, 367-81. 1954.

--- Pearyland-Eskimoerne. Fra Nationalmuseets Arbejdsmark 1948, 29-36. København.

Koch, L. Ethnographical Observations from the Southern Coast of Washington Land. AA, n.s., XXIV, 484-7. 1922.

Kroeber, A.L. Tales of the Smith Sound Eskimo. JAFL, XII, 166-82. 1899.

Laughlin, W.S. and Jørgenson, J.B. Isolate Variation in Greenlandic Eskimo Crania. Acta Genetica et Statistica Medica, VI, 3-12. 1956.

Leden, C. Musik und Tänze der grönländischen Eskimos, ZE, XLIII, 260-70. 1911.

--- Über die Musik der Smith Sund Eskimos. MG, CLII, iii, 92 pp. 1952.

Lynge, H. Inegpait. 187 pp. Copenhagen, 1955.

MacMillan, D.B. Food Supply of the Smith Sound Eskimo. AMJ, XVIII, 161-92. 1918.

Malaurie, J. Amours et Jeux dans le Nuit Polaire. Marco Polo, VIII, 18-29. 1955.

--- Destin des Rois de Thulé. Bulletin de la Société Royale de Géographie d'Anvers, LXVIII, 6-13. 1956.

--- The Last Kings of Thule, 295 pp. New York, 1956.

--- Perspectives Offertes par l'Evolution Économique et Sociale des Eskimos de Thulé. Bulletin International des Sciences Sociales, VI, ·513-19. 1954.

Malaurie, J., et al. L'Isolat Esquimau de Thulé (Groenland). Po, VII, 675-92. 1952.

Markham, C.R. The Arctic Highlanders. TESL, n.s., IV, 125-37. 1866.

--- Papers on the Greenland Eskimos. Arctic Geography and Ethnology, pp. 163-229. London, 1875.

Mathiassen, T. Eskimo Migrations in Greenland. GR, XXV, 408-22. 1935.

--- Eskimo Relics from Washington Land and Hall Land. MG, LXXI, 183-216. 1928.

--- Eskimoernes Sammentraef med Nordboerne i Grønland. Grønland, 1953, 139-42. København.

Mathiassen, T. and Holtved, E. The Archaeology of the Thule District. GT, XLVII, 43-57. 1945.

Meldgaard, J. Grønlaendere i tre tusinde Aar. Grønland, 1958, iv-v, 121-9, 170-8. 1958. København.

Murdock, G.P. The Polar Eskimo. Our Primitive Contemporaries, pp. 192-218. New York, 1934.

Mylius-Erichsen, L., and Moltke, H. Grønland. Kjøbenhavn, 1906.

Nares, G.S. Narrative of a Voyage to the Polar Sea. 2 vols. London, 1878.

Osborn, S. Stray Leaves from an Arctic Journal. London, 1852.

Paterson, T.T. Anthropogeographical Studies in Greenland. JAI, LXIX, 45-76. 1939.

--- Eskimo "Cats' Cradles." Geographical Magazine, IX, 85-91. 1939.

Peary, J.D. My Arctic Journal. New York, 1893.

Peary, R.E. Nearest the Pole. New York, 1907.

--- Northward over the "Great Ice." 2 vols. New York, 1898.

Petersen, C. Erindringer fra polarlandene. Kjøbenhavn, 1857.

Powers, W.E. Polar Eskimos of Greenland and Their Environment. Journal of Geography, XLIX, 186-93. 1950.

Preuss, K.T. Die ethnographische Veränderung der Eskimo des Smith-Sundes. Ethnologisches Notizblatt, II, i, 38-43. 1899.

Rasmussen, K. Greenland by the Polar Sea. London, 1921.

--- Grønland langs Polhavet. Kjøbenhavn, 1919.

--- Myter og sagn fra Grønland, III, 1-340. Kjøbenhavn, 1925.

Ross, J. A Voyage of Discovery. London, 1819.

Schultz-Lorentzen, C.W. Eskimoernes invandring i Grønland. MG, XXVI, 289-330. 1904.

--- Intellectual Culture of the Greenlanders. Greenland, II, 209-70. 1928.

Skeller, E. Øjensgdomme i Grønland. Ugeskrift for Laeger, CXI, 529-32. 1949.

Spitzka, E.A. Three Eskimo Brains from Smith's Sound. American Journal of Anatomy, II, 25-71. 1902.

Stein, R. Eskimo Music. The White World, ed. R. Kersting, pp. 337-56. New York, 1902.

--- Geographische Nomenklatur bei den Eskimos des Smith-Sundes. PMJP, XLVIII, 195-201. 1902.

Thalbitzer, W. Nordboerne ved Uparnavik. Det Grønlandske Selskabs Aarsskrift, 1945, 28-37. København.

Thomsen, T. Eskimo Archaeology. Greenland, II, 271-329. 1928.

Vibe, C. The Marine Mammals and the Marine Fauna in the Thule District. MG, CL, vi, 115 pp. 1950.

Wells, J.R. The Origin of Immunity to Diphtheria in Central and Polar Eskimos. American Journal of Hygiene, XVIII, 629-73. 1933.

Wells, J.R. and Dixon, E. Hemophilus influenzae from the Throats of Polar Eskimos. Journal of Infectious Diseases, LI, 412-15. 1932.

Wells, J.R. and Heinbecker, P. Further Studies on Immunity to Diphtheria among Central and Polar Eskimos. Proceedings of the Society for Experimental Biology and Medicine, XXIX, 1028-30. 1932.

Whitaker, W.L. The Question of Season Sterility among the Eskimos. Science, LXXXVIII, 214-15. 1938.

Wissler, C. Archaeology of the Polar Eskimo. APAM, XXII, 105-66. 1918.

12. SOUTH ALASKA ESKIMO

Birket-Smith, K. The Chugach Eskimo. Nationalmuseets Skrifter, Etnografisk Raekke, VI, 270 pp.
Kϕbenhavn, 1953.

Anderson, H.D., and Eells, W.C. Alaska Natives.
472 pp. Stanford, 1935.

Bancroft, H.H. The Native Races of the Pacific
States, I, 37-94. New York, 1875.

Birket-Smith, K. Forelϕbig beretning om den Dansk-
Amerikanske Ekspedition til Alaska. GT, XXXVII,
187-227. 1934.

Burg, A. North Star Cruises Alaska's Wild West.
NGM, CII, 57-86. 1952.

Collins, H.B. Archaeology of the Bering Sea Region.
PPSC, V, iv, 2825-39. 1934.

Cook, J. A Voyage to the Pacific Ocean. 2d edit.
3 vols. London, 1785.

Coxe, W. Account of the Russian Discoveries between
Asia and America. 4th edit. London, 1804.

Cumming, J.R. Metaphysical Implications of the
Folktales of the Eskimos of Alaska. UAAP, III, i,
37-63. 1954.

Dall, W.H. Alaskan Mummies. AN, IX, 433-40.
1875.

--- The Native Tribes of Alaska. PAAAS, XXXIV,
363-79. 1885.

--- On the Distribution and Nomenclature of the Native Tribes of Alaska. CNAE, I, 7-40. 1877.

--- On the Distribution of the Native Tribes of Alaska.
PAAAS, XVIII, 263-73. 1869.

Disselhoff, H. Bemerkungen zu einigen Eskimo-
Masken. BA, XVIII, 130-7. 1935.

Eells, W.C. Mechanical, Physical, and Musical Ability of the Native Races of Alaska. JAP, XVII, 493-
506. 1933.

--- Mental Ability of the Native Races of Alaska.
JAP, XVII, 417-38. 1933.

Elliott, C.P. Salmon Fishing Grounds and Canneries.
Compilation of Narratives of Explorations in Alaska,
pp. 738-41. Washington, 1900.

Emmons, G.T. Jade in British Columbia and Alaska.
INM, XXXV, 11-53. 1923.

Erman, A. Ueber die Reise und Entdeckungen des
Lieutenant L. Sagoskin. AWKR, VI, 499-522, 613-
72; VII, 429-512. 1848-49.

Gibbs, G. Vocabulary of the Kaniag'mut. CNAE, I,
136-42. 1877.

Gillham, C.E. Beyond the Clapping Mountains, 134 pp.
New York, 1943.

Golder, F.A. Eskimo and Aleut Stories from Alaska.
JAFL, XXII, 10-24. 1909.

Golder, F.A. A Kodiak Island Story. JAFL, XX, 296-
9. 1907.

--- Tales from Kodiak Island. JAFL, XVI, 16-31, 85-
103. 1903.

Gordon, G.B. The Double Axe and Some Other Symbols. MJ, VII, 46-68. 1916.

Hammerich, L.L. Russian Loan-Words in Alaska. ICA,
XXX, 114-26. 1955.

--- The Russian Stratum in Alaskan Eskimo. Slavic
Word, X, 401-28. 1954.

--- The Western Eskimo Dialects. ICA, XXXII, 632-
9. 1958.

Heizer, R.F. Aconite Poison Whaling in Asia and
America. BBAE, CXXXIII, 415-68. 1943.

--- Incised Slate Figurines from Kodiak Island. AAn,
XVII, 266. 1952.

--- Notes on Koniag Material Culture. UAAP, I, 11-
19. 1952.

--- Petroglyphs from Southwestern Kodiak Island, Alaska. PAPS, XCI, 284-93. 1947.

--- Pottery from the Southern Eskimo Region. PAPS,
XCIII, 48-56. 1949.

--- The Sickle in Aboriginal Western North America.
AAn, XVI, 247-52. 1951.

Himmelheber, H. Eskimokünstler. 111 pp. Stuttgart, 1938.

Holmberg, H.J. Ethnographische Skizzen über die
Völker des russischen Amerika. ASSF, IV, 355-421.
1856.

Hrdlicka, A. Anthropological Explorations on Kodiak
Island. EFWSI, 1932, 41-4.

--- Anthropological Work in Alaska. EFWSI, 1931,
91-102.

--- The Anthropology of Kodiak Island. 486 pp.
Philadelphia, 1944.

--- Archeological Excavations on Kodiak Island.
EFWSI, 1934, 47-52.

--- Artifacts on Human and Seal Skulls from Kodiak
Island. AJPA, XXVIII, 411-21. 1941.

--- Catalogue of Human Crania in the United States
National Museum Collections. PUSNM, XCIV, 1-
172. 1944.

--- Diseases of and Artifacts on Skulls and Bones from
Kodiak Island. SMC, CI, iv, 1-14. 1941.

--- Ritual Ablation of Front Teeth in Siberia and
America. SMC, XCIX, iii, 1-32. 1940.

Jacobi, A. Carl Heinrich Mercks ethnographische
Beobachtungen über die Völker des Beringsmeers.
BA, XX, 113-37. 1937.

Laguna, F. de. The Archaeology of Cook Inlet.
Philadelphia, 1934.

Laguna, F. de. Chugach Prehistory. UWPA, XIII,
308 pp. 1956.

--- Peintures rupestres Eskimo. JSAP, n.s., XXV,
17-30. 1933.

--- A Pottery Vessel from Kodiak Island. AAn, IV,
334-43. 1939.

Langsdorff, G.H. von. Voyages and Travels in Various
Parts of the World. London, 1813.

Lantis, M. Alaskan Eskimo Ceremonialism. MAES,
XI, 1-127. 1947.

--- The Mythology of Kodiak Island. JAFL, LI, 123-
72. 1938.

Larsen, H. Archaeological Investigations in Alaska
Since 1939. Polar Record, VI, 593-607. 1953.

Lisiansky, U. A Voyage round the World, pp. 190-
215. London, 1814.

Mason, J.A. Eskimo Pictorial Art. MJ, XVIII, 248-
83. 1927.

--- A Remarkable Stone Lamp from Alaska. MJ, XIX,
170-94. 1928.

Petroff, I. The Limit of the Innuit Tribes on the
Alaskan Coast. AN, XVI, 567-75. 1882.

--- The Population and Resources of Alaska. Compilation of Narratives of Explorations in Alaska,
pp. 210-39. Washington, 1900.

--- Report on the Population, Industries and Resources
of Alaska. U. S. Department of the Interior, Tenth
Census, VIII, 124-46. 1881.

Pinart, A.L. Eskimaux et Koloches. RA, II, 673-80.
1873.

Portlock, N. A Voyage round the World. London,
1789.

Radloff, L. Ueber die Sprache der Ugalachmut. Bulletin de l'Académie Impériale des Sciences de St.
Pétersbourg, Classe Historico-philologique, XV, 26-
38, 48-63, 126-39. 1858.

Riddell, F. Climate and the Aboriginal Occupation of
the Pacific Coast of Alaska. PKAS, XI, 60-123.
1954.

Schott, W. Ueber ethnographische Ergebnisse der
Sagoskinschen Reise. AWKR, VII, 480-512. 1849.

Tarenetzky, A. Beiträge zur Skelet- und Schädelkunde
der Aleuten, Konaegen, Kenai und Koljuschen.
Mémoires de l'Académie Impériale des Sciences de
St. -Pétersbourg, ser. 8, Classe Physico-Mathématique, IX, iv, 1-73. 1900.

Totter, J.R. and Shukers, C.F. Nutrition Surveys of
Eskimos. Alaska's Health, VI, x, 4-6. 1948.

Veniáminov, I. Remarks on the Koloshian and Kadiak
Languages [in Russian]. 83 pp. St. Petersburg, 1846.

Woldt, A., ed. Capitain Jacobsen's Reise an der
Nordwestküste Amerikas. Leipzig, 1884.

Wrangell, F.P. Statistische und ethnographische
Nachrichten über die russischen Besitzungen an der
Nordwestküste von Amerika. BKRR, I, 1-332. 1839.

13. SOUTHAMPTON ESKIMO

Also called Sagdlirmiut.

Boas, F. The Eskimo of Baffin Land and Hudson Bay.
BAMNH, XV, 1-570. 1901-7.

Brown, M. Queen's University Expedition to Southampton Island, 1948. Arctic Circular, I, vii, 81-
82. 1948.

Comer, G. A Geographical Description of Southampton Island and Notes upon the Eskimo. RAGS, XLII,
84-90. 1910.

--- Notes on the Natives of the Northern Shores of Hudson Bay. AA, n.s., XXIII, 243-4. 1921.

Cooch, G. Techniques for Mass Capture of Flightless
Blue and Lesser Snow Geese. Journal of Wildlife
Management, XVII, 460-5. 1953.

Ferguson, R. Arctic Harpooner, ed. L.D. Stair. 216
pp. Philadelphia, 1938.

Hamelin, L.E. Genre de Vie à l'Ile de Southhampton
d'après le Journal d'un Esquimau. Cahiers de Géographie de Quebec, n.s., I, 49-54. 1956.

Hrdlicka, A. Contribution to the Anthropology of Central and Smith Sound Eskimo. APAM, V, 177-280.
1910.

Lyon, G.F. A Brief Narrative of an Unsuccessful Attempt to reach Repulse Bay. London, 1825.

Manning, T.H. Remarks on the Physiography, Eskimo, and Mammals of Southampton Island. CGJ,
XXIV, 16-33. 1942.

Mathiassen, T. Archaeology of the Central Eskimos.
RFTE, IV, 1-533. 1927.

--- Southampton Island og dens oprindelige beboere.
GT, XXX, 39-56. 1927.

Popham, R.E. A Comparative Analysis of the Digital
Patterns of Eskimo from Southampton Island. AJPA,
n.s., XI, 203-13. 1953.

Radwanski, P. Anthropological Structure of 101 Eskimo. An, I, 72-83. 1955.

Robinson, J.L. Eskimo Population in the Canadian
Eastern Arctic. CGJ, XXIX, 128-42. 1944.

Service, E.R. The Canadian Eskimo. PPC, 64-85.
1958.

Teicher, M.I. Adoption Practices among the Eskimos
on Southampton Island. Canadian Welfare, XXIX,
ii, 32-7. 1953.

Teicher, M.I. Three Cases of Psychosis among the Eskimos. Journal of Mental Science, C, 527-35. 1954.

Thibert, A. Le Journal Quotidien d'un Esquimau de Southampton. An, I, 144-97. 1955.

Tocher, J.F. Note on Some Measurements of Eskimo of Southampton Island. Man, II, 165-7. 1902.

Tweedsmuir, J.N.S.B. Hudson's Bay Trade. 195 pp. New York, 1951.

Waterman, T.T. Hudson Bay Eskimo, ed. R.H. Lowie. APAM, IV, 299-307. 1910.

14. WEST ALASKA ESKIMO

Curtis, E.S. The North American Indian, XX, 1-320, Norwood, 1930.

Lantis, M. The Social Culture of the Nunivak Eskimo. TAPS, n.s., XXXV, 153-323. 1946.

Nelson, E.W. The Eskimo about Bering Strait. ARBAE, XVIII, i, 3-518. 1899.

Thornton, H.R. Among the Eskimos of Wales, Alaska. Baltimore, 1931.

Albee, W. Kangut: A Boy of Bering Strait. 116 pp. Boston, 1939.

Anderson, H.D., and Eells, W.C. Alaska Natives. 472 pp. Stanford, 1935.

Andrews, C.L. The Eskimo and His Reindeer in Alaska. 253 pp. Caldwell, 1939.

Bancroft, H.H. The Native Races of the Pacific States, I, 37-94. New York, 1875.

Barnum, F. Grammatical Fundamentals of the Innuit Language. Boston, 1901.

Bartels, P. Kasuistische Mitteilung über den Mongolenfleck bei Eskimo. ZE, XLI, 721-5. 1909.

Beechey, F.W. Narrative of a Voyage to the Pacific and Beering's Strait. 2 vols. London, 1831.

Birker-Smith, K. Early Collections from the Pacific Eskimo. Nationalmuseets Skrifter, Etnografisk Raekke, I, 121-63. 1941.

Boas, F. A.J. Stone's Measurements of Natives of the Northwest Territories. BAMNH, XIV, 53-68. 1901.
--- Decorative Designs of Alaskan Needlecases. PUSNM, XXXIV, 321-44. 1908.
--- Notes on the Eskimo of Port Clarence. JAFL, VII, 205-8. 1894.
--- Property Marks of the Alaskan Eskimo. AA, n.s., I, 601-13. 1899.

Burg, A. North Star Cruises Alaska's Wild West. NGM, CII, 57-86. 1952.

Carrighar, S. Unalakleet, Alaska. Saturday Evening Post, CCXXIII, Jan. 12, pp. 32, 42-43, 45-46. 1952.

Collins, H.B. Archeological Excavations at Bering Strait. EFWSI, 1936, 63-8.
--- Check-stamped Pottery from Alaska. JWAS, XVIII, 254-6. 1928.
--- Culture Migrations and Contacts in the Bering Sea Region. AA, n.s., XXXIX, 375-84. 1937.

Coxe, W. Account of the Russian Discoveries between Asia and America. 4th edit. London, 1804.

Cross, J.F. Eskimo Children. SW, XXXVII, 433-7. 1908.

Cumming, J.R. Metaphysical Implications of the Folktales of the Eskimos of Alaska. UAAP, III, i, 37-63. 1954.

Dale, G.A. Northwest Alaska and the Bering Sea Coast. I.T. Sanders, ed., Societies Around the World, I, 111-30. 1952.

Dall, W.H. Alaska and Its Resources. 627 pp. Boston, 1870.
--- The Native Tribes of Alaska. PAAAS, XXXIV, 363-79. 1885.
--- On the Distribution and Nomenclature of the Native Tribes of Alaska. CNAE, I, 7-40. 1877.
--- On the Distribution of the Native Tribes of Alaska. PAAAS, XVIII, 263-73. 1869.
--- Social Life among our Aborigines. AN, XII, 1-10. 1878.

Dall, W.H., Dawson, G.M., and Ogilvie, W. The Yukon Territory. 438 pp. London, 1898.

Disselhoff, H.D. Bemerkungen zu einigen Eskimo-Masken. BA, XVIII, 130-7. 1935.

Eells, W.C. Mechanical, Physical, and Musical Ability of the Native Races of Alaska. JAP, XVII, 493-506. 1933.
--- Mental Ability of the Native Races of Alaska. JAP, XVII, 417-38. 1933.

Erman, A. Ueber die Reise und Entdeckungen des Lieutenant L. Sagoskin im russischen Amerika. AWKR, VI, 499-522, 613-72; VII, 429-512. 1848-49.

Fritz, M.H. Corneal Opacities among Alaska Natives. Alaska's Health, V, xii, 3-7. 1947.

Fulcomer, A. An Eskimo "Kashim." NH, XI, 55-8. 1898.

Garber, C.M. Eating with Eskimos. Hygeia, XVI, 242-5, 272, 278-9. 1938.
--- Marriage and Sex Customs of the Western Eskimos. SM, XLI, 215-27. 1935.
--- Some Mortuary Customs of the Western Alaska Eskimos. SM, XXXIX, 203-20. 1934.
--- Stories and Legends of the Bering Strait Eskimos. 260 pp. Boston, 1940.

Gillham, C.E. Beyond the Clapping Mountains. 134 pp. New York, 1943.

Giraux, L. Gravures coloriees sur dents de morse des
    Esquimaux de l'Alaska. JSAP, n.s., XVIII, 91-
    102. 1926.
Gordon, G.B. The Double Axe and Some Other Sym-
    bols. MJ, VII, 46-68. 1916.
--- In the Alaskan Wilderness. 247 pp. Philadelphia,
    1917.
--- Notes on the Western Eskimo. TFMSA, II, 69-
    101. 1906.
Hammerich, L.L. The Dialect of Nunivak. ICA,
    XXX, 110-3. 1955.
--- Russian Loan-Words in Alaska. ICA, XXX, 114-
    26. 1955.
--- The Russian Stratum in Alaskan Eskimo. Slavic
    Word, X, 401-28. 1954.
--- The Western Eskimo Dialects. ICA, XXXII, 632-
    9. 1958.
Hawkes, E.W. The Dance Festivals of the Alaskan
    Eskimo. TFMSA, VI, ii. 41 pp. 1914.
--- The "Inviting-in" Feast of the Alaskan Eskimo.
    MCDM, XLV, 1-20. 1913.
Healy, M.A. Report of the Cruise of the Revenue
    Marine Steamer Corwin in the Arctic Ocean. Wash-
    ington, 1887.
Heinrich, A. Some Present-day Acculturative Innova-
    tions in a Nonliterate Society. AA, n.s., LII, 235-
    242. 1950.
Heizer, R.F. Aconite Poison Whaling in Asia and
    America. BBAE, CXXXIII, 415-68. 1943.
Himmelheber, H. Eskimokünstler. 111 pp. Stutt-
    gart, 1938.
--- Der Gefrorene Pfad. 135 pp. Eisenach, 1951.
Hinz, J. Grammar and Vocabulary of the Eskimo Lan-
    guage. 194 pp. Bethlehem, 1944.
Hitchcock, D.J. Parasitological Study on the Eskimos
    in the Bethel Area of Alaska. Journal of Parasitology,
    XXXVI, 232-4. 1950.
--- Parasitological Study on the Eskimos in the Kotzebue
    Area of Alaska. Journal of Parasitology, XXXVII,
    309-11. 1951.
Hrdlicka, A. The Ancient and Modern Inhabitants of
    the Yukon. EFWSI, 1929, 137-46.
--- Anthropological Survey of Alaska. ARBAE, XLVI,
    19-374. 1930.
--- Anthropological Work in Alaska. SMC, LXXVIII,
    vii, 137-58. 1927.
--- Anthropological Work on the Kuskokwim River.
    EFWSI, 1930, 123-34.
--- The Eskimo of the Kuskokwim. AJPA, XVIII, 93-
    145. 1933.
--- Fecundity of Eskimo Women. AJPA, XXII, 91-5.
    1936.

Hrdlicka, A. Height and Weight of Eskimo Children.
    AJPA, XXVIII, 331-41. 1941.
--- Puberty in Eskimo Girls. PNAS, XXII, 355-7.
    1936.
--- Ritual Ablation of Front Teeth in Siberia and
    America. SMC, XCIX, iii, 1-32. 1940.
Ivanov, S.V. O Znachenii Dvukh. ANMAE, XI, 162-
    70. 1949.
Jacobsen, J.A. Leben und Treiben der Eskimo. Aus-
    land, LXIV, 593-8, 636-9, 656-8. 1891.
Jenness, D. Archaeological Investigations in Bering
    Strait. BCDM, L, 71-80. 1926.
--- Little Diomede Island. GR, XIX, 78-86. 1929.
--- Notes on the Phonology of the Eskimo Dialect of
    Cape Prince of Wales. IJAL, IV, 168-80. 1927.
Krause, E. Die Schraube, eine Eskimo-Erfindung?
    Globus, LXXIX, 8-9. 1901.
Laguna, F. de. The Prehistory of Northern North
    America as seen from the Yukon. MSAA, III, 1-
    360. 1947.
Lantis, M. Alaskan Eskimo Ceremonialism. MAES,
    XI, 1-127. 1947.
--- Mme. Eskimo Proves Herself an Artist. NH, LIX,
    68-71. 1950.
--- No Wonder They Worship the Seal. NH, XLVIII,
    166-72. 1941.
Larsen, H. Archaeological Investigations in Alaska
    Since 1939. Polar Record, VI, 593-607. 1953.
--- Archaeological Investigations in Southwestern
    Alaska. AAn, XV, 177-86. 1949.
--- De Dansk-amerikanske Alaska-ekspeditioner 1949-
    50. GT, LI, 63-93. 1951.
--- Et Naturfolk Fortaeller. Vor Viden, XXXVI, 183-
    8. 1951.
Levine, V.E. Dental Caries, Attrition and Crowding
    in the Eskimos of the Coasts of the Bering Sea and
    Arctic Ocean. Journal of Dental Research, XVIII,
    255-6. 1939.
Lucier, C. Buckland Eskimo Myths. UAAP, II, 215-
    33. 1954.
--- Noatagmiut Eskimo Myths. UAAP, VI, 89-118.
    1958.
Mason, J.A. Eskimo Pictorial Art. MJ, XVIII, 248-
    83. 1927.
Mathiassen, T. Some Specimens from the Bering Sea
    Culture. IN, VI, 33-56. 1929.
Matson, G.A., and Roberts, H.J. Distribution of the
    Blood Groups, M-N and Rh Types among Eskimos of
    the Kuskokwim Basin in Western Alaska. AJPA, VII,
    109-22. 1949.

Mayokok, R. I Was a Failure as a Polar Bear Hunter. Alaska Sportsman, XVI, ii, 6-9.

--- Seals. Alaska Sportsman, XVI, iv, 20-1, 29-31. 1950.

--- We Caught a Whale. Alaska Sportsman, XVI, vii, 10-3. 1950.

Mickey, B.H. The Family among the Western Eskimo. UAAP, IV, i, 13-22. 1955.

Muir, J. The Cruise of the Corwin. Boston, 1917.

Muñoz, J. Cliff Dwellers of the Bering Sea. NGM, CV, 129-46. 1954.

Murdoch, J. On the Siberian Origin of Some Customs of the Western Eskimo. AA, I, 325-36. 1888.

Murie, M.E. Modern Eskimo Art. NH, XLIV, 49-52. 1939.

Nordenskiöld, A.E. The Voyage of the Vega. New York, 1882.

Orchard, W.C. Present-day Pictography. IN, I, 70-3. 1924.

Ostermann, H. The Alaskan Eskimos. RFTE, X, iii, 291 pp. 1952.

Oswalt, W.H. The Archaeology of Hooper Bay Village, Alaska. UAAP, I, 47-91. 1952.

--- Pottery from Hooper Bay Village, Alaska. AAn, XVIII, 18-29. 1952.

--- Recent Pottery from the Bering Strait Region. UAAP, II, 5-18. 1953.

--- A Western Eskimo Ethnobotany. UAAP, V, 17-36. 1957.

Pedersen, P.O. Eine Besondere Form der Abnutzung von Eskimozähnen aus Alaska. Deutsche Zahnärztliche Zeitschrift, X, 41-6. 1955.

Petroff, I. The Population and Resources of Alaska. Compilation of Narratives of Explorations in Alaska, pp. 210-39. Washington, 1900.

--- Report on the Population, Industries, and Resources of Alaska. United States Department of the Interior, Tenth Census, VIII, 124-46. 1881.

Price, W.A. New Light on the Etiology of Facial Deformity and Dental Irregularities from Field Studies among Eskimos and Indians in Various Stages of Modernization. Journal of Dental Research, XIV, 229-30. 1934.

--- Relation of Nutrition to Dental Caries among Eskimos and Indians in Alaska and Northern Canada. Journal of Dental Research, XIV; 227-9. 1934.

--- Some Causes for Change in Susceptibility of Eskimos and Indians to Acute and Chronic Infections upon Contact with Modern Civilization. Journal of Dental Research, XIV, 230-31. 1934.

Rainey, F.G. Native Economy and Survival in Arctic Alaska. HO, I, i, 9-14. 1941.

Richet, E. Les Esquimaux de l'Alaska. Bulletin de la Société Royale Géographique d'Anvers, XLI, 5-51, 103-53, 197-245; XLII, 5-50, 185-231. 1921-22.

Rosebury, T. Dental Caries and Related Mouth Conditions among Eskimos of the Kuskokwim Region. Journal of Dental Research, XVI, 305-6. 1936.

Santos, A. Jesuitos en el Polo Norte. 546 pp. Madrid, 1943.

Schott, W. Ueber ethnographische Ergebnisse der Sagoskinschen Reise. AWKR, VII, 480-512. 1849.

Schultze, A. Grammar and Vocabulary of the Eskimo Language. 21 pp. Bethlehem, 1894.

Schwatka, F. Report of a Military Reconnaissance made in Alaska in 1883, pp. 104-11. Washington, 1900.

Shapiro, H.A. The Alaskan Eskimo. APAM, XXXI, 347-84. 1931.

Simpson, R. de E. Eskimo Art in Ivory. M, XXII, 183-8. 1948.

Steinen, K. von den. Die Schraube, keine Eskimo-Erfindung. Globus, LXXIX, 125-7. 1901.

Stepanova, M.V. Dva Eskimosskikh Poiasa iz Sobraniia MAE. ANMAE, XI, 62-72. 1949.

Totter, J.R. and Shukers, C.F. Nutrition Surveys of Eskimos. Alaska's Health, VI, x, 4-6. 1948.

Van Valin, W.B. Eskimoland speaks. 242 pp. Caldwell, 1941.

Walton, W.B. Eskimo or Innuit Dictionary. 32 pp. Seattle, 1901.

Waugh, L.M. Influences of Diet on the Development of the Jaw and Face of the American Eskimo. Journal of Dental Research, XIII, 149-51. 1933.

--- Survey of Mouth Conditions, Nutritional Study and Gnathodynamometer Data in Most Primitive and Populous Native Villages in Alaska. Journal of Dental Research, XVI, 355-6. 1936.

Whymper, F. Russian America. TESL, n.s., VII, 167-85. 1869.

Wiedemann, T. Cheechako into Sourdough. 266 pp. Portland, 1942.

Woldt, A., ed. Capitain Jacobsen's Reise an der Nordwestküste Amerikas. Leipzig, 1884.

Zagoskin, L.A. Peshexodnaa opic chasti russkix vladenii v Amerike. 2 vols. St. Petersburg, 1847-48.

--- Puteshestvie i otkrytia v russkoi Amerike. St. Petersburg, 1847.

15. WEST GREENLAND ESKIMO

Birket-Smith, K. Ethnography of the Egesmind District. MG, LXVI, 1-484. 1924.

Nansen, F. Eskimo Life. London, 1893.

--- Eskimoliv. Christiania, 1891.

Porsild, M.P. Studies on the Material Culture of the Eskimo in West Greenland. MG, LI,113-250. 1915.

Ahrengot, V. and Eldon, K. Distribution of ABO-MN and Rh types among Eskimos in Southwest Greenland. Nature, CLXIX, 1065. 1952.

Anderson, J. Nachrichten von Island, Grönland und der Strasse Davis. Hamburg, 1746.

Anonymous. Kaladlit okalluktualliait. 4 vols. Godthaab, 1859-63.

Anonymous. New Herrnhut. MCM, I, 81-90. 1850.

Barfod, H.P. Dansk-grønlandsk ordliste til skolebrug. 2nd ed. 34 pp. Godthaab, 1952.

Bartels, M.C.A. Ein Eismesser der Eskimo in Groenland. ZE, XXXI, 747-8. 1899.

--- Geräthe der Eskimo aus Neu-Herrnhut bei Godhaab. VBGA, 1900, 542-3.

Bay-Schmith, E. Versuche über die Schicksche Reaction bei Eskimos in Grönland. Klinische Wochenschrift, VIII, 974-6. 1929.

Behrens, W. Ethnografisk beskrivelse over Nord Grønland. 46 pp. Kjøbenhavn, 1860.

Bertelsen, A. Folkemedicinen i Grønland i aeldre og nyere tid. Grønlandske Selskabs Aarsskrift, 1914.

--- Grønlandsk medicinsk Statistik og Nosografi. MG, CXVII, iii, 1-234; iv, 1-246. 1940-43.

--- Navnegivning i Grønland. MG, LVI, 221-87. 1918.

Birket-Smith, K. Det eskimoiske slaegtskabs-system. GT, XXX, 96-111. 1927.

--- Etnografiske problemer i Grønland. GT, XXV, 179-97. 1920.

--- Foreløbigt bidrag til Kap Farvel-Distrikternes kulturhistorie. MG, LIII, 1-38. 1917.

--- The Greenland Bow. MG, LVI, i, 1-28. 1918.

--- The Greenlanders of the Present Day. Greenland, II, 1-207. 1928.

--- Opdagelse og Udforskning. Grønlandsbogen, 15-40. København.

Bistrup, A. Eskimo Women in Greenland. Century Magazine, LXXXII, 667-74. 1911.

Brierley, J., and Parsons, F. Notes on a Collection of Ancient Eskimo Skulls. JAI, XXXVI, 104-20. 1906.

Brun, E. Grønland after Krigen. Grønlandsbogen, II, 5-16. 1950.

Bruun, D. Arkaeologiske undersøgelser i Julianehaabs Distrikt. MG, XVI, 171-461. 1896.

Bugge, A. The Native Greenlander. Arctic, V, 45-53. 1952.

Carmichael, D.M. Psychology and Ethnology. The Cambridge Expedition to West Greenland, by H.I. Drever. GJ, XCIV, 398-401. 1939.

Cranz, D. Historie von Grönland. 2d edit. 3 vols. Barby, 1770.

--- The History of Greenland. 2 vols. London, 1767.

Cummins, H., and Fabricus-Hansen, V. Dermatoglyphics in Eskimos of West Greenland. AJPA, n.s., IV, 395-402. 1946.

Dalager, L. Grønlandske relationer. Kiebenhavn, 1752.

Egede,P. Ausführliche und wahrhafte Nachricht vom Anfange und Fortgange der grönländischen Mission. Hamburg, 1740.

--- Continuation af relationerne betreffende den grønlandske missions tilstand og beskaffenhed. 184 pp. Kjøbenhavn, 1741.

--- Description et histoire naturelle du Groenland. Copenhague, 1763.

--- A Description of Greenland. London, 1745.

--- Det gamle Grønlands nye perlustration eller naturel-historie. MG, LIV, 305-431. 1925.

--- Dictionarium Groenlandico-Danico-Latinum. Hafniae, 1750.

--- Efterretninger om Grønland. Kjøbenhavn, 1788.

--- Grammatica grönlandico-danico-latina. Havniae, 1760.

--- Nachrichten von Grönland. Kopenhagen, 1790.

--- Omstaendelig og udførlig relation angaaende den grønlandske missions begyndelse og fortsaettelse. Kjøbenhavn, 1738.

--- Relationer fra Grønland. MG, LXIV, 1-304. 1925.

Elgström, O. Moderna Eskimaer. Stockholm, 1916.

Fabricius, O. Den grønlandske ordbog. Kjøbenhavn, 1804.

--- Nöiagtig beskrivelse over alle Grönlaendernes fange-redskaber ved saelhundefangsten. KDVSS, V, ii, 125-78. 1810.

--- Nöiagtig beskrivelse over Grönlaendernes landdyr-, figle-, og fiskefangst med dertil hörende redskaber. KDVSS, VI, ii, 231-72. 1818.

--- Udførlig beskrivelse over de grønlandske saele. Skrivter af Naturhistorie-Selskabet, I, i, 79-157. 1790.

Fabricus-Hansen, V. Blood Groups and MN Types of Eskimos. Journal of Immunology. XXXVIII, 405-11. 1940.

Finck, F.N. Die Grundbedeutung des grönländischen Subjektivs. Sitzungsberichte der Berliner Akademie, 1905, i, 280-7.

Fischer-Möller, K. Skeletons from Ancient Greenland Graves. MG, CXIX, iv, 1-30. 1938.

Frederiksen, S. Aspects of European Influence in West Greenlandic Poetry. MWF, II, 251-61. 1952.

--- European Influences in the Poetry of Greenland. Georgetown College Journal, LXXIX, vi, 3-12. 1951.

--- Henrik Lund. PAPS, XCVI, 653-9. 1952.

--- Stylistic Forms in Greenland Eskimo Literature. 40 pp. Copenhagen, 1954.

Fries, T.M. Grönland, dess natur och innevanare. Upsala, 1872.

Funch, J.C.W. Syv aar i Nordgrønland. Viborg, 1840.

Fürst, C.M., and Hansen, F.C.C. Crania groenland- ica. 234 pp. Copenhagen, 1915.

Giesecke, K.L. Mineralogisches Reisejournal über Grönland. MG, XXXV, 1-478. 1910.

Glahn, H.C. Anmaerkninger over de tre første bøger af Hr. David Crantzes Historie om Grønland. Kjøben- havn, 1771.

--- Dagbøger, ed. H. Ostermann. Grønlandske Selskabs Skrifter, IV. 1921.

--- Forsøg til en afhandling om Grønlaendernes skikke ved hvalfiskeriet. Nye Samling af det Kgl. Norske Videnskabers Selskabs Skrifter, I, 273-96. 1874.

--- Om den grønlandske hund. Nye Samling af det Kgl. Norske Videnskabers Selskabs Skrifter, I, 485- 96. 1874.

Gosch, C.C.A., ed. Danish Arctic Expeditions, 1605 to 1620. 2 vols. London, 1897.

Haan, L.F. Beschryving van de Straat Davids. Amster- dam, 1720.

Hansen, P.M. Jagt og Fiskeri. Grønlands Bogen, II, 59-82. 1950.

Hansen, S. Bidrag til Eskimoernes kraniologi. MG, XVII, 347-56. 1895.

--- Bidrag til Vestgrønlaendernes anthropologi. MG, VII, 163-248. 1893.

Harris, Z.S. Structural Restatements. IJAL, XIII, 47-55. 1947.

Holm, G. Beskrivelse af ruiner i Julianehaabs Distrikt. MG, VI, 57-145. 1894.

Holtved, E. Archaeological Investigations in the Thule District. MG, CXLI, i, 1-492. 1944.

Jackson, N. With the "Doctor Boat" along the Green- land Coast. GR, XXXIII, 545-68. 1943.

Jørgensen, J.B. The Eskimo Skeleton. MG, CXLVI, ii, 154 pp. 1953.

Jørgensen, J.B. De Første Eskimoes pa Grønland. Grønland, 1954, vii, 265-71. København.

--- Hvad Skeletfund Kan Berette om Sygdonsme Hos de Første Eskimoer pa Grønland. Grønland, 1954, viii, 306-11. København.

Kane, E.K. Walrus Hunting a Century Ago. B, CCLXXXIV, Dec., 35. 1953.

Kjer, J., and Rasmussen, C. Dansk-Grønlandsk ordbog. Kjøbenhavn, 1893.

Klausen, L.A. Greenlandic Dictionary of Useful Phrases. 58 pp. Washington, 1942.

Kleinschmidt, S. Grammatik der grönlandischen Sprache. 182 pp. Berlin, 1851.

--- Den grønlandske ordbog. Kjøbenhavn, 1871.

Koegels, J. Letters. MCM, I, 249-50, 356-9; II, 191-2. 1850-51.

Kragh, P. Udtog af missionair P. Kraghs dagbog. 2 vols. Haderslev, 1875.

Larsen, H. and J. Meldgaard. Paleo-Eskimo Cultures in Disko Bugt, West Greenland. MG, CLXI, ii. 1958.

Laughlin, W.S. and Jørgenson, J.B. Isolate Variation in Greenlandic Eskimo Crania. Acta Genetica et Statistica Medica, VI, 3-12. 1956.

Lauridsen, P. Bibliographia groenlandica. MG, XII, 137-61, 199-217. 1890.

MacMillan, M. Far North with "Captain Mac." NGM, C, 465-513. 1951.

Marcussen, P.V. and Rendal, J. En Studie over Syph- ilis i en Grønlandsk Boplads. Ugeskrift for Laeger, CXI, 1-4. 1949.

Markham, A.H., ed. The Voyages and Works of John Davis the Navigator. 373 pp. London, 1880.

Mathiassen, T. Ancient Eskimo Settlements in the Kangamiut Area. MG, XCI, 1-150. 1931.

--- Arkaeologiske undersøgelser i Sukkertoppens Dis- trikt. GT, XXXIII, 189-97. 1930.

--- Arkaeologiske undersøgelser i Uperniviks Distrikt. GT, XXXIII, 2-17. 1930.

--- Contributions to the Archaeology of Disko Bay. MG, XCIII, ii, 1-192. 1934.

--- The Eskimo Archeology of Greenland. ARSI, 1936, 397-404.

--- Eskimo Finds from the Kangerdlugssuaq Region. MG, CIV, ix, 1-25. 1934.

--- Eskimo Migrations in Greenland. GR, XXV, 408- 22. 1935.

--- Inugsuk, a Mediaeval Eskimo Settlement. MG, LXXVII, 145-340. 1930.

Mathiassen, T., and Holtved, E. The Eskimo Archae- ology of Julianhaab District. MG, CXVIII, i, 1- 141. 1936.

Meldgaard, J. Fra en Grønlandsk Mumiehule. Fra Nationalmuseets Arbejdsmark, 1953, 14-20. Køben- havn.

Meldgaard, J. Grønlaendere i tre tusinde Aar. Grøn-
    land, 1958, iv-v, 121-9, 170-8. 1958. København.

--- A Paleo-Eskimo Culture in West Greenland. AAn,
    XVII, 222-30. 1952.

Morgan, L.H. Systems of Consanguinity and Affinity.
    SCK, XVII, 291-382. 1871.

Paterson, T.T. Anthropological Studies in Greenland.
    JAI, LXIX, 45-76. 1939.

Pedersen, P.O. Investigations into Dental Conditions
    of about 3,000 Ancient and Modern Greenlanders.
    Dental Record, LVIII, 191-8. 1938.

Pedersen, P.O., and Hinsch, E. Numerical Variations
    in Greenland Eskimo Dentition. Acta Odontologica
    Scandinavica, I, 93-134. 1939.

Poincy, L. de. The Eskimos of Davis Straits in 1656.
    Scottish Geographical Magazine, XXVIII, 281-94.
    1912.

Porsild, M.P. On Eskimo Stone Rows in Greenland.
    GR, VI, 297-309. 1918.

--- Über einige Geräte der Eskimo. ZE, XLIV, 600-
    23. 1912.

Rasmussen, C. Grønlandsk sproglaere. 201 pp.
    Kjøbenhavn, 1888.

Rasmussen, K. Myter og sagn fra Grønland, II, 1-356.
    Kjøbenhavn, 1924.

--- The People of the Polar North. London, 1908.

Rink, H. Danish Greenland. London, 1877.

--- Eskimoiske eventyr og sagn. 2 vols. Kjøbenhavn,
    1866-71.

--- Grønland geografisk og statistisk beskrevet. 2 vols.
    Kjøbenhavn, 1857.

--- Om Grønlaendernes gamle tro og hvad der af
    samme er bevaret under Kristendommen. ANOH,
    III, 192-256. 1868.

--- Tales and Traditions of the Eskimo. 472 pp.
    Edinburgh, 1875.

Ryberg, C. Dansk-Grønlandsk tolk. Kjøbenhavn, 1891.

--- Om erhvervs- og befolkningsforholdene i Grønland.
    GT, XVII, 69-92. 1904.

Saabye, H.E. Brudstykker af en dagbog holden i Grøn-
    land. Odense, 1816.

--- Fragmenter af en dagbok. Stockholm, 1817.

--- Greenland. London, 1818.

Schultz-Lorentzen, C.W. Dictionary of the West
    Greenland Eskimo Language. MG, LXIX, 1-303.
    1927.

--- Eskimoernes indvandring i Grønland. MG, XXVI,
    289-330. 1904.

--- Den grønlandske ordbog. Kjøbenhavn, 1926.

--- Intellectual Culture of the Greenlanders. Green-
    land, II, 209-70. 1928.

Schultz-Lorentzen, D.L. A Grammar of the West
    Greenland Language. MG, CXXIX, iii,1-103. 1945.

Skeller, E. Øjensgdomme i Grønland. Ugeskrift for
    Laeger, CXI, 529-32. 1949.

Solberg, O. Beiträge zur Vorgeschichte der Osteskimo.
    Videnskabs-Selskabets Skrifter, Historisk-Filosofisk
    Klasse, 1907, ii, 1-92.

Steensby, H.P. Ethnografiske og antropogeografiske
    rejsestudier i Nord-Grønland. MG, L, 133-73. 1912.

Steenstrup, K.J.V. Beretning om undersøgelsesrejserne
    i Nord-Grønland. MG, V, 1-41. 1893.

Stefansson, V., ed. The Three Voyages of Martin
    Frobisher. 2 vols. London, 1938.

Stiasny, G. Volkslieder und Sagen der westgrönländi-
    schen Eskimo. Mitteilungen der Kaiserlich-Königli-
    chen Geographischen Gesellschaft in Wien, LI, 327-
    35. 1908.

Swadesh, M. South Greenlandic. VFPA, VI, 30-54.
    1946.

--- South Greenlandic Paradigms. IJAL, XIV, 29-36.
    1948.

Swenander, G. Harpun-, kastpil- och lansspetsar fran
    Väst-Grönland. Kungliga Svenska Vetenskapsakade-
    miens Handlingar, XL, iii, 1-45. 1906.

Thalbitzer, W.C. The Aleutian Language compared
    with Greenlandic. IJAL, II, 40-57. 1921.

--- Cultic Games and Festivals in Greenland. ICA,
    XXI, ii, 236-55. 1924.

--- Fólklore from West Greenland. MG, XL, 496-564.
    1921.

--- Grønlandsk Litteraturhistorie. Grønlands Bogen, II,
    225-50. 1950.

--- Inuit sange og danse fra Grönland. 75 pp. Kjø-
    benhavn, 1939.

--- A Phonetical Study of the Eskimo Language. MG,
    XXXI, 1-405. 1904.

Thomsen, T. Eskimo Archaeology. Greenland, II,
    271-329. 1928.

Thorhallesen, E. Beskrivelse over missionerne i Grøn-
    lands søndre distrikt, ed. L. Bobe. Grønlandske
    Selskabs Skrifter, I. 1914.

Thuren, H. On the Eskimo Music of Greenland. MG,
    XL, 1-45. 1911.

Trebitsch, R. Bei den Eskimos in Westgrönland. Ber-
    lin, 1909.

--- Die "blauen Geburtsflecke" bei den Eskimos in
    Westgrönland. AFA, XXXIV, 237-42. 1907.

Tylor, E.B. Old Scandinavian Civilisation among the
    Modern Esquimaux. JAI, XIII, 348-57. 1884.

Whitaker, W.L. The Question of Season Sterility
    among the Eskimos. Science, LXXXVIII, 214-15.
    1938.

Worster, W.W. Eskimo Folklore and Myths. Edinburgh
    Review, CCXLII, 94-107. 1925.

Zorgdrager, C.G. Bloeyende opkomst der aloude en hedendaagsche groenlandsche visschery. Amsterdam, 1728.

--- Histoire des peches, des découvertes et des établissemens des Hollandois dans les mers du nord. 3 vols. Paris, 1801.

16. YUIT

Including the Eskimo of Siberia and of St. Lawrence Island.

Bogoras, W.G. Materialy po Iazyku Aziatskikh Eskimosov. 255 pp. Leningrad, 1949.

Rubcova, E.S. Materialy po Jazyku i Fol'kloru Eskimosov. Čast 1. 556 pp. Moscow, 1954.

Antropova, V.V. Sovremannaia Cukotskaia i Eskimosskaia Reznaia Kosti. ANMAE, XV, 5-122. 1953.

Bogoras, W.G. The Chukchee. MAMNH, XI. 2 vols. 1904-09.

--- Early Migrations of the Eskimo between Asia and America. ICA, XXI, ii, 216-35. 1924.

--- The Eskimo of Siberia. MAMNH, XII, 417-56. 1910.

--- Igry Malykh Narodnostei Severa. ANMAE, XI, 237-54. 1949.

--- Osnovnye Tipy Fol'klora Severnoi Evrazu-i Severnoi Ameriki. Sovetskii Fol'klor, IV-V, 29-50. 1936.

Burnham, J.B. Siwashing in Siberia. American Wildlife, XI, iii, 6-9, 15. 1922.

Cadzow, D.A. Objects from St. Lawrence Island. IN, II, 122-5. 1925.

Cameron, J. Correlations between Cranial Capacity and Cranial Length, Breadth, and Height. AJPA, XI, 259-99. 1928.

Chard, C.S. Eskimo Archaeology in Siberia. SJA, XI, 150-77. 1955.

Collins, H.B. Ancient Culture of St. Lawrence Island. EFWSI, 1930, 135-44.

--- The Ancient Eskimo Culture of Northwestern Alaska. EFWSI, 1928, 141-50.

--- Archaeology of St. Lawrence Island. SMC, XCVI, i, 1-424. 1937.

--- Archaeology of the Bering Sea Region. PPSC, V, iv, 2825-39. 1934.

--- Archeological Investigations in Northern Alaska. EFWSI, 103-12. 1932.

--- Prehistoric Art of the Alaskan Eskimo. SMC, LXXXI, xiv, 1-52. 1929.

Collins, H.B. Prehistoric Eskimo Culture of Alaska. EFWSI, 1929, 147-56.

Coxe, W. Account of the Russian Discoveries between Asia and America. 4th edit. London, 1804.

Dall, W.H. Alaska and Its Resources, pp. 378-85. Boston, 1870.

--- The Native Tribes of Alaska. PAAAS, XXXIV, 363-79. 1885.

Fainberg, L. K Voprosu o Rodovorn Stroe y Eskimosov. SE, 1955, ii, 82-99. 1955.

Friedman, H. Bird Bones from Eskimo Ruins on St. Lawrence Island. JWAS, XXIV, 83-96. 1934.

Geist, O.W., and Rainey, F.G. Archaeological Excavations at Kukulik. Miscellaneous Publications of the University of Alaska, II, 1-391. 1936.

Gerland, G. Zur Ethnographie des äussersten Nordostens von Asien. ZGE, XVIII, 194-222. 1883.

Grinnell, G.B. The Natives of the Alaska Coast Region. Harriman Alaska Expedition, I, 171-8. New York, 1901.

Heinrich, A. Some Present-day Acculturative Innovations in a Nonliterate Society. AA, n.s., LII, 235-42. 1950.

Hodge, F.W. An Eskimo Toboggan. M, XXIV, 193. 1950.

Herzer, R.F. Aconite Poison Whaling in Asia and America. BBAE, CXXXIII, 415-68. 1943.

Hooper, W.H. Ten Months among the Tents of the Tuski. London, 1853.

Hrdlicka, A. Catalogue of Human Crania in the United States National Museum Collections. PUSNM, XCIV, 1-172. 1944.

--- Ritual Ablation of Front Teeth in Siberia and America. SMC, XCIX, iii, 1-32. 1940.

Hughes, C.C. An Eskimo Deviant from the "Eskimo" Type of Social Organization. AA, LX, 1140-7. 1958.

Ivanov, S.V. Chukotsko-Eskimosskaia Graviura na Kosti. SE, 1949, iv, 107-24. 1949.

Jochelson, W. Past and Present Subterranean Dwellings of the Tribes of North Eastern Asia and North Western America. ICA, XIX, ii, 115-23. 1906.

Kirillov, N.V. Sanitarnaia Obstanovka. Vestnik Obshchestoennoi Gigieny, Sudebnoi i Prakticheskoi Meditsiny, XLIV, 1769-99. 1908.

Kuftin, B.A. Spisok Naibolee Malochislennykh Narodnostei SSSR. Antropologicheskii Zhurnal, XIV, iii-iv, 91-3. 1926.

Laguna, F. de. The Prehistory of Northern North America as seen from the Yukon. MSAA, III, 1-360. 1947.

Leighton, A.H. and Hughes, C.C. Notes on Eskimo Patterns of Suicide. SJA, XI, 327-38. 1955.

Lütke, F. Die Tschuktschen. AWKR, III, 446-64. 1843.

Mathiassen, T. Archaeological Collections from the Western Eskimos. RFTE, X, 1-98. 1930.

Moore, R.D. Social Life of the Eskimo of St. Lawrence Island. AA, n.s., XXV, 339-75. 1923.

Muir, J. The Cruise of the Corwin. Boston, 1917.

Nelson, E.W. The Eskimo about Bering Strait. ARBAE, XVIII, i, 3-518. 1899.

Nordenskiöld, A.E. Vega's färd kring Asien og Europa. 2 vols. Stockholm, 1880-81.

--- The Voyage of the Vega round Asia and Europe. New York, 1882.

Paulson, I. New Eskimo Archaeology from the Soviet Union. Ethnos, XVI, 136-40. 1951.

Potosky, N., and R.L. A Unique Specimen of Pressure-flaked Pyrite from St. Lawrence Island. AAn, XIII, 181-2. 1947.

Rainey, F.G. Eskimo Chronology. PNAS, XXII, 357-62. 1936.

Rudenko, S.I. Tatuirovka Aziatskikh Eskimosov. SE, 1949, i, 149-54. 1949.

Sanford, M.H. Sevoonga-Eskimo Village. Am I, VI, ii, 37-40. 1951.

Voblov, I.K. Eskimosskie Prazdniki. ANIET, XVIII, 320-34. 1952.

Watkins, J.A. The Alaskan Eskimo. American Journal of Public Health, IV, 643-8. 1914.

Wells, R., and Kelly, J.W. English-Eskimo and Eskimo-English Vocabularies. Bureau of Education, Circular of Information, II, 1-72. Washington, 1890.

Yarmolinsky, A. Kamchadal and Asiatic Eskimo Manuscript Collections. New York Public Library Bulletin LI, 659-69. 1947.

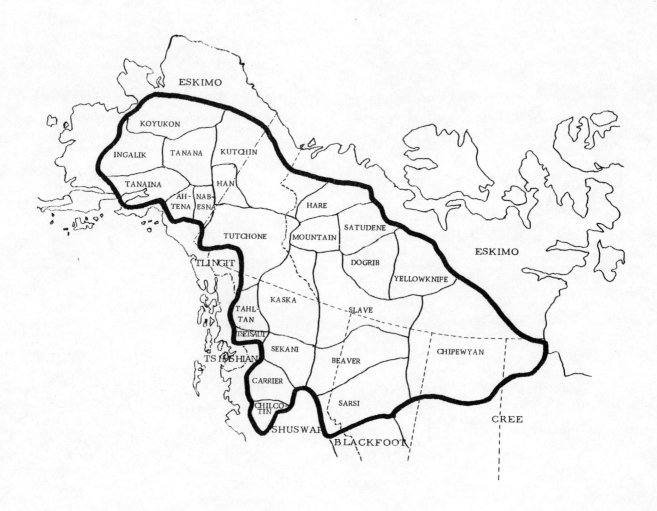

All the tribes of this area belong to the Athapaskan linguistic stock.

Allen, F.H. Summary of Blood Group Phenotypes in Some Aboriginal Americans. AJPA, n.s., XVII, 86. 1959.

Allison, A.C. et al. Urinary B-aminoisobutyric Acid Excretion in Eskimo and Indian Populations of Alaska. Nature, CLXXXIII, 118. 1959.

Anderson, A.A. Notes on the Indian Tribes of British North America. HM, VII, 73-81. 1863.

Aronson, J.D. The History of Disease among the Natives of Alaska. Alaska's Health, V, iii, 1-2; iv, 3-4; v, 5-6; vi, 4-5; vii, 3-4. 1947.

Bancroft, H.H. The Native Races of the Pacific States, I, 114-49. New York, 1875.

Benveniste, E. Le Vocabulaire de la Vie Animale chez les Indiens du Haut Yukon (Alaska). Bulletin de la Société Linguistique de Paris, XLIX, 79-106. 1953.

Boas, F. Die Verbreitung der Indianer-Sprachen in Britisch-Columbien. PMJP, XLII, 21. 1896.

--- Fifth Report on the Indians of British Columbia. BAAS, 1895, 522-92. 1895.

Bompas, W.C. Diocese of Mackenzie River. 108 pp. London, 1888.

Bruet, E. L'Alaska. 451 pp. Paris, 1945.

Buckham, A.F. Indian Engineering. CGJ, XL, 174-81. 1950.

Buschmann, J.C.E. Der athapaskische Sprachstamm. AKAWB, 1855, 149-319.

--- Systematische Worttafel des athapaskischen Sprachstamms. AKAWB, 1859, iii, 501-86.

--- Die Verwandtschafts-Verhältnisse der athapaskischen Sprachen. AKAWB, 1862, ii, 195-252.

--- Die Völker und Sprachen im Innern des britischen Nordamerika's. Monatsberichte der Königlichen Preussischen Akademie der Wissenschaften zu Berlin, 1858, 465-86.

Cameron, J. Correlations between Cranial Capacity and Cranial Length, Breadth, and Height. AJPA, XI, 259-99. 1928.

Canada, Department of Mines and Resources, Indian Affairs Branch. Census of Indians in Canada, 1939 and 1944. Ottawa, 1940, 1944.

Cantwell, G.G. Alaskan Dead Poles. LS, VIII, 214. 1898.

Cooper, J.M. Land Tenure among the Indians of Eastern and Northern North America. PA, VIII, 55-9. 1938.

--- Snares, Deadfalls, and Other Traps of the Northern Algonquians and Northern Athapaskans. CUAS, V, 1-144. 1938.

Dall, W.H. The Native Tribes of Alaska. PAAAS, XXXIV, 363-79. 1885.

--- On the Distribution and Nomenclature of the Native Tribes of Alaska. CNAE, I, 24-36. 1877.

--- On the Distribution of the Native Tribes of Alaska. PAAAS, XVIII, 263-73. 1869.

--- Tribes of the Extreme Northwest. CNAE, I, i, 7-106. 1877.

Dawson, G.M. Note on the Indian Tribes of the Yukon District and Adjacent Northern Portion of British Columbia. ARCGS, ser. 2, III, 191B-213B. 1883.

--- Sketches of the Past and Present Condition of the Indians of Canada. CNG, n.s., IX, 129-59. 1881.

Duchaussois, P.J.B. Mid Snow and Ice. 328 pp. London, 1923.

Fellows, F.S. Mortality in the Native Races of the Territory of Alaska. PHR, XLIX, 289-98. 1934.

Franklin, J. Narrative of a Journey to the Shores of the Polar Sea. London, 1823.

Fraser, S. Journal of a Voyage from the Rocky Mountains to the Pacific Coast. BCNO, I, 156-221. 1889.

Fritz, M.H. Corneal Opacities among Alaska Natives. Alaska's Health, V, xii, 3-7. 1947.

Fritz, M.H. and Thygeson, P. Phlyctenular Keratoconjunctivitis among Alaskan Indians and Eskimos. PHR, LXVI, 934-9. 1951.

Gates, R.R. Blood Groups of Canadian Indians and Eskimos. AJPA, XII, 475-85. 1929.

Gibbs, G. Notes on the Tinneh or Chepewyan Indians. ARSI, 1866, 303-27.

Goddard, P.E. Assimilation to Environment as illustrated by Athapascan Peoples. ICA, XV, i, 337-59. 1906.

--- Similarities and Diversities within Athapascan Linguistic Stocks. ICA, XXII, ii, 489-94. 1926.

Goddard, P.E., and Swanton, J.R. Athapascan Family. BBAE, XXX, i, 108-11. 1907.

Godsell, P.H. Red Hunters of the Snows. 324 pp. Toronto, 1938.

Grantham, E.N. Education Goes North. CGJ, XLII, 44-9. 1951.

Gsovski, V. Russian Administration of Alaska and the Status of the Alaskan Natives. 104 pp. Washington, 1950.

Haldeman, J.C. Problems of Alaskan Eskimos, Indians, Aleuts. PHR, LXVI, 912-7. 1951.

Harrington, J.P. Southern Peripheral Athapaskawan Origins, Divisions and Migrations. SMC, C, 503-32. 1940.

Heller, C.A. Alaska Nutrition Survey Report: Dietary Study. Alaska's Health, VI, x, 7-9. 1948.

Heller, C.A. Food and Dental Health. Alaska's Health, IV, xii, 4-5. 1946.

Hermant, P. Évolution économique et sociale de certaines peuplades de l'Amérique du nord. BSRBG, XXVIII, 341-57. 1904.

Hill-Tout, C. British North America. 263 pp. London, 1907.

Honigmann, J.J. and I. Drinking in an Indian-White Community. QJSA, V, 575-619. 1945.

Hrdlicka, A. Anthropological Survey of Alaska. ARBAE, XLVI, 19-374. 1930.

--- Catalogue of Human Crania in the United States National Museum Collections. PUSNM, XCIV, 1-172. 1944.

Ingstad, H.M. Land of Feast and Famine. 332 pp. New York, 1933.

--- Pelsjegerliv blandt Nord-Kanadas Indianere. 245 pp. Oslo, 1931.

Innis, H.A. The Fur Trade in Canada. 444 pp. New Haven, 1930.

Jenness, D. The Indians of Canada. BNMC, LXV, 3rd ed., 452 pp. 1955.

Kerr, R. For the Royal Scottish Museum. B, CCLXXXIV, June, 32-5. 1953.

Kidd, K.E. Trading into Hudson's Bay. B, CCLXXXVIII, iii, 12-7. 1957.

Korner, I.N. Notes of a Psychologist Fieldworker. An, n.s., I, 91-105. 1959.

Krenov, J. Legends from Alaska. JSAP, XL, n.s., 173-95. 1951.

Kroeber, A.L. Athabascan Kin Term Systems. AA, n.s., XXXIX, 602-9. 1937.

Latham, R.G. On the Ethnography of Russian America. JESL, I, 182-91. 1848.

Laviolette, G. Notes on the Aborigines of the Prairie Provinces. An, II, 107-30. 1956.

Leechman, D. Aboriginal Tree-Felling. BNMC, CXVIII, 44-9. 1950.

--- Yukon Territory. CGJ, XL, 240-67. 1950.

Lindenkohl, A. Das Gebiet des Jukon-Flusses. PMJP, XXXVIII, 134-9. 1892.

Lockhart, J.G. Notes on the Habits of the Moose in the Far North of British America in 1865. PUSNM, XIII, 305-8. 1890.

Mackenzie, A. Voyage from Montreal through the Continent of North America to the Frozen and Pacific Oceans. New edit. 2 vols. New York, 1902.

McLean, J. Notes of a Twenty-Five Years' Service in the Hudson's Bay Territory, ed. W.S.Wallace. PCS, XIX, 1-402. 1932.

McMinimy, D.J. Preliminary Report on Tuberculosis Incidence in Alaska. Alaska's Health, V, x, 4-5. 1947.

MacNeish, J.H. The Poole Field Letters. An, IV, 47-60. 1957.

MacNeish, R.S. A Speculative Framework of Northern North American Prehistory as of April 1959. An, n.s., I, 7-23. 1959.

Mallet, T. Glimpses of the Barren Lands. 146 pp. New York, 1930.

--- Plain Tales of the North. 136 pp. New York, 1926.

Mason, M.H. The Arctic Forests. London, 1924.

Moore, A. Education in the MacKenzie District. The New North-West, ed. C.A.Dawson, pp. 243-69. 1947.

Morice, A.G. Au pays de l'ours noir. Paris, 1897.

--- The Canadian Dénés. AAR, 1905, 187-219.

--- The Déné Languages. TCI, I, 170-212. 1889.

--- Déné Roots. TCI, III, 145-64. 1891.

--- Dénés. Catholic Encyclopedia, IV, 717-19.

--- Dénés. ERE, IV, 636-41. 1912.

--- Les Dénés du nord. BSGQ, XXII, 146-90. 1928.

--- La femme chez les Dénés. ICA, XV, i, 361-94. 1906.

--- The Great Déné Race. A, I, 229-77, 483-508, 695-730; II, 1-34, 181-96; IV, 582-606; V, 113-42, 419-43, 643-53, 969-90. 1906-10.

--- Northwestern Dénés and Northeastern Asiatics. TCI, X, 131-93. 1914.

--- On the Classification of the Déné Tribes. TCI, VI, 75-83. 1899.

--- Smoking and Tobacco among the Northern Dénés. AA, n.s., XXIII, 482-8. 1921.

--- The Unity of Speech among the Northern and the Southern Déné. AA, n.s., IX, 720-37. 1907.

--- Le verbe dans les langues dénées. ICA, XVI, 577-95. 1908.

Olson, R.L. Adze, Canoe, and House Types of the Northwest Coast. UWPA, II, 1-38. 1927.

Osgood, C. The Distribution of the Northern Athapaskan Indians. YUPA, VII, 1-23. 1936.

--- Winter. 255 pp. New York, 1953.

Paulson, I. The "Seat of Honor" in Aboriginal Dwellings in the Circumpolar Zone. ICA, XXIX, iii, 63-5. 1952.

Petitot, E.F.S. Accord des mythologies dans la cosmogonie des Danites arctiques. 493 pp. Paris, 1890.

--- Les Déné-Dindjiés. ICA, I, ii, 13-37, 245-56. 1875.

--- En route pour la mer glaciale. Paris, 1887.

--- Essai sur l'origine des Déné-Dindjié. Paris, 1875.

--- Etude sur la nation Montagnaise ou Tchippewayne. MC, I, 135-6, 144, 151-2, 159-60, 168, 183-4, 199-200, 206-8, 215-16. 1868.

--- Exploration de la région du Grand Lac des Ours. Paris, 1893.

--- Monographie des Dene-Dindjié. 109 pp. Paris, 1876.

--- On the Athabasca District of the Canadian North-West Territory. PRGS, n.s., V, 633-55. 1883.

Petitot, E.F.S. Outils en pierre et en os du Mackenzie.
Matériaux pour l'Histoire Primitive et Naturelle de
l'Homme, 1875, 398-405.

--- Quinze ans sous le cercle polaire. 322 pp. Paris,
1889.

--- Traditions indiennes du Canada nord-ouest. Actes
de la Société Philologique, XVI-XVII, 169-614.
1888.

Pilling, J.C. Bibliography of the Athapascan Languages. BBAE, XIV, 1-125. 1892.

Rae, J. Correspondence with the Hudson's Bay Company on Arctic Exploration 1844-1855. HBRS, XVI,
509 pp. 1953.

Ross, B.R. An Account of the Animals Useful in an
Economic Point of View to the Various Chipewyan
Tribes. CNG, VI, 433-44. 1861.

--- An Account of the Botanical and Mineral Products
Useful to the Chipewyan Tribes of Indians. CNG,
VII, 133-7. 1862.

--- On the Indian Tribes of McKenzie River District
and the Arctic Coast. CNG, IV, 190-7. 1859.

Sapir, E. The Na-dene Languages. AA, n.s., XVII,
535-8. 1915.

--- A Type of Athapascan Relative. IJAL, II, 136-
42. 1923.

Sargent, M. Folk and Primitive Music in Canada.
BNMC, CXXIII, 75-9. 1951.

Schwatka, F. Report of a Military Reconnaissance in
Alaska. 121 pp. Washington, 1885.

Sherwood, A. Some Remarks about the Athapaskan
Indians. An, VI, 51-6. 1958.

Swanton, J.R. The Development of the Clan System
and of Secret Societies among the Northwestern Indians. AA, n.s., VI, 477-85. 1904.

Taché, A.A. Vingt Années de Missions dans le Nord-
ouest de l'Amérique. 239 pp. Montreal, 1888.

Taché, J.C. Esquisse sur le nord-ouest de l'Amérique,
pp. 86-91. Montreal, 1869.

Teit, J.A. Indian Tribes of the Interior. Canada and
Its Provinces, XXI, 283-312. Toronto, 1914.

Teit, J.A. et al. Coiled Basketry in British Columbia.
ARBAE, XLI, 119-484. 1924.

Urquhart, J.A. The Most Northerly Practice in Canada. Canadian Medical Association Journal, XXXIII,
193-6. 1935.

Voegelin, C.F. and E.W. Linguistic Considerations
of Northeastern North America. PRSPF, III, 178-
94. 1946.

Waugh, F.W. Canadian Aboriginal Canoes. CFN,
XXXIII, 23-33. 1919.

White, M.C. David Thompson's Journals Relating to
Montana and Adjacent Regions, 1808-1812. 507 pp.
Missoula, 1950.

Wilson, C. The New North in Pictures. 223 pp.
Toronto, 1947.

Wissler, C. Culture of the North American Indians
occupying the Caribou Area. PNAS, I, 51-4. 1915.

1. AHTENA

Including the Ahtena proper (Ahtna-khotana or
Midnoosky) and the Eyak of the delta of the Copper
River.

Birket-Smith, K., and Laguna, F. de. The Eyak
Indians of the Copper River Delta. 591 pp. København, 1938.

Abercrombie, W.R. A Military Reconnaissance of the
Copper River Valley. Compilation of Narratives of
Explorations in Alaska, pp. 563-91. Washington,
1900.

Allen, H.T. Atnatanas. ARSI, 1886, 258-66.

--- Report of an Expedition to the Copper, Tanana,
and Koyukuk Rivers, pp. 19-23, 127-36. Washington, 1887.

Galitzin, E. Observations recueillies par l'Admiral
Wrangell. NAV, CXXXVII, 195-221. 1853.

Huntington, F. Ahtena. BBAE, XXX, i, 30-1. 1907.

Laguna, F. de. A Preliminary Sketch of the Eyak Indians. PPAS, I, 63-75. 1937.

Learnard, H.G. A Trip from Portage Bay to Turnagain
Arm and up the Sushitna. Compilation of Narratives
of Explorations in Alaska, pp. 648-77. Washington,
1900.

Li, F.-K. A Type of Noun Formation in Athabaskan
and Eyak. IJAL, XXII, 45-8. 1956.

Petroff, I. Report on the Population, Industries, and
Resources of Alaska. U.S. Department of the Interior, Tenth Census, VIII, ii, 164-5. 1880.

Pinart, A.L. A Few Words on the Alaska Déné. A,
I, 907-13. 1906.

--- Sur les Atnahs. Revue de Philologie et d'Ethnographie, II, 1-8. 1875.

Richardson, J. Arctic Searching Expedition, pp. 238-
43. New York, 1852.

2. BEAVER

Also called Tsattine.

Goddard, P.E. The Beaver Indians. APAM, X, 201-
93. 1916.

Anonymous. Tsattine. BBAE, XXX, ii, 822. 1910.

Faraud, H.J. Dix-huit ans chez les sauvages. 456 pp. Paris, 1866.

Garrioch, A.C. A Vocabulary of the Beaver Indian Language. 138 pp. London, 1885.

Goddard, P.E. Beaver Dialect. APAM, X, 399-517. 1917.

--- Beaver Texts. APAM, X, 295-397. 1916.

Grant, J.C.B. Anthropometry of the Beaver, Sekani, and Carrier Indians. BCDM, LXXXI, 1-37. 1936.

--- Progress in an Anthropometric Survey of the Canadian Aborigines. PPSC, V, iv, 2715-21. 1933.

Keith, G. Letters to Mr. Roderic McKenzie. BCNO, II, 1-92. 1890.

3. CARRIER

Including the Carrier proper (Takulli) and the Babine.

Morice, A.G. Notes Archaeological, Industrial, and Sociological on the Western Dénés. TCI, IV, 1-222. 1893.

Anonymous. Takulli. BBAE, XXX, ii, 675-6. 1910.

Barbeau, C.M. Indian Days in the Canadian Rockies. 208 pp. Toronto, 1923.

--- Sons of the Northwest. Musical Quarterly, XIX, 101-11. 1933.

Boas, F. Summary of the Work of the Committee in British Columbia. BAAS, LXVIII, 667-83. 1898.

Cox, R. Adventures on the Columbia River. 335 pp. New York, 1932.

Duff, W. Notes on Carrier Social Organization. ABC, II, 28-34. 1951.

Goldman, I. The Alkatcho Carrier: Historical Background of Crest Prerogatives. AA, n.s., XLIII, 396-418. 1941.

--- The Alkatcho Carrier of British Columbia. ASAIT, 333-89. 1940.

Grant, J.C.B. Anthropometry of the Beaver, Sekani, and Carrier Indians. BCDM, LXXXI, 1-37. 1936.

--- Progress in an Anthropometric Survey of the Canadian Aborigines. PPSC, V, iv, 2715-21. 1933.

Hamilton, G. Customs of the New Caledonian Women belonging to the Nancausky Tine or Stuart's Lake Indians, Natotin Tine or Babine's and Nantley Tine or Fraser Lake Tribes. JAI, VII, 206-8. 1878.

Harmon, D.W. A Journal of Voyages and Travels in the Interior of North America, ed. W.L. Grant, pp. 242-64, 353-64. Toronto, 1911.

Hill-Tout, C. British North America. 263 pp. Toronto, 1907.

Jenness, D. The Ancient Education of a Carrier Indian. BCDM, LXII, 22-7. 1929.

--- The Carrier Indians of the Bulkley River. BBAE, CXXXIII, 469-586. 1943.

--- An Indian Method of treating Hysteria. PM, VI, 13-20. 1933.

--- Indians of Canada. BCDM, LXV, 363-8. 1932.

--- Myths of the Carrier Indians. JAFL, XLVII, 97-257. 1934.

Mackenzie, A. Voyages from Montreal. New edit. 2 vols. New York, 1902.

McLean, J. Notes of a Twenty-Five Years Service in the Hudson's Bay Territory, ed. W.S. Wallace. PCS, XIX, 176-84. 1932.

Morice, A.G. L'abstraction dans la langue des Porteurs. ICA, XXI, i, 323-35. 1924.

--- Are the Carrier Sociology and Mythology Indigenous or Exotic? PTRSC, ser. 1, X, ii, 109-26. 1892.

--- Carrier Indians. ERE, III, 229-30. 1911.

--- The Carrier Language. 2 vols. Wien, 1932.

--- Carrier Onomatology. AA, n.s., XXXV, 632-58. 1933.

--- Carriers and Ainos at Home. AAOJ, XXIV, 88-93. 1902.

--- The Déné Languages. TCI, I, 170-212. 1891.

--- Déné Surgery. TCI, VII, 15-27. 1901.

--- The Great Déné Race. A, I, 229-77, 483-508, 695-730; II, 1-34, 181-96; IV, 582-606; V, 113-42, 416-43, 643-53, 969-90. 1906-10.

--- The History of the Northern Interior of British Columbia. 339 pp. Toronto, 1904.

--- Smoking and Tobacco among the Northern Dénés. AA, n.s., XXIII, 482-8. 1921.

--- Three Carrier Myths. TCI, V, 1-36. 1895.

--- Two Points of Western Déné Ethnography. AA, n.s., XXVII, 478-82. 1925.

--- The Western Dénés. PCI, ser. 3, VII, 109-74. 1889.

Ogden, P.S. Traits of American-Indian Life and Character. 219 pp. London, 1853.

Ray, V.F. Plateau. AR, VIII, 99-257. 1942.

Scott, L. and Leechman, D. The Carriers. B, CCLXXXIII, iii, 26. 1953.

Seligmann, K. Le Mat-totem de Gédem Skanish (Gydaedem Skanees). JSAP, n.s., XXXI, 121-8. 1939.

Smith, H.I. Entomology among the Bellacoola and Carrier Indians. AA, n.s., XXVII, 436-40. 1925.

--- Materia Medica of the Bella Coola and Neighbouring Tribes. BCDM, LVI, 47-68. 1929.

Steward, J.H. Determinism in Primitive Society? SM, LIII, 491-501. 1941.

--- Investigations among the Carrier Indians of British Columbia. SM, LII, 280-3. 1941.

--- Recording Culture Changes among the Carrier Indians of British Columbia. EFWSI, 1940, 83-90. 1941.

--- Variation in Ecological Adoptation. TCC, 173-7. 1955.

Tolmie, W.F., and Dawson, G.M. Comparative Vocabularies of the Indian Tribes of British Columbia, pp. 63B-77B. Montreal, 1884.

4. CHILCOTIN

Morice, A.G. Notes Archaeological, Industrial, and Sociological on the Western Dénés. TCI, IV, 1-222. 1893.

Boas, F. Summary of the Work of the Committee in British America. BAAS, LXVIII, 667-83. 1898.

Boas, F., and Farrand, L. Physical Characteristics of the Tribes of British Columbia. BAAS, LXVIII, 628-44. 1898.

Farrand, L. The Chilcotin. BAAS, LXVIII, 645-8. 1898.

--- Traditions of the Chilcotin Indians. MAMNH, IV, 1-54. 1900.

--- Tsilkotin. BBAE, XX, ii, 826. 1910.

Grant, J.C.B. Progress in an Anthropometric Survey of the Canadian Aborigines. PPSC, V, iv, 2715-21. 1933.

Haeberlin, H.K., Teit, J.A., and Roberts, H.H. Coiled Basketry in British Columbia and Surrounding Regions. ARBAE, XLI, 119-484. 1928.

Harrington, J.P. Pacific Coast Athapascan discovered to be Chilcotin. JWAS, XXXIII, 203-13. 1943.

Morice, A.G. The Great Déné Race. A, I, 229-77, 483-508, 695-730; II, 1-34, 181-96; IV, 582-606; V, 113-42, 419-43, 643-53, 969-90. 1906-10.

--- The History of the Northern Interior of British Columbia. 339 pp. Toronto, 1904.

--- The Western Dénés. PCI, ser. 3, VII, 109-74. 1889.

Ray, V.F. Plateau. AR, VIII, 99-257. 1942.

Teit, J.A. Notes on the Chilcotin Indians. MAMNH, IV, 759-89. 1907.

Tolmie, W.F., and Dawson, G.M. Comparative Vocabularies of the Indian Tribes of British Columbia, pp. 62B-77B. Montreal, 1884.

5. CHIPEWYAN

Birket-Smith, K. Contributions to Chipewyan Ethnology. RFTE, V, iii, 1-114. 1930.

Curtis, E.S. The North American Indian, XVIII, 3-52, 125-9, 147-51, 201-5. Norwood, 1928.

Anonymous. Chipewyan. BBAE, XXX, i, 275-6. 1907.

--- Thilanottine. BBAE, XXX, ii, 742-3. 1910.

Back, G. Narrative of the Arctic Land Expedition. 663 pp. London, 1836.

Birket-Smith, K. The Cultural Position of the Chipewyan within the Circumpolar Culture Region. ICA, XXIV, 97-101. 1930.

Crile, G.W. and Quiring, D.P. Indian and Eskimo Metabolisms. Journal of Nutrition, XVIII, 361-8. 1939.

Dobbs, A. An Account of the Countries adjoining to Hudson's Bay. 211 pp. London, 1744.

Dunn, J. History of the Oregon Territory, pp. 101-11. 2d edit. London, 1846.

Faraud, H.J. Dix-huit ans chez les sauvages. 456 pp. Paris, 1866.

Fidler, P. Journal of a Journey with the Chepawyans or Northern Indians. PCS, XXI, 493-556. 1934.

Franklin, J. Narrative of a Journey to the Shores of the Polar Sea. London, 1823.

Goddard, P.E. Analysis of Cold Lake Dialect, Chipewyan. APAM, X, 67-168. 1912.

--- Chipewyan Texts. APAM, X, 1-65. 1912.

Grant, J.C.B. Anthropometry of the Chipewyan and Cree Indians. BCDM, LXIV, 1-59. 1930.

--- Progress in an Anthropometric Survey of the Canadian Aborigines. PPSC, V, iv, 2715-21. 1933.

Harrington, R. In the Land of the Chipewyans. B, CCLXXVII, 25-33. 1947.

--- Making Moccasins. B, CCLXXXIV, June, 36-7. 1953.

Hearne, S. A Journey from Prince of Wale's Fort in Hudson's Bay to the Northern Ocean, ed. J.B. Tyrrell. PCS, VI, 1-437. 1911.

Henry, A. Travels and Adventures in Canada, ed. M.M. Quaife. Chicago, 1921.

Jenness, D., ed. The Chipewyan Indians. An, III, 15-34. 1956.

Kenney, J.F., ed. The Founding of Churchill, being the Journal of Captain James Knight. 213 pp. Toronto, 1932.

King, R. Narrative of a Journey to the Shores of the Arctic Ocean. 2 vols. London, 1836.

Leechman, D. Caribou for Chipewyans. B, CCLXXVIII, 12-13. 1948.

Leechman, D. The Trappers. B, CCLXXXVIII, iii,
24-31. 1957.
--- The Pointed Skins. B, CCLXXVIII, 14-18. 1948.
Legoff, L. Grammaire de la langue Montagnaise.
351 pp. Montreal, 1889.
Li, F.K. Chipewyan. VFPA, VI, 398-423. 1946.
--- Chipewyan Consonants. Bulletin of the Institute
of History and Philology of the Academica Sinica,
Supplementary Volume I: Ts'ai Yuan Pe'i Anniver-
sary Volume, pp. 429-67. Peiping, 1933.
--- A List of Chipewyan Stems. IJAL, VII, 122-51.
1933.
Lofthouse, J. Chipewyan Stories. TCI, X, 43-51.
1913.
Lowie, R.H. The Chipewyans of Canada. SW,
XXXVIII, 278-83. 1909.
--- Chipewyan Tales. APAM, X, 171-200. 1912.
--- An Ethnological Trip to Lake Athabasca. AMJ,
IX, 10-15. 1909.
--- Windigo, a Chipewyan Story. American Indian
Life, ed. E.C.Parsons, pp. 325-36. New York, 1925.
M'Keevor, T. A Voyage to Hudson's Bay, pp. 48-76.
London, 1819.
MacNeish, J.H. Kin Terms of Arctic Drainage Déné.
AA, LXII, 279-95. 1960.
--- Leadership among the Northeastern Athabascans.
An, II, 131-63. 1956.
Morgan, L.H. The Indian Journals, 1859-62, p. 128.
Ann Arbor, 1959.
--- Systems of Consanguinity and Affinity. SCK,
XVII, 291-382. 1871.
Munsterhjelm, E. The Wind and the Caribou. 234
pp. London, 1953.
Pénard, J.M. Land Ownership and Chieftaincy among
the Chippewayan and Caribou-Eaters. PM, II, 20-
4. 1929.
Petitot, E.F.S. Autour du Grand Lac des Esclaves.
369 pp. Paris, 1891.
--- De Carlton-House au Fort Pitt. Société Neucha-
teloise de Géographie, Bulletin, XI, 176-95. 1899.
--- Dictionnaire de la langue Déné-Dindjié. 367 pp.
Paris, 1876.
--- La femme au serpent. Mélusine, II, 19-20. 1884.
--- On the Athabasca District. Canadian Record of
Science, I, 27-53. 1884.
--- Traditions indiennes du Canada nord-ouest. LPTN,
XXIII, 345-442. 1886.
Richardson, J. Arctic Searching Expedition, II, 33-
60, 387-95. London, 1851.
Robson, J. An Account of Six Years Residence in Hud-
son's Bay. 84 pp. London, 1752.
Ross, B.R. The Eastern Tinneh. ARSI, 1866, 304-11.

Rourke, L. The Land of the Frozen Tide, pp. 90-168.
London, 1924.
Seton, E.T. The Arctic Prairies, pp. 147-58. New
York, 1911.
Simpson, G. Journal of Occurrences in the Athabasca
Department, 1820 and 1821. PCS, I, 557 pp. 1938.
Tyrrell, J.B., ed. David Thompson's Narrative of His
Explorations in Western America. PCS, XII, 1-582.
1916.
West, J. The Substance of a Journal during a Residence
at the Red River Colony. London, 1824.
Whitney, C. On Snow-Shoes to the Barren Grounds.
324 pp. New York, 1896.

6. COYUKON

Allen, H.T. Report of an Expedition to the Copper,
Tananá, and Kóyukuk Rivers, pp. 140-2. Washing-
ton, 1887.
Anonymous. Kaiyukhotana. BBAE, XXX, i, 643-4.
1907.
--- Koyukukhotana. BBAE, XXX, i, 729-30. 1907.
Cantwell, J.C. Report of the Operations of the U.S.
Revenue Steamer Nunivak, pp. 209-36, 281-4.
Washington, 1902.
Dall, W.H. Alaska and Its Resources. 627 pp. Bos-
ton, 1870.
Dall, W.H., Dawson, G.M., and Ogilvie, W. The
Yukon Territory. 438 pp. London, 1898.
Erman, A. Ueber die Reise und Entdeckungen des
Lieutenant L. Sagoskin im russischen Amerika.
AWKR, VI, 499-522, 613-72; VII, 429-512. 1848-
49.
Hrdlicka, A. The Ancient and Modern Inhabitants of
the Yukon. EFWSI, 1929, 137-46.
Jette, J. On Ten'a Folk-Lore. JAI, XXXVIII, 298-367;
XXXIX, 460-505. 1908-09.
--- On the Language of the Ten'a. Man, VII, 51-6;
VIII, 72-3; IX, 21-5. 1907-09.
--- On the Medicine-Men of the Ten'a. JAI, XXXVII,
157-88. 1907.
--- On the Superstitions of the Ten'a Indians. A, VI,
95-108, 241-59, 602-15, 699-723. 1911.
--- L'organisation sociale des Ten'as. ICA, XV, i,
395-409. 1906.
--- Riddles of the Ten'a Indians. VIII, 181-201, 630-
51. 1913.
Laguna, F. de. The Prehistory of Northern North Amer-
ica as seen from the Yukon. MSAA, III, 1-360.
1947.
Rainey, F.G. Archeology of Central Alaska. APAM,
XXXVI, 351-404. 1939.

Santos, A. Jesuitos en el Polo Horte. 546 pp. Madrid, 1943.

Sniffen, M. K., and Carrington, T. S. The Indians of the Yukon and Tanana Valleys. Publications of the Indian Rights Association, ser. 2, XCVIII, 3-35. 1914.

Sullivan, R. J. Temporal Concepts of the Ten'a. PM, XV, 57-65. 1942.

--- The Ten'a Food Quest. CUAS, XI, 1-142. 1942.

Whymper, F. A Journey from Norton Sound, Bering Sea, to Fort Youkon. JRGS, XXXVIII, 219-37. 1868.

--- Russian America. TESL, n.s., VII, 167-85. 1869.

--- Travel and Adventure in the Territory of Alaska, pp. 204-15, 343-4. New York, 1869.

Zagoskin, L.A. Peshexodnaa opic chasti russkix vladenii v Amerike. 2 vols. St. Petersburg, 1847-48.

--- Puteshestvie i otkrytia v russkoi Amerike. St. Petersburg, 1847.

--- Résumé des journaux de l'expedition exécutée dans l'interieur de l'Amérique russe, ed. E. Galitzin. NAV, CXXV, 5-16, 216-29, 249-84; CXVI, 170-86, 241-68. 1850.

7. DOGRIB

Anonymous. Thlingchadinne. BBAE, XXX, ii, 744-5. 1910.

Barbeau, M., and G. Melvin. The Indian Speaks, 49-50. Caldwell, 1943.

Bell, J.M. Fireside Stories of the Chippwyans. JAFL, XVI, 73-84. 1903.

Finnie, R. Dogrib Treaty. NH, XLVI, 52-8. 1940.

Franklin, J. Narrative of a Journey to the Shores of the Polar Sea. London, 1823.

--- Narrative of a Second Expedition to the Shores of the Polar Sea. London, 1828.

Gates, R.R. Blood Groups of Canadian Indians and Eskimos. AJPA, XII, 475-85. 1929.

Jérémie, N. Account of Hudson Strait and Bay, ed. R. Douglas and J.N. Wallace. 42 pp. Ottawa, 1926.

Leechman, D. The Trappers. B, CCLXXXVIII, iii, 24-31. 1957.

MacNeish, J.H. Leadership among the Northeastern Athabascans. An, II, 131-63. 1956.

Mason, J.A. Notes on the Indians of the Great Slave Lake Area. YUPA, XXXIV, 1-46. 1946.

Osgood, C. The Ethnography of the Great Bear Lake Indians. BCDM, LXX, 31-92. 1931.

Petitot, E.F.S. Autour du Grand Lac des Esclaves. 369 pp. Paris, 1891.

--- Traditions indiennes du Canada nordouest. LPTN, XXIII, 307-44. 1886.

Richardson, J. Arctic Searching Expedition, II, 1-31, 395-402. London, 1851.

Ross, B.R. The Eastern Tinneh. ARSI, 1866, 304-11.

Russell, F. Explorations in the Far North, pp. 158-86. Iowa City, 1898.

Wheeler, D.E. The Dog-Rib Indian and His Home. Bulletin of the Geographical Society of Philadelphia, XII, ii. 1914.

Whitney, C. On Snow-Shoes to the Barren Grounds. 324 pp. New York, 1896.

8. HAN

✓Adney, T. Moose Hunting with the Tro-chu-tin. HMM, C, 495-507. 1900.

✓Anonymous. Hankutchin. BBAE, XXX, i, 531. 1907.

--- Vuntakutchin. BBAE, XXX, ii, 882-4. 1910.

✓Murray, A.H. Journal of the Yukon. Publications of the Canadian Archives, IV, 1-125. 1910.

✓Schmitter, F. Upper Yukon Native Customs and Folk-Lore. SMC, LVI, iv, 1-30. 1910.

Schwatka, F. Along Alaska's Great River. 360 pp. New York, 1885.

9. HARE

Anonymous. Kawchodinne. BBAE, XXX, i, 667. 1907.

Bell, J.M. Fireside Stories of the Chippwyans. JAFL, XVI, 73-84. 1903.

Franklin, J. Narrative of a Second Expedition to the Shores of the Polar Sea. London, 1828.

Gates, R.R. Blood Groups of Canadian Indians and Eskimos. AJPA, XII, 475-85. 1929.

MacNeish, J.H. Kin Terms of Arctic Drainage Déné. AA, LXII, 279-95. 1960.

--- Leadership among the Northeastern Athabascans. An, II, 131-63. 1956.

Morgan, L.H. Systems of Consanguinity and Affinity. SCK, XVII, 291-382. 1871.

Morice, A.G. Hare Indians. Catholic Encyclopedia, VII, 136-7. 1910.

Osgood, C. The Ethnography of the Great Bear Lake Indians. BCDM, LXX, 31-92. 1931.

Petitot, E.F.S. Dictionnaire de la langue Dene-Dindjié. Paris, 1876.

--- Exploration du Grand Lac des Ours. Paris, 1893.

--- Quinze ans sous le cercle polaire. Paris, 1889.

--- Traditions indiennes du Canada nord-ouest. LPTN, XXIII, 103-306. 1886.

Richardson, J. Arctic Searching Expedition, II, 1-31. London, 1851.

Ross, B.R. The Eastern Tinneh. ARSI, 1866, 304-11.

Simpson, T. Narrative of the Discoveries on the North Coast of America. 419 pp. London, 1843.

10. INGALIK

Osgood, C. Ingalik Material Culture. YUPA, XXII, 1-500. 1940.

--- Ingalik Mental Culture. YUPA, LVI, 1-195. 1959.

--- Ingalik Social Culture. YUPA, LIII, 1-289. 1958.

Cantwell, J.C. Report of the Operations of the U.S. Revenue Steamer Nunivak, pp. 209-36, 281-4. Washington, 1902.

Chapman, J.W. Athapascan Traditions from the Lower Yukon. JAFL, XVI, 180-5. 1903.

--- Notes on the Tinneh Tribe of Anvik. ICA, XV, ii, 7-38. 1907.

--- Ten'a Texts and Tales from Anvik. PAES, VI, 1-230. 1914.

--- Tinneh Animism. AA, n.s., XXIII, 298-310. 1921.

Chapman, M.S. The Animistic Beliefs of the Ten'a of the Lower Yukon. 15 pp. Hartford, 1939.

Dall, W.H. Alaska and Its Resources. 627 pp. Boston, 1870.

Dall, W.H., Dawson, G.M., and Ogilvie, W. The Yukon Territory. 438 pp. London, 1898.

Disselhoff, H.D. Bemerkungen zu einigen Eskimo-Masken. BA, XVIII, 130-7. 1935.

Erman, A. Ueber die Reise und Entdeckungen des Lieutenant L. Sagoskin im russischen Amerika. AWKR, VI, 499-522, 613-72; VII, 429-512. 1848-49.

Galitzin, E. Observations recueillies par l'Admiral Wrangell sur les habitants des cotes nord-ouest de l'Amérique. NAV, CXXXVII, 195-221. 1853.

Hrdlicka, A. The Ancient and Modern Inhabitants of the Yukon. EFWSI, 1929, 137-46.

--- Anthropological Survey of Alaska. ARBAE, XLVI, 19-374. 1930.

Krieger, H.W. Tinne Indians of the Lower Yukon River Valley. EFWSI, 1927, 125-32.

Laguna, F. de. Indian Masks from the Lower Yukon. AA, n.s., XXXVIII, 569-85. 1936.

Oswalt, W. The Archaeology of Hooper Bay Village, Alaska. UAAP, I, 47-91. 1952.

Parsons, E.C. A Narrative of the Ten'a of Anvik. A, XVI-XVII, 51-71. 1921.

Petroff, I. Report of the Population, Industries, and Resources of Alaska. U.S. Department of the Interior, Tenth Census, VIII, ii, 161-2. 1880.

Reed, T.B., and Parsons, E.C. Cries-for-Salmon, a Ten'a Woman. American Indian Life, ed. E.C. Parsons, pp. 337-61. New York, 1925.

Schott, W. Ueber ethnographische Ergebnisse der Sagoskinschen Reise. AWKR, VII, 480-512. 1849.

Schwatka, F. Report of a Military Reconnaissance made in Alaska in 1883, pp. 96-103. Washington, 1900.

Whymper, F. A Journey from Norton Sound, Bering Sea, to Fort Youkon. JRGS, XXXVIII, 219-37. 1868.

--- Russian America. TESL, n.s., VII, 167-85. 1869.

--- Travel and Adventure in the Territory of Alaska, pp. 174-80. New York, 1869.

Woldt, A. Capitain Jacobsen's Reise an der Nordwestküste Amerikas. Leipzig, 1884.

Zagoskin, L.A. Peshexodnaa opic chasti russkix vladenii v Amerike. 2 vols. St. Petersburg, 1847-48.

--- Puteshestvie i otkrytia v russkoi Amerike. St. Petersburg, 1847.

--- Résumé des journaux de l'expédition exécutée dans l'intérieur de l'Amérique russe, ed. E. Galitzin. NAV, CXXV, 5-16, 216-29, 249-84; CXVI, 170-86, 241-68. 1850.

11. KASKA

Also called Eastern Nahane.

Honigmann, J.J. Culture and Ethos of Kaska Society. YUPA, XL, 1-368. 1949.

--- The Kaska Indians. YUPA, LI, 1-163. 1954.

Teit, J.A. Field Notes on the Tahltan and Kaska Indians, 1912-1915. An, III, 39-171. 1956.

Allard, E. Notes on the Kaska and Upper Liard Indians. PM, II, 24-6. 1929.

Dawson, G.M. Notes on the Indian Tribes of the Yukon District and Adjacent Northern Portion of British Columbia. ARCGS, n.s., III, 199B-201B. 1888.

Honigmann, J.J. Are There Nahani Indians? An, III, 35-8. 1956.

--- Culture Patterns and Human Stress. Psychiatry, XIII, 25-34. 1950.

--- Witch-Fear in Post-contact Kaska Society. AA, n.s., XLIX, 222-43. 1947.

Honigmann, J.J. and I. A Kaska Oracle. Man, XLVII, 139-40. 1947.

McClellan, C. Shamanistic Syncretism in Southern Yukon. TNYAS, ser. 2, XIX, 130-7. 1956.

Morice, A.G. The Great Déné Race. A, I, 229-77, 483-508, 695-730; II, 1-34, 181-96; IV, 582-606; V, 113-42, 419-43, 643-53, 969-90. 1906-10.

Morice, A.G.   The Nah-ane and Their Language. TCI, VII, 517-34. 1903.

--- The Western Dénés. PCI, ser. 3, VII, 109-74. 1889.

Swanton, J.R. Nahane. BBAE, XXX, ii, 10. 1910.

Teit, J.A. Kaska Tales. JAFL, XXX, 427-73. 1917.

Underwood, F.W., and Honigmann, I. A Comparison of Socialization and Personality in Two Simple Societies. AA, n.s., XLIX, 557-77. 1947.

12. KUTCHIN

Also called Loucheux.

Osgood, C. Contributions to the Ethnography of the Kutchin. YUPA, XIV, 1-189. 1936.

Anonymous. Kutchin. BBAE, XXX, i, 739-40. 1907.

Barbeau, M. Loucheux Myths. JAFL, XXVIII, 249-57. 1915.

Benveniste, E. Le Vocabulaire de la Vie Animale chez les Indiens du Haut Yukon. Bulletin de la Société de Linguistique de Paris, XLIX, 79-106. 1953.

Boas, F. A. J. Stone's Measurements of Natives of the Northwest Territories. BAMNH, XIV, 53-68. 1901.

Bompas, W.C. Diocese of Mackenzie River. 108 pp. London, 1922.

Cadzow, D.A. Habitat of Loucheux Bands. IN, II, 172-7. 1925.

--- Old Loucheux Clothing. IN, II, 292-5. 1925.

Camsell, C., and Barbeau, C.M. Loucheux Myths. JAFL, XXVIII, 249-57. 1915.

Corcoran, P.A. et al. Blood Groups of Alaskan Eskimo and Indians. AJPA, n.s., XVII, 187-94. 1959.

Dall, W.H. Alaska and Its Resources. 627 pp. Boston, 1870.

Dawson, G.M. Report on an Exploration in the Yukon District. ARCGS, n.s., III, i, 7B-277B. 1889.

Franklin, J. Narrative of a Second Expedition to the Shores of the Polar Sea. London, 1828.

Gates, R.R. Blood Groups of Canadian Indians and Eskimos. AJPA, XII, 475-85. 1929.

Hardisty, W.L. The Loucheux Indians. ARSI, 1866, 311-20.

Hooper, W.H. Ten Months among the Tents of the Tuski. London, 1853.

Isbester, J.A. On a Short Vocabulary of the Loucheux Language. Proceedings of the Philological Society, IV, 184-5. 1850.

Jones, S. The Kutchin Tribes. ARSI, 1866, 320-7.

Kirby, W.W. A Journey to the Youcan. ARSI, 1864, 416-20.

Leechman, D. Folk-Lore of the Vanta-Kutchin. BNMC, CXXVI, 76-93. 1952.

--- Loucheux Tales. JAFL, LXIII, 158-62. 1950.

--- The Old Crow Altar Cloth. CGJ, XLIII, 204-05. 1951.

--- Old Crow's Village. CGJ, XXXVII, 2-16. 1948.

--- The Vanta Kutchin. BNMC, CXXX, 39 pp. 1954.

Mackenzie, A. Voyage from Montreal through the Continent of North America to the Frozen and Pacific Oceans. New edit. 2 vols. New York, 1902.

Mason, M.H. The Arctic Forests, pp. 21-74. London, 1924.

McKennan, R. Anent the Kutchin Tribes. AA, n.s., XXXVII, 369. 1935.

Morgan, L.H. The Indian Journals, 1859-62, pp. 115-6. Ann Arbor, 1959.

--- Systems of Consanguinity and Affinity. SCK, XVII, 293-382. 1871.

Morice, A.G. Loucheux. Catholic Encyclopedia, IX, 367-8. New York, 1910.

Murray, A.H. Journal of the Yukon. Publications of the Canadian Archives, IV, 1-125. 1910.

Osgood, C. Kutchin Tribal Distribution and Synonymy. AA, n.s., XXXVI, 168-79. 1934.

Petitot, E.F.S. Dictionnaire de la langue Dene-Dindjié. Paris, 1876.

--- Monographie des Déné-Dindjié. 109 pp. Paris, 1876.

--- Quinze ans sous le cercle polaire. Paris, 1889.

--- Six légendes américaines. MC, X, 605-7, 616-20. 1878.

--- Traditions indiennes du Canada nord-ouest. LPTN, XXIII, 13-102. 1886.

Petroff, I. The Population and Resources of Alaska. Compilation of Narratives of Explorations in Alaska, pp. 258-63. Washington, 1900.

Richardson, J. Arctic Searching Expedition, I, 377-401. London, 1851.

Russell, F. Athabascan Myths. JAFL, XIII, 11-18. 1900.

Scott, L. The Loucheux. B, CCLXXXIV, June, 26-7. 1953.

Simpson, T. Narrative of the Discoveries on the North Coast of America. 419 pp. London, 1843.

Slobodin, R. Some Social Functions of Kutchin Anxiety. AA, LXII, 122-33. 1960.

Stewart, E. Early Days at Fort McPherson. B, CCLXXXV, iii, 39-41. 1954/55.

Taylor, P. Tales from the Delta. B, CCLXXXIV, June, 22-5. 1953.

Whymper, F. A Journey from Norton Sound, Bering
    Sea, to Fort Yukon. JRGS, XXXVIII, 219-37. 1868.
--- Travel and Adventure in the Territory of Alaska.
    353 pp. New York, 1869.

13. MOUNTAIN

Franklin, J. Narrative of a Second Expedition to the
    Shores of the Polar Sea. London, 1828.
MacNeish, J.H. Leadership among the Northeastern
    Athabascans. An, II, 131-63. 1956.
--- The Poole Field Letters. An, IV, 47-60. 1957.

14. NABESNA

McKennan, R.A. The Upper Tanana Indians. YUPA,
    LV, 1-223. 1959.

Allen, H.T. Report of an Expedition to the Copper,
    Tananá, and Kóyukuk Rivers, pp. 136-9. Washing-
    ton, 1887.
Murray, A.H. Journal of the Yukon. Publications of
    the Canadian Archives, IV, 1-125. 1910.
Rainey, F.G. Archaeology in Central Alaska. APAM,
    XXXVI, 355-405. 1939.

15. SARSI

Jenness, D. The Sarcee Indians of Alberta. BCDM,
    XC, 1-98. 1938.

Chown, B. and Lewis, M. The Blood Group and
    Secretor Genes of the Stony and Sarcee Indians of
    Alberta, Canada. AJPA, n.s., XIII, 181-9. 1955.
Cronk, H.K. Sarcee Miscellany: 1885. PIA, VII,
    34. 1956.
Curtis, E.S. The North American Indian, XVIII, 91-
    122, 136-44, 158-62, 210-14. Norwood, 1928.
Dorsey, J.O., and Goddard, P.E. Sarsi. BBAE, XXX,
    ii, 467-8. 1910.
Goddard, P.E. Dancing Societies of the Sarsi Indians.
    APAM, XI, 461-74. 1914.
--- Notes on the Sun Dance of the Sarsi. APAM, XVI,
    271-82. 1919.
--- Sarsi Texts. UCP, XI, 189-277. 1915.
Honigmann, J.J. Morale in a Primitive Society.
    Character and Personality, XII, 228-36. 1944.
--- Northern and Southern Athapaskan Eschatology.
    AA, n.s., XLVII, 467-9. 1945.

Honigmann, J.J. Notes on Sarsi Kin Behavior. An,
    II, 17-38. 1956.
--- Parallels in the Development of Shamanism among
    Northern and Southern Athapaskans. AA, n.s., LI,
    512-14. 1949.
Li, F.K. A Study of Sarcee Verb Stems. IJAL, VI,
    3-27. 1930.
Matson, G.A. Blood Groups and Ageusia in Indians of
    Montana and Alberta. AJPA, XXIV, 81-9. 1938.
Morgan, L.H. The Indian Journals, 1859-62, p. 128.
    Ann Arbor, 1959.
Palliser, J. Further Papers. 325 pp. London, 1860.
Petitot, E.F.S. Petit vocabulaire Sarcis. Actes de la
    Société Philologique. XIV, 193-8. 1884.
Sapir, E. A Note on Sarcee Pottery. AA, n.s., XXV,
    247-53. 1923.
--- Personal Names among the Sarcee Indians. AA,
    n.s., XXVI, 109-19. 1924.
--- Pitch Accent in Sarcee. JSAP, n.s., XVII, 185-
    205. 1925.
Simms, S.C. Traditions of the Sarcee Indians. JAFL,
    XVII, 180-2. 1904.
Wilson, E.F. Report on the Sarcee Indians. BAAS,
    LVIII, 242-55. 1888.
--- The Sarcee Indians. OFC, III, 97-102. 1889.

16. SATUDENE

Also called Great Bear Lake Indians.

Osgood, C. The Ethnography of the Great Bear Lake
    Indians. BCDM, LXX, 31-92. 1931.

Franklin, J. Narrative of a Second Expedition to the
    Shores of the Polar Sea. London, 1928.
Keith, G. Letters to Mr. Roderic McKenzie. BCNO,
    II, 111-24. 1890.
MacNeish, J.H. Leadership among the Northeastern
    Athabascans. An, II, 131-63. 1956.
Schaeffer, C.E. The Grasshopper or Children's War —
    a Circumboreal Legend? PA, XII, 60-61. 1942.

17. SEKANI

Jenness, D. The Sekani Indians of British Columbia.
    BCDM, LXXXIV, 1-82. 1937.

Anonymous. Sekani. BBAE, XXX, ii, 498-9. 1910.
Grant, J.C.B. Anthropometry of the Beaver, Sekani,
    and Carrier Indians. BCDM, LXXXI, 1-37. 1936.

Hill-Tout, C. British North America. 263 pp.
Toronto, 1907.

Jenness, D. Indians of Canada. BCDM, LXV, 377-
82. 1932.

--- The Sekani Indians of British Columbia. PTRSC,
ser. 3, XXV, ii, 21-34. 1931.

Morice, A.G. About Cremation. AA, n.s., XXVII,
576-7. 1925.

--- Déné Surgery. TCI, VII, 15-27. 1901.

--- The Great Déné Race. A, I, 229-77, 483-508,
695-730; II, 1-34, 181-96; IV, 582-606; V,
113-42, 419-43, 643-53, 969-90. 1906-10.

--- The History of the Northern Interior of British
Columbia. 339 pp. Toronto, 1904.

--- Notes Archaeological, Industrial and Sociological
on the Western Dénés. TCI, IV, 1-222. 1893.

--- The Western Dénés. PCI, ser. 3, VII, 109-74.
1889.

18. SLAVE

Honigmann, J.J. Ethnography and Acculturation of
the Fort Nelson Slave. YUPA, XXXIII, 1-169. 1946.

Anonymous. Etchareottine. BBAE, XXX, i, 439-40.
1907.

Bell, R. Legends of the Slavey Indians. JAFL, XIV,
26-9. 1901.

Bourget, C. Douze Ans Chez les Sauvages. N.P.,
N.D.

Fidler, P. Journal of a Journey with the Chepawyans
or Northern Indians. PCS, XXI, 493-556. 1934.

Gates, R.R. Blood Groups of Canadian Indians and
Eskimos. AJPA, XII, 475-85. 1929.

Jenness, D. Indians of Canada. BCDM, LXV, 389-
92. 1932.

MacNeish, J.H. Contemporary Folk Beliefs of a Slave
Indian Band. JAFL, LXVII, 185-97. 1954.

--- Folktales of the Slave Indians. An, I, 37-44.
1955.

--- Kin Terms of Arctic Drainage Déné. AA, LXII,
279-95. 1960.

--- Leadership among the Northeastern Athabascans.
An, II, 131-63. 1956.

Mason, J.A. Notes on the Indians of the Great Slave
Lake Area. YUPA, XXXIV, 1-46. 1946.

Morgan, L.H. Systems of Consanguinity and Affinity.
SCK, XVII, 291-382. 1871.

Osgood, C. The Ethnography of the Great Bear Lake
Indians. BCDM, LXX, 31-92. 1931.

Petitot, E.F.S. Autour du Grand Lac des Esclaves.
369 pp. Paris, 1891.

Petitot, E.F.S. Traditions indiennes du Canada nord-
ouest. LPTN, XXIII, 307-44. 1886.

Ross, B.R. The Eastern Tinneh. ARSI, 1866, 304-11.

Wentzel, W.F. Letters to the Hon. Roderic McKenzie.
BCNO, I, 85-105. 1889. (The Slave are here called
the "Beaver.")

Williamson, R.G. Slave Indian Legends. An, I, 119-
43; II, 61-92. 1955-56.

19. TAHLTAN

Also called Western Nahane.

Emmons, G.T. The Tahltan Indians. UPMAP, IV,
1-120. 1911.

Anonymous. Nahane. BBAE, XXX, ii, 10. 1910.

Barbeau, M. Songs of the Northwest. Musical Quarterly, XIX, 101-11. 1933.

Boas, F. A.J. Stone's Measurements of Natives of the
Northwest Territories. BAMNH, XIV, 53-68. 1901.

Callbreath, J.C. Notes on the Tahl-tan Indians.
ARCGS, n.s., III, 195B-199B. 1888.

Dennis, A.P. Life on a Yukon Trail. NGM, X, 384-
7. 1899.

Emmons, G.T. Tahltan. BBAE, XXX, ii, 670-1. 1910.

Jenness, D. Indians of Canada. BCDM, LXV, 370-6.
1932.

MacLachlan, B.B. Notes on Some Tahltan Oral Literature. An, IV, 1-10. 1957.

Morice, A.G. The Great Déné Race. A, I, 229-77,
483-508, 695-730; II, 1-34, 181-96; IV, 582-606;
V, 113-42, 419-43, 643-53, 969-90. 1906-10.

--- The History of the Northern Interior of British
Columbia, pp. 1-32. Toronto, 1904.

--- The Nah·ane and Their Language. TCI, VII, 517-
34. 1903.

--- Nahanes. Catholic Encyclopedia, X, 669-70. 1911.

--- The Western Dénés. PCI, ser. 3, VII, 109-74.
1889.

Teit, J.A. Field Notes on the Tahltan and Kaska Indians, 1912-1915. An, III, 39-171. 1956.

--- Notes on the Tahltan Indians of British Columbia.
Boas Anniversary Volume, pp. 337-49. New York,
1906.

--- On Tahltan (Athabaskan) Work. SRGSC, 1912,
484-7.

--- Tahltan Tales. JAFL, XXXII, 198-250; XXXIV,
223-53, 335-56. 1919-21.

--- Two Tahltan Traditions. JAFL, XXII, 314-18.
1909.

20. TANAINA

Also called Kenai and Knaiakhotana.

Osgood, C. The Ethnography of the Tanaina. YUPA,
 XVI, 1-229. 1937.

Abercrombie, W.R. A Military Reconnaissance of the
 Copper River Valley. Compilation of Narratives of
 Explorations in Alaska, pp. 563-91. Washington,
 1900.
Anonymous. Knaiakhotana. BBAE, XXX, i, 715-17.
 1907.
--- Ueber die Kinaivölker im äussersten Nord-westen
 Amerikas. Globus, XXVI, 87-8. 1874.
Castner, J.C. A Story of Hardship and Suffering in
 Alaska. Compilation of Narratives of Explorations
 in Alaska, pp. 686-709, Washington, 1900.
Cook, F.A. To the Top of the Continent, pp. 269-
 77. New York, 1908.
Galitzin, E. Observations recueillies par l'Admiral
 Wrangell sur les habitants des cotes nord-ouest de
 l'Amérique. NAV, CXXXVII, 195-221. 1853.
Glenn, E.F. Explorations in and about Cooks Inlet.
 Compilation of Narratives of Explorations in Alaska,
 pp. 713-24. Washington, 1900.
Herron, J.S. Explorations in Alaska, 1899, for an All-
 American Overland Route from Cook Inlet, Pacific
 Ocean, to the Yukon. 77 pp. Washington, 1901.
Krusenstern, A.J. von. Wörter-Sammlungen aus den
 Sprachen einiger Völker des östlichen Asien und der
 Nordwest-Küste von Amerika, pp. 59-68. St.
 Petersburg, 1813.
Laguna, F. de. The Archaeology of Cook Inlet. 263
 pp. Philadelphia, 1934.
Learnard, H.G. A Trip from Portage Bay to Turnagain
 Arm and up the Sushitna. Compilation of Narratives
 of Explorations in Alaska, pp. 648-77. Washington,
 1900.
Lisiansky, U. A Voyage round the World. London,
 1814.
Mason, J.A. A Remarkable Stone Lamp from Alaska.
 MJ, XIX, 170-94. 1928.
Osgood, C. Tanaina Culture. AA, n.s., XXXV, 695-
 717. 1933.
Petroff, I. Report on the Population, Industries, and
 Resources of Alaska. U.S. Department of the In-
 terior, Tenth Census, VIII, ii, 162-4. 1881.
Radloff, L. Einige kritische Bemerkungen über Hrn.
 Buschmann's Behandlung der Kinai-Sprache. Acadé-
 mie Impériale des Sciences, Mélanges Russes, III,
 364-99. 1857.

Radloff, L. Wörterbuch der Kinaisprache. Mémoires
 de l'Académie Impériale des Sciences de St. -Péters-
 bourg, ser. 7, XXI, viii, 1-33. 1874.
Richardson, J. Arctic Searching Expedition. London,
 1851.
Woldt, A. Capitain Jacobsen's Reise an der Nordwestküste Amerikas. Leipzig, 1884.
Wrangell, F.P. von. Obitateli severo-zapadyx veregov
 Ameriki. Syn Otechestva, VII, 51-82. St. Petersburg, 1839.
--- Statistische und ethnographische Nachrichten an
 der Nordwestküste von Amerika. BKRR, I, 103-16.
 1838.

21. TANANA

Anonymous. Tenankutchin. BBAE, XXX, ii, 727-8.
 1910.
Cantwell, J.C. Report of the Operations of the U.S.
 Revenue Steamer Nunivak, pp. 209-36, 281-4.
 Washington, 1902.
Dall, W.H. Alaska and Its Resources. 627 pp. Bos-
 ton, 1870.
Gordon, G.B. In the Alaskan Wilderness. 247 pp.
 Philadelphia, 1917.
Hrdlicka, A. Anthropological Survey of Alaska.
 ARBAE, XLVI, 19-374. 1930.
Murray, W.H. Journal of the Yukon. Publications of
 the Canadian Archives, IV, 1-125. 1910.
Rainey, F.G. Archeology in Central Alaska. APAM,
 XXXVI, 351-404. 1939.
Schwatka, F. Report of a Military Reconnaissance
 made in Alaska, pp. 323-62. Washington, 1900.
Sniffen, M.K., and Carrington, T.S. The Indians of
 the Yukon and Tanana Valleys. Publications of the
 Indian Rights Association, ser. 2, XCVIII, 3-35.
 1914.

22. TSETSAUT

Anonymous. Tsetsaut. BBAE, XXX, ii, 825. 1910.
Boas, F. Physical Characteristics of the Tribes of the
 North Pacific Coast. BAAS, LXV, 524-51. 1895.
--- The Tinneh Tribe of Portland Inlet. BAAS, LXV,
 555-69, 587-92. 1895.
--- Traditions of the Ts'ets'aut. JAFL, IX, 257-68;
 X, 35-48. 1896-97.
Boas, F., and Goddard, P.E. Ts'ets'áut. IJAL, III,
 1-35. 1924.
Morice, A.G. The Nah-ane and Their Language. TCI,
 VII, 517-34. 1903.

23. TUTCHONE

Anonymous. Tutchonekutchin. BBAE, XXX, ii, 855. 1910.

Campbell, R. Discovery and Exploration of the Youcon River. Winnipeg, 1885.

Dawson, G.M. Notes on the Indian Tribes of the Yukon District and Adjacent Northern Portion of British Columbia. ARCGS, n.s., III, 191B-213B. 1888.

McClellan, C. Shamanistic Syncretism in Southern Yukon. TNYAS, ser. 2, XIX, 130-7. 1956.

McClellan, C. and Rainier, D. Ethnological Survey of Southern Yukon Territory, 1948. BNMC, CXVIII, 50-3. 1950.

Schwatka, F. Along Alaska's Great River. 360 pp. New York, 1885.

--- Report of a Military Reconnaissance made in Alaska in 1883, pp. 323-62. Washington, 1900.

24. YELLOWKNIFE

Anonymous. Tatsanottine. BBAE, XXX, ii, 698-9. 1910.

Franklin, J. Narrative of a Journey to the Shores of the Polar Sea. London, 1823.

Hearne, S. A Journey from Prince of Wale's Fort in Hudson's Bay to the Northern Ocean, ed. J.B. Tyrrell. PCS, VI, 1-437. 1911.

King, R. Narrative of a Journey to the Shores of the Arctic Ocean. 2 vols. London, 1836.

MacNeish, J.H. Leadership among the Northeastern Athabascans. An, II, 131-63. 1956.

Mason, J.A. Notes on the Indians of the Great Slave Lake Area. YUPA, XXXIV, 1-46. 1946.

Morice, A.G. Yellow-Knives. Catholic Encyclopedia, XV, 733. New York, 1912.

Petitot, E.F.S. La femme aux metaux. Meaux, 1888.

--- De l'origine asiatique des Indiens de l'Amérique arctique. Actes de la Société Philologique, XII, 41-58. 1883.

Pike, W.M. The Barren Ground of Northern Canada. 300 pp. London, 1892.

Ross, B.R. The Eastern Tinneh. ARSI, 1866, 304-11.

Simpson, G. Journal of Occurrences in the Athabasca Department, 1820 and 1821. PCS, I, 557 pp. 1938.

III. NORTHWEST COAST

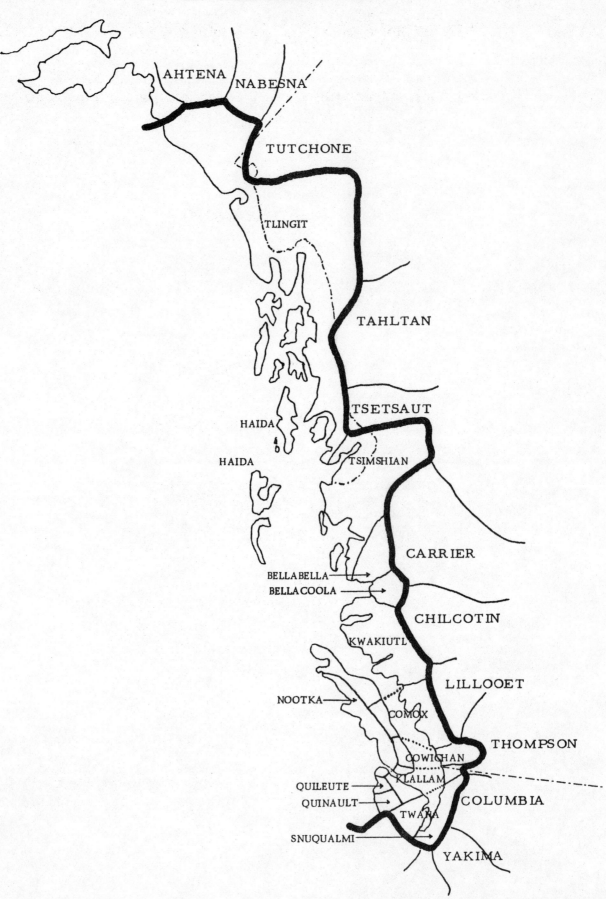

III. NORTHWEST COAST

The tribes of this area are grouped under the following linguistic stocks:

Chimakuan: Chemakum (sub Twana), Quileute.
Chimmesyan: Tsimshian.
Nadene or Great Athapaskan: Haida, Tlingit.
Salishan: Bellacoola, Comox, Cowichan, Klallam,
   Quinault, Snuqualmi, Twana.
Wakashan: Bellabella, Kwakiutl, Nootka.

Adam, L. Nordwest-amerikanische Indianerkunst.
44 pp. Berlin, 1929.
--- North-West American Indian Art and Its Early
Chinese Parallels. Man, XXXVI, 8-11. 1936.
--- Potlatch. Festschrift Eduard Seler, pp. 27-45.
Stuttgart, 1922.
Allen, R.A. The Potlatch and Social Equilibrium.
DJA, II, 43-54. 1956.
Averkieva, U.P. Rabstvo u Indietsev Severnoi
Ameriki. 100 pp. Moscow, 1941.
--- Rabstvo u plemen severo-zapadnogo poberezh'ia
Sev Ameriki. SE, 1935, iv, 40-61.
Bagley, C.B. Indian Myths of the Northwest. 145
pp. Seattle, 1930.
Ballard, A.C. Calendric Terms of the Southern Puget
Sound Salish. SJA, VI, 79-99. 1950.
Bancroft, H.H. History of the Northwest Coast. 2
vols. San Francisco, 1884.
--- The Native Races of the Pacific States, I, 150-
310. New York, 1875.
Bandi, H.G. Einige Gegenstände aus Alaska und
Britisch Kolumbien. ICA, XXXII, 214-20. 1958.
Barbeau, M. Alaska Beckons. 330 pp. Caldwell,
1947.
--- The Aleutian Route of Migration into America.
GR, XXXV, 424-43. 1945.
--- Asiatic Migrations into America. CHR, XIII,
403-17. 1932.
--- Asiatic Survivals in Indian Songs. SM, LIV, 303-
7. 1942.
--- The Bearing of the Heraldry of the Indians of the
North-West Coast of America upon Their Social
Organisation. Man, XII, 83-90. 1912.
--- Bear Mother. JAFL, LIX, 1-12. 1946.
--- The Beaver in Canadian Art. B, CCLXXII, ii,
14-18. 1941.
--- How Totem Poles originated. Queen's Quarterly,
XLVI, 304-11. 1939.
--- Indian Silversmiths on the Pacific Coast. PTRSC,
ser. 3, XXXIII, ii, 23-8. 1939.
--- Medicine Men on the North Pacific Coast. BNMC,
CLII, 95 pp. 1958.
--- Migrations Sibériennes en Amérique. MPR, i,
17-48. 1958.

Barbeau, M. The Modern Growth of the Totem Pole.
ICA, XXIII, 505-11. 1928.
--- The Modern Growth of the Totem Pole. Custom
is King, ed. L.H.D.Buxton, pp. 85-94. London,
1936.
--- The Modern Growth of the Totem Pole. JWAS,
XXVIII, 385-93. 1938.
--- The Modern Growth of the Totem Pole. ARSI,
1939, 491-8. 1940.
--- The Old-world Dragon in America. ICA, XXIX,
iii, 115-24. 1952.
--- Parallel between the Northwest Coast and Iroquo-
ian Clans and Phratries. AA, n.s., XIX, 403-5.
1917.
--- Pathfinders in the North Pacific. 235 pp. Cald-
well, 1958.
--- The Siberian Origin of Our North-Western Indians.
PPSC, V, iv, 2777-89. 1933.
--- Songs of the Northwest. Musical Quarterly, XIX,
101-11. 1933.
--- Totem Poles. ARSI, 1931, 559-70.
--- Totem Poles. SM, LV, 503-14. 1942.
--- Totem Poles. 2 vols. BNMC, CXIX, 892 pp.
1950.
--- "Totemic Atmosphere" on the Northwest Pacific
Coast. JAFL, LXVII, 103-22. 1954.
--- Totemism, a Modern Growth on the North Pacific
Coast. JAFL, LVII, 51-8. 1944.
Barbeau, M., and Melvin, G. The Indian Speaks.
117 pp. Toronto, 1943.
Barnett, H.G. The Coast Salish of British Columbia.
UOSA, IV, 333 pp. 1955.
--- The Nature of the Potlatch. AA, n.s., XL, 349-
58. 1938.
--- The Southern Extent of Totem Pole Carving. PNQ,
XXXIII, 379-89. 1942.
Barrow, F.J. Petroglyphs and Pictographs of the British
Columbian Coast. CGJ, XXIV, 94-101. 1942.
Bastian, A., ed. Amerikas Nordwestküste. Berlin,
1893.
Boas, F. Classification of the Languages of the North
Pacific Coast. MICA, I, 339-46. 1894.
--- Comparative Vocabulary of Eighteen Languages
spoken in British Columbia. BAAS, LX, 692-715.
1890.
--- The Decorative Art of the Indians of the North
Pacific Coast. BAMNH, IX, 123-76. 1897.
--- The Development of the Culture of Northwest
America. Science, XII, 194-6. 1888.
--- Facial Paintings of the Indians of Northern British
Columbia. MAMNH, II, 13-24. 1900.
--- First General Report on the Indians of British
Columbia. BAAS, LIX, 801-900. 1889.

Boas, F. The Growth of American Mythologies. JAFL,
    IX, 1-11. 1896.
--- Indianische Sagen von der Nord-pacifischen Küste
    Amerikas. 363 pp. Berlin, 1895.
--- The Indians of British Columbia. PTRSC, ser. 1,
    VI, ii, 47-57. 1889.
--- The Jessup North Pacific Expedition. ICA, XIII,
    91-100. 1902.
--- Die Mythologie der nordwest-amerikanischen
    Küstenvölker. Globus, LIII, 121-7, 153-7, 299-
    302; LIV, 10-14. 1888.
--- The Physical Characteristics of the Tribes of the
    North Pacific Coast. BAAS, LXI, 424-49; LXV,
    524-51. 1891-95.
--- Preliminary Notes on the Indians of British Colum-
    bia. BAAS, LVIII, 236-42. 1888.
--- Primitive Art, pp. 183-298. Oslo, 1927.
--- Die Resultate der Jesup-Expedition. ICA, XVI,
    3-18. 1908.
--- The Social Organization of the Tribes of the
    North Pacific Coast. AA, n.s., XXVI, 323-32.
    1924.
--- Summary of the Work of the Committee in British
    Columbia. BAAS, LXVIII, 667-83. 1898.
--- The Tribes of the North Pacific Coast. AAR,
    1905, 235-49.
--- Die Verbreitung der Indianer-Sprachen in Britisch-
    Columbien. PMJP, XLII, 21. 1896.
--- Zur Ethnologie von Britisch-Kolumbiens. PMJP,
    XXXIII, 129-33. 1887.
Boas, F., and Farrand, L. Physical Characteristics of
    the Tribes of British Columbia. BAAS, LXVIII,
    628-44. 1898.
Boas, F., and Haeberlin, H.K. Sound Shifts in
    Salishan Dialects. IJAL, IV, 117-36. 1927.
Bogardus, E.S. Symbolism in Totem Poles. Soci-
    ology and Social Research, XXXVI, 247-51. 1951-
    1952.
Borden, C.E. Distribution, Culture, and Origin of
    the Indigenous Population of British Columbia.
    British Columbia Natural Resources Conference,
    Transactions, VII, 186-96. 1954.
Buckham, A.F. Indian Engineering. CGJ, XL, 174-
    81. 1950.
Buschmann, J.C.E. Die Völker und Sprachen Neu-
    Mexico's und der Westseite des britischen Nordamer-
    ika's. AKAWB, 1857, 209-404.
Canada, Dept. of Mines and Resources, Indian Affairs
    Branch. Census of Indians in Canada, 1939 and
    1944. Ottawa, 1940, 1944.
Clark, E.E. George Gibbs' Account of Indian Myth-
    ology in Oregon and Washington Territories. OHQ,
    LVI, 293-325; LVII, 125-67. 1955-56.

Clark, E.E. Indian Legends of the Pacific Northwest.
    233 pp. Berkeley, 1953.
--- Indian Story-telling of Old in the Pacific North-
    west. OHQ, LIV, 91-101. 1953.
--- The Mythology of the Indians in the Pacific North-
    west. OHQ, LIV, 163-89. 1953.
Codere, H. The Swaíxwe Myth of the Middle Fraser
    River. JAFL, LXI, 1-18. 1948.
Collins, J.M. The Indian Shaker Church. SJA, VI,
    399-411. 1950.
--- The Mythological Basis for Attitudes among Salish-
    Speaking Indians. JAFL, LXV, 353-58. 1952.
--- The Oolachan Fishery. BCHQ, V, 25-31. 1941.
Costello, J.A. The Siwash. 169 pp. Seattle, 1895.
Crosby, T. Up and Down the North Pacific Coast by
    Canoe and Mission Ship. 403 pp. Toronto, 1914.
Dall, W.H. On Masks, Labrets and Certain Aborigi-
    nal Customs. ARBAE, III, 106-20. 1884.
Davidson, D.S. Family Hunting Territories in North-
    western North America. INM, XLV, 5-34. 1928.
Davis, R.T. Native Arts of the Pacific Northwest.
    165 pp. Stanford, 1949.
Dawson, G.M. Sketches of the Past and Present Con-
    dition of the Indians of Canada. Canadian Natural-
    ist, n.s., IX, 129-59. 1881.
Densmore, F. Music of the Indians of British Colum-
    bia.BBAE, CXXXVI, 1-99. 1943.
Dixon, R.B. Tobacco Chewing on the Northwest
    Coast. AA, n.s., XXXV, 146-50. 1933.
Douglas, F.H. Northwest Coast Indians. DAMLS, I,
    1-3. 1930.
--- The Northwest Coast Tribes. DAMLS, LXXII, 86-
    8. 1936.
Driver, H.E. Girls' Puberty Rites in Western North
    America. AR, VI, 21-90. 1941.
Drucker, P. The Antiquity of the Northwest Coast
    Totem Pole. JWAS, XXXVIII, 389-97. 1948.
--- Culture Element Distributions: XXVI, Northwest
    Coast. AR, IX, 157-294. 1950.
--- Indians of the Northwest Coast. 220 pp. New
    York, 1955.
--- The Native Brotherhoods. BBAE, CLXVIII, 197
    pp. 1958.
--- Rank, Wealth, and Kinship in Northwest Coast
    Society. AA, n.s., XLI, 55-65. 1939.
--- Sources of Northwest Coast Culture. NIAACH,
    59-81. 1955.
Duff, W. Indian Natural History. VN, VII, 92-4,
    103-6, VIII, 16-17. 1951.
Dunn, J. History of the Oregon Territory. 359 pp.
    London, 1846.
Durham, G. Canoes from Cedar Logs. PNQ, XLVI,
    33-9. 1955.

Eells, M. Aboriginal Geographic Names in the State of Washington. AA, V, 27-35. 1892.

--- History of Indian Missions on the Pacific Coast. 270 pp. Philadelphia, 1882.

Elmendorf, W.W. Word Taboo and Lexical Change in Coast Salish. IJAL, XVII, 205-8. 1951.

Emmons, G.T. The Art of the Northwest Coast Indians. NH, XXX, 282-92. 1930.

--- Jade in British Columbia and Alaska. INM, ser. 2, XXXV, 11-53. 1923.

--- Portraiture among the North Pacific Coast Tribes. AA, n.s., XVI, 59-67. 1914.

Erkes, E. Chinesisch-amerikanische Mythenparallelen. T'oung Pao, XXIV, 32-53. 1926.

Ernst, A.H. Northwest Coast Animal Dancer. Theatre Arts Monthly, XXIII, 661-72. 1939.

--- The Wolf Ritual of the Northwest Coast. 107 pp. Eugene, 1952.

Fellows, F.S. Mortality in the Native Races of the Territory of Alaska. PHR, XLIX, 289-98. 1934.

Franchère, G. Narrative of a Voyage to the Northwest Coast of America. EWT, VI, 167-410. 1904.

Fraser, S. Journal of a Voyage from the Rocky Mountains to the Pacific Coast. BCNO, I, 156-221. 1889.

Galpin, F.W. The Whistles and Reed Instruments of the Northwest Coast. Proceedings of the Musical Association, XXIX, 115-38. 1903.

Garfield, V.E. Antecedents of Totem Pole Carving. ASC, 1953, 242-8. 1956.

--- Possibilities of Genetic Relationship in Northern Pacific Moiety Structures. MSAA, IX, 58-61. 1953.

--- A Research Problem in Northwest Indian Economics. AA, n.s., XLVII, 626-30. 1945.

Gates, R.R., and Darby, G.E. Blood Groups and Physiognomy of British Columbia Coastal Indians. JAI, LXIV, 23-44. 1934.

Gatschet, A.S. Indian Languages of the Pacific States. MAH, I, 145-71. 1877.

Gibbs, G. Tribes of Western Washington and Northwestern Oregon. CNAE, I, 157-241. 1877.

Gjessing, G. Petroglyphs and Pictographs in the Coast Salishan Area of Canada. MPR, i, 257-75. 1958.

Gladstone, P. Native Indians and the Fishing Industry of British Columbia. CJEPS, XIX, 20-34. 1953.

Goddard, P.E. Indians of the Northwest Coast. 176 pp. New York, 1914.

Goldenweiser, A.A. Culture of the Indian Tribes of the Pacific Northwest. OHQ, XLI, 137-46. 1940.

Gormly, M. Spanish Documentary Material Pertaining to the Northwest Coast Indians. DJA, I, 21-41. 1955.

Grasserie, R. de la. Renseignements sur les noms de parenté dans plusieurs langues américaines. JSAP, n.s., II, 333-8. 1905.

Gunther, E. An Analysis of the First Salmon Ceremony. AA, n.s., XXVIII, 605-17. 1926.

--- Ethnobotany of Western Washington. UWPA, X, i, 1-61. 1945.

--- A Further Analysis of the First Salmon Ceremony. UWPA, II, 129-73. 1928.

--- The Indian Background of Washington History. PNQ, XLI, 189-202. 1950.

--- Indians of the Northwest Coast. 48 pp. Colorado Springs, 1952.

--- The Shaker Religion of the Northwest. CUCA, XXXVI, 37-76. 1949.

--- Vancouver and the Indians of Puget Sound. PNQ, LI, 1-12. 1960.

Haeberlin, H.K. Principles of Esthetic Form in the Art of the North Pacific Coast. AA, n.s., XX, 258-64. 1918.

--- Types of Reduplication in the Salish Dialects. IJAL, I, 154-74. 1918.

Haeberlin, H.K., Teit, J.A., and Roberts, H.H. Coiled Basketry in British Columbia and Surrounding Regions. ARBAE, XLI, 119-484. 1928.

Haekel, J. Bestattungsbräuche und Totenerinnerungsmale bei den Indianern Nordwestamerikas. WVM, III, 22-30. 1955.

--- Die Bestattungsformen bei den Stämmen Nordwestamerikas. ZE, LXXX, 103-15. 1955.

--- The Concept of a Supreme Being among the Northwest Coast Tribes of North America. WVM, II, 171-83. 1954.

--- Initiationen und Geheimbünde an der Nordwestküste Nordamerikas. MAGW, LXXXIII, 167-90. 1954.

--- Kosmischer Baum und Pfahl in Mythus und Kult der Stämme Nordwestamerikas. WVM, VI, 33-81. 1958.

--- Zum Problem der Konstanz und des Wandels in den Kulturen Nordwestamerikas. ICA, XXXI, i, 15-26. 1955.

Hale, H. Ethnology and Philology. Narrative of the United States Exploring Expedition, by C. Wilkes, Vol. I. Philadelphia, 1846.

--- Remarks on the Ethnology of British Columbia. BAAS, LX, 553-62. 1890.

d'Harcourt, R. Arts de l'Amerique, pp. 27-34. Paris, 1948.

Harrington, L. Trail of the Candlefish. B, CCLXXXIII, June, 40-44. 1953.

Hawthorn, A.E. People of the Potlatch. 48 pp. Van-
    couver, 1956.

Hawthorn, H.B. et al. The Indians of British Colum-
    bia. 508 pp. Berkeley, 1958.

Heizer, R.F. Aconite Poison Whaling in Asia and
    America. BBAE, CXXXIII. 415-68. 1943.

--- The Botanical Identification of Northwest Coast
    Tobacco. AA, n.s., XLII, 704-6. 1940.

Henking, K.H. Die Südsee-und Alaska-sammlung
    Johann Wäber beschreibender Katalog. Jahrbuch des
    Bernischen Historischen Museums, XXXV-XXXVI,
    325-89. 1955-56.

Hermant, P. Evolution économique et sociale de
    certaines peuplades de l'Amérique du Nord. BSRBG,
    XXVIII, 432-55. 1904-05.

Hewes, G. The Ainu Double Foreshaft Toggle Har-
    poon and Western North America. JWAS, XXXII,
    93-104. 1942.

Hill-Tout, C. British North America. 253 pp. Toron-
    to, 1907.

--- Oceanic Origin of the Kwakiutl-Nootka and Salish
    Stocks. PTRSC, ser. 2, IV, ii, 187-231. 1898.

--- Some Features of the Language and Culture of the
    Salish. AA, n.s., VII, 674-87. 1905.

Hoebel, E.A. The Asiatic Origin of a Myth of the
    Northwest Coast. JAFL, LIV, 1-9. 1941.

Holling, H.C. The Book of Indians, pp. 97-123.
    New York, 1935.

Hough, W. Primitive American Armor. RUSNM,
    1893, 625-51.

Howay, F.W. Indian Attacks upon Maritime Traders
    of the Northwest Coast, 1785-1805. CHR, VI, 287-
    309. 1925.

--- The Dog's Hair Blankets of the Coast Salish. WHQ,
    IX, 83-92. 1918.

--- The Early Literature of the Northwest Coast.
    PTRSC, ser. 3, XVIII, ii, 1-31. 1924.

--- The First Use of Sail by the Indians of the North-
    west Coast. American Neptune, I, 374-80. 1941.

--- The Introduction of Intoxicating Liquors amongst
    the Indians of the Northwest Coast. BCHQ, VI,
    157-69. 1942.

--- The Origin of the Chinook Jargon. BCHQ, VI,
    225-50. 1942.

--- Origin of the Chinook Jargon on the North West
    Coast. OHQ, XLIV, 27-55. 1943.

Hrdlicka, A. Catalogue of Human Crania in the
    United States National Museum Collections.
    PUSNM, XCIV, 1-172. 1944.

Hudson's Bay Company. Masks of the Northwest In-
    dians. Winnipeg, 1955.

Hulse, F.S. Blood Types and Mating Patterns among
    Northwest Coast Indians. SJA, XI, 93-104. 1955.

Inverarity, R.B. Art of the Northwest Coast Indians.
    262 pp. Berkeley, 1950.

--- Movable Masks and Figures of the North Pacific
    Coast Indians. 4 pp, 18 pl. Bloomfield Hills, 1941.

--- Northwest Coast Indian Art. Washington State
    University Museum Series, I, 1-26. 1946.

Jenkins, M. Before the White Man Came. 179 pp.
    Portland, 1951.

Jenness, D. Indians of Canada. BNMC, LXV, 3d ed.,
    452 pp. 1955.

Jochelson, W. Past and Present Subterranean Dwell-
    ings of the Tribes of North Eastern Asia and North
    America. ICA, XV, ii, 115-28. 1907.

Kane, P. Wanderings of an Artist among the Indians.
    455 pp. London, 1859.

Keithahn, E.L. Monuments in Cedar. 160 pp.
    Ketchikan, 1945.

--- The Petroglyphs of Southeastern Alaska. AAn,
    VI, 123-32. 1940.

Kissell, M.L. Organized Salish Blanket Pattern. AA,
    n.s., XXXI, 85-8. 1929.

Krickeberg, W. Malereien auf ledernen Zeremonial-
    kleidern der Nordwestamerikaner. Ipek, 1925, 140-
    50.

Kroeber, A.L. American Culture and the Northwest
    Coast. AA, n.s., XXV, 1-20. 1923.

--- Salt, Dogs, Tobacco. AR, VI, 1-20. 1941.

--- Stepdaughter Marriage. AA, n.s., XLII, 562-70.
    1940.

--- The Tribes of the Pacific Coast of North America.
    ICA, XIX, 385-401. 1915.

Laguna, F. de. The Prehistory of Northern North Amer-
    ica as seen from the Yukon. MSAA, III, 1-360.
    1947.

Landerholm, C., ed. Notices & Voyages of the Famed
    Quebec Mission to the Pacific Northwest. 258 pp.
    Portland, 1956.

Lantis, M. The Alaskan Whale Cult and Its Affinities.
    AA, n.s., XL, 438-64. 1938.

Lapérouse, J.F.de G. de. A Voyage round the World.
    3 vols. London, 1798.

Leechman, D. Abalone Shells from Monterey. AA,
    n.s., XLIV, 159-62. 1942.

--- Aboriginal Paints and Dyes in Canada. PTRSC,
    ser. 3, XXVI, ii, 37-42. 1932.

Lemert, E.M. Alcohol and the Northwest Coast In-
    dians. UCPCS, II, 303-406. 1954.

--- On Alcoholism Among the Northwest Coast Indians.
    (with rejoinder by H. Codere) AA, LVIII, 561-2.
    1958.

Lemert, E.M. Stuttering among the North Pacific Coastal Indians. SJA, VIII, 429-41. 1952.

Lenoir, R. Fete de Boisson et Potlatch. ICA, XXV, i, 173-9. 1934.

--- Sur l'institution du potlatch. Revue Philosophique, XCVII, 233-67. 1924.

Lévi-Strauss, C. The Art of the Northwest Coast at the American Museum of Natural History. Gazette des Beaux-Arts, XXIV, 175-82. 1943.

Lips, E. Bemerkungen zu einigen Stücken von der nordamerikanischen Nordwestküste. JMVL, XIV, 10-30. 1955.

Loeb, E.M. The Social Organization of Oceania and the American Northwest. PPSC, VI, iv, 135-9. 1939.

Lord, J.K. The Naturalist on Vancouver Island and British Columbia, I, 226-61. London, 1866.

Lot-Falck, E. Les masques eskimo et aléoutes de la collection Pinart. JSAP, XLVI, n.s., 5-44. 1957.

Macfie, M. Vancouver Island and British Columbia, pp. 233-92. London, 1865.

MacLean, J. Canadian Savage Folk. 641 pp. Toronto, 1897.

MacLeod, W.C. Certain Aspects of the Social Organisation of the Northwest Coast and of the Algonkian. ICA, XXI, i, 253-65. 1924.

--- Certain Mortuary Aspects of Northwest Coast Culture. AA, n.s., XXVII, 122-48. 1925.

--- Debtor and Chattel Slavery in Aboriginal North America. AA, n.s., XXVII, 70-78. 1925.

--- Economic Aspects of Indigenous American Slavery. AA, n.s., XXX, 632-50. 1928.

--- Mortuary and Sacrificial Anthropophagy on the Northwest Coast. JSAP, n.s., XXV, 335-66. 1933.

--- On the Diffusion of Central American Culture to Coastal British Columbia and Alaska. A, XXIV, 417-39. 1929.

--- The Origin of Servile Labor Groups. AA, n.s., XXXI, 89-113. 1929.

--- Some Social Aspects of Aboriginal American Slavery. JSAP, n.s., XIX, 123-8. 1927.

--- Trade Restrictions in Early Society. AA, n.s., XXIX, 271-8. 1927.

Mayne, R.C. Four Years in British Columbia and Vancouver Island. London, 1862.

Meany, E.S. Origin of Washington Geographic Names. 357 pp. Seattle, 1923.

Meares, J. Voyages made in the Years 1788 and 1789. 2 vols. London, 1791.

Milet-Mureau, M.L.A., ed. Voyage de La Pérouse autour du monde. 4 vols. Paris, 1797.

Newcombe, C.F., ed. Menzies' Journal of Vancouver's Voyage. Archives of British Columbia, Memoir V, 1-171. 1923.

Newcombe, W.A. British Columbia Totem-poles. BCMR, 1930, 8-10. 1931.

--- A Large Salish Earthwork. BCMR, 1931, 7-8. 1932.

--- Thunder-bird and Whale. BCMR, 1929, 10-11. 1930.

Oetteking, B. Craniology of the North Pacific Coast. MAMNH, XV, i, 1-391. 1930.

Olson, R.L. Adze, Canoe, and House Types of the Northwest Coast. UWPA, II, 1-38. 1927.

--- The Indians of the Northwest Coast. NH, XXXV, 183-97. 1935.

--- The Possible Middle American Origin of Northwest Coast Weaving. AA, n.s., XXXI, 114-19. 1929.

Paalen, W. Totem Art. Dyn, IV-V, 7-37. 1943.

Perry, F. Ethno-Botany of the Indians in the Interior of British Columbia. Museum & Art Notes, II, ii, 36-43. 1952.

Phillips, W.S. Totem Tales. 326 pp. Chicago, 1896.

Pickford, A.E. Indian Fish Traps. VN, II, iv, 58. 1945.

Pilling, J.C. Bibliography of the Salishan Languages. BBAE, XVI, 1-86. 1893.

--- Bibliography of the Wakashan Languages. BBAE, XIX, 1-69. 1894.

Pinart, A. La chasses aux animaux marins et les Pecheries chez les indigènes de la cote nord-ouest d'Amerique. 15 pp. Boulogne-sur-Mer. 1875.

Portlock, N. A Voyage round the World. London, 1789.

Pöschl, H. Das Erziehungswesen bei den Indianern im westlichen Nordamerika. WVM, V, 56-7. 1957.

Randall, B.U. The Cinderella Theme in Northwest Coast Folklore. CUCA, XXXVI, 243-86. 1949.

Ravenhill, A. The Native Tribes of British Columbia. 142 pp. Victoria, 1938.

--- Pacific Coast Art. B, CCLXXIII, ii, 4-8. 1942.

Read, C.H. An Account of a Collection of Ethnographical Specimens formed during Vancouver's Voyage. JAI, XXI, 99-108. 1891.

Reid, R.L. The Chinook Jargon and British Columbia. BCHQ, VI, 1-11. 1942.

Relander, C. Drummers and Dreamers. 345 pp. Caldwell, 1956.

Rickard, T.A. The Use of Iron and Copper by the Indians of British Columbia. BCHQ, III, 25-50. 1939.

Riddell, F.A. Climate and the Aboriginal Occupation of the Pacific Coast of Alaska. PKAS, XI, 60-123. 1954.

Sapir, E. Indian Tribes of the Coast. Canada and Its Provinces, ed. A. Shortt and A.G. Doughty, XXI, 315-46. Toronto, 1914.

--- The Social Organization of the West Coast Tribes. PTRSC, ser. 3, IX, ii, 355-74. 1915.

Scouler, J. Observations on the Indigenous Tribes of the N.W. Coast of America. JRGS, XI, 215-50. 1871.

--- On the Indian Tribes inhabiting the North-West Coast of America. JESL, I, 228-52. 1848.

Seler, E. Die Lichtbringer bei den Indianerstämmen der Nordwestküste. Globus, LXI, 195-8, 212-16, 230-5, 243-6. 1892.

Siegel, B.J. Some Methodological Considerations for a Comparative Study of Slavery. AA, n.s., XLVII, 357-92. 1945.

Smith, A.H. The Indians of Washington. RSSCW, XXI, 85-113. 1953.

Smith, C.W. Pacific Northwest Americana. 2d edit. 329 pp. New York, 1921.

Smith, D.A., and Spier, L. The Dot and Circle Design in Northwestern America. JSAP, n.s., XIX, 47-55. 1927.

Smith, H.I. Archeological Investigations on the North Pacific Coast. AA, n.s., II, 563-7. 1900.

--- Kitchen-Middens of the Pacific Coast of Canada. BCDM, LVI, 42-6. 1929.

--- Recent Archaeological Discoveries in North-Western America. BAGS, XXXVIII, 287-95. 1906.

--- Stone Hammers or Pestles of the Northwest Coast. AA, n.s., I, 363-8. 1899.

--- Totem Poles of the North Pacific Coast. AMJ, XI, 77-82. 1911.

--- Trephined Aboriginal Skulls from British Columbia and Washington. AJPA, VII, 447-52. 1924.

Smith, M.W. Continuity in Culture Contact. Man, LV, 100-05. 1955.

--- The Cultural Development of the Northwest Coast. SJA, XII, 272-94. 1956.

--- Culture Area and Culture Depth. ICA, XXIX, iii, 80-96. 1952.

--- Shamanism in the Shaker Religion of Northwest America. Man, LIV, 119-22. 1954.

Smith, M.W. and Gowers, H.J. Basketry Design and the Columbia Valley Art Style. SJA, VIII, 336-41. 1952.

Spier, L. Tribal Distribution in Washington. GSA, III, 1-43. 1936.

Strong, W.D. The Occurrence and Wider Implications of a "Ghost Cult" on the Columbia River suggested by Carvings in Wood, Bone and Stone. AA, n.s., XLVII, 244-61. 1945.

Suttles, W. The "Middle Fraser" and "Foothill" Cultures: a Criticism. SJA, XIII, 156-83. 1957.

Swadesh, M. The Linguistic Approach to Salish Prehistory. CUCA, XXXVI, 161-74. 1949.

Swadesh, M. Mosan. IJAL, XIX, 26-44, 223-36. 1953.

--- Salish Internal Relationships. IJAL, XVI, 157-67. 1950.

--- Salish Phonologic Geography. Lg, XXVIII, 232-48. 1952.

--- Salish-Wakashan Lexical Comparisons. IJAL, XIX, 290-91. 1953.

Swanton, J.R. The Development of the Clan System and of Secret Societies amongst the North-Western Tribes. AA, n.s., VI, 477-85. 1904.

--- Salish. ERE, XI, 97-100. 1921.

Underhill, R. Indians of the Pacific Northwest. ILC, V, 1-232. 1944.

Vancouver, G. Voyage of Discovery to the North Pacific Ocean and round the World. 3 vols. London, 1798.

Wagner, H.R., ed. Journal of Tomás de Suría of His Voyage with Malaspina to the Northwest Coast of America in 1791. Pacific Historical Review, V, 234-76. 1936.

Waterman, T.T. The Geographic Names Used by the Indians of the Pacific Coast. GR, XII, 175-94. 1922.

--- Native Houses of Western North America. INM, ser. 2, XI, 1-97. 1921.

--- Some Conundrums in Northwest Coast Art. AA, n.s., XXV, 435-51. 1923.

Waterman, T.T., and Coffin, G. Types of Canoes of Puget Sound. INM, n.s., V, 1-43. 1920.

Waterman, T.T., and Greiner, R. Indian Houses of Puget Sound. INM, n.s., IX, 7-59. 1921.

Weatherby, H. Tales the Totems tell. 96 pp. Toronto, 1944.

Wike, J. More Puzzles on the Northwest Coast. AA, LIX, 301-17. 1957.

--- Problems in Fur Trade Analysis: The Northwest Coast. AA, LX, 1086-1101. 1958.

--- The Role of the Dead in Northwest Coast Culture. ICA, XXIX, iii, 97-103. 1952.

Willoughby, C.C. A New Type of Ceremonial Blanket from the Northwest Coast. AA, n.s., XII, 1-10. 1910.

Woodcock, G. The Coast Indians of British Columbia. Geographical Magazine, XXVI, 368-81. 1953.

Work, J. The Journal of John Work, 1835. BCHQ, VIII, 127-46, 227-44, 307-18. 1944.

1. BELLABELLA

Including the Bellabella, and the Heiltsuk.

Adam, L. Stammesorganisation und Häuptlingstum der Wakashstämme. ZVR, XXXV, 105-58. 1918.

Anastasi, A., and Foley, J.P. A Study of Animal Drawings by Indian Children of the North Pacific Coast. JSP, IX, 363-74. 1938.

Boas, F. Bella Bella Tales. MAFLS, XXV, 1-178. 1932.

--- Bella Bella Texts. CUCA, V, 1-291. 1928.

--- First General Report on the Indians of British Columbia. BAAS, LIX, 801-900. 1889.

--- The Kwakiutl. BAAS, LX, 604-32, 655-68. 1890.

--- Sagen aus Britisch-Columbien. VBGA, 1893, 444-77.

--- The Social Organization of the Tribes of the North Pacific Coast. AA, n.s., XXVI, 323-32. 1924.

Curtis, E.S. The North American Indian, X, 1-366. Norwood, 1915.

Drucker, P. Kwakiutl Dancing Societies. AR, II, 201-30. 1940.

--- Northwest Coast. AR, IX, 157-294. 1950.

Farrand, L. Myths of the Bellabella. ARBAE, XXXI, 883-8. 1916.

Gibbs, G. Vocabulary of the Ha-ilt'-zukh. CNAE, I, 144-50. 1877.

Lopatin, I.A. Social Life and Religion of the Indians in Kitimat. University of Southern California, Social Science Series, XXVI, 1-107. 1945.

Needham, J.G., and Murphy, H.E. The Social Organization of the Haisla of British Columbia. 31 pp. Berkeley, 1940.

Swanton, J.R. Bellabella. BBAE, XXX, i, 140-1. 1907.

Tolmie, W.F., and Dawson, G.M. Comparative Vocabularies of the Indian Tribes of British Columbia, pp. 27B-37B. Montreal, 1884.

Woldt, A. Capitain Jacobsen's Reise an der Nordwestküste Amerikas. Leipzig, 1884.

2. BELLACOOLA

McIlwraith, T.F. The Bella Coola Indians. 2 vols. Toronto, 1948.

Anastasi, A., and Foley, J.P. A Study of Animal Drawings by Indian Children of the North Pacific Coast. JSP, IX, 363-74. 1938.

Boas, F. The Bilqula. BAAS, LXI, 408-24. 1891.

--- The Bi'lxula. RUSNM, 1895, 646-51.

--- The Language of the Bilhoola in British Columbia. Science, ser. 1, VII, 218. 1886.

Boas, F. Mittheilungen über die Vilxula-Indianer. OMKMB, I, 177-82. 1886.

--- The Mythology of the Bella Coola Indians. MAMNH, II, 25-127. 1900.

--- Sagen aus Britisch-Columbien. VBGA, 1894, 281-306; 1895, 189-95.

--- Salishan Texts. PAPS, XXXIV, 31-48. 1895.

--- Sprache der Bella-Coola-Indianer. VBGA, 1886, 202-6.

--- Terms of Relationship of the Salish Languages. BAAS, LX, 688-92. 1890.

--- The Use of Masks and Head-Ornaments on the North-West Coast. IAE, III, 7-15. 1890.

--- Zur Anthropologie der nordamerikanischen Indianer. VBGA, 1895, 367-411.

Drucker, P. Northwest Coast. AR, IX, 157-294. 1950.

Gibbs, G. Vocabulary of the Belhoola. CNAE, I, 267-83. 1877.

Goeken. Das religiöse Leben der Bella-Coola Indianer. OMKMB, I, 183-6. 1886.

Jacobsen, F. Sissauch-dansen. Ymer, XV, 1-23. 1895.

Jacobsen, J.A. Bella-Coola Sagen. Ausland, LXIII, 352-4. 1890.

--- Geheimbünde der Küstenbewohner Nordwest-America's. VBGA, 1891, 383-95.

--- Der Kosiyut-Bund der Bella-Coola-Indianer. Ausland, LXV, 437-41. 1892.

Kopas, C.R. Bella Coola. B, CCLXXIX, 26-31. 1948.

McIlwraith, T.F. Certain Beliefs of the Bella Coola Indians concerning Animals. AAR, 1924-25, 17-27.

Melançon, C. La Mythologie des Bella-Coula. Revue de l'Université d'Ottawa, XV, 180-97. 1945.

Newcombe, C.F. Guide to the Anthropological Collection in the Provincial Museum, pp. 43-8. Victoria, 1909.

Newman, S. Bella Coola, I: Phonology. IJAL, XIII, 129-34. 1947.

Smith, H.I. Entomology among the Bellacoola and Carrier Indians. AA, n.s., XXVII, 436-40. 1925.

--- Materia Medica of the Bella Coola and Neighbouring Tribes. BCDM, LVI, 47-68. 1929.

--- Sympathetic Magic and Witchcraft among the Bellacoola. AA, n.s., XXVII, 116-21. 1925.

Tolmie, W.F., and Dawson, G.M. Comparative Vocabularies of the Indian Tribes of British Columbia, pp. 62B-72B. Montreal, 1884.

Virchow, R. Die anthropologische Untersuchung der Bella-Coola. VBGA, 1886, 206-15.

3. COMOX

Including the Comox, Homalco, Klahuse, Pentlatch, Seshelt, Slaiamun, and Squamish.

Barnett, H.G. Gulf of Georgia Salish. AR, I, 221-95. 1939.

Barnett, H.G. The Coast Salish of Canada. AA, n. s., XL, 118-41. 1938.

Boas, F. The Mythologies of the Indians. International Quarterly, XII, 157-73. 1905.

--- Myths and Legends of the Catloltq of Vancouver Island. AAOJ, X, 201-11, 366-73. 1888.

--- Sagen aus Britisch-Columbien. VBGA, 1891, 639-43; 1892, 32-66.

--- Terms of Relationship of the Salish Languages. BAAS, LX, 688-92. 1890.

Durieu, P. Polyglott Manual, pp. 61-109, 113-53, 195-248. Kamloops, 1896.

Gibbs, G. Vocabulary of the Ko-mookhs. CNAE, I, 269-83. 1877.

Hill-Tout, C. Notes on the Cosmogony and History of the Squamish Indians. PTRSC, ser. 2, III, ii, 85-90. 1897.

--- Notes on the Sk·qo'mic of British Columbia. BAAS, LXX, 472-549. 1900.

--- Report on the Ethnology of the Siciatl of British Columbia. JAI, XXXIV, 20-91. 1904.

Sapir, E. Noun Reduplication in Comox. MCDM, LXIII, 1-53. 1915.

--- Songs for a Comox Dancing Mask. Ethnos, IV, ii, 49-55. 1939.

Suttles, W. The Early Diffusion of the Potato among the Coast Salish. SJA, VII, 272-88. 1951.

--- The Plateau Prophet Dance among the Coast Salish. SJA, XIII, 352-96. 1957.

--- Private Knowledge, Morality, and Social Classes among the Coast Salish. AA, LX, 497-507. 1958.

Tolmie, W.F., and Dawson, G.M. Comparative Vocabularies of the Indian Tribes of British Columbia, pp. 38B-48B. Montreal, 1884.

Wingert, P.S. American Indian Sculpture. 144 pp. New York, 1948.

4. COWICHAN

Including the Cowichan, Muskwium, Nanaimo, and Sanetch.

Barnett, H.G. Gulf of Georgia Salish. AR, I, 221-95. 1939.

Duff, W. The Upper Stalo Indians of the Fraser Valley, British Columbia. ABCM, I. 135 pp. 1953.

Barnett, H.G. The Coast Salish of Canada. AA, n.s., XL, 118-41. 1938.

Boas, F. The Indian Tribes of the Lower Fraser River. BAAS, LXIV, 454-63. 1894.

--- Notes on the Snanaimuq. AA, II, 321-8. 1889.

--- Sagen aus Britisch-Columbien. VBGA, 1891, 549-76, 628-38.

Codere, H. The Harrison Lake Physical Type. CUCA, XXXVI, 175-84. 1949.

Crosby, T. Among the An-ko-me-nums. 243 pp. Toronto, 1907.

Cryer, B.M. The Flying Canoe. 48 pp. Victoria, 1949.

Curtis, E.S. The North American Indian, IX, 32-137, 157-78, 182-95. Norwood, 1913.

Gibbs, G., Tolmie, W.F., and Mengarini, G. Comparative Vocabularies. CNAE, I, 268-83. 1877.

Grant, W.C. Description of Vancouver Island. JRGS, XXVII, 268-320. 1857.

Harrington, L. The Cowichan Sweater. CGJ, XL, 94-97. 1950.

Harris, M.D. History and Folklore of the Cowichan Indians. 89 pp. Victoria, 1901.

Hill-Tout, C. Ethnological Report of the StsEélis and Sk·aúlits Tribes of the Halkomélem Division of the Salish. JAI, XXXIV, 311-76. 1904.

--- Ethnological Studies of the Mainland Halkomélem. BAAS, LXXII, 355-490. 1902.

--- Report on the Ethnology of the South-Eastern Tribes of Vancouver Island. JAI, XXXVII, 306-74. 1907.

--- The Salish Tribes of the Coast and Lower Fraser Delta. AAR, 1905, 225-35.

Jenness, D. The Faith of a Coast Salish Indian. ABCM, III, 92 pp. 1955.

Kissell, M.L. A New Type of Spinning in North America. AA, n.s., XVIII, 264-70. 1916.

Lane, B.S. The Cowichan Knitting Industry. ABC, II, 14-27. 1951.

Norcross, E.B. The Cowichan Sweater. B, CCLXXVI, 18-19. 1945.

Orchard, W.C. Technique of the Salish Blanket. LMAI, V, 7-15. 1926.

Ravenhill, A. A Corner Stone of Canadian Culture. Occasional Papers of the British Columbia Provincial Museum, V, 103 pp. 1944.

Schriver, J., and Leacock, E.B. Harrison Indian Childhood. CUCA, XXXVI, 195-242. 1949.

Smith, H.I. Shell-Heaps of the Lower Frazer River. MAMNH, IV, i, 133-91. 1903.

--- Shell-Heaps of the Lower Fraser River. RP, IV, 119-27. 1904.

Smith, M.W. House Types of the Middle Fraser River.
AAn, XII, 255-67. 1947.

Suttles, W. Affinal Ties, Subsistence and Prestige
among the Coast Salish. AA, LXII, 296-305. 1960.

--- The Early Diffusion of the Potato among the Coast
Salish. SJA, VII, 272-88. 1951.

--- Katzie Ethnographic Notes. ABCM, II, 31 pp.
1955.

--- Notes on Coast Salish Sea-mammal Hunting.
ABC, III, 10-20. 1952.

--- The Plateau Prophet Dance among the Coast Salish. SJA, XIII, 352-96. 1957.

--- Private Knowledge, Morality, and Social Classes
among the Coast Salish. AA, LX, 497-507. 1958.

Teit, J.A. Tales from the Lower Frazer River.
MAFLS, XI, 129-34. 1917.

Tolmie, W.F., and Dawson, G.M. Comparative
Vocabularies of the Indian Tribes of British Columbia, pp. 39B-49B. Montreal, 1884.

Weber, E.R.C. An Old Kwanthum Village. AAOJ,
XXI, 309-14. 1899.

Wilson, E.F. Report on the Indian Tribes. TESL,
n.s., IV, 275-92. 1866.

Wingert, P.S. American Indian Sculpture. 144 pp.
New York, 1949.

5. HAIDA

Swanton, J.R. Contributions to the Ethnology of the
Haida. MAMNH, VIII, 1-300. 1909.

Adam, L. Stammesorganisation und Häuptlingstum
der Haida und Tsimshian. ZVR, XXX, 161-268.
1913.

Ainsworth, T.H. The Art of the Haidas. Museum
and Art Notes, 2nd series, I, iii, 16-19. 1950.

Allen, R.A. Changing Social Organization and Kinship among the Alaskan Haidas. UAAP, IV, i,
5-11. 1955.

--- Patterns of Preferential Marriage among the Alaskan Haidas. UAAP, II, 195-201. 1954.

Anastasi, A., and Foley, J.P. A Study of Animal
Drawings by Indian Children of the North Pacific
Coast. JSP, IX, 363-74. 1938.

Anonymous. Die Haida-Indianer. Ausland, LVII,
792-7. 1884.

Balfour, H. Haida Portrait Mask. Man, VII, 1-2.
1907.

Barbeau, M. Haida Carvers in Argillite. BNMC,
CXXXIX, 222 pp. 1957.

--- Haida Myths. BNMC, CXXVII, 417 pp. 1953.

Barbeau, M. How the Raven stole the Sun. PTRSC,
ser. 3, XXXVIII, ii, 59-69. 1944.

--- Old Canadian Silver. CGJ, XXII, 150-62. 1941.

Barbeau, M., and G. Melvin. The Indian speaks, pp.
51-3, 112-17. Caldwell, 1943.

Bastian, A. Die Haida's. VBGA, 1882, 278-98.

Benveniste, E. Les Traits Caractéristiques de la Langue
des Indiens Haida. Bulletin de la Société Linguistique
de Paris, XLIX, iii-iv. 1953.

Boas, F. Haida. BAAS, LIX, 867-77. 1889.

--- Sagen aus Britisch-Columbien. VBGA, 1895, 217-
22.

--- The Social Organization of the Haida. BAAS,
LXVIII, 648-54. 1899.

--- Tattooing among the Indians of British Columbia.
TNYAS, VIII, 115-16. 1888.

--- Vocabularies from the Northwest Coast of America.
PAAS, n.s., XXVI, 200-2. 1916.

--- Vocabularies of the Tlingit, Haida and Tsimshian
Languages. PAPS, XXIX, 183-93. 1891.

Boyle, D., ed. British Columbia Specimens. AAR,
1891, 52-6.

Campbell, J. The Origin of the Haidas. PTRSC, ser.
2, III, ii, 91-112. 1897.

Chamberlain, A.F. Haida. ERE, VI, 469-74. 1914.

Charles, P. Testimony from Hydaburg on Fish Traps.
Am I, IV, iii, 45-47.

Collinson, W.H. In the Wake of the War Canoe. London, 1915.

Curtis, E.S. The North American Indian, XI, 115-75,
186-93. Norwood, 1916.

Dall, W.H. On the Distribution and Nomenclature of
the Native Tribes of Alaska. CNAE, I, 7-40. 1877.

Dawson, G.M. The Haidas. HMM, LXV, 401-8.
1882.

--- Report on the Queen Charlotte Islands. Geological
Survey of Canada, Report of Progress for 1878-79,
pp. 1B-239B. 1880.

Deans, J. Carved Columns or Totem Posts of the
Haidas. AAOJ, XIII, 282-7. 1891.

--- Hidery Prayers. AAOJ, XXII, 31-2. 1900.

--- The Hidery Story of Creation. AAOJ, XVII, 61-
7. 1895.

--- The Huida-kwul-ra or Native Tobacco of the
Queen Charlotte Haidas. AAOJ, XII, 48-50. 1890.

--- Inside View of a Huidah Dwelling. AAOJ, IX,
309-10. 1887.

--- Legend of the Fin-back Whale Crest of the
Haidas. JAFL, V, 43-7. 1892.

--- A Little Known Civilization. AAOJ, XVII, 208-
13. 1895.

Deans, J. The Moon Symbol on the Totem Posts on the Northwest Coast. AAOJ, XIII, 341-6. 1891.

--- On the Copper Images of the Haidah Tribes. Proceedings of the Numismatic and Antiquarian Society of Philadelphia, 1885, 14-17.

--- The Raven Myth of the Northwest Coast. AAOJ, XI, 297-301. 1889.

--- The Story of Skaga Belus. AAOJ, XIII, 81-4. 1891.

--- The Story of the Bear and His Indian Wife. JAFL, II, 255-60. 1889.

--- A Strange Way of Preserving Peace amongst Neighbors. AAOJ, X, 42-3. 1888.

--- Tales from the Totems of the Hidery. Archives of the International Folk-Lore Association, II, 1-94. 1899.

--- Totem Posts at the World's Fair. AAOJ, XV, 281-6. 1893.

--- A Weird Mourning Song of the Haidas. AAOJ, XIII, 52-4. 1891.

--- What befell the Slave-seekers. JAFL, I, 123-4. 1888.

--- When Potlatches are observed. AAOJ, XVIII, 329-31. 1896.

Dixon, G. A Voyage round the World. 360 pp. London, 1789.

Drucker, P. Northwest Coast. AR, IX, 157-294. 1950.

Duff, W. A Heritage in Decay. CA, XI, 56-9. 1954.

Duff, W. and Kew, H. Anthony Island, A Home of the Haidas. BCMR, 1957, 37-64. 1958.

Durham, G. Canoes from Cedar Logs. PNQ, XLVI, 33-9. 1955.

Durlach, T.M. The Relationship Systems of the Tlingit, Haida and Tsimshian. PAES, XI, 1-177. 1928.

Emmons, G.T. "Wings" of Haida Ceremonial Canoes. IN, V, 298-302. 1928.

Fuhrmann, E. Tlinkit- und Haida-Indianer. Kulturen der Erde, XXII, 1-61. 1923.

Garfield, V.E. Survey of Southeastern Alaskan Indian Research. ASC, 1950, 20-37. 1952.

Gibbs, G., and Dall, W.H. Comparative Vocabularies. CNAE, I, 135-42. 1877.

Goldschmidt, W.R., and Haas, T.H. Possessory Rights of the Natives of Southeastern Alaska. 173 pp. Washington, 1946.

Gunther, E. The Social Disorganization of the Haida as Reflected in their Slate Carving. DJA, II, 149-53. 1956.

Haeberlin, H.K. Notes on the Composition of the Verbal Complex in Haida. IJAL, II, 159-62. 1923.

Hambleton, J. The Raven, Frog, and Bear Totem Pole. BNMC, CXXIII, 80-83. 1951.

Hamy, M.E.T. Sculptures Haida. ICA, XII, 109-14. 1900.

Harrington, J.P. Southern Peripheral Athapaskawan Origins, Divisions and Migrations. SMC, C, 503-32. 1940.

Harrington, L. Last of the Haida Carvers. NH, LVIII, 200-5. 1949.

Harrington, L. and R. Haida Carver of Argillite. CGJ, XLV, 38-40. 1952.

Harrison, C. Ancient Warriors of the North Pacific. London, 1925.

--- Family Life of the Haidas. JAI, XXI, 470-6. 1892.

--- Haida Grammar. PTRSC, ser. 2, I, ii, 123-226. 1895.

--- Religion and Family among the Haidas. JAI, XXI, 14-29. 1892.

Hill-Tout, C. Haida Stories and Beliefs. BAAS, LXVIII, 700-8. 1898.

Hoffman, W.J. Die Kunst unter den Haida-Indianer. Ausland, LVIII, 701-4. 1885.

--- Remarks on Aboriginal Art in California and Queen Charlotte Island. PDAS, IV, 105-22. 1886.

Honigmann, J.J. Cultural Dynamics of Sex. Psychiatry, X, 37-47. 1947.

Howay, F.W., ed. Voyages of the "Columbia" to the Northwest Coast, 1787-1790 and 1790-1793. MHSC, LXXIX, 207-373. 1941.

Jacobsen, J.A. Die Sintflutsage bei den Haida-Indianer. Ausland, LXV, 170-2, 184-8. 1892.

Jenness, D. Indian Vikings of the North-west Coast. CGJ, VIII, 235-46. 1934.

Keen, J.H. Old Testament Stories in the Haida Language. London, 1893.

Krause, A. Die Tlinkit-Indianer, pp. 303-17. Jena, 1885.

Krieger, H.W. Archeological and Ethnological Studies in Southeast Alaska. SMC, LXXVIII, vii, 174-87. 1927.

--- Indian Villages of Southeast Alaska. ARSI, LXXXII, i, 467-94. 1928.

--- Some Aspects of Northwest Coast Indian Art. SM, XXIII, 211-19. 1926.

La Grasserie, R.de. Cinq langues de la Colombie Brittannique. 530 pp. Paris, 1902.

Leighton, M.W. The Haidah Indians. OM, XXXVII, 1083-6. 1901.

Mackenzie, A. Descriptive Notes on Certain Implements, Weapons, etc., from Graham Island. PTRSC, IX, ii, 45-59. 1891.

Mason, O.T. Overlaying with Copper by the American Aborigines. PUSNM, XVII, 475-7. 1894.

Mayol, L.B. The Big Canoe. 257 pp. New York, 1933.

--- The Talking Totem Pole. 142 pp. Portland, 1943.

Murdock, G.P. Kinship and Social Behavior among the Haida. AA, n.s., XXXVI, 355-85. 1934.

--- Our Primitive Contemporaries, pp. 221-63. New York, 1934.

--- Rank and Potlatch among the Haida. YUPA, XIII, 1-20. 1936.

Newcombe, C.F. Guide to the Anthropological Collection in the Provincial Museum, pp. 1-26. Victoria, 1909.

--- The Haida Indians. ICA, XV, i, 135-49. 1907.

--- The Haida Totem Pole at the Milwaukee Public Museum. YPMCM, II, 194-200. 1922.

--- The McGill Totem Pole. Ottawa Naturalist, XXXII, 99-103. 1918.

Newcombe, W.A. A Haida or Tsimshian Doll. BCMR, 1928, 10-11. 1929.

Niblack, A.P. The Coast Indians of Southern Alaska and Northern British Columbia. RUSNM, 1888, 225-386.

Nieuwenhuis, A.W. The Differences between the Conception of Soul (animus) and of Spirit (spiritus) among the American Indians. ICA, XXI, i, 125-39. 1924.

Orchard, W.C. A Chilkat Blanket and a Haida "Copper." IN, IV, 33-40. 1927.

Poole, F. Queen Charlotte Islands. London, 1872.

Ravenhill, A. A Corner Stone of Canadian Culture. Occasional Papers of the British Columbia Provincial Museum, V, 1-103. 1944.

Ridgeway, W. Notes on the Motives carved on Some Haida Totem Spoons and Pipes. Man, VI, 145-8. 1906.

St. John, M. Description of a Village of the Hydah Indians. JAI, VIII, 426-7. 1879.

Sapir, E. The Na-dene Languages. AA, n.s., XVII, 535-58. 1915.

--- The Phonetics of Haida. IJAL, II, 143-58. 1923.

Swan, J.G. The Haidah Indians of Queen Charlotte's Islands. SCK, XXI, iv, 1-15. 1874.

Swanton, J.R. Haida. BBAE, XXX, i, 520-3. 1907.

--- Haida. BBAE, XL, i, 205-82. 1911.

--- The Haida Calendar. AA, n.s., V, 331-5. 1903.

--- A Haida Food Plant. AA, n.s., XV, 543-4. 1913.

--- Haida Songs. PAES, III, 1-63. 1912.

--- Haida Texts. MAMNH, XIV, 273-812. 1908.

--- Haida Texts and Myths. BBAE, XXIX, 1-448. 1905.

--- Notes on the Haida Language. AA, n.s., IV, 392-403. 1902.

Swanton, J.R. Social Organization of the Haida. ICA, XIII, 327-34. 1902.

--- Types of Haida and Tlingit Myths. AA, n.s., VII, 94-103. 1905.

Tolmie, W.F., and Dawson, G.M. Comparative Vocabularies of the Indian Tribes of British Columbia, pp. 15B-36B, 88B-101B, 126B-7B. Montreal, 1884.

Tylor, E.B. Note on the Haida Totem-Post lately erected in the Pitt Rivers Museum. Man, II, 1-3. 1902.

--- On the Totem-Post from the Haida Village of Masset. JAI, XXVIII, 133-5. 1899.

--- On Two British Columbian House-Posts with Totemic Carvings. JAI, XXVIII, 136-7. 1899.

Waterman, T.T. Observations among the Ancient Indian Monuments of Southeastern Alaska. SMC, LXXIV, v, 115-33. 1925.

Watkins, F.E. Four Haida House-Posts. M, XII, 107-9. 1938.

--- Potlatches and a Haida Potlatch Hat. M, XIII, 11-17. 1939.

Woldt, A. Capitain Jacobsen's Reise an der Nordwestküste Amerikas. Leipzig, 1884.

6. KLALLAM

Including the Klallam, Lummi, Nootsak, Samish, Semiamo, Songish, and Sooke.

Gunther, E. Klallam Ethnography. UWPA, I, 171-314. 1927.

Stern, B.J. The Lummi Indians of Northwest Washington. CUCA, XVII, 1-127. 1934.

Beck, E.F. Lummi Indian How Stories. 124 pp. Caldwell, 1955.

Boas, F. The Lkúngen. BAAS, LX, 563-82. 1890.

--- The Lkúngen. RUSNM, 1895, 644-6.

--- Sagen aus Britisch-Columbien. VBGA, 1891, 643-5.

--- Schädelformen von Vancouver Island. VBGA, 1890, 29-31.

Coleman, E.T. Mountaineering on the Pacific. HMM, XXXIX, 793-817. 1869.

Curtis, E.S. The North American Indian, IX, 19-31, 41-137, 157-75, 179-95. Norwood, 1913.

Douglas, F.H. Puget Sound Indian Houses. DAMLS, XXXIV, 1-3. 1931.

Eells, M. Census of the Clallam and Twana Indians. AAOJ, VI, 35-8. 1884.

--- Indian Music. AAOJ, I, 249-53. 1878.

--- The Indians of Puget Sound. AAOJ, VIII, 40-1; IX, 1-9, 97-104, 211-19, 271-6; X, 26-36, 174-8. 1886-88.

Eells, M. Myths of the Puget Sound Indians. AAOJ, XII, 160-5. 1890.

--- The Religion of the Clallam and Twana Indians. AAOJ, II, 8-14. 1879.

--- The Religion of the Indians of Puget Sound. AAOJ, XII, 69-84. 1890.

--- Ten Years of Missionary Work among the Indians at Skokomish. 271 pp. Boston, 1886.

--- The Twana, Chemakum, and Klallam Indians. ARSI, 1887, 605-81.

Gates, C.M., ed. The Indian Treaty of Point No Point. PNQ, XLVI, 52-8. 1955.

Gibbs, G. Alphabetical Vocabularies of the Clallam and Lummi. 40 pp. New York, 1863.

Grant, W.C. Description of Vancouver Island. JRGS, XXVII, 268-320. 1857.

Gunther, E. Ethnobotany of Western Washington. UWPA, X, 1-62. 1945.

--- Klallam Folk Tales. UWPA, I, 113-69. 1925.

Hill-Tout, C. Report on the Ethnology of the South-Eastern Tribes of Vancouver Island. JAI, XXXVII, 306-74. 1907.

Reagan, A.B. Archaeological Notes on Western Washington. PCAS, ser. 4, VII, 1-31. 1917.

--- Some Notes on the Lummi-Nooksack Indians. TKAS, XXX, 429-37. 1921.

Riley, C.L. The Story of Skalaxt, a Lummi Training Myth. DJA, I, 133-40. 1955.

Smith, H.I. The Cairns or Stone Sepulchers of British Columbia and Washington. RP, III, 243-54. 1904.

Smith, H.I., and Fowke, G. Cairns of British Columbia and Washington. MAMNH, IV, i, 55-75. 1901.

Smith, M.W. The Nooksack, the Chilliwack, and the Middle Fraser. PNQ, XLI, 330-41. 1950.

Suttles, W. Affinal Ties, Subsistence and Prestige among the Coast Salish. AA, LXII, 296-305. 1960.

--- The Early Diffusion of the Potato among the Coast Salish. SJA, VII, 272-88. 1951.

--- The Plateau Prophet Dance among the Coast Salish. SJA, XIII, 352-96. 1957.

--- Post-contact Culture Changes among the Lummi Indians. BCHQ, XVIII, 29-102. 1954.

--- Private Knowledge, Morality, and Social Classes among the Coast Salish. AA, LX, 497-507. 1958.

Tolmie, W.F., and Dawson, G.M. Comparative Vocabularies of the Indian Tribes of British Columbia, pp. 39B-49B. Montreal, 1884.

Wingert, P.S. American Indian Sculpture. 144 pp. New York, 1949.

Winthrop, T. The Canoe and the Saddle, ed. J.H. Williams. Tacoma, 1913.

7. KWAKIUTL

Including the Kitimat or Haisla.

Boas, F. The Kwakiutl of Vancouver Island. MAMNH, VIII, 307-515. 1909.

--- The Social Organization and the Secret Societies of the Kwakiutl Indians. RUSNM, 1895, 311-738.

Codere, H. Fighting with Property. MAES, XVIII, 143 pp. 1950.

Curtis, E.S. The North American Indian, X, 1-366. Norwood, 1915.

Ford, C.S. Smoke from Their Fires. 248 pp. New Haven, 1941.

Müller, W. Weltbild und Kult der Kwakiutl Indianer. SZK, XV, 135 pp. 1955.

Olson, R.L. The Social Organization of the Haisla. AR, II, 169-200. 1940.

Adam, L. Stammesorganisation und Häuptlingstum der Wakashstämme. ZVR, XXXV, 105-351. 1918.

Anastasi, A., and Foley, J.P. A Study of Animal Drawings by Indian Children of the North Pacific Coast. JSP, IX, 363-74. 1938.

Barnett, H.G. Gulf of Georgia Salish. AR, I, 221-95. 1939.

Barrett-Lennard, C.E. Travels in British Columbia. London, 1862.

Bayliss, C.K. A Kwakiutl Fragment. JAFL, XXII, 335. 1909.

Beckwith, M.W. Dance Forms of the Moqui and Kwakiutl Indians. ICA, XV, ii, 79-114. 1906.

Benedict, R. Patterns of Culture, pp. 173-222. Boston, 1934.

Boas, F. Die Ausdrücke für einige religiöse Begriffe der Kwakiutl Indianer. Festschrift Meinhof, pp. 386-92. Hamburg, 1927.

--- Census and Reservations of the Kwakiutl Nation. JAGS, XIX, 225-32. 1887.

--- Contributions to the Ethnology of the Kwakiutl. CUCA, III, 1-357. 1925.

--- Current Beliefs of the Kwakiutl Indians. JAFL, XLV, 177-260. 1932.

--- Dance and Music in the Life of the Northwest Coast Indians of North America. The Function of Dance in Human Society (First Seminar), ed. by F. Boas, pp. 7-18. 1944.

--- Der Einfluss der sozialen Gliederung der Kwakiutl auf deren Kultur. ICA, XIV, i, 141-8. 1904.

--- Die Entwicklung der Geheimbünde der Kwakiutl-Indianer. Festschrift Adolf Bastian, pp. 435-44. Berlin, 1896.

Boas, F. Ethnology of the Kwakiutl. ARBAE, XXXV, 43-1481. 1921.

--- Geographical Names of the Kwakiutl Indians. CUCA, XX, 1-83. 1934.

--- The Houses of the Kwakiutl Indians. PUSNM, XI, 197-213. 1888.

--- The Indians of British Columbia. PTRSC, ser. 1, VI, ii, 47-57. 1889.

--- The Indians of British Columbia. JAGS, XXVIII, 229-43. 1896.

--- The Kwakiutl. BAAS, LX, 604-32, 655-68. 1890.

--- Kwakiutl. BBAE, XL, i, 423-558. 1911.

--- Kwakiutl Culture as reflected in Mythology. MAFLS, XXVIII, 1-190. 1935.

--- Kwakiutl Grammar, ed. H.B. Yampolsky. TAPS, n.s., XXXVII, 201-377. 1947.

--- Kwakiutl Tales. CUCA, II, 1-495. 1910.

--- Kwakiutl Tales, new series. CUCA, XXVI, 1-230. 1935.

--- Metaphorical Expression in the Language of the Kwakiutl Indians. Race, Language and Culture, by F. Boas, pp. 232-9. New York, 1940.

--- Notes on Some Recent Changes in the Kwakiutl Language. IJAL, VII, 90-3. 1932.

--- Notes on the Kwakiutl. BAAS, LXVI, 569-80. 1896.

--- Notes on the Kwakiutl Vocabulary. IJAL, VI, 163-78. 1931.

--- Omeatl und Hálaqa. VBGA, 1888, 18-20.

--- On Certain Songs and Dances of the Kwakiutl. JAFL, I, 49-64. 1888.

--- The Religion of the Kwakiutl Indians. CUCA, X. 2 vols. 1930.

--- Religious Terminology of the Kwakiutl. Race, Language and Culture, by F. Boas, pp. 612-18. New York, 1940.

--- A Revised List of Kwakiutl Suffixes. IJAL, III, 117-31. 1924.

--- Sagen aus Britisch-Columbien. VBGA, 1892, 383-410; 1893, 228-65, 430-44.

--- The Social Organization of the Kwakiutl. AA, n.s., XXII, 111-26. 1920.

--- Songs of the Kwakiutl Indians. IAE, IX, Supplement, 1-9. 1896.

--- Tsimshian Mythology. ARBAE, XXXI, 494-5. 1916.

--- The Use of Masks and Head-Ornaments on the North-West Coast. IAE, III, 7-15. 1890.

--- Vocabulary of the Kwakiutl Language. PAPS, XXXI, 34-82. 1893.

Boas, F., and Hunt, G. Kwakiutl Texts. MAMNH, V, 1-532. 1902-05.

Boas, F., and Hunt, G. Kwakiutl Texts--Second Series. MAMNH, XIV, 1-269. 1906.

British and Foreign Bible Society. The Gospel according to Saint Luke. 138 pp. London, 1894.

Carmichael, A. Indian Legends of Vancouver Island. 97 pp. Toronto, 1922.

Codere, H. The Amiable Side of Kwakiutl Life. AA, LVIII, 334-51. 1956.

--- Kwakiutl Society: Rank without Class. AA, LIX, 473-86. 1957.

Curtis, N., ed. The Indians' Book, pp. 297-307. New York, 1907.

Dawson, G.M. Customs and Arts of the Kwakiool. PSM, XXXIII, 345-52. 1888.

--- Notes and Observations on the Kwakiool People. PTRSC, V, ii, 63-98. 1888.

Deans, J. Lineage of a Tribe on Vancouver Island. JAFL, I, 164. 1888.

--- The Thunder-Bird. AAOJ, VII, 357-8. 1885.

Densmore, F. The Origin of a Siwash Song. AA, n.s., XLVII, 173-5. 1945.

Dorsey, G.A. The Long Bones of Kwakiutl and Salish Indians. AA, X, 174-82. 1897.

--- Wormian Bones in artificially Deformed Kwakiutl Crania. AA, X, 169-73. 1897.

Douglas, G. Revenge at Guayasdums. B, CCLXXXIII, 6-9. Sept. 1952.

Drucker, P. Kwakiutl Dancing Societies. AR, II, 201-30. 1940.

--- Northwest Coast. AR, IX, 157-294. 1950.

Fillmore, J.C. A Woman's Song of the Kwakiutl Indians. JAFL, VI, 285-90. 1893.

Gibbs, G. Vocabulary of the Kwa'kiutl'. CNAE, I, 144-50. 1877.

Goldman, I. The Kwakiutl Indians of Vancouver Island. Cooperation and Competition among Primitive Peoples, ed. M. Mead, pp. 180-209. New York, 1937.

Grant, R.V. The Konikillah--a Kwakiutl Tale. JAFL, LIX, 194-6. 1946.

Grant, W.C. Description of Vancouver Island. JRGS, XXVII, 268-320. 1857.

Hall, A.J. A Grammar of the Kwagiutl Language. PTRSC, VI, ii, 59-105. 1888.

Halliday, W.M. Potlatch and Totem. 240 pp. London, 1935.

Hayward, V. The Indians of Alert Bay. Canadian Magazine, LI, 371-82. 1918.

Henshaw, H.K. Kwakiool Indians. AA, I, 184-6. 1888.

Hodge, F.W. Kwakiutl Sword. IN, I, 200-4. 1924.

Howay, F.W., ed. Voyages of the "Columbia" to the Northwest Coast, 1787-1790 and 1790-1793. MHSC, LXXIX, 32-400. 1941.

Hunt, G. The Rival Chiefs. Boas Anniversary Volume, pp. 108-36. New York, 1906.

Jacobsen, J.A. Geheimbünde der Küstenbewohner Nordwest-Amerika's. VBGA, 1891, 383-95.

Jenness, D. Fading Scenes on Quatsino Inlet. CGJ, VIII, 88-97. 1934.

La Grasserie, R.de. Cinq langues de la Colombie Brittannique. 530 pp. Paris, 1902.

Large, R.G. Soogwilis, 87 pp. Toronto, 1951.

Leeson, B.W. A Quatsino Legend. CGJ, VII, 23-39. 1933.

Lincoln, J.S. The Dream in Primitive Cultures. 359 pp. London, 1935.

Lindblom, G. A Kwakiutl Totem Pole in Stockholm. Ethnos, I, 137-41. 1936.

Locher, G.W. The Serpent in Kwakiutl Religion. 118 pp. Leiden, 1932.

Lopatin, I.A. Social Life and Religion of the Indians in Kitimat, British Columbia. Univ. of Southern California Social Science Series, XXVI, 1-118. 1945.

Loudon, P. Kwakiutl Totem. CGJ, LIII, 147-9. 1956.

Newcombe, C.F. Guide to the Anthropological Collection in the Provincial Museum, pp. 28-39. Victoria, 1909.

Olson, R.L. Black Market in Prerogatives among the Northern Kwakiutl. PKAS, I, 78-80. 1950.

--- Notes on the Bella Bella Kwakiutl. AR, XIV, 319-48. 1955.

--- Social Life of the Owikeno Kwakiutl. AR, XIV, 213-59. 1954.

Pilling, J.C. Bibliography of the Wakashan Languages. BBAE, XIX, 1-70. 1894.

Ravenhill, A. A Corner Stone of Canadian Culture. Occasional Papers of the British Columbia Provincial Museum, V, 1-103. 1944.

Sapir, E. Glottalized Continuants in Navaho, Nootka, and Kwakiutl. Lg, XIV, 248-74. 1938.

Shotridge, L., and F. Indians of the Northwest. MJ, IV, 71-99. 1913.

Taylor, H.C. and Duff, W. A Post-contact Southward Movement of the Kwakiutl. RSSCW, XXIV, 56-66. 1956.

Teall, G.C. The Salmon Wife. AAOJ, XVI, 140-2. 1894.

Tolmie, W.F., and Dawson, G.M. Comparative Vocabularies of the Indian Tribes of British Columbia, pp. 27B-48B, 117B. Montreal, 1884.

Wardle, H.N. Indian Gifts in Relation to Primitive Law. ICA, XXIII, 463-9. 1928.

Woldt, A. Capitain Jacobsen's Reise an der Nordwestküste Amerikas. Leipzig, 1884.

Zeh, L.E. Grotesque Indian Masks. SW, XLI, 473-7. 1912.

8. NOOTKA

Including the Makah of Cape Flattery and the Nootka tribes of Vancouver Island.

Colson, E. The Makah Indians. 324 pp. Minneapolis, 1953.

Drucker, P. The Northern and Central Nootkan Tribes. BBAE, CXLIV, 490 pp. 1951.

Koppert, V.A. Contributions to Clayoquot Ethnology. CUAS, I, 1-124. 1930.

Sapir, E. and Swadesh, M. Native Accounts of Nootka Ethnography. PRCA, I, 457 pp. 1955.

Swan, J.G. The Indians of Cape Flattery. SCK, XVI, ccxx, 1-108. 1870.

Adam, L. Stammesorganisation und Häuptlingstum der Wakashstämme. ZVR, XXXV, 105-30, 351-430. 1918.

Alcalá Galiano, D. and Valdes, C. A Spanish Voyage to Vancouver and the Northwest Coast of America in 1792. 156 pp. London, 1930.

Andrade, M.J. Relations between Nootka and Quileute. IJAL, XIX, 138-40. 1953.

Barrett-Lennard, C.E. Travels in British Columbia. London, 1862.

Boas, F. The Nootka. BAAS, LX, 582-604, 668-79. 1890.

--- Sagen aus Britisch-Columbien. VBGA, 1892, 314-44.

--- The Social Organization and the Secret Societies of the Kwakiutl Indians. RUSNM, 1895, 632-44.

--- Tsimshian Mythology. ARBAE, XXXI, 888-935. 1916.

--- Vocabularies from the Northwest Coast of America. PAAS, n.s., XXVI, 186-200. 1916.

Brabant, A.J. Vancouver Island and Its Missions. Hesquiat, 1900.

Brown, R. (ed.) A Narrative of the Adventures and Sufferings of John R. Jewitt. 256 pp. London, 1896.

Bushnell, D.I. Drawings by John Webster of Natives of the Northwest Coast. SMC, LXXX, x, 1-12. 1928.

Cook, J. A Voyage to the Pacific Ocean, II, 269-340. London, 1785.

Culin, S. A Summer Trip among the Western Indians. BFMUP, III, 143-52. 1901.

Curtis, E.S. The North American Indian, XI, 3-112, 177-86. Norwood, 1916.

Densmore, F. Conscious Effort toward Physical Perfection among the Makah Indians. AA, n.s., XXV, 564-7. 1923.

--- Field Studies of Indian Music. SMC, LXXVI, x, 119-27; LXXVIII, vii, 247-54. 1925-27.

--- Nootka and Quileute Music. BBAE, CXXIV, 1-358. 1939.

Dorsey, G.A. Games of the Makah Indians. AAOJ, XXIII, 69-73. 1901.

Drucker, P. Northwest Coast. AR, IX, 157-294. 1950.

Durham, G. Canoes from Cedar Logs. PNQ, XLVI, 33-9. 1955.

Gibbs, G. Tribes of Western Washington and Northwestern Oregon. CNAE, I, 157-241. 1877.

Giglioli, E.H. Appunti interno ad una collezione etnografica fatta durante il terzo viaggio di Cook. AAE, XXIII, 102-23. 1895.

Grant, W.C. Description of Vancouver Island. JRGS, XXVII, 268-320. 1857.

Gunther, E. A Preliminary Report on the Zoological Knowledge of the Makah. Essays in Anthropology presented to A.L.Kroeber, pp. 105-18. Berkeley, 1936.

Gunther, E. ed. Reminiscences of a Whaler's Wife. PNQ, XXXIII, 65-9. 1942.

Hodge, F.W. A Nootka Basketry Hat. IN, VI, 254-8. 1929.

Howay, F.W. (ed.) The Journal of Captain James Colnett, 1789. PCS, XXVI, 359 pp. 1940.

--- Voyages of the "Columbia" to the Northwest Coast, 1787-1790 and 1790-1793. MHSC, LXXIX, 32-400. 1941.

Hunt, G. Myths of the Nootka. ARBAE, XXXI, 888-935. 1916.

Irvine, D. How the Makah obtained Possession of Cape Flattery. INM, n.s., VI, 5-11. 1921.

Jacobsen, J.A. Geheimbünde der Küstenbewohner Nordwest-Amerika's. VBGA, 1891, 383-95.

Jewitt, J.R. A Journal kept at Nootka Sound, ed. N. L. Dodge. Boston, 1893.

--- A Narrative of the Adventures and Sufferings of John R. Jewitt. Middletown, 1815.

Knipe, C. Some Account of the Tahkaht Language. 80 pp. London, 1868.

Koppert, V.A. The Nootka Family. PM, III, 49-55. 1930.

La Grasserie, R.de. Cinq langues de la Colombie Brittannique. 530 pp. Paris, 1902.

McKelvie, B.A. Maquinna the Magnificent. 65 pp. Vancouver, 1946.

Miller, B.O. Neah Bay: The Makah in Transition. PNQ, XLIII, 262-72. 1952.

Moser, C. Reminiscences of the West Coast of Vancouver Island. 192 pp. Victoria, 1926.

Mozino, J.M. Noticias de Nutka. 117 pp. Mexico, 1913.

Newcombe, C.F. Guide to the Anthropological Collection in the Provincial Museum, pp. 40-2. Victoria, 1909.

Pilling, J.C. Bibliography of the Wakashan Languages. BBAE, XIX, 1-70. 1894.

Quimby, G.I. Culture Contact on the Northwest Coast, 1785-1795. AA, n.s., L, 247-55. 1948.

Ravenhill, A. A Corner Stone of Canadian Culture. Occasional Papers of the British Columbia Provincial Museum, V, 1-103. 1944.

Roberts, H.H. and Swadesh, M. Songs of the Nootka Indians of Western Vancouver Island. TAPS, XLV, 199-327. 1955.

Sapir, E. Abnormal Types of Speech in Nootka. MCDM, LXII, 1-21. 1915.

--- A Flood Legend of the Nootka Indians. JAFL, XXXII, 351-5. 1919.

--- A Girl's Puberty Ceremony among the Nootka Indians. PTRSC, ser. 3, VII, ii, 67-80. 1913.

--- Glottalized Continuants in Navaho, Nootka, and Kwakiutl. Lg, XIV, 248-74. 1938.

--- Indian Legends from Vancouver Island. JAFL, LXXII, 106-14. 1959.

--- The Life of a Nootka Indian. Queen's Quarterly, XXVIII, 232-43, 351-67. 1921.

--- Nootka Baby Words. IJAL, V, 118-19. 1929.

--- The Rival Whalers, a Nitinat Story. IJAL, III, 76-102. 1924.

--- Sayach'apis, a Nootka Trader. American Indian Life, ed. E.C.Parsons, pp. 297-323. New York, 1925.

--- Some Aspects of Nootka Language and Culture. AA, n.s., XIII, 15-28. 1911.

--- Vancouver Island Indians. ERE, XII, 591-5. 1922.

Sapir, E., and Swadesh, M. Nootka Texts. 334 pp. Philadelphia, 1939.

Service, E.R. The Nootka of British Columbia. PPC, 200-21. 1958.

Sproat, G.M. Scenes and Studies of Savage Life. 317 pp. London, 1868.

Sproat, G.M. The West Coast Indians in Vancouver
Island. TESL, n.s., V, 243-54. 1867.

Strange, J. Journal and Narrative of the Commercial
Expedition from Bombay to the North-West Coast of
America. Madras, 1928.

Swadesh, M. Nootka Internal Syntax. IJAL, IX, 77-
102. 1939.

--- Motivations in Nootka Warfare. SJA, IV, 76-93.
1948.

--- A Structural Trend in Nootka. Word, IV, 106-
19. 1948.

Swadesh, M.H., and M. A Visit to the Other World,
a Nitinat Text. IJAL, VII, 195-208. 1933.

Swanson, E.H. Nootka and the California Gray
Whale. PNQ, XLVII, 52-6. 1956.

Thomas, C. On Certain Stone Images. AA, X, 376-
7. 1897.

Tolmie, W.F., and Dawson, G.M. Comparative
Vocabularies of the Indian Tribes of British Columbia, pp. 50B-60B. Montreal, 1884.

Trotter, C. Extracts from the Diary of Mr. James
Strange. JAI, XXX, Anthropological Reviews and
Miscellanies, pp. 50-62. 1900.

Waterman, T.T. The Whaling Equipment of the
Makah Indians. UWPA, I, 1-67. 1920.

Wickersham, J. Pueblos of the Northwest Coast.
AAOJ, XVIII, 21-4. 1896.

Wike, J. Social Stratification among the Nootka. E,
V, 219-41. 1958.

Willoughby, C.C. Hats from the Nootka Sound Region. AN, XXXVII, 65-8. 1903.

Woldt, A. Capitain Jacobsen's Reise an der Nordwestküste Amerikas. Leipzig, 1884.

9. QUILEUTE

Including the Hoh and the Quileute.

Pettit, G.A. The Quileute of La Push, 1775-1945.
AR, XIV, 1-120. 1950.

Andrade, M.J. Notes on the Relations between
Chemakum and Quileute. IJAL, XIX, 212-15.
1953.

--- Quileute. HAIL, III, 151-292. 1933.

--- Quileute Texts. CUCA, XII, 1-211. 1931.

--- Relations between Nootka and Quileute. IJAL,
XIX, 138-40. 1953.

Collins, J.M. Distribution of the Chemakum Language. CUCA, XXXVI, 147-60. 1949.

Curtis, E.S. The North American Indian, IX, 141-
50, 175, 196-8. Norwood, 1913.

Densmore, F. Nootka and Quileute Music. BBAE,
CXXIV, 1-358. 1939.

Farrand, L. Quileute. BBAE, XXX, ii, 340-1. 1910.

--- Quileute Tales. JAFL, XXXII, 251-79. 1919.

Frachtenberg, L.J. Abnormal Types of Speech in
Quileute. IJAL, I, 295-9. 1920.

--- The Ceremonial Societies of the Quileute Indians.
AA, n.s., XXIII, 320-52. 1921.

--- Eschatology of the Quileute Indians. AA, n.s.,
XXII, 330-40. 1920.

--- Ethnological Researches in Oregon and Washington. SMC, LXVI, xvii, 111-17. 1917.

Hobucket, H. Quillayute Indian Traditions. WHQ,
XXV, 49-59. 1934.

Reagan, A.B. Archaeological Notes on Western Washington and Adjacent British Columbia. PCAS, ser.
4, VII, 1-31. 1917.

--- Hunting and Fishing of Various Tribes of Indians.
TKAS, XXX, 443-8. 1921.

--- Plants used by the Hoh and Quileute Indians. TKAS,
XXXVII, 55-70. 1934.

--- Sketches of Indian Life and Character. TKAS,
XXIII, 141-9. 1911.

--- Some Myths of the Hoh and Quillayute Indians.
TKAS, XXXVIII, 43-85. 1935.

--- Some Notes on the Occult and Hypnotic Ceremonies of Indians. PUA, XI, 65-71. 1934.

--- Various Uses of Plants by West Coast Indians.
WHQ, XXV, 133-7. 1934.

--- Whaling of the Olympic Peninsula Indians. NH,
XXV, 25-32. 1925.

Reagan, A.B., and Walters, L.V.W. Tales from the
Hoh and Quileute. JAFL, XLVI, 297-346. 1933.

Swadesh, M. Chemakum Lexicon Compared with
Quileute. IJAL, XXI, 60-72. 1955.

Swan, J.G. The Surf-Smelt of the Northwest Coast
and the Method of taking them by the Quillehute
Indians. PUSNM, III, 43-6. 1880.

10. QUINAULT

Including the Queets and the Quinault.

Olson, R.L. The Quinault Indians. UWPA, VI, 1-
190. 1936.

Conard, L.M. A Visit to Quinault Indian Graves.
Open Court, XIX, 737-44. 1905.

Farrand, L. Basketry Designs of the Salish Indians.
MAMNH, II, 391-9. 1900.

Farrand, L., and Kahnweiler, W.S. Traditions of the
Quinault Indians. MAMNH, IV, 77-132. 1902.

Hrdlicka, A. Tuberculosis among Certain Indian
Tribes. BBAE, XLII, 14-15. 1909.

Reagan, A.B. Ancient Sites and Burial Grounds in the
Vicinity of Queets. EP, XXV, 296-9. 1928.

Swan, J.G. The Northwest Coast. 435 pp. New York,
1857.

Willoughby, C. Indians of the Quinaielt Agency.
ARSI, 1886, 267-83.

Wingert, P.S. American Indian Sculpture. 144 pp.
New York, 1949.

11. SNUQUALMI

Including the Dwamish, Nisqualli, Puyallup,
Samamish, Skagit, Snohomish, Snuqualmi, and
Squaxon.

Haeberlin, H.K., and Gunther, E. Ethnographische
Notizen über die Indianerstämme des Puget-Sundes.
ZE, LVI, 1-74, 1924.

--- The Indians of Puget Sound. UWPA, IV, 1-83.
1930.

Smith, M.W. The Puyallup-Nisqually. CUCA, XXXII,
1-336. 1940.

Adamson, T. Folk-Tales of the Coast Salish. MAFLS,
XXVII, 351-60. 1934.

Altman, G.J. Guardian-Spirit Dances of the Salish. M,
XXI, 155-60. 1947.

Anderson, E.G. Chief Seattle. 390 pp. Caldwell,
1943.

Ballard, A.C. Calendric Terms of the Southern Puget
Sound Salish. SJA, VI, 79-99. 1950.

--- Mythology of Southern Puget Sound. UWPA, III,
31-150. 1929.

--- The Salmon Weir on Green River in Western Washington. DJA, III, 37-53. 1957.

--- Some Tales of the Southern Puget Sound Salish.
UWPA, II, 57-81. 1927.

--- Southern Puget Sound Salish Kinship Terms. AA,
n.s., XXXVII, 111-16. 1935.

Boas, F. Zur Mythologie der Indianer von Washington
und Oregon. Globus, LXIII, 154-7, 172-5, 190-3.
1893.

Boas, F. and Haeberlin, H. Sound Shifts in Salishan
Dialects. IJAL, IV, 117-36. 1926.

Buchanan, C.M. Some Medical Customs, Beliefs and
Practices of the Snokomish Indians. St. Louis Courier of Medicine, XXI, 277, 355. 1889.

Calhoun, F. Four Puget Sound Folktales. JAFL, LIX,
40-44. 1946.

Collins, J.M. Growth of Class Distinctions and Political Authority among the Skagit Indians During the
Contact Period. AA, LII, 331-42. 1950.

--- An Interpretation of Skagit Intragroup Conflict
During Acculturation. AA, LIV, 347-55. 1952.

--- John Fornsby: The Personal Document of a Coast
Salish Indian. CUCA, XXXVI, 287-342. 1949.

Curtis, E.S. The North American Indian, IX, 14-19,
41-137, 157-75, 182-95. Norwood, 1913.

Denny, E.I. Blazing the Way. Seattle, 1909.

Dorsey, G.A. The Dwamish Indian Spirit Boat and Its
Use. BFMUP, III, 227-38. 1902.

--- The Long Bones of Kwakiutl and Salish Indians.
AA, X, 174-82. 1897.

Douglas, F.H. Puget Sound Indian Houses. DAMLS,
XXXIV, 1-3. 1931.

--- The Puget Sound Indians. DAMLS, XXXII, 1-3.
1931.

Eells, M. The Indians of Puget Sound. AAOJ, VIII,
40-1; IX, 1-9, 97-104, 211-19, 271-6; X, 26-
36, 174-8. 1886-88.

--- The Religion of the Indians of Puget Sound. AAOJ,
XII, 69-84. 1890.

Gibbs, G. Dictionary of the Niskwalli. CNAE, I,
285-361. 1877.

Gunther, E. The Shaker Religion of the Northwest.
CUCA, XXXVI, 37-76. 1949.

Haeberlin, H.K. Mythology of Puget Sound. JAFL,
XXXVII, 371-438. 1924.

--- SbEtStdáq, a Shamanistic Performance of the
Coast Salish. AA, n.s., XX, 249-57. 1918.

Herzog, G. Salish Music. CUCA, XXXVI, 93-110.
1949.

Hulse, F.S. Linguistic Barriers to Gene-Flow. AJPA,
n.s., XV, 235-46. 1957.

King, A.R. Archaeology of the San Juan Islands.
CUCA, XXXVI, 133-46. 1949.

Leacock, E.B. The Seabird Community. CUCA,
XXXVI, 185-94. 1949.

Mooney, J. The Ghost-Dance Religion. ARBAE,
XIV, ii, 746-63. 1893.

Rakestraw, C.D. The Shaker Indians of Puget Sound.
SW, XXIX, 703-9. 1900.

Randall, B.U. The Cinderella Theme in Northwest
Coast Folklore. CUCA, XXXVI, 243-86. 1949.

Ransom, J.E. Notes on Duwamish Phonology and Morphology. IJAL, XI, 204-10. 1945.

Rivera, T. Diet of a Food-Gathering People. CUCA,
XXXVI, 19-36. 1949.

Roberts, H.H., and Haeberlin, H.K. Some Songs of
the Puget Sound Salish. JAFL, XXXI, 496-520.
1918.

St. John, L.H. The Present Status and Probable Future of the Indians of Puget Sound. WHQ, V, 12-21.
1914.

Smith, H.I. Archaeology of the Gulf of Georgia and
Puget Sound. MAMNH, IV, 301-441. 1907.

Smith, M.W. The Coast Salish of Puget Sound. AA,
n.s., XLIII, 197-211. 1941.

--- The Puyallup of Washington. ASAIT, 3-38. 1940.

Smith, M.W., ed. Indians of the Urban Northwest.
CUCA, XXXVI, 370 pp. 1949.

Smith, M.W. and Leadbeater, D. Salish Coiled Baskets. CUCA, XXXVI, 111-32. 1949.

Suttles, W. The Early Diffusion of the Potato among
the Coast Salish. SJA, VII, 272-88. 1951.

--- The Plateau Prophet Dance among the Coast Salish.
SJA, XIII, 352-96. 1957.

--- Private Knowledge, Morality, and Social Classes
among the Coast Salish. AA, LX, 497-507. 1958.

Tolmie, W.F., and Dawson, G.M. Comparative
Vocabularies of the Indian Tribes of British Columbia, pp. 50B-60B. Montreal, 1884.

Tweddell, C.E. The Snoqualmie-Duwamish Dialects
of Puget Sound Salish. UWPA, XII, 78 pp. 1950.

Waterman, T.T. The Paraphernalia of the Duwamish
"Spirit-Canoe" Ceremony. IN, VII, 129-48, 295-
312, 535-61. 1930.

--- The Shake Religion of Puget Sound. ARSI, 1922,
499-507.

Wickersham, J. Nusqually Mythology. OM, n.s.,
XXXII, 345-51. 1898.

Wingert, P.S. American Indian Sculpture. 144 pp.
New York, 1949.

--- Coast Salish Painting. CUCA, XXXVI, 77-92.
1949.

12. TLINGIT

Also called Kolosh.

Jones, L.F. A Study of the Thlingets of Alaska. New
York, 1914.

Krause, A. Die Tlinkit-Indianer. Jena, 1885.

--- The Tlingit Indians, translated by Erna Gunther.
325 pp. Seattle, 1956.

Laguna, F. de. The Story of a Tlingit Community.
BBAE, CLXXII, 264 pp. 1960.

Swanton, J.R. Social Condition, Beliefs and Linguistic Relationship of the Tlingit Indians. ARBAE,
XXVI, 391-486. 1908.

Adam, L. Stammesorganisation und Häuptlingstum
der Tlinkitindianer Nordwestamerikas. ZVR, XXIX,
86-120. 1913.

Allen, F.H. Summary of Blood Group Phenotypes in
Some Aboriginal Americans. AJPA, n.s., XVII,
86. 1959.

Anonymous. Cremation among the Sitka Indians. AN,
XI, 372-4. 1877.

--- Masks. UPMB, XIII, i, 1-29. 1947.

Bancroft, H.H. The Native Races of the Pacific States,
I, 94-114. New York, 1875.

Barbeau, M. Old Canadian Silver. CGJ, XXII, 150-
62. 1941.

--- Pathfinders in the North Pacific. 235 pp. Caldwell, 1958.

Boas, F. Einige Mythen der Tlingit. ZGE, XXIII,
159-72. 1888.

--- Grammatical Notes on the Language of the Tlingit
Indians. UPMAP, VIII, 1-179. 1917.

--- The Mythologies of the Indians. International
Quarterly, XII, 157-73. 1905.

--- Sagen aus Britisch-Columbien. VBGA, 1895, 222-
34.

--- Tlingit. BAAS, LIX, 856-67. 1889.

--- Vocabularies of the Tlingit, Haida and Tsimshian
Languages. PAPS, XXIX, 174-83. 1891.

Breysig, K. Die Entstehung des Staates aus der
Geschlechtsverfassung bei Tlinkit und Irokesen. SJG,
XXVIII, 483-527. 1904.

--- Ueber die Entstehung des Gottesgedanken. ZE,
XXXVII, 216-21. 1905.

Bugbee, A.M. The Thlinkets of Alaska. OM, n.s.,
XXII, 185-96. 1893.

Buschmann, J.K.E. Die Pima-Sprache und die
Sprache der Koloschen. AKAWB, 1856, 321-432.

Chase, W.G. Notes from Alaska. JAFL, VI, 51-3.
1893.

Corcoran, P.A. et al. Blood Groups of Alaskan Eskimos and Indians. AJPA, n.s., XVII, 187-94. 1959.

Corser, H.P. Intellectual Life of the Thlinket Indians.
Alaska-Yukon Magazine, XIII, 151-8. 1912.

Dall, W.H. Alaska and Its Resources, pp. 411-28.
Boston, 1870.

--- The Native Tribes of Alaska. PAAAS, XXXIV,
363-79. 1885.

--- On the Distribution and Nomenclature of the Native Tribes of Alaska. CNAE, I, 7-40. 1877.

Davidson, D.S. Family Hunting Territories in Northwestern North America. INM, XLVI, 5-34. 1928.

Davis, C.B. Songs of the Totem. 43 pp. Juneau,
1939.

Deans, J. The Doom of the Katt-a-quins. JAFL, V, 232-5. 1892.

Dixon, G. A Voyage round the World. 360 pp. London, 1789.

Dorsey, G.A. A Cruise among Haida and Tlingit Villages. PSM, LIII, 160-74. 1898.

Douglas, F.H. A Tlinkit Stone Mortar. MCN, VIII, 31-3. 1938.

Drucker, P. Northwest Coast. AR, IX, 157-294. 1950.

Durlach, T.M. The Relationship Systems of the Tlingit, Haida and Tsimshian. PAES, XI, 1-177. 1928.

Eifert, V.S. Lincoln on a Totem Pole. NH, LVI, 64-6. 1947.

Emmons, G.T. The Basketry of the Tlingit. MAMNH, III, 229-77. 1903.

--- The Chilkat Blanket. MAMNH, III, 329-400. 1903.

--- Copper Neck-Rings of Southern Alaska. AA, n.s., X, 644-9. 1908.

--- Native Account of the Meeting between La Perouse and the Tlingit. AA, n.s., XIII, 294-8. 1911.

--- Petroglyphs in Southeastern Alaska. AA, n.s., X, 221-30. 1908.

--- The Potlatch of the North Pacific Coast. AMJ, X, 229-34. 1910.

--- The Use of the Chilcat Blanket. AMJ, VII, 65-70. 1907.

--- The Whale House of the Chilkat. APAM, XIX, 1-33. 1916.

--- The Whale House of the Chilkat. AMJ, XVI, 451-60. 1916.

Erman, A. Ethnographische Wahrnehmungen und Erfahrungen an den Küsten des Berings-Meeres. ZE, II, 295-327, 369-93; III, 149-59. 1870-71.

Fernhelm, H. Notes on the Natives of Alaska. CNAE, I, 111-16. 1877.

Fleurieu, C.P.C.de. Voyage autour du monde pendant les années 1790, 1791 et 1792, par Étienne Marchand. New edit. 4 vols. Paris, 1841.

Fuhrmann, E. Tlinkit- und Haida-Indianer. Kulturen der Erde, XXII, 1-61. 1923.

Garfield, V.E. Historical Aspects of Tlingit Clans in Angoon, Alaska. AA, n.s., XLIX, 438-52. 1947.

--- Survey of Southeastern Alaskan Indian Research. ASC, 1950, 20-37. 1952.

Garfield, V.E., and Forrest, L.A. The Wolf and the Raven. 151 pp. Seattle, 1948.

Gatschet, A. Alaska und seine Bewohner. Aus Allen Welttheilen, VI, 195-204. 1875.

Gibbs, G., and Dall, W.H. Comparative Vocabularies. CNAE, I, 121-42. 1877.

Goddard, P.E. Has Tlingit a Genetic Relation to Athapascan? IJAL, I, 266-79. 1920.

Golder, F.A. Tlingit Myths. JAFL, XX, 290-5. 1907.

Goldschmidt, W.R., and T.H.Haas. Possessory Rights of the Natives of Southeastern Alaska. 173 pp. Washington, 1946.

Grinnell, G.B. The Natives of the Alaska Coast Region. Harriman Alaska Expedition, I, 137-64. New York, 1901.

Halpern, J.M. Arctic Jade. Rocks and Minerals, XXXVIII, 237-42. 1953.

Harrington, J.P. A Field Comparison of Northwestern with Southwestern Indians. EFWSI, 1940, 91-4. 1941.

--- Phonematic Daylight in Lhiinkit, Navajo of the North. JWAS, XXXV, 1-6. 1945.

--- Southern Peripheral Athapaskawan Origins, Divisions and Migrations. SMC, C, 503-32. 1940.

Harrington, M.R. The Northwest Coast Collection. MJ, III, 10-15. 1912.

Henshaw, H.W., and Swanton, J.R. Tlingit. BBAE, XXX, ii, 764-5. 1910.

Hirabayashi, J. The Chilkat Weaving Complex. DJA, I, 43-61. 1955.

Holmberg, H.J. Ethnographische Skizzen über die Völker des russischen Amerika. ASSF, IV, 289-354. 1856.

Jackson, S. Alaska and Missions on the North Pacific Coast, pp. 63-323. New York, 1880.

Jones, L.F. Indian Vengeance. 68 pp. Boston, 1920.

Keithahn, E.L. Human Hair as a Decorative Feature in Tlingit Ceremonial Paraphernalia. UAAP, III, i, 17-20. 1954.

--- The Petroglyphs of Southeastern Alaska. AAn, VI, 123-32. 1940.

Kenyon, K.W. Last of the Tlingit Sealers. NH, LXIV, 294-98. 1955.

Kissell, M.L. The Early Geometric Patterned Chilkat. AA, n.s., XXX, 116-20. 1928.

Knapp, F., and Childe, R.L. The Thlinkets of Southeastern Alaska. Chicago, 1896.

Krieger, H.W. Indian Villages of Southeast Alaska. ARSI, LXXXII, i, 467-94. 1928.

--- Some Aspects of Northwest Coast Indian Art. SM, XXIII, 211-19. 1926.

Krusenstern, A.J.von. Wörter-Sammlungen aus den Sprachen einiger Völker des östlichen Asien und der Nordwest-Küste von Amerika, pp. 47-55. St. Petersburg, 1813.

Laguna, F.de. Some Problems in the Relationship between Tlingit Archaeology and Ethnology. MSAA, IX, 53-57. 1953.

Laguna, F.de. Some Dynamic Forces in Tlingit Society. SJA, VIII, 1-12. 1952.

--- Tlingit Ideas about the Individual. SJA, X, 172-
91. 1954.

La Grasserie, R.de. Cinq langues de la Colombie
Brittanique. 530 pp. Paris, 1902.

Langsdorff, G.H. von. Voyages and Travels in Various
Parts of the World, pp. 395-415. Carlisle, 1817.

Leechman, D. The Chilkat Blanket. CGJ, XLVII,
83. 1953.

Lipshits, B.A. Etnograficheskie Issledovaniia v Ruskikh
Krugosvetnykh Ekspeditsiiakh Pervoi Poloviny XIX v.
ANIET, n.s., XXX, 299-322. 1956.

Lisiansky, U. A Voyage round the World, pp. 235-44.
London, 1814.

Lutké, F. Voyage autour du monde. 3 vols. Paris,
1835.

McClellan, C. The Inland Tlingit. MSAA, IX,
47-51. 1953.

--- The Interrelations of Social Structure with Northern Tlingit Ceremonialism. SJA, X, 75-96. 1954.

Marchand, E. A Voyage round the World. London,
1801.

Marchand, J.F. Tribal Epidemics in the Yukon.
American Medical Association, Journal, CXXIII,
1019-20. 1943.

Maury, J.W. Old Raven's World. 284 pp. Boston,
1931.

Meany, E.S. Attu and Yakutat Basketry. Pacific
Monthly, X, 211-19. 1903.

Miller, R.E. A Strobophotographic Analysis of a
Tlingit Indian's Speech. IJAL, VI, 47-68. 1930.

Miner, L.R. With the Thlingets in Alaska. SW,
XXVIII, 130-3, 218-20, 428-9. 1899.

Müller, F. Bemerkungen ueber das Verbum der
koloschischen Sprache. 12 pp. Wien, 1884.

Niblack, A.P. The Coast Indians of Southern Alaska
and Northern British Columbia. RUSNM, 1888,
225-386. 1890.

Oberg, K. A Comparison of Three Systems of Primitive Economic Organization. AA, n.s., XLV,
572-88. 1943.

--- Crime and Punishment in Tlingit Society. AA,
n.s., XXXVI, 145-56. 1934.

Oliver, N.N. Alaskan Indian Legends. 67 pp. New
York, 1947.

Olson, R.L. Some Trading Customs of the Chilkat
Tlingit. Essays in Anthropology presented to A.L.
Kroeber, pp. 211-14. Berkeley, 1936.

Orchard, W.C. A Chilkat Blanket and a Haida "Copper." IN, IV, 33-40. 1927.

Paul, F. Spruce-root Basketry of the Alaska Tlingit.
IH, VIII, 1-80. 1944.

Petroff, I. The Population and Resources of Alaska.
Compilation of Narratives of Explorations in Alaska,
pp. 264-81. Washington, 1900.

--- Report on the Population, Industries and Resources
of Alaska. U.S.Department of the Interior, Tenth
Census, VIII, 165-77. 1881.

Pfizmaier, A. Aufklärungen über die Sprache der
Koloschen. SKAW, CV, 169-234. 1883.

Pinart, A.L. Notes sur les Koloches. BSAP, ser. 2,
VII, 788-811. 1872.

Ratner-Shternberg, S.A. Muzeinye Materialy po
Tlingitam. ANMAE, VI, 79-114, VIII, 270-301;
IX, 167-86. 1927, 1929-1930.

Santos, A. Jesuitos en el Polo Norte. 546 pp. Madrid,
1943.

Sapir, E. The Na-dene Languages. AA, n.s., XVII,
535-8. 1915.

Schabelski, A. Voyage aux colonies russes de l'Amérique. BSG, ser. 2, IV, 201-20. 1835.

Schott, W. Etwas über die Sprache der Koloschen.
AWKR, III, 439-45. 1843.

Schwatka, F. Report of a Military Reconnaissance in
Alaska. 121 pp. Washington, 1885.

--- A Summer in Alaska. St. Louis, 1894.

Shotridge, F. The Life of a Chilkat Indian Girl. MJ,
IV, 101-3. 1913.

Shotridge, L. The Bride of Tongass. MJ, XX, 131-
56. 1929.

--- The Emblems of the Tlingit Culture. MJ, XIX,
350-77. 1928.

--- Ghost of Courageous Adventurer. MJ, XI, 11-26.
1920.

--- How Ats-ha followed the Hide of His Comrade to
Yek Land. MJ, XXI, 215-26. 1930.

--- Keyt-Gooshe. MJ, X, 213-16. 1919.

--- Land Otter-Man. MJ, XIII, 55-9. 1922.

--- My Northland revisited. MJ, VIII, 105-15. 1917.

--- Tlingit Woman's Root Basket. MJ, XII, 162-78.
1921.

--- War Helmets and Clan Hats of the Tlingit Indians.
MJ, X, 43-8. 1919.

Shotridge, L., and F. Chilkat Houses. MJ, IV, 81-
100. 1913.

--- Indians of the Northwest. MJ, IV, 71-99. 1913.

Swanton, J.R. Explanation of the Seattle Totem Pole.
JAFL, XVIII, 108-10. 1905.

--- Tlingit. BBAE, XL, i, 159-204. 1911.

--- Tlingit. ERE, XII, 351-3. 1922.

--- Tlingit Myths and Texts. BBAE, XXXIX, 1-451.
1909.

Swanton, J.R. Types of Haida and Tlingit Myths. AA, n.s., VII, 94-103. 1905.

Tarenetzky, A. Beiträge zur Skelet- und Schädel-kunde der Aleuten, Konaegen, Kenai und Koljus-chen. Mémoires de l'Académie Impériale des Sciences de St.-Pétersbourg, ser. 8, Classe Physico-Mathématique, IX, iv, 1-73. 1900.

Thorne, J.F. In the Time that was. 30 pp. Seattle, 1909.

Tolmie, W.F., and Dawson, G.M. Comparative Vocabularies of the Indian Tribes of British Columbia, pp. 14B-24B, 126B-127B. Montreal, 1884.

Velten, H.L. Two Southern Tlingit Tales. IJAL, X, 65-74. 1939.

Velten, H.V. Three Tlingit Stories. IJAL, X, 168-80. 1944.

Veniaminov, I. Mitologicheskiya predaniya i suevriya Koloshei. Sin Otechestva, XI, iii, 40-82. 1838.

--- Remarks on the Koloshian and Kadiak Languages [in Russian]. 83 pp. St. Petersburg, 1846.

--- Zapiski ob ostrovakh Unalaskinskago otdiela. Vol. III, 26-154. St. Petersburg, 1840.

Wardle, H.N. Certain Rare West-Coast Baskets. AA, n.s., XIV, 287-313. 1912.

Waterman, T.T. Observations among the Ancient Indian Monuments of Southeastern Alaska. SMC, LXXIV, v, 115-33. 1925.

Woldt, A. Capitain Jacobsen's Reise an der Nordwest-küste Amerikas. Leipzig, 1884.

Wood, C.E.S. Among the Thlinkits in Alaska. Century Magazine, XXIV, 323-39. 1882.

13. TSIMSHIAN

Including the Gitksan, the Niska, and the Tsimshian.

Boas, F. Tsimshian Mythology. ARBAE, XXXI, 29-979. 1916.

Garfield, V.E. Tsimshian Clan and Society. UWPA, VII, 167-349. 1939.

Garfield, V.E. et al. The Tsimshian: Their Arts and Music. PAES, XVIII, 302 pp. 1951.

Adam, L. Stammesorganisation und Häuptlingstum der Haida und Tsimshian. ZVR, XXX, 161-268. 1913.

Anastasi, A., and Foley, J.P. A Study of Animal Drawings by Indian Children of the North Pacific Coast. JSP, IX, 363-74. 1938.

Anonymous. A Short Story of the Metlakatla Christian Mission. 32 pp. Palo Alto, 1954.

--- Masks. UPMB, XIII, i, 1-29. 1947.

Barbeau, M. The Aleutian Route of Migration into America. GR, XXXV, 424-43. 1945.

--- Growth and Federation of the Tsimshian Phratries. ICA, XIX, 402-8. 1915.

--- Old Canadian Silver. CGJ, XXII, 150-62. 1941.

--- Pathfinders in the North Pacific. 235 pp. Caldwell, 1958.

--- Songs of the Northwest. Musical Quarterly, XIX, 101-11. 1933.

--- Totems and Songs. CGJ, L, 176-81. 1955.

--- Totem Poles. GR, XX, 258-72. 1930.

--- Totem Poles of the Gitksan. BCDM, LXI, 1-275. 1929.

Barnett, H.G. Applied Anthropology in 1860. HO, I, iii, 19-32. 1942.

--- Invention and Cultural Change. AA, n.s., XLIV, 14-30. 1942.

--- Personal Conflicts and Social Change. SF, XX, 160-71. 1941.

Beynon, W. The Tsimshians of Metlakatla. AA, n.s., XLIII, 83-8. 1941.

Boas, F. The Houses of the Tsimshian and Nisk·á. BAAS, LXVI, 580-3. 1896.

--- The Nass River Indians. BAAS, LXV, 569-92. 1895.

--- Nisk·a. BAAS, LXVI, 586-91. 1896.

--- Sagen aus Britisch-Columbien. VBGA, 1895, 195-216.

--- The Social Organization and the Secret Societies of the Kwakiutl Indians. RUSNM, 1895, 651-60.

--- Eine Sonnensage der Tsimschian. ZE, XL, 776-97. 1908.

--- Die Tsimshian. ZE, XX, 231-47, 398-405. 1888.

--- Tsimshian. BAAS, LIX, 877-89. 1889.

--- Tsimshian. BBAE, XL, i, 283-422. 1911.

--- Tsimshian Texts. BBAE, XXVII, 1-244. 1902.

--- Tsimshian Texts (New Series). PAES, III, 65-284. 1912.

--- Vocabularies of the Tlingit, Haida and Tsimshian Languages. PAPS, XXIX, 193-208. 1891.

Breton, A.C. Tsimshian Crest Poles at Hazleton and Kishpiox. Man, XVII, 137-9. 1917.

Deans, J. A Creation Myth of the Tsimshians. JAFL, IV, 34. 1891.

--- The Daughter of the Sun. JAFL, IV, 32-3. 1891.

Dorsey, G.A. The Geography of the Tsimshian Indians. AAOJ, XIX, 276-82. 1897.

--- Up the Skeena River to the Home of the Tsimshians. PSM, LIV, 181-93. 1898.

Drucker, P. Kwakiutl Dancing Societies. AR, II,
    221-3. 1940.
--- Northwest Coast. AR, IX, 157-294. 1950.
Duff, W. Gitksan Totem-Poles. ABC, III, 21-30.
    1952.
Duff, W., ed. Histories, Territories, and Laws of the
    Kitwancool. ABCM, IV, 45 pp. 1959.
Dunn, J.H. Puppets of the Skeena. CGJ, XLVII, 248-
    52. 1953.
Durlach, T.M. The Relationship Systems of the
    Tlingit, Haida and Tsimshian. PAES, XI, 1-177.
    1928.
Emmons, G.T. The Kitikshan and Their Totem
    Poles. NH, XXV, 33-48. 1925.
--- The Kitselas of British Columbia. AA, n.s.,
    XIV, 467-71. 1912.
--- Niska. BBAE, XXX, ii, 75-6. 1910.
--- Slate Mirrors of the Tsimshian. INM, n.s., XV,
    5-21. 1921.
--- Some Kitksan Totem Poles. AMJ, XIII, 362-9.
    1913.
--- Tsimshian Stories in Carved Wood. AMJ, XV,
    363-6. 1915.
Garfield, V.E. Making a Bird or Chief's Rattle. DJA,
    I, 155-64. 1955.
--- Making a Box Design. DJA, I, 165-8. 1955.
--- Survey of Southeastern Alaskan Indian Research.
    ASC, 1950, 20-37. 1952.
Gibbs, G. Notes on the Use of Numerals among the
    T'sim Si-an'. CNAE, I, 155-6. 1877.
Gibbs, G., and Dall, W.H. Comparative Vocabu-
    laries. CNAE, I, 143-50. 1877.
Gordon, G.B. Legends of the Kit-selas. MJ, IX, 39-
    49. 1918.
Halliday, W.M. Potlatch and Totem. 240 pp. Lon-
    don, 1935.
Hamy, E.T. Note sur un masque en pierre des Indiens
    de la rivière Nass. JSAP, I, 167-70. 1897.
Huber, L.R. Alaskan Indians build a Utopia. Travel,
    LXXXVIII, 22-26, 32. 1947.
Kerr, R. A Totem-Pole from the Nass River. Man,
    XXXI, 20-1. 1931.
Krappe, A.H. A Solomon Legend among the Indians
    of the North Pacific. JAFL, LIX, 309-14. 1946.
La Grasserie, R.de. Cinq langues de la Colombie
    Brittannique. 530 pp. Paris, 1902.
Mayne, R.C. Four Years in British Columbia and Van-
    couver Island. London, 1862.
McCullagh, J.B. Red Indians I have known. 47 pp.
    London, 1919.
Morison, Mrs. O. Tsimshian Proverbs. JAFL, II,
    285-6. 1889.

Newcombe, C.F. Guide to the Anthropological Col-
    lection in the Provincial Museum, pp. 26-8. Vic-
    toria, 1909.
Newcombe, W.A. A Haida or Tsimshian Doll. BCMR,
    1928, 10-11. 1929.
Niblack, A.P. The Coast Indians of Southern Alaska
    and Northern British Columbia. RUSNM, 1888,
    225-386.
Ogden, P.S. Traits of American-Indian Life and
    Character. 218 pp. London, 1853.
Ravenhill, A. A Corner Stone of Canadian Culture.
    Occasional Papers of the British Columbia Provincial
    Museum, V, 1-103. 1944.
Robinson, G. Tales of Kitimaat. Kitimat, 1956.
Sapir, E. A Haida Kinship Term among the Tsimshian.
    AA, n.s., XXIII, 233-4. 1921.
--- Nass River Terms of Relationship. AA, n.s.,
    XXII, 261-71. 1920.
--- A Sketch of the Social Organization of the Nass
    River Indians. MBCDM, XIX, 1-30. 1915.
Schulenburg, A.C. Die Sprache der Zimshian-
    Indianer. 372 pp. Braunschweig, 1894.
Scott, L. and Leechman, D. The Tsimshian. B,
    CCLXXXIV, ii, 26-27. 1953.
Shotridge, L. A Visit to the Tsimshian Indians. MJ,
    X, 49-67, 117-48. 1919.
Smith, H.I. Materia Medica of the Bella Coola and
    Neighbouring Tribes. BCDM, LVI, 47-68. 1927.
Swanton, J.R. Chimmesyan Family. BBAE, XXX, i,
    270-1. 1907.
--- Tsimshian. ERE, XII, 465-6. 1922.
Tolmie, W.F., and Dawson, G.M. Comparative
    Vocabularies of the Indian Tribes of British Colum-
    bia, pp. 14B-25B, 126B-127B. Montreal, 1884.
Wellcome, H.S. The Story of Metlakahtla. 483 pp.
    New York, 1887.
Woldt, A. Capitain Jacobsen's Reise an der Nordwest-
    küste Amerikas. Leipzig, 1884.

14. TWANA

Including the Twana or Skokomish tribe of the
Salishan linguistic stock and the Chemakum tribe
of the Chimakuan stock.

Eells, M. Twana Indians of the Skokomish Reserva-
    tion. BGGST, III, 57-114. 1877.

Adamson, T. Folk-Tales of the Coast Salish. MAFLS,
    XXVII, 364-78. 1934.

Andrade, M. Notes on Relations between Chemakum
and Quileute. IJAL, XIX, 212-15. 1953.

Boas, F. Notes on the Chemakum Language. AA, V,
37-44. 1892.

Collins, J.M. Distribution of the Chemakum Language. CUCA, XXXVI, 147-60. 1949.

Curtis, E.S. The North American Indian, IX, 11-
13, 141-50. Norwood, 1913.

Eells, M. Census of the Clallam and Twana Indians.
AAOJ, VI, 35-8. 1884.

--- The Chemakum Language. AAOJ, III, 52-4.
1880.

--- Do-ki-batt, or the God of the Puget Sound Indians. AAOJ, VI, 389-93. 1884.

--- Indian Music. AAOJ, I, 249-53. 1878.

--- The Indians of Puget Sound. AAOJ, VIII, 40-1;
IX, 1-9, 97-104, 211-19, 271-6; X, 26-36, 174-
8. 1886-88.

--- Myths of the Puget Sound Indians. AAOJ, XII,
160-5. 1890.

--- The Potlatches of Puget Sound. AAOJ, V, 135-
47. 1883.

Eells, M. The Religion of the Clallam and Twana Indians. AAOJ, II, 8-14. 1879.

--- The Religion of the Indians of Puget Sound. AAOJ,
XII, 69-84. 1890.

--- Ten Years of Missionary Work among the Indians at
Skokomish. 271 pp. Boston, 1886.

--- The Twana, Chemakum, and Klallam Indians.
ARSI, 1887, 605-81.

--- The Twana Language. AAOJ, III, 296-303. 1880.

Elmendorf, W.W. The Cultural Setting of the Twana
Secret Society. AA, n.s., L, 625-33. 1948.

--- Twana Kinship Terminology. SJA, II, 420-32.
1946.

Gates, C.M., ed. The Indian Treaty of Point No
Point. PNQ, XLVI, 52-8. 1955.

Quimby, L.W. Among the Skokomish Indians. SW,
XXX, 511-13. 1901.

Squier, E.L. Children of the Twilight, pp. 1-30,
138-67. New York, 1926.

Swadesh, M. Chemakum Lexicon Compared with
Quileute. IJAL, XXI, 60-72. 1955.

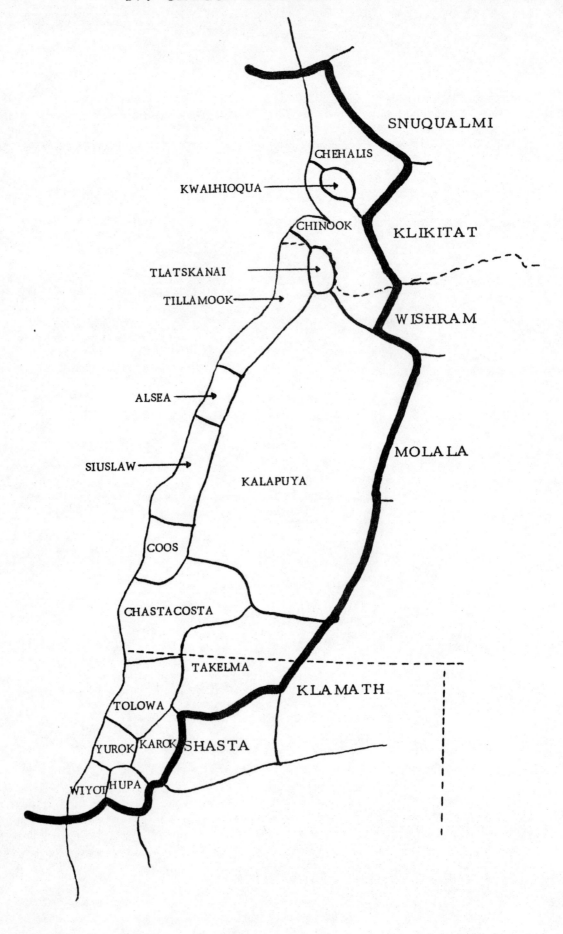

The tribes of this area are grouped under the follow-
ing linguistic stocks:
Athapaskan: Chastacosta, Hupa, Kwalhiokwa,
   Tlàtskanai, Tolowa.
Chinookan: Chinook.
Hokan: Karok.
Kusan: Coos.
Ritwan: Wiyot, Yurok (probably).
Salishan: Chehalis, Tillamook.
Takelman: Kalapuya (probably), Takelma.
Yakonan: Alsea, Siuslaw (probably).

Aberle, D.F. The Prophet Dance and Reactions to
   White Contact. SJA, XV, 74-83. 1959.

Anonymous. Dictionary of the Chinook Jargon as
   spoken on Puget Sound and the Northwest. 38 pp.
   Washington, 1894.

Bagley, C.B. Indian Myths of the Northwest. 145 pp.
   Seattle, 1930.

Bancroft, H.A. The Native Races of the Pacific
   States, I, 222-49, 322-61. New York, 1875.

Barnett, H.G. The Southern Extent of Totem Pole
   Carving. PNQ, XXXIII, 379-89. 1942.

Barry, J.N. The Indians of Oregon. OHQ, XXVIII,
   49-61. 1927.

Bartlett, L.B. Dictionary of the Intertribal Indian
   Language. 91 pp. Tacoma, 1924.

Berreman, J.V. Tribal Distribution in Oregon. MAAA,
   XLVII, 7-65. 1937.

Bledsoe, A.J. The Indian Wars of the Northwest.
   505 pp. San Francisco, 1885.

Caughey, J.W. The Indians of California in 1852.
   188 pp. San Marino, 1952.

Clark, E.E. George Gibbs' Account of Indian Mythology in Oregon and Washington Territories. OHQ,
   LVI, 293-325; LVII, 125-67. 1955-56.

--- Indian Story-Telling of Old in the Pacific Northwest. OHQ, LIV, 91-101. 1953.

--- The Mythology of the Indians in the Pacific Northwest. OHQ, LIV, 163-89. 1953.

Cook, S.F. The Aboriginal Population of the North
   Coast of California. AR, XVI, 81-130. 1956.

--- The Epidemic of 1830-1833 in California and
   Oregon. UCP, XLIII, 303-26. 1954.

Costley, J. and L. Rosen. Indians on Federal Reservations in the United States: Portland Area. U.S.
   Public Health Service Publication, DCXV, i, 1-
   41. 1959.

Cressman, L.S. Aboriginal Burials in Southwestern
   Oregon. AA, n.s., XXXV, 116-30. 1933.

--- Petroglyphs of Oregon. UOSA, II, 1-78. 1937.

Culley, J. The California Indians: Their Medical
   Practices and Their Drugs. Journal of the American
   Pharmaceutical Association, XXV, 332-9. 1936.

Dale, H.E., ed. The Ashley-Smith Explorations and
   the Discovery of a Central Route to the Pacific.
   Cleveland, 1918.

Demers, M. Chinook Dictionary, Catechism, Prayers,
   and Hymns. 68 pp. Montreal, 1871.

Dixon, R.B. Numerical Systems of the Languages of
   California. AA, n.s., IX, 663-90. 1907.

Douglas, F.H. Main Types of Basketry in Washington
   and Northwestern Oregon. DAMLS, SCVIII, 190-2.
   1940.

Driver, H.E. Girls' Puberty Rites in Western North
   America. AR, VI, 21-90. 1941.

Driver, E.H., and Kroeber, A.L. Quantitative Expressions of Cultural Relationships. UCP, XXXI, 236-43.
   1932.

Du Bois, C. The 1870 Ghost Dance. AR, III, 1-151.
   1939.

Durieu, P. Chinook Vocabulary. 16 pp. Kamloops,
   1892.

Eells, M. The Chinook Jargon. AA, VII, 300-12.
   1894.

--- The Stone Age of Oregon. ARSI, 1886, 283-95.

--- The Thunder Bird. AA, II, 329-36. 1889.

Elmendorff, W.W. Word Taboo and Lexical Change
   in Coast Salish. IJAL, XVII, 205-8. 1951.

Fee, C.A. Oregon's Historical Esperanto—the Chinook
   Jargon. OHQ, XLII, 176-85. 1941.

French, K. and D. The Warm Springs Indian Community. AmI, VII, ii, 3-16. 1955.

Gatschet, A.S. Indian Languages of the Pacific States
   and Territories. MAH, VIII, 254-63. 1882.

Gibbs, G. Journal of the Expedition of Colonel Redick
   M'Kee. HCPIT, III, 99-177. 1853.

--- Report on the Indian Tribes of the Territory of
   Washington. RESRR, I, 402-36. 1855.

--- Tribes of Western Washington and Northwestern
   Oregon. CNAE, I, 157-240. 1877.

--- Vocabularies of Indian Languages of Northwest
   California. HCPIT, III, 428-45. 1853.

Gifford, E.W. Californian Bone Artifacts. AR, III,
   153-237. 1940.

Gifford, E.W., and Harris, G.B. Californian Indian
   Nights Entertainments. Glendale, 1930.

Gill, J.K. Dictionary of the Chinook Jargon. 84 pp.
   Portland, 1909.

Goddard, P.E. Assimilation to Environment as illustrated by Athapascan Peoples. ICA, XV, i, 337-59.
   1906.

Goddard, P.E. Wayside Shrines in Northwestern California. AA, n.s., XV, 702-3. 1913.

Good, J.B. Dictionary of the Chinook and Thompson River Tongue. 1880.

Grant, R.V. Chinook Jargon. IJAL, XI, 225-33. 1945.

--- The Chinook Jargon, Past and Present. California Folklore Quarterly, III, 259-76. 1944.

Gunther, E. An Analysis of the First Salmon Ceremony. AA, n.s., XXVIII, 605-17. 1926.

--- A Further Analysis of the First Salmon Ceremony. UWPA, II, 129-73. 1928.

--- The Shaker Religion of the Northwest. CUCA, XXXVI, 37-76. 1949.

Haekel, J. Das Männerhaus im nördlichen Kalifornien. MAGW, LXX, 144-258. 1940.

Hale, H. Ethnology and Philology. Narrative of the United States Exploring Expedition, by C. Wilkes, Vol. VI. Philadelphia, 1846.

--- Indians of North-West America. TAES, II, 1-24. 1848.

--- The Oregon Trade Language or "Chinook Jargon." 63 pp. London, 1890.

Heizer, R.F. Aboriginal California and Great Basin Cartography. RUCAS, XLI, 1-9. 1958.

Heizer, R.F. and Whipple, M.A. The California Indians. 487 pp. Berkeley, 1951.

Hewes, G.W. The Ainu Double Foreshaft Toggle Harpoon and Western North America. JWAS, XXXII, 93-104. 1942.

Howay, F.W. The Origin of the Chinook Jargon. BCHQ, VI, 225-50. 1942.

Jacobs, M. Historic Perspectives in Indian Languages of Oregon and Washington. PNQ, 1937, 55-74.

Jochelson, W. Past and Present Subterranean Dwellings of the Tribes of North Eastern Asia and North Western America. ICA, XV, ii, 115-28. 1907.

Jones, S.J. Some Regional Aspects of Native California. Scottish Geographical Magazine, LXVII, 19-30. 1951.

Kane, P. Wanderings of an Artist among the Indians of North America. 455 pp. London, 1859.

Kelley, H.J. A Geographical Sketch of That Part of North America called Oregon. Boston, 1831.

Krause, F. Die Kultur der kalifornischen Indianer. Leipzig, 1921.

Kroeber, A.L. Area and Climax. UCP, XXXVII, 101-16. 1936.

--- Athabascan Kin Term Systems. AA, n.s., XXXIX, 602-9. 1937.

--- California Culture Provinces. UCP, XVII, 151-69. 1920.

Kroeber, A.L. Elements of Culture in Native California. UCP, XIII, 259-328. 1922.

--- Handbook of the Indians of California. BBAE, LXXVIII, 1-995. 1925.

--- Salt, Dogs, Tobacco. AR, VI, 1-20. 1941.

--- Stepdaughter Marriage. AA, n.s., XLII, 562-70. 1940.

Kroeber, T. The Inland Whale. 205 pp. Bloomington, 1959.

Landerholm, C., ed. Notices & Voyages of the Famed Quebec Mission to the Pacific Northwest. 258 pp. Portland, 1956.

Latham, R.G. On the Languages of the Oregon Territory. JESL, I, 154-66. 1848.

Leechman, D. Indian Summer. 182 pp. Toronto, 1949.

Le Jeune, J.M. Chinook and Shorthand Rudiments. 15 pp. Kamloops, 1898.

Lewis, A.B. Tribes of the Columbia Valley and the Coast of Washington and Oregon. MAAA, I, 147-209. 1906.

Long, F.J. Dictionary of the Chinook Jargon. 41 pp. Seattle, 1909.

Lyman, W.D. Indian Myths of the Northwest. PAAS, n.s., XXV, 375-95. 1915.

MacLeod, W.C. Marriage, Divorce and Illegitimacy in a Primitive Pecuniary Culture. SF, V, 109-17. 1926.

Morice, A.G. The Great Déné Race. A, I, 229-77, 483-508, 695-730; II, 1-34, 181-96; IV, 582-606; V, 113-42, 419-43, 643-53, 969-90. 1906-10.

Osborne, D.H. Northwest Indians' Berry Rights. Nature Magazine, XLVI, 482-4. 1953.

Peery, W.K. And There was Salmon. 100 pp. Portland, 1949.

Rero, R.L. The Chinook Jargon and British Columbia. BCHQ, VI, 1-11. 1942.

Rust, H.N. The Obsidian Blades of California. AA, n.s., VII, 688-95. 1905.

Schulz, P.E. Indians of Lassen Volcanic National Park and Vicinity. Mineral, 1954.

Scouler, J. On the Indian Tribes inhabiting the North-West Coast of America. JESL, I, 228-52. 1848.

Smith, A.H. The Indians of Washington. RSSCW, XXI, 85-113. 1953.

Smith, H.I. Noteworthy Archeological Specimens from the Lower Columbia Valley. AA, n.s., VIII, 298-307. 1906.

Smith, M.W. Shamanism in the Shaker Religion of Northwest America. Man, LIV, 119-22. 1954.

Smith, S.B. Primitive Customs and Beliefs of the Indians of the Pacific Northwest Coast. OHQ, II, 255-65. 1901.

Spier, L. Tribal Distribution in Washington. GSA, III, 1-43. 1936.

Steward, J.H. A New Type of Carving from Columbia Valley. AA, n.s., XXIX, 255-61. 1927.

Strong, W.D. The Occurrence and Wider Implications of a "Ghost Cult" on the Columbia River suggested by Carvings in Wood, Bone and Stone. AA, n.s., XLVII, 244-61. 1945.

Sullivan, M.S. The Travels of Jedediah Smith. Santa Ana, 1934.

Tate, C.M. Chinook as spoken by the Indians. 47 pp. Victoria, 1889.

Thomas, E.H. Chinook. 179 pp. Portland, 1935.

Underhill, R. Indians of the Pacific Northwest. ILC, V, 1-232. 1944.

Victor, F.F. The Early Indian Wars of Oregon. 719 pp. Salem, 1894.

Voegelin, C.F. and E.W. Linguistic Considerations of Northeastern North America. PRSPP, III, 178-94. 1946.

Walling, A.G. History of Southern Oregon. 545 pp. Portland, 1884.

Waterman, T.T. The Geographic Names Used by the Indians of the Pacific Coast. GR, XII, 175-94. 1922.

Winthrop, T. A Partial Vocabulary of the Chinook Jargon. The Canoe and the Saddle, pp. 299-302. Boston, 1863.

1. ALSEA

Including the Alsea and the Yaquina.

Drucker, P. Contributions to Alsea Ethnography. UCP, XXXV, 81-102. 1939.

Barnett, H.G. Oregon Coast. AR, I, 155-204. 1937.

Dorsey, J.O. Gentile System of the Siletz Tribes. JAFL, III, 227-37. 1890.

--- Indians of Siletz Reservation. AA, II, 55-61. 1889.

Farrand, L. Notes on the Alsea Indians. AA, n.s., II, 239-47. 1901.

--- Yakonan Family. BBAE, XXX, ii, 984. 1910.

Frachtenberg, L.J. Alsea Texts and Myths. BBAE, LVIII, 1-304. 1920.

--- Myths of the Alsea Indians. IJAL, I, 64-75. 1917.

Gatschet, A.S. Volk und Sprache der Máklaks. Globus, XXXV, 167-71, 187-9. 1879.

Schmidt, W. Die Joshua-Indianer und einige benachbarte Stämme. UG, II, 330-47. 1929.

2. CHASTACOSTA

Including the Chastacosta, Coquille, Galice, Tututni, and Umpqua.

Anonymous. Umpqua. BBAE, XXX, ii, 866. 1910.

Barnett, H.G. Oregon Coast. AR, I, 155-204. 1937.

Curtis, E.S. The North American Indian, XIII, 91-102, 228-30, 243-53. Norwood, 1924.

Dorsey, J.O. Gentile System of the Siletz Tribes. JAFL, III, 227-37. 1890.

--- Indians of Siletz Reservation. AA, II, 55-61. 1889.

--- Tututni. BBAE, XXX, ii, 857-8. 1910.

--- The Verb "to Have" or "Possess." AA, I, 340. 1888.

Du Bois, C. The Wealth Concept as an Integrative Factor in Tolowa-Tututni Culture. Essays in Anthropology presented to A.L. Kroeber, pp. 49-65. Berkeley, 1936.

Farrand, L., and Frachtenberg, L.J. Shasta and Athapascan Myths from Oregon. JAFL, XXVIII, 224-42. 1915.

Goddard, P.E. Chastacosta. BBAE, XXX, i, 236. 1907.

Hines, G. Wild Life in Oregon, pp. 103-17. New York, 1881.

Morice, A.G. Chasta Costa and the Dene Languages of the North. AA, n.s., XVII, 559-72. 1915.

Sapir, E. Notes on Chasta Costa Phonology and Morphology. UPMAP, II, 273-340. 1914.

Schmidt, W. Die Joshua-Indianer und einige benachbarte Stämme. UG, II, 330-47. 1929.

Schumacher, P. Researches in the Kjökkenmöddings and Graves of a Former Population of the Coasts of Oregon. BGGST, III, 27-37. 1877.

Spier, L. Tribal Distribution in Southwestern Oregon. OHQ, XXVIII, 358-65. 1927.

Young, K., and Cutsforth, T.D. Hunting Superstitions in the Cow Creek Region. JAFL, XLI, 293-5. 1928.

3. CHEHALIS

Including the Copalis, Cowlitz, Humptulip, Lower Chehalis, Oyhut, Satsop, Shoalwater Salish, and Upper Chehalis.

Adamson, T. Folk-Tales of the Coast Salish. MAFLS, XXVIII, 1-350. 1934.

Ballard, A.C. Calendric Terms of the Southern Puget Sound Salish. SJA, VI, 79-99. 1950.

Boas, F. A Chehalis Text. IJAL, VIII, 103-10. 1934.
--- Zur Mythologie der Indianer von Washington und Oregon. Globus, LXIII, 154-7, 172-5, 190-3. 1893.
Curtis, E.S. The North American Indian, IX, 5-9. Norwood, 1913.
Eells, M. The Indians of Puget Sound. AAOJ, VIII, 40-1; IX, 1-9, 97-104, 211-19, 271-6; X, 26-36, 174-8. 1886-88.
Gibbs, G. Report on the Indian Tribes of the Territory of Washington. RESRR, I, 428-33. 1855.
Lee, D., and Frost, J.H. Ten Years in Oregon. 344 pp. New York, 1844.
Lemert, E. M. The Life and Death of an Indian State. HO, XIII, iii, 23-7. 1954.
Palmer, K.E.H. Honne, the Spirit of the Chehalis. 204 pp. Geneva, 1925.
Swan, J.G. The Northwest Coast. 435 pp. New York, 1857.
Tolmie, W.F., and Dawson, G.M. Comparative Vocabularies of the Indian Tribes of British Columbia, pp. 51B-61B. Montreal, 1884.

4. CHINOOK

Including the Lower Chinook tribes (Chinook, Clatsop, Shoalwater Chinook) and the Middle Chinook tribes (Clackamas, Kathlamet, Wahkiakum). The Upper Chinook tribes (Wasco, Wishram) are included under the Wishram in the Plateau area.

Ray, V.F. Lower Chinook Ethnographic Notes. UWPA, VII, 29-165. 1938.

Bartlett, L.B. Chinook-English Songs. 39 pp. Portland, 1914.
Boas, F. Chinook. BBAE, XL, i, 559-678. 1911.
--- Chinook Songs. JAFL, I, 220-26. 1888.
--- Chinook Texts. BBAE, XX, 1-278. 1894.
--- The Doctrine of Souls and Disease among the Chinook Indians. JAFL, VI, 39-42. 1893.
--- Kathlamet Texts. BBAE, XXVI, 1-261. 1901.
--- Notes on the Chinook Language. AA, VI, 55-63. 1893.
--- The Vocabulary of the Chinook Language. AA, n.s., VI, 118-47. 1904.
--- Zur Mythologie der Indianer von Washington und Oregon. Globus, LXIII, 154-7, 172-5, 190-3. 1893.
Colbert, M. Kutkos—Chinook Tyee. 228 pp. Boston, 1942.
Corney, P. Voyages in the Northern Pacific, pp. 58-68. Honolulu, 1896.

Coues, E., ed. Manuscript Journals of Alexander Henry and David Thompson. 3 vols. New York, 1897.
Cox, R. Adventures on the Columbia River, pp. 146-59. New York, 1832.
Curtis, E.S. The North American Indian, VIII, 85-6, 180-3, 198-205. Norwood, 1911.
Donaldson, T. The George Catlin Indian Gallery. RUSNM, 1885, 99-101.
Dunn, J. History of the Oregon Territory, pp. 114-40. London, 1846.
Durieu, P. Chinook Bible History. 112 pp. Kamloops, 1899.
Emmons, G.F. Replies to Inquiries respecting the Indian Tribes of Oregon and Washington. HCPIT, III, 200-25. 1853.
Farrand, L. Chinookan Family. BBAE, XXX, i, 273-4. 1907.
Frachtenberg, L.J. Comparative Studies in Takelman, Kalapuyan and Chinookan Lexicography. IJAL, I, 175-82. 1918.
Gass, P. A Journal of the Voyages and Travels of a Corps of Discovery. Pittsburgh, 1807.
Gibbs, G. Alphabetical Vocabulary of the Chinook Language. 23 pp. New York, 1863.
--- A Dictionary of the Chinook Jargon. New York, 1863.
--- Report on the Indian Tribes of the Territory of Washington. RESRR, I, 402-36. 1855.
--- Tribes of Western Washington and Northwestern Oregon. CNAE, I, 157-241. 1877.
Gunther, E. Ethnobotany of Western Washington. UWPA, X, i, 1-62. 1945.
Hymes, D.H. Myth and Tale Titles of the Lower Chinook. JAFL, LXXII, 139-45. 1959.
Jacobs, M. Clackamas Chinook Texts. MIJL, VIII, 293 pp. 1958.
--- The Content and Style of an Oral Literature. VFPA, XXVI, 293 pp. 1959.
--- A Few Observations on the World View of the Clackamas Chinook Indians. JAFL, LXVIII, 283-9. 1955.
--- Notes on the Structure of Chinook Jargon. Lg, VIII, 27-50. 1932.
--- Notes on the Structure of the Chinook Jargon. ICA, XXIV, 257. 1934.
--- Psychological Inferences from a Chinook Myth. JAFL, LXV, 121-37. 1952.
--- Texts in Chinook Jargon. UWPA, VII, 1-13. 1936.
Kane, P. The Chinook Indians. CJ, III, 273-9. 1855.
--- Wanderings of an Artist among the Indians of North America. London, 1859.

Lee, D., and Frost, J.H. Ten Years in Oregon. 344 pp. New York, 1844.

Lewis, M., and Clark, W. Travels. 3 vols. London, 1815.

Lyman, W.D. Myths and Superstitions of the Oregon Indians. PAAS, n.s., XVI, 221-51. 1904.

Meany, E.S., ed. Diary of Dr. W. F. Tolmie. WHQ, XXIII, 205-27. 1931.

Merk, F. Fur Trade and Empire, pp. 96-105. Cambridge, 1931.

Oetteking, B. Declination of the Pars Basilaris in Normal and in artificially Deformed Skulls. INM, XXVII, 1-25. 1924.

Palmer, J. Journal of Travels over the Rocky Mountains to the Columbia River. Cincinnati, 1847.

Parker, S. Journal of an Exploring Tour beyond the Rocky Mountains, pp. 178-85, 242-52. Ithaca, 1838.

Pilling, J.C. Bibliography of the Chinookan Languages. BBAE, XV, 1-81. 1893.

Ray, V.F. The Historical Position of the Lower Chinook in the Native Culture of the Northwest. PNQ, XXVIII, 363-72. 1937.

--- Plateau. AR, VIII, 99-257. 1942.

Rollins, P.A., ed. The Discovery of the Oregon Trail, pp. 7-16. New York, 1935.

Ross, A. Adventures of the First Settlers on the Oregon or Columbia River, ed. M.M. Quaife. Chicago, 1923.

Sapir, E. A Chinookan Phonetic Law. IJAL, IV, 105-10. 1927.

Spence, L. Chinooks. ERE, III, 560-3. 1911.

Strong, T.N. Cathlamet on the Columbia. London, 1844.

Swan, J.G. The Northwest Coast. 435 pp. New York, 1857.

Swanton, J.R. Morphology of the Chinook Verb. AA, n.s., II, 199-237. 1900.

Thwaites, R.G., ed. Original Journals of the Lewis and Clark Expedition. 7 vols. New York, 1904-05.

Tolmie, W.F., and Dawson, G.M. Comparative Vocabularies of the Indian Tribes of British Columbia, pp. 51B-61B. Montreal, 1884.

Townsend, J.K. Narrative of a Journey across the Rocky Mountains to the Columbia River. Philadelphia, 1839.

5. COOS

Barnett, H.G. Oregon Coast. AR, I, 155-204. 1937.

Dorsey, J.O. Gentile System of the Siletz Tribes. JAFL, III, 227-37. 1890.

Farrand, L. Kusan Family. BBAE, XXX, i, 737. 1907.

Frachtenberg, L.J. Coos. BBAE, XL, ii, 279-430. 1922.

--- Coos Texts. CUCA, I, 1-216. 1913.

--- Lower Umpqua Texts and Notes on the Kusan Dialects. CUCA, IV, 1-156. 1914.

Gatschet, A.S. Volk und Sprache der Máklaks. Globus, XXXV, 167-71, 187-9. 1879.

Jacobs, M. Coos Myth Texts. UWPA, VIII, 127-260. 1940.

--- Coos Narrative and Ethnologic Texts. UWPA, VIII, 1-125. 1939.

Leatherman, K.E., and Krieger, A.D. Contributions to Oregon Coast Prehistory. AAn, VI, 19-28. 1940.

St. Clair, H.H., and Frachtenberg, L.J. Traditions of the Coos Indians. JAFL, XXII, 25-41. 1909.

Schmidt, W. Die Joshua-Indianer und einige benachbarte Stämme. UG, II, 330-47. 1929.

6. HUPA

Including the Chilula, Hupa, Tlelding, and Whilkut.

Goddard, P.E. Life and Culture of the Hupa. UCP, I, 1-88. 1903.

Baumhoff, M.A. California Athabascan Groups. AR, XVI, 157-237. 1958.

Benham, A.M. Hupa Indians and Their Ideal Location. Papoose, I, v, 3-11. 1902.

Cook, S.F. The Aboriginal Population of the North Coast of California. AR, XVI, 81-130. 1956.

--- The Conflict between the California Indian and White Civilization. IA, XXIII, 1-115; XXIV, 1-29. 1943.

Culin, S. A Summer Trip among the Western Indians. BFMUP, III, 102-17. 1901.

Curtis, E.S. The North American Indian, XIII, 3-34, 183-5, 217-20, 243-53. Norwood, 1924.

Driver, H.E. Northwest California. AR, I, 297-433. 1939.

Fry, W.S. Humboldt Indians. OW, XXI, 503-14. 1904.

Gifford, E.W. Californian Anthropometry. UCP, XXII, 255-9. 1926.

--- Californian Kinship Terminologies. UCP, XVIII, 17-19. 1922.

Goddard, P.E. Athapascan (Hupa). BBAE, XL, i, 85-158. 1911.

--- Chilula Texts. UCP, X, 289-379. 1914.

Goddard, P.E. Hon-sitch-a-til-ya (a Hupa Dance).
   BFMUP, III, 117-22. 1901.
--- Hupa. BBAE, XXX, i, 581-4. 1907.
--- Hupa. ERE, VI, 880-3. 1914.
--- Hupa Texts. UCP, I, 89-368. 1904.
--- The Morphology of the Hupa Language. UCP, III,
   3-344. 1905.
--- Notes on the Chilula Indians. UCP, X, 265-88.
   1914.
--- The Phonology of the Hupa Language. UCP, V,
   1-20. 1907.
--- Pitch Accent in Hupa. UCP, XXIII, 333-8. 1928.
Goldschmidt, W. Ethics and the Structure of Society.
   AA, LIII, 506-24. 1951.
Goldschmidt, W.R., and Driver, H.E. The Hupa
   White Deerskin Dance. UCP, XXXV, 103-42. 1940.
Harrington, J.P. Southern Peripheral Athapaskawan
   Origins, Divisions and Migrations. SMC, C, 503-
   32. 1940.
Hrdlicka, A. Tuberculosis among Certain Indian
   Tribes. BBAE, XLII, 1-48. 1909.
Kelly, I.T. The Carver's Art of the Indians of North-
   western California. UCP, XXIV, 343-60. 1936.
Kroeber, A.L. Basket Designs of the Indians of North-
   western California. UCP, II, 105-64. 1905.
--- Handbook of the Indians of California. BBAE,
   LXXVIII, 128-41. 1925.
--- Yurok and Neighboring Kin Term Systems. UCP,
   XXXV, 15-22. 1934.
Kroeber, A.L., and Gifford, E.W. World Renewal.
   A Cult System of Native Northwest California. AR,
   XIII, 1-155. 1949.
Kroeber, T.K. A Note on a California Theme. JAFL,
   LXX, 72-4. 1957.
Mason, O.T. The Ray Collection from Hupa Reserva-
   tion. ARSI, 1886, 205-39.
Powers, S. The Northern California Indians. OM, IX,
   155-64. 1872.
--- Tribes of California. CNAE, III, 72-95. 1877.
Ray, P.H. Manufacture of Bows and Arrows among the
   Natano (Hupa) and Kenuck (Klamath) Indians. AN,
   XX, 832-3. 1886.
Sapir, E. Hupa Tattooing. Essays in Anthropology
   presented to A.L. Kroeber, pp. 273-7. Berkeley,
   1936.
Taylor, E. Hupa Birth Rites. PIAS, LVII, 24-7. 1948.
Wallace, W.J. Hupa Child-Training. Educational
   Administration and Supervision, XXXIII, 25 pp.
   1947.
--- Hupa Indian Dogs. M, XXV, 83-7. 1951.
--- Hupa Narrative Tales. JAFL, LXI, 345-55. 1948.
--- Hupa Warfare. M, XXIII, 71-7, 101-6. 1949.

Wallace, W.J. Personality Variation in a Primitive
   Society. Journal of Personality, XV, 321-8. 1947.
--- The Role of Humor in the Hupa Indian Tribe.
   JAFL, LXVI, 135-42. 1953.
--- The Role of the Aged in Hupa Society. M, XXII,
   86-92. 1948.
Wallace, W.J. and Taylor, E.S. Hupa Sorcery. SJA,
   VI, 188-96. 1950.
Woodruff, C.E. Dances of the Hupa Indians. AA, V,
   53-61. 1892.

7. KALAPUYA

Eells, M. The Stone Age of Oregon. ARSI, 1886,
   283-95.
Farrand, L. Kalapooian Family. BBAE, XXX, i, 645-
   6. 1907.
Frachtenberg, L.J. Comparative Studies in Takelman,
   Kalapuyan and Chinookan Lexicography. IJAL, I,
   175-82. 1918.
--- Ethnological Researches among the Kalapuya In-
   dians. SMC, LXV, vi, 85-9. 1916.
--- Kalapuya Texts. UWPA, XI, 143-369. 1945.
Gatschet, A.S. Adjectives of Color in Indian Lan-
   guages. AN, XIII, 475-85. 1879.
--- The Kalapuya People. JAFL, XII, 212-14. 1899.
--- Oregonian Folk-Lore. JAFL, IV, 139-43. 1891.
Jacobs, M. Santiam Kalapuya Ethnologic Texts.
   UWPA, XI, 3-81. 1945.
--- Santiam Kalapuya Myth Texts. UWPA, XI, 83-
   142. 1945.
--- Texts in Chinook Jargon. UWPA, VII, 14-19.
   1936.
Jacobs, M., Frachtenberg, L.J. and Gatschet, A.S.
   Kalapuya Texts. 394 pp. Seattle, 1945.
Laughlin, W.S. Excavations in the Calapuya Mounds
   of the Willamett Valley, Oregon. AAn, VII, 147-
   55. 1941.
Minto, J. The Number and Condition of the Native
   Race in Oregon. OHQ, I, 296-315. 1900.
Parker, S. Journal of an Exploring Tour beyond the
   Rocky Mountains. Ithaca, 1838.
Ross, A. Adventures of the First Settlers on the Oregon
   or Columbia River, ed. M.M. Quaife. Chicago,
   1923.
Rumberger, J.P. Ethnolinguistic Observations based
   on Kalapuya Texts. IJAL, XV, 158-62. 1949.
Strong, W.D., Schenck, W.E., and Steward, J.H.
   Archaeology of the Dalles-Deschutes Region. UCP,
   XXIX, 1-154. 1930.

8. KAROK

Angulo, J. de, and Freeland, L.S. Karok Texts. IJAL, VI, 194-226. 1931.

Angulo, J. de, and Harcourt, B. d'. La musique des Indiens de la Californie du Nord. JSAP, n.s., XXIII, 189-228. 1931.

Anonymous. Karok. BBAE, XXX, i, 659. 1907.

Arnold, M.E. and M. Reed. In the Land of the Grasshopper Song. 313 pp. New York, 1957.

Bright, W.L. The Karok Language. UCPL, XIII, 468 pp. 1957.

--- Karok Names. Names, VIII, iii, 172-9. 1958.

--- Linguistic Innovations in Karok. IJAL, XVIII, 53-62. 1952.

--- Some Northern Hokan Relationships. UCPL, X, 63-7. 1954.

--- The Travels of Coyote. PKAS, XI, 1-59. 1954.

Cook, S.F. The Aboriginal Population of the North Coast of California. AR, XVI, 81-130. 1956.

--- The Conflict between the California Indian and White Civilization. IA, XXIII, 1-115; XXIV, 1-29. 1943.

Curtis, E.S. The North American Indian, XIII, 57-64, 222-4, 253-62. Norwood, 1924.

Denny, M.B. Orleans Indian Legends. OW, XXV, 37-40, 161-6, 268-71, 373-5, 452-4; XXVI, 73-80, 168-70, 267-8. 1906-07.

Dixon, R.B., and Kroeber, A.L. New Linguistic Families in California. AA, n.s., XV, 647-55. 1913.

Driver, H.E. Northwest California. AR, I, 297-433. 1939.

Drucker, P. A Karuk World-Renewal Ceremony at Panaminik. UCP, XXXV, 23-8. 1936.

Gifford, E.W. Californian Kinship Terminologies. UCP, XVIII, 31-3. 1922.

--- Karok Confessions. MPR, i, 245-55. 1958.

Hamp, E.P. Karok Syllables. IJAL, XXIV, 240-1. 1958.

Harrington, J.P. Chainfern and Maidenhair, Adornment Materials of Northwestern California Basketry. So Live the Works of Men, ed. D.D. Brand and F.E. Harvey, pp. 159-62. Albuquerque, 1939.

--- Karuk Indian Myths. BBAE, CVII, 1-34. 1932.

--- Karuk Texts. IJAL, VI, 121-61, 194-226. 1930-31.

--- The Karuk Tribe. EP, XXVI, 316-19. 1929.

--- Tobacco among the Karuk Indians. BBAE, XCIV, 1-284. 1932.

Jacobsen, W.H. Washo and Karok. IJAL, XXIV, 195-212. 1958.

Kelley, I.T. The Carver's Art of the Indians of Northwestern California. UCP, XXIV, 343-60. 1936.

Kroeber, A.L. Basket Designs of the Indians of Northwestern California. UCP, II, 105-64. 1905.

--- A Ghost-Dance in California. JAFL, XVII, 32-5. 1904.

--- Handbook of the Indians of California. BBAE, LXXVIII, 98-108. 1925.

--- A Karok Orpheus Myth. JAFL, LIX, 13-19. 1946.

--- Karok Towns. UCP, XXV, 29-38. 1936.

--- The Languages of the Coast of California North of San Francisco. UCP, IX, 427-35. 1911.

--- Yurok and Neighboring Kin Term Systems. UCP, XXXV, 15-22. 1934.

Kroeber, A.L., and Gifford, E.W. World Renewal: A Cult System of Native Northwest California. AR, XIII, 1-155. 1949.

Olden, S.E. Karoc Indian Stories. 191 pp. San Francisco, 1923.

O'Neale, L.M. Yurok-Karok Basket Weavers. UCP, XXXII, 1-184. 1932.

Powers, S. The Northern California Indians. OM, VIII, 325-33, 425-35. 1872.

--- Tribes of California. CNAE, III, 19-43. 447-59. 1877.

Roberts, H.H. The First Salmon Ceremony of the Karuk Indians. AA, n.s., XXXIV, 426-40. 1932.

Schenck, S.M. and Gifford, E.W. Karok Ethnobotany. AR, XIII, 377-92. 1952.

Woodward, A. Karok Dance Paraphernalia. IN, IV, 257-71. 1927.

9. KWALHIOKWA

Boas, F. Fifth Report on the Indians of British Columbia. BAAS, LXV, 588-92. 1895.

Boas, F., and Goddard, P.E. Vocabulary of an Athapascan Dialect of the State of Washington. IJAL, III, 39-45. 1924.

Curtis, E.S. The North American Indian, IX, 153-4. Norwood, 1913.

Gibbs, G. Tribes of Western Washington and Northwestern Oregon. CNAE, I, 157-241. 1877.

Harrington, J.P. Southern Peripheral Athapaskawan Origins, Divisions and Migrations. SMC, C, 503-32. 1940.

10. SIUSLAW

Including the Kuitsh or Lower Umpqua and the Siuslaw.

Barnett, H.G. Oregon Coast. AR, I, 155-204. 1937.

Dorsey, J.O. Gentile System of the Siletz Tribes.
     JAFL, III, 227-37. 1890.

--- Indians of Siletz Reservation. AA, II, 55-61. 1889.

--- The Verb "to Have" or "Possess." AA, I, 340.
     1888.

Frachtenberg, L.J. Lower Umpqua Texts and Notes on
     the Kusan Dialects. CUCA,IV, 1-156. 1914.

--- Siuslawan. BBAE, XL, ii, 431-630. 1922.

Gatschet, A.S. Volk und Sprache der Máklaks. Globus,
     XXXV, 167-71, 187-9. 1879.

Hines, G. Wild Life in Oregon, pp. 103-17. New
     York, 1881.

11. TAKELMA

Dorsey, J.O. Gentile System of the Siletz Tribes.
     JAFL, III, 227-37. 1890.

--- Indians of Siletz Reservation, Oregon. AA, II,
     55-61. 1889.

Drucker, P. The Tolowa and Their Southwest Oregon
     Kin. UCP, XXXVI, 221-300. 1936.

Frachtenberg, L.J. Comparative Studies in Takelman,
     Kalapuyan and Chinookan Lexicography. IJAL, I,
     175-82. 1918.

Sapir, E. Notes on the Takelma Indians. AA, n.s.,
     IX, 251-75. 1907.

--- Religious Ideas of the Takelma Indians. JAFL, XX,
     33-49. 1907.

--- Takelma. BBAE, XXX, ii, 673-4. 1910.

--- The Takelma Language. BBAE, XL, ii, 1-296.
     1922.

--- Takelma Texts. UPMAP, II, 1-267. 1909.

--- Upper Takelma. BBAE, XXX, ii, 872. 1910.

Schmidt, W. Die Joshua-Indianer und einige benach-
     barte Stämme. UG, II, 330-47. 1929.

Spier, L. Tribal Distribution in Southwestern Oregon.
     OHQ, XXVIII, 358-65. 1927.

12. TILLAMOOK

Including the Nehalem, Nestucca, Siletz, and
Tillamook.

Barnett, H.G. Oregon Coast. AR, I, 155-204. 1937.

Boas, F. Notes on the Tillamook. UCP, XX, 3-16.
     1923.

--- Traditions of the Tillamook Indians. JAFL, XI,
     23-38, 133-50. 1898.

--- Zur Mythologie der Indianer von Washington und
     Oregon. Globus, LXIII, 154-7, 172-5, 190-3. 1893.

Boas, F., and Haeberlin, H. Sound Shifts in Salishan
     Dialects. IJAL, IV, 117-36. 1926.

Dorsey, J.O. The Gentile System of the Siletz Tribes.
     JAFL, III, 227-37. 1890.

Edel, M.M. Stability in Tillamook Folklore. JAFL,
     LVII, 116-27. 1944.

--- The Tillamook Language. IJAL, X, 1-57. 1939.

Frachtenberg, L.J. A Siletz Vocabulary. IJAL, I,
     45-6. 1917.

Jacobs, M. The Romantic Role of Older Women in a
     Culture of the Pacific Northwest Coast. PKAS,
     XVIII, 79-86. 1958.

Lee, D., and Frost, J.H. Ten Years in Oregon. 344
     pp. New York, 1844.

Lemert, E.M. The Life and Death of an Indian State.
     HO, XIII, iii, 23-7. 1954.

13. TLATSKANAI

Baumhoff, M.A. California Athabascan Groups. AR,
     XVI, 157-237. 1958.

Curtis, E.S. The North American Indian, IX, 153-4.
     Norwood, 1913.

14. TOLOWA

Including the Chetco and the Tolowa.

Drucker, P. The Tolowa and Their Southwest Oregon
     Kin. UCP, XXXVI, 221-300. 1936.

Anonymous. Chetco. BBAE, XXX, i, 249. 1907.

Barnett, H.G. Oregon Coast. AR, I, 155-204. 1937.

Baumhoff, M.A. California Athabascan Groups. AR,
     XVI, 157-237. 1958.

Cook, S.F. The Aboriginal Population of the North
     Coast of California. AR, XVI, 81-130. 1956.

Curtis, E.S. The North American Indian, XIII, 91-
     102, 199-201, 228-30, 243-53. Norwood, 1924.

Dorsey, J.O. The Gentile System of the Siletz Tribes.
     JAFL, III, 227-37. 1890.

Driver, H.E. Northwest California. AR, I, 297-433.
     1939.

DuBois, C. Tolowa Notes. AA, n.s., XXXIV, 248-
     62. 1932.

--- The Wealth Concept as an Integrative Factor in
     Tolowa-Tututni Culture. Essays in Anthropology pre-
     sented to A.L.Kroeber, pp. 49-65. Berkeley, 1936.

Gifford, E.W. Californian Kinship Terminologies.
     UCP, XVIII, 15-17. 1922.

Harrington, E. The Driftwood Witch and the Tolowa
  Adze Handle. M, XIV, 13-16. 1940.
Kroeber, A.L. Handbook of the Indians of California.
  BBAE, LXXVIII, 121-7. 1925.
--- Yurok and Neighboring Kin Term Systems. UCP,
  XXXV, 15-22. 1934.
Powers, S. Tribes of California. CNAE, III, 65-71.
  1877.
Waterman, T.T. Village Sites in Tolowa and Neigh-
  boring Areas. AA, n.s., XXVII, 528-43. 1925.
Woodward, A. Some Tolowa Specimens. IN, IV,
  137-50. 1927.

15. WIYOT

Buchanan, R.C. Report. H.R.Ex.Doc., No. 76
  (Serial No. 906), 34th Congress, 3d Session, pp. 23-
  6. 1857.
Cook, S.F. The Aboriginal Population of the North
  Coast of California. AR, XVI, 81-130. 1956.
--- The Conflict between the California Indian and
  White Civilization. IA, XXIII, 1-115. 1943.
Curtis, E.S. The North American Indian, XIII, 67-
  87, 191-8, 225-8, 263-76. Norwood, 1924.
Driver, H.E. Northwest California. AR, I, 297-433.
  1939.
Gifford, E.W. Californian Kinship Terminologies.
  UCP, XVIII, 29-30. 1922.
Kroeber, A.L. Handbook of the Indians of California.
  BBAE, LXXVIII, 112-20. 1925.
--- The Languages of the Coast of California North of
  San Francisco. UCP, IX, 384-412. 1911.
--- Wishosk. BBAE, XXX, ii, 964. 1910.
--- Wishosk Myths. JAFL, XVIII, 85-107. 1905.
--- Wiyot Folk-Lore. JAFL, XXI, 37-9. 1908.
--- Yurok and Neighboring Kin Term Systems. UCP,
  XXXV, 15-22. 1934.
Kroeber, A.L., and Gifford, E.W. World Renewal:
  A Cult System of Native Northwest California. AR,
  XIII, 1-155. 1949.
Loud, L.L. Ethnogeography and Archaeology of the
  Wiyot Territory. UCP, XIV, 221-436. 1918.
Nomland, G., and Kroeber, A.L. Wiyot Towns. UCP,
  XXXV, 39-48. 1936.
Powers, S. Tribes of California. CNAE, III, 96-106,
  478-82. 1877.
Reichard, G.W. Wiyot Grammar and Texts. UCP,
  XXII, 1-215. 1925.
Sapir, E. The Algonkin Affinity of Yurok and Wiyot
  Kinship Terms. JSAP, n.s., XV, 37-74. 1923.
--- Wiyot and Yurok, Algonkin Languages of California.
  AA, n.s., XV, 617-46. 1913.

Schmidt, W. Die Wiyot. UG, II, 36-41. 1929.
Uhlenbeck, C.C. Algonkisch-klinkende woorden in
  het Wiyot. MKAW, LXIII, A, ix, 233-58. 1927.
--- Grammatische invloed van het Algonkisch op het
  Wiyot en het Yurok. MKAW, n.s., II, iii, 41-9.
  1939.

16. YUROK

Heizer, R.F. and Mills, J.E. The Four Ages of Tsurai.
  207 pp. Berkeley, 1952.
Kroeber, A.L. Handbook of the Indians of California.
  BBAE, LXXVIII, 1-97. 1925.

Anonymous. Yurok. BBAE, XXX, ii, 1012-14. 1910.
Cody, B.P. Some Yurok Customs and Beliefs. M,
  XVI, 157-62; XVII, 81-7. 1942-3.
--- Yurok Fish-Dam Dance. M, XVI, 81-6. 1942.
--- Yurok Tales. M, XV, 228-31. 1941.
Cook, S.F. The Aboriginal Population of the North
  Coast of California. AR, XVI, 81-130. 1956.
--- The Conflict between the California Indian and
  White Civilization. IA, XXIII, 1-115; XXIV, 1-
  29. 1943.
Curtis, E.S. The North American Indian, XIII, 37-
  54, 185-91, 220-1, 263-76. Norwood, 1924.
Driver, H.E. Northwest California. AR, I, 297-433.
  1939.
Erikson, E.H. Observations on the Yurok: Childhood
  and World Image. UCP, XXXV, 257-302. 1943.
Gifford, E.W. Californian Anthropometry. UCP,
  XXII, 261-5. 1926.
--- Californian Kinship Terminologies. UCP, XVIII,
  27-29. 1922.
Goldschmidt, W. Ethics and the Structure of Society.
  AA, LIII, 506-24. 1951.
Heizer, R.F. A Prehistoric Yurok Ceremonial Site.
  RUCAS, XI, 1-4. 1951.
Heye, G.G. Objects illustrating Yurok Ethnology.
  IN, I, 91-3. 1924.
Kelly, I.T. The Carver's Art of the Indians of North-
  western California. UCP, XXIV, 343-60. 1936.
Kroeber, A.L. Ad hoc Reassurance Dreams. UCP,
  XLVII, 205-8. 1957.
--- Basket Designs of the Indians of Northwestern
  California. UCP, II, 105-64. 1905.
--- California Kinship Systems. UCP, XII, 374-6.
  1917.
--- A Ghost-Dance in California. JAFL, XVII, 32-5.
  1905.
--- The Languages of the Coast of California North
  of San Francisco. UCP, IX, 414-26. 1911.

Kroeber, A.L. Law of the Yurok Indians. ICA,XXII,
    ii, 511-16. 1926.
--- Yurok and Neighboring Kin Term Systems. UCP,
    XXXV, 15-22. 1934.
--- A Yurok War Reminiscence. SJA, I, 318-32.
    1945.
Kroeber, A.L., and Gifford, E.W. World Renewal:
    A Cult System of Native Northwest California. AR,
    XIII, 1-155. 1949.
Kroeber, T.K. A Note on a California Theme. JAFL,
    LXX, 72-74. 1957.
Loeffelholz, K. von, ed. Die Zoreisch-Indianer der
    Trinidad-Bai. MAGW, XXIII, 101-23. 1893.
O'Neale, L.M. Yurok-Karok Basket Weavers. UCP,
    XXXII, 1-184. 1932.
Posinsky, S.H. The Problem of Yurok Anality.
    American Imago, XIV, 3-31. 1957.
--- Yurok Shell Money and "Pains." Psychiatric
    Quarterly, XXX, 598-632. 1956.
Powers, S. The Northern California Indians. OM, VIII,
    530-9. 1872.
--- Tribes of California. CNAE, III, 44-64. 460-
    73. 1877.
Ring, M. Flora for an Indian Garden. M, IV, 69-77.
    1930.
Robins, R.H. The Yurok Language. UCPL, XV, 314
    pp. 1958.

Robins, R.H. and MacLeod, N. A Yurok Song without
    Words. Bulletin of the School of Oriental and African
    Studies of the University of London, XX, 501-6.
    1957.
Sapir, E. The Algonkin Affinity of Yurok and Wiyot
    Kinship Terms. JSAP, n.s., XV, 37-74. 1923.
--- Wiyot and Yurok, Algonkin Languages of Califor-
    nia. AA, n.s., XV, 617-46. 1913.
Sapir, J. Yurok Tales. JAFL, XLI, 253-61. 1928.
Spott, R., and Kroeber, A.L. Yurok Narratives. UCP,
    XXXV, 143-56. 1942.
Thompson, L. To the American Indian. 214 pp.
    Eureka, 1916.
Uhlenbeck, C.C. Grammatische invloed van het
    Algonkisch op het Wiyot en het Yurok. MKAW, n.s.,
    II, iii, 41-9. 1939.
Waterman, T.T. All is Trouble along the Klamath.
    American Indian Life, ed. E.C. Parsons, pp. 289-
    96. New York, 1925.
--- Yurok Affixes. UCP, XX, 369-86. 1923.
--- Yurok Geography. UCP, XVI, 174-314. 1920.
Waterman, T.T., and Kroeber, A.L. The Kepel Fish
    Dam. UCP, XXXV, 49-80. 1938.
--- Yurok Marriages. UCP, XXXV, 1-14. 1934.

V. CALIFORNIA

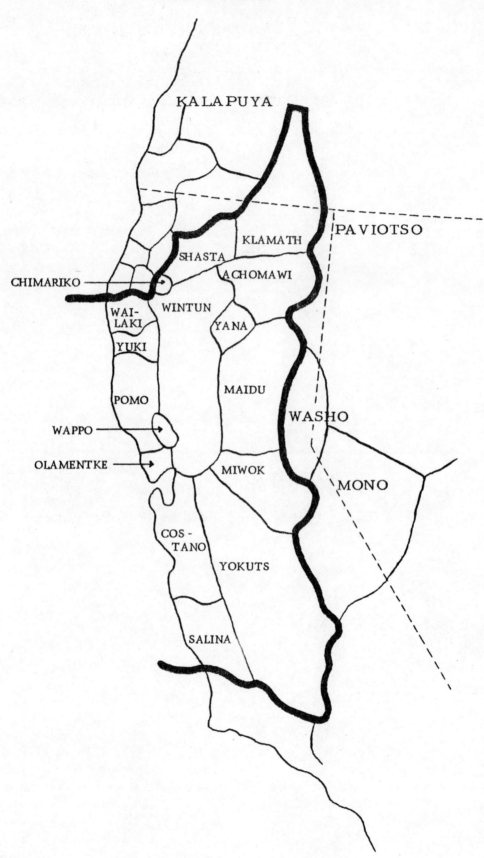

KALAPUYA

SHASTA

KLAMATH

PAVIOTSO

CHIMARIKO

ACHOMAWI

WINTUN

WAI-
LAKI

YANA

YUKI

POMO

MAIDU

WASHO

WAPPO

OLAMENTKE

MIWOK

MONO

COS-
TANO

YOKUTS

SALINA

The tribes in this area are grouped under the following linguistic stocks:

Athapaskan: Wailaki.

Hokan: Achomawi, Chimariko, Pomo, Salina, Shasta, Yana.

Lutuamian: Klamath.

Penutian: Costano, Maidu, Miwok, Olamentke, Wintun, Yokuts.

Yukian: Wappo, Yuki.

Armsby, E.R., and Rockwell, J.G. New Directions among Northern California Indians. AmI, IV, iii, 12-23. 1948.

Bancroft, H.H. The Native Races of the Pacific States, I, 361-401. New York, 1875.

Bennyhoff, J.A. Californian Fish Spears and Harpoons. AR, IX, 295-337. 1950.

Bleeker, S. The Mission Indians of California. 142 pp. New York, 1956.

Bolton, H.E., ed. Spanish Exploration in the Southwest, 1542-1706. New York, 1916.

Bonnerjea, B. California Indian Fishing. Salmon and Trout Magazine, LXXXVII, 130-33. 1937.

Bright, W. Some Northern Hokan Relationships. UCPL, X, 63-7. 1954.

Browne, J.R. The Indians of California. 73 pp. San Francisco, 1944.

Buschmann, J. Die Spuren der aztekischen Sprache im nordlichen Mexico und höheren amerikanischen Norden. AKAWB, 1854, Supplement-Band, II, 512-76.

Callaghan, C.A. California Penutian. IJAL, XXIV, 189-94. 1958.

Caughey, J.W. The Indians of California in 1852. 188 pp. San Marino, 1952.

Cessac, L. de. Rapport sur une Mission au Pérou et en Californie. Archives des Missions Scientifiques et Littéraires, Ser. 3, IX, 333-4. 1882.

Chever, E.E. The Indians of California. AN, IV, 129-48. 1870.

Cody, B.P. California Indian Baby Cradles. M, XIV, 89-96. 1940.

Cook, S.F. The Conflict between the California Indian and White Civilization. IA, XXI, 1-194, XXII, 1-55; XXIII, 1-115. 1943.

--- The Epidemic of 1830-1833 in California and Oregon. UCP, XLIII, 303-26. 1954.

--- Migration and Urbanization of the Indians of California. HB, XV, 33-45. 1943.

--- Population Trends among the California Mission Indians. IA, XVII, 1-48. 1940.

Cook, S.F. Racial Fusion among the California and Nevada Indians. HB, XV, 153-65. 1943.

Culley, J. The California Indians: Their Medical Practices and Their Drugs. Journal of the American Pharmaceutical Association, XXV, 332-9. 1936.

Dalton, O.M. Notes on an Ethnographical Collection from the West Coast of North America. IAE, X, 225-45. 1897.

Dangel, R. Die Schöpfergestalten Nordcentralcaliforniens. ICA, XXII, i, 481-504. 1928.

Demetracopoulou, D. The Loon Woman Myth. JAFL, XLVI, 101-28. 1933.

Dixon, R.B. Basketry Designs of the Indians of Northern California. BAMNH, XVII, 1-32. 1902.

--- Numerical Systems of the Languages of California. AA, n.s., IX, 663-90. 1907.

Dixon, R.B., and Kroeber, A.L. Linguistic Families of California. UCP, XVI, 47-118. 1919.

--- The Native Languages of California. AA, n.s., V, 1-26. 1903.

--- New Linguistic Families in California. AA, n.s., XV, 647-55. 1913.

Douglas, F.H. The Main Divisions of California Indian Basketry. DAMLS, LXXXIII, 130-6. 1937.

Driver, H.E. Girls' Puberty Rites in Western North America. AR, VI, 21-90. 1941.

DuBois, C. The 1870 Ghost Dance. AR, III, i, 1-151. 1939.

Duflot de Mofras, E. Exploration du territoire de l'Orégon, II, 21-35. Paris, 1844.

Engelhardt, Z. Franciscans in California. Harbor Springs, 1897.

--- The Missions and Missionaries of California. 4 vols. San Francisco, 1908-15.

Essig, E.O. The Value of Insects to the California Indians. SM, XXXVIII, 181-6. 1934.

Fages, P. Diary. Publications of the Academy of Pacific Coast History, II, 141-59. 1911.

Fisher, A. Stories California Indians Told. 109 pp. Berkeley, 1957.

Frémont, J.C. Narrative of the Exploring Expedition to the Rocky Mountains. 186 pp. New York, 1846.

Gatschet, A.S. Indian Languages of the Pacific States and Territories. MAH, I, 145-71. 1877.

Gayton, A.H. Areal Affiliations of California Folktales. AA, n.s., XXXVII, 582-99. 1935.

Geary, G.J. The Secularization of the California Indian Missions. Catholic University of America, Studies in American Church History, XVII, 204 pp. 1934.

Gibbs, G. Journal of the Expedition of Colonel Redick M'Kee. HCPIT, III, 99-177. 1853.

Gibbs, G. Vocabularies of Indian Languages in Northwest California. HCPIT, III, 428-45. 1853.

Gifford, E.W. California Indian Types. NH, XXVI, 50-60. 1926.

--- Californian Balanophagy. Essays in Anthropology presented to A.L. Kroeber, pp. 87-98. Berkeley, 1936.

--- Californian Bone Artifacts. AR, III, 153-237. 1940.

--- Composition of California Shellmounds. UCP, XII, 1-29. 1916.

--- Miwok Lineages and the Political Unit in Aboriginal California. AA, n.s., XXVIII, 389-401. 1926.

Gifford, E.W., and Harris, G.B. Californian Indian Nights Entertainments. Glendale, 1930.

Greengo, R.E. Shellfish Foods of the California Indians. PKAS, VII, 63-114. 1952.

Grinnell, E. Making Acorn Bread. RUCAS, XLII, 93-97. 1958.

Heizer, R.F. Aboriginal California and Great Basin Cartography. RUCAS, XLI, 1-9. 1958.

--- Baked-Clay Objects of the Lower Sacramento Valley. AAn, III, 34-50. 1937.

--- Francis Drake and the California Indians, 1579. UCP, XLII, 251-302. 1947.

--- The Occurrence and Significance of Southwestern Grooved Axes in California. AAn, XI, 187-93. 1946.

Heizer, R.F., and Hewes, G.W. Animal Ceremonialism in Central California in the Light of Archaeology. AA, n.s., XLII, 587-603. 1940.

Heizer, R.F. and Massey, W.C. Aboriginal Navigation off the Coasts of Upper and Baja California. BBAE, CLI, 285-312. 1953.

Heizer, R.F., and Treganza, A.E. Mines and Quarries of the Indians of California. California Journal of Mines and Geology, XL, 291-359. 1944.

Heizer, R.F., and Whipple, M.A. The California Indians. 487 pp. Berkeley, 1951.

Henshaw, H.W., ed. Translation from the Spanish of the Account of the Pilot Ferrel of the Voyage of Cabrillo. RUSGS, VI, 293-314. 1879.

Hewes, G.W. The Ainu Double Foreshaft Toggle Harpoon and Western North America. JWAS, XXXII, 93-104. 1942.

--- Economic and Geographical Relations of Aboriginal Fishing in Northern California. California Fish and Game, XXVIII, 103-10. 1942.

Holmes, W.H. Anthropological Studies in California. RUSNM, 1900, 155-87.

Hrdlicka, A. Catalogue of Human Crania in the United States National Museum Collections. PUSNM, LXIX, v, 1-127. 1927.

Hrdlicka, A. Contributions to the Physical Anthropology of California. UCP, IV, 49-64. 1906.

--- Ritual Ablation of Front Teeth in Siberia and America. SMC, XCIX, iii, 1-32. 1940.

Jones, S.J. Some Regional Aspects of Native California. Scottish Geographical Magazine, LXVII, 19-30. 1951.

Klimek, S. The Structure of California Indian Culture. UCP, XXXVII, 1-70. 1935.

Kotzebue, O. von. Entdeckungs-Reise in die Süd-See und nach der Berings-Strasse, pp. 17-29. Weimar, 1821.

--- Voyage of Discovery in the South Sea and to Behring's Straits. London, 1821.

Krause, F. Die Kultur der kalifornischen Indianer. Leipzig, 1921.

Kroeber, A.L. Anthropology, pp. 296-316. New York, 1923.

--- The Anthropology of California. Science, n.s., XXVII, 281-90. 1908.

--- The Archaeology of California. Putnam Anniversary Volume, pp. 1-42. New York, 1909.

--- Area and Climax. UCP, XXXVII, 101-16. 1936.

--- California. ERE, III, 141-5. 1911.

--- California Basketry and the Pomo. AA, n.s., XI, 233-49. 1909.

--- California Culture Provinces. UCP, XVII, 151-69. 1920.

--- California Indian Population about 1910. UCP, XLVII, 218-25. 1957.

--- California Kinship Systems. UCP, XII, 339-96. 1917.

--- California Place Names of Indian Origin. UCP, XII, 31-69. 1916.

--- Catch-Words in American Mythology. JAFL, XXI, 222-7. 1908.

--- Elements of Culture in Native California. UCP, XIII, 259-328. 1922.

--- Games of the California Indians. AA, n.s., XXII, 272-7. 1920.

--- Handbook of the Indians of California. BBAE, LXXVIII, 1-995. 1925.

--- The History of Native Culture in California. UCP, XX, 125-42. 1923.

--- The Phonetic Constituents of the Native Languages of California. UCP, X, 1-12. 1911.

--- Prospects in California Prehistory. AAn, II, 108-16. 1936.

--- The Religion of the Indians of California. UCP, IV, 319-56. 1907.

--- Salt, Dogs, Tobacco. AR, VI, 1-20. 1941.

--- Serian, Tequistlatecan, and Hokan. UCP, XI, 279-90. 1915.

Kroeber, A.L. Stepdaughter Marriage. AA, n.s., XLII, 562-70. 1940.

--- Types of Indian Culture in California. UCP, II, 81-103. 1904.

Kroeber, T. The Inland Whale. 205 pp. Bloomington, 1959.

Leigh, R.W. Dental Pathology of Aboriginal California. UCP, XXIII, 399-440. 1928.

Loud, L.L. The Stege Mounds at Richmond, California. UCP, XVII, 355-72. 1924.

MacGregor, G. The Social and Economic Adjustment of the Indians of the Sacramento Jurisdiction of California. PPSC, VI, iv, 53-8. 1939.

Meredith, H.C. Archaeology of California. Prehistoric Implements, ed. W.K.Moorehead, pp. 258-94. Cincinnati, 1900.

Merriam, C.H. The Indian Population of California. AA, n.s., VII, 594-606. 1905.

--- Studies of California Indians. 251 pp. Berkeley, 1955.

Merrill, R.E. Plants used in Basketry by the California Indians. UCP, XX, 215-42. 1923.

Milet-Mureau, M.L.A., ed. Voyage de La Pérouse autour du monde. 4 vols. Paris, 1797.

Nelson, N.C. The Ellis Landing Shellmound. UCP, VII, 357-402. 1910.

--- Shellmounds of the San Francisco Bay Region. UCP, VII, 309-56. 1909.

Park, W.Z. Shamanism in Western North America. Northwestern University Studies in the Social Sciences, II, 1-166. 1938.

Pettazzoni, R. L'Idée de Création et La Notion d'un Etre Créateur chez les Californiens. ICA, XXXII, 238-44. 1958.

Pitkin, H. and Shipley, W. A Comparative Survey of California Penutian. IJAL, XXIV, 174-88. 1958.

Powers, S. Tribes of California. CNAE, III, 1-635. 1877.

Robinson, E. Vancouver's California Bows. RUCAS, XXVIII, 1-5. 1955.

Romero, J.B. The Botanical Lore of the California Indians. 82 pp. New York, 1954.

Sanchez, N. van de G. Spanish and Indian Place Names in California. 445 pp. San Francisco, 1914.

Sapir, E. The Hokan and Coahuiltecan Languages. IJAL, I, 280-90. 1920.

--- The Position of Yana in the Hokan Stock. UCP, XIII, 1-34. 1917.

Schenck, W.E. The Emeryville Mound. UCP, XXIII, 147-282. 1926.

Schmidt, W. Die Altstämme Nordamerikas. Festschrift Eduard Seler, pp. 471-502. Stuttgart, 1922.

Schmidt, W. Die zentralkalifornischen Indianer. UG, II, 21-326; V, 1-389. 1929, 1934.

Spier, L. Havasupai Ethnography. APAM, XXIX, 81-392. 1928.

Stearns, R.E.C. Aboriginal Shell Money. AN, XI, 344-8. 1877.

Steward, J.H. Petroglyphs of California and Adjoining States. UCP, XXIV, 47-239. 1929.

Strong, W.D. An Analysis of Southwestern Society, AA, n.s., XXIX, 1-61. 1927.

Sullivan, M.S. The Travels of Jedediah Smith. Santa Ana, 1934.

Swadesh, M. Problems of Long-Range Comparison in Penutian. Lg, XXXII, 17-41. 1956.

Taylor, A.S. Indianology of California. California Farmer and Journal of Useful Sciences, Vols. XIII-XX. 1860-63.

Uhle, M. The Emoryville Shellmound. UCP, VII, 1-106. 1907.

Venegas, M. A Natural and Civil History of California. 2 vols. London, 1759.

Waterman, T.T. Native Musical Instruments of California. OW, XXVIII, 276-86. 1908.

Webb, E.B. Indian Life at the Old Missions. 356 pp. Los Angeles, 1952.

Yates, L.G. Aboriginal Weapons of California. OM, ser. 2, XXVII, 337-42. 1896.

--- Archaeology of California. Prehistoric Implements, ed. W.K.Moorehead, pp. 230-52. Cincinnati, 1900.

--- Notes on the Aboriginal Money of California. AN, XI, 30-2. 1877.

1. ACHOMAWI

Including the Achomawi and the Atsugewi.

Garth, T.R. Atsugewi Ethnography. AR, XIV, 123-212. 1953.

Angulo, J. de. The Background of the Religious Feeling in a Primitive Tribe. AA, n.s., XXVIII, 352-60. 1926.

--- Indians in Overalls. Hudson Review, III, 327-77. 1950.

--- La psychologie religieuse des Achumawi. A, XXIII, 141-66, 561-89. 1928.

Angulo, J. de, and Freeland, L.S. The Achumawi Language. IJAL, VI, 77-120. 1930.

--- Two Achomawi Tales. JAFL, XLIV, 125-36. 1931.

Boas, F. Anthropometry of Central California. BAMNH, XVII, 347-80. 1905.

Cook, S.F. The Mechanism and Extent of Dietary
   Adaptation among Certain Groups of California and
   Nevada Indians. IA, XVIII, 1-59. 1941.
Curtin, J., and Dixon, R.B. Achomawi Myths. JAFL,
   XXII, 283-7. 1909.
Curtis, E.S. The North American Indian, XIII, 129-
   58, 206-10, 234-6, 253-62. Norwood, 1924.
Dixon, R.B. Achomawi and Atsugewi Tales. JAFL,
   XXI, 159-77. 1908.
--- Linguistic Relationships within the Shasta-
   Achomawi Stock. ICA, XV, ii, 255-63. 1906.
--- The Mythology of the Shasta-Achomawi. AA,
   n.s., VII, 607-12. 1905.
--- Notes on the Achomawi and Atsugewi Indians.
   AA, n.s., X, 208-20. 1908.
--- The Pronominal Dual in the Languages of Cali-
   fornia. Boas Anniversary Volume, pp. 80-4. New
   York, 1906.
--- The Shasta-Achomawi. AA, n.s., VII, 213-17.
   1905.
--- Some Shamans of Northern California. JAFL, XVII,
   23-7. 1904.
Dixon, R.B., and Hodge, F.W. Palaihnihan. BBAE,
   XXX, ii, 192-3. 1910.
Garth, T.R. Emphasis on Industriousness among the
   Atsugewi. AA, n.s., XLVII, 554-66. 1945.
--- Kinship Terminology, Marriage Practices, and
   Behavior toward Kin among the Atsugewi. AA, n.s.,
   XLVI, 348-61. 1944.
Gifford, E.W. Californian Anthropometry. UCP, XXII,
   273-7. 1926.
--- Californian Kinship Terminologies. UCP, XVIII,
   37-40. 1922.
Kniffen, F.B. Achomawi Geography. UCP, XXIII,
   297-332. 1928.
Kroeber, A.L. Handbook of the Indians of California.
   BBAE, LXXVIII, 305-17. 1925.
Merriam, C.H. An-nik-a-del. 166 pp. Boston, 1928.
--- The Classification and Distribution of the Pit River
   Indian Tribes. SMC, LXXVIII, iii, 1-52. 1927.
Olmsted, D.L. Achumawi-Atsugewi Non-Reciprocal
   Intelligibility. IJAL, XX, 181-4. 1954.
--- Atsugewi Phonology. IJAL, XXIV, 215-20. 1958.
--- Palaihnihan and Shasta. Lg, XXXII, 73-7;
   XXXIII, 136-8. 1956-1957.
Powers, S. The California Indians. OM, XII, 412-
   26. 1874.
--- Tribes of California. CNAE, III, 267-74, 601-6.
   1877.
Schmidt, W. Die Achomawi und Atsugewi. UG, II,
   182-207. 1929.

Uldall, H.J. A Sketch of Achomawi Phonetics. IJAL,
   VIII, 73-7. 1933.
Voegelin, C.F. Notes on Klamath-Modoc and Achu-
   mawi Dialects. IJAL, XII, 96-101. 1946.
Voegelin, E.W. Northeast California. AR, VII, 47-
   251. Berkeley, 1942.
Wheeler-Voegelin, E. (ed.) E.A. Stevenson to Thomas
   W. Healy, Red Bluffs, September 30, 1857. E, IV,
   66-95. 1957.

2. CHIMARIKO

Dixon, R.B. The Chimariko Indians and Language.
   UCP, V, 295-380. 1910.

Dixon, R.B., and Kroeber, A.L. New Linguistic Fam-
   ilies in California. AA, n.s., XV, 647-55. 1913.
Driver, H.E. Northwest California. AR, I, 297-433.
   1939.
Gifford, E.W. Californian Kinship Terminologies.
   UCP, XVIII, 34. 1922.
Kroeber, A.L. Chimariko. BBAE, XXX, i, 270. 1907.
--- Handbook of the Indians of California. BBAE,
   LXXVIII, 109-12. 1925.
Powers, S. Tribes of California. CNAE, III, 474-7.
   1877.
Sapir, E. A Note on the First Person Plural in Chima-
   riko. IJAL, I, 291-4. 1920.

3. COSTANO

Anonymous. Costanoan Family. BBAE, XXX, i, 351.
   1907.
Arroyo de la Cuesta, F. Grammar of the Mutsun Lan-
   guage. 48 pp. New York, 1861.
--- A Vocabulary or Phrase Book of the Mutsun Lan-
   guage. 96 pp. New York, 1861.
Broadbent, S.M. Rumsen. IJAL, XXIII, 275-80. 1957.
Cook, S.F. The Aboriginal Population of Alameda
   and Contra Costa Counties, California. AR, XVI,
   131-55. 1957.
Dixon, R.B., and Kroeber, A.L. New Linguistic
   Families in California. AA, n.s., XV, 647-55.
   1913.
Gatschet, A.S. Specimen of the Chúmeto Language.
   AAOJ, V, 71-3, 173-80. 1883.
Gifford, E.W. Californian Kinship Terminologies.
   UCP, XVIII, 74-6. 1922.
Harrington, J.P. Central California Coast. AR, VII,
   1-46. 1942.

Heizer, R.F. The Mission Indian Vocabularies of Alphonse Pinart. AR, XV, 1-84. 1953.

--- The Mission Indian Vocabularies of H.W. Henshaw. AR, XV, 85-202. 1955.

Kroeber, A.L. The Chumash and Costanoan Languages. UCP, IX, 237-63. 1910.

--- Handbook of the Indians of California. BBAE, LXXVIII, 462-73. 1925.

--- Indian Myths of South Central California. UCP, IV, 167-250. 1907.

--- The Languages of the Coast of California South of San Francisco. UCP, II, 29-80. 1904.

--- A Mission Record of the California Indians. UCP, VIII, 20-7. 1908.

Mason, J.A. The Mutsun Dialect of Costanoan. UCP, XI, 399-472. 1916.

Powers, S. Tribes of California. CNAE, III, 535-59. 1877.

Schmidt, W. Die Costano. UG, II, 283-6. 1929.

Shafer, R. Penutian. IJAL, XIII, 205-19. 1947.

4. KLAMATH

Including the Klamath and the Modoc.

Gatschet, A.S. The Klamath Indians of Southwestern Oregon. CNAE, II. 2 vols. 1890.

Spier, L. Klamath Ethnography. UCP, XXX, 1-338. 1930.

Ames, M.M. Reaction to Stress. DJA, III, 17-30. 1957.

Angulo, J.de, and Freeland, L.S. The Lutuami Language. JSAP, n.s., XXIII, 1-45. 1931.

Angulo, J.de, and Harcourt, B.d'. La musique des Indiens de la Californie du Nord. JSAP, n.s., XXIII, 189-228. 1931.

Barrett, S.A. The Material Culture of the Klamath Lake and Modoc Indians. UCP, V, 239-60. 1910.

Boas, F. Physical Characteristics of the Tribes of the North Pacific Coast. BAAS, LXI, 424-49. 1891.

Brady, C.T. Northwestern Fights and Fighters. 373 pp. New York, 1907.

Burbank, E.A., and Royce, E. Burbank among the Indians, pp. 117-21. Caldwell, 1946.

Carlson, R.L. Klamath Henwas and Other Stone Sculpture. AA, LXI, 88-96. 1959.

Clarke, W.J. Rock Piles and Ancient Dams in the Klamath Valley. AAOJ, VII, 40-1. 1855.

Colville, F.V. Notes on the Plants used by the Klamath Indians. Contributions from the U.S. National Herbarium, V, 87-108. 1897.

Colville, F.B. Wokas, a Primitive Food of the Klamath Indians. RUSNM, 1902, 725-39.

Cook, S.F. The Mechanism and Extent of Dietary Adaptation among Certain Groups of California and Nevada Indians. IA, XVIII, 1-59. 1941.

Cressman, L.S. Klamath Prehistory. TAPS, XLVI, 375-513. 1956.

Cressman, L.S., Williams, H., and Krieger, A.D. Early Man in Oregon. UOSA, III, 1-78. 1940.

Curtin, J. Myths of the Modocs. Boston, 1912.

Curtis, E.S. The North American Indian, VIII, 161-78, 210-14, 237-9. Norwood, 1924.

Dorsey, G.A. Certain Gambling Games of the Klamath Indians. AA, n.s., III, 14-27. 1901.

Douglas, F.H. The Klamath Indians. DAMLS, XLVIII, 1-3. 1932.

Farrand, L. Lutuamian Family. BBAE, XXX, i, 778-9. 1907.

Foreman, G. The Last Trek of the Indians, pp. 314-6. Chicago, 1946.

Franks, A.W. A Bow and Two Arrows of the Modoc. JAI, III, 204-5. 1873.

Gates, M.E. A Visit to the Northern Reservations in Oregon and Montana. LMCI, XVII, 57-61. 1900.

Gatschet, A.S. Adjectives of Color in Indian Languages. AN, XIII, 475-85. 1879.

--- Mythologic Text in the Klamath Language. AAOJ, I, 161-6. 1879.

--- The Numeral Adjective in the Klamath Language. AAOJ, II, 210-17. 1880.

--- Oregonian Folk-Lore. JAFL, IV, 139-43. 1891.

--- Sketch of the Klamath Language. AAOJ, I, 81-4. 1878.

--- Songs of the Modoc Indians. AA, VII, 26-31. 1894.

--- Volk und Sprache der Máklaks. Globus, XXXV, 167-71, 187-9. 1879.

--- Die Windhose: ein Mythus der Modoc-Indianer. Am Ur-Quell, II, 1-3. 1891.

Gifford, E.W. Californian Anthropometry. UCP, XXII, 268-73. 1926.

--- Californian Kinship Terminologies. UCP, XVIII, 41-3. 1922.

Graves, C.S. Lore and Legends of the Klamath River Indians. Eureka, 1929.

Hale, H. The Klamath Nation. Science, XIX, 6-7, 20-1, 29-31. 1892.

Hall, J.C. and Nettl, B. Musical Style of the Modoc. SJA, XI, 58-66. 1955.

Heffernan, W.J. E.M. Kern, The Travels of an Artist-Explorer. 120 pp. Bakersfield, 1953.

Howard, O.O. My Life and Experiences among Our Hostile Indians. 570 pp. Hartford, 1907.

Hrdlicka, A. Head Deformation among the Klamath.
    AA, n.s., VII, 360-1. 1905.
Kroeber, A.L. Handbook of the Indians of California.
    BBAE, LXXVIII, 318-35. 1925.
Kroeber, T.K. A Note on a California Theme. JAFL,
    LXX, 72-4. 1957.
Meacham, A.B. Wi-Ne-Ma (the Woman Chief) and
    Her People. 168 pp. Hartford, 1876.
Miller, J. Life amongst the Modocs. 400 pp. London,
    1873.
Murray, K.A. The Modocs and Their War. 359 pp.
    Norman, 1959.
Nash, P. The Place of Religious Revivalism in the
    Formation of the Intercultural Community on Kla-
    math Reservation. SANAT, 377-442. 1955.
O'Callaghan, J.A. Klamath Indians and the Oregon
    Wagon Road Grant. OHQ, LIII, 23-28. 1952.
Pearsall, M. Klamath Childhood and Education. AR,
    IX, 339-51. 1950.
Powers, S. The California Indians. OM, X, 535-45.
    1873.
--- Tribes of California. CNAE, III, 252-66. 1877.
Ray, P.H. Manufacture of Bows and Arrows among the
    Natano (Hupa) and Kenuck (Klamath) Indians. AN,
    XX, 832-3. 1886.
Riddle, J.C. The Indian History of the Modoc War.
    295 pp. San Francisco, 1914.
Schmidt, M.F., and Brown, D. Fighting Indians of the
    West, pp. 229-50. New York, 1948.
Spencer, R.F. Exhortation and the Klamath Ethos.
    PAPS, C, 77-86. 1956.
--- Native Myth and Modern Religion among the Kla-
    math Indians. JAFL, LXV, 217-25. 1952.
--- Sklaven und Sklavenbesitz unter den Klamath-
    Indianern. ZE, LXXVII, 1-6. 1952.
Spier, L. The Ghost Dance of 1870 among the Kla-
    math. UWPA, II, 43-55. 1927.
Stern, T. The Klamath Indians and the Treaty of 1864.
    OHQ, LVII, 229-73. 1956.
--- Some Sources of Variability in Klamath Mythology.
    JAFL, LXIX, 1-12, 135-46, 377-86. 1956.
--- The Trickster in Klamath Mythology. WF, XII,
    158-74. 1953.
Thompson, L. To the American Indian. 214 pp.
    Eureka, 1916.
Turner, W.M. Scraps of Modoc History. OM, XI, 21-
    5. 1873.
Voegelin, C.F. Notes on Klamath-Modoc and Achu-
    mawi Dialects. IJAL, XII, 96-101. 1946.
Voegelin, E.W. Northeast California. AR, VII, 47-
    251. 1942.

Wheeler-Voegelin, E. (ed.) E.A. Stevenson to Thomas
    W. Healy, Red Bluffs, September 30, 1857. E, IV,
    66-95. 1957.
--- Official Report of the Owyhee Reconnaissance Made
    by Lieut. Colonel C.S. Drew. E, II, 146-82. 1955.
Young, C.A. A Walking Tour in the Indian Territory.
    CO, XXXVI, 167-80. 1958.

5. MAIDU

Including the Maidu proper or Northern Maidu and
the Nisenan or Southern Maidu.

Beals, R.L. Ethnology of the Nisenan. UCP, XXXI,
    835-410. 1933.
Dixon, R.B. The Northern Maidu. BAMNH, XVII,
    119-346. 1905.

Boas, F. Anthropometry of Central California.
    BAMNH, XVII, 347-80. 1905.
Clark, C.U. Excerpts from the Journals of Prince Paul
    of Wurtemberg, Year 1850. SJA, XV, 291-9. 1959.
Cook, S.F. The Mechanism and Extent of Dietary
    Adaptation among Certain Groups of California and
    Nevada Indians. IA, XVIII, 1-59. 1941.
Curtis, E.S. The North American Indian, XIV, 99-124,
    173-7, 192-5, 229-37. Norwood, 1924.
Densmore, F. Music of the Maidu Indians of Califor-
    nia. PHAPF, VII, 77 pp. 1958.
--- Musical Instruments of the Maidu Indians. AA,
    n.s., XLI, 113-18. 1939.
Dixon, R.B. Basketry Designs of the Indians of North-
    ern California. BAMNH, XVII, 2-14. 1902.
--- Basketry Designs of the Maidu Indians. AA, n.s.,
    II, 266-76. 1900.
--- Maidu. BBAE, XL, i, 679-734. 1911.
--- Maidu Myths. BAMNH, XVII, 33-118. 1902.
--- Maidu Texts. PAES, IV, 1-241. 1912.
--- The Musical Bow in California. Science, n.s.,
    XIII, 274-5. 1901.
--- The Pronominal Dual in the Languages of Califor-
    nia. Boas Anniversary Volume, pp. 80-4. New
    York, 1906.
--- Pujunan Family. BBAE, XXX, ii, 326-7. 1910.
--- Some Coyote Stories from the Maidu Indians.
    JAFL, XIII, 267-70. 1900.
--- Some Shamans of Northern California. JAFL, XVII,
    23-7. 1904.
--- System and Sequence in Maidu Mythology. JAFL,
    XVI, 32-6. 1903.

Dixon, R.B., and Kroeber, A.L. New Linguistic Families in California. AA, n.s., XV, 647-55. 1913.

Fassin, A.G. The Con-Cow Indians. OM, ser. 2, IV, 7-14. 1884.

--- Un-koi-to, the Savior. OM, ser. 2, IV, 141-50. 1884.

Faye, P.L. Notes on the Southern Maidu. UCP, XX, 35-53. 1923.

Fontana, B.L. Three Ethnohistoric References to the Maidu. E, III, 34-45. 1956.

Gatschet, A.S. Adjectives of Color in Indian Languages. AN, XIII, 475-85. 1879.

Gifford, E.W. Californian Kinship Terminologies. UCP, XVIII, 43-8. 1922.

--- Southern Maidu Religious Cermonies. AA, n.s., XXIX, 214x-257x. 1927.

Heizer, R.F. Introduced Spearthrowers (Atlatls) in California. M, XIX, 109-12. 1945.

King, A.R. The Dream Biography of a Mountain Maidu. Character and Personality, XI, 227-34. 1943.

Kroeber, A.L. Handbook of the Indians of California. BBAE, LXXVIII, 391-441. 1925.

--- Indian Myths of South Central California. UCP, IV, 167-250. 1907.

--- The Patwin and Their Neighbors. UCP, XXIX, 266-9, 375-91, 407. 1932.

--- The Valley Nisenan. UCP, XXIV, 253-90. 1929.

Kroeber, A.L. and Barrett, S.A. Fishing among the Indians of Northwestern California. AR, XXI, i, 1-210. 1960.

Loeb, E.M. The Eastern Kuksu Cult. UCP, XXXIII, 140-206. 1933.

Miller, M.L. The So-called California "Diggers." PSM, L, 201-14. 1896.

--- Der Untergang der Maidu oder Digger-Indianer. Globus, LXXII, 111-13. 1897.

Powers, S. Aboriginal Botany. PCAS, V, 373-9. 1874.

--- The California Indians. OM, XII, 21-31, 420-4. 1874.

--- Tribes of California. CNAE, III, 282-345, 584-99. 1877.

Preston, W.D. Maidu Macrophonemes. IJAL, XVI, 185-92. 1950.

Schmidt, W. Die Maidu. UG, II, 102-71; V, 98-169. 1929, 1934.

Shafer, R. Penutian. IJAL, XIII, 205-19. 1947.

Shipley, W. The Phonemes of Northeastern Maidu. IJAL, XXII, 233-37. 1956.

Spencer, D.L. Notes on the Maidu Indians. JAFL, XXI, 242-5. 1908.

Stearns, R.E.C. On the Nishinam Game of "Ha" and the Boston Game of "Props." AA, III, 353-8. 1890.

Swartz, B.K. A Study of Material Aspects of Northeastern Maidu Basketry. PKAS, XIX, 67-84. 1958.

Thurston, B.P. A Night in a Maidu Shaman's House. M, VII, 111-15. 1933.

Uldall, H.J. Maidu Phonetics. IJAL, XX, 8-16. 1954.

Voegelin, E.W. Northeast California. AR, VII, 47-251. 1942.

Willoughby, C.C. Feather Mantles of California. AA, n.s., XXIV, 432-7. 1922.

6. MIWOK

Only the Interior Miwok are classed here, the Coast Miwok and the Lake Miwok being classed under Olamentke.

Barrett, S.A., and Gifford, E.W. Miwok Material Culture. BPMCM, II, 117-376. 1933.

Gifford, E.W. Central Miwok Ceremonies. AR, XIV, 261-318. 1955.

Aginsky, B.W. Central Sierra. AR, VIII, 393-468. 1943.

Angulo, J. de, and Freeland, L.S. Miwok and Pomo Myths. JAFL, XLI, 232-52. 1928.

Angulo, J. de, and Harcourt, B. d'. La musique des Indiens de la Californie du Nord. JSAP, n.s., XXIII, 189-228. 1931.

Barrett, S.A. The Geography and Dialects of the Miwok Indians. UCP, VI, 333-68. 1908.

--- Myths of the Southern Sierra Miwok. UCP, XVI, 1-28. 1919.

--- Totemism among the Miwok Indians. JAFL, XXI, 237. 1908.

Beeler, M.S. Saclan. IJAL, XXI, 201-9. 1955.

Clark, C.U. Excerpts from the Journals of Prince Paul of Wurtemberg, Year 1850. SJA, XV, 291-9. 1959.

Clark, G. Indians of the Yosemite Valley and Vicinity. 109 pp. Yosemite, 1904.

Cook, S.F. The Aboriginal Population of Alameda and Contra Costa Counties, California. AR, XVI, 131-55. 1957.

--- The Aboriginal Population of the North Coast of California. AR, XVI, 81-130. 1956.

--- The Aboriginal Population of the San Joaquin Valley, California. AR, XVI, 31-80. 1955.

Curtis, E.S. The North American Indian, XIV, 129-47, 176-7, 195-7, 237-43. Norwood, 1924.

Dixon, R.B., and Kroeber, A.L. New Linguistic Families in California. AA, n.s., XV, 647-55. 1913.

Freeland, L.S. Language of the Sierra Miwok. MIJL, VI, 200 pp. 1951.

Gifford, E.W. Californian Anthropometry. UCP, XXII, 286-8. 1926.

--- Californian Kinship Terminologies. UCP, XVIII, 86-91. 1922.

--- Miwok Cults. UCP, XVIII, 391-408. 1926.

--- Miwok Lineages. AA, n.s., XLVI, 376-81. 1944.

--- Miwok Lineages and the Political Unit in Aboriginal California. AA, n.s., XXVIII, 389-401. 1926.

--- Miwok Moieties. UCP, XII, 139-94. 1916.

--- Miwok Myths. UCP, XII, 283-338. 1917.

Heizer, R.F. Executions by Stoning among the Sierra Miwok and Northern Paiute. PKAS, XII, 45-54. 1955.

Henshaw, H.W., and Kroeber, A.L. Moquelumnan Family. BBAE, XXX, i, 941-2. 1907.

Hutchings, J.M. In the Heart of the Sierras, pp. 421-37. Oakland, 1888.

Kroeber, A.L. California Kinship Systems. UCP, XII, 356-8. 1917.

--- The Dialectic Divisions of the Moquelumnan Family. AA, n.s., VIII, 652-63. 1906.

--- Handbook of the Indians of California. BBAE, LXXVIII, 442-61. 1925.

--- Indian Myths of South Central California. UCP, IV, 167-250. 1907.

--- The Languages of the Coast of California North of San Francisco. UCP, IX, 278-91. 1911.

--- On the Evidences of the Occupation of Certain Regions by the Miwok Indians. UCP, VI, 369-80. 1908.

Lillard, J.B., and Purves, W.K. The Archaeology of the Deer Creek-Cosumnes Area. Sacramento Junior College Department of Anthropology Bulletin, I, 1-21. 1936.

Merriam, C.H. The Dawn of the World. 273 pp. Cleveland, 1910.

--- Distribution and Classification of the Mewan Stock. AA, n.s., IX, 338-57. 1907.

--- Indian Village and Camp Sites in Yosemite Valley. Sierra Club Bulletin, X, 202-9. 1917.

--- Totemism in California. AA, n.s., X, 558-62. 1908.

Mooney, J. Notes on the Cosumnes Tribes. AA, III, 259-62. 1890.

Powers, S. The California Indians. OM, X, 322-33. 1873.

--- Tribes of California. CNAE, III, 346-68. 1877.

Riley, J.H. Vocabulary of the Kah-we'-yak and Kah-so'-wah Indians. HM, ser. 3, III, 238-40. 1868.

Schenck, W.E. Historic Aboriginal Groups of the California Delta Region. UCP, XXIII, 123-46. 1926.

Schenck, W.E., and Dawson, E.J. Archaeology of the Northern San Joaquin Valley. UCP, XXV, 289-413. 1929.

Schmidt, W. Die Miwok. UG, II, 260-71; V, 221-64. 1929, 1934.

Shafer, R. Penutian. IJAL, XIII, 203-19. 1947.

Smith, E.S. Po-ho-no and the Legends of the Yosemite. Carmel, 1927.

7. OLAMENTKE

Including the Lake Miwok and the Olamentke or Coast Miwok.

Angulo, J. de, and Freeland, L.S. Miwok and Pomo Myths. JAFL, XLI, 232-52. 1928.

Barrett, S.A. The Ethno-Geography of the Pomo and Neighboring Indians. UCP, VI, 68-80, 108-9, 301-18. 1908.

--- The Geography and Dialects of the Miwok Indians. UCP, VI, 333-68. 1908.

--- A New Moquelumnan Territory in California. AA, n.s., V, 730. 1903.

Callaghan, C.A. Note on Lake Miwok Numerals. IJAL, XXIV, 247. 1958.

Freeland, L.S. Western Miwok Texts with Linguistic Sketch. IJAL, XIII, 31-46. 1947.

Kroeber, A.L. Handbook of the Indians of California. BBAE, LXXVIII, 272-8. 1925.

--- The Languages of the Coast of California North of San Francisco. UCP, IX, 291-319. 1911.

--- The Patwin and Their Neighbors. UCP, XXIX, 366-9. 1932.

Loeb, E.M. The Western Kuksu Cult. UCP, XXIII, 113-24. 1932.

Merriam, C.H. The Dawn of the World. 273 pp. Cleveland, 1910.

--- Distribution and Classification of the Mewan Stock. AA, n.s., IX, 338-57. 1907.

--- Totemism in California. AA, n.s., X, 558-62. 1908.

Schmidt, W. Die Küsten Miwok. UG, V, 251-9. 1934.

Shafer, R. Penutian. IJAL, XIII, 205-19. 1947.

8. POMO

Barrett, S.A. Material Aspects of Pomo Culture. BPMCM, XX, i-ii, 508 pp. 1952.

Essene, F. Round Valley. AR, VIII, 1-97. 1942.

Gifford, E.W. Clear Lake Pomo Society. UCP, XVIII, 287-390. 1926.

Loeb, E.M. Pomo Folkways. UCP, XIX, 149-405. 1926.

Stewart, O.C. Notes on Pomo Ethnography. UCP, XL, 29-62. 1943.

Aginsky, B.W. An Indian's Soliloquy. AJS, XLVI, 43-4. 1940.

--- The Interaction of Ethnic Groups. ASR, XIV, 288-93. 1949.

--- The Mechanics of Kinship. AA, n.s., XXXVII, 450-7. 1935.

--- Population Control in the Shanel (Pomo) Tribe. ASR, IV, 209-16. 1939.

--- Psychopathic Trends in Culture. Character and Personality, VII, 331-43. 1939.

--- The Socio-Psychological Significance of Death among the Pomo Indians. American Imago, I, iii, 1-18. 1940.

Aginsky, E.G. and B.W. The Process of Change in Family Types. AA, LI, 611-4. 1949.

Angulo, J.de. Pomo Creation Myth. JAFL, XLVIII, 203-62. 1935.

--- Textes en langue Pomo. JSAP, n.s., XIX, 129-44. 1927.

Angulo, J.de, and Benson, W.R. The Creation Myth of the Pomo Indians. A, XXVII, 261-74, 779-96. 1932.

Angulo, J.de, and Freeland, L.S. Miwok and Pomo Myths. JAFL, XLI, 232-52. 1928.

Angulo, J.de, and Harcourt, B.d'. La musique des Indiens de la Californie du Nord. JSAP, n.s., XXIII, 189-228. 1931.

Barrett, S.A. The Army Worm: a Food of the Pomo Indians. Essays in Anthropology presented to A.L. Kroeber, pp. 1-5. Berkeley, 1936.

--- Basket Designs of the Pomo Indians. AA, n.s., VII, 648-53. 1905.

--- Ceremonies of the Pomo Indians. UCP, XII, 397-441. 1917.

--- A Composite Myth of the Pomo Indians. JAFL, XIX, 37-51. 1906.

--- The Ethno-Geography of the Pomo and Neighboring Indians. UCP, VI, 1-245. 1908.

--- Pomo. BBAE, XXX, ii, 276-7. 1910.

--- Pomo Bear Doctors. UCP, XII, 443-65. 1917.

--- Pomo Buildings. Holmes Anniversary Volume, pp. 1-17. Washington, 1916.

--- The Pomo in the Sacramento Valley. AA, n.s., VI, 189-90. 1904.

Barrett, S.A. Pomo Indian Basketry. UCP, VII, 134-308. 1908.

--- Pomo Myths. BPMCM, XV, 1-608. 1933.

Boas, F. Anthropometry of Central California. BAMNH, XVII, 347-80. 1905.

Chestnut, V.K. Plants used by the Indians of Mendocino County. Contributions from the U.S. National Herbarium, VII, 295-408. 1902.

Clark, C. and Williams, T.B. Pomo Indian Myths. 146 pp. New York, 1954.

Cody, B.P. Pomo Bear Impersonators. M, XIV, 132-7. 1940.

Cook, S.F. The Aboriginal Population of the North Coast of California. AR, XVI, 81-130. 1956.

Curtis, E.S. The North American Indian, XIV, 55-70, 170-3, 188-9, 214-20. Norwood, 1924.

Dixon, R.B., and Kroeber, A.L. New Linguistic Families in California. AA, n.s., XV, 647-55. 1913.

Freeland, L.S. Pomo Doctors and Poisoners. UCP, XX, 57-73. 1923.

Gifford, E.W. Californian Anthropometry. UCP, XXII, 278-80. 1926.

--- Californian Kinship Terminologies. UCP, XVIII, 104-15. 1922.

--- Notes on Central Pomo and Northern Yana Society. AA, n.s., XXX, 675-84. 1928.

--- Pomo Lands on Clear Lake. UCP, XX, 77-92. 1923.

Gifford, E.W., and Kroeber, A.L. Pomo. UCP, XXXVII, 117-254. 1937.

Halpern, A.M. A Dualism in Pomo Cosmology. PKAS, VIII/IX, 151-59. 1953.

Harrington, M.R. A Glimpse of Pomo Archaeology. M, XVII, 9-12. 1942.

Hudson, J.W. Pomo Basket Makers. OM, n.s., XXI, 561-78. 1893.

--- Pomo Wampum Makers. OM, n.s., XXX, 101-8. 1897.

Kniffen, F.B. Pomo Geography. UCP, XXXVI, 353-400. 1939.

Kroeber, A.L. California Basketry and the Pomo. AA, n.s., XI, 233-49. 1909.

--- California Kinship Systems. UCP, XII, 370-2. 1917.

--- Handbook of the Indians of California. BBAE, LXXVIII, 222-71. 1925.

--- The Languages of the Coast of California North of San Francisco. UCP, IX, 320-47. 1911.

--- The Patwin and Their Neighbors. UCP, XXIX, 264, 364-6, 403. 1932.

Kroeber, A.L. and Barrett, S.A. Fishing among the Indians of Northwestern California. AR, XXI, i, 1-210. 1960.

Loeb, E.M. The Creator Concept among the Indians
    of North Central California. AA, n.s., XXVIII,
    467-93. 1926.
--- The Western Kuksu Cult. UCP, XXXIII, 3-13,
    101-5, 125-31. 1932.
Merwin, B.W. The Patty Stuart Jewett Collection.
    MJ, IX, 225-43. 1918.
Muensterberger, W. Über Einige Beziehungen zwischen
    Individuum und Umwelt. Sociologus, n.s., I, 126-
    38. 1951.
Orchard, W.C. A Pomo Headdress. IN, IV, 170-
    5. 1927.
--- An Unuaual Pomo Basket. IN, II, 102-9. 1925.
Oswalt, R.L. Russian Loanwords in Southwestern
    Pomo. IJAL, XXIV, 245-7. 1958.
Powers, S. The Northern California Indians. OM,
    IX, 498-507. 1872.
--- Tribes of California. CNAE, III, 146-95, 204-
    17, 491-517. 1877.
Purdy, C. The 'Dau' in Pomo Basketry. OW, XVIII,
    317-25. 1903.
--- The Pomo Indian Baskets and Their Makers. OW,
    XV, 438-49; XVI, 9-19, 151-8, 262-73. 1901-
    02.
Schmidt, W. Die Pomo. UG, II, 208-44; V, 49-
    55, 221-96. 1929, 1934.
Simoons, F.J. Changes in Indian Life in the Clear
    Lake Area. AI, XIII, 103-8. 1953.
Treganza, A.E., et al. The Hindil, a Pomo Indian
    Dance in 1946. M, XXI, 119-25. 1947.
Woodward, A. An Immense Pomo Basket. IN, V,
    178-83. 1928.
Wrangell, K.P. von. Einige Bemerkungen über die
    Wilden an der Nordwestküste von Amerika. BKRR,
    I, 66-96. 1839.

9. SALINA

Including the Esselen and the Salina.

Mason, J.A. The Ethnology of the Salinan Indians.
    UCP, X, 97-240. 1912.

Anonymous. Esselen. BBAE, XXX, i, 438. 1907.
Dixon, R.B., and Kroeber, A.L. New Linguistic
    Families in California. AA, n.s., XV, 647-55.
    1913.
Gifford, E.W. Californian Kinship Terminologies.
    UCP, XVIII, 73. 1922.
Harrington, J.P. Central California Coast. AR, VII,
    1-46. 1942.

Heizer, R.F. The Mission Indian Vocabularies of
    Alphonse Pinart. AR, XV, 1-84. 1953.
Henshaw, H.W. A New Linguistic Family in Califor-
    nia. AA, III, 45-9. 1890.
Henshaw, H.W., and Kroeber, A.L. Salinan Family.
    BBAE, XXX, ii, 415. 1910.
Kroeber, A.L. Handbook of the Indians of California.
    BBAE, LXXVIII, 544-9. 1925.
--- The Languages of the Coast of California South of
    San Francisco. UCP, II, 29-80. 1904.
--- A Mission Record of the California Indians. UCP,
    VIII, 18-24. 1908.
Mason, J.A. The Language of the Salinan Indians.
    UCP, XIV, 1-154. 1918.
Sapir, E. A Supplementary Note on Salinan and
    Washo. IJAL, II, 68-72. 1921.
Schmidt, W. Die Salina-Indianer. UG, II, 287-96.
    1929.
Sitjar, B. Vocabulario de la lengua de los naturales
    de la mision de San Antonio. 53 pp. New York,
    1861.

10. SHASTA

Dixon, R.B. The Shasta. BAMNH, XVII, 381-498.
    1907.
Holt, C. Shasta Ethnography. AR, III, 299-349. 1946.

Angulo, J. de, and Harcourt, B. d'. La musique des
    Indiens de la Californie du Nord. JSAP, n.s.,
    XXIII, 189-228. 1931.
Boas, F. Physical Characteristics of the Tribes of the
    North Pacific Coast. BAAS, LXI, 424-9. 1891.
Burns, L.M. Digger Indian Legends. LS, XIV, 130-
    4, 223-6, 310-14, 397-402. 1901.
Curtis, E.S. The North American Indian, XIII, 105-
    26, 201-6, 230-4, 253-62. Norwood, 1924.
Dixon, R.B. Linguistic Relationships within the
    Shasta-Achomawi Stock. ICA, XV, ii, 255-63.
    1906.
--- Mythology of the Shasta-Achomawi. AA, n.s.,
    VII, 607-12. 1905.
--- Shasta. BBAE, XXX, ii, 527-8. 1910.
--- The Shasta-Achomawi. AA, n.s., VII, 213-17.
    1905.
--- Shasta Myths. JAFL, XXIII, 8-37, 364-70. 1910.
--- Some Shamans of Northern California. JAFL,
    XVII, 23-7. 1904.
Dixon, R.B., and Kroeber, A.L. New Linguistic Fam-
    ilies in California. AA, n.s., XV, 647-55. 1913.
Farrand, L., and Frachtenberg, L.J. Shasta and
    Athapascan Myths from Oregon. JAFL, XXVIII,
    207-23. 1915.

Gifford, E.W. Californian Kinship Terminologies. UCP, XVIII, 35-7. 1922.

Kroeber, A.L. Handbook of the Indians of California. BBAE, LXXVIII, 279-304. 1925.

Kroeber, A.L. and Barrett, S.A. Fishing among the Indians of Northwestern California. AR, XXI, i, 1-210. 1960.

Merriam, C.H. The New River Indians Tló-hom-tah´-hoi. AA, n.s., XXXII, 280-93. 1930.

Olmsted, D.L. Palaihnihan and Shasta. Lg, XXXII, 73-7; XXXIII, 136-8. 1956-1957.

Powers, S. Tribes of California. CNAE, III, 243-51, 607-13. 1877.

Voegelin, E.W. Northeast California. AR, VII, 47-251. 1942.

--- Three Shasta Myths, including "Orpheus." JAFL, LX, 52-8. 1947.

11. WAILAKI

Including the Kato, Lassik, Mattole, Nongatl, Sinkyone, and Wailaki.

Baumhoff, M.A. California Athabascan Groups. AR, XVI, 157-237. 1958.

Nomland, G.A. Bear River Ethnography. AR, II, 91-123. 1938.

--- Sinkyone Notes. UCP, XXXVI, 149-78. 1935.

Cook, S.F. The Aboriginal Population of the North Coast of California. AR, XVI, 81-130. 1956.

Curtis, E.S. The North American Indian, XIV, 3-18, 21-35, 165-9, 183-6, 201-7. Norwood, 1924.

Driver, H.E. Northwest California. AR, I, 297-433. 1939.

Essene, F. Round Valley. AR, VIII, 1-97. 1942.

Foster, G.M. String-Figure Divination. AA, n.s., XLIII, 126-7. 1941.

Gifford, E.W. Californian Anthropometry. UCP, XXII, 260-1. 1926.

--- Californian Kinship Terminologies. UCP, XVIII, 19-27. 1922.

Goddard, P.E. The Bear River Dialect of Athapascan. UCP, XXIV, 291-324. 1929.

--- Elements of the Kato Language. UCP, XI, 1-176. 1912.

--- Habitat of the Pitch Indians. UCP, XVII, 217-25. 1924.

--- Habitat of the Wailaki. UCP, XX, 95-109. 1923.

--- The Kato Pomo not Pomo. AA, n.s., V, 375-6. 1903.

Goddard, P.E. Kato Texts. UCP, V, 65-238. 1909.

--- Lassik. BBAE, XXX, i, 761. 1907.

--- Lassik Tales. JAFL, XIX, 133-40. 1906.

--- Wailaki. BBAE, XXX, ii, 893-4. 1910.

--- Wailaki Texts. IJAL, II, 77-135. 1923.

Kroeber, A.L. Handbook of the Indians of California. BBAE, LXXVIII, 132-58. 1925.

--- A Kato War. Festschrift Publication d'Hommage offerte au P.W. Schmidt, pp. 394-400. Wien, 1928.

--- Sinkyone Tales. JAFL, XXXII, 346-51. 1919.

Kroeber, A.L. and Barrett, S.A. Fishing among the Indians of Northwestern California. AR, XXI, i, 1-210. 1960.

Li, F.K. Mattole, an Athapascan Language. 152 pp. Chicago, 1930.

Loeb, E.M. The Western Kuksu Cult. UCP, XXXIII, 14-54, 73-95. 1932.

Nomland, G.A. A Bear River Shaman's Curative Dance. AA, n.s., XXXIII, 38-41. 1931.

Powers, S. Tribes of California. CNAE, III, 107-24, 150-5. 1877.

Schmidt, W. Die Wailaki. UG, II, 42-56; V, 1-36, 87-97. 1929, 1934.

12. WAPPO

Driver, H.E. Wappo Ethnography. UCP, XXXVI, 179-220. 1936.

Barrett, S.A. The Ethno-Geography of the Pomo and Neighboring Tribes. UCP, VI, 68-80, 111-17, 263-78. 1908.

Cook, S.F. The Aboriginal Population of the North Coast of California. AR, XVI, 81-130. 1956.

Curtis, E.S. The North American Indian, XIV, 207-14. Norwood, 1924.

Gifford, E.W. Californian Kinship Terminologies. UCP, XVIII, 115-18. 1922.

Heizer, R.F., ed. The Archaeology of the Napa Region. AR, XII, 225-358. 1953.

Kroeber, A.L. Handbook of the Indians of California. BBAE, LXXVIII, 217-21. 1925.

--- Some New Group Boundaries in Central California. UCP, XLVII, 215-17. 1957.

--- Wappo Myths. JAFL, XXI, 231-3. 1908.

Loeb, E.M. The Western Kuksu Cult. UCP, XXXIII, 106-12. 1932.

Powers, S. Tribes of California. CNAE, III, 196-203. 1877.

Radin, P. A Grammar of the Wappo Language. UCP, XXVII, 1-94. 1929.

Radin, P. Wappo Texts. UCP, XIX, 1-147. 1924.
Schmidt, W. Die Wappo. UG, II, 245-7; V,
    250-1. 1929, 1934.

13. WINTUN

Including the Nomlaki, the Patwin, the Wintu,
and the Wintun.

DuBois, C. Wintu Ethnography. UCP, XXXVI, 1-
    148. 1935.
Goldschmidt, U. Nomlaki Ethnography. UCP, XLII,
    303-443. 1951.
Kroeber, A.L. The Patwin and Their Neighbors. UCP,
    XXIX, 253-423. 1932.

Angulo, J.de, and Harcourt, B.d'. La musique des
    Indiens de la Californie du Nord. JSAP, n.s., XXIII,
    189-228. 1931.
Anonymous. Patwin. BBAE, XXX, ii, 211. 1910.
Barrett, S.A. The Ethno-Geography of the Pomo and
    Neighboring Indians. UCP, VI, 81-7, 109-10, 284-
    300. 1908.
--- The Wintu Hesi Ceremony. UCP, XIV, 437-88.
    1919.
Bartlett, J.R. Personal Narrative of Explorations and
    Incidents, II, 29-34. New York, 1854.
Boas, F. Anthropometry of Central California. BAMNH,
    XVII, 347-80. 1905.
Curtin, J. Creation Myths of Primitive America.
    530 pp. Boston, 1898.
Curtis, E.S. The North American Indian, XIV, 73-
    96, 173, 189-92, 220-9. Norwood, 1924.
Demetracopoulou, D. Wintu Songs. A, XXX, 483-
    94. 1935.
--- Wintu War Dance. PPSC, VI, iv, 141-3. 1939.
Demetracopoulou, D., and DuBois, C. A Study of
    Wintu Mythology. JAFL, XLV, 375-500. 1932.
Dixon, R.B. Outlines of Wintun Grammar. Putnam
    Anniversary Volume, pp. 461-76. New York, 1909.
Dixon, R.B., and Kroeber, A.L. New Linguistic
    Families in California. AA, n.s., XV, 647-55.
    1913.
DuBois, C., and Demetracopoulou, D. Wintu Myths.
    UCP, XXVIII, 279-403. 1931.
Gatschet, A.S. Classification into Seven Linguistic
    Stocks of Western Indian Dialects. RUSGS, VII, 403-
    85. 1879.
Gifford, E.W. Californian Anthropometry. UCP, XXII,
    283-4. 1926.
--- Californian Kinship Terminologies. UCP, XVIII, 94-
    104. 1922.

Goldschmidt, W. Social Organization in Native Cali-
    fornia and the Origin of Clans. AA, n.s., L, 444-
    56. 1948.
Goldschmidt, W., Foster, G., and Essene, F. War
    Stories from Two Enemy Tribes. JAFL, LII, 141-
    54. 1939.
Heizer, R.F., ed. The Archaeology of the Napa Re-
    gion. AR, XII, 225-358. 1953.
Kroeber, A.L. Basket Designs of the Indians of North-
    western California. UCP, II, 105-64. 1905.
--- California Kinship Systems. UCP, XII, 368-70.
    1917.
--- Handbook of the Indians of California. BBAE,
    LXXVIII, 351-90. 1925.
--- Recent Ethnic Spreads. UCP, XLVII, 259-81. 1959.
--- Some New Group Boundaries in Central California.
    UCP, XLVII, 215-17. 1957.
Kroeber, A.L. and Barrett, S.A. Fishing among the In-
    dians of Northwestern California. AR, XXI, i, 1-210.
    1960.
Kroeber, T.K. A Note on a California Theme. JAFL,
    LXX, 72-4. 1957.
Lee, D.D. Categories of the Generic and the Particu-
    lar in Wintu. AA, n.s., XLVI, 362-9. 1944.
--- The Linguistic Aspect of Wintu Acculturation. AA,
    XLV, 435-40. 1943.
--- Linguistic Reflection of Wintu Thought. IJAL, X,
    181-7. 1944.
--- Notes on the Concept of the Self among the Wintu
    Indians. Journal of Abnormal and Social Psychology,
    XLV, 538-43. 1951.
--- The Place of Kinship Terms in Wintu Speech. AA,
    n.s., XLII, 604-16. 1940.
--- Some Indian Texts Dealing with the Supernatural.
    Review of Religion, V, 403-11. 1941.
--- Stylistic Use of the Negative in Wintu. IJAL, XII,
    79-81. 1946.
--- A Wintu Girls' Puberty Ceremony. NMA, V, 57-
    60. 1940.
Loeb, E.M. The Eastern Kuksu Cult. UCP, XXXIII,
    208-31. 1933.
McKern, W.C. Functional Families of the Patwin.
    UCP, XIII, 235-58. 1922.
--- Patwin Houses. UCP, XX, 159-71. 1923.
Powers, S. The California Indians. OM, XII, 416-17,
    530-40; XIII, 542-50. 1874.
--- Tribes of California. CNAE, III, 218-42, 518-34.
    1877.
Schenck, W.E. Historic Aboriginal Groups of the Cali-
    fornia Delta Region. UCP, XXIII, 123-46. 1926.
Schmidt, W. Die Patwin. UG, II, 248-59; V, 170-
    202. 1929, 1934.

Schmidt, W. Die Wintun. UG, II, 72-101; V, 203-
  20. 1929, 1934.
Shafer, R. Penutian. IJAL, XIII, 205-19. 1947.
Voegelin, E.W. Northeast California. AR, VII, 47-
  251. 1942.
--- Suicide in Northeastern California. AA, n.s.,
  XXXIX, 445-56. 1937.
Washington, F.B. Notes on the Northern Wintun In-
  dians. JAFL, XXII, 92-5. 1909.
Wheeler-Voegelin, E., (ed.). E.A.Stevenson to
  Thomas W. Healy, Red Bluffs, September 30, 1857.
  E, IV, 66-95. 1957.

14. YANA

Including the Yahi and the Yana.

Baumhoff, M.A. An Introduction to Yana Archaeology.
  RUCAS, XXXVIII, 1-5. 1957.
Curtin, J. Creation Myths of Primitive America. 530
  pp. Boston, 1898.
Dixon, R.B., and Kroeber, A.L. New Linguistic Fam-
  ilies in California. AA, n.s., XV, 647-55. 1913.
Gifford, E.W. Californian Kinship Terminologies.
  UCP, XVIII, 41. 1922.
--- Notes on Central Pomo and Northern Yana Society.
  AA, n.s., XXX, 675-84. 1928.
Gifford, E.W., and Klimek, S. Yana. UCP, XXXVII,
  71-100. 1936.
Kroeber, A.L. Handbook of the Indians of California.
  BBAE, LXXVIII, 336-46. 1925.
Nelson, N.C. Flint Working by Ishi. Holmes Anni-
  versary Volume, pp. 397-402. Washington, 1916.
Pope, S.T. The Medical History of Ishi. UCP, XIII,
  174-213. 1920.
--- Yahi Archery. UCP, XIII, 103-52. 1918.
Powers, S. Tribes of California. CNAE, III, 275-82.
  1877.
Sapir, E. The Fundamental Elements of Northern Yana.
  UCP, XIII, 214-34. 1922.
--- Luck-Stones among the Yana. JAFL, XXI, 42.1908.
--- Male and Female Forms of Speech in Yana. Donum
  Natalicium Schrijnen, ed. St. W.J.Teeuven, pp.
  79-85. Nijmegen-Utrecht, 1929.
--- The Position of Yana in the Hokan Stock. UCP,
  XIII, 1-34. 1917.
--- Terms of Relationship and the Levirate. AA, n.s.,
  XVIII, 327-37. 1916.
--- Text Analyses of Three Yana Dialects. UCP, XX,
  263-94. 1923.
Sapir, E. Yana Terms of Relationship. UCP, XIII,
  153-73. 1918.

Sapir, E. Yana Texts. UCP, IX, 1-235. 1910.
Sapir, E., and Spier, L. Notes on the Culture of the
  Yana. AR, III, 239-97. 1943.
Schmidt, W. Die Yana. UG, II, 172-81. 1929.
Waterman, T.T. The Yana Indians. UCP, XIII, 35-
  70. 1918.

15. YOKUTS

Gayton, A.H. Northern Foothills Yokuts and Western
  Mono. AR, X, 143-302. 1948.
--- Tulare Lake, Southern Valley, and Central Foot-
  hills Yokuts. AR, X, 1-140. 1948.
Kroeber, A.L. Handbook of the Indians of California.
  BBAE, LXXVIII, 474-534. 1925.
Latta, F.F. Handbook of Yokuts Indians. 300 pp.
  Oildale, California, 1949.

Aginsky, B.W. Central Sierra. AR, VIII, 393-468. 1943.
Anonymous. Mariposan Family. BBAE, XXX, i, 807-
  8. 1907.
Beals, R.L. and Hester, J.A. A Lacustrine Economy
  in California. MPR, i, 211-7. 1958.
Boas, F. Anthropometrical Observations on the Mis-
  sion Indians. PAAAS, XLIV, 261-6. 1895.
Cook, S.F. The Aboriginal Population of the San
  Joaquin Valley, California. AR, XVI, 31-80. 1955.
--- The Mechanism and Extent of Dietary Adaptation
  among Certain Groups of California and Nevada
  Indians. IA, XVIII, 1-59. 1941.
Curtis, E.S. The North American Indian, XIV, 151-
  62, 177-9, 197-8, 243-7. Norwood, 1924.
Dixon, R.B., and Kroeber, A.L. New Linguistic Fam-
  ilies in California. AA, n.s., XV, 647-55. 1913.
Driver, H.E. Southern Sierra Nevada. AR, I, 53-
  154. 1937.
Fenenga, F. The Archaeology of the Slick Rock Vil-
  lage, Tulare County, California. AAn, XVII, 339-
  47. 1952.
Gayton, A.H. Culture-Environment Integration. SJA,
  II, 252-68. 1946.
--- Estudillo among the Yokuts. Essays in Anthropol-
  ogy presented to A.L.Kroeber, pp. 67-85. Berkeley,
  1936.
--- The Ghost Dance of 1870. UCP, XXVIII, 57-82.
  1930.
--- Yokuts and Western Mono Pottery-Making. UCP,
  XXIV, 239-55. 1929.
--- Yokuts and Western Mono Social Organization.
  AA, n.s., XLVII, 409-26. 1945.
--- Yokuts-Mono Chiefs and Shamans. UCP, XXIV,
  361-420. 1930.

Gayton, A.H., and Newman, S.S. Yokuts and West-
    ern Mono Myths. AR, V, i, 1-109. 1940.

Gifford, E.W. Californian Anthropometry. UCP,
    XXII, 288-90. 1926.

--- Californian Kinship Terminologies. UCP, XVIII,
    77-85. 1922.

--- Dichotomous Social Organization in South Central
    California. UCP, XI, 291-6. 1916.

Gifford, E.W., and Schenck, W.E. Archaeology of
    the Southern San Joaquin Valley. UCP, XXIII, 1-
    122. 1926.

Harris, Z.S. Structural Restatements. IJAL, XIII,
    47-58. 1947.

--- Yokuts Structure and Newman's Grammar. IJAL,
    X, 196-211. 1944.

Hatch, J. Tachi Yokuts Music. PKAS, XIX, 47-66.
    1958.

Hinds, M.G. A Report on Indian Sites and Trails,
    Huntington Lake Region, California. RUCAS, XLVIII,
    1-15. 1959.

Hudson, J.W. An Indian Myth of the San Joaquin
    Basin. JAFL, XV, 104-6. 1902.

Kroeber, A.L. California Kinship Systems. UCP, XII,
    352-8. 1917.

--- Indian Myths of South Central California. UCP,
    IV, 167-250. 1907.

--- Northern Yokuts. Anthropological Linguistics,
    I, viii, 1-19. 1959.

--- Recent Ethnic Spreads. UCP, XLVII, 259-81. 1959.

--- The Yokuts and Yuki Languages. Boas Anniversary
    Volume, pp. 64-79. New York, 1906.

--- The Yokuts Language. UCP, II, 165-377. 1907.

--- Yokuts Names. JAFL, XIX, 142-3. 1906.

Kroeber, A.L. and Barrett, S.A. Fishing among the
    Indians of Northwestern California. AR, XXI, i, 1-
    210. 1960.

Latta, F.F. San Joaquin Primeval, Uncle Jeff's Story,
    A Tale of a San Joaquin Valley Pioneer and his
    Life with the Yokuts Indians. Tulare, 1929.

Merriam, C.H. Distribution of Indian Tribes in the
    Southern Sierra. Science, n.s., XIX, 912-17. 1904.

Newman, S.S. The Yawelmani Dialect of Yokuts.
    IJAL, VII, 85-9. 1932.

--- The Yawelmani Dialect of Yokuts. VFPA, VI,
    222-48. 1946.

--- Yokuts Language in California. VFPA, II, 1-
    247. New York, 1944.

Pilling, A.R. The Archeological Implications of an
    Annual Coastal Visit for Certain Yokuts Groups. AA,
    LII, 438-440. 1950.

Powers, S. The California Indians. OM, XI, 105-16.
    1873.

Powers, S. Tribes of California. CNAE, III, 369-92.
    427-9, 570-85. 1877.

Riddell, F.A. Notes on Yokuts Weather Shamanism
    and the Rattlesnake Ceremony. M, XXIX, 94-8.
    1955.

Rogers, B.T., and Gayton, A.H. Twenty-seven
    Chukchansi Yokuts Myths. JAFL, LVII, 190-207.
    1944.

Schenck, W.E. Historic Aboriginal Groups of the
    California Delta Region. UCP, XXIII, 123-46.
    1926.

Schenck, W.E., and Dawson, E.J. Archaeology of
    the Northern San Joaquin Valley. UCP, XXV, 289-
    413. 1929.

Schmidt, W. Die Yokuts. UG, II, 271-82; V, 297-
    307. 1929, 1934.

Shafer, R. Penutian. IJAL, XIII, 205-19. 1947.

Stewart, G.W. Two Yokuts Traditions. JAFL, XXI,
    237-9. 1908.

--- The Yokut Indians of the Kaweah Region. Sierra
    Club Bulletin, XII, 385-400. 1927.

--- A Yokuts Creation Myth. JAFL, XIX, 322. 1906.

Walker, E.F. Excavations of a Yokuts Indian Cemetery.
    57 pp. Bakersfield, 1947.

--- A Yokuts Cemetery at Elk Hills. M, IX, 145-50.
    1935.

16. YUKI

Including the Coast Yuki, the Huchnom, and the
Interior Yuki.

Foster, G.M. A Summary of Yuki Culture. AR, V,
    155-244. 1944.

Gifford, E.W. The Coast Yuki. A, XXXIV, 292-375.
    1939.

Kroeber, A.L. Handbook of the Indians of California.
    BBAE, LXXVIII, 159-216. 1925.

Barrett, S.A. The Ethno-Geography of the Pomo and
    Neighboring Indians. UCP, VI, 68-80, 111-17,
    246-63. 1908.

Boas, F. Anthropometry of Central California. BAMNH,
    XVII, 347-80. 1905.

Chestnut, V.K. Plants used by the Indians of Mendocino
    County. Contributions from the U.S. National
    Herbarium, VII, 295-408. 1902.

Cook, S.F. The Aboriginal Population of the North
    Coast of California. AR, XVI, 81-130. 1956.

Curtin, L.S.M. Some Plants Used by the Yuki In-
    dians of Round Valley, Northern California. M,
    XXXI, 40-48, 85-94. 1957.

Curtis, E.S. The North American Indian, XIV, 39-52, 169-70, 186-8, 207-14. 1924.

Driver, H.E. Northwest California. AR, I, 297-433. 1939.

Essene, F. Round Valley. AR, VIII, 1-97. 1942.

Gifford, E.W. Californian Anthropometry. UCP, XXII, 265-8. 1926.

--- Californian Kinship Terminologies. UCP, XVIII, 118-22. 1922.

--- Coast Yuki Myths. JAFL, L, 115-27. 1937.

Goldschmidt, W., Foster, G., and Essene, F. War Stories from Two Enemy Tribes. JAFL, LII, 141-54. 1939.

Heizer, R.F., ed. The Archaeology of the Napa Region. AR, XII, 225-358. 1953.

Kelly, I.T. Yuki Basketry. UCP, XXIV, 421-44. 1930.

Kroeber, A.L. California Kinship Systems. UCP, XII, 372-3. 1917.

--- The Coast Yuki of California. AA, n.s., V, 729-30. 1903.

Kroeber, A.L. The Languages of the Coast of California North of San Francisco. UCP, IX, 348-83. 1911.

--- The Patwin and Their Neighbors. UCP, XXIX, 370-4, 408. 1932.

--- The Yokuts and Yuki Languages. Boas Anniversary Volume, pp. 64-79. New York, 1906.

--- Yuki Myths. A, XXVII, 905-39. 1932.

--- Yukian Family. BBAE, XXX, ii, 1008-9. 1910.

Loeb, E.M. The Western Kuksu Cult. UCP, XXXIII, 55-72. 1932.

Powers, S. The Northern California Indians. OM, IX, 305-13. 1872.

--- Tribes of California. CNAE, III, 125-45. 1877.

Schmidt, W. Donner und Regenbogen beim höchsten Wesen der Yuki. Essays in Anthropology presented to A.L.Kroeber, pp. 299-308. Berkeley, 1936.

--- Die Yuki. UG, II, 57-72; V, 37-86. 1929, 1934.

Shipley, W. Some Yukian-Penutian Lexical Resemblances. IJAL, XXIII, 269-74. 1957.

Treganza, A.E. et al. An Archaeological Survey of the Yuki Area. AR, XII, 112-24. 1950.

VI. PENINSULA

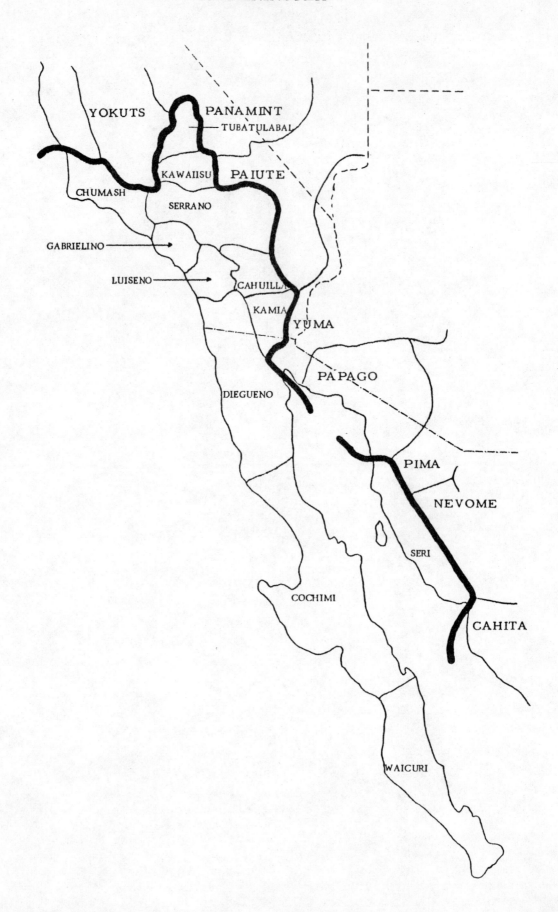

The tribes of this area are grouped under the follow-
ing linguistic stocks:
Hokan: Chumash, Cochimi, Diegueno, Kamia,
Seri, Waicuri (uncertain).
Uto-Aztekan (Shoshonean branch): Cahuilla,
Gabrielino, Kawaiisu, Luiseno, Serrano, Tubatula-
bal.

Aschmann, H. A Primitive Food Preparation Technique in Baja California. SJA, VIII, 36-9. 1952.

Bancroft, H.H. The Native Races of the Pacific States,
I, 402-22. New York, 1875.

Bartlett, J.R. Personal Narrative of Explorations and
Incidents. 2 vols. New York, 1854.

Bleeker, S. The Mission Indians of California. 142 pp.
New York, 1956.

Buschmann, J.C.E. Die Spuren der aztekischen Sprache
im nördlichen Mexico und höheren amerikanischen
Norden. AKAWB, 1854, Supplement-Band, II, 455-
511.

Caughey, J.W. The Indians of California in 1852.
188 pp. San Marino, 1952.

Cook, S.F. The Conflict between the California Indian and White Civilization. IA, XXI, 1-194;
XXIV, 1-29. 1943.

--- The Extent and Significance of Disease among the
Indians of Baja California. IA, XII, 1-39. 1937.

--- Population Trends among the California Mission
Indians. IA, XVII, 1-48. 1940.

--- Racial Fusion among the California and Nevada
Indians. HB, XV, 153-65. 1943.

Coues, E., ed. On the Trail of a Spanish Pioneer:
Francisco Garcés' Diary. 2 vols. New York, 1900.

Culley, J. The California Indians: Their Medical
Practices and Their Drugs. Journal of the American
Pharmaceutical Association, XXV, 332-9. 1936.

Dixon, R.B. Numerical Systems of the Languages
of California. AA, n.s., IX, 663-90. 1907.

Driver, H.E. Girls' Puberty Rites in Western North
America. AR, VI, 21-90. 1941.

Dunne, P.M. Black Robes in Lower California. 550
pp. Berkeley, 1952.

Engelhardt, Z. The Missions and Missionaries of California. 4 vols. San Francisco, 1908-15.

Fages, P. Diary. Publications of the Academy of
Pacific Coast History, II, 141-59. 1911.

--- A Historical, Political and Natural Description
of California. 83 pp. Berkeley, 1937.

Gatschet, A.S. Analytical Report on Eleven Idioms.
ARCE, 1876, iii, 550-63.

Geary, G.J. The Secularization of the California Indian Missions. Catholic University of America,
Studies in American Church History, XVII, 204 pp.
1934.

Gifford, E.W. Californian Anthropometry. UCP, XXII,
217-390. 1926.

--- Californian Kinship Terminologies. UCP, XVIII,
1-285. 1922.

--- Miwok Lineages and the Political Unit in Aboriginal California. AA, n.s., XXVIII, 389-401. 1926.

Harrington, M.R. California Eagle Dance. M, XIX,
5-6. 1945.

Heizer, R.F. Aboriginal California and Great Basin
Cartography. RUCAS, XLI, 1-9. 1958.

--- The Frameless Plank Canoe of the California
Coast. PM, XIII, 80-89. 1940.

--- Historical North Pacific Culture Influences in the
Santa Barbara Region. M, XXI, 150-2. 1947.

--- Honey-Dew "Sugar" in Western North America.
M, XIX, 140-4. 1945.

Heizer, R.F. and Massey, W.C. Aboriginal Navigation Off the Coasts of Upper and Baja California.
BBAE, CLI, 285-312. 1953.

Heizer, R.F. and Whipple, M.A. The California Indians. 487 pp. Berkeley, 1951.

Henshaw, H.W., ed. Translation from the Spanish of
the Account of the Pilot Ferrel of the Voyage of
Cabrillo. RUSGS, VI, 293-314. 1879.

Jackson, H.M.H., and Kinney, A. Report on the
Condition and Needs of the Mission Indians. Washington, 1883.

Jones, S.J. Some Regional Aspects of Native California. Scottish Geographical Magazine, LXVII, 19-
30. 1951.

Krause, F. Die Kultur der kalifornischen Indianer.
Leipzig, 1921.

Kroeber, A.L. Anthropology, pp. 296-316. New
York, 1923.

--- Area and Climax. UCP, XXXVII, 101-16. 1936.

--- Elements of Culture in Native California. UCP,
XIII, 259-328. 1922.

--- Handbook of the Indians of California. BBAE,
LXXVIII, 1-995. 1925.

--- Salt, Dogs, Tobacco. AR, VI, 1-20. 1941.

--- Shoshonean Dialects of California. UCP, IV, 65-
165. 1906.

--- Supposed Shoshoneans in Lower California. AA,
n.s., VII, 570-1. 1905.

Loew, O. Notes upon Ethnology of Southern California. ARCE, 1876, iii, 541-7.

Lowie, R.H. The Cultural Connection of Californian
and Plateau Shoshonean Tribes. UCP, XX, 145-56.
1923.

Massey, W.C. The Dart-Thrower in Baja California.
DJA, III, 55-62. 1957.

North, A.W. The Mother of California. 169 pp.
San Francisco, 1908.

Pfefferkorn, I. Beschreibung der Landschaft Sonora.
2 vol. Köln, 1794/95.

Putnam, F.W., ed. Reports upon Archaeological and
Ethnological Collections from the Vicinity of Santa
Barbara. RUSGS, VII, 1-485. 1879.

Sales, L. Observations on California, 1772-1790.
ECTS, XXXVII, 231 pp. 1956.

Shimkin, D.B. The Uto-Aztecan System of Kinship
Terminology. AA, n.s., XLIII, 223-45. 1941.

Simpson, L.B., ed. California in 1792: the Expedition of Jose Longinos Martinez. 111 pp. San
Marino, 1938.

Steward, J.H. Ecological Aspects of Southwestern
Society. A, XXXII, 87-104. 1937.

Strong, W.D. An Analysis of Southwestern Society.
AA, n.s., XXIX, 1-61. 1927.

Walker, E.F. Indians of Southern California. M, XI,
184-94; XII, 24-9; XVII, 201-16. 1937-38, 1943.

Webb, E.B. Indian Life at the Old Missions. 356 pp.
Los Angeles, 1952.

Yates, L.G. Archaeology of California. Prehistoric
Implements, ed. W.K.Moorehead, pp. 230-52.
Cincinnati, 1900.

1. CAHUILLA

Including the Cahuilla and the Cupeno.

Hooper, L. The Cahuilla Indians. UCP, XVI, 316-80.
1920.

Kroeber, A.L. Ethnography of the Cahuilla Indians.
UCP, VIII, 29-68. 1908.

Strong, W.D. Aboriginal Society in Southern California. UCP, XXVI, 36-273. 1929.

Barrows, D.P. The Ethno-Botany of the Coahuilla Indians. 82 pp. Chicago, 1900.

--- Some Coahuia Songs and Dances. LS,IV,38-41.
1895.

Beattie, H.P. Indians of San Bernadino Valley and
Vicinity. HSSCQ, XXXV, 239-64. 1953.

Benedict, R. A Brief Sketch of Serrano Culture. AA,
n.s., XXVI, 366-92. 1924.

--- Serrano Tales. JAFL, XXXIX, 1-17. 1926.

Boas, F. Anthropometrical Observations on the Mission
Indians. PAAAS, XLIV, 261-6. 1895.

Caballeria, J. History of San Bernardino Valley. San
Bernardino, 1902.

Curtis, E.S. The North American Indian, XV, 21-37,
106-21, 161-5, 173-9. Norwood, 1926.

Davis, E.H. Early Cremation Ceremonies. INM, VII,
93-110. 1921.

Drucker, P. Southern California. AR, I, 1-52. 1937.

Faye, P.L. Christmas Fiestas of the Cupeno. AA,
n.s., XXX, 651-8. 1928.

Foote, K. Mission Indians. RIT, 1890, 207-16.

Gatschet, A.S. Classification into Seven Linguistic
Stocks of Western Indian Dialects. RUSGS, VII,
403-85. 1879.

Gifford, E.W. Californian Kinship Terminologies.
UCP, XVIII, 56-60. 1922.

--- Clans and Moieties in Southern California. UCP,
XIV, 186-201. 1918.

Kroeber, A.L. Basket Designs of the Mission Indians.
APAM, XX, 149-83. 1922.

--- Basketry Designs of the Mission Indians. AMGLS,
LV, 1-10. 1926.

--- Handbook of the Indians of California. BBAE,
LXXVIII, 689-708. 1925.

--- Notes on Shoshonean Dialects of Southern California. UCP, VIII, 236-46. 1909.

Lummis, C.F. The Exiles of Cupa. OW, XVI, 465-
79, 602-12. 1902.

Rush, E.M. The Indians of the Coachella Valley
Celebrate. EP, XXXII, 1-19. 1932.

Schumacher, P. The Method of manufacturing Pottery
and Baskets among the Indians of Southern California. RPM, XII, 521-5. 1879.

Seiler, H. Die Phonetischen Grundlagen der Vokal-
phoneme des Cahuilla. ZPAS, X, 204-23. 1957.

Shinn, G.H. Shoshonean Days. 183 pp. Glendale,
1941.

Studley, C.A. Notes upon Human Remains from Caves
in Coahuila. RPM, XVI-XVII, 233-59. 1884.

Underhill, R. Indians of Southern California. ILC, II,
1-73. 1941.

Woolsey, D.J. Cahuilla Tales. JAFL, XXI, 239-40.
1908.

2. CHUMASH

Including the Chumash of the mainland and the inhabitants of Santa Cruz, Santa Rosa, and San Miguel
Islands.

Bowers, S. Santa Rosa Island. ARSI, 1877, 316-20.

Bryan, B. Excavations at Mishopsnow. AAA, XXXI,
176-85. 1931.

Caballeria y Collel. History of the City of Santa Barbara, tr. E. Burke. 111 pp. Santa Barbara, 1892.

Carr, L. Measurements of Crania from California.
RPM, XII, 497-505. 1880.

Costanso, M. Early California History. LS, XIV, 486-
96; XV, 38-49. 1901.

Eisen, G. An Account of the Indians of the Santa Barbara Islands. SKBGW, 1904, i, 1-30.

Gatschet, A.S. Classification into Seven Linguistic Stocks of Western Indian Dialects. RUSGS, VII, 403-85. 1879.

Gifford, E.W. Californian Bone Artifacts. AR, III, 153-237. 1940.

--- Californian Kinship Terminologies. UCP, XVIII, 72-3. 1922.

Harrington, J.P. Central California Coast. AR, VII, 1-46. 1942.

--- The Mission Indians. EFWSI, 1927, 173-8.

--- Researches on the Archeology of Southern California. SMC, LXXVIII, i, 106-11. 1927.

--- Studies of the Kiowa, Tewa, and California Indians. SMC, LXX, ii, 118-20. 1919.

--- Studying the Mission Indians. EFWSI, 1928, 169-78.

Heizer, R.F. A Californian Messianic Movement of 1801 among the Chumash. AA, n.s., XLIII, 128-9. 1941.

--- The Distribution and Name of the Chumash Plank Canoe. M, XV, 59-61. 1941.

--- An Inquiry into the Status of the Santa Barbara Spearthrower. AAn, IV, 137-41. 1938.

--- Introduced Spearthrowers (Atlatls) in California. M, XIX, 109-12. 1945.

--- The Mission Indian Vocabularies of Alphonse Pinart. AR, XV, 1-84. 1953.

--- The Mission Indian Vocabularies of H.W. Henshaw. AR, XV, 85-202. 1955.

--- The Plank Canoe of the Santa Barbara Region. ES, VII, 193-227. 1938.

--- Two Chumash Legends. JAFL, LXVIII, 34, 56, 72. 1955.

Henshaw, H.W., and Kroeber, A.L. Chumashan Family. BBAE, XXX, i, 296-7. 1907.

Heye, G.G. Certain Artifacts from San Miguel Island. INM, VII, iv, 5-184. 1921.

--- Chumash Objects from a California Cave. IN, III, 193-8. 1926.

Holder, C.F. The Ancient Islanders of California. PSM, XLVIII, 658-62. 1896.

Kroeber, A.L. Basket Designs of the Mission Indians. APAM, XX, 149-83. 1922.

--- The Chumash and Costanoan Languages. UCP, IX, 264-71. 1910.

--- Handbook of the Indians of California. BBAE, LXXVIII, 550-68. 1925.

--- The Languages of the Coast of California South of San Francisco. UCP, II, 29-80. 1904.

--- A Mission Record of the California Indians. UCP, VIII, 15-17. 1908.

Matiegka, H. Ueber Schädel und Skellete von Santa Rosa. SKBGW, 1904, ii, 1-121.

Mohr, A. and Sample, L.L. The Religious Importance of the Swordfish in the Santa Barbara Channel Area. M, XXIX, 62-68. 1955.

Nelson, N.C. Notes on the Santa Barbara Culture. Essays in Anthropology presented to A.L.Kroeber, pp. 199-209. Berkeley, 1936.

Oetteking, B. Declination of the Pars Basilaris in Normal and in Artificially Deformed Skulls. INM, XXVII, 1-25. 1924.

--- Morphological and Metrical Variation in Skulls from San Miguel Island. INM, VII, 49-85; XLV, 1-54. 1920-28.

--- Skeletal Remains from Santa Barbara. INM, ser. 2, XXXIX, 11-168. 1925.

Olson, R.L. Chumash Prehistory. UCP, XXVIII, 1-21. 1930.

Orr, P.C. Archaeology of Mescalitan Island and Customs of the Chumash. Santa Barbara Museum of Natural History, Occasional Papers, V, 1-61. 1943.

Powers, S. Tribes of California. CNAE, III, 560-6. 1877.

Robinson, E. Fishing Arrowpoints from Southern California. M, VII, 147-50. 1933.

--- Plank Canoes of the Chumash. M, XVI, 202-9; XVII, 13-19. 1942-43.

--- Shell Fishhooks of the California Coast. Occasional Papers of the Bernice P. Bishop Museum, XVII, 57-65. 1942.

Rogers, D.B. Prehistoric Man on the Santa Barbara Coast. 452 pp. Santa Barbara, 1929.

Schumacher, P. Researches in the Kjökkenmöddings and Graves of a Former Population of the Santa Barbara Islands and the Adjacent Mainland. BGGST, III, 37-56. 1877.

Virchow, R. Beiträge zur Craniologie der Insulaner von der Westküste Nordamerikas. VBGA, 1889, 382-403.

Wardle, H.N. Stone Implements of Surgery (?) from San Miguel Island. AA, n.s., XV, 656-60. 1913.

Woodward, A. Chumash Village Site excavated. EP, XXVII, 224-6. 1929.

--- An Early Account of the Chumash. M, VIII, 118-23. 1934.

--- Shell Fish Hooks of the Chumash. Bulletin of the Southern California Academy of Sciences, XXVIII, 41-6. 1929.

--- Shells used by the Indians in the Village of Muwu. Bulletin of the Southern California Academy of Sciences, XXX, 105-14. 1931.

Yates, L.G. The Deserted Homes of a Lost People. OM, ser. 2, XXVII, 538-44. 1896.

Yates, L.G. Fragments of the History of a Lost Tribe.
AA, IV, 373-6. 1891. [Repr. RUCAS, XXXVIII, 36-
9. 1957.]

3. COCHIMI

Baegert, J. An Account of the Aboriginal Inhabitants
of the Californian Peninsula. ARSI, 1863, 352-69;
1864, 378-99.
--- Nachrichten von der amerikanischen Halbinsel
Californien. Mannheim, 1772.
Beals, R.L. The Comparative Ethnology of Northern
Mexico. IA, II, 93-225. 1932.
Clavigero, F.X. Historia de la Antigua o Baja Califor-
nia. Mexico, 1852.
--- The History of [Lower] California. 440 pp. Palo
Alto, 1937.
--- Storia della California. 2 vols. Venezia, 1789.
Engelhardt, Z. The Missions and Missionaries of Cali-
fornia. 4 vols. San Francisco, 1908-15.
Gatschet, A.S. Der Yuma-Sprachstamm. ZE, IX,
385-8, 393-407. 1887.
Henshaw, H.W. Cochimi. BBAE, XXX, i, 316-17.
1907.
Kate, H.F.C.ten. Materiaux pour servir à l'anthro-
pologie de la Presqu'ile Californienne. BSAP, ser.
3, VII, 551-69. 1884.
Meigs, P. The Dominican Mission Frontier of Lower
California. University of California Publications in
Geography, VII, 1-232. 1935.
North, A.W. The Native Tribes of Lower California.
AA, n.s., X, 236-50. 1908.
Serra, J. Diary. OW, XVI, 293-6, 399-406, 513-18,
635-42; XVII, 69-76. 1902.
Venegas, M. A Natural and Civil History of Califor-
nia, I, 52-109. London, 1759.

4. DIEGUENO

Including the Akwa'ala, Diegueno, Kiliwa, and
Pipai.

Meigs, P. The Kiliwa Indians of Lower California.
IA, XV, 1-114. 1939.
Spier, L. Southern Diegueno Customs. UCP, XX,
297-358. 1923.

Boas, F. Anthropometrical Observations on the Mission Indians. PAAAS, XLIV, 261-6. 1895.
Curtis, E.S. The North American Indian, XV, 39-52,
121-2, 166-7, 179-82. Norwood, 1926.

Davis, E.H. The Diegueno Ceremony of the Death
Images. CMAI, V, ii, 7-33. 1919.
--- Early Cremation Ceremonies of the Luiseno and
Diegueno Indians. INM, VII, 93-110. 1921.
--- Modern Pottery Vessels from San Diego County.
IN, V, 93-7. 1928.
Drucker, P. Southern California. AR, I, 1-52. 1937.
--- Yuman-Piman. AR, VI, 91-230. 1941.
DuBois, C.G. Diegueno Mortuary Ollas. AA, n.s.,
IX, 484-6. 1907.
--- Diegueno Myths and Their Connections with the
Mohave. ICA, XV, ii, 129-33. 1906.
--- The Mythology of the Dieguenos. JAFL, XIV,
101-6. 1902.
--- The Mythology of the Diegenos. ICA, XIII, 101-
6. 1905.
--- The Religion of the Luiseno Indians. UCP, VIII,
167-73. 1908.
--- Religious Ceremonies and Myths of the Mission
Indians. AA, n.s., VII, 620-9. 1905.
--- The Story of the Chaup. JAFL, XVII, 217-42.
1905.
--- Two Types or Styles of Diegueno Religious Dancing.
ICA, XV, ii, 135-8. 1906.
Foote, K. Mission Indians. RIT, 1890, 207-16.
Forbes, A.S.C. Lace Making by Indian Women. OW,
XVI, 613-16. 1902.
Gatschet, A.S. Classification into Seven Linguistic
Stocks of Western Indian Dialects. RUSGS, VII,
403-85. 1879.
--- Der Yuma-Sprachstamm. ZE, IX, 383-5, 392-
407. 1887.
Gifford, E.W. Californian Kinship Terminologies.
UCP, XVIII, 68-71. 1922.
--- Clans and Moieties in Southern California. UCP,
XIV, 167-74. 1918.
Gifford, E.W., and Lowie, R.H. Notes on the Akwa'ala
Indians. UCP, XXIII, 339-52. 1928.
Hayes, A.S. Field Procedures While Working with the
Diegueno. IJAL, XX, 185-94. 1954.
Henshaw, H.W., and Hodge, F.W. Comeya. BBAE,
XXX, i, 329-30. 1907.
Herzog, G. The Yuman Musical Style. JAFL, XLI,
183-231. 1928.
Heye, G.G. Certain Aboriginal Pottery from Southern
California. INM, VII, i, 7-46. 1919.
--- Shaman's Cache from Southern California. IN, IV,
315-23. 1927.
Hinton, T.B. and Owen, R.C. Some Surviving Yuman
Groups in Northern Baja California. AI, XVII, 87-
102. 1957.

Hohenthal, W.D. Southern Diegueno Use and Knowledge of Lithic Materials. PKAS, II, 6-8. 1950.

Kroeber, A.L. Basket Designs of the Mission Indians. APAM, XX, 149-83. 1922.

--- The Classification of the Yuman Languages. UCPL, I, 21-40. 1943.

--- Handbook of the Indians of California. BBAE, LXXVIII, 709-25. 1925.

--- A Mission Record of the California Indians. UCP, VIII, 2-6. 1908.

--- Yuman Tribes of the Lower Colorado. UCP, XVI, 475-6.

Kroeber, A.L., and Harrington, J.P. Phonetic Elements of the Diegueno Language. UCP, XI, 177-88. 1914.

Lee, M.H. Indians of the Oaks. 153 pp. San Diego, 1937.

--- The Ancient House of the San Diegueno Indian. AAA, XXV, 100-5, 108. 1928.

Meigs, P. The Dominican Mission Frontier of Lower California. UCPG, VII, 1-232. 1935.

Mykrantz, J.W. Indian Burial in Southern California. IN, IV, 154-63. 1927.

North, A.W. The Native Tribes of Lower California. AA, n.s., X, 236-50. 1908.

Pantin, A.M. and Kallsen, R. The Blood Groups of the Diegueno Indians. AJPA, n.s., XI, 91-96. 1953.

Rust, H.N. A Puberty Ceremony of the Mission Indians. AA, n.s., VIII, 28-32. 1906.

Taffelmeier, G., and Luomala, K. Dreams and Dream Interpretation of the Diegueno Indians. Psychoanalytic Quarterly, V, 195-225. 1936.

Treganza, A.E. Possibilities of an Aboriginal Practice of Agriculture among the Southern Diegueno. AAn, XII, 169-73. 1947.

Underhill, R. Indians of Southern California. ILC, II, 1-73. 1941.

Waterman, T.T. Analysis of the Mission Indian Creation Story. AA, n.s., XI, 41-55. 1909.

--- Diegueno Identification of Color with the Cardinal Points. JAFL, XXI, 40-2. 1908.

--- The Religious Practices of the Diegueno Indians. UCP, VIII, 271-358. 1910.

Woodward, A., ed. Notes on the Indians of San Diego County. M, VIII, 140-50. 1934.

5. GABRIELINO

Including the Fernandeno, the Gabrielino, the Nicoleno of San Nicolas Island, and the Santa Catalina Islanders.

Johnston, B.J. The Gabrielino Indians of Southern California. M, XXIX, 180-91; XXX, 6-21, 44-56, 76-89, 125-32, 146-56. 1955-1956.

Reid, H. Account of the Indians of Los Angeles County. BEI, XVII, 1-33. 1885.

Boscana, G. Chinigchinich. New edit. 246 pp. Santa Ana, 1933.

Buschmann, J. Die Sprachen Kizh und Netela von Neu-Californien. AKAWB, 1855, 501-31.

Gatschet, A.S. Classification into Seven Linguistic Stocks of Western Indian Dialects. RUSGS, VII, 403-85. 1879.

Gifford, E.W. Californian Kinship Terminologies. UCP, XVIII, 61-2. 1922.

Harrington, J.P. Central California Coast. AR, VII, 1-46. 1942.

Hodge, Z.P. Tomar of Siba. 48 pp. Los Angeles, 1933.

Kroeber, A.L. Basket Designs of the Mission Indians. APAM, XX, 149-83. 1922.

--- Basketry Designs of the Mission Indians. AMGLS, LV, 1-10. 1926.

--- Handbook of the Indians of California. BBAE, LXXVIII, 620-35. 1925.

--- A Mission Record of the California Indians. UCP, VIII, 11-15. 1908.

--- Notes on Shoshonean Dialects of Southern California. UCP, VIII, 251-3. 1909.

Meighan, C.W. The Nicoleno. Pacific Discovery, VII, 22-7. Feb., 1954.

Nelson, N.C. Notes on the Santa Barbara Culture. Essays in Anthropology presented to A.L.Kroeber, pp. 199-209. Berkeley, 1936.

Reid, H. The Indians of Los Angeles County. 70 pp. Los Angeles, 1926.

Roberts, H.H. Form in Primitive Music. 180 pp. New York, 1933.

Schumacher, P. The Method of Manufacture of Several Articles by the Former Indians of Southern California. RPM, XI, 258-68. 1878.

Woodward, A. Gabrielino Indian Language. M, XVIII, 145-9. 1944.

6. KAMIA

Gifford, E.W. The Kamia of Imperial Valley. BBAE, XCVII, 1-88. 1931.

Anonymous. Kamia Nose Piercing Ceremony. EP, XXXI, 177. 1931.

Gifford, E.W. Californian Kinship Terminologies.
   UCP, XVIII, 65-6. 1922.
--- Clans and Moieties in Southern California. UCP,
   XIV, 157-67. 1918.
Kroeber, A.L. The Classification of the Yuman Lan-
   guages. UCPL, I, 21-40. 1943.
--- Yuman Tribes of the Lower Colorado. UCP, XVI,
   478. 1920.

7. KAWAIISU

Driver, H.E. Southern Sierra Nevada. AR, I, 53-
   154. 1937.
Gifford, E.W. Tübatulabal and Kawaiisu Kinship
   Terms. UCP, XII, 219-48. 1917.
Kroeber, A.L. Handbook of the Indians of California.
   BBAE, LXXVIII, 601-5. 1925.
--- Recent Ethnic Spreads. UCP, XLVII, 259-81.
   1959.
Steward, J.H. Some Observations on Shoshonean Dis-
   tributions. AA, n.s., XLI, 261-5. 1939.
Zigmond, M.L. Kawaiisu Territory. AA, n.s., XL,
   634-8. 1938.

8. LUISENO

Including the Agua Caliente, the Juaneno, and the
Luiseno.

Sparkman, P.S. The Culture of the Luiseno Indians.
   UCP, VIII, 187-234. 1908.

Boas, F. Anthropometrical Observations on the Mission
   Indians. PAAAS, XLIV, 261-6. 1895.
Boscana, G. Chinigchinich. New edit. 246 pp. Santa
   Ana, 1933.
Curtis, E.S. The North American Indian, XV, 5-21,
   101-6, 159-61, 173-9. Norwood, 1926.
Davis, E.H. Early Cremation Ceremonies of the
   Luiseno and Diegueno Indians. INM, VII, 93-110.
   1921.
Drucker, P. Southern California. AR, I, 1-52. 1937.
DuBois, C.G. Mythology of the Mission Indians. JAFL,
   XIX, 52-60. 1904.
--- The Religion of the Luiseno Indians. UCP, VIII,
   69-186. 1908.
Foote, K. Mission Indians. RIT, 1890, 207-16.
Gatschet, A.S. Classification into Seven Linguistic
   Stocks of Western Indian Dialects. RUSGS, VII, 403-
   85. 1897.

Gifford, E.W. Californian Kinship Terminologies.
   UCP, XVIII, 60-1. 1922.
--- Clans and Moieties in Southern California. UCP,
   XIV, 201-14. 1918.
Harrington, J.P. A New Original Version of Boscana's
   Historical Account of the San Juan Capistrano In-
   dians. SMC, XCII, iv, 1-62. 1934.
Harrington, M.R. Ancient Life among the Southern
   California Indians. M, XXIX, 79-88, 117-29,
   153-67. 1955.
James, G.F. The Legend of Tauquitch and Algoot.
   JAFL, XVI, 153-9. 1903.
--- A Saboba Origin Myth. JAFL, XV, 36-9. 1902.
Kroeber, A.L. Basket Designs of the Mission Indians.
   APAM, XX, 149-83. 1922.
--- Basketry Designs of the Mission Indians. AMGLS,
   LV, 1-10. 1926.
--- California Kinship Systems. UCP, XII, 348-52.
   1917.
--- Handbook of the Indians of California. BBAE,
   LXXVIII, 636-67. 1925.
--- Notes on Shoshonean Dialects of Southern Califor-
   nia. UCP, VIII, 247-50. 1909.
--- Notes on the Luiseno. UCP, VIII, 174-86. 1908.
--- Problems on Boscana. UCP, XLVII, 282-93. 1959.
--- Two Myths of the Mission Indians. JAFL, XIX,
   309-21. 1906.
Kroeber, A.L. and Grace, G.W. The Sparkman
   Grammar of Luiseno. UCPL, XVI, 257 pp. 1960.
Meighan, C.W. A Late Complex in Southern Califor-
   nia Prehistory. SJA, X, 215-27. 1954.
Roberts, H.H. Form in Primitive Music. 180 pp.
   New York, 1933.
Rust, H.N. A Puberty Ceremony of the Mission Indians.
   AA, n.s., VIII, 28-32. 1906.
Sparkman, P.S. A Luiseno Tale. JAFL, XXI, 35-6.
   1908.
--- A Sketch of the Grammar of the Luiseno Language.
   AA, n.s., VII, 656-62. 1905.
Strong, W.D. Aboriginal Society in Southern Califor-
   nia. UCP, XXVI, 274-328. 1929.
Tagliavini, C. L'evangelizzazione e i costumi degli
   Indi Luisenos. ICA, XXIII, 633-48. 1928.
--- Frammento d'un dizionarietto Luiseno-Spagnuolo.
   ICA, XXIII, 905-17. 1928.
--- Osservazioni sul dialetto Shoshone di S. Luis Rey.
   ICA, XXII, ii, 539-49. 1926.
Underhill, R. Indians of Southern California. ILC, II,
   1-73. 1941.
Waterman, T.T. Analysis of the Mission Indian Crea-
   tion Story. AA, n.s., XI, 41-55. 1909.

White, R.C. The Luiseno Theory of "Knowledge."
AA, LIX, 1-19. 1957.

--- Two Surviving Luiseno Indian Ceremonies. AA,
LV, 569-78. 1953.

9. SERI

Kroeber, A.L. The Seri. SWMP, VI, 1-60. 1931.

McGee, W J. The Seri Indians. ARBAE, XVII, i,
9-298. 1898.

Anonymous. Rudo ensayo. RACHS, V, ii, 193-200.
1894.

Beals, R.L. The Comparative Ethnology of Northern
Mexico. IA, II, 93-225. 1932.

Cook de Leonard, C. Los Seris, antes y hoy. YAN,
I, 18-28. 1953.

Coolidge, D., and M.R. The Last of the Seris. 264
pp. New York, 1939.

Davis, E.H., and Dawson, E.Y. The Savage Seris
of Sonora. SM, LX, 193-202, 261-8. 1945.

Dawson, E.Y. Some Ethnobotanical Notes on the
Seri Indians. Desert Plant Life, XVI, 133-8. 1944.

Fay, G.E. A Seri Fertility Figurine from Bahia Kino,
Sonora. K, XXI, iii/iv, 11-12. 1956.

Forbes, J.D. Historical Survey of the Indians of
Sonora, 1821-1910. E, IV, 335-68. 1957.

Gatschet, A.S. The Waikuru, Seri and Yuma Languages. Science, n.s., XII, 556-8. 1900.

Genna, G. I Seri, AAE, LXXIV, 5-24. 1944.

Gini, C. Premiers Résultats d'une Expedition Italo-
Mexicaine. Genus, I, 147-76. 1934.

Gonzalez Bonilla, L.A. Los Seris. Revista Mexicana
de Sociologia, III, ii, 93-107. 1941.

Hardy, R.W.H. Travels in the Interior of Mexico in
1825, 1826, 1827 and 1828. London, 1829.

Hernandez, F. Las razas indigenas de Sonora, pp. 3-
74, 237-95. Mexico, 1902.

Hrdlicka, A. Notes on the Indians of Sonora. AA,
n.s., VI, 51-89. 1904.

Kroeber, A.L. Serian, Tequistlatecan, and Hokan.
UCP, XI, 279-90. 1915.

Lindig, W. Über die Bestattung bei den Seri in
Sonora, Mexico. BA, n.f., VII, 191-200. 1959.

--- "Zahme" und "Wilde" Seri. Ethnos, XXIV, 45-
51. 1959.

Masturzi, G. Una expedición a la isla del Tiburón.
Memorias y Revista de la Sociedad Cientifica
"Antonio Alzate," LII, 267-77. 1930.

McGee, W J. Expedition to Papagueria and Seriland.
AA, IX, 93-8. 1896.

McGee, W J. Germe d'industrie de la pierre en Amérique. BSAP, ser 5, III, 82-8. 1902.

--- The Wildest Tribe in North America. LS, XIV,
364-76, 463-74. 1901.

Malkin, B. Seri Ethnozoology. DJA, II, 73-83. 1956.

Monzon, A. La estructura social de los Seris. La
Sociologia en Mexico, I, 89-92. 1953.

Mühlenpfordt, E. Versuch einer getreuen Schilderung
der Republik Mejico. Hannover, 1844.

Sauer, C. The Distribution of Aboriginal Tribes and
Languages in Northwestern Mexico. IA, V, 42-5.
1934.

Spicer, E. Parentescos Uto-Aztecas de la Lengua Seri.
YAN, I, 37-40. 1953.

Watkins, F.E. Seri Indian Pelican-skin Robes. M, XIII,
210-13. 1939.

Xavier, G.H. Seri Face Painting. K, XI, 15-20. 1946.

10. SERRANO

Including the Alliklik, Kitanemuk, Serrano, and
Vanyume.

Anonymous. Serranos. BBAE, XXX, ii, 512-13. 1910.

Beattie, H.P. Indians of San Bernadino Valley and
Vicinity. HSSCQ, XXXV, 239-64. 1953.

Benedict, R. A Brief Sketch of Serrano Culture. AA,
n.s., XXVI, 366-92. 1924.

--- Serrano Tales. JAFL, XXXIX, 1-17. 1926.

Boas, F. Anthropometrical Observations on the Mission
Indians. PAAAS, XLIV, 261-6. 1895.

Drucker, P. Southern California. AR, I, 1-52. 1937.

Foote, K. Mission Indians. RIT, 1890, 207-16.

Gifford, E.W. Californian Kinship Terminologies. UCP,
XVIII, 53-6. 1922.

--- Clans and Moieties in Southern California. UCP,
XIV, 178-86. 1918.

--- Dichotomous Social Organization in South Central
California. UCP, XI, 291-6. 1916.

Harrington, J.P. Central California Coast. AR, VII,
1-46. 1942.

Kroeber, A.L. Handbook of the Indians of California.
BBAE, LXXVIII, 611-19. 1925.

--- Indian Myths of South Central California. UCP, IV,
167-250. 1907.

--- A New Shoshonean Tribe in California. AA, n.s.,
XVII, 773-5. 1915.

--- Notes on Shoshonean Dialects of Southern California. UCP, VIII, 253-6. 1909.

Shinn, G.H. Shoshonean Days. 183 pp. Glendale,
1941.

Smith, G.A. Rancheria Amuscopiabit. M, XXVII, 123-
7. 1953.

Strong, W.D. Aboriginal Society in Southern California. UCP, XXVI, 5-35. 1929.
Underhill, R. Indians of Southern California. ILC, II,
1-73. 1941.

11. TUBATULABAL

Voegelin, E.W. Tübatulabal Ethnography. AR, II,
1-84. 1938.

Driver, H.E. Southern Sierra Nevada. AR, I, 53-154.
1937.
Gifford, E.W. Dichotomous Social Organization in
South Central California. UCP, XI, 291-6. 1915.
--- Tübatulabal and Kawaiisu Kinship Terms. UCP,
XII, 219-48. 1917.
Kroeber, A.L. California Kinship Systems. UCP, XII,
366-8. 1917.
--- Handbook of the Indians of California. BBAE,
LXXVIII, 605-10. 1925.
--- Notes on Shoshonean Dialects of Southern Califor-
nia. UCP, VIII, 262-5. 1909.
Merwin, B.W. The Patty Stuart Jewett Collection.
MJ, IX, 225-43. 1918.
Powers, S. Tribes of California. CNAE, III, 393-5.
1877.
Swadesh, M., and Voegelin, C.F. A Problem in
Phonological Alternation. Lg, XV, 1-10. 1939.
Voegelin, C.F. Tübatulabal Grammar. UCP, XXXIV,
55-190. 1935.
--- Tübatulabal Texts. UCP, XXXIV, 191-246. 1935.
--- Working Dictionary of Tübatulabal. IJAL, XXIV,
221-8. 1958.
Voegelin, E.W. Initial and Final Elements in Tübatu-
labal Myths. SJA, IV, 71-5. 1948.
Whorf, B.L. Notes on the Tübatulabal Language. AA,
n.s., XXXVIII, 341-4. 1936.

12. WAICURI

Including the Pericu and the Waicuri.

Baegert, J. An Account of the Aboriginal Inhabitants
of the Californian Peninsula. ARSI, 1863, 352-69;
1864, 378-99.
--- Nachrichten von der amerikanischen Halbinsel
Californien. Mannheim, 1772.
Beals, R.L. The Comparative Ethnology of Northern
Mexico. IA, II, 93-225. 1932.
Diguet, L. Anciennes sépultures indigènes de la Basse-
Californie méridionale. JSAP, n.s., II, 329-33.
1905.
--- Note sur la pictographie de la Basse-Californie.
Ane, VI, 160-75. 1895.
--- Rapport sur une mission scientifique dans la Basse
Californie. Nouvelles Archives des Missions Sci-
entifiques, IX, 1-53. 1899.
Engelhardt, Z. The Missions and Missionaries of Cali-
fornia. 4 vols. San Francisco, 1908-15.
Gatschet, A.S. The Waikuru, Seri and Yuma Lan-
guages. Science, n.s., XII, 556-8. 1900.
Kate, H.F.C. ten. Materiaux pour servir à l'anthro-
pologie de la Presque'ile Californienne. BSAP, ser.
3, VII, 551-69. 1884.
--- Quelques observations ethnographiques recueillies
dans la Presque'ile Californienne et en Sonora. RE,
1883, 321-6.
Massey, W.C. The Dart-Thrower in Baja California.
DJA, III, 55-62. 1957.
North, A.W. The Native Tribes of Lower California.
AA, n.s., X, 236-50. 1908.
Rivet, P. Recherches anthropologiques sur la Basse-
Californie. JSAP, n.s., VI, 147-253. 1909.
Serra, J. Diary. OW, XVI, 293-6, 399-406, 513-
18, 635-42; XVII, 69-76. 1902.
Venegas, M. A Natural and Civil History of Califor-
nia, I, 52-109. London, 1759.

VII. BASIN

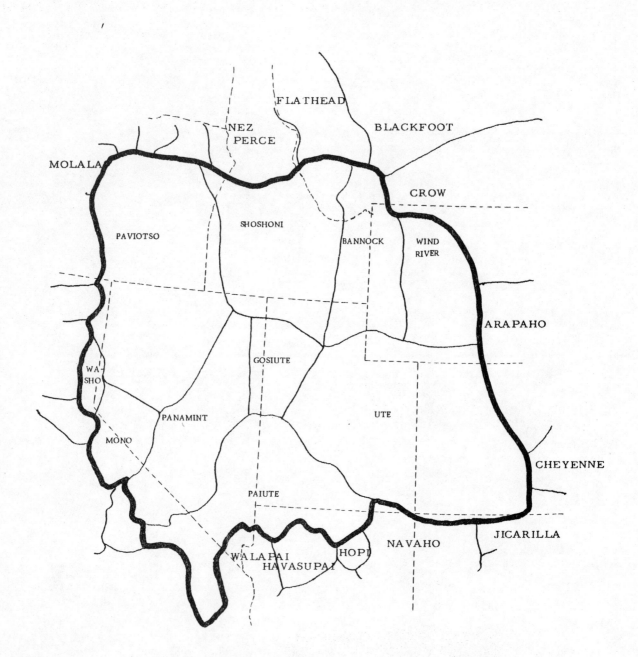

With the exception of the Washo, who are Hokan, all the tribes of this area belong to the Shoshonean branch of the Uto-Aztekan linguistic stock.

Bancroft, H.H. History of Utah. San Francisco, 1889.

--- The Native Races of the Pacific States, I, 422-42, 460-70. New York, 1875.

Barber, B. A Socio-Cultural Interpretation of the Payote Cult. AA, n.s., XLIII, 673-5. 1941.

Bartlett, K. The Distribution of the Indians of Arizona in 1848. P, XVII, 41-5. 1945.

Beauvais, L. Primitive People of the Gunnison Basin. SWL, XXI, iii, 29-34. 1955.

Bolton, H.E. Pageant in the Wilderness. UHQ, XVIII, 283 pp. 1950.

Cappannari, S.C. The Concept of Property among the Shoshoneans. Essays in the Science of Culture in Honor of Leslie A. White, 133-44. New York, 1960.

Chamberlin, R.V. Man and Nature in Early Utah. PUA, XXIV, 3-22. 1947.

Clark, E.E. George Gibbs' Account of Indian Mythology in Oregon and Washington Territories. OHQ, LVI, 293-325; LVII, 125-67. 1955-56.

Colorado State Historical Society. The Indians of Colorado. 52 pp. Denver, 1957.

Crampton, C.G. (ed.). The Mariposa Indian War 1850-1851. 175 pp. Salt Lake City, 1957.

Cressman, L.S. Petroglyphs of Oregon. UOSA, II, 1-78. 1937.

Cressman, L.S., et al. Early Man in Oregon. UOSA, III, 1-78. 1940.

Dale, H.E,, ed. The Ashley-Smith Explorations and the Discovery of a Central Route to the Pacific. Cleveland, 1918.

Douglas, F.H., and Marriott, A. Metal Jewelry of the Peyote Cult. MCN, XVII, 17-82. 1942.

Driver, H.E. Girls' Puberty Rites in Western North America. AR, VI, 21-90. 1941.

DuBois, C. The 1870 Ghost Dance. AR, III, 1-151. 1939.

Erwin, R.P. Indian Rock Writing in Idaho. State Historical Society of Idaho, Biennial Report, XII, 35-111. 1930.

Fremont, J.C. Narrative of the Exploring Expedition to the Rocky Mountains. 186 pp.

Fuller, H.M. and Hafen, L.R., eds. The Journal of Captain John R. Bell. FWRHS, VI, 349 pp. 1957.

Gatschet, A.S. Analytical Report on Eleven Idioms. ARCE, 1876, iii, 557-9.

--- Classification into Seven Linguistic Stocks of Western Indian Dialects. RUSGS, VII, 403-85. 1879.

Goddard, P.E. The Cultural and Somatic Correlations of Uto Aztecan. AA, n.s., XXII, 244-7. 1920.

Gottfredson, P. History of Indian Depredations in Utah. Salt Lake City, 1919.

Hafen, L.R. and A.W. Old Spanish Trail. FWRHS, I, 377 pp. 1954.

Hafen, L.R. and A.W., eds. Rufus B. Sage, His Letters and Papers, 1836-1847. FWRHS, IV, 354 pp.; V, 360 pp. 1956.

--- To the Rockies and Oregon, 1839-42. FWRHS, III, 315 pp. 1955.

--- The Utah Expedition, 1857-1858. FWRHS, VII, 375 pp. 1958.

Hamblin, J. Jacob Hamblin, A Narrative of His Personal Experiences. 151 pp. Salt Lake City, 1909.

Harris, W.R. The Catholic Church in Utah. 350 pp. Salt Lake City, 1909.

Hebard, G.R. Sacajawea. 340 pp. Glendale, 1933.

Heizer, R.F. Aboriginal California and Great Basin Cartography. RUCAS, XLI, 1-9. 1958.

--- Honey-Dew "Sugar" in Western North America. M, XIX, 140-4. 1945.

--- Kutsavi, a Great Basin Indian Food. PKAS, II, 35-41. 1950.

Herzog, G. Plains Ghost Dance and Great Basin Music. AA, n.s., XXXVII, 403-19. 1935.

Hunter, M.R. Utah Indian Stories. 282 pp. Springville, 1946.

Jennings, J.D. Danger Cave. MSAA, XIV, 340 pp. 1957.

Jones, J.A. A Reinterpretation of the Ute-Southern Paiute Classification. AQ, II, 53-58. 1954.

Jones, V.H. The Use of Honey-Dew as Food by Indians. M, XIX, 145-9. 1945.

Kennedy, K.A.R. The Aboriginal Population of the Great Basin. RUCAS, XLV, 1-84. 1959.

Korns, J.R. West From Fort Bridges. UHQ, XIX, 317 pp. 1951.

Kroeber, A.L. Salt, Dogs, Tobacco. AR, VI, 1-20. 1941.

--- Shoshonean Dialects of California. UCP, IV, 65-165. 1906.

--- Stepdaughter Marriage. AA, n.s., XLII, 562-70. 1940.

Lamb, S.M. Linguistic Prehistory in the Great Basin. IJAL, XXIV, 95-100. 1958.

Lewis, M., and Clark, W. Travels. 3 vols. London, 1815.

Lowie, R.H. The Cultural Connection of Californian and Plateau Shoshonean Tribes. UCP, XX, 145-56. 1923.

Lowie, R.H. The Northern Shoshone. APAM, II, 169-306. 1908.

Mack, E.M. Nevada, pp. 39-57. Glendale, 1936.

Mooney, J. The Ghost-Dance Religion. ARBAE, XIV, ii, 641-1110. 1896.

Neumann, G. On the Physical Types of the Shoshonean-speaking Tribes. PIAS, LV, 23-8. 1946.

New Mexico State Planning Board. Indian Lands in New Mexico. 176 pp. Santa Fe, 1936.

Palmer, W.P. An Etymological and Historical Study of Tribes and Tribal Names from Original Sources. UHQ, I, 35-56. 1928.

Park, W.Z. Shamanism in Western North America. Northwestern University Studies in the Social Sciences, II, 1-166. 1938.

Powell, J.W., and Ingalls, G.W. Report. ARCIA, 1873, 41-6.

Quaife, M.M. Narrative of the Adventures of Zenas Leonard. 278 pp. Chicago, 1934.

Remy, J. A Journey to Great-Salt-Lake City. 2 vols. London, 1861.

Rollins, P.A., ed. The Discovery of the Oregon Trail. 391 pp. New York, 1935.

Ross, A. The Fur Hunters of the Far West, ed. M.M. Quaife, pp. 238-66. Chicago, 1924.

Schmidt, M.F., and Brown, D. Fighting Indians of the West, pp. 273-300. New York, 1948.

Schmidt, W. Die Schoschone. UG, V, 308-22. 1934.

Shimkin, D.B. Shoshone-Comanche Origins and Migrations. PPSC, VI, iv, 17-25. 1940.

--- The Uto-Aztecan System of Kinship Terminology. AA, n.s., XLIII, 223-45. 1941.

Simpson, J.H. Report of Explorations across the Great Basin. Washington, 1876.

--- The Shortest Route to California, pp. 45-55. Philadelphia, 1861.

Spier, L. Havasupai Ethnography. APAM, XXIX, 81-392. 1928.

Steward, J.H. Basin-Plateau Aboriginal Socio-political Groups. BBAE, CXX, 1-346. 1938.

--- Changes in Shoshonean Indian Culture. SM, XLIX, 524-37. 1939.

--- Linguistic Distributions and Political Groups of the Great Basin Shoshoneans. AA, n.s., XXXIX, 625-34. 1937.

--- Native Cultures in the Intermontane (Great Basin) Area. SMC, C, 445-502. 1940.

--- Petroglyphs of California and Adjoining States. UCP, XXIV, 67-239. 1929.

--- Some Observations on Shoshonean Distributions. AA, n.s., XLI, 261-5. 1939.

Strong, W.D. An Analysis of Southwestern Society. AA, n.s., XXIX, 1-61. 1927.

Sullivan, M.S. The Travels of Jedediah Smith. Santa Ana, 1934.

Taylor, E.F. Indian Reservations in Utah. UHQ, IV, 29-32. 1931.

Townsend, J.K. Narrative of a Journey across the Rocky Mountains. Philadelphia, 1905.

Train, P. et al. Medicinal Uses of Plants by Indian Tribes of Nevada. Washington, U.S.D.A., 1941.

Victor, F.F. The Early Indian Wars of Oregon. 719 pp. Salem, 1894.

Wallace, W.J. A Basket Weaver's Kit from Death Valley. M, XXVIII, 216-21. 1954.

White, M.C. David Thompson's Journals Relating to Montana and Adjacent Regions, 1808-1812. 507 pp. Missoula, 1950.

Whorf, B.L. The Comparative Linguistics of Uto-Aztecan. AA, n.s., XXXVII, 600-8. 1935.

Wright, C. and G. Indian-White Relations in the Uintah Basin. Utah Humanities Review, II, 319-46. 1948.

Wyeth, N.J. Indian Tribes of the South Pass of the Rocky Mountains, the Salt Lake Basin, the Valley of the Great Säaptin, or Lewis' River, and the Pacific Coasts of Oregon. HCPIT, I, 204-28. 1851.

Zingg, R.M. A Reconstruction of Uto-Aztekan History. University of Denver Contributions to Ethnography, II, 1-274. 1939.

--- The Ute Indians in Historical Relation to Proto-Azteco-Tanoan Culture. Colorado Magazine, XV, 134-52. 1938.

1. BANNOCK

Boas, F. Anthropometry of Shoshonean Tribes. AA, n.s., I, 751-8. 1899.

Brimlow, G.F. The Bannock Indian War of 1878. 231 pp. Caldwell, 1938.

Henshaw, H.W., and Thomas, C. Bannock. BBAE, XXX, i, 129-30. 1907.

Hoffman, W.J. Remarks on Indian Tribal Names. PAPS, XXIII, 298-9. 1886.

--- Die Shoshoni- und Banak-Indianer. Globus, LXIX, 57-60. 1896.

Hultkranz, A. Indianerna i Yellowstone Park. Ymer, LXXIV, 112-40. 1954.

Jones, D.W. Forty Years among the Indians. 400 pp. Salt Lake City, 1890.

Kroeber, A.L. The Bannock and Shoshoni Languages. AA, n.s., XI, 266-77. 1909.

Liljeblad, S. Bannack. IJAL, XVI, 126-31. 1950.

Lowie, R.H. The Kinship Terminology of the Bannock
Indians. AA, n.s., XXXII, 294-9. 1930.

Madsen, B.D. The Bannock of Idaho. 382 pp. Caldwell, 1958.

Steward, J.H. Basin Plateau Aboriginal Socio-political Groups. BBAE, CXX, 1-346. 1938.

Stewart, O.C. The Northern Paiute Bands. AR, II,
127-49. 1939.

2. GOSIUTE

Anonymous. Gosiute. BBAE, XXX, i, 496-7. 1907.

Chamberlain, R.V. Animal Names and Anatomical
Terms of the Goshute Indians. Proceedings of the
Academy of Natural Sciences of Philadelphia, LX,
75-103. 1908.

--- The Ethno-Botany of the Gosiute Indians. MAAA,
II, 329-405. 1911.

Chamberlain, R.V. Place and Personal Names of the
Gosiute Indians. PAPS, LII, 1-20. 1913.

Hayes, A. Peyote Cult on the Goshiute Reservation.
NMA, IV, 34-6. 1940.

Malouf, C. The Gosiute Indians. University of Utah
Museum, Archaeology and Ethnology Papers, III,
1-10. 1940.

--- Gosiute Peyotism. AA, n.s., XLIV, 93-103.
1942.

Malouf, C., and Smith, E.R. Some Gosiute Mythological Characters and Concepts. Utah Humanities
Review, I, 369-77. 1942.

Reagan, A.B. The Gosiute. PUA, XI, 43-54. 1934.

--- The Shoshoni-Goship Indians. TKAS, XXVIII, 227-
32. 1918.

Steward, J.H. Northern and Gosiute Shoshoni. AR,
VIII, 203-392. 1943.

3. MONO

Including the Eastern Mono or Owens Valley Paiute
and the Western Mono, who are culturally akin to
the Yokuts of California.

Gayton, A.H. Northern Foothill Yokuts and Western
Mono. AR, X, 143-301. 1948.

Gifford, E.W. The Northfork Mono. UCP, XXXI, 15-
65. 1932.

Steward, J.H. Ethnography of the Owens Valley
Paiute. UCP, XXXIII, 233-350. 1933.

Aginsky, B.W. Central Sierra. AR, VIII, 393-468.
1943.

Chalfant, W.A. The History of Inyo. Chicago, 1922.

--- Medicine Men of the Eastern Mono. M, V, 50-4.
1931.

Cook, S.F. The Conflict between the California Indian and White Civilization. IA, XXIV, 1-29.
1943.

--- The Mechanism and Extent of Dietary Adaptation
among Certain Groups of California and Nevada Indians. IA, XVIII, 1-59. 1941.

Curtis, E.S. The North American Indian, XV, 55-66,
123-9, 167-9, 182-8. Norwood, 1926.

Driver, H.E. Southern Sierra Nevada. AR, I, 53-154.
1937.

Gayton, A.H. The Ghost Dance of 1870. UCP, XXVIII,
57-82. 1930.

--- Yokuts and Western Mono Pottery-Making. UCP,
XXIV, 239-55. 1929.

--- Yokuts and Western Mono Social Organization.
AA, n.s., XLVII, 409-26. 1945.

--- Yokuts-Mono Chiefs and Shamans. UCP, XXIV,
361-420. 1930.

Gayton, A.H., and Newman, S.S. Yokuts and Western Mono Myths. AR, V, 1-109. 1940.

Gifford, E.W. Californian Anthropometry. UCP, XXII,
291-4. 1926.

--- Californian Kinship Terminologies. UCP, XVIII,
49-52. 1922.

--- Dichotomous Social Organization in South Central
California. UCP, XI, 291-6. 1916.

--- Western Mono Myths. JAFL, XXXVI, 301-67. 1923.

Hindes, M.G. A Report on Indian Sites and Trails,
Huntington Lake Region, California. RUCAS, XLVIII,
1-15, 1959.

Hoffman, W.J. Miscellaneous Ethnographic Observations. ARGGS, X, 461-78. 1876.

Hutchings, J.M. In the Heart of the Sierras, pp. 421-
37. Oakland, 1888.

Kroeber, A.L. Handbook of the Indians of California.
BBAE, LXXVIII, 584-9. 1925.

--- Recent Ethnic Spreads. UCP, XLVII, 259-81.
1959.

Lowie, R.H. The Kinship Terminology of the Bannock
Indians. AA, n.s., XXXII, 294-9. 1930.

Merriam, C.H. Distribution of Indian Tribes in the
Southern Sierra. Science, n.s., XIX, 912-17. 1904.

--- The Em´-tim´-bitch, a Shoshonean Tribe. AA,
n.s., XXXII, 496-9. 1930.

Noble, W.B. A Day with the Mono Indians. OW, XX,
413-21. 1904.

Parcher, F.M. The Indians of Inyo County. M, IV,
146-53. 1930.

Powers, S. Tribes of California. CNAE, III, 396-8. 1877.

Randle, M.C. A Shoshone Hand Gambling Song. JAFL, LXVI, 155-59. 1953.

Rush, E.M. Legends of the Paiutes of the Owens River Valley. EP, XXVIII, 72-87. 1930.

Steward, J.H. Irrigation without Agriculture. PMA, XII, 149-56. 1929.

--- Myths of the Owens Valley Paiute. UCP, XXXIV, 355-440. 1936.

--- Panatübiji', an Owens Valley Paiute. BBAE, CXIX, 183-95. 1938.

--- Two Paiute Autobiographies. UCP, XXXIII, 423-38. 1934.

Wheeler-Voegelin, E. On the Meaning of the Name Mono. E, IV, 62-65. 1957.

4. PAIUTE

Including the Chemehuevi of southeastern California and other Southern Paiute bands in southeastern Nevada, southwestern Utah, and northwestern Arizona. The Northern Paiute bands are classed under Paviotso.

Lowie, R.H. Notes on Shoshonean Ethnography. APAM, XX, 185-314. 1924.

Aberle, D.F. and Stewart, O.C. Navaho and Ute Peyotism. UCSSA, VI, 138 pp. 1957.

Alter, J.C. Father Escalante and the Utah Indians. UHQ, I, 75-86, 106-13; II, 18-25, 46-54. 1928-29.

--- Some Useful Early Utah Indian References. UHQ, I, 26-32, 52-6. 1928.

Bailey, P. Wovoka. 223 pp. Los Angeles, 1957.

Baldwin, G.C. The Pottery of the Southern Paiute. AAn; XVI, 50-56. 1950.

Cummings, B. Indians I Have Known. 75 pp. Tucson, 1952.

Dangberg, G.M. Letters to Jack Wilson, the Paiute Prophet. BBAE, CLXIV, 279-96. 1957.

Dellenbaugh, F.S. A Canyon Voyage, pp. 177-9, 250-2. New York, 1908.

Driver, H.E. Southern Sierra Nevada. AR, I, 53-154. 1937.

Drucker, P. Southern California. AR, I, 1-52. 1937.

--- Yuman-Piman. AR, VI, 91-230. 1941.

Ellison, W.H. Adventures of George Nidever. New Spain and the Anglo-American West, ed. C.W. Hackett, G.P. Hammond, et al, II, 21-45. Los Angeles, 1932.

Gatschet, A.S. Classification into Seven Linguistic Stocks of Western Indian Dialects. RUSGS, VII, 403-85. 1879.

Gifford, E.W. Tübatulabal and Kawaiisu Kinship Terms. UCP, XII, 219-48. 1917.

Harrington, M.R. Bug Sugar. M, XIX, 95-6. 1945.

--- Hand-Game Song. WF, IX, 159. 1950.

--- Southern Nevada Pit-Dwellings. M, XXVII, 136-42. 1953.

Henshaw, H.W., and Kroeber, A.L. Chemehuevi. BBAE, XXX, i, 242-3. 1907.

Henshaw, H.W., and Mooney, J. Paiute. BBAE, XXX, ii, 186-8. 1910.

Hoffman, W.J. Pah-Ute Cremation. PAPS, XIV, 297-8. 1874.

Ives, J.C. Report upon the Colorado River of the West. 131 pp. Washington, 1861.

Jones, D.W. Forty Years among the Indians. 400 pp. Salt Lake City, 1890.

Jones, V.H. Notes of Frederick S. Dellenbaugh on the Southern Paiute from Letters of 1927 and 1928. M, XXII, 177-82. 1948.

Kelly, I.T. Band Organization of the Southern Paiute. AA, n.s., XL, 633-4. 1938.

--- Chemehuevi Shamanism. Essays in Anthropology presented to A.L. Kroeber, pp. 129-42. Berkeley, 1936.

--- Southern Paiute Bands. AA, n.s., XXXVI, 548-60. 1934.

--- Southern Paiute Shamanism. AR, II, 151-67. 1939.

Kroeber, A.L. California Kinship Systems. UCP, XII, 366-8. 1917.

--- Desert Mohave: Fact or Fancy. UCP, XLVII, 294-307. 1959.

--- Handbook of the Indians of California. BBAE, LXXVIII, 593-600. 1925.

--- Notes on Shoshonean Dialects of Southern California. UCP, VIII, 256-62. 1909.

--- Origin Tradition of the Chemehuevi Indians. JAFL, XXI, 240-2. 1908.

--- Recent Ethnic Spreads. UCP, XLVII, 259-81. 1959.

Liebling, A.J. A Reporter at Large. New Yorker, XXX, xlvi, 25-41; xlvii, 33-61; xlviii, 32-69; xlix, 37-73. 1955.

Loew, O. Notes upon Ethnology of Southern California. ARCE, 1876, iii, 541-7.

Lowie, R.H. Shoshonean Tales. JAFL, XXXVII, 92-200. 1924.

Lyman, A.R. Pahute Biscuits. UHQ, III, 118-20. 1930.

Malouf, C., and A.A. The Effects of Spanish Slavery on the Indians of the Intermountain West. SJA, I, 378-91. 1945.

O'Neill, S. Americana. WF, XI, 109-13. 1952.

Palmer, W.R. Pahute Indian Government and Laws. UHQ, II, 35-42. 1929.

--- Pahute Indian Homelands. UHQ, VI, 88-102. 1933.

--- Pahute Indian Legends. 134 pp. Salt Lake City, 1946.

--- Utah Indians Past and Present. UHQ, I, 35-52. 1928.

--- Why the North Star Stands Still. 118 pp. Englewood Cliffs, 1957.

Pendergast, D.M. and Meighan, C.W. Folk Traditions as Historical Fact. JAFL, LXXII, 128-33. 1959.

Phister, N.P. The Indian Messiah. AA, IV, 105-8. 1891.

Powell, J.W. Exploration of the Colorado River. 291 pp. Washington, 1875.

Sapir, E. A Note on Reciprocal Terms of Relationship. AA, n.s., XV, 132-8. 1913.

--- Some Fundamental Characteristics of the Ute Language. Science, n.s., XXXI, 350-2. 1910.

--- Song Recitative in Paiute Mythology. JAFL, XXIII, 455-72. 1910.

--- Southern Paiute. PAA, LXV, 1-296. 1930.

--- Southern Paiute and Nahuatl. JSAP, n.s., X, 379-425; XI, 443-88. 1913-19.

--- Southern Paiute and Nahuatl. AA, n.s., XVII, 98-120, 306-28. 1915.

--- Southern Paiute Dictionary. PAA, LXV, 537-730. 1931.

--- Texts of the Kaibab Paiutes and Uintah Utes. PAA, LXV, 297-535. 1930.

--- Two Paiute Myths. MJ, I, 15-18. 1910.

Severance, M.S., and Yarrow, H.C. Notes upon Human Crania and Skeletons. RUSGS, VII, 391-7. 1879.

Shutler, D. A Pinon Nut Cache near Tonopah, Nevada. P, XXVIII, 70-72. 1956.

Steward, J.H. Nevada Shoshone. AR, IV, 209-59. 1941.

--- Notes on Hiller's Photographs of the Paiute and Ute Indians. SMC, XCVIII, xviii, 1-23. 1939.

Stewart, O.C. Navaho Basketry as made by Ute and Paiute. AA, n.s., XL, 758-9. 1938.

--- Ute-Southern Paiute. AR, VI, 231-355. 1942.

Stuart, B.R. Paiute Mourners. M, XIX, 108. 1945.

--- Paiute Surprise the Mohave. M, XVII, 217-19. 1943.

--- Southern Paiute Staff of Life. M, XIX, 133-4. 1945.

Watkins, F.E. Moapa Paiute Winter Wickiup. M, XIX, 13-18. 1945.

Wetherill, M.A. A Paiute Trap Corral on Skeleton Mesa, Arizona. P, XXVI, 116. 1954.

5. PANAMINT

Including the Panamint or Koso of southeastern California and the Western Shoshoni of Nevada.

Steward, J.H. Nevada Shoshone. AR, IV, 209-59. 1941.

Burbank, E.A., and Royce, E. Burbank among the Indians, pp. 121-5. Caldwell, 1946.

Coville, F.V. The Panamint Indians of California. AA, V, 351-61. 1892.

Driver, H.E. Southern Sierra Nevada. AR, I, 53-154. 1937.

Dutcher, B.H. Pinon Gathering among the Panamint Indians. AA, VI, 377-80. 1893.

Harris, J. Western Shoshoni. AA, n.s., XL, 407-10. 1938.

Humfreville, J.L. Twenty Years among Our Savage Indians. 674 pp. Hartford, 1897.

Kirk, R.E. Panamint Basketry. M, XXVI, 76-86. 1952.

Kroeber, A.L. Handbook of the Indians of California. BBAE, LXXVIII, 589-92. 1925.

Mayhugh, J.S. Western Shoshone Agency. RIT, 1890, 382-8.

Merwin, B.W. The Patty Stuart Jewett Collection. MJ, IX, 225-43. 1918.

Nelson, E.W. The Panamint and Saline Valley Indians. AA, IV, 371-2. 1891.

Steward, J.H. Basin-Plateau Aboriginal Sociopolitical Groups. BBAE, CXX, 1-346. 1938.

--- The Great Basin Shoshonean Indians. TCC, 101-21. 1955.

--- Shoshoni Polyandry. AA, n.s., XXXVIII, 561-4. 1936.

--- Some Western Shoshoni Myths. BBAE, CXXXVI, 249-99. 1943.

6. PAVIOTSO

Including the various Northern Paiute bands of Oregon, Nevada, and northeastern California.

Kelly, I.T. Ethnography of the Surprise Valley Paiute. UCP, XXXI, 67-210. 1932.

Lowie, R.H. Notes on Shoshonean Ethnography. APAM, XX, 185-314. 1924.

Stewart, O.C. Northern Paiute. AR, IV, 361-446. 1941.

Voegelin, E.W. and Steward, J.H. The Northern Paiute Indians. 313 pp. Washington, 1954.

Underhill, R. The Northern Paiute Indians. ILC, I, 1-78. 1941.

Wheeler-Voegelin, E. The Northern Paiute of Central Oregon. E, II, 95-132, 241-72; III, 1-10. 1955-1956.

Whiting, B.B. Paiute Sorcery. VFPA, XV, 1-110. 1950.

Angulo, J.de, and Freeland, L.S. Notes on the Northern Paiute of California. JSAP, n.s., XXI, 313-35. 1929.

Angulo, J.de, and Harcourt, B.d'. La musique des Indiens de la Californie du Nord. JSAP, n.s., XXIII, 189-228. 1931.

Berreman, J.V. Tribal Distribution in Oregon. MAAA, XLVII, 7-65. 1937.

Blyth, B. Northern Paiute Bands in Oregon. AA, n.s., XL, 402-5. 1938.

Cressman, L.S. Archaeological Survey of the Guano Valley Region in Southeastern Oregon. UOSA, I, 1-48. 1936.

Cressman, L.S., et al. Early Man in Oregon. UOSA, III, 1-78. 1940.

Curtis, E.S. The North American Indian, XV, 66-85, 129-49, 169-71, 182-8. Norwood, 1926.

Gates, M.E. A Visit to the Northern Reservations in Oregon and Montana. LMCI, XVII, 57-61. 1900.

Gifford, E.W. Californian Anthropometry. UCP, XXII, 290-1. 1926.

Harrington, M.R. A Cat-tail Eater. M, VII, 147-9. 1933.

Hart, C.P. Piute Herbalists. PAAAS, XXXV, 330-1. 1886.

Heizer, R.F. Executions by Stoning among the Sierra Miwok and Northern Paiute. PKAS, XII, 45-54. 1955.

--- Notes on Some Paviotso Personalities and Material Culture. Nevada State Museum Anthropological Papers, I, i, 7 pp. 1959.

Hoffman, W.J. Miscellaneous Ethnographic Observations. ARGGS, X, 461-78. 1876.

Hopkins, S.W. Life among the Paiutes. Boston, 1883.

Kelly, I.T. Northern Paiute Tales. JAFL, LI, 363-438. 1939.

Kober, G.M. Reminiscences. Washington, 1930.

Kroeber, A.L. California Kinship Systems. UCP, XII, 358-64. 1917.

--- Coefficients of Cultural Similarity of Northern Paiute Bands. UCP, XLVII, 209-14. 1957.

--- Handbook of the Indians of California. BBAE, LXXVIII, 581-4. 1925.

--- Recent Ethnic Spreads. UCP, XLVII, 259-81. 1959.

Loud, L.L. Notes on the Northern Paiute. UCP, XXV, 152-64. 1929.

Lowie, R.H. Shoshonean Tales. JAFL, XXXVII, 200-42. 1924.

Marsden, W.L. The Northern Paiute Language of Oregon. UCP, XX, 175-91. 1923.

Mooney, J. The Ghost-Dance Religion. ARBAE, XIV, ii, 764-91, 1048-57. 1893.

Murdock, G.P. Notes on the Tenino, Molala, and Paiute of Oregon. AA, n.s., XL, 395-402. 1938.

Nash, P. The Place of Religious Revivalism in the Formation of the Intercultural Community on Klamath Reservation. SANAT, 377-442. 1955.

Natches, G. Northern Paiute Verbs. UCP, XX, 245-59. 1923.

Park, W.Z. The Organization and Habitat of Paviotso Bands. AA, n.s., XL, 622-6. 1938.

--- Paviotso Polyandry. AA, n.s., XXXIX, 366-8. 1937.

--- Paviotso Shamanism. AA, n.s., XXXVI, 98-113. 1934.

--- Shamanism in Western North America. Northwestern University Studies in the Social Sciences, II, 1-166. 1938.

Powers, S. Centennial Mission to the Indians of Western Nevada and California. ARSI, 1876, 449-54. 1877.

Steward, J.H. The Great Basin Shoshonean Indians. TCC, 101-21. 1955.

--- Nevada Shoshone. AR, IV, 209-59. 1941.

--- Some Western Shoshoni Myths. BBAE, CXXXVI, 249-99. 1943.

Stewart, O.C. Northern Paiute. AA, n.s., XL, 405-7. 1938.

--- Northern Paiute. AR, IV, 361-446. 1941.

--- The Northern Paiute Bands. AR, II, 127-49. 1939.

--- Northern Paiute Polyandry. AA, n.s., XXXIX, 368-9. 1937.

--- Three Gods for Joe. Tomorrow, IV, iii, 71-6. 1956.

--- Washo-Northern Paiute Peyotism. PPSC, VI, iv, 65-8. 1939.

--- Washo-Northern Paiute Peyotism. UCP, XL, 63-142. 1944.

Waterman, T.T. The Phonetic Elements of the Northern Paiute Language. UCP, X, 13-44. 1911.

Wheat, M.M. Notes on Paviotso Material Culture. Nevada State Museum Anthropological Papers, I, i, 13 pp. 1959.

Wheeler-Voegelin, E. (ed.) J.W.Perit Huntington to Hon. N.S.Taylor, Umatilla Reservation. E, III, 163-79. 1956.

Wheeler-Voegelin, E. The "Yahooskin Snakes" of
    South Central Oregon. PIAS, LXIV, 49-50. 1954.
Woodruff, J. Indian Oasis, pp. 159-221. Caldwell,
    1939.

7. SHOSHONI

Including the Northern Shoshoni bands of Idaho and
northern Nevada. The Western Shoshoni are classed
under Panamint, and the Eastern Shoshoni under
Wind River.

Lowie, R.H. The Northern Shoshone. APAM, II,
    169-306. 1908.

Boas, F. Anthropometry of Shoshonean Tribes. AA,
    n.s., I, 751-8. 1899.
Farnham, T.J. Travels in the Great Western Prairies.
    New York, 1843.
Harris, J.S. The White Knife Shoshoni of Nevada.
    ASAIT, 39-118. 1940.
Henshaw, H.W. Shoshoni. BBAE, XXX, ii, 556-8.
    1910.
Hoebel, E.A. Bands and Distributions of the Eastern
    Shoshone. AA, n.s., XL, 410-13. 1938.
--- Comanche and Hekandika Shoshone Relationship
    Systems. AA, n.s., XLI, 440-57. 1939.
--- The Sun Dance of the Hekandika Shoshone. AA,
    n.s., XXXVII, 570-81. 1935.
Hoffman, W.J. Remarks on Indian Tribal Names.
    PAPS, XXIII, 296-8. 1886.
--- Die Shoshoni- und Banak-Indianer. Globus, LXIX,
    57-60. 1896.
Hultkranz, A. Indianerna i Yellowstone Park. Ymer,
    LXXIV, 112-40. 1954.
--- Shoshonerna i Klippiga Bergsomradet. Ymer,
    LXXVI, 161-89. 1956.
Kroeber, A.L. The Bannock and Shoshoni Languages.
    AA, n.s., XI, 266-77. 1909.
Le Sieur, T.B. The Shoshone Sun Dance. The Red
    Man, IV, 107-10. 1911.
Malouf, C., and A.A. The Effects of Spanish Slavery
    on the Indians of the Intermountain West. SJA, I,
    378-91. 1945.
Ross, A. The Fur Hunters of the Far West, ed. M. M.
    Quaife, pp. 238-66. Chicago, 1924.
Steward, J.H. Basin-Plateau Aboriginal Sociopolitical
    Groups. BBAE, CXX, 1-346. 1938.
--- Lemhi Shoshoni Physical Therapy. BBAE, CXIX,
    177-81. 1938.
--- Nevada Shoshone. AR, IV, 209-59. 1941.

Steward, J.H. Northern and Gosiute Shoshoni. AR,
    VIII, 263-392. 1943.
Swanson, E.H. Problems in Shoshone Chronology.
    Idaho Yesterdays, I, iv, 21-6. 1958.
Tuohy, D.R. Horseshoes and Handstones. Idaho
    Yesterdays, II, ii, 20-7. 1958.
--- Shoshoni Ware from Idaho. DJA, II, 55-71. 1956.
Wyeth, N.J. Indian Tribes of the South Pass of the
    Rocky Mountains. HCPIT, I, 204-28. 1851.

8. UTE

Lowie, R.H. Notes on Shoshonean Ethnography.
    APAM, XX, 185-314. 1924.

Aberle, D.F. and Stewart, O.C. Navaho and Ute
    Peyotism. UCSSA, VI, 138 pp. 1957.
Alter, J.C. Black Hawk's Last Raid. UHQ, IV, 99-
    108. 1931.
--- Father Escalante and the Utah Indians. UHQ, I,
    75-86, 106-13; II, 18-25, 46-54. 1928-29.
--- Some Useful Early Utah Indian References. UHQ,
    I, 26-32, 52-6. 1928.
Anonymous. Ute. BBAE, XXX, ii, 874-6. 1910.
Bailey, P. Walkara. 185 pp. Los Angeles, 1954.
Barber, E.A. Comparative Vocabulary of Utah Dia-
    lects. BGGST, III, 533-45. 1877.
--- Gaming among the Utah Indians. AN, XI, 351-3.
    1877.
--- Language and Utensils of the Modern Utes. BGGST,
    II, 71-6. 1876.
Beals, R.L. Ethnology of Rocky Mountain Park: the
    Ute and Arapaho. 27 pp. Berkeley, 1935.
Beidleman, R.G. A Partial, Annotated Bibliography
    of Colorado Ethnology. Colorado College Studies,
    II, 55 pp. 1958.
Boas, F. Anthropometry of Shoshonean Tribes. AA,
    n.s., I, 751-8. 1899.
--- Zur Anthropologie der nordamerikanischen Indianer.
    VBGA, 1895, 367-411.
Boyd, H.H. Saguache Antelope Traps. SWL, VI, 28-
    34. 1940.
Burbank, E.A., and Royce, E. Burbank among the
    Indians, pp. 192-6. Caldwell, 1946.
Burton, R.F. The City of the Saints, pp. 575-82.
    London, 1861.
Calef, W.C. Land Associations and Occupance Prob-
    lems in the Uinta Country. 179 pp. Chicago, 1949.
Campion, J.S. On the Frontier, pp. 224-32. 2d edit.
    London, 1878.

Chamberlain, R.V. Some Plant Names of the Ute Indians. AA, n.s., XI, 27-40. 1909.

Cooke, A.M. The Northern Ute. AA, n.s., XL, 627-30. 1938.

Covington, J.W. Ute Scalp Dance in Denver. Colorado Magazine, XXX, 119-24. 1953.

Cummings, B. Indians I Have Known. 75 pp. Tucson, 1952.

Densmore, F. Northern Ute Music. BBAE, LXXV, 1-210. 1922.

--- Preservation of Indian Music. SMC, LXV, vi, 81-5. 1915.

--- Study of Indian Music. SMC, LXVI, xvii, 108-11. 1917.

Douglas, F.H. The Ute Indians. DAMLS, X, 1-4. 1930.

Emmitt, R. The Last War Trail. 343 pp. Norman, 1954.

Euler, R.C. and Naylor, H.L. Southern Ute Rehabilitation Planning. HO, XI, iv, 27-32. 1952.

Gatschet, A.S. Classification into Seven Linguistic Stocks of Western Indian Dialects. RUSGS, VIII, 403-85. 1879.

--- Zwölf Sprachen aus dem Südwesten Nordamerikas. 150 pp. Weimar, 1876.

Gibbs, J.F. Moshoquop the Avenger. UHQ, II, 3-8. 1929.

Gifford, E.W. Apache-Pueblo. AR, IV, 1-207. 1940.

--- Tübatulabal and Kawaiisu Kinship Terms. UCP, XII, 219-48. 1917.

Gilbertson, A.N. Negro-Ute Métis. AA, n.s., XV, 363-4. 1913.

Harmon, E.M. The Story of the Indian Fort near Granby, Colorado. Colorado Magazine, XXII, 167-71. 1945.

Harrington, J.P. The Phonetic System of the Ute Language. University of Colorado Studies, VIII, 199-222. 1910.

Hauck, P.A. Ute Rorschach Performances. APUU, XXIII, 20 pp. 1955.

Hawley, F.L., et al. Culture Process and Change in Ute Adaptation. EP, LVII, 311-31, 345-61. 1950.

Haydon, W. Uintah and Ouray Agency. RIT, 1890, 597-601.

Heap, G.H. Central Route to the Pacific. 136 pp. Philadelphia, 1854.

Heizer, R.F. Notes on the Utah Utes by Edward Palmer, 1866-1877. APUU, XVII, 1-8. 1954.

Hoffmeister, H. The Consolidated Ute Indian Reservation. GR, XXXV, 601-23. 1945.

Hrdlicka, A. Physiological and Medical Observations among the Indians of Southwestern United States and Northern Mexico. BBAE, XXXIV, 1-425. 1908.

--- Southern Ute. BBAE, XXX, ii, 619-20. 1910.

Humfreville, J.L. Twenty Years among Our Savage Indians. 674 pp. Hartford, 1897.

Humphrey, N.B. The Mock Battle Greeting. JAFL, LIV, 186-90. 1941.

Hurst, C.T. Colorado's Old-Timers. SWL, XII, 19-26. 1946.

--- A Ute Shelter. SWL, V, 57-64. 1939.

Jones, D.W. Forty Years among the Indians. 400 pp. Salt Lake City, 1890.

Jones, J.A. The Sun Dance of the Northern Ute. BBAE, CLVII, 203-64. 1955.

Kane, F.F., and Riter, F.M. Proposed Removal of the Southern Utes. 32 pp. Philadelphia, 1892.

Kate, H.F.C. ten. Reizen en onderzoekingen in Noord-Amerika, pp. 313-29. Leiden, 1885.

King, W.G. Our Ute Indians. Colorado Magazine, XXXVII, 128-32. 1960.

Kroeber, A.L. California Kinship Systems. UCP, XII, 366-8. 1917.

--- Notes on the Ute Language. AA, n.s., X, 74-87. 1908.

--- Ute Tales. JAFL, XIV, 252-85. 1901.

Lang, G.O. A Study in Culture Contact and Culture Change. APUU, XV, 82 pp. 1953.

Lang, G.O. and Kunstadter, P. Survey Research on the Uintah and Ouray Ute Reservation. AA, LIX, 527-32. 1957.

Lowie, R.H. Dances and Societies of the Plains Shoshone. APAM, XI, 823-35. 1915.

--- Shoshonean Tales. JAFL, XXXVII, 1-91. 1924.

--- The Sun Dance of the Wind River Shoshoni and Ute. APAM, XVI, 405-10. 1919.

Malouf, C., and A.A. The Effects of Spanish Slavery on the Indians of the Intermountain West. SJA, I, 378-91. 1945.

Mason, J.A. Myths of the Uintah Utes. JAFL, XXIII, 299-363. 1910.

Matson, G.A., and Piper, C.L. Distribution of the Blood Groups, M-N, Rh Types, and Secretors among the Ute Indians of Utah. AJPA, n.s., V, 357-68. 1947.

Matson, G.A., and Shrader, H.F. The Distribution of the Four Blood Groups among the Ute Indians of Utah. PUA, XVIII, 101-3. 1941.

Meeker, N.C. The Utes of Colorado. AAOJ, I, 224-6. 1879.

Meston, G.D. Southern Ute Agency. RIT, 1890, 226-30.

Moomaw, J.C. Aborigines of the Colorado Highlands. SWL, XXIII, iii, 35-7. 1957.

Morgan, L.H. Systems of Consanguinity and Affinity. SCK, XVII, 291-382. 1871.

Opler, M.K. The Character and History of the Southern Ute Peyote Rite. AA, n.s., XLII, 463-78. 1940.

--- A Colorado Ute Indian Bear Dance. SWL, VII, 21-30. 1941.

--- Fact and Fancy in Ute Peyotism. AA, n.s., XLIV, 151-9. 1942.

--- The Origins of Commanche and Ute. AA, n.s., XLV, 155-63. 1943.

--- The Southern Ute. AA, n.s., XL, 632-3. 1938.

--- The Southern Ute Dog-Dance and Its Reported Transmission to Taos. NMA, III, 66-72. 1939.

--- The Southern Ute of Colorado. ASAIT, 119-206. 1940.

--- Southern Ute Pottery Types. M, XIII, 161-3. 1939.

--- The Ute Indian War of 1879. EP, XLVI, 255-62. 1939.

Palmer, W.R. Pahute Indian Homelands. UHQ, VI, 88-102. 1933.

--- Utah Indians Past and Present. UHQ, I, 35-52. 1928.

Powell, J.W. Exploration of the Colorado River. 291 pp. Washington, 1875.

Reagan, A.B. The Bear Dance of the Ouray Utes. WA, n.s., IX, 148-50. 1929.

--- Mortuary Customs of the Ouray Utes. EP, XXXI, 411-13. 1931.

--- Some Games of the Northern Ute. Northwest Science, VIII, 12-16. 1934.

--- Some Names of the Ute Indians. PUA, XII, 1-39. 1935.

--- Some Notes on the History of the Uintah Basin. PUA, XI, 55-64. 1934.

--- The Sun God Moccasin Tales. 33 pp. Provo, 1935.

--- Ute Dwellings. EP, XXXI, 410-11. 1931.

Reed, V.Z. The Ute Bear Dance. AA, IX, 237-44. 1896.

Richie, E. General Mano Mocha of the Utes. Colorado Magazine, IX, 150-7. 1932.

Rockwell, W. The Utes: A Forgotten People. 307 pp. Denver, 1956.

Sapir, E. A Note on Reciprocal Terms of Relationship. AA, n.s., XV, 132-8. 1913.

--- Texts of the Kaibab Paiutes and Uintah Utes. PAA, LXV, 297-535. 1930.

Sonne, C.B. Royal Blood of the Utes. UHQ, XXII, 271-96. 1954.

Sprague, M. Massacre. 382 pp. Boston, 1957.

Stacher, S.F. Ouray and the Utes. Colorado Magazine, XXVII, 134-40. 1950.

Steward, J.H. The Great Basin Shoshonean Indians. TCC, 101-21. 1955.

--- Notes on Hiller's Photographs of the Paiute and Ute Indians. SMC, XCVIII, xviii, 1-23. 1939.

--- A Uintah Ute Bear Dance. AA, n.s., XXXIV, 263-73. 1932.

Stewart, O.C. Escalante and the Ute. SWL, XVIII, 47-51. 1952.

--- Navaho Basketry as made by Ute and Paiute. AA, n.s., XL, 758-9. 1938.

--- Southern Ute Adjustment to Modern Living. ICA, XXIX, ii, 80-7. 1952.

--- The Southern Ute Peyote Cult. AA, n.s., XLIII, 303-8. 1941.

--- Ute Peyotism. UCSSA, I, 1-42. 1948.

--- Ute-Southern Paiute. AR, VI, 231-355. 1942.

Turenne, L. de. Une légende indienne. JSAP, I, 61-71. 1896.

Tyler, S.L. The Spaniard and the Ute. UHQ, XXII, 343-61. 1954.

Zingg, R.M. The Ute Indians in Historical Relation to Proto-Azteco-Tanoan Culture. Colorado Magazine, XV, 134-52. 1938.

9. WASHO

Barrett, S.A. The Washo Indians. BPMCM, II, 1-52. 1917.

Lowie, R.H. Ethnographic Notes on the Washo. UCP, XXXVI, 301-52. 1939.

Cartwright, W.D. A Washo Girl's Puberty Ceremony. ICA, XXX, 136-42. 1955.

Cohn, C.A. Arts and Crafts of the Nevada Indians. Nevada Historical Society Biennial Reports, I, 75-9. 1909.

Cook, S.F. The Conflict between the California Indian and White Civilization. IA, XXIV, 1-29. 1943.

--- The Mechanism and Extent of Dietary Adaptation among Certain Groups of California and Nevada Indians. IA, XVIII, 1-59. 1941.

Curtis, E.S. The North American Indian, XV, 89-98, 149-56, 171-2, 188-92. Norwood, 1926.

Dangberg, G. Washo Texts. UCP, XXII, 391-443. 1927.

Gifford, E.W. Californian Anthropometry. UCP, XXII, 281-2. 1926.

Gordon, G.B. The Richard Waln Meirs Collection. MJ, X, 26-8. 1919.

Jacobsen, W.H. Washo and Karok. IJAL, XXIV, 195-212. 1958.

Kroeber, A.L. California Kinship Systems. UCP, XII, 362-5. 1917.

--- Handbook of the Indians of California. BBAE, LXXVIII, 569-73. 1925.

--- The Washo Language. UCP, IV, 251-318. 1907.

Mack, E.M. Nevada, pp. 39-57. Glendale, 1936.

Merriam, A.P. and d'Azevedo, W.L. Washo Peyote Songs. AA, LIX, 615-41. 1957.

Sapir, E. A Supplementary Note on Salinan and Washo. IJAL, II, 68-72. 1921.

Schellbach, L. A Bone Implement of the Washo. IN, IV, 400-3. 1927.

Simpson, J.H. Report of Explorations across the Great Basin, pp. 459-74. Washington, 1876.

Siskin, E.E. Washo Territory. AA, n.s., XL, 626-7. 1938.

Stewart, O.C. Northern Paiute. AR, IV, 361-446. 1941.

--- Washo-Northern Paiute Peyotism. PPSC, VI, iv, 65-8. 1939.

--- Washo-Northern Paiute Peyotism. UCP, XL, 63-142. 1944.

10. WIND RIVER

Including the Eastern or Wind River Shoshoni of Wyoming.

Lowie, R.H. Notes on Shoshonean Ethnography. APAM, XX, 185-314. 1924.

Shimkin, D.B. Wind River Shoshone Ethnogeography. AR, V, 245-88. 1947.

--- The Wind River Shoshone Sun Dance. BBAE, CLI, 397-484. 1953.

Bourke, J.G. On the Border with Crook. 491 pp. New York, 1892.

Brackett, A.G. The Shoshonis. ARSI, 1879, 328-33.

Culin, S. A Summer Trip among the Western Indians. BFMUP, III, 10-17. 1901.

Dorsey, G.A. The Shoshonean Game of Na-wá-ta-pi. JAFL, XIV, 24-5. 1901.

Hebard, G.R. Washakie. 337 pp. Cleveland, 1930.

Hultkrantz, A. The Concept of the Soul Held by the Wind River Shoshone. Ethnos, XVI, 18-44. 1951.

--- Configurations of Religious Belief among Wind River Shoshoni. Ethnos, XXI, 194-215. 1956.

--- Indianerna i Yellowstone Park. Ymer, LXXIV, 112-40. 1954.

--- The Origin of Death Myth as Found among the Wind River Shoshoni Indians. Ethnos, XX, 127-36. 1955.

--- Shoshonerna i Klippigga Bergsomradet. Ymer, LXXVI, 161-89. 1956.

--- Tribal Divisions within the Eastern Shoshoni of Wyoming. ICA, XXXII, 148-54. 1958.

Lowie, R.H. Dances and Societies of the Plains Shoshone. APAM, XI, 813-22. 1915.

--- The Northern Shoshone. APAM, II, 169-306. 1908.

--- The Sun Dance of the Wind River Shoshoni and Ute. APAM, XVI, 387-404. 1919.

Moran, P. Shoshone Agency. RIT, 1890, 629-34.

Morgan, D.L., ed. Washakie and the Shoshoni. Annals of Wyoming, XXV, 141-90; XXVI, 65-80, 141-90; XXVII, 61-88, 198-220; XXVIII, 80-93, 193-207; XXIX, 86-102, 195-228; XXX, 53-89. 1953-58.

Olden, S.E. Shoshone Folk Lore. 103 pp. Milwaukee, 1923.

St. Clair, H.H., and Lowie, R.H. Shoshone and Comanche Tales. JAFL, XXII, 265-73. 1909.

Shimkin, D.B. Childhood and Development among the Wind River Shoshone. AR, V, v, 289-325. 1947.

--- Dynamics of Recent Wind River Shoshone History. AA, n.s., XLIV, 451-62. 1942.

--- Shoshone. IJAL, XV, 175-94, 203-12. 1949.

--- Wind River Shoshone Geography. AA, n.s., XL, 413-15. 1938.

--- Wind River Shoshone Literary Forms. JWAS, XXXVII, 329-52. 1947.

Sprague, M. Massacre. 382 pp. Boston, 1957.

Voget, F. Current Trends in the Wind River Shoshone Sun Dance. BBAE, CLI, 485-500. 1953.

--- Individual Motivation in the Diffusion of the Wind River Shoshone Sundance to the Crow Indians. AA, n.s., L, 634-45. 1948.

--- A Shoshone Innovator. AA, n.s., LII, 53-63. 1950.

Williams, P.L. Personal Recollections of Wash-a-kie. UHQ, I, 101-6. 1928.

Wilson, E.N. The White Indian Boy, ed. H.R. Driggs. Yonkers, 1919.

VIII. PLATEAU

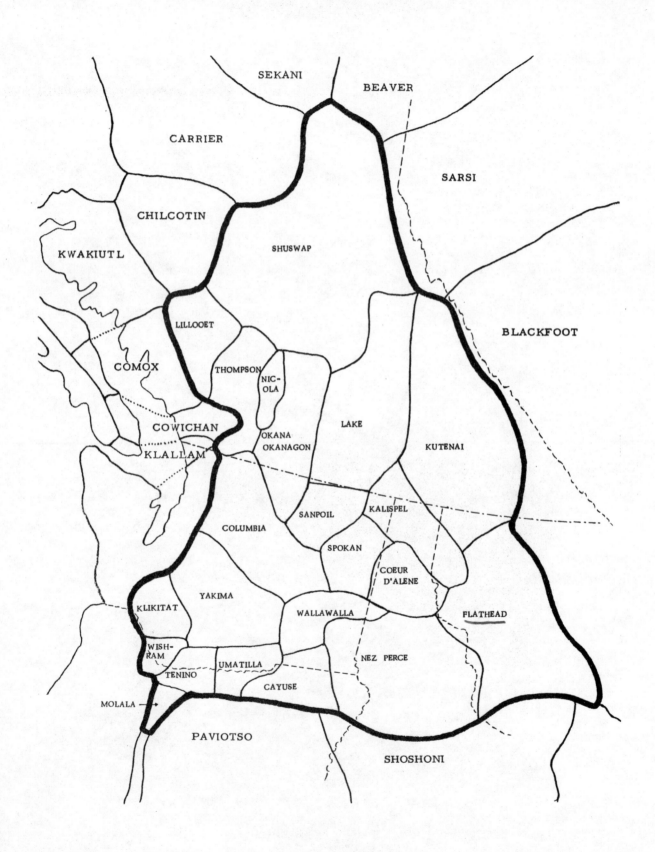

The tribes of this area are grouped under the follow-
ing linguistic stocks:
Athapaskan: Nicola.
Chinookan: Wishram.
Kitunahan: Kutenai.
Sahaptin: Klikitat, Nez Perce, Tenino, Umatilla,
   Wallawalla, Yakima.
Salishan: Coeur d'Alene, Columbia, Flathead,
   Kalispel, Lake, Lillooet, Okanagon, Sanpoil,
   Shuswap, Spokan, Thompson.
Waiilatpuan: Cayuse, Molala.

Alvord, B. Report concerning the Indians in the Territories of Oregon and Washington. H.R.Ex.Doc. No.
   75 (Serial No. 906), 34th Cong., 3d Session, pp.
   10-22. 1857.

Arnold, R.R. Indian Wars of Idaho. 268 pp. Caldwell, 1932.

Bancroft, H.H. The Native Races of the Pacific
   States, I, 250-91, 310-21. New York, 1875.

Barbeau, M. Indian Days in the Canadian Rockies.
   209 pp. Toronto, 1923.

Barry, J.N. The Indians of Oregon. OHQ, XXVIII,
   49-61. 1927.

Berreman, J.V. Tribal Distribution in Oregon.
   MAAA, XLVII, 7-65. 1937.

Boas, F. Comparative Vocabulary of Eighteen Languages spoken in British Columbia. BAAS, LX,
   692-715. 1890.

--- Physical Characteristics of the Tribes of the North
   Pacific Coast. BAAS, LXV, 524-51. 1895.

--- The Salish Tribes of the Interior of British Columbia. AAR, 1905, 219-25.

--- Summary of the Work of the Committee in British Columbia. BAAS, LXVIII, 667-83. 1898.

--- Die Verbreitung der Indianer-Sprachen in Britisch-
   Columbien. PMJP, XLII, 21. 1896.

--- Zur Anthropologie der nordamerikanischen Indianer. VBGA, 1895, 367-411.

Boas, F., and Farrand, L. Physical Characteristics
   of the Tribes of British Columbia. BAAS, LXVIII,
   628-44. 1898.

Boas, F., and Haeberlin, H.K. Sound Shifts in
   Salishan Dialects. IJAL, IV, 117-36. 1927.

Butler, B.R. The Prehistory of the Dice Game in the
   Southern Plateau. Tebiwa, II, 65-71. 1958.

Canada, Dept. of Mines and Resources, Indian Affairs Branch. Census of Indians in Canada, 1939
   and 1944. 33 pp. Ottawa, 1940, 1944.

Childears, L. Montana Place-Names from Indian
   Myth and Legend. WF, IX, 263-4. 1950.

Chittenden, H.M., and Richardson, A.T., eds. Life,
   Letters and Travels of Father Pierre-Jean De Smet.
   4 vols. New York, 1905.

Clark, E.E. George Gibbs' Account of Indian Mythology in Oregon and Washington Territories. OHQ,
   LVI, 293-325; LVII, 125-67. 1955-56.

Coues, E., ed. Manuscript Journals of Alexander
   Henry and David Thompson. 3 vols. New York,
   1897.

Cox, R. Adventures on the Columbia River. 2d edit.
   335 pp. New York, 1832.

Cressman, L.S. Petroglyphs of Oregon. UOSA, II,
   1-78. 1937.

DeVoto, B.A. Across the Wide Missouri. 483 pp.
   New York, 1947.

Driver, H.E. Girls' Puberty Rites in Western North
   America. AR, VI, 21-90. 1941.

DuBois, C. The Feather Cult of the Middle Columbia. GSA, VII, 1-45. 1938.

Eells, M. Aboriginal Geographic Names in the State
   of Washington. AA, V, 27-35. 1892.

Erwin, R.P. Indian Rock Writing in Idaho. State
   Historical Society of Idaho, Biennial Report, XII,
   35-111. 1930.

Farrand, L. Sahaptin Tales. MAFLS, XI, 135-79.
   1917.

Franchère, G. Narrative of a Voyage to the Northwest Coast of America. EWT, VI, 167-410. 1904.

Fraser, S. Journal of a Voyage from the Rocky Mountains to the Pacific Coast. BCNO, I, 156-221.
   1889.

French, K. and D. The Warm Springs Indian Community. AmI, VII, ii, 3-16. 1955.

Gass, P. A Journal of the Voyages and Travels of a
   Corps of Discovery. Pittsburgh, 1807.

Gatschet, A.S. Indian Languages of the Pacific
   States and Territories. MAH, I, 145-71. 1877.

Gibbs, G. Report on the Indian Tribes of the Territory of Washington. RESRR, I, 402-36. 1855.

Grasserie, R. de la. Renseignements sur les noms de
   parenté dans plusieurs langues américaines. JSAP,
   n.s., II, 333-8. 1905.

Gunther, E. An Analysis of the First Salmon Ceremony. AA, n.s., XXVIII, 605-17. 1926.

--- A Further Analysis of the First Salmon Ceremony.
   UWPA, II, 129-73. 1928.

--- The Indian Background of Washington History.
   PNQ, XLI, 189-202. 1950.

--- The Westward Movement of Some Plains Traits.
   AA, n.s., LII, 174-80. 1950.

Haeberlin, H.K. Types of Reduplication in the Salish Dialects. IJAL, I, 154-74. 1918.

Haeberlin, H.K., Teit, J.A., and Roberts, H.H. Coiled Basketry in British Columbia and Surrounding Regions. ARBAE, XLI, 119-484. 1928.

Hafen, L.R. and A.W., eds. Rufus B. Sage, His Letters and Papers, 1836-1847. FWRHS, IV, 354 pp.; V, 360 pp. 1956.

--- To the Rockies and Oregon, 1839-1842. FWRHS, III, 315 pp. 1955.

Hale, H. Ethnology and Philology. Narrative of the United States Exploring Expedition, by C. Wilkes, Vol. VI. Philadelphia, 1846.

--- Indians of North-West America. TAES, II, 1-24. 1848.

Hewes, C.W. The Ainu Double Foreshaft Toggle Harpoon and Western North America. JWAS, XXXII, 93-104. 1942.

Hill-Tout, C. British North America. London, 1907.

--- Some Features of the Language and Culture of the Salish. AA, n.s., VII, 674-87. 1905.

Huggins, E.L. Smohalla, the Prophet of Priest Rapids. OM, ser. 2, XVII, 208-15. 1891.

Hultkrantz, A. The Indians and the Wonders of Yellowstone. Ethnos, XIX, 34-68. 1954.

--- The Indians in Yellowstone Park. Annals of Wyoming, XXIX, 125-50. 1957.

Jacobs, M. Historic Perspectives in Indian Languages of Oregon and Washington. PNQ, 1937, 55-74.

Jenness, D. Indians of Canada. BCDM, LXV, 351-8. 1932.

Kane, P. Wanderings of an Artist among the Indians of North America. London, 1859.

Krieger, H.W. Archeological Investigations in the Columbia River Valley. SMC, LXXVIII, vii, 187-200. 1927.

--- A Prehistoric Pit House Village Site on the Columbia River. PUSNM, LXXIII, xi, 1-29. 1928.

Kroeber, A.L. Salt, Dogs, Tobacco. AR, VI, 1-20. 1941.

Leighton, C.C. Life at Puget Sound. Boston, 1884.

Lewis, A.B. Tribes of the Columbia Valley and the Coast of Washington and Oregon, MAAA, I, 147-209. 1906.

Lewis, M., and Clark, W. Travels. 3 vols. London, 1815.

Lord, J.K. The Naturalist in Vancouver Island and British Columbia, I, 226-61. London, 1866.

Lyman, W.D. Indian Myths of the Northwest. PAAS, n.s., XXV, 375-95. 1915.

MacMurray, J.W. The "Dreamers" of the Columbia River Valley. Transactions of the Albany Institute, XI, 241-8. 1887.

Mayne, R.C. Four Years in British Columbia and Vancouver Island, pp. 242-304. London, 1862.

Meany, E.S. Origin of Washington Geographic Names. 357 pp. Seattle, 1923.

Mooney, J. The Ghost-Dance Religion. ARBAE, XIV, ii, 641-1110. 1896.

Olson, R.L. Adze, Canoe, and House Types of the Northwest Coast. UWPA, II, 1-38. 1927.

Park, W.Z. Shamanism in Western North America. Northwestern University Studies in the Social Sciences, II, 1-166. 1938.

Parker, S. Journal of an Exploring Tour beyond the Rocky Mountains. Ithaca, 1838.

Pilling, J.C. Bibliography of the Salishan Languages. BBAE, XVI, 1-86. 1893.

Randall, B.U. The Cinderella Theme in Northwest Coast Folklore. CUCA, XXXVI, 243-86. 1949.

Ray, V.F. The Bluejay Character in the Plateau Spirit Dance. AA, n.s., XXXIX, 593-601. 1937.

--- Cultural Relations in the Plateau of Northwestern America. PHAPF, III, 1-154. 1939.

--- Historic Backgrounds of the Conjuring Complex in the Plateau and the Plains. Language, Culture, Personality, Essays in Memory of E. Sapir, pp. 204-16. Menasha, 1941.

--- The Kolaskin Cult. AA, n.s., XXXVIII, 67-75. 1936.

--- Native Villages and Groupings of the Columbia Basin. PNQ, XXVII, ii, 1-54. 1936.

--- Tribal Distribution in Northeastern Oregon. AA, n.s., XL, 384-95. 1938.

Ross, A. The Fur Hunters of the Far West, ed. M.M. Quaife. 317 pp. Chicago, 1924.

Scouler, J. Observations on the Indigenous Tribes of the N.W. Coast of America. JRGS, XI, 215-50. 1841.

Smet, P.J. de. Western Missions and Missionaries. New York, 1863.

Smith, A.H. The Indians of Washington. RSSCW, XXI, 85-113. 1953.

Smith, D.A., and Spier, L. The Dot and Circle Design in Northwestern America. JSAP, n.s., XIX, 47-55. 1927.

Smith, H.I. Recent Archaeological Discoveries in North-Western America. BAGS, XXXVIII, 287-95. 1906.

Smith, M.W. House Types of the Middle Fraser River. AAn, XII, 255-67. 1947.

--- Shamanism in the Shaker Religion of Northwest America. Man, LIV, 119-22. 1954.

Spier, L. An Analysis of Plains Indian Parfleche Decoration. UWPA, I, 89-112. 1925.

Spier, L. Plains Indian Parfleche Designs. UWPA,
    IV, 293-322. 1931.
--- The Prophet Dance of the Northwest and Its Deri-
    vatives. GSA, I, 1-74. 1935.
--- Tribal Distribution in Washington. GSA, III, 1-
    43. 1936.
Strong, W.D., and Schenck, W.E. Petroglyphs on
    the Columbia River. AA, n.s., XXVII, 76-90.
    1925.
Swanton, J.R. Salish. ERE, XI, 97-100. 1921.
Teit, J.A. Indian Tribes of the Interior. Canada
    and Its Provinces, XXI, 283-312. Toronto, 1914.
--- The Middle Columbia Salish. UWPA, II, 98-
    108. 1928.
Teit, J.S., Haeberlin, H.K., and Roberts, H.
    Coiled Basketry in British Columbia and Surround-
    ing Region. ARBAE, XLI, 119-484. 1924.
Thwaites, R.G., ed. Original Journals of the Lewis
    and Clark Expedition. 7 vols. New York, 1904-05.
Townsend, J.K. Narrative of a Journey across the
    Rocky Mountains to the Columbia River. EWT, XXI,
    111-369. 1905.
Tyrrell, J.B., ed. David Thompson's Narrative of
    His Explorations in Western America. PCS, XII,
    1-582. 1916.
Victor, F.F. The Early Indian Wars of Oregon. 719
    pp. Salem, 1894.
Wallace, W.S. The Intermontane Corridor. SWL,
    XVIII, 38-46. 1952.
Wardle, H.N. Certain Rare West-Coast Baskets.
    AA, n.s., XIV, 287-313. 1912.
White, M.C. David Thompson's Journals Relating to
    Montana and Adjacent Regions, 1808-1812. 507
    pp. Missoula, 1950.
Wilson, E.F. Report on the Indian Tribes. TESL,
    n.s., IV, 292-532. 1866.
Wyeth, N.J. Indian Tribes of the South Pass of the
    Rocky Mountains, the Salt Lake Basin, the Valley
    of the Great Säaptin, or Lewis' River, and the Paci-
    fic Coasts of Oregon. HCPIT, I, 204-28. 1851.
Young, F.G., ed. The Correspondence and Journals
    of Captain Nathaniel J. Wyeth. Sources of the His-
    tory of Oregon, I, 1-256. 1899.

1. CAYUSE

Alvord, B. Concerning the Manners and Customs, the
    Superstitions, &c., of the Indians of Oregon.
    HCPIT, V, 651-7. 1855.
Culin, S. A Summer Trip among the Western Indians.
    BFMUP, III, 159-64. 1901.
Curtis, E.S. The North American Indian, VIII, 79-
    82. Norwood, 1911.
Farrand, L. Cayuse. BBAE, XXX, i, 224-5. 1907.
Gairdner. Notes on the Geography of the Columbia
    River. JRGS, XI, 250-7. 1841.
Townsend, J.K. Narrative of a Journey across the
    Rocky Mountains. EWT, XXI, 349-51. 1905.
Whitman, Mrs. M. Letters written by Mrs. Whitman
    from Oregon to Her Relations in New York. Trans-
    actions of the Oregon Pioneer Association, XIX,
    79-179; XXI, 53-219. 1891-93.

2. COEUR D'ALENE

Also called Skitswish.

Teit, J.A. The Salishan Tribes of the Western Pla-
    teaus. ARBAE, XLV, 37-197. 1930.

Cody, E.R. History of the Coeur d'Alene Mission of
    the Sacred Heart. 45 pp. Caldwell, 1930.
Curtis, E.S. The North American Indian, VII, 53-4,
    79-114. Norwood, 1911.
Manring, B.F. The Conquest of the Coeur d'Alenes,
    Spokanes and Palouses. 280 pp. Spokane, 1912.
Mengarini, G. Vocabulary of the Schit-zui. CNAE,
    I, 267-82. 1877.
Owen, J. Journals and Letters, ed. S. Dunbar and
    P.C. Phillips. 2 vols. New York, 1927.
Ray, V.F. Plateau. AR, VIII, 99-257. 1942.
Reichard, G.A. An Analysis of Coeur d'Alene Indian
    Myths. MAFLS, XLI, 1-218. 1947.
--- Coeur d'Alene. HAIL, III, 517-707. New York,
    1938.
--- Composition and Symbolism of Coeur d'Alene
    Verb-stems. IJAL, XI, 47-63. 1945.
--- Imagery in an Indian Vocabulary. American
    Speech, IX, 96-102. 1943.
--- Stem-List of the Coeur d'Alene Language. IJAL,
    X, 92-108. 1939.
--- The Style of Coeur d'Alene Mythology. ICA,
    XXIV, 243-53. 1930.
Teit, J.A. Coeur d'Alene Tales. MAFLS, XI, 119-
    28. 1917.
Vogt, H. Salishan Studies. Skrifter utgitt av det
    Norske Videnskaps-Akademi, Historisk-filosofisk
    klasse, II, 1-19. 1940.

3. COLUMBIA

Including the Chelan, Methow, Sinkaquaiius,
Sinkiuse, and Wenatchi or Pisquow.

Teit, J.A. The Middle Columbia Salish. UWPA,
II, 83-128. 1928.

Curtis, E.S. The North American Indian, VII, 65-
114, 179-89. Norwood, 1911.
Gibbs, G. Vocabulary of the Piskwaus. CNAE, I,
249-65. 1877.
Ray, V.F. Plateau. AR, VIII, 99-257. 1942.
Smith, H.I. The Archaeology of the Yakima Valley. APAM, VI, 1-171. 1910.

4. FLATHEAD

Also called Salish.

Teit, J.A. The Salishan Tribes of the Western Plateaus. ARBAE, XLV, 295-396. 1930.
Turney-High, H.H. The Flathead Indians of Montana. MAAA, XLVIII, 1-161. 1937.

Bischoff, W.N. The Jesuits in Old Oregon (1840-
1940). 258 pp. Caldwell, 1945.
Cox, R. Adventures on the Columbia River, pp. 118-
29. New York, 1832.
Curtis, E.S. Indian Days of the Long Ago. Yonkers,
1915.
--- The North American Indian, VII, 43-51, 69-
114, 179-89. Norwood, 1911.
Dorsey, G.A. The Long Bones of the Kwakiutl and
Salish Indians. AA, X, 174-82. 1893.
Dusenberry, V. Gabriel Nattau's Soul Speaks. JAFL,
LXII, 155-60. 1959.
Ewers, J.C. Gustavus Sohon's Portraits of Flathead
and Pend d'Oreille Indians, 1854. SMC, CX, vii,
1-68. 1948.
Forbis, R.G. The Flathead Apostasy. MMH, I, iv,
35-40. 1951.
Hoffman, W.J. Selish Myths. BEI, XV, 24-40.
1883.
--- Vocabulary of the Selish Language. PAPS,
XXIII, 361-71. 1886.
Matson, G.A. Blood Groups and Ageusia in Indians
of Montana and Alberta. AJPA, XXIV, 81-9.
1938.
McDermott, L. Myths of the Flathead Indians. JAFL,
XIV, 240-51. 1901.

Mengarini, G. Indians of Oregon. Journal of the
Anthropological Institute of New York, I, 81-8.
1871-72.
--- A Selish or Flat-head Grammar. 122 pp. New
York, 1861.
--- Vocabulary of the Selish Proper. CNAE, I, 267-
82. 1877.
Merriam, Alan P. Flathead Indian Instruments and
Their Music. Musical Quarterly, XXXVII, 368-75.
1951.
--- The Hand Game of the Flathead Indians. JAFL,
LXVIII, 313-24. 1955.
--- Music of the Flathead Indian. Tomorrow, IV,
iii, 103-7. 1956.
Morgan, L.H. Systems of Consanguinity and Affinity.
SCK, XVII, 246. 1871.
Ogden, P.S. Traits of American-Indian Life and
Character. London, 1853.
Owen, J. Journals and Letters, ed. S. Dunbar and
P.C. Phillips. 2 vols. New York, 1927.
Palladino, L.B. Indian and White in the Northwest.
411 pp. Baltimore, 1894.
Partoll, A.J. The Flathead-Salish Name in Mon-
tana Nomenclature. MMH, I, i, 37-48. 1951.
Ray, V.F. Plateau. AR, VIII, 99-257. 1942.
Ronan, P. Historical Sketch of the Flathead Indian
Nation. Helena, c. 1890.
Schaeffer, C. The First Jesuit Mission to the Flat-
head. PNQ, XXVIII, 227-50. 1937.
Smet, P.J.de. Letters and Sketches. Philadelphia,
1843.
--- Oregon Missions. New York, 1847.
--- Voyages aux Montagnes Rocheuses. New edit.
Paris, 1873.
--- Western Missions and Missionaries, pp. 296-303.
New York, 1863.
Turney-High, H.H. The Bluejay Dance. AA, n.s.,
XXXV, 103-7. 1933.
--- Cooking Camas and Bitter Root. SM, XXXVI,
262-3. 1933.
--- The Diffusion of the Horse to the Flatheads. Man,
XXXV, 183-5. 1935.
Weisel, G.F. Animal Names, Anatomical Terms,
and Some Ethnozoology of the Flathead Indians.
JWAS, XLII, 345-55. 1952.
--- A Flathead Indian Tale. JAFL, LXV, 359-60.
1952.
--- The Rams Horn Tree and Other Medicine Trees
of the Flathead Indians. MMH, I, iii, 5-14. 1951.
Wingert, P.S. American Indian Sculpture. 144 pp.
New York, 1949.

5. KALISPEL

Including the Kalispel, the Pend d'Oreille, and the Semteuse.

Teit, J.A. The Salishan Tribes of the Western Plateaus. ARBAE, XLV, 295-396. 1930.

Boas, F. Terms of Relationship of the Salish Languages. BAAS, LX, 688-92. 1890.

Curtis, E.S. The North American Indian, VII, 51-3, 69-114, 179-89. Norwood, 1911.

Dusenberry, V. Visions among the Pend d'Oreille Indians. Ethnos, XXIV, 52-7. 1959.

Ewers, J.C. Gustavus Sohon's Portraits of Flathead and Pend d'Oreille Indians, 1854. SMC, CX, vii, 1-68. 1948.

Gibbs, G. Vocabulary of the Kalispelm. CNAE, I, 267-82. 1877.

Giorda, J. A Dictionary of the Kalispel or Flat-head Indian Language. 644 pp. St. Ignatius Mission, 1877-79.

Jones, J.A. Kalispel Law. PIAS, LXV, 50. 1955.

Ray, V.F. Plateau. AR, VIII, 99-257. 1942.

Smalley, E.V. The Kalispel Country. Century Illustrated Magazine, XXIX, 447-55. 1885.

Smet, P.J.de. Letters and Sketches. Philadelphia, 1843.

Teit, J.A. Pend d'Oreille Tales. MAFLS, XI, 114-18. 1917.

Tolmie, W.F. Vocabulary of the Kulleespelm. CNAE, I, 267-82. 1877.

Tolmie, W.F., and Dawson, G.M. Comparative Vocabularies of the Indian Tribes of British Columbia, pp. 78B-86B. Montreal, 1884.

Vogt, H. The Kalispel Language. 178 pp. Oslo, 1940.

--- Salishan Studies. Skrifter utgitt av det Norske Videnskaps-Akademi, Historisk-filosofisk klasse, II, 1-19. 1940.

6. KLIKITAT

Including the Klikitat, the Mical, and the Taidnapam.

Ballard, A.C. Mythology of Southern Puget Sound. UWPA, III, 31-150. 1929.

Bunnell, C.O. Legends of the Klickitats. 64 pp. Portland, 1933.

Clark, E.E. The Bridge of the Gods in Fact and Fancy. OHQ, LIII, 29-38. 1952.

Curtis, E.S. The North American Indian, VII, 37-40, 161-2. Norwood, 1911.

Farrand, L. Klikitat. BBAE, XXX, i, 713-14. 1907.

Gibbs, G. Tribes of Western Washington and Northwestern Oregon. CNAE, I, 157-241. 1877.

Haeberlin, H.K., Teit, J.A., and Roberts, H.H. Coiled Basketry in British Columbia and Surrounding Regions. ARBAE, XLI, 119-484. 1928.

Jacobs, M. Northern Sahaptin Kinship Terms. AA, n.s., XXXIV, 688-93. 1932.

--- Northwest Sahaptin Texts. UWPA, II, 175-244. 1929.

--- Northwest Sahaptin Texts. CUCA, XIX, 1-291. 1934.

--- A Sketch of Northern Sahaptin Grammar. UWPA, IV, 85-292. 1931.

Lyman, W.D. Myths and Superstitions of the Oregon Indians. PAAS, n.s., XVI, 221-51. 1904.

Parker, S. Journal of an Exploring Tour beyond the Rocky Mountains. Ithaca, 1838.

Ray, V.F. Plateau. AR, VIII, 99-257. 1942.

Rea, E.M. Ordeal of a Klickitat Family under Klickitat Mores. OHQ, XLII, 186-91. 1941.

Scouler, J. On the Indian Tribes inhabiting the North-West Coast of America. JESL, I, 228-52. 1848.

Tolmie, W.F., and Dawson, G.M. Comparative Vocabularies of the Indian Tribes of British Columbia, pp. 78B-86B. Montreal, 1884.

Winthrop, T. The Canoe and the Saddle, ed. J.H. Williams. Tacoma, 1913.

7. KUTENAI

Chamberlain, A.F. Report on the Kootenay Indians. BAAS, LXII, 549-617. 1892.

Turney-High, H.H. Ethnography of the Kutenai. MAAA, LVI, 1-202. 1941.

Baillie-Grohman, W.A. The Kootenay Country. GJ, LII, 44-51. 1918.

Boas, F. Additional Notes on the Kutenai Language. IJAL, IV, 85-104. 1927.

--- Einige Sagen der Kootenay. VBGA, 1891, 161-2.

--- First General Report on the Indians of British Columbia. BAAS, LIX, 801-900. 1889.

--- Kinship Terms of the Kutenai Indians. AA, n.s., XXI, 98-101. 1919.

--- Kutenai Tales. BBAE, LIX, 1-387. 1918.

--- Kutonáqa. BAAS, LIX, 889-93. 1889.

Campbell, J. The Kootenay and Tsimshian Languages. PTRSC, ser. 2, IV, ii, 23-42. 1898.

Canestrelli, P. Grammar of the Kutenai Language.
IJAL, IV, 1-84. 1927.

Chamberlain, A.F. Beitrag zur Pflanzenkunde der
Naturvölker Amerika's. VBGA, 1895, 551-6.

--- The Coyote and the Owl. MICA, 1893, 282-4.

--- Earlier and Later Kootenay Onomatology. AA,
n.s., IV, 229-36. 1902.

--- Geographic Terms of Kootenay Origin. AA, n.s.,
IV, 348-50. 1902.

--- Incorporation in the Kootenay Language. PAAAS,
XLIII, 346-8. 1894.

--- Der "Kartensinn" der Kitonaqa-Indianer. Globus,
XCV, 270-1. 1909.

--- Kootenay Group-Drawings. AA, n.s., III, 248-
56. 1901.

--- Kootenay Indian Drawings. BAAS, LXVII, 792-
3. 1897.

--- Kootenay Indian Personal Names. PAAAS, XLIV,
260-1. 1895.

--- The Kootenay Indians. AAR, 1905, 178-87.

--- A Kootenay Legend. JAFL, VII, 195-6. 1894.

--- Kootenay "Medicine Man." JAFL, XIV, 95-9.
1901.

--- Kutenai. BBAE, XXX, i, 740-2. 1907.

--- Kutenai Basketry. AA, n.s., XI, 318-19. 1909.

--- Kutenaian and Shoshonean. AA, n.s., XI, 535-
6. 1909.

--- New Words in the Kootenay Language. AA, VII,
186-92. 1894.

--- Note sur l'association des idées chez un peuple
primitif. BSAP, ser. 5, X, 132-4. 1909.

--- Note sur l'influence exercée sur les Indiens
Kitonaqa par les missionnaires catholiques. REES,
II, 155-7. 1909.

--- Notes on the Kootenay Indians. AAOJ, XV, 292-
4; XVI, 271-4; XVII, 68-72. 1893-95.

--- Noun Composition in the Kootenay Language. A,
V, 787-90. 1910.

--- Sagen vom Ursprung der Fliegen und Moskiten.
Am Urquell, IV, 129-31. 1893.

--- Some Kutenai Linguistic Material. AA, n.s., XI,
13-26. 1909.

--- Sulle significazioni nella lingua degli indigeni
Americani detti Kitonaqa (Kootenay) dei termini
che denotano gli stati e le condizioni del corpo e
dell'animo. AAE, XXIII, 393-9. 1893.

--- Terms for the Body, Its Parts, Organs, etc., in
the Language of the Kootenay Indians. Boas
Anniversary Volume, pp. 94-107. New York, 1906.

--- Über Personennamen der Kitonaqa-Indianer.
ZE, XLI, 378-80. 1909.

--- Der Wettlauf. Am Urquell, III, 212-13. 1892.

Chamberlain, A.F. Word-Formation in the Kootenay
Language. PAAAS, XLIV, 259-60. 1895.

--- Words Expressive of Cries and Noises in the Kootenay Language. AA, VII, 68-70. 1894.

Curtis, E.S. The North American Indian, VII, 117-55,
167-79. 1911.

Duboc, J.L. Cordage of the Early Northwest Indians.
MMH, III, ii, 42-7. 1953.

Garvin, P.L. Christian Names in Kutenai. IJAL, XIII,
69-77. 1947.

--- Colloquial Kutenai Text. IJAL, XX, 316-34. 1954.

--- Kutenai. IJAL, XIV, 37-42, 87-90, 171-87; XVII,
84-97. 1948, 1951.

--- Kutenai Lexical Innovations. Word, IV, 120-6.
1948.

--- L'Obviation en Kutenai. Bulletin de la Société
Linguistique de Paris, XLVII, 166-212. 1951.

--- Short Kutenai Texts. IJAL, XIX, 305-11. 1953.

--- Structure and Variation in Language and Culture.
ICA, XXIX, iii, 216-21. 1951.

Graham, C. Fur and Gold in the Kootenays. 206 pp.
Vancouver, 1945.

Haugen, E. Syllabification in Kutenai. IJAL, XXII,
196-201. 1956.

Kissell, M.L. A Kutenai Berry-basket. AA, n.s., XI,
529-31. 1909.

Linderman, F.B. Kootenai Why Stories. 166 pp. New
York, 1926.

Malouf, C.A. Early Kutenai History. MMH, II, ii,
5-10. 1952.

Malouf, C.A. and White, T. Kutenai Calendar
Records. MMH, III, ii, 34-39. 1953.

--- Recollections of Lasso Stasso. MSASP, XII, 8 pp.
1952.

Mason, O.T. Pointed Bark Canoes of the Kutenai and
Amur. RUSNM, 1899, 523-37.

Mathias, C.B. "Firsts" among the Flathead Lake Kutenai. MSASP, VIII, 4 pp. 1952.

Morgan, L.H. Systems of Consanguinity and Affinity.
SCK, XVII, 291-382. 1871.

Palliser, J. Further Papers. 325 pp. London, 1860.

Ray, V.F. Plateau. AR, VIII, 99-257. 1942.

Sapir, E. Kinship Terms of the Kootenay Indians.
AA, n.s., XX, 414-18. 1918.

Schaeffer, C.E. The Bear Foster Parent Tale: A
Kutenai Version. JAFL, LX, 286-8. 1947.

--- Molded Pottery among the Kutenai Indians.
MSASP, VI, 8 pp. 1952.

Smyth, F.J. Tales of the Kootenays. 205 pp. Cranbrook, B.C., 1938.

Sperlin, O.B. Two Kootenay Women masquerading as
Men. WHQ, XXI, 120-30. 1930.

Teit, J.A. Traditions and Information Regarding
the Tona'xa. AA, n.s., XXXII, 624-32. 1930.

Tolmie, W.F., and Dawson, G.M. Comparative
Vocabularies of the Indian Tribes of British Columbia, pp. 79B-87B, 102B-111B. Montreal, 1884.

Turney-High, H.H. Two Kutenai Stories. JAFL,
LIV, 191-6. 1941.

White, T. Kutenai Pipes. Western Anthropology, I,
1-11. Missoula, 1955.

Wilson, E.F. The Kootenay Indians. OFC, III, xiii.
1890.

--- The Kootenay Indians. JAFL, III, 10-12. 1890.

--- Report on the Indian Tribes. TESL, n.s., IV,
304-6. 1866.

8. LAKE

Also called Senijextee.

Curtis, E.S. The North American Indian, VII, 69-
114. Norwood, 1911.

Teit, J.A. The Salishan Tribes of the Western Plateaus. ARBAE, XLV, 37-396. 1930.

9. LILLOOET

Teit, J.A. The Lillooet Indians. MAMNH,
IV, 193-300. 1906.

Boas, F. Physical Characteristics of the Tribes of the
North Pacific Coast. BAAS, LXI, 424-49. 1891.

--- Terms of Relationship of the Salish Languages.
BAAS, LX, 688-92. 1890.

Dawson, G.M. Notes on the Shuswap People. PTRSC,
IX, ii, 3-44. 1891.

Durieu, P. Polyglott Manuel, pp. 380-411. Kamloops, 1896.

Elliott, W.C. Lake Lillooet Tales. JAFL, XLIV,
166-81. 1931.

Farrand, L. Basketry Designs of the Salish Indians.
MAMNH, II, 391-9. 1900.

Gibbs, G. Vocabulary of the Lilowat. CNAE, I,
268-83. 1877.

Hill-Tout, C. Report on the Ethnology of the
StlatlumH. JAI, XXXV, 126-218. 1905.

Ray, V.F. Plateau. AR, VIII, 99-257. 1942.

Schmidt, W. Die Inland-Selish Stämme. UG, II,
348-77; V, 391-471. 1929, 1934.

Teit, J.A. Traditions of the Lillooet Indians. JAFL,
XXV, 287-371. 1912.

Tolmie, W.F., and Dawson, G.M. Comparative Vocabularies of the Indian Tribes of British Columbia,
pp. 63B-73B. Montreal, 1884.

Wingert, P.S. American Indian Sculpture. 144 pp.
New York, 1949.

10. MOLALA

Curtis, E.S. The North American Indian, VIII, 195-8.
Norwood, 1911.

Farrand, L. Molala. BBAE, XXX, i, 930. 1907.

Murdock, G.P. Notes on the Tenino, Molala, and
Paiute of Oregon. AA, n.s., XL, 395-402. 1938.

11. NEZ PERCE

Also called Sahaptin.

Spinden, H.J. The Nez Percé Indians. MAAA, II,
165-274. 1908.

Ainslie, G. Notes on the Grammar of the Nez Percés
Language. BGGST, II, 271-7. 1876.

Alvord, B. Concerning the Manners and Customs, the
Superstitions, &c., of the Indians of Oregon. HCPIT,
V, 651-7. 1855.

Burbank, E.A., and Royce, E. Burbank among the Indians, pp. 175-84. Caldwell, 1946.

Brady, C.T. Northwestern Fights and Fighters. 373 pp.
New York, 1907.

Burns, R.I. A Jesuit in the War against the Northern
Indians. RACHS, LXI, 9-54. 1950.

--- The Jesuits, the Northern Indians, and the Nez Perce
War of 1877. PNQ, XLII, 40-76. 1951.

Bushnell, D.I. Sketches by Paul Kane in the Indian
Country, 1845-1848. SMC, XCIX, i, 1-25. 1940.

Butterfield, G. Romantic Historical Tale of the Nez
Perces. OHQ, XLIII, 150-7. 1942.

Cataldo, J.M., tr. Jesus-Christ-nim kinne vetas-pa
kut kaᵻkala time-nin i-ues pilep-eza-pa taz-pa
tamtai-pa numipu-timt-ki. 386 pp. Portland, 1915.

Clark, E.E. The Pleiades: Indian and Greek Versions.
RSSCW, XIX, 203-4. 1951.

--- Some Nez Perce Traditions Told by Chief Armstrong.
OHQ, LIII, 181-91. 1952.

--- Watkuese and Lewis and Clark. WF, XII, 175-8.
1953.

Clark, J.S. The Nez Percés in Exile. PNQ, XXXVI,
213-32. 1945.

Coale, G.L. Ethnohistorical Sources for the Nez Percé
Indians. E, III, 246-55, 346-60. 1956.

Coale, G.L. Notes on the Guardian Spirit Concept among the Nez Perce. IAE, XLVIII, 135-48. 1958.

Curtis, E.S. The North American Indian, VIII, 3-76, 157-72, 183-5, 191-5. Norwood, 1911.

Daugherty, R.D. and Dammel, E.A. Preliminary Excavations of a Burial Site on the Snake River. RSSCW, XX, 122-34. 1952.

Donaldson, T. The George Catlin Indian Gallery. RUSNM, 1885, 94-9.

Farrand, L. Notes on the Nez Percé Indians. AA, n.s., XXIII, 244-6. 1921.

Foreman, G. The Last Trek of the Indians, pp. 322-30. Chicago, 1946.

Gatschet, A.S. Adjectives of Color in Indian Languages. AN, XIII, 475-85. 1879.

Haines, F. Chief Joseph and the Nez Perce Warriors. PNQ, XLV, 1-7. 1954.

--- The Nez Percés. 346 pp. Norman, 1955.

--- Red Eagles of the Northwest. 361 pp. Portland, 1939.

Henshaw, H.W., and Farrand, L. Nez Percés. BBAE, XXX, ii, 65-8. 1910.

Howard, H.A., and McGrath, D.L. War Chief Joseph. 362 pp. Caldwell, 1941.

Howard, O.O. My Life and Experiences among Our Hostile Indians. 570 pp. Hartford, 1907.

--- Nez Percé Joseph. 274 pp. Boston, 1881.

Irving, W. The Adventures of Captain Bonneville. Rev. edit. 428 pp. New York, 1850.

Leepar, R.D., and Beall, T. Legends of the Nez Perces. 23 pp. n.d.

McBeth, K.C. The Nez Perces since Lewis and Clark. 272 pp. New York, 1850.

McWhorter, L.V. Yellow Wolf. 324 pp. Caldwell, 1940.

Morvillo. A Numipu or Nez Percé Grammar. De Smet, 1891.

Osborne, D. Nez Perce Horse Castration. DJA, I, 113-22. 1955.

Packard, R.L. Notes on the Mythology and Religion of the Nez Percé. JAFL, IV, 327-30. 1891.

Parker, S. Journal of an Exploring Tour beyond the Rocky Mountains. Ithaca, 1838.

Phinney, A. Nez Percé Texts. CUCA, XXV, 1-497. 1934.

Schmidt, M.F., and Brown, D. Fighting Indians of the West, pp. 251-72. New York, 1948.

Scouler, J. On the Indian Tribes inhabiting the North-West Coast of America. JESL, I, 228-52. 1848.

Skeels, D. A Classification of Humor in Nez Perce Mythology. JAFL, LXVII, 57-64. 1954.

Skeels, D. The Function of Humor in Three Nez Perce Indian Myths. American Imago, XI, 248-61. 1954.

Spinden, H.J. Myths of the Nez Percé Indians. JAFL, XXI, 13-23, 149-58. 1908.

--- Nez Percé Tales. MAFLS, XI, 180-201. 1917.

Velten, H.V. The Nez Percé Verb. PNQ, XXXIV, 271-92. 1943.

Wallace, W.S. An Early North to South Journey in the Intermountain Area of Western America. SWL, XV, iv, 54-57. 1950.

White, E. Testimonials and Records. Washington, 1861.

Wyman, A. Cornhusk Bags of the Nez Percé Indians. M, IX, 89-95. 1935.

12. NICOLA

Allison, Mrs. S.S. Account of the Similkameen Indians. JAI, XXI, 305-18. 1892.

Anonymous. Stuichamukh. BBAE, XXX, ii, 645. 1910.

Boas, F. The Tinneh Tribe of Nicola Valley. BAAS, LXV, 551-5. 1895.

--- Vocabulary of the Athapascan Tribe of Nicola Valley. IJAL, III, 36-8. 1924.

Harrington, J.P. Southern Peripheral Athapaskawan Origins, Divisions and Migrations. SMC, C, 503-32. 1940.

Leechman, J.D., and Harrington, M.R. String Records of the Northwest. IN, n.s., XVI, 1-64. 1921.

Morice, A.G. The Great Déné Race. A, I, 504-6. 1906.

13. OKANAGON

Including the Northern Okanagon and the Sinkaietk or Southern Okanagon.

Cline, W., Commons, R.S., Mandelbaum, M., Post, R.H., and Walters, L.V.W. The Sinkaietk or Southern Okanagon of Washington, ed. L. Spier, GSA, VI, 1-262. 1938.

Teit, J.A. The Salishan Tribes of the Western Plateaus. ARBAE, XLV, 198-294. 1930.

Allison, Mrs. S.S. Account of the Similkameen Indians. JAI, XXI, 305-18. 1892.

Boas, F. Terms of Relationship of the Salish Languages. BAAS, LX, 688-92. 1890.

Dawson, G.M.   Notes on the Shuswap People of British Columbia. PTRSC, IX, ii, 3-44. 1891.

Gibbs, G.   Vocabulary of the Okinaken. CNAE, I, 248-64. 1877.

Gould, M.K.   Okanagon Tales. MAFLS, XI, 98-100. 1917.

Hill-Tout, C.   Report on the Ethnology of the Okanǎk·rn. JAI, XLI, 130-61. 1911.

Hulse, F.S.   Linguistic Barriers to Gene-Flow. AJPA, n.s., XV, 235-46. 1957.

Lerman, N.H.   An Okanagan Winter Dance. ABC, IV, 35-36. 1953/54.

Morgan, L.H.   Systems of Consanguinity and Affinity. SCK, XVII, 291-382. 1871.

Mourning Dove (Humishuma).   Coyote Stories, ed. H.D.Bure. 228 pp. Caldwell, 1933.

Ross, A.   Adventures of the First Settlers on the Oregon or Columbia River, ed. M.M.Quaife, pp. 308-56. Chicago, 1923.

Teit, J.A.   Okanagon Tales. MAFLS, XI, 65-97. 1917.

Tolmie, W.F.   Vocabulary of the Wa-ky-na-kaine. CNAE, I, 248-65. 1877.

Wade, M.S.   The Thompson Country. 136 pp. Kamloops, 1907.

14. SANPOIL

Including the Colville, the Nespelem, and the Sanpoil.

Ray, V.F.   The Sanpoil and Nespelem. UWPA, V, 1-237. 1932.

Clark, E.E.   The Bridge of the Gods in Fact and Fancy. OHQ, LIII, 29-38. 1952.

Curtis, E.S.   The North American Indian, VII, 62-5, 69-114, 179-89. Norwood, 1911.

Gibbs, G.   Vocabulary of the Shwoyelpi. CNAE, I, 248-65. 1877.

Gould, M.K.   Sanpoil Tales. MAFLS, XI, 101-13. 1917.

Gwydir, R.D.   A Record of the San Poil Indians. WHQ, VIII, 243-50. 1917.

Mengarini, G.   Vocabulary of the Skoylpeli. CNAE, I, 248-65. 1877.

Mills, J.E. and Osborne, C.   Material Culture of an Upper Coulee Rockshelter. AAn, XVII, 352-9. 1952.

Ray, V.F.   The Kolaskin Cult. AA, n.s., XXXVIII, 67-75. 1936.

Ray, V.F.   Pottery on the Middle Columbia. AA, n.s., XXXIV, 127-33. 1932.

--- Plateau. AR, VIII, 99-257. 1942.

--- Sanpoil Folk Tales. JAFL, XLVI, 129-87. 1933.

Schmidt, W.   Die Sanpoil und Nespelem. UG, V, 857-75. 1934.

Teit, J.A.   The Salishan Tribes of the Western Plateaus. ARBAE, XLV, 37-396. 1930.

Vogt, H.   Salishan Studies. Skrifter utgitt av det Norske Videnskaps-Akademi, Historisk-filosofisk klasse, II, 1-19. 1940.

15. SHUSWAP

Teit, J.A.   The Shuswap. MAMNH, IV, 447-758. 1909.

Boas, F.   Sagen aus Britisch-Columbien. VBGA, 1891, 532-46.

--- The Shuswap. BAAS, LX, 632-47, 683-5. 1890.

--- Terms of Relationship of the Salish Languages. BAAS, LX, 688-92. 1890.

--- Zur Anthropologie der nordamerikanischen Indianer. VBGA, 1895, 367-411.

Dawson, G.M.   Notes on the Shuswap People. PTRSC, IX, ii, 3-44. 1891.

Gibbs, G.   Vocabulary of the Shihwapmukh. CNAE, I, 247-64. 1877.

Mackenzie, A.   Voyages from Montreal, ed. M.M. Quaife, pp. 268-94. Chicago, 1931.

Ray, V.F.   Plateau. AR, VIII, 99-257. 1942.

Schmidt, W.   Die Inland-Selish Stämme. UG, II, 348-77; V, 391-471. 1929, 1934.

Smith, H.I.   Some Indians of British Columbia. SW, XLI, 477-83. 1912.

Tolmie, W.F.   Vocabulary of the Shooswaap. CNAE, I, 247-64. 1877.

Wade, M.S.   The Thompson Country. 136 pp. Kamloops, 1907.

16. SPOKAN

Teit, J.A.   The Salishan Tribes of the Western Plateaus. ARBAE, XLV, 295-396. 1930.

Burns, R.I.   A Jesuit in the War against the Northern Indians. RACHS, LXI, 9-54. 1950.

Curtis, E.S.   The North American Indian, VII, 54-62, 69-114, 179-89. Norwood, 1911.

Gibbs, G.   Vocabulary of the Spokan. CNAE, I, 249-65. 1877.

Gwydir, R.D. Prehistoric Spokane--an Indian legend. WHQ, I, 136-7. 1907.

Manring, B.F. The Conquest of the Coeur d'Alenes, Spokanes, and Palouses. 280 pp. Spokane, 1912.

Morgan, L.H. Systems of Consanguinity and Affinity. SCK, XVII, 293-382. 1871.

Vogt, H. Salishan Studies. Skrifter utgitt av det Norske Videnskaps-Akademi, Historisk-filosofisk klasse, II, 1-19. 1940.

17. TENINO

Including the John Day, the Tenino, the Tygh, and the Wayam or Deschutes, known collectively as the Warmsprings Sahaptin.

Farrand, L. Des Chutes. BBAE, XXX, i, 387-8. 1907.

--- Tyigh. BBAE, XXX, ii, 859-60. 1910.

Mooney, J. The Ghost-Dance Religion. ARBAE, XIV, ii, 739-44. 1893.

Murdock, G.P. Notes on the Tenino, Molala, and Paiute of Oregon. AA, n.s., XL, 395-402. 1938.

--- Social Organization of the Tenino. MPR, i, 299-315. 1958.

--- Social Structure, pp. 111-12, 229. New York, 1949.

Ray, V.F. Plateau. AR, VIII, 99-257. 1942.

Strong, W.D., Schenck, W.E., and Steward, J.H. Archaeology of the Dalles-Deschutes Region. UCP, XXIX, 1-154. 1930.

Terry, J. Sculptured Anthropoid Ape Heads found in or near the Valley of the John Day River. 15 pp. New York, 1891.

18. THOMPSON

Also called Nitlakapamuk.

Teit, J.A. The Thompson Indians. MAMNH, II, 163-392. 1900.

Abraham, O., and Hornbostel, E.M. von. Phonographirte Indianermelodieen aus British Columbia. Boas Anniversary Volume, pp. 447-74. New York, 1906.

Barbeau, M. On Interior Salish Work, 1912. SRGSC, 1912, 461-3.

Boas, F. The NtlakyápamuQ. BAAS, LXVIII, 654-62. 1898.

Boas, F. Sagen aus Britisch-Columbien. VBGA, 1891, 546-9.

Farrand, L. Basketry Designs of the Salish Indians. MAMNH, II, 391-9. 1900.

Gibbs, G. Vocabulary of the Nitkutemukh. CNAE, I, 248-64. 1877.

Good, J.B. A Vocabulary and Outlines of Grammar of the Nitlakapamuk or Thompson Tongue. 46 pp. Victoria, 1880.

Hill-Tout, C. Notes on the N'tlakápamuq Indians. BAAS, LXIX, 500-85. 1899.

--- "Sqaktktquaclt," or the Benign-faced. FL, X, 195-216. 1899.

Jenness, D. The "Snare" Indians. PTRSC, ser. 3, XXXIII, ii, 103-5. 1939.

Kissell, M.L. A New Type of Spinning in North America. AA, n.s., XVIII, 264-70. 1916.

Ray, V.F. Plateau. AR, VIII, 99-257. 1942.

Schmidt, W. Die Inland-Selish Stämme. UG, II, 348-77; V, 391-471. 1929, 1934.

Smith, H.I. Archaeology of Lytton. MAMNH, II, 129-61. 1900.

--- Archaeology of Lytton. RP, I, 205-18. 1902.

--- Archaeology of the Thompson River Region. MAMNH, II, 401-42. 1900.

--- The Thompson Indians. SW, XL, 23-36. 1911.

Steedman, E.V. The Ethnobotany of the Thompson Indians. ARBAE, XLV, 441-522. 1928.

Stewart, N., and Ravenhill, A. Meet Mr. Coyote. 28 pp. Victoria, 1941.

Teit, J.A. European Tales from the Upper Thompson Indians. JAFL, XXIX, 301-29. 1916.

--- More Thompson Indian Tales. JAFL, L, 173-90. 1937.

--- Mythology of the Thompson Indians. MAMNH, XII, 199-416. 1912.

--- A Rock Painting of the Thompson River Indians. BAMNH, VIII, 227-30. 1896.

--- Tattooing and Face and Body Painting of the Thompson Indians. ARBAE, XLV, 397-439. 1930.

--- Thompson Tales. MAFLS, XI, 1-64. 1917.

--- Traditions of the Thompson River Indians. MAFLS, VI, 1-137. 1898.

Wade, M.S. The Thompson Country. 136 pp. Kamloops, 1907.

Wingert, P.S. American Indian Sculpture. 144 pp. New York, 1949.

19. UMATILLA

Culin, S. A Summer Trip among the Western Indians. BFMUP, III, 159-64. 1901.

Curtis, E.S. The North American Indian, VIII, 79-82. 1911.

Jacobs, M. A Sketch of Northern Sahaptin Grammar. UWPA, IV, 85-292. 1931.

Ray, V.F. Plateau. AR, VIII, 99-257. 1942.

--- Tribal Distribution in Northeastern Oregon. AA, n.s., XL, 384-95. 1938.

Stern, T. A Umatilla Prophet Cult. ACISA, V, 346-50. 1960.

20. WALLAWALLA

Including the Palus, the Wallawalla, and the Wauyukma.

Curtis, E.S. The North American Indian, VIII, 79-82. Norwood, 1911.

Gairdner. Notes on the Geography of the Columbia River. JRGS, XI, 250-7. 1841.

Kane, P. Notes of Travel among the Walla-Walla Indians. CJ, n.s., I, 417-24. 1856.

Manring, B.F. The Conquest of the Coeur d'Alenes, Spokanes and Palouses. 280 pp. Spokane, 1912.

Scouler, J. On the Indian Tribes inhabiting the North-West Coast of America. JESL, I, 228-52. 1848.

21. WISHRAM

Including the Wasco and the Wishram.

Spier, L., and Sapir, E. Wishram Ethnography. UWPA; III, 151-300. 1930.

Alvord, B. Concerning the Manners and Customs, the Superstitions, &c., of the Indians of Oregon. HCPIT, V, 651-7. 1855.

Biddle, H.J. Wishram. OHQ, XXVII, 113-30. 1926.

Boas, F. Chinook. BBAE, XL, i, 638-45, 650-4. 1911.

Curtis, E.S. The North American Indian, VIII, 86-154, 172-81, 185-91, 198-205. Norwood, 1911.

Dyk, W. and Hymes, D.H. Stress Accent in Wishram Chinook. IJAL, XXII, 238-41. 1956.

Hymes, D.H. Two Wasco Motifs. JAFL, LXVI, 69-70. 1953.

Lee, D., and Frost, J.H. Ten Years in Oregon. 344 pp. New York, 1844.

Sapir, E. A Chinookan Phonetic Law. IJAL, IV, 105-10. 1926.

--- Preliminary Report on the Language and Mythology of the Upper Chinook. AA, n.s., IX, 533-44. 1907.

Sapir, E. Terms of Relationship and the Levirate. AA, n.s., XVIII, 327-37. 1916.

--- Wasco. BBAE, XXX, ii, 917-18. 1910.

--- Wishram Texts. PAES, II, 1-314. 1909.

Strong, W.D., and Schenck, W.E. Petroglyphs near the Dalles of the Columbia River. AA, n.s., XXVII, 76-90. 1925.

Strong, W.D., Schenck, W.E., and Steward, J.H. Archaeology of the Dalles-Deschutes Region. UCP, XXIX, 1-154. 1930.

22. YAKIMA

Burns, R.I. A Jesuit in the War Against the Northern Indians. RACHS, LXI, 9-54. 1950.

Clark, E.E. The Bridge of the Gods in Fact and Fancy. OHQ, LIII, 29-38. 1952.

Curtis, E.S. The North American Indian, VII, 3-34, 159-61, 172-9. Norwood, 1911.

Desmond, G.R. Gambling among the Yakima. CUAS, XIV, 56 pp. 1952.

Hulse, F.S. Linguistic Barriers to Gene-Flow. AJPA, n.s., XV, 235-46. 1957.

Leechman, J.D., and Harrington, M.R. String Records of the Northwest. INM, ser. 2, XVI, 1-64. 1921.

Lyman, W.D. Myths and Superstitions of the Oregon Indians. PAAS, n.s., XVI, 221-51. 1904.

McWhorter, L.V. The Crime against the Yakimas. 56 pp. North Yakima, 1913.

Mooney, J. The Ghost-Dance Religion. ARBAE, XIV, ii, 708-45. 1893.

--- Yakima. BBAE, XXX, ii, 983-4. 1910.

Morgan, L.H. Systems of Consanguinity and Affinity. SCK, XVII, 291-382. 1871.

Pandosy, M.C. Grammar and Dictionary of the Yakama Language. 56 pp. New York, 1862.

Relander, C. et al. The Yakimas, Treaty Centennial, 1855-1955. Yakima, Washington, 1955.

St. Onge, L.N. Alphabet Yakama. 101 pp. Montreal, 1872.

Smith, H.I. An Archaeological Expedition to the Columbia Valley. RP, IV, 119-27. 1905.

--- The Archaeology of the Yakima Valley. APAM, VI, 1-171. 1910.

--- A Costumed Human Figure from Tampico. BAMNH, XX, 195-203. 1904.

Splawn, A.J. Ka-mi-akin. 500 pp. Portland, 1944.

Steward, J.H. A Peculiar Type of Stone Implement. AA, n.s., XXX, 314-16. 1928.

Strong, J.C. Wah-kee-nah and Her People, 275 pp. New York, 1893.

IX. PLAINS

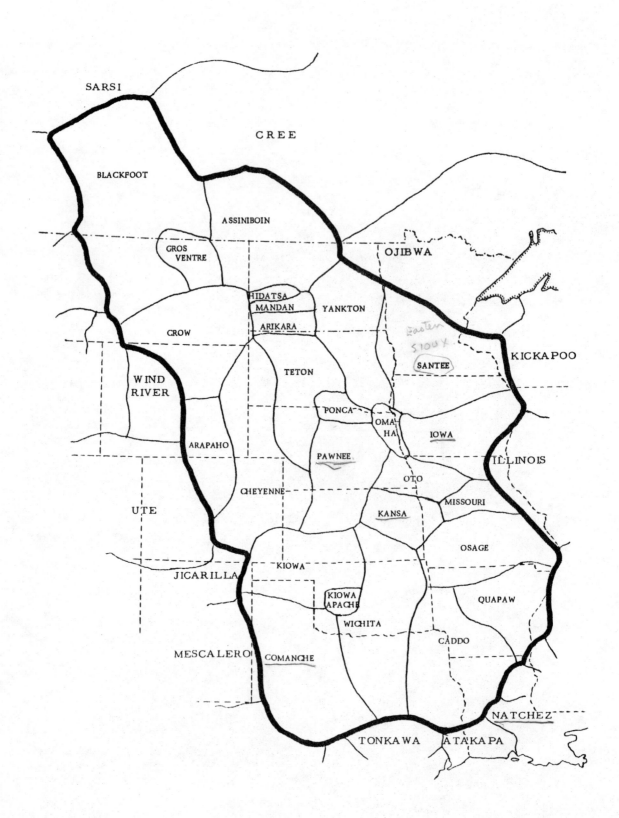

The tribes of this area are grouped under the following linguistic stocks:

Algonkian: Arapaho, Blackfoot, Cheyenne, Gros Ventre.

Athapaskan: Kiowa Apache.

Caddoan: Arikara, Caddo, Pawnee, Wichita.

Kiowan: Kiowa.

Siouan: Assiniboin, Crow, Hidatsa, Iowa, Kansa, Mandan, Missouri, Omaha, Osage, Oto, Ponca, Quapaw, Santee, Teton, Yankton.

Uto-Aztekan (Shoshonean branch): Comanche.

Abel, A.H. The History of Events that Resulted in Indian Consolidation West of the Mississippi River. Annual Report of the American Historical Association, I, 233-450. 1908.

--- Indian Reservations in Kansas. CKSHS, VIII, 72-109. 1902.

Alexander, H.B. The Horse in American Indian Culture. So Live the Works of Men, ed. D. D. Brand and F.E. Harvey, pp. 65-74. Albuquerque, 1939.

Allen, L. Siouan and Iroquoian. IJAL, VI, 185-93. 1931.

Anderson, R. Reduction of Variants as a Measure of Cultural Integration. Essays in the Science of Culture in Honor of Leslie A. White, 50-62. New York, 1960.

Anonymous. Indians on Federal Reservations in the United States. U.S. Public Health Service, Publication, DCXV, ii, 17 pp; iii, 73 pp. 1958-59.

Artichoker, J. Indians of South Dakota. South Dakota Department of Public Instruction, Bulletin 67A. 1956.

Averkieva, J.P. and Zolotorevskaia, I.A. Indejcy Prerij. Trudy Instituta Etnografii Imena N.N. Mikhluho-Maklaia, XXV, 98-110. 1955.

Barbeau, M., and Melvin, G. The Indian Speaks. 117 pp. Toronto, 1943.

Barber, B. A Socio-Cultural Interpretation of the Peyote Cult. AA, n.s., XLIII, 673-5. 1941.

Beidleman, R.G. A Partial, Annotated Bibliography of Colorado Ethnology. Colorado College Studies, II, 55 pp. 1958.

Benedict, R.F. The Vision in Plains Culture. AA, n.s., XXIV, 1-23. 1922.

Biasutti, R. Le Razzi e i Popoli della Terra, 2nd ed., IV, 402-24. Torino, 1957.

Blankinship, J.W. Native Economic Plants of Montana. Montana State Agricultural Experiment Station Bulletin, LVI, 38 pp. 1905.

Boller, H.A. Among the Indians. 428 pp. Philadelphia, 1868.

Bolton, H.E., ed. Spanish Exploration in the Southwest, 1542-1706. 487 pp. New York, 1916.

Bourke, J.G. MacKenzie's Last Fight with the Cheyennes. Journal of the Military Service Institution of the United States, XI, 29-49, 198-221. 1890.

Braasch, W.F. et al. Survey of Medical Care among the Upper Midwest Indians. Journal of the American Medical Association, CXXXIX, 220-5. 1949.

Brackenridge, H.M. Views of Louisiana. 304 pp. Pittsburgh, 1814.

Bushnell, D.I. Ethnographical Material from North America in Swiss Collections. AA, n.s., X, 1-15. 1908.

--- The Various Uses of Buffalo Hair by the North American Indians. AA, n.s., XI, 401-25. 1909.

Cameron, W.B. Costumes of the Plains Indians. B, CCLXXIV, iii, 33-7. 1943.

Campbell, T.N. Origin of the Mescal Bean Cult. AA, LX, 156-58. 1958.

Carroll, H.B. The Texan Santa Fe Trail. PPHR, XXIV, 1-201. 1954.

Carter, R.G. On the Border with MacKenzie, pp. 253-300. Washington, 1935.

Catlin, G. North American Portfolio. 16 pp. New York, 1845.

Childears, L. Montana Place-Names from Indian Myth and Legend. WF, IX, 263-4. 1950.

Chittenden, H.M. The American Fur Trade of the Far West, II, 841-81. New York, 1902.

Chittenden, H.M., and Richardson, A.T., eds. Life, Letters and Travels of Father Pierre-Jean De Smet. 4 vols. New York, 1905.

Clark, W.P. The Indian Sign Language. 443 pp. Philadelphia, 1885.

Clements, F. Plains Indian Tribal Correlations with Sun Dance Data. AA, n.s., XXXIII, 216-27. 1931.

Collier, D. The Sun Dance of the Plains Indians. AI, III, 359-64. 1943.

Colorado State Historical Society. The Indians of Colorado. 52 pp. Denver, 1957.

Crockett, B.N. Health Conditions in Indian Territory. CO, XXXV, 80-90; XXXVI, 21-39. 1957-58.

Cutler, J. A Topographical Description of the State of Ohio, Indiana Territory, and Louisiana. 219 pp. Boston, 1812.

Dale, H.E., ed. The Ashley-Smith Explorations and the Discovery of a Central Route to the Pacific. Cleveland, 1918.

DeBarthe, J. Life and Adventures of Frank Grouard. 296 pp. Norman, 1958.

Devoto, B. Across the Wide Missouri. 511 pp. Boston, 1947.

Dobie, J.F. Indian Horses and Horsemanship. Southwest Review, XXXV, 265-75. 1950.

Dodge, H. Report on the Expedition of Dragoons. American State Papers, Military Affairs, VI, 130-46. 1861.

Dodge, R.I. The Plains of the Great West and Their Inhabitants. 448 pp. New York, 1877.

Domenech, E. Seven Years Residence in the Great Deserts of North America. 2 vols., 469, 477 pp. London, 1860.

Donaldson, T. The George Catlin Indian Gallery in the U.S. National Museum. RUSNM, 1885, 1-939.

Dorsey, J.O. Camping Circles of Siouan Tribes. AA, II, 175-7. 1889.

--- Migrations of Siouan Tribes. AN, XX, 211-22. 1886.

--- Nanibozhu in Siouan Mythology. JAFL, V, 293-304. 1892.

--- The Place of Gentes in Siouan Camping Circles. AA, II, 375-9. 1889.

--- Siouan Onomatopes. AA, V, 1-8. 1892.

Douglas, F.H. The Buffalo and the Indian. DAMLS, VII, 1-4. 1930.

--- An Incised Bison Rawhide Parfleche. MCN, VI, 23-5. 1938.

--- Plains Beads and Beadwork Designs. DAMLS, LXXIII-LXXIV, 90-6. 1936.

--- Plains Indian Clothing. DAMLS, XXIV, 1-4. 1931.

--- The Plains Indian Earth Lodge. DAMLS, XX, 1-4. 1931.

--- The Plains Indian Tipi. DAMLS, XIX, 1-4. 1931.

--- Plains Indian Tribes. DAMLS, XXIII, 1-4. 1931.

--- Two Plains Bison Hair Ropes. MCN, V, 19-22. 1938.

Douglas, F.H., and A. Marriott. Metal Jewelry of the Peyote Cult. MCN, XVII, 17-82. 1942.

Driver, H.E. The Measurement of Geographical Distribution Form. AA, n.s., XLI, 583-8. 1939.

Driver, H.E., and Kroeber, A.L. Quantitative Expression of Cultural Relationships. UCP, XXXI, 226-36. 1932.

Dunn, D. The Development of Modern American Indian Painting in the Southwest and Plains Areas. EP, LVIII, 331-53. 1951.

--- Oscar Howe: Sioux Artist. EP, LXIV, 167-73. 1957.

Eisenstadt, S.N. Plains Indian Age Groups. Man, LIV, 6-8. 1954.

Ewers, J.C. Hair Pipes in Plains Indian Adornment. BBAE, CLXIV, 29-86. 1957.

Ewers, J.C. The Indian Trade of the Upper Missouri before Lewis and Clark. BMHS, X, 429-46. 1954.

--- Plains Indian Painting. 84 pp. Palo Alto, 1939.

--- Plains Indian War Medicine. Tomorrow, IV, iii, 85-90. 1956.

--- Selected References on the Plains Indians. Smithsonian Anthropological Bibliographies, I, 36 pp. 1960.

Farabee, W.C. Dress among the Plains Indian Women. MJ; XII, 239-51. 1921.

Farber, W.O., et al. Indians, Law Enforcement, and Local Government. State University of South Dakota, Government Research Bureau Report, XXXVII, 1-92. 1951.

Farnham, T.J. Travels in the Great Western Prairies. EWT, Vols. XXVIII-XXIX. 1906.

Fletcher, A.C. The Emblematic Use of the Tree in the Dakotan Group. PAAAS, XLV, 191-209. 1896.

Forsyth, T. Thomas Forsyth to Lewis Cass, October 29, 1831. E, IV, 198-210. 1957.

Fowke, G. Antiquities of Central and Southeastern Missouri. BBAE, XXXVII, 1-116. 1910.

Fowler, J. The Journal of Jacob Fowler. 183 pp. New York, 1898.

Frederikson, O.F. The Liquor Question among the Indian Tribes in Kansas, 1804-1881. University of Kansas, Bulletin, Humanistic Studies, IV, iv, 103 pp. 1932.

Frémont, D. Les Aborigènes du Nord-Ouest Canadien au Temps de La Vérendrye. Mémoires de la Société Royale du Canada, XLIII, 3e série, Sect. I, 7-21. 1949.

Fremont, J.C. Narrative of the Exploring Expedition to the Rocky Mountains. 186 pp. New York, 1846.

Fuller, H.M. and Hafen, L.R., ed. The Journal of Captain John R. Bell. FWRHS, VI, 349 pp. 1957.

Gallagher, O.R. and Powell, L.H. Time Perspective in Plains Indian Beaded Art. AA, LV, 609-13. 1953.

Garth, T.R. A Comparison of the Intelligence of Mexican and Mixed and Full Blood Indian Children. Psychological Review, XXX, 388-401. 1923.

--- The Intelligence of Full Blood Indians. Journal of Applied Psychology, IX, 382-9. 1925.

Gass, P. A Journal of the Voyages and Travels of a Corps of Discovery. Pittsburgh, 1807.

Gilmore, M.R. The Aboriginal Geography of the Nebraska Country. PMVHA, VI, 317-31. 1913.

--- Some Indian Ideas of Property. IN, V, 137-44. 1928.

Gladwin, T. Personality Structure in the Plains. PM, XXX, 111-24. 1957.

Gregg, J. Commerce of the Prairies. 2 vols. New York, 1844.

Grinnell, G.B. The Story of the Indian. 268 pp. New York, 1895.

Gunther, E. The Westward Movement of Some Plains Traits. AA, LII, 174-80. 1950.

Haekel, J. Totemismus und Zweiklassen-System bei den Sioux-Indianern. A, XXXII, 210-38, 450-501, 795-848. 1937.

--- Zum Ethnologischen Aussagewert von Kultur- parallelen. WVM, III, 176-90. 1955.

Hafen, L.R. and A.W., eds. Rufus B. Sage, His Letters and Papers, 1836-1847. FWRHS, IV, 354 pp.; V, 360 pp. 1956.

--- To the Rockies and Oregon, 1839-1842. FWRHS, III, 315 pp. 1955.

--- The Utah Expedition, 1857-1858. FWRHS, VII, 375 pp. 1958.

Haines, F. The Northward Spread of Horses among the Plains Indians. AA, n.s., XL, 429-37. 1938.

--- Where did the Plains Indians get Their Horses? AA, n.s., XL, 112-17. 1938.

Hall, H.U. A Buffalo Robe Biography. MJ, XVII, 5-35. 1926.

--- Some Shields of the Plains and Southwest. MJ, XVII, 37-61. 1926.

Hamilton, W.T. My Sixty Years on the Plains. 244 pp. New York, 1905.

Hammond, G.P. and Rey, A., eds. Narratives of the Coronado Expedition, 1540-1542. 413 pp. Albuquerque, 1940.

d'Harcourt, R. Arts de l'Amerique, pp. 35-42. Paris, 1948.

Harrington, M.R. Indian Tribes of the Plains. M, XV, 116-28, 168-77, 213-20; XVI, 5-15, 86- 93. 1941-42.

Haskell, M.L. Rubi's Inspection of the Frontier Presidios of New Spain, 1766-1768. Publications of the Southern California Historical Society, V, 33-43. 1917.

Hermant, P. Evolution économique et sociale de certaines peuplades de l'Amérique du Nord. BSRBG, XXIX, 5-30. 1905.

Herzog, G. Plains Ghost Dance and Great Basin Music. AA, n.s., XXXVII, 403-19. 1935.

Hewitt, J.N.B., ed. Journal of Rudolph Friederich Kurz. BBAE, CXV, 1-382. 1937.

Holling, H.C. The Book of Indians, pp. 45-72. New York, 1935.

Holmer, N.M. Lexical and Morphological Contacts between Siouan and Algonquian. Lunds Universitets Arsskrift, n.s., XLV, 1-36. 1949.

Hornaday, W.T. The Extermination of the Ameri- can Bison. RUSNM, 1887, ii, 369-548.

Houck, L., ed. The Spanish Régime in Missouri. 2 vols. Chicago, 1909.

Hough, W. Ceremonial and Other Practices on the Human Body among the Indians. ICA, XIX, 283- 5. 1915.

Howard, J.H. The Mescal Bean Cult of the Central and Southern Plains. AA, LIX, 75-87. 1957.

--- Pan-Indian Culture of Oklahoma. SM, LXXXI, 215-20. 1955.

--- Plains Indian Feathered Bonnets. PIA, II, 23-26. 1954.

Hrdlicka, A. Catalogue of Human Crania in the United States National Museum Collections. PUSNM, LXIX, v, 1-127. 1927.

Humphrey, N.D. A Characterization of Certain Plains Associations. AA, n.s., XLIII, 428-36. 1941.

Hunter, J.O. Manners and Customs of the Several Indian Tribes. 407 pp. Minneapolis, 1957.

Hyde, G.E. Indians of the High Plains. 231 pp. Nor- man, 1959.

Irving, W. The Adventures of Captain Bonneville. 428 pp. New York, 1851.

Jennings, J.D. The Archeology of the Plains: an Assessment. 180 pp. Salt Lake City, 1955.

--- Plainsmen of the Past. Washington, 1948.

Kane, P. Wanderings of an Artist among the Indians. 455 pp. London, 1859.

Krause, F. Zur Besiedelungsgeschichte der nord- amerikanischen Prärie. KBDGA, XLIV, 66-70. 1913.

Kroeber, A.L. The Ceremonial Organization of the Plains Indians. ICA, XV, ii, 53-63. 1906.

Lange, C.H. Plains-Southwestern Inter-Cultural Re- lations During the Historic Period. E, IV, 150-73. 1957.

--- A Reappraisal of Evidence of Plains Influences among the Rio Grande Pueblos. SJA, IX, 212-30. 1953.

Larpenteur, C. Forty Years a Fur Trader on the Upper Missouri, ed. E. Coues. 2 vols. New York, 1898.

Laviolette, G. Notes on the Aborigines of the Prairie Provinces. An, II, 107-30. 1956.

Leland, J.A.C. Indian Names in Missouri. Names, I, 266-73. 1953.

Lesser, A. Some Aspects of Siouan Kinship. ICA, XXIII, 563-71. 1928.

Lewis, M., and Clark, W. Travels. 3 vols. London, 1815.

Linton, R. The Origin of the Plains Earth Lodge. AA, n.s., XXVI, 247-57. 1924.

Long, J. Journal, 1768-1782. EWT, II, 329 pp. 1904.

Lowie, R.H. Indians of the Plains. 222 pp. New York, 1954.

--- Marriage and Family Life among the Plains Indians. SM, XXXIV, 462-4. 1932.

--- Plains Indian Age-Societies. APAM, XI, 877-992. 1916.

--- Reflections on the Plains Indians. AQ, III, 63-86. 1955.

--- Some Problems in Plains Indian Folklore. JAFL, LX, 401-3. 1947.

--- Studies in Plains Indian Folklore. UCP, XL, 1-28. 1942.

McCracken, H. George Catlin and the Old Frontier. 216 pp. New York, 1959.

McFarling, L. Exploring the Northern Plains, 1804-1878. 452 pp. Caldwell, 1955.

MacKenzie, A. Voyages. 498 pp. Toronto, 1927.

MacLean, J. Canadian Savage Folk. 641 pp. Toronto, 1897.

Mallery, G. Sign Language among North American Indians. ARBAE, I, 263-552. 1880.

--- The Sign Language of the Indians of the Upper Missouri. AAOJ, II, 218-28. 1880.

Marcy, R.B. Adventure on Red River. 199 pp. Norman, 1937.

Margry, P. Découvertes et Etablissements des Français. Parts 1-60. Paris, 1875-86.

Matthews, G.H. Proto-Siouan Kinship Terminology. AA, LXI, 252-78. 1959.

Matthews, W. The Earth Lodge in Art. AA, n.s., IV, 1-12. 1902.

Mattison, R.H. The Indian Reservation System on the Upper Missouri, 1865-1890. NeH, XXXVI, 141-72. 1955.

Michelson, T. Algonquian Notes. IJAL, IX, 103-12. 1939.

Mishkin, B. Rank and Warfare among the Plains Indians. MAES, III, 1-65. 1940.

Möllhausen, B. Diary of a Journey from the Mississippi to the Coasts of the Pacific. 2 vols. London, 1858.

Mooney, J. The Ghost-Dance Religion. ARBAE, XIV, 640-1136. 1896.

Morris, A. The Treaties of Canada with the Indians of Manitoba, the North-West Territories, and Keewa-tin. Toronto, 1880.

Morse, J. Report to the Secretary of War. 400 pp. New Haven, 1822.

Mulloy, W. The Northern Plains. AEUS, 124-38. 1952.

--- A Preliminary Historical Outline for the Northwestern Plains. UWP, XXII, i-ii, 1-235. 1958.

Mulvaney, C.P. The History of the North-West Rebellion of 1885. 424 pp. Toronto, 1885.

Muntsch, A. The Relations between Religion and Morality among the Plains Indians. PM, IV, 22-9. 1931.

Nasatir, A.P. Before Lewis and Clark. 2 vols. 882 pp. St. Louis, 1952.

Neumann, G. The Origin of the Prairie Physical Type of American Indian. PMA, XXVII, 539-42. 1941.

Newcomb, W.W. A Re-Examination of the Causes of Plains Warfare. AA, LII, 317-30. 1950.

Newman, T.M. Documentary Sources on the Manufacture of Pottery by the Indians of the Central Plains and Middle Missouri. PIA, IV, 13-20. 1955.

Nydahl, T.L. The Pipestone Quarry and the Indians. MiH, XXXI, 193-208. 1950.

Over, W.H. Indian Picture Writing in South Dakota. University of South Dakota Archaeological Studies, IV, 1-59. 1941.

Ozee, D.W. An Historic Indian Cache in Clay County. BTAPS, XXVI, 256-8. 1955.

Paget, A.M. The People of the Plains. Toronto, 1909.

Paul Wilhelm, Duke of Wuerttemburg. First Journey to North America. SDHC, XIX, 7-473. 1938.

Perrin du Lac, M. Travels through the Two Louisianas. 106 pp. London, 1807.

--- Voyage dans les deux Louisianes. 472 pp. Lyon, 1805.

Pike, Z.M. Account of Expeditions to the Sources of the Mississippi. 2 vols. Philadelphia, 1810.

Pilling, J.C. Bibliography of the Siouan Languages. BBAE, V, 1-87. 1887.

Powell, L.H. A Study of Indian Beadwork of the North Central Plains. ILSPSM, V-VII, 1-8. 1953.

Provinse, J.H. The Underlying Sanctions of Plains Indian Culture. SANAT, pp. 341-76. 1955.

Rauch, J.W. Report [on the Medical and Economical Botany of Iowa]. Proceedings of the Iowa State Medical and Chirurgical Society, II, 11-52. 1851.

Ray, V.F. Historic Backgrounds of the Conjuring Complex in the Plateau and the Plains. Essays in Memory of E. Sapir, pp. 204-16. Menasha, 1941.

Renaud, E.B. Indian Petroglyphs of the Plains. So Live the Works of Men, ed. D.D. Brand and F.E. Harvey, pp. 295-310. Albuquerque, 1939.

Rickett, H.W. John Bradbury's Explorations in Missouri Territory. PAPS, XCIV, 59-90. 1950.

Ridley, F. Cultural Contacts of Iroquoian and Plains. PA, XXVII, 33-38. 1957.

Röder, J. Der Wissenschaftliche Nachlass von Maximilian, Prinz zu Wied. ICA, XXX, 187-92. 1955.

Roe, F.G. From Dogs to Horses among the Western Indian Tribes. PTRSC, ser. 3, XXXIII, ii, 209-75. 1939.

--- White Buffalo. PTRSC, ser. 3, XXXVIII, ii, 155-73. 1944.

Rollins, P.A., ed. The Discovery of the Oregon Trail. 391 pp. New York, 1935.

Sandoz, M. The Look of the West - 1854. NeH, XXXV, 243-54. 1954.

Scott, H.L. The Sign Language of the Plains Indians. Archives of the International Folk-Lore Association, I, 1-206. 1893.

Secoy, F.R. Changing Military Patterns on the Great Plains. MAES, XXI, 120 pp. 1953.

Shelby, C.C. St. Denis's Declaration Concerning Texas in 1717. SWHQ, XXVI, 165-83, 1923.

--- St. Denis's Second Expedition to the Rio Grande, 1716-1719. SWHQ, XXVII, 190-216. 1924.

Shonle, R. Peyote. AA, n.s., XXVII, 53-75. 1925.

Siiger, H. Indianerne og Bisonen. GT, XLVII, 155-74. 1945.

--- Praerieindianerne og Piben. Fra Nationalmuseets Arbejdsmark, 1946, 24-9. København.

Slotkin, J.S. Early Eighteenth Century Documents on Peyotism North of the Rio Grande. AA, LIII, 420-27. 1951.

Smet, P.J. de. Letters and Sketches. Philadelphia, 1843.

--- Voyages aux Montagnes Rocheuses. New edit. Paris, 1873.

Smith, M.G. Political Organization of the Plains Indians. University of Nebraska Studies, XXIV, 1-84. 1925.

Smith, M.W. The War Complex of the Plains Indians. PAPS, LXXVIII, 425-64. 1938.

South Dakota. Department of Public Instruction. Indians of South Dakota. 63 pp. Pierre, 1954.

Spier, L. An Analysis of Plains Indian Parfleche Decoration. UWPA, I, 89-112. 1925.

--- Plains Indian Parfleche Designs. UWPA, IV, 293-322. 1931.

--- The Sun Dance of the Plains Indians. APAM, XVI, 451-527. 1921.

Stenberg, M.P. The Peyote Culture among Wyoming Indians. UWP, XII, 85-156. 1946.

Stewart, E.I. Custer's Luck. 538 pp. Norman, 1955.

Stirling, M.W. Indians of Our Western Plains. NGM, LXXXVI, 73-108. 1944.

Strong, W.D. From History to Prehistory in the Northern Great Plains. SMC, C, 353-94. 1940.

--- An Introduction to Nebraska Archeology. SMC, XCIII, x, 323 pp. 1935.

Strong, W.D. The Plains Culture Area in the Light of Archaeology. AA, n.s., XXXV, 271-87. 1933.

Sullivan, L.R. Anthropometry of the Siouan Tribes. PNAS, VI, 131-4. 1920.

Taylor, V.H. and Hammons, J. The Letters of Antonio Martinez. 379 pp. Austin, 1957.

Thomas, A.B. The Plains Indians and New Mexico, 1751-1778. 232 pp. Albuquerque, 1940.

Thomas, A.B., ed. After Coronado. 307 pp. Albuquerque, 1935.

Tibbles, T.H. Buckskin and Blanket Days. 336 pp. Garden City, 1957.

Tilghman, Z.A. Source of the Buffalo Origin Legend. AA, n.s., XLIII, 487-8. 1941.

Tomkins, W. Universal Sign Language of the Plains Indians. 77 pp. San Diego, 1926.

Truteau, J.B. Journal. American Historical Review, XIX, 299-333. 1914.

Vatter, E. Historienmalerei und heraldische Bilderschrift der nordamerikanischen Präriestämme. Ipek, 1927, 46-81. 1927.

Vestal, S. Warpath and Council Fire. 338 pp. New York, 1948.

Voegelin, C.F. Internal Relationships of Siouan Languages. AA, n.s., XLIII, 246-9. 1941.

--- A Problem in Morpheme Alternants and Their Distribution. Lg, XXIII, 245-54. 1947.

Wagner, G. Entwicklung und Verbreitung des Peyote-Kultes. BA, XV, 59-144. 1932.

Wagner, H.R. The Plains and the Rockies, 3rd edition. 601 pp. Columbus, 1953.

Wake, C.S. Mythology of the Plains Indians. AAOJ, XXVII, 9-16, 73-80, 323-8; XXVIII, 205-12. 1905-06.

Walker, J.R. Sign Language of the Plains Indians. CO, XXXI, 168-77. 1953.

Webb, W.P. The Great Plains, pp. 47-84. Boston, 1931.

Wedel, W.R. Environment and Native Subsistence Economies in the Central Great Plains. SMC, CI, iii, 1-30. 1941.

--- An Introduction to Kansas Archeology. BBAE, CLXXIV, 723 pp. 1959.

--- Prehistory and Environment in the Central Great Plains. TKAS, L, 1-18. 1947.

--- Some Aspects of Human Ecology in the Central Plains. AA, LV, 499-514. 1953.

Weer, P. Preliminary Notes on the Caddoan Family. PRS, I, iv, 111-30. 1938.

--- Preliminary Notes on the Siouan Family. Indiana History Bulletin, XIV, 99-120. 1937.

Weltfish, G. The Question of Ethnic Identity. E, VI, 321-46. 1959.

White, M.C. David Thompson's Journals Relating to Montana and Adjacent Regions, 1808-1812. 507 pp. Missoula, 1950.

Williamson, A.W. The Dakotan Languages. AAOJ, IV, 110-28. 1882.

Wissler, C. Changes in Population Profiles among the Northern Plains Indians. APAM, XXXVI, 1-67. 1936.

--- Costumes of the Plains Indians. APAM, XVII, 39-91. 1915.

--- Diffusion of Culture in the Plains. ICA, XV, ii, 39-52. 1906.

--- The Distribution and Functions of Tribal Societies among the Plains Indians. PNAS, I, 401-3. 1915.

--- Distribution of Moccasin Decorations among the Plains Tribes. APAM, XXIX, 1-23. 1927.

--- Ethnographical Problems of the Missouri Saskatchewan Area. AA, n.s., X, 197-207. 1908.

--- General Discussion of Shamanistic and Dancing Societies. APAM, XI, 853-76. 1916.

--- The Influence of the Horse in the Development of Plains Culture. AA, n.s., XVI, 1-25. 1914.

--- North American Indians of the Plains. 147 pp. New York, 1912.

--- Population Changes among the Northern Plains Indians. YUPA, I, 1-20. 1936.

--- Riding Gear of the North American Indians. APAM, XVII, 1-38. 1915.

--- Structural Basis to the Decoration of Costumes among the Plains Indians. APAM, XVII, 93-114. 1916.

--- Types of Dwellings and Their Distribution in Central North America. ICA, XVI, 477-87. 1908.

Wolff, H. Comparative Siouan. IJAL, XVI, 61-6. 1950.

Wright, M.H. A Guide to the Indian Tribes of Oklahoma. 300 pp. Norman, 1951.

1. ARAPAHO

Hilger, M.I. Arapaho Child Life and Its Cultural Background. BBAE, CXLVIII, 269 pp. 1952.

Kroeber, A.L. The Arapaho. BAMNH, XVIII, 1-229, 279-454. 1902-07.

Anonymous. Arapaho and Cheyenne Indians. H.R. 11359, 70th Congress, 1st Session, March 1 and 15, 1928.

Beals, R.L. Ethnology of Rocky Mountain Park: the Ute and Arapaho. 27 pp. Berkeley, 1935.

Berthrong, D.J. Federal Indian Policy and the Southern Cheyennes and Arapahoes, 1887-1907. E, III, 138-53. 1956.

Boas, F. Zur Anthropologie der nordamerikanischen Indianer. VBGA, 1895, 367-411.

Bushnell, D.I. Villages of the Algonquian, Siouan and Caddoan Tribes. BBAE, LXXVII, 33-7. 1922.

Carter, J.G. The Northern Arapaho Flat Pipe and the Ceremony of covering the Pipe. BBAE, CXIX, 69-102. 1938.

Curtis, E.S. The North American Indian, VI, 138-50, 159-64, 167-73. Norwood, 1911.

Curtis, N., ed. The Indians' Book, pp. 197-217. New York, 1907.

Dangberg, G.M. Letters to Jack Wilson, the Paiute Prophet. BBAE, CLXIV, 279-96. 1957.

Densmore, F. Cheyenne and Arapaho Music. SWMP, X, 9-111. 1936.

Dodge, R.I. Our Wild Indians. 650 pp. Hartford, 1882.

Dorsey, G.A. The Arapaho Sun Dance. FMAS, IV, 1-228. 1903.

Dorsey, G.A., and Kroeber, A.L. Traditions of the Arapaho. FMAS, V, 1-475. 1903.

Douglas, F.H. A Northern Arapaho Quilled Cradle. MCN, I, 53-9. 1941.

Dyer, D.B. Fort Reno or Picturesque Cheyenne-Arapaho Army Life before the Opening of Oklahoma. 216 pp. New York, 1896.

Edwards, T.A. Early Days in the C & A. CO, XXVII, 148-61. 1949.

Eggan, F. The Cheyenne and Arapaho Kinship System. SANAT, 35-98. 1955.

Elkin, H. The Northern Arapaho of Wyoming. ASAIT, 207-58. 1940.

Fisher, M.C. On the Arapahoes, Kiowas, and Comanches. JESL, n.s., I, 274-87. 1869.

Fletcher, A.C. Indian Story and Song from North America. 126 pp. Boston, 1907.

Foreman, G. The Last Trek of the Indians, pp. 296-302. Chicago, 1946.

Gross, F. Language and Value Changes among the Arapaho. IJAL, XVII, 10-17. 1951.

--- Nomadism of the Arapaho Indians of Wyoming. UWP, XV, iii, 35-55. 1950.

Harmon, E.M. The Story of the Indian Fort near Granby, Colorado. Colorado Magazine, XXII, 167-71. 1945.

Hayden, F.V. Contributions to the Ethnography and Philology of the Indian Tribes of the Missouri Valley. TAPS, n.s., XII, 321-39. 1863.

Hockett, C.F. Sapir on Arapaho. IJAL, XII, 243-5.
    1946.

Hultkrantz, A. Some Notes on the Arapaho Sun
    Dance. Ethnos, XVII, 24-38. 1952.

Hurst, C.T. Colorado's Old-Timers. SWL, XII, 19-
    26. 1946.

Kate, H.F.C. ten. Reizen en onderzoekingen in
    Noord-Amerika. 464 pp. Leiden, 1885.

Kroeber, A.L. Arapaho Dialects. UCP, XII, 71-
    138. 1916.

--- Decorative Symbolism of the Arapaho. AA, n.s.,
    III, 308-36. 1901.

--- Symbolism of the Arapaho Indians. BAMNH,
    XIII, 69-86. 1900.

--- The Symbolism of the Arapaho Indians. Sci-
    entific American Supplement, 1297. 1900.

Meserve, C.F. The First Allotment of Lands in
    Severalty among the Oklahoma Cheyenne and
    Arapaho Indians. CO, XI, 1040-3. 1933.

Michelson, T. Narrative of an Arapaho Woman.
    AA, n.s., XXXV, 595-610. 1933.

--- Phonetic Shifts in Algonquian Languages. IJAL,
    VIII, 131-71. 1935.

--- Some Arapaho Kinship Terms and Social Usages.
    AA, n.s., XXXVI, 137-9. 1934.

Mooney, J. Arapaho. BBAE, XXX, i, 72-4. 1907.

--- The Ghost-Dance Religion. ARBAE, XIV, ii,
    953-1023. 1893.

Moran, P. Shoshone Agency. RIT, 1890, 629-34.

Muntsch, A. Notes on Age-Classes among the North-
    ern Arapaho. PM, V, 49-52. 1932.

Nettl, B. Musical Culture of the Arapaho.Musical
    Quarterly, XLI, 325-31. 1955.

--- Text-Music Relationships in Arapaho Songs. SJA,
    X, 192-99. 1954.

Painter, C.C.G. Cheyenne and Arapaho Revisited.
    62 pp. Philadelphia, 1893.

Pajeken, F.J. Religion und religiöse Vorstellungen
    der Arrapahoë-Indianer. Ausland, LXIII, 1011-
    15. 1890.

Peery, D.W. The Indians' Friend, John H. Seger.
    CO, X, 348-68, 570-91; XI, 709-32, 845-68,
    967-94. 1933.

Radin, P. Jessie Clay's Account of the Arapaho Man-
    ner of Giving the Peyote Ceremony. ARBAE,
    XXXVII, 415-19. 1923.

Roberts, J., tr. Hethadence waunauyaunee vadan
    Luke vanenana. 102 pp. New York, 1903.

Salzmann, Z. Arapaho. IJAL, XXII, 49-56, 151-
    58, 266-72. 1956.

--- Arapaho Kinship Terms and Two Related Ob-
    servations. Anthropological Linguistics, I, ix, 6-
    10. 1959.

Salzmann, Z. An Arapaho Version of the Star Hus-
    band Tale. HF, IX, 50-58. 1950.

--- Contrastive Field Experience with Language and
    Values of the Arapaho. IJAL, XVII, 98-101. 1951.

--- Arapaho Tales III. MWF, VII, 27-37. 1957.

Salzmann, Z. and J. Arapaho Tales I. HF, IX, 80-
    96. 1950.

--- Arapaho Tales II. MWF, II, 21-42. 1952.

Schmidt, W. Die Arapaho. UG, II, 680-756; V,
    664-76. 1929, 1934.

Scott, H.L. The Early History and Names of the
    Arapaho. AA, n.s., IX, 545-60. 1907.

Seger, J.H. Early Days among the Cheyenne and
    Arapahoe Indians, ed. S. Vestal. 155 pp.; 164 pp.
    Norman, 1934, 1956.

Smith, J.S. Arapahoes. HCPIT, III, 446-59. 1853.

Stewart, D.D. Cheyenne-Arapaho Assimilation.
    Phylon, XIII, 120-26. 1952.

Stoller, M.L. A Sacred Bundle of the Arapaho In-
    dians. ACM, XXXV, 11-25. 1957.

Thayer, B.H. Additional Arapaho Moccasin Charac-
    teristics. MA, VIII, 30-40. 1942.

Uhlenbeck, C.C. Additional Blackfoot-Arapaho
    Comparisons. IJAL, IV, 227-8. 1927.

Underhill, R.M. Peyote. ICA, XXX, 143-48. 1955.

Underhill, R.M. et al. Modern Arapaho. SWL, XVII,
    38-42. 1951.

Voth, H.R. Arapaho Tales. JAFL, XXV, 43-50.
    1912.

--- Funeral Customs among the Cheyenne and Arapa-
    ho Indians. Folklorist, Vol. I. 1893.

Wake, C.S. Nihacan, the White Man. AAOJ, XXVI,
    225-31. 1904.

Wedel, W.R. The Arapaho and Cheyenne. BBAE,
    CLXXIV, 80-1. 1959.

Wildschut, W. Arapaho Medicine Bundle, IN, IV,
    83-8. 1927.

--- Arapaho Medicine-Mirror. IN, IV, 252-7. 1927.

2. ARIKARA

Deland, C.E. The Aborigines of South Dakota.
    SDHC, III, 267-586. 1906.

Ewers, J.C. Edwin T. Denig's "Of the Arickaras."
    BMHS, VI, 189-215. 1950.

Macgowan, E.S. The Arikara Indians. MA, VIII,
    83-122. 1942.

Abel, A.H., ed. Tabeau's Narrative of Loisel's Ex-
    pedition to the Upper Missouri. 286 pp. Norman,
    1939.

Anonymous. Arikara Creation Myth. JAFL, XXII, 90-2. 1909.

--- South Dakota Physical Types. WHO, XII, v, 1. 1952.

Archaeological Project, South Dakota Works Project Administration. Arikara Indians of South Dakota. 62 pp. Vermillion, 1941.

Boas, F. Zur Anthropologie der nordamerikanischen Indianer. VBGA, 1895, 367-411.

Brackenridge, H.M. Views of Louisiana, pp. 245-58. Pittsburgh, 1814.

Bradbury, J. Travels in the Interior of America. Liverpool, 1817.

Bruner, E.M. Assimilation among Fort Berthold Indians. AmI, VI, iv, 21-9. 1953.

Bushnell, D.I. Villages of the Algonquian, Siouan and Caddoan Tribes. BBAE, LXXVII, 167-79. 1922.

Culbertson, T.A. Journal of an Expedition to the Mauvaises Terres and the Upper Missouri in 1850. BBAE, CXLVII, 172 pp. 1952.

Curtis, E.S. The North American Indian, V, 59-100, 148-52, 155-63, 169-80. Cambridge, 1909.

Dorsey, G.A. An Arikara Story-telling Contest. AA, n.s., VI, 240-3. 1904.

--- Traditions of the Arikara. 202 pp. Washington, 1904.

Fenenga, F. The Interdependence of Archaeology and Ethnology as Illustrated by the Ice-Glider Game of the Northern Plains. PlA, I, 31-38. 1954.

Fletcher, A.C. Arikara. BBAE, XXX, i, 83-6. 1907.

Fort Berthold Mission, ed. A Few Bible Translations and Hymns. 27 pp. Fort Berthold, 1900.

Gilmore, M.R. Arikara Account of the Origin of Tobacco and Catching of Eagles. IN, VI, 26-33. 1929.

--- Arikara Basketry. IN, II, 89-95. 1925.

--- The Arikara Book of Genesis. PMA, XII, 95-120. 1929.

--- Arikara Commerce. IN, III, 13-18. 1926.

--- Arikara Consolation Ceremony. IN, III, 256-74. 1926.

--- Arikara Fish-Trap. IN, I, 120-34. 1924.

--- Arikara Genesis and Its Teachings. IN, III, 188-93. 1926.

--- Arikara Household Shrine to Mother Corn. IN, II, 31-4. 1925.

--- The Arikara Method of Preparing a Dog for a Feast. PMA, XIX, 37-8. 1933.

--- The Arikara Tribal Temple. PMA, XIV, 47-70. 1930.

--- Arikara Units of Measure. IN, II, 64-6. 1925.

Gilmore, M.R. Arikara Uses of Clay and of Other Earth Products. IN, II, 283-9. 1925.

--- Buffalo-Skull from the Arikara. IN, III, 75-9. 1926.

--- The Cattail Game of Arikara Children. IN, V, 316-18. 1928.

--- The Coyote's Boxelder Knife. IN, IV, 214-16. 1927.

--- Glass Bead Making by the Arikara. IN, I, 20-1. 1924.

--- The Making of a New Head Chief by the Arikara. IN, V, 411-18. 1928.

--- Months and Seasons of the Arikara Calendar. IN, VI, 246-50. 1929.

--- Notes on Arikara Tribal Organization. IN, IV, 332-50. 1927.

--- Notes on Gynecology and Obstetrics of the Arikara Tribe. PMA, XIV, 71-81. 1930.

---Origin of the Arikara Silverberry Drink. IN, IV, 125-7. 1927.

--- The Plight of Living Scalped Indians. PMA, XIX, 39-45. 1933.

--- The Sacred Bundles of the Arikara. PMA, XVI, 33-50. 1931.

--- Some Games of Arikara Children. IN, III, 9-12. 1926.

--- Use of Cat-tails by Arikara. EP, XXIV, 114,116. 1928.

Goddard, P.E. Indian Ceremonies of the Long Ago. NH, XXII, 559-64. 1922.

Hayden, F.V. Contributions to the Ethnography and Philology of the Indian Tribes of the Missouri Valley. TAPS, n.s., XII, 351-63. 1863.

Hilger, M.I. Some Customs Related to Arikara Indian Child Life. PM, XXIV, 67-71. 1951.

Hoffman, W.-J. La Fête annuelle des Indiens Arikaris. BSAP, ser. 3, VII, 526-32. 1884.

--- Remarks on Indian Tribal Names. PAPS, XXIII, 294-6. 1886.

--- The Water Babies, an Arickaree Story. AAOJ, XIV, 167-9. 1892.

Holder, P. Social Stratification among the Arikara. E, V, 210-18. 1958.

Hyde, G.E. The Mystery of the Arikaras. North Dakota History, XVIII, 187-218; XIX, 25-58. 1951-1952.

Kohlepp, H.W. A Missionary Trip to the Land of the Arikara. MA, III, 90-3. 1937.

Leigh, R.W. Dental Pathology of Indian Tribes. AJPA, VIII, 179-99. 1925.

Libby, O.G., ed. The Arikara Narrative of the Campaign against the Hostile Dakotas. SDHC, VI, 1-276. 1920.

Libby, O.G. Typical Villages of the Mandan, Arikara and Hidatsa in the Missouri Valley. SDHC, IV, 498-508. 1908.

Lowie, R.H. Societies of the Arikara Indians. APAM, XI, 645-78. 1915.

--- Some Problems in the Ethnology of the Crow and Village Indians. AA, n.s., XIV, 60-71. 1912.

Morgan, L.H. The Indian Journals, 1859-62, pp. 146, 161-4. Ann Arbor, 1959.

--- The Stone and Bone Implements of the Arickarees. ARUNY, XXI, 25-46. 1871.

--- Systems of Consanguinity and Affinity. SCK, XVII, 291-382. 1871.

Mulloy, W. The Northern Plains. AEUS, 124-38. 1952.

Nasatir, A.P. Before Lewis and Clark. 2 vols. 882 pp. St. Louis, 1952.

Over, W.H. Lewis and Clark Site. NWHOM, XVI, i, 1-4. 1955.

Reid, R. The Earth Lodge. NDHQ, IV, 174-85. 1930.

Smith, G.H. J.B. Trudeau's Remarks on the Indians of the Upper Missouri. AA, n.s., XXXVIII, 565-8. 1936.

Stirling, M.W. Archaeological Investigations in South Dakota. EFWSI, 1924, 66-71.

--- Arikara Glassworking. JWAS, XXXVII, 257-63. 1947.

Strong, W.D. Studying the Arikara and Their Neighbors. EFWSI, 1932, 73-6.

Swanton, J.R. Arikara Pottery Making. AAn, X, 100-1. 1944.

Trudeau, J.B. Description of the Upper Missouri. MVHR, VIII, 149-79. 1921.

--- Journal. SDHC, VII, 453-62. 1914.

Wedel, W.R. Archeological Materials from the Vicinity of Mobridge, South Dakota. BBAE, CLVII, 69-188. 1955.

--- Observations on Some Nineteenth-Century Pottery Vessels from the Upper Missouri. BBAE, CLXIV, 87-114. 1957.

Wied-Neuwied, M.zu. Reise in das innere Nordamerika. 2 vols. Coblenz, 1839-41.

--- Travels in the Interior of North America. EWT, XXII, 335-6; XXIII, 386-95; XXIV, 210-14. 1906.

Will, G.F. Archaeology of the Missouri Valley. APAM, XXII, 285-344. 1924.

--- Arikara Ceremonials. NDHQ, IV, 247-65. 1930.

--- Indian Agriculture at Its Northern Limits. ICA, XX, i, 203-5. 1922.

--- Notes on the Arikara Indians and Their Ceremonies. OWS, III, 5-48. 1934.

Will, G.F., and Hyde, G.E. Corn among the Indians of the Upper Missouri. 317 pp. St. Louis, 1917.

Wood, W.R. Historical and Archaeological Evidence for Arikara Visits to the Central Plains. PIA, IV, 27-39. 1955.

3. ASSINIBOIN

Also called Stoney.

Denig, E.T. Indian Tribes of the Upper Missouri, ed. J.N.B. Hewitt. ARBAE, XLVI, 375-628. 1930.

Ewers, J.C. Edwin T. Denig's "Of the Assiniboine." BMHS, VIII, 121-50. 1952.

Lowie, R.H. The Assiniboine. APAM, IV, 1-270. 1910.

Rodnick, D. The Fort Belknap Assiniboine of Montana. 125 pp. New Haven, 1938.

Barbeau, M. Indian Days in the Canadian Rockies. 208 pp. Toronto, 1923.

Breton, A.C. The Stoney Indians. Man, XX, 65-7. 1920.

Burpee, L.J., ed. Journals and Letters of Pierre Gaultier de Varennes de la Vérendrye and His Sons. PCS, XVI, 1-548. 1927.

Bushnell, D.I. Burials of the Algonquian, Siouan and Caddoan Tribes. BBAE, LXXXIII, 42-9. 1927.

--- Sketches by Paul Kane in the Indian Country, 1845-1848. SMC, XCIX, i, 1-25. 1940.

--- Villages of the Algonquian, Siouan and Caddoan Tribes. BBAE, LXXVII, 71-7. 1922.

Chown, B. and Lewis, M. The Blood Group and Secretor Genes of the Stony and Sarcee Indians of Alberta, Canada. AJPA, n.s., XIII, 181-89. 1955.

Cocking, M. An Adventurer from Hudson Bay, ed. L.J. Burpee. PTRSC, ser. 3, II, ii, 89-121. 1908.

Coues, E., ed. Manuscript Journals of Alexander Henry and of David Thompson. 3 vols. New York, 1897.

Culbertson, T.A. Journal of an Expedition to the Mauvaises Terres and the Upper Missouri in 1850. BBAE, CXLVII, 172 pp. 1952.

Curtis, E.S. The North American Indian, III, 125-33, 152-9; XVIII, 163-76, 214-18. Cambridge, 1908. Norwood, 1928.

Dangberg, G.M. Letters to Jack Wilson, the Paiute Prophet. BBAE, CLXIV, 279-96. 1957.

Denig, E.T. Assiniboine. HCPIT, IV, 416-31. 1854.

Dorsey, J.O. Preface. CNAE, IX, xi-xxxii. 1893.

--- Siouan Sociology. ARBAE, XV, 222-6. 1894.

Doughty, A.G., and Martin, C., eds. The Kelsey Papers. Ottawa, 1929.

Ewers, J.C. The Assiniboin Horse Medicine Cult. PM, XXIX, 57-68. 1956.

--- The Bear Cult among the Assiniboin and Their Neighbors of the Northern Plains. SJA, XI, 1-14. 1955.

Fenenga, F. An Early Nineteenth Century Account of Assiniboine Quillwork. PlA, III, 19-22. 1955.

Gilmore, M.R. Old Assiniboin Buffalo-Drive in North Dakota. IN, I, 204-11. 1924.

Hassrick, R.B. Assiniboin Succession. North Dakota History, XIV, 146-67. 1947.

Hayden, F.V. Contributions to the Ethnography and Philology of the Indian Tribes of the Missouri Valley. TAPS, n.s., XII, 379-91. 1863.

Hector, J., and Vaux, W.S.W. Notice of Indians seen by the Exploring Expedition under the Command of Captain Palliser. TESL, n.s., I, 245-61. 1861.

Henry, A. Travels and Adventures, ed. M.M.Quaife, pp. 266-97. Chicago, 1921.

Jenks, A.E. The Wild Rice Gatherers of the Upper Lakes. ARBAE, XIX, ii, 1013-137. 1898.

Leechman, D. The Trappers. B, CCLXXXVIII, iii, 24-31. 1957.

Long, J.L. Land of Nakoda. 296 pp. Helena, 1942.

Matson, G.A. Blood Groups and Ageusia in Indians of Montana and Alberta. AJPA, XXIV, 81-9. 1938.

McDonnell, J. Some Account of the Red River. BCNO, I, 265-95. 1889.

McGee, W.J. The Siouan Indians. ARBAE, XV, 157-204. 1894.

Mooney, J., and Thomas, C. Assiniboin. BBAE, XXX, i, 102-5. 1907.

Morgan, L.H. The Indian Journals, 1859-62, p. 166. Ann Arbor, 1959.

--- Systems of Consanguinity and Affinity. SCK, XVII, 291-382. 1871.

Nasatir, A.P. Before Lewis and Clark. 2 vols. 882 pp. St. Louis, 1952.

Orchard, W.C. Porcupine Quill Ornamentation. IN, III, 59-68. 1926.

Paget, A.M. The People of the Plains. 199 pp. Toronto, 1909.

Palliser, J. Further Papers. 325 pp. London, 1860.

Potts, W.J. Creation Myth of the Assinaboines. JAFL, V, 72-3. 1892.

Riggs, S.R. Dakota Grammar, Texts and Ethnography. CNAE, IX, 1-232. 1893.

Rodnick, D. An Assiniboine Horse-raiding Expedition. AA, n.s., XLI, 611-16. 1939.

--- Political Structure and Status among the Assiniboine Indians. AA, n.s., XXXIX, 408-16. 1937.

Smet, P.J.de. Western Missions and Missionaries, pp. 130-205. New York, 1863.

Sullivan, L.R. Anthropometry of the Siouan Tribes. APAM, XXIII, 81-174. 1920.

Weekes, M. An Indian's Description of the Making of a Buffalo Pound. Saskatchewan History, I, 14-17. 1948.

Wied-Neuwied, M. zu. Reise in das innere Nordamerika. 2 vols. Coblenz, 1839-41.

--- Travels in the Interior of North America. EWT, XXII, 370-1; XXIII, 14-24; XXIV, 215-17. 1906.

4. BLACKFOOT

Including the Blackfoot or Siksika, the Blood, and the Piegan.

Devereux, G. Reality and Dream. 464 pp. New York, 1951.

Ewers, J.C. The Blackfeet. 366 pp. Norman, 1958.

--- The Horse in Blackfoot Indian Culture. BBAE, CLIX, 390 pp. 1955.

McClintock, W. The Old North Trail. 532 pp. London, 1910.

Wissler, C. Material Culture of the Blackfoot Indians. APAM, V, 1-175. 1910.

--- The Social Life of the Blackfoot Indians. APAM, VII, 1-64. 1912.

Barrett, S.A. The Blackfoot Iniskim or Buffalo Bundle. YPMCM, I, 80-4. 1921.

--- The Blackfoot Sweat Lodge. YPMCM, I, 73-80. 1921.

--- The Painted Lodge or Ceremonial Tipi of the Blackfoot. YPMCM, I, 85-8. 1921.

Barry, G.L. The Whoop-up Trail. Edmonton, 1953.

Boas, F. Zur Anthropologie der nordamerikanischen Indianer. VBGA, 1895, 367-411.

Bradley, J.H. Characteristics, Habits, and Customs of the Blackfeet Indians. Contributions of the Historical Society of Montana, IX, 255-87. 1923.

Brown, A. Prairie Totems. CGJ, XXIII, 148-51. 1941.

Browne, J.M. Indian Medicine. Indian Miscellany, ed. W.W.Beach, pp. 74-85. Albany, 1877.

Bull Plume. Blackfoot Legends. M, VII, 41-6, 70-73. 1933.

Burpee, L.J. Henday Discovers the Blackfoot. CGJ, XXXIII, 188-9. 1946.

Burpee, L.J., ed. An Adventurer from Hudson Bay. PTRSC, ser. 3, II, ii, 109-12. 1908.

--- York Factory to the Blackfeet Country. PTRSC, ser. 3, I, ii, 307-54. 1907.

Bushnell, D.I. Burials of the Algonquian, Siouan and Caddoan Tribes. BBAE, LXXXIII, 10-13. 1927.

--- Sketches by Paul Kane in the Indian Country, 1845-1848. SMC, XCIX, i, 1-25. 1940.

--- Villages of the Algonquian, Siouan and Caddoan Tribes. BBAE, LXXVII, 25-33. 1922.

Canada, Dept. of Mines and Resources, Indian Affairs Branch. Census of Indians in Canada, 1939 and 1944. Ottawa, 1940, 1944.

Catlin, G. Illustrations of the Manners, Customs and Condition of the North American Indians, I, 29-43, 51-3. New York, 1841.

Chown, B. and Lewis, M. The ABO, MNSs, P, Rh, Lutheran, Kell, Lewis, Duffy and Kidd Blood Groups and the Secretor Status of the Blackfoot Indians of Alberta, Canada. AJPA, n.s., XI, 369-83. 1953.

Cocking, M. An Adventurer from Hudson Bay, ed. L.J. Burpee. PTRSC, ser. 3, II, ii, 89-121. 1908.

Conn, R. Blackfeet Soumak Necklaces. DJA, I, 99-112. 1955.

Cooper, J.M. The Shaking Tent Rite among Plains and Forest Algonquians. PM, XVII, 60-84. 1944.

Coues, E., ed. Manuscript Journals of Alexander Henry and of David Thompson. 3 vols. New York, 1897.

Culbertson, T.A. Journal of an Expedition to the Mauvaises Terres and the Upper Missouri in 1850. BBAE, CXLVII, 172 pp. 1952.

Curtis, E.S. The North American Indian, VI, 3-83, 153-5, 167-73; XVIII, 176-98. Norwood, 1911-28.

Dempsey, H.A. The Amazing Death of Calf Shirt. MMH, III, i, 65-72. 1953.

--- Social Dances of the Blood Indians. JAFL, LXIX, 47-52. 1956.

--- Stone "Medicine Wheels." JWAS, XLVI, 177-82. 1956.

Denny, C. Blackfoot Magic. B, CCLXXV, ii, 14-15. 1944.

Devereux, G. Three Technical Problems in the Psychotherapy of Plains Indian Patients. American Journal of Psychotherapy, V, 411-23. 1951.

Donaldson, T. The George Catlin Indian Gallery. RUSNM, 1885, 101-6.

Douglas, F.H. The Blackfoot Indians. DAMLS, XXXVII-XXXVIII, 1-8. 1931.

Ellison, W.H. Adventures of George Nidever. New Spain and the Anglo-American West, ed. C.W. Hackett, G.P. Hammond, et al, II, 21-45. Los Angeles, 1932.

Ewers, J.C. Blackfeet Crafts. IH, IX, 1-66. 1945.

--- The Blackfoot War Lodge: Its Construction and Use. AA, n.s., XLVI, 182-92. 1944.

--- The Case for Blackfoot Pottery. AA, n.s., XLVII, 289-99. 1945.

--- Food Rationing is Nothing New to the Blackfoot. M, XVIII, 73-80. 1944.

--- Identification and History of the Small Robes Band of Piegan Indians. JWAS, XXXVI, 397-401. 1946.

--- The Last Bison Drives of the Blackfoot Indians. JWAS, XXXIX, 355-60. 1949.

--- The Medicine Rock of the Marias. MMH, II, iii, 51-55. 1952.

--- Primitive American Commandos. M, XVII, 117-25. 1943.

--- Self-Torture in the Blood Indian Sun Dance. JWAS, XXXVIII, 166-73. 1948.

--- Some Winter Sports of Blackfoot Indian Children. M, XVII, 180-87. 1944.

--- The Story of the Blackfeet. ILC, VI, 1-66. 1944.

--- Were the Blackfoot Rich in Horses? AA, n.s., XLV, 602-10. 1943.

Gates, M.E. A Visit to the Northern Reservations in Oregon and Montana. LMCI, XVII, 62-6. 1900.

Gaudst, V. Au pays des Peaux-rouges. 238 pp. Lille, 1911.

Geers, G.J. The Adverbial and Prepositional Prefix in Blackfoot. Leiden, 1917.

Goldfrank, E.S. Administrative Programs and Changes in Blood Society during the Reserve Period. HO, II, ii, 18-23. 1943.

--- Changing Configurations in the Social Organization of a Blackfoot Tribe during the Reserve Period. MAES, VIII, 1-73. 1945.

--- The Different Patterns of Blackfoot and Pueblo Adaptation to White Authority. ICA, XXIX, ii, 74-9. 1952.

--- Observations on Sexuality among the Blood Indians of Alberta. PSS, III, 71-98. 1951.

--- "Old Man" and the Father Image in Blood (Blackfoot) Society. PAC, 132-41. 1951.

Grinnell, G.B. Blackfeet Indian Stories. 214 pp. New York, 1913.

--- Blackfoot Lodge Tales. New York, 1892.

--- A Blackfoot Sun and Moon Myth. JAFL, VI, 44-7. 1893.

Grinnell, G.B. The Butterfly and the Spider among the Blackfeet. AA, n.s., I, 194-6. 1899.

--- Childbirth among the Blackfeet. AA, IX, 286-7. 1896.

--- Early Blackfoot History. AA, V, 153-74, 582-3. 1892.

--- The Lodges of the Blackfeet. AA, n.s., III, 650-68. 1901.

--- The Punishment of the Stingy, pp. 127-235. New York, 1901.

Hale, H. Report on the Blackfoot Tribes. BAAS, LV, 696-708. 1885.

Hanks, L.M. A Psychological Exploration in the Blackfoot Language. IJAL, XX, 195-205. 1954.

Hanks, L.M. and J.R. Tribe under Trust. 220 pp. Toronto, 1950.

Hanks, L.M., and Richardson, J. Observations on Northern Blackfoot Kinship. MAES, IX, 1-31. 1945.

Hayden, F.V. Contributions to the Ethnography and Philology of the Indian Tribes of the Missouri Valley. TAPS, n.s., XII, 248-73. 1863.

Hendry, A. York Factory to the Blackfoot Country, ed. L.J.Burpee. PTRSC, ser. 3, I, ii, 307-60. 1907.

Hyde, G.E. The Early Blackfeet and Their Neighbors. OWS, II, 5-45. 1933.

Josselin de Jong, J.P.B. de. Blackfoot Texts. UKAW, n.s., XIV, iv, 1-154. 1914.

--- Prof. C.C.Uhlenbeck's Latest Contribution to Blackfoot Ethnology. IAE, XXI, 105-15. 1913.

--- Social Organization of the Southern Peigans. IAE, XX, 191-7. 1912.

Kane, P. Wanderings of an Artist among the Indians of North America. 329 pp. London, 1859.

Kehoe, T.F. Stone "Medicine Wheels" in southern Alberta and the Adjacent Portion of Montana. JWAS, XLIV, 133-37. 1954.

--- Tipi Rings. AA, LX, 861-73. 1958.

Kehoe, T.F. and A.B. Boulder Effigy Monuments in the Northern Plains. JAFL, LXXII, 115-27. 1959.

--- A Historical Marker, Indian Style. AHR, V, iv, 6-10. 1957.

Kennedy, G.A. The Last Battle. Alberta Folklore Quarterly, I, 57-60. 1945.

Knox, R.H. A Blackfoot Version of the Magic Flight. JAFL, XXXVI, 401-3. 1923.

Laidlaw, G.E. The Sun Dance among the Blackfeet. AAOJ, VIII, 169-70. 1886.

Lanning, C.M. A Grammar and Vocabulary of the Blackfoot Language. 143 pp. Fort Benton, 1882.

Legal, E.J. Au nord-ouest canadien: les Pieds-Noirs. BSG, ser. 7, XX, 450-61. 1899.

Levine, P. Distribution of Blood Groups and Agglutinogen M among "Blackfeet" and "Blood" Indians. Proceedings of the Society for Experimental Biology and Medicine, XXXIII, 297-9. 1935.

Lewis, O. The Effects of White Contact upon Blackfoot Culture with Special Reference to the Role of the Fur Trade. MAES, VI, 1-73. 1942.

--- Manly-Hearted Women among the North Piegan. AA, n.s., XLIII, 173-87. 1941.

L'Heureux, J. Ethnological Notes on the Astronomical Customs and Religious Ideas of the Chokitapia or Blackfeet Indians. JAI, XV, 301-4. 1885.

--- The Kekip-Sesoators, or Ancient Sacrificial Stone, of the North-West Tribes of Canada. JAI, XV, 161-4. 1885.

Lincoln, J.S. The Dream in Primitive Cultures. 359 pp. London, 1935.

Linderman, F.B. American. 324 pp. New York, 1930.

--- Blackfeet Indians. 65 pp. St. Paul, 1935.

--- Indian Why Stories. 236 pp. New York, 1915.

Long Lance, Buffalo Child. Long Lance. 278 pp. New York, 1928.

McAllester, D. Water as a Disciplinary Agent among the Crow and Blackfoot. AA, n.s., XLIII, 593-604. 1941.

McClintock, W. The Blackfoot. M, X, 85-96. 1936.

--- The Blackfoot Beaver Bundle. M, IX, 77-84, 108-17. 1935.

--- A Blackfoot Circle-Camp. M, I, 5-12. 1927.

--- Blackfoot Legends. M, VI, 41-6, 70-3. 1933.

--- Blackfoot Medicine-Pipe Ceremony. SWML, XXI, 1-9. 1948.

--- The Blackfoot Tipi. M, X, 85-96. 1936.

--- Blackfoot Warrior Societies. M, XI, 148-58, 198-204; XII, 11-23. 1937-38.

--- Bräuche und Legenden der Schwarzfuss-indianer. ZE, XL, 606-14. 1908.

--- Dances of the Blackfoot Indians. M, XI, 77-86, 111-21. 1937.

--- Medizinal- und Nutzpflanzen der Schwarzfuss-Indianer. ZE, XLI, 273-9. 1909.

--- Old Indian Trails. 336 pp. London, 1923.

--- Painted Tipis and Picture-Writing of the Blackfoot Indians. M, X, 121-33, 169-79. 1936.

--- Saitsiko, the Blackfoot Doctor. M, XV, 80-6. 1941.

--- The Thunderbird Motive in Blackfoot Art. M, XV, 129-34. 1941.

--- The Thunderbird Myth. M, XV, 164-8, 224-7; XVI, 16-18. 1941-42.

--- The Tragedy of the Blackfoot. M, IV, 22-6. 1930.

McClintock, W. The Tragedy of the Blackfoot.
SWMP, III, 1-53. 1930.

McLean, J. Blackfoot Amusements. AAOJ, XXIII,
163-9. 1901.

--- Blackfoot Indian Legends. JAFL, III, 296-8.
1890.

--- The Blackfoot Language. TCI, V, 128-65. 1898.

--- Blackfoot Mythology. JAFL, VI, 165-72. 1893.

--- The Blackfoot Sun-Dance. PCI, ser. 3, VI, 231-
7. 1888.

--- Canadian Savage Folk. Toronto, 1896.

--- The Gesture Language of the Blackfeet. TCI,
V, 44-8. 1898.

--- The Indians of Canada. 3d edit. 351 pp. London,
1892.

--- The Mortuary Customs of the Blackfeet Indians.
PCI, ser. 3, V, 20-4. 1887.

--- Picture-Writing of the Blackfeet. TCI, V, 114-
20. 1898.

--- Social Organization of the Blackfoot Indians.
TCI, IV, 249-60. 1895.

McQuesten, C. The Sun Dance of the Blackfoot.
Rod and Gun in Canada, XIII, 1169-77. 1912.

Matson, G.A. Blood Groups and Ageusia in Indians
of Montana and Alberta. AJPA, XXIV, 81-9. 1938.

--- Unexpected Differences in Distribution of Blood
Groups among American Indians. Proceedings of
the Society for Experimental Biology and Medicine,
XXX, 1380-2. 1933.

Matson, G.A., et al. Distribution of the Sub-groups
of A and Agglutinogens among the Blackfeet Indians. Proceedings of the Society for Experimental
Biology and Medicine, XXXIII, 25, 46-7. 1936.

Matson, G.A., and Schrader, H.F. Blood Grouping
among the "Blackfeet" and "Blood" Tribes. Journal
of Immunology, XXV, 155-63. 1933.

Meeker, L.L. Piegan Fortune-Telling. AA, IX, 368.
1896.

Michelson, T. Notes on Some Word-Comparisons between Blackfoot and Other Algonquian Languages.
IJAL, III, 233-5. 1925.

--- Notes on the Piegan System of Consanguinity.
Holmes Anniversary Volume, pp. 320-33. Washington, 1916.

--- Phonetic Shifts in Algonquian Languages. IJAL,
VIII, 131-71. 1935.

--- A Piegan Tale. JAFL, XXIX, 408-9. 1916.

--- Piegan Tales. JAFL, XXIV, 238-48. 1911.

Middleton, S.H. Kainai Chieftainship. 179 pp.
Lethbridge, 1951.

--- The Story of the Blood Indians. Alberta Folklore
Quarterly, I, 85-8. 1945.

Mooney, J. Siksika. BBAE, XXX, ii, 570-1. 1910.

Morgan, L.H. The Indian Journals, 1859-62, pp.
98, 128-9, 144-5, 200. Ann Arbor, 1959.

--- Systems of Consanguinity and Affinity. SCK,
XVII, 282-391. 1871.

Owen, J. Journals and Letters, ed. S. Dunbar and
P.C. Phillips. New York, 1927.

Palliser, J. Further Papers. 325 pp. London, 1860.

Petitot, E.F.S. Traditions indiennes du Canada nord-
ouest. LPTN, XXIII, 489-507. 1886.

--- Vocabulaire piéganie. Actes de la Société Philologique, XIV, 170-98. 1885.

Richardson, J., and Hanks, L.M. Water Discipline
and Water Imagery among the Blackfoot. AA, n.s.,
XLIV, 331-3. 1942.

Sanders, H.F. The White Quiver. 344 pp. New
York, 1913.

Schaeffer, C.E. Bird Nomenclature and Principles
of Avian Taxonomy of the Blackfeet Indians. JWAS,
XL, 37-46. 1950.

--- Was the California Condor Known to the Blackfoot Indians? JWAS, XLI, 181-91. 1951.

Schemm, M.W. The Major's Lady: Natawista. MMH,
II, i, 5-16. 1952.

Schmidt, W. Die Blackfeet. UG, II, 659-70. 1929.

Schultz, J.W. Apank, Caller of Buffalo. 226 pp.
Boston, 1916.

--- Blackfeet Tales. 241 pp. Boston, 1916.

--- Friends of My Life as an Indian. 299 pp. Boston,
1923.

--- My Life as an Indian. 426 pp. New York, 1907.

--- Signposts of Adventure. 225 pp. Boston, 1926.

Schultz, J.W., and Donaldson, J.L. The Sun God's
Children. 255 pp. Boston, 1930.

Smet, P.J. de. Western Missions and Missionaries.
New York, 1863.

Smith, DeC. Indian Experiences. 387 pp. Caldwell,
1943.

Spier, L. Blackfoot Relationship Terms. AA, n.s.,
XVII, 603-7. 1915.

Stanley, J.M. Visit to the Piegan Camp. RESRR, I,
447-9. 1855.

Steward, J.H. The Blackfoot. 92 pp. Berkeley,
1934.

Tims, J.W. Grammar and Dictionary of the Blackfoot Language. 191 pp. London, 1889.

Tyrrell, J.B., ed. David Thompson's Narrative of
His Explorations in Western America. PCS, XII,
345-71. 1916.

Uhlenbeck, C.C. Additional Blackfoot-Arapaho
Comparisons. IJAL, IV, 227-8. 1927.

--- Blackfoot Imità(ua), Dog. IJAL, III, 236. 1925.

Uhlenbeck, C.C. Blackfoot kimmat. Scriti in
    onore de Alfredo Trombetti, xiv. Milano, 1936.

--- Blackfoot Notes. IJAL, II, 181; V, 119-20; IX,
    76, 119. 1923-39.

--- A Concise Blackfoot Grammar. VKAW, n.s.,
    XLI, 1-240. 1938.

--- Het emphatisch gebruik van relatief-promominale
    uitgangen in het Blackfoot. Festschrift Publication
    d'Hommage offerte au P.W. Schmidt, ed. W.
    Koppers, pp. 148-56. Wien, 1928.

--- Flexion of Substantives in Blackfoot. VKAW, n.
    s., XIV, i, 1-40. 1913.

--- Geslachts- en persoonsnamen der Peigans. MKAW,
    ser. 4, XI, 4-29. 1912.

--- A New Series of Blackfoot Texts. VKAW, n.s.,
    XIII, i, 1-264. 1912.

--- Ontwerp van eene vergelijkende vormleer van
    eenige Algonkin-talen. VKAW, n.s., XI, iii,
    1-67. 1910.

--- The Origin of the Otter-Lodge. Festschrift Vilhelm
    Thomsen, pp. 74-7. Leipzig, 1912.

--- Original Blackfoot Texts. VKAW, n.s., XII, i,
    1-106. 1911.

--- Philological Notes to Dr. J.P.B. de Josselin de
    Jong's Blackfoot Texts. VKAW, n.s., XVI, i,
    1-43. 1915.

--- Some Blackfoot Song Texts. IAE, XXIII, 241-
    2. 1916.

--- Some General Aspects of Blackfoot Morphology.
    VKAW, n.s., XIV, v, 1-61. 1914.

--- Some Word-Comparisons between Blackfoot and
    Other Algonquian Languages. IJAL, III, 103-8.
    1924.

--- A Survey of the Non-pronominal and Non-forma-
    tive Affixes of the Blackfoot Verb. VKAW, XX, ii,
    1-130. 1920.

Uhlenbeck, C.C., and Gulick, R.H. van. A Black-
    foot-English Vocabulary. VKAW, n.s., XXXIII,
    ii, 1-380. 1934.

--- An English-Blackfoot Vocabulary. VKAW, n.s.,
    XXIX, iv, 1-261. 1930.

Voegelin, C.F. The Position of Blackfoot among
    the Algonquian Languages. PMA, XXIV, 505-12.
    1941.

Walton, E.L. Dawn Boy; Blackfoot and Navaho
    Songs. 82 pp. New York, 1926.

Wied-Neuwied, M. zu. Reise in das innere Nord-
    amerika. 2 vols. Coblenz, 1839-41.

--- Travels in the Interior of North America. EWT,
    XXIII, 86-164; XXIV, 217-20. 1906.

Wildschut, W. Blackfoot Beaver Bundle. IN, I,
    138-41. 1924.

Wildschut, W. Blackfoot Pipe Bundles. IN, V, 419-
    33. 1928.

Wilson, E.F. Report on the Blackfoot Tribes. BAAS,
    LVII, 183-200. 1887.

Wilson, R.N. Blackfoot Star Myths. AAOJ, XV,
    149-50, 200-3. 1893.

--- The Sacrificial Rite of the Blackfoot. PTRSC,
    ser. 3, III, ii, 3-21. 1909.

Wissler, C. The Blackfoot Indians. AAR, 1905, 162-
    78.

--- Ceremonial Bundles of the Blackfoot Indians.
    APAM, VII, 65-289. 1912.

--- Comparative Study of Pawnee and Blackfoot
    Rituals. ICA, XIX, 335-9. 1915.

--- Decorative Art of the Sioux Indians. BAMNH,
    XVIII, 276-7. 1904.

--- Smoking Star, a Blackfoot Shaman. American
    Indian Life, ed. E.C.Parsons, pp. 45-62. New
    York, 1925.

--- Societies and Dance Associations of the Black-
    foot Indians. APAM, XI, 359-460. 1913.

--- The Sun Dance of the Blackfoot Indians. APAM,
    XVI, 223-70. 1918.

Wissler, C., and Duvall, D.C. Mythology of the
    Blackfoot Indians. APAM, II, 1-163. 1908.

5. CADDO

Including the Adai, the Caddo (Ceni, Teja), and
the Hinai.

Griffith, W.J. The Hasinai Indians of East Texas as
    Seen by Europeans, 1687-1772. PDS, II, 43-165.
    1954.

Parsons, E.C. Notes on the Caddo. MAAA, LVII,
    1-76. 1941.

Swanton, J.R. Source Material on the History and
    Ethnology of the Caddo Indians. BBAE, CXXXII,
    1-332. 1942.

Antle, H.R. Excavation of a Caddoan Earth Lodge.
    CO, XII, 444-6. 1934.

Bell, R.E. Caddoan Prehistory. BTAPS, XIX, 148-
    54. 1948.

Boas, F. Zur Anthropologie der nordamerikanischen
    Indianer. VBGA, 1895, 367-411.

Bolton, H.E. Athanase de Mesières and the Louisiana-
    Texas Frontier. 2 vols. Cleveland, 1914.

--- Nabedache. BBAE, XXX, ii, 1-4. 1910.

--- Nacogdoche. BBAE, XXX, ii, 6-8. 1910.

--- The Native Tribes about the East Texas Missions.
    TSHAQ, XI, 249-76. 1908.

Bolton, H.E. Neche. BBAE, XXX, ii, 49-50. 1910.

--- Texas in the Middle Eighteenth Century. UCPH, IV, 1-501. 1915.

--- Xinesi. BBAE, XXX, ii, 981. 1910.

Castaneda, C. Myths and Customs of the Tejas Indians. PTFLS, IX, 167-74. 1931.

Clark, R.C. The Beginnings of Texas. Texas State Historical Quarterly, I, iii, 171-205. 1902.

Connelley, W.E. Notes on the Early Indian Occupancy of the Great Plains. CKSHS, XIV, 438-70. 1918.

Dickinson, S.D. Notes on the Decoration and Form of Arkansas Caddo Pottery. BTAPS, XV, 9-29. 1943.

Dormon, C. Caddo Pottery. AAA, XXXV, 59-68. 1934.

Dorsey, G.A. Caddo Customs of Childhood. JAFL, XVIII, 226-8. 1905.

--- Traditions of the Caddo. 136 pp. Washington, 1905.

Douglas, F.H. The Grass House of the Wichita and Caddo. DAMLS, I, xlii, 1-4. 1932.

Ethridge, A.N. Indians of Grant Parish. LHQ, XXIII, 1108-31. 1940.

Fletcher, A.C. Adai. BBAE, XXX, i, 12-13. 1907.

--- Bidai. BBAE, XXX, i, 145-6. 1907.

--- Caddo. BBAE, XXX, i, 179-82. 1907.

--- Kadohadacho. BBAE, XXX, i, 638-9. 1907.

Ford, J.A. Analysis of Indian Village Site Collections from Louisiana and Mississippi. Louisiana Department of Conservation, Anthropological Studies, II, 1-285. 1936.

Foreman, G. The Last Trek of the Indians, pp. 282-6, 291-5. Chicago, 1946.

Glover, W.B. A History of the Caddo Indians. LHQ, XVIII, 872-946. 1935.

Griffith, W.J. The Spanish Occupation of the Hasinai Country, 1690 to 1737. Middle American Research Institute, Studies, III, 147 pp. 1954.

Harby, Mrs. L.C. The Tejas. Annual Report of the American Historical Association, 1894, 63-82.

Harrington, M.R. Certain Caddo Sites in Arkansas. INM, n.s., X, 1-349. 1920.

Hatcher, M.A. Descriptions of the Tejas or Asinai Indians. SWHQ, XXX, 206-18, 283-304; XXXI, 50-62, 150-80. 1927.

--- Myths of the Tejas Indians. PTFLS, VI, 107-18. 1927.

Heflin, E. The Oashuns or Dances of the Caddo. BOAS, I, 39-42. 1953.

Hilder, F.F. A Texas Indian Myth. AA, n.s., I, 592-4. 1899.

Hodges, T.L. The Cahinnio-Caddo. BTAPS, XXVIII, 190-97. 1957.

--- Suggestion for Identification of Certain Mid-Ouachita Pottery as Cahinnio Caddo. BTAPS, XVI, 98-116. 1945.

Humble, S.L. The Ouachita Valley Expedition of DeSoto. LHQ, XXV, 611-43. 1942.

Hungate, M. Religious Beliefs of the Nebraska Indian. NeH, XIV, iii, 207-26. 1938.

Hyde, G.E. The Pawnee Indians. OWS, IV, 5-54; V, 3-50. 1934.

Jackson, A.T. Fire in East Texas Burial Rites. BTAPS, X, 77-113. 1938.

Jennings, J.D. Prehistory of the Lower Mississippi Valley. AEUS, 256-71. 1952.

Joutel, H. Journal of La Salle's Last Voyage. New edit. 258 pp. Albany, 1906.

--- Relation. DEFAS, III, 91-534. 1879.

Kunkel, P.A. The Indians of Louisiana about 1700. LHQ, XXXIV, 175-204. 1951.

Lesser, A., and Weltfish, G. Composition of the Caddoan Linguistic Stock. SMC, LXXXVII, vi, 1-15. 1932.

Lyon, O. The Trail of the Caddo. ArHQ, XI, 124-30. 1952.

Mansanet, D. Carta. TSHAQ, II, 254-312. 1899.

Mooney, J. The Ghost-Dance Religion. ARBAE, XIV, ii, 1092-1102. 1893.

Morfi, J.H. de. Memorias for the History of the Province of Texas, ed. F.M. Chabot. 85 pp. San Antonio, 1932.

Nasatir, A.P. Before Lewis and Clark. 2 vols. 882 pp. St. Louis, 1952.

Newell, H.P. and Krieger, A.D. The George C. Davis Site, Cherokee County, Texas. MSAA, V, 271 pp. 1949.

Orr, K.G. Survey of Caddoan Area Archeology. AEUS, 239-54. 1952.

Padilla, J.A. Texas in 1820, tr. M.A. Hatcher. SWHQ, XXIII, 47-68. 1919.

Peck, W.M. Caddolina. 45 pp. Denison, 1917.

Sayles, E.B. An Archaeological Survey of Texas. Medallion Papers, XVII, 1-164. 1935.

Shea, J.G., ed. Early Voyages up and down the Mississippi. 191 pp. Albany, 1861.

Sibley, J. A Report from Natchitoches. INM, n.s., XXV, 5-102. 1922.

--- Vocabulary of the Caddoquis or Caddo Language. AN, 1879, 787-90.

Smith, R.A. Account of the Journey of Bénard de la Harpe. SWHQ, LXII, 75-86, 246-59, 371-85, 525-41. 1958-59.

Spier, L. Wichita and Caddo Relationship Terms.
    AA, n.s., XXVI, 258-63. 1924.

Swanton, J.R. The Caddo Social Organization and
    Its Possible Historical Significance. JWAS, XXI,
    203-6. 1931.

--- Indians of the Southeastern United States. BBAE,
    CXXXVII, 11-832. 1946.

Walker, W.M. A Caddo Burial Site at Natchitoches.
    SMC, XCIV, xiv, 1-15. 1935.

--- A Variety of Caddo Pottery from Louisiana.
    JWAS, XXIV, 99-104. 1934.

Webb, C.H. The Belcher Mound. MSAA, XVI, 225
    pp. 1959.

--- House Types among the Caddo Indians. BTAPS,
    XII, 49-75. 1940.

--- A Second Historic Caddo Site at Natchitoches.
    BTAPS, XVI, 52-83. 1945.

Weer, P. Preliminary Notes on the Caddoan Family.
    PRS, I, 111-30. 1938.

Zavala, A. de. Religious Beliefs of the Tejas or
    Hasanias Indians. PTFLS, I, 39-43. 1916.

6. CHEYENNE

Grinnell, G.B. The Cheyenne Indians. 2 vols. New
    Haven, 1923.

--- The Fighting Cheyennes. 2nd ed. 470 pp. Nor-
    man, 1956.

Jablow, J. The Cheyenne in Plains Indian Trade Re-
    lations, 1795-1840. MAES, XIX, 110 pp. 1951.

Llewellyn, K.N., and Hoebel, E.A. The Cheyenne
    Way. 360 pp. Norman, 1941.

Abel, A.H., ed. Tabeau's Narrative of Loisel's Ex-
    pedition to the Upper Missouri. 272 pp. Norman,
    1939.

Alexander, T. and Anderson, R. Children in a So-
    ciety under Stress. Behavioral Science, II, 46-55.
    1957.

Anderson, R. The Buffalo Men. SJA, XII, 92-104.
    1956.

--- The Northern Cheyenne War Mothers. AQ, IV,
    82-90. 1956.

--- Notes on Northern Cheyenne Corn Ceremonialism.
    M, XXXII, 57-63. 1958.

Anonymous. Arapaho and Cheyenne Indians. H.R.
    11359, 70th Congress, 1st Session, March 1 and
    15, 1928.

Barrett, S.M. Hoistah, an Indian Girl. 136 pp.
    New York, 1913.

Berthrong, D.J. Federal Indian Policy and the South-
    ern Cheyennes and Arapahoes, 1887-1907. E, III,
    138-53. 1956.

Boas, F. Zur Anthropologie der nordamerikanischen
    Indianer. VBGA, 1895, 367-411.

Bonnerjea, B. Reminiscences of a Cheyenne Indian.
    JSAP, n.s., XXVII, 129-43. 1935.

Bourke, J.G. MacKenzie's Last Fight with the Chey-
    ennes. Journal of the Military Service Institution of
    the United States, XI, 29-49, 198-221. 1890.

Brant, C.S. Peyotism among the Kiowa-Apache and
    Neighboring Tribes. SJA, VI, 212-22. 1950.

Brown, D.N. The Ghost Dance Religion among the
    Oklahoma Cheyenne. CO, XXX, 408-16. 1952.

Burbank, E.A., and Caldwell, E. Burbank among the
    Indians, pp. 164-74. Caldwell, 1946.

Bushnell, D.I. Burials of the Algonquian, Siouan and
    Caddoan Tribes. BBAE, LXXXIII, 7-10. 1927.

--- Villages of the Algonquian, Siouan and Caddoan
    Tribes. BBAE, LXXVII, 21-5. 1922.

Campbell, S. The Cheyenne Tipi. AA, n.s., XVII,
    685-94. 1915.

--- Two Cheyenne Stories. JAFL, XXIX, 406-8. 1916.

Curtis, E.S. The North American Indian, VI, 89-134,
    155-8, 167-73; XIX, 107-48, 224-6, 230-8. Nor-
    wood, 1911-30.

Curtis, N., ed. The Indians' Book, pp. 147-93. New
    York, 1907.

Densmore, F. Cheyenne and Arapaho Music. SWMP,
    X, 9-111. 1936.

Devereux, G. Cultural Factors in Psychoanalytic Ther-
    apy. Journal of the American Psychoanalytic As-
    sociation, I, 629-55. 1953.

Dodge, R.I. Our Wild Indians. 650 pp. Hartford,
    1882.

Donaldson, T. The George Catlin Indian Gallery.
    RUSNM, 1885, 88-94.

Dorsey, G.A. The Cheyenne. FMAS, IX, 1-186.
    1905.

Douglas, F.H. A Cheyenne Peyote Fan. MCN, XII,
    47-52. 1939.

Dyer, D.B. Fort Reno or Picturesque Cheyenne-
    Arapaho Army Life before the Opening of Oklahoma.
    216 pp. New York, 1896.

Eggan, F. The Cheyenne and Arapaho Kinship Sys-
    tem. SANAT, 35-98. 1955.

Flying Eagle Goodbear, P. Southern Cheyenne Ghost
    Narratives. PM, XXIV, 10-20. 1951.

Foreman, G. The Last Trek of the Indians, pp.
    296-302. Chicago, 1946.

Garrard, L.H. Wa-to-yah and the Taos Trail. Cin-
    cinnati, 1850; Norman, 1955.

Goggin, J.M. A Note on Cheyenne Peyote. NMA, III, 26-30. 1939.

Grinnell, G.B. Account of the Northern Cheyennes concerning the Messiah Superstition. JAFL, IV, 61-9. 1891.

--- A Buffalo Sweatlodge. AA, n.s., XXI, 361-75. 1919.

--- By Cheyenne Campfires. 305 pp. New Haven, 1926.

--- The Cheyenne Medicine Lodge. AA, n.s., XVI, 245-56. 1914.

--- A Cheyenne Obstacle Myth. JAFL, XVI, 108-15. 1903.

--- Cheyenne Stream Names. AA, n.s., VIII, 15-22. 1906.

--- Cheyenne Woman Customs. AA, n.s., IV, 13-16. 1902.

--- Coup and Scalp among the Plains Indians. AA, n.s., XII, 296-310. 1910.

--- Early Cheyenne Villages. AA, n.s., XX, 359-80. 1918.

--- Falling-Star. JAFL, XXXIV, 308-15. 1921.

--- The Fighting Cheyennes. New York, 1915.

--- The Great Mysteries of the Cheyenne. AA, n.s., XII, 542-75. 1910.

--- Lone Wolf's Last War Trip. M, XVII, 162-7, 219-24. 1943.

--- Notes on Some Cheyenne Songs. AA, n.s., V, 312-22. 1903.

--- Social Organization of the Cheyennes. ICA, XIII, 135-46. 1902.

--- Some Cheyenne Plant Medicines. AA, n.s., VII, 37-43. 1905.

--- Some Early Cheyenne Tales. JAFL, XX, 169-94; XXI, 269-320. 1907-08.

--- When Buffalo Ran. 114 pp. New Haven, 1920.

Hafen, L.R. A Report from the First Indian Agent of the Upper Platte and Arkansas. New Spain and the Anglo-American West, ed. C.W.Hackett, G.P. Hammond, et al, II, 121-37. Los Angeles, 1932.

Harmon, E.M. The Story of the Indian Fort near Granby, Colorado. Colorado Magazine, XXII, 167-71. 1945.

Hayden, F.V. Contributions to the Ethnography and Philology of the Indian Tribes of the Missouri Valley. TAPS, n.s., XII, 274-320. 1863.

Hilger, M.I. Notes on Cheyenne Child Life. AA, n.s., XLVIII, 60-69. 1946.

Hoebel, E.A. Associations and the State in the Plains. AA, n.s., XXXVIII, 433-8. 1936.

--- The Cheyennes. 103 pp. New York, 1960.

Hurst, C.T. Colorado's Old-Timers. SWL, XII, 19-28. 1946.

Kate, H.F.C.ten. Reizen en onderzoekingen in Noord-Amerika. 464 pp. Leiden, 1885.

Kroeber, A.L. Cheyenne Tales. JAFL, XIII, 161-90. 1900.

McCracken, H. The Sacred White Buffalo. NH, LV, 304-9. 1946.

Marquis, T.B. A Warrior who Fought Custer. 384 pp. Minneapolis, 1931.

Meserve, C.F. The First Allotment of Lands in Severalty among the Oklahoma Cheyenne and Arapaho Indians. CO, XI, 1040-3. 1933.

Michelson, T. Field-Work among the Catawba, Fox, Sutaio and Sauk Indians. SMC, LXIII, viii, 836. 1914.

--- The Narrative of a Southern Cheyenne Woman. SMC, LXXXVII, v, 1-13. 1932.

Mooney, J. The Cheyenne Indians. MAAA, I, 357-442. 1907.

--- A Cheyenne Tree Burial. SW, XXXVI, 95-7. 1907.

--- The Ghost-Dance Religion. ARBAE, XIV, ii, 1023-42. 1893.

Morgan, L.H. The Indian Journals, 1859-62, pp. 95-7, 110. Ann Arbor, 1959.

--- Systems of Consanguinity and Affinity. SCK, XVII, 291-382. 1871.

Mulloy, W. The Northern Plains. AEUS, 124-38. 1952.

Nasatir, A.P. Before Lewis and Clark. 2 vols. 882 pp. St. Louis, 1952.

Painter, C.C.G. Cheyennes and Arapahoes Revisited. 62 pp. Philadelphia, 1893.

Peery, D.W. The Indians' Friend, John H. Seger. CO, X, 348-68, 570-91; XI, 709-32, 845-68, 967-94. 1933.

Petter, R.C. Cheyenne Grammar. 196 pp. Newton, Kansas, 1952.

--- English-Cheyenne Dictionary. Kettle Falls, 1913-15.

--- Sketch of the Cheyenne Grammar. MAAA, I, 443-78. 1907.

Petter, R.C., tr. The Kingdom of God. 282 pp. Lame Deer, Montana, 1926.

--- Nivova-pavhosto. 273 pp. Lame Deer, Montana, 1928.

Randolph, R.W. Sweet Medicine. 196 pp. Caldwell, 1937.

Sapir, E. Algonkin p and s in Cheyenne. AA, n.s., XV, 538-9. 1913.

Schmidt, M.F., and Brown, D. Fighting Indians of the West, pp. 41-62, 113-228. New York, 1948.

Schmidt, W. Die Cheyenne. UG, II, 757-74; V, 677-715. 1929, 1934.

Scully, B. The Cheyenne and Peyote. Mission Almanac of the Seraphic Mass Association, 6-14. Ashland, Montana. May, 1941.

Seger, J.H. Cheyenne Marriage Customs. JAFL, XI, 298-301. 1898.

--- Early Days among the Cheyenne and Arapahoe Indians, ed. S. Vestal. 155 pp.; 164 pp. Norman, 1934, 1956.

Service, E.R. The Cheyenne of the North American Plains. PPC, 110-35. 1958.

Smith, J.S. Cheyennes. HCPIT, III, 446-59. 1853.

Smith, W.B.S. Some Cheyenne Forms. Studies in Linguistics, VII, 77-85. 1949.

Spence, L. Cheyenne. ERE, III, 513-14. 1911.

Stewart, D.D. Cheyenne-Arapaho Assimilation. Phylon, XIII, 120-26. 1952.

Swanton, J.R. Some Neglected Data Bearing on Cheyenne, Chippewa, and Dakota History. AA, n.s., XXXII, 156-60. 1930.

Thunderbird, Chief. Cheyenne Ceremony for Girls. M, XXIII, 178-9. 1949.

Tomkins, W. Universal Indian Sign Language. 96 pp. San Diego, 1927.

Voth, H.R. Funeral Customs among the Cheyenne and Arapaho Indians. Folklorist, I. 1893.

Wedel, W.R. The Arapaho and Cheyenne. BBAE, CLXXIV, 80-1. 1959.

Wildschut, W. Cheyenne Medicine Blanket. IN, III, 33-6. 1926.

Will, G.F., and Hyde, G.E. Corn among the Indians of the Upper Missouri. 317 pp. St. Louis, 1917.

7. COMANCHE

Wallace, E. and Hoebel, E.A. The Comanches. 400 pp. Norman, 1952.

Atkinson, M.J. The Texas Indians, pp. 227-332. San Antonio, 1935.

Bancroft, H.H. The Native Races of the Pacific States, I, 473-525. New York, 1875.

Becker, D.M. The Comanches, Their Philosophy and Religion. SS, VI, iv, 4-5. 1954.

Boas, F. Zur Anthropologie der nordamerikanischen Indianer. VBGA, 1895, 367-411.

Bollaert, W. Observations on the Indian Tribes in Texas. JESL, II, 262-83. 1850.

Bolton, H.E. Athanase de Mézières and the Louisiana-Texas Frontier. 2 vols. Cleveland, 1914.

Brant, C.S. Peyotism among the Kiowa-Apache and Neighboring Tribes. SJA, VI, 212-22. 1950.

Burbank, E.A., and Royce, E. Burbank among the Indians, pp. 185-91. Caldwell, 1946.

Burnet, D.G. The Comanches and Other Tribes of Texas. HCPIT, I, 229-41. 1851.

Canonge, E.D. Comanche Texts. 169 pp. Norman, 1958.

--- Voiceless Vowels in Comanche. IJAL, XXIII, 63-67. 1957.

Carlson, G.A., and Jones, V.H. Some Notes on Uses of Plants by the Comanche Indians. PMA, XXV, 517-42. 1939.

Carroll, H.B., and Haggard, J.V., eds. Three New Mexico Chronicles. 342 pp. Albuquerque, 1942.

Casagrande, J.B. Comanche Baby Language. IJAL, XIV, 11-14. 1948.

--- Comanche Linguistic Acculturation. IJAL, XX, 140-51, 217-37; XXI, 8-25. 1954-55.

Catlin, G. Illustrations of the Manners, Customs and Condition of the North American Indians, II, 64-9. New York, 1841.

Cessac, L. de. Renseignements ethnographiques sur les Comanches. RE, I, 94-118. 1882.

Clark, C.U. Excerpts from the Journals of Prince Paul of Wurtemberg, Year 1850. SJA, XV, 291-9. 1959.

Cummins, H., and Goldstein, M.S. Dermatoglyphics in Comanche Indians. AJPA, XVII, 229-35. 1932.

Curtis, E.S. The North American Indian, XIX, 181-96, 228-38. Norwood, 1930.

Eagleton, N.E. An Historic Indian Cache in Pecos County. BTAPS, XXVI, 200-17. 1955.

Eastman, E. Seven and Nine Years among the Camanches and Apaches. 309 pp. Jersey City, 1874.

Espinosa, A.M., ed. Los Comanches. University of New Mexico Bulletin, Language Series, I, i, 1-46. 1907.

Fisher, M.C. On the Arapahoes, Kiowas, and Comanches. JESL, n.s., I, 274-87. 1869.

Foreman, G., ed. Adventure on Red River. 199 pp. Norman, 1937.

Garcia Rejon, M. Vocabulario del idioma comanche. 29 pp. Mexico, 1866.

Gatschet, A.S. Zwölf Sprachen aus dem Südwesten Nordamerikas. 150 pp. Weimar, 1876.

Gladwin, T. Comanche Kin Behavior. AA, n.s., L, 73-94. 1948.

Goldstein, M.S. Anthropometry of the Comanches. AJPA, XIX, 289-321. 1934.

Gregg, J. Commerce of the Prairies. EWT, XX, 342-52. 1905.

Grinnell, G.B. Who Were the Padouca? AA, n.s.,
    XXII, 248-60. 1920.

Griswold, G. Old Fort Sill. CO, XXXVI, 2-15. 1958.

Haley, J.E. The Comanchero Trade. SWHQ,
    XXXVIII, 157-76. 1936.

--- The Great Comanche War Trail. PPHR, XXIII,
    11-21. 1950.

Hasskarl, R.A. An Unusual Historic Indian House in
    Washington County, Texas. BTAPS, XXVIII, 232-
    39. 1957.

Hoebel, E.A. Comanche and Hekandika Shoshone
    Relationship Systems. AA, n.s., XLI, 440-57.
    1939.

--- The Comanche Sun Dance and Messianic Out-
    break of 1873. AA, n.s., XLIII, 301-3. 1941.

--- The Political Organization and Law-Ways of the
    Comanche Indians. MAAA, LIV, 1-149. 1940.

Hoffman, W.J. Remarks on Indian Tribal Names.
    PAPS, XXIII, 299-301. 1886.

Howard, J.H. A Comanche Spear Point Used in a
    Kiowa-Comanche Peyote Ceremonial. MNUSD,
    VII, 3-6. 1950.

Humfreville, J.L. Twenty Years among Our Savage
    Indians. 674 pp. Hartford, 1897.

Jenkins, J.H., ed. Recollections of Early Texas.
    333 pp. Austin, 1958.

Jones, J.H. A Condensed History of the Apache and
    Comanche Indian Tribes. San Antonio, 1899.

Kate, H.F.C. ten. Notes ethnographiques sur les
    Comanches. RE, IV, 120-36. 1885.

--- Reizen en onderzoekingen in Noord-Amerika,
    pp. 377-94. Leiden, 1885.

Lee, N. Three Years among the Camanches. 224
    pp., Albany, 1860; 179 pp., Norman, 1957.

Lehmann, H. Nine Years among the Indians. 235
    pp. Austin, 1927.

Levy, J.E. Kiowa and Comanche: Report from the
    Field. Anthropology Tomorrow, VI, ii, 30-44.
    1958.

Linton, R. The Comanche Sun Dance. AA, n.s.,
    XXXVII, 420-8. 1935.

--- The Study of Man. 497 pp. New York, 1936.

Lowie, R.H. The Comanche, a Sample of Accultura-
    tion. Sociologus, n.s., III, 122-27. 1953.

--- Dances and Societies of the Plains Shoshone.
    APAM, XI, 809-12. 1915.

Marcy, R.B. Exploration of the Red River of Louisi-
    ana. 320 pp. Washington, 1853.

--- Thirty Years of Army Life on the Border. 442 pp.
    New York, 1866.

Mooney, J. Comanche. BBAE, XXX, i, 327-9. 1907.

Morfi, J.A.de. Memorias for the History of the
    Province of Texas, ed. F.M.Chabot. 85 pp. San
    Antonio, 1932.

Nasatir, A.P. Before Lewis and Clark. 2 vols. 882
    pp. St. Louis, 1952.

Neighbors, K.F. The Marcy-Neighbors Exploration
    of the Headwaters of the Brazos and Wichita Rivers
    in 1854. PPHR, XXVII, 27-46. 1954.

Neighbors, R.S. The Na-ü-ni or Comanches of
    Texas. HCPIT, II, 125-34. 1852.

Newcomb, W.W. An Historic Burial from Yellow-
    house Canyon, Lubbock County. BTAPS, XXVI,
    186-99. 1955.

Nye, W.S. Carbine and Lance. 441 pp. Norman,
    1937.

Opler, M.K. The Origins of Comanche and Ute. AA,
    n.s., XLV, 155-63. 1943.

Osborn, H., and Smalley, W.A. Formulae for
    Comanche Stem and Word Formation. IJAL, XV,
    93-9. 1949.

Parker, W.B. Manners, Customs, and History of the
    Indians of South-western Texas. HCPIT, V, 682-
    5. 1855.

--- Notes taken during the Expedition Commanded by
    Capt. R.B.Marcy, pp. 188-203, 230-41. Phila-
    delphia, 1856.

Peters, J.H. Dyeing, Spinning and Weaving by the
    Comanches, Navajoes, and Other Indians of New
    Mexico. Indian Miscellany, ed. W.W. Beach,
    pp. 352-60. Albany, 1877.

Porter, K.W. Negroes and Indians on the Texas
    Frontier, 1831-1876. JNH, XLI, 185-214, 285-
    310. 1956.

Richardson, R.N. The Comanche Barrier to South
    Plains Settlement. 424 pp. Glendale, 1933.

--- The Culture of the Comanche Indians. BTAPS, I,
    58-73. 1929.

Riggs, V. Alternate Phonemic Analyses of Comanche.
    IJAL, XV, 229-31. 1949.

Rister, C.C. Comanche Bondage. 210 pp. Glen-
    dale, 1955.

St. Clair, H.H., and Lowie, R.H. Shoshone and
    Comanche Tales. JAFL, XXII, 273-82. 1909.

Schmidt, M.F., and Brown, D. Fighting Indians of
    the West, pp. 63-88. New York, 1948.

Secoy, F.R. The Identity of the "Paduca." AA,
    LIII, 525-42. 1951.

Shimkin, D.B. Shoshone-Comanche Origins and Mi-
    grations. PPSC, VI, iv, 17-25. 1940.

Shirk, G.H. Peace on the Plains. CO, XXVIII, 2-
    41. 1950.

Smalley, W.A. Phonemic Rhythm in Comanche.
IJAL, XIX, 297-301. 1953.

Smith, C.L., and Jeff, D. The Boy Captives, ed.
J.M. Hunter. Bandera, 1927.

Smith, R.A. Account of the Journey of Bénard de la
Harpe. SWHQ, LXII, 75-86, 246-59, 371-85,
525-41. 1958-59.

Thomas, A.B. After Coronado. 307 pp. Norman,
1935.

--- An Eighteenth Century Comanche Document. AA,
n.s., XXXI, 289-98. 1929.

Tilghman, Z.A. Quanah, the Eagle of the Comanches. 196 pp. Oklahoma City, 1938.

Underhill, R.M. Peyote. ICA, XXX, 143-48. 1955.

Vigness, D.M. Indian Raids on the Lower Rio Grande,
1836-1837. SWHQ, LIX, 14-23. 1955.

Wallace, E. The Comanche Eagle Dance. BTAPS,
XVIII, 83-6. 1947.

--- The Comanches on the White Man's Road.
WTHAY, XXIX, 3-32. 1953.

--- David G. Burnett's Letters Describing the Comanche Indians. WTHAY, XXX, 115-40. 1954.

Wedel, W.R. The Comanche. BBAE, CLXXIV, 75-
7. 1959.

8. CROW

Also called Apsaroke.

Ewers, J.C. "Of the Crow Nation," by Edwin Thompson Denig. BBAE, CLI, 1-74. 1953.

Lowie, R.H. The Crow Indians. 350 pp. New York,
1935, 1956.

--- The Material Culture of the Crow Indians. APAM,
XXI, 201-70. 1922.

--- Social Life of the Crow Indians. APAM, IX, 179-
248. 1912.

Anonymous. Crows. BBAE, XXX, i, 367-9. 1907.

Beckwourth, J.P. Life and Adventures, ed. T.D.
Bonner. 405 pp. New York, 1931.

Boas, F. Zur Anthropologie der nordamerikanischen
Indianer. VBGA, 1895, 367-411.

Bonner, T.D., ed. The Life and Adventures of James
P. Beckwourth. 537 pp. New York, 1856.

Bradley, J.H. Indian Traditions. Contributions to the
Historical Society of Montana, IX, 288-99. 1923.

Burbank, E.A., and Royce, E. Burbank among the
Indians, pp. 147-63. Caldwell, 1946.

Bushnell, D.I. Villages of the Algonquian, Siouan
and Caddoan Tribes. BBAE, LXXVII, 150-5. 1922.

Campbell, W.S. The Tipis of the Crow Indians.
AA, n.s., XXIX, 87-104. 1927.

Catlin, G. Illustrations of the Manners, Customs
and Condition of the North American Indians, I,
42-51. New York, 1841.

Corson, E.F. Long Hair, Chief of the Crows. Archives of Dermatology and Syphilology, LVI,
443-7. 1947.

Culbertson, T.A. Journal of an Expedition to the
Mauvaises Terres and the Upper Missouri in 1850.
BBAE, CXLVII, 172 pp. 1952.

Curtis, E.S. The North American Indian, IV, 3-
126, 175-80, 189-210. Cambridge, 1909.

Donaldson, T. The George Catlin Indian Gallery.
RUSNM, 1885, 106-15.

Douglas, F.H. A Crow Beaded Horse Collar. MCN,
II, 5-8. 1937.

--- An Incised Bison Rawhide Parfleche. MCN, I,
25-35. 1938.

Dunraven, W.T.W., Earl of. The Great Divide,
pp. 59-128. London, 1876.

Ehrlich, C. Tribal Culture in Crow Mythology.
JAFL, L, 307-408. 1937.

Ewers, J.C. Three Ornaments Worn by Upper Missouri Indians a Century and a Quarter Ago. NYHSQ,
XLI, 24-33. 1957.

Goldenweiser, A.A. Remarks on the Social Organization of the Crow Indians. AA, n.s., XV, 281-
94. 1913.

Hayden, F.V. Contributions to the Ethnography and
Philology of the Indian Tribes of the Missouri Valley. TAPS, n.s., XII, 391-420. 1863.

Hoffman, W.J. An Absaroka Myth. JAI, X, 239-40.
1880.

Kaschube, D. Examples of Tone in Crow. IJAL,
XX, 34-36. 1954.

Kehoe, T.F. and A.B. Boulder Effigy Monuments
in the Northern Plains. JAFL, LXXII, 115-27.1959.

Koch, P. A Trading Expedition among the Crow Indians, 1873-1874. MVHR, XXXI, 407-30. 1944.

Laroque, F.A. Journal. Publications of the Canadian Archives, III, 55-70. 1910.

Leonard, Z. Adventures of Zenas Leonard. 189 pp.
Norman, 1959.

Lincoln, J.S. The Dream in Primitive Cultures.
359 pp. London, 1935.

Linderman, F.B. American. 313 pp. New York,
1930.

--- Old Man Coyote. 254 pp. New York, 1931.

--- Red Mother. 256 pp. New York, 1932.

Lowie, R.H. Alleged Kiowa-Crow Affinities. SJA,
IX, 357-68. 1953.

Lowie, R.H. Crow Curses. JAFL, LXXII, 105.1959.

--- Crow Indian Art. APAM, XXI, 271-322. 1922.

--- Crow Indian Clowns . AMJ, XII, 74. 1912.

--- The Crow Language. UCP, XXXIX, 1-142. 1941.

--- Crow Prayers. AA, n.s., XXXV, 433-42. 1933.

--- The Crow Sun Dance. JAFL, XXVII, 94-6. 1914.

--- A Crow Tale. AQ, II, 1-22. 1954.

--- A Crow Text. UCP, XXIX, 155-75. 1930.

--- Crow Texts. 564 pp. Berkeley, 1960.

--- A Crow Woman's Tale. American Indian Life,
ed. E.C.Parsons, pp. 35-40. New York, 1925.

--- Indian Theologians. EP, XXXV, 217-31. 1933.

--- The Kinship Systems of the Crow and Hidatsa.
ICA, XIX, 340-3. 1915.

--- Marriage and Society among the Crow Indians.
Source Book in Anthropology, by A.L.Kroeber and
T.T.Waterman, rev. ed., pp. 304-9. New York,
1931.

--- Military Societies of the Crow Indians. APAM,
XI, 143-217. 1913.

--- Minor Ceremonies of the Crow Indians. APAM,
XXI, 323-65. 1924.

--- Myths and Traditions of the Crow Indians. APAM,
XXV, 1-308. 1918.

--- A Note on Aesthetics. AA, n.s., XXIII, 170-4.
1921.

--- Observations on the Literary Style of the Crow Indians. Beiträge zur Gesellungs- und Völkerwissen-
schaft, 271-83. Berlin, 1950.

--- The Omaha and Crow Kinship Terminologies.
ICA, XXIV, 102-8. 1934.

--- The Oral Literature of the Crow Indians. JAFL,
LXXII, 97-104. 1959.

--- Primitive Religion, pp. 2-32. New York, 1925.

--- Proverbial Expressions among the Crow Indians.
AA, n.s., XXXIV, 739-40. 1932.

--- The Relations between the Kiowa and the Crow
Indians. BSSA, VII, 1-5. 1953.

--- The Religion of the Crow Indians. APAM, XXV,
309-444. 1922.

--- Some Problems in the Ethnology of the Crow and
Village Indians. AA, n.s., XIV, 60-71. 1912.

--- Studies in Plains Indian Folklore. UCP, XL,
1-28. 1942.

--- The Sun Dance of the Crow Indians. APAM, XVI,
1-50. 1915.

--- Supplementary Notes on the Social Life of the
Crow. APAM, XXI, 53-99. 1917.

--- Takes-the-Pipe, a Crow Warrior. American Indian Life, ed. E.C.Parsons, pp. 17-33. New York,
1925.

Lowie, R.H. The Tobacco Society of the Crow Indians. APAM, XXI, 101-200. 1919.

--- A Trial of Shamans. American Indian Life, ed.
E.C.Parsons, pp. 41-3. New York, 1925.

McAllester, D. Water as a Disciplinary Agent among
the Crow and Blackfoot. AA, n.s., XLIII, 593-
604. 1941.

McGee, W.J. The Siouan Indians. ARBAE, XV, 157-
204. 1894.

Marquis, T.B. Memoirs of a White Crow Indian. 356
pp. New York, 1928.

Mason, J.A. A Collection from the Crow Indians. MJ,
XVII, 393-413. 1926.

Morgan, L.H. The Indian Journals, 1859-62, pp.
167-76, 183-90, 197. Ann Arbor, 1959.

--- Systems of Consanguinity and Affinity. SCK,
XVII, 291-382. 1871.

Mulloy, W. The Northern Plains. AEUS, 124-38.
1952.

Murdock, G.P. Our Primitive Contemporaries, pp.
264-90. New York, 1934.

Nasatir, A.P. Before Lewis and Clark. 2 vols. 882
pp. St. Louis, 1952.

Nevins, A., ed. Narratives of Exploration and Adventure by John Charles Frémont. 542 pp. New
York, 1956.

Pierce, J.E. Crow vs. Hidatsa in Dialect Distance
and Glottochronology. IJAL, XX, 134-36. 1954.

Quaife, M.M., ed. Narrative of the Adventures of
Zenas Leonard, pp. 227-52. Chicago, 1934.

Quivey, A.M., ed. Bradley Manuscript, Book "F".
Contributions to the Historical Society of Montana,
VIII, 197-250. 1917.

Simms, S.C. Crow Indian Hermaphrodites. AA,
n.s., V, 580-1. 1903.

--- A Crow Monument to Shame. AA, n.s., V,
374-5. 1903.

--- Cultivation of "Medicine Tobacco" by the Crows.
AA, n.s., VI, 331-5. 1904.

--- Traditions of the Crows. FMAS, II, 281-324.
1903.

--- Water Transportation by the Early Crows. AA,
n.s., VI, 191-2. 1904.

Smith, DeC. Indian Experiences. 387 pp. Caldwell, 1943.

Voegelin, C.F. Historical Results of Crow-Hidatsa
Comparisons. PIAS, L, 39-42. 1941.

--- Kiowa-Crow Mythological Affiliations. AA, n.s.,
XXXV, 470-4. 1933.

Voget, F. Crow Socio-Cultural Groups. ICA, XXIX,
ii, 88-93. 1952.

Voget, F. Individual Motivation in the Diffusion of the Wind River Shoshone Sundance to the Crow Indians. AA, n.s., L, 634-45. 1948.

Wagner, G.D., and Allen, W.A. Blankets and Moccasins. 304 pp. Caldwell, 1933.

Ward, R.E. et al. Indians in Agriculture. Montana State Agricultural Experiment Station Bulletin, DXXII, 52 pp. 1956.

Wied-Neuwied, M. zu. Reise in das innere Nordamerika. 2 vols. Coblenz, 1839-41.

--- Travels in the Interior of North America. EWT, XXII, 346-55. 1906.

Wildschut, W. Crow Love Medicine. IN, II, 211-14. 1925.

--- A Crow Pictographic Robe. IN, III, 28-32. 1926.

--- A Crow Shield. IN, II, 315-20. 1925.

--- The Crow Skull Medicine Bundle. IN, II, 119-22. 1925.

--- Crow Sun-Dance Bundle. IN, III, 99-107. 1926.

--- Crow War Bundle of Two-Leggings. IN, III, 284-8. 1926.

--- Moccasin-Bundle of the Crows. IN, III, 201-5. 1926.

Wildschut, W. and Ewers, J.C. Crow Indian Beadwork. CMAI, XVI, 55 pp. 1959.

Woodruff, J. Indian Oasis, pp. 21-157. Caldwell, 1939.

Yellowtail, R. Fine Horses, Pride of the Sioux. IW, IV, 36-9. 1937.

9. GROS VENTRE

Also called Atsina.

Cooper, J.M. The Gros Ventres of Montana. II. Religion and Ritual. CUAS, XVI, 500 pp. 1956.

Flannery, R. The Gros Ventres of Montana. Part I: Social Life. CUAS, XV, 234 pp. 1953.

Kroeber, A.L. Ethnology of the Gros Ventre. APAM, I, 145-281. 1907.

Barry, L. With the First U.S. Cavalry in Indian Country, 1859-1861. KHQ, XXIV, 257-84. 1958.

Boas, F. Zur Anthropologie der nordamerikanischen Indianer. VBGA, 1895, 367-411.

Cooper, J.M. The Shaking Tent Rite among Plains and Forest Algonquians. PM, XVII, 60-84. 1944.

Curtis, E.S. The North American Indian, V, 103-39, 152-4, 164-77, 180-4. Cambridge, 1909.

Flannery, R. The Changing Form and Functions of the Gros Ventre Grass Dance. PM, XX, 39-70. 1947.

Flannery, R. The Dearly-Loved Child among the Gros Ventres of Montana. PM, XIV, 33-8. 1941.

--- The Gros Ventre Shaking Tent. PM, XVII, 54-9. 1944.

--- Individual Variation in Culture. ACISA, V, 87-92. 1960.

--- Men's and Women's Speech in Gros Ventre. IJAL, XII, 133-5. 1946.

Flannery, R., and Cooper, J.M. Social Mechanisms in Gros Ventre Gambling. SJA, II, 391-419. 1946.

Hayden, F.V. Contributions to the Ethnography and Philology of the Indian Tribes of the Missouri Valley. TAPS, n.s., XII, 340-5. 1863.

Kroeber, A.L. Arapaho Dialects. UCP, XII, 71-138. 1916.

--- Gros Ventre Myths and Tales. APAM, I, 55-139. 1907.

Mooney, J. Atsina. BBAE, XXX, i, 113. 1907.

Morgan, L.H. The Indian Journals, 1859-62, pp. 165-6. Ann Arbor, 1959.

--- Systems of Consanguinity and Affinity. SCK, XVII, 291-382. 1871.

Schmidt, W. Die Gros Ventres. UG, II, 671-9. 1929.

Scott, H.L. The Early History and Names of the Arapaho. AA, n.s., IX, 545-60. 1907.

Wied-Neuwied, M. zu. Reise in das innere Nordamerika. 2 vols. Coblenz, 1839-41.

--- Travels in the Interior of North America. EWT, XXIII, 70-7; XXIV, 226-7. 1906.

10. HIDATSA

Also called Minitari.

Matthews, W. Ethnography and Philology of the Hidatsa Indians. U.S. Geological and Geographical Survey, Miscellaneous Publications, VII, 1-239. 1877.

Beckwith, M.W. Mandan and Hidatsa Tales. PFLF, XIV, 269-320. 1934.

--- Mandan-Hidatsa Myths and Ceremonies. MAFLS, XXXII, 1-320. 1938.

--- Myths and Ceremonies of the Mandan and Hidatsa. PFLF, XII, 117-267. 1932.

--- Myths and Hunting Stories of the Mandan and Hidatsa Sioux. PFLF, X, 1-116. 1930.

Bruner, E.M. Assimilation among Fort Berthold Indians. AmI, VI, iv, 21-9. 1953.

--- Cultural Transmission and Cultural Change. SJA, XII, 191-9. 1956.

Bruner, E.M. Primary Group Experience and the Processes of Acculturation. AA, LVIII, 605-23. 1956.

--- Two Processes of Change in Mandan-Hidatsa Kinship Terminology. AA, LVII, 840-50. 1955.

Bushnell, D.I. Burials of the Algonquian, Siouan and Caddoan Tribes. BBAE, LXXXIII, 73-8. 1927.

--- Villages of the Algonquian, Siouan, and Caddoan Tribes. BBAE, LXXVII, 140-50. 1922.

Catlin, G. Illustrations of the Manners, Customs, and Condition of the North American Indians, I, 185-202. New York, 1841.

Culbertson, T.A. Journal of an Expedition to the Mauvaises Terres and the Upper Missouri in 1850. BBAE, CXLVII, 172 pp. 1952.

Curtis, E.S. The North American Indian, IV, 129-72, 180-96, 210-11. Cambridge, 1909.

DeLand, C.E. The Aborigines of South Dakota. South Dakota Historical Collections, III, 269-586. 1906.

Densmore, F. Mandan and Hidatsa Music. BBAE, LXXX, 1-186. 1923.

Dorsey, J.O. Preface. CNAE, IX, xviii-xxx. 1893.

--- A Study of Siouan Cults. ARBAE, XI, 513-18. 1890.

--- Siouan Sociology. ARBAE, XV, 242-3. 1894.

Douglas, F.H. An Hidatsa Burden Basket. MCN, I, 60-5. 1941.

Gilmore, M.R. Being an Account of an Hidatsa Shrine and the Beliefs respecting It. AA, n.s., XXVIII, 572-3. 1926.

Harris, Z.S. Culture and Style in Extended Discourse. ICA, XXIX, iii, 210-15. 1951.

Hayden, F.V. Contributions to the Ethnography and Philology of the Indian Tribes of the Missouri Valley. TAPS, n.s., XII, 420-6. 1863.

Kehoe, T.F. and A.B. Boulder Effigy Monuments in the Northern Plains. JAFL, LXXII, 115-27. 1959.

Libby, O.G. Typical Villages of the Mandans, Arikara, and Hidatsa. Collections of the State Historical Society of North Dakota, II, 498-508. 1908.

Lowie, R.H. The Hidatsa Sun Dance. APAM, XVI, 411-31. 1919.

--- Hidatsa Texts. PRS, I, 173-239. 1939.

--- The Kinship Systems of the Crow and Hidatsa. ICA, XIX, 340-3. 1915.

--- Social Life of the Hidatsa. APAM, XXI, 17-52. 1917.

--- Societies of the Hidatsa and Mandan Indians. APAM, XI, 221-93, 323-54. 1913.

--- Some Problems in the Ethnology of the Crow and Village Indians. AA, n.s., XIV, 60-71. 1912.

--- Studies in Plains Indian Folklore. UCP, XL, 1-28. 1942.

McGee, W J. The Siouan Indians. ARBAE, XV, 157-204. 1894.

Matthews, W. Grammar and Dictionary of the Language of the Hidatsa. 169 pp. New York, 1873-74.

Mooney, J. Hidatsa. BBAE, XXX, i, 547-9. 1907.

Morgan, L.H. The Indian Journals, 1859-62, pp. 155-60, 163, 169, 189-90, 195-6, 200. Ann Arbor, 1959.

--- Systems of Consanguinity and Affinity. SCK, XVII, 291-382. 1871.

Nasatir, A.P. Before Lewis and Clark. 2 vols. 882 pp. St. Louis, 1952.

Pepper, G.H., and Wilson, G.L. An Hidatsa Shrine and the Beliefs respecting it. MAAA, II, 275-328. 1908.

Pierce, J.E. Crow vs. Hidatsa in Dialect Distance and Glottochronology. IJAL, XX, 134-36. 1954.

Riggs, S.R. Dakota Grammar, Texts, and Ethnography. CNAE, IX, xviii-xxix. 1893.

Robinett, F.M. Hidatsa. IJAL, XXI, 1-7, 160-77, 210-16. 1955.

Romney, A.K. and Metzger, D. On the Processes of Change in Kinship Terminology [with rejoinder by E.M.Bruner]. AA, LVIII, 551-56. 1956.

Smith, C.S. An Analysis of the Firearms and Related Specimens from Like-A-Fishhook Village and Fort Berthold I. PIA, IV, 3-12. 1955.

Stetson, R.H. An Experimentalist's View of Hidatsa Phonology. IJAL, XII, 136-8. 1946.

Voegelin, C.F. Historical Results of Crow-Hidatsa Comparisons. PIAS, L, 39-42. 1941.

Voegelin, C.F. and Robinett, F.M. 'Mother Language' in Hidatsa. IJAL, XX, 65-70. 1954.

Wied-Neuwied, M. zu. Reise in das innere Nordamerika. 2 vols. Coblenz, 1839-41.

--- Travels in the Interior of North America. EWT, XXII, 357-66; XXIII, 252-385; XXIV, 24-35, 67-8, 261-76. 1906.

Will, G.F. Archaeology of the Missouri Valley. APAM, XXII, 285-344. 1924.

--- Some Hidatsa and Mandan Tales. JAFL, XXV, 93-4. 1912.

Will, G.F., and Hyde, G.E. Corn among the Indians of the Upper Missouri. 317 pp. St. Louis, 1917.

Wilson, G.L. Agriculture of the Hidatsa Indians. University of Minnesota Studies in the Social Sciences, IV, 1-129. 1917.

--- Goodbird the Indian. 80 pp. New York, 1914.

--- Hidatsa Eagle Trapping. APAM, XXX, 99-245. 1928.

Wilson, G.L. The Hidatsa Earthlodge, ed. B.
    Weitzner. APAM, XXXIII, 341-420. 1934.
--- The Horse and the Dog in Hidatsa Culture. APAM,
    XV, 127-311. 1924.
--- Waheenee. 189 pp. St. Paul, 1921.

11. IOWA

Skinner,A. Ethnology of the Ioway Indians.
    BPMCM, V, 181-354. 1926.

Ashby, D. Anecdotes. Glimpses of the Past, VIII,
    105-12. 1941.
Carman, J.N. and Pond, K.S. The Replacement of
    the Indian Languages of Kansas by English. TKAS,
    LVIII, 137-50. 1955.
Catlin, G. Notice sur les Indiens Ioways. 24 pp.
    Paris, 1845.
Donaldson, T. The George Catlin Indian Gallery.
    RUSNM, 1885, 142-53.
Dorsey, J.O. On the Comparative Phonology of
    Four Siouan Languages. ARSI, 1881, 919-29.
--- Preface. CNAE, IX, xviii-xxx. 1893.
--- Siouan Sociology. ARBAE, XV, 238-40. 1894.
--- The Sister and Brother: an Iowa Tradition.
    AAOJ, IV, 286-8. 1882.
--- The Social Organization of the Siouan Tribes.
    JAFL, IV, 336-40. 1891.
--- A Study of Siouan Cults. ARBAE, XI, 423-30.
    1890.
Dorsey, J.O., and Thomas, C. Iowa. BBAE,XXX,
    i, 612-14. 1907.
Foster, T. The Iowa. 100 pp. Cedar Rapids, 1911.
Griffin, J.B. The Archaeological Remains of the
    Chiwere Sioux. AAn, II, 180-1. 1937.
Hamilton, W. Remarks on the Iowa Language.
    HCPIT, IV, 397-406. 1854.
Hamilton, W., and Irvin, S.M. An Ioway Grammar.
    152 pp. 1848.
Harrington, M.R. An Archaic Iowa Tomahawk. INM,
    X, 55-8. 1920.
Hayden, F.V. Contributions to the Ethnography and
    Philology of the Indian Tribes of the Missouri Val-
    ley. TAPS,n.s.,XII,444-56. 1863.
Irvin, S.M. The Waw-ru-haw-a: the Decline and
    Fall of Indian Superstitions. Philadelphia, 1871.
Irvin, S.M., and Hamilton, W. Iowa and Sac Tribes.
    HCPIT, III, 259-77. 1853.
McGee, W J. The Siouan Indians. ARBAE, XV, 157-
    204. 1894.
Miner, W.H. The Iowa. 100 pp. Cedar Rapids, 1911.

Morgan, L.H. The Indian Journals, 1859-62, pp.
    67-70, 99, 137-8. Ann Arbor, 1959.
--- Systems of Consanguinity and Affinity. SCK,
    XVII, 291-382. 1871.
Nasatir, A.P. Before Lewis and Clark. 2 vols. 882
    pp. St. Louis, 1952.
Plank, P. The Iowa, Sac and Fox Indian Mission.
    TKSHS, X, 312-25. 1908.
Schmidt, W. Die Iowa. UG, II, 648-53. 1929.
Skinner, A. Medicine Ceremony of the Menomini,
    Iowa and Wahpeton Dakota. INM, IV, 189-261.
    1920.
--- Societies of the Iowa. APAM, XI, 679-740.
    1915.
--- Some Unusual Ethnological Specimens. YPMCM,
    III, 103-9. 1925.
--- A Summer among the Sauk and Ioway Indians.
    YPMCM, II, 16-22. 1922.
--- Traditions of the Iowa Indians. JAFL, XXXVIII,
    425-506. 1925.
Whitman, W. Descriptive Grammar of Ioway-Oto.
    IJAL, XIII, 233-48. 1947.
Will, G.F., and Hyde, G.E. Corn among the In-
    dians of the Upper Missouri. 317 pp. St. Louis,
    1917.

12. KANSA

Adams, F.G. Reminiscences of Frederick Chouteau.
    TKSHS, VIII, 423-34. 1904.
Anonymous. Extracts from the Diary of Major Sibley.
    CO, V, 196-218. 1927.
--- Kansa. BBAE, XXX, i, 653-6. 1907.
Barry, L. With the First U.S.Cavalry in Indian Coun-
    try, 1859-1861. KHQ, XXIV, 257-84. 1958.
Bushnell, D.I. Villages of the Algonquian, Siouan
    and Caddoan Tribes. BBAE, LXXVII, 89-97. 1922.
Chapman, B.B. Charles Curtis and the Kaw Reserva-
    tion. KHQ, XV, 337-51. 1947.
Connelley, W.E. Notes on the Early Indian Occu-
    pancy of the Great Plains. CKSHS, XIV, 438-70.
    1918.
Dorsey, J.O. Mourning and War Customs of the Kan-
    sas. AN, XIX, 671-80. 1885.
--- On the Comparative Phonology of Four Siouan Lan-
    guages. ARSI, 1883, 919-29.
Dorsey, J.O. Preface. CNAE, IX, xviii-xxx. 1893.
--- Siouan Sociology. ARBAE,XV, 230-3. 1894.
--- The Social Organization of the Siouan Tribes.
    JAFL, IV, 333-4. 1891.
--- A Study of Siouan Cults. ARBAE, XI, 361-422.
    1890.

Finney, F.F. The Kaw Indians and Their Indian Territory Agency. CO, XXXV, 416-24. 1957.

Foreman, G. The Last Trek of the Indians, pp. 277-82. Chicago, 1946.

Hunter, J.D. Manners and Customs of Several Indian Tribes. Philadelphia, 1823.

James, E. Account of an Expedition from Pittsburgh to the Rocky Mountains. EWT, XIV, 186-209; XVII, 290-8. 1905.

Long, S.H. The Kansas Indians. TKSHS, I-II, 280-301. 1881.

McGee, W J. The Siouan Indians. ARBAE, XV, 157-204. 1894.

Morehouse, G.P. History of the Kansa or Kaw Indians. TKSHS, X, 327-68. 1908.

Morgan, L.H. The Indian Journals, 1859-62, pp. 29, 34-5, 82-3. Ann Arbor, 1959.

--- Systems of Consanguinity and Affinity. SCK, XVII, 291-382. 1871.

Nasatir, A.P. Before Lewis and Clark. 2 vols. 882 pp. St. Louis, 1952.

Remsburg, G.J. An Old Kansas Indian Town on the Missouri. 11 pp. Plymouth, Iowa, 1919.

Riggs, S.R. Dakota Grammar, Texts and Ethnography. CNAE, IX, xviii-xxix. 1893.

Skinner, A. Kansa Organizations. APAM, XI, 741-75. 1915.

Spencer, J. The Kaw or Kansas Indians. TKSHS, X, 373-82. 1908.

Voe, C. de. Legends of the Kaw. 215 pp. Kansas City, 1904.

Wedel, W.R. The Kansa. BBAE, CLXXIV, 50-4. 1959.

--- The Kansa Indians. TKAS, XLIX, 1-35. 1946.

13. KIOWA

Barry, L. With the First U.S. Cavalry in Indian Country, 1859-1861. KHQ, XXIV, 257-84.

Battey, T.C. The Life and Adventures of a Quaker among the Indians. 339 pp. Boston, 1875.

Boas, F. Zur Anthropologie der nordamerikanischen Indianer. VBGA, 1895, 367-411.

Brant, C.S. Indian and White Relations, Southwestern Oklahoma. CO, XXXVII, 433-9. 1959/60.

--- Peyotism among the Kiowa-Apache and Neighboring Tribes. SJA, VI, 212-22. 1950.

Burbank, E.A., and Caldwell, E. Burbank among the Indians, pp. 185-91. Caldwell, 1946.

Collier, D. Conjuring among the Kiowa. PM, XVII, 45-9. 1944.

Crowell, E.E. A Preliminary Report on Kiowa Structure. IJAL, XV, 163-7. 1949.

Curtis, N., ed. The Indians' Book, pp. 221-40. New York, 1907.

Fisher, M.C. On the Arapahoes, Kiowas, and Comanches. JESL, n.s., I, 274-87. 1869.

Gamble, J.I. Changing Patterns in Kiowa Indian Dances. ICA, XXIX, ii, 94-104. 1952.

Gatschet, A.S. Phonetics of the Kayowe Language. AAOJ, IV, 280-5. 1882.

--- Sinti, der erste Mensch. Ausland, LXIII, 901-4. 1890.

--- Zwölf Sprachen aus dem Südwesten Nordamerikas. 150 pp. Weimar, 1876.

Griswold, G. Old Fort Sill. CO, XXXVI, 2-15. 1958.

Harrington, J.P. Kiowa Memories of the Northland. So Live the Works of Men, ed. D.D.Brand and F.E.Harvey, pp. 162-76. Albuquerque, 1939.

--- On Phonetic and Lexical Resemblances between Kiowa and Tanoan. AA, n.s., XII, 119-23. 1910.

--- Three Kiowa Texts. IJAL, XII, 237-42. 1946.

--- Vocabulary of the Kiowa Language. BBAE, LXXXIV, 1-255. 1928.

Harrington, M.R. Peyote Outfit. M, XVIII, 143-4. 1944.

Howard, J.H. A Comanche Spear Point Used in a Kiowa-Comanche Peyote Ceremonial. MNUSD, VII, 3-6. 1950.

Jacobsen, O.B. Kiowa Indian Art. Nice, 1929.

Jensen, D.O. Wo-Haw: Kiowa Warrior. BMHS, VII, 76-88. 1950.

La Barre, W. Kiowa Folk Sciences. JAFL, LX, 105-14. 1947.

Levy, J.E. Kiowa and Comanche: Report from the Field. Anthropology Tomorrow, VI, ii, 30-44. 1958.

Lowie, R.H. Alleged Kiowa-Crow Affinities. SJA, IX, 357-68. 1953.

--- A Note on Kiowa Kinship Terms and Usages. AA, n.s., XXV, 279-81. 1923.

--- Notes on the Kiowa Indians. Tribus, IV/V, 131-38. 1956.

--- The Relations between the Kiowa and the Crow Indians. BSSA, VII, 1-5. 1953.

--- Societies of the Kiowa. APAM, XI, 837-51. 1916.

McKenzie, P., and Harrington, J.P. Popular Account of the Kiowa Language. Monographs of the School of American Research, XII, 1-21. 1948.

Marriott, A. Greener Fields. 274 pp. New York, 1953.

--- The Ten Grandmothers. 306 pp. Norman, 1945.

Marriott, A. Winter-telling Stories. 84 pp. New York, 1947.

Merrifield, W. Classification of Kiowa Nouns. IJAL, XXV, 269-71. 1959.

--- The Kiowa Verb Prefix. IJAL, XXV, 168-76. 1959.

Methvin, J.J. Andele, or the Mexican-Kiowa Captive. Louisville, 1899.

Miller, W.R. A Note on Kiowa Linguistic Affiliations. AA, LXI, 102-105. 1959.

Mishkin, B. Rank and Warfare among the Plains Indians. MAES, III, 1-65. 1940.

Mooney, J. Calendar History of the Kiowa Indians. ARBAE, XVII, i, 141-447. 1896.

--- Field-Work among the Kiowa. SMC, LXX, ii, 99-103. 1919.

--- The Ghost-Dance Religion. ARBAE, XIV, ii, 1078-91. 1893.

--- Indian Shield Heraldry. SW, XXX, 500-4. 1901.

--- Kiowa. BBAE, XXX, i, 699-701. 1907.

--- A Kiowa Mescal Rattle. AA, V, 64-5. 1892.

Nye, W.S. Carbine and Lance. 441 pp. Norman, 1937.

Olmsted, O. On the Linguistic Classification of Kiowa. SWL, XVII, 15-17. 1951.

Parsons, E.C. Kiowa Tales. MAFLS, XXII, 1-151. 1929.

Prentice, R.A. Pictograph Story of Koñate. EP, LVIII, 90-6. 1951.

Richardson, J. Law and Status among the Kiowa Indians. MAES, I, 1-136. 1940.

Schmidt, M.F., and Brown, D. Fighting Indians of the West, pp. 63-88. New York, 1948.

Schmitt, K. Wichita-Kiowa Relations and the 1874 Outbreak. CO, XXVIII, 154-60. 1950.

Scott, H.L. Notes on the Kado, or Sun Dance of the Kiowa. AA, n.s., XIII, 345-79. 1911.

Shirk, G.H. Peace on the Plains. CO, XXVIII, 2-41. 1950.

Sivertsen, E. Pitch Problems in Kiowa. IJAL, XXII, 117-30. 1956.

Spier, L. Notes on the Kiowa Sun Dance. APAM, XVI, 433-50. 1921.

Tsa Toke, M., et al. The Peyote Ritual. 84 pp. San Francisco, 1957.

Vestal, P.A., and Schultes, R.E. The Economic Botany of the Kiowa Indians. 110 pp. Cambridge, 1939.

Vigness, D.M. Indian Raids on the Lower Rio Grande, 1836-1837. SWHQ, LIX, 14-23. 1955.

Voegelin, E.W. Kiowa-Crow Mythological Affiliations. AA, n.s., XXXV, 470-4. 1933.

Wedel, W.R. The Kiowa and Kiowa Apache. BBAE, CLXXIV, 78-80. 1959.

Wharton, C. Satanta, the Great Chief of the Kiowas and His People. 239 pp. Dallas, 1935.

Wonderly, W.L. et al. Number in Kiowa. IJAL, XX, 1-7. 1954.

14. KIOWA APACHE

Battey, T.C. The Life and Adventures of a Quaker among the Indians. 339 pp. Boston, 1875.

Boatright, M.C., ed. The Sky is My Tipi. Texas Folklore Society, XXII, 1-243. 1949.

Brant, C.S. The Cultural Position of the Kiowa-Apache. SJA, V, 56-61. 1949.

--- Kiowa Apache Culture History. SJA, IX, 195-202. 1953.

--- Peyotism among the Kiowa-Apache and Neighboring Tribes. SJA, VI, 212-22. 1950.

Hoijer, H. The Apachean Verb. IJAL, XI, 193-203; XII, 1-13, 51-9; XIV, 247-59; XV, 12-22. 1945-49.

--- Phonetic and Phonemic Change in the Athapaskan Languages. Lg, XVIII, 218-20. 1942.

--- Pitch Accent in the Apachean Languages. Lg, XIX, 38-41. 1943.

James, E. Account of an Expedition from Pittsburgh to the Rocky Mountains. EWT, XVI, 109-19, 194-212. 1905.

McAllister, J.G. Kiowa-Apache Social Organization. SANAT, 99-172. 1955.

Mooney, J. Calendar History of the Kiowa Indians. ARBAE, XVII, i, 245-53. 1896.

--- Kiowa Apache. BBAE, XXX, i, 701-3. 1907.

Nye, W.S. Carbine and Lance. 441 pp. Norman, 1937.

Opler, M.E. The Kinship Systems of the Southern Athabaskan-speaking Tribes. AA, n.s., XXXVIII, 620-33. 1936.

Smith, R.A. Account of the Journey of Bénard de la Harpe. SWHQ, LXII, 75-86, 246-59, 371-85, 525-41. 1958-59.

Wedel, W.R. The Kiowa and Kiowa Apache. BBAE, CLXXIV, 78-80. 1959.

15. MANDAN

Bowers, A.W. Mandan Social and Ceremonial Organization. 512 pp. Chicago, 1950.

DeLand, C.E. The Aborigines of South Dakota. SDHC, III, 267-586; IV, 273-730. 1906-08.

Will, G.F., and Spinden, H.J. The Mandans. PMP,
III, 81-219. 1906.

Anonymous. South Dakota Physical Types. WHO,
XII, v, 1. 1952.

Beckwith, M.W. Mandan and Hidatsa Tales. PFLF,
XIV, 269-320. 1934.

--- Mandan-Hidatsa Myths and Ceremonies. MAFLS,
XXXII, 1-320. 1938.

--- Myths and Ceremonies of the Mandan and Hidatsa.
PFLF, XII, 117-267. 1932.

--- Myths and Hunting Stories of the Mandan and
Hidatsa Sioux. PFLF, X, 1-116. 1930.

Boas, F. Zur Anthropologie der nordamerikanischen
Indianer. VBGA, 1895, 367-411.

Brower, J.V. Mandan. 158 pp. St. Paul, 1904.

Brown, C.E. The Huff Mandan Village Site. WA,IX,
120-2. 1930.

Bruner, E.M. Assimilation among Fort Berthold Indians. AmI, VI, iv, 21-9. 1953.

--- Cultural Transmission and Cultural Change. SJA,
XII, 191-9. 1956.

--- Primary Group Experience and the Processes of
Acculturation. AA, LVIII, 605-23. 1956.

--- Two Processes of Change in Mandan-Hidatsa Kinship Terminology. AA, LVII, 840-50. 1955.

Bushnell, D.I. Burials of the Algonquian, Siouan and
Caddoan Tribes. BBAE, LXXXIII, 65-73. 1927.

--- Villages of the Algonquian, Siouan and Caddoan
Tribes. BBAE, LXXVII, 122-40. 1922.

Catlin, G. An Account of an Annual Religious Ceremony practised by the Mandan Tribe. Miscellanies of the Philobiblon Society, VIII, x, 1-67. 1864.

--- Illustrations of the Manners, Customs and Condition of the North American Indians, I, 80-184. New
York, 1841.

--- O-Kee-Pa. 52 pp. Philadelphia, 1867.

Coues, E., ed. Manuscript Journals of Alexander
Henry and of David Thompson. 3 vols. New York,
1897.

Crawford, K. A Brief Sketch of the Mandan Indians.
MA, II, iii, 1-5. 1936.

Crawford, L.F. Flint Quarries on Knife River. MA,
II, iv, 1-4. 1936.

Culbertson, T.A. Journal of an Expedition to the
Mauvaises Terres and the Upper Missouri in 1850.
BBAE, CXLVII, 172 pp. 1952.

Curtis, E.S. The North American Indian, V, 3-55,
143-8, 169-77. Cambridge, 1909.

Densmore, F. Mandan and Hidatsa Music. BBAE,
LXXX, 1-186. 1923.

Donaldson, T. The George Catlin Indian Gallery.
RUSNM, 1885, 80-8, 349-83, 398-406.

Dorsey, J.O. Preface. CNAE, IX, xviii-xxx. 1893.

--- A Study of Siouan Cults. ARBAE, XI, 501-13.
1890.

Dorsey, J.O., and Thomas, C. Mandan. BBAE, XXX,
i, 796-9. 1907.

Eschambault, A. d'. La voyage de Vérendrye au
pays des Mandannes. Revue de l'Histoire de
l'Amérique Française, II, 424-31. 1948.

Ewers, J.C. Early White Influence upon Plains Indian Painting. SMC, CXXXIV, vii, 11 pp. 1957.

--- Three Ornaments Worn by Upper Missouri Indians a Century and a Quarter Ago. NYHSQ, XLI,
24-33. 1957.

Frobenius, L. Geographische Kulturkunde, pp. 581-
602. Leipzig, 1904.

Gaskin, L. A Rare Pamphlet on the Mandan Religious Ceremony. Man, XXXIX, 141-2. 1939.

Gesner, A.T. Prehistoric Mandan Remains in North
Dakota. RP, IV, 363-7. 1905.

Gilmore, M.R. A Mandan Monument to a National
Hero. IN, VI, 147-51. 1929.

Goplen, A.O. The Mandan Indians. North Dakota
History, XIII, 153-75. 1946.

Hayden, F.V. Contributions to the Ethnography and
Philology of the Indian Tribes of the Missouri Valley. TAPS, n.s., XII, 426-44. 1863.

--- A Sketch of the Mandan Indians. American
Journal of Science and Arts, XXXIV, 57-66. 1862.

Hiller, W.R. Indian Village at Fort Berthold. MA,
XVII, 3-9, 1951.

--- The Manufacture of Bone Fish-hooks and Stone
Net Sinkers by the Mandans. MA, VI, 144-8. 1940.

--- X-marked Mandan Game Pieces. MA, VIII,
126-7. 1942.

Hopkins, W.J. The Indian Book. 239 pp. Boston,
1911.

Kennard, E. Mandan Grammar. IJAL, IX, i, 1-43.
1936.

Kipp, J. Mandan. HCPIT, III, 446-59. 1853.

--- On the Accuracy of Catlin's Account of the Mandan Ceremonies. ARSI, 1872, 436-8.

Kruse, H. A Remarkable Aerial Photograph of a
Mandan Village Site. MA, VIII, 80-1. 1942.

Lewis, M., and Clark, W. Travels. 3 vols. London, 1815.

Libby, O.G. Typical Villages of the Mandans,
Arikara, and Hidatsa. Collections of the State Historical Society of North Dakota, II, 498-508. 1908.

Lowie, R.H. Social Life of the Mandan. APAM, XXI,
7-16. 1917.

--- Societies of the Hidatsa and Mandan Indians.
APAM, XI, 294-358. 1913.

Lowie, R.H. Some Problems in the Ethnology of the Crow and Village Indians. AA, n.s., XIV, 60-71. 1912.

McGee, W J. The Siouan Indians. ARBAE, XV, 157-204. 1894.

Matthews, W. The Catlin Collection of Indian Paintings. RUSNM, 1890, 593-610.

--- Two Mandan Chiefs. AAOJ, X, 269-72. 1888.

Morgan, L.H. The Indian Journals, 1859-62, p.169. Ann Arbor, 1959.

--- Systems of Consanguinity and Affinity. SCK, XVII, 291-382. 1871.

Morice, A.G. Disparus et survivants. BSGQ, XXI, 11-49. 1927.

Mulloy, W. The Northern Plains. AEUS, 124-38. 1952.

Nasatir, A.P. Before Lewis and Clark. 2 vols. 882 pp. St. Louis, 1952.

Neill, E.D. Life among the Mandans Eighty Years ago. AAOJ, VI, 248-53, 377-84. 1884.

Newman, M.T. The Blond Mandan. SJA, VI, 255-72. 1950.

Powell, W. Mandan Village Visited by Verendrye in 1738. MA, II, x, 4-6. 1936.

Preuss, K.T. Das Frühlingsfest im alten Mexiko und bei den Mandan Indianern. Donum natalicium Schrijnen, pp. 825-37. Nijmegen-Utrecht, 1929.

Reid, R. The Earth Lodge. NDHQ, IV, 174-85. 1930.

Riggs, S.R. Dakota Grammar, Texts and Ethnography. CNAE, IX, xviii-xxix. 1893.

Romney, A.K. and Metzger, D. On the Processes of Change in Kinship Terminology [with rejoinder by E.M. Bruner]. AA, LVIII, 551-6. 1956.

Simpson, R. de E. A Mandan Bull-Boat. M, XXIII, 174-5. 1949.

Smith, C.S. An Analysis of the Firearms and Related Specimens from Like-A-Fishhook Village and Fort Berthold I. PlA, IV, 3-12. 1955.

Soulen, H. A Resume of Bone Materials Found in Our Mandan Site Exploratory Trip. MA, VI, 82-7. 1940.

Steinbreuck, E.R. Indian Fireplaces and Pots. Archaeological Bulletin, III, 22-3. 1912.

Strong, W.D. An Unusual Side-bladed Knife from a Proto-historic Mandan Site. AAn, XI, 60-61. 1945.

Tyrrell, J.B., ed. David Thompson's Narrative of His Explorations in Western America. PCS, XII, 225-37. 1916.

Vérendrye, P.G. La Verendrye's Journal. MA, II, x, 7-10. 1936.

Wedel, W.R. Observations on Some Nineteenth-Century Pottery Vessels from the Upper Missouri. BBAE, CLXIV, 87-114. 1957.

Wied-Neuwied, M. zu. Reise in das innere Nord-amerika. 2 vols. Coblenz, 1839-41.

--- Travels in the Interior of North America. EWT, XXII, 345-51; XXIII, 252-366; XXIV, 39-53, 73-5, 234-61. 1906.

Will, G.F. Archaeology of the Missouri Valley. APAM, XXII, 285-344. 1924.

--- The Bourgeois Village Site. AA, XII, 473-6. 1910.

--- The Mandan Lodge at Bismarck. NDHQ, V, 38-48. 1930.

--- No-Tongue, a Mandan Tale. JAFL, XXVI, 331-7; XXIX, 402-6. 1913-16.

Will, G.F., and Hyde, G.E. Corn among the Indians of the Upper Missouri. 317 pp. St. Louis, 1917.

16. MISSOURI

Berry, J.B. The Missouri Indians. Southwestern Social Science Quarterly, XVII, 113-24. 1936.

Bushnell, D.I. Burials of the Algonquian, Siouan and Caddoan Tribes. BBAE, LXXXIII, 63-5. 1927.

Chapman, C.H. Culture Sequence in the Lower Missouri Valley. AEUS, 139-51. 1952.

Dorsey, J.O., and Thomas, C. Missouri. BBAE, XXX, i, 911-12. 1907.

Foreman, G. The Last Trek of the Indians, pp. 258-62. Chicago, 1946.

McGee, W.J. The Siouan Indians. ARBAE, XV, 157-204. 1894.

Nasatir, A.P. Before Lewis and Clark. 2 vols. 882 pp. St. Louis, 1952.

17. OMAHA

Dorsey, J.O. Omaha Sociology. ARBAE, III, 205-370. 1882.

Fletcher, A.C., and La Flesche, F. The Omaha Tribe. ARBAE, XXVII, 17-654. 1906.

Anonymous. South Dakota Physical Types. WHO, XII, v, 1. 1952.

Arth, M.J. A Functional View of Peyotism in Omaha Culture. PlA, VII, 25-29. 1956.

Bibaud, F.M. Biographie des sagamos illustrés de l'Amérique Septentrionale, pp. 271-4. Montreal, 1848.

Boas, F. Zur Anthropologie der nordamerikanischen Indianer. VBGA, 1895, 367-411.

Brown, C. Omaha Arrowmakers. WA, X, 123-4. 1911.

Bushnell, D.I. Burials of the Algonquian, Siouan and Caddoan Tribes. BBAE, LXXXIII, 50-2. 1927.

--- Villages of the Algonquian, Siouan, and Caddoan Tribes. BBAE, LXXVII, 77-87. 1922.

Densmore, F. The Survival of Omaha Songs. AA, n.s., XLVI, 418-20. 1944.

Dorsey, J.O. Abstracts of Omaha and Ponka Myths. JAFL, I, 74-8, 204-8. 1888.

--- The Ȼegiha Language. CNAE, VI, 1-783. 1890.

--- How the Rabbit caught the Sun in a Trap. ARBAE, I, 581-3. 1880.

--- How the Rabbit killed the (Male) Winter. AAOJ, II, 128-32. 1879.

--- Indian Personal Names. PAAAS, XXXIV, 393-9. 1886.

--- Omaha and Ponca Letters. BBAE, XI, 1-123. 1891.

--- Omaha Clothing and Personal Ornaments. AA, III, 71-8. 1890.

--- Omaha Dwellings, Furniture, and Implements. ARBAE, XIII, 263-88. 1892.

--- Omaha Folk-Lore Notes. JAFL, I, 213-14; II, 190. 1888-89.

--- Omaha Songs. JAFL, I, 209-13. 1888.

--- On the Gentile System of the Omahas. AAOJ, V, 312-18. 1883.

--- The Orphan and the Buffalo Woman. TASW, I, 69. 1883.

--- Ponka and Omaha Songs. JAFL, II, 271-6. 1889.

--- Preface. CNAE, IX, xviii-xxx. 1893.

--- The Religion of the Omahas and Ponkas. AAOJ, V, 271-5. 1883.

--- Siouan Folk-Lore and Mythologic Notes. AAOJ, VI, 174-6; VII, 105-8. 1884-85.

--- The Social Organization of the Siouan Tribes. JAFL, IV, 264-6. 1891.

--- Songs of the Heȼucka Society. JAFL, I, 65-8. 1888.

--- A Study of Siouan Cults. ARBAE, XI, 361-422. 1890.

--- The Young Chief and the Thunders. JASW, I, 52-5. 1883.

--- The Young Chief and the Thunders. AAOJ, III, 303-7. 1883.

Dorsey, J.O., and Thomas, C. Omaha. BBAE, XXX, ii, 119-21. 1910.

Fletcher, A.C. The Child and the Tribe. PNAS, I, 569-74. 1915.

--- The Emblematic Use of the Tree in the Dakotan Group. PAAAS, XLV, 191-209. 1896.

Fletcher, A.C. The Emblematic Use of the Tree in the Dakotan Group. Science, n.s., IV, 475-87. 1896.

--- Glimpses of Child-Life among the Omaha Tribe of Indians. JAFL, I, 115-23. 1888.

--- Hae-thu-ska Society of the Omaha Tribe. JAFL, V, 135-44. 1892.

--- Häusliches Leben bei den Indianern. Globus, LXXIII, 252-9. 1898.

--- Historical Sketch of the Omaha Tribe. 12 pp. Washington, 1885.

--- Home Life among the Indians. Century Magazine, LIV, 252-63. 1897.

--- The Indian and Nature. PNAS, I, 467-73. 1915.

--- Indian Story and Song from North America. 126 pp. Boston, 1900.

--- Lands in Severalty to Indians. PAAAS, XXXIII, 654-65. 1884.

--- The "Lazy Man" in Indian Lore. JAFL, XIV, 100-4. 1901.

--- Leaves from My Omaha Note-Book: Courtship and Marriage. JAFL, II, 219-26. 1889.

--- Love Songs among the Omaha Indians. MICA, 1893, 153-7.

--- Nature and the Indian Tribe. AAA, IV, 291-6. 1916.

--- Observations on the Laws and Privileges of the Gens in Indian Society. PAAAS, XXXII, 395-6. 1883.

--- Observations on the Usage, Symbolism and Influence of the Sacred Pipes of Fellowship among the Omahas. PAAAS, XXXIII, 615-17. 1884.

--- The Sacred Pole of the Omaha Tribe. PAAAS, XLIV, 270-80. 1895.

--- The Sacred Pole of the Omaha Tribe. AAOJ, XVII, 257-68. 1895.

--- The Significance of the Scalp-Lock. JAI, XXVII, 436-50. 1897.

--- A Study from the Omaha Tribe: the Import of the Totem. PAAAS, XLVI, 325-34. 1897.

--- A Study from the Omaha Tribe: the Import of the Totem. ARSI, 1897, 577-86.

--- A Study of Omaha Indian Music. PMP, I, v, 7-152. 1893.

--- Tribal Life among the Omahas. Century Magazine, LI, 450-7. 1896.

--- Tribal Structure. Putnam Anniversary Volume, pp. 252-67. New York, 1909.

--- Wakondagi. AA, n.s., XIV, 106-8. 1912.

--- The "Wawan," or Pipe Dance of the Omahas. RPM, XVI-XVII, 308-33. 1883.

Fletcher, A.C., and La Flesche, F. A Study of
    Omaha Indian Music. PMP, I, v, 1-152. 1893.
Fontenelle, H. History of the Omaha Indians.
    TRNHS, I, 76-83. 1885.
Fortune, R.F. Omaha Secret Societies. CUCA, XIV,
    1-193. 1932.
Giffen, F.R. Oo-mah-ha Ta-wa-tha (Omaha City).
    94 pp. Lincoln, 1898.
Gilmore, M.R. Indian Tribal Boundary-lines and
    Monuments. IN, V, 59-63. 1928.
--- The Mescal Society among the Omaha Indians.
    Publications of the Nebraska State Historical So-
    ciety, XIX, 163-7. 1919.
--- Methods of Indian Buffalo Hunts. PMA, XVI, 17-
    32. 1931.
--- A Study in the Ethnobotany of the Omaha Indians.
    Collections of the Nebraska State Historical Society,
    XVII, 314-57. 1913.
--- Teokanha's Sacred Bundle. IN, I, 52-62. 1924.
--- Uses of Plants by the Indians of the Missouri River
    Region. ARBAE, XXXIII, 43-154. 1912.
Hayden, F.V. Brief Notes on the Pawnee, Winnebago,
    and Omaha Languages. PAPS, X, 406-11. 1868.
--- Contributions to the Ethnography and Philology of
    the Indian Tribes of the Missouri Valley. TAPS,
    n.s., XII, 444-52. 1863.
Holmer, N.M. Sonant- Surds in Ponca-Omaha. IJAL,
    XI, 75-85. 1945.
Howard, J.H. An Oto-Omaha Peyote Ritual. SJA,
    XII, 432-6. 1956.
James, E. Account of an Expedition from Pittsburgh
    to the Rocky Mountains. EWT, XIV, 288-321;
    XV, 11-130; XVII, 290-8. 1905.
Kercheval, G.T. An Otoe and an Omaha Tale. JAFL,
    VI, 199-204. 1893.
Kobelt, W. Das Volk der Omaha. Globus, L, 347-
    51. 1886.
La Flesche, F. Death and Funeral Customs among
    the Omahas. JAFL, II, 3-11. 1889.
--- Omaha and Osage Traditions of Separation. ICA,
    XIX, 459-62. 1915.
--- Omaha Bow and Arrow-Makers. ICA, XX, i, 111-
    16. 1922.
--- Omaha Bow and Arrow Makers. ARSI, 1926, 487-
    94.
--- The Omaha Buffalo Medicine-Men. JAFL, III,
    215-21. 1890.
--- The Sacred Pipes of Friendship. PAAAS, XXXIII,
    613-15. 1884.
--- Who Was the Medicine Man? Annual Report of
    the Fairmount Park Art Association, XXXII, 3-13.
    1904.

Lowie, R.H. The Omaha and Crow Kinship Termi-
    nologies. ICA, XXIV, 102-8. 1934.
McGee, W J. The Siouan Indians. ARBAE, XV, 157-
    204. 1894.
Matson, G.A. Distribution of Blood Groups among
    the Sioux, Omaha, and Winnebago Indians. AJPA,
    XXVIII, 313-18. 1941.
Mead, M. The Changing Culture of an Indian Tribe.
    CUCA, XV, 1-313. 1932.
Morgan, L.H. The Indian Journals, 1859-62, pp. 66,
    87-92, 138. Ann Arbor, 1959.
--- Systems of Consanguinity and Affinity. SCK,
    XVII, 291-382. 1871.
Myer, W.E. Archeological Field-Work in South
    Dakota and Missouri. SMC, LXXII, xv, 117-25.
    1922.
Nasatir, A.P. Before Lewis and Clark. 2 vols. 882
    pp. St. Louis, 1952.
Nebraska Writers' Project. Indian Place Legends.
    Nebraska Folklore Pamphlets, II, 1-15. 1937.
Omaha Tribe of Indians. Code of Laws. 4 pp.
    Omaha, 1860.
Riggs, S.R. Dakota Grammar, Texts and Ethnog-
    raphy. CNAE, IX, xviii-xxix. 1893.
Schmidt, W. Die Omaha und die Ponca. UG, II,
    657-8. 1929.
Wardle, H.N. Indian Gifts in Relation to Primitive
    Law. ICA, XXIII, 463-9. 1928.
Will, G.F., and Hyde, G.E. Corn among the In-
    dians of the Upper Missouri. 317 pp. St. Louis,
    1917.

18. OSAGE

Anonymous. Extracts from the Diary of Major Sib-
    ley. CO, V, 196-218. 1927.
--- The Lord's Prayer in Osage. AmI, III, xii, 4.
    1929.
Ashley-Montagu, M.F. An Indian Tradition relating
    to the Mastodon. AA, XLVI, 569-71. 1944.
Barney, R.A. Laws relating to Osage Tribe of In-
    dians. 112 pp. Pawhuska, 1929.
Berry, B., Chapman, C., and Mack, J. Archaeo-
    logical Remains of the Osage. AAn, X, 1-12.
    1944.
Boas, F. Zur Anthropologie der nordamerikanischen
    Indianer. VBGA, 1895, 367-411.
Bradbury, J. Travels in the Interior of America.
    EWT, V, 1-320. 1904.
Burbank, E.A., and Royce, E. Burbank among the
    Indians, pp. 197-200. Caldwell, 1946.

Bushnell, D. I. Burials of the Algonquian, Siouan and Caddoan Tribes. BBAE, LXXXIII, 55-60. 1927.

--- Villages of the Algonquian, Siouan, and Caddoan Tribes. BBAE, LXXVII, 98-108. 1922.

Chapman, B. B. Dissolution of the Osage Reservation. CO, XX, 244-54, 375-86; XXI, 78-87, 171-82. 1942-43.

--- Removal of the Osages from Kansas. KHQ, VII, 287-305. 1938.

Chapman, C. H. Culture Sequence in the Lower Missouri Valley. AEUS, 139-51. 1952.

Connelley, W. E. Notes on the Early Indian Occupancy of the Great Plains. CKSHS, XIV, 438-70. 1918.

Cutler, J. A Topographical Description of the State of Ohio, Indiana Territory, and Louisiana, pp. 115-20. Boston, 1812.

Dickerson, P. J. History of the Osage Nation. 144 pp. 1906.

Donaldson, T. The George Catlin Indian Gallery. RUSNM, 1885, 42-6.

Dorsey, G. A. The Osage Mourning-War Ceremony. AA, n.s., IV, 404-11. 1902.

--- Traditions of the Osage. FMAS, VII, 9-60. 1904.

Dorsey, J. O. An Account of the War Customs of the Osages. AN, XVIII, 113-33. 1884.

--- On the Comparative Phonology of Four Siouan Languages. ARSI, 1883, 919-29.

--- An Osage Secret Society. JASW, III, 3-4. 1885.

--- Osage Traditions. ARBAE, VI, 373-97. 1885.

--- Preface. CNAE, IX, xviii-xxx. 1893.

--- Siouan Sociology. ARBAE, XV, 233-8. 1894.

--- The Social Organization of the Siouan Tribes. JAFL, IV, 334-6. 1891.

--- A Study of Siouan Cults. ARBAE, XI, 361-422. 1890.

Douglas, F. H. An Osage Yarn Bag. MCN, VII, 26-30. 1938.

Finney, F. F. Old Osage Customs Die with the Last Pah-hue-skah. CO, XXXVI, 131-36. 1958.

--- The Osage Indians and the Liquor Problem before Statehood. CO, XXXIV, 456-64. 1956.

--- The Osages and Their Agency. CO, XXXVI, 416-28. 1958-59.

FitzGerald, M. P. Beacon on the Plains. 297 pp. Leavenworth, 1939.

Fletcher, A. C., and La Flesche, F. The Omaha Tribe. ARBAE, XXVIII, 57-66. 1906.

Foreman, G. Indians and Pioneers. Rev. edit. 285 pp. Norman, 1936.

--- The Last Trek of the Indians, pp. 266-77. Chicago, 1946.

Gatschet, A. S. Die Osageindianer. Globus, LXXIII, 349-55. 1898.

Graves, W. W. The First Protestant Osage Missions, 1820-1837. 272 pp. Oswego, Kansas, 1949.

Gregg, K. L. Westward with Dragoons. 97 pp. Fulton, 1937.

Hargrett, L. A Bibliography of the Constitutions and Laws of the American Indians, pp. 99-100. Cambridge, 1947.

Harner, J. The Village of the Big Osage. Missouri Archaeologist, V, 19-20. 1939.

Hunter, J. D. Memoirs of a Captivity among the Indians of North America. 447 pp. London, 1823.

La Barre, W. A Cultist Drug Addiction in an Indian Alcoholic. Bulletin of the Menninger Clinic, V, 40-46. 1941.

La Flesche, F. Ceremonies and Rituals of the Osage. SMC, LXIII, viii, 66-9. 1914.

--- A Dictionary of the Osage Language. BBAE, CIX, 1-406. 1932.

--- Ethnology of the Osage Indians. SMC, LXXVI, x, 104-7. 1924.

--- Omaha and Osage Traditions of Separation. ICA, XIX, 459-62. 1915.

--- Osage Marriage Customs. AA, n.s., XIV, 127-30. 1912.

--- Osage Songs and Rituals. SMC, LXV, vi, 78-81. 1915.

--- Osage Tribal Rites. SMC, LXXII, i, 71-3. 1920.

--- The Osage Tribe. ARBAE, XXXVI, 35-604; XXXIX, 31-630; XLIII, 23-164; XLV, 529-833. 1921-30.

--- Researches among the Osage. SMC, LXX, ii, 110-13. 1919.

--- Right and Left in Osage Ceremonies. Holmes Anniversary Volume, pp. 278-87. Washington, 1916.

---The Symbolic Man of the Osage Tribe. AAA, IX, 68-72. 1920.

--- Tribal Rites of Osage Indians. SMC, LXVIII, xii, 84-90. 1918.

--- War Ceremony and Peace Ceremony of the Osage Indians. BBAE, CI, 1-280. 1939.

--- Work among the Osage Indians. SMC, LXVI, xvii, 118-21. 1917.

Lamb, A. H. The Osage People. 31 pp. Pawhuska, 1930.

McDermott, J. F., ed. Tixier's Travels on the Osage Prairies. 309 pp. Norman, 1940.

McGee, W J. The Siouan Indians. ARBAE, XV, 157-204. 1894.

MacRitchie, D. A Red Indian Coiffure. Man, XVII,
7-9. 1917.

Mathews, J.J. Talking to the Moon. 243 pp. Chicago, 1945.

--- Wah'kon-tah: the Osage and the White Man's
Road. 359 pp. Norman, 1932.

Mead, J.R. The Little Arkansas. TKSHS, X, 7-14.
1908.

Montgomery, W.B. Washashe wageressa pahvgreh
tse. 126 pp. Boston, 1834.

Morfi, J.A.de. Memorias for the History of the Province of Texas, ed. F.M.Chabot. 85 pp. San
Antonio, 1932.

Morgan, L.H. The Indian Journals, 1859-62, p. 82.
Ann Arbor, 1959.

--- Systems of Consanguinity and Affinity. SCK,
XVII, 291-382. 1871.

Morse, J. A Report to the Secretary of War. 400 pp.
New Haven, 1822.

Nasatir, A.P. Before Lewis and Clark. 2 vols. 882
pp. St. Louis, 1952.

Nett, B.R. Historical Changes in the Osage Kinship
System. SJA, VIII, 164-81. 1952.

Nuttall, T. A Journal of Travels into the Arkansa
Territory. 296 pp. Philadelphia, 1821.

Riggs, S.R. Dakota Grammar, Texts and Ethnography.
CNAE, IX, xviii-xxix. 1893.

Rohrer, J.H. The Test Intelligence of Osage Indians.
JSP, XVI, 99-105. 1942.

Sebbelov, G. The Osage War Dance. MJ, II, 71-4.
1911.

Skinner, A.B. An Osage War Party. YPMCM, II,
165-9. 1923.

Synder, J.F. Were the Osages Mound Builders? ARSI,
1888, 587-96.

Speck, F.G. Notes on the Ethnology of the Osage Indians. TFMSA, II, 159-71. 1907.

Swanton, J.R. Osage. BBAE, XXX, ii, 156-8. 1910.

Vissier, P. Histoire de la tribu des Osages. 92 pp.
Paris, 1827.

Wedel, W.R. The Osage. BBAE, CLXXIV, 54-8.
1959.

White Horse Eagle. We Indians. 255 pp. New York,
1931.

Williams, A.M. The Giants of the Plain. Lippin-
cott's Magazine, Oct. 1883.

Wolff, H. Osage. IJAL, XVIII, 63-8, 231-37. 1952.

--- An Osage Graphemic Experiment. IJAL, XXIV,
30-5. 1958.

19. OTO

Whitman, W. The Oto. CUCA, XXVIII, 1-32.
1937.

Anderson, B.G. Indian Sleep Man Tales. 145 pp.
Caldwell, 1940.

Anonymous. Extracts from the Diary of Rev. Moses
Merrill. TRNHS, IV, 160-91. 1892.

--- Oto. BBAE, XXX, ii, 164-6. 1910.

Bushnell, D.I. Villages of the Algonquian, Siouan
and Caddoan Tribes. BBAE, LXXVII, 114-21.
1922.

Culbertson, T.A. Journal of an Expedition to the
Mauvaises Terres and the Upper Missouri in 1850.
BBAE, CXLVII, 172 pp. 1952.

Curtis, E.S. The North American Indian, XIX, 25-
6, 151-77, 226-8, 230-8. Norwood, 1930.

Dorsey, J.O. On the Comparative Phonology of Four
Siouan Languages. ARSI, 1883, 919-29.

--- Preface. CNAE, IX, xviii-xxx. 1893.

--- The Rabbit and the Grasshopper. AAOJ, III, 24-
7. 1880.

Fletcher, A.C. A Birthday Wish from Native America. Holmes Anniversary Volume, pp. 118-22.
Washington, 1916.

Foreman, G. The Last Trek of the Indians, pp. 258-
62. Chicago, 1946.

Green, T.L. (ed.) Notes on a Buffalo Hunt – The
Diary of Mordecai Bartram. NeH, XXXV, 193-
222. 1954.

Griffin, J.B. The Archaeological Remains of the
Chiwere Sioux. AAn, II, 180-81. 1937.

Harrington, M.R. A Sacred Warclub of the Oto.
INM, X, 25-7. 1920.

--- A Visit to the Otoe Indians. MJ, IV, 107-13.
1913.

Hayden, F.V. Brief Notes on the Present Condition
of the Otoe Indians. ARGGS, I, 32-5. 1867.

--- Contributions to the Ethnography and Philology
of the Indian Tribes of the Missouri Valley. TAPS,
n.s., XII, 444-56. 1863.

Howard, J.H. An Oto-Omaha Peyote Ritual. SJA,
XII, 432-6. 1956.

Irving, J.T. Indian Sketches. 2 vols. Philadelphia,
1835.

--- Indian Sketches Taken During an Expedition to
the Pawnee Tribes (1833). 317 pp. Norman, 1955.

Kercheval, G.T. An Otoe and an Omaha Tale. JAFL,
VI, 199-204. 1893.

Lieberkühn, S. The History of Our Lord and Saviour
Jesus Christ, tr. into Oto by M. Merrill and L.
Dorion. 32 pp. Rochester, 1888.

McGee, W J. The Siouan Indians. ARBAE, XV, 157-204. 1894.

Merrill, M. Extracts from the Diary of Rev. Moses Merrill. TRNHS, IV, 160-91. 1892.

Möllhausen, B. Diary of a Journey from the Mississippi to the Coasts of the Pacific, I, 171-81, 198-212, 243-9. London, 1858.

Morgan, L.H. The Indian Journals, 1859-62, pp. 67, 99. Ann Arbor, 1959.

--- Systems of Consanguinity and Affinity. SCK, XVII, 291-382. 1871.

Nasatir, A.P. Before Lewis and Clark. 2 vols. 882 pp. St. Louis, 1952.

Nebraska Writers' Project. Indian Place Legends. Nebraska Folklore Pamphlets, II, 1-15. 1937.

Riggs, S.R. Dakota Grammar, Texts and Ethnography. CNAE, IX, xviii-xxix. 1893.

Shunatona, R. Otoe Indian Lore. Nebraska History and Record of Pioneer Days, V, 60-4. 1922.

Skinner, A. Remarkable Oto Necklace. IN, II, 36-8. 1925.

Whitman, W. Descriptive Grammar of Ioway-Oto. IJAL, XIII, 233-48. 1947.

--- Origin Legends of the Oto. JAFL, LI, 173-205. 1938.

Wied-Neuwied, M. zu. Reise in das innere Nordamerika. 2 vols. Coblenz, 1839-41.

--- Travels in the Interior of North America. EWT, XXIV, 101-12, 285-93, 313-14. 1906.

20. PAWNEE

Hyde, G.E. Pawnee Indians. 318 pp. Denver, 1951.

Allis, S. Forty Years among the Indians. TRNHS, II, 133-66. 1887.

Anonymous. Extracts from the Diary of Major Sibley. CO, V, 196-218. 1927.

Boas, F. Zur Anthropologie der nordamerikanischen Indianer. VBGA, 1895, 367-411.

Bruce, R., ed. Pawnee Naming Ceremonial. 36 pp. New York, 1933.

Buckstaff, R.N. Stars and Constellations of a Pawnee Sky Map. AA, n.s., XXIX, 279-85. 1927.

Bushnell, D.I. Buriels of the Algonquian, Siouan and Caddoan Tribes. BBAE, LXXXIII, 79-82. 1927.

Clark, J.S. A Pawnee Buffalo Hunt. CO, XX, 387-95. 1942.

Clayton, L., ed. William Clayton's Journal. 376 pp. Salt Lake City, 1921.

Connelley, W.E. Notes on the Early Indian Occupancy of the Great Plains. CKSHS, XIV, 438-70. 1918.

Culbertson, T.A. Journal of an Expedition to the Mauvaises Terres and the Upper Missouri in 1850. BBAE, CXLVII, 172 pp. 1952.

Curtis, N., ed. The Indians' Book, pp. 93-143. New York, 1907.

Dangel, R. Tirawa, der höchste Gott der Pawnee. ARW, XXVII, 113-44. 1929.

Densmore, F. Communication with the Dead as practised by the American Indians. Man, L, 40-41. 1950.

--- Pawnee Music. BBAE, XCIII, 1-129. 1929.

Dodge, H. Journal of Colonel Dodge's Expedition from Fort Gibson to the Pawnee Pict Village (1834). American State Papers, Military Affairs, V, 373-82. 1860.

--- Report on the Expedition of Dragoons, under Colonel Henry Dodge, to the Rocky Mountains in 1835. American State Papers, Military Affairs, VI, 130-46. 1861.

Dorsey, G.A. How the Pawnee captured the Cheyenne Medicine Arrows. AA, n.s., V, 644-58. 1903.

--- One of the Sacred Altars of the Pawnee. ICA, XIII, 67-74. 1902.

--- The Pawnee: Mythology. 546 pp. Washington, 1906.

--- A Pawnee Personal Medicine Shrine. AA, n.s., VII, 496-8. 1905.

--- A Pawnee Ritual of Instruction. Boas Anniversary Volume, pp. 350-3. New York, 1906.

--- Pawnee War Tales. AA, n.s., VIII, 337-45. 1906.

--- The Skidi Rite of Human Sacrifice. ICA, XV, ii, 65-70. 1906.

--- Social Organization of the Skidi Pawnee. ICA, XV, ii, 71-7. 1906.

--- Traditions of the Skidi Pawnee. MAFLS, VIII, 1-366. 1904.

Dorsey, G.A., and Murie, J.R. Notes on Skidi Pawnee Society. FMAS, XXVII, 67-119. 1940.

Dunbar, J. Journal. CKSHS, XIV, 578-619. 1918.

--- The Pawnee Indians. MAH, IV, 241-81; V, 321-42; VIII, 734-54. 1880-82. Repr. New York, 1883.

--- The Pawnee Language. In, G.B. Grinnell, Pawnee Hero Stories and Folk-Tales, 2nd ed., 409-37. New York, 1893.

--- The Presbyterian Mission among the Pawnee Indians. CKSHS, XI, 323-32. 1910.

Fletcher, A.C. Giving Thanks: a Pawnee Ceremony. JAFL, XIII, 261-6. 1900.

--- The Hako: a Pawnee Ceremony. ARBAE, XXII,
  ii, 5-372. 1904.

--- Indian Story and Song from North America. 126
  pp. Boston, 1900.

--- Pawnee. BBAE, XXX, ii, 213-16. 1910.

--- Pawnee. ERE, IX, 698-700. 1917.

--- A Pawnee Ritual used when changing a Man's
  Name. AA, n.s., I, 82-97. 1899.

--- Pawnee Star Lore. JAFL, XVI, 10-15. 1903.

--- Skidi. BBAE, XXX, ii, 589-91. 1910.

--- Star Cult among the Pawnee. AA, n.s., IV,
  730-6. 1902.

Foreman, G. The Last Trek of the Indians, pp. 237-
  47. Chicago, 1946.

Gilmore, M.R. Methods of Indian Buffalo Hunts.
  PMA, XVI, 17-32. 1931.

--- Uses of Plants by the Indians of the Missouri River
  Region. ARBAE, XXXIII, 43-154. 1912.

Grinnell, G.B. Development of a Pawnee Myth.
  JAFL, V, 127-34. 1892.

--- Marriage among the Pawnees. AA, IV, 275-81.
  1891.

--- Pawnee Hero Stories and Folk-Tales. 417 pp.
  New York, 1889.

--- Pawnee Mythology. JAFL, VI, 113-30. 1893.

--- A Pawnee Star Myth. JAFL, VII, 197-200. 1894.

--- The Punishment of the Stingy, pp. 49-113. New
  York, 1901.

--- Two Pawnian Tribal Names. AA, IV, 197-9.
  1891.

--- The Young Dog's Dance. JAFL, IV, 307-13.
  1891.

Hamilton, J.C. The Panis. PCI, n.s., I, 19-27.
  1896.

Hayden, F.V. Brief Notes on the Pawnee, Winnebago,
  and Omaha Languages. PAPS, X, 389-406. 1868.

--- Contributions to the Ethnography and Philology
  of the Indian Tribes of the Missouri Valley. TAPS,
  n.s., XII, 345-51. 1863.

Hodge, F.W. Pitalesharu and His Medal. M, XXIV,
  111-19. 1950.

Hotz, G. Indianische Bilderschriftszenen auf einer
  Wapitihaut. BA, n.f., V, 209-24. 1957.

Hungate, M. Religious Beliefs of the Nebraska Indian. NeH, XIV, iii, 207-26. 1938.

Hyde, G.E. The Pawnee Indians. OWS, IV, 5-54;
  V, 3-50. 1934.

Irving, J.T. Indian Sketches. 2 vols. Philadelphia,
  1835.

Irving, J.T. Indian Sketches Taken During an Expedition to the Pawnee Tribes. 317 pp. Norman,
  1955.

Lesser, A. Cultural Significance of the Ghost Dance.
  AA, n.s., XXXV, 108-15. 1933.

--- Levirate and Fraternal Polyandry among the
  Pawnees. Man, XXX, 98-101. 1930.

--- The Pawnee Ghost Dance Hand Game. CUCA,
  XVI, 1-337. 1933.

Lesser, A., and Weltfish, G. Composition of the
  Caddoan Linguistic Stock. SMC, LXXXVII, vi,
  1-15. 1932.

Lillie, G.W. Indian Burials. AAOJ, VIII, 28-30.
  1886.

--- Sacred Dance of the Pawnees. AAOJ, VII, 208-
  12. 1885.

Linton, R. Annual Ceremony of the Pawnee Medicine Men. FMDAL, VIII, 1-20. 1923.

--- The Origin of the Skidi Pawnee Sacrifice to the
  Morning Star. AA, n.s., XXVIII, 457-66. 1926.

--- Purification of the Sacred Bundles. FMDAL, VII,
  1-11. 1923.

--- The Sacrifice to the Morning Star by the Skidi
  Pawnee. FMDAL, VI, 1-18.

--- The Thunder Ceremony of the Pawnee. FMDAL,
  V, 1-19. 1922.

Lounsbury, F.G. A Semantic Analysis of the Pawnee Kinship Usage. Lg, XXXII, 158-94. 1956.

Mead, J.R. The Pawnees as I knew them. TKSHS,
  X, 106-11. 1908.

Meleen, E.E. A Report on the Investigation of the
  La Roche Site. University of South Dakota Archaeological Studies, V, 1-35. 1948.

Moore, G.R. Pawnee Traditions and Customs. CO,
  XVII, 151-69. 1939.

Morgan, L.H. The Indian Journals, 1859-62, pp.
  66, 90, 135-6, 141. Ann Arbor, 1959.

--- Systems of Consanguinity and Affinity. SCK,
  XVII, 291-382. 1871.

Morse, J. A Report to the Secretary of War. 400 pp.
  New Haven, 1822.

Mullin, C.P. Pita-le-Sharu and the Hako. 72 pp.
  Omaha, 1931.

Murie, J.R. Pawnee Indian Societies. APAM, XI,
  543-644. 1914.

Murray, C.A. Travels in North America. 2 vols.
  New York, 1839.

Nasatir, A.P. Before Lewis and Clark. 2 vols. 882
  pp. St. Louis, 1952.

Nebraska History Magazine. The War between
  Nebraska and Kansas. NeH, X, iii, 155-261. 1927.

Nebraska Writers' Project. Animal Legends. Nebraska Folklore Pamphlets, VI, 1-11. 1937.

--- Indian Ghost Legends. Nebraska Folklore Pamphlets, XII, 1-11. 1937.

--- Indian Place Legends. Nebraska Folklore Pamphlets, II, 1-15. 1937.

Oehler, G.F. and Smith, D.Z. Description of a Journey and Visit to the Pawnee Indians. MCM, II, 217-25; III, 55-69. 1851-52.

--- Description of a Journey and Visit to the Pawnee Indians. 32 pp. New York, 1914.

Parsons, E.C. Ritual Parallels in Pueblo and Plains Cultures. AA, n.s., XXXI, 642-54. 1929.

Platt, E.G. Reminiscences of a Teacher among the Nebraska Indians. TRNHS, III, 125-43. 1892.

--- Some Experiences as a Teacher among the Pawnees. CKSHS, XIV, 784-94. 1918.

Pruitt, O.J. Some Iowa Indian Tales. Annals of Iowa, 3rd series, XXXII, 203-16. 1953-55.

Shirk, G.H. Peace on the Plains. CO, XXVIII, 2-41. 1950.

Smith, D.Z. Description of the Manners and Customs of the Pawnee Indians. MCM, III, 86-94. 1852.

Strong, W.D. Introduction to Nebraska Archaeology. SMC, XCIII, x, 1-315. 1935.

Wedel, W.R. The Direct-Historical Approach to Pawnee Archaeology. SMC, XCVII, vii, 1-21. 1938.

--- An Introduction to Pawnee Archeology. BBAE, CXII, 1-122. 1936.

--- The Pawnee. BBAE, CLXXIV, 58-60. 1959.

Weltfish, G. Caddoan Texts: Pawnee. PAES, XVII, 1-251. 1937.

--- Coiled Gambling Baskets of the Pawnee and Other Plains Tribes. IN, VII, 277-95. 1930.

--- The Question of Ethnic Identity. E, VI, 321-46. 1959.

--- The Vision Story of a Fox-Boy. IJAL, IX, 44-76. 1936.

Will, G.F., and Hyde, G.E. Corn among the Indians of the Upper Missouri. 317 pp. St. Louis, 1917.

Wissler, C. Comparative Study of Pawnee and Blackfoot Rituals. ICA, XIX, 335-9. 1915.

--- The Sacred Bundles of the Pawnee. NH, XX, 569-71. 1920.

Wissler, C., and Spinden, H.J. The Pawnee Human Sacrifice to the Morningstar. AMJ, XVI, 49-55. 1916.

21. PONCA

Anonymous. South Dakota Physical Types. WHO, XII, v, 1. 1952.

Boas, F. Notes on the Ponka Grammar. ICA, XV, ii, 317-37. 1906.

Boas, F., and Swanton, J.R. Siouan. BBAE, XL, i, 875-966. 1911.

Dorsey, G.A. The Ponca Sun Dance. FMAS, VII, 67-88. 1905.

Dorsey, J.O. Abstracts of Omaha and Ponka Myths. JAFL, I, 74-8, 204-8. 1888.

--- The Çegiha Language. CNAE, VI, 1-783. 1890.

--- The Myths of the Raccoon and the Crawfish. AAOJ, VI, 237-40. 1884.

--- Omaha and Ponca Letters. BBAE, XI, 1-123. 1891.

--- On the Comparative Phonology of Four Siouan Languages. ARSI, 1883, 919-29.

--- Ponka and Omaha Songs. JAFL, II, 271-6. 1889.

--- Ponka Stories. JAFL, I, 73. 1888.

--- Preface. CNAE, IX, xviii-xxx. 1893.

--- The Religion of the Omahas and Ponkas. AAOJ, V, 271-5. 1883.

--- The Social Organization of the Siouan Tribes. JAFL, IV, 331-2. 1891.

--- A Study of Siouan Cults. ARBAE, XI, 361-422. 1890.

Dorsey, J.O., and Thomas, C. Ponca. BBAE, XXX, ii, 278-9. 1910.

Fletcher, A.C. The Emblematic Use of the Tree in the Dakotan Group. Science, n.s., IV, 475-87. 1896.

--- Indian Story and Song from North America. 126 pp. Boston, 1907.

Fletcher, A.C., and La Flesche, F. The Omaha Tribe. ARBAE, XXVII, 37-57. 1906.

Foreman, G. The Last Trek of the Indians, pp. 247-58. Chicago, 1946.

Gilmore, M.R. Uses of Plants by the Indians of the Missouri River Region. ARBAE, XXXIII, 43-154. 1912.

Holmer, N.M. Sonant-Surds in Ponca-Omaha. IJAL, XI, 75-85. 1945.

Howard, J.H. and Kurath, G.P. Ponca Dances, Ceremonies and Music. Ethnomusicology, III, i, 1-14. 1959.

McGee, W J. Ponka Feather Symbolism. AA, XI, 156-9. 1898.

--- The Siouan Indians. ARBAE, XV, 157-204. 1894.

Morgan, L.H. The Indian Journals, 1859-62, p.147.
Ann Arbor, 1959.
--- Systems of Consanguinity and Affinity. SCK,
XVII, 291-382. 1871.
Nasatir, A.P. Before Lewis and Clark. 2 vols. 882
pp. St. Louis, 1952.
Riggs, S.R. Dakota Grammar, Texts and Ethnography.
CNAE, IX, 1-232. 1893.
Schmidt, W. Die Omaha und die Ponca. UG, II,
657-8. 1929.
Skinner, A.B. Medicine Ceremony of the Menomi-
ni, Iowa, and Wahpeton Dakota. INM, IV, 306-
8. 1920.
--- Ponca Societies and Dances. APAM, XI, 777-
801. 1915.
Welsh, W. Report of a Visit to the Sioux and Ponka
Indians of the Missouri River. 36 pp. Philadelphia,
1872.
Whitman, W. Xube, a Ponca Autobiography. JAFL,
LII, 180-93. 1939.
Wied-Neuwied, M. zu. Reise in das innere Nord-
amerika. 2 vols. Coblenz, 1839-41.
--- Travels in the Interior of North America. EWT,
XXII, 283-90. 1906.
Will, G.F., and Hyde, G.E. Corn among the In-
dians of the Upper Missouri. 317 pp. St. Louis,
1917.
Wood, W.R. Notes on Ponca Ethnohistory. E, VI,
1-27. 1959.
Zimmerman, C.L. White Eagle, 273 pp. Harris-
burg, 1941.

22. QUAPAW

Also called Arkansa.

Bossu, J.B. Nouveaux voyages aux Indes Occiden-
tales, I, 108-24. Paris, 1768.
--- Travels through That Part of North America for-
merly called Louisiana, II, 91-109. London, 1771.
Bushnell, D.I. Villages of the Algonquian, Siouan
and Caddoan Tribes. BBAE, LXXVII, 108-12.
1922.
Dorsey, J.O. Kwapa Folk-Lore. JAFL, VIII, 130-1.
1895.
--- Preface. CNAE, IX, xviii-xxx. 1893.
--- Siouan Sociology. ARBAE, XV, 229-30. 1894.
Fletcher, A.C., and La Flesche, F. The Omaha
Tribe. ARBAE, XXVII, 67-8. 1906.
Foreman, G. The Last Trek of the Indians, pp. 308-
14. Chicago, 1946.

Joutel, H. Journal of La Salle's Last Voyage. New
edit. 258 pp. Albany, 1906.
--- Relation. DEFAS, III, 91-534. 1879.
La Flesche, F. Omaha and Osage Traditions of Sep-
aration. ICA, XIX, 459-62. 1915.
Lane, J. Federal-Ouapaw Relations, 1800-1833.
ArHQ, XIX, 61-74. 1960.
Laurence, M. A Trip to Quapaw in 1903. CO, XXXI,
142-67. 1953.
Lyon, O. The Trail of the Quapaw. ArHQ, IX, 205-
13. 1950.
McGee, W J. The Siouan Indians. ARBAE, XV, 157-
204. 1894.
Mereness, N.D., ed. Travels in the American
Colonies, pp. 57-8. New York, 1916.
Nasatir, A.P. Before Lewis and Clark. 2 vols. 882
pp. St. Louis, 1952.
Nieberding, V. St. Mary's of the Quapaws. CO,
XXXI, 2-14. 1953.
Nuttall, T. A Journal of Travels into the Arkansa
Territory. 296 pp. Philadelphia, 1821.
Phillips, P. et al. Archaeological Survey of the
Lower Mississippi Alluvial Valley, 1940-1947.
PMP, XXV, 392-421. 1951.
Riggs, S.R. Dakota Grammar, Texts and Ethnog-
raphy. CNAE, IX, xviii-xxix. 1893.
Swanton, J.R. Indians of the Southeastern United
States. BBAE, CXXXVII, 11-832. 1946.
Thomas, C. Quapaw. BBAE, XXX, ii, 333-6.
1910.
Thompson, V.H. A History of the Quapaw. CO,
XXXIII, 360-83. 1955.
Tonti, H. de. An Account of Monsieur de la Salle's
Last Expedition. CNYHS, II, 217-341. 1814.
Weer, P. Passamaquoddy and Quapaw Mnemonic
Records. PIAS, LV, 29-32. 1946.
Wilson, C.B. Quapaw Agency Indians. 38 pp.
Miami, Oklahoma, 1947.
Wright, M.H. American Indian Corn Dishes. CO,
XXXVI, 155-66. 1958.

23. SANTEE

Including the Mdewakanton, the Santee, the
Sisseton, the Wahpekute, and the Wahpeton, col-
lectively known as the Eastern Dakota or Eastern
Sioux.

Riggs, S.R. Dakota Grammar, Texts and Ethnography. CNAE, IX, 1-232. 1893.

Wallis, W.D. The Canadian Dakota. APAM, XLI, i,
1-225. 1947.

Winchell, N.H. The Aborigines of Minnesota. 761
pp. St. Paul, 1911.

Adams, M.N. The Sioux Outbreak in the Year 1862.
CMHS, IX, 431-52. 1901.

Ames, J.H. The Sioux or Nadouesis. Macalester
College Contributions, I. 229-40. 1890.

Andros, F. The Medicine and Surgery of the Winnebago and Dakota Indians. Journal of the American
Medical Association, I, 116-8. 1883.

Anonymous. Dakota. BBAE, XXX, i, 376-80. 1907.

--- Wahpeton. BBAE, XXX, ii, 891-3. 1910.

Atwater, C. Remarks made on a Tour to Prairie du
Chien. 296 pp. Columbus, 1831.

Babcock, W.M. Sioux Villages in Minnesota prior to
1837. MA, XI, 126-46. 1945.

Beckwith, P. Notes on Customs of the Dakotahs.
ARSI, 1886, 245-57.

Beltrami, J.C. A Pilgrimage in Europe and America,
II, 206-300. London, 1828.

Bibaud, F.M. Biographie des sagamos illustrés de
l'Amérique Septentrionale, pp. 257-64. Montreal,
1848.

Boas, F., and Deloria, E. Dakota Grammar. Memoirs of the National Academy of Sciences, XXIII, ii,
1-183. 1941.

Boas, F., and Swanton, J.R. Siouan. BBAE, XL, i,
875-966. 1911.

Bradley, J.H. History of the Sioux. Contributions
of the Historical Society of Montana, IX, 29-140.
1923.

Brown, D.M. Wisconsin Indian Corn Origin Myths.
WA, n.s., 19-27. 1940.

Bushnell, D.I. Burials of the Algonquian, Siouan and
Caddoan Tribes. BBAE, LXXXIII, 17-27. 1927.

--- Villages of the Algonquian, Siouan and Caddoan
Tribes. BBAE, LXXVII, 44-55. 1922.

Carver, J. Travels through the Interior Parts of North
America. 2d edit. London, 1779.

Crooker, G. George Crooker's Letter to President
Abraham Lincoln Concerning the Sioux Outbreak,
October 7, 1862. MA, XIX, iii, 3-17. 1954.

Culbertson, T.A. Journal of an Expedition to the
Mauvaises Terres and the Upper Missouri in 1850.
BBAE, CXLVII, 172 pp. 1952.

Dally, N. Tracks and Trails. 138 pp. Walker, 1931.

Daniels, A.W. Reminiscences of Little Crow.
CMHS, XII, 513-30. 1908.

Deloria, E.C. Speaking of Indians. 163 pp. New
York, 1944.

Donaldson, T. The George Catlin Indian Gallery.
RUSNM, 1885, 53-63.

Dorsey, J.O. Preface. CNAE, IX, xi-xxxii. 1893.

--- The Social Organization of the Siouan Tribes.
JAFL, IV, 257-60. 1891.

--- A Study of Siouan Cults. ARBAE, XI, 351-544.
1890.

Dorsey, J.O., and Thomas, C. Mdewakanton.
BBAE, XXX, i, 826-8. 1907.

Douglas, F.H. The Sioux or Dakota Indians. DAMLS,
XLI, 1-4. 1932.

Duratschek, M.C. Crusading along Sioux Trails.
334 pp. St. Meinrad, Indiana, 1947.

Eastman, C.A. From the Deep Woods to Civilization. 206 pp. Boston, 1916.

--- Indian Boyhood. 289 pp. New York, 1902.

--- Indian Child Life. 162 pp. Boston, 1913.

--- Indian Heroes and Great Chieftains. 241 pp.
Boston, 1918.

--- Old Indian Days. 275 pp. New York, 1907.

--- The Soul of the Indian. 171 pp. Boston, 1911.

Eastman, C.A. and E.G. Wigwam Evenings. 253
pp. Boston, 1909.

Eastman, M. Dacotah. 268 pp. New York, 1849.

Federal Writers' Projects. Wisconsin Indian Place
Legends, 28-9. Milwaukee, 1936.

Fernberger, S.W., and Speck, F.G. Two Sioux
Shields and Their Psychological Interpretation.
Journal of Abnormal and Social Psychology, XXXIII,
168-78. 1938.

Fletcher, A.C. The Religious Ceremony of the Four
Winds or Quarters, as observed by the Santee Sioux.
RPM, XVI-XVII, 289-95. 1883.

Forbes, W.H. Traditions of Sioux Indians. CMHS,
VI, 413-16. 1894.

Gabetentz, H.G.C. von der. Grammatik der Dakota-
Sprache. 64 pp. Leipzig, 1852.

Gardner, W.H. Ethnology of the Indians of the Valley of the Red River. ARSI, 1870, 369-73.

Garvie, J. Abraham Lincoln toni Kin. 17 pp.
Santee Agency, 1893.

Gates, C.M. The Lac qui Parle Indian Mission.
MiH, XVI, 133-51. 1935.

Gates, C.M., ed. Five Fur Traders of the Northwest. 298 pp. Minneapolis, 1933.

Gatschet, A.S. Adjectives of Color in Indian Languages. AN, XIII, 475-85. 1879.

Gilmore, M.R. Uses of Plants by the Indians of the
Missouri River Region. ARBAE, XXXIII, 43-154.
1912.

Goodrich, A.M. Early Dakota Trails and Settlements at Centerville, Minn. CMHS, XV, 315-22.
1915.

Gordon, H.H. Legends of the Northwest. 143 pp. St. Paul, 1881.

Hans, F.M. The Great Sioux Nation. 575 pp. Chicago, 1907.

Heard, I.V.D. History of the Sioux War and Massacres of 1862 and 1863. 354 pp. New York, 1863.

Heilbron, B.L. Some Sioux Legends in Pictures. MiH, XXXVI, i, 18-23. 1958.

Hennepin, L. A New Discovery of a Vast Country in America, ed. R.G.Thwaites. 2 vols. Chicago, 1903.

--- Nouvelle decouverte d'un tres grand pays situé dans l'Amérique. Utrecht, 1697.

Hofmann, C. American Indian Music in Wisconsin. JAFL, LX, 289-93. 1947.

Howard, J.H. The Cultural Position of the Dakota: A Reassessment. Essays in the Science of Culture in Honor of Leslie A. White, 249-68. New York, 1960.

Huggan, N. The Story of Nancy McClure. CMHS, VI, 439-60. 1894.

Hurt, W.R. House Types of the Santee Indians. MNUSD, XIV, xi, 1-3. 1953.

Jenks, A.E. The Wild Rice Gatherers of the Upper Lakes. ARBAE, XIX, ii, 1013-137. 1898.

Keating, W.H. Narrative of an Expedition to the Source of St. Peter's River, I, 376-439. Philadelphia, 1824.

Landes, R. Dakota Warfare. SJA, XV, 43-52. 1959.

Lockwood, J.H. Early Times in Wisconsin. CSHSW, II, 178-95. 1855.

Long, S.H. Voyage in a Six-Oared Skiff to the Falls of Saint Anthony in 1817. CMHS, II, i, 9-88. 1860.

Lowie, R.H. Dance Associations of the Eastern Dakota. APAM, XI, 101-42. 1913.

Lynd, J.W. The Religion of the Dakotas. CMHS, II, 63-84. 1864.

McGee, W J. The Siouan Indians. ARBAE XV, 157-204. 1894.

McLaughlin, J. My Friend the Indian. 417 pp. Boston, 1910.

McLaughlin, M.L. Myths and Legends of the Sioux. 200 pp. Bismarck, 1916.

Matson, G.A. Distribution of Blood Groups among the Sioux, Omaha, and Winnebago Indians. AJPA, XXVIII, 313-18. 1941.

Mayer, F.B. With Pen and Pencil on the Frontier. Minnesota Historical Society Narratives and Documents, I, 1-214. 1932.

Morgan, L.H. The Indian Journals, 1859-62, pp. 60-1, 110-1, 151-2, 198. Ann Arbor, 1959.

Morgan, L.H. Systems of Consanguinity and Affinity. SCK, XVII, 291-382. 1871.

Nebraska Writers' Project. Santee-Sioux Indian Legends. Nebraska Folklore Pamphlets. XXI, 1-15; XXIII, 1-14. 1937.

Neill, E.D. Dakota Land and Dakota Life. CMHS, I, 254-94. 1872.

--- The History of Minnesota, pp. 49-98. Philadelphia, 1858.

--- Memoir of the Sioux. Macalester College Contributions, I, 223-40. 1890.

Newton, R. The King's Highway. 427 pp. Yankton Agency, 1879.

Oehler, C.M. The Great Sioux Uprising. 272 pp. New York, 1959.

Peet, S.D. The Snake Clan among the Dakotas. AAOJ, XII, 237-42. 1890.

Pike, Z.M. Pike's Explorations in Minnesota, 1825-6. CMHS, I, 368-416. 1872.

Pond, G.H. Dakota Superstitions. CMHS, II, 32-62. 1867.

--- Power and Influence of Dakota Medicine-Men. HCPIT, IV, 641-51. 1854.

Pond, S.W. The Dakotas or Sioux in Minnesota. CMHS, XII, 319-501. 1908.

--- Indian Warfare in Minnesota. CMHS, III, 129-38. 1880.

Prescott, P. Contributions to the History, Customs and Opinions of the Dacota Tribe. HCPIT, II, 168-99; III, 225-46; IV, 59-72. 1852-54.

Riggs, S.R. The Dakota Language. CMHS, I, 89-107. 1872.

--- The Dakota Mission. CMHS, III, 114-28.1870.

--- Dakota Portraits. Minnesota History Bulletin, II, 481-568. 1918.

--- Mary and I. 388 pp. Chicago, 1880.

--- Mythology of the Dakotas. AAOJ, V, 147-9. 1883.

--- Protestant Missions in the Northwest. CMHS, VI, 117-88. 1894.

--- Tah-koo Wah-kan. 491 pp. Boston, 1869.

--- The Theogony of the Sioux. AAOJ, II, 265-70. 1880.

Ritzenthaler, R.E. Evidence of the Ancestors of the Chiwere Sioux. WA, n.s., XXVII, 89. 1946.

Robinson, D. A History of the Dakota or Sioux Indians. SDHC, II, 1-523. 1904.

Roddis, L.H. The Indian Wars of Minnesota. 329 pp. Cedar Rapids, 1956.

Roehrig, F.L.O. On the Language of the Dakota or Sioux Indians. ARSI, 1871, 434-50.

Schmidt, W. Die Wahpeton-Dakota. UG, II, 653-7. 1929.

Seymour, E.S. Sketches of Minnesota. 281 pp. New York, 1850.

Shea, J.G., ed. Early Voyages up and down the Mississippi. 191 pp. Albany, 1861.

Skinner, A. Medicine Ceremony of the Menomini, Iowa, and Wahpeton Dakota. INM, IV, 262-305. 1920.

--- Notes on the Sun Dance of the Sisseton Dakota. APAM, XVI, 381-5. 1919.

--- A Sketch of Eastern Dakota Ethnology. AA, n.s., XXI, 164-74. 1919.

--- Tree-Dweller Bundle of the Wahpeton Dakota. IN, II, 66-73. 1925.

Snelling, W.J. Tales of the North-West. 288 pp. Boston, 1830.

Telford, C.W. Test Performance of Full and Mixed-Blood North Dakota Indians. Journal of Comparative Psychology, XIV, 123-45. 1932.

Thayer, B.W. A Comparison of Dakota and Ojibway Steel Implements with Their Prehistoric Equivalents. MA, I, vi, 1-6. 1935.

Thwaites, R.G., ed. Radisson and Groseilliers in Wisconsin. CSHSW, XI, 64-96. 1888.

Upham, W. Mounds built by the Sioux in Minnesota. AAOJ, XXVII, 217-23. 1905.

Wallis, R.S. The Changed Status of Twins among the Eastern Dakota. AQ, III, 116-20. 1955.

--- The Overt Fears of Dakota Indian Children. Child Development, XXV, 185-92. 1954.

Wallis, R.S. and W.D. The Sins of the Fathers. SJA, IX, 431-6. 1953.

Wallis, W.D. Beliefs and Tales of the Canadian Dakota. JAFL, XXXVI, 36-101. 1923.

--- The Sun Dance of the Canadian Dakota. APAM, XVI, 317-80. 1921.

Wamditanka, Big Eagle. A Sioux Story of the War. CMHS, VI, 382-400. 1894.

Warren, G.K. Explorations in the Dacota Country. 79 pp. Washington, 1856.

White, N.D. Captivity among the Sioux. CMHS, IX, 396-426. 1901.

Williamson, A.W. The Dakotas and Their Traditions. AAOJ, XIII, 54-5. 1891.

Williamson, J.P. An English-Dakota Dictionary. New York, 1902.

--- The Letters of John P. Williamson. MA, XX, i, 2-21. 1956.

Williamson, T.S. Dacotas of the Mississippi. HCPIT, I, 247-56. 1851.

Winchell, N.H. Habitations of the Sioux in Minnesota. WA, VII, 155-64. 1908.

Wissler, C. Decorative Art of the Sioux Indians. BAMNH, XVIII, 231-77. 1904.

24. TETON

Including the Brulé, the Hunkpapa, the Kuluwitcatca, the Minneconjou, the Oglala, the Sans Arc, the Teton, and the Two Kettle, collectively known as the Western Dakota or Western Sioux.

Curtis, E.S. The North American Indian, III, 3-118, 137-90. Cambridge, 1908.

Macgregor, G. Warriors without Weapons. 228 pp. Chicago, 1946.

Malan, V.D. The Dakota Indian Family. South Dakota Agricultural Experiment Station Bulletin, CCCCLXX, 71 pp. 1958.

Abel, A.H., ed. Tabeau's Narrative of Loisel's Expedition to the Upper Missouri. 272 pp. Norman, 1939.

Anderson, H. An Investigation of the Early Bands of the Saone Group of Teton Sioux. JWAS, XLVI, 87-94. 1956.

Anonymous. Dakota. BBAE, XXX, i, 376-80. 1907.

--- The Dakota Indian Feast at the Big Bend. WHO, XIII, vii, 3. 1952.

--- An Oglala Ghost Story. WHO, XVIII, i-ii, 2. 1956.

--- Oglala Tales. WHO, XVIII, iii-iv, 4-5. 1956.

Beckwith, M.W. Mythology of the Oglala Dakota. JAFL, XLIII, 339-442. 1930.

Beckwith, P. Notes on Customs of the Dakotahs. ARSI, 1886, 245-57.

Bessaignet, P. Histoires Sioux. JSAP, n.s., XLIV, 49-54. 1955.

Blakeslee, C. Some Observations on the Indians of Crow Creek Reservation, South Dakota. PIA, V, 31-35. 1955.

Blish, H.H. The Ceremony of the Sacred Bow of the Oglala Dakota. AA, n.s., XXXVI, 180-7. 1934.

--- Ethical Conceptions of the Oglala Dakota. University of Nebraska Studies, XXVI, iii-iv, 1-47. 1926.

Boas, F. Some Traits of the Dakota Language. Lg, XIII, 137-41. 1937.

--- Teton Sioux Music. JAFL, XXXVIII, 319-24. 1925.

Boas, F., and Deloria, E. Notes on the Dakota, Teton Dialect. IJAL, VII, 97-121. 1933.

Boas, F., and Swanton, J.R. Siouan. BBAE, XL, i, 875-966. 1911.

Brackett, A.G. The Sioux or Dakota Indians. ARSI, XXXI, 466-72. 1876.

Bradley, J.H. History of the Sioux. Contributions of the Historical Society of Montana, IX, 29-140. 1923.

Brady, C.T. Indian Fights and Fighters. 423 pp. New York, 1904.

Brininstool, E.A. Fighting Red Cloud's Warriors. 241 pp. Columbus, 1926.

Brininstool, E.A. et al. Chief Crazy Horse, His Career and Death. NeH, XII, i, 4-78. 1929.

Brown, J.E. The Sacred Pipe. 164 pp. Norman, 1953.

Buechel, E. A Grammar of Lakota. 374 pp. St. Louis, 1939.

Burbank, E.A., and Royce, E. Burbank among the Indians, pp. 126-46. Caldwell, 1946.

Burdick, U.L. The Last Battle of the Sioux Nation. 164 pp. Fargo, 1929.

Bushnell, D.I. Burials of the Algonquian, Siouan and Caddoan Tribes. BBAE, LXXXIII, 29-42. 1927.

--- Villages of the Algonquian, Siouan, and Caddoan Tribes. BBAE, LXXVII, 59-71. 1922.

Bushotter, G. Oath-taking among the Dakota. IN, IV, 81-3. 1927.

--- A Teton Dakota Ghost Story. JAFL, I, 68-72. 1888.

Byrne, P.E. Soldiers of the Plains. 260 pp. New York, 1926.

Catlin, G. Illustrations of the Manners, Customs and Condition of the North American Indians, I, 208-46. New York, 1841.

Clark, A. About the Pine Ridge Porcupine. ILR, Sioux Series, I, 1-73. 1941.

--- Brave Against the Enemy. ILR, Sioux Series, VII, 1-215. 1944.

--- Bringer of the Mystery Dog. ILR, Sioux Series, VI, 1-84. 1944.

--- Buffalo Caller. 36 pp. Evanston, 1942.

--- The Grass Mountain Mouse. ILR, Sioux Series, III, 1-108. 1943.

--- The Hen of Wahpeton. ILR, Sioux Series, IV, 1-97. 1943.

--- Singing Sioux Cowboy Reader. ILR, Sioux Series, IX, 1-114. 1947.

--- The Slim Butte Raccoon. ILR, Sioux Series, II, 1-81. 1942.

--- There still are Buffalo. ILR, Sioux Series, V, 1-86. 1942.

Clark, D.W. A Note on the Function of Christianity among Indians. The Changing Indian, ed. O. La Farge, pp. 163-5. Norman, 1942.

Colby, L.W. The Ghost Songs of the Dakotas. PCNHS, ser. 2, I, 131-50. 1895.

Culbertson, T.A. Journal of an Expedition to the Mauvaises Terres and the Upper Missouri in 1850. BBAE, CXLVII, 172 pp. 1952.

Curtis, N., ed. The Indians' Book, pp. 37-90. New York, 1907.

Dangberg, G.M. Letters to Jack Wilson, the Paiute Prophet. BBAE, CLXIV, 279-96. 1957.

DeLand, C.E. The Aborigines of South Dakota. South Dakota Historical Collections, III, 269-586.

Deloria, E. Dakota Texts. PAES, XIV, 1-279. 1932.

--- Short Dakota Texts Including Conversation. IJAL, XX, 17-22. 1954.

--- The Sun Dance of the Oglala Sioux. JAFL, XLII, 354-413. 1929.

Densmore, F. A Collection of Specimens from the Teton Sioux. INM, XI, 163-204. 1948.

--- The Importance of the Mental Concept in Indian Art. M, XXII, 96-9. 1948.

--- Music in Its Relation to the Religious Thought of the Teton Sioux. Holmes Anniversary Volume, pp. 67-79. Washington, 1916.

--- Poems from Sioux and Chippewa Songs. 24 pp. Washington, 1917.

--- The Rhythm of Sioux and Chippewa Music. AAA, IX, 59-67. 1920.

--- Teton Sioux Music. BBAE, LXI, 1-533. 1918.

Donaldson, T. The George Catlin Indian Gallery. RUSNM, 1885, 53-63.

Dorsey, G.A. Legend of the Teton Sioux Medicine Pipe. JAFL, XIX, 326-9. 1906.

Dorsey, J.O. Games of Teton Dakota Children. AA, IV, 329-45. 1891.

--- Preface. CNAE, IX, xi-xxxii. 1893.

--- Siouan Sociology. ARBAE, XV, 218-22. 1894.

--- The Social Organization of the Siouan Tribes. JAFL, IV, 260-3. 1891.

--- A Study of Siouan Cults. ARBAE, XI, 351-544. 1890.

--- Teton Folk-Lore. AA, II, 143-58. 1889.

--- Teton Folk-Lore Notes. JAFL, II, 133-9. 1889.

Dorsey, J.O., and Thomas, C. Brulé. BBAE, XXX, i, 166-7. 1907.

--- Oglala. BBAE, XXX, ii, 109-11. 1910.

Douglas, F.H. The Sioux or Dakota Indians. DAMLS, XLI, 1-4. 1932.

Duratschek, M.C. Crusading along Sioux Trails. 334 pp. St. Meinrad, Indiana, 1947.

Erikson, E.H. Observations on Sioux Education. Journal of Psychology, VII, 101-56. 1939.

Ewers, J.C. Edwin T. Denig's "Of the Sioux." BMHS, VII, 185-215. 1951.

--- Teton Dakota Ethnology and History. 108 pp. Berkeley, 1938.

Farrell, R.C. The Burial of Sitting Bull. WHO, XV, i, 1-2. 1954.

Fenenga, F. The Interdependence of Archaeology and Ethnology as Illustrated by the Ice-Glider Game of the Northern Plains. PlA, I, 31-38. 1954.

Fletcher, A.C. The Elk Mystery or Festival. RPM, XVI-XVII, 276-88. 1883.

--- Indian Story and Song from North America. 126 pp. Boston, 1907.

--- The Shadow or Ghost Lodge. RPM, XVI-XVII, 296-307. 1883.

--- The White Buffalo Festival of the Uncpapas. RPM, XVI-XVII, 260-75. 1883.

Gaul, G. Standing Rock Agency. RIT, 1890, 519-26.

Gauvreau, E. Les Dakotas. ICA, XV, i, 311-13. 1907.

Gilmore, M.R. The Dakota Ceremony of Hunka. IN, VI, 75-9. 1929.

--- The Dakota Ceremony of presenting a Pipe. PMA, XVIII, 15-21. 1932.

--- Dakota Mourning Customs. IN, III, 295-6. 1926.

--- Oath-taking among the Dakota. IN, IV, 81-3. 1927.

--- The Old-Time Method of rearing a Dakota Boy. IN, VI, 367-72. 1929.

--- Prairie Smoke. 208 pp. New York, 1929.

--- Some Native Nebraska Plants with Their Uses by the Dakota. Nebraska State Historical Society Collections, XVII, 358-70. 1913.

--- Uses of Plants by the Indians of the Missouri River Region. ARBAE, XXXIII, 43-154. 1912.

--- The Victory Dance of the Dakota Indians. PMA, XVIII, 23-30. 1932.

Goldfrank, S. Historic Change and Social Character: A Study of the Teton Dakota. AA, n.s., XLV, 67-83. 1943.

Hallam, J. A Sioux Vision. Indian Miscellany, ed. W.W.Beach, pp. 127-44. Albany, 1877.

Hans, F.W. The Great Sioux Nation. 575 pp. Chicago, 1907.

Hassrick, R.B. Teton Dakota Kinship System. AA, n.s., XLVI, 338-47. 1944.

Hayden, F.V. Contributions to the Ethnography and Philology of the Indian Tribes of the Missouri Valley. TAPS, n.s., XII, 364-78. 1863.

Hebard, G.R. and Brininstool, E.A. The Bozeman Trail. 2 vols. Cleveland, 1922.

Heilbron, B.L. Some Sioux Legends in Pictures. MiH, XXXVI, i, 18-23. 1958.

Hennepin, L., et al. The Dakota Bark House. ILSPSC, I-IV, 1951.

Howard, J.H. The Cultural Position of the Dakota: A Reassessment. Essays in the Science of Culture in Honor of Leslie A. White, 249-68. New York, 1960.

--- Dakota Fishing Practices. MNUSD, XII, v, 1-4. 1951.

--- The Dakota Heyota Cult. SM, LXXVIII, 254-8.

--- Dakota Winter Counts as a Source of Plains History. BBAE, CLXXIII, 335-416. 1960.

--- New Notes on the Dakota Earth Lodge. NLPAC, IV, i, 4-10. 1951.

--- Notes on the Dakota Grass Dance. SJA, VII, 82-5. 1951.

--- Two Dakota Dream Headdresses. MNUSD, XII, iv, 1-4. 1951.

--- Dakota Fishing Practices. University of South Dakota, Museum News, XII, v, 1-4. 1951.

--- Two Dakota Winter Count Texts. PlA, V, 13-30. 1955.

--- The Tree Dweller Cults of the Dakota. JAFL, LXVIII, 462-72. 1955.

Hrdlicka, A. Anthropology of the Sioux. AJPA, XVI, 123-70. 1931.

--- Ritual Ablation of Front Teeth in Siberia and America. SMC, XCIX, iii, 1-32. 1940.

--- Tuberculosis among Certain Indian Tribes. BBAE, XLII, 11-14. 1909.

Hulsizer, A. Region and Culture in the Curriculum of the Navaho and the Dakota. 344 pp. Federalsburg, 1940.

Humfreville, J.L. Twenty Years among Our Savage Indians. 674 pp. Hartford, 1897.

Hurt, W.R. Additional Notes on Dakota House Types of South Dakota. WHO, XV, i, 3. 1954.

Hurt, W.R. and Howard, J.H. A Dakota Conjuring Ceremony. SJA, VIII, 286-96. 1952.

--- Two Newly-Recorded Dakota House Types. SJA, VI, 423-6. 1950.

Hyde, G.E. Red Cloud's Folk: A History of the Oglala Sioux Indians. 331 pp. Norman, 1937.

--- A Sioux Chronicle. 353 pp. Norman, 1956.

Hyer, J.K. Dictionary of the Sioux Language. 34 pp. New York, 1931.

Johnson, W.F. Life of Sitting Bull and History of the Indian War. 545 pp. Edgewood, 1891.

Johnston, M.A. Federal Relations with the Great Sioux Indians of South Dakota, 1887-1933. 137 pp. Washington, 1949.

Kane, L.M. The Sioux Treaties and the Traders. MiH, XXXII, 65-80. 1951.

Keegan, J.J. The Indian Brain. AJPA, III, 25-62. 1920.

Kelly, F. Narrative of My Captivity among the Sioux Indians. 304 pp. Toronto, 1872.

Kroeber, A.L. Recent Ethnic Spreads. UCP,XLVII, 259-81. 1959.

Laymon, O.F. Tribal Law for Oglala Sioux. Pierre, 1953.

Lee, D.D. Freedom and Culture, pp. 59-69. Englewood Cliffs, 1959.

Leigh, R.W. Dental Pathology of Indian Tribes. AJPA, VIII, 179-99. 1925.

Lesser, A. Some Aspects of Siouan Kinship. ICA, XXIII, 563-71. 1928.

Lord, M.P. Wowapi wakan kin token eya he, What saith the Scripture. 45 pp. Santee, 1894.

Lyford, C.A. Quill and Beadwork of the Western Sioux. IH, I, 1-116. 1940.

McGee, W J. The Siouan Indians. ARBAE, XV, 157-204. 1894.

McGillycuddy, J.B. McGillycuddy Agent. 291 pp. Stanford, 1941.

McLaughlin, J. My Friend the Indian. 417 pp. Boston, 1910.

Malan, V.D. and Jesser, C.J. The Dakota Indian Religion. South Dakota Agricultural Experiment Station Bulletin, CCCCLXXIII, 64 pp. 1959.

Malan, V.D. and Kallich, M. Changing Dakota Indian Culture. South Dakota Agricultural Experiment Station, Farm and Home Research, VIII, 11-15. May, 1957.

Mallery, G. A Calendar of the Dakota Nation. BGGST, III, 3-25. 1877.

Mathews, G.H. Phonemic Analysis of a Dakota Dialect. IJAL, XXI, 56-9. 1955.

Matson, G.A. Distribution of Blood Groups among the Sioux, Omaha, and Winnebago Indians. AJPA, XXVIII, 313-18. 1941.

Meeker, L.L. Oglala Games. BFMUP, III, 23-46. 1901.

--- Siouan Mythological Tales. JAFL, XIV, 161-4. 1901.

--- White Man, a Siouan Myth. JAFL, XV, 84-7. 1902.

Mekeel, S. A Discussion of Culture Change as illustrated by Material from a Teton-Dakota Community. AA, n.s., XXXIV, 274-85. 1932.

--- The Economy of a Modern Teton Dakota Community. YUPA, VI, 1-14. 1936.

Mekeel, S. A Short History of the Teton-Dakota. NDHQ, X, 136-205. 1943.

Mirsky, J. The Dakota. Cooperation and Competition among Primitive Peoples, ed. M. Mead, pp. 382-427. New York, 1937.

Montgomery, G. A Method of studying the Structure of Primitive Verse applied to the Songs of the Teton-Sioux. University of California Publications in Modern Philology, XI, 269-83. 1922.

Mooney, J. The Ghost-Dance Religion. ARBAE, XIV, ii, 796-927, 1058-78. 1893.

Moorehead, W.K. The Indian Messiah and the Ghost Dance. AAOJ, XIII, 161-7. 1891.

--- The Passing of Red Cloud. TKSHS, X, 295-311. 1908.

--- Sioux Women at Home. Illustrated American, V, 481-4. 1891.

--- Wanneta, the Sioux. New York, 1890.

Morgan, A. A Description of a Dakotan Calendar. Proceedings of the Literary and Philosophical Society of Liverpool, XXXIII, 233-53. 1879.

Morgan, L.H. The Indian Journals, 1859-62, pp. 60-1, 198. Ann Arbor, 1959.

--- Systems of Consanguinity and Affinity. SCK, XVII, 291-382. 1871.

Nasatir, A.P. Before Lewis and Clark. 2 vols. 882 pp. St. Louis, 1952.

Neihardt, J.G. When the Tree Flowered. New York, 1951.

Nevins, A., ed. Narratives of Exploration and Adventure by John Charles Frémont. 542 pp. New York, 1956.

Norton, A. The Sioux Spaceman. 133 pp. New York, 1960.

Parkman, F. The Oregon Trail. 5th edit. 381 pp. Boston, 1873.

Plant, W.G. A Hebrew-Dakota Dictionary. PAJHS, XLII, 361-70. 1953.

Pond, S.W. Two Volunteer Missionaries among the Dakotas. 287 pp. Chicago, 1893.

Poole, D.C. Among the Sioux of Dakota. 235 pp. New York, 1881.

Primbs, C. The Sunflower Dance of the Sioux Indians of the Upper Missouri. 15 pp. Norfolk, 1876.

Riggs, M.A.C. An English and Dakota Vocabulary. 120 pp. New York, 1852.

Riggs, S.R. A Dakota-English Dictionary. CNAE, VII, 1-665. 1890.

--- Dakota Grammar, Texts and Ethnography.CNAE, IX, 1-232. 1893.

--- Grammar and Dictionary of the Dakota Language. SCK, IV, 1-338. 1852.

Roberts, W.O. Successful Agriculture within the Reservation Framework. HO, II, iii, 37-44. 1943.

Robinson, D. A History of the Dakota or Sioux Indians. SDHC, II, 1-523. 1904 . [Reprinted, 1956.]

--- Sioux Indians. Cedar Rapids, 1908.

--- The Sioux of the Dakotas. Home Geographic Monthly, II, v, 7-12. 1932.

Ruby, R.H. The Oglala Sioux. 115 pp. New York, 1955.

Saint-Paul, C. Die Dakotahs oder Sioux. Ausland, LXIV, 121-6. 1891.

Sandoz, M. Crazy Horse. 428 pp. New York, 1942.

Schmidt, M.F., and Brown, D. Fighting Indians of the West, pp. 15-40, 113-228. New York, 1948.

Schwarzer, H. Die Heilige Pfeife. 234 pp. Olten, 1956.

Schwatka, F. The Sun-Dance of the Sioux. Century Magazine, XXXIX, 753-9. 1890.

Smith, DeC. Indian Experiences. 387 pp. Caldwell, 1943.

Snelling, W.J. Tales of the Northwest. 294 pp. Boston, 1830.

South Dakota Writers' Project, Work Projects Administration. Legends of the Mighty Sioux. 158 pp. Chicago, 1941.

Speck, F.G. Notes on the Functional Basis of Decoration and the Feather Technique of the Oglala Sioux. IN, V, 1-42. 1928.

Speck, F.G. and Fernberger, S.W. Two Sioux Shields and Their Psychological Interpretation. Journal of Abnormal and Social Psychology, XXXV, 168-78. 1938.

Speck, F.G., and Hassrick, R.B. A Plains Indian Shield and its Interpretation. PM, XXI, 74-9. 1948.

Spindler, W.H. Tragedy Strikes at Wounded Knee. 80 pp. Gordon, Nebraska, 1955.

Standing Bear, L. Land of the Spotted Eagle. 259 pp. Boston, 1933.

--- My People the Sioux. 288 pp. Boston, 1928.

--- Stories of the Sioux. Boston, 1934.

Sullivan, L.R. Anthropometry of the Siouan Tribes. APAM, XXIII, 81-174. 1920.

Thomas, C. Teton. BBAE, XXX, ii, 736-7. 1910.

Thompson, L. Attitudes and Acculturation. AA, n. s., L, 200-15. 1948.

Tomkins, W. Universal Indian Sign Language. 96 pp. San Diego, 1927.

Trudeau, J.B. Description of the Upper Missouri. MVHR, VIII, 149-79. 1921.

Useem, J., MacGregor, G., and Useem, R.H. Wartime Employment and Cultural Adjustments of the Rosebud Sioux. HO, II, ii, 1-9. 1943.

Vestal, S. New Sources of Indian History. 351 pp. Norman, 1934.

--- Sitting Bull. 2nd ed. 376 pp. Norman, 1957.

--- Warpath. 291 pp. Boston, 1934.

Vogt, K. The Dakota-Sioux. SS, V, ii, 4-7. 1953.

Walker, J.D. Tuberculosis among the Oglala Sioux Indians. SW, XXXV, 378-84. 1906.

Walker, J.R. Dakota Offering Sticks. IN, III, 199-200. 1926.

--- Oglala Kinship Terms. AA, n.s., XVI, 96-109. 1914.

--- Sioux Games. JAFL, XVIII, 277-90; XIX, 29-36. 1905-06.

--- The Sun Dance and Other Ceremonies of the Oglala. APAM, XVI, 51-221. 1917.

Wedel, W.R. and Griffenhagen, G.B. An English Balsam among the Dakota Aborigines. American Journal of Pharmacy, CXXVI, xii, 409-15. 1954.

Welsh, H. Civilization among the Sioux Indians. 58 pp. Philadelphia, 1893.

--- Four Weeks among Some of the Sioux Tribes of Dakota and Nebraska. 31 pp. Philadelphia, 1882.

--- Report of a Visit to the Great Sioux Reserve. 49 pp. Philadelphia, 1883.

Weygold, F. Die Hunkazeremonie. AFA, XXXIX, 145-60. 1912.

Wilson, E.P. The Story of Oglala and Brule Sioux in the Pine Ridge Country of Northwest Nebraska in the Middle Seventies. NeH, XXII, 15-33. 1941.

Wissler, C. Decorative Art of the Sioux Indians. BAMNH, XVIII, 231-75. 1905.

--- Distribution of Deaths among American Indians. HB, VIII, 223-31. 1936.

--- Measurements of Dakota Indian Children. ANYAS, XX, 355-64. 1911.

--- Societies and Ceremonial Associations in the Oglala Division of the Teton Dakota. APAM, XI, 1-97. 1912.

--- Some Dakota Myths. JAFL, XX, 121-31, 195-206. 1907.

--- Some Protective Designs of the Dakota. APAM, I, 21-53. 1907.

--- Symbolism in the Decorative Art of the Sioux. ICA, XIII, 339-45. 1902.

--- The Whirlwind and the Elk in the Mythology of the Dakotas. JAFL, XVIII, 257-68. 1905.

Yarrow, H.C. Some Superstitions of the Live Indians. AAOJ, IV, 136-44. 1882.

25. WICHITA

Including the Kichai, the Waco, and the Wichita.

Schmitt, K. and I.A. Wichita Kinship Past and Present. 82 pp. Norman, 1952.

Barry, L. With the First U.S. Cavalry in Indian Country, 1859-1861. KHQ, XXIV, 257-84. 1958.

Boas, F. Zur Anthropologie der nordamerikanischen Indianer. VBGA, 1895, 367-411.

Bolton, H.E. Athanase de Mezières and the Louisiana-Texas Frontier. 2 vols. Cleveland, 1914.

--- Tawakoni. BBAE, XXX, ii, 701-4. 1910.

--- Tawehash. BBAE, XXX, ii, 705-7. 1910.

--- Waco. BBAE, XXX, ii, 887-8. 1910.

--- Yscanis. BBAE, XXX, ii, 1002-3. 1910.

Bushnell, D.I. Villages of the Algonquian, Siouan and Caddoan Tribes. BBAE, LXXVII, 179-82. 1922.

Chapman, B.B. Dissolution of the Wichita Reservation. CO, XXII, 192-209, 300-14. 1944.

Curtis, E.S. The North American Indian, XIX, 35-104, 223-4, 230-8. Norwood, 1930.

Dorsey, G.A. Hand or Guessing Game among the Wichitas. AAOJ, XXIII, 363-70. 1901.

--- The Mythology of the Wichita. 351 pp. Washington, 1904.

--- Wichita Tales. JAFL, XV, 215-39; XVI, 160-79; XVII, 153-60. 1902-04.

Douglas, F.H. The Wichita Indians and Allied Tribes. DAMLS, XL, 1-4. 1932.

--- The Grass House of the Wichita and Caddo. DAMLS, XLII, 1-4. 1932.

Ethridge, A.N. Indians of Grant Parish. LHQ, XXIII, 1108-31. 1940.

Fletcher, A.C. Kichai. BBAE, XXX, i, 682-3. 1907.

Foreman, G. The Last Trek of the Indians, pp. 282-6, 290-91, 302-4. Chicago, 1946.

Garvin, P.L. Wichita. IJAL, XVI, 179-84. 1950.

Gatschet, A.S. Migration of the Wichita Indians. AAOJ, XIII, 249-52. 1891.

--- Two Indian Documents. AAOJ, XIII, 249-54. 1891.

Haas, M.R. Comments on the Name "Wichita." AA, n.s., XLIV, 164-5. 1942.

Harper, E.A. The Taovayas Indians in Frontier Trade and Diplomacy. CO, XXXI, 268-89. 1953.

--- The Taovayas Indians in Frontier Trade and Diplomacy, 1769-1779. SWHQ, LVII, 181-201. 1953.

--- The Taovayas Indians in Frontier Trade and Diplomacy, 1779-1835. PPHR, XXVI, 41-72. 1953.

Hungate, M. Religious Beliefs of the Nebraska Indian. NeH, XIV, iii, 207-26. 1938.

Lesser, A. Levirate and Fraternal Polyandry among the Pawnees. Man, XXX, 98-101. 1930.

Lesser, A., and Weltfish, G. Composition of the Caddoan Linguistic Stock. SMC, LXXXVII, vi, 1-15. 1932.

Mead, J.R. The Little Arkansas. TKSHS, X, 7-14. 1908.

Mooney, J. Wichita. BBAE, XXX, ii, 947-50. 1910.

Nasatir, A.P. Before Lewis and Clark. 2 vols. 882 pp. St. Louis, 1952.

Nye, W.S. Carbine and Lance. 441 pp. Norman, 1937.

O'Bryant, A. Differences in Wichita Indian Camp Sites as revealed by Stone Artifacts. KHQ, XV, 143-50. 1947.

Sayles, E.B. An Archaeological Survey of Texas. Medallion Papers, XVII, 1-164. 1935.

Scarborough, D. Traditions of the Waco Indians. PTFLS, I, 50-4. 1916.

Schmitt, K. Wichita Death Customs. CO, XXX, 200-06. 1952.

--- Wichita-Kiowa Relations and the 1874 Outbreak. CO, XXVIII, 154-60. 1950.

Smith, R.A. The Tawehash in French, Spanish, English, and American Imperial Affairs. WTHAY, XXVIII, 18-49. 1952.

--- Account of the Journey of Bénard de la Harpe. SWHQ, LXII, 75-86, 246-59, 371-85, 525-41. 1958-59.

Spier, L. Wichita and Caddo Relationship Terms. AA, n.s., XXVI, 258-63. 1924.

Steen, C.R. Two Early Historic Sites on the Southern Plains. BTAPS, XXIV, 177-88. 1953.

Tilghman, Z.A. Origin of the Name Wichita. AA, n.s., XLIII, 488-9. 1941.

Wedel, W.R. The Wichita. BBAE, CLXXIV, 60-8. 1959.

26. YANKTON

Including the Yankton and the Yanktonnai.

Anonymous. Dakota. BBAE, XXX, i, 376-80. 1907.

Belden, G.P. Belden, the White Chief. 511 pp. Cincinnati, 1870.

Bradley, J.H. History of the Sioux. Contributions of the Historical Society of Montana, IX, 29-140. 1923.

Culbertson, T.A. Journal of an Expedition to the Mauvaises Terres and the Upper Missouri in 1850. BBAE, CXLVII, 172 pp. 1952.

Culin, S. A Summer Trip among the Western Indians. BFMUP, III, 166-72. 1901.

Curtis, E.S. The North American Indian, III, 121-3, 152-9. Cambridge, 1908.

Dangberg, G.M. Letters to Jack Wilson, the Paiute Prophet. BBAE, CLXIV, 279-96. 1957.

Dorsey, J.O. Preface. CNAE, IX, xi-xxxii. 1893.

--- Siouan Sociology. ARBAE, XV, 217-18. 1894.

--- A Study of Siouan Cults. ARBAE, XI, 431-500. 1890.

Douglas, F.H. The Sioux or Dakota Indians. DAMLS, XLI, 1-4. 1932.

Ducheneaux, F. The Cheyenne River Sioux. AmI, VII, iii, 20-29. 1956.

Duratschek, M.C. Crusading along Sioux Trails. 334 pp. St. Meinrad, Indiana, 1947.

Gaul, G. Standing Rock Agency. RIT, 1890, 519-26.

Hayden, F.V. Contributions to the Ethnography and Philology of the Indian Tribes of the Missouri Valley. TAPS, n.s., XII, 364-78. 1863.

Hayes, J. Christ Church? Dakota People of Yankton. The B.C.U. Digest, I, iii, 1-3. Yankton, 1957.

Heilbron, B.L. Some Sioux Legends in Pictures. MiH, XXXVI, i, 18-23. 1958.

Howard, J.H. The Cultural Position of the Dakota: A Reassessment. Essays in the Science of Culture in Honor of Leslie A. White, 249-68. New York, 1960.

--- Dakota Winter Counts as a Source of Plains History. BBAE, CLXXIII, 335-416. 1960.

--- Drifting Goose's Village. WHO, XV, i, 2. 1954.

--- Notes on Two Dakota "Holy Dance" Medicines and Their Uses. AA, LV, 608-09. 1953.

--- Yanktonai Dakota Eagle Trapping. SJA, X, 69-74. 1954.

--- A Yanktonai Dakota Mide Bundle. NDHQ, XIX, ii, 132-39. 1952.

Hurt, W.R. The Yankton Dakota Church. Essays in the Science of Culture in Honor of Leslie A. White, 269-87. New York, 1960.

Keating, W.H. Narrative of an Expedition to the Source of St. Peter's River, I, 376-439. Philadelphia, 1824.

Laviolette, G. The Sioux Indians in Canada. 138 pp. Regina, 1944.

Lockwood, J.H. Early Times and Events in Wisconsin. CSHSW, II, 98-196. 1855.

McGee, W J. The Siouan Indians. ARBAE, XV, 157-204. 1894.

McLaughlin, J. My Friend the Indian. 417 pp. Boston, 1910.

Morgan, L.H. The Indian Journals, 1859-62, pp. 60-1, 110-1, 148-9, 151-2, 195, 198. Ann Arbor, 1959.

--- Systems of Consanguinity and Affinity. SCK, XVII, 167-76, 291-382. 1871.

Olden, S.E. The People of Tipi Sapa. 158 pp. Milwaukee, 1918.

Pruitt, O.J. Smutty Bear Tribe. Annals of Iowa, 3rd series, XXXI, 544-47, 1953.

Riggs, S.R. A Dakota-English Dictionary. CNAE, VII, 1-665. 1890.

--- Dakota Grammar, Texts and Ethnography. CNAE, IX, 1-232. 1893.

--- Grammar and Dictionary of the Dakota Language. SCK, IV, 1-338. 1852.

Robinson, D. A History of the Dakota or Sioux Indians. SDHC, II, 1-523. 1904.

Roddis, L.H. The Indian Wars of Minnesota. 329 pp. Cedar Rapids, 1956.

Shields, J. Thrilling Adventures among the Sioux and Chippewas. BMHS, XIII, 275-82. 1957.

Sibley, H.H. Iron Face. 230 pp. Chicago, 1950.

Snelling, W.J. Tales of the North-West. 288 pp. Boston, 1830.

Sullivan, L.R. Anthropometry of the Siouan Tribes. APAM, XXIII, 81-174. 1920.

Thomas, C. Yankton. BBAE, XXX, ii, 988-90. 1910.

--- Yanktonai. BBAE, XXX, ii, 990-1. 1910.

Weston, M.C., and Cook, J.W. Calvary wiwicawangapi kin, qa wokiksuye anpetu kin koya. 32 pp. Madison, S.D., 1893.

Wied-Neuwied, M.zu. Reise in das innere Nordamerika. 2 vols. Coblenz, 1839-41.

--- Travels in the Interior of North America. EWT, XXII, 304-11, 341-4; XXIV, 223-6. 1906.

Williamson, J.P. An English-Dakota Dictionary. New York, 1902.

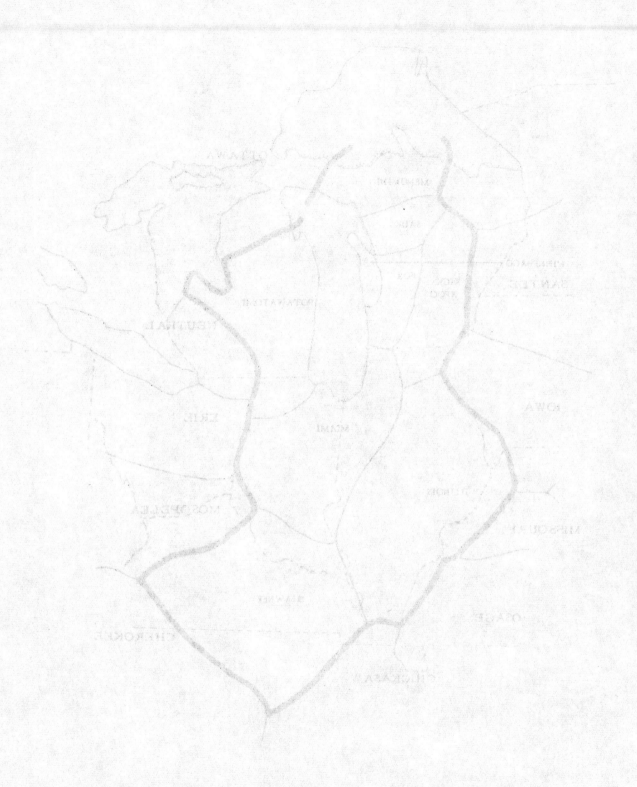

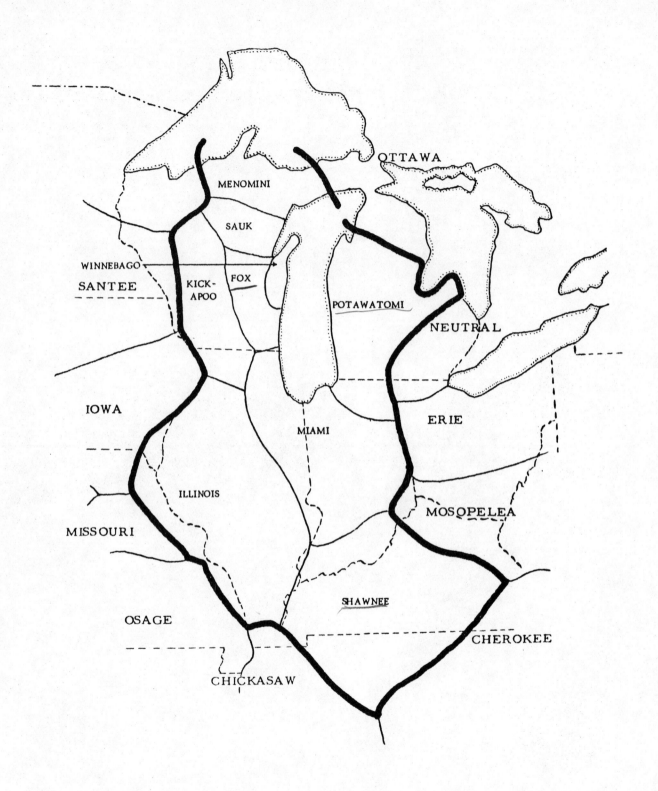

OTTAWA

MENOMINI

SAUK

WINNEBAGO

SANTEE

KICK-
APOO

FOX

POTAWATOMI

NEUTRAL

IOWA

ERIE

MIAMI

ILLINOIS

MOSOPELEA

MISSOURI

SHAWNEE

OSAGE

CHEROKEE

CHICKASAW

With the exception of the Winnebago, who are Siouan, all the tribes of this area belong to the Algonkian linguistic stock.

Alberts, R.C. Trade Silver and Indian Silver Work in the Great Lakes Region. WA, XXXIV, 1-121. 1953.

Aller, W.F. Aboriginal Food Utilization of Vegetation by the Indians of the Great Lakes Region as Recorded in the Jesuit Relations. WVA, XXXV, iii, 59-73. 1954.

Atwater, C. Remarks made on a Tour to Prairie du Chien. 296 pp. Columbus, 1831.

Baerreis, D.A. Trade Silver and Indian Silversmiths. Wisconsin Magazine of History, XXXIV, 76-82. 1950.

Bauman, R.F., ed. The Last Gathering under the Old Council Elm. NOQ, XXIX, 145-60. 1957.

--- The Removal of Indians from the Maumee Valley. NOQ, XXX, 10-25. 1958.

Beardsley, G. The Groundnut as used by the Indians of Eastern North America. PMA, XXV, iv, 507-15. 1939.

Beatty, C. The Journal of a Two-Months Tour. 110 pp. London, 1768.

Beauchamp, W.M. Indian Nations of the Great Lakes. AAOJ, XVII, 321-5. 1895.

Beckner, L. The Moundbuilders. Filson Club History Quarterly, XXIX, 203-25. 1955.

Birket-Smith, K. A Geographic Study of the Early History of the Algonquian Indians. IAE, XXIV, 174-222. 1918.

Bloomfield, L. Proto-Algonquian -i•t- 'Fellow.' Lg, XVII, 292-7. 1941.

Braasch, W.F., et al. Survey of Medical Care among the Upper Midwest Indians. Journal of the American Medical Association, CXXXIX, 220-5. 1949.

Brown, C.E. Indian Village and Camp Sites on the Lower Rock River in Wisconsin. WA, n.s., IX, 7-93. 1929.

--- The Native Copper Implements of Wisconsin. WA, III, 49-85. 1904.

--- The Native Copper Ornaments of Wisconsin. WA, III, 101-21. 1904.

--- The Use of Earthenware Vessels by the Old Northwest Indians. WA, n.s., VIII, 69-75. 1929.

--- Winabozho. 7 pp. Madison, 1944.

Bushnell, D.I. Native Cemeteries and Forms of Burial East of the Mississippi. BBAE, LXXI, 1-160. 1920.

--- Native Villages and Village Sites East of the Mississippi. BBAE, LXIX, 1-111. 1919.

Byers, D.S. The Environment of the Northeast. PRSPF, III, 3-32. 1946.

Carr, L. The Mounds of the Mississippi Valley. ARSI, 1891, 503-99.

Carver, J. Travels through the Interior Parts of North America. 2d edit. London, 1779.

Chamberlain, L.S. Plants used by the Indians of Eastern North America. AN, XXXV, 1-10. 1901.

Chambliss, C.E. The Botany and History of Zizania aquatica L. ("Wild Rice"). JWAS, XXX, 185-205. 1940.

Charlevoix, P.F.X.de. Histoire de la Nouvelle France. 3 vols. Paris, 1894.

--- History and General Description of New France, ed. J.M.Shea. 6 vols. New York, 1866-72.

--- Journal of a Voyage to North America, ed. L. P. Kellogg. 2 vols. Chicago, 1923.

Clarke, P.D. Origin and Traditional History of the Wyandotts. 158 pp. Toronto, 1870.

Covington, J.W. The Indian Liquor Trade at Peoria, 1824. JISHS, XLVI, 142-50. 1953.

Deuel, T. Basic Cultures of the Mississippi Valley. AA, n.s., XXXVII, 429-45. 1935.

Dixon, R.B. The Mythology of the Central and Eastern Algonkins. JAFL, XXII, 1-9. 1909.

Douglas, F.H. Tribes of the Great Lakes Region. DAMLS, LXXXI, 121-4. 1937.

Essington, J.H. Early Inhabitants of the Ohio Valley. WVH, XIII, 277-85. 1952.

Fisher, M.W. The Mythology of the Northern and Northeastern Algonkians in Reference to Algonkian Mythology as a Whole. PRSPF, III, 226-62. 1946.

Ford, J.A., and Willey, G.R. An Interpretation of the Prehistory of the Eastern United States. AA, n.s., XLIII, 325-63. 1941.

Foreman, G. The Last Trek of the Indians, pp. 18-88, 159-81, 229-36. Chicago, 1946.

Frémont, D. Les Aborigènes du Nord-Ouest Canadien au Temps de La Vérendrye. Mémoires de la Société Royale du Canada, XLIII, 3e série, Sect. I, 7-21. 1949.

Geary, J.A. Algonquian nasaump and napõpi. Language, XXI, 40-45. 1945.

--- Proto-Algonquian *ck. Lg, XVII, 304-10. 1941.

--- The Proto-Algonquian Form for 'I-Thee.' Lg, XIX, 147-51. 1943.

Gille, J. Der Mamabozho-Flutzyklus der Nord-, Nordost-, und Zentral-Algonkin. 86 pp. Göttingen, 1939.

--- Zur Lexikologie des Alt-Algonkin. ZE, LXXI, 71-86. 1939.

Governor's Commission on Human Rights. Handbook on Wisconsin Indians. Madison, 1952.

Hawley, F. Tree-Ring Analysis and Dating in the Mississippi Drainage. University of Chicago Publications in Anthropology, Occasional Papers, II, 1-110. 1941.

Hibbard, B.H. Indian Agriculture in Southern Wisconsin. PSHSW, LII, 145-55. 1904.

Hinsdale, W.B. Distribution of the Aboriginal Population of Michigan. OCMA, II, 1-35. 1932.

--- Indian Corn Culture in Michigan. PMA, VIII, 31-49. 1927.

Hockett, C.F. Central Algonquian /t/ and /c/. IJAL, XXII, 202-7. 1956.

--- Central Algonquian Vocabulary Stems in /k/. IJAL, XXIII, 247-68. 1957.

--- Implications of Bloomfield's Algonquian Studies. Lg, XXIV, 117-35. 1948.

Holmer, N.M. Lexical and Morphological Contacts between Siouan and Algonquian. Lunds Universitets Arsskrift, n.s., XLV, 1-36. 1949.

Holmes, W.H. Prehistoric Textile Fabrics of the United States. ARBAE, III, 393-425. 1882.

Horsman, R. British Indian Policy in the Northwest, 1807-1818. MVHR, XLV, 51-66. 1958.

Hrdlicka, A. Catalogue of Human Crania in the United States National Museum Collections. PUSNM, LXIX, v, 1-127. 1927.

Hulbert, A.B., and Schwarze, W.N., eds. Zeisberger's History of Northern American Indians. OAHQ, XIX, 1-189. 1910.

Hunter, W.A. The Ohio, the Indian's Land. PH, XXI, 338-50. 1954.

Johnson, F., ed. Man in Northeastern North America. PRSPF, III, 1-347. 1946.

Jones, V.H. Notes on the Preparation and the Uses of Basswood Fiber by the Indians of the Great Lakes Region. PMA, XXII, 1-14. 1936.

Jones, W. Some Principles of Algonquian Word-Formation. AA, n.s., VI, 369-411. 1904.

Kellogg, L.P., ed. Early Narratives of the Northwest. 382 pp. New York, 1917.

Kinietz, V. Notes on the Algonquian Family Hunting Ground System. AA, n.s., XLII, 179. 1940.

--- Notes on the Roached Headdress of Animal Hair among the North American Indians. PMA, XXVI, 463-7. 1940.

Knowles, N. The Torture of Captives by the Indians of Eastern North America. PAPS, LXXXII, 151-225. 1940.

Kuhm, H.W. Indian Place-Names in Wisconsin. WA, XXXIII, 1-157. 1952.

Kuhm, H.W. The Mining and Use of Lead by the Wisconsin Indians. WA, XXXII, 25-38. 1951.

--- Wisconsin Indian Fishing. WA, n.s., VII, 61-114. 1928.

Kurath, G.P. Algonquian Ceremonialism and Natural Resources of the Great Lakes. Indian Institute of Culture, Reprint XXII. Bangalore, 1957.

--- Antiphonal Songs of Eastern Woodlands Indians. Musical Quarterly, XLII, 520-6. 1956.

--- Blackrobe and Shaman. PMA, XLIV, 209-15. 1959.

--- Catholic Hymns of Michigan Indians. AQ, XXX, 31-44. 1957.

--- Ceremonies, Songs and Dances of Michigan Indians. MHM, XXXIX, 466-68. 1955.

--- Pan-Indianism in Great Lakes Tribal Festivals. JAFL, LXX, 179-82. 1957.

Lahontan, A.L.de D. New Voyages to North-America, ed. R.G.Thwaites. 2 vols. Chicago, 1905.

Laviolette, G. Notes on the Aborigines of the Prairie Provinces. An, II, 107-30. 1956.

Loskiel, G.H. Geschichte der Mission der evangelischen Brüder unter den Indianern in Nordamerika. 783 pp. Barby, 1789.

--- History of the Mission of the United Brethren among the Indians of North America. London, 1794.

Lyons, E.J. Isaac McCoy: His Plan of and Work for Indian Colonization. Fort Hayes Kansas State College Bulletin, XXXV, xvii, 61 pp. 1945.

McKern, W.C. An Hypothesis for the Asiatic Origin of the Woodland Culture. AAn, III, 138-43.1937.

Marquette, J., and Joliet, L. An Account of the Discovery of Some New Countries and Nations in North America. HCL, II, 277-97. 1850.

Matthews, G.H. Proto-Siouan Kinship Terminology. AA, LXI, 252-78. 1959.

Michelson, T. Algonquian Notes. IJAL, IX, 103-12. 1939.

--- Contributions to Algonquian Linguistics. IJAL, X, 75-85. 1939.

--- Phonetic Shifts in Algonquian Languages. IJAL, VIII, 131-71. 1935.

--- Preliminary Report on the Linguistic Classification of Algonquian Tribes. ARBAE, XXVIII, 221-90. 1907.

--- Some Algonquian Kinship Terms. AA, n.s., XXXIV, 357-9. 1932.

--- Terms of Relationship and Social Organization. PNAS, II, 297-300. 1916.

Nasatir, A.P. Before Lewis and Clark. 2 vols. 882 pp. St. Louis, 1952.

Nydahl, T.L. The Pipestone Quarry and the Indians. MiH, XXXI, 193-208. 1950.

Parkins, A.E. The Indians of the Great Lakes Region and Their Environment. GR, VI, 504-12. 1918.

Pearce, N.O. Tuberculosis among Minnesota's Indians. AmI, IV, i, 20-23. 1947.

Peet, S.D. The Location of the Indian Tribes. AAOJ, I, 85-98. 1878.

Perrot, N. Mémoire sur les moeurs, coustumes et religion des sauvages de l'Amérique septentrionale. 341 pp. Paris, 1864.

--- Memoir on the Manners, Customs, and Religion of the Savages of North America. ITUMV, I, 25-272. 1911.

Pilling, J.C. Bibliography of the Algonquian Languages. BBAE, XIII, 1-614. 1891.

Potherie, B. de la. History of the Savage Peoples who are Allies of New France. ITUMV, I, 273-372; II, 13-136. 1911-12.

Quimby, G.I. The Archeology of the Upper Great Lakes Area. AEUS, 99-107. 1952.

Reynolds, H.L. Algonkin Metal-Smiths. AA, I, 341-52. 1888.

Ritzenthaler, R.E. Prehistoric Indians of Wisconsin. PSHPMCM, IV, 43 pp. 1953.

Rogers, R. A Concise Account of North America. 264 pp. London, 1765.

Schermerhorn, J.F. Report respecting the Indians inhabiting the Western Parts of the United States. MHSC, ser. 2, II, 1-45. 1814.

Shea, J.G. Discovery and Exploration of the Mississippi Valley. 2d edit. Albany, 1903.

--- Early Voyages up and down the Mississippi. 191 pp. Albany, 1861.

--- The Indian Tribes of Wisconsin. CSHSW, III, 125-38. 1856.

Shetrone, H.C. The Mound Builders. 508 pp. New York, 1930.

Shippen, H.H. A Woven Bulrush Mat from an Indian Tribe of the Great Lakes Region. PMA, XXXIX, 399-406. 1954.

Siebert, F.T. Certain Proto-Algonquian Consonant Clusters. Lg, XVII, 298-303. 1941.

Siiger, H. Praerieindianerne og Piben. Fra Nationalmuseets Arbejdsmark, 1946, 24-9. København.

Skinner, A. The Algonkin and the Thunderbird. AMJ, XIV, 71-3. 1914.

--- Some Aspects of the Folk-Lore of the Central Algonkin. JAFL, XXVII, 97-100. 1914.

--- Traces of the Stone Age among the Eastern and Northern Tribes. AA, n.s., XIV, 391-5. 1912.

Steeves, T.A. Wild Rice. Economic Botany, VI, 107-42. 1952.

Stickney, G.P. The Use of Maize by Wisconsin Indians. Parkman Club Publications, XIII, 63-87. 1897.

Surrey, F.M., ed. Calendar of Manuscripts in Paris Archives and Libraries relating to the History of the Mississippi Valley to 1803. 2 vols. Washington, 1926-28.

Temple, W.C. Indian Villages of the Illinois Country. SPISM, II, ii, 218 pp. 1958.

Terry, F.T. Aborigines of the Northwest. Parkman Club Publications, IV, 59-72. 1896.

Thomas, C. Burial Mounds in the Northern Sections of the United States. ARBAE, V, 9-119. 1884.

Thwaites, R.G., ed. The French Regime in Wisconsin. CSHSW, Vols. XVI-XVIII. 1902-08.

Tonti, H. de. Relation de la Louisianne, et du Mississipi. RVN, V, 35-195. 1734.

Trumbull, J.H. On the Algonkin Verb. Transactions of the American Philological Association, VII, 147-71. 1877.

Turner, F.J. The Character and Influence of the Indian Trade in Wisconsin. Johns Hopkins University Studies in Historical and Political Science, IX, xi-xii, 3-75. 1891.

Ueck, L.P. Material Used by the Southwest Michigan Indians in the Flaking of Stone Artifacts. Earth Science Digest, VI, vi, 31-33. 1953.

Verwyst, C. Missionary Labors of Fathers Marquette, Menard, and Allouez. 262 pp. Chicago, 1886.

Voegelin, C.F. and E.W. Linguistic Considerations of Northeastern North America. PRSPF, III, 178-94. 1946.

Voegelin, E.W. Indians of Indiana. PIAS, L, 27-32. 1941.

--- Mortuary Customs of the Shawnee and Other Eastern Tribes. PRS, II, 227-444. 1944.

Walker, L.J. Indian Camp Meeting at Greensky Hill. JAFL, LXIII, 96-7. 1950.

Walton, I. Indian Place Names in Michigan. MWF, V, 23-34. 1955.

West, G.A. Copper: Its Mining and Use by the Aborigines of the Lake Superior Region. BPMCM, X, 1-184. 1929.

--- Uses of Tobacco and the Calumet by Wisconsin Indians. WA, X, 5-64. 1911.

Wilson, H.C. A New Interpretation of the Wild Rice District of Wisconsin. AA, LVIII, 1059-64. 1956.

1. FOX

Also called Musquaki and Outagami.

Gearing, F., Netting, R.M., and Peattie, L.R., eds. Documentary History of the Fox Project, 1948-1959. 426 pp. Chicago, 1960.

Hagan, W.T. The Sac and Fox Indians. 301 pp. Norman, 1958.

Jones, W. Ethnography of the Fox Indians. BBAE, CXXV, 1-156. 1939.

Anonymous. Cha kǎ ta ko si: a Collection of Meskwaki Manuscripts. Iowa City, 1907.

Armstrong, P.A. The Sauks and the Black Hawk War. 726 pp. Springfield, 1887.

Beckwith, H.W. The Illinois and Indiana Indians. FHS, XXVII, 146-62. 1884.

Berthrong, D.J. John Beach and the Removal of the Sauk and Fox from Iowa. IJHP, LIV, 313-34. 1956.

Bicknell, A.D. The Tama County Indians. Annals of Iowa, ser. 3, IV, 196-208. 1899.

Bloomfield, L. Notes on the Fox Language. IJAL, III, 219-32; IV, 181-219. 1925-27.

Brown, D.M. Wisconsin Indian Corn Origin Myths. WA, n.s., 19-27. 1940.

Burford, C.C. Sauk and Fox Indian Ceremonials attract Large Audience and Wide-spread Interest. Journal of the Illinois State Archaeological Society, V, 24-30. 1947.

Busby, A.B. Two Summers among the Musquakies. Vinton, 1886.

Bushnell, D.I. Villages of the Algonquian, Siouan and Caddoan Tribes. BBAE, LXXVII, 37-41. 1922.

Carman, J.N. and Pond, K.S. The Replacement of the Indian Languages of Kansas by English. TKAS, LVIII, 131-50. 1955.

English, E.H. A Mesquakie Chief's Burial. Annals of Iowa, 3rd series, XXX, 545-50. 1951.

Ferris, I.M. The Sauks and Foxes. CKSHS, XI, 333-95. 1910.

Flannery, R. Two Concepts of Power. ICA, XXIX, iii, 185-9. 1952.

Flom, G.T. Syllabus of Vowel and Consonantal Sounds in Meskwaki Indian. Iowa City, 1906.

Foreman, G. The Last Trek of the Indians, pp. 133-58, 222-9. Chicago, 1946.

Forsyth, T. Account of the Manners and Customs of the Sauk and Fox Nations. ITUMV, II, 183-245. 1912.

Galland, I. The Indian Tribes of the West. Annals of Iowa, VII, 347-66. 1869.

Gates, C.M., ed. Five Fur Traders of the Northwest. 296 pp. Minneapolis, 1933.

Gearing, F. Today's Mesquakies. AmI, VII, ii, 24-37. 1955.

Geary, J.A. The Changed Conjunct (with -ni) and the Interrogative in Fox. IJAL, XII, 66-78. 1946.

--- The Changed Conjunct Verb (without NI) in Fox. IJAL, XI, 169-81. 1945.

--- The Subjunctive in Fox. IJAL, XII, 198-203. 1946.

Green, O.J. The Mesquaki Indians. Red Man, V, 47-52, 104-9. 1912.

Hargrett, L. A Bibliography of the Constitutions and Laws of the American Indians, pp. 102-3. Cambridge, 1947.

Harrington, M.R. A Bird-Quill Belt of the Sauk and Fox Indians. INM, X, 47-50. 1920.

--- Old Sauk and Fox Beaded Garters. INM, X, 39-41. 1920.

--- Sacred Bundles of the Sac and Fox. UPMAP, IV, 125-262. 1914.

Hunter, W.A. Refugee Fox Settlements among the Senecas. E, III, 11-20. 1956.

Huot, M.C. Peyote Songs. Transition, XXIV, 117-19. 1936.

Jenks, A.E. The Wild Rice Gatherers of the Upper Lakes. ARBAE, XIX, ii, 1013-137. 1898.

Joffe, N.F. The Fox of Iowa. ASAIT, 259-332. 1940.

Jones, W. The Algonkin Manitou. JAFL, XVIII, 183-90. 1905.

--- Algonquian (Fox). BBAE, XL, i, 735-873. 1911.

--- An Algonquin Syllabary. Boas Anniversary Volume, pp. 88-93. New York, 1906.

--- Episodes in the Culture-Hero Myth of the Sauks and Foxes. JAFL, XIV, 225-39. 1901.

--- Fox Texts. PAES, I, 1-383. 1907.

--- The Heart of the Brave. Harvard Monthly, XXX, 99-106. 1900.

--- Mortuary Observances and the Adoption Rites of the Algonkin Foxes of Iowa. ICA, XV, i, 263-77. 1906.

--- Notes on the Fox Indians. JAFL, XXIV, 209-37. 1911.

--- Some Principles of Algonquian Word-Formation. AA, n.s., VI, 369-411. 1904.

Kellogg, L.P. The Fox Indians during the French Regime. PSHSW, LV, 142-88. 1907.

Lasley, M. Sac and Fox Tales. JAFL, XV, 170-8. 1902.

Lawson, P.V. The Outagamie Village at West Menasha. PSHSW, XLVII, 204-11. 1900.

McGee, W J. A Muskwaki Bowl. AA, XI, 88-91. 1898.

Marsh, C. Expedition to the Sacs and Foxes. CSHSW, XV, 104-55. 1900.

Marston, M. Letter to Reverend Dr. Jedediah Morse. ITUMV, II, 139-82. 1912.

Michelson, T. Algonquian Linguistic Miscellany. JWAS, IV, 402-9. 1914.

--- The Autobiography of a Fox Indian Woman. ARBAE, XL, 291-349. 1919.

--- The Changing Character of Fox Adoption-Feasts. AJS, XXXIV, 890-2. 1929.

--- Contributions to Algonquian Grammar. AA, n.s., XV, 470-6. 1913.

--- Contributions to Fox Ethnology. BBAE, LXXXV, 1-162; XCV, 1-183. 1927-30.

--- Field-Work among the Catawba, Fox, Sutaio and Sauk Indians. SMC, LXIII, viii, 836. 1914.

--- Fox Linguistic Notes. Festschrift Meinhof, pp. 403-8. Hamburg, 1927.

--- Fox Miscellany. BBAE, CXIV, 1-124. 1937.

--- How Meskwaki Children should be brought up. American Indian Life, ed. E.C.Parsons, pp. 81-6. New York, 1925.

--- Miss Owen's "Folk-Lore of the Musquakie Indians." AA, n.s., XXXVIII, 143-5. 1936.

--- The Mythical Origin of the White Buffalo Dance of the Fox Indians. ARBAE, XL, 23-289. 1919.

--- Note on Fox Gens Festivals. ICA, XXIII, 545-6. 1928.

--- Note on the Hunting Territories of the Sauk and Fox. AA, n.s., XXIII, 238-9. 1921.

--- Notes on Algonquian Languages. IJAL, I, 50-7. 1919.

--- Notes on Fox Mortuary Customs and Beliefs. ARBAE, XL, 351-496. 1919.

--- Notes on the Buffalo-Head Dance of the Thunder Gens of the Fox Indians. BBAE, LXXVII, 1-94. 1928.

--- Notes on the Folklore and Mythology of the Fox Indians. AA, n.s., XV, 699-700. 1913.

--- Notes on the Fox Society known as Those who worship the Little Spotted Buffalo. ARBAE, XL, 497-539. 1919.

--- Notes on the Fox Wapanowiweni. BBAE, CV, 1-195. 1932.

--- Notes on the Great Sacred Pack of the Thunderbird Gens of the Fox Indians. BBAE, XCV, 43-183. 1930.

--- Notes on the Social Organization of the Fox Indians. AA, n.s., XV, 691-3. 1913.

Michelson, T. Observations on the Thunder Dance of the Bear Gens of the Fox Indians. BBAE, LXXXIX, 1-73. 1929.

--- On the Future of the Independent Mode in Fox. AA, n.s., XIII, 171-2. 1911.

--- On the Origin of the So-called Dream Dance of the Central Algonkians. AA, n.s., XXV, 277-8. 1923.

--- The Owl Sacred Pack of the Fox Indians. BBAE, LXXII, 1-83. 1921.

--- Revision of Wm. Jones' Sketch of Algonquian. BBAE, XL, i, 737-873. 1911.

--- Ritualistic Origin Myths of the Fox Indians. JWAS, VI, 209-11. 1916.

--- The So-called Stems of Algonquian Verbal Complexes. ICA, XIX, 541-4. 1915.

--- Sol Tax on the Social Organization of the Fox Indians. AA, n.s., XL, 177-9. 1938.

--- Some General Notes on the Fox Indians. JWAS, IX, 483-94, 521-8, 593-6. 1919.

--- Studies on the Fox and Ojibwa Indians. SMC, LXXVIII, i, 111-13. 1926.

--- The Traditional Origin of the Fox Society known as "The singing around Rite." ARBAE, XL, 541-658. 1919.

--- Vocalic Harmony in Fox. AJP, XLI, 181-3. 1920.

--- What happened to Green Bear who was blessed with a Sacred Pack. BBAE, CXIX, 161-76. 1938.

Miller, W.B. Two Concepts of Authority. AA, LVII, 271-89. 1955.

Mooney, J., and Thomas, C. Foxes. BBAE, XXX, i, 472-4. 1907.

Morgan, L.H. The Indian Journals, 1859-62, pp. 40, 76-7, 80-1, 83. Ann Arbor, 1959.

Morse, J. A Report to the Secretary of War. 400 pp. New Haven, 1922.

Nasatir, A.P. Before Lewis and Clark. 2 vols. 882 pp. St. Louis, 1952.

Owen, M.A. Algonquins. ERE, I, 319-26. 1908.

--- Folk-Lore of the Musquakie Indians. 147 pp. London, 1904.

Polgar, S. Biculturation of Mesquakie Teenage Boys. AA, LXII, 217-35. 1960.

Rebok, H.M. The Last of the Mus-qua-kies. Iowa Historical Record, XVII, 305-35. 1901.

Schmidt, W. Die Foxes. UG, II, 574-80; V, 583-663; VII, 761-3. 1929, 1934, 1940.

Smith, H.H. Ethnobotany of the Meskwaki Indians. BPMCM, IV, 175-326. 1928.

--- The Red Earth Indians. YPMCM, III, 27-38. 1923.

Steward, J.F. Lost Maramech and Earliest Chicago.
    390 pp. Chicago, New York, etc., 1903.
Tax, S. The Fox Project. HO, XVII, i, 17-19. 1958.
--- The Social Organization of the Fox Indians.
    SANAT, pp. 243-84. 1955.
Thwaites, R.G., ed. The Jesuit Relations and Allied
    Documents. 74 vols. Cleveland, 1896-1901.
Ward, D.J.H. The Meskwaki People of To-day.
    IJHP, IV, 190-219. 1906.
--- Meskwakia. IJHP, IV, 179-89. 1906.
Wied-Neuwied, M. zu. Reise in das innere Nord-
    amerika. 2 vols. Coblenz, 1839-41.
--- Travels in the Interior of North America. EWT,
    XXII, 217-30; XXIV, 276-7, 294-5. 1906.

2. ILLINOIS

Including the Cahokia, Kaskaskia, Mascouten,
Michigamea, Moingwena, Peoria, and Tamaroa.

Anonymous. Illinois and Miami Vocabulary and
    Lord's Prayer. U.S. Catholic Historical Magazine,
    III, 1-9. 1891.
Beckwith, H.W. The Illinois and Indiana Indians.
    FHS, XXVII, 99-106. 1884.
Belting, N.M. Illinois Names for Themselves and
    Other Groups. E, V, 285-91. 1958.
Blasingame, E.J. The Depopulation of the Illinois
    Indians. E, III, 193-224, 361-412. 1956.
Bushnell, D.I. Native Cemeteries and Forms of
    Burial East of the Mississippi. BBAE, LXXI, 39-
    43. 1920.
Carr, L. The Mascoutins. PAAS, n.s., XIII, 448-62.
    1900.
Caton, J.D. The Last of the Illinois. FHS, III, 1-
    55. 1876.
Charlevoix, P.F.X. de. Journal of a Voyage to North
    America. 2 vols. Chicago, 1923.
Deliette, L. Memoir concerning the Illinois Country,
    ed. T.C. Pease and R.C. Werner. Collections of
    the Illinois State Historical Library, XXIII, 302-95.
    1934.
Federal Writers' Projects. Wisconsin Indian Place
    Legends, pp. 2-3, 17-18. Milwaukee, 1936.
Foreman, G. The Last Trek of the Indians, pp. 204-
    6. Chicago, 1946.
Hamy, E.T. Note sur d'anciennes peintures sur peaux
    des Indiens Illinois. JSAP, II, 185-95. 1897.
Hennepin, L. A New Discovery of a Vast Country in
    America, ed. R.G. Thwaites. 2 vols. Chicago,
    1903.

Henson, C.E. Ritual Elements in Mississippi River
    Petroglyphs. FL, LXVIII, 405-10. 1957.
Jones, A.E. The Site of the Mascoutin. PSHSW, LIV,
    175-82. 1906.
Joutel, H. Journal of La Salle's Last Voyage. New
    edit. 258 pp. Albany, 1906.
--- Relation. DEFAS, III, 91-534. 1879.
Kellogg, L.P., ed. Early Narratives of the North-
    west, pp. 223-57. New York, 1917.
Kelly, A.R. Some Problems of Recent Cahokia Ar-
    chaeology. Transactions of the Illinois State
    Academy of Sciences, XXV, 101-3. 1933.
Kenton, E., ed. The Indians of North America, II,
    269-74, 287-9, 356-63, 374-9. New York, 1927.
Kinietz, W.V. The Indian Tribes of the Western
    Great Lakes. OCMA, X, 161-225, 383-408. 1940.
Marquette, J., and Joliet, L. An Account of the
    Discovery of Some New Countries and Nations in
    North America. HCL, II, 277-97. 1850.
Mereness, N.D., ed. Travels in the American Colo-
    nies, pp. 71-4. New York, 1916.
Michelson, T. The Identification of the Mascoutens.
    AA, n.s., XXXVI, 226-33. 1934.
--- Notes on Peoria Folk-Lore and Mythology. JAFL,
    XXX, 493-5. 1917.
--- Once more Mascoutens. AA, n.s., XXXVII,
    163-4. 1935.
Mooney, J., and Thomas, C. Illinois. BBAE, XXX,
    i, 597-9. 1907.
--- Kaskaskia. BBAE, XXX, i, 661-3. 1907.
--- Mascoutens. BBAE, XXX, i, 810-12. 1907.
--- Michigamea. BBAE, XXX, i, 856-7. 1907.
--- Peoria. BBAE, XXX, ii, 228. 1910.
Morgan, L.H. The Indian Journals, 1859-62, pp.
    40-1. Ann Arbor, 1959.
--- Systems of Consanguinity and Affinity. SCK,
    XVII, 291-382. 1871.
Nasatir, A.P. Before Lewis and Clark. 2 vols. 882
    pp. St. Louis, 1952.
Peithmann, I.M. Echoes of the Red Man. 134 pp.
    New York, 1955.
Schmidt, W. Die Mascoutens oder Prärie-Potawato-
    mie. UG, II, 516-38; V, 580-2. 1929, 1934.
Shea, J.G. Discovery and Exploration of the Missis-
    sippi Valley. 2d edit. Albany, 1903.
Silvy, A. Relation par lettres de l'Amérique sep-
    tentrionale, ed. C. de Rochemonteix, pp. 138-
    73. Paris, 1904.
Skinner, A. An Illinois Quilled Necklace. INM, X,
    33-4. 1920.
Strong, W.D. The Indian Tribes of the Chicago Re-
    gion. FMDAL, XXIV, 1-13. 1926.

Thwaites, R.G., ed. The Jesuit Relations and Allied Documents. 74 pp. Cleveland, 1896-1901.

--- Radisson and Groseilliers in Wisconsin. CSHSW, XI, 64-96. 1888.

Tonti, H. de. An Account of Monsieur de la Salle's Last Expedition. CNYHS, II, 217-341. 1814.

Villiers, M. de. Recettes médicales employées dans la région des Illinois vers 1724. JSAP, n.s., XVIII, 15-20. 1926.

Winslow, C.S., ed. Indians of the Chicago Region. 210 pp. Chicago, 1946.

Wray, D.E. Archeology of the Illinois Valley: 1950. AEUS, 152-64. 1952.

Wray, D.E., and Smith, H. An Hypothesis for the Identification of the Illinois Confederacy with the Middle Mississippi Culture in Illinois. AAn, X, 23-7. 1944.

3. KICKAPOO

Ritzenthaler, R.E. and Peterson, F.A. The Mexican Kickapoo Indians. PAMPM, II, 91 pp. 1956.

Silverberg, J. The Kickapoo Indians. WA, XXXVIII, 61-181. 1957.

Beckwith, H.W. The Illinois and Indiana Indians. FHS, XXVII, 117-37. 1884.

Carman, J.N. and Pond, K.S. The Replacement of the Indian Languages of Kansas by English. TKAS, LVIII, 131-50. 1955.

Fabila, A. La tribu Kikapoo de Coahuiha. 94 pp. Mexico, 1945.

Foreman, G. The Last Trek of the Indians, pp. 206-17. Chicago, 1946.

Goggin, J.M. The Mexican Kickapoo Indians. SJA, VII, 314-27. 1951.

Hoad, L.G. Kickapoo Indian Trails. 129 pp. Caldwell, 1944.

Hunter, J.D. Memoirs of a Captivity among the Indians of North America. 447 pp. London, 1823.

Jones, W. The Algonkin Manitou. JAFL, XVIII, 183-90. 1905.

--- Kickapoo Ethnological Notes. AA, n.s., XV, 332-5. 1913.

--- Kickapoo Tales. PAES, IX, 1-142. 1915.

Michelson, T. Algonquian Tribes of Oklahoma and Iowa. EFWSI, 1928, 183-8.

--- The Punishment of Impudent Children among the Kickapoo. AA, n.s., XXV, 281-3. 1923.

--- Studies of the Algonquian Tribes of Iowa and Oklahoma. EFWSI, 1929, 207-12.

Mooney, J., and Jones, W. Kickapoo. BBAE, XXX, i, 684-6. 1907.

Morgan, L.H. Systems of Consanguinity and Affinity. SCK, XVII, 291-382. 1871.

Neighbors, K.F. The Marcy-Neighbors Exploration of the Headwaters of the Brazos and Wichita Rivers in 1854. PPHR, XXVII, 27-46. 1954.

Owen, M.A. Algonquins. ERE, I, 322-6. 1908.

Patton, W. Journal of a Visit to the Indian Missions, Missouri Conference. BMHS, X, 167-80. 1954.

Peterson, F.A. and R.E. Ritzenthaler. The Kickapoos Are Still Kicking. NH, LXIV, 200-06, 224. 1955.

Pope, R.K. The Withdrawal of the Kickapoo. AmI, VIII, ii, 17-26. 1958-59.

Schmidt, W. Die Kickapoo und die Shawnee. UG, II, 599-601. 1929.

4. MENOMINI

Hoffman, W.J. The Menomini Indians. ARBAE, XIV, i, 11-328. 1893.

Skinner, A. Material Culture of the Menomini. INM, n.s., XX, 1-478. 1921.

--- Social Life and Ceremonial Bundles of the Menomini Indians. APAM, XIII, 1-165. 1913.

Slotkin, J.S. The Menomini Powwow. PAMPM, IV, 166 pp. 1957.

Spindler, G.D. Sociological and Psychological Processes in Menomini Acculturation. UCPCS, V, 276 pp. 1955.

Ames, D.W. and Fisher, B.R. The Menominee Termination Crisis. HO, XVIII, iii, 101-11. 1959.

Barrett, S.A. The Dream Dance of the Chippewa and Menominee Indians. BPMCM, I, 251-406. 1911.

Bloomfield, L. The Menomini Language. ICA, XXI, 336-43. 1924.

--- Menomini Texts. PAES, XII, 1-607. 1928.

Boas, F. Zur Anthropologie der nordamerikanischen Indianer. VBGA, 1895, 367-411.

Brown, D.M. Indian Winter Legends. WA, n.s., XXII, 49-53. 1941.

Bruce, W.H. Menomonee. HCPIT, II, 470-81. 1852.

Bushnell, D.I. Sketches by Paul Kane in the Indian Country, 1845-1848. SMC, XCIX, i, 1-25. 1940.

Curtis, M.E. The Black Bear and the White-tailed Deer. MWF, II, 177-90. 1952.

--- Folklore of Feast and Famine among the Menomini. PMA, XXXIX, 407-19. 1954.

Densmore, F. Menominee Music. BBAE, CII, 1-
230. 1932.

--- Music of the Winnebago and Menominee Indians.
EFWSI, 1928-189-98.

--- Studies of Indian Music among the Menomini.
SMC, LXXVIII, i, 119-25. 1926.

--- Tribal Customs of the Menominee Indians. EFWSI,
1929, 217-22.

Douglas, F.H. The Menomini Indians. DAMLS,
XXV, 1-4. 1931.

Federal Writers' Projects. Wisconsin Indian Place
Legends, pp. 33-8. Milwaukee, 1936.

Favre, B. La Grammaire de la Langue Ménomonie
du P. Antoine-Marie Gachet. A, XLIX, 1094-
1100. 1954.

Gachet, A.M. Grammaire de la Langue Ménomonie.
Micro-Bibliotheca Anthropos, XXI, 456 pp. 1954.

Hilger, M.I. Menomini Child Life. JSAP, n.s.,
XL, 167-71. 1951.

Hoffman, W.J. The Mythology of the Menomini Indians. AA, III, 243-58. 1890.

Hrdlicka, A. Tuberculosis among Certain Indian
Tribes. BBAE, XLII, 8-10. 1909.

Jenks, A.E. The Wild Rice Gatherers of the Upper
Lakes. ARBAE, XIX, ii, 1013-137. 1898.

Keesing, F.M. The Menomini Indians of Wisconsin.
MAPS, X, 1-261. 1939.

Krautbauer, F.X. Short Sketch of the History of the
Menominee Indians. American Catholic Historical
Researches, IV, 152-8. 1887.

Kurath, G.P. Menomini Indian Dance Songs in a
Changing Culture. MWF, IX, 31-8. 1959.

--- Wild Rice Gatherers of Today. AA, LIX, 713.
1957.

McAllester, D.P. Menomini Peyote Music. TAPS,
XLII, 681-700. 1952.

Michelson, T. Fruther Remarks on the Origin of the
So-called Dream Dance of the Central Algonkians.
AA, n.s., XXVI, 293-4. 1924.

--- Menominee Tales. AA, n.s., XIII, 68-88. 1911.

Mooney, J., and Thomas, C. Menominee. BBAE,
XXX, i, 842-4. 1907.

Morgan, L.H. Systems of Consanguinity and Affinity.
SCK, XVII, 291-382. 1871.

Peet, S.O. Mythology of the Menominees. AAOJ,
XXXI, 1-14. 1909.

Ritzenthaler, R.E. The Menominee Indian Sawmill.
WA, XXXII, 39-44. 1951.

Ritzenthaler, R. and Sellars, M. Indians in an Urban
Situation. WA, XXXVI, 147-61. 1955.

Robinson, C.D. Legend of the Red Banks. Annual Report of the Wisconsin State Historical Society, II,
491-4. 1855.

Sady, R.R. The Menominee. HO, VI, ii, 1-14.
1947.

Schmidt, W. Die Menomini. UG, II, 539-73.
1929.

Skinner, A. Associations and Ceremonies of the
Menomini Indians. APAM, XIII, 167-215. 1915.

--- Collecting among the Menomini. WA, n.s., III,
135-42. 1924.

--- A Comparative Sketch of the Menomini. AA,
n.s., XIII, 551-65. 1911.

--- Little-Wolf joins the Medicine Lodge. American
Indian Life, ed. E.C.Parsons, pp. 63-73. New
York, 1925.

--- Medicine Ceremony of the Menomini, Iowa, and
Wahpeton Dakota. INM, IV, 15-188. 1920.

--- The Menomini Game of Lacrosse. AMJ, XI,
139-41. 1911.

--- The Menomini Word "Häwătuk." JAFL, XXVIII,
258-61. 1915.

--- Recollections of an Ethnologist among the Menomini Indians. WA, XX, 41-74. 1921.

--- Some Menomini Indian Place Names in Wisconsin. WA, XVIII, iii, 97-102. 1919.

--- Songs of the Menomini Medicine Ceremony. AA,
n.s., XXVII, 290-314. 1925.

--- War Customs of the Menomini Indians. AA, n.s.,
XIII, 299-312. 1911.

Skinner, A., and Satterlee, J.V. Folklore of the
Menomini Indians. APAM, XIII, 217-546. 1915.

Slotkin, J.S. A Case of Paranoid Schizophrenia
among the Menomini Indians of Wisconsin. Micro-
card Publications of Primary Records in Culture
and Personality, III. Madison, 1959.

--- Social Psychiatry of a Menomini Community.
Journal of Abnormal and Social Psychology, XLVIII,
10-16. 1953.

Smith, H.H. Ethnobotany of the Menomini Indians.
BPMCM, IV, 1-174. 1923.

--- Uses of Native Plants by the Menomini. WA,
n.s., III, 24-6. 1924.

Spindler, G.D. Personal Documents in Menomini
Peyotism. Primary Records in Culture and Personality, II. 1956.

--- Personality and Peyotism in Menomini Indian
Acculturation. Psychiatry, XV, 151-59. 1952.

Spindler, G.D. and Goldschmidt, W. Experimental
Design in the Study of Culture Change. SJA, VIII,
68-83. 1952.

Spindler, L.S. Witchcraft in Menomini Acculturation. AA, LIV, 593-602. 1952.

Spindler, L.S. and G.D. Male and Female Adapta-
tions in Culture Change. AA, LX, 217-33. 1958.

5. MIAMI

Including the Miami, the Piankashaw, and the Wea.

Kinietz, W.V. The Indian Tribes of the Western Great Lakes. OCMA, X, 161-225. 1940.

Trowbridge, C.C. Meearmeear Traditions, ed. W. V. Kinietz. OCMA, VII, 1-91. 1938.

Anonymous. Illinois and Miami Vocabulary and Lord's Prayer. U.S. Catholic Historical Magazine, III, 1-9. 1891.

Baldwin, C.C. Early Indian Migration in Ohio. AAOJ, I, 227-39. 1879.

Beckwith, H.W. The Illinois and Indiana Indians. FHS, XXVII, 107-17. 1884.

Bibaud, F.M. Biographie des sagamos illustrés de l'Amérique Septentrionale, pp. 236-42. Montreal, 1848.

Blasingame, E.J. The Miami Prior to the French and Indian War. E, II, 1-10. 1955.

Brice, W.A. History of Fort Wayne. 324 pp. Fort Wayne, 1868.

Deliette, L. Memoir concerning the Illinois Country, ed. T.C. Pease and R.C. Werner. Collections of the Illinois State Historical Library, XXIII, 302-95. 1934.

Dillon, J.B. The National Decline of the Miami Indians. Indiana Historical Society Publications, I, 121-43. 1897.

Dunn, C. Jacob Piatt Dunn: His Miami Language Studies and Indian Manuscript Collection. PRS, I, ii, 31-59. 1937.

Dunn, J.P. True Indian Stories. 320 pp. Indianapolis, 1909.

Foreman, G. The Last Trek of the Indians, pp. 125-32, 201-4. Chicago, 1946.

Handy, C.N. Miami. HCPIT, II, 470-81. 1852.

Harrison, W.H. A Discourse on the Aborigines of the Ohio Valley. FHS, XXVI, 1-95. 1883.

Henson, C.E. Ritual Elements in Mississippi River Petroglyphs. FL, LXVIII, 405-10, 1957.

Hill, L.U. John Johnston and the Indians in the Land of the Three Miamis. 207 pp. Piqua, 1957.

Hooton, E.A. Indian Village Site and Cemetery near Madisonville Ohio. PMP, VIII, i, 1-137. 1920.

Hosmer, H.L. Early History of the Maumee Valley. Toledo Directory, pp. 9-70. Toledo, 1858.

Hundley, W.M. Squawtown. 209 pp. Caldwell, 1939.

Mary Celeste. The Miami Indians prior to 1700. Mid-America, n.s., XVI, 225-34. 1934.

Mooney, J. Piankashaw. BBAE, XXX, ii, 240-1. 1910.

--- Wea. BBAE, XXX, ii, 925-6. 1910.

Mooney, J., and Thomas, C. Miami. BBAE, XXX, i, 852-5. 1907.

Moorehead, W.K. The Indian Tribes of Ohio. OAHQ, VII, 1-109. 1898.

Morgan, L.H. The Indian Journals, 1859-62, p. 78. Ann Arbor, 1959.

--- Systems of Consanguinity and Affinity. SCK, XVII, 291-382. 1871.

Quimby, G.I. European Trade Articles as Chronological Indicators for the Archaeology of the Historic Period in Michigan. PMA, XXIV, iv, 25-31. 1938.

Robertson, R.S. Burial among the Miamis. AAOJ, II, 54-5. 1879.

Shetrone, H.C. The Indian in Ohio. OAHQ, XXVII, 273-510. 1918.

Smith, G.H. Three Miami Tales. JAFL, LII, 194-208. 1939.

Strong, W.D. The Indian Tribes of the Chicago Region. FMDAL, XXIV, 14-16. 1926.

Taylor, E.L. The Ohio Indians. OAHQ, VI, 72-94. 1898.

Thornton, W. Miamis. TCAAS, II, 305-67. 1836.

Voegelin, C.F. Shawnee Stems and the Jacob P. Dunn Miami Dictionary. PRS, I, 63-108, 135-67, 345-406, 409-78. 1938-40.

Volney, C.F.C. Tableau du climat et du sol des Etats-Unis d'Amérique. 2 vols. Paris, 1803.

--- View of the Climate and Soil of the United States of America, pp. 393-503. London, 1804.

Winter, G. Journals and Indian Paintings, 1837-1839. 208 pp. Indianapolis, 1948.

6. POTAWATOMI

Deale, V.B. The History of the Potawotamies before 1722. E, V, 305-60. 1958.

Ritzenthaler, R.E. The Potawatomi Indians of Wisconsin. BPMCM, XIX, 99-174. 1953.

Skinner, A. The Mascoutens or Prairie Potawatomi Indians. BPMCM, VI, 1-411. 1924-27.

Beckwith, H. The Illinois and Indiana Indians. FHS, XXVII, 162-83. 1884.

Bloodworth, J. Social and Economic Survey of Potawatomie Jurisdiction. 58 pp. Bureau of Indian Affairs, Washington, 1957.

Brown, D.M. Indian Winter Legends. WA, n.s., XXII, 49-53. 1941.

--- Wisconsin Indian Corn Origin Myths. WA, n.s., XXI, 19-27. 1940.

Buechner, C.B. The Pokagons. Indiana Historical Society Publications, X, 281-340. 1933.

Carman, J.N. and Pond, K.S. The Replacement of the Indian Languages of Kansas by English. TKAS, LVIII, 131-50. 1955.

Caton, J.D. The Last of the Illinois and a Sketch of the Pottawatomies. FHS, III, 3-30. 1876.

Chapman, B.B. The Pottawatomie and Absentee Shawnee Reservation. CO, XIV, 292-305. 1946.

Faben, W.W. Indians of the Tri-State Area: the Potowattamis. NOQ, XXX, 49-53, 100-05. 1958.

Federal Writers' Projects. Wisconsin Indian Place Legends, pp. 13-14, 17-25, 30-32, 39. Milwaukee, 1936.

Foreman, G. The Last Trek of the Indians, pp. 100-125, 218-22. Chicago, 1946.

Hockett, C.F. The Conjunct Modes in Ojibwa and Potawatomi. Lg, XXVI, 278-82. 1950.

--- The Position of Potawatomi in Central Algonkian. PMA, XXVIII, 537-42. 1942.

--- Potawatomi. IJAL, XIV, 1-10, 63-73, 139-49, 213-25. 1948.

--- Potawatomi Syntax. Lg, XV, 235-48. 1939.

Jacobs, H. The Potawatomi Mission 1854. Mid-America, XXXVI, 220-48. 1954.

Johnson, F. Notes on the Ojibwa and Potawatomi of the Parry Island Reservation. IN, VI, 193-216. 1929.

Jones, J.A. The Political Organization of the Three Fires. PIAS, LXIII, 46. 1953.

Keating, W.H. Narrative of an Expedition to the Source of St. Peter's River, I, 91-138. Philadelphia, 1824.

Kinietz, W.V. The Indian Tribes of the Western Great Lakes. OCMA, X, 308-16. 1940.

Kurath, G.P. Wild Rice Gatherers of Today. AA, LIX, 713. 1957.

Lawson, P.V. The Potawatomi. WA, XIX, 41-116. 1920.

Lykins, J., tr. The Gospel according to Matthew and Acts of the Apostles. 240 pp. Louisville, 1844.

McDonald, D. Removal of the Pottawattomie Indians from Northern Indiana. 59 pp. Plymouth, 1899.

Metzdorf, W. The Pottawatomi. ITUMV, II, 287-97. 1912.

Meyer, A.H. Circulation and Settlement Patterns of the Calumet Region of Northwest Indiana and Northeast Illinois. AAAG, XLIV, 245-74. 1954.

Michelson, T. The Identification of the Mascoutens. AA, n.s., XXXVI, 226-33. 1934.

Michelson, T. The Linguistic Classification of Potawatomi. PNAS, I, 450-2. 1915.

Mooney, J., and Hewitt, J.N.B. Potawatomi. BBAE, XXX, ii, 289-93. 1910.

Morgan, L.H. The Indian Journals, 1859-62, pp. 35-6, 58, 84. Ann Arbor, 1959.

--- Systems of Consanguinity and Affinity. SCK, XVII, 291-382. 1871.

Morse, J. A Report to the Secretary of War. 400 pp. New Haven, 1822.

Nasatir, A.P. Before Lewis and Clark. 2 vols. 882 pp. St. Louis, 1952.

Nichols, P.V. Wisconsin - what does it mean? AI, VIII, 171-6. 1948.

Patton, W. Journal of a Visit to the Indian Missions, Missouri Conference. BMHS, X, 167-80. 1954.

Pokagon, S. O-gi-maw-kwe mit-i-gwä-ki: Queen of the Woods. Hartford, 1899.

Pruitt, O.J. Some Iowa Indian Tales. Annals of Iowa, 3rd series, XXXII, 203-16. 1953-55.

Quimby, G.I. European Trade Articles as Chronological Indicators for the Archaeology of the Historic Period in Michigan. PMA, XXIV, iv, 25-31. 1938.

--- Some Notes on Kinship and Kinship Terminology among the Potawatomi of the Huron. PMA, XXV, 553-63. 1939.

Ragland, H.D. Potawatomi Day Schools. CO, XXX, 270-78. 1952.

Ritzenthaler, R. and Sellars, M. Indians in an Urban Situation. WA, XXXVI, 147-61. 1955.

Schmidt, W. Die Potawatomie (und Ottawa). UG, II, 508-15. 1929.

Schoewe, C.G. Uses of Wood and Bark among the Wisconsin Indians. WA, n.s., XI, 148-52. 1932.

Skinner, A. Medicine Ceremony of the Menomini, Iowa, and Wahpeton Dakota. INM, IV, 327-30. 1920.

--- A Trip to the Potawatomi. WA, n.s., III, 143-50. 1924.

Smet, P.J. de. Legend of the Potawotomie Indians. EWT, XXIX, 373-80. 1906.

Smith, H.H. Among the Potawatomi. YPMCM, V, 68-76. 1925.

--- Ethnobotany of the Forest Potawatomi Indians. BPMCM, VII, 1-230. 1933.

Strong, W.D. The Indian Tribes of the Chicago Region. FMDAL, XXIV, 17-34. 1926.

Thwaites, R.G., ed. The Jesuit Relations and Allied Documents. 74 vols. Cleveland, 1896-1901.

--- Radisson and Groseilliers in Wisconsin. CSHSW, XI, 64-96. 1888.

Tiedke, K.E. A Study of the Hannahville Indian Community. Michigan State Agricultural Experiment Station, Special Bulletin, CCCLXIX, 43 pp. 1951.

Webb, J.W., ed. Altowan. 2 vols. New York, 1846.

7. SAUK

Hagan, W.T. The Sac and Fox Indians. 301 pp. Norman, 1958.

Skinner, A. Observations on the Ethnology of the Sauk Indians. BPMCM, V, 1-180. 1923-25.

Armstrong, P.A. The Sauks and the Black Hawk War. 726 pp. Springfield, 1887.

Beckwith, H.W. The Illinois and Indiana Indians. FHS,XXVII, 146-62. 1884.

Beltrami, J.C. A Pilgrimage in Europe and America, II, 138-59. London, 1828.

Berthrong, D.J. John Beach and the Removal of the Sauk and Fox from Iowa. IJHP, LIV, 313-34. 1956.

Black Hawk. Autobiography. 208 pp. St. Louis, 1882.

Brown, D.M. Wisconsin Indian Corn Origin Myths. WA, n.s., XXI, 19-27. 1940.

Burford, C.C. Sauk and Fox Indian Ceremonials attract Large Audience and Wide-spread Interest. Journal of the Illinois State Archaeological Society, V, 24-30. 1947.

Bushnell, D.I. Villages of the Algonquian, Siouan and Caddoan Tribes. BBAE, LXXVII, 37-41. 1922.

Carman, J.N. and Pond, K.S. The Replacement of the Indian Languages of Kansas by English. TKAS, LVIII, 131-50. 1955.

Donaldson, T. The George Catlin Indian Gallery. RUSNM, 1885, Appendix, 13-39.

Ferris, I.M. The Sauks and Foxes. CKSHS, XI, 333-95. 1910.

Foreman, G. The Last Trek of the Indians, pp. 133-58, 222-9. Chicago, 1946.

Forsyth, T. Account of the Manners and Customs of the Sauk and Fox Nations. ITUMV, II, 183-245. 1912.

Galland, I. The Indian Tribes of the West. Annals of Iowa, VII, 347-66. 1869.

Hargrett, L. A Bibliography of the Constitutions and Laws of the American Indians, pp. 102-3. Cambridge, 1947.

Harrington, M.R. A Bird-Quill Belt of the Sauk and Fox Indians. INM, X, 47-50. 1920.

Harrington, M.R. Old Sauk and Fox Beaded Garters. INM, X, 39-41. 1920.

--- Sacred Bundles of the Sac and Fox. UPMAP,IV, 125-262. 1914.

Hewitt, J.N.B. Sauk. BBAE, XXX, ii, 471-80. 1910.

Jackson, D. Ma-ka-tai-me-she-kia-kiak, Black Hawk. 206 pp. Urbana, 1955.

Jenks, A.E. The Wild Rice Gatherers of the Upper Lakes. ARBAE, XIX, ii, 1013-137. 1898.

Johnston, G. Osawgenong – A Soc Tradition. CSHSW, XV, 448-51. 1900.

Jones, W. The Algonkin Manitou. JAFL, XVIII, 183-90. 1905.

--- Episodes in the Culture-Hero Myth of the Sauks and Foxes. JAFL, XIV, 225-39. 1901.

Keating, W.H. Narrative of an Expedition to the Source of St. Peter's River, I, 218-32. Philadelphia, 1824.

Lasley, M. Sac and Fox Tales. JAFL, XV, 170-8. 1902.

Marsh, C. Expedition to the Sacs and Foxes. CSHSW, XV, 104-55. 1900.

Marston, M. Letter to Reverend Dr. Jedediah Morse. ITUMV, II, 139-82. 1912.

Michelson, T. Ethnological Researches among the Fox Indians. SMC, LXXVII, ii, 133-6. 1925.

--- Field-Work among the Catawba, Fox, Sutaio and Sauk Indians. SMC, LXIII, viii, 836. 1914.

--- Note on the Hunting Territories of the Sauk and Fox. AA, n.s., XXIII, 238-9. 1921.

--- Review. AA, n.s., XXVI, 93-100. 1924.

Morgan, L.H. The Indian Journals, 1859-62, pp. 40, 76-7; 80-1, 83. Ann Arbor, 1959.

--- Systems of Consanguinity and Affinity. SCK, XVII, 291-382. 1871.

Morse, J. A Report to the Secretary of War. 400 pp. New Haven, 1822.

Nasatir, A.P. Before Lewis and Clark. 2 vols. 882 pp. St. Louis, 1952.

Schmidt, W. Die Sauk. UG, II, 581-98. 1929.

Skinner, A. Sauk Tales. JAFL, XLI, 147-71. 1928.

--- Sauk War Bundles. WA, n.s., II, 148-50. 1923.

--- Some Unusual Ethnological Specimens. YPMCM, III, 103-9. 1923.

--- Summer among the Sauk and Ioway Indians. YPMCM, II, 6-15. 1922.

Steward, J.F. Lost Maramech and Earliest Chicago. 390 pp. Chicago, 1903.

Thwaites, R.G., ed. The Jesuit Relations and Allied Documents. 74 vols. Cleveland, 1896-1901.

Thwaites, R.G., ed. The Jesuit Relations and Allied Documents. 74 vols. Cleveland, 1896-1901.

Wied-Neuwied, M. zu. Reise in das innere Nordamerika. 2 vols. Coblenz, 1839-41.

--- Travels in the Interior of North America. EWT, XXII, 217-30; XXIV, 276-7, 294-5. 1906.

8. SHAWNEE

Trowbridge, C.C. Shawnese Traditions, ed. W.V. Kinietz and E.W. Voegelin. OCMA, IX, 1-71. 1939.

Alford, T.W. Civilization, ed. F. Drake. 203 pp. Norman, 1936.

Alford, T.W., tr. The Four Gospels of Our Lord Jesus Christ. 200 pp. Xenia, 1929.

Baldwin, C.C. Early Indian Migration in Ohio. AAOJ, I, 227-39. 1879.

Beckner, L. Eskippakithiki, the Last Indian Town in Kentucky. Filson Club Historical Quarterly, VI, 355-82. 1932.

Bibaud, F.M. Biographie des sagamas illustrés de l'Amérique Septentrionale, 243-52. Montreal, 1848.

Brinton, D.G. The Shawnees and Their Migrations. HM, X, 1-4. 1866.

Butler, R. Shawnoes. TCAAS, II, 305-67. 1836.

Chapman, B.B. The Potawatomie and Absentee Shawnee Reservation. CO, XIV, 293-305. 1946.

Cummings, R.W. Shawnee. HCPIT, II, 470-81. 1852.

Curtis, E.S. The North American Indian, XIX, 19-21. Norwood, 1930.

Downes, R.C. Council Fires on the Upper Ohio, 367 pp. Pittsburgh, 1940.

Drake, B. Life of Tecumseh, and of His Brother the Prophet. 235 pp. Cincinnati, 1841.

Dunn, J.P. True Indian Stories. 320 pp. Indianapolis, 1909.

Galloway, W.A. Old Chillicothe, pp. 18-23, 170-206. Xenia, 1834.

Gibson, A.M. Wyandotte Mission. CO, XXXVI, 137-54. 1958.

Hanna, C.A. The Wilderness Trail, I, 119-60. New York, 1911. .

Harvey, H. History of the Shawnee Indians. 316 pp. Cincinnati, 1855.

Hickerson, N.P. An Acoustic Analysis of Shawnee. IJAL, XXIV, 20-9, 130-42; XXV, 22-31, 97-104. 1958-59.

Howe, H. Historical Collections of Ohio. 3 vols. Cincinnati, 1848.

Howerton, E.H. Logan, the Shawnee Indian Capital of West Virginia 1760 to 1780. WVH, XVI, 313-33. 1955.

Hunter, W.A. John Hays' Diary and Journal of 1760. PA, XXIV, 63-84. 1954.

Johnston, J. Account of the Present State of the Indian Tribes inhabiting Ohio. TCAAS, I, 269-99. 1820.

Jones, D. A Journal of Two Visits made to Some Nations of Indians on the West Side of the River Ohio. 95 pp. Burlington, 1774.

Joutel, H. Journal of La Salle's Last Voyage. New edit. 258 pp. Albany, 1906.

--- Relation. DEFAS, III, 89-534. 1879.

Klopfenstein, C.G. Westward Ho: Removal of Ohio Shawnees, 1832-1833. BHPSO, XV, 3-32. 1957.

Miller, W.R. An Outline of Shawnee Historical Phonology. IJAL, XXV, 16-21. 1959.

Milling, C.J. Red Carolinians. 438 pp. Chapel Hill, 1940.

Mooney, J. The Ghost-Dance Religion. ARBAE, XIV, ii, 670-91. 1893.

--- Shawnee. BBAE, XXX, ii, 530-8. 1910.

Moorehead, W.K. The Indian Tribes of Ohio. OAHQ, VII, 1-109. 1898.

Morgan, L.H. Ancient Society, pp. 168-70. New York, 1877.

--- The Indian Journals, 1859-62, pp. 28, 44-8, 56, 74-8, 144. Ann Arbor, 1959.

--- Systems of Consanguinity and Affinity. SCK, XVII, 291-382. 1871.

Morse, J. A Report to the Secretary of War. 400 pp. New Haven, 1822.

Nasatir, A.P. Before Lewis and Clark. 2 vols. 882 pp. St. Louis, 1952.

Nettl, B. The Shawnee Musical Style. SJA, IX, 277-85. 1953.

Neumann, G.K. Population Statistics Bearing on a Fort Ancient— Shawnee Linkage. PIAS, LXVI, 45. 1956.

Patton, W. Journal of a Visit to the Indian Missions, Missouri Conference. BMHS, X, 167-80. 1954.

Perrin du Lac, M. Travels through the Two Louisianas. 106 pp. London, 1807.

--- Voyage dans les deux Louisianes. 472 pp. Lyon, 1805.

Richardson, J. Tecumseh and Richardson. 124 pp. Toronto, 1924.

Royce, C.C. An Inquiry into the Identity and History of the Shawnee Indians. AAOJ, III, 178-89. 1881.

Royce, C.C. An Inquiry into the Identity and History of the Shawnee Indians. AAOJ, III, 178-89. 1881.

Schaeffer, C.E. The Grasshopper or Children's War - a Circumboreal Legend? PA, XII, 60-1. 1942.

Schmidt, W. Die Kickapoo und die Shawnee. UG, II, 599-601. 1929.

Shetrone, H.C. The Indian in Ohio. OAHQ, XXVII, 273-510. 1918.

Sipe, C.H. The Principal Indian Towns in Western Pennsylvania. WPHM, XIII, 104-22. 1930.

Smith, D.L. Shawnee Captivity Ethnography. E, II, 29-41. 1955.

Spencer, J. Shawnee Folk-Lore. JAFL, XXII, 319-26. 1909.

--- The Shawnee Indians. TKSHS, X, 382-402. 1908.

Swanton, J.R. Early History of the Creek Indians and Their Neighbors. BBAE, LXXIII, 317-20. 1922.

--- Indians of the Southeastern United States. BBAE, CXXXVII, 71-832. 1946.

Thomas, C. The Story of a Mound; or, the Shawnees in Pre-Columbian Times. AA, IV, 109-159, 237-73. 1891.

Tucker, G. Tecumseh: Vision of Glory. 399 pp. Indianapolis, 1956.

Uhler, S.P. Pennsylvania's Indian Relations to 1754. 144 pp. Allentown, 1951.

Voegelin, C.F. From FL (Shawnee) to TL (English). IJAL, XIX, 1-25. 1953.

--- Productive Paradigms in Shawnee. Essays in Anthropology presented to A.L.Kroeber, pp. 391-403. Berkeley, 1936.

--- The Shawnee Female Deity. YUPA, X, 1-21. 1936.

--- Shawnee Phonemes. Lg, XI, 23-37. 1935.

--- Shawnee Stems and the Jacob P. Dunn Miami Dictionary. PRS, I, 63-108, 135-67, 345-406, 409-79. 1938-40.

Voegelin, C.F. and E.W. The Shawnee Female Deity in Historical Perspective. AA, n.s., XLVI, 370-5. 1944.

--- Shawnee Name Groups. AA, n.s., XXXVII, 617-35. 1935.

Voegelin, C.F. et al. From FL (Shawnee) to TL (English). IJAL, XIX, 106-17. 1953.

--- Shawnee Laws. MAAA, LXXIX, 32-46. 1954.

Voegelin, C.F. and Yegerlehner, J. Toward a Definition of Formal Style. IUPFS, IX, 141-50. 1957.

Voegelin, E.W. Indians of Indiana. PIAS, L, 27-32. 1941.

Voegelin, E.W. Mortuary Customs of the Shawnee and Other Eastern Tribes. PRS, II, 227-444. 1944.

--- The Place of Agriculture in the Subsistence Economy of the Shawnee. PMA, XXIV, 513-20. 1941.

--- Some Possible Sixteenth and Seventeenth Century Locations of the Shawnee. PIAS, XLVIII, 13-18. 1939.

--- Shawnee Musical Instruments. AA, n.s., XLIV, 463-75. 1942.

Voegelin, E.W., and Neumann, G.K. Shawnee Pots and Pottery Making. PA, XVIII, 3-12. 1948.

Weslager, C.A. Monongahela Woodland Culture and the Shawnee. PA, XVIII, 19-22. 1948.

Whorf, B.L. Gestalt Technique of Stem Composition in Shawnee. PRS, I, 391-406. 1940.

Witthoft, J. and Hunter, W.A. The Seventeenth-Century Origin of the Shawnee. E, II, 42-57. 1955.

Wright, M.H. and Shirk, G.H. Artist Möllhausen in Oklahoma, 1853. CO, XXXI, 392-441. 1953.

9. WINNEBAGO

Radin, P. The Evolution of an American Prose Epic. SPBF, III, V, 99 pp., pp. 103-48. 1954, 1956.

--- The Road of Life and Death. 345 pp. New York, 1945.

--- Winnebago Culture as described by Themselves. MIJAL, III, 1-78. 1950.

--- The Winnebago Tribe. ARBAE, XXXVII, 33-550. 1916.

Radin, P. et al. Der Göttliche Schelm. 219 pp. Zürich, 1954.

Andros, F. The Medicine and Surgery of the Winnebago and Dakota Indians. Journal of the American Medical Association, I, 116-8. 1883.

Atwater, C. Remarks made on a Tour to Prairie du Chien, pp. 75-180. Columbus, 1831.

Baerreis, D.A. A Note on a Winnebago Medical Technique. WA, XXXIV, 139-43. 1953.

Beauchamp, W.M. Indian Nations of the Great Lakes, AAOJ, XVII, 321-5. 1895.

Beckwith, H.W. The Illinois and Indiana Indians. FHS, XXVII, 138-45. 1884.

Behncke, N. Winnebagoland Legends. WA, n.s., XX, 31-4. 1939.

Bergen, F.D. Some Customs and Beliefs of the Winnebago Indians. JAFL, IX, 51-4. 1896.

Boas, F. Zur Anthropologie der nordamerikanischen Indianer. VBGA, 1895, 367-411.

Boas, F., and Swanton, J.R. Siouan. BBAE, XL, i, 875-966. 1911.

Brown, C.E. Lake Mendota Indian Legends. Madison, 1927.

Brown, D.M. Indian Winter Legends. WA, n.s., XXII, 49-53. 1941.

--- Wisconsin Indian Corn Origin Myths. WA, n.s., XXI, 19-27. 1940.

Buckstaff, R.N. Painted and Incised Pottery Fragments of the Winnebagos. WA, n.s., XXII, 84-6. 1941.

--- Serrated Shells of the Winnebago. WA, n.s., XX, 23-8. 1939.

Bushnell, D.I. Sketches by Paul Kane in the Indian Country, 1845-1848. SMC, XCIX, i, 1-25. 1940.

Carter, B.F. The Weaving Technic of Winnebago Bags. WA, n.s., XII, 33-47. 1933.

Curtis, N., ed. The Indians' Book, pp. 243-93. New York, 1907.

DeKaury, S. Narrative of Spoon Decorah. CSHSW, XIII, 448-62. 1895.

Densmore, F. Music of the Winnebago Indians. EFWSI, 1927, 183-8.

Dorsey, J.O. On the Comparative Phonology of Four Siouan Languages. ARSI, 1883, 919-29.

--- A Study of Siouan Cults. ARBAE, XI, 423-30. 1890.

--- Winnebago Folk-Lore Notes. JAFL, II, 140. 1889.

Dorsey, J.O., and Radin, P. Winnebago. BBAE, XXX, ii, 958-61. 1910.

Federal Writers' Projects. Wisconsin Indian Place Legends, pp. 4-7, 10, 15-16. Milwaukee, 1936.

Flannery, R. Algonquian Indian Folklore. JAFL, LX, 397-401. 1947.

Fletcher, A.C. Phonetic Alphabet of the Winnebago Indians. PAAAS, XXXVIII, 354-7. 1889.

--- Symbolic Earth Formations of the Winnebagoes. PAAAS, XXXII, 396-7. 1883.

Fletcher, J.E. Manners and Customs of the Winnebagoes. HCPIT, IV, 51-9. 1854.

--- Origin and History of the Winnebagoes. HCPIT, IV, 227-43. 1854.

Gilmore, M.R. Uses of Plants by the Indians of the Missouri River Region. ARBAE, XXXIII, 43-154. 1912.

Greenman, E.F. Chieftainship among Michigan Indians. MHM, XXIV, 361-79. 1940.

Hayden, F.V. Brief Notes on the Pawnee, Winnebago, and Omaha Languages. PAPS, X, 411-21. 1868.

Hofmann, C. American Indian Music in Wisconsin. JAFL, LX, 289-93. 1947.

Jenks, A.E. The Wild Rice Gatherers of the Upper Lakes. ARBAE, XIX, ii, 1013-137. 1898.

Jipson, N.W. Winnebago Villages and Chieftains. WA, n.s., II, 125-39. 1923.

Kellogg, L.P. Removal of the Winnebago. Transactions of the Wisconsin Academy of Sciences, Arts and Letters, XXI, 23-9. 1924.

Koenig, M.W. Tuberculosis among the Nebraska Winnebago. 48 pp. Lincoln, 1921.

Kurath, G.P. Algonquian Ceremonialism and Natural Resources of the Great Lakes. Indian Institute of Culture, Reprint XXII. Bangalore, 1957.

--- Modern Ottawa Dancers. MWF, V, 15-22. 1955.

Lamere, O., and Radin, P. Description of a Winnebago Funeral. AA, n.s., XIII, 437-44. 1911.

Lamere, O., and Shinn, H.B. Winnebago Stories. 165 pp. New York, 1928.

Lawson, P.V. Habitat of the Winnebago, 1632-1832. PSHSW, LIV, 144-66. 1906.

--- The Winnebago Tribe. WA, VI, 78-162. 1907.

Lenders, E.W. Myth des "Wah-ru-hap-ah-rah" oder des heiligen Kriegskeulenbündels. ZE, XLVI, 404-20. 1914.

Lipkind, W. Winnebago Grammar. 68 pp. New York, 1945.

Lowie, R.H., ed. Notes concerning New Collections. APAM, IV, 289-97. 1910.

Lurie, N.O. Winnebago Berdache. AA, LV, 708-12. 1953.

McGee, W J. The Siouan Indians. ARBAE, XV, 157-204. 1894.

McKern, W.C. Winnebago Dog Myths. YPMCM, X, 317-22. 1930.

--- A Winnebago Myth. YPMCM, IX, 215-30. 1929.

--- A Winnebago War-Bundle Ceremony. YPMCM, VIII, i, 146-55. 1928.

Matson, G.A. Distribution of Blood Groups among the Sioux, Omaha, and Winnebago Indians. AJPA, XXVIII, 313-18. 1941.

Merrill, R.H. The Calendar Stick of Tshi-zun-haukau. BCIS, XXIV, 1-11. 1945.

Michelson, T. Some Notes on Winnebago Social and Political Organization. AA, n.s., XXXVII, 446-9. 1935.

Morgan, L.H. The Indian Journals, 1859-62, pp. 60-1. Ann Arbor, 1959.

--- Systems of Consanguinity and Affinity. SCK, XVII, 291-382. 1871.

Oestreich, N. Culture Change among the Wisconsin Winnebago. WA, n.s., XXV, 119-25. 1944.

--- Trends of Change in Patterns of Child Care and Training among the Wisconsin Winnebago. WA, n.s., XXIX, 39-140. 1948.

Radin, P. The Autobiography of a Winnebago Indian. UCP, XVI, 381-473. 1920.

--- The Clan Organization of the Winnebago. AA, n.s., XII, 209-19. 1910.

--- Crashing Thunder. 202 pp. New York, 1926.

--- The Influence of the Whites on Winnebago Culture. PSHSW, 1913, 137-45.

--- Literary Aspects of Winnebago Mythology. JAFL, XXXIX, 18-52. 1926.

--- Monotheistic Tendencies among the Winnebago Indians. ICA, XXXII, 176. 1958.

--- Personal Reminiscences of a Winnebago Indian. JAFL, XXVI, 293-318. 1913.

--- The Ritual and Significance of the Winnebago Medicine Dance. JAFL, XXIV, 149-208. 1911.

--- A Semi-Historical Account of the War of the Winnebago and the Foxes. PSHSW, 1914, 191-207.

--- A Sketch of the Peyote Cult of the Winnebago. Journal of Religious Psychology, VII, 1-22. 1914.

--- The Social Organization of the Winnebago Indians. MBCDM, X, 1-40. 1915.

--- Some Aspects of Winnebago Archeology. AA, n.s., XIII, 517-38. 1911.

--- Thunder-Cloud, a Winnebago Shaman, relates and prays. American Indian Life, ed. E.C. Parsons, pp. 75-80. New York, 1925.

--- The Thunderbird Warclub, a Winnebago Tale. JAFL, XLIV, 143-65. 1931.

--- The Trickster. 221 pp. New York, 1956.

Radin, P. Winnebago Hero Cycles. MIJAL, I, 1-168. 1948.

--- Winnebago Myth Cycles. Primitive Culture, I, 8-86. 1926.

--- Winnebago Tales. JAFL, XXII, 288-313. 1909.

Riggs, S.R. Dakota Grammar, Texts and Ethnography. CNAE, IX, xviii-xxix. 1893.

Ritzenthaler, R. and Sellars, M. Indians in an Urban Situation. WA, XXXVI, 147-61. 1955.

Schmidt, W. Die Winnebago. UG, II, 602-47. 1929.

Sebeok, T.A. Two Winnebago Texts. IJAL, XIII, 167-70. 1947.

Smith, H.H. Among the Winnebago. YPMCM, VIII, 76-82. 1928.

Snelling, W.J. Early Days at Prairie du Chien. Reports and Collections of the Wisconsin State Historical Society, V, i, 123-53. 1868.

Stacy, J., tr. Bible Selections. 483 pp. New York, 1907.

Stout, A.B., and Skavlem, H.L. The Archaeology of the Lake Koshkonong Region. WA, VII, 47-102. 1908.

Susman, A. The Accentual System of Winnebago. 149 pp. New York, 1943.

--- Word Play in Winnebago. Lg, XVII, 342-4. 1941.

Voegelin, C.F. A Problem in Morpheme Alternants and Their Distribution. Lg, XXIII, 245-54. 1947.

Webb, J.W., ed. Altowan. 2 vols. New York, 1846.

Weer, P. Preliminary Notes on the Siouan Family. Indiana History Bulletin, XIV, 99-120. 1937.

Winnebago Tribe of Indians. Laws and Regulations. 6 pp. Omaha, 1868.

Winter, G. Journals and Indian Paintings, 1837-1839. 208 pp. Indianapolis, 1948.

Wolff, H. Comparative Siouan. IJAL, XVI, 61-6. 1950.

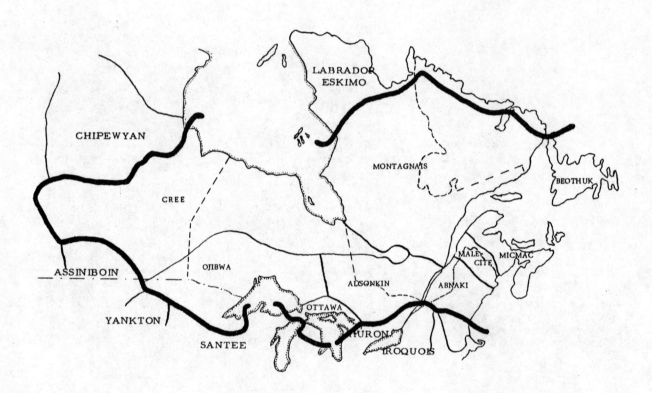

With the possible exception of the Beothuk, who may constitute a distinct stock, all the tribes of this area belong to the Algonkian linguistic stock.

Alberts, R.C. Trade Silver and Indian Silver Work in the Great Lakes Region. WA, XXXIV, 1-121. 1953.

Aller, W.F. Aboriginal Food Utilization of Vegetation by the Indians of the Great Lakes Region as Recorded in the Jesuit Relations. WVA, XXXV, iii, 59-73. 1954.

Anonymous. Supplementary Materials on Location, Numbers and Socio-Economic Conditions of Indians and Eskimos. ECAS, I, 103-16. 1955.

Bailey, A.G. The Conflict of European and Eastern Algonkian Cultures. Publications of the New Brunswick Museum, Monograph Series, III, 1-206. 1937.

Beers, H.P. The French in North America. Baton Rouge, 1957.

Biasutti, R. Le Razzi e i Popoli della Terra, 2nd ed., IV, 425-37. Torino, 1957.

Biggar, H.P., ed. The Works of Samuel de Champlain. 6 vols. Toronto, 1922-36.

Birket-Smith, K. A Geographic Study of the Early History of the Algonquian Indians. IAE, XXIV, 174-222. 1918.

Bloomfield, L. Algonquian. VFPA, VI, 85-129. 1946.

--- Proto-Algonquian -i·t- 'Fellow'. Lg, XVII, 292-7. 1941.

Boucher, P. Histoire veritable et naturelle des moeurs et productions du pays de la Nouvelle France. Paris, 1664.

Braasch, W.F., et al. Survey of Medical Care among the Upper Midwest Indians. Journal of the American Medical Association, CXXXIX, 220-5. 1949.

Braunholtz, H.J. The Sloane Collection: Ethnography. British Museum Quarterly, XVIII, i, 23-6. 1953.

Brown, C.E. Winabozho. 7 pp. Madison, 1944.

Brown, L.A. Early Maps of the Ohio Valley. Pittsburgh, 1960.

Burgesse, J.A. Snow Shoes. B, CCLXXI, ii, 24-8. 1941.

--- Tribal Laws of the Woodlands. B, CCLXXII, iv, 18-21. 1942.

Byers, D.S. The Environment of the Northeast. PRSPF, III, 3-32. 1946.

Canada, Dept. of Mines and Resources, Indian Affairs Branch. Census of Indians in Canada, 1939 and 1944. Ottawa, 1940, 1944.

Chamberlain, A.F. Indians of the Eastern Provinces of Canada. AAR, XVI, 122-36. 1905.

--- The Maple amongst the Algonkian Tribes. AA, IV, 39-43. 1891.

--- Maple Sugar and the Indians. AA, IV, 381-3. 1891.

--- Signification of Certain Algonquian Animal-Names. AA, n.s., III, 669-83. 1901.

--- The Thunder-Bird amongst the Algonkians. AA, III, 51-4. 1890.

Charency, H. de. Etudes algiques. JSAP, IV, 8-54. 1903.

Charlevoix, P.F.X. de. Histoire de la Nouvelle France. 3 vols. Paris, 1894.

--- History and General Description of New France, ed. J.M. Shea. 6 vols. New York, 1866-72.

--- Journal of a Voyage to North America, ed. L.P. Kellogg. 2 vols. Chicago, 1923.

Cooper, J.M. The Culture of the Northeastern Indian Hunters. PRSPF, III, 272-305. 1946.

--- Is the Algonquian Family Hunting Ground System Pre-Columbian? AA, n.s., XLI, 66-90. 1939.

--- Land Tenure among the Indians of Eastern and Northern North America. PA, VIII, 55-9. 1938.

--- Snares, Deadfalls, and Other Traps of the Northern Algonquians and northern Athapaskans. CUAS, V, 1-144. 1938.

Covington, J.W. The Indian Liquor Trade at Peoria, 1824. JISHS, XLVI, 142-50. 1953.

Dawson, G.M. Sketches of the Past and Present Condition of the Indians of Canada. Canadian Naturalist, n.s., IX, 129-59. 1881.

Dixon, R.B. The Mythology of the Central and Eastern Algonkins. JAFL, XXII, 1-9. 1909.

Dobbs, A. An Account of the Countries Adjoining to Hudson's Bay. 211 pp. London, 1744.

Dodge, E.S. Ethnology of Northern New England and the Maritime Provinces. BMAS, XVIII, 68-71. 1957.

Du Creux, F. The History of Canada or New France. PCS, XXX, 776 pp. 1951-52.

Eiseley, L.C. Land Tenure in the Northeast. AA, n.s., XLIX, 680-1. 1947.

Fewkes, V.J. Aboriginal Potsherds from Red River, Manitoba. AAn, III, 143-55. 1937.

Fisher, M.W. The Mythology of the Northern and Northeastern Algonkians. PRSPF, III, 226-62. 1946.

Flannery, R. Algonquian Indian Folklore. JAFL, LX, 397-401. 1947.

--- An Analysis of Coastal Algonquian Culture. CUAS, VII, 1-219. 1939.

Flannery, R. The Culture of the Northeastern Indian
    Hunters. PRSPF, III, 263-71. 1946.

Frémont, D. Les Aborigènes du Nord-Ouest Canadien
    au Temps de La Vérendrye. Mémoires de la So-
    ciété Royale du Canada, XLIII, 3e série, Sect. I,
    7-21. 1949.

Fried, J. (ed.) A Survey of the Aboriginal Popula-
    tions of Quebec and Labrador. ECAS, I, 125 pp.
    1955.

Geary, J.A. Algonquian nasaump and napopi. Lg,
    XXI, 40-5. 1945.

--- Proto- Algonquian *ck. Lg, XVII, 304-10. 1941.

--- The Proto-Algonquian Form for "I-Thee." Lg,
    XIX, 147-51. 1943.

Gerard, W.R. The Root Kompau, Its Form and Mean-
    ing. AA, n.s., XIV, 574-6. 1912.

Gille, J. Das "Geistertier" als Urbild des Zentral-
    algonkin "manetoua." Veröffentlichungen aus
    dem Museum für Natur- Völker- und Handelskunde
    in Bremen, Reihe B, I, 17-23. 1950.

--- Der Manabozho-Flutzyklus der Nord-, Nordost-,
    and Zentralalgonkin. 86 pp. Göttingen, 1939.

--- Weskarini und Ur-Algonkin. 16 pp. Göttingen,
    1939.

--- Zur Lexikologie des Alt-Algonkin. ZE, LXXI,
    71-86. 1939.

Haas, M.R. A New Linguistic Relationship in North
    America. SJA, XIV, 231-64. 1958.

Hadlock, W.S. Warfare among the Northeastern
    Woodland Indians. AA, n.s., XLIX, 204-221.
    1947.

Hallowell, A.I. The Size of Algonkian Hunting
    Territories: A Function of Ecological Adjustments.
    AA, n.s., LI, 35-45. 1949.

--- Some Psychological Characteristics of the North-
    eastern Indians. PRSPF, III, 195-225. 1946.

Hamilton, J.C. The Algonquin Manabozho and
    Hiawatha. JAFL, XVI, 229-33. 1903.

Harris, W.R. Practice of Medicine and Surgery by
    the Canadian Tribes in Champlain's Time. AAR,
    1915, 35-54.

Herman, M.W. Wampum as a Money in Northeast-
    ern North America. E, V, 21-33. 1958.

Hockett, C.F. Central Algonquian Vocabulary: Stems
    in /k-/. IJAL, XXIII, 247-68. 1957.

--- Implications of Bloomfield's Algonquian Studies.
    Lg, XXIV, 117-35. 1948.

Holmer, N.M. Lexical and Morphological Contacts
    between Siouan and Algonquian. Lunds Universitets
    Arsskrift, n.s., XLV, 1-36. 1949.

Howells, W.W. Physical Types of the Northeast.
    PRSPF, III, 168-77. 1946.

Innis, H.A. The Fur Trade in Canada. 444 pp. New
    Haven, 1930.

Jeancon, J.A., and Douglas, F.H. Iroquoian and
    Algonkin Wampum. DAMLS, XXXI, 1-4. 1931.

Jenness, D. Indians of Canada. BCDM, LXV, 1-
    446. 1932.

Johnson, F., ed. Man in Northeastern North Ameri-
    ca. PRSPF, III, 1-347. 1946.

Joblin, E.E.M. The Education of the Indians of West-
    ern Ontario. Ontario College of Education, Bul-
    letin of the Department of Educational Research,
    XIII, 138 pp. 1947.

Kennedy, J.H. Jesuit and Savage in New France.
    206 pp. New Haven, 1950.

Kidd, K.E. Sixty Years of Ontario Archeology.
    AEUS, 71-82. 1952.

Kinietz, V. Notes on the Algonquian Family Hunt-
    ing Ground System. AA, n.s., XLII, 179. 1940.

--- Notes on the Roached Headdress of Animal Hair
    among the North American Indians. PMA, XXVI,
    463-7. 1940.

Kurath, G.P. Algonquian Ceremonialism and Na-
    tural Resources of the Great Lakes. Indian Institute
    of Culture, Reprint XXII. Bangalore, 1957.

--- Antiphonal Songs of Eastern Woodlands Indians.
    Musical Quarterly, XLII, 520-6. 1956.

--- Blackrobe and Shaman. PMA, XLIV, 209-15.
    1959.

--- Ceremonies, Songs and Dances of Michigan In-
    dians. MHM, XXXIX, 466-68. 1955.

--- Pan- Indianism in Great Lakes Tribal Festivals.
    JAFL, LXX, 179-82. 1957.

Laguna, F. de. The Prehistory of Northern North
    America as seen from the Yukon. MSAA, III,
    1-360. 1947.

Lahontan, A.L. de D. New Voyages to North Ameri-
    ca, ed. R.G. Thwaites. 2 vols. Chicago, 1905.

--- Nouveaux voyages dans l'Amérique septentrionale.
    220 pp. La Haye, 1703.

Laverdière, C.H., ed. Oeuvres de Champlain. 2d
    edit. 6 vols. Quebec, 1870.

Laviolette, G. Indian Bands of the Province of
    Quebec. ECAS, I, 90-6. 1955.

--- Notes on the Aborigines of the Province of On-
    tario. An, IV, 79-106. 1957.

--- Notes on the Aborigines of the Prairie Provinces.
    An, II, 107-30. 1956.

--- Notes on the Aborigines of the Province of Que-
    bec. An, I, 198-211. 1955.

Le Clercq, C. First Establishment of the Faith in
    New France, ed. J.G. Shea. 2 vols. New York,
    1881.

Leechman, D. Aboriginal Paints and Dyes in Canada. PTRSC, ser. 3, XXVI, ii, 37-42. 1932.

Loewenthal, J.W.J. Die Religion der Ostalgonkin. 219 pp. Berlin, 1913.

Lowther, G. Archeology in the Province of Quebec. ECAS, I, 65-73. 1955.

MacLean, J. Canadian Savage Folk. 641 pp. Toronto, 1897.

MacNeish, R.S. The Archeology of the Northeastern United States. AEUS, 46-58. 1952.

Michelson, T. Algonquian Notes. IJAL, IX, 103-12. 1939.

--- Contributions to Algonquian Linguistics. IJAL, X, 75-85. 1939.

--- Phonetic Shifts in Algonquian Languages. IJAL, VIII, 131-71. 1935.

--- Preliminary Report on the Linguistic Classification of Algonquian Tribes. ARBAE, XXVIII, 221-90. 1907.

--- Some Algonquian Kinship Terms. AA, n.s., XXXIV, 357-9. 1932.

Morris, A. The Treaties of Canada with the Indians of Manitoba, the North-West Territories, and Keewa-tin. Toronto, 1880.

Morris, J.L. Indians of Ontario. 75 pp. Toronto, 1943.

Müller, F. Der grammatische Bau der Algonkin-Sprachen. SKAW, LVI, 132-54. 1867.

Mulvaney, C.P. The History of the North-West Rebellion of 1885. 424 pp. Toronto, 1885.

Murray, H. Historical and Descriptive Account of British America, I, 73-127. Edinburgh, 1840.

Orr, R.B. North American Indian Games –Dice. AAR, XXVII, 20-34. 1915.

Pilling, J.C. Bibliography of the Algonquian Languages. BBAE, XIII, 1-614. 1891.

Quimby, G.I. The Archeology of the Upper Great Lakes Area. AEUS, 99-107. 1952.

--- A Subjective Interpretation of Some Design Similarities between Hopewell and Northern Algonkian. AA, n.s., XLV, 630-3. 1943.

Radwanski, P. Physical Anthropological Problems in the Province of Quebec. ECAS, I, 85-9. 1955.

Rogers, R. A Concise Account of North America. 264 pp. London, 1765.

Rousseau, J.J. Chez les Indiens de la Foret et de la Toundra Québecoise. EUO, I, 237-51. 1951.

--- Le Couteau Croche des Indiens de la Foret Boréale. Technique, XXI, 447. 1946.

--- L'Indien de la Foret Boreale. RSCSV, 37-51. 1958.

Rousseau, J.J. L'Origine du Motif de la Double Courbe dans l'Art Algonkin. An, II, 218-21. 1956.

Rousseau, M. and J. Le Dualisme Religieux des Peuples de la Foret Boréale. ICA, XXIX, ii, 118-26. 1952.

Sargent, M. Folk and Primitive Music in Canada. BNMC, CXXIII, 75-79. 1951.

Siebert, F.T. Certain Proto- Algonquian Consonant Clusters. Lg, XVII, 298-303. 1941.

Silvy, A. Relation par lettres de l'Amérique septentrionale, ed. C. de Rochemonteix. 221 pp. Paris, 1904.

Skinner, A. The Algonkin and the Thunderbird. AMJ, XIV, 71-3. 1914.

--- Some Aspects of the Folk-Lore of the Central Algonkin. JAFL, XXVII, 97-100. 1914.

--- Traces of the Stone Age among the Eastern and Northern Tribes. AA, XIV, 391-5. 1912.

Slotkin, J.S., and Schmitt, K. Studies of Wampum. AA, n.s., LI, 223-36. 1949.

Speck, F.G. Concerning Iconology and the Masking Complex in Eastern North America. UPMB, XV, 6-57. 1950.

--- Culture Problems in Northeastern North America. PAPS, LXV, 272-311. 1926.

--- The Family Hunting Band as the Basis of Algonkian Social Organization. AA, n.s., XVII, 289-305. 1915.

--- The Historical Approach to Art in Archaeology in the Northern Woodlands. AAn, VIII, 173-5. 1942.

--- More Algonkian Scapulimancy from the North, and the Hunting Territory Question. Ethnos, IV, 21-8. 1939.

--- Northern Elements in Iroquois and New England Art. IN, II, 1-12. 1925.

--- The Social Structure of the Northern Algonkian. PASS, XII, 82-100. 1917.

Speck, F.G., and Eiseley, L.C. Significance of Hunting Territory Systems of the Algonkian in Social Theory. AA, n.s., XLI, 269-80. 1939.

Stanley, G.F.G. The Indians and the Brandy Trade during the Ancien Régime. Revue d'Histoire de l'Amérique Française, VI, 489-505. 1953.

Steeves, T.A. Wild Rice. Economic Botany, VI, 107-42. 1952.

Stillfried, I. Studie zu Kosmogonischen und Kultischen Elementen der Algonkonischen und Irokesischen Stämme. WVM, IV, 82-85. 1956.

Thomas, C. Historical Account. AAR, 1905, 71-83.

Thomas, W.J. The Art of the Canadian Indians.
   AAR, XXXIII, 75-82. 1922.
Trumbull, J.H. On the Algonkin Verb. Transactions
   of the American Philological Association, VII, 147-
   71. 1877.
Vinay, J.P. Les Manuscrits Amerindiens de Québec.
   ECAS, I, 74-84. 1955.
Voegelin, C.F. and E.W. Linguistic Considerations
   of Northeastern North America. PRSPF, III, 178-94.
   1946.
Voegelin, E.W. Mortuary Customs of the Shawnee
   and Other Eastern Tribes. PRS, II, 227-444. 1944.
Waugh, F.W. Canadian Aboriginal Canoes. CFN,
   XXXIII, 23-33. 1919.
--- Notes on Canadian Pottery. AAR, XIV, 108-
   15. 1901.
White, P.C.T. Lord Selkirk's Diary, 1803-04.
   PCS, XXXV, 391 pp. 1958.
Wintemberg, W.J. Distinguishing Characteristics of
   Algonkian and Iroquoian Cultures. BCDM, LXVII,
   65-124. 1931.

1. ABNAKI

Including the Arosaguntacook, Kennebec, Norridgewock, Penobscot, Sokoki, and Wawenock.

Speck, F.G. Penobscot Man. 325 pp. Philadelphia,
   1940.
Vetromile, E. The Abnakis and Their History. 171
   pp. New York, 1866.

Alger, A.L. The Creation, a Penobscot Indian Myth.
   PSM, XLIV, 195-6. 1893.
--- In Indian Tents. 139 pp. Boston, 1897.
Allen, F.H. Summary of Blood Group Phenotypes in
   some Aboriginal Americans. AJPA, n.s., XVII,
   86. 1959.
Anonymous. How the Indians Learned to Call Moose.
   SS, VI, v, 11-12. 1954.
--- Numbers, in the Norridgwog Language. MNSC,
   ser. 1., X, 137-8. 1809.
Baxter, J.P. The Abnakis and Their Ethnic Relations.
   CPMHS, ser. 2, III, 13-40. 1892.
Bibaud, F.M. Biographie des sagamos illustrés de
   l'Amérique Septentrionale, pp. 191-4. Montreal,
   1848.
Boas, F. Zur Anthropologie der nordamerikanischen
   Indianer. VBGA, 1895, 367-411.
Bolton, R.P. Indian Remains in Northern Vermont.
   IN, VII, 57-69. 1930.

Brown, Mrs. W.W. Some Indoor and Outdoor Games
   of the Wabanaki Indians. PTRSC, VI, ii, 41-6.
   1888.
--- Wa-ba-ba-nal, or Northern Lights. JAFL, III,
   213-14. 1890.
Browne, G.W. Indian Legends of Acadia. Acadien-
   sis, II, 54-64. 1902.
Burrage, H.S., ed. Early English and French Voy-
   ages, pp. 367-81. New York, 1906.
Chamberlain, A.F. Indians of the Eastern Provinces
   of Canada. AAR, 1905, 122-36.
Chamberlain, M. The Primitive Life of the Wapanaki
   Women. Acadiensis, II, 75-86. 1902.
Curtis, N., ed. The Indians' Book, pp. 3-27. New
   York, 1907.
Day, G.M. Dartmouth and St. Francis. Dartmouth
   Alumni Magazine, 28-30. November, 1959.
--- Note on St. Francis Nomenclature. IJAL, XXV,
   272-3. 1959.
Deming, E.W. Abenaki Witchcraft Story. JAFL, XV,
   62-3. 1902.
Dexter, H.M. The New England Indians. Sabbath
   at Home, II, 193-206. 1868.
Dixon, R.B. The Early Migrations of the Indians of
   New England and the Maritime Provinces. PAAS,
   n.s., XXIV, 65-76. 1914.
Eckstorm, F.H. Handicrafts of the Modern Indians
   of Maine. Bulletins of the Abbe Museum, III, 1-
   72. 1932.
--- The Indians of Maine. Maine, a History, ed.
   L.C.Hatch, I, 43-64. New York, 1919.
--- Katahdin Legends. Appalachia, n.s., XVI, 39-
   52. 1924.
--- Old John Neptune and Other Maine Shamans.
   209 pp. Portland, 1945.
Evans, G.H. Pigwacket. New Hampshire Historical
   Society, Publications, I, 135 pp. 1939.
Frost, H.K. Two Abnaki Legends. JAFL, XXV, 188-
   90. 1912.
Godfrey, J.E. The Ancient Penobscot of Panawan-
   skek. CPMHS, VII, 1-22. 1876.
--- The Ancient Penobscot of Panawanskik. HM,
   ser. 3, I, 85-92. 1872.
Hadlock, W.S., and Dodge, E.S. A Canoe from
   the Penobscot River. American Neptune, VIII, 289-
   301. 1948.
Hallowell, A.I. Recent Changes in the Kinship
   Terminology of the St. Francis Abenaki. ICA, XXII,
   ii, 97-145. 1926.
Hanson, J.W. History of Gardiner, Pittston and West
   Gardiner, pp. 13-28. Gardiner, 1852.

Hanson, J.W. History of the Old Towns Norridgewock and Canaan. 373 pp. Boston, 1849.

Harrington, M.R. An Abanaki "Witch-Story." JAFL,
XIV, 160. 1901.

Hoffman, B.G. The Souriquois, Etechemin and
Wegesh. E, II, 65-87. 1955.

Hubbard, L.L. Some Indian Place-Names in Northern
Maine. Boston, 1884.

Jack, D.R. The Indians of Acadia. Acadiensis, I,
187-201. 1901.

Jack, E. Day with the Abenakis. Acadiensis, I,
191-94. 1901.

--- The Abenakis of Saint John River. TCI, III,
195-205. 1892.

Jackson, E.P. Indian Occupation and Use of the
Champlain Lowland. PMA, XIV, 113-60. 1931.

Johnson, F. Indians of New Hampshire. Appalachia,
n.s., VI, vii, 3-15. 1940.

Kenton, E., ed. The Indians of North America, II,
364-92, 484-7. New York, 1927.

Kidder, F. The Abenaki Indians. CPMHS, VI, 229-
63. 1859.

Laurent, J. New Familiar Abenakis and English Dialogues. 230 pp. Quebec, 1884.

--- The Abenakis. Vermont History, XXIII, 286-95.
1955.

Leger, M.C. The Catholic Indian Missions in Maine,
1611-1820. Catholic University of America, Studies in American Church History, VIII, 184 pp. 1929.

Leland, C.G. The Algonquin Legends of New England. 379 pp. Boston, 1884.

Leland, C.G., and Prince, J.D. Kulóskap the Master and Other Algonkin Poems. 370 pp. New York,
1902.

Le Sueur, J. History of the Calumet and of the
Dance. CMAI, XII, v, 26 pp. 1952.

Lincoln, E. Remarks on the Indian Languages.
CPMHS, I, 310-23. 1831.

McGuire, J.D. Ethnological and Archeological Notes
on Moosehead Lake. AA, n.s., X, 549-57. 1908.

Mallery, G. The Fight with the Giant Witch: An
Abanaki Myth. AA, III, 65-70. 1890.

Masta, H.L. Abenaki Indian Legends, Grammar, and
Place Names. 110 pp. Victoriaville, 1932.

Maurault, J.P.A. Histoire des Abenakis. 631 pp.
Quebec, 1866.

Merlet, L.V.C. Histoire des relations des Hurons et
des Abnaquis du Canada avec Notre-Dame de
Chartres. 78 pp. Chartres, 1858.

Mooney, J. Penobscot. BBAE, XXX, ii, 226-7. 1910.

Mooney, J., and Thomas, C. Abnaki. BBAE, XXX,
i, 2-6. 1907.

Moorehead, W.K. A Report on the Archaeology of
Maine. 272 pp. Andover, 1922.

Nicolar, J. Life and Traditions of the Red Man. 147
pp. Bangor, 1893.

O'Brien, M.C. Grammatical Sketch of the Ancient
Abnaki. CPMHS, IX, 259-94. 1887.

Orchard, W.C. Notes on Penobscot Houses. AA, n.s.,
XI, 601-6. 1909.

Perkins, G.H. Some Relics of the Indians of Vermont.
AN, V, 11-17. 1871.

Prince, J.D. The Differentiation between the
Penobscot and the Canadian Abenaki Dialects. AA,
n.s., IV, 17-32. 1902.

--- The Modern Dialect of the Canadian Abenaki.
Miscellanea Linguistica in Onore di Graziadio
Ascoli, pp. 343-62. Torino, 1901.

--- Notes on Passamaquoddy Literature. ANYAS, XIII,
381-6. 1901.

--- Notes on the Language of the Eastern Algonquin
Tribes. AJP, IX, 310-16. 1888.

--- The Penobscot Language of Maine. AA, n.s.,
XII, 183-208. 1910.

Provost, H. Les Abénaquis sur la Chaudière. Publication de la Société Historique de la Chaudière,
I, 27 pp. 1958.

Rasles, S. A Dictionary of the Abnaki Language.
Memoirs of the American Academy of Sciences
and Arts, n.s., I, 375-574. 1833.

Reade, J. Some Wabanaki Songs. PTRSC, ser. 1,
V, ii, 1-8. 1887.

Rosier, J. Relation of Waymouth's Voyage to the
Coast of Maine. 176 pp. Portland, 1887.

Rousseau, J. Ethnobotanique abénakise. Archives de
folklore, XI, 145-82. 1947.

Sabine, L. Indian Tribes of New England. Christian
Examiner, LXII, 27-54, 210-37. 1857.

Schmidt, W. Die Nordost Algonkin. UG, II, 449-
58; VII, 522-30. 1929, 1940.

Sewall, R.K. Wawenoc Numerals. HM, ser. 2, III,
179-80. 1868.

Sieber, S.A. The Saulteaux, Penobscot-Abenaki,
and the Concept of Totemism. ACISA, IV, ii,
325-9. 1955.

Siebert, F.T. Mammoth or "Stiff-legged Bear."
AA, n.s., XXXIX, 721-5. 1937.

Silvy, A. Relation par lettres de l'Amérique septentrionale, ed. C. de Rochemonteix, pp. 196-201.
Paris, 1904.

Smith, N.N. Premonition Spirits among the Wabanaki.
BMAS, XV, 52-6. 1954.

--- Smoking Habits of the Wabanaki. BMAS, XVIII,
76-7. 1957.

Smith, N. N.   The Survival of the Red Paint Com-
plex in Maine. BMAS, XVII, 4-6. 1955.
--- Wabanaki Dances. BMAS, XVI, 29-37. 1955.
--- Wabanaki Uses of Greases and Oils. BMAS, XXI,
ii, 19-21. 1960.
Smith, R. V.   New Hampshire Remembers the Indians.
Historical New Hampshire, VIII, ii, 1-36. 1952.
Speck, F. G.   "Abenaki" Clans--Never! AA, n.s.,
XXXVII, 528-30. 1935.
--- Abnaki Text. IJAL, XI, 45-6. 1945.
--- Bird-Lore of the Northern Indians. University of
Pennsylvania, University Lectures, VII, 349-80.
1920.
--- Correction to Kinship Terms among the North-
eastern Algonkian. AA, n.s., XXII, 85. 1920.
--- Culture Problems in Northeastern North America.
PAPS, LXV, 282-7. 1926.
--- The Double-Curve Motive in Northeastern Algon-
kian Art. MCDM, XLII, 1-17. 1914.
--- The Eastern Algonkian Wabanaki Confederacy.
AA, n.s., XVII, 492-508. 1915.
--- European Folktales among the Penobscot. JAFL,
XXVI, 81-4. 1913.
--- The Family Hunting Band as the Basis of Algon-
kian Social Organization. AA, n.s., XVII, 289-
305. 1915.
--- The Functions of Wampum among the Eastern Al-
gonkian. MAAA, VI, 3-71. 1919.
--- Game Totems among the Northeastern Algonkians.
AA, n.s., XIX, 9-18. 1917.
--- Kinship Terms and the Family Band among the
Northeastern Algonkian. AA, n.s., XX, 143-61.
1918.
--- Mammoth or "Stiff-Legged Bear." AA, n.s.,
XXXVII, 159-63. 1935.
--- Medicine Practices of the Northeastern Algon-
quians. ICA, XIX, 303-21. 1915.
--- The Penobscot Indians of Maine. GM, XXXIX,
396-405. 1937.
--- Penobscot Shamanism. MAAA, VI, 237-88. 1919.
--- Penobscot Tales. JAFL, XXVIII, 52-8. 1915.
--- Penobscot Tales and Religious Beliefs. JAFL,
XLVIII, 1-107. 1935.
--- Penobscot Transformer Tales. IJAL, I, 187-244.
1918.
--- Reptile-Lore of the Northern Indians. JAFL,
XXXVI, 273-80. 1923.
--- Some Uses of Birch Bark by Our Eastern Indians.
MJ, I, 33-6. 1910.
--- Symbolism in Penobscot Art. APAM, XXIX, 25-
80. 1927.
--- A Visit to the Penobscot Indians. MJ, II, 21-6.
1911.

Speck, F. G.   Wawenock Myth Texts from Maine.
ARBAE, XLIII, 165-97. 1926.
Stamp, H.   The Water-Fairies. JAFL, XXVIII, 310-
16. 1915.
Sullivan, J.   The History of the Penobscott Indians.
MHSC, IX, 206-32. 1804.
Swadesh, M.   Sociologic Notes on Obsolescent Lan-
guages. IJAL, XIV, 226-35. 1948.
Thwaites, R. G., ed.   The Jesuit Relations and Al-
lied Documents. 74 vols. Cleveland, 1896-1901.
Trumbull, J. H.   A Mode of Counting, said to have
been used by the Wawenoc Indians of Maine. Pro-
ceedings of the American Philological Association,
III, 13-15. 1871.
Vetromile, E.   The Abnaki Indians. CPMHS, VI,
203-26. 1859.
--- Acadia and Its Aborigines. CPMHS, VII, 337-49.
1876.
--- Indian Good Book. 449 pp. New York, 1856.
Williamson, W. D.   The History of the State of Maine,
I, 453-514. Hallowell, 1832.
Willis, W.   The Language of the Abnaquies. CPMHS,
IV, 93-117. 1856.
Willoughby, C. C.   The Adze and Ungrooved Axe of
the New England Indians. AA, n.s., IX, 296-306.
1907.
--- Antiquities of the New England Indians. 314 pp.
Cambridge, 1935.
--- Dress and Ornaments of the New England Indians.
AA, n.s., VII, 499-508. 1905.
--- Houses and Gardens of the New England Indians.
AA, n.s., VIII, 115-32. 1906.
--- Pottery of the New England Indians. Putnam
Anniversary Volume, pp. 83-101. New York, 1909.
--- Textile Fabrics of the New England Indians.
AA, n.s., VII, 85-93. 1905.
Wilson, C. B.   Indian Relics and Encampments in
Maine. AAOJ, V, 181-3. 1883.
Wilson, G. L.   Indian Hero Tales. 203 pp. New
York, 1906.
Wzokhilain, P. P.   Wawasi lagidamwoganek mdala
chowagidamwoganal tabtagil. 35pp. Boston, 1830.

2. ALGONKIN

Including the Abitibi, Algonkin, Kitcisagi (Grand
Lake Victoria), Maniwaki (River Desert), Nipissing, and Temiscaming.

Anonymous. Muggahmaht'adem. SS, IV, iii, 5.
1952.

Beck, H.P. Algonquin Folklore from Maninaki.
JAFL, LX, 259-264. 1947.

Bibaud, F.M. Biographie des sagamos illustrés de
l'Amérique Septentrionale, pp. 115-19. Montreal,
1848.

Brinton, D.G. The Chief God of the Algonkins.
AAOJ, VII, 137-9. 1885.

--- The Hero-God of the Algonkins as a Cheat and a
Liar. Essays of an Americanist, pp. 130-34. Philadelphia, 1890.

Carr, L.G.K. Interesting Animal Foods, Medicines,
and Omens of the Eastern Indians. JWAS, XLI,
229-35. 1951.

Chamberlain, A.F. The Algonkian Indians of Baptist Lake. Annual Report of the Canadian Institute,
IV, 83-9. 1891.

Champlain, S. de. Voyages and Discoveries, ed. H.
H. Langton and W.F.Ganong. The Works of Sam-
uel de Champlain, ed. H.P.Biggar, Vol. III.
Toronto, 1929.

Conard, E.L.M. Les idees des Indiens Algonquins
relatives à la vie d'outre-tombe. Revue d'Histoire
et Religion, LXII, 9-81, 220-74. 1900.

Cooper, J.M. Field Notes on Northern Algonkian
Magic. ICA, XXIII, 513-18. 1928.

--- Northern Algonkian Scrying and Scapulimancy.
Festschrift P.W.Schmidt, pp. 205-17. Wien, 1928.

Cuoq, J.A. Chrestomathie Algonquine, Actes de la
Société Philologique, III, ii, 39-50. 1873.

--- Etudes philologiques sur quelques langues sauvages
de l'Amérique. 160 pp. Montreal, 1866.

--- Grammaire de la langue Algonquine. PTRSC, IX,
i, 85-114; X, i, 41-119. 1891-92.

--- Lexique de la langue Algonquine. 446 pp. Montreal, 1886.

Davidson, D.S. The Family Hunting Territories of
the Grand Lake Victoria Indians. ICA, XXII, ii,
69-95. 1926.

--- Folk Tales from Grand Lake Victoria. JAFL, XLI,
275-82. 1928.

Hallowell, A.I. Was Cross-Cousin Marriage practised by the North-Central Algonkian? ICA, XXIII,
519-44. 1928.

Hunter, A.F. Indian Village Sites in North and South
Orillia Townships, AAR, 1903, 105-25.

Jenkins, W.H. Notes on the Hunting Economy of the
Abitibi Indians. CUAS, IX, 1-31. 1939.

Johnson, F. An Algonkian Band at Lac Barriere. IN,
VII, 27-39. 1930.

--- The Algonquin at Golden Lake. IN, V, 173-8.
1928.

Keppler, J. The Peace Tomahawk Algonkian Wampum. IN, VI, 130-8. 1929.

Lemoine, G. Dictionnaire Français-Algonquin. Quebec, 1911.

--- Le génie de la langue Algonquine. ICA, XV, ii,
225-42. 1906.

Long, J.K. Voyages and Travels of an Indian Interpreter and Trader. 295 pp. London, 1791.

McGee, J.T. Family Hunting Grounds in the Kippewa
Area. PM, XXIV, 47-53. 1951.

Mooney, J. Nipissing. BBAE, XXX, II, 73-4. 1910.

Mooney, J., and Thomas, C. Algonkin. BBAE, XXX,
i, 38. 1907.

Orr, R.B. Algonquin Subtribes and Clans of Ontario.
AAR, 1921-22, 24-31.

--- The Nipissings. AAR, 1917, 9-23.

Petrullo, V.M. Decorative Art on Birch-Bark from the
Algonquin River du Lièvre Band. IN, VI, 225-42. 1929.

Speck, F.G. Art Processes in Birchbark of the River
Desert Algonquin. BBAE, CXXVIII, 229-74. 1941.

--- Speck, F.G. Boundaries and Hunting Groups of the
River Desert Algonquin. IN, VI, 97-120. 1929.

--- Divination by Scapulimancy among the Algonquin
of River Desert. IN, V, 167-73. 1928.

--- The Family Hunting Band as the Basis of Algonkian
Social Organization. AA, n.s., XVII, 289-305. 1915.

--- Family Hunting Territories and Social Life of Various Algonkian Bands of the Ottawa Valley. MCDM,
LXX, 1-10. 1915.

--- Myths and Folk-Lore of the Timiskaming Algonquin
and Timiskaming Ojibwa. MCDM, LXXI, 1-27. 1915.

--- River Desert Indians of Quebec. IN, IV, 240-52. 1927.

Squair, J. The Indian Tribes on the St. Lawrence at the
Time of the Arrival of the French. AAR, XXXIV, 82-
8. 1923.

Thwaites, R.G., ed. The Jesuit Relations and Allied
Documents. 74 vols. Cleveland, 1896-1901.

Wake, C.S. Migrations of the Algonkins. AAOJ, XVI,
127-39. 1894.

3. BEOTHUK

Howley, J.P. The Beothucks or Red Indians. 345 pp.
Cambridge, 1915.

Blake, E. The Beothuks of Newfoundland. Nineteenth
Century, XXIV, 899-918. 1888.

Burrage, H.S., ed. Early English and French Voyages,
pp. 4-24. New York, 1906.

Busk, G. Description of Two Beothuc Skulls. JAI, V,
230-2. 1875.

Chamberlain, A.F. The Beothuks of Newfoundland. AAR,
1905, 117-22.

Chappell, E. Voyage of His Majesty's Ship Rosa-
mond to Newfoundland, pp. 69-87. London, 1818.

Gatschet, A.S. The Beothuk Indians. PAPS, XXII,
408-24; XXIII, 411-32; XXVIII, 1-16. 1885-90.

Harp, E. An Archaeological Survey in the Strait of
Belle Isle Area. AAn, XVI, 203-20. 1951.

Hewitt, J.N.B., and Gatschet, A.S. Beothukan
Family. BBAE, XXX, i, 141-2. 1907.

Jenness, D. Notes on the Beothuk Indians of Newfoundland. BCDM, LVI, 36-7. 1929.

Klittke, M. Die Beothuk-Indianer von Neufundland.
Aus Allen Welttheilen, XXV, 235-47. 1894.

Lloyd, T.G.B. A Further Account of the Beothucs of
Newfoundland. JAI, V, 222-30. 1875.

--- On the "Beothucs." JAI, IV, 21-39. 1874.

--- On the Stone Implements of Newfoundland. JAI,
V, 233-48. 1875.

Macdougall, A. The Boeothic Indians. TCI, II,
98-102. 1891.

Morice, A.G. Disparus et survivants. BSGQ, XX,
78-94. 1926.

Murray, C.A. The Red Indians of Newfoundland.
176 pp. Philadelphia, 1854.

Patterson, G. Beothik Vocabularies. PTRSC, X, ii,
19-32. 1892.

--- The Beothiks or Red Indians of Newfoundland.
PTRSC, IX, ii, 123-71. 1891.

Pilot, W., and Gray, L.H. Beothuks. ERE, II, 501-
3. 1910.

Ryan, D.W.S. Relics of a Lost Race. Atlantic Guardian, V, 41-4. 1948.

Speck, F.G. Beothuk and Micmac. INM, ser. 2,
XXII, 1-187. 1921.

--- The Beothuks of Newfoundland. SW, XLI, 559-
63. 1913.

--- Eskimo Jacket Ornaments of Ivory suggesting
Function of Bone Pendants Found in Beothuk Sites
in Newfoundland. AAn, V, 225-8. 1940.

Townsend, C.W., ed. Captain Cartwright and His
Labrador Journal, pp. 16-25. Boston, 1911.

Willoughby, C.C. Antiquities of the New England
Indians, pp. 11-15. Cambridge, 1935.

Wintemberg, W.J. Shell Beads of the Beothuk Indians. PTRSC, ser. 2, XXX, ii, 23-6. 1936.

4. CREE

Including the Maskegon, Plains Cree, Swampy
Cree, and Tete-de-Boule.

Honigmann, J.J. The Attawapiskat Swampy Cree.
UAAP, V, i, 23-82. 1956.

Mandelbaum, D.G. The Plains Cree. APAM,
XXXVII, 155-316. 1940.

Skinner, A. Notes on the Eastern Cree and Northern
Saulteaux. APAM, IX, 1-116. 1911.

Adam, L. Esquisse d'une grammaire comparée de
la langue des Chippeways et de la langue des Crees.
ICA, I, ii, 88-148. 1875.

--- Examen grammatical comparé de seize langues
américaines. ICA, II, ii, 161-244. 1877.

Adams, J. Sketches of the Tete de Boule Indians.
TLHSQ, II, 25-39. 1831.

Ahenakew, E. Cree Trickster Tales. JAFL, XLII,
309-53. 1929.

Anonymous. Anthropological Studies among the
Attawapiskat Indians. Arctic Circular, IX, i, 9-
10. 1956.

--- Tuberculosis Survey: James and Hudson Bays.
Arctic Circular, IV, 45-47. 1951.

Ballantyne, R.M. Hudson's Bay, pp. 41-69. 2d
edit. Edinburgh, 1848.

Beardsley, G. Notes on Cree Medicines. PMA,
XXVII, 483-96. 1941.

Bell, C.N., ed. Journal of Henry Kelsey. Transactions of the Historical and Scientific Society of
Manitoba, n.s., IV, 1-43. 1928.

Bell, R. The History of the Che-che-puy-ew-tis.
JAFL, X, 1-8. 1897.

--- Report on an Exploration of Portions of the At-
ta-wa-pish-kat and Albany Rivers, Lonely Lake to
James Bay, 1886. RPCGS, 1886, G, 38 pp. 1887.

Bloomfield, L. The Plains Cree Language. ICA,
XXII, ii, 427-31. 1926.

--- Plains Cree Texts. PAES, XVI, 1-309. 1934.

--- Sacred Stories of the Sweet Grass Cree. BCDM,
LX, 1-346. 1930.

--- The Story of the Bad Owl. ICA, XXII, ii, 23-34.
1926.

Boas, F. Zur Anthropologie der nordamerikanischen
Indianer. VBGA, 1895, 367-411.

Boyle, D. The Killing of Moostoos, the Wehtigoo.
AAR, 1903, 126-38.

Burpee, L.J., ed. Journals and Letters of Pierre
Gaultier de Varennes de la Vérendrye and His Sons.
PCS, XVI, 1-548. 1927.

Bushnell, D.I. Sketches by Paul Kane in the Indian
Country, 1845-1848. SMC, XCIX, i, 1-25. 1940.

Cadzow, D.A. Peace-Pipe of the Prairie Cree. IN,
III, 82-9. 1926.

Cadzow, D.A. The Prairie Cree Tipi. IN, III, 19-27. 1926.

--- Smoking Tipi of Buffalo-Bull the Cree. IN, IV, 271-80. 1927.

Cameron, D. The Nipigon Country. BCNO, II, 231-65. 1890.

Cameron, W.B. Blood Red the Sun. 225 pp. Calgary, 1950.

Campbell, H.C. Radisson's Journal: Its Value in History. PSHSW, XLIII, 88-116. 1896.

Chappell, E. Narrative of a Voyage to Hudson's Bay. 279 pp. London, 1817.

Chown, B. and Lewis, M. The Blood Group Genes of the Cree Indians and the Eskimos of the Ungava District of Canada. AJPA, n.s., XIV, 215-24. 1956.

Clay, C. The Cree Legend of Creation. Alberta Folklore Quarterly, II, 69-71. 1946.

--- Indians as I know them. CGJ, VIII, 43-50. 1934.

--- Swampy Cree Legends. 95 pp. Toronto, 1938.

Cocking, M. An Adventurer from Hudson Bay, ed. L.J. Burpee. PTRSC, ser. 3, II, ii, 89-121. 1908.

Cooper, J.M. The Cree Witiko Psychosis. PM, VI, 20-4. 1933.

--- Field Notes on Northern Algonkian Magic. ICA, XXIII, 513-18. 1928.

--- Is the Algonquian Family Hunting Ground System Pre-Columbian? AA, n.s., XLI, 66-90. 1939.

--- Northern Algonkian Scrying and Scapulimancy. Festschrift P.W. Schmidt, pp. 205-17. Wien, 1928.

--- The Northern Algonquian Supreme Being. CUAS, II, 1-78. 1934.

--- The Shaking Tent Rite among Plains and Forest Algonquians. PM, XVII, 60-84. 1944.

--- Tete-de-Boule Cree. IJAL, XI, 36-44. 1945.

Corrigan, C. Medical Practice among the Bush Indians of Northern Manitoba. Canadian Medical Association Journal, LIV, 220-23. 1946.

Coues, E., ed. Manuscript Journals of Alexander Henry and of David Thompson. 3 vols. New York, 1897.

Cresswell, J.R. Folk-Tales of the Swampy Cree. JAFL, XXXVI, 404-6. 1923.

Curtis, E.S. The North American Indian, XVIII, 55-87, 129-35, 152-8, 205-10. Norwood, 1928.

Darby, tr. The Epistle to the Romans in the Cree Language. 67 pp. Oonikup, N.W. Territory, 1897.

Davidson, D.S. Decorative Art of the Tetes de Boule of Quebec. INM, X, 115-53. 1928.

--- Notes on Tete de Boule Ethnology. AA, n.s., XXX, 18-46. 1928.

--- Some Tete de Boule Tales. JAFL, XLI, 262-74. 1928.

Denmark, D.E. James Bay Beaver Conservation. B, CCLXXIX, 38-43. 1948.

Dunn, J. History of the Oregon Territory, pp. 88-100. London, 1846.

Ellis, C.D. A Note on Okima·hka·n. Anthropological Linguistics, II, iii, 1. 1960.

Ellis, H. A Voyage to Hudson's-Bay, pp. 181-98. London, 1748.

Ewers, J.C. Edwin T. Denig's "Of the Crees or Kristeneau." BMHS, IX, 37-69. 1952.

--- Three Ornaments Worn by Upper Missouri Indians a Century and a Quarter Ago. NYHSQ, XLI, 24-33. 1957.

Faraud, H.J. Dix-huit ans chez les sauvages. 456 pp. Bruxelles, 1866.

Faries, R., ed. A Dictionary of the Cree Language. 530 pp. Toronto, 1938.

Flannery, R. Cross-Cousin Marriage among the Cree and Montagnais of James Bay. PM, XI, 29-33. 1938.

--- Gossip as a Clue to Attitudes. PM, VII, 8-12. 1934.

--- The Position of Women among the Eastern Cree. PM, VIII, 81-6. 1935.

--- Some Aspects of James Bay Recreative Culture. PM, IX, 49-56. 1937.

Fortescue, J. Les Indiens Cris de l'Amérique du Nord. Archives de la Société Américaine de France, n.s., III, 31-66. 1883.

Francine, J. The Forgotten Land. CGJ, XVIII, 52-7. 1939.

Franklin, J. Narrative of a Journey to the Shores of the Polar Sea. London, 1823.

Gates, R.R. Pedigree Study of Amerindian Crosses in Canada. JAI, LXVIII, 511-32. 1928.

Goddard, P.E. Notes on the Sun Dance of the Cree in Alberta. APAM, XVI, 295-310. 1919.

Godsell, P.H. Red Hunters of the Snows. 324 pp. Toronto, 1938.

Grant, J.C.B. Anthropometry of the Chipewyan and Cree Indians of the Neighborhood of Lake Athabaska. BCDM, LXIV, 1-59. 1930.

--- Anthropometry of the Cree and Saulteaux Indians in Northeastern Manitoba. BCDM, LIX, 1-73. 1929.

--- Anthropometry of the Lake Winnipeg Indians. AJPA, VII, 299-315. 1924.

--- Progress in an Anthropometric Survey of the Canadian Aborigines. PPSC, V, iv, 2715-21. 1933.

Greenlees, S. The Caribou Hunters. Forest and Outdoors, XLVIII, xi, 12-13, 20.

--- Indian Canoe Makers. B, CCLXXXV, 46-9. Summer, 1954.

Guinard, J.E. Witiko among the Tete-de-Boule.
PM, III, 69-71. 1930.

Hallowell, A.I. Cross-Cousin Marriage in the Lake
Winnipeg Area. PPAS, I, 95-110. 1937.

--- The Incidence, Character, and Decline of
Polygyny among the Lake Winnipeg Cree and
Saulteaux. AA, n.s., XL, 235-56. 1938.

--- Kinship Terms and Cross-Cousin Marriage of the
Montagnais-Naskapi and the Cree. AA, n.s.,
XXXIV, 171-99. 1932.

--- Was Cross-Cousin Marriage practised by the
North-Central Algonkian? ICA, XXIII, 519-44.
1928.

Hamilton, H. Life at Eastmain. B, CCLXXIV, 42.
1943.

Hamilton, J.C. Two Algonquin Legends. JAFL, VII,
201-4. 1894.

Hardisty, R.G. The Last Sun Dance. Alberta Folk-
lore Quarterly, II, 57-61. 1946.

Harmon, D.W. A Journal of Voyages and Travels in
the Interior of North America, ed. W.L.Grant, pp.
269-353. Toronto, 1911.

Hayden, F.V. Contributions to the Ethnography and
Philology of the Indian Tribes of the Missouri Valley. TAPS, n.s., XII, 234-48. 1862.

Hector, J., and Vaux, W.S.W. Note of the Indians
seen by the Exploring Expedition under the Command of Captain Palliser. TESL, n.s., I, 245-61.
1861.

Henry, A. Travels and Adventures in Canada, ed.
M.M.Quaife, pp. 339-42. Chicago, 1921.

Hind, H.Y. Narrative of the Canadian Red River Exploring Expedition. 2 vols. London, 1860.

--- North-West Territory. 201 pp. Toronto, 1859.

--- Of Some of the Superstitions and Customs common among the Indians in the Valley of the Assiniboine and Saskatchewan. CJ, n.s., XXII, 253-
62. 1859.

Holmes, E.M. Medicinal Plants used by the Cree Indians. Pharmaceutical Journal and Transactions,
ser. 3, XV, 302-4. 1884.

Honigmann, J.J. Attawapiskat—Blend of Traditions.
An, VI, 57-67. 1958.

--- Culture Patterns and Human Stress. Psychiatry,
XIII, 25-34. 1950.

--- European and Other Tales from the Western Woods
Cree. JAFL, LXVI, 309-31. 1953.

--- Incentives to Work in a Canadian Indian Community. HO, VIII, iv, 23-8. 1949.

--- Intercultural Relations at Great Whale River. AA,
LIV, 510-22. 1952.

Honigmann, J.J. The Logic of the James Bay Survey.
DR, XXX, 378-86. 1951.

--- Social Organization of the Attawapiskat Cree Indians. A, XLVIII, 809-16. 1953.

Honigmann, J.J. and Carrera, R. Another Experiment in Sample Reliability. SJA, XIII, 99-102.
1957.

--- Cross-cultural Use of Machover's Figure Drawing
Test. AA, LIX, 650-54. 1957.

Horden, J. A Grammar of the Cree Language. 238
pp. London, 1881.

Horden, J., tr. Bible and Gospel History. 64 pp.
London, 1892.

Howse, J. A Grammar of the Cree Language. 324
pp. London, 1844.

Hunter, J. A Lecture on the Grammatical Construction of the Cree Language. 267 pp. London, 1875.

Jefferson, R. Fifty Years on the Saskatchewan. Publications of the Canadian North-West Historical
Society, I, v, 1-160. 1929.

Jérémie, N. Account of Hudson Strait and Bay, ed.
R. Douglas and J.N.Wallace. 42 pp. Ottawa,
1926.

Kennedy, G.A. The Last Battle. Alberta Folklore
Quarterly, I, 57-60. 1945.

Kidd, K.E. Trading into Hudson's Bay. B,
CCLXXXVIII, iii, 12-17. 1957.

Lacombe, A. Dictionnaire de la langue des Cris.
709 pp. Montreal, 1874.

--- Grammaire de la langue des Cris. 190 pp. Montreal, 1874.

Laidlaw, G.E. Gambling amongst the Crees with
Small Sticks. AAOJ, XXIII, 275-6. 1901.

Lance, B.C.L. When the Crees moved West. AAR,
XXXIV, 25-34. 1923.

Lane, C. The Sun Dance of the Cree Indians. Canadian Record of Science, II, 22-6. 1887.

Latourelle, R. Étude sur les Écrits de Saint Jean de
Brébeuf. 271 pp. Montreal, 1953.

Leden, C. Unter den Indianern Canadas. ZE, XLIV,
811-31. 1912.

Leechman, D. The Savages of James Bay. B,
CCLXXVI, 14-17. 1945.

--- The Trappers. B, CCLXXXVIII, iii, 24-31. 1957.

Linderman, F.B. Indian Old-man Stories. 169 pp.
New York, 1920.

--- Indian Why Stories. 236 pp. New York, 1915.

Logan, R.A. The Precise Speakers. B, CCLXXXII,
i, 40-43. 1951.

Longacre, R.E. Quality and Quantity in Cree Vowels.
Journal of the Canadian Linguistic Association,
III, 66-70. 1957.

Long Lance, B.C. When the Crees moved West.
AAR, 1923, 25-34.

Lowie, R.H. The Military Societies of the Plains
Cree. ICA, XXXI, i, 3-9. 1955.

McDonnell, J. Some Account of the Red River.
BCNO, I, 265-95. 1889.

McDougall, J. Pathfinding on Plain and Prairie.
277 pp. Toronto, 1898.

Macfie, J. Crafts of the Cree. B, CCLXXXVIII, ii,
53-7. 1957.

Mackenzie, A. Voyage from Montreal, ed. M.M.
Quaife. Chicago, 1931.

Mackintosh, W.A. Prairie Settlement. Toronto,
1934.

McLean, J. Notes of a Twenty-five Years' Service
in the Hudson's Bay Territory, ed. W.S. Wallace.
PCS, XIX, 1-402. 1932.

Mandelbaum, D.G. Boom Periods in the History of
an Indian Tribe. SF, XVI, 117-19. 1937.

--- Friendship in North America. Man, XXXVI,
205-6. 1936.

Matson, G.A. Blood Groups and Ageusia in Indians
of Montana and Alberta. AJPA, XXIV, 81-9. 1938.

Michelson, T. Linguistic Classification of Cree and
Montagnais-Naskapi Dialects. BBAE, CXXIII, 67-
95. 1939.

--- The Linguistic Classification of the Tete de
Boule. AA, n.s., XXXV, 396. 1933.

--- Plains Cree Kinship Terms. AA, n.s., XL, 531-
2. 1938.

--- Tetes de Boule. BBAE, XXX, ii, 735-6. 1910.

Millar, J. Some Observations on Haemoglobin Levels
of an Indian Population. Journal of the Canadian
Medical Association, LXVII, v, 414-17. 1952.

Mooney, J. Maskegon. BBAE, XXX, i, 813-14. 1907.

--- Tetes de Boule. BBAE, XXX, ii, 735-6. 1910.

Mooney, J., and Thomas, C. Cree. BBAE, XXX,
i, 359-62. 1907.

Moore, P.E., et al. Medical Survey of Nutrition
among the Northern Manitoba Indians. Canadian
Medical Association Journal, LIV, 223-33. 1946.

Morgan, L.H. The Indian Journals, 1859-62, pp.
111-3, 115, 117, 120. Ann Arbor, 1959.

--- Systems of Consanguinity and Affinity. SCK,
XVII, 291-382. 1871.

Neilson, J.M. The Mistassini Territory of Northern
Quebec. CGJ, XXXVII, 144-57. 1948.

Orchard, W.C. Old Porcupine-Quillwork. IN, I,
157-61. 1924.

Orr, R.B. The Crees of New Ontario. AAR, 1923,
9-24.

Palliser, J. Further Papers. 325 pp. London, 1860.

--- Papers. 325 pp. London, 1859.

Peeso, F.E. The Cree Indians. MJ, III, 50-7. 1912.

Perrot, N. Memoir on the Manners, Customs and Religion of the Savages of North America. ITUMV, I,
25-272. 1911.

--- Mémoire sur les moeurs, coustumes et relligion
des sauvages de l'Amérique septentrionale. 341 pp.
Paris, 1864.

Petitot, E.F.S. De Carlton-House au Fort Pitt. Société Neuchateloise de Géographie, Bulletin, XI,
176-95. 1899.

--- Légendes et traditions des Cris. LPTN, XXIII,
445-88. 1886.

--- On the Athabasca District of the Canadian North-
West Territory. Canadian Record of Science, I,
27-53. 1884.

Prud'homme, L.A. Carmel, une légende de la tribu
des Cris. PTRSC, ser. 3, XIII, i, 95-100.

Raymond, M. Notes Ethnobotaniques sur les Tetes-
de-boule de Manouan. Contributions de l'Institut
Botanique de l'Université de Montréal, LV, 113-
35. 1945.

Raynor, W. Windigo Woman. B, CCLXXXVIII, i,
32-3. 1957.

Richardson, J. Arctic Searching Expedition, II, 33-
60, 387-95. London, 1851.

Rogers, E.S. Down the Rupert's River. B, CCLXXIX,
29-33. 1948.

Rossignol, M. Cross-Cousin Marriage among the
Saskatchewan Cree. PM, XI, 26-8. 1938.

--- Property Concepts among the Cree of the Rocks.
PM, XII, 61-70. 1939.

--- The Religion of the Saskatchewan and Western
Manitoba Cree. PM, XI, 67-71. 1939.

Rousseau, J.J. Mokouchan. Foret et Conservation,
II, 683-87. 1950.

--- Persistance Paiennes chez les Amerindiens de la
Foret Boréale. CD, XVII, 183-208. 1952.

--- Les Voyages du Père Albanel au Lac Mistassini et
la Baie James. RHAF, III, 556-86. 1950.

Russell, F. Explorations in the Far North, pp. 21-40,
168-86, 201-20. Iowa City, 1898.

Saindon, J.E. Mental Disorders among the James Bay
Cree. PM, VI, 1-12. 1933.

Schmidt, W. Die Ostzentral-Algonkin. UG, II, 459-
74; V, 531-54, 887. 1929, 1934.

Schoolcraft, H.R. Kenistenos. HCPIT, V, 164-72.
1855.

Scull, G.D. Voyages of Peter Esprit Radisson. 385 pp.
Boston, 1885.

Shave, H. John West, Peguis and P. Rindisbacher.
    B, CCLXXXVIII, i, 14-19. 1957.
Shipley, N. Frances and the Crees. 181 pp. Toron-
    to, 1957.
Simms, S.C. The Metawin of the Bungees or Swampy
    Indians of Lake Winnipeg. JAFL, XIX, 330-3.
    1906.
--- Myths of the Bungees or Swampy Indians of Lake
    Winnipeg. JAFL, XIX, 334-40. 1906.
Skinner, A. Bear Customs of the Cree and Other
    Algonkin Indians of Northern Ontario. Papers and
    Records of the Ontario Historical Society, XII, 203-
    9. 1914.
--- Notes on the Plains Cree. AA, n.s., XVI, 68-
    87. 1914.
--- Ojibway and Cree of Central Canada. AMJ, X,
    9-18. 1908.
--- Plains Cree Tales. JAFL, XXIX, 341-67. 1916.
--- Political Organization, Cults and Ceremonies of
    the Plains-Cree. APAM, XI, 513-42. 1914.
--- The Sun Dance of the Plains-Cree. APAM, XVI,
    283-93. 1919.
--- A Visit to the Ojibway and Cree of Central Cana-
    da. AMJ, X, 9-18. 1910.
Stewart, J. Rupert's Land Indians in the Olden Time.
    AAR, 1904, 89-100.
Swindlehurst, F. Folk-Lore of the Cree Indians.
    JAFL, XVIII, 139-43. 1905.
Teeter, K.V. Consonant Harmony in Wiyot. IJAL,
    XXV, 41-3. 1960.
Teit, J.A. Two Plains Cree Tales. JAFL, XXXIV,
    320-1. 1921.
Thwaites, R.G., ed. The Jesuit Relations and Al-
    lied Documents. 74 vols. Cleveland, 1896-1901.
--- Radisson and Groseilliers in Wisconsin. CSHSW,
    XI, 64-96. 1888.
Tyrrell, J.B., ed. David Thompson's Narrative of
    His Explorations in Western America. PCS, XII,
    78-127. 1916.
--- Documents relating to the Early History of Hudson
    Bay. PCS, XVIII, 1-419. 1931.
Uhlenbeck, C.C. Ontwerp van eene vergelijkende
    vormleer van eenige Algonkin-talen. VKAW, n.
    s., XI, iii, 1-67. 1910.
Umfreville, E. The Present State of Hudson's Bay.
    London, 1790.
Vivian, R.P., et al. The Nutrition and Health of the
    James Bay Indian. Canadian Medical Association
    Journal, LIX, 505-18. 1948.
Watkins, E.A. A Dictionary of the Cree Language.
    460 pp., London, 1865. 534 pp., Toronto, 1938.

White, M.C. David Thompson's Journals Relating
    to Montana and Adjacent Regions, 1808-1812.
    507 pp. Missoula, 1950.
Whitney, C. On Snow-Shoes to the Barren Grounds.
    324 pp. New York, 1896.
Wissler, C. The Excess of Females among the Cree
    Indians. PNAS, XXII, 151-3. 1936.
Wood, W.J. Tularemia. Manitoba Medical Associ-
    ation, Review, XXXI, x, 641-4. 1951.
Young, E.R. By Canoe and Dog-Train among the
    Cree and Salteaux Indians. 267 pp. London, 1890.
--- On the Indian Trail. 214 pp. New York, 1897.
--- Stories from Indian Wigwams and Northern Camp-
    Fires. 293 pp. New York, 1893.

5. MALECITE

Including the Etchimin, the Malecite, and the
Passamaquoddy.

Mechling, W.H. The Malecite Indians, with Notes
    on the Micmacs. An, VII, 1-160; VIII, 161-274.
    1958-59.
Smith, N.N. Notes on the Malecite of Woodstock,
    New Brunswick. An, V, 1-40. 1957.
Wallis, W.D. and R.S. The Malecite Indians of
    New Brunswick. BNMC, CXLVIII, 58 pp. 1957.

Adney, E.T. The Malecite Indian's Names for Na-
    tive Berries and Fruits. Acadian Naturalist, I,
    103-10. 1944.
Alger, A.L. A Collection of Words and Phrases taken
    from the Passamaquoddy Tongue. PAPS, XXI,
    240-55. 1885.
--- In Indian Tents. 139 pp. Boston, 1897.
Anonymous. Ontario Indians: Their Fisheries and
    Fishery Appliances. AAR, 1917, 24-43.
--- Superstitions of the Passamaquoddies. JAFL, II,
    229-31. 1889.
--- Wood and Wood Products: Their Uses by the Pre-
    historic Indians of Ontario. AAR, 1918, 25-48.
Barratt, J. The Indians of New England. 24 pp.
    Middletown, 1851.
Brown, Mrs. W.W. "Chief-making" among the
    Passamaquoddy Indians. JAFL, V, 57-9. 1892.
Chamberlain, M. Indians in New Brunswick in
    Champlain's Time. Acadiensis, IV, 280-95. 1904.
--- The Origin of the Maliseets. New Brunswick
    Magazine, I, 41-5. 1898.

Dionne, N.E. Etude Archeologique: le Fort Jacques-Cartier et la Petite Hermine. Montreal, 1891.

Dodge, E.S. An Early Nineteenth Century Passamaquoddy Bark Box. BMAS, XIV, 77-8. 1953.

Eckstorm, F.H. Old John Neptune and Other Maine Indian Shamans. 209 pp. Portland, 1945.

Fewkes, J.W. A Contribution to Passamaquoddy Folk-Lore. JAFL, III, 257-80. 1890.

Ganong, W.F. The Economic Mollusca of Acadia: Wampum among the New Brunswick Indians. Bulletin of the Natural History Society of New Brunswick, VIII, 3-116, 1889.

--- Historical-Geographical Documents Relating to New Brunswick. Collections of the New Brunswick Historical Society, V, xiii, 76-128. 1930.

Goodwin, W.L. Notes on an Old Indian Encampment. Canadian Record of Science, V, v, 284-5. 1893.

Hadlock, W.S., and Dodge, E.S. A Canoe from the Penobscot River. American Neptune, VIII, 289-301. 1948.

Hoffman, B.G. The Souriquois, Etechemin and Wegesh. E, II, 65-87. 1955.

Jack, E. Maliseet Legends. JAI, VIII, 193-208. 1895.

Kellogg, E. Vocabulary of Words in the Language of the Quoddy Indians. MHSC, ser. 3, III, 181-2. 1833.

Leland, C.G. The Algonquin Legends of New England. 379 pp. Boston, 1884.

Leland, C.G., and Prince, J.D. Kulóskap the Master, and Other Algonquin Poems. 370 pp. New York, 1902.

Lescarbot, M. Histoire de la Nouvelle-France. 888 pp. Paris, 1609.

--- The History of New France, ed. L. Grant. PCS, Vols. I, VII, XI. 1907-14.

--- Nova Francia, pp. 145-330. New edit. London, 1928.

Maillard, A.S. Account of the Customs and Manners of the Micmakis and Maricheets. 138 pp. London, 1758.

Mechling, W.H. Malecite Tales. MCDM, XLIX, 1-133. 1914.

--- Maliseet Tales. JAFL, XXVI, 219-58. 1913.

Michelson, T. The Passamaquoddy Indians of Maine. EFWSI, 1934, 85-8.

Mooney, J., and Thomas, C. Malecite. BBAE, XXX, i, 793-4. 1907.

Morgan, L.H. Systems of Consanguinity and Affinity. SCK, XVII, 291-382. 1871.

Prince, J.D. Algonquins (Eastern). ERE, I, 319-21. 1908.

Prince, J.D. The Morphology of the Passamaquoddy Language. PAPS, LIII, 92-117. 1914.

--- Notes on Passamaquoddy Literature. ANYAS, XIII, 381-6. 1901.

--- Notes on the Language of the Eastern Algonkin Tribes. AJP, IX, 310-16. 1888.

--- A Passamaquoddy Aviator. AA, n.s., XI, 628-50. 1909.

--- Passamaquoddy Texts. PAES, X, 1-85. 1921.

--- A Passamaquoddy Tobacco Famine. IJAL, I, 58-63. 1917.

--- The Passamaquoddy Wampum Records. PAPS, XXXVI, 479-95. 1897.

--- The Passamaquoddy Wampum Records. NYSMB, CLXXXIV, 119-25. 1916.

--- Some Passamaquoddy Documents. ANYAS, XI, 369-77. 1898.

--- Some Passamaquoddy Witchcraft Tales. PAPS, XXXVIII, 181-9. 1899.

Raymond, W.O. The Old Meductic Fort. Collections of the New Brunswick Historical Society, I, 221-72. 1896.

Reade, J. Some Wabanaki Songs. PTRSC, V, ii, 1-8. 1887.

Speck, F.G. An Algonkian Myth. MJ, I, 49-52. 1910.

--- The Eastern Algonkian Wabanaki Confederacy. AA, n.s., XVII, 492-508. 1915.

--- Game Totems among the Northeastern Algonkians. AA, n.s., XIX, 9-18. 1917.

--- Kinship Terms and the Family Band among the Northeastern Algonkian. AA, n.s., XX, 143-61. 1918.

--- Malecite Tales. JAFL, XXX, 479-85. 1917.

--- Reptile-Lore of the Northern Indians. JAFL, XXXVI, 273-80. 1923.

Speck, F.G. and Dexter, R.W. Utilization of Animals and Plants by the Malecite Indians of New Brunswick. JWAS, XLII, 1-7. 1952.

Speck, F.G., and Hadlock, W.S. A Report on Tribal Boundaries and Hunting Areas of the Malecite Indian of New Brunswick. AA, n.s., XLVIII, 355-74. 1946.

Stamp, H. A Malecite Tale. JAFL, XXVIII, 243-8. 1915.

Tenesles, N. The Indian of New England and the North Eastern Provinces. 24 pp. Middletown, 1851.

Thwaites, R.G., ed. The Jesuit Relations and Allied Documents. 74 vols. Cleveland, 1896-1901.

Treat, J. Etchemins. TCAAS, II, 305-67. 1836.

Van Wart, A.F. The Indians of the Maritime Provinces, Their Diseases and Native Cures. Canadian Medical Association Journal, LIX, 573-7. 1948.

Vetromile, E. The Abnakis and Their History. 171
    pp. New York, 1866.
Watson, L.W. The Origin of the Melicites. JAFL,
    XX, 160-62. 1907.
Weer, P. Passamaquoddy and Quapaw Mnemonic
    Records. PIAS, LV, 29-32. 1946.
Williamson, W.D. The History of the State of Maine,
    I, 453-514. Hallowell, 1832.
Wilson, G.L. Indian Hero Tales. 203 pp. New York,
    1906.

                        6. MICMAC

Denys, N. The Description and Natural History of
    the Coasts of North America, ed. W.F. Ganong.
    PCS, II, 399-452, 572-606. 1908.
LeClercq, G. New Relation of Gaspesia, ed. W.F.
    Ganong. PCS, V, 1-452. 1910.
Wallis, W.D. and R.S. The Micmac Indians of East-
    ern Canada. 530 pp. Minneapolis, 1955.

Adrien, P. Conservatisme et Changement chez les
    Indiens Micmacs. An, II, 1-16. 1956.
Alger, A.L. In Indian Tents. 139 pp. Boston, 1897.
Barratt, J. The Indians of New England. 24 pp.
    Middletown, 1851.
Baxter, J.P. A Memoir of Jacques Cartier. 464 pp.
    New York, 1906.
Boas, F. Zur Anthropologie der nordamerikanischen
    Indianer. VBGA, 1895, 367-411.
Bromley, W. A General Description of Nova Scotia,
    pp. 44-58. Halifax, 1823.
Cameron, J. A Craniometric Study of the Micmac
    Skull. PNSIS, XV, 1-31. 1919.
Campbell, D. Nova Scotia, pp. 17-26. Montreal, 1873.
Chamberlain, A.F. Indians of the Eastern Provinces
    of Canada. AAR, 1905, 122-36.
Chamberlain, M. Indians in New Brunswick in Cham-
    plain's Time. Acadiensis, IV, 280-95. 1904.
Clark, J.S. Uktce-bal-lok, a Micmac Legend.
    Acadiensis, III, 301-3. 1903.
Dixon, R.B. The Migrations of the Indians of New
    England and the Maritime Provinces. PAAS, n.s.,
    XXIV, 65-76. 1914.
Eckstorm, F.H. Old John Neptune and Other Maine
    Indian Shamans. 209 pp. Portland, 1945.
Elder, W. The Aborigines of Nova Scotia. North
    American Review, CXII, 1-30. 1871.
Fauset, A.H. Folklore from the Halfbreeds in Nova
    Scotia. JAFL, XXXVIII, 300-15. 1925.
Fewkes, J.W. A Pictograph from Nova Scotia. AN,
    XXIV, 995-9. 1890.

Frye, Col. Indians in Acadie, A.D.1760. MHSC,
    ser. 1, X, 115-16. 1809.
Ganong, W.F. The Economic Mollusca of Acadia:
    Wampum among the New Brunswick Indians. Bul-
    letin of the Natural History Society of New Bruns-
    wick, VIII, 3-116. 1889.
--- Upon Aboriginal Pictographs from New Brunswick.
    Bulletin of the Natural History Society of New
    Brunswick, 1904, 175-8.
Gates, R.R. The Blood Groups and Other Features of
    the Micmac Indians. JAI, LXVIII, 283-98. 1938.
Gatschet, A.S. Micmac Fans and Games. BFMUP,
    II, 190-4. 1900.
Gilpin, J.B. Indians of Nova Scotia. PNSIS, IV,
    260-81. 1877.
--- On the Stone Age of Nova Scotia. PNSIS, III,
    220-31. 1873.
Hagar, S. The Celestial Bear. JAFL, XIII, 92-103.
    1900.
--- A Melange of Micmac Notes. PAAAS, XLIV,
    257-8. 1895.
--- Micmac Customs and Traditions. AA, VIII, 31-
    42. 1895.
--- Micmac Magic and Medicine. JAFL, IX, 170-
    7. 1896.
--- Weather and the Seasons in Micmac Mythology.
    JAFL, X, 101-5. 1897.
Haliburton, R.G. On the Festival on the Dead.
    PNSIS, I, i, 61-85. 1863.
Harper, J.R. Micmac Arm Bands. PA, XXVII, 135-
    36. 1957.
--- Two Seventeenth Century Micmac "Copper Ket-
    tle" Burials. An, IV, 11-36. 1957.
Hoffman, B.G. Historical Ethnography of the Mic-
    mac of the Sixteenth and Seventeenth Centuries.
    E, III, 190-91. 1956.
--- The Souriquois, Etechemin and Wegesh. E, II,
    65-87. 1955.
Johnson, F. Notes on Micmac Shamanism. PM, XVI,
    53-80. 1943.
Kroeber, A.L. Micmac. Encyclopaedia Britannica,
    14th ed., XV, 426. 1929.
Le Clercq, C. Language of the Gaspesians. HM,
    ser. 1, V, 284-5. 1861.
--- Nouvelle relation de la Gaspesie. 572 pp. Paris,
    1691.
Leland, C.G. The Algonquin Legends of New Eng-
    land. 379 pp. Boston, 1884.
Leland, C.G., and Prince, J.D. Kulóskap the Mas-
    ter and Other Algonkin Poems. 370 pp. New York,
    1902.

Lescarbot, M. Histoire de la Nouvelle-France. 3 vols. Paris, 1866.

--- The History of New France, ed. L. Grant. PCS, Vols. I, VII, XI. 1907-14.

McLeod, R.R. In the Acadian Land, pp. 140-55. Boston, 1899.

--- Markland or Nova Scotia, pp. 166-75. Chicago, 1903.

Maillard, A.S. An Account of the Customs and Manners of the Micmakis and Maricheets. 138 pp. London, 1758.

--- Grammar of the Mikmaque Language. 101 pp. New York, 1864.

Maillard, A.S., and Pacifique. Le catéchisme Micmac. 128 pp. Ristigouche, P.Q., 1906.

Mechling, W.H. The Malecite Indians, with Notes on the Micmacs. An, VII, 1-160; VIII, 161-274. 1958-59.

Michelson, T. Micmac Tales. JAFL, XXXVIII, 33-54. 1925.

Mooney, J., and Thomas, C. Micmac. BBAE, XXX, i, 858-9. 1907.

Morgan, L.H. Systems of Consanguinity and Affinity. SCK, XVII, 291-382. 1871.

Pacifique. Leçons grammaticales théoriques et pratiques de la langue Micmaque. Ristigouche, P.Q. 1939.

--- Notes supplémentaires sur les traités de langue Micmaque. ACFAS, VI, 271-7. 1940.

--- Le Pays des Micmacs. BSGQ, XXI, 111-7, 165-85; XXII, 43-5, 140-5, 270-7; XXIII, 37-45; XXV, 96-106; XXVII, 34-50, 51-64; XXVIII, 105-47. 1927-34.

--- Quelques traits caracteristiques de la tribu des Micmacs. ICA, XV, i, 315-28. 1906.

--- Traité theorique et pratique de la langue Micmaque. ACFAS, IV, 213-333; V, 159-276. 1938-39.

Parsons, E.C. Half-Breed. SM, XVIII, 144-8. 1924.

--- Micmac Folklore. JAFL, XXXVIII, 55-133. 1925.

--- Micmac Notes. JAFL, XXXIX, 460-85. 1926.

Patterson, G. Antiquities of Nova Scotia. ARSI, 1881, 673-7.

--- History of the County of Pictou, Nova Scotia, pp. 26-37. Montreal, 1877.

--- The Stone Age in Nova Scotia. PNSIS, VII, 231-52. 1889.

Peterson, M.S. Some Scandinavian Elements in a Micmac Swan Maiden Story. Scandinavian Studies and Notes, XI, 135-8. 1930.

Pierronet, T. Specimen of the Mountaineer or Sheshatapooshshoish, Skoffie, and Micmac Languages. MHSC, VI, 16-33. 1798.

Piers, H. Aboriginal Remains of Nova Scotia. PNSIS, VII, 276-90. 1889.

--- Brief Account of the Micmac Indians. PNSIS, XIII, 99-125. 1912.

--- Relics of the Stone Age in Nova Scotia. PNSIS, IX, 26-58. 1895.

Prince, J.D. A Micmac Manuscript. ICA, XV, i, 87-124. 1906.

--- Notes on the Language of the Eastern Algonquin Tribes. AJP, IX, 310-16. 1888.

Rand, S.T. The Beautiful Bride. AAOJ, XIII, 156-9. 1890.

--- The Coming of the White Man Revealed. AAOJ, XIII, 155-6. 1890.

--- Dictionary of the Language of the Micmac Indians. 286 pp. Halifax, 1888.

--- Glooscap, Cuhkw and Coolpurjot. AAOJ, XII, 283-6. 1890.

--- The Legends of the Micmacs. AAOJ, XII, 3-14. 1890.

--- Legends of the Micmacs. 452 pp. New York, 1894.

--- The Micmac Indians. OFC, II, 10-12. 1888.

--- The Micmac Language. Canadian Science Monthly, III, 142-6. 1885.

--- Micmac Place-Names in the Maritime Provinces and Gaspé Peninsula. Ottawa, 1919.

--- Rand's Micmac Dictionary. Charlottetown, P.E.I., 1902.

--- A Short Statement of Facts relating to the History, Manners, Customs, Language, and Literature of the Micmac Tribe of Indians. 40 pp. Halifax, 1850.

Rousseau, J.J. Ethnobotanique et Ethnozoologie Gaspéssienne. Archives de Folklore, III, 51-64. 1948.

--- Notes sur l'Ethnobotanique d'Anticosti. Archives de Folklore, I, 60-71. 1946.

St. Croix, S. The Micmacs of Newfoundland. In J.R. Smallwood, ed., The Book of New Foundland, I, 284-6. St. John's, 1937.

Schmidt, W. Die Nordost Algonkin. UG, II, 449-58. 1929.

Shaw, A. A Micmac Glengarry. Art Bulletin of the New Brunswick Museum, II, iii, 3-4. 1954.

Shaw, B.H.H. The Indians of the Maritimes. Canadian Magazine, LVIII, 343-50. 1922.

Shea, J.G. Micmac or Recollect Hieroglyphics. HM, ser. 1. V, 289-92.

Smith, H.I., and Wintemberg, W.J. Some Shell-Heaps in Nova Scotia. BCDM, XLVII, 1-192. 1929.

Speck, F.G. Beothuk and Micmac. INM, ser. 2,
XXII, 1-187. 1921.

--- The Eastern Algonkian Wabanaki Confederacy.
AA, n.s., XVII, 492-508. 1915.

--- The Family Hunting Band as the Basis of Algonkian Social Organization. AA, n.s., XVII, 289-
305. 1915.

--- Kinship Terms and the Family Band among the
Northeastern Algonkian. AA, n.s., XX, 143-61.
1918.

--- Micmac Slate Image. IN, I, 153-4. 1924.

--- Reptile-Lore of the Northern Indians. JAFL,
XXXVI, 273-80. 1923.

--- Some Micmac Tales from Cape Breton Island.
JAFL, XXVIII, 59-69. 1915.

Speck, F.G. and Dexter, R.W. Utilization of Animals and Plants by the Micmac Indians of New
Brunswick. JWAS, XLI, 250-59. 1951.

Tenesles, N. The Indian of New-England and the
North-Eastern Provinces. 24 pp. Middletown, 1851.

Thwaites, R.G., ed. The Jesuit Relations and Allied Documents. 74 vols. Cleveland, 1896-1901.

Uhlenbeck, C.C. Ontwerp van eene vergelijkende
vormleer van eenige Algonkin-talen. VKAW, n.
s., XI, iii, 1-67. 1910.

Van Wart, A.F. The Indians of the Maritime Provinces, Their Diseases and Native Cures. Canadian
Medical Association Journal, LIX, 573-7. 1948.

Vernon, C.W. Indians of St. John Island. Acadiensis, III, 110-15. 1903.

Vetromile, E. The Abnakis and Their History. 171
pp. New York, 1866.

Wallis, W.D. Medicines used by the Micmac Indians.
AA, n.s., XXIV, 24-30. 1922.

Wallis, W.D. and R.S. Culture Loss and Culture
Change among the Micmac of the Canadian Maritime Provinces, 1912-1950. PKAS, VIII/IX, 100-
29. 1953.

Watson, L.W. The Origin of the Malicites. JAFL,
XX, 160-62. 1907.

West, J. A Journal of a Mission to the Indians of the
British Provinces of New Brunswick and Nova
Scotia, pp. 235-55. London, 1827.

Wilson, G.L. Indian Hero Tales. 203 pp. New
York, 1906.

Witthoft, J., et al. Micmac Pipes, Vase-Shaped
Pipes, and Calumets. PA, XXIII, 89-107. 1953.

7. MONTAGNAIS

Including the Montagnais and the Naskapi.

Lane, K.S. The Montagnais Indians, 1600-1640.
PKAS, VII, 1-62. 1952.

Leacock, E. The Montagnais Hunting Territory and
the Fur Trade. MAAA, LXXVIII, 71 pp. 1954.

Lips, J.E. Naskapi Law. TAPS, n.s., XXXVII, 379-
492. 1947.

--- Naskapi Trade. JSAP, XXXI, 129-95. 1939.

--- Notes on Montagnais-Naskapi Economy, Ethnos,
XII, 1-78. 1947.

Speck, F.G. Naskapi. 236 pp.   Norman, 1935.

Turner, L.M. Ethnology of the Ungava District.
ARBAE, XI, 159-84, 267-350. 1890.

Anonymous. Nascapee. BBAE, XXX, ii, 30-2.1910.

--- Tuberculosis Survey: James and Hudson Bays.
Arctic Circular, IV, 45-47. 1951.

Arkle, P.W. A Study of the Nascapi in Labrador.
Oral Hygiene, XXXIII, 202-6. 1943.

Barbeau, M. The Kingdom of Saguenay. 170 pp.
Toronto, 1936.

Biays, P. Conditions et Genres de Vie au Labrador
Septentrionale. 33 pp. Quebec, 1955.

Boas, F. Zur Anthropologie der nordamerikanischen
Indianer. VBGA, 1895, 367-411.

Bond, E.W. How to Build a Birchbark. NH, LXIV,
242-6. 1955.

Bruet, E. Le Labrador et Le Nouveau-Québec. 346
pp. Paris, 1949.

Burgesse, J.A. Les Indiens du Saguenay. Bulletin
de la Société historique du Saguenay. II, 2-11.
1946.

--- Lake St. John and the Big Beaver. B,CCLXXXIV,
Dec., 48-9. 1953.

--- Montagnais Cross-Bows. B, CCLXXIV, iv, 37-
9. 1943.

--- The Montagnais Hunter. B, CCLXXIII, ii, 43-
5. 1942.

--- Montagnais - Naskapi Nomenclature. PM, XVI,
44-8. 1943.

--- Property Concepts of the Lac-St-Jean Montagnais.
PM, XVIII, 1-25. 1945.

--- The Spirit Wigwam. PM, XVII, 50-53. 1944.

--- Tribal Laws of the Woodlands. B, CCLXXII, 18-
21. 1942.

--- The Woman and Child among the Lac-St-Jean
Montagnais. PM, XVII, 1-18. 1944.

Cabot, W.B. In Northern Labrador. 292 pp. Boston,
1912.

Chamberlain, A.F. Indians of the Eastern Provinces
of Canada. AAR, 1905, 122-36.

Chambers, E.T.D. The Ouananiche and Its Canadian
Environment, pp. 301-29. New York, 1896.

Comeau, N.A. Life and Sport on the North Shore of the Lower St. Lawrence and Gulf. 2d edit. 440 pp. Quebec, 1923.

Cooper, J.M. Field Notes on Northern Algonkian Magic. ICA, XXIII, 413-18. 1928.

--- Northern Algonkin Scrying and Scapulimancy. Festschrift P.W.Schmidt, pp. 205-17. Wien, 1928.

--- The Northern Algonquian Supreme Being. CUAS, II, 1-78. 1934.

--- The Shaking Tent Rite among Plains and Forest Algonquians. PM, XVII, 60-84. 1944.

--- Some Notes on the Waswanipi. ICA, XXII, ii, 459-61. 1926.

David, C.E. Les Montagnais du Labrador. ICA, XV, i, 205-11. 1906.

Davidson, D.S. Family Hunting Territories of the Waswanipi Indians. IN, V, 42-59. 1928.

Davies, W.H.A. Notes on Ungava Bay and Its Vicinity. TLHSQ, IV, 119-37. 1854.

Douglas, F.H. A Naskapi Painted Skin Shirt. MCN, X, 38-42. 1939.

Flannery, R. Cross-Cousin Marriage among the Cree and Montagnais of James Bay. PM, XI, 29-33. 1938.

--- The Shaking-Tent Rite among the Montagnais of James Bay. PM, XII, 11-16. 1939.

--- Some Aspects of James Bay Recreative Culture. PM, IX, 49-56. 1937.

Francine, J. The Forgotten Land. CGJ, XVIII, 52-7. 1939.

Gaines, R. A Montagnais Prayer-Book and a Mohawk Primer. IN, VI, 138-47. 1929.

Garigue, P. The Social Organization of the Montagnais-Naskapi. An, IV, 107-36. 1957.

Gille, J. Die Montagnais in 1535. Göttingen Völkerkundliche Studien, ed. H. Plischke, pp. 263-7. Leipzig, 1939.

--- Montagnais und Canadiens. A, XXXV, 153-65. 1940.

Grenfell, W.T. Labrador, pp. 184-225. New York, 1909.

Hallowell, A.I. Kinship Terms and Cross-Cousin Marriage of the Montagnais-Naskapi and the Cree. AA, n.s., XXXIV, 171-99. 1932.

--- The Physical Characteristics of the Indians of Labrador. JSAP, n.s., XXI, 337-71. 1929.

Harp, E. An Archaeological Survey in the Strait of Belle-Isle Area. AAn, XVI, 203-20. 1951.

Hind, H.Y. Explorations in the Interior of the Labrador Peninsula. 2 vols. London, 1863.

Kenton, E., ed. The Indians of North America, I, 103-210; II, 412-24. New York, 1927.

Kleivan, H. Labrador i Støpeskjeen, Polarboken, 65-98. 1956.

Knowles, N. The Torture of Captives by the Indians of Eastern North America. PAPS, LXXXII, 151-225. 1940.

Leacock, E. Matrilocality in a Simple Hunting Economy. SJA, XI, 31-47. 1955.

--- Status among the Montagnais-Naskapi of Labrador. E, V, 200-09. 1958.

Legoff, L. Dictionnaire français-montagnais. 1058 pp. Lyon, 1916.

--- Histoire de l'Ancien Testament racontée aux Montagnais. 214 pp. Montreal, 1889.

Le Jeune, P. Relation. The Jesuit Relations and Allied Documents, ed. R.G.Thwaites, XI, 27-279; XII, 1-277. Cleveland, 1898.

Lemoine, G. Dictionnaire Français-Montagnais. Boston, 1901.

Lips, J.E. Public Opinion and Mutual Assistance among the Montagnais-Naskapi. AA, n.s., XXXIX, 222-8. 1937.

--- Tents in the Wilderness. 297 pp. Philadelphia. 1942.

--- Trap Systems among the Montagnais-Naskapi Indians of Labrador. SEMSM, XIII, 1-28. 1936.

Low, A.P. Report on Explorations in the Labrador Peninsula. ARCGS, n.s., VIII, 44L-51L. 1896.

McKenzie, J. The King's Posts. BCNO, II, 401-54. 1890.

McLean, J. Notes of a Twenty-five Year's Service in the Hudson's Bay Territory, ed. W.S.Wallace. PCS, XIX, 258-65. 1932.

Michelson, T. Linguistic Classification of Cree and Montagnais-Naskapi Dialects. BBAE, CXXIII, 67-95. 1939.

--- Some Linguistic Features of Speck's "Naskapi." AA, n.s., XXXIX, 370-2. 1937.

--- Studies among the Montagnais-Naskapi Indians of the Northern Shore of the St. Lawrence River. EFWSI, 1937, 119-22.

Miller, E.C. Aksunai. CGJ, LI, 256-63. 1955

Mooney, J. and Thomas, C. Mistassin. BBAE, XXX, i, 912. 1907.

--- Montagnais. BBAE, XXX, i, 933-4. 1907.

Neilson, J.M. The Mistassini Territory of Northern Quebec. CGJ, XXXVII, 144-57. 1948.

Pierronet, T. Specimen of the Mountaineer or Sheshatapooshshoish, Skoffie, and Micmac Languages. MHSC, VI, 16-33. 1798.

Quimby, G.I. Habitat, Culture, and Archaeology. Essays in the Science of Culture in Honor of Leslie A. White, 380-9. New York, 1960.

Ritzenthaler, R. and Sellars, M. Indians in an Urban Situation. WA, XXXVI, 147-61. 1955.

Rousseau, J.J. A Travers l'Ungava. L'Actualité Economique, XXV, 83-131. 1949.

--- Autour de la Marmite des Mistassini. Gastronomie, VIII, 9-12. 1946.

--- Le Caribou et Le Renne dans la Québec Arctique et Hémiarctique. Revue Canadienne de Géographie, IV, 60-89. 1950.

--- Chez les Mistassini. Revue de 'Institut Français d'Amérique Latine, II, 64-91. 1945.

--- La Crainte des Iroquois. Revue d'Histoire de l'Amérique Française, II, 13-26. 1948.

--- Dans l'Ungava. L'Explorateur, LXXIX, 25-28; LXXX, 25-28, LXXXI, 25-28, LXXXII, 25-28, LXXXIII, 25-29. 1951.

--- Le dualisme religieux chez les Mistassini. ACFAS, XIII, 118-9. 1947.

--- Ethnobotanique des Mistassini. ACFAS, XIII, 118. 1947.

--- Mistassini Calendar. B, CCLXXX, 33-37. 1949.

--- Le Nom du Caribou chez les Montagnais-Naskapi et les Esquimaux de l'Ungava. An, I, 212-14. 1955.

--- Notes Ethnologiques. Foret et Conservation, II, 683-87. 1950.

--- On Human and Animal Adaptation. Canadian Geographer, VI, 17-20. 1955.

--- Le Partage du Gibier dans la Cuisine des Montagnais-Naskapi. An I, 215-17. 1955.

--- La Religion Primitive des Montagnais et des Hurons. ICA, XXX, 151-54. 1955.

--- Rites Paiens de la Foret Quebecoise. CD, XVIII, 129-55. 1953.

Rousseau, J.J., and Currier, J.P. Notes sur le folklore zoologique des Mistassini et particulièrement la peche. ACFAS, XIII, 117-8. 1947.

Rousseau, J.J. and Raymond, M. Le Folklore Botanique de Caughnawaga. Contributions de l'Institut Botanique de l'Université Montréal, LV, 7-74. 1945.

Rousseau, M. La Crainte de l'Iroquois au Lac Mistassini. ACFAS, XIII, 119-20. 1947.

Rousseau, M. and J.J. La Ceremonie de la Tente Agitée chez les Mistassini. ICA, XXVIII, 307-15. 1947.

Schmidt, W. Die Ostzentral-Algonkin. UG, II, 459-74; V, 531-54; VII, 727-60. 1929, 1934, 1940.

Sirois, L. Montagnais sans maitre: Ilnoimun e kakatshishkotomoakent. 135 pp. Saguenay, 1936.

Speck, F.G. Analysis of Eskimo and Indian Skin-dressing Methods in Labrador. Ethnos, II, 345-53. 1937.

--- Central Eskimo and Indian Dot Ornamentation. IN, II, 151-72. 1925.

--- Culture Problems in Northeastern North America, PAPS, LXV, 274-82. 1926.

--- Dogs of the Labrador Indians. NH, XXV, 58-64. 1925.

--- The Double-Curve Motive in Northeastern Algonkian Art. MCDM, XLII, 1-17. 1914.

--- Eskimo and Indian Backgrounds in Southern Labrador. GM, XXXVIII, 1-17, 143-63. 1935-36.

--- Ethical Attributes of the Labrador Indians. AA, n.s., XXXV, 559-94. 1933.

--- Family Hunting Territories of the Lake St. John Montagnais. A, XXII, 387-403. 1927.

--- Family Hunting Territories of the Waswanipi Indians. IN, V, 42-59. 1928.

--- Game Totems among the Northeastern Algonkians. AA, n.s., XIX, 9-18. 1917.

--- Hunting Charms of the Montagnais and Mistassini. INM, Ser. 2, XIII, 19 pp. 1921.

--- In Montagnais Country. American Indian Life, ed. E.C.Parsons, pp. 87-97. New York, 1925.

--- An Incident in Montagnais Winter Life. NH, XXVI, 61-7. 1926.

--- Indian and Eskimo Backgrounds in Southern Labrador. GM, XXXVIII, 1-17, 143-63. 1935.

--- Kinship Terms and the Family Band among the Northeastern Algonkian. AA, n.s., XX, 143-61. 1918.

--- Mammoth or "Stiff-Legged Bear." AA, n.s., XXXVII, 159-63. 1935.

--- Medicine Practices of the Northeastern Algonquians. ICA, XIX, 303-21. 1915.

--- Mistassini Hunting Territories. AA, n.s., XXV, 452-71. 1923.

--- Mistassini Notes. IN, VII, 410-57. 1930.

--- Modern and Classical Soul Philosophy among Stone Age Savages of Labrador. GM, XXVIII, 112-17. 1926.

--- Montagnais and Naskapi Tales. JAFL, XXXVIII, 1-32. 1925.

--- Montagnais Art in Birch-Bark. INM, XI, 45-157. 1937.

--- The Montagnais Indians. SW, XXXVIII, 148-54. 1909.

--- Montagnais-Naskapi Bands and Early Eskimo Distribution in the Labrador Peninsula. AA, n.s., XXXIII, 557-600. 1931.

Speck, F.G. The Montagnais of Labrador. Home
Geographic Monthly, II, i, 7-12. 1932.

--- More Algonkian Scapulimancy from the North.
Ethnos, IV, 21-8. 1939.

--- Myths from Little Whale River. JAFL, XXVIII,
70-7. 1915.

--- Reptile-Lore of the Northern Indians. JAFL,
XXXVI, 273-80. 1923.

--- Some Naskapi Myths from Little Whale River.
JAFL, XXVIII, 70-7. 1915.

--- Spiritual Beliefs among the Labrador Indians.
ICA, XXI, i, 266-75. 1924.

--- Swimming-Paddles among Northern Indians. AA,
n.s., XXXIX, 726-7. 1937.

Speck, F.G., and Eiseley, L.C. Montagnais-Naskapi Bands and Family Hunting of the Central and
Southeastern Labrador Peninsula. PAPS, LXXXV,
215-42. 1942.

Speck, F.G., and Heye, G.G. Hunting Charms of
the Montagnais and the Mistassini. INM, ser. 2,
XIII, 5-19. 1921.

Stearns, W.A. Labrador, pp. 259-68. Boston, 1884.

Stephen, C.N. Kosoak River Brigade. B, CCLXXII,
36-43. 1941.

Stewart, T.D. Anthropometric Observations on the
Eskimos and Indians of Labrador. FMAS, XXXI,
1-163. 1939.

Strong, W.D. Cross-Cousin Marriage and the Culture
of the Northeastern Algonkian. AA, n.s., XXXI,
277-88. 1929.

--- A Stone Age Culture from Northern Labrador. AA,
n.s., XXXII, 126-44. 1930.

Tanner, V. Folkrörelser och kulturväxlingar pa
Labrador-halvön. Svensk Geografisk Arsbok, XV,
80-126. 1939.

--- Outlines of the Geography; Life and Customs of
Newfoundland-Labrador. Acta Geographica, VIII,
i, 437-891. 1944.

Tantaquidgeon, G. Notes on the Origin and Uses of
Plants of the Lake St. John Montagnais. JAFL,
XLV, 265-67. 1932.

Thwaites, R.G., ed. The Jesuit Relations and Allied
Documents. 74 vols. Cleveland, 1896-1901.

Townsend, C.W., ed. Captain Cartwright and His
Labrador Journal. 385 pp. Boston, 1911.

Turner, L.M. On the Indians and Eskimos of the
Ungava District. PTRSC, V, ii, 108-19. 1887.

--- Scraper of the Naskopie (Naynaynots) Indians.
AA, I, 186-8. 1888.

--- The Single-headed Drum of the Naskopie.
PUSNM, XI, 433-4. 1888.

Walker, L.J. Jawinikom's Tale. MWF, V, 35-36.
1955.

Walker, L.J. Indian Burial Customs. JAFL, LXIII,
239-40. 1950.

Wallace, D. The Long Labrador Trail. 315 pp.
New York, 1907.

Waugh, F. The Naskopi Indians of Labrador and
Their Neighbors. Transactions of the Women's
Canadian Historical Society of Ottawa, IX, 126-
36. 1925.

8. OJIBWA

Including the Bungi, Chippewa, Missisauga, Plains
Ojibwa, and Saulteaux.

Densmore, F. Chippewa Customs. BBAE, LXXXVI,
1-204. 1929.

Dunning, R.W. Social and Economic Change among
the Northern Ojibwa. 227 pp. Toronto, 1959.

Hallowell, A.I. Culture and Experience. 450 pp.
Philadelphia, 1955.

Hilger, I. Chippewa Child Life and its Cultural
Background. BBAE, CXLVI, 218 pp. 1951.

Holmer, N.M. The Ojibway on Walpole Island, Ontario. Upsala Canadian Studies, IV, 91 pp. 1954.

Jenness, D. The Ojibwa Indians of Parry Island.
BCDM, LXXVIII, 1-115. 1935.

Landes, R. Ojibwa Sociology. CUCA, XXIX, 1-
144. 1937.

--- The Ojibwa Woman. CUCA, XXXI, 1-247. 1938.

Lips, E. Die Reisernte der Ojibwa-Indianer. 406 pp.
Berlin, 1956.

Müller, W. Die Blaue Hütte. 145 pp. Wiesbaden,
1954.

Skinner, A. Notes on the Eastern Cree and Northern
Saulteaux. APAM, IX, 117-77. 1911.

Adam, L. Esquisse d'une grammaire comparée de la
langue des Chippeways et de la langue des Crees.
ICA, I, ii, 88-148. 1875.

--- Examen grammatical comparé de seize langues
américaines. ICA, II, ii, 161-244. 1877.

Armstrong, H.G. Early Life among the Indians. 266
pp. Ashland, 1892.

Astrov, M., ed. The Winged Serpent, pp. 75-9.
New York, 1946.

Atwater, C. Remarks made on a Tour to Prairie du
Chien. 296 pp. Columbus, 1831.

Babbitt, F.E. Illustrative Notes concerning the
Minnesota Odjibwas. PAAAS, XXXVI, 303-7.
1887.

Babcock, W.M. The Minnesota Indian and His History. MA, XIX, 18-25. 1954.

Baldwin, W.W. Social Problems of the Ojibwa Indians in the Collins Area in Northwestern Ontario.
An, V, 51-124. 1957.

Balikci, A. Note sur le Midewiwin. An, II, 165-
217. 1956.

Ball, A.E. White Earth Consolidated Agency. RIT,
1890, 339-51.

Baner, J.G.R., and Bellaire, J.L. Kitch-iti-ki-pi.
61 pp. Manistique. Michigan, 1933.

Baraga, F. A Dictionary of the Otchipwe Language.
New edit. 2 vols. Montreal, 1878-80.

--- A Lecture Delivered in 1863. Acta et Dicta, V,
St. Paul, 1917.

--- A Theoretical and Practical Grammar of the
Otchipwe Language. 2d edit. 422 pp. Montreal,
1878.

Barnouw, V. Acculturation and Personality among
the Wisconsin Chippewa. MAAA, LXXII, 1-152.
1950.

--- The Phantasy World of a Chippewa Woman.
Psychiatry, XII, i, 67-76. 1949.

--- A Psychological Interpretation of a Chippewa
Origin Legend. JAFL, LXVIII, 73-85, 211-23,
341-55. 1955.

--- Reminiscences of a Chippewa Mide Priest. WA,
XXXV, 83-112. 1954.

Barrett, S.A. The Dream Dance of the Chippewa
and Menominee Indians of Northern Wisconsin.
BPMCM, I, 251-406. 1911.

Beauchamp, W.M. Indian Nations of the Great Lakes.
AAOJ, XVII, 321-5. 1895.

Belcourt, G.A. Department of Hudson's Bay.CMHS,
I, 227-36. 1872.

--- Principles de la langue des sauvages appelés
Sauteux. 146 pp. Quebec, 1839.

Beltrami, J.C. A Pilgrimage in Europe and America,
II, 227-300. London, 1828.

Bernard, M. Religion and Magic among the Cass
Lake Ojibwa. PM, II, 52-5. 1929.

Blackbird, A.J. History of the Ottawa and Chippewa
Indians of Michigan. 128 pp. Ypsilanti, 1887.

Blackwood, B. Tales of the Chippewa Indians. FL,
XL, 315-44. 1929.

Bleeker, S. The Chippewa Indians. 157 pp. New
York, 1955.

Blessing, F.K. Contemporary Costuming of Minnesota Chippewa Indians. MA, XX, iv, 1-8. 1956.

--- An Exhibition of Mide Magic. MA, XX, iv, 9-
13. 1956.

--- Miscellany. MA, XX, iv, 14-17. 1956.

--- The Physical Characteristics of Southern Ojibwa
Woodcraft. MA, XVIII, iv, 9-21. 1952.

Blessing, F.K. Some Observations on the Use of
Bark by the Southern Ojibwa Indians. MA, XIX,
iv, 3-14. 1954.

--- Some Uses of Bone, Horn, Claws and Teeth by
Minnesota Ojibwa Indians. MA, XX, iii, 1-11.
1956.

--- A Southern Ojibwa Glossary. MA, XIX, i, 2-57.
1954.

Bloomfield, L. Eastern Ojibwa. 282 pp. Ann Arbor,
1957.

Boas, F. Zur Anthropologie der nordamerikanischen
Indianer. VBGA, 1895, 367-411.

Boggs, S.T. Culture Change and the Personality of
Ojibwa Children. AA, LX, 47-58. 1958.

--- An Interactional Study of Ojibwa Socialization.
ASR, XXI, 191-8. 1956.

Breck, J.L. Chippeway Pictures from the Territory of
Minnesota. 29 pp. Hartford, 1910.

Brogan, D. Wild Rice Harvest. Frontiers, XX, v,
131-5. 1956.

Brown, D.M. Wisconsin Indian Corn Origin Myths.
WA, n.s., XXI, 19-27. 1940.

Brown, T.T. Plant Games and Toys of Chippewa
Children. WA, n.s., IX, 185-6. 1930.

Burden, H.N. Manitoulin. 164 pp. London, 1895.

Burton, F.R. American Primitive Music. 281 pp.
New York, 1909.

Bushnell, D.I. Burials of the Algonquian, Siouan
and Caddoan Tribes. BBAE, LXXXIII, 2-6. 1927.

--- An Ojibway Ceremony. AA, n.s., VII, 69-73.
1905.

--- Ojibway Habitations and Other Structures. ARSI,
1917, 609-17.

--- Sketches by Paul Kane in the Indian Country,
1845-1848. SMC, XCIX, i, 1-25. 1940.

--- Villages of the Algonquian, Siouan and Caddoan
Tribes. BBAE, LXXVII, 8-17. 1922.

Cadzow, D.A. Bark Records of the Bungi Midewin
Society. IN, III, 123-34. 1926.

Calkins, H. Indian Nomenclature of Northern Wisconsin, with a Sketch of the Manners and Customs of
the Chippewas. CSHSW, I, 119-26. 1854.

Cameron, D. The Nipigon Country. BCNO, II, 231-
65. 1890.

Campbell, G.M. Original Indian Dictionary of the
Ojibway or Chippewa Language. 80 pp. Minneapolis, 1940.

Cappel, J.L'S. Chippewa Tales. 64 pp. Los Angeles, 1928.

Carlson, E.J. Indian Rice Camps. Indians at Work,
II, vii, 16-23. 1934.

Carson, W. Ojibway Tales. JAFL, XXX, 491-3.
1917.

Carver, J. Travels through the Interior Parts of North America. 360 pp. London, 1778.

Casagrande, J.B. John Mink, Ojibwa Informant. WA, XXXVI, 106-27. 1955.

--- Ojibwa Bear Ceremonialism. ICA, XXIX, ii, 113-17. 1952.

--- The Ojibwa's Psychic Universe. Tomorrow, IV, iii, 33-40. 1956.

Caudill, W. Psychological Characteristics of Acculturated Wisconsin Ojibwa Children. AA, n.s., LI, 409-27. 1949.

Chamberlain, A.F. The Language of the Mississagas of Skugog. 84 pp. Philadelphia, 1892.

--- Maple Sugar and the Indians. AA, o.s., IV, 381-84. 1891.

--- A Mississaga Legend of Naniboju. JAFL, V, 291-2. 1892.

--- Nanibozhu amongst the Otchipwe, Mississagas, and Other Algonkian Tribes. JAFL, IV, 193-213. 1891.

--- Notes on the History, Customs, and Beliefs of the Mississagua Indians. JAFL, I, 150-60. 1888.

--- Tales of the Mississaguas. JAFL, II, 141-7; III, 149-54. 1889-90.

--- The Two Brothers: a Mississagua Legend. PAAAS, XXXVIII, 353. 1889.

Chatfield, W. The Midewiwin Songs of Fine-Day. WHO, XV, x, 1-2. 1954.

Coatsworth, E.S. The Indians of Quetico. 68 pp. Toronto, 1956.

Coleman, B. Decorative Designs of the Ojibwa of Northern Minnesota. CUAS, XII, 1-125. 1947.

--- The Ojibwa and the Wild Rice Problem. AQ, I, 79-88. 1953.

--- Religion and Magic among the Cass Lake Ojibwa. PM, II, 52-3. 1929.

--- The Religion of the Ojibwa of Northern Minnesota. PM, X, 33-57. 1937.

Cooper, J.M. Field Notes on Northern Algonkian Magic. ICA, XXIII, 513-18. 1928.

--- Notes on the Ethnology of the Otchipwe of the Lake of the Woods and of Rainy Lake. CUAS, III, 1-29. 1936.

--- The Shaking Tent Rite among Plains and Forest Algonquians. PM, XVII, 60-84. 1944.

Copway, G. Indian Life and Indian History. 266 pp. Boston, 1860.

--- The Life, Letters and Speeches of Kah-ge-ga-gah-bowh, pp. 11-48. New York, 1850.

--- The Traditional History and Characteristic Sketches of the Ojibway Nation. 298 pp. London, 1850.

Coues, E., ed. Manuscript Journals of Alexander Henry and of David Thompson. 3 vols. New York, 1897.

Culkin, W.E. Tribal Dance of the Ojibway Indians. Minnesota History Bulletin, I, 83-93. 1915.

Dally, N. Tracks and Trails. 138 pp. Walker, 1931.

Davidson, J.F. Ojibwa Songs. JAFL, LVIII, 303-5. 1945.

Davidson, J.N. In Unnamed Wisconsin. 314 pp. Milwaukee, 1895.

Delorme, D.P. Emancipation and the Turtle Mountain Chippewas. AmI, VII, i, 11-20. 1954.

Densmore, F. Chippewa Music. BBAE, XLV, 1-209; LIII, 1-334. 1910-13.

--- The Importance of the Mental Concept in Indian Art. M, XXII, 96-9. 1948.

--- Material Culture among the Chippewa. SMC, LXX, ii, 114-18. 1919.

--- Music of the Winnebago, Chippewa, and Pueblo Indians. EFWSI, 1930, 217-24.

--- The Native Art of the Chippewa. AA, n.s., XLIII, 678-81. 1941.

--- An Ojibwa Prayer Ceremony. AA, n.s., IX, 443-4. 1907.

--- Poems from Sioux and Chippewa Songs. 23 pp. Washington, 1917.

--- The Rhythm of Sioux and Chippewa Music. AAA, IX, 59-67. 1920.

--- Study of Chippewa Material Culture. SMC, LXVIII, xii, 95-100. 1918.

--- Uses of Plants by the Chippewa Indians. ARBAE, XLIV, 275-397. 1927.

Doty, J. Northern Wisconsin in 1820. CSHSW, VII, 195-206. 1876.

Dougherty, P. A Chippewa Primer. 84 pp. New York, 1844.

--- Ojibwa of Grand Traverse Bay. HCPIT, II, 458-69. 1852.

Douglas, F.H. The Ojibwa or Chippewa Indians. DAMLS, XXXVI, 1-4. 1931.

Ducatel, J.J. A Fortnight among the Chippewas of Lake Superior. Indian Miscellany, ed. W.W. Beach, pp. 361-78. Albany, 1877.

Dunning, R.W. Ethnic Relations and Marginal Man in Canada. HO, XVIII, iii, 117-22.

--- Rules of Residence and Ecology among the Northern Ojibwa. AA, LXI, 806-16. 1959.

--- Some Implications of Economic Change in Northern Ojibwa Social Structure. CJEPS, XXIV, 562-6. 1958.

Eastman, C.A. Life and Handicrafts of the Northern Ojibwas. SW, XL, 273-8. 1911.

Elliott, R.R. The Chippewas and Ottawas. American
    Catholic Quarterly Review, XXII, 18-46. 1897.

--- The Chippewas of Lake Superior. American
    Catholic Quarterly Review, XXI, 354-73. 1896.

Engelhardt, Z. Anishinabe Neganiod. Harbor Springs,
    Michigan, 1901.

Evatt, H. The Red Canoe. 137 pp. Indianapolis,
    1940.

Federal Writers' Projects. Wisconsin Indian Place
    Legends, pp. 26-7, 40-50. Milwaukee, 1936.

Flannery, R. The Cultural Position of the Spanish
    River Indians. PM, XIII, 1-25. 1940.

Friedl, E. A Note on Birchbark Transparencies. AA,
    n.s., XLVI, 149-50. 1944.

--- Persistence in Chippewa Culture and Personality.
    AA, LVIII, 814-25. 1956.

Gates, R.R. Pedigree Study of Amerindian Crosses
    in Canada. JAI, LVIII, 511-32. 1928.

Gilfillan, J.A. Ojibwa Characteristics. SW, XXXI,
    260-62. 1902.

--- The Ojibways of Minnesota. CMHS, IX, 55-128.
    1901.

Gillin, J. Acquired Drives in Culture Contact. AA,
    n.s., XLIV, 545-54. 1942.

Gillin, J. and Raimy, V. Acculturation and Per-
    sonality. ASR, V, 371-80. 1940.

Gilmore, M.R. Some Chippewa Uses of Plants.
    PMA, XVII, 119-43. 1933.

Godsell, P.H. The Ojibwa Indian. Canadian Ge-
    ological Journal, IV, 51-66. 1932.

Grant, J.C.B. Anthropometry of the Cree and Sault-
    eaux Indians in Northeastern Manitoba. BCDM,
    LIX, 1-73. 1929.

--- Anthropometry of the Lake Winnipeg Indians.
    AJPA, VII, 299-315. 1924.

Grant, P. The Sauteux Indians. BCNO, II, 303-
    66. 1890.

Greenlees, S. Indian Canoe Makers. B, CCLXXXV,
    i, 46-9. 1954.

Greenman, E.F. Chieftainship among Michigan In-
    dians. MHM, XXIV, 361-79. 1940.

Hall, G.L. Me Papoose Sitter. 243 pp. New York,
    1955.

Hallowell, A.I. Acculturation Processes and Per-
    sonality Changes as Indicated by the Rorschach Tech-
    nique. Rorschach Research Exchange, VI, 42-50.
    1942.

--- Aggression in Saulteaux Society. Psychiatry, III,
    395-407. 1940.

--- Concordance of Ojibwa Narratives in the Pub-
    lished Works of Henry R. Schoolcraft. JAFL, LIX,
    136-53. 1946.

Hallowell, A.I. Cross-Cousin Marriage in the Lake
    Winnipeg Area. PPAS, I, 95-110. 1937.

--- Culture and Mental Disorder. Journal of Abnor-
    mal and Social Psychology, XXIX, 1-9. 1934.

--- Fear and Anxiety as Cultural and Individual Vari-
    ables in a Primitive Society. JSP, IX, 25-47. 1938.

--- Freudian Symbolism in the Dream of a Saulteaux
    Indian. Man, XXXVIII, 47-8. 1938.

--- The Incidence, Character, and Decline of Poly-
    gyny among the Lake Winnipeg Cree and Saulteaux.
    AA, n.s., XL, 235-56. 1938.

--- Magic: the Role of Conjuring in Saulteaux So-
    ciety. Papers presented before the Monday Night
    Group, 1939-40, ed. M.A.May, pp. 94-115. New
    Haven, 1940.

--- Myth, Culture and Personality. AA, n.s., XLIX,
    544-56. 1947.

--- Notes on the Material Culture of the Island Lake
    Saulteaux. JSAP, n.s., XXX, 129-40. 1938.

--- Notes on the Northern Range of Zizania in Mani-
    toba. Rhodora, XXXVII, 302-4. 1935.

--- Ojibwa Personality and Acculturation. ICA, XXIX,
    ii, 105-12. 1952.

--- Pagan Tribe in Ontario. EP, XXXIII, 204-5.
    1932.

--- The Passing of the Midewiwin in the Lake Winni-
    peg Region. AA, n.s., XXXVIII, 32-51. 1928.

--- "Popular" Responses and Cultural Differences.
    Rorschach Research Exchange, IX, 153-68. 1945.

--- Psychic Stresses and Culture Patterns. American
    Journal of Psychiatry, XCII, 1291-310. 1936.

--- The Role of Conjuring in Saulteaux Society.
    PPAS, II, 1-96. 1942.

--- The Rorschach Method as an Aid in the Study of
    Personalities in Primitive Society. Character and
    Personality, IX, 235-45. 1941.

--- The Rorschach Technique in the Study of Per-
    sonality and Culture. AA, n.s., XLVII, 195-210.
    1945.

--- Shabwan: a Dissocial Indian Girl. American
    Journal of Orthopsychiatry, VIII, 329-40. 1938.

--- Sin, Sex and Sickness in Saulteaux Belief. Brit-
    ish Journal of Medical Psychology, XVIII, 191-7.
    1939.

--- The Social Function of Anxiety in a Primitive
    Society. ASR, VI, 869-81. 1941.

--- Some Empirical Aspects of Northern Saulteaux
    Religion. AA, n.s., XXXVI, 389-404. 1934.

--- Some European Folktales of the Berens River
    Saulteaux. JAFL, LII, 155-79. 1939.

--- Some Psychological Aspects of Measurement
    among the Saulteaux. AA, n.s., XLIV, 62-77. 1942.

Hallowell, A.I. The Spirits of the Dead in Saulteaux Life and Thought. JAI, LXX, 29-51. 1940.

--- Temporal Orientation in Western Civilization and in a Preliterate Society, AA, n.s., XXXIX, 647-70. 1937.

--- The Use of Projective Techniques in the Study of the Socio-psychological Aspects of Acculturation. Journal of Projective Techniques, XV, 27-44. 1951.

--- Values, Acculturation and Mental Health. American Journal of Orthopsychiatry, XX, 732-43. 1950.

--- Was Cross-Cousin Marriage practised by the North-Central Algonkian? ICA, XXIII, 519-44. 1928.

Hamilton, J.C. The Algonquin Manabozho and Hiawatha. JAFL, XV, 229-33. 1903.

Hammond, J.H. The Ojibway of Lakes Huron and Simcoe. AAR, 1904, 71-3.

Harmon, D.W. A Journal of Voyages and Travels in the Interior of North America, ed. W.L. Grant, pp. 269-334. Toronto, 1911.

Harrington, M.R. You Can't Rush an Indian. M, XXVII, i, 29-30. 1953.

Hart, I.H. The Story of Beengwa. MiH, IX, 319-30. 1928.

Hasketh, J. History of the Turtle Mountain Chippewa. North Dakota State Historical Society Collections, V, 85-124. 1923.

Henry, A. Travels and Adventures in Canada, ed. M.M. Quaife. 340 pp. Chicago, 1921.

Hickerson, H. The Feast of the Dead among the Seventeenth Century Algonkians of the Upper Great Lakes. AA, LXII, 81-107. 1960.

--- The Genesis of a Trading Post Band: the Pembina Chippewa. E, III, 289-345. 1956.

Hickerson, H., ed. Journal of Charles Jean Baptiste Chaboillez, 1797-1798. E, VI, 265-320, 363-427. 1959.

Hilger, M.I. Ceremonia para dar nombre a un niño Indio Chippewa. AI, IV, 237-42. 1944.

--- Ceremonia para dar nombre a un niño Chippewa. Anales de la Sociedad de Geografía e Historia, XXII, 166-71. 1947.

--- Chippewa Burial and Mourning Customs. AA, n.s., XLVI, 564-8. 1944.

--- Chippewa Customs. PM, IX, 17-24. 1936.

--- Chippewa Hunting and Fishing Customs. Minnesota Conservationist, ii-iii, 17-9. April, 1936.

--- Chippewa Interpretations of Natural Phenomena. SM, XLV, 178-9. 1937.

--- Chippewa Pre-natal Food and Conduct Taboos. PM, IX, 46-8. 1936.

Hilger, M.I. In the Early Days of Wisconsin. WA, XVI, n.s., 32-49. 1936.

--- Indian Women Making Birch-bark Receptacles. Indians at Work, III, iii, 19-21. 1935.

--- Indian Women Preparing Bulrush Mats. Indians at Work, II, ii, 41. 1935.

--- Letters and Documents of Bishop Baraga Extant in the Chippewa Country. RACHS, XLVII, 292-302. 1936.

--- Naming a Chippewa Indian Child. WA, XXXIX, 120-6. 1958.

--- A Social Study of One Hundred Fifty Chippewa Indian Families. 251 pp. Washington, 1939.

--- Some Phases of Chippewa Material Culture. A, XXXII, 780-2. 1937.

Hill, H.C., ed. A Dictionary of the Chippewa Indian Language. 16 pp. Flint, 1943.

Hind, H.Y. Narrative of the Canadian Red River Exploring Expedition. 2 vols. London, 1860.

--- North-West Territory. 201 pp. Toronto, 1859.

Hindley, J.I. Indian Legends. 22 pp. Barrie, Ont., 1885.

Hockett, C.F. The Conjunct Modes in Ojibwa and Potawatomi. Lg, XXVI, 278-82. 1950.

Hoffman, W.J. The Midewiwin or "Grand Medicine Society" of the Ojibwa. ARBAE, VII, 143-300. 1886.

--- Notes on Ojibwa Folk-Lore. AA, II, 215-23. 1889.

--- Pictography and Shamanistic Rites of the Ojibwa. AA, I, 209-29. 1888.

--- Remarks on Ojibwa Ball Play. AA, III, 133-5. 1890.

Honigmann, J.J. Attawapiskat-Blend of Traditions. An, VI, 57-68. 1957.

Houghton, F. The Indian Occupancy of the Niagara Frontier. BBSNS, IX, 263-374. 1909.

Howard, J.H. The Sun Dance of the Turtle Mountain Ojibwa. NDHQ, XIX, 249-64. 1952.

Hrdlicka, A. Anthropological Work among the Sioux and Chippewa. SMC, XLVI, xvii, 92-9. 1917.

--- Anthropology of the Chippewa. Holmes Anniversary Volume, pp. 198-227. Washington, 1916.

--- Trip to the Chippewa Indians of Minnesota. SMC, LXVI, iii, 71-5. 1916.

Hugolin. L'idée spiritualiste et l'idée morale chez les Chippewas. ICA, XV, i, 329-35. 1906.

Hurlburt, T. A Memoir on the Inflections of the Chippewa Tongue. HCPIT, IV, 385-96. 1854.

James, E., ed. A Narrative of the Captivity and Adventures of John Tanner. 426 pp. New York, 1830.

Jenks, A.E. The Bear-Maiden. JAFL, XV, 33-5. 1902.

Jenks, A.E. The Childhood of Ji-shib, the Ojibwa. Madison, 1900.

--- Indian-White Amalgamation. University of Minnesota Studies in the Social Sciences, VI, 1-24. 1916.

--- The Wild Rice Gatherers of the Upper Lakes. ARBAE, XIX, ii, 1013-137. 1898.

Joblin, E.E.M. The Education of the Indians of Western Ontario. Ontario College of Education Bulletin, XIII, 1-138. 1948.

Johnson, F. Notes on the Ojibwa and Potawatomi of the Parry Island Reservation. IN, VI, 193-216. 1929.

Johnston, G. Ojibwa of St. Mary's. HCPIT, II, 458-69. 1852.

Jones, J.A. The Political Organization of the Three Fires. PIAS, LXIII, 46. 1953.

Jones, P. History of the Ojebway Indians. 278 pp. London, 1861.

--- Life and Journals of Kah-ke-wa-quo-na-by. 435 pp. Toronto, 1860.

Jones, V.H. A Chippewa Method of manufacturing Wooden Brooms. PMA, XX, 23-30. 1934.

--- Notes on the Manufacture of Cedar-bark Mats by the Chippewa Indians. PMA, XXXII, 341-63. 1946.

--- Notes on the Preparation and the Uses of Basswood Fiber by the Indians of the Great Lakes Region. PMA, XXII, 1-14. 1936.

--- Some Chippewa and Ottawa Uses of Sweet Grass. PMA, XXI, 21-31. 1935.

Jones, W. Central Algonkin. AAR, 1905, 136-46.

--- Ojibwa Tales from North Shore of Lake Superior. JAFL, XXIX, 368-91. 1916.

--- Ojibwa Texts. PAES, VII, i, 1-501; ii, 1-771. 1917-19.

Josselin de Jong, J.P.B. de. A Few Otchipwe-Songs. IAE, XX, 189-90. 1912.

--- Original Odzibwe-Texts. BA, Beiheft V, 1-54. 1913.

Keating, W.H. Narrative of an Expedition to the Source of St. Peter's River, II, 151-73. Philadelphia, 1824.

Kidd, K.E. Burial of an Ojibwa Chief, Muskoka District, Ontario. PA, XXI, i-ii, 3-8, 31-32. 1951.

Kinietz, W.V. Birch Bark Records among the Chippewa. PIAS, XLIX, 38-40. 1940.

--- Chippewa Village. BCIS, XXV, 1-259. 1947.

--- The Indian Tribes of the Western Great Lakes. OCMA, X, 317-29. 1940.

Kinietz, W.V., and Jones, V.H. Notes on the Manufacture of Rush Mats among the Chippewa. PMA, XXVII, 525-37. 1941.

Koeninger, R.C. An Experiment in Intercultural Education. PMA, XXXIII, 407-12. 1947.

Kohl, J.G. Kitchi-Gami. 428pp. London, 1860; 451 pp., Minneapolis, 1956.

--- Kitschi-Gami. 2 vols. Bremen, 1859.

Kurath, G.P. Chippewa Sacred Songs in Religious Metamorphosis. SM, LXXIX, 311-17. 1954.

--- Wild Rice Gatherers of Today. AA, LIX, 713. 1957.

Lafleur, L.J. On the Midé of the Ojibway. AA, n. s., XLII, 705-7. 1940.

Laidlaw, G.E. Ojibwa Myths and Tales. AAR, 1914, 77-9; 1915, 71-90; 1916, 84-92; 1918, 74-110; 1920, 66-85; 1921-22, 84-99; 1924-25, 34-80.

--- Ojibway Myths and Tales. WA, n.s., I, 28-38. 1922.

Landes, R. The Abnormal among the Ojibwa. Journal of Abnormal and Social Psychology, XXXIII, 14-33. 1938.

--- The Ojibwa of Canada. Cooperation and Competition among Primitive Peoples, ed. M. Mead, pp. 87-126. New York, 1937.

--- The Personality of the Ojibwa. Character and Personality, VI, 51-60. 1937.

Lathrop, S.E. A Historical Sketch of the Old Mission. Ashland, Wisconsin, 1905.

Leitch, A. Porcupine Crafts. CGJ, LI, 128-9. 1955.

Levi, M.C. Chippewa Indians of Yesterday and Today. 385 pp. New York, 1956.

Lincoln, J.S. The Dream in Primitive Cultures. 359 pp. London, 1935.

Linderman, F.B. Indian Old-man Stories. 169 pp. New York, 1920.

--- Indian Why Stories. 236 pp. New York, 1915.

Lips, E. Das Indianerbuch. 443 pp. Leipzig, 1956.

--- Wanderungen und Wirtschaftsformen der Ojibwa-Indianer. Wissenschaftliche Zeitschrift der Universität Leipzig, Gesellschafts- und Sprachwissenschaftliche Reihe, I, 1-38. 1951-52.

--- Zizania Aquatica als bestimmender Faktor im Leben der Ojibwa-Indianer von Nett Lake (Minnesota). Huitième Congrès Internationale de Botanique, Rapports et Communications parvenus avant le congrès au Sections 14, 15 et 16, pp. 45-9. Paris, 1954.

Lips, J.E. Notes on Some Ojibway-Traps. Ethnos, II, 354-60. 1937.

Lloyd, T. Wild Rice in Canada. CGJ, XIX, 288-300. 1939.

Long, J.K. Voyages and Travels of an Indian Interpreter and Trader, ed. M.M. Quaife. 238 pp. Chicago, 1922.

Lowie, R.H. Ojibwa. ERE, IX, 454-8. 1917.

Lyford, C.A. The Crafts of the Ojibwa. IH, V, 1-216. 1943.

McDonnell, J. Some Account of the Red River. BCNO, I, 265-95. 1889.

McGee, W J. Ojibwa Feather Symbolism. AA, XI, 177-80. 1898.

McKenney, T.L. Memories, Official and Personal. 490 pp. New York, 1846.

--- Sketches of a Tour of the Lakes. 493 pp. Baltimore, 1827.

McLean, J. Notes of a Twenty-five Years' Service in the Hudson's Bay Territory, ed. W.S. Wallace. PCS, XIX, 1-402. 1932.

Matson, G.A. et al. A Study of the Hereditary Blood Factors among the Chippewa Indians of Minnesota. AJPA, n.s., XII, 413-26. 1954.

Meakins, C. Old Albert of Chemung. Forest and Stream, XCI, 5-7, 34-8, 64-5, 85-7. 1921.

Means, P.A. Preliminary Survey of the Remains of the Chippewa Settlements on La Pointe Island. SMC, LXVI, xiv, 1-15. 1917.

Merwin, B.W. Some Ojibway Buffalo Robes. MJ, VII, 93-6. 1916.

Michelson, T. Maiden Sacrifice among the Ojibwa. AA, n.s., XXXVI, 628-9. 1934.

--- Ojibwa Tales. JAFL, XXIV, 249-50. 1911.

--- Studies of the Fox and Ojibwa Indians. SMC, LXXVIII, i, 111-13. 1926.

Monckton, E. The White Canoe. 138 pp. New York, 1904.

Mooney, J., and Thomas, C. Chippewa. BBAE, XXX, i, 277-81. 1907.

--- Missisauga. BBAE, XXX, i, 909-10. 1907.

Moran, G. Ojibwa of Saganaw. HCPIT, II, 458-69. 1852.

Morgan, L.H. The Indian Journals, 1859-62, pp. 82-4, 114-5. Ann Arbor, 1959.

--- Systems of Consanguinity and Affinity. SCK, XVII, 291-382. 1871.

Morse, J. A Report to the Secretary of War. 400 pp. New Haven, 1822.

Morse, R.F. The Chippewas of Lake Superior. CSHSW, III, 338-69. 1856.

Myers, F.A. The Bear-Walk. Inland Seas, IX, 12-18, 98-103, 169-74, 250-54. 1953.

Nasatir, A.P. Before Lewis and Clark. 2 vols. 882 pp. St. Louis, 1952.

Neill, E.D. History of the Ojibways. CMHS, V, 395-510. 1885.

O'Brien, F.G. Minnesota Pioneer Sketches. 372 pp. Minneapolis, 1904.

Orr, R.B. The Chippewa Indians. AAR, 1918, 9-23.

--- The Mississaugas. AAR, 1915, 7-18.

Owl, F.M. Seven Chiefs Rule the Red Lake Band. AmI, VI, iii, 3-12. 1952.

Perrot, N. Memoir on the Manners, Customs, and Religion of the Savages of North America. ITUMV, I, 25-272. 1911.

--- Mémoire sur les moeurs, coustumes et relligion des sauvages de l'Amérique septentrionale. 341 pp. Paris, 1864.

Piper, W.S. The Eagle of Thunder Cape. 235 pp. New York, 1924.

Plischke, H. Eine Bilderschrift auf Birkenrinde, Odjibeway-Indianer. ZE, LXXXII, 171-73. 1957.

Potherie, B. de la. History of the Savage Peoples who are Allies of New France. ITUMV, I, 273-372; II, 13-136. 1911-12.

Pruitt, O.J. A Tribe of Chippewa Indians. Annals of Iowa, 3rd series, XXXIII, 295-97. 1955-57.

Quimby, G.I. New Evidence Links Chippewa to Prehistoric Cultures. Bulletin of the Chicago Natural History Museum, XXIX, iv, 7-8. 1958.

Radin, P. Ethnological Notes on the Ojibwa of Southeastern Ontario. AA, n.s., XXX, 659-68. 1928.

--- An Introductive Enquiry in the Study of Ojibwa Religion. Papers and Records of the Ontario Historical Society, XII, 210-18. 1914.

--- Ojibwa and Ottawa Puberty Dreams. Essays in Anthropology presented to A.L. Kroeber, pp. 233-64. Berkeley, 1936.

--- Ojibwa Ethnological Chit-Chat. AA, n.s., XXVI, 491-533. 1924.

--- Some Aspects of Puberty Fasting among the Ojibwa. MBCDM, II, 69-78. 1914.

--- Some Myths and Tales of the Ojibwa of Southeastern Ontario. MCDM, XLVIII, 1-83. 1914.

Radin, P., and Reagan, A.B. Ojibwa Myths and Tales. JAFL, XLI, 61-146. 1928.

Reagan, A.B. The Bois Fort Chippewa. WA, n.s., III, 101-32. 1924.

--- The Flood Myth of the Chippewas. PIAS, XXIX, 347-52. 1919.

--- Flood Myths of the Bois Fort Chippewas. TKAS, XXX, 437-43. 1921.

--- Hunting and Fishing of Various Tribes of Indians. TKAS, XXX, 443-8. 1921.

--- Medicine Songs of George Farmer. AA, n.s., XXIV, 332-69. 1922.

--- The O-ge-che-dah or Head-Men Dance of the Bois Fort Indians. Americana, XXVIII, 302-6. 1934.

Reagan, A.B. Picture Writings of the Chippewa In-
    dians. WA, n.s., VI, 80-3. 1927.
--- Plants used by the Bois Fort Chippewa. WA, n.
    s., VII, 230-48. 1928.
--- Rainy Lakes Indians. WA, n.s., II, 140-7.
    1923.
--- Some Chippewa Medicinal Receipts. AA, n.s.,
    XXIII, 246-9. 1921.
--- Some Games of the Bois Fort Ojibwa. AA, n.s.,
    XXI, 264-78. 1919.
--- Some Plants of the Bois Fort Indian Reservation
    and Vicinity in Minnesota. Transactions of the
    Illinois State Academy of Science, XIV, 61-70.
    1921.
Reid, A.P. Religious Beliefs of the Ojibois or Sau-
    teux Indians. JAI, III, 106-13. 1873.
Richardson, J. Arctic Searching Expedition, pp. 262-
    77. New York, 1852.
Riggs, S.R. Protestant Missions in the Northwest.
    CMHS, VI, 117-88. 1894.
Ritzenthaler, R. The Acquisition of Surnames by the
    Chippewa Indians. AA, n.s., XLVII, 175-7. 1945.
--- The Building of a Chippewa Indian Birch-Bark
    Canoe. BPMCM, XIX, 53-99. 1950.
--- The Ceremonial Destruction of Sickness by the
    Wisconsin Chippewa. AA, n.s., XLVII, 320-2.
    1945.
--- Chippewa Preoccupation with Health. BPMCM,
    XIX, 175-258. 1953.
--- The Chippewa Indian Method of securing and
    tanning Deerskin. WA, n.s., XXVIII, 6-13. 1947.
--- Impact of War on an Indian Community. AA, n.
    s., XLV, 325-6. 1943.
--- Totemic Insult among the Wisconsin Chippewa.
    AA, n.s., XLVII, 322-4. 1945.
Roddis, L.H. The Indian Wars of Minnesota. 329 pp.
    Cedar Rapids, 1956.
Rohr, J.F. Ojibway Trails. 33 pp. Ottawa, Illinois,
    1928.
Sagatoo, M.A. Wah Sash Kah Moqua. 140 pp. Bos-
    ton, 1897.
Schmidt, W. Die Ojibwa. UG, II, 475-507; V,
    555-64. 1929, 1934.
Schoolcraft, H.R. Algic Researches. 2 vols. New
    York, 1839.
--- The Myth of Hiawatha. 343 pp. Philadelphia,
    1856.
--- Mythology, Superstitions and Languages of the
    North American Indians. New York Theological
    Review, II, 96-121. 1835.
--- Narrative Journal of Travels from Detroit North-
    west through the Great Chain of American Lakes.
    419 pp. Albany, 1821.

Schoolcraft, H.R. Narrative of an Expedition through
    the Upper Mississippi to Itasca Lake. 307 pp. New
    York, 1834.
--- Oneóta, or Characteristics of the Red Race of
    America. 512 pp. New York, 1845.
--- Personal Memoirs of a Residence of Thirty Years
    with the Indian Tribes on the American Frontiers.
    703 pp. Philadelphia, 1851.
--- Summary Narrative of an Exploratory Expedition to
    the Sources of the Mississippi River. 596 pp. Phil-
    adelphia, 1855.
--- Travels in the Central Portions of the Mississippi
    Valley. 459 pp. New York, 1825.
Shields, J. Thrilling Adventures among the Sioux and
    Chippewas. BMHS, XIII, 275-82. 1957.
Sieber, S.A. The Saulteaux Indians. 160 pp. St.
    Boniface, Man., 1948.
--- The Saulteaux, Penobscot-Abenaki, and the Con-
    cept of Totemism. ACISA, IV, ii, 325-9. 1955.
Simms, S.C. The Metawin Society of the Bungees or
    Swampy Indians of Lake Winnipeg. JAFL, XIX, 330-3.
--- Myths of the Bungees or Swampy Indians of Lake
    Winnipeg. JAFL, XIX, 334-40. 1906.
Skinner, A. Bear Customs of the Cree and Other Al-
    gonkin Indians of Northern Ontario. Papers and
    Records of the Ontario Historical Society, XII, 203-
    9. 1914.
--- The Cultural Position of the Plains Ojibway. AA,
    n.s., XVI, 314-18. 1914.
--- European Tales from the Plains Ojibwa. JAFL, XXIX,
    330-40. 1916.
--- Medicine Ceremony of the Menomini, Iowa and
    Wahpeton Dakota. INM, IV, 309-26. 1920.
--- Ojibway and Cree of Central Canada. AMJ, X, 9-
    18. 1908.
--- Plains Ojibwa Tales. JAFL, XXXII, 280-305. 1919.
--- Political and Ceremonial Organization of the
    Plains-Ojibway. APAM, XI, 475-511. 1914.
--- The Sun Dance of the Plains-Ojibway. APAM, XVI,
    311-15. 1919.
--- A Visit to the Ojibway and Cree of Central Canada.
    AMJ, X, 9-18. 1910.
Slight, B. Indian Researches. 179 pp. Montreal,
    1844.
Smith, H.H. Botanizing among the Ojibwe. YPMCM,
    III, 38-47. 1923.
--- Ethnobotany of the Ojibwe Indians. BPMCM, IV,
    327-525. 1932.
Smith, H.I. Certain Shamanistic Ceremonies among
    the Ojibwas. AAOJ, XVIII, 282-4. 1896.
--- The Monster in the Tree: an Ojibwa Myth. JAFL,
    X, 324-5. 1897.
--- An Ojibwa Cradle. AAOJ, XVI, 302-3. 1894.

Smith, H.I. Some Ojibwa Myths and Traditions. JAFL, XIX, 215-30. 1906.

Snelling, W.J. Early Days at Prairie du Chien. Reports and Collections of the Wisconsin State Historical Society, V, i, 123-53. 1868.

--- Tales of the Northwest. 294 pp. Boston, 1830.

Speck, F.G. The Family Hunting Band as the Basis of Algonkian Social Organization. AA, n.s., XVII, 289-305. 1915.

--- Family Hunting Territories and Social Life of Various Algonkian Bands of the Ottawa Valley. MCDM, LXX, 11-30. 1915.

--- Kinship Terms and the Family Bands among the Northeastern Algonkian. AA, n.s., XX, 143-61. 1918.

--- Myths and Folk-Lore of the Timiskaming Algonquin and Timiskaming Ojibwa. MCDM, LXXI, 28-87. 1915.

Speck, F.G., and F.I. Ojibwa, Hiawatha's People. Home Geographic Monthly, II, iv, 7-12. 1932.

Spindler, G.D. Research Design and Ojibwa Personality Persistence. AA, LX, 934-36. 1958.

Stewart, O.C. Cart-Using Indians of the American Plains. ACISA, V, 351-5. 1960.

Stickney, G.P. Indian Use of Wild Rice. AA, IX, 115-21. 1896.

Stowe, G.C. Plants used by the Chippewa. WA, n.s., XXI, 8-13. 1940.

Summerfield, J. Sketch of Grammar of the Chippeway Language. 35 pp. Cazenovia, 1834.

Swanton, J.R. Some Neglected Data bearing on Cheyenne, Chippewa, and Dakota History. AA, n.s., XXXII, 156-60. 1930.

Sweet, G.W. Incidents of the Threatened Outbreak of Hole-in-the-Day. CMHS, VI, 401-8. 1894.

Telford, C.W. Test Performance of Full and Mixed-Blood North Dakota Indians. Journal of Comparative Psychology, XIV, 123-45. 1932.

Thompson, L. Attitudes and Acculturation. AA, n.s., L, 200-15. 1948.

Thompson, S. The Indian Legend of Hiawatha. Publications of the Modern Language Association, XXXVII, 128-40. 1928.

Thwaites, R.G., ed. The French Regime in Wisconsin. CSHSW, Vols. XVI-XVIII. 1902-08.

--- The Jesuit Relations and Allied Documents. 74 vols. Cleveland, 1896-1901.

Tomkins, W. Universal Indian Sign Language. 96 pp. San Diego, 1927.

Uhlenbeck, C.C. Ontwerp van eene vergelijkende vormleer van eenige Algonkin-talen. VKAW, n.s., XI, iii, 1-67. 1910.

Van Dusen, C. The Indian Chief. 216 pp. London, 1867.

Verwyst, F.C. Chippewa Exercises. Harbor Springs, 1901.

--- Geographical Names in Wisconsin, Minnesota and Michigan Having a Chippewa Origin. CSHSW, XII, 390-8. 1892.

--- Life and Labors of Rt. Rev. Frederic Baraga. 476 pp. Milwaukee, 1900.

--- Missionary Labors of Fathers Marquette, Menard, and Allouez. 262 pp. Chicago, 1886.

Voegelin, E.W. Notes on Ojibwa-Ottawa Pictography. PIAS, LI, 44-7. 1941.

Warren, W.W. History of the Ojibways. CMHS, V, 21-394. 1885.

--- Oral Traditions respecting the History of the Ojibwa Nation. HCPIT, II, 135-67. 1852.

West, G.A. Uses of Tobacco and the Calumet by Wisconsin Indians. WA, X, 5-64. 1911.

Whipple, H.B. Civilization and Christianization of the Ojibways of Minnesota. CMHS, IX, 129-42. 1901.

Wilcox, A.T. The Chippewa Sugar Camp. MHM, XXXVII, 276-85. 1953.

Wilford, L. History of the Chippewa. MA, XVII, ii, 3-10. 1951.

Wilson, E.F. Missionary Work among the Ojebway Indians. 255 pp. London, 1886.

--- The Ojebway Language. 412 pp. Toronto, 1874.

Winchell, N.H. The Aborigines of Minnesota, pp. 580-743. St. Paul, 1911.

Wood, W.J. Tularemia. Manitoba Medical Association, Review, XXXI, x, 641-4. 1951.

Wright, J.C. The Great Myth. 170 pp. Lansing, 1922.

Young, E.R. Algonquin Indian Tales. 256 pp. New York, 1903.

--- By Canoe and Dog-Train among the Cree and Salteaux Indians. 267 pp. London, 1890.

--- On the Indian Trail. 214 pp. New York, 1897.

--- Stories from Indian Wigwams and Northern Camp-Fires. 293 pp. New York, 1893.

Zschokke, H. Ein Besuch bei den Chippewas-Indianern in der Reservation White Earth in Nordamerika. Berichte der Leopoldinenstiftung in Kaiserthume Oesterreich, LI. 1881.

9. OTTAWA

Kinietz, W.V. The Indian Tribes of the Western Great Lakes. OCMA, X, 226-307. 1940.

Perrot, N. Memoir on the Manners, Customs, and Religion of the Savages of North America. ITUMV, I, 25-272. 1911.

--- Mémoire sur les moeurs, coustumes et relligion des sauvages de l'Amerique septentrionale.. 341 pp. Paris, 1864.

Bauman, R.F. The Last Ottawa. NOQ, XXIV, 4-9. 1951-52.

--- The Migration of the Ottawa Indians from the Maumee Valley to Walpole Island. NOQ, XXI, 86-112. 1949.

--- Pontiac's Successor. NOQ, XXVI, 8-38. 1954.

Beauchamp, W.M. Indian Nations of the Great Lakes. AAOJ, XVII, 321-5. 1895.

Bibaud, F.M. Biographie des sagamos illustrés de l'Amérique Septentrionale, pp. 213-21. Montreal, 1848.

Blackbird, A.J. History of the Ottawa and Chippewa Indians of Michigan. 128 pp. Ypsilanti, 1887.

Boas, F. Zur Anthropologie der nordamerikanischen Indianer. VBGA, 1895, 367-411.

Chamberlain, A.F. Nanibozhu amongst the Otchipwe, Mississagas, and Other Algonkian Tribes. JAFL, IV, 193-213. 1891.

Chamberlain, M.E. The Twenty-one Precepts of the Ottawa Indians. JAFL, V, 332-4. 1892.

Downes, R.C. The Ottawa Indians and the Erie and Kalamazoo Railroad. NOQ, XXIV, 136-38. 1952.

Elliott, R.R. The Chippewas and Ottawas. American Catholic Quarterly Review, XXII, 18-46. 1897.

Engelhardt, Z. Anishinabe Neganiod. Harbor Springs, Michigan, 1901.

Ettawageshik, F. Ghost Suppers. AA, n.s., XLV, 491-3. 1943.

Ettawageshik, J. Three True Tales from L'Arbre Croche. MWF, VII, 38-40. 1957.

Foreman, G. The Last Trek of the Indians, pp. 89-92, 190-93. Chicago, 1946.

Greenman, E.F. Chieftainship among Michigan Indians. MHM, XXIV, 361-79. 1940.

Hallowell, A.I. Was Cross-Cousin Marriage practised by the North-Central Algonkian? ICA, XXIII, 519-44. 1928.

Hamelin. Ottawas. TCAAS, II, 305-67. 1836.

Hamilton, J.C. The Algonquin Manabozho and Hiawatha. JAFL, XV, 229-33. 1903.

Hickerson, H. The Feast of the Dead among the Seventeenth Century Algonkians of the Upper Great Lakes. AA, LXII, 81-107. 1960.

Hilger, M.I. In the Early Days of Wisconsin. WA, XVI, 32-49. 1936.

Hootkins, H. Some Notes on the Ottawa Dialect. PMA, XXVI, 557-60. 1940.

Humphrey, N.B. The Mock Battle Greeting. JAFL, LIV, 186-90. 1941.

Hunter, A.F. Wampum Records of the Ottawas. AAR, 1901, 52-6.

James, E., ed. A Narrative of the Captivity and Adventures of John Tanner. 426 pp. New York, 1830.

Jenks, A.E. The Wild Rice Gatherers of the Upper Lakes. ARBAE, XIX, ii, 1013-137. 1898.

Jones, J.A. The Political Organization of the Three Fires. PIAS, LXIII, 46. 1953.

Jones, V.H. Some Chippewa and Ottawa Uses of Sweet Grass. PMA, XXI, 21-31. 1935.

Kenton, E., ed. The Indians of North America, II, 164-7, 371-4. New York, 1927.

Kurath, G.P. Catholic Hymns of Michigan Indians. PM, XXX, 31-44. 1957.

Lincoln, J.S. The Dream in Primitive Cultures. 359 pp. London, 1935.

McCoy, I. History of Baptist Missions. 611 pp. Washington, 1840.

Maxwell, T.J. Pontiac Before 1763. E, IV, 41-46. 1957.

Meeker, J. Ottawa First Book. 2d edit. 128 pp. 1850.

Michelson, T. Note on the Gentes of the Ottawa. AA, n.s., XIII, 338. 1911.

--- Three Ottawa Tales. JAFL, XLIV, 191-5. 1932.

Mooney, J., and Hewitt, J.N.B. Ottawa. BBAE, XXX, ii, 167-72. 1910.

Morgan, L.H. The Indian Journals, 1859-62, pp. 37-40. Ann Arbor, 1959.

--- Systems of Consanguinity and Affinity. SCK, XVII, 291-382. 1871.

Myers, F.A. The Bear-Walk. Inland Seas, IX, 12-18, 98-103, 169-74, 250-54. 1953.

Nasatir, A.P. Before Lewis and Clark. 2 vols. 882 pp. St. Louis, 1952.

Orr, R.B. The Ottawas. AAR, 1916, 7-25.

Parkman, F. The Conspiracy of Pontiac and the Indian War after the Conquest of Canada. 2 vols. Boston, 1886.

Peckham, H.H. Pontiac and the Indian Uprising. 346 pp. Princeton, 1947.

Radin, P. Ojibwa and Ottawa Puberty Dreams. Essays in Anthropology presented to A.L. Kroeber, pp. 233-64. Berkeley, 1936.

Schmidt, W. Die Potawatomie (und Ottawa). UG. II, 508-15; V, 565-79. 1929, 1934.

Schoolcraft, H.R. Algic Researches. 2 vols. New York, 1839.

Smith, J. An Account of the Remarkable Occurrence in the Life and Travels of Col. James Smith, ed. W.M.Darlington. Ohio Valley Historical Series, Vol. V. 1870.

Thwaites, R.G., ed. The French Regime in Wisconsin. CSHSW, Vols. XVI-XVIII. 1902-08.

--- The Jesuit Relations and Allied Documents. 74 vols. Cleveland, 1896-1901.

Voegelin, E.W. Notes on Ojibwa-Ottawa Pictography. PIAS, LI, 44-7. 1941.

Watkins, F.E. Ottawa Indian Quill-Decorated Birchbark Boxes. IX, 123-7. 1935.

Weer, P. Ethnological Notes on the Ottawa. PIAS, XLIX, 23-7. 1940.

Wilson, E.F. The Ottawa Indians. OFC, III, 1-6. 1889.

Wright, J.C. The Crooked Tree. 3d edit. 148 pp. Harbor Springs, 1917.

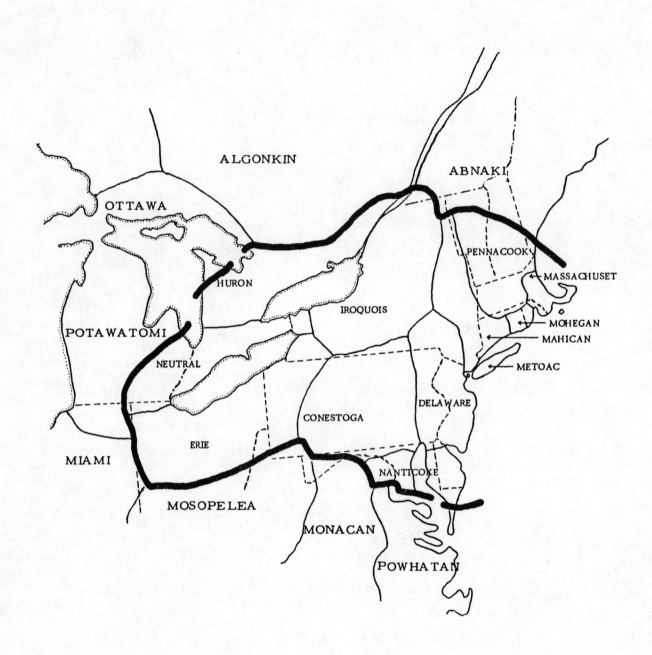

The tribes of this area are grouped under the following linguistic stocks:

Algonkian: Delaware, Mahican, Massachuset, Metoac, Mohegan, Nanticoke, Pennacook.

Iroquoian: Conestoga, Erie, Huron, Iroquois, Neutral.

Abbott, C.C. Primitive Industry. 560 pp. Salem, 1881.

Adams, J.A. English Institutions and the American Indian. Johns Hopkins University Studies in Historical and Political Science, XII, x, 4-59.1894.

Alberts, R.C. Trade Silver and Indian Silver Work in the Great Lakes Region. WA, XXXIV, 1-121. 1953.

Allen, F.H., et al. Blood Groups of Eastern American Indians. Proceedings of the International Congress of Genetics, X, ii, 5. 1958.

Allen, L. Siouan and Iroquoian. IJAL, VI, 185-93.

Anonymous. New Jersey's Place in Cultural History. 37 pp. Trenton, 1957.

--- The Number of Indians in Connecticut, 1774. MHSC, ser. 1, X, 117-18. 1809.

--- Number of Indians in Rhode-Island, 1774. MHSC, ser. 1, X, 119. 1809.

--- References on American Indians within the Present Limits of the State of Delaware. BASD, I, v, 18-19. 1934.

Armbruster, E.L. The Indians of New England and New Netherland. 11 pp. New York, 1918.

Barbeau, M. Indian Captivities. PAPS, XCIV, 522-48. 1950.

--- Indian Trade Silver. PTRSC, ser. 3, XXXIV, ii, 27-41. 1940.

Barbeau, M., and Melvin, G. The Indian Speaks. 117 pp. Toronto, 1943.

Barber, J.W. The History and Antiquities of New England, New York, New Jersey and Pennsylvania, pp. 69-120. Hartford, 1843.

Beardsley, G. The Groundnut as used by the Indians of Eastern North America. PMA, XXV, iv, 507-15. 1939.

Beauchamp, W.M. Indian Nations of the Great Lakes. AAOJ, XVII, 321-5. 1895.

Beers, H.P. The French in North America. Baton Rouge, 1957.

Benedict, A.L. A Medical View of the American Indians of the Northeast. Medical Age, XIX, 767-71. 1901.

Bennett, M.K. The Food Economy of the New England Indians, 1605-1675. Journal of Political Economy, LXIII, 369-97. 1955.

Biasutti, R. Le Razzi e i Popoli della Terra, 2nd ed., IV, 425-37. Torino, 1957.

Birket-Smith, K. Ancient Artefacts from Eastern United States. JSAP, n.s., XII, 141-69. 1920.

--- A Geographic Study of the Early History of the Algonquian Indians. IAE, XXIV, 174-222. 1918.

Bisbee, E.E. et al. White Mountain Scrap Heap. 64 pp. Lumenburg, Vt., 1956.

Blasingham, E.J. The "New England Indians" in the Western Great Lakes Region. PIAS, LXVI, 47-49. 1956.

Bloomfield, L. Algonquian. VFPA, VI, 85-129. 1946.

Bradley, W.T. Medical Practices of the New England Aborigines. Journal of the American Pharmaceutical Association, XXV, 138-47. 1936.

Braunholtz, H.J. The Sloane Collection: Ethnography. British Museum Quarterly, XVIII, i, 23-6. 1953.

Bushnell, D.I. Native Villages and Village Sties East of the Mississippi. BBAE, LXIX, 1-111. 1919.

--- Tribal Migrations East of the Mississippi. SMC, LXXXIX, xii, 1-9. 1934.

--- The Use of Soapstone by the Indians of the Eastern United States. ARSI, 1939, 471-89.

Butler, E.L. Algonkian Culture and the Use of Maize in Southern New England. BASC, XXII, 3-39. 1948.

--- The Brush or Stone Memorial Heaps of Southern New England. BASC, XIX, 3-12. 1946.

--- Some Early Indian Basket Makers of Southern New England. Archaeological Society of New Jersey Research Series, I, 34-55. 1947.

--- Sweat-Houses in the Southern New England Area. BMAS, VII, 11-15, 1945.

Butler, E.L., and Hadlock, W.S. Dogs of the Northeastern Woodland Indians. BMAS, X, 17-36. 1949.

--- Some Uses of Birch Bark in Northern New England. BMAS, XVIII, 72-75. 1957.

Byers, D.S. The Environment of the Northeast. PRSPF, III, 3-32. 1946.

Carpenter, E.S., and Hassrick, R.B. Some Notes on Arrow Poisoning among the Tribes of the Eastern Woodlands. Proceedings of the Delaware County Institute of Science, X, 45-52. 1947.

Carr, L.G.K. Interesting Animal Foods, Medicines, and Omens of the Eastern Indians. JWAS, XLI, vii, 229-35. 1951.

Chamberlain, A.F. The Maple amongst the Algonkian Tribes. AA, IV, 39-43. 1891.

--- Maple Sugar and the Indians. AA, IV, 381-3. 1891.

Chamberlain, L.S. Plants used by the Indians of Eastern North America. AN, XXXV, 1-10. 1901.

Charlevoix, P.F.X.de. Histoire de la Nouvelle France. 3 vols. Paris, 1894.

--- History and General Description of New France, ed. J.M.Shea. 6 vols. New York, 1866-72.

Chatard, F.E. An Early Description of Birch-Bark Canoes. American Neptune, VIII, 91-8. 1948.

Clauser, C.E. The Relationship between a Coastal Algonkin and a Karankawa Cranial Series. PIAS, LVII, 18-23. 1948.

Cooper, J.M. Land Tenure among the Indians of Eastern and Northern North America. PA, VIII, 55-9. 1938.

Day, G.M. The Indian as an Ecologic Factor in the Northeastern Forest. Ecology, XXXIV, 329-46. 1953.

Delabarre, E.B., and Wilder, H.H. Indian Corn Hills in Massachusetts. AA, n.s., XXII, 203-25. 1920.

Dexter, F. Extracts from the Itineraries and Other Miscellanies of Ezra Stiles. New Haven, 1916.

Dixon, R.B. The Early Migrations of the Indians of New England and the Maritime Provinces. PAAS, n.s., XXIV, 65-76. 1914.

--- The Mythology of the Central and Eastern Algonkins. JAFL, XXII, 1-9. 1909.

Dodge, E.S. Ethnology of Northern New England and the Maritime Provinces. BMAS, XVIII, 68-71. 1957.

--- Some Thoughts on the Historic Art of the Indians of Northeastern North America. BMAS, XIII, i, 1-4. 1951.

Douglas, F.H. Iroquoian and Algonkin Wampum. DAMLS, XXXI, 1-4. 1931.

--- New England Indian Houses, Forts and Villages. DAMLS, XXXIX, 1-4, 1932.

--- The New England Tribes. DAMLS, XXVII-XXVIII, 1-8. 1931.

Douglas-Lithgow, R.A. Dictionary of American Indian Place and Proper Names in New England. 400 pp. Salem, 1909.

Drake, S.G. Indian Captivities. 367 pp. Auburn, 1850.

Du Creux, F. The History of Canada or New France. PCS, XXX-XXXI, 776 pp. 1951-52.

Dunlap, A.R. and Weslager, C.A. Indian Place-Names in Delaware. 82 pp. Wilmington, 1951.

Engberg, R.M. Algonkian Sites of Westmoreland and Fayette Counties, Pennsylvania. WPHM, XIV, 143-90. 1931.

Essington, J.H. Early Inhabitants of the Ohio Valley. WVH, XIII, 277-85. 1952.

Fenton, W.N. The Present State of Anthropology in Northeastern North America. AA, n.s., L, 494-515. 1948.

Flannery, R. Algonquian Indian Folklore. JAFL, LX, 397-401. 1947.

--- An Analysis of Coastal Algonquian Culture. CUAS, VII, 1-219. 1939.

Foreman, G. The Last Trek of the Indians, 17-88, 159-81, 229-36. Chicago, 1946.

Fowler, W.S. Primitive Woodworking in the Connecticut Valley. BMAS, VII, 72-5. 1946.

Gerard, W.R. Algonquian Names for Pickeral. AA, n. s., V, 581-2. 1903.

Gilbert, W.H., Jr. Surviving Indian Groups of the Eastern United States. ARSI, 1948, 407-38.

Gille, J. Der Manabozho-Flutzyklus der Nord-, Nordost-, und Zentralalgonkin. 86 pp. Göttingen, 1939.

--- Weskarini und Ur-Algonkin. 17 pp. Göttingen, 1939.

--- Zur Lexikologie des Alt-Algonkin. ZE, LXXI, 71-86. 1939.

Gillingham, H.E. Indian Ornaments made by Philadelphia Silversmiths. 26 pp. New York, 1936.

Griffin, J.B. Aboriginal Methods of Pottery Manufacture in the Eastern United States. PA, V, 19-24. 1935.

Haas, M.R. A New Linguistic Relationship in North America. SJA, XIV, 231-64. 1958.

Hadlock, W.S. Warfare among the Northeastern Woodland Indians. AA, n.s., XLIX, 204-21. 1947.

Hallett, L.F. Medicine and Pharmacy of the New England Indians. BMAS, XVII, 46-9. 1956.

Hallowell, A.I. Some Psychological Characteristics of the Northeastern Indians. PRSPF, III, 195-225. 1946.

Hamilton, K.G. Cultural Contributions of Moravian Missions among the Indians. PH, XVIII, 1-15. 1951.

Herman, M.W. Wampum as a Money in Northeastern North America. E, V, 21-33. 1958.

Holling, H.C. The Book of Indians, pp. 17-44. New York, 1935.

Holmes, W.H. Aboriginal Pottery of the Eastern United States. ARBAE, XX, 1-201. 1899.

Howe, H.F. Sources of New England Indian History prior to 1620. BMAS, III, 19-24. 1942.

Howells, W.W. Physical Types of the Northeast. PRSPF, III, 168-77. 1946.

Howes, W.J. The Importance of the Connecticut Valley Territory of Western Massachusetts to the Indians. BMAS, I, iv, 4-10. 1940.

Hrdlicka, A. Catalogue of Human Crania in the United States National Museum Collections. PUSNM, LXIX, v, 1-127. 1927.

--- Physical Anthropology of the Lenape or Delawares, and of the Eastern Indians in General. BBAE, LXII, 110-30. 1916.

Huden, J.C. Indian Place Names in Vermont. 32
pp. Burlington, 1957.

Hunter, W.A. The Ohio, the Indian's Land. PH,
XXI, 338-50. 1954.

Jacobs, W.R. The Indian Frontier of 1763. WPHM,
XXXIV, 185-98. 1951.

Jeançon, J.A., and Douglas, F.H. Iroquoian and
Algonkin Wampum. DAMLS, XXXI, 1-4. 1931.

Jacobsson, N. Svenskai och Indianer. Stockholm,
1922.

Johnson, F., ed. Man in Northeastern North America. PRSPF, III, 1-347. 1946.

Josselyn, J. New England's Rarities Discovered.
Transactions and Collections of the American Antiquarian Society, IV, 105-238. 1860.

Kinietz, V. Notes on the Roached Headdress of Animal Hair among the North American Indians. PMA,
XXVI, 463-7. 1940.

Kurath, G.P. Algonquian Ceremonialism and Natural Resources of the Great Lakes. Indian Institute
of Culture, Reprint XXII. Bangalore, 1957.

--- Antiphonal Songs of Eastern Woodlands Indians.
Musical Quarterly, XLII, 520-6. 1956.

Lahontan, A.L. de D. New Voyages to North America, ed. R.G.Thwaites. 2 vols. Chicago, 1905.

--- Nouveaux voyages. 220 pp. La Haye, 1703.

Leach, D.E. Flintlock and Tomahawk. 318 pp.
New York, 1958.

Lincoln, C.H., ed. Narratives of the Indian Wars,
1675-1699. 316 pp. New York, 1913.

Loskiel, G.H. Geschichte der Mission der evangelischen Brüder unter den Indianern in Nordamerika.
783 pp. Barby, 1789.

--- History of the Mission of the United Brethren
among the Indians in North America. London, 1794.

MacNeish, R.S. The Archeology of the Northeastern
United States. AEUS, 46-58. 1952.

Merwin, B.W. Wampum. MJ, VII, 125-33. 1916.

Michelson, T. Algonquian Notes. IJAL, IX, 103-
12. 1939.

--- Preliminary Report on the Linguistic Classification
of Algonquian Tribes. ARBAE, XXVIII, 221-90.
1907.

Morris, J.L. Indians of Ontario. 75 pp. Toronto,
1943.

Orr, R.B. North American Indian Games — Dice.
AAR, XXVII, 20-34. 1915.

Parker, A.C. The Role of Wampum in the Colonial
Era. The Galleon, XIV, 1-5. 1954.

Peet, S.D. The Location of the Indian Tribes. AAOJ,
I, 85-98. 1878.

Philhower, C.A. Indian Currency and Its Manufacture.
PNJHS, n.s., XIII, 310-18. 1928.

Philhower, C.A. Wampum, Its Use and Value.
PNJHS, n.s., XV, 216-23. 1930.

Pilling, J.C. Bibliography of the Algonquian Languages. BBAE, XIII, 1-614. 1891.

--- Bibliography of the Iroquoian Languages. BBAE, VI,
1-208. 1888.

Potherie, B. de la. History of the Savage People who
are Allies of New France, ed. E.H.Blair. ITUMV, I,
273-372; II, 13-136. 1911-12.

Putnam, F.W. The Manufacture of Soapstone Pots by
the Indians of New England. RPM, XI, ii, 273-6.
1878.

Reynolds, H.L. Algonkin Metal-Smiths. AA, I, 341-
52. 1888.

Ritchie, W.A. An Algonkin-Iroquois Contact Site on
Castle Creek. RRRMAS, II, 1-58. 1934.

--- An Algonkian Village Site near Lavanna. RRRMAS,
I, 1-27. 1928.

--- Indian History of New York State. Part III — The
Algonkian Tribes. New York State Museum Educational Leaflet Series. 1956.

--- A Perspective of Northeastern Archeology. AAn,
IV, 94-112. 1938.

Rogers, R. A Concise Account of North America. 264
pp. London, 1765.

Rouse, I. Ceramic Traditions and Sequences in Connecticut. BASC, XXI, 10-25. 1947.

--- Styles of Pottery in Connecticut. BMAS, VII, 1-
8. 1945.

Rouse, I., and Horton, D., eds. A Preliminary Archaeological Bibliography of the Eastern United States.
BASC, Vols. IX-X. 1939-40.

Russell, F., and Huxley, H.M. A Comparative Study
of the Physical Structure of the Labrador Eskimos and
the New England Indians. PAAAS, XLVIII, 365-79.
1899.

Schmitt, K. Archeological Chronology of the Middle
Atlantic States. AEUS, 59-70. 1952.

Schusky, E. Pan-Indianism in the Eastern United States.
Anthropology Tomorrow, VI, 116-23. 1957.

Sherman, C.F. Habitations, Summer and Winter Sites,
and Reasons for Same. BMAS, VI, 10-14. 1944.

--- Winslow's Reports of the Indians. BMAS, III, 43-51.
1942.

Skinner, A. The Algonkin and the Thunderbird. AMJ,
XIV, 71-3. 1914.

--- Traces of the Stone Age among the Eastern and
Northern Tribes. AA, n.s., XIV, 391-5. 1912.

Slotkin, J.S., and Schmitt, K. Studies of Wampum.
AA, n.s., LI, 223-36. 1949.

Smith, C.S. The Archaeology of Coastal New York.
APAM, XLIII, ii, 105 pp. 1950.

Smith, C.S. An Outline of the Archaeology of Coastal New York. BASC, XXI, 3-9. 1947.

Snyderman, G.S. The Functions of Wampum. PAPS, XCVIII, 469-94. 1954.

Speck, F.G. Concerning Iconology and the Masking Complex in Eastern North America. UPMB, XV, 6-57. 1950.

--- Dream Symbolism and the Desire Motive in Floral Designs of the Northeast. The Guardian, I, 124-7. 1925.

--- Eastern Algonkian Block-Stamp Decoration. Archaeological Society of New Jersey, Research Series, I, 1-34. Trenton, 1947.

--- The Family Hunting Band as the Basis of Algonkian Social Organization. AA, n.s., XVII, 289-305. 1915.

--- The Functions of Wampum among the Eastern Algonkian. MAAA, VI, 3-71. 1919.

--- The Historical Approach to Art in Archaeology in the Northern Woodlands. AAn, VIII, 173-5. 1942.

--- The Memorial Brush Heap in Delaware and Elsewhere. BASD, IV, ii, 17-23. 1945.

--- Wampum in Indian Tradition and Currency. Proceedings of the Numismatic and Antiquarian Society of Philadelphia, XXVII, 121-30. 1916.

Spier, L. The Trenton Argillite Culture. APAM, XXII, 167-226. 1918.

Sylvester, H.M. Indian Wars of New England. 3 vols. Boston, 1910.

Tooker, W.W. The Algonquian Terms Patawomeke and Massawomeke. AA, VII, 174-85. 1894.

Trumbull, B. A Compendium of the Indian Wars in New England, ed. F.B.Hartranft. 61 pp. Hartford, 1926.

Trumbull, J.H. The Composition of Indian Geographical Names. Collections of the Connecticut Historical Society, II, 1-50. 1870.

--- On the Algonkin Verb. Transactions of the American Philological Association, VII, 147-71. 1877.

Uhler, S.P. Pennsylvania's Indian Relations to 1754. 144 pp. Allentown, 1951.

Voegelin, C.F. and E.W. Linguistic Considerations of Northeastern North America. PRSPF, III, 178-94. 1946.

Voegelin, E.W. Mortuary Customs of the Shawnee and Other Eastern Tribes. PRS, II, 227-444. 1944.

Wallace, A.F.C. Political Organization and Land Tenure among the Northeastern Indians, 1600-1830. SJA, XIII, 301-21. 1957.

Wallace, P.A.W. Historic Indian Paths of Pennsylvania. PMHB, LXXVI, 411-39. 1952.

Waugh, F.W. Notes on Canadian Pottery. AAR, XIV, 108-15. 1901.

Weslager, C.A. A Discussion of the Family Hunting Territory Question in Delaware. In, L. DeValinger, Indian Land Sales in Delaware, pp. 14-24. Wilmington, 1941.

--- The Non-food Use of Corn in the Domestic Economy of the Eastern Indians. Proceedings of the Delaware County Institute of Science, X, 3-22. 1947.

--- Robert Evelyn's Indian Tribes and Place-names of New Albion. BASNJ, IX.

Wherry, E.T. Some Little-Known Food Plants of Pennsylvania. Proceedings of the Delaware County Institute of Science, X, ii, 23-7. 1947.

White, P.C.T. Lord Selkirk's Diary, 1803-04. PCS, XXXV, 391 pp. 1958.

Willoughby, C.C. The Adze and the Ungrooved Axe of New England. AA, n.s., IX, 296-306. 1907.

--- Dress and Ornaments of the New England Indians. AA, n.s., VII, 499-508. 1905.

--- Houses and Gardens of the New England Indians. AA, n.s., VIII, 115-32. 1906.

--- Textile Fabrics of the New England Indians. AA, n.s., VII, 85-93. 1905.

--- Wooden Bowls of the Algonquian Indians. AA, n.s., X, 423-34. 1908.

Winsor, J. The Earliest Printed Books connected with the Aborigines of New England, 1630-1700. Massachusetts Historical Society, Proceedings, X, 327-59. 1895.

Wintemberg, W.J. Archaeological Evidence of Algonkian Influence on Iroquoian Culture. PTRSC, XXIX, ii, 331-42. 1935.

--- Distinguishing Characteristics of Algonkian and Iroquoian Cultures. BCDM, LXVII, 65-124. 1931.

--- The Use of Shells by the Ontario Indians. AAR, 1907, 38-90.

Woodward, A. Wampum. 2d edit. 56 pp. Albany, 1880.

Young, R.F. Comenius and the Indians of New England. 27 pp. London, 1929.

1. CONESTOGA

Also called Andaste and Susquehannock.

Alsop, G. A Character of the Province of Maryland, ed. J.G.Shea, pp. 71-81. New York, 1869.

Benson, E.A. The Story of the Susquehannocks. Lancaster, Pa., 1958.

Bozman, J.L. The History of Maryland, I, 103-93. Baltimore, 1837.

Cadzow, D.A. Archaeological Studies of the Susquehannock Indians. PPHC, III, ii, 1-217. 1936.

Crozier, A. Indian Towns near Wilmington, Delaware. BASD, II, vi, 2-4. 1938.

--- Notes on the Archaeology of Newcastle County, Delaware. BASD, I, iv, 1-6. 1934.

Donehoo, G.P. A Short Sketch of the Indian Trails of Pennsylvania. PWHGS, XVII, 67-94. 1919.

Dunlap, A.R. and Weslager, C.A. Toponymy of the Delaware Valley as Revealed by an Early Seventeenth-Century Dutch Map. BASNJ, XV-XVI, 1-13. 1958.

Eshleman, H.F. Annals of the Susquehannocks. 415 pp. Lancaster, 1908.

--- Lancaster County Indians. 28 pp. Lancaster, 1909.

Goldsborough, E.R. The Aborigines of the Lower Potomac River Valley. PA, VIII, 27-36. 1938.

Guss, A.L. Early Indian History on the Susquehanna. 32 pp. Harrisburg, 1883.

Hanna, C.A. The Wilderness Trail, I, 26-87. New York, 1911.

Henretta, J.E., ed. Kane and the Upper Allegheny. 357 pp. Philadelphia, 1929.

Hewitt, J.N.B. Conestoga. BBAE, XXX, i, 335-7. 1907.

--- Susquehanna. BBAE, XXX, ii, 653-9. 1910.

Hill, J. My People the Delawares. BASD, IV, i, 9-13. 1943.

Holzinger, C.H. The Ibaugh Site: A Susquehannock Cemetery. BESAF, XVII, 12. 1958.

Kinsey, W.F. The Oscar Leibhart Site. A Susquehannock Village of 1650-1675. BESAF, XVI, 13. 1957.

--- A Preliminary Report on Susquehannock Pottery Types. BESAF, XVII, 12. 1958.

Landis, D.H. A Brief Description of Indian Life and Indian Trade of the Susquehannock Indians. 48 pp. Lancaster, 1929.

Lucy, C.L. Notes on a Small Andaste Burial Site and Andaste Archaeology. PA, XXI, 53-56. 1951.

Macaulay, P.S. The Legendary Susquehannocks. PA, VI, 43-7. 1936.

MacCord, H.A. The Susquehannock Indians in West Virginia, 1630-77. WVH, XIII, 239-53. 1952.

Mercer, H.C. Distribution of Indian Tribes in Central Pennsylvania in Prehistoric Times. Antiquarian, I, 215-16. 1897.

Moorehead, W.K. A Report of the Susquehanna River Expedition. 142 pp. Andover, 1938.

Murray, E. The "Noble Savage." SM, XXXVI, 251-7. 1933.

Murray, L.W. Excavating an Andasta Chief. Proceedings and Collections of the Tioga Point Historical Society, I, 28-32. 1896.

--- Selected Manuscripts of General John S. Clark relating to the Aboriginal History of the Susquehanna. 150 pp. Athens, 1931.

Parker, A.C. The Influence of the Iroquois on the History and Archaeology of the Wyoming Valley. PWHGS, XI, 65-102. 1910.

Schrabisch, M. Aboriginal Rock Shelters and Other Archeological Notes of Wyoming Valley and Vicinity. PWHGS, XIX, 47-218. 1926.

Shea, J.G. The Identity of the Andastes, Minquas, Susquehannas, & Conestogues. HM, II, 294-7. 1858.

Stephenson, R.L. The Prehistoric People of Accokeek Creek. 35 pp. Accokeek, Md., 1959.

Stewart, T.B. Andaste Camp Site. Now and Then, IV, 76-8. 1930.

Strachey, W. The Historie of Travaile into Virginia Britannia, pp. 39-41. London, 1849.

Streeter, S.F. The Fall of the Susquehannocks. HM, I, 65-73. 1857.

Tooker, W.W. The Names Susquehanna and Chesapeake, with Historical and Ethnological Notes. 63 pp. New York, 1901.

Uhler, S.P. Pennsylvania's Indian Relations to 1754. 144 pp. Allentown, 1951.

Weslager, C.A. The Minquas and Their Early Relations with the Delaware Indians. BASD, IV, i, 14-23. 1943.

--- Susquehannock Indian Religion from an Old Document. JWAS, XXXVI, 302-5. 1946.

Witthoft, J. Archaeological History of Susquehannock Indians [and] A Note on the Map-locations of Susquehannock Towns. 9 pp., unpaginated, mimeographed issued with: Newsletter of the Archeological Society of Maryland, IV, i, ii, iv. 1958.

Witthoft, J. and Kinsey, W.F. Susquehannock Miscellany. 167 pp. Harrisburg, 1959.

Wren, C. Aboriginal Pottery of the Wyoming Valley. PWHGS, IX, 137-70. 1905.

--- Some Indian Graves. PWHGS, XII, 199-214. 1912.

--- The Stone Age. PWHGS, VIII, 93-115. 1904.

--- A Study of North Appalachian Indian Pottery. PWHGS, XIII, 131-222. 1914.

Wren, C. Turtle Shell Rattles and Other Implements from Indian Graves. PWHGS, X, 195-210. 1909.

Wysong, T.T. The Rocks of Deer Creek. 78 pp. Baltimore, 1879.

2. DELAWARE

Including the Munsee, the Unalachtigo, and the Unami, also known collectively as the Lenape.

Heckewelder, J.G.E. An Account of the History Manners, and Customs, of the Indian Nations, who once inhabited Pennsylvania and the Neighbouring States. THLC, I, 1-348. 1819.

Hulbert, A.B., and Schwarze, W.N., eds. Zeisberger's History of Northern American Indians. OAHQ, XIX, 1-189. 1910.

Kinietz, W.V. Delaware Culture Chronology. PRS, III, 1-143. 1946.

Newcomb, W.W. The Culture and Acculturation of the Delaware Indians. APMA, X, 144 pp. 1956.

Tantaquidgeon, G. A Study of Delaware Indian Medicine Practices and Folk Beliefs. 91 pp. Harrisburg, 1942.

Abbott, C.C. The Delaware Indian as an Artist. PSM, XLI, 586-94. 1892.

--- Idols and Idol Worship of the Delaware Indians. AN, XVI, 799-802. 1882.

--- Indians of New Jersey. New Jersey as a Colony and as a State, ed. F.B. Lee, I, 53-71. New York, 1902.

--- The Stone Age in New Jersey. ARSI, 1875, 246-380.

--- Ten Years' Diggings in Lenape Land. 191 pp. Trenton, 1912.

--- The Use of Copper by the Delaware Indians. AN, XIX, 774-7. 1885.

Adams, R.C. The Adoption of Mew-seu-qua. 52 pp. Washington, 1917.

--- The Ancient Religion of the Delaware Indians. 43 pp. Washington, 1904.

--- A Brief History of the Delaware Indians. U.S. Senate, 59th Congress, 1st Session, Document 501, pp. 1-70. 1906.

--- A Delaware Indian Legend. 75 pp. Washington, 1899.

--- History of the Delaware Indians. RIT, 1890, 297-300.

Adams, R.C. Legends of the Delaware Indians and Picture Writing. Washington, 1905.

Allinson, S. Fragmentary History of the New Jersey Indians. PNJHS, ser. 2, IV, 33-50. 1875.

Anderson, W. de la R. The Indian Legend of Watchung. PNJHS, ser. 4, XI, 45-8. 1926.

Anonymous. Walam Olum or Red Score. 393 pp. Indianapolis, 1954.

Barber, E.A. Notes on the Lenni Lenape. AAOJ, VI, 385-9. 1884.

Berlin, A.F. Mode of Fishing by the Delaware Indians. AAOJ, IX, 167-9. 1887.

Bibaud, F.M. Biographie des sagamos illustrés de l'Amérique Septentrionale, pp. 223-6, 231-3. Montreal, 1848.

Bliss, E.F., ed. Diary of David Zeisberger. 2 vols. Cincinnati, 1885.

Boas, F. Zur Anthropologie der nordamerikanischen Indianer. VBGA, 1895, 367-411.

Bolton, R.P. Indian Life of Long Ago in the City of New York. 167 pp. New York, 1934.

--- Indian Paths in the Great Metropolis. INM, XXIII, 1-279. 1922.

--- New York City in Indian Possession. INM, II, 225-395. 1920.

Brant, C.S. Peyotism among the Kiowa-Apache and Neighboring Tribes. SJA, VI, 212-22. 1950.

Brickell, J. Narrative of John Brickell's Captivity among the Delaware Indians. American Pioneer, I, 43-56. 1842.

Brinton, D.G. Folk-Lore of the Modern Lenape. Essays of an Americanist, pp. 181-92. Philadelphia, 1890.

--- The Lenapé and Their Legends. 262 pp. Philadelphia, 1885.

--- Lenape Conversations. JAFL, I, 37-43. 1888.

Brinton, D.G., and Anthony, A.S., eds. A Lenapé-English Dictionary. 236 pp. Philadelphia, 1888.

Brooks, S.T. The Question of a Minquas Indian Fort on Iron Hill. BASD, IV, iv, 27-33. 1947.

Brunner, D.B. The Indians of Berks County. 177 pp. Reading, 1881.

Buck, W.J. Lappawinzo and Tishcohan, Chiefs of the Lenni Lenape. PMHB, VII, 215-18. 1883.

Bushnell, D.I. Native Cemeteries and Forms of Burial East of the Mississippi. BBAE, LXXI, 20-4. 1920.

Butler, M. Two Lenape Rock Shelters near Philadelphia. AAn, XII, 246-55. 1947.

Cross, D. Canoes of the Lenni Lenape. Archaeological Society of New Jersey Newsletter, III, 10. 1941.

Cross, D. Houses of the Lenni Lenape. Archaeological Society of New Jersey Newsletter, II, 11-12. 1940.

--- Pottery Making. Archaeological Society of New Jersey Newsletter V, 7-9. 1941.

Crozier, A. Fishing Methods of the Indians of the Delmarva Region. BASD, IV, iv, 16-9. 1947.

Cummings, R.W. Delaware. HCPIT, II, 470-81. 1852.

Dencke, C.F., tr. Nek nechenenawachgissitschik bambilak naga geschiechauchsitpanna Johannessa elekhangup. 21 pp. New York, 1818.

De Roo, P. Linape National Songs. History of America before Columbus, I, 585-91. Philadelphia, 1900.

De Valinger, L. Indian Land Sales in Delaware. BASD, III, iii, 29-32; iv, 25-33. 1940-41.

Donehoo, G.P. A Short Sketch of the Indian Trails of Pennsylvania. PWHGS, XVII, 67-94. 1919.

Doren, C. van, and Boyd, J.P. Indian Treaties printed by Benjamin Franklin. 340 pp. Philadelphia, 1938.

Downes, R.C. Council Fires on the Upper Ohio. 367 pp. Pittsburgh, 1940.

Dunlap, A.R. A Bibliographical Discussion of the Indian Languages of the Delmarva Peninsula. BASD, IV, v, 2-5. 1949.

Dunlap, A.R. and Weslager, C.A. Indian Place Names in Delaware. Wilmington, 1950.

--- Toponymy of the Delaware Valley as Revealed by an Early Seventeenth-Century Dutch Map. BASNJ, XV-XVI, 1-13. 1958.

Dunn, J.P. True Indian Stories. 320 pp. Indianapolis, 1909.

Ely, A.G. A Summary of Delaware Indian Culture. EP, LII, 14-19. 1945.

Farley, A.W. The Delaware Indians in Kansas, 1829-1867. 16 pp. Kansas City, 1955.

Foreman, G. The Last Trek of the Indians, pp. 182-90. Chicago, 1946.

Gifford, A. The Aborigines of New Jersey. PNJHS, IV, 165-98. 1850.

Hanna, C.A. The Wilderness Trail, I, 88-118. New York, 1911.

Hannum, M.F., and F.D. Scull. A Study of the Lenni Lenape or Delaware Indians. 25 pp. New York, 1941.

Harrington, M.R. Dickon among the Lenape Indians. 353 pp. Chicago, 1938.

--- The Life of a Lenape Boy. PA, III, iv, 3-8. 1933.

--- A Preliminary Sketch of Lenape Culture. AA, n.s., XV, 208-35. 1913.

Harrington, M.R. Religion and Ceremonies of the Lenape. INM, ser. 2, XIX, 1-249. 1921.

--- Some Customs of the Delaware Indians. MJ, I, 52-60. 1910.

--- The Thunder Power of Rumbling Wings. PA, IV, i, 3-9; ii, 7-12. 1934.

--- The Thunder Power of Rumbling-Wings. American Indian Life, ed. E.C. Parsons, pp. 107-25. New York, 1925.

--- Vestiges of Material Culture among the Canadian Delawares. AA, n.s., X, 408-18. 1908.

Harris, Z.S. Structural Restatements. IJAL, XIII, 175-86. 1947.

Heckewelder, J.G.E. Names which the Lenni Lenape or Delaware Indians, who once inhabited This Country, had given to Rivers, Streams, Places, &c. TAPS, n.s., IV, 351-96. 1834.

--- A Narrative of the Mission of the United Brethren among the Delaware and Mohegan Indians. Philadelphia, 1820.

--- Words, Phrases, and Short Dialogues, in the Language of the Lenni Lenape or Delaware Indians. THLC, I, 450-64. 1819.

Heckewelder, J.G.E., and Duponceau, P.S. Correspondence. THLC, I, 351-448. 1819.

Heller, W.J. The Disappearance of the Lenni Lenape from the Delaware and Their Subsequent Migrations. Penn Germania, n.s., I, 711-17. 1912.

Herman, M.W. A Reconstruction of Aboriginal Delaware Culture from Contemporary Sources. PKAS, I, 45-77. 1950.

Heye, G.G., and Pepper, G.H. Exploration of a Munsee Cemetery. CMAI, II, i, 1-78. 1915.

Holm, T.C. A Short Description of the Province of New Sweden. Memoirs of the Historical Society of Pennsylvania, III, 112-56. 1834.

Hrdlicka, A. Physical Anthropology of the Lenape or Delawares. BBAE, LXII, 1-130. 1916.

Hunter, W.A. John Hays' Diary and Journal of 1760. PA, XXIV, 63-84. 1954.

--- Provincial Negotiations with the Western Indians, 1754-58. PH, XVIII, 213-19. 1951.

--- Pymatuning. PA, XXVI, 174-7. 1956.

Joblin, E.E.M. The Education of the Indians of Western Ontario. Ontario College of Education Bulletin, XIII, 1-138. 1948.

Johnson, A. The Indians and Their Culture as described in Swedish and Dutch Records. ICA, XIX, 277-82. 1915.

Kinietz, W.V. European Civilization as a Determinant of Native Indian Customs. AA, n.s., XLII, 116-21. 1940.

Leslie, V.E. An Archaeological Reconnaissance of Upper Delaware Valley Sites. PA, XVI, 20-30, 59-78, 95-112, 131-41. 1946.

--- A Tentative Catalogue of Minsi Material Culture. PA, XXI, 9-20. 1951.

Lilly, E. Remarks regarding the Pictographs of the Walum Olum. PIAS, XLIX, 32-3. 1940.

--- Tentative Speculations on the Chronology of the Walam Olum and the Migration Route of the Lenape. PIAS, LIV, 33-40. 1945.

Lincoln, A.T. Our Indians of Early Delaware. Delaware Citizens Association Historical Bulletin, I, 1-42. 1932.

Lindeström, P. Geographia Americae, with an Account of the Delaware Indians. 418 pp. Philadelphia, 1925.

Loskiel, G.H. Geschichte der Mission der evangelischen Brüder unter den Indianern in Nordamerika. 783 pp. Barby, 1789.

--- History of the Mission of the United Brethren among the Indians of North America. London, 1794.

Luckenbach, A., tr. Forty-six Select Scripture Narratives from the Old Testament. 304 pp. New York, 1838.

McCracken, H.L. The Delaware Big House. CO, XXXIV, 183-92. 1956.

MacLeod, W.C. The Family Hunting Territory and Lenape Political Organization. AA, n.s., XXIV, 448-63. 1922.

Mahr, A.C. Aboriginal Culture Traits as Reflected in 18th Century Delaware Indian Tree Names. OJS, LIV, 380-87. 1954.

--- Anatomical Terminology of the Eighteenth-Century Delaware Indians. Anthropological Linguistics, II, v, 1-65. 1960.

--- Eighteenth Century Terminology of Delaware Indian Cultivation and Use of Maize. E, II, 209-40. 1955.

--- Semantic Analysis of Eighteenth-Century Delaware Indian Names for Medicinal Plants. E, II, 11-28. 1955.

--- Walam Olum, I, 17: A Proof of Rafinesque's Integrity. AA, LIX, 705-708, 1957.

Meeussen, A.E. Prefix Pluralizers in Delaware. IJAL, XXV, 188-9. 1959.

Mercer, H.C. The Lenape Stone. 95 pp. New York, 1885.

Mooney, J. Delaware. BBAE, XXX, i, 385-7. 1907.

--- Munsee. BBAE, XXX, i, 957-8. 1907.

--- Passing of the Delaware Nation. PMVHA, III, 329-40. 1911.

Morgan, L.H. The Indian Journals, 1859-62, pp. 28, 49-57, 59. Ann Arbor, 1959.

Morgan, L.H. Systems of Consanguinity and Affinity. SCK, XVII, 291-382. 1871.

Myers, A.C., ed. Narratives of Early Pennsylvania, Western New Jersey, and Delaware. 476 pp. New York, 1912.

Nelson, W. The Indians of New Jersey. 168 pp. Paterson, 1894.

--- Indian Words, Personal Names and Place Names in New Jersey. AA, n.s., IV, 183-92. 1902.

Newcomb, W.W. A Note on Cherokee-Delaware Pan-Indianism. AA, LVII, 1041-45. 1955.

--- The Peyote Cult of the Delaware Indians. TJS, VIII, 202-11. 1956.

--- The Walam Olum of the Delaware Indians in Perspective. TJS, VII, 57-63. 1955.

Omwake, H.G. Delaware Indians in the Far West. BASD, IV, iv, 20-1. 1947.

Orchard, W.C. Porcupine Quill Ornamentation. IN, III, 59-68. 1926.

Patton, W. Journal of a Visit to the Indian Missions, Missouri Conference. BMHS, X, 168-80. 1954.

Peet, S.D. The Delaware Indians in Ohio. AAOJ, II, 132-44. 1879.

Penn, W. Account of the Lenni Lennape, ed. A.C. Myers. 107 pp. Moylan, 1937.

Petrullo, V. The Diabolic Root: a Study of Peyotism, the New Indian Religion, among the Delawares. 185 pp. Philadelphia, 1934.

Philhower, C.A. The Aboriginal Inhabitants of Monmouth County. PNJHS, ser. 4, IX, 22-40. 1924.

--- Aboriginal Inhabitants of New Jersey. New Jersey, a History, ed. I.S.Kull, I, 14-53. New York, 1930.

--- The Aboriginal Inhabitants of Union County. PNJHS, ser. 4, VIII, 124-38. 1923.

--- The Aborigines of Hunterdon County. PNJHS, ser. 4, XI, 508-25. 1926.

--- Agriculture and Food of the Indians of New Jersey. PNJHS, LVIII, 93-102, 192-202. 1940.

--- The Art of the Lenape. Leaflets of the Archaeological Society of New Jersey, I, 1-4. 1932.

--- The Earliest Account of the Lenape and Narragansett Indians. BASNJ, V, 10-11. 1952.

--- Foods of the Indians of New Jersey. Archaeological Society of New Jersey Newsletter, IV, 5-10. 1941.

--- Indian Days in Middlesex County, New Jersey. PNJHS, ser. 4, XII, 385-405. 1927.

--- The Indians of the Morris County Area. PNJHS, LIV, 249-67. 1936.

--- The Indians of Somerset County. PNJHS, ser. 4, X, 28-41. 1925.

Philhower, C.A. Minisink--Its Use and Significance. PNJHS, ser. 4, XI, 186-90. 1926.

--- The Munsee-Lenape Site, Sussex County, New Jersey. BESAF, XII, 9. 1953.

--- Some Personal Characteristics of the Lenape Indians. PNJHS, n.s., XVI, 138-61. 1931.

--- South Jersey Indians. PNJHS, n.s., XVI, 1-21. 1931.

Prince, J.D. An Ancient New Jersey Indian Jargon. AA, n.s., XIV, 508-24. 1912.

--- A Modern Delaware Tale. PAPS, XLI, 20-34. 1902.

--- Notes on the Modern Minsi-Delaware Dialect. AJP, XXI, 295-302. 1900.

Raynaud, G. Walam Olum (livre des legendes Lenapes). Archives de la Société Americaine de France, n.s., VII, 129-36. 1888.

Rupp, I.D. History of the Counties of Berks and Lebanon, pp. 16-32. Lancaster, 1844.

Ruttenber, E.M. History of the Indian Tribes of Hudson's River. 415 pp. Albany, 1872.

--- Indian Geographical Names in the Valley of Hudson's River. the Valley of the Mohawk, and on the Delaware. Proceedings of the New York State Historical Association, VI. 241 pp. 1906.

Schmidt, W. Die Lenape. UG, II, 408-48; V, 475-521, 876-82; VII, 705-26. 1929, 1934, 1940.

Schrabisch, M. Indian Rock-Shelters in Northern New Jersey and Southern New York. APAM, III, 141-65. 1909.

--- The Indians of New Jersey. Americana, V, 877-87. 1910.

--- Mountain Haunts of the Coastal Algonquian. AA, n.s., XXI, 139-52. 1919.

Scot, G. The Model of the Government of the Province of East New Jersey. 2d edit. Collections of the New Jersey Historical Society, I, 359-475. 1874.

Shetrone, H.C. The Indian in Ohio. OAHQ, XXVII, 273-510.

Sipe, C.H. The Principal Indian Towns in Western Pennsylvania. WPHM, XIII, 104-22. 1930.

Skinner, A. Another Indian Village-Site on Staten Island. IN, II, 296-7. 1925.

--- Archaeology of the New York Coastal Algonkin. APAM, III, 213-35. 1909.

--- The Indians of Greater New York. Cedar Rapids, 1915.

--- The Indians of Manhattan Island and Vicinity. AMGLS, XXIX, 5-54; XLI, 5-54. 1909-15.

--- The Indians of Newark before the White Men came. 16 pp. Newark, 1915.

Skinner, A. The Lenapé Indians of Staten Island. APAM, III, 1-62. 1909.

--- Two Lenape Stone Masks. INM, n.s., III, 5-7. 1920.

Skinner, A., and Schrabisch, M., eds. A Preliminary Report of the Archaeological Survey of the State of New Jersey. Bulletin of the Geological Survey of New Jersey, IX, 1-94. 1913.

Smet, P.J.de. Western Missions and Missionaries, pp. 218-30. New York, 1863.

Speck, F.G. Bird Nomenclature and Song Interpretation of the Canadian Delaware. JWAS, XXXVI, 249-58. 1946.

--- The Boy-bear (The Bear Abductor). A, XXXVI, 973-4. 1941.

--- Critical Comments on "Delaware Culture Chronology." AA, n.s., L, 723-4. 1948.

--- The Delaware Indians as Women. PMHB, LXX, 377-89. 1946.

--- Gourds of the Southeastern Indians. 113 pp. Boston, 1941.

--- The Grasshopper War in Pennsylvania. PA, XII, 31-4. 1942.

--- The Great Pennsylvania Earthquake of Indian Days. PA, XII, 57-9. 1942.

--- Indian Life in Bergen County. Papers and Proceedings of the Bergen County Historical Society, III, 19-28. 1907.

--- Notes on the Life of John Wilson, the Revealer of Peyote. GM, XXV, 539-56. 1933.

--- Oklahoma Delaware Ceremonies, Dances and Feasts. MAPS, VII, 1-161. 1937.

--- Speaking of the Delawares. PA, IV, iv, 3-9. 1935.

--- A Study of the Delaware Big House Ceremony. PPHC, II, 5-192. 1931.

--- The Wapanachki Delawares and the English. PMHB, LXVII, 319-44. 1943.

Speck, F.G., and J. Moses. The Celestial Bear comes down to Earth. Reading Public Museum Scientific Publications, VII, 1-91. 1945.

Speck, F.G., and Orchard, W.C. The Penn Wampum Belts. LMAI, IV, 7-20. 1925.

Squier, E.G. Historical and Mythological Traditions of the Algonquins. American Review, n.s., III, 173-93. 1849.

--- Historical and Mythological Traditions of the Algonquins. Indian Miscellany, ed. W.W.Beach, pp. 9-42. Albany, 1877.

Stiegerwalt, H.J. Some Lenape History. Archeological Bulletin, VIII, 3-4. 1917.

Tantaquidgeon, G. Delaware Indian Art Designs. PA, XX, i-ii, 24-30. 1950.

Thomas, C. Migrations of the Lenni Lenape or Delawares. AAOJ, XIX, 73-80. 1897.

Thomas, G. An Historical and Geographical Account of the Province and Country of Pensilvania. 55 pp. London, 1698.

Troost, G. Extracts from the Voyages of David Pieterszen de Vries. CNYHS, n.s., I, 243-80. 1841.

Uhler, S.P. Pennsylvania's Indian Relations to 1754. 144 pp. Allentown, 1951.

Voegelin, C.F. Delaware, an Eastern Algonquian Language. VFPA, VI, 130-57. 1946.

--- Delaware Texts. IJAL, XI, 105-119. 1945.

--- The Lenape and Munsee Dialects of Delaware. PIAS, XLIX, 34-7. 1940.

--- Proto-Algonkian Clusters in Delaware. Lg, XVII, 143-7. 1941.

--- Word Distortions in Delaware Big House and Walam Olum Songs. PIAS, LI, 48-54. 1942.

Voegelin, E.W. Culture Parallels to the Delaware Walum Olum. PIAS, XLIX, 28-31. 1940.

Volkman, A.G. Lenape Basketry in Delaware. BASD, IV, v, 15-18. 1949.

Wake, C.S. Migrations of the Algonkins. AAOJ, XVI, 127-39. 1894.

--- The Migrations of the Lenape. AAOJ, XXX, 221-3. 1908.

Walker, E.R. The Lenni-Lenape or Delaware Indians. PNJHS, ser. 4, II, 193-218. 1917.

Wallace, A.F.C. King of the Delawares. 305 pp. Philadelphia, 1949.

--- New Religions among the Delaware Indians, 1600-1900. SJA, XII, 1-21. 1956.

--- Some Psychological Characteristics of the Delaware Indians during the 17th and 18th Centuries. PA, XX, i-ii, 33-39. 1950.

--- Woman, Land, and Society. PA, XVII, 1-35. 1947.

Weer, P. Provenience of the Walam Olum. PIAS, LI, 55-9. 1942.

Weslager, C.A. The Anthropological Position of the Indian Tribes of the Delmarva Peninsula. BASD, IV, iv, 3-7. 1947.

--- Delaware Indian Villages. PA, XII, 53-6. 1942.

--- Delaware Indian Villages at Philadelphia. PA, XXVI, 178-80. 1956.

--- The Delaware Indians as Women. JWAS, XXXIV, 381-8. 1944.

--- Further Light on the Delaware Indians as Women. JWAS, XXXVII, 298-304. 1947.

--- The Indians of Lewes, Delaware. BASD, IV, v, 6-14. 1949.

--- The Minquas and Their Early Relations with the Delaware Indians. BASD, IV, i, 14-23. 1943.

Westervelt, F.A. The Indians of Bergen County, New Jersey, 26 pp. Hackensack, 1923.

Wheeler-Voegelin, E., ed. Some Remarks Concerning the Traditions, Customs, Languages &c.of the Indians in North America. E, VI, 42-69, 186. 1959.

Widen, A. Om gudsbegreppet hos Lenape. Ethnos, II, 252-65. 1937.

Wigglesworth, J. A Brief Archaeology of the Leni Lenape. 12 pp. Wilmington, Delaware.

Witthoft, J. Green Corn Ceremonialism in the Eastern Woodlands. OCMA, XIII, 11-21. 1949.

--- The Grasshopper War in Lenape Land. PA, XVI, 91-4. 1946.

Wren, C. A Study of North Appalachian Indian Pottery. PWHGS, XIII, 131-222. 1914.

Wright, M.H. and Shirk, G.H. Artist Möllhausen in Oklahoma, 1853. CO, XXXI, 392-441. 1953.

Zeisberger, D. Delaware Indian and English Spelling Book. 179 pp. Philadelphia, 1806.

--- A Grammar of the Language of the Lenni Lenape or Delaware Indians. TAPS, n.s., III, 65-250. 1830.

--- Indian Dictionary. 236 pp. Cambridge, 1887.

--- Some Remarks and Annotations concerning the Traditions, Customs, Languages, &c. of the Indians of North America. Olden Time, I, 271-81. 1846.

3. ERIE

Baldwin, C.C. Early Indian Migration in Ohio. AAOJ, I, 227-39. 1879.

Braden, J.A. Little Brother of the Hudson. 279 pp. New York, 1928.

Edson, W.H. The Eries, the Nation of the Cat. Proceedings of the New York State Historical Association, XXXIII, 36-44. 1935.

Hewitt, J.N.B. Erie. BBAE, XXX, i, 430-2. 1907.

Houghton, F. The Indian Occupancy of the Niagara Frontier. BBSNS, IX, 263-374. 1908.

Moorehead, W.K. The Indian Tribes of Ohio. OAHQ, VII, 1-109. 1898.

Mosely, E.L. Some Plants That Were Probably Brought to Northern Ohio from the West by the Indians. PMA, XIII, 169-72. 1931.

Parker, A.C. Excavations in an Erie Indian Village and Burial Site. NYSMB, CXVII, 459-554. 1907.

--- The Origin of the Iroquois as suggested by Their Archeology. AA, n.s., XVIII, 479-507. 1916.

--- The Ripley Erie Site. NYSMB, CCXXXV-CCXXXVIII, 246-306. 1920.

Schmitz, E. Les Eriés on Ka-Kwaks et leur Destruction par les Sénécas. ICA, II, i, 360-61. 1878.

Silver, D.M. The Location of the Nations of Indians
called the Wenroes or Wenrohronons and the Eries.
19 pp. Buffalo, 1923.

Thwaites, R.G., ed. The Jesuit Relations and Allied Documents. 74 vols. Cleveland, 1896-1901.

Vietzen, R.C. The Immortal Eries. 387 pp. Elyria,
1945.

4. HURON

Including the Ataronchronon, Huron, Tionontati
or Tobacco, Wenrohonronon, and Wyandot.

Brébeuf, J. de. Relation of the Hurons, 1636. The
Jesuit Relations and Allied Documents, ed. R.G.
Thwaites, X, 124-317. Cleveland, 1897.

Kinietz, W.V. The Indian Tribes of the Western
Great Lakes. OCMA, X, 1-160. 1940.

Sagard-Théodat, G. Le grand voyage du pays des
Huron. New edit. Paris, 1865.

--- The Long Journey to the Country of the Hurons,
ed. G.M.Wrong. PCS, XXV, 1-411. 1939.

Anonymous. Grammar of the Huron Language. Report of the Ontario Bureau of Archives, XV, 25-
77. 1920.

Bailey, A.G. The significance of the Identity and
Disappearance of the Laurentian Iroquois. PTRSC,
ser. 3, XXVII, ii, 97-108. 1933.

Barbeau, M. Classification of Iroquoian Radicals
with Subjective Pronominal Prefixes. MCDM,
XLVI, 1-30. 1915.

--- La Croix de Cartier. Revue de l'Université
d'Ottawa, XI, 440-43. 1941.

--- How the Huron-Wyandot Language was saved
from Oblivion. PAPS, XCIII, 226-32. 1949.

--- Huron and Wyandot Mythology. MCDM, XLVI,
1-30. 1915.

--- Iroquoian Clans and Phratries. AA, n.s., XIX,
392-402. 1917.

--- Le mythe de la création chez les Hurons. Revue
Franco-américaine, X, 492-502. 1913.

--- Supernatural Beings of the Huron and Wyandot.
AA, n.s., XVI, 288-313. 1914.

--- Wyandot Tales. JAFL, XXVIII, 83-95. 1915.

Barbeau, M., and Melvin, G. The Indian Speaks,
pp. 17-44, 102-4. Caldwell, 1943.

Beauchamp, W.M. Indian Nations of the Great Lakes.
AAOJ, XVII, 321-5. 1895.

Beaugrand-Champagne, A. Le Chemin et l'Emplacement de la Bourgade d'Hochelaga. CD, XII, 115-
60. 1947.

--- Les Hurons. CD, XI, 52-61. 1946.

--- Le Peuple d'Hochelaga. CD, XI, 93-114. 1946.

Bibaud, F.M. Biographie des sagamos illustrés de
l'Amérique Septentrionale, pp. 107-10, 185-90.
Montreal, 1848.

Biggar, H.P., ed. The Works of Samuel de Champlain, III, 114-58. Toronto, 1929.

Boucher, P. Histoire véritable et naturelle des
moeurs et productions du pays de la Nouvelle
France. Paris, 1864.

Bourne, E.G., ed. The Voyages and Explorations of
Samuel de Champlain, II, 119-44. New York, 1906.

Brebeuf, J. de. Burial Ceremonies of the Hurons.
ARBAE, V, 110-19. 1884.

Bushnell, D.I. Native Cemeteries and Forms of Burial East of the Mississippi. BBAE, LXXI, 73-83.
1920.

Campbell, T.S. Pioneer Priests of North America,
1642-1710. 2 vols. New York, 1908, 1910.

Carr, L. On the Social and Political Position of Woman among the Huron-Iroquois Tribes. RPM, III,
207-32. 1887.

Charlevoix, P.F.X. de. Journal of a Voyage to North
America. 2 vols. Chicago, 1923.

Chaumonot, J.M. Grammar of the Huron Language.
TLHSQ, II, 94-198. 1831.

Clarke, P.D. Origin and Traditional History of the
Wyandotts. 158 pp. Toronto, 1870.

Connelley, W.E. Indian Myths. 167 pp. New York,
1928.

--- Notes on the Folk-Lore of the Wyandots. JAFL,
XII, 116-25. 1899.

--- The Sword and Belt of Orion. AAR, 1905, 68-70.

--- Wyandot Folk-Lore. 116 pp. Topeka, 1899.

--- The Wyandots. AAR, 1899, 92-141.

Devine, E.J. Old Fort Ste. Marie. 56 pp. Mid-
land, 1942.

Emerson, J.N. The Old Indian Fort Site. Ontario
History, L. 1958.

Faillon. The Indian Tribes on the St. Lawrence.
AAR, 1923, 82-8.

Finley, J.B. History of the Wyandott Mission. 432
pp. Cincinatti, 1840.

--- Life among the Indians, ed. D.W. Clark. 548 pp.
1868.

Foreman, G. The Last Trek of the Indians, pp. 92-
9, 193-200. Chicago, 1946.

Gendron. Quelques particularitez du pays des Hurons.
New edit. 26 pp. Albany, 1868.

Gérin, L. The Hurons of Lorette. BAAS, LXX, 549-68. 1900.

Gibson, A.M. Wyandotte Mission. CO, XXXVI, 137-54. 1958.

Girault de Villeneuve, E.P.T. Des missions. 9 pp. Quebec, 1902.

Gray, L.H. Huron. ERE, VI, 883-6. 1914.

Greene, W. On Some Processes in Use Among the Huron Indians in Dyeing. TLHSQ, II, 23-5. 1831.

Gruber, J.W. Preliminary Notes on Huron Dentition. BESAF, XVII, 9. 1958.

Haldeman, S.S. Phonology of the Wyandots. PAPS, IV, 268-9. 1846.

Hale, H. The Fall of Hochelaga, a Study of Popular Tradition. JAFL, VII, 1-14. 1894.

--- Four Huron Wampum Records. JAI, XXVI, 221-54. 1896.

--- Huron Folk-Lore. JAFL, I, 177-83; II, 249-54. 1888-1889.

--- A Huron Historical Legend. MAH, 1883, 475-83.

Hammond, J.H. Explanation of the Ossuary Burial of the Huron Nation. AAR, 1923, 95-102.

Hamy, E.T. Note sur un wampum représentant les quatre-nations des Hurons. JSAP, I, 163-6. 1897.

Herman, M.W. The Social Aspect of Huron Property. AA, LVIII, 1044-58. 1956.

Hewitt, J.N.B. Blood Cement used by the Ancient Hurons. AA, VI, 322. 1893.

--- The Cosmogonic Gods of the Iroquois. PAAAS, XLIV, 241-50. 1895.

--- Huron. BBAE, XXX, i, 584-91. 1907.

Hickerson, H. The Feast of the Dead among the Seventeenth Century Algonkians of the Upper Great Lakes. AA, LXII, 81-107. 1960.

Hirschfelder, C.A. Burial Customs of the Hurons. PAAAS, XL, 363-5. 1891.

Holland, C.P. From Paganism to Mysticism: René Tsondiwane. Martyr's Shrine Message, XVII, i, 20-21, 23, 1953.

Houghton, F. The Indian Occupancy of the Niagara Frontier. BBSNS, IX, 263-374. 1909.

Hrdlicka, A. Ritual Ablation of Front Teeth in Siberia and America. SMC, XCIX, III, 1-32. 1940.

Hunter, A.F. Indian Village Sites in North and South Orillia Townships. AAR, 1903, 105-25.

--- National Characteristics and Migrations of the Hurons. TCI, III, 225-8. 1893.

--- Notes on Sites of Huron Villages. AAR, 1899, 51-82; 1901, 56-100; 1902, 153-83.

James, C.C. The Downfall of the Huron Nation. PTRSC, ser. 2, XII, ii, 311-46. 1906.

Jenness, D. Indians of Canada. BCDM, LXV, 289-99. 1932.

Jones, A.E. Huron Indians. Catholic Encyclopedia, VII, 565-83. New York, 1910.

--- "8endake Ehen," or Old Huronia. Report of the Bureau of Archives for the Province of Ontario, V, 1-505. 1908.

--- Topography of Huronia. ICA, XV, i, 299-30. 1907.

Jury, W. Flanagan Prehistoric Huron Village Site. University of Western Ontario, Bulletin of Museums, VI, 1-9. 1948.

--- Huron Area Archaeology. Ontario History, L. 1958.

Jury, W. and E.M. Saint Louis: Huron Indian Village and Jesuit Mission Site. MBMIA, X, 1-76, 1955.

Jury, W., and Fox, W.S. A Pre-White Huron Village in Simcoe County, Ontario. PTRSC, ser. 3, XLII, ii, 85-9. 1948.

--- St. Ignace. PTRSC, ser. 3, XLI, ii, 55-78. 1947.

Kennedy, J.H. Jesuit and Savage in New France. 206 pp. New Haven, 1950.

Kenton, E., ed. The Indians of North America, I, 211-31, 234-312, 498-523; II, 29-46. New York, 1927.

Kerans, P. Murder and Atonement in Huronia. Martyrs' Shrine Message, XVII, ii, 46-7, 52-3. 1953.

Kidd, K.E. Excavation and Historical Identification of a Huron Ossuary. AAn, XVIII, 359-79. 1953.

--- Orr Lake Pottery. TCI, 165-185. 1951.

--- Sixty Years of Ontario Archeology. AEUS, 71-82. 1952.

Knowles, F.H.S. Physical Anthropology of the Roebuck Iroquois. BCDM, LXXXVII, 1-75. 1937.

Lahontan, L.A. New Voyages to North America, ed. R.G. Thwaites. 2 vols. Chicago, 1905.

Laverdière, C.H., ed. Oeuvres de Champlain. 2d edit. 6 vols. Quebec, 1870.

Le Beau, C. Avantures du Sr. C. Le Beau. 2 vols. Amsterdam, 1738.

Le Jeune, P. Relation. The Jesuit Relations and Allied Documents, ed. R.G. Thwaites, XI, 27-279; XII, 1-277. Cleveland, 1898.

Lighthall, W.D. Hochelagans and Mohawks. PTRSC, ser. 2, V, ii, 199-211. 1899.

--- Hochelaga and the "Hill of Hochelaga." PTRSC, 3rd ser., XVIII, ii, 95. 1924.

--- A New Hochelaga Burial Ground. Montreal, July-September 1898, 5. 1898.

--- New Hochelaga Finds in 1933. PTRSC, XXVIII, 103-8. 1934.

McIlwraith, T.F. The Feast of the Dead. An, VI, 83-6. 1958.

--- On the Location of Cahiagué. PTRSC, ser. 3, XLI, ii, 99-102. 1947.

Martin, F. Hurons et Iroquois. Paris, 1877.

Merlet, L.V.C. Histoire des relations des Hurons et des Abnaquis du Canada avec Notre-Dame de Chartres. 78 pp. Chartres, 1858.

Merwin, B.W. The Art of Quillwork. MJ, IX, 50-5. 1918.

Mooney, J. Tionontati. BBAE, XXX, ii, 755-6. 1910.

Morgan, L.H. The Indian Journals, 1859-62, pp. 28, 58-9. Ann Arbor, 1959.

--- Systems of Consanguinity and Affinity. SCK, XVII, 291-382. 1871.

Orr, R.B. The Hurons. AAR, 1921-22, 9-24.

--- The Iroquois in Canada. AAR, XXXI, 9-55. 1919.

--- The Masks or False Faces of our Ontario Indians. AAR, XXXIII, 32-7. 1922.

--- Tionnontates. AAR, 1914, 7-18.

Parkman, F. The Jesuits in North America. 463 pp. Boston, 1867.

Peckham, H.H. Thomas Gist's Indian Captivity, 1758-1759. PMHB, LXXX, 285-311. 1956.

Perrot, N. Memoir on the Manners, Customs, and Religion of the Savages of North America. ITUMV, I, 25-272. 1911.

--- Mémoire sur les moeurs, coustumes et relligion des sauvages de l'Amérique septentrionale. 341 pp. Paris, 1864.

Popham, R.E. Late Huron Occupations in Ontario. Ontario History, XLII, ii, 81-90. 1950.

Potier, P. Elementa grammaticae huronicae. Report of the Ontario Bureau of Archives, XV, 1-157. 1920.

--- Extraits de l'Evangelé. Report of the Ontario Bureau of Archives, XV, 457-688. 1920.

--- Radices huronicae. Report of the Ontario Bureau of Archives, XV, 159-455. 1920.

Powell, J.W. Wyandot Government. ARBAE, I, 57-69. 1880.

Read, D.B. The Hurons. TCI, ser. 4, I, 86-95. 1890.

Richardie, F., and Potier, P. Account Book of the Huron Mission at Detroit and Sandwich (1740-1751). Report of the Ontario Bureau of Archives, XV, 689-724. 1920.

Rioux, M. Les Hurons-Iroquois Pratiquaient- ils le Totemisme? PTRSC, ser. B, XXXIX, i, 173-6. 1945.

Robinson, P.J. The Huron Equivalents of Cartier's Second Vocabulary. PTRSC, ser. 3, XLII, 127-46. 1948.

Robinson, P.J. Huron Place-Names on Lake Erie. PTRSC, ser. 3, XL, ii, 191-207. 1946.

--- The Origin of the Name Hochelaga. CHR, XXIII, 295-6. 1942.

Rousseau, J.J. La Religion Primitive des Montagnais et des Hurons. ICA, XXX, 151-54. 1955.

--- Les Hochelagas. ICA, XV, i, 279-97. 1907.

Sagard-Théodat, C. Dictionnaire de la langue Huronne. New edit. Paris, 1866.

--- Histoire du Canada. Paris, 1836; new ed., 1866.

Sargent, M. Seven Songs from Lorette. JAFL, LXIII, 175. 1950.

Schlup, E. The Wyandot Mission. OAHQ, XV, 163-81. 1906.

Scull, G.D., ed. Voyages of Peter Esprit Radisson. Boston, 1885.

Shaw, J.G. Brother Sagard's Huronian Triangle. Culture, III, 17-30. 1942.

Shea, J.G. An Historical Sketch of the Tionontates. HM, V, 262-9. 1861.

Shetrone, H.C. The Indian in Ohio. OAHQ, XXVII, 273-510. 1918.

Skinner, A. Some Wyandot Corn Foods. YPMCM, III, 109-12.

Smith, J. An Account of the Remarkable Occurrences in the Life and Travels of Col. James Smith, ed. W.M. Darlington. Ohio Valley Historical Series, V. 1870.

Speck, F.G. Huron Hunting Territories in Quebec. IN, IV, 1-12. 1927.

--- Huron Moose Hair Embroidery. AA, n.s., XIII, 1-14. 1911.

--- Notes on the Material Culture of the Huron. AA, n.s., XIII, 208-28. 1911.

--- Some Huron Treaty Belts. MJ, II, 26-7. 1911.

Squair, J., tr. The Indian Tribes on the St. Lawrence at the Time of the Arrival of the French. AAR, XXXIV, 82-8. 1923.

Talbot, F.X. Saint among the Hurons. 351 pp. New York, 1949.

Thomas, E.H. Tionnontates (Petun or Tobacco Indian) Tools. PA, XXVI, 43-47. 1956.

Thomson, M.M. Excavating Ontario History. Toronto, 1948.

Thwaites, R.G., ed. The French Regime in Wisconsin. CSHSQ, Vols. XVI-XVIII. 1902-08.

--- The Jesuit Relations and Allied Documents. 74 vols. Cleveland, 1896-1901.

Tylor, E.B. The Hale Series of Huron Wampum Belts. JAI, XXVI, 248-54. 1896.

Walker, B.N. Tales of the Bark Lodges. 107 pp. Oklahoma City, 1919.

Walker, B. N. O. Mon-dah-min and the Redman's
Old Uses of Corn as Food. CO, XXXV, 194-203.
1957.

Wallace, A. F. C. Mazeway Disintegration. HO,
XV, ii, 23-7. 1957.

Waugh, F. W. Notes on Canadian Pottery. AAR, 1901,
108-15.

Weer, P. T. Preliminary Notes on the Iroquoian Family. PRS, I, 1-59. 1937.

Wilkie, J. Grammar of the Huron Language. TLHSQ,
II, 94-198. 1831.

Wilson, D. The Huron-Iroquois of Canada. PTRSC,
II, ii, 55-106. 1884.

--- The Huron Race and Its Head-Form. CJ, n.s.,
XIII, 113-34. 1871.

Wintemberg, W. J. Bone and Horn Harpoon Heads of
the Ontario Indians. AAR, 1905, 33-56.

--- The Sidey-Mackay Village Site. AAn, XI, 154-
82. 1946.

5. IROQUOIS

Including the Cayuga, Mohawk, Oneida, Onondaga,
and Seneca.

Fenton, W. N. The Iroquois Eagle Dance. BBAE,
CLVI, 330 pp. 1953.

MacNeish, R. S. Iroquois Pottery Types. BNMC,
CXXIV, 166 pp. 1952.

Morgan, L. H. League of the Ho-Dé-No-Sau-Nee
or Iroquois, ed. H. M. Lloyd. 2 vols. New York,
1901; reprint, New Haven, 1954.

Noon, J. A. Law and government of the Grand River
Iroquois. VFPA, XII, 1-186. 1949.

Ritzenthaler, R. E. The Oneida Indians of Wisconsin.
BPMCM, XIX, 1-52. 1950.

Speck, F. G. The Iroquois. BCIS, XXIII, 1-94. 1945.

Adams, S. L. The Longhouse of the Iroquois. 175 pp.
Chicago, 1944.

Akweks, A. Legend of the Wampum Bird. SS, VI,
iii, 9. 1954.

--- A Mohawk Adoption.   NYFQ, VI, 44-6. 1950.

Allen, H. E. An Oneida Tale. JAFL, LVII, 280-1.
1944.

Anonymous. Interpretation of Three Belts of Wampum
sent to Canada by the Mohawks in 1639. Canadian
Antiquarian and Numismatic Journal, III, 110-12.
1874-75.

--- A Seneca Adoption. M, XXVI, 94-6. 1952.

--- Supplementary Materials on Location, Numbers
and Socio-Economic Conditions of Indians and Eskimos. ECAS, I, 103-16. 1955.

Bailey, A. G. The Significance of the Identity and
Disappearance of the Laurentian Iroquois. PTRSC,
ser. 3, XXVII, ii, 97-107. 1933.

Bailey, J. H. An Analysis of Iroquoian Ceramic Types.
AAn, III, 333-8. 1938.

Baldwin, C. C. The Iroquois in Ohio. Western Reserve Historical Society, II, xl, 25-32. 1878.

Barbeau, M. Assomption Sash. BCDM, XCIII, 1-
51. 1937.

--- Classification of Iroquoian Radicals with Subjective Pronominal Prefixes. MCDM, XLVI, 1-30.
1915.

--- The Dragon Myths and Ritual Songs of the Iro-
quoians. Journal of the International Folk Music
Council, III, 81-85. 1951.

--- Iroquoian Clans and Phratries. AA, n.s., XIX,
392-405. 1917.

Bartram, J. Observations on the Inhabitants, Climate, Soil, Rivers, Productions, Animals, and
Other Matters Worthy of Notice. 94 pp. London,
1751.

Bates, E. Our First New York Co-Operators. Bureau
Farmer, VI, ii, 3-25. 1930.

Baxter, J. P. A Memoir of Jacques Cartier. 464 pp.
New York, 1906.

Beauchamp, W. M. Aboriginal Chipped Stone Implements of New York. NYSMB, XVI, 5-84. 1897.

--- Aboriginal Occupation of New York. NYSMB,
XXXII, 5-187. 1900.

--- Aboriginal Place Names of New York. NYSMB,
CVIII, 5-333. 1907.

--- Aboriginal Use of Wood in New York. NYSMB,
LXXXIX, 87-272. 1905.

--- Cayuga Indian Relics. AN, XXIII, 401-6. 1889.

--- Champlain and the Oneidas in 1615. Annual
Report of the American Scenic and Historic Preservation Society, XXIII, 625-43. 1918.

--- Civil, Religious, and Mourning Councils and
Ceremonies of Adoption of the New York Indians.
NYSMB, CXIII, 341-451. 1907.

--- The Early Religion of the Iroquois. AAOJ, XIV,
344-9. 1892.

--- Earthenware of the New York Aborigines. NYSMB,
XXII, 75-146. 1898.

--- Earthworks and Stockades. AAOJ, XIII, 42-51.
1891.

--- The Founders of the New York Iroquois League
and Its Probable Date. RNYAS, III. 1921.

--- The Good Hunter and the Iroquois Medicine.
JAFL, XIV, 153-9. 1901.

--- Hi-a-wat-ha. JAFL, IV, 295-306. 1891.

--- A History of the New York Iroquois. NYSMB,
LXXVIII, 125-461. 1905.

Beauchamp, W.M. Horn and Bone Implements of
the New York Indians. NYSMB, L, 243-350. 1902.

--- Indian Names in New York. 148 pp. Fayetteville, 1893.

--- Indian Nations of the Great Lakes. AAOJ, XVII,
321-5. 1895.

--- An Iroquois Condolence. JAFL, VIII, 313-16.
1895.

--- Iroquois Folk Lore. 247 pp. Syracuse, 1922.

--- Iroquois Games. JAFL, IX, 269-77. 1896.

--- Iroquois Notes. JAFL, IV, 39-46; V, 223-9.
1891-2.

--- Iroquois Pottery and Wampum. PWHGS, XII, 55-
68. 1912.

--- The Iroquois Trail. 150 pp. Fayetteville, 1892.

--- The Iroquois White Dog Feast. AAOJ, VII, 235-
9. 1885.

--- Iroquois Women. JAFL, XIII, 81-91. 1900.

--- The Life of Conrad Weiser. 122 pp. Syracuse,
1925.

--- Metallic Implements of the New York Indians.
NYSMB, LV, 3-92. 1902.

--- Metallic Ornaments of the New York Indians.
NYSMB, LXXIII, 3-120. 1903.

--- Mohawk Notes. JAFL, VIII, 217-21. 1895.

--- The New Religion of the Iroquois. JAFL, X,
169-80. 1897.

--- Notes on Onondaga Dances. JAFL, VI, 181-4.
1893.

--- Onondaga Customs. JAFL, I, 195-203. 1888.

--- Onondaga Indian Names of Plants. Bulletin of
the Torrey Botanical Club, XV, 262-6. 1888.

--- Onondaga Names of Months. JAFL, II, 160-61.
1889.

--- Onondaga Notes. JAFL, VIII, 209-16. 1895.

--- Onondaga Plant Names. JAFL, XV, 91-103.
1902.

--- Onondaga Tale of the Pleiades. JAFL, XIII,
281-2. 1900.

--- Onondaga Tales. JAFL, I, 44-8; II, 261-70;
VI, 173-80. 1888-93.

--- The Origin and Antiquity of the New York Iroquois. AAOJ, VIII, 358-66. 1886.

--- The Origin and Early Life of the New York Iroquois. Transactions of the Oneida Historical Society, 1887-89, 119-42.

--- The Origin of the Iroquois. AAOJ, XVI, 61-9.
1894.

--- Permanence of Early Iroquois Clans and Sachem-
ships. PAAAS, XXXIV, 381-92. 1885.

--- Permanency of Iroquois Clans and Sachemship.
AAOJ, VIII, 82-91. 1886.

Beauchamp, W.M. Polished Stone Articles used by
the New York Aborigines. NYSMB, XVIII, 3-102.
1897.

--- The Principal Founders of the Iroquois League
and its Probable Date. Proceedings of the New
York State Historical Association. XXIV, 27-36.
1926.

--- Wampum and Shell Articles used by the New York
Indians. NYSMB, XLI, 328-480. 1901.

--- Wampum Belts of the Six Nations. ARSI, 1879,
389-90.

--- Wampum used in Council and as Currency.
AAOJ, XX, 1-13. 1898.

Beaugrand-Champagne, A.L. Les Anciens Iroquois
de Québec. CD, I, 171-99. 1936.

--- Le chemin et l'emplacement de la bourgade
d'Hochelaga. CD, XII, 115-60. 1947.

--- Croyances des anciens Iroquois. CD, VI, 195-
210. 1941.

--- Les Maladies et la Médicine des Anciens Iroquois.
CD, IX, 227-42. 1944.

--- L'organisation sociale des anciens Iroquois. CD,
IV, 271-89. 1939.

--- La poterie iroquoise. CD, VIII, 267-84. 1943.

--- Le régime politique des anciens Iroquois. CD,
V, 217-29. 1940.

--- La stratégie,la tactique et l'armement des anciens
Iroquois. CD, X, 21-40. 1945.

Belknap, J. Report on the Oneida, Stockbridge and
Brotherton Indians, 1796. INAM, series 2, LIV,
39 pp. 1955.

Bibaud, F.M. Biographie des sagamos illustrés de
l'Amérique Septentrionale, pp. 101-5, 133-4,
161-84, 207-10, 227-30, 265-70. Montreal,
1848.

Biggar, H.P., ed. The Works of Samuel de Champlain. 6 vols. Toronto, 1929.

Bleeker, S. Indians of the Longhouse. 160 pp. New
York, 1950.

Blomkvist, E.E. Irokezy. Trudy Instituta Etnografii
Imena N.N. Mikhluvo-Maklaia, XXV, 67-97. 1955.

Boas, F. Notes on the Iroquois Language. Putnam
Anniversary Volume, pp. 427-60. New York, 1909.

--- Zur Anthropologie der nordamerikanischen Indianer.
VBGA, 1895, 367-411.

Bond, R.P. Queen Anne's American Kings. 160 pp.
Oxford, 1952.

Bourne, E.G., ed. The Voyages and Explorations of
Samuel de Champlain. 2 vols. New York, 1906.

Boyle, D. Big Corn Feast. AAR, 1899, 34-40.

--- The Iroquois. AAR, 1905, 146-58.

--- Iroquois Medicine Man's Mask. AAR, 1899, 27-
9.

Boyle, D. The Making of a Cayuga Chief. AAR, 1905, 56-9.

--- On the Paganism of the Civilised Iroquois of Ontario. JAI, XXX, 263-73. 1900.

Brant-Sero, J.O. Dekanawideh. Man, I, 166-70. 1901.

Breysig, K. Die Entstehung des Staates aus der Geschlechtsverfassung bei Tlinkit und Irokesen. SJG, XXVIII, 483-527. 1904.

Brigham, A.P. Sites and Trails of the Mohawk Indians. NYSMB, CCLXXX, 86-9. 1929.

Brodhead, J.R. Wentworth Greenhalgh's Journal of a Tour to the Indians of Western New York. Documents relative to the Colonial History of the State of New York, ed. E.B.O'Callaghan, III, 250-2. Albany, 1853.

Brown, D.M. Indian Winter Legends. WA, n.s., XXII, 49-53. 1941.

--- Wisconsin Indian Corn Origin Myths. WA, n.s., XXI, 19-27. 1940.

Bruyas, J. Radical Words of the Mohawk Language with Their Derivatives. ARUNY, XVI, Appendix E, 1-123. 1863.

Buck, J. What is Wampum? AAR, XXXVI, 48-50. 1928.

Burke, C. The Indian and His River. 45 pp. Rochester, 1933.

Burtin, N.V. Histoire de l'Ancien Testament traduite en Iroquois. 706 pp. Montreal, 1890.

Bushnell, D.I. Native Cemeteries and Forms of Burial East of the Mississippi. BBAE, LXXI, 70-3, 83-9. 1920.

Campbell, T.S. Pioneer Priests of North America, 1642-1710. 2 vols. New York, 1908, 1910.

Canfield, W.W. The Legends of the Iroquois. 211 pp. New York, 1902.

Carpenter, E.S. Iroquoian Figurines. AAn, VIII, 105-13. 1942.

--- Iroquois Prehistory. PA, XXIII, 72-78. 1953.

Carr, L. On the Social and Political Position of Woman among the Huron-Iroquois Tribes. RPM, III, 207-32. 1887.

Carse, M.R. The Mohawk Iroquois. BASC, XXIII, 3-53. 1949.

Caswell, H.S. Our Life among the Iroquois Indians. 321 pp. Boston, 1892.

Chadwick, E.M. The People of the Longhouse. 166 pp. Toronto, 1897.

Chafe, W.L. The Classification of Morphs in Seneca. Anthropological Linguistics, I, v, 1-6. 1959.

--- Seneca Morphology. IJAL, XXVI, 11-22, 123-30. 1960.

Chalmers, H. and Monture, E.B. Joseph Brant: Mohawk. 368 pp. Toronto, 1955.

Chamberlain, A.F. Iroquois in Northwestern Canada. AA, n.s., VI, 459-63. 1904.

--- A Mohawk Legend of Adam and Eve. JAFL, II, 228. 1889.

--- Notes on Indian Child-Language. AA, III, 237-41. 1890.

Charlevoix, P.F.X.de. Journal of a Voyage to North America, ed. L.P.Kellogg. 2 vols. Chicago, 1923.

Clark, J.V.H. Lights and Lines of Indian Character. 375 pp. Syracuse, 1854.

--- Onondaga. 2 vols. Syracuse, 1849.

Clarke, J.M. Report on the Archeology Section. ARUNY, LXI, i, 85-111. 1908.

--- Wampums of the Iroquois Confederacy. ARUNY, LXI, 85-111. 1908.

Clarke, N.T. The Thacher Wampum Belts. NYSMB, CCLXXIX, 53-8. 1929.

--- The Wampum Belt Collection of the New York State Museum. NYSMB, CCLXXXVIII, 85-122. 1931.

Clarke, T.W. The Bloody Mohawk. 372 pp. New York, 1940.

Colden, C. History of the Five Indian Nations, Continuation, 1707-1720. CNYHS, 1935, 359-434. 1937.

--- The History of the Five Indian Nations of Canada. New edit. 2 vols. New York, 1922.

Conklin, H.C. and Sturtevant, W.C. Seneca Indian Singing Tools at Coldspring Longhouse. PAPS, XCVII, 262-90. 1953.

Conover, G.S. Sayerqueraghta, King of the Senecas. Waterloo, Vt., 1885.

--- Seneca Indian Villages. 12 pp. Geneva, 1889.

Conservation Society of New York County. Seneca Indians. 125 pp. York, 1944.

Converse, H.M. The Iroquois Silver Brooches. ARUNY, LIV, i, r231-r254. 1900.

--- Myths and Legends of the New York State Iroquois, ed. A.C.Parker. NYSMB, CXXV, 5-195. 1908.

--- The Seneca New-Year Ceremony and Other Customs. IN, VII, 69-89. 1930.

Cook, F. Journals of the Military Expedition of Major General John Sullivan. 580 pp. Auburn, 1887.

Cooke, C.A. Iroquois Personal Names. PAPS, XCVI, 424-38. 1952.

Cornplanter, J.J. Legends of the Longhouse. 216 pp. Philadelphia, 1938.

Cringan, A.T. Iroquois Folk Songs. AAR, 1902, 137-52.

Cringan, A.T. Pagan Dance Songs of the Iroquois. AAR, 1899, 168-89.

Crowell, S. The Dog Sacrifice of the Seneca. Indian Miscellany, ed. W.W.Beach, pp. 323-32. Albany, 1877.

Cuoq, J.A. Etudes philologiques sur quelques langues sauvages de l'Amérique. 160 pp. Montreal, 1866.

--- Kaiatonsera iontewaienstakwa kaiatonseraso: Nouveau syllabaire iroquois. 69 pp. Tiohtiake, 1873.

--- Lexique de la langue Iroquoise. 215 pp. Montreal, 1882.

Curtin, J. Seneca Indian Myths. 516 pp. New York, 1923.

Curtin, J., and Hewitt, J.N.B. Seneca Fiction, Legends, and Myths. ARBAE, XXXII, 37-819. 1911.

Cusick, D. Sketches of Ancient History of the Six Nations. 35 pp. Lockport, 1848.

--- Sketches of the Ancient History of the Six Nations. HCPIT, V, 631-46. 1855.

Deardorff, M.H. The Cornplanter Grant in Warren County. WPHM, XXIV, 1-22. 1941.

--- The Religion of Handsome Lake. BBAE, CXLIX, 77-108. 1951.

--- Zeisberger's Allegheny River Indian Towns: 1767-1770. PA, XVI, 2-19. 1946.

Deardorff, M.H. and Snyderman, G.S. A Nineteenth Century Journal of a Visit to the Indians of New York. PAPS, C, 582-612. 1956.

Densmore, F. An Onondaga Thanksgiving Song. Indian School Journal, VII, 23-4. 1907.

Deserontyon, J. A Mohawk Form of Ritual of Condolence. INM, X, 87-110. 1928.

Desrosiers, L.P. Iroquoisie, Terre Française. CD, XX, 35-59. 1955.

--- Iroquoisie, 1534-1646. 351 pp. Montreal, 1947.

--- Les Onnantagués. CD, XVIII, 45-66. 1953.

--- Premières missions iroquoises. Revue de l'Histoire de l'Amérique Française, I, 21-38. 1947.

Dodge, E.S. A Cayuga Bear Society Curing Rite. PM, XXII, 65-71. 1949.

--- Notes from the Six Nations on the Hunting and Trapping of Wild Turkeys and Passenger Pigeons. JWAS, XXXV, 342-3. 1945.

Donaldson, T. The George Catlin Indian Gallery. RUSNM, 1885, 154-96.

--- The Six Nations of New York. RIT, 1890, 447-98.

Donohue, T. The Iroquois and the Jesuits. 276 pp. Buffalo, 1895.

Doren, C. van, and Boyd, J.P. Indian Treaties printed by Benjamin Franklin. 340 pp. Philadelphia, 1938.

Doty, L.L. A History of Livingston County, pp. 19-127. Genesee, 1876.

Douglas, F.H. Iroquois Foods. DAMLS, XXVI, 1-4. 1931.

--- Iroquois Long House. DAMLS, XII, 1-4. 1930.

Downes, R.C. Council Fires on the Upper Ohio. 367 pp. Pittsburgh, 1940.

Dunning, R.W. Iroquois Feast of the Dead. An, VI, 87-118. 1958.

Eccles, W.J. Frontenac and the Iroquois. CHR, XXXVI, 1-16. 1955.

Echeverria, D. The Iroquois Visit Rochambeau at Newport in 1780. Rhode Island History, XI, 73-81. 1952.

Eggen, D. Indian Tales from Western New York. NYFQ, VI, 240-5. 1950.

Emerson, J.N. Castellation Development among the Iroquois. Ontario Archeological Society, Research Guide, I. 1955.

--- Understanding Iroquois Pottery in Ontario. 64 pp. Toronto, 1956.

Ewers, J.C. Gustavus Sohon's Portraits of Flathead and Pend d'Oreille Indians. SMC, CX, vii, 54-62. 1948.

Fadden, R. The Visions of Handsome Lake. PH, XXII, 341-58. 1955.

Fenstermaker, G.B. Good Luck Hunting Charms. National Archaeological News, I, iv, 27-9. 1937.

--- Iroquois Animal Gods or Hunting Charms. PA, VI, 76-8. 1936.

--- Iroquois Pottery. National Archaeological News, I, iii, 3-6, 16-17. 1937.

--- Iroquois Pottery. PA, VI, 79-82. 1936.

Fenton, W.N. A Calendar of Manuscript Materials Relating to the History of the Six Nations. PAPS, XCVII, 578-95. 1953.

--- Collecting Materials for a Political History of the Six Nations. PAPS, XCIII, 233-7. 1949.

--- The Concept of Locality and the Program of Iroquois Research. BBAE, CXLIX, 1-12. 1951.

--- Contacts Between Iroquois Herbalism and Colonial Medicine. ARSI, 1941, 503-26.

--- Fish Drives among the Cornplanter Seneca. PA, XII, 48-52. 1942.

--- A Further Quest for Iroquois Medicines. EFWSI, 1939, 93-6.

--- An Herbarium from the Allegheny Senecas. Historical Annals of Southwestern New York, ed. Doty, Congdon, and Thornton, 787-96. New York, 1940.

Fenton, W.N. The Hiawatha Wampum Belt of the Iroquois League for Peace. ACISA, V, 3-7. 1960.

--- The Hyde de Neuville Portraits of New York Savages in 1807-1808. NYHSQ, XXXVIII, 118-37. 1954.

--- An Iroquois Condolence Council for installing Cayuga Chiefs in 1945. JWAS, XXXVI, 110-27. 1946.

--- Iroquois Indian Folklore. JAFL, LX, 383-97. 1947.

--- Iroquois Studies at the Mid-Century. PAPS, XCV, 296-310. 1951.

--- Iroquois Suicide. BBAE, CXXVIII, 80-137. 1941.

--- Locality as a Basic Factor in the Development of Iroquois Social Structure. BBAE, CXLIX, 35-54. 1951.

--- Long-term Trends of Change among the Iroquois. In V.F.Ray, ed., Cultural Stability and Cultural Change, 30-35. Seattle, 1957.

--- The Maple and the Passenger Pigeon in Iroquois Indian Life. Bulletin to Schools, University of the State of New York, March, 7 pp. 1955.

--- Masked Medicine Societies of the Iroquois. ARSI, 1940, 397-430.

--- Medicinal Plant Lore of the Iroquois. Bulletin to the Schools, XXXV, vii, 233-7. Albany, 1949.

--- Museum and Field Studies of Iroquois Masks and Ritualism. EFWSI, 1940, 95-100.

--- An Outline of Seneca Ceremonies at Coldspring Longhouse. YUPA, IX, 1-23. 1936.

--- Place Names and Related Activities of the Cornplanter Senecas. PA, XV, 25-29, 42-50, 88-96, 108-18; XVI, 42-57. 1945-46.

--- Pennsylvania's Remaining Indian Settlement. Pennsylvania Park News, XLIV, 2 pp. 1945.

--- Problems arising from the Historic Northeastern Position of the Iroquois. SMC, C, 159-251. 1940.

--- The Roll Call of the Iroquois Chiefs. 103 pp. Detroit, 1950.

--- The Roll Call of the Iroquois Chiefs. SMC,CXI, xv, 1-75. 1950.

--- Samuel Crowell's Account of a Seneca Dog Sacrifice. NOQ, XVI, 158-63. 1944.

--- Seneca Indians by Asher Wright. E, IV, 302-21. 1957.

--- The Seneca Society of Faces. SM, XLIV, 215-38. 1937.

--- Seneca Songs from Coldspring Longhouse. Library of Congress, Music Division, Recording Laboratory, 16 pp. and Record Album XVII.

--- Seth Newhouse's Traditional History and Constitution of the Iroquois Confederacy. PAPS, XCIII, 185-206. 1949.

Fenton, W.N. Simeon Gibson: Iroquois Informant, 1889-1943. AA, n.s., XLVI, 231-234. 1944.

--- Some Social Customs of the Modern Seneca. Social Welfare Bulletin, VII, i, 4-7. 1936.

--- Songs from the Iroquois Longhouse. Smithsonian Publication 3691, 34 pp. 1942.

--- Tonawanda Longhouse Ceremonies. BBAE, CXXVIII, 140-66. 1941.

--- Toward the Gradual Civilization of the Indian Natives. PAPS, C, 567-81. 1956.

--- Twi'yendagon' (Wood-eater) Takes the Heavenly Path. AmI, III, iii, 11-15. 1946.

Fenton, W.N., and Deardorff, M.H. The Last Passenger Pigeon Hunts of the Cornplanter Senecas. JWAS, XXXIII, 289-315. 1943.

Fenton, W.N. and Dodge, E.S. An Elm Bark Canoe in the Peabody Museum of Salem. American Neptune, IX, 185-206. 1949.

Fenton, W.N. and Kurath, G.P. The Feast of the Dead, or Ghost Dance at Six Nations Reserve, Canada. BBAE, CXLIX, 139-66. 1951.

Follett, H.C. Seneca Burial Sites in New York State. Archeological Bulletin, VI, 36-7. 1915.

Freilich, M. Cultural Persistence among the Modern Iroquois. A, LIII, 473-83. 1958.

French, M.J. Samuel de Champlain's Incursion against the Onondaga Nation. 23 pp. Ann Arbor, 1949.

Frey, S.L. The Mohawks.Oneida Historical Society Transactions, VIII, 1-41. 1898.

--- The Historic and Prehistoric Mohawks. AA, VI, 277-8. 1893.

Gibson, A.M. Wyandotte Mission. CO,XXXVI, 137-54. 1958.

Goldenweiser, A.A. The Clan and Maternal Family of the Iroquois League. AA, n.s., XV, 696-7. 1913.

--- Early Civilization, pp. 70-82. New York, 1922.

--- Hanging-Flower, the Iroquois. American Indian Life, ed. E.C.Parsons, pp. 99-106. New York, 1925.

--- On Iroquois Work. SRGSC, 1912, 464-75; 1913, 365-72.

Grassman, T. The Mohawk-Caughnawaga Excavations. PA, XXII, 33-6. 1952.

--- The Question of the Locations of Mohawk Indian Village Sites Existing during the Historic Period. PA, XXII, 98-111. 1952.

Gray, L.H. Iroquois. ERE, VII, 420-2. 1915.

Griffin, J.B. The Iroquois in American Prehistory. PMA, XXIX, 357-74. 1943.

Guthe, A. K. The Cultural Background of the Iro-
quois. Essays in the Science of Culture in Honor of
Leslie A. White, 202-15. New York, 1960.
--- The Hummel Site, An Early Iroquois Occupation.
BESAF, XIV, 11. 1955.
--- A Possible Seneca House Site, A.D.1600. PA,
XXVIII, 33-8. 1958.
--- A Possible Seneca House Site: 1600 A.D. BESAF,
XVI, 13. 1957.
Hale, H. "Above" and "Below." JAFL, III, 178-90.
1890.
--- Hiawatha and the Iroquois Confederation. 20 pp.
Salem, 1881.
--- Indian Etymologies. AA, I, 290-1. 1888.
--- Indian Migrations as evidenced by Language.
AAOJ, V, 18-28. 1883.
--- The Iroquois Book of Rites. 222 pp. Philadel-
phia, 1883.
--- An Iroquois Condoling Council. PTRSC, ser. 2,
I, ii, 45-65. 1895.
--- The Iroquois Sacrifice of the White Dog. AAOJ,
VII, 7-14. 1885.
--- A Lawgiver of the Stone Age. PAAAS, XXX, 324-
41. 1881.
--- On Some Doubtful or Intermediate Articulations.
JAI, XIV, 233-43. 1885.
Hamilton, M. W. Guy Johnson's Opinions on the
American Indian. PMHB, LXXVII, 311-27. 1953.
Hanna, C.A. The Wilderness Trail, pp. 26-87. New
York, 1911.
Hargrett, L. A Bibliography of the Constitutions and
Laws of the American Indians, pp. 106-9. Cam-
bridge, 1947.
Harrington, M.R. The Dark Dance of Ji-gé-onh. M,
VII, 76-9. 1933.
--- Hiawatha's Peace League. PA, XV, 70-74. 1945.
--- Iroquois Silverwork. APAM, I, 351-69. 1908.
--- The Origin of Iroquois Silversmithing. AA, n.s.,
XII, 349-57. 1910.
--- Some Seneca Corn-Foods and Their Preparation.
AA, n.s., X, 575-90. 1908.
--- Some Unusual Iroquois Specimens. AA, n.s.,
XI, 85-91. 1909.
--- The Story Bag. M, V, 147-52, 179-83. 1931-32.
Harris, G.H. The Indian Bread Root of the Senecas.
8 pp. Waterloo, 1890.
--- Root Foods of the Seneca Indians. PRAS, I, 106-
17. 1891.
Hatt, R.T. Installing a Cayuga Chief. Cranbrook
Institute of Science, Newsletter, XV, 65-71.1946.
Hawley, C. Early Chapters of Cayuga History. 106
pp. Auburn, 1879.

Hawley, C. Early Chapters of Seneca History. Au-
burn, 1884.
Hawley, G. Mohawk Numbers. MHSC, ser. 1, X, 137. 1809.
Heckewelder, J. An Account of the History, Manners,
and Customs of the Indian Nations. THLC, I, 1-
348. 1819.
Hennepin, L. Description de la Louisiane. Paris,
1683.
--- Description of Louisiana, ed. J.M.Shea. 407 pp.
New York, 1880.
--- A New Discovery of a Vast Country in America,
ed. R.G.Thwaites. 2 vols. Chicago, 1903.
--- Nouvelle decouverte d'un tres grand pays situé
dans l'Amérique. Utrecht, 1697.
Henning, C.L. Die Onondaga-Indianer. Globus,
LXXVI, 197-202, 222-6. 1899.
--- The Origin of the Confederacy of the Five Na-
tions. PAAAS, XLVII, 477-80. 1898.
Henry, T.R. Wilderness Messiah. 285 pp. New York,
1955.
Hewitt, J.N.B. A Constitutional League of Peace in
the Stone Age of America. ARSI, 1918, 527-45.
--- The Cosmogonic Gods of the Iroquois. PAAAS,
XLIV, 241-50. 1895.
--- Era of the Formation of the Historic League of
the Iroquois. AA, VII, 61-7. 1894.
--- Ethnological Researches among the Iroquois and
Chippewa. SMC, LXXVIII, i, 114-17. 1925.
--- Ethnological Studies among the Iroquois Indians.
SMC, LXXVIII, vi, 237-47. 1926.
--- Ethnology of the Iroquois. SMC, LXVIII, xii,
106-7. 1917.
--- Field Researches among the Six Nations of the
Iroquois. EFWSI, 1930, 201-6.
--- Field Studies among the Iroquois Tribes. EFWSI,
1931, 175-8.
--- Field-Work among the Iroquois. SMC, LXX, ii,
103-7. 1911.
--- Field-Work among the Iroquois Indians. EFWSI,
1932, 81-4.
--- The Iroquoian Concept of the Soul. JAFL, VIII,
107-16. 1895.
--- Iroquoian Cosmology. ARBAE, XXI, 127-339;
XLIII, 449-819. 1900-26.
--- Iroquoian Mythologic Notes. AA, III, 290-1.
1890.
--- Iroquois. BBAE, XXX, i, 617-20. 1907.
--- Iroquois Game of LaCrosse. AA, V, 189-91.
1892.
--- Iroquois Superstitions. AA, III, 388-9. 1890.
--- The League of Nations of the Iroquois Indians in
Canada. EFWSI, 1929, 201-6.

Hewitt, J.N.B. Legend of the Founding of the Iroquois League. AA, V, 131-48. 1892.

--- Mohawk. BBAE, XXX, i, 921-6. 1907.

--- New Fire among the Iroquois. AA, II, 319.1889.

--- Oneida. BBAE, XXX, ii, 123-7. 1910.

--- Onondaga. BBAE, XXX, ii, 129-35. 1910.

--- Orenda and a Definition of Religion. AA, n.s.,
IV, 33-46. 1902.

--- Oyaron. BBAE, XXX, ii, 178-80. 1910.

--- The Requickening Address of the League of the
Iroquois. Holmes Anniversary Volume, pp. 163-
79. Washington, 1916.

--- The Requickening Address of the Iroquois Condolence Council, ed. W.N.Fenton. JWAS, XXXIV,
65-85. 1944.

--- Sacred Numbers among the Iroquois. AA, II,
165-6. 1889.

--- Seneca. BBAE, XXX, ii, 502-8. 1910.

--- Sexual Tradition. AA, II, 346. 1889.

--- Some Esoteric Aspects of the League of the Iroquois. ICA, XIX, 322-6. 1915.

--- Status of Woman in Iroquois Polity before 1784.
ARSI, 1932, 475-88.

--- A Sun-myth and the Tree of Language of the
Iroquois. AA, V, 61-2. 1892.

--- Teharonhiawagon. BBAE, XXX, ii, 718-23.
1910.

--- White Dog Sacrifice. BBAE, XXX, ii, 939-44.
1910.

Hewitt, J.N.B., and Fenton, W.N. Some Mnemonic
Pictographs relating to the Iroquois Condolence
Council. JWAS, XXXV, 301-15. 1945.

Heye, G.G. Wampum Collection. IN, VII, 320-4.
1930.

Hinsdale, W.G. Old Iroquois Needles of Brass.
IN, IV, 174-6. 1927.

Hoffman, B.G. Iroquois Linguistic Classification
from Historical Materials. E, VI, 160-85. 1959.

Holmer, N.M. The Character of the Iroquoian Languages. Uppsala Canadian Studies, I, 39 pp. 1952.

--- Seneca. IJAL, XVIII, 217-22, 281-91; XIX,
281-89. 1952-1953.

--- The Seneca Language. Upsala Canadian Studies,
III, 116 pp. 1954.

Hough, W. Games of Seneca Indians. AA, I, 134.
1888.

Houghton, F. The Characteristics of Iroquoian Village Sites of Western New York. AA, n.s., XVIII,
508-20. 1916.

--- The Indian Inhabitants of the Niagara Frontier.
Journal of American History, XVI, 213-28. 1922.

Houghton, F. The Indian Occupancy of the Niagara
Frontier. BBSNS, IX, 263-374. 1909.

--- The Migrations of the Seneca Nation. AA, n.s.,
XXIX, 241-50. 1927.

--- The Seneca Nation from 1655 to 1687. BBSNS,
X, 363-476. 1912.

--- The Traditional Origin and the Naming of the
Seneca Nation. AA, n.s., XXIV, 31-43. 1922.

Hrdlicka, A. Ritual Ablation of Front Teeth in Siberia and America. SMC, XCIX, iii, 1-32.1940.

Hubbard, J.N. An Account of Sa-go-ye-wat-ha, or
Red-Jacket, and His People. 356 pp. Albany,
1886.

Huden, J.C. Iroquois Place Names in Vermont.
Vermont History, XXV, 66-76. 1957.

Huguenin, C.A. The Sacred Stone of the Oneidas.
NYFQ, XIII, 16-22. 1957.

Hulbert, A.B., and Schwarze, W.N., eds. Zeisberger's History of Northern American Indians.
OAHQ, XIX, 1-189. 1910.

Hunt, G.T. The Wars of the Iroquois. 209 pp. Madison, 1940.

Hunter, W.A. John Hays' Diary and Journal of 1760.
PA, XXIV, 63-84. 1954.

--- Refugee Fox Settlements among the Senecas. E,
III, 11-20. 1956.

Huot, M.C. Some Mohawk Words of Acculturation.
IJAL, XIV, 150-4. 1948.

Jackson, E.P. Indian Occupation and Use of the
Champlain Lowland. PMA, XIV, 113-60. 1931.

Jackson, H. Civilization of the Indian Natives. 120
pp. Philadelphia, 1830.

Jamieson, N.E. Indian Arts and Crafts. Ontario, 1942.

Jamieson, E. and Sandiford, P. The Mental Capacity
of Southern Ontario Indians. Journal of Educational
Psychology, XIX, 313-28, 536-51. 1928.

Jansen, J.V. Oorlog in een Primitieve Maatschappij
(de Iroquois). 160 pp. Rotterdam, 1955.

Jeancon, J.A., and F.H.Douglas. Iroquois and Algonkin Wampum. DAMLS, XXXI, 1-4. 1931.

Jenness, D. Indians of Canada. BCDM, LXV, 300-
7. 1932.

--- Three Iroquois Wampum Records. BCDM, LXX,
25-9. 1932.

Joblin, E.E.M. The Education of the Indians of Western Ontario. Ontario College of Education Bulletin.
XIII, 1-138. 1948.

Johnson, E. Legends, Traditions, and Laws of the
Iroquois. Lockport, 1881.

Kennedy, J.H. Jesuit and Savage in New France.
206 pp. New Haven, 1950.

Kenton, E., ed. The Indians of North America, II, 62-91, 176-81, 186-9. New York, 1927.

Keppler, J. Cayuga Adoption Custom. IN, III, 73-5. 1926.

--- Comments on Certain Iroquois Masks. CMAI, XII, iv, 1-40. 1941.

--- The Peach Tomahawk Algonkian Wampum. IN, VI, 130-8. 1929.

--- Some Seneca Stories. IN, VI, 372-6. 1929.

Kidd, K.E. Fashions in Tobacco Pipes among the Iroquois Indians of Ontario. BROMA, XXII, 15-21. 1954.

Kimm, S.C. The Iroquois. 122 pp. Middleburgh, 1900.

Knowles, F.H.S. Physical Anthropology of the Roebuck Iroquois. BCDM, LXXXVII, 1-75. 1937.

Knowles, N. The Torture of Captives by the Indians of Eastern North America. PAPS, LXXXII, 151-225. 1940.

Kraus, B.S. Acculturation. AAn, IX, 302-18. 1944.

Kurath, G.P. An Analysis of the Iroquois Eagle Dance and Songs. BBAE, CLVI, 223-306. 1953.

--- Iroquois Midwinter Medicine Rites. Journal of the International Music Council, III, 96-100. 1951.

--- The Iroquois Ohgiwe Death Feast. JAFL, LXIII, 361-62. 1950.

--- Local Diversity in Iroquois Music and Dance. BBAE, CXLIX, 109-138. 1951.

--- Matriarchal Dances of the Iroquois. ICA, XXIX, iii, 123-30. 1952.

--- Onondaga Ritual Parodies. JAFL, LXVII, 404-6. 1954.

--- The Tutelo Fourth Night Spirit Release Singing. Midwest Folklore, IV, 87-105. 1955.

Lafitau, J.F. Moeurs des sauvages amériquains. 2 vols. Paris, 1724.

Laft, F. The Snow-snake and the Indian Game of Snow-snaking. AAR, XXIV, 69-71. 1912.

Laviolette, G. Indian Bands of the Province of Quebec. ECAS, I, 90-6. 1955.

Leder, L.H., ed. The Livingston Indian Records. PH, XXIII, 1-240. 1956.

Leonard, A.L. The Presque Isle Portage and the Venango Trail. PA, XV, 59-64. 1945.

Lighthall, W.D. Hochelagans and Mohawks. PTRSC, ser. 2, V, ii, 199-211. 1899.

Lismer, M. Seneca Splint Basketry. IH, IV, 1-39. 1941.

Loewenthal, J. Der Heilbringer in der irokesischen und der algonkinischen Religion. ZE, XLV, 65-82. 1913.

--- Irokesische Wirtschaftsaltertümer. ZE, LII-LIII, 171-233. 1920-21.

Long, J.K. Voyages and Travels of an Indian Interpreter and Trader. 295 pp. London, 1791.

Loskiel, G.H. Geschichte der Mission der evangelischen Brüder unter den Indianern in Nordamerika. Barby, 1789.

---History of the Mission of the United Brethren among the Indians of North America. 3 pts. London, 1794.

Lounsbury, F.G. Oneida Verb Morphology. YUPA, XLVIII, 111 pp. 1953.

--- Stray Number Systems among Certain Indian Tribes. AA, n.s., XLVIII, 672-5. 1946.

Lucy, C.L. Notes on a Seneca Mask. PM, XXIV, 35-6. 1951.

Lydekker, J.W. The Faithful Mohawks. 206 pp. New York, 1938.

Lyford, C.A. Iroquois Crafts. IH, VI, 1-97. 1943.

McIlwraith, T.F. The Feast of the Dead. An, VI, 83-6. 1958.

McKelvey, B. The Seneca "Time of Trouble." Rochester History, XIII, iii, 1-24. 1951.

Mackenzie, J.B. The Six-Nations Indians in Canada. 151 pp. Toronto, 1896.

MacLeod, W.C. Trade Restrictions in Early Society. AA, n.s., XXIX, 271-8. 1927.

Manley, H.S. Buying Buffalo from the Indians. New York History, XXVIII, 313-29. 1947.

Marcoux, J. Catechism in the Mohawk Language. 50 pp. Tiohtiake, 1904.

--- Kaiatonsera ionterennaientakwa ne teieiasontha onkwe onwe. 568 pp. Caughnawaga, P.Q., 1903.

Martin, F. Hurons et Iroquois. Paris, 1877.

Marye, W.B. Warriors' Paths. PA, XIII, 4-26; XIV, 4-22. 1943-44.

Mayer, J.R. Flintlocks of the Iroquois, 1620-1687. RRRMAS, VI, 1-59. 1943.

Megapolensis, J. Short Sketch of the Mohawk Indians in New Netherlands. CNYHS, ser. 2, III, 137-60. 1857.

Merrill, A. Have They Kept that Pledge? AmI, I, i, 4-14. 1943.

Métais, P. Marriage et Equilibre Social dans les Sociétés Primitives. Travaux et Mémoires de l'Institut d'Ethnologie, LIX, 545 pp. 1956.

Mitchell, J. The Mohawks in High Steel. The New Yorker, XXV, xxx, 38-52. 1949. [Reprinted in Wilson, 1960.]

Mooney, J. Cherokee and Iroquois Parallels. JAFL, II, 67. 1889.

Mooney, J., and Hewitt, J.N.B. Cayuga. BBAE, XXX, i, 223-4. 1907.

Morgan, L.H. Ancient Society, pp. 62-150. New York, 1877.

Morgan, L.H. Communications. ARUNY, II, 81-91. 1849.

--- The Fabrics of the Iroquois. American Quarterly Register and Magazine, IV, 319-43. 1850.

--- Government and Institutions of the Iroquois, ed. A.C.Parker. RNYAS, VII, 5-30. 1928.

--- Houses and House-Life of the American Aborigines. CNAE, IV, 1-281. 1881.

--- Laws of Descent of the Iroquois. PAAAS, XI, ii, 132-48. 1857.

--- Letters on the Iroquois, by Skenandoah. American Review, V, 177-90, 242-57, 447-61; VI, 477-90, 626-33. 1847.

--- Report on the Fabrics, Inventions, Implements and Utensils of the Iroquois. ARUNY, V, 67-117. 1851.

--- Report to the Regents of the University upon the Articles furnished the Indian Collection. ARUNY, III, 65-97. 1850.

--- Systems of Consanguinity and Affinity. SCK, XVII, 150-69, 291-382, 511-14. 1871.

Mulkearn, L. Half King, Seneca Diplomat of the Ohio Valley. WPHM, XXXVII, 65-81. 1954.

Murdock, G.P. Our Primitive Contemporaries, pp. 291-323. New York, 1934.

Murray, H. Historical and Descriptive Account of British America, I, 73-127. Edinburgh, 1840.

Myrtle, M. The Iroquois. 317 pp. New York, 1855.

Newman, M.T. The Physique of the Seneca Indians of Western New York. JWAS, XLVII, 357-62. 1957.

Nieberding, V. Seneca-Cayuga Green Corn Feast. CO, XXXIV, 231-4. 1956.

O'Callaghan, E.B., ed. Documentary History of the State of New York. 4 vols. Albany, 1849-51.

Orchard, W.C. Mohawk Burden-Straps. IN, VI, 351-9. 1929.

--- Porcupine-Quill Ornamentation. IN, III, 59-68. 1926.

Oronhyatekha. The Mohawk Language. CJ, n.s., X, 182-94; XV, 1-12. 1865-76.

Orr, R.B. The Iroquois in Canada. AAR, XXXI, 9-55. 1919.

Owl, W.D. The Iroquois Temperance League. Narragansett Dawn, I, 183-5. 1935.

Painter, L.K. Jacob Taylor, Quaker Missionary Statesman. Niagara Frontier, VI, ii, 33-40. 1959.

Palmer, R.A. The North American Indians. Smithsonian Scientific Series, IV, 70-105. 1929.

Parker, A.C. Aboriginal Cultures and Chronology of the Genesee Country. PRAS, VI, 243-83. 1929.

--- Aboriginal Inhabitants. History of the Genesee Country, ed. L.R.Doty, I, 145-65. Chicago, 1925.

Parker, A.C. Additional Notes on Iroquois Silversmithing. AA, n.s., XIII, 283-93. 1911.

--- The Amazing Iroquois. AAA, XXIII, 99-108. 1927.

--- An Analytical History of the Seneca Indians. RNYAS, VI, 11-158. 1926.

--- The Archeological History of New York. NYSMB, CCXXXV-CCXXXVIII, 5-743. 1920.

--- Certain Iroquois Tree Myths and Symbols. AA, n.s., XIV, 608-20. 1912.

--- Champlain's Assault on the Fortified Town of the Oneidas. NYSMB, CCVII-CCVIII, 165-73. 1918.

--- The Civilization of the Red Man. History of the State of New York, ed. A.C.Flick, I, 99-131. New York, 1933.

--- The Code of Handsome Lake, the Seneca Prophet. NYSMB, CLXIII, 5-148. 1912.

--- The Constitution of the Five Nations. NYSMB, CLXXXIV, 7-158. 1916.

--- The Constitution of the Five Nations: a Reply. AA, n.s., XX, 120-4. 1918.

--- An Early Colonial Seneca Site. RNYAS, I, ii, 3-36. 1919.

--- Fundamental Factors in Seneca Folk Lore. NYSMB, CCLIII, 49-66. 1924.

--- Indian Medicine and Medicine Men. AAR, 1928, 9-17.

--- The Influence of the Iroquois on the History and Archaeology of the Wyoming Valley. PWHGS, XI, 65-102. 1910.

--- The Iroquois. History of the State of New York, ed. A.C.Flick, I, 67-97. New York, 1933.

--- Iroquois Sun Myths. JAFL, XXIII, 473-8. 1910.

--- Iroquois Uses of Maize and Other Food Plants. NYSMB, CXLIV, 5-119. 1910.

--- The Iroquois Wampums. Proceedings of the New York State Historical Association, VIII, 205-8. 1909.

--- League of the Iroquois. Home Geographic Monthly, II, ii, 7-12. 1932.

--- The Origin of Iroquois Silversmithing. AA, n.s., XII, 349-57. 1910.

--- The Origin of the Iroquois as suggested by Their Archeology. AA, n.s., XVIII, 479-507. 1916.

--- The Peace Policy of the Iroquois. SW, XL, 691-9. 1911.

--- The Rise of the Seneca Nation. History of the Genesee Country, ed. L.R.Doty, I, 167-89. Chicago, 1925.

--- Rumbling Wings and Other Indian Tales. 279 pp. Garden City, 1928.

Parker, A.C. Secret Medicine Societies of the Seneca. AA, n.s., XI, 161-85. 1909.

--- Seneca Myths and Folk-Tales. Buffalo Historical Society Publications, XXVII, 1-465. 1923.

--- The Senecas in Their Own Home Land. History of the Genesee Country, ed. L.R.Doty, I, 192-222. Chicago, 1925.

--- Skunny Wundy and Other Indian Tales. 262 pp. New York, 1926.

--- Snow-Snake as played by the Seneca-Iroquois. AA, n.s., XI, 250-6. 1909.

--- The Status of New York Indians. NYSMB, CCLIII, 67-82. 1924.

Parkman, F. The Jesuits in North America. 463 pp. Boston, 1867.

Peck, M.A. Caughnawaga. CGJ, X, 92-100. 1935.

Peck, W.F. Semi-Centennial History of the City of Rochester. 736 pp. Syracuse, 1884.

Perrot, N. Memoir on the Manners, Customs, and Religion of the Savages of North America. ITUMV, I, 25-272. 1911.

--- Mémoire sur les moeurs, coustumes et relligion des sauvages de l'Amérique septentrionale. 341 pp. Paris, 1864.

Peterson, G.W. An Iroquoian Story of the Beginning of the World. 69 pp. Torrington, 1937.

Pilling, J.C. Bibliography of the Iroquoian Languages. BBAE, VI, 208 pp. 1888.

Powers, M. El primer ensayo de paz en América. AI, VI, 105-25. 1946.

Preston, W.D., and Voegelin, C.F. Seneca I. IJAL, XV, 23-44. 1949.

Quain, B.H. The Iroquois. Cooperation and Competition among Primitive Peoples, ed. M. Mead, pp. 240-81. New York, 1937.

Randle, M.C. Educational Problems of Canadian Indians. Food for Thought, XIII, vi, 10-14.1953.

--- Iroquois Women, Then and Now. BBAE, CXLIX, 167-80. 1951.

--- Psychological Types from Iroquois Folktales. JAFL, LXV, 13-22. 1952.

--- The Waugh Collection of Iroquois Folktales. PAPS, XCVII, 611-33. 1953.

Reid, W.M. Calumet. RP, VIII, 97-101. 1909.

--- Mohawk Pottery. RP, III, 184-8. 1904.

Rhoades, G.E. Prehistoric Iroquois Culture. AAR, 1923, 89-95.

Richards, C.B. Matriarchy or Mistake: The Role of Iroquois Women through Time. In V.F.Ray, ed., Cultural Stability and Cultural Change, 36-45. Seattle, 1957.

Ridley, F. Cultural Contacts of Iroquian and Plains. PA, XXVII, 33-38. 1957.

Rioux, M. Les Hurons-Iroquois pratiquaient-ils le totemisme? PTRSC, ser. 3, XXXIX, i, 173-6. 1945.

--- Notes Autobiographiques d'un Iroquois Cayuga. An, I, 18-36. 1955.

--- Persistence of a Tutelo Cultural Trait among the Contemporary Cayuga. BNMC, CXXIII, 72-4. 1951.

--- Relations between Religion and Government among the Longhouse Iroquois of Grand River, Ontario. BNMC, CXXVI, 94-98. 1952.

--- Some Medical Beliefs and Practices of the Contemporary Iroquois Longhouse of the Six Nations Reserve. JWAS, XLI, 152-58. 1951.

Ritchie, W.A. Algonkin-Iroquois Contacts in New York State. BASD, I, ii, 2-6. 1934.

--- Dutch Hollow. RRNYSAA, XIII, i, 102 pp. 1954. [Also RRRMAS, X, 102 pp. 1954.]

--- Indian History of New York State. Part II - The Iroquoian Tribes. 2nd ed. New York State Museum Educational Leaflet Series, VII, 20 pp. 1953.

Ritzenthaler, R.E. The Wisconsin Oneida Wake. WA, n.s., XXII, 1-2. 1941.

Ritzenthaler, R. and Sellars, M. Indians in an Urban Situation. WA, XXXVI, 147-61. 1955.

Rousseau, J.J. L'Aurore de l'Agriculture. L'Actualité Economique, II, 344-61. 1944.

--- La Crainte des Iroquois. Revue d'Histoire de l'Amérique Française, II, 13-26. 1948.

Rousseau, J.J. and Raymond, M. Le Folklore Botanique de Caughnawaga. Contributions de l'Institut Botanique de l'Université Montréal, LV, 7-74. 1945.

Rousseau, M. La Crainte de l'Iroquois au Lac Mistassini. ACFAS, XIII, 119-20. 1947.

Rousseau, M.A. and J. La crainte des Iroquois chez les Mistassini. Revue de l'Histoire de l'Amérique Française, II, 13-26. 1948.

Rousseau, P. Les Hochelagas. ICA, XV, 279-97. 1906.

Ruttenber, E.M. History of the Indian Tribes of Hudson's River. 415 pp. Albany, 1872.

--- Indian Geographical Names in the Valley of Hudson's River, the Valley of the Mohawk, and on the Delaware. Proceedings of the New York State Historical Association, VI. 241 pp. 1906.

Sanborn, J.W. Day-yu-da-gont. 18 pp. Friendship, 1904.

--- Hymnal in the Seneca Language. 48 pp. Batavia, 1884.

--- Indian Stories. 38 pp. Friendship, 1915.

--- Legends, Customs, and Social Life of the Seneca Indians. Gowanda, 1878.

Schellbach, L. An Historic Iroquois Warclub. IN, V, 157-66. 1928.

Schoolcraft, H.H. Notes on the Iroquois. 498 pp. New York, 1846.

Scott, D.C. Traditional History of the Confederacy of the Six Nations. PTRSC, ser. 3, V, ii, 195-246. 1912.

Scull, G.D., ed. Voyages of Peter Esprit Radisson. Boston, 1885.

Seaver, J.E. A Narrative of the Life of Mary Jemison. 4th edit. New York, 1856.

Setzler, F.M. Samuel Crowell's Account of a Seneca Dog Sacrifice. NOQ, XVI, 144-6. 1944.

Shea, J.G., ed. A French-Onondaga Dictionary. 103 pp. New York, 1860.

Shipman, C.M. Iroquois Village Site at Fairport, Ohio. National Archaeological News, I, xi, 2-4. 1937.

Silvy, A. Relation par lettres de l'Amérique septentrionale, ed. C. de. Rochemonteix, pp. 182-96. Paris, 1904.

Sipa, C.H. The Principal Indian Towns in Western Pennsylvania. WPHM, XIII, 104-22. 1930.

Skinner, A. An Antique Tobacco-Pouch of the Iroquois. INM, II, 103-8. 1920.

--- An Iroquois Antler Figurine. INM, II, 109-14. 1920.

--- Iroquois Falseface Pipe. IN, II, 321-2. 1925.

--- The Iroquois Indians of Western New York. SW, XXXVIII, 206-11. 1909.

--- Notes on Iroquois Archeology. INM, n.s., XVIII, 5-216. 1921.

--- An Old Seneca Warclub. IN, III, 45-7. 1926.

--- Seneca Charm Canoes. IN, III, 36-8. 1926.

--- Some Seneca Masks and Their Uses. IN, II, 191-207. 1925.

--- Some Seneca Tobacco Customs. IN, II, 127-30. 1925.

Smith, De C. Additional Notes on Onondaga Witchcraft and Hoⁿ do'-i. JAFL, II, 277-81. 1889.

--- Indian Experiences. 387 pp. Caldwell, 1943.

--- Onondaga Superstitions. JAFL, II, 282-3. 1889.

--- Witchcraft and Demonism of the Modern Iroquois. JAFL, I, 184-94. 1888.

Smith, E.A. Comparative Differences in the Iroquois Group of Dialects. PAAAS, XXX, 315-19. 1881.

--- The Customs and the Language of the Iroquois. JAI, XIV, 244-53. 1884.

--- Disputed Points concerning Iroquois Pronouns. PAAAS, XXXIII, 606-9. 1884.

--- Life among the Mohawks. PAAAS, XXXII, 398-9. 1883.

Smith, E.A. Myths of the Iroquois. ARBAE, II, 47-116. 1881.

--- Myths of the Iroquois. AAOJ, IV, 31-9. 1882.

--- The Significance of Flora to the Iroquois. PAAAS, XXXIV, 404-11. 1885.

--- Studies in the Iroquois concerning the Verb to be and Its Substitutes. PAAAS, XXXII, 399-402. 1883.

Smith, J. Life and Travels. 162 pp. Philadelphia, 1831.

Snyderman, G.S. Behind the Tree of Peace. PA, XVIII, 2-93. 1948.

--- Concepts of Land Ownership among the Iroquois and Their Neighbors. BBAE, CXLIX, 13-34. 1951.

--- The Functions of Wampum. PAPS, XCVIII, 469-94. 1954.

--- Halliday Jackson's Journal of a Visit Paid to the Indians of New York. PAPS, CI, 565-88. 1957.

--- The Manuscript Collections of the Philadelphia Yearly Meeting of Friends Pertaining to the American Indian. PAPS, CII, 613-20. 1958.

--- A Preliminary Survey of American Indian Manuscripts in Repositories of the Philadelphia Area. PAPS, XCVII, 596-610. 1953.

--- Some Ideological Aspects of Present Day Seneca Folklore. PM, XXIV, 37-46. 1951.

Society of Friends. The Case of the Seneca Indians. Philadelphia, 1840.

Speck, F.G. Algonkian Influence upon Iroquois Social Organization. AA, n.s., XXV, 217-27. 1923.

--- The Cayuga Indian Snake Game. GM, XLIII, 416-19. 1941.

--- How the Dew Eagle Society of the Allegany Seneca Cured Gahéhdagowa. PM, XXII, 39-59. 1949.

--- Indian Apostates. GM, XLIV, 24-7. 1941.

--- The Iroquois. Cranbrook Institute of Science Newsletter, XV, 33-6. 1945.

--- Midwinter Rites of the Cayuga Long House. 192 pp. Philadelphia, 1949.

--- Niagara Falls and Cayuga Indian Medicine. NYFQ, I, 205-8. 1945.

--- Northern Elements in Iroquois and New England Art. IN, II, 1-13. 1925.

Speck, F.G. and Beck, H.P. Old World Tales among the Mohawks. JAFL, LXIII, 285-308. 1950.

Speck, F.G., and Dodge, E.S. Amphibian and Reptile Lore of the Six Nations Cayuga. JAFL, LVIII, 306-9. 1945.

Speck, F.G., and Orchard. The Penn Wampum Belts. LMAI, IV, 7-20. 1925.

Speck, F.G., and Schaeffer, C.E. The Mutual Aid and Volunteer Company of the Eastern Cherokee ... compared with Mutual-Aid Societies of the Northern Iroquois. JWAS, XXXV, 169-79. 1945.

Squair, J., tr. The Indian Tribes on the St. Lawrence at the Time of the Arrival of the French.
AAR, XXXIV, 82-8. 1923.

Squier, E.G. Aboriginal Monuments of the State of
New York. SCK, II, ix, 9-188. 1849.

--- Antiquities of the State of New York. 343 pp.
Buffalo, 1851.

Stephens, B.W. Iroquoian Pottery Pipes. CSAJ, II,
6-9. 1956.

Stern, B.J. The Letters of Asher Wright to Lewis
Henry Morgan. AA, n.s., XXXV, 138-45. 1933.

Stewart, A.M. French Pioneers in North America.
Occasional Papers of the New York State Archaeological Association, I-II. 1958-59.

Stillfried, I. Studie zu Kosmogonischen und Kultischen Elementen der Algonkonischen und Irokesischen Stämme. WVM, IV, 82-85. 1956.

Stites, S.H. Economics of the Iroquois. 159 pp.
Lancaster, 1905.

Stone, W.L. The Life and Times of Red Jacket or
Sa-go-ye-wat-ha. 488 pp. New York, 1841.

--- Life of Joseph Brant. 2 vols. New York, 1838.

Strong, J.C. Report of the Commissioners of the
Land Office in the Matter of the Cayuga Indians re-
siding in Canada. 8 pp. Buffalo, 1889.

Sulte, B. The War of the Iroquois. AAR, 1899, 124-
51.

Taft, G.E. Cayuga Indemnity. RP, XIII, 96-101.
1914.

--- Cayuga Notes. 23 pp. Benton Harbor, 1913.

--- An Onondaga Festival. RP, XIII, 101-2. 1914.

--- Tarenyagon. RP, XII, 169-70. 1913.

Thompson, S. The Indian Legend of Hiawatha. Publications of the Modern Language Association,
XXXVII, i, 128-40. 1922.

Uhler, S.P. Pennsylvania's Indian Relations to 1754.
144 pp. Allentown, 1951.

Vail, R.W.G., ed. The Western Campaign of 1779.
NYHSQ, XLI, i, 34-69. 1952.

Voget, F. Acculturation at Caughnawaga. AA, LIII,
220-31. 1951.

--- Kinship Changes at Caughnawaga. AA, LV, 385-
94. 1953.

Wainwright, N.B. George Croghan and the Indians
Uprising of 1747. PH, XXI, 21-31. 1954.

Wallace, A.F.C. The Dekanawidah Myth Analyzed
as the Record of a Revitalization Movement. E, V,
118-30. 1958.

--- Dreams and Wishes of the Soul. AA, LX, 234-
48. 1958.

--- Halliday Jackson's Journal to the Seneca Indians.
PH, XIX, 117-47, 325-49. 1952.

Wallace, A.F.C. Handsome Lake and the Great Revival in the West. American Quarterly, IV, 149-
65. 1952.

--- Mazeway Resynthesis. TNYAS, ser. 2, XVIII,
626-38. 1956.

--- Origins of Iroquois Neutrality. PH, XXIV, 223-
35. 1957.

--- Some Psychological Determinants of Culture
Change in an Iroquoian Community. BBAE,
CXLIX, 55-76. 1951.

--- Woman, Land and Society. PA, XVII, 1-35.
1947.

Wallace, P.A.W. Conrad Weiser, 1696-1760, Friend
of Colonist and Mohawk. 648 pp. Philadelphia,
1945.

--- The Five Nations of New York and Pennsylvania.
NYHSQ, XXXVII, 228-50. 1953.

--- The Iroquois: A Brief Outline of Their History.
PH, XXIII, 15-28, 1956.

--- The Return of Hiawatha. New York History,
XXIX, 385-403. 1948.

--- The White Roots of Peace. 57 pp. Philadelphia,
1946.

Waugh, F.W. Iroquois Foods and Food Preparation.
MCDM, LXXXVI, 1-235. 1916.

--- On Work in Material Culture of the Iroquois, 1912.
SRGSC, 1912, 476-80.

--- Some Notes on Ethnobotany. Ottawa Naturalist,
XXXI, 27-9. 1917.

Weslager, C.A. The Delaware Indians as Women.
JWAS, XXXIV, 381-8. 1944.

--- Further Light on the Delaware Indians as Women.
JWAS, XXXVII, 298-304. 1947.

Wheeler-Voegelin, E., ed. John Heckewelder to
Peter S. Du Ponceau. E, VI, 70-81. 1959.

--- Some Remarks Concerning the Traditions, Customs, Languages &c. of the Indians in North America. E, VI, 42-69, 186. 1959.

White, M.E. An Iroquois Sequence in New York's
Niagara Frontier. BESAF, XVI, 14. 1957.

--- An Iroquois Sequence in New York's Niagara Frontier. PA, XXVIII, 145-150. 1958.

Wilcox, R. Feathers in a Dark Sky. 223 pp. Woodstock, 1941.

Willoughby, C.C. A Mohawk (Caughnawaga) Halter
for leading Captives. AA, n.s., XL, 49-50. 1938.

Wilson, D. The Huron-Iroquois of Canada, PTRSC,
II, ii, 55-106. 1884.

Wilson, J.G. Arent van Curler and His Journal of
1634-35. Annual Report of the American Historical Association, 1895, 81-101.

Wintemberg, W.J. Culture of a Prehistoric Iroquoian Site in Eastern Ontario. ICA, XIX, 37-42. 1915.

Witthoft, J. Cayuga Midwinter Festival. NYFQ, II, 24-39. 1946.

--- Green Corn Ceremonialism in the Eastern Woodlands. OCMA, XIII, 21-31. 1949.

--- Iroquois Archaeology at the Mid-Century. PAPS, XCV, 311-21. 1951.

Witthoft, J., and Hadlock, W.S. Cherokee-Iroquois Little People. JAFL, LIX, 413-22. 1946.

Wolf, M. Iroquois Religion and Its Relation to Their Morals. New York, 1919.

Wray, C.F. Archaeological Evidence of the Mask among the Seneca. BNYSAA, VII, 7-8. 1956.

--- Index Traits of the Historic Seneca-1550-1687. BESAF, XIII, 6. 1954.

--- Seneca Tobacco Pipes. BNYSAA, VI, 15-6. 1956.

Wray, C.F. and H.L.Schoff. A Preliminary Report on the Seneca Sequence in Western New York-1550-1687. PA, XXIII, 55-63. 1957.

Wren, C. A Study of North Appalachian Indian Pottery. PWHGS, XIII, 131-222. 1914.

--- Turtle Shell Rattles and Other Implements from Indian Graves. PWHGS, X, 195-210. 1909.

Yawger, R.N. The Indian and the Pioneer. 2 vols. Syracuse, 1893.

Zeisberger, D. Essay of an Onondaga Grammar. PMHB, XI, 442-53; XII, 65-75, 233-9, 325-40. 1887-88.

--- Indian Dictionary. 236 pp. Cambridge, 1887.

6. MAHICAN

Including the Mahican of the Hudson River and the Wappinger tribes of southern New York and western Connecticut.

Allen, C. Report on the Stockbridge Indians. Massachusetts Legislature of 1870, House Document 13. Boston, 1870.

Armbruster, E.L. The Indians of New England and New Netherlands. Brooklyn, 1918.

Belknap, J. Report on the Oneida, Stockbridge and Brotherton Indians, 1796. INAM, series 2, LIV, 39 pp. 1955.

Birdsey, N. An Account of the Indians in and about Stratford. MHSC, ser. 1, X, 111-12. 1809.

Bolton, R.P. Indian Life of Long Ago in the City of New York. 167 pp. New York, 1934.

Bolton, R.P. Indian Paths in the Great Metropolis. INM, ser. 2, XXIII, 1-280. 1922.

--- The Indians of Washington Heights. APAM, III, 77-109. 1909.

--- New York City in Indian Possession. INM, II, 225-395. 1920.

Brown, R.H. The Housatonic Indians. BMAS, XIX, iii, 44-50. 1958.

Canning, E.W.B. The Aborigines of the Housatonic Valley. MAH, II, 734-40. 1878.

Coffin, C.C. Excavations in Southwest Connecticut. BASC, X, 33-49. 1940.

--- Impressed Shell Designs on Connecticut Indian Pottery. BASC, IV, 2-6. 1936.

--- An Indian Village Site at Cedar Ridge. BASC, VII, 9-11. 1938.

--- A Prehistoric Shell Heap at the Mouth of the Housatonic. BASC, V, 10-19. 1937.

Curtis, W.C. The Basketry of the Pautatucks and Scatacooks. SW, XXXIII, 385-90. 1904.

Davidson, J.N. Muh-he-ka-ne-ok, a History of the Stockbridge Nation. 66 pp. Milwaukee, 1893.

DeForest, J.W. History of the Indians of Connecticut. 509 pp. Hartford, 1851.

Denton, D. A Brief Description of New York, ed. G. Gurman. 57 pp. New York, 1845.

Donck, A. van der. Beschryvinge van Nieuw-Nederlant. 100 pp. Amsterdam, 1655.

--- Description of the New Netherlands. CNYHS, ser. 2, I, 125-242. 1841.

Edwards, J. Observations on the Language of the Muhhekaneew Indians. 17 pp. New Haven, 1788.

Finch, J.K. Aboriginal Remains on Manhattan Island. APAM, III, 65-73. 1909.

Hargrett, L. A Bibliography of the Constitutions and Laws of the American Indians, pp. 111-12. Cambridge, 1947.

Harrington, M.R. Ancient Shell Heaps near New York City. APAM, III, 169-79. 1909.

--- The Rock-Shelters of Armonk, New York. APAM, III, 125-38. 1909.

Heye, G.G. A Mahican Wooden Cup. INM, V, 15-18. 1921.

Hodge, F.W., and Orchard, W.C. John W. Quinney's Coat. IN, VI, 343-51. 1929.

Hopkins, S. Historical Memoirs relating to the Housatonic Indians. Magazine of History, Extra Numbers, XVII, 7-198. 1911.

Jackson, E.P. Indian Occupation and Use of the Champlain Lowland. PMA, XIV, 113-60. 1931.

--- Mountains and the Aborigines of the Champlain Lowland. Appalachia, XXIV, 131-36. 1930.

Juet, R. Extract from the Journal of the Voyage of the Half-Moon. CNYHS, ser. 2, I, 317-32. 1841.

Laet, J. de. Extracts from the New World, or a Description of the West Indies. CNYHS, ser. 2, I, 281-316. 1841.

Leder, L.H., ed. The Livingston Indian Records, 1666-1723. PH, XXIII, 1-240. 1956.

Michelson, T. Investigations among the Stockbridge, Brotherton, and Fox Indians. SMC, LXV, vi, 90-4. 1915.

Montanus, A. Description of New Netherland. Documentary History of the State of New York, ed. E.B. O'Callaghan, IV, 113-32. Albany, 1851.

Mooney, J. Quinnipiac. BBAE, XXX, ii, 344-5. 1910.

--- Wappinger. BBAE, XXX, ii, 913. 1910.

Mooney, J., and Thomas, C. Mahican. BBAE, XXX, i, 786-9. 1907.

Morgan, L.H. The Indian Journals, 1859-62, p. 57. Ann Arbor, 1959.

Orcutt, S. The Indians of the Housatonic and Naugatuck Valleys. 220 pp. Hartford, 1882.

Orcutt, S., and Beardsley, A. The History of the Old Town of Derby, pp. xvii-xcvii. Springfield, 1880.

Prince, J.D. A Tale in the Hudson River Indian Language. AA, n.s., VII, 74-84. 1905.

Prince, J.D., and Speck, F.G. Dying American Speech-Echoes from Connecticut. PAPS, XLII, 346-52. 1903.

Rainey, F.G. A Compilation of Historical Data contributing to the Ethnography of Connecticut and Southern New England Indians. BASC, 1936, iii, 1-89.

Ray, L. The Aboriginal Inhabitants of Connecticut. Indian Miscellany, ed. W.W. Beach, pp. 280-302. Albany, 1877.

Ruttenber, E.M. History of the Indian Tribes of Hudson's River. 415 pp. Albany, 1872.

--- Indian Geographical Names in the Valley of Hudson's River, the Valley of the Mohawk, and on the Delaware. Proceedings of the New York State Historical Association, VI. 241 pp. 1906.

Scott, K. and Baker, C.E. Renewals of Governor Nicolls' Treaty of 1665 with the Esopus Indians. NYHSQ, XXXVII, 251-72. 1953.

Skinner, A. Archaeology of Manhattan Island. APAM, III, 113-21. 1909.

--- Archaeology of the New York Coastal Algonkin. APAM, III, 213-35. 1909.

--- The Indians of Greater New York. Cedar Rapids, 1915.

Skinner, A. The Indians of Manhattan Island and Vicinity. AMGLS, XXIX, 5-54; XLI, 5-54. 1909-15.

--- The Manhattan Indians. NYSMB, CLVIII, 199-212. 1912.

--- Notes on Mahican Ethnology. BPMCM, II, 87-116. 1925.

--- Objects from New York City. IN, I, 236-8. 1924.

Smith, C.P. The Housatonic. 532 pp. New York, 1946.

Smith, W.F. The Quest of an Indian Garden. BASC, XIX, 13-17. 1946.

Speck, F.G. Bird Nomenclature and Song Interpretation of the Canadian Delaware. JWAS, XXXVI, 249-58. 1946.

--- Decorative Art of the Indian Tribes of Connecticut. MCDM, LXXV, 1-73. 1915.

Speck, F.G., and J. Moses. The Celestial Bear comes down to Earth. Reading Public Museum Scientific Publications, VII, 1-91. 1945.

Spiess, M. The Indians of Connecticut. Committee on Historical Publications, Tercentenary Commission of the State of Connecticut. 33 pp. New Haven, 1933.

Townshend, C.H. The Quinnipiack Indian and Their Reservation. 79 pp. New Haven, 1900.

Troost, G. Extracts from the Voyages of David Pieterszen de Vries. CNYHS, ser. 2, I, 243-80. 1841.

Trumbull, B. A Complete History of Connecticut, I, 39-57. New Haven, 1818.

Wassenaer, N. van. Description and First Settlement of New Netherland. Documentary History of the State of New York, ed. E.B. O'Callaghan, III, 27-48. Albany, 1850.

Wheeler-Voegelin, E., ed. Some Remarks Concerning the Traditions, Customs, Languages &c. of the Indians in North America. E, VI, 42-69, 186. 1959.

Willoughby, C.C. Antiquities of the New England Indians. 314 pp. Cambridge, 1935.

--- Textile Fabrics of the New England Indians. AA, n.s., VII, 85-93. 1905.

--- The Wilderness and the Indian. Commonwealth History of Massachusetts, ed. A.B. Hart, I, 127-58. Cambridge, 1927.

Wissler, C., ed. The Indians of Greater New York and the Lower Hudson. APAM, III, 3-237. 1909.

Wolley, C. A Two Years Journal in New York, ed. E.B. O'Callaghan. 97 pp. New York, 1860.

Woodward, A. Antler Implements from New York City. IN, IV, 226-31. 1927.

7. MASSACHUSET

Including the Massachuset, Nauset, Nipmuc, and Wampanoag.

Allen, Z. Native Indians of America. 55 pp. Providence, 1881.

Anonymous. A Description of Mashpee. MHSC, ser. 2, III, 1-12. 1846.

--- Saconet Indians. MHSC, ser. 1, X, 114. 1809.

--- Wunnashowetuckoog. BBAE, XXX, ii, 975. 1910.

Archer, G. The Relation of Captain Gosnold's Voyage. MHSC, ser. 3, VIII, 72-81. 1843.

Bacon, O.N. A History of Natick, pp. 21-39. Boston, 1856.

Badger, S. Historical and Characteristic Traits of the American Indians in General and Those of the Natick in Particular. MHSC, ser. 1, V, 32-45. 1835.

Banks, C.E. History of Martha's Vineyard, 3 vols. Boston, 1911.

Bassett, B. Fabulous Traditions and Customs of the Indians of Martha's Vineyard. MHSC, I, 139-40. 1792.

Bibaud, F.M. Biographie des sagamos illustrés de l'Amérique Septentrionale, pp. 91-100. Montreal, 1848.

Biggar, H.P., ed. The Works of Samuel de Champlain, I, 338-61. Toronto, 1922.

Bradford, W. History of the Plymouth Plantation. 2 vols. Boston, 1912.

Brereton, J. A Brief and True Relation of the Discovery of the North Part of Virginia. MHSC, ser. 3, VIII, 83-94. 1843.

Burrage, H.S., ed. Early English and French Voyages, pp. 330-9, 347-51. New York, 1906.

Burton, A.H. Massasoit. 270 pp. New York, 1896.

Byers, D.S., and Johnson, F. Two Sites on Marthas Vineyard. PRSPF, I, i, 1940.

Carr, L. Notes on the Crania of New England Indians. 10 pp. Boston, 1880.

Chase, H.E. Notes on the Wampanoag Indians. ARSI, 1883, 878-907.

Cheever, G.B. The Journal of the Pilgrims at Plymouth, 2d edit. New York, 1849.

Cotton, J. Vocabulary of the Massachusetts (or Natick) Indian Language. MHSC, ser. 3, II, 147-257. 1830.

Crane, J.C. The Nipmucks and their Country. Collections of the Worcester Society of Antiquity, XVI, 3-19. 1912.

DeForest, J.W. History of the Indians of Connecticut. 509 pp. Hartford, 1851.

Dexter, H.M. The New England Indians. Sabbath at Home, II, 193-206. 1868.

Dexter, H.M., ed. Mourt's Relation. 176 pp. Boston, 1865.

Dixon, R.B. The Early Migrations of the Indians of New England and the Maritime Provinces. PAAS, n.s., XXIV, 65-76. 1914.

Drake, S.G., ed. The Old Indian Chronicle. 333 pp. Boston, 1867.

Dunn, G.C. Indians in Bridgewater. BMAS, III, 31-3. 1942.

Durocher, F. Aiamieu kukuetshimitun misinaigan. 72 pp. Quebec, 1856.

Dwight, T. Travels in New-England and New-York, I, 84-102. London, 1823.

Eliot, J. A Grammar of the Massachusetts Indian Language. New edit. 66 pp. Boston, 1822.

--- The Indian Grammar Begun. Old South Leaflets, III, lii, 1-16. 1896.

--- The Indian Primer. Edinburgh, 1877.

--- The Logick Primer. 94 pp. Cambridge, 1672; Cleveland, 1904.

Ellis, G.E. The Indians of Eastern Massachusetts. The Memorial History of Boston, ed. J. Winsor, I, 241-74. Boston, 1880.

Ellis, G.W. and Morris, J.E. King Philip's War. 326 pp. New York, 1906.

Ferguson, C.C. Some Observations in Regard to our Earliest Indian Inhabitants. Proceedings of the Worcester Historical Society, n.s., II, 193-204. 1939.

Freeman, F. Civilization and Barbarism. 186 pp. Cambridge, 1878.

Gahan, L.K. The Nipmucks and their Territory. BMAS, II, iv, 2-6. 1941.

Gookin, D. An Historical Account of the Doings and Sufferings of the Christian Indians in New England. Archaeologia Americana, Transactions and Collections, II, 423-534. 1836.

--- Historical Collections of the Indians of New England. MHSC, ser. 1, I, 141-227. 1792.

Gregory, J.H. Some Essex County Indians. Essex Antiquarian, V, 39-40. 1901.

Guernsey, S.J. Notes on Explorations of Martha's Vineyard. AA, n.s., XVIII, 81-97. 1915.

Hale, E.E. The Language of the Massachusetts Indians. RP, IV, 361-3. 1905.

Hallet, L.F. Cultural Traits of the Southern New England Indians. BMAS, XV, 59-64. 1954.

Hawley, G. Mashpee Indians. MHSC, ser. 1, X, 113-14. 1809.

Haynes, H.W. Agricultural Implements of the New England Indians. Proceedings of the Boston Society of Natural History, XXII, 437-43. 1883.

Higginson, F. New England's Plantation. MHSC, I, 117-24. 1806.

Hooton, E.A. Notes on Skeletal Remains from Martha's Vineyard. AA, n.s., XVIII, 98-104. 1915.

Hosmer, J.K., ed. Winthrop's Journal. 2 vols. New York, 1908.

Jones, J.W., ed. The Relation of John Verarzanus. Divers Voyages touching the Discovery of America, ed. R. Hakluyt, pp. 55-90. London, 1850.

Josselyn, J. An Account of Two Voyages to New England. 211 pp. Boston, 1865.

LaBrosse, J.B. de. Nehiro-iriniui aiamihe massina-higan. 96 pp. Quebec, 1767.

Kittredge, G.L. Letters of Samuel Lee and Samuel Sewell relating to New England and the Indians. Publications of the Colonial Society of Massachusetts, XV, 142-86. 1912.

Knight, M.F. Wampanoag Indian Tales. JAFL, XXXVIII, 134-7. 1925.

Knight, M.V. The Craniometry of Southern New England Indians. Memoirs of the Connecticut Academy of Arts and Sciences, IV, 1-36. 1915.

Leach, D.E. Flintlock and Tomahawk. 304 pp. New York, 1958.

Lechford, T. Plain Dealing: or Newes from New-England. MHSC, ser. 3, III, 101-5. 1833.

Macy, Z. A Short Journal of the First Settlement of the Island of Nantucket. MHSC, ser. 1, III, 155-60. 1794.

Mawen, T. A List of the Names of the Indians... which live in or belong to Natick. MHSC, ser. 1, X, 134-6. 1809.

Mayhew, D. Observations on the Indian Language. 12 pp. Boston, 1884.

Michelson, T. On the Etymology of the Natick Word Kompaw. AA, n.s., XIII, 339. 1911.

Miller, W.J. Notes concerning the Wampanoag Tribe of Indians. 148 pp. Providence, 1880.

Mooney, J. Martha's Vineyard Indians. BBAE, XXX, i, 810. 1907.

--- Nipmuc. BBAE, XXX, ii, 74-5. 1910.

--- Wampanoag. BBAE, XXX, ii, 903-4. 1910.

Mooney, J., and Thomas, C. Massachuset. BBAE, XXX, i, 816-17. 1907.

Mooney, J., and Thomas, C. Nauset. BBAE, XXX, ii, 40-1. 1910.

Morton, T. New England Canaan. Tracts and Other Papers relating principally to the Origin, Settlement, and Progress of the Colonies in North America, ed. P. Force, II, v, 1-125. Washington, 1838.

Phelps, M. Indians of Old Brookfield. BMAS, IX, 80-82. 1948.

Prince, J.D. Last Living Echoes of the Natick. AA, n.s., IX, 493-8. 1907.

Rainey, F.G. A Compilation of Historical Data contributing to the Ethnography of Connecticut and Southern New England Indians. BASC, 1936, iii, 1-89.

Robbins, M. Historical Approach to Titicut. BMAS, XI, 48-73. 1950.

--- Indians of the Old Colony. BMAS, XVII, 59-73. 1956.

Saville, M.H. The John Eliot Indian Bible. IN, III, 120-3. 1926.

Schoolcraft, H.R. Massachusetts Indians. HCPIT, I, 284-99. 1851.

Shepard, T. The Day-Breaking, if not the Sun-Rising of the Gospell with the Indians of New-England. MHSC, ser. 3, IV, 1-23. 1834.

Sherman, C.F. Winslow's Reports of the Indians. BMAS, III, 43-52; IV, 15-16. 1942.

Silver, S. Natick Consonants in Reference to Proto-Central Algonquian. IJAL, XXV, 112-20. 1960.

Speck, F.G. Mythology of the Wampanoag. EP, XXV, 83-6. 1928.

--- A Note on the Hassanamisco Band of Nipmuc. BMAS, IV, 49-57. 1943.

--- Territorial Subdivisions and Boundaries of the Wampanoag, Massachusett, and Nauset Indians. INM, ser. 2, XLIV, 7-152. 1928.

Speck, F.G., and Dexter, R.W. Utilization of Marine Life by the Wampanoag Indians of Massachusetts. JWAS, XXXVIII, 257-65. 1948.

Stiles, E. An Account of the Potenummecut Indians. MHSC, ser. 1, X, 112-3. 1809.

Swadesh, M. Sociologic Notes on Obsolescent Languages. IJAL, XIV, 226-35. 1948.

Tantaquidgeon, G. Newly Discovered Straw Basketry of the Wampanoag Indians. IN, VII, 475-84. 1930.

--- Notes on the Gay Head Indians of Massachusetts. IN, VII, 1-26. 1930.

Tooker, W.W. The Significance of John Eliot's Natick. AA, o.s., X, 281-7. 1897.

Travers, M.A. The Wampanoag Indian Federation of the Algonquin Nation. 245 pp. New Bedford, 1957.

Trumbull, J.H. Natick Dictionary. BBAE, XXV,
     1-349. 1903.

--- Origin and Early Progress of Indian Missions in
     New England. 50 pp. Worcester, 1874.

Uhlenbeck, C.C. Ontwerp van eene vergelijkende
     vormleer van eenige Algonkin-talen. VKAW, n.
     s., XI, iii, 1-67. 1910.

Wall, C.A. The Nipmuck Indians. 21 pp. Wor-
     cester, 1898.

Weeks, A.G. Massasoit of the Wampanoags. 270
     pp. Fall River, 1920.

Wilder, H.H. Notes on the Indians of Southern
     Massachusetts. AA, n.s., XXV, 197-218. 1923.

Willoughby, C.C. The Adze and the Ungrooved
     Axe of the New England Indians. AA, n.s., IX,
     296-306. 1907.

--- Antiquities of the New England Indians. 314
     pp. Cambridge, 1935.

--- Certain Earthworks of Eastern Massachusetts.
     AA, n.s., XIII, 566-76. 1911.

--- Dress and Ornaments of the New England Indians.
     AA, n.s., VII, 499-508. 1905.

--- Houses and Gardens of the New England Indians.
     AA, n.s., VIII, 115-32. 1906.

--- Indian Burial Place at Winthrop. PMP, XI, 1-
     37. 1924.

--- Pottery of the New England Indians. Putnam
     Anniversary Volume, pp. 83-101. New York,
     1909.

--- Textile Fabrics of the New England Indians. AA,
     n.s., VII, 85-93. 1905.

--- The Wilderness and the Indian. Commonwealth
     History of Massachusetts, ed. A.B.Hart, I, 127-
     58. New York, 1927.

--- Wooden Bowls of the Algonquian Indians. AA,
     n.s., X, 423-34. 1908.

Winslow, E. Good News from New England. The
     Story of the Pilgrim Fathers, ed. E. Arber, pp.
     581-92. London, 1897.

Winthrop, J. The History of New England., 2 vols.
     Boston, 1825.

Wood, W. New England Prospect. BMAS, VIII,
     17-22. 1947.

--- New-England's Prospect, pp. 63-110. New edit.
     Boston, 1865.

Wright, H.A. Two Letters to the Editor concerning
     the Boundaries of the Nipmucks. BMAS, II, iv,,
     14-16. 1941.

8. METOAC

Including the Montauk, the Shinnecock, and
other small tribes of Long Island.

Bolton, R.P. Indian Life of Long Ago in the City of
     New York, 167 pp. New York, 1934.

--- New York City in Indian Possession. INM, II,
     225-395. 1920.

Carr, L.G., and Westez, C. Surviving Folktales
     and Herbal Lore among the Shinnecock Indians of
     Long Island. JAFL, LVIII, 113-23. 1945.

Denton, D. A Brief Description of New York, ed.
     G. Furman. 57 pp. New York, 1845.

Douglas, F.H. Long Island Indian Culture. DAMLS,
     L, 1-4. 1932.

--- Long Island Indian Tribes. DAMLS, XLIX, 1-4.
     1932.

Furman, G. Antiquities of Long Island. 478 pp. New
     York, 1875.

Harrington, M.R. Ancient Shell Heaps near New
     York City. APAM, III, 169-79. 1909.

--- An Ancient Village Site of the Shinnecock In-
     dians. APAM, XXII, 227-83. 1924.

--- Past and Present of the Shinnecock Indians. SW,
     XXXII, 282-9. 1903.

--- Shinnecock Notes. JAFL, XVI, 37-9. 1903.

Hayne, C. The Lost Tribes. Narragansett Dawn,
     I, 164-7. 1935.

Hunter, L.M. The Shinnecock Indians. 90 pp.
     Islip, 1950.

Jefferson, T. Long Island. TCAAS, II, 305-67.
     1836.

Macauley, J. The Natural, Statistical and Civil
     History of the State of New York, II, 252-75. Al-
     bany, 1829.

Mooney, J. Metoac. BBAE, XXX, i, 851. 1907.

--- Montauk. BBAE, XXX, i, 934-5. 1907.

Morice, J.H., and Speck, F.G. Concerning "An
     Ethnological Introduction to the Long Island In-
     dians." BMAS, VII, 59-62. 1946.

Occum, S. An Account of the Montauk Indians.
     MHSC, ser. 1, X, 106-11. 1809.

Orchard, F.P. A Matinecoc Site on Long Island. IN,
     V, 217-31. 1928.

Ruttenber, E.M. History of the Indian Tribes of Hud-
     son's River. 415 pp. Albany, 1872.

Saville, F.H. Cache of Blades from Long Island. IN,
     III, 41-5. 1926.

--- Indian Wells on Long Island. IN, II, 207-11.
     1925.

--- A Montauk Cemetery at Easthampton. INM, II,
     65-102. 1920.

Skinner, A. Archaeology of the New York Coastal
    Algonkin. APAM, III, 213-35. 1909.

Solecki, R.S. The Archaeological Position of His-
    toric Fort Corchaug. BASC, XXIV, 3-40. 1950.

Tooker, W.W. John Eliot's First Indian Teacher and
    Interpreter. 60 pp. New York, 1896.

--- Some Indian Fishing Stations upon Long Island.
    Algonquian Series, VII, 7-62. 1901.

Westez, C.A.H. An Ethnological Introduction to the
    Long Island Indians. BMAS, VI, 39-42. 1945.

--- A Study of the Long Island Indian Problem.
    BMAS, V, 17-20. 1944.

Wolley, C. A Two Years Journal in New York, ed.
    E.B.O'Callaghan. 97 pp. New York, 1860.

9. MOHEGAN

Including the Mohegan or Pequot, the Narraganset,
and the Niantic.

Williams, R. A Key into the Language of America.
    197 pp. London, 1643.

Adams, F.P. Pipe of Peace. Narragansett Dawn, I,
    157. 1935.

Allen, Z. Native Indians of America. 55 pp. Provi-
    dence, 1881.

Anonymous. Extract from an Indian History. MHSC,
    ser. 1, IX, 99-102. 1804.

--- The Mohegans. Bostonian Magazine, 1895, 369-
    85, 503-13, 671-8.

--- A Southern New England Village. Bulletin of the
    Roger Williams Park Museum, III, ii-iii. 1911.

Apes, W. A Son of the Forest. 216 pp. New York,
    1829.

Bacchiani, A. Giovanni da Verrazzano and His Dis-
    coveries in North America. Annual Report of the
    American Scenic and Historic Preservation Society,
    XV, 190-4. 1910.

Bartlett, J.R., ed. Letters of Roger Williams. Pub-
    lications of the Narragansett Club, VI, 1-420.
    1874.

Beardsley, E.E. The Mohegan Land Controversy.
    Papers of the New Haven Colony Historical Society,
    III, 205-25. 1882.

Bibaud, F.M. Biographie des sagamos illustrés de
    l'Amérique Septentrionale, pp. 111-14, 121-31,
    135-60. Montreal, 1848.

Boissevain, E. The Detribalization of the Narragan-
    sett Indians. E, III, 225-45. 1956.

Boissevain, F. Factors of Narragansett Survival.
    BESAF, XIV, 12. 1955.

Bradshaw, H.C. The Indians of Connecticut: the
    Effect of English Colonization. 64 pp. Deep River,
    1935.

Brown, M.W. Narragansett Words. Narragansett
    Dawn, II, vi, 6. 1936.

Butler, E.L. Notes on Indian Ethnology and History.
    BASC, XXVII, 35-47. 1953.

--- Sweat-Houses in the Southern New England Area.
    BMAS, VII, 11-16. 1945.

Champlin, E. From Old Medicine Records Marked
    1831. Narragansett Dawn, II, 35-6. 1936.

Chapin, H.M. Indian Graves. RIHSC, XX, 14-32.
    1927.

--- Indian Implements found in Rhode Island. RIHSC,
    XVII, 105-24; XVIII, 22-32. 1924-25.

--- Sachems of the Narragansetts. Providence, 1931.

--- Unusual Indian Implements found in Rhode Island.
    RIHSC, XIX, 117-28. 1926.

DeForest, J.W. History of the Indians of Connecticut.
    509 pp. Hartford, 1851.

Dexter, H.M. The New England Indians. Sabbath at
    Home, II, 193-206. 1868.

Dixon, R.B. The Early Migrations of the Indians of
    New England and the Maritime Provinces. PAAAS,
    n.s., XXIV, 65-76. 1914.

Dorr, H.C. The Narragansett. RIHSC, VII, 135-
    233. 1885.

Drake, S.G., ed. The Old Indian Chronicle. 333
    pp. Boston, 1867.

Dwight, T. Travels in New-England and New-York,
    I, 84-102. London, 1823.

Edwards, J. Observations on the Mohegan Language.
    MHSC, ser. 2, X, 81-160. 1823.

Ellis, G.W. and Morris, J.E. King Philip's War.
    326 pp. New York, 1906.

Ferguson, H.L. Archeological Exploration of Fishers
    Island. INM, XI, 1-44. 1935.

Fielding, F.A.H. Text of the Pequot Sermon. AA,
    n.s., V, 199-212. 1903.

Forbes, A. Indian Games. GM, XLIV, 27-30. 1941.

Freeman, F. Civilization and Barbarism. 186 pp.
    Cambridge, 1878.

Gardner, L.L. Relation of the Pequot Warres. MHSC,
    ser. 3, III, 131-60. 1833.

Glasko, F. The Narragansett Mothers Many Years ago
    were Proud Home Makers. Narragansett Dawn, I,
    93-4. 1935.

--- Succotash. Narragansett Dawn, I, 22-3. 1935.

Gookin, D. An Historial Account of the Doings and Sufferings of the Christian Indians in New England. Archaeologia Americana, Collections and Transactions, II, 423-534. 1836.

--- Historical Collections of the Indians of New England. MHSC, I, 141-227. 1792.

Gookin, W.F. Indian Deeds on the Vineyard. BMAS, XIII, ii, 6-7. 1952.

--- Metsoo'onk. BMAS, XII, 58-60. 1951.

Hallet, L.F. Cultural Traits of the Southern New England Indians. BMAS, XV, 59-64. 1954.

Hayne, C. The Lost Tribes. Narragansett Dawn, I, 164-7. 1935.

Holmes, A.A. Additional Memoir of the Moheagans. MHSC, ser. 1, IX, 75-99. 1804.

Jones, J.W., ed. The Relation of John Verarzanus. Divers Voyages touching the Discovery of America, ed. R. Hakluyt, pp. 55-90. London, 1850.

Kittredge, G.L. Letters of Samuel Lee and Samuel Sewall relating to New England and the Indians. Publications of the Colonial Society of Massachusetts, XIV, 142-86. 1912.

Knight, M.V. The Craniometry of Southern New England Indians. Memoirs of the Connecticut Academy of Arts and Sciences, IV, 1-36. 1915.

Leach, D.E. Flintlock and Tomahawk. 304 pp. New York, 1958.

--- A New View of the Declaration of War against the Narragansetts, November, 1675. Rhode Island History, XV, 33-41. 1956.

Little Bear. Narragansett Fires. Narragansett Dawn, I, 115. 1935.

Lone Wolf. The Baby Name. Narragansett Dawn, I, 118. 1935.

--- Birds of Prey. Narragansett Dawn, I, 119-20. 1935.

Lossing, B.J. The Last of the Pequods. Indian Miscellany, ed. W.W. Beach, pp. 452-60. Albany, 1877.

Mason, J. A Brief History of the Pequot War. MHSC, ser. 2, VIII, 120-53. 1819.

Mason, V.W. Bermuda's Pequots. Harvard Alumni Bulletin, XXXIX, 616-20. 1937.

Means, C.A. Mohegan-Pequot Relationships. BASC, XXI, 26-34. 1947.

Mooney, J. Mohegan. BBAE, XXX, i, 926-7. 1907.

--- Narraganset. BBAE, XXX, ii, 28-30. 1910.

--- Niantic. BBAE, XXX, ii, 68-9. 1910.

--- Pequot. BBAE, XXX, ii, 229-31. 1910.

Morgan, L.H. Ancient Society, pp. 173-4. New York, 1877.

Morgan, L.H. The Indian Journals, 1859-62, p. 135. Ann Arbor, 1959.

--- Systems of Consanguinity and Affinity. SCK, XVII, 291-382. 1871.

Morton, T. New England Canaan. Tracts and Other Papers relating principally to the Origin, Settlement, and Progress of the Colonies in North America, ed. P. Force, II, v, 1-125. Washington, 1838.

Neesqutton. The Children of Gitche Manitou. Narragansett Dawn, I, 187-9. 1935.

Orr, C. History of the Pequot War. 149 pp. Cleveland, 1897.

Parsons, U. Indian Names of Places in Rhode-Island. 32 pp. Providence, 1861.

--- Indian Relics recently found in Charlestown. HM, ser. 1, VII, 41-4. 1863.

Peale, A.L. Uncas and the Mohegan-Pequot. Boston, 1939.

Peckham, P. The Narragansett Indian Church. Narragansett Dawn, I, 8-9. 1935.

Philhower, C.A. The Earliest Account of the Lenape and Narragansett Indians. BASNJ, V, 10-11. 1952.

Pickering, J., ed. Dr. Edwards' Observations on the Mohegan Language. MHSC, ser. 2, X, 135-60. 1823.

Pine Tree, Chief. A Feast for an Indian Scout. Narragansett Dawn, I, 179. 1935.

--- An Old Indian Cure in Measles. Narragansett Dawn, I, 159-60. 1935.

Prince, J.D., and Speck, F.G. Dying American Speech Echoes from Connecticut. PAPS, XLII, 346-52. 1903.

--- Glossary of the Mohegan-Pequot Language. AA, n.s., VI, 18-45. 1904.

--- The Modern Pequots and Their Language. AA, n.s., V, 193-212. 1903.

Rainey, F.G. A Compilation of Historical Data contributing to the Ethnography of Connecticut and Southern New England Indians. BASC, III, 1-89. 1936.

Ray, L. The Aboriginal Inhabitants of Connecticut. Indian Miscellany, ed. W.W. Beach, pp. 280-302. Albany, 1877.

Redwing, P. Art. Narragansett Dawn, I, 234-5. 1935.

--- The Corn Dance. Narragansett Dawn, I, 96-8. 1935.

--- History of the Indian's Religion. Narragansett Dawn, I, 195-9. 1935.

Redwing, P. Lessons in the Narragansett Tongue. Narragansett Dawn, I, 18, 44-5, 68, 88-9, 122-3, 138-9, 185-7, 204, 232-3, 259-60, 287; II, 5, 29. 1935-36.

--- Old Beliefs. Narragansett Dawn, I, 161. 1935.

--- Sign Language. Narragansett Dawn, I, 255-6. 1935.

--- Totems. Narragansett Dawn, II, 12. 1936.

--- Youth learns the Mysteries of Life from Gitche Manitou, the Great Spirit. Narragansett Dawn, I, 25-7. 1935.

Rider, S.S. The Lands of Rhode Island as They were known to Caunounicus and Miantunnomu when Roger Williams came in 1636. 297 pp. Providence, 1904.

Sherman, C.F. Habitations, Summer and Winter Sites, and Reasons for Same. BMAS, VI, 10-14. 1944.

Smith, De C. Martyrs of the Oblong and Little Nine. 310 pp. Caldwell, 1948.

Solecki, R.S. The Archaeological Position of Historic Fort Corchaug. BASC, XXIV, 3-40. 1950.

Speck, F.G. Decorative Art of the Indian Tribes of Connecticut. MCDM, LXXV, 1-73. 1915.

--- Medicine Practices of the Northeastern Algonquians. ICA, XIX, 303-21. 1915.

--- A Modern Mohegan-Pequot Text. AA, n.s., VI, 469-76. 1904.

--- Mohegan Beadwork on Birch-Bark. IN, V, 295-8. 1928.

--- A Mohegan-Pequot Witchcraft Tale. JAFL, XVI, 104-6. 1903.

--- Mohegan Traditions of Muhkeahweesug, "the Little Men." Papoose, I, vii, 11-14. 1903.

--- Native Tribes and Dialects of Connecticut. ARBAE, XLIII, 199-287. 1926.

--- Northern Elements in Iroquois and New England Art. IN, II, 1-13. 1925.

--- Notes on the Mohegan and Niantic Indians. APAM, III, 183-210. 1909.

--- A Pequot-Mohegan Witchcraft Tale. JAFL, XVI, 104-7. 1903.

--- Remnants of the Nehantics. SW, XLVII, 65-9. 1918.

--- Some Mohegan-Pequot Legends. JAFL, XVII, 183-4. 1904.

Spiess, M. The Indians of Connecticut. Committee on Historical Publications, Tercentenary Commission of the State of Connecticut. 33 pp. New Haven, 1933.

--- Podunk Indian Sites. BASC, V, 2-6. 1937.

Stiles, E. Memoir of the Pequots. MHSC, ser. 1, X, 101-3. 1809.

--- The Number of the Nyhantic Tribe of Indians. MHSC, ser. 1, X, 103-4; ser. 4, X, 103-4. 1809, 1857.

Swadesh, M. Sociologic Notes on Obsolescent Languages. IJAL, XIV, 226-35. 1948.

Tantaquidgeon, G. Mohegan Medicinal Practices, Weather Lore, and Superstitions. ARBAE, XLIII, 264-79. 1926.

--- Notes on Mohegan-Pequot Basketry Designs. Indians at Work, II, 43-5. 1935.

Trumbull, B. A Compendium of the Indian Wars in New England, ed. F.B.Hartranft. 61 pp. Hartford, 1926.

--- A Complete History of Connecticut, I, 39-57. New Haven, 1818.

Wahana. Ancient Narragansett Bath Houses. Narragansett Dawn, I, 265. 1935.

Wheeler, R.A. The Pequot Indians. 23 pp. Westerly, 1877.

Wilder, H.H. Notes on the Indians of Southern Massachusetts. AA, n.s., XXV, 197-218. 1923.

--- The Physiognomy of the Indians of Southern New England. AA, n.s., XIV, 415-36. 1912.

Willoughby, C.C. Antiquities of the New England Indians. 314 pp. Cambridge, 1935.

--- Dress and Ornaments of the New England Indians. AA, n.s., VII, 499-508. 1905.

--- Houses and Gardens of the New England Indians. AA, n.s., VIII, 115-32. 1906.

--- Wooden Bowls of the Algonquian Indians. AA, n.s., X, 423-34. 1908.

Wood, G.A. The Mohegan Indians East and West. PMVHA, X, 440-53. 1920-21.

10. NANTICOKE

Including the Conoy or Piscataway and the Nanticoke.

Anonymous. Choptank. BBAE, XXX, i, 291. 1907.

Babcock, W.H. The Nanticoke Indians of Indian River. AA, n.s., I, 277-82. 1899.

Bender, H.E. The Nanticoke Indians in Lancaster County. Publications of the Lancaster County Historical Association, XXIII, 121-30. 1929.

Bozman, J.L. The History of Maryland, I, 103-93. Baltimore, 1837.

Brinton, D.G. The Lenapé and Their Legends, pp. 22-9. Philadelphia, 1885.

Brinton, D.G. A Vocabulary of the Nanticoke Dialect. PAPS, XXXI, 325-33. 1893.

Bushnell, D.I. Native Cemeteries and Forms of Burial East of the Mississippi. BBAE, LXXI, 24-6. 1920.

Carr, L.G. Native Drinks in the Southeast and Their Values, with Special Emphasis on Persimmon Beer. Proceedings of the Delaware County Institute of Science, X, 29-43. 1947.

Crozier, A. Fishing Methods of the Indians of the Delmarva Region. BASD, IV, iv, 16-9. 1947.

--- The Nanticokes of the Delmarva Peninsula. BASD, I, v, 2-6. 1934.

Davidson, D.S. Burial Customs in the Delmarva Peninsula and the Question of Their Chronology. AAn, I, 84-97. 1935.

Denny, E.R. Indians of Kent Island. 20 pp. [Stevensville, Md.?], [1959].

Dunlap, A.R. A Bibliographical Discussion of the Indian Languages of the Delmarva Peninsula. BASD, IV, v, 2-5. 1949.

Ferguson, A.L.L. Moyaone and the Piscataway Indians. 44 pp. Washington, 1937.

--- An Ossuary near Piscataway Creek. AAn, V, 4-13. 1940.

Gilbert, W.H.Jr. The Wesorts of Southern Maryland. JWAS, XXXV, 237-46. 1945.

Goldsborough, E.R. The Aborigines of the Lower Potomac River Valley. PA, VIII, 27-36. 1938.

Hassrick, R.B. A Visit with the Nanticoke. BASD, IV, i, 7-8. 1943.

Holmes, W.H. Aboriginal Shell-Heaps of the Middle Atlantic Tidewater Region. AA, n.s., IX, 113-28. 1907.

--- Stone Implements of the Potomac-Chesapeake Tidewater Province. ARBAE, XV, 3-152. 1897.

Lincoln, A.T. Our Indians of Early Delaware. Delaware Citizens Association Historical Bulletin, I, 1-42. 1932.

MacLeod, W.C. Piscataway Royalty. JWAS, XVI, 301-9. 1926.

Marye, W.B. Indian Paths of the Delmarva Peninsula. BASD, II, iii, 5-22; iv, 4-27; v, 2-15; vi, 4-11. 1936-38.

--- Indian Towns of the Southeastern Part of Sussex County. BASD, III, ii, 18-25; iii, 21-8. 1939-40.

--- A Quiakeson House in Eastern Maryland. AAn, IX, 456. 1944.

--- The Wiccomiss Indians of Maryland. AAn, IV, ii, 146-52; V, i, 51-5. 1938-39.

Mooney, J. Indian Tribes of the District of Columbia. AA, II, 259-66. 1889.

Mooney, J., and Thomas, C. Conoy. BBAE, XXX, i, 339-41. 1907.

--- Nanticoke. BBAE, XXX, ii, 24-6. 1910.

Murray, W.V. Nanticokes. TCAAS, II, 305-67. 1836.

Parker, A.C. The Nanticoke. PA, V, 83-90; VI, 3-12. 1935-36.

Semmes, R. Aboriginal Maryland, 1608-1689. Maryland Historical Magazine, XXIV, 157-72, 195-209. 1929.

Speck, F.G. Back again to Indian River, Its People and Their Games. BASD, III, v, 17-24. 1942.

--- "Cudgelling Rabbits," an Old Nanticoke Hunting Tradition and its Significance. BASD, IV, iv, 9-12. 1946.

--- The Frolic among the Nanticoke of Indian River Hundred, Delaware. BASD, IV, i, 2-4. 1943.

--- Gourds of the Southeastern Indians. 113 pp. Boston, 1941.

--- Indians of the Eastern Shore of Maryland. 15 pp. Baltimore, 1922.

--- A Maker of Eel-Pots among the Nanticokes of Delaware. BASD, IV, v, 25-7. 1949.

--- Medicine Practices of the Northeastern Algonquians. ICA, XIX, 303-21. 1915.

--- The Nanticoke and Conoy Indians. Papers of the Historical Society of Delaware, n.s., I, 1-77. 1927.

--- The Nanticoke Community of Delaware. CMAI, II, iv, 1-43. 1915.

Speck, F.G. and Schaeffer, C.E. The Deer and the Rabbit Hunting Drive in Virginia and the Southeast. SIS, II, 3-20. 1950.

Stewart, T.D. A Report on Skeletal Remains. AAn, V, 13-18. 1940.

Tantaquidgeon, G. A Study of Delaware Indian Medicine Practice and Folk Beliefs. 91 pp. Harrisburg, 1942.

Uhler, S.P. Pennsylvania's Indian Relations to 1754. 144 pp. Allentown, 1951.

Weslager, C.A. The Anthropological Position of the Indian Tribes of the Delmarva Peninsula. BASD, IV, iv, 3-7. 1947.

--- Delaware's Forgotten Folk. 215 pp. Philadelphia, 1943.

--- Folklore among the Nanticokes of Indian River Hundred. Delaware Folklore Bulletin, I, v, 17-18. 1955.

--- The Nanticoke Indians. 159 pp. Harrisburg, 1948.

Weslager, C.A. The Nanticoke Indians in Early
Pennsylvania. PMHB, LXVII, 345-355. 1943.
--- Nanticokes and the Buzzard Song. BASD, IV,
ii, 14-17. 1945.
--- Wynicaco – a Choptank Indian Chief. PAPS,
LXXXVII, 398-402. 1944.

11. NEUTRAL

Also called Attiwandaron.

Anderson, R.T. Malahide, Yarmouth and Bayham
Townships. AAR, 1902, 79-92.
Beauchamp, W.M. Indian Nations of the Great Lakes.
AAOJ, XVII, 321-5. 1895.
--- The Neutral Nation. AAOJ, XVI, 193-200. 1894.
Coyne, J.H. The Southwold Earthwork and the Coun-
try of the Neutrals. Annual Report of the Canad-
ian Institute, VI, 22-34. 1893.
Harris, W.R. The Flint Workers. AAR, 1900, 28-
36.
Herriott, W. Aboriginal Agriculture in Southwestern
Ontario. Waterloo Historical Society, Annual Re-
port, XI, 18-21. 1923.
Hewitt, J.N.B. Neutrals. BBAE, XXX, ii, 60-2.
1910.
Houghton, F. The Characteristics of Iroquoian Vil-
lage Sites of Western New York. AA, n.s., XVIII,
508-20. 1916.
--- The Indian Inhabitants of the Niagara Frontier.
Journal of American History, XVI, 213-28. 1922.
--- The Indian Occupancy of the Niagara Frontier.
BBSNS, IX, 263-374. 1909.
--- Report on the Neuter Cemetery, Grand Island,
N.Y. BBSNS, IX, 377-85. 1909.
Kenton, E., ed. The Indians of North America, I,
417-27. New York, 1927.
Knowles, F.H.S. Physical Anthropology of the Roe-
buck Iroquois. BCDM, LXXXVII, 1-75. 1937.
--- The Torture of Captives by the Indians of Eastern
North America. PAPS, LXXXII, 151-225. 1940.
Kraus, B.S. Acculturation. AAn, IX, 302-18. 1944.
Orr, R.B. The Attiwandarons. AAR, 1913, 7-20.
--- The Iroquois in Canada. AAR, XXXI, 9-55. 1919.
Parker, A.C. The Origin of the Iroquois as suggested
by Their Archeology. AA, n.s., XVIII, 479-507.
1916.
Reville, F.D. History of the County of Brant, I, 15-
68. Brantford, 1920.
Ritchie, W.A. Early Huron and Neutral Sand Knoll
Sites in Western New York. RNYAS, VII, iii, 62-
78. 1930.

Skinner, A. An Unusual Canadian Disc Pipe. IN, III,
39-41. 1926.
Thwaites, R.G., ed. The Jesuit Relations and Allied
Documents. 74 vols. Cleveland, 1896-1901.
Waugh, F.W. Attiwandaron or Neutral Village-Sites
in Brant County. AAR, 1902, 70-9.
Wintemberg, W.J. Bone and Horn Harpoon Heads of
the Ontario Indians. AAR, 1905, 33-56.
--- The Middleport Prehistoric Village Site. MBCDM,
CIX, 1-79. 1948.
--- Relics of the Attiwandarons. RP, IV, 266-75.
1905.
Young, A.W. History of Chautauqua County, pp.
20-34. Buffalo, 1875.

12. PENNACOOK

Including the Pennacook of New Hampshire and
the Pocumtuc of western Massachusetts.

Allen, W. The History of Chelmsford. 192 pp.
Haverhill, 1820.
Ballard, E. Indian Mode of Applying Names. Collec-
tions of the New Hampshire Historical Society,
VIII, 446-52. 1866.
--- Character of the Penacooks. Collections of the
New Hampshire Historical Society, VIII, 428-45.
1866.
Eckstorm, F.H. The Indians of Maine. Maine, A
History, ed. L.C. Hatch, I, 43-64. New York,
1919.
Fowler, W.S. Stone Age Methods of Woodworking in
the Connecticut Valley. BASC, XX, 1-32. 1946.
Gookin, D. Historical Collection of the Indians in
New England. MHSC, ser. 1, I, 141-227; ser. 4,
I, 141-227. 1792; 1859.
Johnson, F. Indians of New Hampshire. Appalachia,
n.s., VI, vii, 3-15. 1940.
Knight, M.V. The Craniometry of Southern New
England Indians. Memoirs of the Connecticut
Academy of Arts and Sciences, IV, 1-36. 1915.
Mooney, J. Pocumtuc. BBAE, XXX, ii, 270. 1910.
Mooney, J., and Thomas, C. Pennacook. BBAE,
XXX, ii, 225-6. 1910.
Potter, C.E. Indians of New England. History of
Manchester, New Hampshire, pp. 22-100. Man-
chester, 1856.
Proctor, M.A. The Indians of the Winnipesaukee
and Pemigewasset Valleys. 67 pp. Franklin, N.
H., 1930.
Robbins, M. Indians of the Old Colony. BMAS,
XVII, 59-74. 1956.

Schoolcraft, H.R. Pennacooks. HCPIT, V, 217-37. 1855.

Stiles, E. Indians on the Connecticut River. MHSC, ser. 1, X, 104-5; ser. 4, X, 104-5. 1809, 1857.

Wilder, H.H. Excavation of Indian Graves in Western Massachusetts. AA, n.s., VII, 295-300. 1905.

--- Notes on the Indians of Southern Massachusetts. AA, n.s., XXV, 197-218. 1923.

Wilder, H.H. The Physiognomy of the Indians of Southern New England. AA, n.s., XIV, 415-36. 1912.

Wilder, H.H., and Whipple, R.W. The Position of the Body in Aboriginal Interments in Western Massachusetts. AA, n.s., XIX, 372-87. 1917.

Willoughby, C.C. Antiquities of the New England Indians. 314 pp. Cambridge, 1935.

--- The Wilderness and the Indian. Commonwealth History of Massachusetts, ed. A.B.Hart, I, 127-58. Cambridge, 1927.

XIII. SOUTHEAST

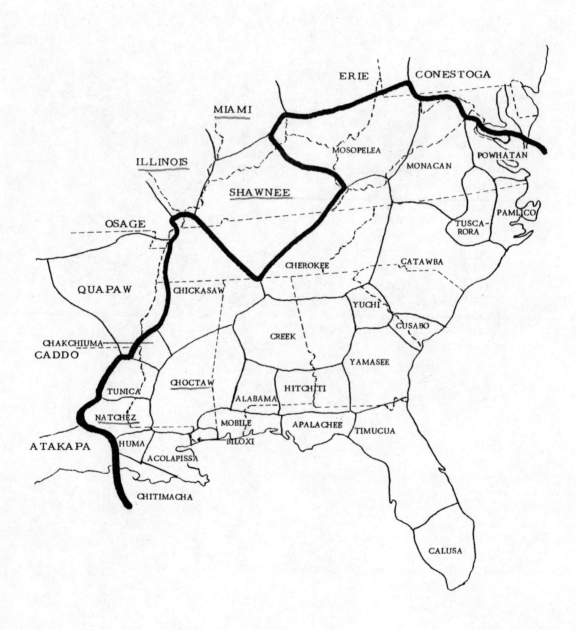

The tribes of this area are grouped under the following linguistic stocks:

Algonkian: Pamlico, Powhatan.
Iroquoian: Cherokee, Tuscarora.
Muskhogean: Acolapissa, Alabama, Apalachee, Chakchiuma, Chickasaw, Choctaw, Creek, Cusabo, Hitchiti, Huma, Mobile, Natchez, Seminole, Yamasee.
Siouan: Biloxi, Catawba, Monacan, Mosopelea.
Timucuan: Calusa (uncertain), Timucua.
Tunican: Tunica.
Uchean: Yuchi.

Abel, A.H. The Slaveholding Indians. 3 vols. Cleveland, 1915-25.

Adair, J. The History of the American Indians. 464 pp. London, 1775.

Adams, J.A. English Institutions and the American Indian. Johns Hopkins University Studies in Historical and Political Science. XII, x, 4-59. 1894.

Alden, J.R. John Stuart and the Southern Colonial Frontier. 384 pp. Ann Arbor, 1944.

Anonymous. Mémoire sur la Louisiane, ou le Mississippi. Recueil A-Z, II (B), 123-52. Luxembourg, 1752.

Barcia Carballido y Zuniga, A.G. Ensayo cronológico para la historia general de la Florida. 366 pp. Madrid, 1723.

Battle, H.B. The Domestic Use of Oil among the Southern Aborigines. AA, n.s., XXIV, 171-82. 1922.

Beers, H.P. The French in North America. Baton Rouge, 1957.

Bennett, J.W. Middle American Influences upon the Cultures of the Southeastern United States. AAm, II, 25-50. 1944.

--- Southeastern Culture Types and Middle American Influences. In, El Norte de Mexico y el Sur de Estados Unidos, 223-41. Mexico, 1943.

Berquin-Duvallon. Travels in Louisiana and the Floridas. 181 pp. New York, 1806.

Beverly, R. The History and Present State of Virginia. Chapel Hill, 1947. Original Edition, 1705.

Biasutti, R. Le Razzi e i Popoli della Terra, 2nd ed., IV, 437-40. Torino, 1957.

Biedma, L.F.de. A Narrative of the Expedition of Hernando de Soto. HCL, II, 97-109. 1850.

Blume, G.W.J. Present-day Indians of Tidewater Virginia. QBASV, VI, iv, 1-11. 1951.

Boyd, M.F. Historic Sites in and around the Jim Woodruff Reservoir Area, Florida-Georgia. BBAE, CLXIX, 195-314. 1958.

Brackenridge, H.M. Views of Louisiana. 304 pp. Pittsburgh, 1814.

Brannon, P.A. Indian Treaties. AHQ, XII, 242-50. 1950.

--- The Pensacola Indian Trade. FHSQ, XXXI, 1-15. 1952.

--- Removal of Indians from Alabama. AHQ, XII, 91-117. 1950.

--- The Southern Indian Trade. 87 pp. Montgomery, 1935.

Bullen, R.P. Six Sites near the Chattahoochee River in the Jim Woodruff Reservoir Area, Florida. BBAE, CLXIX, 315-58. 1958.

Bushnell, D.I. Aboriginal Forms of Burial in Eastern United States. Holmes Anniversary Volume, pp. 31-43. Washington, 1916.

--- Native Villages and Village Sites East of the Mississippi. BBAE, LXIX, 1-111. 1919.

--- Tribal Migrations East of the Mississippi. SMC, LXXXIX, xii, 1-9. 1934.

--- The Use of Soapstone by the Indians of the Eastern United States. ARSI, 1939, 471-89.

Carr, L. Dress and Ornaments of Certain American Indians. PAAS, n.s., XI, 381-454. 1897.

--- The Mounds of the Mississippi Valley. ARSI, 1891, 503-99.

Carr, L.G. Native Drinks in the Southeast and their Values. Proceedings of the Delaware County Institute of Science, X, ii, 29-42. 1947.

Chard, T. Did the First Spanish Horses landed in Florida and Carolina leave Progeny? AA, n.s., XLII, 90-106. 1940.

Charlevoix, P.F.X.de. Histoire de la Nouvelle France. 3 vols. Paris, 1894.

--- History and General Description of New France, ed. J.M.Shea. 6 vols. New York, 1866-72.

--- Journal of a Voyage to North America, ed. L. P. Kellogg. 2 vols. Chicago, 1923.

Clark, T.D., ed. Travels in the Old South; a Bibliography. 2 vols. 622 pp. Norman, 1956.

Coxe, D. A Description of the English Province of Carolana. HCL, II, 223-76. 1850.

Crane, V.W. The Southern Frontier. 391 pp. Philadelphia, 1929.

Crockett, B.N. Health Conditions in Indian Territory. CO, XXXVI, 21-39. 1958.

--- Health Conditions in Indian Territory, 1830 to Civil War. CO, XXXV, 80-90. 1957.

Crump, B.L.M. The Educability of Indian Children in Reservation Schools. Southeastern State Teachers' College, Contributions to Education, III, 58 pp. 1932.

Debo, A. The Five Civilized Tribes. 35 pp. Philadelphia, 1951.

Delanglez, J. The French Jesuits in Lower Louisiana. Catholic University of America, Studies in American Church History, XXI, 573 pp. 1935.

Densmore, F. Traces of Foreign Influence in the Music of American Indians. AA, n.s., XLVI, 106-13. 1944.

Deuel, T. Basic Cultures of the Mississippi Valley. AA, n.s., XXXVII, 429-45. 1935.

Dunn, W.E. Spanish and French Rivalry in the Gulf Region of the United States, 1678-1702. University of Texas Studies in History, I, 238 pp. 1917.

Fairbanks, G.R. History of Florida. 350 pp. Philadelphia, 1871.

Ford, J.A., and Willey, G.R. An Interpretation of the Prehistory of the Eastern United States. AA, n.s., XLIII, 325-63. 1941.

Foreman, G. Indian Removal. Norman, 1932.

--- A Traveler in Indian Territory. 270 pp. Cedar Rapids, 1930.

Fuller, A.W.F. An Original Sixteenth Century Painting of Natives of Florida. ICA, XX, ii, 191-93. 1928.

Fundaburk, E.L. Southeastern Indians, Life Portraits. 136 pp. Luverne, Ala., 1958.

Fundaburk, E.L. and Foreman, M.D.F. Sun Circles and Human Hands. 232 pp. Luverne, Ala., 1957.

Garth, T.R. A Comparison of the Intelligence of Mexican and Mixed and Full Blood Indian Children. Psychological Review, XXX, 388-401. 1923.

--- The Intelligence of Full Blood Indians. JAP, IX, 382-9. 1925.

Garcilaso de la Vega. La Florida del Inca. Madrid, 1723.

Geary, J.A. The Language of the Carolina Algonkian Tribes. HSS, CV, 873-900. 1955.

--- Strachey's Vocabulary of Indian Words used in Virginia, 1612. HSS, CIII, 208-14. 1953.

Gentleman of Elvas. A Narrative of the Expedition of Hernando de Soto. HCL, II, 113-220. 1850.

--- True Relation of the Hardships suffered by Governor Fernando de Soto, ed. J.E.Robertson. 2 vols. Deland, 1933.

Gifford, J.C. Five Native Florida Plants. Tequesta, IV, 36-44. 1944.

Gilbert, W.H. Surviving Indian Groups of the Eastern United States. ARSI, 1948, 403-38.

Goggin, J.M. Florida's Indians. Economic Leaflets, College of Business Administration, University of Florida, X, viii. 1951.

--- Style Areas in Historic Southeastern Art. ICA, XXIX, iii, 172-6. 1951.

Gore, J.H. Tuckahoe, or Indian Bread. ARSI, 1881, 687-701.

Gosselin, A. Les Sauvages du Mississipi (1698-1708). ICA, XV, i, 31-51. 1907.

Gray, L.H. Muskhogeans. ERE, IX, 61-2. 1917.

Griffin, J.B. Aboriginal Methods of Pottery Manufacture in the Eastern United States. PA, V, 19-24. 1935.

Griffin, J.W., ed. The Florida Indian and His Neighbors. 168 pp. Winter Park, 1949.

Haas, M.R. The Classification of the Muskogean Languages. Essays in Memory of Edward Sapir, pp. 41-6. Menasha, 1941.

--- Development of Proto-Muskogean *k^W. IJAL, XIII, 135-7. 1947.

--- A New Linguistic Relationship in North America. SJA, XIV, 231-64. 1958.

--- Noun Incorporation in the Muskogean Languages. Lg, XVII, 311-5. 1941.

--- A Proto-Muskogean Paradigm. Lg, XXII, 326-32. 1946.

--- Southeastern Indian Folklore. JAFL, LX, 403-6. 1947.

Haggard, J.V. The Neutral Ground between Louisiana and Texas. LHQ, XXVIII, 1001-1128. 1945.

Hale, E.M. Ilex cassine, the Aboriginal North American Tea. U.S. Department of Agriculture, Division of Botany, Bulletin, XIV, 22 pp. 1891.

Harpe, B. de la. Historical Journal of the Establishment of the French in Louisiana. HCL, III, 9-118. 1851.

--- Journal historique de l'établissement des Français a la Louisiane. 412 pp. Nouvelle-Orléans, 1831.

Hawley, F. Tree-Ring Analysis and Dating in the Mississippi Drainage. University of Chicago Publications in Anthropology, Occasional Papers, II, 1-110. 1941.

Haywood, J. The Natural and Aboriginal History of Tennessee. 390 pp. Nashville, 1823.

Hendren, S.R. Government and Religion of the Virginia Indians. Johns Hopkins University, Studies in History and Political Science, series 13, XI-XII, 58 pp. 1895.

Holmes, W.H. Aboriginal Pottery of the Eastern United States. ARBAE, XX, 1-201. 1899.

--- Earthenware of Florida. Journal of the Academy of Natural Sciences of Philadelphia, ser. 2, X, 105-28. 1894.

--- Prehistoric Textile Art of the Eastern United States. ARBAE, XIII, 9-46. 1896.

--- Prehistoric Textile Fabrics of the United States. ARBAE, III, 393-425. 1882.

Hough, W. Ceremonial and Other Practices in the Human Body among the Indians. ICA, XIX, 283-5. 1915.

Householder, J.C. Virginia's Indian Neighbors in 1712. PIAS, LV, 23-5. 1946.

Howard, J.H. Pan-Indian Culture of Oklahoma. SM, LXXXI, 215-20. 1955.

Hrdlicka, A. Ritual Ablation of Front Teeth in Siberian and America. SMC, XCIX, iii, 1-32. 1940.

Jackson, W.R. Early Florida Through Spanish Eyes. 179 pp. Coral Gables, 1954.

Jefferson, T. Notes on the State of Virginia. 315 pp. Chapel Hill, 1955.

Jimenez Moreno, W. Relaciones Etnologicas entre Mesoamerica y el Sur de Estados Unidos. In, El Norte de Mexico y el Sur de Estados Unidos, 286-300. Mexico, 1943.

Johnson, J.G. The Colonial Southeast, 1732-1763. University of Colorado Studies, XIX, 163-225. 1932.

Johnston, R.B. Remarks on the Physical Type of Certain Middle Mississippi and Southeastern Groups. PIAS, LXVI, 50-52. 1956.

Jones, C.C. Antiquities of the Southern Indians. 532 pp. New York, 1873.

Joutel, H. Journal of La Salle's Last Voyage. New edit. 258 pp. Albany, 1906.

Knowles, N. The Torture of Captives by the Indians of Eastern North America. PAPS, LXXXII, 151-225. 1940.

Kunkel, P.A. The Indians of Louisiana about 1700. LHQ, XXXIV, 175-204. 1951.

Kurath, G.P. Antiphonal Songs of Eastern Woodlands Indians. Musical Quarterly, XLIII, 520-6. 1956.

Lawson, J. The History of Carolina. 390 pp. Raleigh, 1860.

Le Page du Pratz. Histoire de la Louisiane. 3 vols. Paris, 1758.

--- The History of Louisiana. 2 vols. London, 1763.

Lewis, T.M.N., and Kneberg, M. The Prehistory of the Chickamauga Basin in Tennessee. Tennessee Anthropology Papers, I, 1-42. 1941.

--- Tribes that Slumber. 207 pp. Knoxville, 1958.

Lowery, W. The Spanish Settlements within the Present Limits of the United States. 2 vols. New York, 1901-05.

McCary, B.C. Indians in Seventeenth-Century Virginia. 93 pp. Williamsburg, 1957.

MacLeod, W.C. Debtor and Chattel Slavery in Aboriginal North America. AA, n.s., XXVII, 70-78. 1925.

MacLeod, W.C. Economic Aspects of Indigenous American Slavery. AA, n.s., XXX, 632-50. 1928.

--- Priests, Temples, and the Practice of Mummification in Southeastern North America. ICA, XXII, ii, 207-30. 1926.

Matthews, G.H. Proto-Siouan Kinship Terminology. AA, LXI, 252-78. 1959.

Maxwell, H. The Use and Abuse of Forests by the Virginia Indians. William and Mary College Quarterly Historical Magazine, XIX, 73-103. 1910.

Miller, C.F. Revaluation of the Eastern Siouan Problem. BBAE, CLXIV, 115-212. 1957.

Milling, C.J. Red Carolinians. 469 pp. Chapel Hill, 1940.

Moore, J.R. The Five Great Indian Nations. CO, XXIX, 324-36. 1951.

Morgan, L.H. Ancient Society, pp. 160-5. New York, 1877.

Morton, O. Confederate Government Relations with the Five Civilized Tribes. CO, XXXI, 189-204, 299-322. 1953.

Myer, W.E. Indian Trails of the Southeast. ARBAE, XLII, 727-857. 1925.

Myron, R. L'Art Symbolique dans les Groupements Indiens du Sud-Est des Etats-Unis. JSAP, n.s., XLVII, 47-54. 1958.

Neill, W.T. Coracles or Skin Boats of the Southeastern Indians. FA, VII, 119-26. 1954.

--- The Identity of Florida's "Spanish Indians." FA, VIII, 43-58. 1955.

O'Callaghan, M.A. An Indian Removal Policy in Spanish Louisiana. In, Greater America: Essays in Honor of Herbert Eugene Bolton, pp. 281-94. Berkeley, 1945.

Omaechevarria, I. Martires Franciscanoes de Georgia. MH, XII, 5-93, 291-370. 1955.

Owen, M.B. Indians in Alabama. AHQ, XII, 2-90. 1950.

--- Alabama Indian Chiefs. AHQ, XIII, 5-90. 1951.

--- Indian Trading Houses. AHQ, XIII, 136-39. 1951.

--- Indian Tribes and Towns in Alabama. AHQ, XII, 118-241. 1950.

--- Indian Wars in Alabama. AHQ, XIII, 92-131. 1951.

Pierce, R.G. Bibliographical List of Articles, Books and References to Virginia Indians, with Particular Emphasis on Archeology. 3 vols. Archeological Society of Virginia, 1944, 1945, 1947.

Pilling, J.C. Bibliography of the Muskhogean Languages. BBAE, IX, 1-114. 1889.

Posey, W.B. The Development of Methodism in the Old Southwest, 1783-1824. 151 pp. Tuscaloosa, 1933.

Quinn, D.B., ed. The Roanoke Voyages, 1584-1590. HSS, CIV-CV, 1040 pp. 1955.

Read, W.A. Indian Place Names in Alabama. Louisiana State University Studies, IX, 84 pp. 1937.

--- Indian Place-names in Louisiana. LHQ, XI, 445-62. 1928.

--- Indian Stream-names in Georgia. IJAL, XV, 128-32; XVI, 203-7. 1949.

--- Louisiana-French. Louisiana State University Studies, V, 152-8. 1931.

--- Louisana Place Names of Indian Origin. Louisiana State University Bulletin, XIX, n.s., II, 72 pp. 1927.

Reynolds, B.D. Indians of Virginia 350 Years Ago. VJS, n.s., VIII, 3-18. 1957.

Rights, D.L. The American Indian in North Carolina. 296 pp., Durham, 1947; 318 pp. Winston-Salem, 1957.

Rights, D.L. and Cumming, W.P. The Discoveries of John Lederer. 159 pp. Winston-Salem, 1958.

Robinson, W.S. The Legal Status of the Indian in Colonial Virginia. VM, LXI, 247-59. 1953.

Rogers, R. A Concise Account of North America. 264 pp. London, 1765.

Rouse, I., and Horton, D., eds. A Preliminary Archaeological Bibliography of the Eastern United States. BASC, Vols. IX-X. 1939-40.

Schermerhorn, J.F. Report respecting the Indians inhabiting the Western Parts of the United States. MHSC, ser. 2, II, 1-45. 1814.

Shaw, H.L. British Administration of the Southern Indians, 1756 to 1783. 225 pp. Lancaster, 1931.

Shea, J.G. Discovery and Exploration of the Mississippi Valley. 2d edit. Albany, 1903.

Shetrone, H.C. The Mound Builders. 508 pp. New York, 1930.

Shipp, B. The History of Hernando de Soto and Florida. 689 pp. Philadelphia, 1881.

Sibley, J. A Report from Natchitoches in 1807. INM, n.s., XXV, 5-102. 1922.

Silver, J.W. Edmund Pendleton Gaines and Frontier Problems. Journal of Southern History, I, 320-44. 1935.

Simsa, P. Indianische Königreiche im südöstlichen Nordamerika. ACISA, IV, ii, 341-6. 1955.

Sleight, F.W. Kunti; a Food Staple of Florida Indians. FA, VI, 46-52. 1953.

Slotkin, J.S., and Schmitt, K. Studies of Wampum. AA, n.s., LI, 223-36. 1949.

Small, J.G. Seminole Bread. Journal of the New York Botanical Garden, XXII, 121-37. 1921.

Smith, H.G. The Ethnological and Archaeological Significance of Zamia. AA, LIII, 238-44. 1951.

--- The European and the Indian. PFAS, IV, 158 pp. 1956.

Speck, F.G. Addendum to "Gourds of the Southeastern Indians." Gourd Seed, IX, 15; X, 3-6, 8, 11, 16, 24. 1948-49.

--- Gourds of the Southeastern Indians. 113 pp. Boston, 1941.

--- Some Comparative Traits of the Maskogian Languages. AA, n.s., IX, 470-84. 1907.

--- Some Outlines of Aboriginal Culture in the Southeastern States. AA, n.s., IX, 287-95. 1907.

Stirling, M.W. Florida Cultural Affiliations in Relation to Adjacent Areas. Essays in Anthropology presented to A.L. Kroeber, pp. 351-7. Berkeley, 1936.

--- The Historic Method as applied to Southeastern Archaeology. SMC, C, 117-23. 1940.

Strachey, W. The Historie of Travell into Virginia Britanica. HSS, CIII, 253 pp. 1953.

Sturtevant, W.C. Accomplishments and Opportunities in Florida Indian Ethnology. Florida Anthropology, II, 15-56. 1958.

--- Chakaika and the Spanish Indians. Tequesta, XIII, 35-73. 1953.

Surrey, F.M., ed. Calendar of Manuscripts in Paris Archives and Libraries relating to the History of the Mississippi Valley to 1803. 2 vols. Washington, 1926-8.

Swanton, J.R. Aboriginal Culture of the Southeast. ARBAE, XLII, 673-726. 1925.

--- De Soto's Line of March from the Viewpoint of an Ethnologist. PMVHA, V, 147-57. 1912.

--- Early History of the Eastern Siouan Tribes. Essays in Anthropology presented to A.L. Kroeber, pp. 371-81. Berkeley, 1936.

--- Ethnological Value of the De Soto Narratives. AA, n.s., XXXIV, 570-90. 1932.

--- Indian Place Names. American Speech, 212-15. October, 1937.

--- Indians of the Southeastern United States. BBAE, CXXXVII, 1-943. 1946.

--- Notes on the Cultural Province of the Southeast. AA, n.s., XXXVII, 373-85. 1935.

--- A Point of Resemblance between the Ball Game of the Southeastern Indians and the Ball Games of Mexico and Central America. JWAS, XIX, 304-7. 1929.

Swanton, J.R. The Relation of the Southeast to General Cultural Problems of American Pre-History. National Research Council, Conference on Southern Pre-History, pp. 60-74. Washington, 1932.

--- Relations between Northern Mexico and the Southeast of the United States from the Point of View of Ethnology and History. In, El Norte de Mexico y el Sur de Estados Unidos, 259-76. Mexico, 1943.

--- Southeastern Indians of History. National Research Council, Conference on Southern Pre-History, pp. 5-20. Washington, 1932.

--- The Southern Contacts of the Indians North of the Gulf of Mexico. ICA, XX, i, 53-9. 1922.

--- Sun Worship in the Southeast. AA, n.s., XXX, 206-13. 1928.

--- Unclassified Languages of the Southeast. IJAL, I, 47-9. 1917.

Taylor, L.A. Plants used as Curatives by Certain Southeastern Tribes. 88 pp. Cambridge, 1940.

Thomas, C. Prehistoric Migrations in the Atlantic Slope. AAOJ, XVIII, 346-58; XIX, 11-19. 1896-97.

Tonti, H. de. Relation de la Louisianne, et du Mississipi. RVN, V, 35-195. 1734.

Toomey, T.N. Proper Names from the Muskhogean Languages. BHLAL, III, 1-31. 1917.

Torrey, J. Observations on the Tuckahoe or Indian Bread of the Southern States. Medical Repository, XXI, 34-44. 1821.

Uhler, S.P. Pennsylvania's Indian Relations to 1754. 144 pp. Allentown, 1951.

Varner, J.G. and J.J. The Florida of the Inca. 713 pp. Austin, 1951.

Villiers du Terrage, M. de. Rapport du Chevalier de Kerlérec. ICA, XV, i, 61-86. 1906.

Voegelin, C.F. Corrigenda and Addenda to Thirty Extinct Languages. AA, n.s., XLVIII, 289. 1946.

--- Internal Relationships of Siouan Languages. AA, n.s., XLIII, 246-9. 1941.

Voegelin, C.F. and E.W. Linguistic Considerations of Northeastern North America. PRSPF, III, 178-94. 1946.

Voegelin, E.W. Mortuary Customs of the Shawnee and Other Eastern Tribes. PRS, II, 227-444. 1944.

Weer, P. Preliminary Notes on the Muskhogean Family. PRS, I, 245-86. 1939.

--- Preliminary Notes on the Siouan Family. Indiana History Bulletin, XIV, 99-120. 1937.

Weitlaner, R.J. Las Lenguas del Sur de Estados Unidos y el Norte de Mexico. In, El Norte de Mexico y el Sur de Estados Unidos, 181-5. Mexico, 1943.

Wenhold, L.L. A 17th Century Letter of Gabriel Diaz Vara Calderon. SMC, XCV, xvi, 1-14. 1936.

Willey, G.R. Archeology of the Florida Gulf Coast. SMC, CXIII, 624 pp. 1949.

Willoughby, C.C. Antler-pointed Arrows of the South-Eastern Indians. AA, n.s., III, 431-7. 1901.

--- Notes on the History and Symbolism of the Muskhogeans. Etowah Papers, ed. W.C. Moorehead, pp. 7-67. New Haven, 1932.

Winston, S. Indian Slavery in the Carolina Region. Bulletin of the Archaeological Society of North Carolina, III, i, 3-9. 1936.

Withers, A.S. Chronicles of Border Warfare. 447 pp. Cincinnati, 1895.

Witthoft, J. Green Corn Ceremonialism in the Eastern Woodlands. OCMA, XIII, 31-77. 1949.

Wolf, F.A. The Fruiting Stage of the Tuckahoe Pachyma cocas. Elisha Mitchell Scientific Society Journal, XXXVIII, 127-37. 1922.

Wolff, H. Comparative Siouan. IJAL, XVI, 61-6. 1950.

Wright, M.H. A Guide to the Indian Tribes of Oklahoma. 300 pp. Norman, 1951.

1. ACOLAPISSA

Including the Acolapissa, Bayogoula, Chawasha, Mugulasha, Quinipissa, Okelousa, Tangipahoa, and Washa.

Albrechts, A.C. Ethnohistorical Data Pertaining to the Bayogoula. NLSAC, II, iv, 26-29. 1941.

Burch, M.C. The Indigenous Indians of the Lower Trinity Area of Texas. SWHQ, LX, 36-52. 1956.

Bushnell, D.I. Drawings by A. deBatz in Louisiana. SMC, LXXX, v, 1-14. 1927.

Le Moyne d'Iberville, P. Historical Journal. HCL, ser. 2, II, 31-103. 1875.

Margry, P., ed. Découvertes et établissements des Français dans l'Amérique septentrionale, V, 463-70. Paris, 1883.

Quimby, G.I. The Natchezan Culture Type. AAn, VII, 255-75. 1942.

Swanton, J.R. Indian Tribes of the Lower Mississippi Valley and Adjacent Coast of the Gulf of Mexico. BBAE, XLIII, 274-84, 297-302. 1911.

Villiers du Terrage, M. de. Documents concernant l'histoire des Indiens de la région orientale de la Louisiane. JSAP, n.s., XIV, 127-40. 1922.

2. ALABAMA

Including the Alabama, Kaskinampo, Koasati, Muklasa, Pawokti, and Tawasa.

Bludworth, G.T. How the Alabamas came south.
PTFLS, XIII, 298-9. 1937.

Bossu, M. Nouveaux voyages aux Indes Occidentales,
II, 17-72. Paris, 1768.

--- Travels through That Part of North America formerly called Louisiana, I, 229-77. London, 1771.

Densmore, F. The Alabama Indians and Their
Music. PTFLS, XIII, 270-93. 1937.

Gatschet, A.S. A Migration Legend of the Creek
Indians, pp. 85-90. Philadalphia, 1884.

Gatschet, A.S., and Thomas, C. Alibamu. BBAE,
XXX, i, 43-4. 1907.

Haas, M.R. Men's and Women's Speech in Koasati.
Lg, XX, 142-9. 1944.

Harrington, M.R. Among Louisiana Indians. SW,
XXXVII, 656-61. 1908.

Heard, E. Two Tales from the Alabamas. PTFLS,
XIII, 294-8. 1937.

Jacobson, D. The Origin of the Koasati Community
of Louisiana. E, VII, 97-120. 1960.

Martin, H.N. Folktales of the Alabama-Coushatta
Indians. 75 pp. Livingston, 1946.

Smither, H. The Alabama Indians of Texas. SWHQ,
XXXVI, 83-108. 1932.

Swanton, J.R. Animal Stories from the Indians of
the Muskhogean Stock. JAFL, XXVI, 209-14.
1913.

--- Early History of the Creek Indians and Their
Neighbors. BBAE, LXXIII, 137-41, 191-207. 1922.

--- Indian Language Studies in Louisiana. EFWSI,
1930, 195-200.

--- The Kaskinampo Indians and Their Neighbors.
AA, n.s., XXXII, 405-18. 1930.

--- Koasati. BBAE, XXX, i, 719-20. 1907.

--- Modern Square Grounds of the Creek Indians.
SMC, LXXXV, viii, 1-46. 1931.

--- Myths and Tales of the Southeastern Indians.
BBAE, LXXXVIII, 118-213. 1929.

--- Religious Beliefs and Medical Practices of the
Creek Indians. ARBAE, XLII, 473-672. 1925.

--- Social Organization and Social Usages of the
Indians of the Creek Confederacy. ARBAE, XLII,
23-472. 1925.

Taylor, L.A. Plants used as Curatives by Certain
Southeastern Tribes. 88 pp. Cambridge, 1940.

Villiers du Terrage, M. de. Documents concernant
l'histoire des Indiens de la région orientale de la
Louisiane. JSAP, n.s., XIV, 127-40. 1922.

Wade, M.D. The Alabama Indians of East Texas.
Livingston, 1936.

3. APALACHEE

Boyd, M.F., et al. Here Once They Stood. 189 pp.
Gainesville, Fla., 1951.

Bandelier, A.F., ed. The Journey of Alvar Nunez
Cabeza de Vaca, pp. 25-34. New York, 1922.

Boyd, M.F. Diego Peña's Expedition to Apalachee
and Apalachicolo in 1716. FHSQ, XXVIII, 1-27.
1949.

--- Documents Describing the Second and Third Expedition of Lieutenant Diego Peña to Apalachee and
Apalachicolo in 1717 and 1718. FHSQ, XXXI,
109-39. 1952.

--- Further Considerations of the Apalachee Missions.
Americas, IX, 459-79. 1953.

Brinton, D.G. Notes on the Floridian Peninsula, pp.
92-110. Philadelphia, 1859.

Fontaneda, H. de Escalante. Mémoire sur la Floride.
Voyages, ed. H. Ternaux-Compans, XX, 9-42.
Paris, 1841.

--- Memoir. HCL, ser. 2, II, 235-65. 1875.

Haas, M.R. The Position of Apalachee in the Muskogean Family. IJAL, XV, 121-7. 1949.

Harrison, B. Indian Races of Florida. FHSQ, III,
29-37. 1924.

Klingberg, F.J., ed. The Carolina Chronicle of
Dr. Francis Le Jau, 1706-1717. UCPH, LIII,
228 pp. 1956.

La Roncière, C.G., ed. La Floride française. 139
pp. Paris, 1928.

Milling, C.J. Red Carolinians. 438 pp. Chapel
Hill, 1940.

Mooney, J. Apalachee. BBAE, XXX, i, 67-8. 1907.

--- Pensacola. BBAE, XXX, ii, 227. 1910.

Oviedo y Valdez, G.F. de. Historia general y natural de las Indias, III, 578-86. Madrid, 1853.

Palerm, A. San Carlos de Chachalacas, una
fundación de los indios de Florida en Veracruz.
Cuadernos Americanos, año 11, LXI, i, 165-184.

Smith, B. Documents in the Spanish and Two of the
Early Tongues of Florida. 12 pp. Washington, 1860.

--- Letter of Hernando de Soto and Memoir of
Hernando de Escalante Fontaneda. 67 pp. Washington, 1854.

--- Specimen of the Appalachian Language. HM,
IV, 40-1. 1860.

Swanton, J.R. Early History of the Creek Indians and Their Neighbors. BBAE, LXXIII, 109-29. 1922.

Toomey, T.N. Analysis of a Text in the Apalachi Language. BHLAL, VI, 1-8. 1918.

Wenhold, L.L., ed. The Trials of Captain Don Isidoro De Leon. FHSQ, XXXV, 246-65. 1957.

Willey, G.R. Archeology of the Florida Gulf Coast. SMC, CXIII, 624 pp. 1949.

4. BILOXI

Anonymous. Biloxi. BBAE, XXX, i, 147-8. 1907.

Bass, A. James Mooney in Oklahoma. CO, XXXII, 246-62. 1954.

Bushnell, D.I. Native Cemeteries and Forms of Burial East of the Mississippi. BBAE, LXXI, 135-7. 1920.

Dorsey, J.O. The Biloxi Indians of Louisiana. PAAAS, XLII, 267-87. 1893.

--- Preface. CNAE, IX, xviii-xxx. 1893.

--- Siouan Sociology. ARBAE, XV, 243-4. 1894.

--- Two Biloxi Tales. JAFL, VI, 48-50. 1893.

Dorsey, J.O., and Swanton, J.R. A Dictionary of the Biloxi and Ofo Languages. BBAE, XLVII, 1-340. 1912.

Dumont de Montigny. Memoires historiques sur la Louisiane, I, 240-3. Paris, 1753.

Ethridge, A.N. Indians of Grant Parish. LHQ, XXIII, 1108-31. 1940.

Miller, C.F. Revaluation of the Eastern Siouan Problem, BBAE, CLXIV, 115-212. 1957.

Mooney, J. The Siouan Tribes of the East. BBAE, XXII, 5-101. 1894.

Porter, K.W. A Legend of the Biloxi. JAFL, LIX, 168-73. 1946.

Sturtevant, W.C. Siouan Languages in the East. AA, LX, 738-43. 1958.

Swanton, J.R. New Light on the Early History of the Siouan Peoples. JWAS, XIII, 33-43. 1923.

Voegelin, C.F. Ofo-Biloxi Sound Correspondences. PIAS, XLVIII, 23-6. 1939.

5. CALUSA

Including the Ais, Calusa, Guacara, and Tequesta.

Alegre, F.J. Historia de la Provincia de la Compañia de Jesús de Nueva España. New ed. 2 vols. Rome, 1956-58.

Andrews, C.M. The Florida Indians in the Seventeenth Century. Tequesta, I, iii, 36-48. 1943.

Brinton, D.G. Notes on the Floridian Peninsula, pp. 111-19. Philadelphia, 1859.

Collins, H.B. Burial of the Calusa Indians. EP, XXIV, 223-4. 1928.

--- The "Lost" Calusa Indians. EFWSI, 1928, 151-6.

Covington, J.W. Trade Relations between Southwestern Florida and Cuba - 1600-1840. FHSQ, XXXVIII, 114-28. 1959.

Cushing, F.H. Exploration of Ancient Key Dwellers' Remains on the Gulf Coast of Florida. PAPS, XXXV, 329-448. 1896.

Dickenson, J. God's Protecting Providence. 7th edit. 136 pp. London, 1790.

--- Journal, ed. E.W. and C.M. Andrews. Yale Historical Publications, Manuscripts and Edited Texts, XIX, 1-252. 1945.

--- Narrative of a Shipwreck in the Gulph of Florida. 6th edit. New York, 1803.

Fewkes, J.W. Aboriginal Wooden Objects from Southern Florida. SMC, LXXX, ix, 1-2. 1928.

Fontenada, D. de Escalante. Mémoire sur la Floride. Voyages, ed. H. Ternaux-Compans, XX, 9-42. Paris, 1941.

--- Memoir. HCL, ser. 2, II, 235-65. 1875.

--- Memoir Respecting Florida. Coral Gables, 1945.

--- Memoria de las cosas y costa y Indios de la Florida. Colección de Documentos Inéditos, relativos al Descubrimiento, Conquista y Colonización de las Posesiones Espanolas en América y Oceanía, V, 532-48. Madrid, 1866.

Goggin, J.M. The Indians and History of the Matecumbe Region. Tequesta, X, 13-24. 1950.

--- The Tekesta Indians of Southern Florida. FHSQ, XVIII, 274-84. 1940.

Goggin, J.M. and Sommer, F.H. Excavations on Upper Matecumbe Key, Florida. YUPA, XLI, 104 pp. 1949.

Griffin, J.W. The Antillean Problem in Florida Archaeology. FHSQ, XXII, 86-91. 1943.

Harrison, B. Indian Races of Florida. FHSQ, III, 29-37. 1924.

Hrdlicka, A. The Anthropology of Florida. PFSHS, I, 1-140. 1922.

Keegan, G.J., and Tormo Sanz, L. Experiencia Misionera en la Florida (siglos XVI y XVII). MH, series B, vol. VII, 404 pp. 1957.

Kenworthy, C.J. Ancient Canals in Florida. ARSI, 1881, 631-5.

McNicoll, R. E. The Caloosa Village Tequesta.
    Tequesta, I, i, 11-20. 1941.
Mooney, J. Ais. BBAE, XXX, i, 31. 1907.
--- Calusa. BBAE, XXX, i, 195-6. 1907.
--- Tequesta. BBAE, XXX, ii, 733. 1910.
Moore, C.B. Certain Antiquities of the Florida West-
    Coast. Journal of the Academy of Natural Sci-
    iences of Philadelphia, ser. 2, XI, 353-94. 1900.
Morfi, J.A. de. Memorias for the History of the
    Province of Texas, ed. F.M. Chabot. 85 pp. San
    Antonio, 1932.
Neill, W.T. The Identity of Florida's "Spanish In-
    dians." FA, VIII, ii, 43-57. 1955.
Pinart, A.L. Geroglificos entre los indios de la
    Florida. A, II, 133-4. 1907.
Read, C.H. Note on Ethnological Objects excavated
    at Marco. JAI, XXV, 406-7. 1896.
Rouse, I. B. A Survey of Indian River Archeology,
    Florida. YUPA, XLIV, 1-296. 1951.
Smith, B., ed. Letter of Hernando de Soto and
    Memoir of Hernando de Escalante Fontaneda. 67
    pp. Washington, 1854.
Smith, R.M. Anthropology in Florida. FHSQ, XI,
    151-72. 1933.
Stirling, M.W. Florida Cultural Affiliations in Rela-
    tion to Adjacent Areas. Essays in Anthropology pre-
    sented to A.L.Kroeber, pp. 351-7. Berkeley, 1936.
--- Mounds of the Vanished Calusa Indians of Florida.
    EFWSI, 1930, 167-72. 1931.
Sturtevant, W.C. Chakaika and the "Spanish Indians."
    Tequesta, XIII, 35-73. 1953.
Swanton, J.R. Early History of the Creek Indians and
    Their Neighbors. BBAE, LXXIII, 27-31, 387-98.
    1922.
Walker, S.T. The Aborigines of Florida. ARSI, 1881,
    677-80.
Zubillaga, F. La Florida. 473 pp. Rome, 1941.

6. CATAWBA

Including the Adshusheer, Backhook, Cape Fear,
Catawba or Issa, Cheraw or Sara, Congaree, Eno,
Hook, Keyauwee, Peedee, Santee, Sewee, Shoccoree, Sissipahaw, Sugaree, Waccamaw, Warrennuncock, Wateree, Waxhaw, Winyaw, and Woccon.

Adair, J. The History of the American Indians. 464
    pp. London, 1775.
Alvord, C.W., and Bidgood, L. First Explorations
    of the Trans-Allegheny Region by the Virginians,
    1650-1674. 275 pp. Cleveland, 1912.

Anghierra, P. M. de. De orbe novo, tr. F.A.
    MacNutt. 2 vols. New York, 1912.
Anonymous. Eno. BBAE, XXX, i, 425-6. 1907.
Ardrey, W.B. The Catawba Indians. AAOJ, XVI,
    266-9. 1894.
Barton, B.S. New Views of the Origin of the Tribes
    and Nations of America. 2nd ed., 77-133. Phil-
    adelphia, 1798.
Bradford, W.R. The Catawba Indians of South Caro-
    lina. Bulletin of the University of South Carolina,
    n.s., XXXIV, 1-31. 1946.
Brickell, J. The Natural History of North-Carolina,
    pp. 277-408. Dublin, 1737.
Brown, D.S. Catawba Land Records, South Caro-
    lina Historical Magazine, LIX, 64-77, 171-6,
    226-33. 1958.
Bushnell, D.I. Native Cemeteries and Forms of Bur-
    ial East of the Mississippi. BBAE, LXXI, 131-5.
    1920.
Catesby, M. The Natural History of Carolina, Flori-
    da, and Bahama Islands. 2 vols. London, 1731-43.
Chamberlain, A.F. The Catawba Language. 3 pp.
    Toronto, 1888.
Coe, J.L. The Cultural Sequence of the Carolina
    Piedmont. AEUS, 301-11. 1952.
Fewkes, V.J. Catawba Pottery-Making. PAPS,
    LXXXVIII, 69-124. 1944.
Foreman, G. The Last Trek of the Indians, pp. 316-
    20. Chicago, 1946.
Gatschet, A.S. Grammatic Sketch of the Catawba
    Language. AA, n.s., II, 527-49. 1900.
--- Onomatology of the Catawba River Basin. AA,
    n.s., IV, 52-6. 1902.
Gregg, A. History of the Old Cheraws, pp. 1-30.
    New York, 1867.
Gregorie, A.K. Notes on Sewee Indians. Contribu-
    tions from the Charleston Museum, V, 1-23. 1925.
Griffin, J.B. An Interpretation of Siouan Archaeology
    in the Piedmont of North Carolina and Virginia.
    AAn, X, 321-30. 1945.
Harrington, M.R. Catawba Potters and Their Work.
    AA, n.s., X, 399-407. 1908.
Holmes, W.H. Aboriginal Pottery of the Eastern
    United States. ARBAE, XX, 53-55. 1903.
Howe, G. An Essay on the Antiquities of the Con-
    garee Indians. HCPIT, IV, 155-69. 1854.
Kirkland, T.J. and Kennedy, R.M. Historic Cam-
    den. Columbia, S.C., 1905.
Kingberg, F.J., ed. The Carolina Chronicle of Dr.
    Francis Le Jau, 1706-1717. UCPH, LIII, 228 pp.
    1956.

Lanman, C. Adventures in the Wilds of the United States and British American Provinces. I, 452; II, 410-12. Philadelphia, 1856.

Lawson, J. The History of Carolina, pp. 24-75, 87-93, 277-390. New edit. Raleigh, 1860.

Lewis, E. Ceramic Analysis of a Proto-historic Siouan Village. BESAF, XI, 9. 1953.

Lieber, O.M. Vocabulary of the Catawba Language. Collections of the South Carolina Historical Society, II, 327-42. 1858.

Michelson, T. Field-Work among the Catawba, Fox, Sutaio and Sauk Indians. SMC, LXIII, viii, 836. 1914.

Miller, C.F. Revaluation of the Eastern Siouan Problem. BBAE, CLXIV, 115-212. 1957.

Milling, C.J. Red Carolinians. 438 pp. Chapel Hill, 1940.

Mills, R. Statistics of South Carolina, p. 111. 1826.

Mooney, J. Catawba. BBAE, XXX, i, 213-16. 1907.

--- Cheraw. BBAE, XXX, i, 244-5. 1907.

--- The Siouan Tribes of the East. BBAE, XXII, 5-101. 1894.

Pennypacker, S.W. A Note on Catawba Ceramics. PA, VII, 55-6. 1937.

Pepper, G.H. Wateree Artifacts. IN, I, 74-5. 1924.

Pickens, A.L. Contribution to Catawba Ethnozoology. Neighborhood Research, Spring 1957, 1-5. Queens College, Charlotteville, N.C.

--- Dictionary of Indian-Place Names in Upper South Carolina. South Carolina Natural History, LI-LIII, 1-10. 1937.

--- Supplementary List for the Dictionary of Indian Place-Names in Upper South Carolina. Neighborhood Research, II, 1. 1938.

--- Seeking Carolina Indian Names for Beasts. Neighborhood Research, February, 1954, 3-6.

--- Studies in Catawba Verse. Neighborhood Research, XI, 1-2.

Potter, E. An Account of Several Nations of Southern Indians. MHSC, ser. 1, X, 119-21. 1809.

Rights, D.L. The American Indian in North Carolina. 296 pp., Durham, 1947; 318 pp., Winston-Salem, 1957.

--- Indian Occupation of the Charlotte Area. Bulletin of the Archaeological Society of North Carolina, II, i, 10-13. 1935.

Scaife, H.L. History and Condition of the Catawba Indians. Publications of the Indian Rights Association, ser. 2, XXI, 1-24. Philadelphia, 1896.

Siebert, F.T., Jr. Linguistic Classification of Catawba. IJAL, XI, 100-104, 211-18. 1945.

Smyth, J.F.D. A Tour in the United States of America. 2 vols., I, 184-95, 347. London, 1784.

Speck, F.G. The Cane Blowgun in Catawba and Southeastern Ethnology. AA, n.s., XL, 198-204. 1938.

Speck, F.G. Catawba Games and Amusements. PM, XVII, 19-28. 1944.

--- Catawba Herbals and Curative Practices. JAFL, LVII, 37-50. 1944.

--- Catawba Hunting, Trapping and Fishing. PPAS, II, 1-33. 1946.

--- Catawba Medicines and Curative Practices. PPAS, I, 179-97. 1937.

--- The Catawba Nation and Its Neighbors. North Carolina Historical Review, XVI, iv, 404-17. 1939.

--- Catawba Religious Beliefs, Mortuary Customs, and Dances. PM, XII, 21-57. 1939.

--- Catawba Text. IJAL, XII, 64-5. 1946.

--- Catawba Texts. CUCA, XXIV, 1-91. 1934.

--- Eggan's Yuchi Kinship Interpretations. AA, n.s., XLI, 171-2. 1939.

--- Ethnoherpetology of the Catawba and Cherokee Indians. JWAS, XXXVI, 355-60. 1946.

--- The Possible Siouan Identity of the Words recorded from Francisco of Chicora on the South Carolina Coast. JWAS, XIV, 303-6. 1924.

--- The Question of Matrilineal Descent in the Southeastern Siouan Area. AA, n.s., XL, 1-12. 1938.

--- Recording the Catawba Language. EP, XXIV, 307-8. 1928.

--- Siouan Tribes of the Carolinas. AA, n.s., XXXVII, 201-25. 1935.

--- Some Catawba Texts and Folk-Lore. JAFL, XXVI, 319-30. 1913.

Speck, F.G., and Carr, L.G. Catawba Folk Tales from Chief Sam Blue. JAFL, LX, 79-84. 1947.

Speck, F.G., and Schaeffer, C.E. Catawba Kinship and Social Organization. AA, n.s., XLIV, 555-75. 1942.

--- The Deer and the Rabbit Hunting Drive in Virginia and the Southeast. SIS, II, 3-20. 1950.

Sturtevant, W.C. Siouan Languages in the East. AA, LX, 738-43. 1958.

Swadesh, M. Sociologic Notes on Obsolescent Languages. IJAL, XIV, 226-38. 1948.

Swanton, J.R. Catawba Notes. JWAS, VIII, 623-9. 1918.

--- Early History of the Eastern Siouan Tribes. Essays in Anthropology presented to A.L. Kroeber, pp. 371-81. Berkeley, 1936.

--- The First Description of an Indian Tribe in the Territory of the Present United States. In, Studies for William A. Read, 326-38. Baton Rouge, 1940.

--- New Light on the Early History of the Siouan Peoples. JWAS, XIII, 33-43. 1923.

Talbot, W., ed. The Discoveries of John Lederer. New edit. 30 pp. Rochester, 1902.

Uhler, S.P. Pennsylvania's Indian Relations to 1754. 144 pp. Allentown, 1951.

7. CHAKCHIUMA

Including the Chakchiuma, the Ibitoupa, and the Taposa.

Halbert, H.S. The Small Indian Tribes of Mississippi. PMHS, V, 302-8. 1902.

Swanton, J.R. Indian Tribes of the Lower Mississippi Valley and Adjacent Coast of the Gulf of Mexico. BBAE, XLIII, 292-7. 1911.

8. CHEROKEE

Adair, J. The History of the American Indians, pp. 226-56. London, 1775.

Allen, I.E. The Cherokee Nation: Fort Mountain, Vann House, Chester Inns, New Echota. 59 pp. Atlanta, [1958?]

Anonymous. Cherokee Stickball. Life, 11 Nov. 1946, pp. 90-92.

--- The Sam Houston Shoulder Pouch. TA, XI, ii, 88-9. 1955.

Bailey, C.S. Stories from an Indian Cave. 217 pp. Chicago, 1924.

Baillou, C.D. The Chief Vann House at Spring Place, Georgia. EG, II, ii, 3-11. 1957.

--- The Excavations at New Echota in 1954. EG, I, iv, 18-29. 1955.

Ballenger, T.L. The Andrew Nave Letters. CO, XXX, 2-5. 1952.

--- Joseph Franklin Johnson. CO, XXX, 285-91. 1952.

Barrett, S.M. Joe the Cherokee. 124 pp. Kansas City, 1944.

Barry, A.L. Yunini's Story of the Trail of Tears. 230 pp. London, 1932.

Bartram, W. Observations on the Creek and Cherokee Indians. TAES, III, 1-81. 1853.

--- Travels in Georgia and Florida, 1773-74, ed. F. Harper. TAPS, n.s., XXXIII, 126, 172-205, 225. 1943.

--- The Travels of William Bartram, Naturalist's Edition. 788 pp. New Haven, 1958.

--- Travels through North and South Carolina. London, 1792.

Bass, A. Cherokee Messenger. 348 pp. Norman, 1936.

Bell, C. John Rattling-Gourd of Big Cove. 103 pp. New York, 1955.

Bell, M.W. Chick-a-liel-lih. SFQ, XVII, 255-58. 1953.

Bender, E. Cherokee. IJAL, XV, 223-8. 1949.

Bender, E., and Harris, Z.S. The Phonemes of North Carolina Cherokee. IJAL, XII, 14-21. 1946.

Bibaud, F.M. Biographie des sagamos illustrés de l'Amérique Septentrionale, pp. 199-205, 274-81. Montreal, 1848.

Bloom, L. The Acculturation of the Eastern Cherokee. NCHR, XIX, 323-58. 1942.

--- The Cherokee Clan. AA, n.s., XLI, 266-8. 1939.

--- A Measure of Conservatism. AA, n.s., XLVII, 630-5. 1945.

Boas, F. Zur Anthropologie der nordamerikanischen Indianer. VBGA, 1895, 367-411.

Boozer, J.D. The Legend of Yalloo Falls. TA, XI, ii, 66-7. 1955.

Boyd, G.A. Elias Boudinot. Princeton, 1952.

Brown, J.P. Old Frontiers. 570 pp. Kingsport, 1938.

Brown, T.S. By Way of Cherokee. 127 pp. Atlanta, 1944.

Bushnell, D.I. Native Cemeteries and Forms of Burial East of the Mississippi. BBAE, LXXI, 90-3. 1920.

--- Virginia before Jamestown. SMC, C, 125-58. 1940.

Buttrick, D.S. Antiquities of the Cherokee Indians. 20 pp. Vinita, 1884.

Cameron, C.M. Cherokee Indian Health Survey. PHR, LXXI, 1086-8. 1956.

Cassel, J., Gulick, J. and Smith, H.L. The Cherokee Project. Research Reviews, IV, ii, 10-18. 1956.

Caywood, E.R. The Administration of William C. Rogers. CO, XXX, 29-37. 1952.

Coleman, K. Federal Indian Relations in the South, 1781-1789. CO, XXV, 435-58. 1947.

Corkran, D.H. A Cherokee Migration Fragment. SIS, IV, 27-8. 1952.

--- Cherokee Prehistory. NCHR, XXXIV, 455-66. 1957.

--- Cherokee Sun and Fire Observances. SIS, VII, 33-8. 1955.

--- The Nature of the Cherokee Supreme Being. SIS, VIII, 27-35. 1956.

--- The Sacred Fire of the Cherokees. SIS, V, 21-6. 1953.

Cotterill, R.S. The Southern Indians. 268 pp. Norman, 1954.

Dale, E. E., and Litton, G. Cherokee Cavaliers. 308 pp. Norman, 1940.

Davis, J. B. The Liver-Eater: a Cherokee Story. Annals of Archaeology and Anthropology, II, 134-8. 1909.

--- Some Cherokee Stories. Annals of Archaeology and Anthropology, III, 26-49. 1910.

--- Two Cherokee Charms. Annals of Archaeology and Anthropology, II, 131-3. 1909.

Debo, A. And still the Waters run. 417 pp. Princeton, 1940.

--- Southern Refugees of the Cherokee Nation. SWHQ, XXXV, 255-66. 1932.

Donaldson, T. Eastern Band of Cherokees of North Carolina. U.S. Census Office, Eleventh Census, Extra Census Bulletin, pp. 7-21. 1892.

Downing, A. The Cherokee Indians and Their Neighbors. AAOJ, XVII, 307-16. 1895.

Eaton, R. C. John Ross and the Cherokee Indians. 212 pp, Menasha, 1914; 153 pp., Muskogee, 1921.

Fewkes, V. J. Catawba Pottery-making. PAPS, LXXXVIII, 69-124. 1944.

Field, C. Fine Root Runner Basketry among the Oklahoma Cherokee Indians. Philbrook Art Center, I, 1-10. 1943.

Foreman, C. T. An Early Account of the Cherokees. CO, XXXIV, 141-58. 1956.

--- Park Hill. 186 pp. Muskogee, Oklahoma, 1948.

Foreman, G. The Five Civilized Tribes, pp. 281-426. Norman, 1934.

--- Indians and Pioneers. Rev. edit. 285 pp. Norman, 1936.

--- Sequoyah. 90 pp. Norman, 1938.

Foreman, G., ed. A Traveler in Indian Territory. 270 pp. Cedar Rapids, 1930.

Foster, G. E. Literature of the Cherokees. 138 pp. Ithaca, 1889.

--- Se-quo-yah. 244 pp. Philadelphia, 1885.

--- Story of the Cherokee Bible. 89 pp. Ithaca, 1899.

Gabelentz, H. G. C. von der. Kurze Grammatik der tscherokesischen Sprache. Zeitschrift für die Wissenschaft der Sprache, III, 257-300. 1852.

Gabriel, R. H. Elias Boudinot, Cherokee, and His America. Norman, 1941.

Gatschet, A. S. On the Affinity of the Cheroki to the Iroquois Dialects. Transactions of the American Philological Association, XVI, xl-xlv. 1886.

Gearing, F. The Structural Poses of 18th Century Cherokee Villages. AA, LX, 1148-1157. 1958.

Gilbert, W. H. The Cherokees of North Carolina. ARSI, CXII, 529-56. 1957.

Gilbert, W. H. Eastern Cherokee Social Organization. SANAT, 285-340. 1955.

--- The Eastern Cherokees. BBAE, CXXXIII, 169-414. 1943.

Graebner, N. A. Pioneer Indian Agriculture in Oklahoma. CO, XXIII, 232-48. 1945.

--- Provincial Indian Society in Eastern Oklahoma. CO, XXIII, 323-37. 1945-6.

--- The Public Land Policy of the Five Civilized Tribes. CO, XXIII, 107-18. 1945.

Groff, J. F. Some Major Indian Trading Paths Across Georgia. Mineral News Letter, VI, 1v. 1953.

Gulick, J. The Acculturation of Eastern Cherokee Community Organization. SF, XXXVI, 246-50. 1958.

--- Language and Passive Resistance among the Eastern Cherokees. E, V, 60-81. 1958.

--- Problems of Cultural Communication — the Eastern Cherokees. AmI, VIII, i, 20-31. 1958.

--- The self-corrective circuit and trait-persistence in conservative Eastern Cherokee Culture. Research Reviews, VI, iii, 1-10. 1959.

Hagar, S. Cherokee Star-Lore. Boas Anniversary Volume, pp. 354-66. New York, 1906.

Hale, H. Indian Migrations as evidenced by Language. AAOJ, V, 18-28. 1883.

Hargrett, L. A Bibliography of the Constitutions and Laws of the American Indians, pp. 3-40. Cambridge, 1947.

Harrington, M. R. Cherokee and Earlier Remains on Upper Tennessee River. INM, n.s., XXIV, 5-321. 1922.

--- The Last of the Iroquois Potters. ARUNY, LXII, i, 222-7. 1909.

Hawkins, B. Letters, 1796-1806. CGHS, IX, 1-500. 1916.

Haywood, J. The Natural and Aboriginal History of Tennessee. 390 pp. Nashville, 1823.

Hensley, J. C. My Father is Rich. 214 pp. Nashville, 1956.

Hewes, L. The Oklahoma Ozarks as the Land of the Cherokees. GR, XXXII, 269-81. 1942.

Hinkle, L. E. The Cherokee Language. Bulletin of the Archaeological Society of North Carolina, II, i, 1-9. 1935.

Holt, E. O. Life with the Cherokee. 30 pp. Cranfills Gap, Texas, 1950.

Howard, J. H. Altamaha Cherokee Folklore and Customs. JAFL, LXXII, 134-8. 1959.

Irvine, A. How the Turkey Got His Beard. SWL, XVI, ii, 35-6. 1950.

Jacobs, W.R. Indians of the Southern Colonial Frontier. Columbia, S.C., 1954.

Jarrett, R.F. Occoneechee. 284 pp. New York, 1916.

Klingberg, F.J., ed. The Carolina Chronicle of Dr. Francis Le Jau, 1706-1717. UCPH, LIII, 228 pp. 1956.

Kate, H.F.C. ten. Legends of the Cherokee. JAFL, II, 53-5. 1889.

Kephart, H. The Cherokees of the Smoky Mountains. 36 pp. Ithaca, 1938.

King, V.O. The Cherokee Nation of Indians. TSHAQ, 1898, 58-72.

Knepler, A.E. Education in the Cherokee Nation. CO, XXI, 378-401. 1943.

--- Eighteenth Century Cherokee Educational Efforts. CO, XX, 55-61. 1942.

Knight, O. Cherokee Society under the Stress of Removal. CO, XXXII, 414-28. 1954.

--- History of the Cherokees. CO, XXXIV, 159-82. 1956.

Kutsche, P. Report on a Summer Field Project in Cherokee, North Carolina. BPAS, X, i, 8-11. 1956.

Lanman, C. Adventures in the Wilds of the United States and British American Provinces, I, 407-30. Philadelphia, 1856.

--- Letters from the Alleghany Mountains, pp. 84-114. New York, 1849.

Lewis, T.M.N. Early Historic Cherokee Data. NLSAC, III, iii, 28-30. 1953.

Lewis, T.M.N. and Kneberg, M. The Cherokee "Hothouse." TA, IX, i, 2-5. 1953.

--- Ocanaluftee Village. 103 pp. Cherokee, 1954.

Logan, J.H. A History of the Upper Country of South Carolina. 521 pp. Charleston, 1859.

Lounsbury, F.G. Stray Number Systems among Certain Indian Tribes. AA, n.s., XLVIII, 672-5. 1946.

McGinty, J.R. Symbols of a Civilization that Perished in Its Infancy. EG, I, iv, 14-7. 1955.

McGowan, D.J. Indian Secret Societies. HM, ser. 1, X, 139-41. 1866.

Mahoney, J.W. and Foreman, R. The Cherokee Physician or Complete Guide to Health. Asheville, N.C., 1842.

Malone, H.T. The Cherokees Become a Civilized Tribe. EG, II, ii, 12-15. 1957.

--- The Cherokee Phoenix. GHQ, XXXIV, 163-88. 1950.

--- Cherokee-White Relations on the Southern Frontier in the Early Nineteenth Century. NCHR, XXXIV, 1-14. 1957.

Malone, H.T. Cherokees of the Old South. 251 pp. Athens, 1956.

--- New Echota-Capital of the Cherokee Nation, 1525-1830. EG, I, iv, 6-13. 1955.

Marriott, A. Greener Fields. 274 pp. New York, 1953.

Martin, R.G. The Cherokee Phoenix. CO, XV, 102-19. 1947.

Mason, R.L. Tree Myths of the Cherokees. American Forests and Forest Life, XXXV, 259-62, 300. 1929.

Milam, J.B. The Great Seal of the Cherokee Nation. CO, XXI, 8-9. 1943.

Milling, C.J. Red Carolinians. 438 pp. Chapel Hill, 1940.

Mooney, J. Among the East Cherokee Indians. SMC, LXIII, viii, 61-4. 1913.

--- Cherokee. BBAE, XXX, i, 245-9. 1907.

--- Cherokee and Iroquois Parallels. JAFL, II, 67. 1889.

--- Cherokee Ball Play. AA, III, 105-32. 1890.

--- Cherokee Mound-Building. AA, II, 167-71. 1889.

--- Cherokee Plant Lore. AA, II, 223-4. 1889.

--- The Cherokee River Cult. JAFL, XIII, 1-10. 1900.

--- Cherokee Theory and Practice of Medicine. JAFL, III, 44-50. 1890.

--- Evolution in Cherokee Personal Names. AA, II, 61-2. 1889.

--- Improved Cherokee Alphabets. AA, V, 63-4. 1892.

--- Myths of the Cherokee. ARBAE, XIX, i, 3-548. 1898.

--- Myths of the Cherokees. JAFL, I, 97-108. 1888.

--- The Sacred Formulas of the Cherokees. ARBAE, VII, 301-97. 1886.

--- The Swimmer Manuscript, ed. F.M. Olbrechts. BBAE, XCIX, 1-319. 1932.

Morgan, L.H. Systems of Consanguinity and Affinity. SCK, XVII, 291-382. 1871.

Nuttall, T. A Journal of Travels into the Arkansa Territory, pp. 123-37. Philadelphia, 1821.

Olbrechts, F.M. Cherokee Belief and Practice with Regard to Childbirth. A, XXVI, 17-33. 1931.

--- Prophylaxis in Cherokee Medicine. A, XXIV, 271-80. 1929.

--- Some Cherokee Methods of Divination. ICA, XXIII, 547-52. 1928.

--- Some Notes on Cherokee Treatment of Disease. Janus, XXXIII, 272-80. 1928.

--- Two Cherokee Texts. IJAL, VI, 179-84. 1931.

Painter, C.C. The Eastern Cherokees. 16 pp. Philadelphia, 1888.

Parker, T.V. The Cherokee Indians. 116 pp. New York, 1907.

Pickens, A.L. A Comparison of Cherokee and Pioneer Bird-Nomenclature. SFQ, VII, 213-21. 1943.

Pickering, J. A Grammar of the Cherokee Language. 48 pp. Boston, 1830.

Pickett, A.J. History of Alabama, I, 154-63. Charleston, 1851.

Pilling, J.C. Bibliography of the Iroquoian Languages. BBAE, VI, 1-208. 1888.

Potter, E. An Account of Several Nations of Southern Indians. MHSC, ser. 1, X, 119-21. 1809.

Powell, J.W. The Cherokees probably Mound Builders. ARBAE, V, 87-107. 1884.

Reyburn, W.D. Cherokee Verb Morphology. IJAL, XIX, 172-80, 259-73; XX, 44-64. 1953-54.

Richardson, W. An Account of the Presbyterian Mission to the Cherokees, 1757-1759. Tennessee Historical Magazine, ser. 2, I, 125-8. 1931.

Rights, D.L. The American Indian in North Carolina. 296 pp. Durham, 1947; 318 pp., Winston-Salem, 1957.

Ross, Mrs. W.P. Life and Times of Wm. P. Ross. 272 pp. Fort Smith, 1893.

Royce, C.C. The Cherokee Nation of Indians. ARBAE, V, 121-378. 1884.

Schmitt, K. and Bell, R.E. Historic Indian Pottery from Oklahoma. BOAS, II, 19-30. 1954.

Sears, W.H. Creek and Cherokee Culture in the 18th Century. AAn, XXI, 143-9. 1955.

Self, R.D. Chronology of New Echota. EG, I, iv, 3-5. 1955.

Siler, M.R. Cherokee Indian Lore and Smoky Mountain Stories. 111 pp. Bryson City, 1938.

Simon, C.M. Younger Brother. 182 pp. New York, 1942.

Speck, F.G. Decorative Art and Basketry of the Cherokee. BPMCM, II, 53-86. 1920.

--- Ethnoherpetology of the Catawba and Cherokee Indians. JWAS, XXXVI, 355-60. 1946.

--- Some Eastern Cherokee Texts. IJAL, IV, 111-13. 1926.

Speck, F. and Broom, L. Cherokee Dance and Drama. 121 pp. Berkeley, 1951.

Speck, F.G. and Schaeffer, C.E. The Mutual-aid and Volunteer Company of the Eastern Cherokee. JWAS, XXXV, 169-79. 1945.

Spence, L. Cherokees. ERE, III, 503-8. 1911.

Spoehr, A. Changing Kinship Systems. FMAS, XXXIII, 153-235. 1947.

Starkey, M.L. The Cherokee Nation. 355 pp. New York, 1946.

Starr, E. History of the Cherokee Indians. 680 pp. Oklahoma City, 1921.

Steen, C.T. The Home for the Insane, Deaf, Dumb and Blind of the Cherokee Nation. CO, XXI, 402-19. 1943.

Story, I.F. Our Eastern Cherokee Indians. Home Geographic Monthly, V, vi, 7-12. 1932.

Street, O.D. The Indians of Marshall County, Alabama. Transactions of the Alabama Historical Society, IV, 193-210. 1904.

Stringfield, W.W. North Carolina Cherokee Indians. 24 pp. Raleigh, 1903.

Stuart, J. A Sketch of the Cherokee and Choctaw Indians. 42 pp. Little Rock, 1837.

Terrell, J.W. The Demon of Consumption. JAFL, V, 125-6. 1892.

Thomas, C. Burial Mounds in the Northern Sections of the United States. ARBAE, V, 87-107. 1884.

--- The Cherokees in Pre-Columbian Times. 97 pp. New York, 1890.

Timberlake, H. Memoirs. London, 1762.

Tinnin, I.W. Influences of the Cherokee National Seminaries. CO, XXXVII, 59-67. 1959.

Tooker, W.W. The Problems of the Rechaheerian Indians of Virginia. AA, XI, 261-70. 1898.

Ulmer, M. and Beck, S.E., eds. To Make My Bread. 72 pp. Cherokee, 1951.

Walker, R.S. Torchlights to the Cherokees. 339 pp. New York, 1931.

Wardell, M.L. A Political History of the Cherokee Nation. 383 pp. Norman, 1938.

Washburn, C. Reminiscences of the Indians. 236 pp., Richmond, 1869; 209 pp., Van Buren, Ark., 1955.

Watts, W.J. Cherokee Citizenship. 144 pp. Muldrow, 1895.

Webster, C.L. Prof. D.W.C. Duncan's Analysis of the Cherokee Language. AN, XXIII, 775-81. 1889.

Wilburn, H.C. Judaculla Place-Names and the Judaculla Tales. SIS, IV, 23-6. 1952.

--- Judaculla Rock. SIS, IV, 19-22. 1952.

--- Nununyi, the Kituhwas, or Mountain Indians and the State of North Carolina. SIS, II, 54-64. 1950.

Winkler, E.W. The Cherokee Indians in Texas. TSHAQ, VII, 95-165. 1903.

Witthoft, J. Bird Lore of the Eastern Cherokee. JWAS, XXXVI, 372-84. 1946.

--- The Cherokee Green Corn Medicine and the Green Corn Festival. JWAS, XXXVI, 213-19. 1946.

--- An Early Cherokee Ethnobotanical Note. JWAS, XXXVII, 73-5. 1947.

Witthoft, J. Green Corn Ceremonialism in the East-
    ern Woodlands. OCMA, XIII, 31-50. 1949.
--- Notes on a Cherokee Migration Story. JWAS,
    XXXVII, 304-5. 1947.
--- Some Eastern Cherokee Bird Stories. JWAS,
    XXXVI, 177-80. 1946.
--- Stone Pipes of the Historic Cherokee. SIS, I,
    ii, 43-69. 1949.
--- Will West Long, Cherokee Informant. AA, n.s.,
    L, 355-9. 1948.
Witthoft, J., and Hadlock, W.S. Cherokee-Iroquois
    Little People. JAFL, LIX, 413-22. 1946.
Wood, W.W. War and the Eastern Cherokee. SIS,
    II, 47-53. 1950.
Wright, M.H. American Indian Corn Dishes. CO,
    XXXVI, 155-66. 1958.

9. CHICKASAW

Swanton, J.R. Social and Religious Beliefs and Us-
    ages of the Chickasaw Indians. ARBAE, XLIV, 169-
    273. 1927.

Abbott, M. Indian Policy and Management in the
    Mississippi Territory, 1798-1817. JMH, XIV, 153-
    69. 1952.
Adair, J. The History of the American Indians, pp.
    352-73. London, 1775.
Bartram, W. The Travels of William Bartram, Na-
    turalist's Edition. 788 pp. New Haven, 1958.
--- Travels through North and South Carolina. Lon-
    don, 1792.
Bell, R.E. and Baerreis, D.A. A Survey of Oklahoma
    Archeology. BTAPS, XXII, 7-100. 1951.
Boas, F. Zur Anthropologie der nordamerikanischen
    Indianer. VBGA, 1895, 367-411.
Braden, G.B. The Colberts and the Chickasaw Na-
    tion. THQ, XVII, 222-49, 318-35. 1958-59.
Brinton, D.G. National Legend of the Chahta-Musko-
    kee Tribes. 13 pp. Morrisania, 1870.
Bushnell, D.I. Native Cemeteries and Forms of Bur-
    ial East of the Mississippi. BBAE, LXXI, 105-8.
    1920.
Campbell, T.N. Medicinal Plants Used by Choctaw,
    Chickasaw and Creek Indians. JWAS, XLI, 285-90.
    1951.
Cotterill, R.S. The Southern Indians. 268 pp. Nor-
    man, 1954.
Cushman, H.B. History of the Choctaw, Chickasaw,
    and Natchez Indians. 607 pp. Greenville, 1899.
Debo, A. And still the Waters run. 417 pp. Princeton,
    1940.

Dumont de Montigny. L'etablissement de la province
    de la Louisiane. JSAP, n.s., XXIII, 273-440.
    1931.
Foreman, G. The Five Civilized Tribes, pp. 97-
    144. Norman, 1934.
--- Indians and Pioneers. Rev. edit. 285 pp. Nor-
    man, 1936.
Foreman, G., ed. A Traveler in Indian Territory.
    270 pp. Cedar Rapids, 1930.
Gatschet, A.S. A Migration Legend of the Creek
    Indians, pp. 90-7. Philadelphia, 1884.
Gatschet, A.S., and Thomas, C. Chickasaw. BBAE,
    XXX, i, 260-2. 1907.
Graebner, N.A. Pioneer Indian Agriculture in Okla-
    homa. CO, XXIII, 232-48. 1945.
--- Provincial Indian Society in Eastern Oklahoma.
    CO, XXIII, 323-37. 1945-46.
--- The Public Land Policy of the Five Civilized
    Tribes. CO, XXIII, 107-18. 1945.
Hargrett, L. A Bibliography of the Constitutions and
    Laws of the American Indians, pp. 41-53. Cam-
    bridge, 1947.
Hawkins, B. Letters, 1796-1806. CGHS, IX, 1-
    500. 1916.
Haywood, J. The Natural and Aboriginal History of
    Tennessee. 390 pp. Nashville, 1823.
Hiemstra, W.L. Presbyterian Mission Schools Among
    the Choctaws and Chickasaws, 1845-1861. CO,
    XXVII, 33-40. 1949.
Howard, J.H. Some Chickasaw Fetishes. FA, XII,
    ii, 47-56. 1959.
Jennings, J.D. Chickasaw and Earlier Indian Cul-
    tures of Northeast Mississippi. JMH, III, iii, 155-
    226. 1941.
--- Prehistory of the Lower Mississippi Valley. AEUS,
    256-71. 1952.
Malone, J.H. The Chickasaw Nation. 537 pp.
    Louisville, 1922.
Milling, C.J. Red Carolinians. 438 pp. Chapel
    Hill, 1940.
Morgan, L.H. Systems of Consanguinity and Affinity.
    SCK, XVII, 291-382. 1871.
Nuttall, T. A Journal of Travels into the Arkansa
    Territory. 296 pp. Philadelphia, 1821.
Osborn, G.C. Relations with the Indians in West
    Florida during the Administration of Governor Peter
    Chester, 1770-1781. FHSQ, XXXI, 239-72. 1953.
Parsons, J.E. Letters on the Chickasaw Removal of
    1837. NYHSQ, XXXVII, 273-83. 1953.
Phelps, D.A. The Chickasaw Agency. JMH, XIV,
    119-37. 1952.
--- The Chickasaw Council House. JMH, XIV, 170-
    76. 1952.

Phelps, D.A. The Chickasaw, the English, and the
    French, 1699-1744. THQ, XVI, 117-33. 1957.
Pickett, A.J. History of Alabama, I, 146-53.
    Charleston, 1851.
Potter, E. An Account of Several Nations of Southern
    Indians. MHSC, ser. 1, X, 119-21. 1809.
Romans, B. A Concise Natural History of East and
    West Florida, pp. 59-71. New York, 1775.
Smith, H.K. Chickasaws in Humphreys and Benton
    Counties, Tennessee. TA, XIV, i, 26-30. 1958.
Smyth, J.F.D. A Tour in the United States of Amer-
    ica. I, 360-4. London, 1784.
Speck, F.G. Notes on Chickasaw Ethnology and
    Folk-Lore. JAFL, XX, 50-8. 1907.
Swanton, J.R. Early History of the Creek Indians and
    Their Neighbors. BBAE, LXXIII, 414-20. 1922.
--- Social Organization and Social Usages of the In-
    dians of the Creek Confederacy. ARBAE, XLII, 23-
    472. 1925.
Villiers du Terrage, M. de. Documents concernant
    l'histoire des Indiens de la région orientale de la
    Louisiane. JSAP, n.s., XIV, 127-40. 1922.
--- Note sur deux cartes dessinées par les Chickachas.
    JSAP, n.s., XIII, 7-9. 1921.
Warren, H. Chickasaw Traditions, Customs, etc.
    PMHS, VIII, 543-53. 1904.
--- Some Chickasaw Chiefs and Prominent Men.
    PMHS, VIII, 555-70. 1904.
Williams, S.C. Beginnings of West Tennessee. 311
    pp. Johnson City, Tenn., 1930.
Wright, J.B. Ranching in the Choctaw and Chicka-
    saw Nations. CO, XXXVII, 294-300. 1959.
Wright, M.H. American Indian Corn Dishes. CO,
    XXXVI, 155-66. 1958.
Young, C.A. A Walking Tour in the Indian Territory.
    CO, XXXVI, 167-80. 1958.

10. CHITIMACHA

Burch, M.C. The Indigenous Indians of the Lower
    Trinity Area of Texas. SWHQ, LX, 36-52. 1956.
Bushnell, D.I. The Chitimacha Indians of Bayou
    La Fourche, Louisiana. JWAS, VII, x, 301-7. 1917.
--- Some New Ethnologic Data from Louisiana. JWAS,
    XII, xiii, 303-7. 1922.
Densmore, F. A Search for Songs among the Chiti-
    macha Indians in Louisiana. BBAE, CXXXIII, 1-
    16. 1943.
Dumont de Montigny. Memoires historiques sur la
    Louisiane, I, 106-14. Paris, 1753.
Ethridge, A.N. Indians of Grant Parish. LHQ, XXIII,
    1108-31. 1940.
Gatschet, A.S. Chitimacha. BBAE, XXX, i, 286.
    1907.
--- Die Schetimascha-Indianer im südlichen
    Luisiana. Ausland, LVII, 581-9. 1884.
--- The Shetimasha Indians of St. Mary's Parish.
    Transactions of the Anthropological Society of
    Washington, II, 148-58. 1883.
Haas, M.R. Natchez and Chitimacha Clans and
    Kinship Terminology. AA, n.s., XLI, 597-610.
    1939.
Harrington, M.R. Among Louisiana Indians. SW,
    XXXVII, 656-61. 1908.
Le Page du Pratz, A.S. Histoire de la Louisiane, I,
    105-17. Paris, 1758.
Merwin, B.W. Basketry of the Chitimacha Indians.
    MJ, X, 29-34. 1919.
Quimby, G.I. The Bayou Goula Site. FMAS, XLVII,
    ii. 1957.
Swadesh, M. Atakapa-Chitimacha *k^w. IJAL, XIII,
    120-1. 1947.
--- Chitimacha Verbs of Derogatory or Abusive Con-
    notation. Lg, IX, 192-201. 1933.
--- The Phonetics of Chitimacha. Lg, X, 345-62.
    1934.
--- Phonologic Formulas for Atakapa-Chitimacha.
    IJAL, XII, 113-32. 1946.
--- Sociologic Notes on Obsolescent Languages. IJAL,
    XIV, 226-35. 1948.
Swanton, J.R. Historic Use of the Spear-Thrower in
    Southeastern North America. AAn, III, 356-8.
    1938.
--- Indian Tribes of the Lower Mississippi Valley and
    Adjacent Coast of the Gulf of Mexico. BBAE,
    XLIII, 337-60. 1911.
--- Mythology of the Indians of Louisiana and the
    Texas Coast. JAFL, XX, 285-9. 1907.
--- Chitimacha Myths and Beliefs. JAFL, XXX, 474-
    8. 1917.
--- A Structural and Lexical Comparison of the
    Tunica, Chitimacha, and Atakapa Languages.
    BBAE, LXVIII, 1-56. 1919.
Toomey, T.N. Relationships of the Chitimachan
    Linguistic Family. BHLAL, IV, 1-12. 1914.

11. CHOCTAW

Swanton, J.R. Source Material for the Social and
    Ceremonial Life of the Choctaw Indians. BBAE,
    CIII, 1-282. 1931.

Abbott, M. Indian Policy and Management in the
    Mississippi Territory, 1798-1817. JMH, XIV,
    153-69. 1952.

Adair, J. The History of the American Indians, pp. 282-351. London, 1775.

Bartram, W. The Travels of William Bartram, Naturalist's Edition. 788 pp. New Haven, 1958.

--- Travels through North and South Carolina. London, 1792.

Baudry des Lozières, L. H. Voyage à la Louisiane. 382 pp. Paris, 1802.

Bell, R. E. and Baerreis, D. A. A Survey of Oklahoma Archeology. BTAPS, XXII, 7-100. 1951.

Benson, H. C. Life among the Choctaw Indians. 314 pp. Cincinnati, 1860.

Bossu, M. Nouveaux voyages aux Indes occidentales, II, 87-106. Paris, 1768.

--- Travels through That Part of North America formerly called Louisiana, I, 292-309. London, 1771.

Brinton, D. G. National Legend of the Chahta-Muskokee Tribes. 13 pp. Morrisania, 1870.

Brown, C. S. Archeology of Mississippi, Mississippi Geological Survey, University, Miss., 1926.

Bryan, F. A Choctaw Throwing Club. M, VI, 178-9. 1933.

Buckner, H. F. Burial among the Choctaws. AAOJ, II, 55-8. 1879.

Bushnell, D. I. The Choctaw of Bayou Lacomb. BBAE, XLVIII, 1-37. 1909.

--- The Choctaw of St. Tammany. LHQ, I, i, 11-20. 1917.

--- Myths of the Louisiana Choctaw. AA, n.s., XII, 526-35. 1910.

--- Native Cemeteries and Forms of Burial East of the Mississippi. BBAE, LXXI, 94-101. 1920.

Byington, C. A Dictionary of the Choctaw Language. BBAE, XLVI, 1-611. 1915.

--- Grammar of the Choctaw Language, ed. D. G. Brinton. PAPS, XI, 317-67. 1870.

Campbell, T. N. The Choctaw Afterworld. JAFL, LXXII, 146-54. 1959.

--- Choctaw Subsistence. FA, XII, i, 9-24. 1959.

--- Medicinal Plants Used by Choctaw, Chickasaw and Creek Indians. JWAS, XLI, 285-90. 1951.

Catlin, G. Illustrations of the Manners, Customs and Condition of the North American Indians, II, 122-8. New York, 1841.

Claiborne, J. F. H. Mississippi as a Province, Territory, and State, pp. 483-526. Jackson, 1880.

Collins, H. B. Additional Anthropometric Observations on the Choctaw. AJPA, XI, 353-5. 1928.

--- Anthropometric Observations on the Choctaw. AJPA, VIII, 425-36. 1925.

--- Archeological and Anthropometrical Work in Mississippi. SMC, LXXVIII, i, 89-95. 1927.

Collins, H. B. Potsherds from Choctaw Village Sites in Mississippi. JWAS, XVII, 259-63. 1927.

Copeland, C. C. A Choctaw Tradition. TAES, III, i, 169-71. 1853.

Cotterill, R. S. The Southern Indians. 268 pp. Norman, 1954.

Cushman, H. B. History of the Choctaw, Chickasaw and Natchez Indians. 607 pp. Greenville, 1899.

Debo, A. And still the Waters run. 417 pp. Princeton, 1940.

--- The Rise and Fall of the Choctaw Republic. 314 pp. Norman, 1934.

Densmore, F. Choctaw Music. BBAE, CXXXVI, 101-88. 1943.

DeRosier, A. H. Pioneers with Conflicting Ideals. JMH, XXI, 174-189. 1959.

Donaldson, T. The George Catlin Indian Gallery. RUSNM, 1885, 212-4.

Douglas, F. H. A Choctaw Pack Basket. MCN, IV, 15-18. 1937.

Edwards, J. The Choctaw Indians in the Middle of the Nineteenth Century. CO, X, 392-425. 1932.

Edwards, T. A. Early Developments in the C & A. CO, XXVII, 148-61. 1949.

Eggan, F. Historical Changes in the Choctaw Kinship System. AA, n.s., XXXIX, 34-52. 1937.

Ethridge, A. N. Indians of Grant Parish. LHQ, XXIII, 1108-31. 1940.

Ford, J. A. Analysis of Indian Village Site Collections from Louisiana and Mississippi. Louisiana Department of Conservation, Anthropological Studies, II, 1-285. 1936.

Foreman, G. The Five Civilized Tribes, pp. 17-94. Norman, 1934.

--- Indians and Pioneers. Rev. edit. 285 pp. Norman, 1936.

Foreman, G., ed. A Traveler in Indian Territory. 270 pp. Cedar Rapids, 1930.

Gatschet, A. S. A Migration Legend of the Creek Indians, pp. 100-18. Philadelphia, 1884.

Goggin, J. M. Louisiana Choctaw Basketry. EP, XLVI, 121-3. 1939.

Graebner, N. A. Pioneer Indian Agriculture in Oklahoma. CO, XXIII, 232-48. 1945.

--- Provincial Indian Society in Eastern Oklahoma. CO, XXIII, 323-37. 1945-6.

--- The Public Land Policy of the Five Civilized Tribes. CO, XXIII, 107-18. 1945.

Haag, W. G. Choctaw Archeology. NLSAC, III, iii, 25-8. 1953.

Haas, M. R. The Choctaw Word for "Rattlesnake." AA, n.s., XLIII, 129-32. 1941.

Halbert, H.S. The Choctaw Achahpih (Chungkee) Game. AAOJ, X, 283-4. 1888.

--- The Choctaw Creation Legend. PMHS, IV, 267-70. 1901.

--- A Choctaw Migration Legend. AAOJ, XVI, 215-16. 1894.

--- The Choctaw Robin Goodfellow. AAOJ, XVII, 157. 1895.

--- Courtship and Marriage among the Choctaws. AN, XVI, 222-4. 1882.

--- District Divisions of the Choctaw Nation. Publications of the Alabama Historical Society, Miscellaneous Collections, I, 375-85. 1901.

--- Funeral Customs of the Mississippi Choctaws. PMHS, III, 353-66. 1900.

--- Nanih Waiya, the Sacred Mound of the Choctaws. PMHS, II, 223-34. 1899.

--- Okla Hannali; or the Six Towns District of the Choctaws. AAOJ, XV, 146-9. 1893.

--- Pyramid and Old Road in Mississippi. AAOJ, XIII, 348-9. 1891.

Hargrett, L. A Bibliography of the Constitutions and Laws of the American Indians, pp. 54-77. Cambridge, 1947.

Hawkins, B. Letters, 1796-1806. CGHS, IX, 1-500. 1916.

Hensley, J.C. My Father is Rich. 214 pp. Nashville, 1956.

Hiemstra, W.L. Presbyterian Mission Schools among the Choctaws and Chickasaws, 1845-1861. CO, XXVII, 33-40. 1949.

Hodgson, A. Letters from North America, I, 215-24, 240-50. London, 1824.

Jennings, J.D. Prehistory of the Lower Mississippi Valley. AEUS, 256-71. 1952.

Knight, O. Fifty Years of Choctaw Law. CO, XXXI, 76-95. 1953.

Lanman, C. Adventures in the Wilds of the United States and British American Provinces, II, 429-35. Philadelphia, 1856.

Lewis, A. Pushmataha, American Patriot. 204 pp. New York, 1959.

Lincecum, G. Choctaw Traditions about Their Settlement in Mississippi and the Origin of Their Mounds. PMHS, VIII, 521-42. 1904.

Marriott, A. Greener Fields. 274 pp. New York, 1953.

Milford, L.L. de. Mémoire ou coup-d'oeil rapide sur les différens voyages et mon séjour dans la nation Crëck, pp. 288-317. Paris, 1802.

Morgan, L.H. Systems of Consanguinity and Affinity. SCK, XVII, 291-382. 1871.

Morrison, J.D. News for the Choctaws. CO, XXVII, 207-22. 1949.

--- Problems in the Industrial Progress and Development of the Choctaw Nation. CO, XXXII, 70-91. 1954.

Nuttall, T. A Journal of Travels into the Arkansa Territory. 296 pp. Philadelphia, 1821.

Osborn, G.C. Relations with the Indians in West Florida during the Administration of Governor Peter Chester, 1770-1781. FHSQ, XXXI, 239-72. 1953.

Petitot, E.F.S. Six légendes américaines. MC, XI, 21-2, 32-5, 45-8. 1879.

Phelps, D.A. The Choctaw Mission. JMH, XIV, 35-62. 1952.

Pickett, A.J. History of Alabama, I, 134-46. Charleston, 1851.

Plaisance, A. The Choctaw Trading House — 1803-1822. AHQ, XVI, 393-423. 1954.

Potter, E. An Account of Several Nations of Southern Indians. MHSC, ser. 1, X, 119-21. 1809.

Read, W.A. Louisiana Place Names of Indian Origin. Louisiana State University Bulletin, XIX, n.s., II, 72 pp. 1927.

--- Notes on an Opelousas Manuscript of 1862. AA, XLII, 546-8. 1940.

Ridaught, H.G. Hell's Branch Office. 240 pp. Citra, Fla., 1957.

Romans, B. A Concise Natural History of East and West Florida, pp. 59-71. New York, 1775.

Smyth, J.F.D. A Tour in the United States of America. II, 7 ff. London, 1784.

Speck, F.G. and Schaeffer, C.E. The Deer and the Rabbit Hunting Drive in Virginia and the Southeast. SIS, II, 3-20. 1950.

Spence, L. Choctaws. ERE, III, 567-9. 1911.

Spoehr, A. Changing Kinship Systems. FMAS, XXXIII, 153-235. 1947.

Stuart, J. A Sketch of the Cherokee and Choctaw Indians. 42 pp. Little Rock, 1837.

Swanton, J.R. An Early Account of the Choctaw Indians. MAAA, V, 53-72. 1918.

Swanton, J.R., and Thomas, C. Choctaw. BBAE, XXX, i, 288-9. 1907.

Taylor, L.A. Plants used as Curatives by Certain Southeastern Tribes. 88 pp. Cambridge, 1940.

Villiers du Terrage, M. de. Documents concernant l'histoire des Indiens de la région orientale de la Louisiane. JSAP, n.s., XIV, 397-426. 1904.

--- Notes sur les Chactas. JSAP, n.s., XV, 223-50. 1923.

Wade, J.W. The Removal of the Mississippi Choctaws. PMHS, VIII, 397-426. 1904.

Walker, B. N. O. Mon-dah-min and the Red Man's
    Uses of Corn as Food. CO, XXXV, 194-203. 1957.

Watkins, J. A. The Choctaws in Mississippi. AAOJ,
    XVI, 69-77. 1894.

--- A Contribution to Chacta History. AAOJ, XVI,
    257-65. 1894.

West, R. T. Pushmataha's Travels. CO, XXXVII,
    162-74. 1959.

Willis, W. S. The Nation of Bread. E, IV, 125-49.
    1957.

Wright, A. Choctaws. Missionary Herald, XXV,
    182-3. 1828.

Wright, J. B. Ranching in the Choctaw and Chicka-
    saw Nations. CO, XXXVII, 294-300. 1959.

Wright, M. H. American Indian Corn Dishes. CO,
    XXXVI, 155-66. 1958.

Wright, M. H. and Shirk, G. H. Artist Möllhausen in
    Oklahoma, 1853. CO, XXXI, 392-441. 1953.

Young, F. B. Notices of the Chactaw or Choktah
    Tribe. Edinburgh Journal of Natural and Geographi-
    cal Science, II, 13-17. 1830.

12. CREEK

Including the Coweta, Kasihta, and other Lower
Creek tribes and the Abihka, Coosa, and other
Upper Creek tribes, also known collectively as
Muskogee.

Swanton, J. R. Social Organization and Social Us-
    ages of the Indians of the Creek Confederacy.
    ARBAE, XLII, 23-472. 1925.

Adair, J. The History of the American Indians, pp.
    257-81. London, 1775.

Anonymous. Creeks. BBAE, XXX, i, 362-5. 1907.

--- The Pole Cat, or Shell Dance. Southern Liter-
    ary Messenger, III, 390-1. 1837.

Ashley, M. E. A Creek Site in Georgia. IN, IV,
    221-6. 1927.

Bareis, C. Two Historic Indian Burials from Pitts-
    burg County, Oklahoma. CO, XXIX, 408-14.
    1951.

Barton, B. S. New Views of the Origin of the Tribes
    and Nations of America. 2d edit. Philadelphia,
    1798.

Bartram, W. Observations on the Creek and Chero-
    kee Indians. TAES, III, 1-81. 1853.

--- Travels in Georgia and Florida, 1773-74, ed.
    F. Harper. TAPS, n.s., XXXIII, 126, 172-209,
    225. 1943.

Bartram, W. The Travels of William Bartram, Na-
    turalist's Edition. 788 pp. New Haven, 1958.

--- Travels through North and South Carolina. Lon-
    don, 1792.

Bell, R. E. and Baerreis, D. A. A Survey of Oklahoma
    Archeology. BTAPS, XXII, 7-100. 1951.

Boas, F. Zur Anthropologie der nordamerikanischen
    Indianer. VBGA, 1895, 367-411.

Bolster, M. H. "The Smoked Meat Rebellion." CO,
    XXXI, 37-55. 1953.

Bonner, J. C. Tustunugee Hutkee and Creek Faction-
    alism on the Georgia-Alabama Frontier. AIR, X,
    111-25. 1957.

Boyd, M. F. Historic Sites in and around the Jim
    Woodruff Reservoir Area, Florida-Georgia. BBAE,
    CLXIX, 195-314. 1958.

Boyd, M. F. and Navarro Latorne, J. Spanish Interest
    in British Florida. FHSQ, XXXII, 92-130. 1953.

Brannon, P. A. Creek Indian War, 1836-37. AHQ,
    XIII, 156-58. 1951.

--- The Dress of the Early Indians of Alabama. Arrow
    Points, V, v, 84-92. 1922.

Brinton, D. G. Contributions to a Grammar of the
    Muskokee Language. PAPS, XI, 301-9. 1870.

--- The National Legends of the Chahta-Muskokee
    Tribes. HM, ser. 2, VII, 118-26. 1870.

--- National Legend of the Chahta-Muskokee Tribes.
    13 pp. Morrisania, 1870.

Buckner, H. F., and Herrod, G. A Grammar of the
    Maskoke or Creek Language. 138 pp. Marion,
    1860.

Bullen, R. P. An Archaeological Survey of the Chatt-
    ahoochee River Valley in Florida. JWAS, L, 100-
    125. 1950.

Bushnell, D. I. An Account of Lamhatty. AA, n.s.,
    X, 568-74. 1908.

--- Native Cemeteries and Forms of Burial East of
    the Mississippi. BBAE, LXXI, 110-14. 1920.

Campbell, J. B. Campbell's Abstract of Creek Indian
    Census Cards and Index. Muskogee, Okl., 1915.

Campbell, T. N. Medicinal Plants Used by Choctaw,
    Chickasaw and Creek Indians. JWAS, XLI, 285-
    90. 1951.

Caughey, J. W. McGillivray of the Creeks. 385 pp.
    Norman, 1938.

Chamberlain, A. F. Busk. BBAE, XXX, i, 176-8.
    1907.

Coleman, K. Federal Indian Relations in the South,
    1781-1789. CO, XXV, 435-58. 1947.

Corry, J. P. Indian Affairs in Georgia, 1732-1756.
    197 pp. Philadelphia, 1936.

Cotterill, R. S. The Southern Indians. 268 pp. Nor-
    man, 1954.

Debo, A. And still the Waters run. 417 pp. Princeton, 1940.

--- The Road to Disappearance. 399 pp. Norman, 1941.

DeJarnette, D.L. and Hansen, A.T. The Archeology of the Childersburg Site, Alabama. Florida State University, Department of Anthropology, Notes in Anthropology, IV, 65 pp. 1960.

Douglas, F.H. Three Creek Baskets. MCN, XV, 66-9. 1941.

Eakins, D.W. Some Information respecting the Creeks. HCPIT, I, 265-83. 1851.

Eggleston, G.C. Red Eagle and the Wars with the Creek Indians of Alabama. 346 pp. New York, 1878.

Fairbanks, C.H. Archeology of the Funeral Mound, Ocmulgee National Monument, Georgia. Archeological Research Series, III. Washington, 1956.

--- Creek and Pre-Creek. AEUS, 285-300. 1952.

--- The Protohistoric Creek of Georgia. NLSAC, III, iii, 21-22. 1953.

--- Some Problems of the Origin of Creek Pottery. FA, XI, 53-64. 1958.

Fleming, J. The Maskoke Semahayeta. 54 pp. Union, 1836.

Foreman, G. The Five Civilized Tribes, pp. 147-219. Norman, 1934.

Foreman, G., ed. A Traveler in Indian Territory. 270 pp. Cedar Rapids, 1930.

Gatschet, A.S. Adjectives of Color in Indian Languages. AN, XIII, 475-85. 1879.

--- La Langue Maskõki et ses dialèctes. ICA, III, ii, 742-58. 1880.

--- A Migration Legend of the Creek Indians. 251 pp. Philadelphia, 1884.

--- Tchikilli's Kasi'hta Legend in the Creek and Hitchiti Languages. Transactions of the Academy of Science of St. Louis, V, 33-239. 1888.

--- Towns and Villages of the Creek Confederacy. PAHS, I, 386-415. 1901.

Graebner, N.A. Pioneer Indian Agriculture in Oklahoma. CO, XXIII, 232-48. 1945.

--- The Public Land Policy of the Five Civilized Tribes. CO, XXIII, 107-18. 1945.

Haas, M.R. Ablaut and Its Function in Muskogee. Lg, XVI, 141-50. 1940.

--- Classificatory Verbs in Muskogee. IJAL, XIV, 244-6. 1948.

--- Creek Inter-Town Relations. AA, n.s., XLII, 479-89. 1940.

--- Dialects of the Muskogee Language. IJAL, XI, 69-74. 1945.

Haas, M.R. Geminate Consonant Clusters in Muskogee. Lg, XIV, 61-5. 1938.

--- Natchez and Chitimacha Clans and Kinship Terminology. AA, XLI, n.s., 597-610. 1939.

--- Natchez and the Muskogean Languages. Lg, XXXII, 61-72. 1956.

--- On the Historical Development of Certain Long Vowels in Creek. IJAL, XVI, 122-25. 1950.

--- A Popular Etymology in Muskogee. Lg, XVII, 340-1. 1941.

Haekel, J. Mannerhäuser und Festplatzanlagen in Ozeanien und im östlichen Nordamerika. BA, XXIII, 8-18. 1940.

Halbert, H.S. and Ball, T.H. The Creek War of 1813 and 1814. 331 pp. Chicago, 1895.

Hall, A.H. The Red Stick War. CO, XII, 264-93. 1934.

Hargrett, L. A Bibliography of the Constitutions and Laws of the American Indians, pp. 78-90. Cambridge, 1947.

Harris, W.A. Here the Creeks Sat Down. 166 pp. Macon, 1958.

Hawkins, B.H. Letters. CGHS, IX, 1-500. 1916.

--- A Sketch of the Creek Country. CGHS, III, i, 19-85. 1848.

Hewitt, J.N.B. Notes on the Creek Indians, ed. J. R. Swanton. BBAE, CXXIII, 119-59. 1939.

Hodgson, A. Letters from North America, I, 117-36. London, 1824.

Hodgson, W.B. The Creek Confederacy. CGHS, III, i, 13-18. 1848.

Jacobs, W.R. Indians of the Southern Colonial Frontier. Columbia, S.C., 1954.

Jones, C.C. Historical Sketch of Tomo-chi-chi. 133 pp. Albany, 1868.

--- Primitive Storehouse of the Creek Indians. ARSI, 1885, 900-1.

Ketcham, H.E. Three Sixteenth Century Spanish Chronicles Relating to Georgia. GHQ, XXXVIII, i, 66-82. 1954.

Klingberg, F.J., ed. The Carolina Chronicle of Dr. Francis Le Jau, 1706-1717. UCPH, LIII, 228 pp. 1956.

Loughridge, R.M., and Hodge, D.M. English and Muskokee Dictionary. St. Louis, 1890.

Milford, L.L.D. Memoir or a Cursory Glance at my Different Travels, J.F. McDermott, ed. 313 pp. Chicago, 1956.

--- Mémoire ou coup-d'oeil rapide sur mes différens voyages et mon séjour dans la nation Crëck. 331 pp. Paris, 1802.

Morgan, L.H. Systems of Consanguinity and Affinity. SCK, XVII, 291-382. 1871.

Motte, J.R. Journey into Wilderness. 361 pp. Gainesville, 1953.

Nunez, T.A. Creek Nativism and the Creek War of 1813-1814. E, V, 1-47, 131-75, 292-301. 1958.

Opler, M.E. The Creek "Town" and the Problem of Creek Indian Political Organization. HPTC, 165-82. 1952.

Osborn, G.C. Relations with the Indians in West Florida during the Administration of Governor Peter Chester, 1770-1781. FHSQ, XXXI, 239-72. 1953.

Payne, J.H. The Green Corn Dance. Continental Monthly, I, 17-29. 1862.

Pickett, A.J. History of Alabama, I, 74-127. Charleston, 1851.

Pope, G.A., Jr. Ocmulgee Old Fields Creeks. NLSAC, III, iii, 20-1. 1953.

Pope, J. A Tour through the Southern and Western Territories of the United States, pp. 52-66. New edit. New York, 1888.

Potter, E. An Account of Several Nations of Southern Indians, MHSC, ser. 1, X, 119-21. 1809.

Pound, M.B. Benjamin Hawkins - Indian Agent. 280 pp. Athens, 1951.

Quimby, G.I. and Spoehr, A. Historic Creek Pottery from Oklahoma. AAn, XV, 249-51. 1950.

Read, W.A. Indian Place Names in Alabama. Louisiana State University Studies, IX, 84 pp. 1937.

--- Indian Stream-names in Georgia. IJAL, XV, 128-32; XVI, 203-7. 1949.

Romans, B. A Concise Natural History of East and West Florida. New York, 1775.

Schmitt, K. Two Creek Pottery Vessels from Oklahoma. FA, III, 3-8. 1950.

Schmitt, K. and Bell, R.E. Historic Indian Pottery from Oklahoma. BOAS, II, 19-30. 1954.

Sears, W.H. Creek and Cherokee Culture in the 18th Century. AAn, XXI, 143-9. 1955.

Speck, F.G. Ceremonial Songs of the Creek and Yuchi Indians. UPMAP, I, 157-245. 1911.

--- The Creek Indians of Taskigi Town. MAAA, II, 99-164. 1907.

--- The Negroes and the Creek Nation. SW, XXXVII, 106-10. 1908.

--- Notes on Social and Economic Conditions among the Creek Indians of Alabama in 1941. AI, VII, 195-8. 1947.

Spoehr, A. Changing Kinship Systems. FMAS, XXXIII, 153-235. 1947.

--- Creek Inter-Town Relations. AA, n.s., XLIII, 132-3. 1941.

Swan, C. Position and State of Manners and Arts of the Creek or Muscogee Nation. HCPIT, V, 251-83. 1855.

Swanton, J.R. Animal Stories from the Indians of the Muskhogean Stock. JAFL, XXVI, 193-218. 1913.

--- Coonti. AA, n.s., XV, 141. 1913.

--- The Creek Indians as Mound Builders. AA, n.s., XIV, 320-4. 1912.

--- Early History of the Creek Indians and Their Neighbors. BBAE, LXXIII, 207-86. 1922.

--- Ethnological Value of the De Soto Narratives. AA, n.s., XXXIV, 570-90. 1932.

--- A Foreword on the Social Organization of the Creek Indians. AA, n.s., XIV, 593-9. 1912.

--- The Green Corn Dance. CO, X, 170-95. 1932.

--- Indian Place Names. American Speech, 212-15. October, 1937.

--- Indian Recognition of Return Discharge in Lightning. JAFL, LXIX, 46. 1956.

--- An Indian Social Experiment and Some of Its Lessons. SM, XXXI, 368-76. 1930.

--- The Interpretation of Aboriginal Mounds by Means of Creek Indian Customs. ARSI, 1927, 495-506.

--- Modern Square Grounds of the Creek Indians. SMC, LXXXV, viii, 1-46. 1931.

--- Myths and Tales of the Southeastern Indians. BBAE, LXXXVIII, 1-86. 1929.

--- Religious Beliefs and Medical Practices of the Creek Indians. ARBAE, XLII, 473-672. 1925.

--- The Social Significance of the Creek Confederacy. ICA, XIX, 327-34. 1915.

--- Tokulki of Tulsa. American Indian Life, ed. E. C. Parsons, pp. 127-45. New York, 1925.

Tarvin, M.E. The Muscogees or Creek Indians from 1519 to 1893. AHQ, XVII, 125-45. 1955.

Villiers du Terrage, M.de. Documents concernant l'histoire des Indiens de la région orientale de la Louisiane. JSAP, n.s., XIV, 127-40. 1922.

Watson, I.A. Creek Indian Burial Customs Today. CO, XXVIII, 95-102. 1950.

Wenhold, L.L. A Seventeenth Century Letter of Gabriel Diaz Vara Calderón. SMC, XCV, xvi. 1936.

Willey, G.R. and Sears, W.H. The Kasita Site. SIS, IV, 3-18. 1952.

Witthoft, J. Green Corn Ceremonialism in the Eastern Woodlands. OCMA, XIII, 52-70. 1949.

Woodward, T.S. Reminiscences of the Creek or Muscogee Indians. Montgomery, 1859.

Wright, M.H. American Indian Corn Dishes. CO, XXXVI, 155-66. 1958.

13. CUSABO

Including the Ashipoo, Combahee, Edisto, Etiwaw,
Kiawaw, Stono, Wapoo, and Wimbee.

Anghiera, P.M.d' (Peter Martyr). De orbe novo,
ed. F.A.MacNutt, II, 255-71. New York, 1912.

Anonymous. Cusabo. BBAE, XXX, i, 373. 1907.

--- Edisto. BBAE, XXX, i, 414. 1907.

--- Etiwaw. BBAE, XXX, i, 443-4. 1907.

Gomara, F.L.de. Historia de las Indias. Madrid,
1749.

Hewatt, A. An Historical Account of the Rise and
Progress of the Colonies of South Carolina and
Georgia, I, 64-73. London, 1779.

Hilton, W. A True Relation of a Voyage upon Discovery of a Part of the Coast of Florida. Collections of the South Carolina Historical Society, V,
18-28. 1897.

Lanning, J.T. The Spanish Missions of Georgia,
pp. 9-32. Chapel Hill, 1935.

Laudonnière, R. L'histoire notable de la Floride.
Paris, 1586.

Milling, C.J. Red Carolinians. 438 pp. Chapel
Hill, 1940.

Mooney, J. The Siouan Tribes of the East. BBAE,
XXII, 5-101. 1894.

Oviedo y Valdez, G.F.de. Historia general y natural de las Indias, III, 624-33. Madrid, 1853.

Quattlebaum, P. The Land Called Chicora. 153 pp.
Gainesville, 1956.

Sandford, R. The Port Royall Discovery. Collections
of the South Carolina Historical Society, V, 57-
81. 1897.

Swanton, J.R. Early History of the Creek Indians and
Their Neighbors. BBAE, LXXIII, 16-25, 31-80.
1922.

14. HITCHITI

Including the Apalachicola, Chatot, Chiaha,
Oconee, Okmulgee, Sawokli, and Tamali.

Caldwell, J.R. The Archeology of Eastern Georgia
and South Carolina. AEUS, 312-21. 1952.

Gatschet, A.S. Hitchiti. BBAE, XXX, i, 551. 1907.

--- A Migration Legend of the Creek Indians, pp.
77-85. Philadelphia, 1884.

--- Tchikilli's Kasi'hta Legend in the Creek and
Hitchiti Languages. Transactions of the Academy
of Science of St. Louis, V, 33-239. 1888.

Smith, B. Comparative Vocabularies of the Seminole
and Mikasuke Tongues. Indian Miscellany, ed. W.
W. Beach, pp. 120-6. Albany, 1877.

Swanton, J.R. Animal Stories from the Indians of the
Muskhogean Stock. JAFL, XXVI, 214-16. 1913.

--- Early History of the Creek Indians and Their Neighbors. BBAE, LXXIII, 129-37, 141-3, 167-84. 1922.

--- Myths and Tales of the Southeastern Indians.
BBAE, LXXXVIII, 87-117. 1929.

--- Religious Beliefs and Medical Practices of the
Creek Indians. ARBAE, XLII, 473-672. 1925.

--- Social Organization and Social Usages of the Indians of the Creek Confederacy. ARBAE, XLII, 23-
472. 1925.

15. HUMA

Harrington, M.R. Among Louisiana Indians. SW,
XXXVII, 656-61. 1908.

Margry, P., ed. Découvertes et établissements des
Francais dans l'ouest et dans le sud de l'Amérique
septentrionale, IV, 174-7. Paris, 1880.

Parenton, V. and Pellegrin, R.J. The "Sabines."
SF, XXIX, 148-154. 1950.

Quimby, G.I. The Bayou Goula Site. FMAS, XLVII,
ii, 1957.

--- The Natchezan Culture Type. AAn, VII, 255-
75. 1942.

Shea, J.G., ed. Early Voyages up and down the
Mississippi, pp. 143-8. Albany, 1861.

Speck, F.G. A List of Plant Curatives obtained from
the Houma Indians of Louisiana. PM, XIV, 49-
73. 1941.

--- A Social Reconnaissance of the Creole Houma
Indian Trappers of the Louisiana Bayous. AI, III,
134-46, 210-20. 1943.

Speck, F.G. and Dexter, R.W. Molluscan Food
Items of the Houma Indians. Nautilus, LX, 34.
1946.

Swanton, J.R. Indian Tribes of the Lower Mississippi
River and Adjacent Coast of the Gulf of Mexico.
BBAE, XLIII, 285-92. 1911.

Thwaites, R.G., ed. The Jesuit Relations and Allied
Documents, LXV, 146-55. Cleveland, 1900.

16. MOBILE

Including the Mobile, Moctobi, Naniba, Pascagoula, Pensacola, and Tomome.

Bandelier, A.F., ed. The Journey of Alvar Nunez Cabeza de Vaca, pp. 41-9. New York, 1905.

Bass, A. James Mooney in Oklahoma. CO, XXXII, 246-62. 1954.

Bourne, E.G., ed. Narratives of the Career of Hernando de Soto, I, 87-98; II, 16-21, 120-8. New York, 1904.

Dumont de Montigny. Memoires historiques sur la Louisiane, I, 243-6. Paris, 1753.

Gatschet, A.S., and Thomas, C. Mobile. BBAE, XXX, i, 916. 1907.

Hamilton, P.J. Colonial Mobile. 2d edit. 594 pp. Boston, 1910.

Lewis, T.M.N. A Florida Burial. WA, n.s., X, 123-8. 1931.

Margry, P., ed. Découvertes et établissements des Français dans l'ouest et dans le sud de l'Amerique septentrionale, V, 388-91. Paris, 1883.

Swanton, J.R. Early History of the Creek Indians and Their Neighbors. BBAE, LXXIII, 143-65. 1922.

--- Indian Tribes of the Lower Mississippi Valley and Adjacent Coast of the Gulf of Mexico. BBAE, XLIII, 302-6. 1911.

Villiers du Terrage, M. de. Documents concernant l'histoire des Indiens de la région orientale de la Louisiane. JSAP, n.s., XIV, 127-40. 1922.

17. MONACAN

Including the Hassinunga, Manahoac, Monacan, Ocaneechi, Ontponea, Saponi, Shackaconia, Stegaraki, Tauxitania, Tegninateo, Tutelo, and Whonkenti.

Alvord, C.W., and Bidgood, L. First Explorations of the Trans-Allegheny Region by the Virginians. 275 pp. Cleveland, 1912.

Anderson, J. The Newly Discovered Relationship of the Tuteloes to the Dakotan Stock. Proceedings of the American Philological Association, III, 15-16. 1872.

Binford, L.R. Comments on the "Siouan Problem." E, VI, 27-41. 1959.

Bushnell, D.I. Discoveries beyond the Appalachian Mountains. AA, n.s., IX, 45-56. 1907.

--- The Five Monacan Towns in Virginia. SMC, LXXXII, xii, 1-38. 1930.

--- Indian Sites below the Falls of the Rappahannock. SMC, XCVI, iv, 1-65. 1937.

--- The Manahoac Tribes in Virginia. SMC, XCIV, viii, 1-56. 1935.

--- Monacan Sites in Virginia. EFWSI, 1930, 211-16.

Bushnell, D.I. Native Cemeteries and Forms of Burial East of the Mississippi. BBAE, LXXI, 122-31. 1920.

--- Virginia before Jamestown. SMC, C, 125-58. 1940.

Byrd, W. The History of the Dividing Line between Virginia and North Carolina. 2 vols. Richmond, 1866.

Coe, J.L. The Cultural Sequence of the Carolina Piedmont. AEUS, 301-11. 1952.

Cringan, A.T. Iroquois Folk Songs. AAR, 1902, 137-52.

Dorsey, J.O. Preface. CNAE, IX, xviii-xxx. 1893.

--- A Study of Siouan Cults. ARBAE, XI, 518-19. 1890.

Douglas, F.H. The Virginia Indian Tribes. DAMLS, LVII, 1-4. 1933.

Frachtenberg, L.J. Contributions to a Tutelo Vocabulary. AA, n.s., XV, 477-9. 1913.

Griffin, J.B. An Interpretation of Siouan Archaeology in the Piedmont of North Carolina and Virginia. AAn, X, 321-30. 1945.

--- On the Historic Location of the Tutelo and the Mohetan in the Ohio Valley. AA, n.s., XLIV, 275-80. 1942.

Hale, H. The Tutelo Tribe and Language. PAPS, XXI, 1-45. 1883.

Hendren, S.R. Government and Religion of the Virginia Indians. Johns Hopkins University Studies in Historical and Political Science, XIII, xi-xii, 3-58. 1895.

Jefferson, T. Notes on the State of Virginia. 244 pp. Philadelphia, 1788.

Kurath, G.P. The Tutelo Fourth Night Spirit Release Singing. MWF, IV, 87-105. 1955.

--- The Tutelo Harvest Rites. SM, LXXVI, 153-62. 1953.

Lawson, J. The History of Carolina, pp. 80-6. New edit. Raleigh, 1860.

Maxwell, H. The Use and Abuse of Forests by the Virginia Indians. William and Mary College Quarterly, XIX, 73-104. 1910.

Miller, C.F. Revaluation of the Eastern Siouan Problem. BBAE, CLXIV, 115-212. 1957.

Milling, C.J. Red Carolinians. 438 pp. Chapel Hill, 1940.

Mooney, J. Monacan. BBAE, XXX, i, 930-1. 1907.

--- Saponi. BBAE, XXX, ii, 464-5. 1910.

--- The Siouan Tribes of the East. BBAE, XXII, 5-101. 1894.

--- Tutelo. BBAE, XXX, ii, 855-6. 1910.

Rights, D.L. The American Indian in North Carolina. 296 pp., Durham, 1947; 318 pp., Winston-Salem, 1957.

Rioux, M. Persistence of a Tutelo Cultural Trait
among the Contemporary Cayuga. BNMC,CXXIII,
72-74. 1951.

Sapir, E. A Tutelo Vocabulary. AA, n.s., XV, 295-
7. 1913.

Smith, J. The Generall Historie of Virginia, New-
England, and the Summer Isles, pp. 129-48. Richmond, 1819.

Speck, F.G. The Question of Matrilineal Descent in
the Southeastern Siouan Area. AA, n.s., XL, 1-
12. 1938.

--- Siouan Tribes of the Carolinas. AA, n.s.,
XXXVII, 201-25. 1935.

--- Tutelo Rituals. Bulletin of the Archeological Society of North Carolina, II, ii, 1-7. 1935.

Speck, F.G., and Herzog, G. The Tutelo Spirit
Adoption Ceremony. 125 pp. Harrisburg, 1942.

Speck, F.G., and Schaeffer, C.E. Catawba Kinship
and Social Organization with a Resume of Tutelo
Kinship Terms. AA, n.s., XLIV, 555-75. 1942.

Strachey, W. The Historie of Travaile into Virginia
Britannia. 203 pp. London, 1849.

--- The Historie of Travell into Virginia Britania.
HSS, CIII, 253 pp. 1953.

Sturtevant, W.C. Siouan Languages in the East.
AA, LX, 738-43. 1958.

Swanton, J.R. Early History of the Eastern Siouan
Tribes. Essays in Anthropology presented to A.L.
Kroeber, pp. 371-81. Berkeley, 1936.

--- New Light on the Early History of the Siouan Peoples. JWAS, XIII, 33-43. 1923.

--- Siouan Tribes and the Ohio Valley. AA, n.s.,
XLV, 49-66. 1943.

Talbot, W,, ed. The Discoveries of John Lederer.
New edit. 30 pp. Rochester, 1902.

Tooker, W.W. The Algonquian Appellatives of the
Siouan Tribes of Virginia. AA, VIII, 376-92. 1895.

--- The Algonquian Names of the Siouan Tribes of
Virginia. 83 pp. New York, 1901.

Wyth (White), J. Portraits to the Life and Manners
of the Inhabitants of that Province in America
called Virginia, 15 pp. New York, 1841.

Willoughby, C.C. The Virginia Indians in the Seventeenth Century. AA, n.s., IX, 57-86. 1907.

18. MOSOPELEA

Including the Chonque, Mosopelea, Ofo, and
Ushpee.

Dorsey, J.O., and Swanton, J.R. A Dictionary of
the Biloxi and Ofo Languages. BBAE, XLVII, 1-
340. 1912.

Griffin, J.B. The Fort Ancient Aspect. 407 pp. Ann
Arbor, 1943.

Holmer, N.M. An Ofo Phonetic Law. IJAL, XIII,
1-8. 1947.

Miller, C.F. Revaluation of the Eastern Siouan Problem. BBAE, CLXIV, 115-212. 1957.

Sturtevant, W.C. Siouan Languages in the East. AA,
LX, 738-43. 1958.

Swanton, J.R. Early History of the Eastern Siouan
Tribes. Essays in Anthropology presented to A.L.
Kroeber, pp. 371-81. Berkeley, 1936.

--- New Light on the Early History of the Siouan Peoples. JWAS, XIII, 33-43. 1923.

--- A New Siouan Dialect. Putnam Anniversary Volume, pp. 477-86. New York, 1909.

--- Siouan Tribes and the Ohio Valley. AA, n.s.,
XLV, 49-66. 1943.

Voegelin, C.F. Ofo-Biloxi Sound Correspondences.
PIAS, XLVIII, 23-6. 1939.

19. NATCHEZ

Including the Avoyel, the Natchez, and the Taensa.

Swanton, J.R. Indian Tribes of the Lower Mississippi
Valley and Adjacent Coast of the Gulf of Mexico.
BBAE, XLIII, 1-274. 1911.

Albrecht, A.C. Ethical Precepts among the Natchez
Indians. LHQ, XXXI, 569-97. 1948.

--- Indian-French Relations at Natchez. AA, n.s.,
XLVIII, 321-54. 1946.

--- The Location of the Historic Natchez Villages.
JMH, VI, 67-8. 1944.

Anonymous. Memoire sur la Louisiane, ou le Mississippi. Recueil A-Z, II (B), 123-52. Luxembourg,
1752.

Baudry des Lozières, L.N. Voyage à la Louisiane.
382 pp. Paris, 1802.

Berthond, A.M. A Sketch of the Natchez Indians.
11 pp. Golden, 1886.

Bossu, M. Nouveaux voyages aux Indes occidentales, I, 37-79. Paris, 1768.

--- Travels through That Part of North America formerly called Louisiana, I, 37-67. London, 1771.

Brinton, D.G. On the Language of the Natchez.
PAPS, XIII, 483-99. 1873.

Brinton, D.G. The Taensa Grammar and Dictionary. AAOJ, VII, 108-13. 1885.

Bushnell, D.I. Native Cemeteries and Forms of Burial East of the Mississippi. BBAE, LXXI, 101-5. 1920.

Calhoun, R.D. The Taensa Indians. LHQ, XVII, 411-35, 642-79. 1934.

Charlevoix, P.F.X.de. Historical Journal. HCL,III, 140-70. 1851.

--- History and General Description of New France, ed. J.M.Shea. 6 vols. New York, 1866-72.

Chateaubriand, F.A.R. Les Natchez. 554 pp. Baltimore, 1932.

Cushman, H.B. History of the Choctaw, Chickasaw and Natchez Indians. 607 pp. Greenville, 1899.

Dumont de Montigny. L'etablissement de la province de la Louisiane. JSAP, n.s., XXIII, 273-440. 1931.

--- Mémoires historiques sur la Louisiane. 2 vols. Paris, 1753.

Ethridge, A.N. Indians of Grant Parish. LHQ,XXIII, 1108-31. 1940.

Ford, J.A. Analysis of Indian Village Site Collections from Louisiana and Mississippi, Louisiana Department of Conservation, Anthropological Studies, II, 1-285. 1936.

Foreman, G. The Last Trek of the Indians, pp. 320-22. Chicago, 1946.

Gatschet, A.S. Removal of the Taensa Indians. AAOJ, XIII, 252-4. 1891.

--- Two Indian Documents. AAOJ, XIII, 249-54. 1891.

Gosselin, A. Les sauvages du Mississipi. ICA, XV, i, 31-51. 1906.

Haas, M.R. Natchez and Chitimacha Clans and Kinship Terminology. AA, n.s., XLI, 597-610. 1939.

--- Natchez and the Muskogean Languages. Lg, XXXII, 61-72. 1956.

Haekel, J. Männerhäuser und Festplatzanlagen in Ozeanien und im östlichen Nordamerika. BA,XXIII, 8-18. 1940.

Hart, C.W.M. A Reconsideration of the Natchez Social Structure. AA, n.s., XLV, 374-86. 1943.

Haumonté, J.D., Parisot, M.J., and Adam, L. Grammaire et vocabulaire de la langue Taensa. 111 pp. Paris, 1882. (A famous forgery.)

Henshaw, H.W., and Swanton, J.R. Natchez. BBAE, XXX, ii, 35-6. 1910.

Humble, S.L. The Ouachita Valley Expedition of DeSoto. LHQ, XXV, 611-43. 1942.

Imbelloni, J. Intorno ai crani "incredibili" degli Indiani Natchez. ICA,XXII, 391-406. 1926.

Jennings, J.D. Prehistory of the Lower Mississippi Valley. AEUS, 256-71. 1952.

Josselin de Jong, J.P.B.de. The Natchez Social System. ICA, XXIII, 553-62. 1928.

Kenton, E., ed. The Indians of North America, II, 425-50. New York, 1927.

Le Page du Pratz. Histoire de la Louisiane. 3 vols. Paris, 1758.

--- The History of Louisiana. 2 vols. London,1763.

Le Petit, M. Relation des Natchez. RVN, IX, 1-79. 1737.

Lounsbury, F.G. Stray Number Systems among Certain Indian Tribes. AA, n.s., XLVIII, 672-5. 1946.

MacLeod, W.C. Natchez Political Evolution. AA, n.s., XXVI, 201-29. 1924.

--- On Natchez Culture Origins. AA, n.s., XXVIII, 409-13. 1926.

Margry, P., ed. Découvertes et établissements des Français dans l'ouest et dans le sud de l'Amérique septentrionale, V, 444-55. Paris, 1883.

Mereness, N.D., ed. Travels in the American Colonies, pp. 47-9. New York, 1916.

Mooney, J. The End of the Natchez. AA, n.s., I, 510-21. 1899.

Morfi, J.A.de. Memorias for the History of the Province of Texas, ed. F.M.Chabot. 85 pp. San Antonio, 1932.

Morice, A.G. Disparus et survivants. BSGQ, XX, 199-221. 1926.

Nuttall, T. A Journal of Travels into the Arkansa Territory, pp. 268-82. Philadelphia, 1821.

Parish, J.C. The Lake of the Taensa. LHQ, V, 201-7. 1922.

Quimby, G.I. Natchez Archaeology. NLSAC, III, iii, 22-4. 1953.

--- Natchez Social Structure as an Instrument of Assimilation. AA, n.s., XLVIII, 134-7. 1946.

--- The Natchezan Culture Type. AAn, VII, 255-75. 1942.

Ross, E.H. and Phelps, O.A., eds. A Journey over the Natchez Trace in 1792. JMH, XV, 252-73. 1953.

Shea, J.G., ed. Early Voyages up and down the Mississippi, pp. 76-86, 136-42. Albany, 1861.

Swadesh, M. Sociologic Notes on Obsolescent Languages. IJAL, XIV, 226-35. 1948.

Swanton, J.R. Animal Stories from the Indians of the Muskhogean Stock. JAFL, XXVI, 192-209. 1913.

--- Early History of the Creek Indians and Their Neighbors. BBAE, LXXIII, 312-16. 1922.

Swanton, J.R. Ethnological Position of the Natchez Indians. AA, n.s., IX, 513-28. 1907.

--- The Language of the Taënsa. AA, n.s., X, 24-32. 1908.

--- The Muskhogean Connection of the Natchez Language. IJAL, III, 46-75. 1924.

--- Myths and Tales of the Southeastern Indians. BBAE, LXXXVIII, 213-66. 1929.

--- Natchez. ERE, IX, 187-91. 1917.

--- Social Organization and Social Usages of the Indians of the Creek Confederacy. ARBAE, XLII, 23-472. 1925.

--- Taensa. BBAE, XXX, ii, 668-9. 1910.

Thwaites, R.G., ed. The Jesuit Relations and Allied Documents, LXV, 134-45; LXVIII, 120-63. Cleveland, 1900.

Tonti, H.de. An Account of Monsieur de la Salle's Last Expedition. CNYHS, II, 217-341. 1814.

--- Relation de la Louisiane, et du Mississippi. RVN, V, 35-195. 1734.

Vinson, J. La langue Taensa. RLPC, XIX, 147-69. 1886.

Walker, W.M. The Troyville Mounds. BBAE, CXIII, 1-73. 1936.

Witthoft, J. Green Corn Ceremonialism in the Eastern Woodlands. OCMA, XIII, 70-77. 1949.

20. PAMLICO

Including the Lumbee (Croatan) and Pamlico.

Anonymous. Moratoc. BBAE, XXX, 942. 1910.

Baxter, J.P. Raleigh's Lost Colony. New England Magazine, n.s., XI, v, 565-87. 1895.

Brickell, J. The Natural History of North-Carolina. Dublin, 1737.

Burrage, H.S., ed. Early English and French Voyages, pp. 230-9. New York, 1906.

Coates, J.R. Native Indians of the Old Dominion State. AmI, II, iv, 22-5. 1945.

Dillard, R. Indian Tribes of Eastern Carolina. North Carolina Booklet, VI, 4-26. 1906.

Estabrook, A.H. and McDougle, I.E. Mongrel Virginians, pp. 188-94. Baltimore, 1926.

Hariot, T. A Brief and True Report of the New Found Land of Virginia. 46 pp. London, 1893.

Harper, R.M. The Most Prolific People in the United States. Eugenical News, XXIII, ii, 29-31. 1938.

--- A Statistical Study of the Croatans. Rural Sociology, II, 444-57. 1937.

Jenkins, P.B. American Indian Cross-Bow. WA, n.s., VIII, iv, 132-5. 1929.

Johnson, G.B. Personality in a White-Indian-Negro Community. ASR, IV, 516-23. 1939.

Kuhm, H.W. The Indians of Virginia. WA, n.s., XI, 91-9. 1932.

Lawrence, R.C. The State of Robeson, pp. 111-20. Lumberton, S.C., 1939.

Lawson, J. The History of Carolina, pp. 277-390. Raleigh, 1860.

McMillan, H. Sir Walter Raleigh's Lost Colony. Wilson, N.C., 1888.

McPherson, O.M. Indians of North Carolina. 252 pp. 63d Congress, 3d Session, Senate Document 677, Washington.

Mook, M.A. The Aboriginal Population of Tidewater Virginia. AA, n.s., XLVI, 193-208. 1944.

--- Algonkian Ethnohistory of the Carolina Sound. JWAS, XXXIV, 181-228. 1944.

--- The Anthropological Position of the Indian Tribes of Tidewater Virginia. William and Mary College Quarterly, n.s., XXIII, 27-40. 1943.

--- A Newly Discovered Algonkian Tribe of Carolina. AA, n.s., XLV, 635-7. 1943.

Mooney, J. Coree. BBAE, XXX, i, 349. 1907.

--- Croatan Indians. BBAE, XXX, i, 365. 1907.

--- Secotan. BBAE, XXX, ii, 494-5. 1910.

--- Weapemeoc. BBAE, XXX, ii, 926-7. 1910.

Ningler, L., ed. Voyages en Virginie et en Floride. 311 pp. Paris, 1927.

Parsons, E.C. Folklore of the Cherokee of Robeson County, North Carolina. JAFL, XXXII, 384-93. 1919.

Rights, D.L. The American Indian in North Carolina. 296 pp., Durham, 1947; 318 pp., Winston-Salem, 1957.

Sams, C.W. The Conquest of Virginia: the Forest Primeval. 432 pp. New York, 1916.

Smith, J. The Generall Historie of Virginia, New-England, and the Summer Isles, pp. 94-9. New edit. Richmond, 1819.

Speck, F.G. The Catawba Nation and its Neighbors. NCHR, XVI, 404-17. 1939.

--- The Ethnic Position of the Southeastern Algonkian. AA, n.s., XXVI, 184-200. 1924.

--- Remnants of the Machapunga Indians of North Carolina. AA, n.s., XVIII, 271-6. 1916.

Swanton, J.R. Probable Identity of the "Croatan" Indians. 5 pp. Office of Indian Affairs, Washington, 1933.

--- Siouan Indians of Lumber River. 6 pp. 73d Congress, 2d Session, House Document 1752, 1934.

Tyler, L.G., ed. Narratives of Early Virginia. New York, 1907.

Willoughby, C.C. The Virginia Indians in the Seventeenth Century. AA, n.s., IX, 57-86. 1907.

Wyth (White), J. Portraits to the Life and Manners of the Inhabitants of That Province in America called Virginia. New edit. New York, 1841.

21. POWHATAN

Speck, F.G. Chapters on the Ethnology of the Powhatan Tribes. INM, I, 227-455. 1928.

--- The Rappahannock Indians of Virginia. INM, V, 25-83. 1925.

Stern, T. Chickahominy. PAPS, XCVI, 157-225. 1952.

Beverley, R. The History and Present State of Virginia. 366 pp. Chapel Hill, 1947.

--- The History of Virginia. 284 pp. London, 1722.

Bibaud, F.M. Biographie des sagamos illustrés de l'Amérique Septentrionale, pp. 65-85. Montreal, 1848.

Blume, G.W.S. Present-day Indians of Tidewater Virginia. QBASV, VI, ii, 1-11. 1951.

Bozman, J.L. The History of Maryland, I, 103-93. Baltimore, 1837.

Burk, J.D. The History of Virginia. 4 vols. Petersburg, 1822.

Bushnell, D.I. Indian Sites below the Falls of the Rappahannock. SMC, XCVI, iv, 1-65. 1937.

--- Virginia before Jamestown. SMC, C, 125-58. 1940.

--- Virginia--from Early Records. AA, n.s., IX, 31-44. 1907.

Coates, J.R. Native Indians of the Old Dominion State. AmI, II, iv, 22-5. 1945.

Cooke, J.E. Virginia, pp. 26-33. 5th edit. Boston, 1884.

Davidson, D.S. Some String Figures of the Virginia Indians. IN, IV, 384-95. 1927.

Douglas, F.H. The Virginia Indian Tribes. DAMLS, LVII, 1-4. 1933.

Dunlap, A.R. A Bibliographical Discussion of the Indian Languages of the Delmarva Peninsula. BASD, IV, v, 2-5. 1949.

Fewkes, V.J. Catawba Pottery-making. PAPS, LXXXVIII, 69-124. 1944.

Forbes, J.D. Anglo-Powhatan Relations to 1676. M, XXX, 179-83; XXXI, 4-7. 1956-1957.

Geary, J.A. The Language of the Carolina Algonkian Tribes. HSS, CV, 873-900. 1955.

Geary, J.A. Strachey's Vocabulary of Indian Words used in Virginia, 1612. HSS, CIII, 208-14. 1953.

Gerard, W.R. The Tapehanek Dialect of Virginia. AA, n.s., VI, 313-30. 1904.

--- Virginia's Contributions to English. AA, n.s., IX, 87-112. 1907.

Gilliam, C.E. Powhatan Algonkian Bird Names. JWAS, XXXVII, 1-2. 1947.

--- Powhatan Sun Worship. QBASV, XII, i, 1-4. 1957.

Harrington, J.P. The Original Strachey Vocabulary of the Virginia Indian Language. BBAE, CLVII, 189-202. 1955.

Hassrick, R., and Carpenter, E. Rappahannock Games and Amusements. PM, XVII, 29-39. 1944.

Hendren, S.R. Government and Religion of the Virginia Indians. Johns Hopkins University Studies in Historical and Political Science, XIII, xi-xii, 3-58. 1895.

Holmes, W.H. Stone Implements of the Potomac-Chesapeake Tidewater Province. ARBAE, XV, 3-152. 1897.

Hough, W. The Indians of the District of Columbia. SM, XXXII, 537-9. 1931.

Howe, H. Historical Collections of Virginia, pp. 135-41. Charleston, 1845.

Jefferson, T. Notes on the State of Virginia. 244 pp. Philadelphia, 1788.

Kuhm, H.W. The Indians of Virginia. WA, n.s., XI, 91-9. 1932.

Lewis, C.M. and Loomie, A.J. The Spanish Jesuit Mission in Virginia, 1570-1572, pp. 231-72. Chapel Hill, 1953.

Lorant, S. The New World. New York, 1946.

Lurie, N.O. Indian Cultural Adjustment to European. In J.M.Smith, ed., Seventeenth-century America, 33-60. Chapel Hill, 1959.

McCary, B.C. Indians in Seventeenth Century Virginia. 93 pp. Williamsburg, 1957.

--- The Kiskiack (Chiskiack) Indians. QBASV, XIII, iii, 7-12. 1959.

Mason, O.T. Anthropological News. AN, XL, 624. 1877.

Maxwell, H. The Use and Abuse of Forests by the Virginia Indians. William and Mary College Quarterly. XIX, 73-104. 1910.

Michelson, T. The Linguistic Classification of Powhatan. AA, n.s., XXXV, 549. 1933.

Mook, M.A. The Aboriginal Population of Tidewater Virginia. AA, n.s., XLVI, 193-208. 1944.

--- The Anthropological Position of the Indian Tribes of Tidewater Virginia. William and Mary College Quarterly, n.s., XXIII, 27-40. 1943.

Mook, M.A. The Ethnological Significance of Tindall's Map of Virginia, 1608. William & Mary College Quarterly, n.s., XXIII, 371-408. 1943.

--- Virginia Ethnology from an Early Relation. William and Mary College Quarterly, n.s., XXIII, 101-29. 1943.

Mooney, J. Chickahominy. BBAE, XXX, i, 259-60. 1907.

--- Indian Tribes of the District of Columbia. AA, II, 259-66. 1889.

--- Pamunkey. BBAE, XXX, ii, 197-9. 1910.

--- Powhatan. BBAE, XXX, ii, 299-302. 1910.

--- The Powhatan Confederacy. AA, n.s., IX, 129-52. 1907.

--- Queene Anne, of the Pamunkeys. BBAE, XXX, ii, 338. 1910.

Newport, C. A Relatyon of the Discovery of Our River. TCAAS, IV, 40-65. 1860.

Pollard, J.G. The Pamunkey Indians of Virginia. BBAE, XVII, 1-19. 1894.

Quinn, D.B., ed. The Roanoke Voyages, 1584-1590. HSS, CIV-CV, 1040 pp. 1955.

Robinson, W.S. Indian Education and Missions in Colonial Virginia. Journal of Southern History, XVIII, 152-68. 1952.

--- Tributary Indians in Colonial Virginia. VM, LXVII, i, 49-64. 1959.

Rose, C.B. The Indians of Arlington. 30 pp. Arlington, Va., 1957.

Rowell, M.K. Pamunkey Indian Games and Amusements. JAFL, LVI, 203-7. 1943.

Sams, C.W. The Conquest of Virginia: the First Attempt. 547 pp. Norfolk, 1924.

--- The Conquest of Virginia: the Forest Primeval. 432 pp. New York, 1916.

Semmes, R. Aboriginal Maryland, 1608-1689. Maryland Historical Magazine, XXIV, 157-72, 195-209. 1929.

Shiner, J.L. A Jamestown Indian Site. QBASV, X, 14-15. 1955.

Smith, J. The Generall Historie of Virginia, New-England, and the Summer Isles, pp. 129-48. New edit. Richmond, 1819.

--- A True Relation of Virginia, ed. C. Deane. 88 pp. Boston, 1866.

--- Works, 1608-1631. 2 vols., revised edition. Edinburgh, 1910.

Speck, F.G. The Ethnic Position of the Southeastern Algonkian. AA, n.s., XXVI, 184-200. 1924.

--- The Gourd Lamp among the Virginia Indians. AA, n.s., XLIII, 676-8. 1941.

Speck, F.G., Hassrick, R.B., and Carpenter, E.S. Rappahannock Herbals, Folk-Lore and Science of Cures. Proceedings of the Delaware County Institute of Science, X, 1-55. 1942.

--- Rappahannock Taking Devices: Traps, Hunting and Fishing. PPAS, I, 1-28. 1946.

Speck, F.G. and Schaeffer, C.E. The Deer and the Rabbit Hunting Drive in Virginia and the Southeast. SIS, II, 3-20. 1950.

Stern, T. Pamunkey Pottery Making. SIS, III, 78 pp. 1951.

Stewart, T.D. Excavating the Indian Village of Patawomeke. EFWSI, 1938, 87-90.

--- Further Excavations at the Indian Village of Patawomeke. EFWSI, 1939, 79-82.

Strachey, W. The Historie of Travaile into Virginia Britannia. 203 pp. London, 1849.

--- The Historie of Travell into Virginia Britania. HSS, CIII, 253 pp. 1953.

Swanton, J.R. Newly Discovered Powhatan Bird Names. JWAS, XXIV, 96-9. 1934.

Tooker, W.W. The Mystery of the Name Pamunkey. AAOJ, XVII, 289-93. 1895.

--- The Names Chickahominy, Pamunkey and the Kuskarawokes of Captain John Smith. 90 pp. New York, 1901.

--- The Powhatan Name for Virginia. AA, n.s., VIII, 23-7. 1906.

Tyler, L.G., ed. Narratives of Early Virginia. New York, 1907.

Tylor, E.B. Notes on Powhatan's Mantle. IAE, I, 215-17. 1888.

Uhler, S.P. Pennsylvania's Indian Relations to 1754. 144 pp. Allentown, 1951.

Weslager, C.A. Indian Tribes of the Delmarva Peninsula. BASD, III, No. v. 1942.

Willoughby, C.C. The Virginia Indians in the Seventeenth Century. AA, n.s., IX, 57-86. 1907.

Wyth (White), J. Portraits to the Life and Manners of the Inhabitants of That Province in America called Virginia. 15 pp. New York, 1841.

22. SEMINOLE

Being a post-Columbian tribe, partly Hitchiti but mainly Creek in origin, the Seminole are not shown on the tribal map.

Capron, L. The Medicine Bundles of the Florida Seminole and the Green Corn Dance. BBAE, CLI, 155-210. 1953.

MacCauley, C. The Seminole Indians of Florida. ARBAE, V, 469-531. 1884.

Spoehr, A. The Florida Seminole Camp. FMAS, XXXIII, 117-150. 1944.

--- Kinship System of the Seminole. FMAS, XXXIII, 31-113. 1942.

Sturtevant, W.C. Accomplishments and Opportunities in Florida Indian Ethnology. PFAS, V; Florida State University Department of Anthropology, Notes in Anthropology, II, 15-55. 1958.

--- The Medicine Bundles and Busks of the Florida Seminole. FA, VII, 31-72. 1954.

Anonymous. Billy Bowlegs and Suite. Gleason's Pictorial Drawing Room Companion, III, xvii, 257. Boston, 1852.

--- Improved Sanitary and Social Conditions of the Seminoles of Florida. American Medical Association Journal, XXVI, 683-4. 1896.

--- Los Indios Seminoles de Florida. Boletin Indigenista, XVII, 140-4. 1957.

--- The Pole Cat, or Shell Dance. Southern Literary Messenger, III, 390-391. 1837.

--- A Sketch of the Indian Tribes known under the Appellation of Muskogees (Seminoles), etc... Monthly Magazine of Religion and Literature, I, 137-47. 1840.

Antle, H.R. Interpretation of Seminole Clan Relationship Terms. CO, XIV, 343-8. 1936.

--- The Legend of Abuska. CO, XX, 255-6. 1942.

Arnett, W.T. Seminole Indian Clues for Contemporary House Form in Florida. FA, VI, 145-48. 1953.

Bartram, W. Observations on the Creek and Cherokee Indians. TAES, III, 3-81. 1853.

--- Travels in Georgia and Florida, 1773-74, ed. F. Harper. TAPS, n.s., XXXIII, 126, 190, 209, 223-6. 1943.

--- The Travels of William Bartram, Naturalist's Edition. 788 pp. New Haven, 1958.

--- Travels through North and South Carolina. London, 1792.

Bell, R.E. and Baerreis, D.A. A Survey of Oklahoma Archeology. BTAPS, XXII, 7-100. 1951.

Blassingame, W. Seminoles of Florida. 48 pp. [Fla. State Dept. of Agriculture, Tallahassee], [1959].

Boyd, M.F. Asi-Yaholo or Osceola. FHSQ, XXXIII, 249-305. 1955.

--- Florida Aflame. 115 pp. Tallahassee, 1951.

--- Historic Sites in and Around the Jim Woodruff Reservoir Area, Florida -Georgia. BBAE, CLXIX, 195-314. 1958.

Boyd, M.F. Horatio S. Dexter and Events Leading to the Treaty of Moultrie Creek with the Seminole Indians. FA, XI, 65-94. 1958.

--- The Seminole War. FHSQ, XXX, 3-115. 1951.

[Brooks, A.M.] "Sylvia Sunshine". Petals Plucked from Sunny Climes. 2d. ed. 495 pp. Nashville, 1886.

Bullen, R.P. An Archaeological Survey of the Chattahoochee River Valley in Florida. JWAS, XL,100-25. 1950.

--- Notes on the Seminole Archaeology of West Florida. NLSAC, III, iii, 18-19. 1953.

Bushnell, D.I. Native Cemeteries and Forms of Burial East of the Mississippi. BBAE, LXXI, 114-16. 1920.

Capron, L. Floridas "Wild" Indians, the Seminole. NGM, CX, 819-40. 1956.

--- Notes on the Hunting Dance of the Cow Creek Seminole. FA, IX, 67-78. 1956.

Casey, R.R. Free Kings of the Everglades. SWL, XVIII, 20-24. 1942.

Church, A. A Dash Through the Everglades. Tequesta, IX, 15-41. 1949.

Coe, C.H. Koontee, the Seminole Bread Root. Scientific American Supplement. Aug. 20, 1898, p. 18929.

--- The Parentage and Birthplace of Osceola. FHSQ, XXVII, 304-11. 1939.

--- Red Patriots. 298 pp. Cincinnati, 1898.

Cohen, M.M. Notices of Florida and the Campaigns. 240 pp. Charleston, 1836.

Cory, C.B. Hunting and Fishing in Florida. 2nd ed. 304 pp. Boston, 1896.

Cotterill, R.S. The Southern Indians. 268 pp. Norman, 1954.

Covington, J.W. Cuban Bloodhounds and the Seminoles. FHSQ, XXXIII, 111-19. 1954.

--- The Story of Southwestern Florida. Vol. 1. New York, 1957.

Covington, J.W. ed. A Petition from Some Latin-American Fishermen, 1838. Tequesta, XIV, 61-65. 1954.

Curtis, E.S. The North American Indian, XIX, 8-11. Norwood, 1930.

Davis, H.J. The History of Seminole Clothing and its Multicolored Designs. AA, LVII, 974-80. 1955.

Davis, H.N. Designs from the Seminoles [and] Sewing Art of the Seminoles. McCall's Needlework and Crafts Annual, VI, 61-3. 1955.

Debo, A. And still the Waters run. 417 pp. Princeton, 1940.

Densmore, F. Recording Indian Music. EFWSI, 1931, 183-90.

--- Recording Seminole Songs in Florida. EFWSI, 1932, 93-6.

--- The Seminole Indian Today. SFQ, XVIII, 212-21. 1954.

--- Seminole Music. BBAE, CLXI, 251 pp. 1956.

--- Seminole Music related to Cocopa. EP, XXXII, 172-3. 1932.

Dimock, A.W., and J.A. Florida Enchantments. New York, 1908.

Drew, F. Notes on the Origin of the Seminole Indians of Florida. FHSQ, VI, 21-4. 1927.

Duncan, A.J. Report of A.J. Duncan, United States Indian Inspector, to the Honorable Secretary of the Interior, in Regard to the Reservation of Lands for the Use of the Seminole Indians of Florida. Report of the Secretary of the Interior for the Fiscal Year Ending June 30, 1898, 204-42. 1898.

Ellis, L.B. The Seminoles of Florida. Gunton's Magazine, XXV, 495-505. New York, 1903.

Emerson, W.C. The Seminoles. 72 pp. New York, 1954.

Erwin, A.T. and Lana, E.P. The Seminole Pumpkin. Economic Botany, X, i, 33-37. 1956.

Foreman, C.T. John Jumper. CO, XXIX, 137-52. 1951.

--- The Jumper Family of the Seminole Nation. CO, XXXIV, 272-85. 1956.

Foreman, G. The Five Civilized Tribes, pp. 223-78. Norman, 1934.

--- Report of Cherokee Deputation into Florida. CO, IX, iv. 1931.

Foster, L. Negro-Indian Relationships in the Southeast. 86 pp. Philadelphia, 1935.

Freeman, E.C. Culture Stability and Change among the Seminoles of Florida. ACISA, V, 248-54. 1960.

--- The Seminole Woman of the Big Cypress and Her Influence in Modern Life. AI, IV, 123-8. 1944.

--- Our Unique Indians the Seminoles of Florida. AmI, II, ii, 14-28. 1944-45.

--- We live with the Seminoles. NH, XLIX, 226-37. 1942.

Gatschet, A.S. A Migration Legend of the Creek Indians, pp. 66-73. Philadelphia, 1884.

Giddings, J.R. The Exiles of Florida. Columbus, O., 1858.

Gifford, J.C. Billy Bowlegs and the Seminole War, 79 pp. Coconut Grove, 1925.

Goggin, J.M. Beaded Shoulder Pouches of the Florida Seminole. FA, IV, 3-17. 1951.

Goggin, J.M. A Florida Indian Trading Post, Circa 1763-1784. SIS, I, ii, 35-37. 1949.

--- Florida's Indians. Economic Leaflets, X, viii. Gainesville, 1951.

--- Osceola. FHSQ, XXXIII, 161-92. 1955.

--- The Present Condition of the Florida Seminoles. NMA, I, 37-9. 1937.

--- Seminole Archaeology in East Florida. NLSAC, III, iii, 16, 19. 1953.

--- The Seminole Negroes of Andros Island, Bahamas. FHSQ, XXIV, 201-6. 1946.

--- Seminole Pottery. In, Prehistoric Pottery of the Eastern United States, [J.B.Griffin, ed.]. 37 pp. [Ann Arbor, 1958.]

--- Silver Work of the Florida Seminole. EP, XLVII, 25-32. 1940.

--- Source Materials for the Study of the Florida Seminole Indians. University of Florida, Anthropology Laboratory, Laboratory Notes, III, 1-19. 1959.

Goggin, J.M. et al. An Historic Indian Burial, Alachua County, Florida. FA, II, i-ii, 10-25. 1949.

Graebner, N.A. Pioneer Indian Agriculture in Oklahoma. CO, XXIII, 232-48. 1945.

--- The Public Land Policy of the Five Civilized Tribes. CO, XXIII, 107-18. 1945.

Greenlee, R.F. Aspects of Social Organization and Material Culture of the Seminole of Big Cypress Swamp. FA, V, 25-32. 1952.

--- Ceremonial Practices of the Modern Seminoles. Tequesta, I, ii, 25-33. 1942.

--- Eventful Happenings among the Modern Florida Seminoles. SFQ, IX, 145-52. 1945.

--- Folktales of the Florida Seminole. JAFL, LVIII, 138-44. 1945.

--- Medicine and Curing Practices of the Modern Florida Seminoles. AA, n.s., XLVI, 317-28. 1944.

Griffin, J.W. Some Comments on the Seminole in 1818. FA, X, iii/iv, 41-49. 1957.

Griffin, J.W., ed. The Florida Indian and His Neighbors, 45-54. Winter Park, 1949.

Hadley, J.N. Notes on the Socio-Economic Status of the Oklahoma Seminoles. Publicazioni del Comitato Italiano per lo Studio dei Problemi della Popolazioni, ser. 3, II, 133-59. 1935.

Hamlin, H. A Health Survey of the Seminole Indians. Yale Journal of Biology and Medicine, VI, 155-77. 1933.

Harrington, M.R. Bad Injun Boy—He Fix 'Em. M, XXVII, v, 185. 1953.

Harrington, M.R. Funko the Slave. M, XX, 169-
  70. 1946.
--- Seminole Adventure. M, XX, 157-9. 1946.
--- Seminole Oranges. M, XX, iv, 112. 1946.
--- Seminole Surgeon. M, XXVII, 122. 1953.
Henshall, J.A. Camping and Cruising in Florida,
  pp. 153-67. Cincinnati, 1884.
Hough, W. Seminoles of the Florida Swamps. Home
  Geographic Monthly, II, iii, 7-12. 1932.
Hoxie, W.J. A Seminole Vocabulary. Atlantic
  Slope Naturalist, I, 64-5. 1903.
Hrdlicka. A. The Anthropology of Florida. PFSHS,
  I, 1-140. 1922.
Huston, W. Los indios Seminolas. Revista Geográfi-
  ca Española, VII, 49-58. 1940.
Krogman, W.M.   The Cephalic Type of the
  Full-Blood and Mixed-Blood Seminole Indians.
  Zeitschrift für Rassenkunde, III, 176-90. 1936.
--- The Physical Anthropology of the Seminole In-
  dians. Publicazioni del Comitato Italiano per lo
  Studio dei Problemi della Popolazione, ser. 3,
  II, 1-199. 1935.
--- The Racial Composition of the Seminole Indians
  of Florida and Oklahoma. JNH, XIX, 412-30.
  1934.
--- The Racial Type of the Seminole Indians of Flori-
  da and Oklahoma. FA, I, iii/iv, 61-73. 1948.
--- Vital Data on the Population of the Seminole In-
  dians. HB, VII, 335-49. 1935.
Laxson, D.D. An Historic Seminole Burial in a
  Hialeah Midden. FA, VII, 111-118. 1954.
McCarthy, J.E. Portraits of Osceola and the Artists
  Who Painted Them. Papers of the Jacksonville His-
  torical Society, II, 23-44. 1949.
McKenzie, B. and Fish, R. The Indian Ball Game as
  Played by the Seminoles. Indian School Journal,
  XVII, ii, 79-81. Chilocco, Okla., 1916.
McReynolds, E.C. The Seminoles. 412 pp. Nor-
  man, 1957.
Madigan, L.V. The Most Independent People. In-
  dian Affairs, XXXI. 1959.
Marchman, W.P. The Ingraham Everglades Exploring
  Expedition, 1892. Tequesta, VII, 3-43. 1947.
[Marmon, K.A.] The Seminole Indians of Florida.
  20 pp. Sherman Institute, Riverside, Calif.,
  1956.
Mercer, H.C. Recent Pile Structures made by Semi-
  nole Indians. AN, XXXI, 357-9. 1897.
Mooney, J. Seminole. BBAE, XXX, ii, 500-2.
  1910.
Moore-Willson, M. History of Osceola County. 59
  pp. Orlando, 1935.

Moore-Willson, M. The Seminole Indians of Florida.
  FHSQ II, 75-87. 1928.
--- Seminoles. ERE, XI, 376-8. 1921.
--- The Seminoles of Florida. New edit. 235 pp.
  New York, 1914.
Morice, A.G. Autres Muskokis. BSGQ, XXI, 211-
  31. 1927.
Motte, J.R. Journey into Wilderness. 361 pp.
  Gainesville, 1953.
Munroe, K. Alligator Hunting with the Seminoles.
  Cosmopolitan, XIII, 576-81. 1892.
--- A Forgotten Remnant. Scribner's Magazine,
  VII, 303-17. 1890.
Nash, R.C. Survey of the Seminole Indians of Flori-
  da. 88 pp. 71st Congress, 3d Session, Senate
  Document 314, Washington, 1931.
N.Y.A. Project. Bibliography on Seminole Indians.
  24 pp. Gainesville, 1940.
Neill, W.T. The Calumet Ceremony of the Semi-
  nole Indians. FA, VIII, 83-8. 1955.
--- Dugouts of the Mikasuki Seminole. FA, VI, 77-
  84. 1953.
--- Florida's Seminole Indians. 81 pp. Silver
  Springs, 1952.
--- Graters of the Mikasuki Seminole. FA, VII, 75-
  6. 1954.
--- The Identity of Florida's "Spanish Indians." FA,
  VIII, ii, 43-57. 1955.
--- A Note on the Seminole Burial from Hialeah,
  Florida. FA, X, iii-iv, 11-13. 1957.
--- Preparation of Rubber by the Florida Seminole.
  FA, IX, 25-28. 1956.
--- Sailing Vessels of the Florida Seminole. FA, IX,
  79-86. 1956.
--- The Site of Osceola's Village. FHSQ, XXXIII,
  240-46. 1955.
--- The Story of Florida's Seminole Indians. Silver
  Springs, 1952.
New Orleans Correspondent. Billy Bowlegs at New
  Orleans. Harper's Weekly, II, lxxvi, 376-378.
  1858.
Ober, F.P. Ten Days with the Seminoles. Apple-
  tons' Journal, XIV, 142-4, 171-3. 1875.
Osceola, B. Operations of the Seminole Tribe of
  Florida as of January 1, 1959. Dania, Florida,
  1959.
Palerm, A. San Carlos de Chachalacas. Cuadernos
  Americanas, LXI, 165-84. 1952.
Peithmann, I.M. The Unconquered Seminole In-
  dians. 95 pp. St. Petersburg, 1956.

Pierce, J. Notices of the Agriculture, Scenery, Geology, and Animal, Vegetable and Mineral Productions of the Floridas, and of the Indian Tribes. American Journal of Science, IX, 119-36. 1825.

Porter, K.W. The Cowkeeper Dynasty of the Seminole Nation. FHSQ, XXX, 341-49. 1952.

--- Farewell to John Horse. Phylon, VIII, 265-273. 1947.

--- Florida Slaves and Free Negroes in the Seminole War, 1835-1842. JNH, XXVIII, 390-421. 1943.

--- The Founder of the "Seminole Nation." FHSQ, XXVII, 362-84. 1949.

--- John Caesar: Seminole Negro Partisan. JNH, XXXI, 190-207. 1946.

--- The Negro Abraham. FHSQ, XXV, 1-43. 1946.

--- Negroes and the Seminole War, 1817-1818. JNH, XXXVI, 249-80. 1951.

--- Notes on Seminole Negroes in the Bahamas. FHSQ, XXIV, 56-60. 1945.

--- Origins of the St. John's River Seminole. FA, IV, 39-45. 1951.

--- Osceola and the Negroes. FHSQ, XXXIII, 235-9. 1955.

--- Seminole Flight from Fort Marion. FHSQ, XXII, 112-133. 1944.

--- Seminole in Mexico, 1850-1861. CO, XXIX, 153-72. 1951.

--- The Seminole in Mexico, 1850-1861. HAHR, XXXI, 1-36. 1951.

--- The Seminole Negro-Indian Scouts, 1870-1881. SWHQ, LV, 358-377. 1952.

Price, W.A. Dental-Caries Incidence in Relation to Nutrition among Past and Present Indians of Florida. Journal of Dental Research, XV, 179-80. 1935.

Read, W.A. Florida Place Names of Indian Origin and Seminole Personal Names. Louisiana State University, University Studies, XI. 1934.

Roberts, A.H. The Dade Massacre. FHSQ, V, 123-138. 1927.

Sears, W.H. A-296 - A Seminole Site in Alachua County. FA, XII, i, 25-30. 1959.

Self, R.D. Chronology of New Echota. EG, I, iv, 3-5. 1955.

Simmons, W.H. Notices of East Florida. 105 pp. Charleston, 1822.

Simpson, J.C. A Provisional Gazetteer of Florida Place-Names of Indian Derivation. Florida Geological Survey, Special Publication, I. Tallahassee, 1956.

Skinner, A. The Florida Seminoles. SW, XL, 154-63. 1911.

--- Notes on the Florida Seminole. AA, n.s., XV, 63-77. 1913.

Small, J.K. Seminole Bread- the Conti. Journal of the New York Botanical Garden, XXII, 121-137. 1921.

Smith, B. Comparative Vocabularies of the Seminole and Mikasuke Tongues. Historical Magazine, 1st ser., X, 239-243. Morrisania, N.Y., 1866.

--- Comparative Vocabularies of the Seminole and Mikasuke Tongues. Indian Miscellany, ed. W.W. Beach, pp. 120-6. Albany, 1877.

[Smith, W.W.] A Lieutenant of the Left Wing. Sketches of the Seminole War. 311 pp. Charleston, 1836.

Spoehr, A. Camp, Clan, and Kin among the Cow Creek Seminole. FMAS, XXXIII, 1-27. 1941.

--- "Friends" among the Seminole. CO, XIX, 252. 1941.

--- Oklahoma Seminole Towns. CO, XIX, 377-80. 1941.

Sprague, J.T. The Origin, Progress, and Conclusion of the Florida War. 559 pp. New York, 1848.

Stephan, L.L. Geographic Role of the Everglades in the Early History of Florida. SM, LV, 515-26. 1942.

Stirling, G. Report on the Seminole Indians of Florida. 9 pp. Applied Anthropology Unit, Office of Indian Affairs, Washington, 1936.

Stirling, R.B. Some Psychological Mechanisms Operative in Gossip. SF, XXXIV, 262-7. 1956.

Sturtevant, W.C. Chakaika and the "Spanish Indians." Tequesta, XIII, 35-73. 1953.

--- Notes on Modern Seminole Traditions of Osceola. FHSQ, XXXIII, 206-217, 1955.

--- Osceola's Coats? FHSQ, XXXIV, 315-28. 1956.

--- R.H. Pratt's Report on the Seminole in 1879. FA, IX, i, 1-24. 1956.

--- A Seminole Personal Document. Tequesta, XVI, 55-75. 1956.

Swanton, J.R. Coonti. AA, XV, 141. 1913.

--- Early History of the Creek Indians and Their Neighbors. BBAE, LXXIII, 398-414. 1922.

--- Modern Square Grounds of the Creek Indians. SMC, LXXXV, viii, 1-46. 1931.

--- Religious Beliefs and Medical Practices of the Creek Indians. ARBAE, XLII, 477-672. 1925.

--- Social Organization and Social Usages of the Indians of the Creek Confederacy. ARBAE, XLII, 23-472. 1925.

Tebeau, C.W. Florida's Last Frontier. Miami, 1957.

Tozier, M.M. Report on the Florida Seminole. 25 pp. Washington, 1954.

U.S. Office of Indian Affairs. Special Report of the Florida Seminole Agency. 67th U.S. Congress, 2nd Session, Senate Document 102. 1921.

Ward, M.M. The Disappearance of the Head of Osceola. FHSQ, XXXIII, 193-201, 1955.

Webb, W.S. The Indian as I Knew Him. E, II, 181-198. 1954.

White, F.F. Macomb's Mission to the Seminoles. FSHQ, XXXV, 130-93. 1956.

Williams, J.L. The Territory of Florida, pp. 209-78. New York, 1837.

W.P.A. Writers' Program. The Seminole Indians in Florida. Florida State Department of Agriculture, Bulletin CVII, ii. 1941.

Yonge, J.C. The White Flag. FHSQ, XXXIII, 218-34. 1955.

23. TIMUCUA

Swanton, J.R. Early History of the Creek Indians and Their Neighbors. BBAE, LXXIII, 320-87. 1922.

Andrews, C.M. The Florida Indians in the Seventeenth Century. Tequesta, I, iii, 36-48. 1943.

Bartram, J. A Description of East Florida. 3d edit. 40 pp. London, 1769.

Bartram, W. Travels in Georgia and Florida, 1773-74, ed. F. Harper. TAPS, n.s., XXXIII, 193-4. 1943.

--- The Travels of William Bartram, Naturalist's Edition. 788 pp. New Haven, 1958.

Basanier, M. L'histoire notable de la Floride. 223 pp. Paris, 1853.

Bourne, E.G., ed. Narratives of the Career of Hernando de Soto, I, 22-30. New York, 1904.

Brinton, D.G. Notes on the Floridian Peninsula, pp. 111-38. Philadelphia, 1859.

Burrage, H.S., ed. Early English and French Voyages, pp. 120-8. New York, 1906.

Bushnell, D.I. Drawing by Jacques Lemoyne de Morgues of Saturioua, a Timucua Chief. SMC, LXXXI, iv, 1-9. 1928.

--- Native Cemeteries and Forms of Burial East of the Mississippi. BBAE, LXXI, 116-22. 1920.

Connor, J.T. Jean Ribault. PFSHS, X, 1-139. 1927.

Dickenson, J. God's Protecting Providence. 7th edit. 136 pp. London, 1790.

--- Narrative of a Shipwreck in the Gulph of Florida. 6th edit. New York, 1803.

Douglass, A.E. A Find of Ceremonial Weapons in a Florida Mound. PAAAS, XXXI, 585-92. 1882.

--- Some Characteristics of the Indian Earth and Shell Mounds on the Atlantic Coast of Florida. AAOJ, VII, 74-82. 1885.

Ehrmann, W.W. The Timucua Indians of Sixteenth Century Florida. FHSQ, XVIII, 168-91. 1940.

Gaffarel, P.L.J. Histoire de la Floride française, pp. 461-3. Paris, 1875.

Gatschet, A.S. The Timucua Language. PAPS, XVI, 626-42; XVII, 490-504; XVIII, 465-502. 1877-80.

--- Volk und Sprache der Timucua. VBGA, 1877, 245-60.

Gatschet, A.S., and Grasserie, R. de la. Textes Timucua. RLPC, XXII, 320-46. 1889.

Geiger, M. The Franciscan Conquest of Florida (1573-1618). Catholic University Studies in Hispanic-American History, I, 1-319. 1937.

Gifford, J.C. Five Plants Essential to the Indians and Early Settlers of Florida. Tequesta, IV, 36-44. 1944.

Goggin, J.M. An Introductory Outline of Timucua Archeology. NLSAC, III, iii, 4-15, 17. 1953.

--- Space and Time Perspective in Northern St. Johns Archeology, Florida. YUPA, XLVII, 1-147. 1952.

Granberry, J. Timucua I. IJAL, XXII, 97-105. 1956.

Grasserie, R. de la. Esquisse d'une grammaire du Timucua. 44 pp. Orleans, n.d.

--- Textes analysés et vocabulaire de la langue Timucua. ICA, VII, 403-37. 1888.

--- Textes en Langue Timucua. 27 pp. Paris, 1890.

--- Vocabulaire Timucua. 16 pp. Orleans, 1892.

Griffin, J.W., and Smith, H.G. Nocoroco. FHSQ, XXVII, 340-61. 1949.

Hakluyt, R. Collection of the Early Voyages, Travels, and Discoveries of the English Nation, III, 612-16. London, 1810.

Harrison, B. Indian Races of Florida. FHSQ, III, 29-37. 1924.

Hrdlicka, A. The Anthropology of Florida. PFSHS, I, 1-140. 1922.

Lanning, J.T. The Spanish Missions of Georgia, pp. 9-32. Chapel Hill, 1935.

La Roncière, C.G., ed. La Floride française. 139 pp. Paris, 1928.

Laudonnière, R. L'histoire notable de la Floride. Paris, 1586.

--- History of Jean Ribault's First Voyage to Florida. HCL, n.s., I, 177-362. 1869.

Laudonnière, R. History of the First Attempt of the French to colonize the Newly Discovered Country of Florida. HCL, n.s., I, 165-75. 1869.

Le Moyne, J. Narrative. Boston, 1875.

Mooney, J. Timucuan Family. BBAE, XXX, ii, 752-4. 1910.

Moore, C.B. Certain Sand Mounds of the St. Johns River. 2 vols. Philadelphia, 1894.

Ningler, L., ed. Voyages en Virginie et en Floride. 311 pp. Paris, 1927.

Pareja, F. Arte de la lengua Timuquana. 129 pp. Paris, 1886.

--- Cathecismo en lengua Castellana y Timuquana. 160 pp. Mexico, 1612.

Pickett, A.J. History of Alabama, I, 54-73. Charleston, 1851.

Ribault, J. Narrative. HCL, ser. 2, II, 170-82. 1875.

Romans, B. A Concise Natural History of East and West Florida. New York, 1775.

Smith, B. Documents in the Spanish and Two of the Early Tongues of Florida. 12 pp. Washington, 1860.

--- The Timuquana Language. HM, II, 1-3. 1858.

Smith, R.M. Anthropology in Florida. FHSQ, XI, 151-72. 1933.

Sparke, J. The Voyage made by Master John Hawkins. Voyages of the Elizabethan Seamen to America, ed. E.J. Payne, I, 55-67. Oxford, 1893.

Stirling, M.W. Florida Cultural Affiliations in Relation to Adjacent Areas. Essays in Anthropology presented to A.L. Kroeber, pp. 351-7. Berkeley, 1936.

Swanton, J.R. The Tawasa Language. AA, XXXI, 435-53. 1929.

--- Terms of Relationship in Timucua. Holmes Anniversary Volume, pp. 451-63. Washington, 1916.

Ternaux-Compans, H. Recueil de pièces sur la Floride. 368 pp. Paris, 1841.

Wenhold, L.L., tr. A 17th Century Letter of Gabriel Diaz Vara Calderon, Bishop of Cuba. SMC, XCV, xvi, 1-14. 1936.

Willey, G.R. Archeology of the Florida Gulf Coast. SMC, CXIII, 624 pp. 1949.

24. TUNICA

Including the Koroa, the Tioux, the Tunica, and the Yazoo.

Anonymous. Tunica. BBAE, XXX, ii, 838-9. 1910.

Bushnell, D.I. Drawings by A. DeBatz in Louisiana. SMC, LXXXV, 1-14. 1927.

Dumont de Montigny. L'établissement de la province de la Louisiane. JSAP, n.s., XXIII, 273-440. 1931.

Ford, J.A. Analysis of Indian Village Site Collections from Louisiana and Mississippi. Louisiana Department of Conservation, Anthropological Studies, II, 1-285. 1936.

Gatschet, A.S. Sex-denoting Nouns in American Languages. Transactions of the American Philological Association, XX, 159-71. 1889.

Gosselin, A. Les sauvages du Mississipi. ICA, XV, i, 31-51. 1906.

Haas, M.R. A Grammatical Sketch of Tunica. VFPA, VI, 337-66. 1946.

--- The Solar Deity of the Tunica. PMA, XXVIII, 531-5. 1942.

--- Tunica. HAIL, IV, 1-143. New York, 1941.

--- Tunica Dictionary. UCPL, VI, 175-332. 1953.

--- Tunica Texts. UCPL, VI, 1-174. 1950.

Harpe, B. de la. Journal historique de l'établissement des Français à la Louisiane, ed. Beaurain. New Orleans, Paris, 1831.

Klingberg, F.J., ed. The Carolina Chronicle of Dr. Francis Le Jau, 1706-1717. UCPH, LIII, 228 pp. 1956.

Margry, P., ed. Découvertes et établissements des Français dans l'ouest et dans le sud de l'Amerique septentrionale. 6 vols. Paris, 1879-88.

Quatrefages, A. de, ed. Les voyages de Moncatch-Apé. RA, X, 593-634. 1881.

Quimby, G.I. The Natchezan Culture Type. AAn, VII, 255-75. 1942.

Shea, J.G. Early Voyages up and down the Mississippi, pp. 77-81, 133-7. Albany, 1861.

Swanton, J.R. Indian Language Studies in Louisiana. EFWSI, 1930, 195-200.

--- Indian Tribes of the Lower Mississippi Valley and Adjacent Coast of the Gulf of Mexico. BBAE, XLIII, 306-36. 1911.

--- Mythology of the Indians of Louisiana and the Texas Coast. JAFL, XX, 285-9. 1907.

--- A Structural and Lexical Comparison of the Tunica, Chitimacha, and Atakapa Languages. BBAE, LXVIII, 1-56. 1919.

--- The Tunica Language. IJAL, II, 1-39. 1921.

Thwaites, R.G., ed. The Jesuit Relations and Allied Documents, LXV, 127-35. Cleveland, 1900.

25. TUSCARORA

Including the Meherrin, the Nottoway, and the Tuscarora.

Wallace, A.F.C. The Modal Personality of the Tuscarora Indians. BBAE, CL, 128 pp. 1951.

Barbeau, M. Iroquoian Clans and Phratries. AA, n. s., XIX, 392-402. 1917.

Barnwell, J. The Tuscarora Expedition. Carolina Historical and Genealogical Magazine, IX, 28-58. 1908.

Bland, E. The Discovery of New Brittaine. Narratives of Early Carolina, ed. A.S. Salley, pp. 1-19. New York, 1911.

Brickell, J. The Natural History of North-Carolina. Dublin, 1737.

Byrd, W. The History of the Dividing Line between Virginia and North Carolina. 2 vols. Richmond, 1866.

Dillard, R. Indian Tribes of Eastern Carolina. North Carolina Booklet, VI, 4-26. 1906.

Douglas, F.H. The Virginia Indian Tribes. DAMLS, LVII, 1-4. 1933.

Fenton, W.N. A Calendar of Manuscript Materials Relating to the History of the Six Nations. PAPS, XCVII, 578-95. 1953.

--- Collecting Materials for a Political History of the Six Nations. PAPS, XCIII, 233-7. 1949.

Goldsborough, E.R. The Aborigines of the Lower Potomac River Valley. PA, VIII, 27-36. 1938.

Graffenried, C. de. Manuscript. The Colonial Records of North Carolina, ed. W.L. Saunders, I, 905-86. Raleigh, 1886.

Hale, H. Indian Migrations as evidenced by Language. AAOJ, V, 18-28. 1883.

Hewitt, J.N.B. Tuscarora. BBAE, XXX, ii, 842-53. 1910.

Johnson, E. Legends, Traditions, and Laws of the Iroquois, or Six Nations, and History of the Tuscarora Indians. Lockport, 1881.

Landy, D. Tuscarora Tribalism and National Identity. E, V, 250-84. 1958.

Lawson, J. The History of Carolina, pp. 277-390. Raleigh, 1860.

Mooney, J. Nottoway. BBAE, XXX, ii, 87. 1910.

Morgan, L.H. The League of the Ho-De-No-Sau-nee or Iroquois, ed. H.M. Lloyd. 2 vols. New York, 1901.

--- Systems of Consanguinity and Affinity. SCK, XVII, 291-382. 1871.

Olbrechts, F.M. De Pronominale Prefixen in het Tuscarora. Donum Natalicium Schrijnen, pp. 154-61. Nimègue-Utrecht, 1929.

Pilling, J.C. Bibliography of the Iroquoian Languages. BBAE, VI, 1-208. 1888.

Rights, D.L. The American Indian in North Carolina. 296 pp., Durham, 1947; 318 pp., Winston-Salem, 1957.

Smith, E.A. Comparative Differences in the Iroquois Group of Dialects. PAAAS, XXX, 315-19. 1881.

--- The Significance of Flora to the Iroquois. PAAAS, XXXIV, 414-11. 1885.

Uhler, S.P. Pennsylvania's Indian Relations to 1754. 144 pp. Allentown, 1951.

Wallace, A.F.C. Some Psychological Determinants of Culture Change in an Iroquoian Community. BBAE, CXLIX, 55-76. 1951.

--- The Tuscaroras. PAPS, XCIII, 159-65. 1949.

Wallace, A.F.C. and Reyburn, W.D. Crossing the Ice. IJAL, XVII, 42-7. 1951.

26. YAMASEE

Including the Guale, the Yamacraw, and the Yamasee.

Barcia Carballido y Zuniga, A.G. Ensayo cronológica para la historia general de la Florida, pp. 170-2. Madrid, 1723.

Bartram, W. Travels in Georgia and Florida, 1773-74, ed. F. Harper. TAPS, n.s., XXXIII, 191-3. 1943.

--- The Travels of William Bartram, Naturalist's Edition. 788 pp. New Haven, 1958.

Caldwell, J.R. The Archeology of Eastern Georgia and South Carolina. AEUS, 312-21. 1952.

Geiger, M. The Franciscan Conquest of Florida (1573-1618). Catholic University Studies in Hispanic-American History. I, 1-319. 1937.

Jones, C.C. Historical Sketch of Tomo-chi-chi, Mico of the Yamacraws. Albany, 1868.

Klingberg, F.J., ed. The Carolina Chronicle of Dr. Francis Le Jau, 1706-1717. UCPH, LIII, 228 pp. 1956.

Lanning, J.T. The Spanish Missions of Georgia, pp. 9-32. Chapel Hill, 1935.

Milling, C.J. Red Carolinians. 438 pp. Chapel Hill, 1940.

Mooney, J. Yamasee. BBAE, XXX, ii, 986-7. 1910.

Palerm, A. San Carlos de Chachalacas. Cuadernos Americanos, Año XI, LXI, i, 165-84. 1952.

Swanton, J.R. Early History of the Creek Indians and Their Neighbors. BBAE, LXXIII, 80-109. 1922.

Zubillaga, F. La Florida. 473 pp. Rome, 1941.

27. YUCHI

Including the Westo and the Yuchi.

Speck, F.G. Ethnology of the Yuchi Indians. UPMAP, I, 1-154. 1909.

Bauxar, J.J. Yuchi Ethnoarchaeology. E, IV, 279-302, 369-464. 1957.

Benveniste, E. La Négation en Yuchi. Word, VI, 99-105. 1950.

Crane, V.S. An Historical Note on the Westo Indians. AA, n.s., XX, 331-7. 1918.

Foreman, C.T. The Yuchi: Children of the Sun. CO, XXXVII, 480-96. 1959/60.

Gatschet, A.S. Some Mythic Stories of the Yuchi Indians. AA, VI, 279-82. 1893.

Haas, M.R. The Proto-Gulf Word for Water. IJAL, XVII, 71-9. 1951.

Hawkins, B.H. A Sketch of the Creek Country. CGHS, III, i, 61-3. 1848.

Milling, C.J. Red Carolinians. 438 pp. Chapel Hill, 1940.

Neill, W.T. An Historic Indian Burial from Columbia County, Georgia. SIS, VII, 3-9. 1955.

Russell, O.B. Notes on Chief Samuel William Brown, Jr., Yuchi. CO, XXXVII, 497-501. 1959/60.

Speck, F.G. Ceremonial Songs of the Creek and Yuchi Indians. UPMAP, I, 157-245. 1911.

--- Eggan's Yuchi Kinship Interpretations. AA, n.s., XLI, 171-2. 1939.

--- Yuchi. BBAE, XXX, ii, 1003-7. 1910.

Swanton, J.R. Early History of the Creek Indians and Their Neighbors. BBAE, LXXIII, 184-91, 286-312. 1922.

--- Identity of the Westo Indians. AA, n.s., XXI, 213-16. 1919.

--- Social Organization and Social Usages of the Indians of the Creek Confederacy. ARBAE, XLII, 23-472. 1925.

Wagner, G. Yuchi. HAIL, III, 293-384. 1934.

--- Yuchi Tales. PAES, XIII, 1-357. 1931.

Wolff, H. Yuchi Phonemes and Morphemes. IJAL, XIV, 240-43. 1948.

--- Yuchi Text with Analysis. IJAL, XVII, 48-53. 1951.

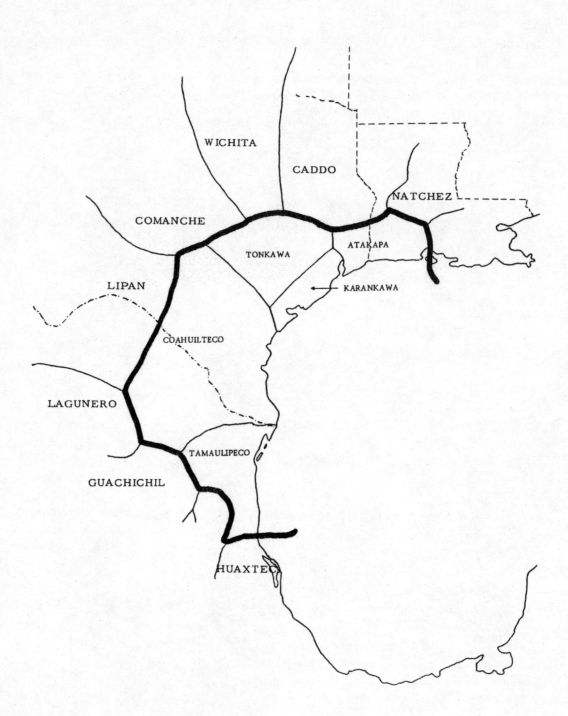

The tribes of this area are grouped under the following linguistic stocks:

Hokan: Coahuilteco, Karankawa, Tonkawa.

Tamaulipecan: Tamaulipeco.

Tunican: Atakapa (probably).

Bancroft, H.H. The Native Races of the Pacific States, I, 615-44. New York, 1875.

Bandelier, A.F., ed. The Journey of Alvar Nunez de Vaca. 230 pp. New York, 1922.

Beals, R.L. The Comparative Ethnology of Northern Mexico. IA, II, 93-225. 1932.

Bollaert, W. Observations on the Indian Tribes in Texas. JESL, II, 262-83. 1850.

Bolton, H.E. Texas in the Middle Eighteenth Century. UCPH, III, 1-501. 1915.

Cortes Alonso, V. Noticias sobre las tribus de las Costas de Tejas durante el Siglo XVIII. Trabajos y Conferencias del Seminario de Estudios Americanistas, IV, 133-40. 1954.

Haas, M.R. A New Linguistic Relationship in North America. SJA, XIV, 231-64. 1958.

--- The Proto-Gulf Word for Land. IJAL, XVIII, 238-40. 1952.

--- The Proto-Gulf Word for Water. IJAL, XVII, 71-9. 1951.

Hrdlicka, A. Catalogue of Human Crania in the United States National Museum Collections. PUSNM, LXXXVII, 315-464. 1940.

Jackson, A.T. Ornaments of East Texas Indians. BTAPS, VII, 11-28. 1935.

--- Picture-Writing of Texas Indians. University of Texas Publications, Anthropological Papers, II, 1-490. 1938.

Jimenez Moreno, W. Tribus e Idiomas del Norte de Mexico. In, El Norte de Mexico y el Sur de Estados Unidos, 121-33. Mexico, 1943.

Kirchhoff, P. Los Recolectores-Cazadores del Norte de Mexico. In, El Norte de Mexico y el Sur de Estados Unidos, 133-44. Mexico, 1943.

Krieger, A.D. Food Habits of Texas Coastal Indians in the Early Sixteenth Century. BTAPS, XXVII, 47-58. 1956.

Kunkel, P.A. The Indians of Louisiana about 1700. LHQ, XXXIV, 175-204. 1951.

Mason, J.A. The Place of Texas in Pre-Columbian Relationships between the United States and Mexico. BTAPS, VII, 29-46. 1935.

Morfi, J.A.de. Memorias for the History of the Province of Texas, ed. F.M.Chabot. 85 pp. San Antonio, 1932.

O'Rourke, T.P. The Franciscan Missions in Texas (1690-1793). Catholic University of America, Studies in American Church History, V, 107pp. 1927.

Sapir, E. The Hokan and Coahuiltecan Languages. IJAL, I, 280-90. 1920.

Sibley, J. A Report from Natchitoches in 1807. INM, n.s., XXV, 5-102. 1922.

Smith, R.A. Account of the Journey of Bénard de la Harpe. SWHQ, LXII, 75-86, 246-59, 371-82, 525-41. 1958-59.

Swanton, J.R. Linguistic Position of the Tribes of Southern Texas and Northeastern Mexico. AA, n.s., XVII, 17-40. 1915.

--- Relations between Northern Mexico and the Southeast of the United States from the Point of View of Ethnology and History. In, El Norte de Mexico y el Sur de Estados Unidos, 259-76. Mexico, 1943.

Taylor, V.H. and Hammons, J. The Letters of Antonio Martinez. 374 pp. Austin, 1957.

Weitlaner, R.J. Las Lenguas del Sur de Estados Unidos y el Norte de Mexico. In, El Norte de Mexico y el Sur de Estados Unidos, 181-5. Mexico, 1943.

1. ATAKAPA

Including the Akokisa, the Atakapa, and the Opelousa.

Bolton, H.E. Athanase de Mézières and the Louisiana-Texas Frontier. 2 vols. Cleveland, 1914.

Bossu, M. Travels through That Part of North America formerly called Louisiana, I, 337-45. London, 1771.

Burch, M.C. The Indigenous Indians of the Lower Trinity Area of Texas. SWHQ, LX, 36-52. 1956.

Bushnell, D.I. Drawings by A. DeBatz in Louisiana. SMC, LXXX, v, 1-14. 1927.

Campbell, T.N. Archeological Investigations at the Caplen Site, Galveston County, Texas. TJS, IX, 448-471. 1957.

Dyer, J.O. The Lake Charles Atakapas. Galveston, 1917.

Gatschet, A.S., and Swanton, J.R. A Dictionary of the Atakapa Language. BBAE, CVIII, 1-181. 1932.

Hewitt, J.N.B. Attacapa. BBAE, XXX, i, 114-15. 1907.

Newcomb, W.W. A Reappraisal of the "Cultural Sink" of Texas. SJA, XII, 145-53. 1956.

Sayles, E.B. An Archaeological Survey of Texas. Medallion Papers, XVII, 1-164. 1935.

Swadesh, M. Atakapa-Chitimacha *k^W. IJAL, XIII, 120-1. 1947.

Swadesh, M. Phonologic Formulas for Atakapa-
Chitimacha. IJAL, XII, 113-32. 1946.

Swanton, J.R. Indian Language Studies in Louisiana.
EFWSI, 1930, 195-200.

--- Indian Tribes of the Lower Mississippi Valley and
Adjacent Coast of the Gulf of Mexico. BBAE, XLIII,
360-4. 1911.

--- Indians of the Southeastern United States. BBAE,
CXXXVII, 11-830. 1946.

--- Mythology of the Indians of Louisiana and the
Texas Coast. JAFL, XX, 285-9. 1907.

--- A Sketch of the Atakapa Language. IJAL, V,
121-49. 1929.

--- A Structural and Lexical Comparison of the Tunica, Chitimacha, and Atakapa Languages. BBAE,
LXVIII, 1-56. 1919.

Villiers du Terrage, M. de, and Rivet, P. Les Indiens du Texas. JSAP, n.s., XI, 403-42. 1919.

Wheat, J.B. The Addicks Dam Site. BBAE, CLIV,
143-252. 1953.

2. COAHUILTECO

Including the Alasapa, Borrado, Comecrudo, Mescale, Orejone, Pakawa, Pampopa, Pausane,
Pihuique, Sanipao, Tacame, Tilijayo, and Venado.

Anderson, A.E. Artifacts of the Rio Grande Delta Region. BTAPS, IV, 29-31. 1932.

Bishop, M. The Odyssey of Cabeza de Vaca. 306
pp. New York, 1933.

Gatschet, A.S., and Thomas, C. Coahuiltecan.
BBAE, XXX, i, 314-15. 1907.

Haas, M.R. The Proto-Hokan-Coahuiltecan Word
for "Water." UCPL, X, 57-62. 1954.

Martin, G.C. The Indian Tribes of the Mission
Nuestra Senora del Refugio. 82 pp. San Antonio,
1936.

Newcomb, W.W. A Reappraisal of the "Cultural
Sink" of Texas. SJA, XII, 145-53. 1956.

Opler, M.E. The Use of Peyote by the Carrizo and
Lipan Apache Tribes. AA, n.s., XL, 271-85.
1938.

Ruecking, F. Bands and Band-Clusters of the Coahuiltecan Indians. Student Papers in Anthropology,
I, ii, 1-24. 1954.

--- Ceremonies of the Coahuiltecan Indians of Southern Texas. TJS, VI, 330-9. 1954.

--- The Economic System of the Coahuiltecan Indians of Southern Texas. TJS, V, 480-97. 1953.

Ruecking, F. The Social Organization of the Coahuiltecan Indians of Southern Texas. TJS, VII,
357-88. 1955.

Sapir, E. The Hokan and Coahuiltecan Languages.
IJAL, I, 280-90. 1920.

Sayles, E.B. An Archaeological Survey of Texas.
Medallion Papers, XVII, 1-164. 1935.

Swanton, J.R. Linguistic Material from the Tribes
of Southern Texas and Northeastern Mexico. BBAE,
CXXVII, 1-145. 1940.

Villiers du Terrage, M. de, and Rivet, P. Les Indiens
du Texas. JSAP, n.s., XI, 403-42. 1919.

3. KARANKAWA

Gatschet, A.S. The Karankawa Indians. PMP, I,
ii, 5-103. 1891.

Atkinson, M.J. The Texas Indians, pp. 193-207.
345 pp. San Antonio, 1935.

Bedichek, R. Karankaway Country. Southwest Review, XXXV, 259-64. 1950.

Bishop, M. The Odyssey of Cabeza de Vaca. 306 pp.
New York, 1933.

Bolton, H.E. Athanase de Mézières and the Louisiana-Texas Frontier. 2 vols. Cleveland, 1914.

Burch, M.C. The Indigenous Indians of the Lower
Trinity Area of Texas. SWHQ, LX, 36-52. 1956.

Clauser, C.E. The Relationship between a Coastal
Algonkin and a Karankawa Cranial Series. PIAS,
LVII, 18-23. 1948.

Fletcher, A.C. Coaque. BBAE, XXX, i, 315-16.
1907.

Fletcher, A.C., and Swanton, J.R. Karankawa.
BBAE, XXX, i, 657-8. 1907.

Gatschet, A.S. Die Karankawa-Indianer. Globus,
XLIX, 123-5. 1886.

Martin, G.C. The Indian Tribes of the Mission
Nuestra Señora del Refugio. 82 pp. San Antonio,
1936.

--- Notes on Some Texas Coast Campsites and Other
Remains. BTAPS, I, 50-7. 1929.

--- Texas Coast Pottery. BTAPS, III, 53-6. 1931.

Newcomb, W.W. A Reappraisal of the "Cultural
Sink" of Texas. SJA, XII, 145-53, 1956.

Potter, W.H. Ornamentation on the Pottery of the
Texas Coastal Tribes. BTAPS, II, 41-4. 1930.

Roessler, A.R. Antiquities and Aborigines of Texas.
ARSI, 1881, 613-16.

Sayles, E.B. An Archaeological Survey of Texas.
Medallion Papers, XVII, 1-164. 1935.

Schaedel, R.P.   The Karankawa of the Texas Gulf
Coast. SJA, V, 117-37. 1949.

Straley, W. The Karankawas. National Archaeological News, I, viii, 5-11. 1937.

Swanton, J.R. Linguistic Material from the Tribes
of Southern Texas and Northeastern Mexico. BBAE,
CXXVII, 124-33. 1940.

Villiers du Terrage, M. de, and Rivet, P. Les Indiens du Texas. JSAP, n.s., XI, 403-42. 1919.

4. TAMAULIPECO

Beals, R.L. The Comparative Ethnology of Northern
Mexico. IA, II, 93-225. 1932.

Lopez Prieto, A. Historia y estadistica del estado de
Tamaulipas. Mexico, 1873.

MacNeish, R.S. Preliminary Archaeological Investigations in the Sierra de Tamaulipas. TAPS, n.s.,
XLIV, vi, 210 pp. 1958.

Martin, G.C. The Indian Tribes of the Mission
Niestra Señora del Refugio. 82 pp. San Antonio,
1936.

Saldivar, G. Historia Compendiada de Tamaulipas.
358 pp. Mexico, 1945.

--- Los Indios de Tamaulipas. In El Norte de Mexico y el Sur de Estados Unidos, 49-52. Mexico,
1943.

--- Los Indios de Tamaulipas. PIPGH, LXX, 36 pp.
1943.

5. TONKAWA

Including the Cava, Emet, Ervipiame, Mayeye,
Sana, Tohaha, Toho, Tonkawa, Yguase, and
Yojuane.

Atkinson, M.J. The Texas Indians, pp. 211-24.
San Antonio, 1935.

Bishop, M. The Odyssey of Cabeza de Vaca. 306
pp. New York, 1933.

Bolton, H.E. Athanase de Mézières and the Louisiana-Texas Frontier. 2 vols. Cleveland, 1914.

--- Sana. BBAE, XXX, ii, 422-3. 1910.

--- Tonkawa. BBAE, XXX, ii, 778-83. 1910.

--- Yojuane. BBAE, XXX, ii, 998-9. 1910.

Borgström, C.H. Tonkawa and Indo-European Vowel
Gradation. Norsk Tidsskrift for Sprogvidenskap,
XVII, 119-28. 1954.

Fletcher, A.C. Yguases. BBAE, XXX, ii, 997. 1910.

Foreman, G. The Last Trek of the Indians, pp. 286-
90. Chicago, 1946.

Gatschet, A.S. Remarks upon the Tónkawa Language. PAPS, XVI, 318-27. 1876.

--- Die Sprache der Tonkawas. ZE, IX, 64-73.
1877.

--- Zwölf Sprachen aus dem Südwesten Nordamerikas. 150 pp. Weimar, 1876.

Haas, M.R. Tonkawa and Algonquian. Anthropological Linguistics, I, ii, 1-6. 1959.

Hoijer, H. Analytical Dictionary of the Tonkawa
Language. UCPL, V, 1-74. 1949.

--- Tonkawa. VFPA, VI, 239-311. 1946.

--- Tonkawa. HAIL, III, 1-148. 1931.

--- Tonkawa Syntactic Suffixes and Anaphoric Parti-
cles. SJA, V, 37-55. 1949.

Howard, J.H. A Tonkawa Peyote Legend. MNUSD,
XII, iv, 1-4. 1951.

Mooney, J. Our Last Cannibal Tribe. Harper's
Magazine. September, 1901.

--- Die Tonkawas. Globus, LXXXII, 76-9. 1902.

Nance, B.H. D.A. Nance and the Tonkawa Indians.
WTHAY, XXVIII, 87-95. 1952.

Newcomb, W.W. A Reappraisal of the "Cultural
Sink" of Texas. SJA, XII, 145-53. 1956.

Opler, M.E. A Description of a Tonkawa Peyote
Meeting. AA, n.s., XLI, 433-9. 1939.

Roessler, A.R. Antiquities and Aborigines of Texas.
ARSI, 1881, 613-16.

Sayles, E.B. An Archaeological Survey of Texas.
Medallion Papers, XVII, 1-164. 1935.

Sjoberg, A.F. The Culture of the Tonkawa. TJS,
V, 280-304. 1953.

Villiers du Terrage, M. de, and Rivet, P. Les Indiens du Texas. JSAP, n.s., XI, 403-42. 1919.

XV. SOUTHWEST

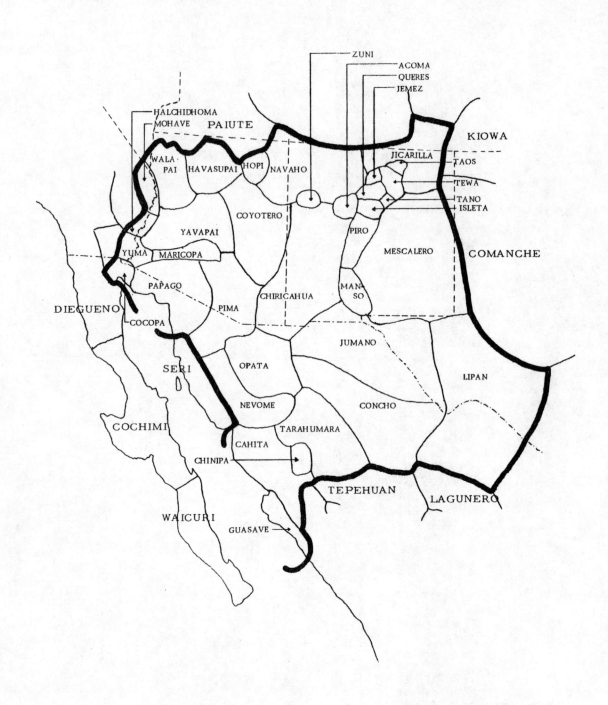

The tribes of this area are grouped under the following linguistic stocks:

Athapaskan: Chiricahua, Coyotero, Jicarilla, Lipan, Mescalero, Navaho.

Hokan (Yuman branch): Cocopa, Halchidhoma, Havasupai, Maricopa, Mohave, Walapai, Yavapai, Yuma.

Keresan: Acoma, Queres.

Tanoan: Isleta, Jemez, Manso (uncertain), Piro, Tano, Taos, Tewa.

Uto-Aztekan: (Piman branch) Nevome, Papago, Pima; (Shoshonean branch) Hopi; (Taracahitian branch) Cahita, Chinipa, Concho, Guasave (probably), Jumano (uncertain), Opata, Tarahumara.

Zunian: Zuni.

Abel, A.H., ed. Indian Affairs in New Mexico under the Administration of William Carr Lane. NMHR, XVI, 206-32, 328-58. 1941.

Aberle, S.D. The Pueblo Indians of New Mexico. MAAA, LXX, 1-93. 1948.

Adair, J. Navaho and Pueblo Silversmiths. 220 pp. Norman, 1944.

--- The Navajo and Pueblo Veteran. AmI, IV, i, 5-11. 1947.

Adams, E.B. Bishop Tamaron's Visitation of New Mexico, 1760. NMHR, XXVIII, 81-114, 192-221, 291-315; XXIX, 41-7. 1953-54.

Alexander, H.B. Pueblo Indian Painting. Nice, 1932.

--- The Ritual Dances of the Pueblo Indians. Denver, 1927.

Allen, F.W., and Larsen, H.D. Heredity of Agglutinogens M and N among Pueblo and Blackfeet Indians. Journal of Immunology, XXXII, 301-5. 1937.

Allen, F.W., and Schaeffer, W. The Distribution of the Human Blood Groups among the Navajo and Pueblo Indians. UNMBB, IV, ii, 3-29. 1935.

Amsden, C.A. Arts and Crafts of the Southwestern Indians. M, XV, 74-80. 1941.

--- Prehistoric Southwesterners from Basketmaker to Pueblo. 163 pp. Los Angeles, 1949.

Anderson, F.G. Intertribal Relations in the Pueblo Kachina Cult. ACISA, V, 377-83. 1960.

--- The Pueblo Kachina Cult. SJA, XI, 404-19. 1955.

Andrews, E. Military Surgery among the Apache Indians. Chicago Medical Examiner, X, 599-601. 1869.

Anonymous. The All-Pueblos Council. United Pueblos Quarterly Bulletin, I, No. vi. 1940.

Applegate, F.G. Native Tales of New Mexico. 263 pp. Philadelphia, 1932.

Ariss, R. Distribution of Smoking Pipes in the Pueblo Area. NMA, III, 53-7. 1939.

Armstrong, S.C. Indian Reservations of the Southwest. 28 pp. Philadelphia, 1884.

Ayer, Mrs. E.E., ed. The Memorial of Fray Alonso de Benavides. LS, XIII, 277-90, 337-40, 345-58, 419-20, 435-44; XIV, 39-52, 137-48, 227-32. 1900-01.

--- The Memorial of Fray Alonso de Benavides. 309 pp. Chicago, 1916.

Baldwin, P.M. Fray Marcos de Niza and His Discovery of the Seven Cities of Cibola. NMHR, I, 193-223, 1926.

Bancroft, H.H. The Native Races of the Pacific States, I, 471-614. New York, 1875.

Bandelier, A.F. Contributions to the History of the Southwestern Portion of the United States. PAIA, V, 1-206. 1890.

--- Documentary History of the Rio Grande Pueblos. Papers of the School of American Research (Archaeology), XIII, 1-27. 1910.

--- Documentary History of the Rio Grande Pueblos. NMHR, IV, 303-34; V, 38-66, 154-85, 240-62, 333-85. 1929-30.

--- Final Report of Investigations among the Indians of the Southwestern United States. PAIA, III, 1-323; IV, 1-591. 1890-92.

--- The Gilded Man. 302 pp. New York, 1893.

--- Historical Introduction to Studies among the Sedentary Indians of New Mexico. PAIA, I, 1-33. 1881.

--- Kin and Clan. NMHR, VIII, 165-75. 1933.

--- The "Montezuma" of the Pueblo Indians. AA, V, 319-26. 1892.

Bandelier, A.F., and F.R. Historical Documents relating to New Mexico, Nueva Viscaya, and Approaches thereto, ed. C.W. Hackett. 3 vols. Washington, 1923-37.

Bandelier, A.F., and Hewitt, E.L. Indians of the Rio Grande Valley. 274 pp. Albuquerque, 1937.

Barber, B. A Socio-Cultural Interpretation of the Peyote Cult. AA, n.s., XLIII, 673-5. 1941.

Barber, E.A. On the Ancient and Modern Pueblo Tribes. AN, XI, 591-9. 1877.

--- Pueblo Pottery. AN, XV, 453-62. 1881.

Barker, G.C. Some Functions of Catholic Processions in Pueblo and Yaqui Culture Change. AA, LX, 449-55. 1958.

Bartlett, K. The Distribution of the Indians of Arizona in 1848. P, XVII, 41-5. 1945.

Bartlett, K. The Indians of Northern Arizona.
  MNMNA, V, 65-71. 1933.

Baumann, G. Frijoles Canyon Pictographs. 43 pp.
  Santa Fe, 1939.

Beals, R.L. The Comparative Ethnology of Northern
  Mexico. IA, II, 93-225. 1932.

--- An Ecological Interpretation of the Southwestern
  Culture Area. EAMG, 255-60. 1956.

--- Northern Mexico and the Southwest. In, El
  Norte de Mexico y el Sur de Estados Unidos, 191-9.
  Mexico, 1943.

--- Preliminary Report on the Ethnography of the
  Southwest. 120 pp. Berkeley, 1935.

--- Relations between Meso America and the Southwest. In, El Norte de Mexico y el Sur de Estados
  Unidos, 245-52. Mexico, 1943.

Beidleman, R.C. Ethno-zoology of the Pueblo Indians in Historic Times. SWL, XXII, 5-13, 17-
  28. 1956.

Bell, W.A. New Tracks in North America. 2 vols.
  London, 1869.

--- On the Native Races of New Mexico. JESL, n.s.,
  I, 222-74. 1869.

Bell, W.H., and Castetter, E.F. The Utilization of
  Mesquite and Screwbean by the Aborigines in the
  American Southwest. UNMBB, V, ii, 3-55. 1937.

--- The Utilization of Yucca, Sotol, and Beargrass
  by the Aborigines in the American Southwest.
  UNMBB, V, v, 74 pp. 1941.

Benedict, R. Psychological Types in the Cultures of
  the Southwest. ICA, XXIII, 572-81. 1928.

Bennett, J.W. The Interpretation of Pueblo Culture.
  SJA, II, 361-374. 1946.

Berry, R.V.S. American Indian Inter-tribal Indian
  Art. AAA, XXXII, v-vi. 1931.

Bewley, M. A Résumé of the Pre-Civil War Indian
  Situation in New Mexico. University of New Mexico, Research, III, i, 33-41. 1939.

Biasutti, R. Le Razzi e i Popoli della Terra, 2nd ed.,
  IV, 445-53. Torino, 1957.

Biggs, B. Testing Intelligibility among Yuman Languages. IJAL, XXIII, 57-62. 1957.

Birket-Smith, K. An Early American Skin Garment
  in the Danish National Museum. MPR, i, 219-26.
  1958.

Blackwood, B. A Study of Mental Testing in Relation
  to Anthropology. Mental Measurement Monographs,
  IV, 1-120. 1927.

Bleeker, S. The Pueblo Indians. New York, 1955.

Bloom, L.B. Bourke on the Southwest. NMHR, VIII,
  1-30; IX, 33-77, 159-83, 273-89, 375-435; X,
  1-35, 271-322; XI, 77-122, 188-207, 217-82;
  XII, 41-77, 337-79; XIII, 192-238. 1933-38.

Bloom, L.B. Early Bridges in New Mexico. EP,
  XVIII, 163-75. 1925.

--- Early Weaving in New Mexico. NMHR, II, 228-
  38. 1927.

Bolton, H.E. Pageant in the Wilderness. UHQ, XVIII,
  283 pp. 1950.

--- Rim of Christendom, a Biography of Eusebio
  Francisco Kino. 627 pp. New York, 1936.

--- Spanish Exploration in the Southwest, 1542-
  1706. New York, 1916.

Bourke, J.G. The Snake Ceremonials at Walpi. AA,
  VIII, 192-6. 1895.

Bradley, C.E. Yerba de la Fleche. Economic Botany, X, 362-6. 1956.

Brayer, H.O. Pueblo Indian Land Grants of the "Rio
  Abajo." University of New Mexico Bulletin, Historical Series, I, i, 1-135. 1938.

Brewer, I.W. Tuberculosis among the Indians of
  Arizona and New Mexico. New York Medical
  Journal, LXXXIV, 981-3. 1906.

Bright, W.L. A Note on Southwestern Words for
  Cat. IJAL, XXVI, 167-8. 1960.

Bryan, K. Pre-Columbian Agriculture in the Southwest as Conditioned by Periods of Alluviation. Proceedings of the Eighth American Scientific Congress, II, 57-74. 1942.

Bunker, R. Other Men's Skies. 256 pp. Bloomington, 1956.

Burbank, E.A., and Royce, E. Burbank among the
  Indians, pp. 57-87. Caldwell, 1946.

Buschmann, J.C.E. Die Verwandtschafts-Verhältnisse der athapaskischen Sprachen. AKAWB, 1862,
  ii, 195-252. 1863.

--- Die Völker und Sprachen Neu-Mexico's und der
  Westseite des britischen Nordamerika. AKAWB,
  1857, 209-404.

Bushnell, G.H.S. and Digby, A. Ancient American
  Pottery. 64 pp. London, 1955.

Byrne, E. The Pueblo Indians of New Mexico. America, LXXXII, 717-19. 1950.

Campa, A.L. Piñon as an Economic and Social Factor. New Mexico Business Review, I, 144-7. 1932.

Carroll, H.B. The Texan Santa Fe Trail. PPHR,
  XXIV, 1-201. 1954.

Carter, G.F. Plant Geography and Culture History in
  the American Southwest. VFPA, 1-140. New York,
  1945.

Carter, G.F., and Anderson, E. A Preliminary Survey of Maize in the South-Western United States.
  AMBG, XXXII, 297-322. 1945.

Cassidy, I.S. Some Pueblo Ideas. WF, X, 78. 1951.

Castetter, E.F. Early Tobacco Utilization and Cultivation in the American Southwest. AA, n.s., XLV,
320-25. 1943.

--- Uncultivated Native Plants used as Sources of
Food. UNMBB, IV, i, 3-62. 1935.

Castetter, E.F., and Bell, W.H. The Aboriginal
Utilization of the Tall Cacti in the American
Southwest. UNMBB, V, i, 1-48. 1937.

Castetter, E.F., Bell, W.H., and Grove, A.R. The
Early Utilization and Distribution of Agave in the
American Southwest. UNMBB, V, iv, 1-92. 1938.

Cazeneuve, J. Indiens du Nouveau-Mexique. Connaissance du Monde, XII, vi, 19-30. 1957.

--- Noël chez les Pueblos du Rio Grande. Ethnographie, L, 163-8. 1955.

Chapin, F.H. The Land of Cliff Dwellers. 188 pp.
Boston, 1892.

Chapman, K.M. Decorative Art of the Indians of
the Southwest. BLA, I, 1-11. 1934.

--- Life Forms in Pueblo Pottery Decoration. AAA,
XIII, 120-2. 1922.

--- Pueblo Indian Pottery. 2 vols. Nice, 1933.

---.Pueblo Indian Pottery of the Post-Spanish Period.
BLA, IV, 1-14. 1938.

Chapman, K.M., and Ellis, B.T. The Line-Break.
EP, LVIII, 251-89. 1951.

Chard, C.S. Distribution and Significance of Ball
Courts in the Southwest. Papers of the Excavators
Club, I, No. ii. 1941.

Chesky, J. Indian Music of the Southwest. K, VII,
9-12. 1941.

Christinger, R. Mythes et Légendes des Pueblos du
Nouveau Mexique et de l'Arizona. BSSA, I, 11-4.
1950.

Collins, G.N. Pueblo Indian Maize Breeding. Journal of Heredity, V, 255-68. 1914.

Colton, H.S. Prehistoric Trade in the Southwest.
SM, LII, 308-19. 1941.

Colton, H.S., and Hargrave, L.L. Handbook of
Northern Arizona Pottery Wares. BMNA, XI, 1-
267. 1937.

Coolidge, M.R. The Rain-Makers. 313 pp. Boston,
1929.

Coues, E., ed. On the Trail of a Spanish Pioneer. 2
vols. New York, 1900.

Coze, P. Southwestern Indian Hair-Dos. AH, XXVI,
vii, 26-35. 1950.

Crane, L. Desert Drums. 393 pp. Boston, 1928.

Crimmins, M.L. The Aztec Influence on the Primitive Culture of the Southwest. BTAPS, IV, 32-9.
1932.

Curtin, L.S.M. Healing Herbs of the Upper Rio
Grande. 381 pp. Santa Fe, 1948.

Curtis, W.E. Education and Morals among the
Navajos and Pueblos. AAOJ, XXVII, 259-64.
1905.

Dale, E.E. The Indians of the Southwest. 283 pp.
Norman, 1949.

Davis, W.W.H. The Pueblo Indians of New Mexico.
EP, XXVI, 259-86. 1929.

DeHuff, J. The Intelligence Quotient of the Pueblo
Indian. EP, XXII, 422-32. 1927.

Dennis, W., and M.G. Cradles and Cradling Practices of the Pueblo Indians. AA, n.s., XLII, 107-
15. 1940.

Densmore, F. A Resemblance between Yuman and
Pueblo Songs. AA, n.s., XXXIV, 694-700. 1932.

DiPeso, C.C. A Guaraheo Potter. K, XVI, iii, 1-
5. 1950.

Dockstader, F.J. The Kachina and the White Man.
BCIS, XXXV, 202 pp. 1954.

Dodge, N.N. and Zim, H.S. The American Southwest. 160 pp. New York, 1955.

Dolch, E.W. and M.P. Pueblo Stories, in Basic Vocabulary. 160 pp. Champaign, 1956.

Dominguez, F.A. The Missions of New Mexico, 1776.
408 pp. Albuquerque, 1956.

Dorsey, G.A. Indians of the Southwest. 223 pp.
1903.

Douglas, F.H. Indian Sand-Painting. DAMLS,
XLIII-XLIV, 1-8. 1932.

--- Kachinas and Kachina Dolls. DAMLS, CXI, 3
pp. 1951.

--- Modern Pueblo Indian Villages. DAMLS, XLV-
XLVI, 1-8. 1932.

--- Modern Pueblo Pottery Types. DAMLS, LIII-LIV,
10-16. 1935.

--- Notes on Distinguishing Similar Objects. DAMLS,
LXXXVI, 141-4. 1939.

--- Periods of Pueblo Culture and History. DAMLS,
XI, 1-4. 1930.

--- Pottery of the Southwestern Tribes. DAMLS,
LXIX-LXX, 74-80. 1935.

--- Pueblo Indian Clothing. DAMLS, IV, 1-4. 1930.

--- Pueblo Indian Foods. DAMLS, VIII, 1-4. 1930.

--- Pueblo Indian Pottery Making. DAMLS, VI, 1-
4. 1930.

--- Southwestern Indian Dwellings. DAMLS, IX, 1-
4. 1930.

--- Southwestern Twined, Wicker, and Plaited Basketry. DAMLS, XCIX-C, 194-9. 1940.

--- Tribes of the Southwest. DAMLS, LV, 1-4. 1933.

--- Types of Southwestern Coiled Basketry. DAMLS,
LXXXVIII, 150-2. 1939.

Douglas, F.H., and Marriott, A. Metal Jewelry of
the Peyote Cult. MCN, XVII, 17-82. 1942.

Douglass, A.E. Dating Pueblo Bonito and Other Ruins of the Southwest. National Geographic Society Contributed Technical Papers, Pueblo Bonito Series, I, 1-74. 1935.

--- The Secret of the Southwest solved by Talkative Tree Rings. NGM, LXV, 737-70. 1929.

--- Tree Rings and Chronology. University of Arizona Bulletin, VIII, iv, 1-36. 1937.

Dozier, E.P. Ethnological Clues for the Sources of Rio Grande Population [with comment by L.A. White]. UASSB, XXVII, 21-32. 1958.

--- Spanish-Catholic Influences on Rio Grande Pueblo Religion. AA, LX, 441-48. 1958.

Driver, H.E. Girls' Puberty Rites in Western North America. AR, VI, 21-90. 1941.

Dunn, D. The Development of Modern American Painting in the Southwest and Plains Areas. EP, LVIII, 331-53. 1951.

--- The Studio of Painting: Santa Fe Indian School. EP, LXVII, 16-27. 1960.

Dutton, B.P. Indian Artistry in Wood and Other Media. EP, LXIV, 3-28. 1957.

--- New Mexico Indians and Their Arizona Neighbors. Santa Fe, 1955.

Eggan, F. Social Organization of the Western Pueblos. 401 pp. Chicago, 1951.

Eickemeyer, C. and L.W. Among the Pueblo Indians. 195 pp. New York, 1895.

Eickhoff, H. Die Kultur der Pueblos in Arizona und New Mexico. SFMV, IV, 1-78. 1908.

Elias, E. El terrible veneno. Tactica guerrera de los Indios Apaches. Boletin de la Sociedad Chihuahuense de Estudios Historicos, VII, 392-93. 1950.

Ellis, F.H. Patterns of Aggression and the War Cult in Southwestern Pueblos. SJA, VII, 177-201. 1951.

--- Pueblo Social Organization and Southwestern Archaeology. AAn, XVII, 148-51. 1951.

Elmore, F.H. Ethnobiology and Climate in the Southwest. EP, LIX, 315-19. 1952.

Espinosa, A.M. Spanish Tradition among the Pueblo Indians. Estudios Hispanicos, Homenaje a Archer M. Huntington, 131-41. Wellesley, 1952.

--- Pueblo Indian Folk Tales. JAFL, XLIX, 69-133. 1936.

Espinosa, J.M., ed. First Expedition of Vargas into New Mexico. 319 pp. Albuquerque, 1940.

Euler, R.C. and Jones, V.H. Hermetic Sealing as a Technique of Food Preservation among the Indians of the American Southwest. PAPS, C, 87-9. 1956.

Evans, B. and M.G. American Indian Dance Steps. 122 pp. New York, 1931.

Fages, P. Diary. Publications of the Academy of Pacific Coast History, III, 133-233. 1913.

--- Voyage en Californie. NAV, CI, 145-82, 311-47. 1844.

Farmer, M.M. A Suggested Typology for Defensive Systems of the Southwest. SJA, XIII, 249-66. 1957.

Fay, G.E. A Calendar of Indian Ceremonies. EP, LVII, 166-72. 1950.

Fewkes, J.W. Ancient Pueblo and Mexican Water Symbol. AA, n.s., VI, 535-8. 1904.

Fisher, R.G. An Outline of Pueblo Government. So Live the Works of Men, ed. D.D. Brand and F.E. Harvey, pp. 147-57. Albuquerque, 1939.

Forbes, A. A Survey of Current Pueblo Indian Painting. EP, LVII, 235-52. 1950.

Forbes, J.D. The Appearance of the Mounted Indian in Northern Mexico and the Southwest, to 1680. SJA, XV, 189-212. 1959.

Forrest, E.R. Missions and Pueblos of the Old Southwest. Cleveland, 1929.

Francis, E.K. Multiple Intergroup Relations in the Upper Rio Grande Region. ASR, XXI, 84-7. 1956.

Frank, M.L., and Elkin, C.A. Scarlet Fever among Pueblo Indians. American Journal of Diseases of Children, LXXI, 477-81. 1946.

Freeman, G.F. Southwestern Beans and Teparies. Arizona State Agricultural Experiment Station Bulletin, LXVIII, 573-619. 1912.

Fynn, A.J. The Pueblo Indian as a Product of Environment. 275 pp. New York, 1907.

Gallenkamp, C. The Pueblo Indians of New Mexico. CGJ, L, 206-15. 1955.

Galvez, B. de. Instructions for Governing the Interior Provinces of New Spain, 1786. PQS, XII, 164 pp. 1951.

Garth, T.R. A Comparison of the Intelligence of Mexican and Mixed and Full Blood Indian Children. Psychological Review, XXX, 388-401. 1923.

--- The Intelligence of Full Blood Indians. JAP, IX, 382-9. 1925.

Garth, T.R., and Barnard, M.A. The Will-Temperament of Indians. JAP, XI, 512-18. 1927.

Gatschet, A.S. Der Yuma-Sprachstamm. ZE, XXIV, 1-18. 1892.

Gerheim, E.B. Incidence of Rh Factor among the Indians of the Southwest. Proceedings of the Society for Experimental Biology and Medicine, LXVI, 419-20. 1947.

Germann, F.E.E. Ceramic Pigments of the Indians of the Southwest. EP, XX, 222-6. 1926.

Gershowitz, H. The Diego Factor among Asiatic Indians, Apaches and West African Negroes. AJPA, n.s., XVII, 195-200. 1959.

Getty, H.T. Some Characteristics of the Folklore of the Indians of Arizona. University of Arizona Bulletin, XVI, i, 29-32. 1945.

Gifford, E.W. Cultural Relations of the Gila River and Lower Colorado Tribes. AA, n.s., XXXVIII, 679-82. 1936.

--- Pottery-making in the Southwest. UCP, XXIII, 253-73. 1928.

Gilpin, L. The Pueblos, a Camera Chronicle. 124 pp. New York, 1941.

Gladwin, H.S. A History of the Ancient Southwest. 403 pp. Portland, Me., 1957.

Goddard, P.E. Assimilation to Environment as illustrated by Athapascan Peoples. ICA, XV, i, 337-59. 1906.

--- The Cultural and Somatic Correlations of Uto-Aztecan. AA, n.s., XXII, 244-7. 1920.

--- Indians of the Southwest. 188 pp. New York, 1931.

--- Pottery of the Southwestern Indians. AMGLS, LXXIII, 1-30. 1928.

--- Similarities and Diversities within Athapascan Linguistic Stocks. ICA, XXII, ii, 489-94. 1926.

Goggin, J.M. Additional Pueblo Ceremonies. NMA, III, 62-3. 1939.

Goldfrank, E.S. The Different Patterns of Blackfoot and Pueblo Adaptation to White Authority. ICA, XXIX, ii, 74-9. 1952.

Goodwin, G. The Southern Athapaskans. K, IV, ii, 5-10. 1938.

Gunnerson, D.A. The Southern Athabascans. EP, LXIII, 346-65. 1956.

Hackett, C.W. The Revolt of the Pueblo Indians of New Mexico in 1680. TSHAQ, XV, 93-147. 1911.

Hackett, C.W., ed. Revolt of the Pueblo Indians of New Mexico and Otermin's Attempted Reconquest, 1680-1682. 2 vols. Albuquerque, 1942.

Hackett, C.W., Hammond, G.P., et al, eds. New Spain and the Anglo-American West. 2 vols. Los Angeles, 1932.

Haeberlin, H.K. Das Flachenornament in der Keramik der alten Pueblo-Kultur. BA, VI, 1-35. 1922.

--- The Idea of Fertilization in the Culture of the Pueblo Indians. MAAA, III, 1-55. 1916.

Haekel, J. Das Mutterrecht bei den Indianerstämmen im südwestlichen Nordamerika. ZE, LXVIII, 227-49. 1936.

Hafen, L.R. and A.W., eds. Rufus B. Sage, His Letters and Papers, 1836-1847. FWRHS, IV, 354 pp; V, 360 pp. 1956.

Hall, E.T. Recent Clues to Athapascan Prehistory in the Southwest. AA, n.s., XLVI, 98-105. 1944.

Hall, H.U. Some Shields of the Plains and Southwest. MJ, XVII, 37-61. 1926.

Halseth, O.S. The Acculturation of the Pueblo Indians. EP, XVIII, 254-68. 1925.

--- The Pueblo Indians. EP, XXII, 238-51. 1927.

--- Revival of Pueblo Pottery-Making. EP, XXI, 135-54. 1926.

Hammond, G.P. Don Juan de Onate and the Founding of New Mexico. NMHR, I, 42-77, 156-92, 292-323, 445-77; II, 37-66, 134-74. 1926-27.

Hammond, G.P., and Rey, A., eds. Expedition into New Mexico by Antonio de Espejo. PQS, I, 1-143. 1929.

--- The Gallegos Relation of the Rodriguez Expedition. NMHR, II, 239-68, 334-62. 1927.

Harcourt, R. d'. Arts de l'Amérique, pp. 43-8. Paris, 1948.

Harrington, J.P. Southern Peripheral Athapaskawan Origins, Divisions and Migrations. SMC, C, 503-32. 1940.

Harris, W.R. The Catholic Church in Utah. 350 pp. Salt Lake City, 1909.

Haskell, M.L. Rubi's Inspection of the Frontier Presidios of New Spain, 1766-1768. Publications of the Southern California Historical Society, V, 33-43. 1917.

Haught, B.F. Mental Growth of the Southwestern Indian. JAP, XVIII, 137-42. 1934.

Hawley, F.M. Big Kivas, Little Kivas, and Moiety Houses in Historical Reconstruction. SJA, VI, 286-302. 1950.

--- Mechanics of Perpetuation of Pueblo Witchcraft. FTD, 143-58, 1950.

--- Pueblo Social Organization as a Lead to Pueblo History. AA, n.s., XXXIX, 504-22. 1937.

--- The Role of Pueblo Social Organization in the Dissemination of Catholicism. AA, n.s., XLVIII, 407-15. 1946.

--- Some Factors in the Indian Problem in New Mexico. University of New Mexico Department of Government Publications, XV, 1-48. 1948.

Heizer, R.F. Ancient Grooved Clubs and Modern Rabbit Sticks. AAn, VIII, 41-56. 1942.

Henderson, A.C. Indian Artists of the Southwest. AmI, II, iii, 21-7. 1945.

--- Why Pueblo Culture is Dying. AmI, V, 13-16. 1949.

Herzog, G. A Comparison of Pueblo and Pima Musical Styles. JAFL, XLIX, 283-417. 1936.

Hewett, E.L. Ancient Life in the American Southwest. 392 pp. Indianapolis, 1930.

Hewett, E.L. My Neighbors, the Pueblo Indians.
AAA, XVI, 3-25. 1924.

--- Native American Artists. AAA, XIII, 103-13.
1922.

--- Pueblo Water Color Painting. AAA, XIII, 103-
11. 1922.

Hewett, E.L., and Dutton, B.P. The Pueblo Indian
World. 176 pp. Albuquerque, 1945.

Hewett, E.L., Henderson, J., and Robbins, W.W.
The Physiography of the Rio Grande Valley, New
Mexico, in Relation to Pueblo Culture. BBAE, LIV,
1-76. 1913.

Hodge, F.W. How Old is Southwestern Indian Silverwork? EP, XXV, 224-32. 1928.

--- Masked Kachinas in Spanish Times. M, XXVI,
17-20. 1952.

--- Pueblo Indian Clans. AA, IX, 345-52. 1896.

--- Pueblo Indian Government. M, VII, 124-6. 1933.

--- Pueblo Names in the Onate Documents. NMHR,
X, 36-47. 1935.

--- Pueblo Snake Ceremonials. AA, IX, 133-6.
1896.

--- Pueblos. BBAE, XXX, ii, 318-24. 1910.

Hodge, G.M. The Kachinas are coming. 129 pp.
Los Angeles, 1937.

Hoffman, W.J. The Practice of Medicine and Surgery by the Aboriginal Races of the Southwest.
Medical and Surgical Reporter, XL, 157-60. 1879.

Hoijer, H. The Southern Athapaskan Languages. AA,
n.s., XL, 75-87. 1938.

--- The Structure of the Noun in Apachean Languages.
ICA, XXVIII, 173-84. 1948.

Holling, H.C. The Book of Indians, pp. 73-96. New
York, 1935.

Hough, W. Pueblo Environment. PAAAS, LV, 447-
54. 1906.

Houghton, N.D. "Wards of the United States" — Arizona Applications. UASSB, XIV, 5-19. 1945.

Howells, W.W., and Hotelling, H. Measurements
and Correlations on Pelves of Indians of the Southwest. AJPA, XXI, 91-106. 1936.

Hrdlicka, A. Catalogue of Human Crania in the
United States National Museum Collections.
PUSNM, LXXVIII, ii, 1-95. 1931.

--- Diseases of the Indians. Washington Medical Annals, IV, 372-82. 1905-06.

--- On the Stature of the Indians of the Southwest and
of Northern Mexico. Putnam Anniversary Volume,
pp. 405-26. New York, 1909.

--- Physiological and Medical Observations among
the Indians of Southwestern United States and Northern Mexico. BBAE, XXIV, 1-425. 1908.

Hrdlicka, A. The Pueblos. AJPA, XX, 235-460.
1935.

--- Ritual Ablation of Front Teeth in Siberia and
America. SMC, XCIX, iii, 1-32. 1940.

Hunt, W.B. Kachina Dolls. PSHPMCM, VII, 36
pp. 1957.

Hurt, W.R. Christmas Eve Ceremonies of the Pueblo Indians of New Mexico. MNUSD, XII, iv, 4-
7. 1951.

Huscher, B.H. and H.A. Athapaskan Migration via
the Intermontane Region. AAn, VIII, 80-8. 1942.

Indian Arts and Crafts Board. Pottery of the Pueblo
Indian. 7 pp. Washington, 1956.

--- Silver Jewelry of the Navajo and Pueblo Indians.
7 pp. Washington, 1956.

Ingstad, H. Apache-Indianerne. 329 pp. Oslo,
1939.

Ives, R.L. Sonoran Mission Languages in 1730. M,
XXII, 93-5. 1948.

Jeancon, J.A. Indian Music of the Southwest. EP,
XXIII, 438-47. 1927.

--- Pueblo Beads and Inlay. DAMLS, XXX, 1-4.
1931.

Jimenez Moreno, W. Tribus e Idiomas del Norte de
Mexico. In, El Norte de Mexico y el Sur de
Estados Unidos, 121-33. Mexico, 1943.

Johnson, J.B. Sonora Dance Regalia. El México
Antiguo, I-II, 54-6. 1940.

Kaplan, L. The Cultivated Beans of the Prehistoric
Southwest. AMBG, XLIII, 189-251. 1956.

Kate, H.F.C. ten. Notes on the Hands and Feet of
American Natives. AA, n.s., XX, 187-202. 1918.

--- Sur la synonymie ethnique et la toponymie chez
les Indiens de l'Amérique du Nord. VMKAW, ser.
3, I, 353-63. 1884.

Keech, R.A. Christianity and the Pueblo Indians.
EP, XXXIV, 143-6. 1933.

--- Pueblo Dwelling Architecture. EP, XXXVI, 49-
53. 1934.

Kelly, W.H. Applied Anthropology in the Southwest. AA, LVI, 709-14. 1954.

--- Indians of the Southwest. RBER, I, 129 pp. 1953.

Kent, K.P. A Comparison of Prehistoric and Modern
Pueblo Weaving. K, X, 14-20. 1945.

--- The Cultivation and Weaving of Cotton in the
Prehistoric Southwestern United States. TAPS,
XLVII, 457-732. 1957.

--- Notes on the Weaving of Prehistoric Pueblo Textiles. P, XIV, 1-11. 1941.

Kidder, A.V. An Introduction to the Study of Southwestern Archaeology. 151 pp. New Haven, 1924.

Kidder, A.V., and Guernsey, S.J. Archeological Explorations in Northeastern Arizona. BBAE, LXV, 1-228. 1919.

Kirchhoff, P. Gatherers and Farmers in the Greater Southwest. AA, LVI, 529-50. 1954.

--- Los Recolectores-Cazadores del Norte de Mexico. In, El Norte de Mexico y el Sur de Estados Unidos, 133-44. Mexico, 1943.

--- Versuch einer Gliederung der Südgruppe des Athapaskischen. ICA, XXIV, 258-63. 1930.

Kirkland, F. A Study of Indian Pictures in Texas. BTAPS, IX, 89-119. 1937.

Kluckhohn, C. Conceptions of Death among the Southwestern Indians. Harvard University Divinity School Bulletin, LXVI, 5-19.

--- Southwestern Studies of Culture and Personality. AA, LVI, 685-97. 1954.

Kraus, B.S. and Jones, B.M. Indian Health in Arizona. RBER, II, 164 pp. 1954.

Krause, F. Die Pueblo-Indianer. 98 pp. Halle, 1907.

Krickeberg, W. Blood-letting and Bloody Castigation among the American Indians. Ciba Symposia, I, 26-34. 1939.

--- The Indian Sweat Bath. Ciba Symposia, I, 19-25. 1939.

Kroeber, A.L. Athabascan Kin Term Systems. AA, n.s., XXXIX, 602-8. 1937.

--- The Classification of the Yuman Languages. UCPL, I, 21-40. 1943.

--- Native Culture of the Southwest. UCP, XXIII, 375-98. 1928.

--- Salt, Dogs, Tobacco. AR, VI, 1-20. 1941.

--- Stepdaughter Marriage. AA, n.s., XLII, 562-70. 1940.

--- Uto-Aztecan Languages of Mexico. IA, VIII, 1-27. 1934.

Kurath, G.P. Game Animal Dances of the Rio Grande Pueblos. SJA, XIV, 438-48. 1958.

--- Notation of a Pueblo Indian Corn Dance. Dance Notation Record, VIII, iv, 9-11. 1957.

--- The Origin of the Pueblo Indian Matachines. EP, LXIV, 259-64. 1957.

Landar, H.J. The Diffusion of Some Southwestern Words for Cat. IJAL, XXV, 273-4. 1959.

--- The Loss of Athapascan Words for Fish in the Southwest. IJAL, XXVI, 75-7. 1960.

Lange, C.H. Comparative Notes on Southwestern Medical Practices. TJS, VI, 62-71. 1954.

--- Education and Leadership in Rio Grande Pueblo Culture Change. AmI, ii, 27-35. 1958-59.

Lange, C.H. The Keresan Component of Southwestern Pueblo Culture. SJA, XIV, 34-50. 1958.

--- Notes on the Use of Turkeys by Pueblo Indians. EP, LVII, 204-09. 1950.

--- Plains-Southwestern Inter-Cultural Relations During the Historic Period. E, IV, 150-73. 1957.

--- A Reappraisal of Evidence of Plains Influences among the Rio Grande Pueblos. SJA, IX, 212-30. 1953.

--- Tablita, or Corn, Dances of the Rio Grande Pueblo Indians. TJS, IX, 59-74. 1957.

Lee, B.J. Cancer among the Indians of the Southwest. Boletin de la Liga Contra el Cancer, Edition Social, I, 234-41. 1930.

--- The Incidence of Cancer among the Indians of the Southwest. Surgery, Gynecology, and Obstetrics, L, 196-9. 1930.

Leonard, I.A., ed. The Mercurio Volante of Don Carlos de Sigüenza y Góngora. 136 pp. Los Angeles, 1932.

Leupp, F.E. Notes of a Summer Tour among the Indians of the Southwest. Philadelphia, 1897.

Linton, R. Nomad Raids and Fortified Pueblos. AAn, X, 28-32. 1944.

Lummis, C.F. Land of Poco Tiempo. 310 pp. New York, 1893.

Lyman, T.S. and Darrel, T.H. Report of Fray Alonso de Posada. NMHR, XXXIII, 285-314. 1958.

McGee, W.J. The Beginning of Zooculture. AA, X, 215-30. 1897.

McGiboney, J.R. Trachoma among Indians of the United States of America. AI, II, iii, 20-3. 1942.

MacGregor, J.C. Southwestern Archaeology. 403 pp. New York, 1941.

Marcson, S. Some Methodological Consequences of Correlational Analysis in Anthropology. AA, n.s., XLV, 588-601. 1943.

Marriott, A.L. Indians of the Four Corners. 229 pp. New York, 1952.

Marti, S. Musica primitiva en Sonora. YAN, I, 10-17. 1953.

Martin, D. D. H. Lawrence and Pueblo Religion. Arizona Quarterly, IX, 219-34. 1953.

Mason, J.A. The Classification of the Sonoran Languages. Essays in Anthropology presented to A.L. Kroeber, pp. 183-98. Berkeley, 1936.

--- Turquoise Mosaics from Northern Mexico. MJ, XX, 157-75. 1929.

Mecham, J.L. The Second Spanish Expedition in New Mexico. NMHR, I, 265-91. 1926.

Mera, H.P. Indian Silverwork of the Southwest. BLA, XVII-XIX, 1-59. 1944-45.

Mera, H.P. Indian Silverwork of the Southwest. 128
     pp. Globe, 1959.
--- Pueblo Indian Embroidery. MLA, IV, 1-73. 1943.
--- The "Rain Bird": a Study in Pueblo Design. MLA,
     II, 1-113. 1937.
--- Style Trends of Pueblo Pottery. MLA, III, 1-165.
     1939.
Mindeleff, C. Aboriginal Architecture in the United
     States. BAGS, XXX, 414-27. 1898.
Milford, S.J. The Twin War God Myth Cycle. EP,
     XLIII, 1-12, 19-28. 1937.
Miller, M.R.T. Pueblo Indian Culture as seen by
     the Early Spanish Explorers. 30 pp. Los Angeles,
     1941.
Mohr, A. The Hunting Crook. M, XXV, 145-54.
     1951.
Möllhausen, B. Diary of a Journey from the Missis-
     sippi to the Coasts of the Pacific. 2 vols. London,
     1858.
Morgan, L.H. Houses and House-Life of the Ameri-
     can Aborigines. CNAE, IV, 1-281. 1881.
Morice, A.G. The Great Déné Race. A, I, 229-77,
     483-508, 695-730; II, 1-34, 181-96; IV, 582-
     606; V, 113-42, 419-43, 643-53, 969-90. 1906-
     10.
Nelson, N.C. The Southwest Problem. EP, VI, 132-
     5. 1919.
Neumann, D.L. Southwestern Indians Enter Modern
     Money Economy. EP, LXIII, 233-35. 1956.
Newman, S. American Indian Linguistics in the
     Southwest. AA, LVI, 626-34. 1954.
New Mexico Association on Indian Affairs. New
     Mexico Indians, 36 pp. Santa Fe, 1941.
New Mexico State Planning Board. Indian Lands in
     New Mexico. 176 pp. Santa Fe, 1936.
Obregón, B. de. History of 16th Century Explorations
     in Western America, ed. G.P. Hammond and A.
     Ray. 351 pp. Los Angeles, 1928.
Ocaranza, F. Parva cronica de la Sierra Madre y les
     Pimerias. Instituto Panamericano de Geografia e
     Historia, LXIV, 1-156. 1942.
Officer, J.E. Indians in School. University of Ari-
     zona, Bureau of Ethnic Research, American Indian
     Series, I, 148 pp. 1956.
Oglesby, C. Modern Primitive Arts, pp. 21-95.
     New York, 1939.
Orozco y Berra, M. Geografia de las lenguas y carta
     ethnográfica de México. Mexico, 1864.
Otis, R. Indian Art of the Southwest. Santa Fe, 1931.
Paloheimo, L.C. The Antelope are Fat in Summer.
     M, XXIV, 73-78, 1950.
Parsons, E.C. The House-Clan Complex of the
     Pueblos. Essays in Anthropology presented to A.L.
     Kroeber, pp. 229-31. Berkeley, 1936.

Parsons, E.C. The Pueblo Indian Clan in Folk-Lore.
     JAFL, XXXIV, 209-16. 1921.
--- Pueblo Indian Religion. 2 vols. Chicago, 1939.
--- The Religion of the Pueblo Indians. ICA, XXI,
     i, 140-61. 1924.
--- Ritual Parallels in Pueblo and Plains Cultures.
     AA, n.s., XXXI, 642-54. 1929.
--- Some Aztec and Pueblo Parallels. AA, n.s.,
     XXXV, 611-31. 1933.
--- Der spanische Einfluss auf die Märchen der
     Pueblo-Indianer. ZE, LVIII, 16-28. 1926.
--- Spanish Elements in the Kachina Cult of the
     Pueblos. ICA, XXIII, 582-603. 1928.
--- Witchcraft among the Pueblos: Indian or Spanish.
     Man, XXVII, 106-12, 125-8. 1927.
Parsons, E.C., and Beals, R.L. The Sacred Clowns
     of the Pueblo and Mayo-Yaqui Indians. AA, n.s.,
     XXXVI, 491-514. 1934.
Peet, S.D. The Cliff Dwellers and Pueblos. Chicago,
     1899.
Pilling, J.C. Bibliography of the Athapascan Lan-
     guages. BBAE, XIV, 1-125. 1892.
Pi-Sunyer, O. Religion and Witchcraft: Spanish Atti-
     tudes and Pueblo Reactions. An, n.s., II, i, 66-
     75. 1960.
Pogue, J.E. The Aboriginal Use of Turquoise in
     North America. AA, n.s., XIV, 437-66. 1912.
Posey, W.C. Trachoma among the Indians of the
     Southwest. Journal of the American Medical As-
     sociation, LXXXVIII, 1618-19. 1927.
Pospisil, F. Etnologické materiálie z jihozápadu U.
     S.A. 256 pp. Brno, 1932.
Powell, J.W. Canyons of the Colorado. 400 pp.
     Meadville, 1895.
Putnam, F.W. Archaeological and Ethnological Col-
     lections. RUSGS, VII, 1-497. 1879.
Reagan, A.B. Don Diego. 352 pp. New York, 1914.
Reed, E.K. Aspects of Acculturation in the Southwest.
     AAm, II, 62-9. 1944.
--- Transition to History in the Pueblo Southwest. AA,
     LVI, 592-603. 1954.
--- Turkeys in Southwestern Archaeology. EP, LVIII,
     195-205. 1951.
Reeve, F.D. Federal Indian Policy in New Mexico,
     1858-80. NMHR, XII, 218-69; XIII, 14-62, 146-
     91, 261-313. 1937-38.
Reichard, G.A. A Few Instances of Cultural Resist-
     ance in Southwest North America. ICA, XXII, ii,
     289-97. 1926.
Renaud, E.B. Evolution of Population and Dwelling
     in the Indian Southwest. SF, VII, 263-70. 1928.
--- Fabrication de la céramique Indienne du sud-
     ouest des Etats-Unis. JSAP, n.s., XVII, 101-17.
     1925.

Renaud, E.B. Notes sur le céramique indienne du sud-ouest des Etats-Unis. JSAP, n.s., XVII, 85-100. 1925.

Robbins, W.J. Some Aspects of Pueblo Indian Religion. Harvard Theological Review, XXXIV, 25-49. 1941.

Roberts, F.H.H. Archaeology in the Southwest. AAn, III, 3-33. 1937.

--- The Ruins at Kiatuthlanna. BBAE, C, 1-195. 1931.

--- A Survey of Southwestern Archaeology. AA, n. s., XXXVII, 1-35. 1935.

Roberts, H.H. Indian Music from the Southwest. NH, XXVII, 257-65. 1927.

Robinson, B. Basketmakers of Arizona. AH, XXVII, viii, 30-9. 1951.

--- The Basket Weavers of Arizona. 176 pp. Albuquerque, 1955.

Roediger, V.M. Ceremonial Costumes of the Pueblo Indians. 136 pp. New York, 1938.

--- Ceremonial Costumes of the Pueblo Indians. 234 pp. Berkeley, 1941.

Rubin de la Borbolla, D.F. La Antropologia Física y el Norte de Mexico. In, El Norte de Mexico y el Sur de Estados Unidos, 166-71. Mexico, 1943.

Sauer, C.O. Aboriginal Population of Northwestern Mexico. IA, X, 1-33. 1935.

--- The Distribution of Aboriginal Tribes and Languages in Northwestern Mexico. IA, V, 1-90. 1934.

--- The Road to Cibola. IA, III, 1-58. 1932.

Sauer, J. Amaranths as Dye Plants among the Pueblo Peoples. SJA, VI, 412-5. 1950.

Saunders, L. A Guide to Materials bearing on Cultural Relations in New Mexico. 528 pp. Albuquerque, 1944.

Scholes, F.V. Civil Government and Society in New Mexico in the Seventeenth Century. NMHR, X, 71-111. 1935.

Secoy, F.R. The Identity of the "Paduca." AA, LIII, 525-42. 1951.

Seltzer, C.C. Racial Prehistory in the Southwest and the Hawikuh Zunis. PMP, XXIII, 1-37. 1944.

Shimkin, D.B. The Uto-Aztecan System of Kinship Terminology. AA, n.s., XLIII, 223-45. 1941.

Sides, D.S. Decorative Art of the Southwestern Indians. Santa Ana, 1936.

Simpson, J.H. Journal of a Military Reconnaissance from Santa Fe, New Mexico, to the Navajo Country. Philadelphia, 1852.

Simpson, R.D. The Coyote in Southwestern Indian Tradition. M, XXXII, ii, 43-54. 1958.

Spencer, F.C. Education of the Pueblo Child. 93 pp. New York, 1899.

Spicer, E.H. Spanish-Indian Acculturation in the Southwest. AA, LVI, 663-78. 1954.

--- Worlds Apart – Cultural Differences in the Modern Southwest. Arizona Quarterly, XIII, 197-229. 1957.

Spier, L. Havasupai Ethnography. APAM, XXIX, 81-392. 1928.

--- Problems arising from the Cultural Position of the Havasuapi. AA, n.s., XXXI, 213-22. 1929.

Spinden, H.J. Indian Dances of the Southwest. AMJ, XV, 103-15. 1915.

Spuhler, J.N. Some Problems in the Physical Anthropology of the American Southwest. AA, LVI, 604-19. 1954.

Standley, P.C. Some Useful Native Plants of New Mexico. ARSI, 1911, 447-63.

Steece, H.M. Corn Culture among the Indians of the Southwest. NH, XXI, 414-24. 1921.

Steward, J.H. Ecological Aspects of Southwestern Society. A, XXXII, 87-104. 1937.

--- Lineage to Clan. TCC, 151-72. 1955.

Stewart, G.R. Conservation in Pueblo Culture. SM, LI, 201-20, 329-40. 1940.

Stewart, G.R., and Donnelly, M. Soil and Water Economy in the Pueblo Southwest. SM, LVI, 31-44, 134-44. 1943.

Strong, W.D. An Analysis of Southwestern Society. AA, n.s., XXIX, 1-61. 1927.

Tanner, C.L. Basketry of the Modern Southwest Indians. K, IX, 18-26. 1944.

--- Contemporary Southwest Indian Silver. K, XXV, iii, 1-22. 1960.

--- Coral among Southwestern Indians. FTD, 117-32. 1950.

--- The Influence of the White Man on Southwest Indian Art. E, VII, 137-50. 1960.

--- Life Forms in Prehistoric Pottery of the Southwest. K, VIII, 26-32. 1943.

--- Pottery of the Modern Southwestern Indians. K, X, 3-12. 1944.

--- Southwest Indian Painting. 175 pp. Tucson, 1957.

Tanner, C.L., and Connolly, F. Petroglyphs in the Southwest. K, III, 13-16. 1938.

Taub, A. Southwestern Indian Poetry. Arizona Quarterly, VI, 236-43. 1950.

Taylor, V.H. and Hammons, J. The Letters of Antonio Martinez. 374 pp. Austin, 1957.

Thomas, A.B. After Coronado. 307 pp. Norman, 1935.

Thomas, A.B. The Plains Indians and New Mexico, 1751-1778. 232 pp. Albuquerque, 1940.

Thomas, C., and Swanton, J.R. Indian Languages of Mexico and Central America. BBAE, XLIV, 1-108. 1911.

Thompson, H. Atoms and the Morning Star. The Land, IX, 41-45. 1950.

Toulouse, J.H., Jr. Cremation among the Indians of New Mexico. AAn, X, 65-74. 1944.

Tower, D.B. The Use of Marine Mollusca and Their Value in reconstructing Prehistoric Trade Routes in the American Southwest. Papers of the Excavators' Club, II, No. iii. 1945.

Trager, G.L. Linguistic History and Ethnologic History in the Southwest. JWAS, XLI, 341-43. 1951.

Twitchell, R.E. Pueblo Indian Land Tenures in New Mexico and Arizona. EP, XII, 31-3, 38-61. 1922.

Underhill, R.M. Ceremonial Patterns in the Greater Southwest. MAES, XIII, 1-62. 1948.

--- First Penthouse Dwellers of America. Rev. ed. 161 pp. Santa Fe, 1946.

--- Intercultural Relations in the Greater Southwest. AA, LVI, 645-56. 1954.

--- Pueblo Crafts. IH, VII, 1-147. 1944.

--- Workaday Life of the Pueblos. ILC, IV, 1-174. (n.d.)

Wadsworth, B. Design Motifs of the Pueblo Indians. 96 pp. San Antonio, 1957.

Wagner, G. Entwicklung und Verbreitung des Peyote-Kultes. BA, XV, 59-144. 1932.

Ward, J. Report. ARCIA, 1864, 187-95.

Warner, H.J. Notes on the Results of Trachoma Work by the Indian Service in Arizona and New Mexico. PHR, XLIV, 2913-20. 1929.

Waterman, T.T. Ornamental Designs in Southwestern Pottery. IN, VII, 497-522. 1930.

Waters, F. Masked Gods. 438 pp. Albuquerque, 1950.

Watkins, F.E. Southwestern Athapascan Women. SWL, X, 32-5. 1944.

Watson, E.L. The Cult of the Mountain Lion. EP, XXXIV, 95-109. 1933.

Wheat, J.B. Kroeber's Formulation of the Southwestern Culture Area. UCSSA, IV, 23-44. 1954.

Wheeler, R.P. Danton, Leslie and Cynoamp English Merchants. ICA, XXVI, ii, 369-72. 1948.

Whipple, A.W., Ewbank, T., and Turner, W.M. Report upon the Indian Tribes. RESRR, III, 7-127. 1855.

White, C.B. A Comparison of Theories on Southern Athapaskan Kinship Systems. AA, LIX, 434-48. 1957.

White, L.A. A Ceremonial Vocabulary among the Pueblos. IJAL, X, 161-7. 1944.

--- The Impersonation of Saints among the Pueblos. PMA, XXVII, 559-64. 1941.

Whorf, B.L. The Comparative Linguistics of Uto-Aztecan. AA, n.s., XXXVII, 600-8. 1935.

Winship, G.P. The Coronado Expedition. ARBAE, XIV, i, 339-613. 1893.

Winter, W. Yuman Languages. IJAL, XXIII, 18-24. 1957.

Wittfogel, K.A., and Goldfrank, E.S. Some Aspects of Pueblo Mythology and Society. JAFL, LVI, 17-30. 1943.

Worcester, D.C. Early Spanish Accounts of the Apache Indians. AA, n.s., XLIII, 308-12. 1941.

Worcester, D.E. The Spread of Spanish Horses in the Southwest. NMHR, XIX, 225-32; XX, 1-13. 1944-45.

Wormington, H.M. The Story of Pueblo Pottery. Denver Museum of Natural History, Museum Pictorial, II, 1-61. 1951.

Yarnell, R.A. Prehistoric Pueblo Use of Datura. EP, LXVI, 176-8. 1959.

Zárate-Salmerón, G. de. Relating all the Things that have been seen and known in New Mexico. LS, XI, 337-56; XII, 39-48, 104-13, 180-7. 1899-1900.

Zingg, R.M. A Reconstruction of Uto-Aztekan History. University of Denver Contributions to Ethnography, II, 1-274. 1939.

Zolotarevskaia, I.A. Indejcy Pueblo. Trudy Instituta Etnografii Imena N.N.Mikluho-Maklaia, XXV, 119-34. 1955.

1. ACOMA

Including the western Keresan pueblos of Acoma and Laguna.

Curtis, E.S. The North American Indian, XVI, 65-248. Norwood, 1926.

Eggan, F. Social Organization of the Western Pueblos, pp. 223-90. Chicago, 1950.

Stirling, M.W. Origin Myth of Acona. BBAE, CXXXV, 1-123. 1942.

White, L.A. The Acoma Indians. ARBAE, XLVII, 17-192. 1930.

--- New Material from Acoma. BBAE, CXXXVI, 301-59. 1943.

Anonymous. Acoma the Sky Pueblo. EP, XLVII, 160-1. 1940.

Bandelier, A.F. Ein Brief über Akoma. Ausland, LVII, 241-3. 1884.

Beckwith, F. A Day in Acoma. EP, XXXV, 201-10. 1933.

Benedict, R. Eight Stories from Acoma. JAFL, XLIII, 59-87. 1930.

Bercovitz, M. Laguna Indian Translations. 27 pp. Laguna, c. 1880.

Bloom, L.B., ed. Bourke on the Southwest. NMHR, XII, 337-79. 1937.

Boas, F. Abstract Characteristics of Keresan Folktales. ICA, XX, i, 223-4. 1922.

--- A Keresan Text. IJAL, II, 171-80. 1923.

--- Keresan Texts. PAES, VIII, i, 1-300. 1928.

Boke, R.L. Laguna Indians pin their Hopes on Better Land Use. Soil Conservation, II, 199-200. 1937.

Brayer, H.O. The Land Grants of Laguna. Research, I, 5-22. 1936.

Bunzel, R.L. The Pueblo Potter. CUCA, VIII, 1-134. 1929.

Curtis, N., ed. The Indians' Book, pp. 447-70. New York, 1907.

--- Two Pueblo Indian Grinding Songs. Craftsman, VII, 35-41. 1904.

DeHuff, E.W. More Pueblo Tales. EP, XI, 140-4. 1921.

--- Myths told by the Pueblos. EP, XI, 86-92. 1921.

--- Taytay's Memories, pp. 25-40, 55-82, 158-60, 187-97, 229-47. New York, 1924.

--- Taytay's Tales, pp. 40-50, 88-91, 95-111, 132-40, 165-7, 172-82, 191-7. New York, 1922.

Densmore, F. Music of Acoma, Isleta, Cochiti and Zuñi Pueblos. BBAE, CLXV, 129 pp. 1957.

Dismuke, D. Acoma and Laguna Indians adjust Their Livestock to Their Range. Soil Conservation, VI, 130-2. 1940.

Donaldson, T. Moqui Indians of Arizona and Pueblo Indians of New Mexico. U.S. Census Office, Eleventh Census, Extra Bulletin, pp. 1-136. Washington, 1893.

Douglas, F.H. Acoma Pueblo Weaving and Embroidery. DAMLS, LXXXIX, 154-6. 1939.

--- An Embroidered Cotton Garment from Acoma. MCN, I, 1-4. 1937.

Dutton, B.P., and Marmon, M.A. The Laguna Calendar. UNMB, I, ii, 1-21. 1936.

Ellis, F.H. An Outline of Laguna Pueblo History and Social Organization. SJA, XV, 325-47. 1959.

--- Laguna Bows and Arrows. EP, LXVI, 91. 1959.

Espinosa, A.M. All-Souls' Day at Zuni, Acoma, and Laguna. JAFL, XXXI, 550-2. 1918.

--- El desarrollo de la palabra castilla en la lengua de los Indios Queres de Nuevo Mejico. Revista de Filologia Española, XIX, 261-77. 1932.

Forde, C.D. A Creation Myth from Acoma. FL, XLI, 370-87. 1930.

Gatschet, A.S. Classification into Seven Linguistic Stocks of Western Indian Dialects. RUSGS, VII, 403-85. 1879.

Goldfrank, E.S. Notes on Deer-hunting Practices at Laguna Pueblo. TJS, VI, 407-21. 1954.

--- Notes on Two Pueblo Feasts. AA, n.s., XXV, 188-96. 1923.

Gunn, J.M. History, Traditions, and Narratives of the Queres Pueblos of Laguna and Acoma. RP, III, 291-310, 323-44. 1904.

--- Schat-chen. 222 pp. Albuquerque, 1917.

Harrington, J.P. Haák'o, Original Form of the Keresan Name of Acoma. EP, LVI, 141-4. 1949.

Hawley, F. Keresan Patterns of Kinship and Social Organization. AA, n.s., LII, 499-512. 1950.

Hodge, F.W. Acoma. BBAE, XXX, i, 10-11. 1907.

--- Laguna. BBAE, XXX, i, 752-3. 1907.

--- Pueblo Snake Ceremonials. AA, IX, 133-6. 1896.

--- The Verification of a Tradition. AA, X, 299-302. 1897.

Hrdlicka, A. A Laguna Ceremonial Language. AA, n.s., V, 730-2. 1903.

Kroeber, A.L. Zuni Kin and Clan. APAM, XVIII, 83-8. 1917.

Lemos, P.J. Marvelous Acoma and Its Craftsmen. EP, XXIV, 234-44. 1928.

Lummis, C.F. A Week of Wonders. LS, XV, 315-32, 425-37. 1901.

Mickey, B.H. Acoma Kinship Terms. SJA, XII, 249-256. 1956.

Miller, W.R. Some Notes on Acoma Kinship Terminology. SJA, XV, 179-84. 1959.

--- Spanish Loanwords in Acoma. IJAL, XXV, 147-53; XXVI, 41-9. 1959-60.

Morgan, L.H. Systems of Consanguinity and Affinity. SCK, XVII, 291-382. 1871.

Parsons, E.C. All-Souls' Day at Zuni, Acoma, and Laguna. JAFL, XXX, 495-6. 1917.

--- The Antelope Clan in Keresan Custom and Myth. Man, XVII, 190-3. 1917.

--- Early Relations between Hopi and Keres. AA, n.s., XXXVIII, 554-60. 1936.

--- The Kinship Nomenclature of the Pueblo Indians. AA, n.s., XXXIV, 377-89. 1932.

--- Laguna Genealogies. APAM, XIX, 133-292. 1923.

--- The Laguna Migration to Isleta. AA, n.s., XXX, 602-13. 1928.

--- Laguna Tales. JAFL, XLIV, 137-42. 1931.

Parsons, E.C. Mothers and Children at Laguna. Man,
     XIX, 34-8. 1919.
--- Nativity Myth at Laguna and Zuni. JAFL, XXXI,
     256-63. 1918.
--- Notes on Acoma and Laguna. AA, n.s., XX, 162-
     86. 1918.
--- Notes on Ceremonialism at Laguna. APAM, XIX,
     85-131. 1920.
--- Notes on Isleta, Santa Ana, and Acoma. AA, n.
     s., XXII, 56-69. 1920.
--- Pueblo-Indian Folk-Tales, probably of Spanish
     Provenience. JAFL, XXXI, 216-55. 1918.
--- Pueblo Indian Religion. 2 vols. Chicago, 1939.
--- War God Shrines of Laguna and Zuni. AA, n.s.,
     XX, 381-405. 1918.
Parsons, E.C., and Boas, F. Spanish Tales from
     Laguna and Zuni. JAFL, XXXIII, 47-72. 1920.
Paytiamo, J. Flaming Arrow's People. 157 pp.
     New York, 1932.
Pradt, G.H. Shakok and Miochin: Origin of Summer
     and Winter. JAFL, XV, 88. 1902.
Reuter, B.A. Restoration of Acoma Mission. EP,
     XXII, 79-87. 1927.
Roberts, H.H. Chakwena Songs of Zuni and Laguna.
     JAFL, XXXVI, 177-84. 1923.
Ruppe, R.J. and Dittert, A.E. Acoma Archaeology.
     EP, LX, 259-74. 1953.
--- The Archaeology of Cebolleta Mesa and Acoma
     Pueblo. EP, LIX, 191-219. 1952.
Schiff, E. A Note on Twins. AA, n.s., XXIII, 387-
     8. 1921.
Sedgwick, Mrs. W.T. Acoma, the Sky City. 295
     pp. Cambridge, 1926.
Smith, D.M. Indian Tribes of the Southwest, pp.
     1-15. Stanford, 1933.
Spencer, R.F. The Phonemes of Keresan. IJAL, XII,
     229-36. 1946.
--- A Sketch of Laguna Land Ways. EP, XLVII, 214-
     27. 1940.
Stevenson, J. Illustrated Catalogue of the Collections
     obtained from the Indians of New Mexico and Ari-
     zona. ARBAE, II, 399-405. 1883.
Toomey, T.N. Grammatical and Lexical Notes on
     the Keres Language. BHLAL, V, 1-11. 1914.
White, L.A. A Comparative Study of Keresan Medi-
     cine Societies, ICA, XXIII, 604-19. 1928.
--- Miscellaneous Notes on the Keresan Pueblos. PMA,
     XXXII, 365-76. 1946.
--- Notes on the Ethnobotany of the Keres. PMA, XXX,
     557-70. 1944.
---Notes on the Ethnozoology of the Keresan Pueblo
     Indians. PMA, XXXI, 223-46. 1945.

White, L.A. "Rohona" in Pueblo Culture. PMA,
     XXIX, 439-43. 1943.
--- Summary Report of Field Work at Acoma. AA,
     n.s., XXX, 559-68. 1928.
Whitener, H.C., tr. Jesus Christo niya tawa-mani.
     72 pp. Albuquerque, 1935.

2. CAHITA

Including the Mayo, Nio, Tehueco, Tepahue,
Yaqui, and Zuaque.

Beals, R.L. The Aboriginal Culture of the Cahita
     Indians. IA, XIX, 1-86. 1943.
--- The Contemporary Culture of the Cahita Indians.
     BBAE, CXLII, 1-244. 1945.
Holden, W.C., Seltzer, C.C., Studhalter, R.A.,
     Wagner, C.J., and McMillan, W.G. Studies of
     the Yaqui Indians of Sonora. Texas Technologi-
     cal College Bulletin, XII, i, 1-142. 1936.
Spicer, E.H. Pascua: a Yaqui Village in Arizona.
     319 pp. Chicago, 1940.
--- Potam. MAAA, LXXVII, 226 pp. 1954.

Altman, G.J. The Yaqui Easter Play of Guadalupe,
     Arizona. M, XX, 181-9; XXI, 19-23, 67-72.
     1946-47.
Barker, G.C. Some Aspects of Penitential Processions
     in Spain and the American Southwest. JAFL, LXX,
     137-42. 1957.
--- Some Functions of Catholic Processions in Pueb-
     lo and Yaqui Culture Change. AA, LX, 449-55.
     1958.
--- The Yaqui Easter Ceremony at Hermosillo. WF,
     XVI, 256-62. 1957.
Beals, R.L. Aboriginal Survivals in Mayo Culture.
     AA, n.s., XXXIV, 28-39. 1932.
Bogan, P.M. Yaqui Indian Dances. 69 pp. Tucson,
     1925.
Bower, B. La fabrication de panela entre los indios
     tepehuas. Boletin Indigenista, VII, 374-9. 1947.
Brown, E. The Passion at Pascua. 28 pp. Tucson,
     1941.
Buschmann, J.C. Grammatik der Sonorischen
     Sprache. AKAWB, XLVII, 369-454; LI, 23-216;
     LIII, i, 67-266. 1863, 1867, 1869.
Cazeneuve, L. Les Indiens de la Région de Tucson.
     Ee, LI, 37-45. 1956.
Chavez, A. The Penitentes of New Mexico. NMHR,
     XXIX, 97-123. 1954.

Clark, C.U. Excerpts from the Journals of Prince Paul of Wurtemberg, Year 1850. SJA, XV, 291-9. 1959.

Collard, H. and B. Folleto Sobre el Paludismo. Mexico, 1956.

Cowan, G. El idioma silbido entre los Mazatecos y los Tepehuas de Hidalgo, Mexico. Tlatoani, I, 31-3. 1952.

Davila Garibi, J.I. Es el Coca un Idioma Tara-Cahita. HDAC, 143-52. 1951.

Dedrick, J.M. How Jobe'eso Ro'i Got His Name. Tlalocan, II, 163-6. 1946.

Densmore, F. Native Songs of Two Hybrid Ceremonies. AA, n.s., XLIII, 77-82. 1941.

--- Yuman and Yaqui Music. BBAE, CX, 1-216. 1932.

Dominguez, F. Costumbres Yaquis. Mexican Folkways, Special Yaqui Number, pp. 6-25. 1937.

--- Musica Yaqui. Mexican Folkways, Special Yaqui Number, pp. 32-44. 1937.

Dozier, E.P. Two Examples of Linguistic Acculturation. Lg, XXXII, 146-57. 1956.

Drucker, P. Yuman-Piman. AR, VI, 91-230. 1941.

Escudero, J.A. de. Noticias estadisticas de Sonora y Sinaloa. Mexico, 1849.

Fabila, A. Los Indios Yaquis del Estado Sonora. Sociologia en Mexico, I, iv, 1-27. 1951.

--- Los Indios Yaquis de Sonora. 87 pp. Mexico, 1945.

--- Las tribus Yaquis de Sonora. 313 pp. Mexico, 1940.

Fay, G.E. Indian House Types of Sonora, I: Yaqui. M, XXIX, 196-99. 1955.

--- Indian House Types of Sonora, II: Mayo. M, XXX, 25-28. 1956.

--- Uses of the Tamarindo Fruit. EP, LXIII, 58. 1956.

Forbes, J.D. Historical Survey of the Indians of Sonora, 1821-1910. E, IV, 335-68. 1957.

Fraenkel, G. Yaqui Phonemics. Anthropological Linguistics, I, v, 7-18. 1959.

Getty, H.T. Some Characteristics of the Folklore of the Indians of Arizona. University of Arizona Bulletin, XVI, i, 29-42. 1945.

González Bonilla, L.A. Los Yaquis. Revista Mexicana de Sociologia, II, i, 57-88. 1940.

Hamy, E.T. Algunas observaciones sobre la distribución geográfica de los ópatas, de los tarahumares y de los pimas. Anales del Museo de Arqueologia, Historia y Etnografia, epoca 4ª, V, 93-8. 1922.

Hernandez, F. Las razas indigenas de Sonora y la guerra del Yaqui, pp. 77-233. Mexico, 1902.

Hodge, F.W. Cahita. BBAE, XXX, i, 184-5. 1907.

Hodge, F.W. Yaqui, BBAE, XXX, ii, 991-2. 1910

Honigmann, J.J. An Interpretation of the Social-Psychological Functions of the Ritual Clown. Character and Personality, X, 220-26. 1942.

Hrdlicka, A. Notes on the Indians of Sonora. AA, n.s., VI, 59-71. 1904.

Johnson, J.B. A Clear Case of Linguistic Acculturation. AA, n.s., XLV, 427-34. 1943.

Kraus, B.S. Occurrence of the Carabelli Trait in Southwest Ethnic Groups. AJPA, n.s., XVII, 117-23. 1959.

Kroeber, A.L. Uto-Aztecan Languages of Mexico. IA, VIII, 1-27. 1934.

Kurath, G.P. The Sena'asom Rattle of the Yaqui Indian Pascolas. Ethnomusicology, IV, ii, 60-3. 1960.

Kurath, W., and Spicer, E.H. A Brief Introduction to Yaqui. UASSB, XV, 1-46. 1947.

MacKenzie, A.S. Yaqui of Mexico. AA, II, 299-300. 1889.

Mason, J.A. A Preliminary Sketch of the Yaqui Language. UCP, XX, 195-212. 1923.

Montell, G. Yaqui Dances. Ethnos, III, vi, 145-66. 1938.

Painter, M.T. The Yaqui Easter Ceremony at Pascua. Tucson, 1950.

Painter, M.T., et al. A Yaqui Easter Sermon. UASSB, XXVI, 89 pp. 1955.

Parsons, E.C., and Beals, R.L. The Sacred Clowns of the Pueblo and Mayo-Yaqui Indians. AA, n.s., XXXVI, 491-514. 1934.

Perez de Ribas, A. Historia de los triumphos de novestra santa fee en los missiones de la provincia de Nueva Espana. Madrid, 1645.

Sauer, C. The Distribution of Aboriginal Tribes and Languages in Northwestern Mexico. IA, V, 23-6, 31-2. 1934.

Spicer, E.H. Linguistic Aspects of Yaqui Acculturation. AA, n.s., XLV, 410-26. 1943.

--- The Military Orientation in Yaqui Culture. FTD, 171-88. 1950.

--- El Problema Yaqui. AI, V, 273-86. 1945.

--- Social Organization and Disorganization in an Arizona Yaqui Village. Chicago, 1946.

--- Social Structure and Cultural Process in Yaqui Religious Acculturation. AA, LX, 433-41. 1958.

--- Yaqui Militarism. Arizona Quarterly, III, 40-8. 1947.

--- Yaqui Villages Past and Present. K, XIII, 2-12. 1947.

Toor, F. Apuntes sobre costumbres Yaquis. Mexican Folkways, Special Yaqui Number, pp. 52-63. 1937.

Velasco, J.B. de. Arte de la lengua Cahita. Mexico, 1890.

Warner, R.E. Yaquis of Mexico and Their Folk Literature. K, VIII, 18-22. 1943.

Whiting, A.F. The Tumacacori Census of 1796. K, XXIX, i, 1-12. 1953.

3. CHINIPA

Including the Chinipa, the Huite, and the Tubar.

Anonymous. Tubare. BBAE, XXX, ii, 830. 1910.

Lumholtz, C. Unknown Mexico, I, 441-4. New York, 1902.

Sauer, C. The Distribution of Aboriginal Tribes and Languages in Northwestern Mexico. IA, V, 28, 32-6. 1934.

4. CHIRICAHUA

Including the Chiricahua Apache and the Mimbreno or Gila Apache.

Opler, M.E. An Apache Life-way. 500 pp. Chicago, 1941.

--- Myths and Tales of the Chiricahua Apache Indians. MAFLS, XXXVII, 1-114. 1942.

Anonymous. Apache. BBAE, XXX, i, 63-7. 1907.

--- Chiricahua. BBAE, XXX, i, 282-5. 1907.

Arnold, E. Blood Brother. 558 pp. New York, 1947.

Ball, E. Chiricahua Legends. WF, XV, 110-12. 1956.

Barrett, S.M., ed. Geronimo's Story of His Life. 216 pp. New York, 1906.

Bartoli, J.F. The Apache "Devil Dance." Musical Courier, CLII, viii, 8-10. 1955.

Bellah, R.N. Apache Kinship Systems. 151 pp. Cambridge, 1952.

Betzinez, J. and Nye, W.S. I Fought with Geronimo. 214 pp. Harrisburg, Pa., 1959.

Bigelow, J. On the Bloody Trail of Geronimo. 237 pp. Los Angeles, 1958.

Bourke, J.G. An Apache Campaign in the Sierra Madre. 112 pp. New York, 1886.

--- The Medicine Men of the Apache. ARBAE, IX, 451-595. 1892.

--- Notes on Apache Mythology. JAFL, III, 209-12. 1890.

--- Notes upon the Gentile Organization of the Apaches of Arizona. JAFL, III, 111-26. 1890.

Bourke, J.G. Notes upon the Religion of the Apache Indians. FL, II, 419-54. 1891.

--- On the Border with Crook. 491 pp. New York, 1892.

--- Vesper Hours of the Stone Age. AA, III, 55-63. 1890.

Castetter, E.F., and Opler, M.E. The Ethnobiology of the Chiricahua and Mescalero Apache. UNMBB, IV, v, 3-63. 1936.

Cremony, J.C. Life among the Apaches. 322 pp. San Francisco, 1868.

Curtis, E.S. The North American Indian, I, 3-51. Cambridge, 1907.

Curtis, N., ed. The Indians' Book, pp. 323-8. New York, 1907.

Dana, R.W. An Echo of Apache Days. IN, VI, 250-4. 1929.

Devereux, G., and Loeb, E.M. Some Notes on Apache Criminality. Journal of Criminal Psychopathology, IV, 424-30. 1943.

East, O.G. and Manucy, A.C. Arizona Apaches as "Guests" in Florida. FHSQ, XXX, 294-300. 1952.

Gardner, H. Philip St. George Cooke and the Apache, 1854. NMHR, XXVIII, 115-32. 1953.

Gatschet, A.S. The Chiricahua Apache "Sun Circle." SMC, XXXIV, ii, 144-7. 1885.

Gershowitz, H. The Diego Factor among Asiatic Indians, Apaches and West African Negroes. AJPA, n.s., XVII, 195-200. 1959.

Gifford, E.W. Apache-Pueblo. AR, IV, 1-207. 1940.

Harrington, J.P. Southern Peripheral Athapaskawan Origins, Divisions, and Migrations. SMC, C, 503-32. 1940.

Harrington, M.R. The Devil Dance of the Apaches. MJ, III, 6-10. 1912.

Hayes, J.G. Apache Vengeance. 185 pp. Albuquerque, 1954.

Hoijer, H. The Apachean Verb. IJAL, XI, 193-203; XII, 1-13, 51-9; XIV, 247-59; XV, 12-22. 1945-49.

--- Chiricahua Apache. VFPA, VI, 9-29. 1946.

--- Chiricahua and Mescalero Apache Texts. 219 pp. Chicago, 1938.

--- Chiricahua Loan-Words from Spanish. Lg, XV, 100-15. 1939.

--- Classificatory Verb Stems in the Apachean Languages. IJAL, XI, 13-23. 1945.

--- Pitch Accent in the Apachean Languages. Lg, XIX, 38-41. 1943.

--- Phonetic and Phonemic Change in the Athapaskan Languages. Lg, XVIII, 218-20. 1942.

Kate, H.F.C. ten. Reizen en onderzoekingen in Noord-Amerika, pp. 165-208. Leiden, 1885.

Kraus, B.S. Indian Health in Arizona. RBER, II, 164 pp. 1954.

Lehmann, H. Nine Years among the Indians. 235 pp. Austin, 1927.

Lockwood, F.C. The Apache Indians. 348 pp. New York, 1938.

Loeb, E.M. A Note on Two Far-Travelled Kachinas. JAFL, LVI, 192-9. 1943.

Matson, D.S. and Schroeder, A.H. Cordero's Description of the Apache—1796. NMHR, XXXII, 335-56. 1957.

Ogle, R.H. The Apache and the Government—1870's. NMHR, XXXIV, 81-102. 1959.

--- Federal Control of the Western Apaches. Historical Society of New Mexico, Publications in History, IX. 1940.

Opler, M.E. An Analysis of Mescalero and Chiricahua Apache Social Organization in the Light of Their Systems of Relationship. 19 pp. Chicago, 1936.

--- Apache Data concerning the Relation of Kinship Terminology to Social Classification. AA, n.s., XXXIX, 201-12. 1937.

--- Chiricahua Apache Material relating to Sorcery. PM, XIX, 81-92. 1946.

--- The Concept of Supernatural Power among the Chiricahua and Mescalero Apache. AA, n.s., XXXVII, 65-70. 1935.

--- Examples of Ceremonial Interchanges among Southwestern Tribes. M, XVI, 77-80. 1942.

--- Further Comparative Anthropological Data bearing on the Solution of a Psychological Problem. JSP, IX, 477-83. 1938.

--- The Identity of the Apache Mansos. AA, n.s., XLIV, 725. 1942.

--- An Interpretation of Ambivalence of Two American Indian Tribes. JSP, VII, 82-116. 1936.

--- The Kinship Systems of Southern Athabaskan-speaking Tribes. AA, n.s., XXXVIII, 620-33. 1936.

--- Mountain Spirits of the Chiricahua Apache. M, XX, 125-31. 1946.

--- A Note on the Cultural Affiliations of Northern Mexican Nomads. AA, n.s., XXXVII, 702-6. 1935.

--- Notes on Chiricahua Apache Culture. PM, XX, 1-14. 1947.

--- An Outline of Chiricahua Apache Social Organization. SANAT, 173-242. 1955.

Opler, M.E. The Sacred Clowns of the Chiricahua and Mescalero Indians. EP, XLIV, 75-9. 1938.

--- Some Points of Comparison and Contrast between the Treatment of Functional Disorders by Apache Shamans and Modern Psychiatric Practice. American Journal of Psychiatry, XCII, 1371-87. 1936.

Opler, M.E., and Hoijer, H. The Raid and War-Path Language of the Chiricahua Apache. AA, n. s., XLII, 617-34. 1940.

Santee, R. Apache Land. 216 pp. New York, 1947.

Sauer, C. The Distribution of Aboriginal Tribes and Languages in Northwestern Mexico. IA, V, 75-6. 1934.

Schmidt, M.F., and Brown, D. Fighting Indians of the West, pp. 301-30. New York, 1948.

Schmitz, O. Die Apachen. Ausland, XLIV, 347-51. 1871.

Woodward, A. John G. Bourke on the Arizona Apache, 1874. P, XVI, 33-44. 1943.

5. COCOPA

Including the Cocopa and the Kohuana.

Gifford, E.W. The Cocopa. UCP, XXXI, 257-334. 1933.

Chittenden, N.H. Among the Cocopahs. LS, XIV, 196-204. 1901.

Densmore, F. Field Work among the Yuma, Cocopa, and Yaqui Indians. SMC, LXXIV, v, 147-54. 1925.

--- Yuman and Yaqui Music. BBAE, CX, 1-216. 1932.

Drucker, P. Yuman-Piman. AR, VI, 91-230. 1941.

Dobyns, H.F., et al. Thematic Changes in Yuman Warfare. In, V.F.Ray, ed., Cultural Stability and Cultural Change, 46-71. 1957.

Gatschet, A.S. Der Yuma-Sprachstamm. ZE, IX, 382-3, 392-406. 1887.

Gifford, E.W. Californian Kinship Terminologies. UCP, XVIII, 67-8. 1922.

--- Clans and Moieties in Southern California. UCP, XIV, 156-67. 1918.

Henshaw, H.W. Cajuenche. BBAE, XXX, i, 187. 1907.

Hodge, F.W. Cocopa. BBAE, XXX, i, 319-20. 1907.

Ives, J.C. Report upon the Colorado River of the West. 131 pp. Washington, 1861.

Kelly, D.S. A Brief History of the Cocopa Indians.
    FTD, 159-170. 1950.
Kelly, W.H. Cocopa Gentes. AA, n.s., XLIV, 675-
    91. 1942.
--- The Place of Scalps in Cocopa Warfare. EP, LVI,
    85-91. 1949.
Kniffen, F.B. The Primitive Cultural Landscape of
    the Colorado Delta. UCPG, V, 43-66. 1931.
Kroeber, A.L. Yuman Tribes of the Lower Colorado.
    UCP, XVI, 475-82. 1920.
North, A.W. The Native Tribes of Lower California.
    AA, n.s., X, 236-50. 1908.

6. CONCHO

Including the Chinarra, the Chizo, and the Concho.

Beals, R.L. The Comparative Ethnology of Northern
    Mexico. IA, II, 93-225. 1932.
Hammond, G.P., and Rey, A., eds. Expedition into
    New Mexico made by Antonio de Espejo, pp. 49-54.
    Los Angeles, 1929.
--- The Gallegos Relation of the Rodriguez Expedition.
    NMHR, II, 251-2. 1927.
Kelley, J.C. The Historic Indian Pueblos of La Junta
    de los Rios. NMHR, XXVII, 257-95; XXVIII, 21-
    51. 1952-53.
Sauer, C. The Distribution of Aboriginal Tribes and
    Languages in Northwestern Mexico. IA, V, 59-64.
    1934.

7. COYOTERO

Including the Arivaipa, Carrizo, Cibecue, Pinaleno,
San Carlos, Tonto, and White Mountain, commonly known collectively as the Western Apache.

Goodwin, G. The Social Organization of the Western
    Apache. 791 pp. Chicago, 1942.
Kaut, C.R. The Western Apache Clan System.
    UNMPA, IX, 99 pp. 1957.

Anonymous. Apache. BBAE, XXX, i, 63-7. 1907.
Arnold, E. The Ceremony of the Big Wickiup. AH,
    XXVII, viii, 8-15. 1951.
Bartoli, J.F. The Apache "Devil Dance." Musical
    Courier, CLII, viii, 8-10. 1955.
Beals, R.L. Material Culture of the Pima, Papago,
    and Western Apache. 44 pp. Berkeley, 1934.
Bellah, R.N. Apache Kinship Systems. 151 pp. Cam-
    bridge, 1952.

Bloom, L.B., ed. Bourke on the Southwest. NMHR,
    IX, 159-83, 375-435; X, 1-35. 1934-35.
Bourke, J.G. The Medicine Men of the Apache.
    ARBAE, IX, 451-595. 1892.
--- Notes upon the Gentile Organization of the
    Apaches of Arizona. JAFL, III, 111-26. 1890.
--- Notes upon the Religion of the Apache Indians.
    FL, II, 419-54. 1891.
--- Vesper Hours of the Stone Age. AA, III, 55-63.
    1890.
Burbank, E.A., and Royce, E. Burbank among the
    Indians, pp. 17-39. Caldwell, 1946.
Buschmann, J.C.E. Die Spuren der aztekischen
    Sprache im nördlichen Mexico und höheren ameri-
    kanischen Norden. AKAWB, 1854, Supplement-
    Band, II, 298-322.
Clum, J.P. Es-kim-in-zin. NMHR, III, 399-420;
    IV, 1-28. 1928-29.
--- The San Carlos Apache Police. NMHR, IV, 203-
    20; V, 67-93. 1929-30.
Clum, W. Apache Agent. 297 pp. Boston, 1936.
Curtis, E.S. The North American Indian, I, 3-51.
    Cambridge, 1907.
Dodge, K.T. White Mountain Apache Baskets. AA,
    n.s., II, 193-4. 1900.
Douglas, F.H. Apache Indian Coiled Basketry.
    DAMLS, LXIV, 54-6. 1934.
--- The Apache Indians. DAMLS, XVI, 1-4. 1930.
East, O.G. and Manucy, A.C. Arizona Apaches as
    "Guests" in Florida. FHSQ, XXX, 294-300. 1952.
Edgerton, F. and Hill, F. Primers I, II. Glendale,
    1958.
Federal Writers' Project. The Apache. Arizona
    State Teachers College Bulletin, XX, i, 1-16.
    1939.
Forbes, J.D. Historical Survey of the Indians of
    Sonora, 1821-1910. E, IV, 355-68. 1957.
Frazer, R. The Apaches of the White Mountain
    Reservation. 22 pp. Philadelphia, 1885.
Gatschet, A.S. Classification into Seven Linguistic
    Stocks of Western Indian Dialects. RUSGS, VII,
    403-85. 1879.
--- Zwölf Sprachen aus dem Südwesten Nord-ameri-
    kas. 150 pp. Weimar, 1876.
Gerald, R.E. Two Wickiups on the San Carlos Indian
    Reservation. K, XXIII, iii, 5-11. 1958.
Gershowitz, H. The Diego Factor among Asiatic In-
    dians, Apaches and West African Negroes. AJPA,
    n.s., XVII, 195-200. 1959.
Gifford, E.W. Apache-Pueblo. AR, IV, 1-207. 1940.
Goddard, P.E. Myths and Tales from the San Carlos
    Apache. APAM, XXIV, 1-86. 1918.

Goddard, P.E. Myths and Tales from the White Mountain Apache. APAM, XXIV, 87-139. 1919.

--- San Carlos Apache Texts. APAM, XXIV, 141-367. 1919.

--- Slender-Maiden of the Apache. American Indian Life, ed. E.C. Parsons, pp. 147-51. New York, 1925.

--- White Mountain Apache Texts. APAM, XXIV, 369-527. 1920.

Goodwin, G. The Characteristics and Function of Clan in a Southern Athapascan Culture. AA, n.s., XXXIX, 394-407. 1937.

--- Clans of the Western Apache. NMHR, VIII, 176-82. 1933.

--- A Comparison of Navaho and White Mountain Ceremonial Forms and Categories. SJA, I, 498-506. 1945.

--- Myths and Tales of the White Mountain Apache. MAFLS, XXXIII, 1-223. 1939.

--- The Social Divisions and Economic Life of the Western Apache. AA, n.s., XXXVII, 55-64. 1935.

--- White Mountain Apache Religion. AA, n.s., XL, 24-37. 1938.

Goodwin, G. and Kaut, C. A Native Religious Movement among the White Mountain and Cibecue Apache. SJA, X, 385-404. 1954.

Harrington, J.P. Southern Peripheral Athapaskawan Origins, Divisions, and Migrations. SMC, C, 503-32. 1940.

Hildburgh, W.L. On the Flint Implements attached to Some Apache "Medicine Cords." Man, XIX, 81-7. 1919.

Hoffman, W.J. Miscellaneous Ethnographic Observations. ARGGS, X, 461-78. 1876.

Hoijer, H. The Apachean Verb. IJAL, XI, 193-203; XII, 1-13, 51-9. 1945-46.

--- Pitch Accent in the Apachean Languages. Lg, XIX, 38-41. 1943.

--- Phonetic and Phonemic Change in the Athapaskan Languages. Lg, XVIII, 218-20. 1942.

Hrdlicka, A. Notes on the San Carlos Apache. AA, n.s., VII, 480-95. 1905.

James, G.W. Basket Makers of the Palomas Apaches. Sunset Magazine, XI, 146-53. 1903.

Kate, H.F.C. ten. Reizen en onderzoekingen in Noord-Amerika, pp. 165-208. Leiden, 1885.

Kaut, C.R. Notes on Western Apache Religious and Social Organization. AA, LXI, 99-102. 1959.

--- Western Apache Clan and Phratry Organization. AA, LVIII, 140-46. 1956.

Keegan, J.J. The Indian Brain. AJPA, III, 25-62. 1920.

Kraus, B.S. Occurrence of the Carabelli Trait in Southwest Ethnic Groups. AJPA, n.s., XVII, 117-23. 1959.

Kraus, B.S. and Jones, B.M. Indian Health in Arizona. RBER, II, 164 pp. 1954.

Kraus, B.S. and White, C.B. Micro-Evolution in a Human Population. AA, LVIII, 1017-43. 1956.

LaFarge, O. Apache Chief–1949 Model. AmI, V, iii, 3-16. 1950.

Lockwood, F.C. The Apache Indians. 348 pp. New York, 1938.

Loew, O. Vocabulary of the Apache and of the Navajo. RUSGS, VII, 424-65, 469. 1879.

McAllester, D.P. The Role of Music in Western Apache Culture. ACISA, V, 468-72. 1960.

Matson, D.S. and Schroeder, A.H. Cordero's Description of the Apache–1796. NMHR, XXXII, 335-56. 1957.

Ogle, R.H. The Apache and the Government–1870's. NMHR, XXXIV, 81-102. 1959.

--- Federal Control of the Western Apaches, 1848-1886. Historical Society of New Mexico, Publications in History, IX, 268 pp. 1940.

Opler, M.E. The Kinship Systems of the Southern Athabaskan-speaking Tribes. AA, n.s., XXXVIII, 620-33. 1936.

Palmer, E. Customs of the Coyotero Apaches. Zoe, I, 161-72. 1890.

--- Notes on Indian Manners and Customs. AN, XII, 308-13. 1878.

Reagan, A.B. Apache Medicine Ceremonies. PIAS, XIV, 275-83. 1904.

--- The Apache Stick Game. PIAS, XIII, 197-9. 1903.

--- Archaeological Notes on the Fort Apache Region. PIAS, XXXIII, 111-31. 1930.

--- Naezhosh, or the Apache Pole Game. PIAS, XII, 68-71. 1902.

--- Notes on the Indians of the Fort Apache Region. APAM, XXXI, 281-345. 1930.

--- Plants used by the White Mountain Apache Indians. WA, n.s., VIII, 143-61. 1929.

--- Sketches of Indian Life and Character. TKAS, XXI, 207-15. 1908.

--- Some Notes on the Occult and Hypnotic Ceremonies of Indians. PUA, XI, 65-71. 1934.

Reed, A.C. Apache Cattle, Horses and Men. AH, XXX, vii, 16-25. 1954.

Roberts, H.H. Basketry of the San Carlos Apache. APAM, XXXI, 121-218. 1929.

--- San Carlos Apache Double Coiled Basket. AA, n.s., XVIII, 601-2. 1916.

Romero, M. Correrias de los Apaches "Los Amarillos."
  Boletin de la Sociedad Chihuahense de Estudios
  Historicos, VII, xi, 567-70. 1952.

Santee, R. Apache Land. 216 pp. New York, 1947.

Sapir, E. An Apache Basket Jar. MJ, I, 13-15. 1910.

Schaeffer, M.W.M. The Construction of a Wickiup
  on the Fort Apache Indian Reservation. K, XXIV,
  ii, 14-20. 1958.

Schmidt, M.F., and Brown, D. Fighting Indians of
  the West, pp. 89-112. New York, 1948.

Schoolcraft, H.R. Apaches. HCPIT, V, 202-14.
  1855.

Smart, C. Notes on the "Tonto" Apaches. ARSI,
  XXII, 417-19. 1867.

Smith, D.M. Indian Tribes of the Southwest, pp.
  16-33. Stanford, 1933.

Stratton, R.B. Captivity of the Oatman Girls. 288 pp.
  New York, 1857.

Wesley, C. From the Apache Indians of San Carlos.
  Boletin Indigenista, XIV, 31-36. March 1954.

White, C.B. The Western Apache and Cross-Cousin
  Marriage. AA, LIX, 131-33. 1957.

Whiting, A.F. The Tumacacori Census of 1796. K,
  XXIX, i, 1-12. 1953.

Woodward, A. John G. Bourke on the Arizona Apache,
  1874. P, XVI, 33-44. 1943.

8. GUASAVE

Ekholm, G.F. Excavations at Guasave, Sinaloa,
  Mexico. APAM, XXXVIII, ii, 23-139. 1942.

Sauer, C. The Distribution of Aboriginal Tribes and
  Languages in Northwestern Mexico. IA, V, 28-30.
  1934.

9. HALCHIDHOMA

Kroeber, A.L. Handbook of the Indians of California. BBAE, LXXVIII, 799-802. 1925.

--- Yuman Tribes of the Lower Colorado. UCP, XVI,
  478-82. 1920.

Spier, L. Yuman Tribes of the Gila River. 433 pp.
  Chicago, 1933.

10. HAVASUPAI

Spier, L. Havasupai Ethnography. APAM, XXIX,
  83-392. 1928.

Berry, S.S. A Shell Necklace from the Havasupai Indians. P, XIX, 29-34. 1946.

Curtis, E.S. The North American Indian, II, 97-102.
  Cambridge, 1908.

Cushing, F.H. The Nation of the Willows. Atlantic
  Monthly, L, 362-74, 541-59. 1882.

Douglas, F.H. The Havasupai Indians. DAMLS,
  XXXIII, 1-4. 1931.

Emerick, R. The Havasupais. BUM, XVIII, iii,
  33-47. 1954.

Henshaw, H.W. Havasupai. BBAE, XXX, i, 537-9.
  1907.

Iliff, F.G. People of the Blue Water. 271 pp. New
  York, 1954.

James, G.W. The Indians of the Painted Desert Region. 268 pp. Boston, 1903.

Montandon, G. Une descente chez les Havazoupai.
  JSAP, n.s., XIX, 145-54. 1927.

--- Gravures et peintures rupestres des Indiens du
  Cataract Canyon. Ane, XXXIII, 347-55. 1923.

Schroeder, A.H. A Brief History of the Havasupai.
  P, XXV, 45-52. 1953.

Schwartz, D.W. Culture Area and Time Depth. AA,
  LXI, 1060-70, 1959.

--- The Havasupai 600 A.D.-1955 A.D. P,
  XXVIII, 77-85. 1956.

Service, Elman. Recent Observations on Havasupai
  Land Tenure. SJA, III, 360-6. 1947.

Shufeldt, R.W. Some Observations on the Havesu-pai
  Indians. PUSNM, XIV, 387-90. 1891.

Spier, L. Comparative Vocabularies and Parallel
  Texts in Two Yuman Languages of Arizona. UNMPA,
  II, 1-150. 1940.

--- Havasupai Days. American Indian Life, ed. E.C.
  Parsons, pp. 179-87. New York, 1925.

--- The Havasupai of Cataract Canyon. AMJ, XVIII,
  637-45. 1918.

--- Havasupai (Yuman) Texts. IJAL, III, 109-16.
  1924.

--- Problems arising from the Cultural Position of the
  Havasupai. AA, n.s., XXXI, 213-22. 1929.

Whiting, A.F. Havasupai Characteristics in the
  Cohonina. P, XXX, 55-60. 1958.

Writers' Program of Work Projects Administration. The
  Havasupai and the Hualapai. Arizona State Teachers College Bulletin, XXI, v, 1-36. 1940.

11. HOPI

Including the pueblos of Mishongnovi, Oraibi, Shipaulovi, Shongopovi, Sichomovi, and Walpi, also
known collectively as the Moqui.

Aberle, D.F. The Psychosocial Analysis of a Hopi
    Life History. CPM, XXI, i, 133 pp. 1951.
Brandt, R.B. Hopi Ethics. 408 pp. Chicago, 1954.
Colton, H.S. Hopi Kachina Dolls. 144 pp. Albu-
    querque, 1949, 1959.
Curtis, E.S. The North American Indian, XII, 1-
    291. Norwood, 1922.
Eggan, F. Social Organization of the Western Pueb-
    los, pp. 17-138. Chicago, 1950.
Emmons, G.L. Hopi Hearings. 412 pp. Washing-
    ton, 1955.
Hack, J.T. The Changing Physical Environment of
    the Hopi Indians. PMP, XXXV, i, 1-85. 1942.
Hough, W. The Hopi Indians. 265 pp. Cedar Rapids,
    1915.
Montgomery, R.G., Smith, W., and Brew, J.O.
    Franciscan Awatowi. PMP, XXXVI, 1-361. 1949.
Simmons, L.W. Sun Chief. 460 pp. New Haven,
    1942.
Stephen, A.M. Hopi Journal, ed. E.C.Parsons.
    CUCA, XXXIII. 2 vols. 1936.
Thompson, L. Culture in Crisis. 221 pp. New York,
    1950.
Titiev, M. Old Oraibi. PMP, XXII, i, 1-277. 1944.

Akin, L. American Artist. AMJ, XIII, 113-18.
    1913.
American Bible Society. Imuy Matthewt, Markt,
    Luket, pu Johnt pumuy lomatuawiamu. 270 pp.
    New York, 1929.
Anderson, E., et al. Observations on Three Varie-
    ties of Hopi Maize. AJB, XXXIX, 597-609. 1952.
Anonymous. Found on Navajo Mountain.Pacific Dis-
    covery, VI, 12-13, 32. September-October 1953.
--- Hopi Snake Dance. AH, XXI, vii, 4-7. 1950.
--- Moqui Pueblos of Arizona. RIT, 1890, 160-98.
Barber, E.A. Habits of the Moqui Tribe. PAAAS,
    XXVI, 340. 1877.
--- Moqui Food Preparations. AN,XII, 456-8.1878.
--- The Seven Towns of Moqui. AN, XI, 728-31.
    1877.
Barrett, S.A. An Observation on Hopi Child Burial.
    AA, n.s., XXXIX, 562-4. 1937.
Bartlett, K. Hopi Indian Costume. P, XXII, 1-10.
    1949.
--- Hopi History, II: The Navajo Wars. MNMNA,
    VIII, 33-7. 1937.
--- Spanish Contacts with the Hopi. MNMNA, VI,
    55-9. 1934.
Baxter, R.H. The Moqui Snake Dance. AAOJ,XVII,
    205-7. 1895.

Beaglehole, E. Hopi Hunting and Hunting Ritual.
    YUPA, IV, 1-26. 1936.
--- Notes on Hopi Economic Life. YUPA, XV, 1-88.
    1937.
Beaglehole, E., and P. Hopi of the Second Mesa.
    MAAA, XLIV, 1-65. 1935.
Beaglehole, P. Census Data from Two Hopi Villages.
    AA, n.s., XXXVII, 41-54. 1935.
Beaver, W.T. Peyote and the Hopi. AA, LIV, 120.
    1952.
Beckwith, M.W. Dance Forms of the Moqui and
    Kwakiutl Indians. ICA,XV,ii, 79-114. 1906.
Bennett, C.N. The Elder Brother of the Hopi Indians.
    SS, IV, v, 4-5. 1952.
Bloom, L.B. Bourke on the Southwest. NMHR, X,
    1-35. 1935.
--- A Campaign against the Moqui Pueblos. NMHR,
    VI, 158-226. 1931.
Boas, F. Zur Anthropologie der nordamerikanischen
    Indianer. VBGA, 1895, 367-411.
Bogert, C.M. The Hopi Snake Dance. NH, XLVII,
    276-83. 1941.
Bourke, J.G. The Snake Ceremonials at Walpi. AA,
    VIII, 192-6. 1895.
--- The Snake-Dance of the Moquis of Arizona. 371
    pp. London, 1884.
Brainerd, M. The Hopi Indian Family. 62 pp.
    Chicago, 1939.
Brew, J.O. The First Two Seasons at Awatovi. AAn,
    III, 122-37. 1937.
Brew, J.O., and Hack, J.T. Prehistoric Use of Coal
    by Indians of Northern Arizona. P, XII, 8-14.1939.
Bunzel, R.L. The Pueblo Potter. CUCA, VIII, 1-
    134. 1929.
Burbank, E.A., and Royce, E. Burbank among the
    Indians, pp. 88-107. Caldwell, 1946.
Buschmann, J.C.E. Die Spuren der aztekischen
    Sprache im nördlichen Mexico und höheren ameri-
    kanischen Norden. AKAWB, 1854, Supplement-
    Band, II, 281-93.
Chapman, K.M. A Feather Symbol of the Ancient
    Pueblos. EP, XXIII, 526-36. 1927.
Coleman, G.E. Rattlesnake Venom Antidote of the
    Hopi Indians. Bulletin of the Antivenin Institute
    of America, Vol. I. 1928.
Collins, G.N. A Drought-resisting Adaptation in
    Seedlings of Hopi Maize. Journal of Agricultural
    Research, I, 293-302. 1914.
--- Pueblo Indian Maize Breeding. Journal of Hered-
    ity, V, 255-68. 1914.
Colton, H.S. A Brief Survey of Hopi Common Law.
    MNMNA, VII, 21-4. 1934.

Colton, H.S. "Fools Names like Fools Faces." P, XIX, 1-8. 1946.

--- Hopi Deities. P, XX, 10-16. 1947.

--- Hopi Number Systems. P, XIV, 33-6. 1941.

--- Hopi Pottery Firing Temperatures. P, XXIV, 73-76. 1951.

--- Kachina Dolls. AH, XXI, vii, 8-13. 1950.

--- Primitive Pottery Making. Faenza, XXXVII, vi, 135-9. 1952.

--- Troy Town on the Hopi Mesas. SM, LVIII, 129-34. 1944.

--- What is a Kachina? P, XIX, 40-7. 1947.

Colton, H.S., Colton, M.R.F., and Nequatewa, E. Hopi Legends of the Sunset Crater Region. MNMNA, V, 17-23. 1932.

Colton, H.S., and Nequatewa, E. The Ladder Dance. MNMNA, V, 4-12. 1932.

Colton, M.R.F. The Arts and Crafts of the Hopi Indians. MNMNA, XI, 1-24. 1938.

--- Hopi Silversmithing. P, XII, 1-8. 1939.

--- Technique of the Major Hopi Crafts. MNMNA, III, xii, 1-7. 1931.

Colton, M.R.F., and E. Nequatewa. Hopi Courtship and Marriage. Museum of Northern Arizona, Notes, V, ix, 41-56. 1933.

Coolidge, M.R. The Rain-Makers. 313 pp. Boston, 1929.

Crane, L. Indians of the Enchanted Desert. 364 pp. Boston, 1925.

Crimmins, M.L. The Rattlesnake in the Art and Life of the American Indian. BTAPS, XVII, 28-41. 1946.

Cummings, B. The Bride of the Sun. K, I, v, 1-4. 1936.

Curtis, N., ed. The Indians' Book, pp. 473-532. New York, 1907.

Cushing, F.H. Origin Myth from Oraibi. JAFL, XXXVI, 163-70. 1923.

Cushing, F.H., Fewkes, J.W., and Parsons, E.C. Contributions to Hopi History. AA, n.s., XXIV, 253-98. 1922.

DeHuff, E.W. Taytay's Memories, pp. 83-90. New York, 1924.

--- Taytay's Tales, pp. 18-21, 25-39, 116-21, 125-31, 141-8, 172-82. New York, 1922.

--- Two Little Hopi. 224 pp. New York, 1936.

--- The Witch. EP, XXXI, 37-9. 1931.

Dellenbaugh, F.S. The Somaikoli Dance at Sichumovi. AMJ, XV, 256-8. 1915.

Dennis, W. Animism and Related Tendencies in Hopi Children. JSAP, XXXVIII, 21-36. 1943.

Dennis, W. Does Culture appreciably affect Patterns of Infant Behavior? JSP, XII, 305-17. 1940.

--- The Hopi Child. 204 pp. New York, 1940, 1945.

Dennis, W., and M.G. The Effect of Cradling Practices upon the Onset of Walking in Hopi Children. Journal of Genetic Psychology, LVI, 77-86. 1940.

Devereux, G. La chasse collective au lapin. JSAP, n.s., XXXIII, 63-90. 1941.

Dienes, A.de. Costumes of the Southwest Indians. NH, LVI, 360-7. 1947.

Dockstader, F.J. Christmas—Hopi Style. SS, III, vi, 2-5. 1951.

--- The Hopi Kachina Cult. Tomorrow, IV, iii, 57-63. 1956.

--- Spanish Loanwords in Hopi. IJAL, XXI, 151-9. 1955.

Donaldson, T. Moqui Indians of Arizona and Pueblo Indians of New Mexico. U.S.Census Office, Eleventh Census, Extra Census Bulletin, pp. 1-136. Washington, 1893.

Dorsey, G.A. The Hopi Indians of Arizona. PSM, LV, 732-50. 1899.

--- Indians of the Southwest. 223 pp. 1903.

Dorsey, G.A., and Voth, H.R. The Mishongnovi Ceremonies of the Snake and Antelope Fraternities. FMAS, III, 165-261. 1902.

--- The Oraibi Soyal Ceremony. FMAS, III, 5-59. 1901.

Douglas, F.H. Hopi Indian Basketry. DAMLS, XVII, 1-4. 1931.

--- Hopi Indian Pottery. DAMLS, XLVII, 1-4. 1932.

--- Hopi Indian Weaving. DAMLS, XVIII, 1-4. 1931.

--- The Hopi Indians. DAMLS, XIII, 1-4. 1930.

--- Hopi Pottery. Enjoy Your Museum Series, IIIa, 15 pp. Pasadena, 1933.

--- Main Types of Pueblo Cotton Textiles. DAMLS, XCII-XCIII, 166-72. 1940.

--- Main Types of Pueblo Woolen Textiles. DAMLS, XCIV-XCV, 174-80. 1940.

--- Notes on Hopi Brocading. MNMNA, XI, 35-8. 1938.

Dozier, E.P. Kinship and Linguistic Change among the Arizona Tewa. IJAL, XXI, 242-51. 1955.

--- Resistance to Acculturation and Assimilation in an Indian Pueblo. AA, n.s., LIII, 56-66. 1951.

Drucker, P. Yuman-Piman. AR, VI, 91-230. 1941.

Earle, E., and Kennard, E.A. Hopi Kachinas. 40 pp. New York, 1938.

Eggan, D. The General Problem of Hopi Adjustment. AA, n.s., XLV, 357-373. 1943.

--- The General Problem of Hopi Adjustment. PNSC, 276-91. 1953.

Eggan, D. Hopi Marriage and Family Traditions. Marriage and Family Living, VI, 1-2. 1944.

--- Instruction and Affect in Hopi Cultural Continuity. SJA, XII, 347-70. 1956.

--- The Manifest Content of Dreams. AA, LIV, 469-485. 1952.

--- The Significance of Dreams for Anthropological Research. AA, n.s., LI, 177-198. 1949.

Eggan, F. The Kinship System of the Hopi Indians. 56 pp. Chicago, 1936.

Ehrenreich, W. Ein Ausflug nach Tusayan. Globus, LXXVI, 53-4, 74-8, 91-5, 138-42, 154-5. 1899.

Farmer, M.F. Awatovi Bows. P, XXVIII, 8-10. 1955.

--- Awatovi Mural Decorations. P, XXVII, ii, 21-24. 1954.

Federal Writers' Project. The Hopi. Arizona State Teachers College Bulletin, XVIII, ii, 1-26. 1937.

Fergusson, E. Dancing Gods, pp. 115-78. New York, 1931.

Fewkes, J.W. The Alósaka Cult of the Hopi Indians. AA, n.s., I, 522-44. 1899.

--- Ancestor Worship of the Hopi Indians. ARSI, 1921, 485-506.

--- The A-wa'-to-bi. AA, VI, 363-76. 1893.

--- The Butterfly in Hopi Myth and Ritual. AA, n.s., XII, 575-94. 1910.

--- A Central American Ceremony which suggests the Snake Dance of the Tusayan Villagers. AA, VI, 285-306. 1893.

--- The Ceremonial Circuit among the Village Indians of North East Arizona. JAFL, V, 33-42. 1892.

--- A Comparison of Sia and Tusayan Snake Ceremonials. AA, VIII, 118-41. 1895.

--- A Contribution to Ethno-Botany. AA, IX, 14-21. 1896.

--- Designs on Prehistoric Hopi Pottery. ARBAE, XXXIII, 207-84. 1919.

--- The Destruction of the Tusayan Monsters. JAFL, VIII, 132-7. 1895.

--- Dolls of the Tusayan Indians. IAE, VII, 45-74. 1894.

--- The Feather Symbol in Ancient Hopi Designs. AA, XI, 1-14. 1898.

--- A Few Summer Ceremonials at the Tusayan Pueblos. JAEA, II, 1-160. 1892.

--- A Few Tusayan Pictographs. AA, V, 9-26. 1892.

--- Fire Worship of the Hopi Indians. ARSI, 1920, 589-610.

--- The Growth of the Hopi Ritual. JAFL, XI, 173-94. 1898.

--- Hopi. BBAE, XXX, i, 560-8. 1907.

Fewkes, J.W. Hopi Basket Dances. JAFL, XII, 81-96. 1899.

--- Hopi Ceremonial Frames. AA, n.s., VIII, 664-70. 1906.

--- Hopi Katcinas. ARBAE, XXI, 3-126. 1903.

--- Hopi Katcinas Drawn by Native Artists. ARBAE, XXI, 3-126. 1900.

--- Hopi Shrines near the East Mesa. AA, n.s., VIII, 346-75. 1906.

--- Hopi Snake-Washing. AA, XI, 313-8. 1898.

--- An Interpretation of Katcina Worship. JAFL, XIV, 81-94. 1901.

--- The Katcina Altars in Hopi Worship. ARSI, 1926, 469-86.

--- The Kinship of the Tusayan Villagers. AA, VII, 394-417. 1894.

--- The Lesser New-Fire Ceremony at Walpi. AA, n.s., III, 438-53. 1901.

--- The Mam-zrau'ti: a Tusayan Ceremony. AA, V, 217-45. 1892.

--- Minor Hopi Festivals. AA, n.s., IV, 482-511. 1902.

--- The Mishongnovi Flute Altars. JAFL, IX, 241-55. 1896.

--- Morphology of Tusayan Altars. AA, X, 129-45. 1897.

--- The New-Fire Ceremony at Walpi. AA, n.s., II, 80-138. 1900.

--- On Certain Personages who appear in a Tusayan Ceremony. AA, VII, 32-52. 1894.

--- The Oraibi Flute Altar. JAFL, VIII, 265-82. 1895.

--- The Owakülti Altar at Sichomovi Pueblo. AA, n.s., III, 211-26. 1901.

--- Pacific Coast Shells from Prehistoric Tusayan Pueblos. AA, IX, 359-67. 1896.

--- The Pa-lü-lü-kon-ti. JAFL, VI, 269-82. 1893.

--- Prehistoric Culture of Tusayan. AA, IX, 151-73. 1896.

--- Preliminary Account of an Expedition to the Cliff Villages of the Red Rock Country and the Tusayan Ruins of Sikyatki and Awatobi. ARSI, 1895, 557-88.

--- Property-Right in Eagles among the Hopi. AA, n.s., II, 690-707. 1900.

--- Provisional List of Annual Ceremonies at Walpi. IAE, VIII, 215-38. 1895.

--- The Sacrificial Element in Hopi Worship. JAFL, X, 187-201. 1897.

--- Sky-God Impersonations in Hopi Worship. JAFL, XV, 14-32. 1902.

--- Snake Ceremonials at Walpi. JAEA, IV, 1-126. 1894.

Fewkes, J.W. Southern Extension of Prehistoric Tusa-
    yan. AA, IX, 253. 1896.
--- Studies in Tusayan Archaeology. IAE, IX, 204-
    5. 1896.
--- A Study of Summer Ceremonials at Zuni and
    Moqui Pueblos. BEI, XXII, 89-113. 1890.
--- A Suggestion as to the Meaning of the Moki Snake
    Dance. JAFL, IV, 129-38. 1891.
--- Sun Worship of the Hopi Indians. ARSI, 1918,
    493-526.
--- The Sun's Influence on the Form of Hopi Pueblos.
    AA, n.s., VIII, 88-100. 1906.
--- A Theatrical Performance at Walpi. PWAS, II,
    605-29. 1900.
--- Tusayan Flute and Snake Ceremonies. ARBAE,
    XIX, ii, 957-1011. 1900.
--- Tusayan Katcinas. ARBAE, XV, 245-313. 1897.
--- Tusayan Migration Traditions. ARBAE, XIX, ii,
    573-633. 1900.
--- The Tusayan New Fire Ceremony. Proceedings
    of the Boston Society of Natural History, XXVI,
    422-58. 1894.
--- The Tusayan Ritual. ARSI, 1895, i, 683-700.
--- Tusayan Snake Ceremonies. ARBAE, XVI, 267-
    312. 1897.
--- Tusayan Totemic Signatures. AA, X, 1-11.
    1897.
--- The Use of Idols in Hopi Worship. ARSI, 1922,
    i, 377-97.
--- Walpi. BBAE, XXX, ii, 901-2. 1910.
--- The Walpi Flute Observance. JAFL, VII, 265-87.
    1894.
--- The Wa-wac-ka-tci-na, a Tusayan Foot Race.
    BEI, XXIV, 113-33. 1892.
--- The Winter Solstice Ceremony at Walpi. AA,
    XI, 65-87, 101-15. 1898.
--- Wüwütcimti: the Tusayan New Fire Ceremony.
    Proceedings of the Boston Society of Natural His-
    tory, XXVI, 422-58. 1895.
Fewkes, J.W., and Owens, J.G. The Lá-la-kon-ta:
    a Tusayan Dance. AA, V, 105-29. 1892.
Fewkes, J.W., and Stephen, A.M. The Ná-ac-nai-
    ya: a Tusayan Initiation Ceremony. JAFL, V,
    189-217. 1892.
Fewkes, J.W., Stephen, A.M., and Owens, J.G.
    The Snake Ceremonials at Walpi. JAEA, IV, 1-
    126. 1894.
Fisher, A.K. A Partial List of Moki Animal Names.
    AA, IX, 174. 1896.
Forde, C.D. Habitat, Economy, and Society, pp.
    220-59. London, 1934.

Forde, C.D. Hopi Agriculture and Land Ownership.
    JAI, LXI, 357-405. 1931.
Gatschet, A.S. Classification into Seven Linguistic
    Stocks of Western Indian Dialects. RUSGS, VII, 403-
    85. 1879.
--- Zwolf Sprachen aus dem Sudwesten Nordamerikas.
    150 pp. Wiemar, 1876.
Gianini, C.A. The Hopi Snake Dance. EP, XXV, 439-
    49. 1928.
Gifford, E.W. Apache-Pueblo. AR, IV, 1-207. 1940.
Gilman, B.I. Hopi Songs. JAEA, V, 1-226. 1908.
Goldfrank, E.S. The Impact of Situation and Personali-
    ty on Four Hopi Emergence Myths. SJA, IV, 241-62.
    1948.
--- Socialization, Personality, and the Structure of
    Pueblo Society. AA, n.s., XLVII, 516-40. 1945.
Gray, L.H. Hopi. ERE, VI, 782-9. 1914.
Hamer, J.H. An Analysis of Aggression in Two Socie-
    ties. Anthropology Tomorrow, V, 87-94. 1956.
Hammond, G.P., and Rey, A., eds. Expedition into
    New Mexico made by Antonio de Espejo, pp. 95-
    104. Los Angeles, 1929.
Hargrave, L.L. First Mesa. MNMNA, III, viii, 1-4.
    1931.
--- The Jeddito Valley and the First Pueblo Towns in
    Arizona to be visited by Europeans. MNMNA, VIII,
    17-32. 1935.
--- Oraibi. MNMNA, IV, vii, 1-8. 1932.
--- Shungopovi. MNMNA, II, x, 1-4. 1931.
Harrington, I.L. "The Good-Bringing," a Tale from
    the Hopi Pueblo of Oraibi. NMHR, VI, 227-30.
    1931.
Harrington, J.P. Note on the Names Moqui and Hopi.
    AA, n.s., XLVII, 177-8. 1945.
Harrington, M.R. Ancient Nevada Pueblo Cotton.
    Masterkey, XI, 5-7. 1937.
Haury, E.W., and Conrad, C.M. The Comparison of
    Fiber Properties of Arizona Cliff-Dweller and Hopi
    Cotton. AAn, III, 224-7. 1938.
Heizer, R.F. The Hopi Snake Dance. Ciba Symposia,
    V, 1681-4. 1944.
Henry, W.E. The Thematic Apperception Technique
    in the Study of Culture-Personality Relations. Genetic
    Psychology Monographs, XXXV, 1-135. 1947.
Hodge, F.W. Hopi Pottery fired with Coal. AA, n.s.,
    VI, 581-2. 1904.
Hodge, G.M. The Kachinas are coming. 129 pp.
    Los Angeles, 1937.
Holterman, J. Mission San Bartolome de Xongopavi.
    P, XXVIII, 29-36. 1955.
Hoover, J.W. Tusayan: the Hopi Indian Country of
    Arizona. GR, XX, 425-44. 1930.

Hough, W. A Collection of Hopi Ceremonial Pigments. RUSNM, 1900, 463-71.

--- Environmental Interrelations in Arizona. AA, XI, 133-55. 1898.

--- Field Work among the Hopi Indians. SMC, LXXII, vi, 94-6. 1922.

--- The Hopi in Relation to Their Plant Environment. AA, X, 33-44. 1897.

--- The Hopi Indian Collection in the United States National Museum. PUSNM, LIV, 235-96. 1919.

--- The Moki Snake Dance. 58 pp. Chicago, 1899.

--- Music of the Hopi Flute Ceremony. AA, X, 162-3. 1897.

--- Sacred Springs in the Southwest. RP, V, 163-70. 1906.

--- The Sio Shalako at the First Mesa. AA, n.s., XIX, 410-15. 1917.

Hubert, V. An Introduction to Hopi Pottery Design. MNMNA, X, 1-4. 1937.

Ives, J.C. Report upon the Colorado River of the West. 131 pp. Washington, 1861.

James, G.W. The Indians of the Painted Desert Region. 268 pp. Boston, 1903.

James, H.C. Haliksai. 28 pp. El Centro, 1940.

--- The Hopi Indians. 236 pp. Caldwell, 1956.

Jones, H. Niman Katcina Dance at Walpi. EP, XXXIII, 68-71. 1932.

Jones, V.H. The Establishment of the Hopi Reservation. P, XXIII, 17-25. 1950.

Judd, N.M. Nampeyo, an Additional Note. P, XXIV, 92-96. 1951.

Kabotie, F. Designs from the Ancient Mimbreños. 83 pp. San Francisco, 1949.

Kate, H.F.C. ten. Reizen en onderzoekingen in Noord-Amerika, pp. 245-67. Leiden, 1885.

Kennard, E.A. Hopi Kachinas. 40 pp. New York, 1938.

--- Hopi Reactions to Death. AA, n.s., XXXIX, 491-6. 1937.

--- Little Hopi Hopihoya. ILR, Pueblo Series, II, 1-201. 1948.

Kent, K.P. The Braiding of a Hopi Wedding Sash. P, XII, 46-52. 1940.

Kewanwytewa, J., and Bartlett, K. Hopi Mocassin Making. P, XIX, 21-8. 1946.

Kewanwytewa, J. A True Story. P, XXIX, 87-88. 1957.

Klauber, L.M. A Herpetological Review of the Hopi Snake Dance. Bulletin of the Zoological Society of San Diego, VI, 1-58. 1930.

--- How the Hopi handle Rattlesnakes. P, XIX, 37-9. 1947.

Kluckhohn, C. Hopi and Navajo. New Mexico Quarterly, III, 56-64. 1933.

Kluckhohn, C. and MacLeish, K. Moencopi Variations from Whorf's Second Mesa Hopi. IJAL, XXI, 150-6. 1955.

Lawrence, B. Mammals found at the Awatovi Site. PMP, XXXV, iii, 44 pp. 1951.

Lee, D.D. Freedom and Culture. 187 pp. Englewood Cliffs, 1959.

Lewton, F.L. The Cotton of the Hopi Indians. SMC, LX, vi, 1-15. 1913.

Linné, S. Prehistoric and Modern Hopi Pottery. Ethnos, XI, 89-98. 1946.

Loeb, S.M. A Note on Two Far-Travelled Kachinas. JAFL, LVI, 192-9. 1943.

Lockett, H.G. The Unwritten Literature of the Hopi. UASSB, II, 1-101. 1933.

Lowie, R.H. Hopi Kinship. APAM, XXX, 361-88. 1929.

--- Noted in Hopiland. AMJ, XVII, 569-74. 1917.

--- Notes on Hopi Clans. APAM, XXX, 303-60. 1929.

--- A Woman's Ceremony among the Hopi. NH, XXV, 178-84. 1925.

McCormick, H. The Artist's Southwest. AMJ, XIII, 119-25. 1913.

McGibbeny, J.H. Hopi Jewelry. AH, XXI, vii, 18-25. 1950.

MacGregor, J.C. Burial of an Early American Magician. PAPS, LXXXVI, 270-92. 1943.

--- Zwei gegensätzliche Indianer-Stämme in Arizona. Natur und Volk, LXVIII, 535-44. 1938.

MacLeish, K. A Few Hopi Songs from Moenkopi. M, XV, 178-84. 1941.

--- Notes on Folk Medicine in the Hopi Village of Moenkopi. JAFL, LVI, 62-8. 1943.

--- Notes on Hopi Belt-Weaving of Moenkopi. AA, n.s., XLII, 291-310. 1940.

McPhee, J.C. Indians in Non-Indian Communities. 68 pp. Window Rock, 1953.

Marcy, R.B. Thirty Years of Army Life on the Border, pp. 104-11. New York, 1866.

Martin, P.S., and Willis, E.S. Anasazi Painted Pottery. Anthropology Memoirs of the Field Museum of Natural History, V, 1-284. 1940.

Mearns, E.A. Ornithological Vocabulary of the Moki Indians. AA, IX, 391-403. 1896.

Milford, S.J. Why the Coyote has a Black Spot on His Tail. EP, XLVIII, 83-4. 1941.

Mindeleff, C. An Indian Dance. Science, VII, 507-14. 1886.

--- Localization of Tusayan Clans. ARBAE, XIX, ii, 635-53. 1900.

Mindeleff, V. A Study of Pueblo Architecture, Tusayan and Cibola. ARBAE, VIII, 13-234. 1887.

Munk, J.A. Arizona Sketches, pp. 181-211. New
York, 1905.

Murdock, G.P. Our Primitive Contemporaries, pp.
324-58. New York, 1934.

Murphy, M.M. The Snake Dance People and Their
Country. 14 pp. Oakland, 1928.

Nelson, J.L. Rhythm for Rain. 272 pp. Boston,
1937.

Nequatewa, E. Chaveyo, the First Kachina. P, XX,
60-2. 1948.

--- The Destruction of Elden Pueblo. P, XXVIII, ii,
37-44. 1955.

--- The Flute Ceremony at Hotevilla. P, XIX, 35-
6. 1946.

--- Hopi Hopiwime: the Hopi Ceremonial Calendar.
MNMNA, III, ix, 1-4. 1931.

--- How the Hopi respect the Game Animals. P,
XVIII, 61-2. 1946.

--- A Mexican Raid on the Hopi Pueblo of Oraibi. P,
XVI, 44-52. 1944.

--- Miniature Pottery. P, XII, 18. 1939.

--- The Place of Corn and Feathers in Hopi Ceremonies. P, XIX, 15-16. 1946.

--- Some Hopi Recipes for the Preparation of Wild
Plant Foods. P, XVI, 18-20. 1943.

--- Truth of a Hopi and Other Clan Stories of Shungopovi. BMNA, VIII, 1-113. 1936.

Nequatewa, E., and Colton, M.R.F. Hopi Courtship
and Marriage. MNMNA, V, 41-54. 1933.

Nusbaum, M.A. Another Tower of Babel, a Hopi
Tale. EP, XVIII, 9-12. 1925.

Oakden, E.C., and Sturt, M. The Snake Dance of
the Hopi Indians. Scottish Geographic Magazine,
XLIII, 41-4. 1927.

O'Kane, W.C. The Hopi. 279 pp. Norman, 1953.

--- Sun in the Sky. 261 pp. Norman, 1950.

Oliver, M.L. The Snake Dance. NGM, XXII, 107-
37. 1911.

Owens, J.G. Natal Ceremonies of the Hopi Indians.
JAEA, II, 163-75. 1892.

Page, G.B. Hopi Land Patterns. P, XIII, 29-36.
1940.

Parry, C.C. On a Form of the Boomerang in Use
among the Moqui-Pueblo Indians. PAAAS, XX,
397-400. 1871.

Parsons, E.C. Early Relations between Hopi and
Keres. AA, n.s., XXXVIII, 554-60. 1936.

--- Getting Married on First Mesa. SM, XIII, 259-
65. 1921.

Parsons, E.C. Hidden Ball on First Mesa. Man, XXII,
89-91. 1922.

--- Hopi and Zuni Ceremonialism. MAAA, XXXIX,
1-108. 1933.

--- The Hopi Buffalo Dance. Man, XXIII, 21-7. 1923.

--- Hopi Mothers and Children. Man, XXI, 98-104.
1921.

--- The Hopi Wöwöchim Ceremony in 1920. AA, n.
s., XXV, 156-87. 1923.

--- The Humpbacked Flute Player of the Southwest.
AA, n.s., XL, 337-8. 1938.

--- The Kinship Nomenclature of the Pueblo Indians.
AA, n.s., XXXIV, 377-89. 1932

--- Naming Practices in Arizona. AA, n.s., XXXIX,
561-2. 1937.

--- A Pueblo Indian Journal. MAAA, XXXII, 1-123.
1925.

--- Pueblo Indian Religion. 2 vols. Chicago, 1939.

Peet, S.D. The Worship of the Rain-God. AAOJ,
XVI, 341-56. 1894.

Phoenix Indian School. The New Trail: a Book of
Creative Writing by Indian Students. 158 pp.
Phoenix, 1941.

Reid, F.A. Hopi Snake Poison. M, XXII, 10-11.
1948.

Renaud, E.B. Kokopelli. SWL, XIV, 25-40. 1948.

Rust, H.N. The Moqui Snake Dance. LS, IV, 70-6.
1896.

Senter, D., and Hawley, F. Hopi and Navajo Child
Burials. AA, n.s., XXXIX, 131-4. 1937.

Shufeldt, R.W. A Maid of Wolpai. PUSNM, XV,
29-33. 1892.

Simpson, R.D. The Hopi Indians. SWML, XXV, 91
pp. 1953.

Singer, O.E. Abbot Sakiestewa-Hopi Doll Maker.
AH, XXXI, viii, 8-15. 1955.

Smith, D.M. Indian Tribes of the Southwest, pp.
39-55. Stanford, 1933.

Smith, W. Kiva Mural Decorations at Awatovi and
Kawaika-a. PMP, XXXVII, 1-348. 1952.

Solberg, O. Gebräuche der Mittelmesa-Hopi (Moqui)
bei Namengebung, Heirat und Tod. ZE, XXXVII,
626-36. 1905.

--- Uber die Báhos der Hopi. AFA, XXII, 48-74.
1906.

Stephen, A.M. Hopi Indians of Arizona. M, XIII,
197-204; XIV, 20-7, 102-9, 143-9, 170-9, 207-
15. 1939-40.

--- Hopi Tales. JAFL, XLII, 2-72. 1929.

--- Legend of the Snake Order of the Moquis. JAFL,
I, 109-14. 1888.

Stephen, A.M. The Po-boc-tu among the Hopi. AAOJ, XVI, 212-15. 1894.

Stephen, A.M., and Fewkes, J.W. The Na-ac-naiya: a Tusayan Initiation Ceremony. JAFL, V, 189-222. 1892.

Stevenson, J. Illustrated Catalogue of the Collections obtained from the Indians of New Mexico and Arizona. ARBAE, II, 375-99. 1883.

--- Illustrated Catalogue of the Collections obtained from the Pueblos of Zuni, New Mexico, and Wolpi, Arizona. ARBAE, III, 587-94. 1884.

Stevenson, M.C. Tusayan Legends of the Snake and Flute People. PAAAS, XLI, 258-71. 1892.

Steward, J.H. Notes on Hopi Ceremonies in Their Initiatory Form. AA, n.s., XXXIII, 56-79. 1931.

Stirling, M.W. Snake Bites and the Hopi Snake Dance. ARSI, 1941, 551-5.

Stocker, J. Indian Country. AH, XXXI, vii, 18-29. 1955.

Thompson, L. Attitudes and Acculturation. AA, n.s., L, 200-15. 1948.

--- Logico-Aesthetic Integration in Hopi Culture. AA, n.s., XLVII, 540-53. 1945.

Thompson, L., and Joseph, A. The Hopi Way. 151 pp. Chicago, 1945.

Titiev, M. Dates of Planting at the Hopi Indian Pueblo of Oraibi. MNMNA, XI, 39-42. 1938.

--- The Hopi Method of baking Sweet Corn. PMA, XXIII, 87-94. 1937.

--- Hopi Snake Handling. SM, LVII, 44-51. 1943.

--- Hopi Racing Customs at Oraibi. PMA, XXIV, iv, 33-42. 1938.

--- A Hopi Salt Expedition. AA, n.s., XXXIX, 244-58. 1937.

--- A Hopi Visit to the Afterworld. PMA, XXVI, 495-504. 1940.

--- Notes on Hopi Witchcraft. PMA, XXVIII, 549-57. 1943.

--- The Problem of Cross-Cousin Marriage among the Hopi. AA, n.s., XL, 105-11. 1938.

--- Shamans, Witches and Chiefs among the Hopi. Tomorrow, IV, iii, 51-6. 1956.

--- The Story of Kokopele. AA, n.s., XLI, 91-8. 1939.

--- Suggestions for the Further Study of Hopi. IJAL, XII, 89-91. 1946.

--- Two Hopi Myths and Rites. JAFL, LXI, 31-43. 1948.

--- Two Hopi Tales from Oraibi. PMA, XXIX, 425-38. 1943.

--- The Use of Kinship Terms in Hopi Ritual. MNMNA, X, 9-11. 1937.

Underhill, R.M. First Penthouse Dwellers of America, pp. 25-55. New York, 1938.

Vestal, P.A. Notes on a Collection of Plants from the Hopi Indian Region. Harvard University Botanical Museum Leaflets, VIII, 153-68. 1940.

Voegelin, C.F. Phonemicizing for Dialect Study with Reference to Hopi. Lg, XXXII, 116-35. 1956.

--- Pregnancy Couvade Attested by Term and Text in Hopi. AA, LXII, 491-4. 1960.

Voegelin, C.F. and F.M. Hopi Domains. MIJL, XIV, 88 pp. 1957.

--- Selection in Hopi Ethics, Linguistics, and Translation. Anthropological Linguistics, II, ii, 48-78. 1960.

Voegelin, C.F. and Euler, R.C. Introduction to Hopi Chants. JAFL, LXX, 115-36. 1957.

Voth, H.R. Four Hopi Tales. FMAS, XI, 139-43. 1912.

--- Hopi Marriage Rites on the Wedding Morning. FMAS, XI, 145-9. 1912.

--- Hopi Proper Names. FMAS, VI, 63-113. 1905.

--- Notes on Modern Burial Customs of the Hopi. FMAS, XI, 99-103. 1912.

--- Notes on the Eagle Cult among the Hopi Indians. FMAS, XI, 105-9. 1912.

--- The Oraibi Marau Ceremony. FMAS, XI, 1-88. 1912.

--- Oraibi Marriage Customs. AA, n.s., II, 238-46. 1900.

--- Oraibi Natal Customs and Ceremonies. FMAS, VI, 47-61. 1905.

--- The Oraibi New Year Ceremony. FMAS, XI, 111-19. 1912.

--- The Oráibi Oáqöl Ceremony. FMAS, VI, 1-46. 1903.

--- The Oraibi Powamu Ceremony. FMAS, III, 67-158. 1901.

--- The Oraibi Summer Snake Ceremony. FMAS, III, 267-358. 1903.

--- Tawa Baholawu of the Oraibi Flute Ceremony. FMAS, XI, 121-36. 1912.

--- The Traditions of the Hopi. FMAS, VIII, 1-319. 1905.

Wallis, W.D. Folk Tales from Shumopovi. JAFL, XLIX, 1-68. 1936.

Wallis, W.D., and Titiev, M. Hopi Notes from Chimopovy. PMA, XXX, 523-56. 1944.

Walton, E.L., and Waterman, T.T. American Indian Poetry. AA, n.s., XXVII, 25-52. 1925.

Watkins, F.E. Indians at Play. M, XVIII, 139-41; XIX, 20-22, 113-5, 162-4; XX, 81-7. 1944-46.

Watson, J.B. How the Hopi classify their Food. P, XV, 49-52. 1943.

Wencker, A. Easy Hopi Sentence Folder. Glendale,
    1959.
--- Primer I-II. Glendale, 1959.
White, L.A. "Rohona" in Pueblo Culture. PMA,
    XXIX, 439-43. 1943.
Whiting, A.F. Ethnobotany of the Hopi. BMNA, XV,
    1-120. 1939.
--- Hopi Indian Agriculture. MNMNA, VIII, x, 51-
    3; X, v, 13-16. 1936-37.
Whitney, R. Idols of Rain. M, I, 14-22. 1927.
Whorf, B.L. An American Indian Model of the Uni-
    verse. IJAL, XVI, 67-72. 1950.
--- The Hopi Language, Toreva Dialect. VFPA, VI,
    150-83. 1946.
--- Linguistic Factors in the Terminology of Hopi Ar-
    chitecture. IJAL, XIX, 141-45. 1953.
--- The Punctual and Segmentative Aspects of Verbs
    in Hopi. Lg, XII, 127-31. 1936.
--- The Relation of Habitual Thought and Behavior
    to Language. Essays in Memory of Edward Sapir,
    pp. 75-93. Menasha, 1941.
--- Some Verbal Categories of Hopi. Lg, XIV, 275-
    86. 1938.
Woodbury, R.B. Prehistoric Stone Implements of
    Northeastern Arizona. PMP, XXXIV, 240 pp. 1954.
Yamada, G. (ed.) The Great Resistance. 79 pp.
    Mexico, 1957.
Yount, G.C. A Sketch of the Hopi in 1828. M,
    XVI, 193-9. 1942.
Zorn, E. Die Hopi-Pueblos in Arizona und ihre
    Bevölkerung. Erdball, I, 108-15. 1927.

12. ISLETA

Including the southern Tiwa pueblos of Isleta,
Isleta del Sur, Sandia, and Senecu del Sur.

Parsons, E.C. Isleta. ARBAE, XLVII, 193-466.
    1930.

Bloom, L.B., ed. Bourke on the Southwest. NMHR,
    XIII, 192-238. 1938.
Curtis, E.S. The North American Indian, XVI, 3-
    27. Norwood, 1926.
Densmore, F. Music of Acoma, Isleta, Cochiti and
    Zuñi Pueblos. BBAE, CLXV, 129 pp. 1957.
Dismuke, D. Range Management brings Success to
    Isleta Indians. Soil Conservation, V, 34-5. 1939.
Dixon, W.H. Isleta – Why the Church has a Wooden
    Floor. Scribner's Magazine, LXX, 193-9. 1921.

Euler, R.C. Notes on Land Tenure at Isleta Pueblo.
    EP, LXI, 368-73. 1954.
Fergusson, E. Dancing Gods, pp. 49-53. New York, 1931.
Fewkes, J.W. The Pueblo Settlements near El Paso.
    AA, n.s., IV, 57-72. 1902.
French, D.H. Factionalism in Isleta Pueblo. MAES,
    XIV, 1-48. 1948.
Gatschet, A.S. Classification into Seven Linguistic
    Stocks of Western Indian Dialects. RUSGS, VII,
    403-85. 1879.
--- A Mythic Tale of the Isleta Indians. PAPS, XXIX,
    207-17. 1891.
--- The Sun Worship of Isleta Pueblo. PAPS, XXIX,
    217-19. 1891.
--- Zwölf Sprachen aus dem Südwesten Nordamerikas.
    150 pp. Weimar, 1876.
Goldfrank, E.S. Isleta Variants: a Study in Flexibil-
    ity. JAFL, XXXIX, 70-8. 1926.
Hammond, G.P., and Rey, A., eds. Expedition into
    New Mexico made by Antonio de Espejo, pp. 79-
    82. Los Angeles, 1929.
Hodge, F.W. Isleta. BBAE, XXX, i, 622-4. 1907.
--- Tigua. BBAE, XXX, ii, 747-9. 1910.
Hurt, W.R. Tortugas. EP, LIX, 104-22. 1952.
Lange, C.H. Notes on a Winter Ceremony at Isleta
    Pueblo, January 7, 1940. EP, LX, 116-23. 1953.
Lummis, C.F. The Man who married the Moon.
    239 pp. New York, 1894.
--- Pueblo Indian Folk-Stories. 257 pp. New York,
    1910.
Parsons, E.C. Further Notes on Isleta. AA, n.s.,
    XXIII, 149-69. 1921.
--- The Kinship Nomenclature of the Pueblo Indians.
    AA, n.s., XXXIV, 377-89. 1932.
--- The Laguna Migration to Isleta. AA, n.s., XXX,
    602-13. 1928.
--- Notes on Isleta, Santa Ana, and Acoma. AA, n.
    s., XXII, 56-69. 1920.
--- Pueblo Indian Religion. 2 vols. Chicago, 1939.
Trager, G.L. The Kinship and Status Terms of the
    Tiwa Languages. AA, n.s., XLV, 557-71. 1943.
White, L.A. Ethnographic Notes on Sandia Pueblo.
    PMA, XXXI, 215-22. 1945.

13. JEMEZ

Including the pueblos of Jemez and Pecos.

Parsons, E.C. The Pueblo of Jemez. 141 pp. New
    Haven, 1925.

Alexander, H.B. Field Notes at Jemez. EP, XXVII, 95-106. 1929.

Bandelier, A.F. A Visit to the Aboriginal Ruins in the Valley of the Rio Pecos. PAIA, I, 37-133. 1883.

Bloom, L.B. Bourke on the Southwest. NMHR, XIII, 192-238. 1938.

--- The West Jemez Culture Area. EP, XII, 19-25. 1922.

--- The West Jemez Culture Area. NMHR, XXI, 120-6. 1946.

DeHuff, E.W. Taytay's Tales, pp. 162-4, 170-71. New York, 1922.

Douglas, F.H. Weaving of the Tiwa Pueblos and Jemez. DAMLS, XCI, 162-4. 1939.

Dutton, B.P. Hopi Dance of the Jemez Indians. Research, I, 70-84. 1936.

Ellis, F.H. Authoritative Control and the Society System in Jemez Pueblo. SJA, IX, 385-94. 1953.

--- Jemez Kiva Magic and its Relation to Features of Prehistoric Kivas. SJA, VIII, 147-63. 1952.

Fergusson, E. Dancing Gods, pp. 61-5. New York, 1931.

Gatschet, A.S. Classification into Seven Linguistic Stocks of Western Indian Dialects. RUSGS, VII, 403-85. 1879.

--- Zwölf Sprachen aus dem Südwesten Nordamerikas. 150 pp. Weimar, 1876.

Hewett, E.L. Studies on the Extinct Pueblo of Pecos. AA, n.s., VI, 426-39. 1904.

Hodge, F.W. Jemez. BBAE, XXX, i, 629-31. 1907.

Holmes, W.H. Notes on the Antiquities of Jemez Valley. AA, n.s., VII, 198-212. 1905.

Hooton, E.A. The Indians of Pecos Pueblo. 391 pp. New Haven, 1930.

Jones, J.R. A Jemez Corn Grinding. EP, LIV, 43-4. 1947.

Judd, N.M. When the Jemez Medicine Men came to Zuni. JAFL, XL, 182-4. 1947.

Keech, R.A. The Pecos Ceremony at Jemez. EP, XXXVI, 129-34. 1934.

--- Two Days and Nights in a Pueblo. EP, XXXV, 185-95. 1933.

Kidder, A.V. The Artifacts of Pecos. 314 pp. New Haven, 1932.

--- Pecos, New Mexico: Archaeological Notes. PRSPF, V, 380 pp. 1958.

--- Pecos Pueblo. EP, LVIII, 83-89. 1951.

Kidder, A.V., and Shepard, A. The Pottery of Pecos. 2 vols. New Haven, 1936.

Kidder, M.A., and A.V. Notes on the Pottery of Pecos. AA, n.s., XIX, 325-60. 1917.

Lambert, M.F. A Rare Stone Humpbacked Figurine from Pecos Pueblo. EP, LXIV, 93-108. 1957.

Loew, O. Lieutenant G.M. Wheeler's zweite Expedition nach Neu-Mexiko und Colorado. PMJP, XXII, 209-11. 1876.

Nelson, C.T. The Teeth of the Indians of Pecos Pueblo. AJPA, XXIII, 261-94. 1938.

Parsons, E.C. The Kinship Nomenclature of the Pueblo Indians. AA, n.s., XXXIV, 377-89. 1932.

--- Pueblo Indian Religion. 2 vols. Chicago, 1939.

Reagan, A.B. The Corn Dance at Jemez. SW, LXIV, 481-4. 1915.

--- Dances of the Jemez Pueblo Indians. TKAS, XXIII, 241-72. 1906.

--- The Jemez Indians. AAR, 1923, 103-8.

--- The Masked Dance of the Jemez Indians. SW, LXIV, 423-7. 1915.

--- Notes on Jemez Ethnography. AA, n.s., XXIX, 719-28. 1927.

--- Sketches of Indian Life and Character. TKAS, XXI, 207-15. 1908.

--- Some Paintings from one of the Estufas in the Indian Village of Jemez. PIAS, XIII, 201-4. 1903.

Reiter, P. The Jemez Pueblo of Unshagi. School of American Research Monographs, V, 1-92; VI, 97-211. 1938.

--- The Jemez Pueblo of Unshagi. University of New Mexico Bulletin, Monograph Series, I, iv-v. 211 pp. 1938.

Rihan, H.Y. Dental and Orthodontic Observations on 289 Adult and 53 Immature Skulls from Pecos. International Journal of Orthodontia and Oral Surgery and Radiography, XVIII, 708-13. 1932.

Stubbs, S.A., et al. "Lost" Pecos Church. EP, LXIV, 67-92. 1957.

Thompson, G. An Indian Dance at Jemez. AA, II, 351-5. 1889.

Twitchell, R.E. The Ancient Pueblo of Pecos. Santa Fe Magazine, IV, 27-32. 1910.

Walter, P. Notes on a Trip to Jemez. EP, XXIX, 206-13. 1930.

Williamson, T.B. The Jemez Yucca Ring Basket. EP, XLII, vii-ix. 1937.

14. JICARILLA

Opler, M.E. The Character and Derivation of Jicarilla Holiness Rites. UNMB, IV, iii, 1-98. 1943.

--- Childhood and Youth in Jicarilla Apache Society. PHAPF, V, 1-170. 1946.

Opler, M.E. A Summary of Jicarilla Apache Culture. AA, n.s., XXXVIII, 202-23. 1936.

Bartoli, J.F. The Apache "Devil Dance." Musical Courier, CLII, viii, 8-10. 1955.

Bellah, R.N. Apache Kinship Systems. 151 pp. Cambridge, 1952.

Curtis, E.S. The North American Indian, I, 53-72. Cambridge, 1907.

Daklugie, A. and Ball, E. Coyote and the Flies. NMFR, X, 12-3. 1955-56.

Dolan, T.A. Report of Council Proceedings with the Jicarilla Apache Indians. NMHR, IV, 59-72. 1929.

Douglas, F.H. Apache Indian Coiled Basketry. DAMLS, LXIV, 54-6. 1934.

--- The Apache Indians. DAMLS, XVI, 1-4. 1930.

--- A Jicarilla Apache Beaded Cape. MCN, IV, 34-7. 1939.

Douglas, F.H., et al. A Jicarilla Apache Man's Skin Shirt. MCN, XXI, 10 pp. 1953.

--- A Jicarilla Apache Man's Skin Leggings. MCN, XXII, 12 pp. 1953.

--- A Jicarilla Apache Woman's Skin Dress. MCN, XX, 10 pp. 1953.

Dunn, D. Nehakije: Apache Artist. EP, LIX, 71-76. 1952.

Fergusson, E. Dancing Gods, pp. 269-76. New York, 1931.

--- Modern Apaches of New Mexico. AmI, VI, i, 3-13. 1951.

Gatschet, A.S. Classification into Seven Linguistic Stocks of Western Indian Dialects. RUSGS, VII, 403-85. 1879.

Goddard, P.E. Jicarilla Apache Texts. APAM, VIII, 1-276. 1911.

Grinnell, G.B. Who were the Padouca? AA, n.s., XXII, 248-60. 1920.

Harrington, J.P. Southern Peripheral Athapaskawan Origins, Divisions, and Migrations. SMC, C, 503-32. 1940.

Hodge, F.W. Jicarilla. BBAE, XXX, i, 631-2. 1907.

Hoijer, H. The Apachean Verb. IJAL, XI, 193-203; XII, 1-13, 51-9; XIV, 247-59; XV, 12-22. 1945-49.

--- Pitch Accent in the Apachean Languages. Lg, XIX, 38-51. 1943.

--- Phonetic and Phonemic Change in the Athapaskan Languages. Lg, XVIII, 218-20. 1942.

Jones, G. A Jicarilla Apache Family. AmI, VI, ii, 32-7. 1951.

Lockwood, F.C. The Apache Indians. 348 pp. New York, 1938.

Matson, D.S. and Schroeder, A.H. Cordero's Description of the Apache—1796. NMHR, XXXII, 335-56. 1957.

Meston, G.D. Jicarilla Apache Reservation. RIT, 1890, 404-7.

Mooney, J. The Jicarilla Genesis. AA, XI, 197-209. 1898.

Ogle, R.H. The Apache and the Government—1870's. NMHR, XXXIV, 81-102. 1959.

Opler, M.E. Adolescence Rite of the Jicarilla. EP, XLIX, 25-38. 1942.

--- Apache Data concerning the Relation of Kinship Terminology to Social Classification. AA, n.s., XXXIX, 201-12. 1937.

--- Dirty Boy: a Jicarilla Tale of Raid and War. MAAA, LII, 1-80. 1938.

--- Further Comparative Anthropological Data bearing on the Solution of a Psychological Problem. JSP, IX, 477-83. 1938.

--- The Jicarilla Apache Ceremonial Relay Race. AA, n.s., XLVI, 75-97. 1944.

--- A Jicarilla Apache Expedition and Scalp Dance. JAFL, LIV, 10-23. 1941.

--- Jicarilla Apache Fertility Aids and Practices for Preventing Conception. AA, n.s., L, 359-61. 1948.

--- The Kinship Systems of the Southern Athabaskan-speaking Tribes. AA, n.s., XXXVIII, 620-33. 1936.

--- Mythology and Folk Belief in the Maintenance of Jicarilla Apache Tribal Endogamy. JAFL, LX, 126-9. 1947.

--- Myths and Tales of the Jicarilla Apache Indians. MAFLS, XXXI, 1-406. 1938.

--- Navaho Shamanistic Practice among the Jicarilla Apache. NMA, VI-VII, 13-18. 1943.

--- Rule and Practice in the Behavior between Jicarilla Apache Affinal Relatives. AA, n.s., XLIX, 453-62. 1947.

Russell, F. An Apache Medicine Dance. AA, XI, 367-72. 1898.

--- Myths of the Jicarilla Apaches. JAFL, XI, 253-71. 1898.

Santee, R. Apache Land. 216 pp. New York, 1947.

Schoolcraft, H.R. Apaches. HCPIT, V, 202-14. 1855.

Sharp, A.W. The Annual Jicarilla Apache Encampment, 1951. EP, LIX, 95-6. 1952.

Thomas, A.B. After Coronado. 307 pp. Norman, 1935.

Wedel, W.R. The Plains Apache. BBAE, CLXXIV, 69-75. 1959.

Woodward, A. John G. Bourke on the Arizona Apache, 1874. P, XVI, 33-44. 1943.

15. JUMANO

Including the Jumano and the Suma.

Bolton, H.E. The Jumano Indians in Texas. TSHAQ, XV, 66-84. 1911.

Forbes, J.D. The Janos, Jocomes, Mansos and Sumas Indians. NMHR, XXXII, 319-34. 1957.

--- Unknown Athapaskans. E, VI, 97-159. 1959.

Hammond, G.P., and Rey, A. Expedition into New Mexico made by Antonio de Espejo, pp. 54-69. Los Angeles, 1929.

--- The Gallegos Relation of the Rodriguez Expedition. NMHR, II, 239-68, 334-62. 1927.

Henshaw, F.W. Suma. BBAE, XXX, ii, 649. 1910.

Hodge, F.W. Jumano. BBAE, XXX, i, 636. 1907.

--- The Jumano Indians. PAAS, n.s., X, 249-68. 1910.

Kelley, J.C. Juan Sabeata and Diffusion in Aboriginal Texas. AA, LVII, 981-95. 1955.

Kubler, G. Gran Quivira-Humanas. NMHR, XIV, 418-21. 1939.

Sauer, C. The Distribution of Aboriginal Tribes and Languages in Northwestern Mexico. IA, V, 65-74. 1934.

Scholes, F.V., and Mera, H.P. Some Aspects of the Jumano Problem. Carnegie Institution Contributions to American Anthropology and History, VI, 265-99. 1940.

16. LIPAN

Opler, M.E. Myths and Legends of the Lipan Apache Indians. MAFLS, XXXVI, 1-296. 1940.

Bartlett, J.R. Personal Narrative of Explorations and Incidents in Texas, New Mexico, California, Sonora, and Chihuahua, I, 323-9. New York, 1854.

Beals, R.L. The Comparative Ethnology of Northern Mexico. IA, II, 93-225. 1932.

Bellah, R.N. Apache Kinship Systems. 151 pp. Cambridge, 1952.

Bollaert, W. Observations on the Indian Tribes in Texas. JESL, II, 262-83. 1850.

Bolton, H.E. Athanase de Mézières and the Louisiana-Texas Frontier. 2 vols. Cleveland, 1914.

--- Texas in the Middle Eighteenth Century. UCPH, III, 1-501. 1915.

Chavez, J.C. Los Apaches de Chihuahua. Boletin de la Sociedad Chihuahuense de Estudios Historicos, IX, ii, 815-20. 1955.

Dunn, W.E. Apache Relations in Texas. TSHAQ, XIV, 198-274. 1910.

Gifford, E.W. Apache-Pueblo. AR, IV, 1-207. 1940.

Gunnerson, J.H. An Introduction to Plains Apache Archeology. BBAE, CLXXIII, 131-260. 1960.

Harrington, J.P. Southern Peripheral Athapaskawan Origins, Divisions, and Migrations. SMC, C, 503-32. 1940.

Hodge, F.W. Lipan. BBAE, XXX, i, 768-9. 1907.

Hoijer, H. The Apachean Verb. IJAL, XI, 193-203; XII, 1-13, 51-9; XIV, 247-59; XV, 12-22. 1945-49.

--- Pitch Accent in the Apachean Languages. Lg, XIX, 38-41. 1943.

--- Phonetic and Phonemic Change in the Athapaskan Languages. Lg, XVIII, 218-20. 1942.

Matson, D.S. and Schroeder, A.H. Cordero's Description of the Apache—1796. NMHR, XXXII, 335-56. 1957.

Morfi, J.A.de. Memorias for the History of the Province of Texas, ed. F.M.Chabot. 85 pp. San Antonio, 1932.

Ogle, R.H. The Apache and the Government—1870's. NMHR, XXXIV, 81-102. 1959.

Opler, M.E. Apache Data concerning the Relation of Kinship Terminology to Social Classification. AA, n.s., XXXIX, 201-12. 1937.

--- An Application of the Theory of Themes in Culture. JWAS, XXXVI, 137-66. 1946.

--- Further Comparative Anthropological Data bearing on the Solution of a Psychological Problem. JSP, IX, 477-83. 1938.

--- The Kinship Systems of the Southern Athabaskan-speaking Tribes. AA, n.s., XXXVIII, 620-33. 1936.

--- The Lipan Apache Death Complex and its Extensions. SJA, I, 122-41. 1945.

--- Myths and Legends of the Lipan Apache Indians. MAFLS, XXXVI, 1-296. 1940.

--- Themes as Dynamic Forces in Culture. AJS, LI, 198-206. 1945.

--- The Use of Peyote by the Carrizo and Lipan Apache Tribes. AA, n.s., XL, 271-85. 1938.

Sayles, E.B. An Archaeological Survey of Texas. Medallion Papers, XVII, 1-164. 1935.

Sjoberg, A.F. Lipan Apache Culture in Historical Perspective. SJA, IX, 76-98. 1953.

Vigness, D.M. Indian Raids on the Lower Rio Grande, 1836-1837. SWHQ, LIX, 14-23. 1955.

17. MANSO

Anonymous. Manso. BBAE, XXX, i, 801-2. 1907.

Bandelier, A.F. Final Report of Investigations among the Indians of the Southwestern United States. PAIA, III, 1-323; IV, 1-591. 1890-92.

Forbes, J.D. The Janos, Jocomes, Mansos and Sumas Indians. NMHR, XXXII, 319-34. 1957.

--- Unknown Athapaskans. E, VI, 97-159. 1959.

Opler, M.E. The Identity of the Apache Mansos. AA, n.s., XLIV, 725. 1942.

18. MARICOPA

Spier, L. Yuman Tribes of the Gila River. 433 pp. Chicago, 1933.

Bartlett, J.R. Personal Narrative of Explorations and Incidents in Texas, New Mexico, California, Sonora, and Chihuahua, II, 221-38. New York, 1854.

Brown, H. A Pima-Maricopa Ceremony. AA, n.s., VIII, 688-90. 1906.

Buschmann, J.C.E. Die Spuren der aztekischen Sprache im nördlichen Mexico und höheren amerikanischen Norden. AKAWB, 1854, Supplement-Band, II, 264-7.

Curtis, E.S. The North American Indian, II, 81-7. Cambridge, 1908.

Dobyns, H.F., et al. Thematic Changes in Yuman Warfare. In, V.F.Ray, ed., Cultural Stability and Cultural Change, 46-71. 1957.

Drucker, P. Yuman-Piman. AR, VI, 91-230. 1941.

Gatschet, A.S. Der Yuma-Sprachstamm. ZE, IX, 375-7, 390-406. 1887.

Gifford, E.W. Clans and Moieties in Southern California. UCP, XIV, 155-219. 1918.

Hodge, F.W. Maricopa. BBAE, XXX, i, 805-7. 1907.

Hrdlicka, A. Maricopa Weaving. AA, n.s., VII, 361. 1905.

Kate, H.F.C.ten. Indiens d'Amérique du Nord. Ane, XXVIII, 369-401. 1917.

--- Somatological Observations on Indians of the Southwest. JAEA, III, 117-44. 1892.

Phoenix Indian School. The New Trail; a Book of Creative Writing by Indian Students. 158 pp. Phoenix, 1941.

Spier, L. Comparative Vocabularies and Parallel Texts in Two Yuman Languages. UNMPA, II, 1-150. 1946.

Spier, L. Cultural Relations of the Gila River and Lower Colorado Tribes. YUPA, III, 1-22. 1936.

Whited, S. Pima Agency. RIT, 1890, 137-46.

19. MESCALERO

Including the Faraon Apache and the Mescalero Apache.

Sonnichsen, C.L. The Mescalero Apaches. 315 pp. Norman, 1958.

Bartoli, J.F. The Apache "Devil Dance." Musical Courier, CLII, viii, 8-10. 1955.

Bellah, Robert N. Apache Kinship Systems. 151 pp. Cambridge, 1952.

Castetter, E.F., and Opler, M.E. The Ethnobiology of the Chiricahua and Mescalero Apache. UNMBB, IV, v, 3-63. 1936.

Curtis, E.S. The North American Indian, I, 3-51. Cambridge, 1907.

Devereux, G., and E.M.Loeb. Some Notes on Apache Criminality. Journal of Criminal Psychopathology, IV, 424-30. 1943.

Dory, W. The Mescalero Apaches' Present Conditions. SW, LI, 413-19, 422.

Douglas, F.H. Apache Indian Coiled Basketry. DAMLS, LXIV, 54-6. 1934.

--- The Apache Indians. DAMLS, XVI, 1-4. 1930.

Dunn, W.E. Apache Relations in Texas. TSHAQ, XIV, 198-274. 1910.

Fergusson, E. Dancing Gods, pp. 249-69. New York, 1931.

--- Modern Apaches of New Mexico. AmI, VI, i, 3-14. 1951.

Flannery, R. The Position of Woman among the Mescalero Apache. PM, V, 26-33. 1932.

Forbes, J.D. Unknown Athapaskans. E, VI, 97-159. 1959.

Gardner, H. Philip St. George Cooke and the Apache, 1854. NMHR, XXVIII, 115-32. 1953.

Gifford, E.W. Apache-Pueblo. AR, IV, 1-207. 1940.

Goddard, P.E. Gotal--a Mescalero Apache Ceremony. Putnam Anniversary Volume, pp. 385-94. New York, 1909.

--- The Masked Dancers of the Apache. Holmes Anniversary Volume, pp. 132-6. Washington, 1916.

Harrington, J.P. Southern Peripheral Athpaskawan Origins, Divisions, and Migrations. SMC, C, 503-32. 1940.

Hodge, F.W. Mescaleros. BBAE, XXX, i, 846. 1907.

Hoijer, H. The Apachean Verb. IJAL, XI, 193-203; XII, 1-13, 51-9; XIV, 247-59; XV, 12-22. 1945-49.

--- Chiricahua and Mesc lero Apache Texts. 219 pp. Chicago, 1938.

--- Pitch Accent in the Apachean Languages. Lg, XIX, 38-41. 1943.

--- Phonetic and Phonemic Change in the Athapaskan Languages. Lg, XVIII, 218-20. 1942.

Lockwood, F.C. The Apache Indians. 348 pp. New York, 1938.

Matson, D.S. and Schroeder, A.H. Cordero's Description of the Apache—1796. NMHR, XXXII, 335-56. 1957.

Mechem, G.B. Mescalero Agency. RIT, 1890, 398-404.

Nicholas, D. Mescalero Apache Girls' Puberty Ceremony. EP, XLVI, 193-204. 1939.

Ogle, R.H. The Apache and the Government—1870's. NMHR, XXXIV, 81-102. 1959.

Opler, M.E. An Analysis of Mescalero and Chiricahua Apache Social Organization in the Light of Their Systems of Relationship. 19 pp. Chicago, 1936.

--- Apache Data concerning the Relation of Kinship Terminology to Social Classification. AA, n.s., XXXIX, 201-12. 1937.

--- The Concept of Supernatural Power among the Chiricahua and Mescalero Apaches. AA, n.s., XXXVII, 65-70. 1935.

--- The Creative Role of Shamanism in Mescalero Apache Mythology. JAFL, LIX, 268-81. 1946.

--- Further Comparative Anthropological Data bearing on the Solution of a Psychological Problem. JSP, IX, 477-83. 1938.

--- The Influence of Aboriginal Pattern and White Contact on a recently introduced Ceremony, the Mescalero Peyote Rite. JAFL, XLIX, 143-66. 1936.

--- An Interpretation of Ambivalence of Two American Indian Tribes. JSP, VII, 82-118. 1936.

--- Kinship Systems of the Southern Athabaskan-speaking Tribes. AA, n.s., XXXVIII, 620-33. 1936.

--- A Mescalero Apache Account of the Origin of the Peyote Ceremony. EP, LII, 210-12. 1945.

--- A Note on the Cultural Affiliations of Northern Mexican Nomads. AA, n.s., XXXVII, 702-6. 1935.

--- Reaction to Death among the Mescalero Apache. SJA, II, 455-67. 1946.

--- The Sacred Clowns of the Chiricahua and Mescalero Indians. EP, XLIV, 75-9. 1938.

--- The Slaying of the Monsters. EP, LIII, 215-25, 242-58. 1946.

Opler, M.E. Some Points of Comparison and Contrast between the Treatment of Functional Disorders by Apache Shamans and Modern Psychiatric Practice. American Journal of Psychiatry, XCII, 1371-87. 1936.

Opler, M.E. and C.H. Mescalero Apache History in the Southwest. NMHR, XXV, 1-36. 1950.

Santee, R. Apache Land. 216 pp. New York, 1947.

Schoolcraft, H.R. Apaches. HCPIT, V, 202-14. 1855.

Thomas, A.B. After Coronado. 307 pp. Norman, 1935.

Vigness, D.M. Indian Raids on the Lower Rio Grande, 1836-1837. SWHQ, LIX, 14-23. 1955.

Woodward, A. John G. Bourke on the Arizona Apache, 1874. P, XVI, 33-44. 1943.

20. MOHAVE

Kroeber, A.L. Handbook of the Indians of California. BBAE, LXXVIII, 726-80. 1925.

Allen, G.A. Manners and Customs of the Mohaves. ARSI, 1890, 615-16.

Boas, F. Zur Anthropologie der nordamerikanischen Indianer. VBGA, 1895, 367-411.

Bourke, J.G. Notes on the Cosmogony and Theogony of the Mojave Indians. JAFL, II, 169-89. 1889.

Burbank, E.A., and Royce, E. Burbank among the Indians, pp. 114-7. Caldwell, 1946.

Campion, J.S. On the Frontier. 2d edit. 372 pp. London, 1878.

Curtis, E.S. The North American Indian, II, 47-61. Cambridge, 1908.

Densmore, F. Yuman and Yaqui Music. BBAE, CX, 1-216. 1932.

Devereux, G. Amusements and Sports of Mohave Children. M, XXIV, 143-52. 1950.

--- Atypical and Deviant Mohave Marriages. S, IV, 200-215. 1951.

--- Der Begriff der Vaterschaft bei den Mohave-Indianer. ZE, LXIX, 72-8. 1937.

--- Cultural and Characterological Traits of the Mohave. Psychoanalytic Quarterly, XX, 398-422. 1951.

--- Dream Learning and Individual Ritual Differences in Mohave Shamanism. AA, LIX, 1036-45. 1957.

--- Education and Discipline in Mohave Society. PM, XXIII, 85-102. 1950.

--- L'envoutement chez les Indiens Mohave. JSAP, n.s., XXIX, 405-12. 1937.

Devereux, G. The Function of Alcohol in Mohave Society. QJSA, IX, 207-51. 1948.

--- Heterosexual Behavior of the Mohave Indians. PSS, II, 85-128. 1950.

--- Institutionalized Homosexuality of the Mohave Indians. HB, IX, 498-527. 1937.

--- Magic Substances and Narcotics of the Mohave Indians. British Journal of Medical Psychology, XXII, 110-16. 1949.

--- Mohave Beliefs Concerning Twins. AA, n.s., XLIII, 573-92. 1941.

--- Mohave Chieftainship in Action. P, XXIII, 33-43. 1951.

--- Mohave Coyote Tales. JAFL, LXI, 233-55. 1948.

--- Mohave Culture and Personality. Character and Personality, VIII, 91-109. 1939.

--- Mohave Dreams of Omen and Power. Tomorrow, IV, iii, 17-24. 1956.

--- Mohave Etiquette. M, XXII, 119-27. 1948.

--- Mohave Indian Autoerotic Behavior. Psychoanalytic Review, XXXVII, 201-20. 1950.

--- Mohave Indian Infanticide. Psychoanalytic Review, XXXV, 126-39. 1948.

--- Mohave Indian Kamaloty. Journal of Clinical Psychopathology, IX, 433-57. 1948.

--- Mohave Indian Obstetrics. AI, V, 95-139. 1948.

--- Mohave Indian Verbal and Motor Profanity. PSS, III, 99-127. 1951.

--- The Mohave Male Puberty Rite. S, III, 11-25. 1949.

--- The Mohave Neonate and Its Cradle. PM, XXI, 1-18. 1948.

--- Mohave Orality. Psychoanalytic Quarterly, XVI, 519-46. 1947.

--- Mohave Paternity. S, III, 162-94. 1949.

--- Mohave Pregnancy. AAm, VI, 89-116. 1948.

--- Mohave Soul Concepts. AA, n.s., XXXIX, 417-22. 1937.

--- Mohave Voice and Speech Mannerisms. Word, V, 268-72. 1949.

--- Mohave Zoophilia. S, II, 227-45. 1948.

--- Notes on the Developmental Pattern and Organic Needs of Mohave Indian Children. TKAS, LIII, 178-85. 1950.

--- Post-Partum Parental Observances of the Mohave Indians. TKAS, LII, 458-65. 1949.

--- The Primal Scene and Juvenile Heterosexuality in Mohave Society. PAC, 90-107. 1951.

--- Primitive Psychiatry. Bulletin of the History of Medicine, VIII, 1194-1213, XI, 522-42. 1940, 1942.

Devereux, G. Psychodynamics of Mohave Gambling. AI, VII, 55-65. 1950.

--- The Psychology of Feminine Genital Bleeding. International Journal of Psycho-Analysis, XXXI, 237-52. 1950.

--- The Social and Cultural Implications of Incest among the Mohave Indians. Psychoanalytic Quarterly, VIII, 510-33. 1939.

--- Some Mohave Gestures. AA, n.s., LI, 325-6. 1949.

--- Status, Socialization and Interpersonal Relations of Mohave Children. Psychiatry, XIII, 489-502. 1950.

Devereux, G., and Loeb, E. M. Antagonistic Acculturation. ASR, VIII, 133-47. 1943.

Dobyns, H.F. A Mohave Potter's Experiment. K, XXIV, iii, 16-17. 1959.

Dobyns, H.F., et al. Thematic Changes in Yuman Warfare. In V.F.Ray, ed., Cultural Stability and Cultural Change, 46-71. 1957.

DuBois, C.G. Diegueno Myths and Their Connections with the Mohave. ICA, XV, ii, 129-33. 1906.

Essig, E.O. The Value of Insects to the California Indians. SM, XXXVIII, 181-6. 1934.

Fathauer, G.H. Religion in Mohave Social Structure. OJS, LI, 273-76. 1951.

--- The Structure and Causation of Mohave Warfare. SJA, X, 97-118. 1954.

Gatschet, A.S. Classification into Seven Linguistic Stocks of Western Indian Dialects. RUSGS, VII, 403-85. 1879.

--- Der Yuma-Sprachstamm. ZE, IX, 378-80, 391-407, 412-18. 1887.

Gifford, E.W. Clans and Moieties in Southern California. UCP, XIV, 156-67. 1918.

Hafen, L.R. and A.W. Old Spanish Trail. FWRHS, I, 377 pp. 1954.

Hall, S.M. The Burning of a Mojave Chief. OW, XVIII, 60-5. 1903.

Harrington, J.P. The Mohave. EP, XXVII, 16-19. 1929.

Henshaw, H.W., and Hodge, F.W. Mohave. BBAE, XXX, i, 919-21. 1907.

Herzog, G. The Yuman Musical Style. JAFL, XLI, 183-231. 1928.

Hoffman, W.J. Miscellaneous Ethnographic Observations. ARGGS, X, 461-77. 1876.

Hrdlicka, A. Tuberculosis among Certain Indian Tribes. BBAE, XLII, 17-19. 1909.

Ives, J.C. Report upon the Colorado River of the West. 131 pp. Washington, 1861.

Kate, H.F.C.ten. Reizen en onderzoekingen in Noord-Amerika, pp. 123-37. Leiden, 1885.

Kroeber, A.L. Ad hoc Reassurance Dreams. UCP, XLVII, 205-8. 1957.

--- California Kinship Systems. UCP, XII, 340-8. 1917.

--- Desert Mohave: Fact or Fancy. UCP, XLVII, 294-307. 1959.

--- Earth-Tongue, a Mohave. American Indian Life, ed. E.C.Parsons, pp. 189-202. New York, 1925.

--- Mohave Clairvoyance. UCP, XLVII, 226-33. 1957.

--- A Mohave Historical Epic. AR, XI, 71-176. 1951.

--- Olive Oatman's Return. PKAS, IV, 1-18. 1951.

--- Phonetic Elements of the Mohave Language. UCP, X, 45-96. 1911.

--- Preliminary Sketch of the Mohave Indians. AA, n.s., IV, 276-85. 1902.

--- Seven Mohave Myths. AR, XI, 1-70. 1948.

--- Two Myths of the Mission Indians. JAFL, XIX, 309-21. 1906.

Kroeber, A.L. and Harner, M.J. Mohave Pottery. AR, XVI, 35 pp. 1955.

Lincoln, J.S. The Dream in Primitive Cultures. 359 pp. London, 1935.

Loew, O. Notes upon Ethnology of Southern California and Adjacent Regions. ARCE, 1876, iii, 541-7.

McNichols, C.L. Crazy Weather. 195 pp. New York, 1944.

Möllhausen, B. Diary of a Journey from the Mississippi to the Coasts of the Pacific, II, 249-71. London, 1858.

Palmer, E. Fish Hooks of the Mohave Indians. AN, XII, 403. 1878.

Pickerell, A.R. Death of Orawthoma. M, XXXI, 166-9. 1957.

Spier, L. Cultural Relations of the Gila River and Lower Colorado Tribes. YUPA, III, 1-22. 1936.

--- Mohave Culture Items. 35 pp. Flagstaff, 1955.

--- Some Observations on Mohave Clans. SJA, IX, 324-42. 1953.

Stewart, K.M. An Account of the Mohave Mourning Ceremony. AA, n.s., XLIX, 146-8. 1947.

--- Mohave Fishing. M, XXXI, 198-203. 1957.

--- Mohave Hunting. M, XXI, 80-4. 1947.

--- Mohave Warfare. SJA, III, 257-78. 1947.

Stratton, R.B. Captivity of the Oatman Girls, 288 pp. New York, 1857.

Stuart, B.R. Paiute surprise the Mohave. M, XVII, 217-19. 1943.

Taylor, E.S., and Wallace, W.J. Mohave Tattooing and Face-Painting. M, XXI, 183-95. 1947.

Wallace, W.J. The Dream in Mohave Life. JAFL, LX, 252-8. 1947.

--- The Girl's Puberty Rite of the Mohave. PIAS, LVII, 37-40. 1948.

--- Infancy and Childhood among the Mohave Indians. PM, XXI, 19-37. 1948.

--- Mohave Fishing Equipment and Methods. AQ, III, 87-94. 1955.

--- Tobacco and Its Use Among the Mohave Indians. M, XXVII, 193-202. 1953.

Waterman, T.T. Analysis of the Mission Indian Creation Story. AA, n.s., XI, 41-55. 1909.

Woodward, A. Irataba — "Chief of the Mohave." P, XXV, 53-68. 1953.

21. NAVAHO

Amsden, C.A. Navaho Weaving. 263 pp. Albuquerque, 1949.

Darby, W.J., et al. Study of the Dietary Background and Nutrition of the Navajo Indian. Journal of Nutrition, LX, supplement 2, 1-85. 1956.

Dyk, W. A Navaho Autobiography. VFPA, VIII, 1-218. 1947.

Elmore, F.H. Ethnobotany of the Navajo. Monograph of the School of American Research, VIII, 1-136. 1944.

Franciscan Fathers. An Ethnologic Dictionary of the Navaho Language. 536 pp. St. Michaels, 1910.

Haile, B. Emergence Myth according to the Hanelthnaye or Upward Reaching Rite. NRS, III, 1-186. 1949.

--- Origin Legend of the Navaho Flintway. 319 pp. Chicago, 1943.

--- Property Concepts of the Navaho Indians. CUAS, XVII, 64 pp. 1954.

Kluckhohn, C. Navaho Witchcraft. PMP, XXII, ii, 1-149. 1944.

Kluckhohn, C., and Leighton, D.C. The Navaho. 258 pp. Cambridge, 1946.

Ladd, J. The Structure of a Moral Code. 489 pp. Cambridge, 1957.

Landgraf, J.L. Land-Use in the Ramah Area of New Mexico. PMP, XLII, i, 105 pp. 1954.

Leighton, A.H. and D.C. Gregorio, the Hand-Trembler. PMP, XL, i, 1-177. 1949.

Leighton, D.C., and Kluckhohn, C. Children of the People. 277 pp. Cambridge, 1947.

Lipps, O.H. The Navajos. 136 pp. Cedar Rapids, 1909.

O'Bryan, A. The Diné. BBAE, CLXIII, 194 pp. 1956.

Reichard, G.A. Navaho Religion. 2 vols. New York, 1950.

--- Social Life of the Navajo Indians. CUCA,VII, 1-239. 1928.

Roberts, J.M. Three Navaho Households. PMP,XL, iii, 101 pp. 1951.

Underhill, R.M. The Navajos. 315 pp. Norman, 1956.

Vestal, P.A. Ethnobotany of the Ramah Navaho. PMP, XL, iv, 104 pp. 1952.

Vogt, E.Z. Navaho Veterans. PMP, XLI, i, 243 pp. 1951.

Wyman, L.C. and Harris, S.K. The Ethnobotany of the Kayenta Navaho. UNMPB, V, 66pp. 1951.

Abel, T.M. Free Designs of Limited Scope as a Personality Index. Character and Personality, VII, 50-63. 1938.

Aberle, D.F. Mythology of the Navaho Game Stick-Dice. JAFL, LV, 144-54. 1942.

Aberle, D.F. and Stewart, O.C. Navaho and Ute Peyotism. UCSSA, VI, 138 pp. 1957.

Adair, J. Navaho and Pueblo Silversmiths. 220 pp. Norman, 1944.

--- The Navajo and Pueblo Veteran. AmI, IV, i, 5-11. 1947.

Adair, J. and Deuschle, K. Some Problems of the Physicians on the Navajo Reservation. HO, XVII, iv, 19-23. 1958.

Adair, J., and Vogt, E. Navaho and Zuni Veterans: A Study of Contrasting Modes of Culture Change. AA, n.s., LI, 547-61. 1949.

Adair, J., et al. Patterns of Health and Disease among the Navahos. APSS, CCCXI, 80-94. 1957.

Adams, W.Y. New Data on Navajo Social Organization. P, XXX, 64-70. 1958.

Albert, E.M. The Classification of Values. AA, LVIII, 221-48. 1956.

Alley, R.D., and M. Pijoan. Salmonella Javiana Food Infection. Yale Journal of Biology and Medicine. XV, 229-39. 1942.

Altman, G.J. A Navaho Wedding. M, XX, 159-64. 1946.

American Bible Society, ed. Mozes bi naltsos alsedihigi Godesziz holyehigi inda yistainilli ba Hani Mark naltsos ye yiki-iscinigi. 46 pp. New York, 1912.

Amsden, C.A. Navaho Origins. NMHR, VII, 193-209. 1932.

--- Navaho Weaving. 261 pp. Santa Ana, 1934.

--- Reviving the Navaho Blanket. M, VI, 137-49. 1932.

Amsden, C.A. When Navaho Rugs were Blankets. School Arts Magazine, XXXIV, 387-96. 1935.

Anderson, H.A. Tribesmen of Tuzigoot. Desert, XIII, 16-19. June 1950.

Anonymous. The Alamos; a Problem in Human Rehabilitation. United Pueblos Quarterly Bulletin, I, No. iii. 1940.

--- Los Indios Navajos. Boletin Indigenista, XVII, 224-31. 1957.

--- Navaho Baby-Carrier. M, XXII, 99. 1948.

--- Navaho Pottery and Basketry. M, XXVI, 109. 1952.

--- Navahos seem Immune to Cancer. Hygeia, IX, 684. 1931.

Armer, L.A. The Crawler, Navaho Healer. M, XXVII, 5-10. 1953.

--- Sand-Paintings of the Navaho Indians. LEITA,V, 1-9. 1931.

--- Two Navaho Sand-Paintings. M, XXIV, 79-83. 1950.

--- Waterless Mountain. 212 pp. New York, 1931.

Astrov, M. The Concept of Motion as the Psychological Leitmotif of Navaho Life and Literature. JAFL, LXIII, 45-56. 1950.

Babington, S.H. Navajos, Gods and Tom-Toms. 256 pp. New York, 1950.

Backus, E. An Account of the Navajoes. HCPIT, IV, 209-15. 1854.

Bailey, F.L. Navaho Foods and Cooking Methods. AA, n.s., XLII, 270-90. 1940.

--- Navaho Motor Habits. AA, n.s., XLIV, 210-234. 1942.

--- Navaho Women and the Sudatory. AA, n.s., XLIII, 484-5. 1941.

--- Some Sex Beliefs and Practices in a Navaho Community. PMP, XL, ii, 108 pp. 1950.

--- Suggested Techniques for Inducing Navaho Women to Accept Hospitalization during Childbirth. American Journal of Public Health, XXXVIII, 1418-23. 1948.

Barber, B. Acculturation and Messianic Movements. ASR, IV, 663-9. 1941.

Bartlett, K. Hopi History, II: the Navajo Wars. MNMNA, VIII, 33-7. 1937.

--- Hopi Yucca Baskets. P, XXI, 33-41. 1949.

--- Recent Trends in Weaving on the Western Navajo Reservation. P, XXIII, 1-5. 1950.

--- Why the Navajos came to Arizona. MNMNA, V, 29-32. 1932.

Beadle, J.H. The Undeveloped West. Philadelphia, 1873.

Bedinger, M. Navajo Indian Silver-Work. OWS, VIII, 1-43. 1936.

Beidleman, R.G. A Partial, Annotated Bibliography of Colorado Ethnology. Colorado College Studies, II, 55 pp. 1958.

Berry, R.V.S. The Navajo Shaman and His Sacred Sand-Paintings. AAA, XXVII, 3-17. 1929.

Blackwood, B. An Anthropologist among the Navaho. NH, XXVII, 223-8. 1927.

Bloom, L.B., ed. Bourke on the Southwest. NMHR, XI, 77-122, 217-82. 1936.

Blount, T., et al. Primers I-III. Phoenix, 1947.

--- Primers I-III, New Series. Phoenix, 1957.

Blunn, C.T. Improvement of the Navajo Sheep. Journal of Heredity, XXXI, 99-112. 1940.

Boas, F. Northern Elements in the Mythology of the Navaho. AA, X, 371-6. 1897.

--- Zur Anthropologie der nordamerikanischen Indianer. VBGA, 1895, 367-411.

Bourke, J.G. The Early Navajo and Apache. AA, VIII, 287-94. 1895.

Boyce, G.A. A Primer of Navajo Economic Problems. 128 pp. Window Rock, 1942.

Boyd, W.C. and L.G. The Blood Groups and Types of the Ramah Navaho. AJPA, n.s., VII, 569-74. 1949.

Brewer, J. Notes on how to build a Hogan. SWMMR, 1936, Supplement, 485-8.

Brewer, S.P. Notes on Navaho Astronomy. FTD, 133-36. 1950.

Brugge, D.M. Navaho Sweat Houses. EP, LXIII, 101-06. 1956.

Bryan, N.G., and Young, S. Navaho Native Dyes. IH, II, 1-75. 1940.

Buckland, A.W. Points of Contact between Old World Myths and Customs and the Navajo Myth entitled "The Mountain Chant." JAI, XXII, 346-55. 1892.

Bunker, R. The Hunger of the Navajos. NMQR, XXVI, 133-46. 1956.

--- Other Men's Skies. 256 pp. Bloomington, 1956.

Burge, M. The Navahos and the Land. American Indian Defense Association and National Association on Indian Affairs, Bulletin XXVI, 1937.

Buschmann, J.C.E. Die Spuren der aztekischen Sprache im nördlichen Mexico und höheren amerikanischen Norden. AKAWB, 1854, Supplement-Band, II, 293-8.

Buxton, L.H.D. Some Navajo Folktales and Customs. FL, XXXIV, 293-313. 1923.

Campbell, I. Navajo Sandpaintings. Southwest Review, XXV, 143-50. 1940.

Carpenter, T.M., and Steggerda, M. The Food of the Present-day Navajo Indians. Journal of Nutrition, XVIII, 297-306. 1939.

Carr, M., Spencer, K., and Woolley, D. Navaho Clans and Marriage at Pueblo Alto. AA, n.s., XLI, 245-57. 1939.

Casagrande, J.B. The Southwest Project in Comparative Psycholinguistics. ACISA, V, 777-82. 1960.

Chapin, G. A Navajo Myth. NMA, IV, 63-7. 1940.

Clark, A. Little Herder in Autumn. ILR, Navaho Series. 97 pp. 1940.

--- Little Herder in Spring. ILR, Navaho Series. 114 pp. 1940.

--- Little Herder in Summer. ILR, Navaho Series. 126 pp. 1942.

--- Little Herder in Winter. ILR, Navaho Series. 111 pp. 1942.

--- Little Navaho Bluebird. ILR, Navaho Series. 143 pp. 1943.

--- Who wants to be a Prairie Dog? ILR, Navaho Series. 63 pp. 1940.

Clute, W.N. Notes on the Navajo Region. American Botanist, XXVI, 39-47. 1920.

Cole, E.P. Navajo Weaving with Two- or Four-Harness Looms. Weaver, II, iv, 11-13. 1937.

Coleman, N.R. Navajo Child Health. National Association on Indian Affairs, Bulletin XXV, 1936.

Collier, C.W. Soil Conservation, I, 1-4. 1935.

Collier, J. Navajos. Survey, II, 332-9; 363-5. 1924.

Collier, M.C. Leadership at Navajo Mountain and Klagetoh. AA, n.s., XLVIII, 137-8. 1946.

Collins, G.N. Pueblo Indian Maize Breeding. Journal of Heredity, V, 255-68. 1914.

Colton, H.S. Troy Town on the Hopi Mesas. SM, LVIII, 129-34. 1944.

Coolidge, D., and M.R. The Navajo Indians. 309 pp. Boston, 1930.

Coolidge, M.R. The Rain-Makers, pp. 245-90. Boston, 1929.

Corbett, J.M. Navajo House Types. EP, XLVII, 97-108. 1940.

Corle, E. People on the Earth. 401 pp. New York, 1937.

Cornell, R.D. Four-Horned Rams. NH, LXIV, 258-9. 1955.

Cowan, J.L. Bedouins of the Southwest. OW, XXXV, 107-16. 1912.

Cozzens, S.W. The Marvellous Country. London, 1874.

Cummings, B. Indians I Have Known. 75 pp. Tucson, 1952.

Cummings, B. Navajo Sand Paintings. K, I, vii, 1-2. 1936.

Cummins, H. Dermatoglyphics in North American Indians and Spanish-Americans. HB, XIII, 177-88. 1941.

Curtis, E.S. The North American Indian, I, 73-129, 136-44. Cambridge, 1907.

--- Vanishing Indian Types. Scribner's Magazine, XXXIX, 513-29. 1906.

Curtis, N., ed. The Indians' Book, pp. 347-421. New York, 1907.

Darby, W.J., et al. A Study of the Dietary Background and Nutriture of the Navajo Indian. Journal of Nutrition, LX, ii, 81 pp. 1956.

Davis, W.H. El Gringo, pp. 389-432. New York, 1857.

DeHuff, E.W. Taytay's Memories, pp. 131-4, 175-86, 224-8, 248-55. New York, 1924.

Denman, L.V.N. Dance with Fire. 8 pp. San Francisco, 1952.

Dennis, W. Does Culture appreciably affect Patterns of Infant Behavior? JSP, XII, 305-17. 1940.

Devereux, G. The Psychological 'Date' of Dreams. Psychiatric Quarterly Supplement, XXIII, 127-30. 1949.

Dietrich, M.S. The Navajo in No-Man's Land. NMQR, XX, 439-50. 1950.

--- Urgent Navajo Problems. 42 pp. Santa Fe, 1940.

Dittmann, A.T., and Moore, H.C. Disturbance in Dreams as Related to Peyotism among the Navaho. AA, LIX, 642-9. 1957.

Dodd, A. Patterns of a Culture – The Navaho. M, XXVIII, 52-62. 1954.

Dory, W. Navajo Land. NH, XXIII, 487-505. 1923.

Douglas, F.H. Navaho Silversmithing. DAMLS, XV, 1-4. 1930.

--- Seven Navajo Pots. MCN, III, 9-14. 1937.

Dutton, B.P. The Navaho Wind Way Ceremonial. EP, XLVIII, 73-82. 1941.

Dyk, W. Notes and Illustrations of Navaho Sex Behavior. PAC, 108-19. 1951.

--- Son of Old Man Hat. 378 pp. New York, 1938.

Eaton, J.H. Vocabulary of the Language of the Navajo. HCPIT, IV, 416-31. 1854.

Ehrenreich, W. Ein Ausflug nach Tusayan. Globus, LXXVI, 172-4. 1899.

Eickemeyer, C. Over the Great Navajo Trail. 270 pp. New York, 1900.

Elmore, F.H. The Deer, and His Importance to the Navaho. EP, LX, 371-84. 1953.

--- Food Animals of the Navajo. EP, XLIV, 149-54. 1938.

Enochs, J.B. Little Man's Family. 78 pp. Phoenix, 1940.

Eubank, L. Legends of Three Navaho Games. EP, LII, 138-40. 1945.

Euler, R.C. Anthropology, Economics, and the Navaho. P, XXIII, 58-60. 1951.

Evans, T. Navajo Folk Lore. SWL, I, 10-16. 1935.

--- Hosteen Bear loses the Second Fall. SWL, XIV, 3-4. 1948.

Evans, W. How Jackrabbit got His Long Ears. SWL, XIII, 41-2. 1947.

--- Navaho Folk Lore. SWL, XIV, 45-68. 1948.

--- The Origins of Navajo Sandpainting. NMFR, IX, 4-7. 1954-1955.

--- The White-haired One wrestles with Hosteen Bear. SWL, XIII, 53-4. 1948.

Falls, A.E. The Culinary Art of the Navajos. Practical Home Economics, XX, 349-50. 1942.

Farmer, M.F. Navaho Archaeology of Upper Blanco and Largo Canyons. AAn, VIII, 65-79. 1942.

Federal Writers' Project. The Navaho. Arizona State Teachers College Bulletin, XVIII, iv, 1-29. 1937.

Fergusson, E. Dancing Gods, pp. 179-247. New York, 1931.

Fewkes, J.W. Clay Figurines made by Navaho Children. AA, n.s., XXV, 559-63. 1923.

Filmore, J.C. Songs of the Navajos. LS, V, 238-41. 1896.

Fishler, S.A. In the Beginning. APUU, XIII, 132 pp. 1953.

--- Navaho Buffalo Hunting. EP, LXII, 43-57. 1955.

--- A Navaho Version of the "Bear's Son" Folktale. JAFL, LXVI, 70-74. 1953.

--- Symbolism of a Navaho "Wedding" Basket. M, XXVIII, 205-15. 1954.

Franciscan Fathers. A Vocabulary of the Navaho Language. 2 vols. St. Michaels, 1912.

Fryer, E.R. Navajo Social Organization and Land Use Adjustment. SM, LV, 408-22. 1942.

Gatschet, A.S. Classification into Seven Linguistic Stocks of Western Indian Dialects. RUSGS, VII, 403-85. 1879.

--- Zwölf Sprachen aus dem Südwesten Nordamerikas. 150 pp. Weimar, 1876.

Gerken, E.A. Development of a Health Education Program: Experiences with Navajo Indians. American Journal of Public Health, XXX, 915-20. 1940.

--- How the Navajos improve Their Health. Childhood Education, XVIII, 315-18. 1942.

Gifford, E.W. Apache-Pueblo. AR, IV, 1-207. 1940.

Gillmor, F., and Wetherill, L.W. Traders to the Navajos. 265 pp. Boston, 1934.

Gilman, M.F. Birds of the Navajo Reservation. Condor, X, 146-52. 1908.

Goddard, P.E. Assimilation to Environment as illustrated by Athapascan Peoples. ICA, XV, i, 337-59. 1906.

--- Navaho Blankets. AMJ, X, 201-11. 1910.

--- Navaho Myths, Prayers, and Songs. UCP, V, No. ii, 1907.

--- Navajo. ERE, IX, 254-6. 1917.

--- Navajo Texts. APAM, XXXIV, 1-179. 1933.

Goldfrank, E.S. Irrigation Agriculture and Navaho Community Leadership. AA, n.s., XLVII, 262-77. 1945.

--- More on Irrigation Agriculture and Navaho Community Leadership. AA, n.s., XLVIII, 473-6. 1946.

Goodwin, G. A Comparison of Navaho and White Mountain Apache Ceremonial Forms and Categories. SJA, I, 498-506. 1945.

Grandstaff, J.O. Wool Characteristics in Relation to Navajo Weaving. Department of Agriculture Technical Bulletin, DCCXC, 1-36. 1942.

Green, E.C. Navajo Rugs. SWL, XXIV, ii, 17-24. 1958.

Gregory, H.E. Geology of the Navajo Country. U.S. Department of the Interior, Professional Papers, XCIII, 1-161. 1917.

--- The Navajo Country. BAGS, XLVII, 561-77, 652-72. 1915.

--- The Navajo Country. U.S. Department of the Interior, Water Supply Papers, CCLXXX, 1-219. 1916.

Guernsey, S.J. Notes on a Navajo War Dance. AA, n.s., XXII, 304-7. 1920.

Haile, B. Aspects of Navaho Life. The Americas, VII, 63-72. July 1950.

--- Head and Face Masks in Navaho Ceremonialism. 122 pp. St. Michaels, 1947.

--- The Holy Gospels for Sunday and Holy Days. 254 pp. St. Michaels, 1938.

--- Learning Navaho. 4 vols. St. Michael's, 1941-48.

--- Legend of the Ghostway Ritual. 372 pp. St. Michaels, 1950.

--- A Manual of Navaho Grammar. 324 pp. St. Michaels, 1926.

--- Navaho Chantways and Ceremonials. AA, n.s., XL, 639-52. 1938.

--- Navaho Country. FMSW, X, 28-38. 1922.

Haile, B. The Navaho Fire Dance or Corral Dance. 57 pp. St. Michael's, 1946.

--- Navaho Games of Chance and Taboo. PM, VI, 35-40. 1933.

--- The Navaho Land Question. FMSW, X, 8-16. 1922.

--- Navaho Sacrificial Figurines. 100 pp. Chicago, 1947.

--- Navaho Upward-reaching Way and Emergence Place. AA, n.s., XLIV, 407-20. 1942.

--- The Navaho War Dance. 50 pp. St. Michael's, 1946.

--- Origin Legend of the Navaho Enemy Way. YUPA, XVII, 1-320. 1938.

--- Prayer Stick Cutting in a Five Night Navaho Ceremonial of the Male Branch of Shootingway. 229 pp. Chicago, 1947.

--- Reichard's Chant of Waning Endurance. AA, n. s., XLV, 307-11. 1943.

--- Religious Concepts of the Navajo Indians. Proceedings of the Catholic Philosophical Association, X, 84-98. 1935.

--- Some Cultural Aspects of the Navajo Hogan. 9 pp. Fort Wingate, 1937.

--- Some Mortuary Customs of the Navaho. FMSW, V, 29-33. 1917.

--- Starlore among the Navajo. 44 pp. Santa Fe, 1947.

--- A Stem Vocabulary of the Navaho Language, 2 vols. 727 pp. St. Michaels, 1950-51.

--- Why the Navaho Hogan? PM, XV, 39-56. 1942.

Hamamsy, L.S. The Role of Women in a Changing Navaho Society. AA, LIX, 101-111. 1957.

Hamer, J.H. An Analysis of Aggression in Two Societies. Anthropology Tomorrow, V, 87-94. 1956.

Hancock, J.C. Diseases among the Indians. Southwestern Medicine, XVII, 126. 1933.

Hannum, A. Paint the Wind. 206 pp. New York, 1958.

--- Spin a Silver Dollar. 193 pp. New York, 1945.

Harrington, J.P. The Apache and Navaho. EP, XXVII, 37-9. 1929.

--- A Field Comparison of Northwestern with Southwestern Indians. EFWSI, 1940, 91-4. 1941.

--- A Key to the Navaho Orthography employed by the Franciscan Fathers. AA, n.s., XIII, 164-6. 1911.

--- Six Common Navaho Nouns accounted for. JWAS, XXXV, 373. 1945.

--- Southern Peripheral Athapaskawan Origins, Divisions, and Migrations. SMC, C, 503-32. 1940.

Harrington, M.R. Swedged Navaho Bracelets. M, VIII, 183-4. 1934.

Harris, Z.S. Navaho Phonology and Hoijer's Analysis. IJAL, XI, 239-46. 1945.

Harrold, L.L. Floods in the Navajo Country. Soil Conservation, VII, 172-3. 1942.

Hartman, L.D. The Life and Customs of the Navajo Women. WA, n.s., XVIII, 100-7. 1938.

Hayes, F. Chee and His Pony. 262 pp. Boston, 1950.

--- Hosh-ki the Navaho. 250 pp. New York, 1943.

Heffernan, W.J. E.M. Kern, the Travels of an Artist-Explorer. 120 pp. Bakersfield, 1953.

Heinecke, R. Der Kampf der Navajos. 94 pp. Hannover, 1955.

Henderson, R. Healing Ceremonies in Monument Valley. Desert, XIII, 24-25. March 1950.

Henry, W.E. Thematic Apperception Technique in the Study of Culture-Personality Relations. Genetic Psychology Monographs, XXXV, 1-135. 1947.

Hill, G. The Art of the Navajo Silversmith. K, II, v, 17-21. 1937.

--- The Use of Turquoise among the Navajo. K, IV, 11-14. 1938.

Hill, W.W. The Agricultural and Hunting Methods of the Navaho Indians. YUPA, XVIII, 1-194. 1938.

--- The Hand Trembling Ceremony of the Navaho. EP, XXXVIII, 65-8. 1935.

--- Navaho Humor. GSA, IX, 1-28. 1943.

--- The Navaho Indians and the Ghost Dance of 1890. AA, n.s., XLVI, 523-7. 1944.

--- Navaho Rites for dispelling Insanity and Delirium. EP, XLI, 71-4. 1936.

--- Navaho Trading and Trading Ritual. SJA, IV, 371-96. 1948.

--- Navaho Warfare. YUPA, V, 1-19. 1936.

--- Navajo Pottery Manufacture. UNMB, II, iii, 5-23. 1937.

--- Navajo Salt Gathering. UNMB, III, iii, 5-23. 1940.

--- Navajo Use of Jimson Weed. NMA, III, 19-21. 1939.

--- Some Aspects of Navajo Political Structure. P, XIII, 23-8. 1940.

--- Some Navaho Culture Changes during Two Centuries. SMC, C, 395-415. 1940.

--- Stability in Culture and Pattern. AA, n.s., XLI, 258-60. 1939.

--- The Status of the Hermaphrodite and Transvestite in Navaho Culture. AA, n.s., XXXVII, 273-9. 1935.

Hill, W.W. and D.W. The Legend of the Navajo Eagle-catching Way. NMA, VI-VII, 31-6. 1943.

Hill, W.W. and D.W. Navaho Coyote Tales and Their Position in the Southern Athabaskan Group. JAFL, LVIII, 317-43. 1945.

--- Two Navajo Myths. NMA, VI-VII, 111-14. 1943.

Hobson, R. Navaho Acquisitive Values. PMP, XLII, iii, 45 pp. 1954.

Hocking, G.M. Some Plant Materials Used Medicinally and Otherwise by the Navaho Indians in the Chaco Canyon, New Mexico. EP, LXIII, 146-65. 1956.

Hodge, F.W. The Early Navajo and Apache. AA, VIII, 223-40. 1895.

--- How Old is Southwest Indian Silverwork? EP, XXV, 224-32. 1928.

Hoffman, F.L. The Navaho Population Problem. ICA, XXIII, 620-33. 1928.

Hogner, D.C. Navaho Winter Nights. 180 pp. New York, 1935.

Hoijer, H. The Apachean Verb. IJAL, XI, 193-203; XII, 1-13, 51-9; XIV, 247-59; XV, 12-22. 1945-49.

--- Cultural Implications of Some Navaho Linguistic Categories. Lg, XXVII, 111-20. 1951.

--- Navaho Phonology. UNMPA, I, 1-59. 1945.

--- Pitch Accent in the Apachean Languages. Lg, XIX, 38-41. 1943.

--- Phonetic and Phonemic Change in the Athapaskan Languages. Lg, XVIII, 218-20. 1942.

Hollister, U.S. The Navajo and His Blanket. 144 pp. Denver, 1903.

Honigmann, J.J. Northern and Southern Athapaskan Eschatology. AA, n.s., XLVII, 467-9. 1945.

Hoover, J.W. Navajo Land Problems. Economic Geography, XIII, 281-300. 1937.

--- Navajo Nomadism. GR, XXI, 429-45. 1931.

Hough, W. Apache and Navaho Fire-making. AA, n.s., III, 585-6. 1901.

Hrdlicka, A. Catalogue of Human Crania in the United States National Museum Collections. PUSNM, LXXVIII, ii, 1-95. 1931.

--- Physical and Physiological Observations on the Navaho. AA, n.s., II, 339-45. 1900.

Hulsizer, A. Region and Culture in the Curriculum of the Navaho and the Dakota. 344 pp. Federalsburg, 1940.

Hung, B.Y.P. On the Phonemic Status of Navaho. Anthropological Linguistics, I, ix, 20-3. 1959.

Hurt, W.R. Eighteenth Century Navaho Hogans from Canyon de Chelly National Monument. AAn, VIII, 89-104. 1942.

Indian Arts and Crafts Board. Navajo Indian Rugs. 7 pp. Washington, 1956.

Indian Arts and Crafts Board. Silver Jewelry of the Navajo and Pueblo Indians. 7 pp. Washington, 1956.

Inman, D. Don't Fence Me In. 167 pp. New York, 1955.

Ives, J.C. Report upon the Colorado River of the West. 131 pp. Washington, 1861.

James, G.W. Indian Blankets and Their Makers. 213 pp. Chicago, 1914.

--- The Indians of the Painted Desert Region. 268 pp. Boston, 1903.

James, M. A Note on Navajo Pottery-making. EP, XLIII, 13-15, 85-6. 1937.

Jeancon, J.A., and Douglas, F.H. The Navaho Indians. DAMLS, XXI, 1-4. 1931.

--- Navaho Spinning, Dyeing, and Weaving. DAMLS, III, 1-4. 1930.

Jewell, D.P. A Case of a "Psychotic" Navaho Indian Male. HO, XI, i, 32-36. 1952.

Johnston, B.E. Navaho Education. M, XXXIII, 4-12. 1959.

--- A Navaho Good Samaritan. M, XXVIII, 138-40. 1954.

Jones, C.R. Spindle-spinning Navajo Style. P, XVIII, 43-51. 1946.

Jones, D.W. Forty Years among the Indians. 400 pp. Salt Lake City, 1890.

Jones, T.J., Allen, H.B., Loram, C.T., and Deloria, E. The Navajo Indian Problem. 127 pp. New York, 1939.

Jones, V.H. A New and Unusual Navajo Dye (Endothia singularis). P, XXI, 17-24. 1948.

Kaplan, B. A Study of Rorschach Responses in Four Cultures. PMP, XLII, ii, 54 pp. 1954.

Kate, H.F.C. ten. Reizen en onderzoekingen in Noord-Amerika, pp. 232-42, 267-70. Leiden, 1885.

Kelly, C. Chief Hoskaninni. UHQ, XXI, 219-26. 1953.

Keur, D.L. Big Bead Mesa. MSAA, I, 1-90. 1941.

--- A Chapter in Navaho-Pueblo Relations. AAn, X, 75-86. 1944.

--- New Light on Navaho Origins. TNYAS, n.s., II, 182-92. 1940.

Kimball, S.T. Future Problems in Navajo Administration. HO, IX, ii, 21-4. 1950.

Kimball, S.T., and Provinse, J.H. Navajo Social Organization and Land Use Planning. HO, I, iv, 18-25. 1942.

King, J. Where the Two came to Their Father, ed. M. Oakes and J. Campbell. Bollingen Series, I, 1-88. 1943.

Kirk, R.F. Southwestern Indian Jewelry. EP, LII, 21-32, 41-50. 1945.

--- Southwestern Indian Jewelry. Papers of the School of American Research, ser. 2, XXXVIII, 1-24. 1945.

Klah, H. Navaho Creation Myth. NRS, I, 237 pp. 1942.

Kluckhohn, C. The Dance of Hasjelti. EP, XV, 187-92. 1923.

--- The Great Chants of the Navajo. Theatre Arts Monthly, XVII, 639-45. 1933.

--- Hopi and Navajo. New Mexico Quarterly, III, 56-64. 1933.

--- Myths and Rituals: A General Theory. Harvard Theological Review, XXXV, 45-79. 1942.

--- A Navaho Personal Document with a Brief Paretian Analysis. SJA, I, 260-83. 1945.

--- Navaho Women's Knowledge of Their Song Ceremonials. EP, XLV, 87-92. 1938.

--- The Navahos in the Machine Age. Technology Review, XLIV, iv, 2-6. 1942.

--- Notes on the Navajo Eagle Way. NMA, V, 6-14. 1941.

--- Participation in Ceremonials in a Navaho Community. AA, n.s., XL, 359-69. 1938.

--- Patterning as exemplified in Navaho Culture. Essays in Memory of Edward Sapir. Menasha, 1941.

--- Personality Formation among the Navaho Indians. Sociometry, IX, 128-32. 1946.

--- The Philosophy of the Navaho Indians. In F.S.C. Northrop, ed., Ideological Differences and World Order, 356-84. New Haven, 1949.

--- Some Aspects of Navaho Infancy and Early Childhood. PSS, I, 37-86. 1947.

--- Some Navaho Value Terms in Behavioral Content. Lg, XXXII, 140-5. 1956.

--- Some Personal and Social Aspects of Navaho Ceremonial Practice. Harvard Theological Review, XXXII, 57-82. 1939.

--- What Modern Parents can learn from the Navajos. AmI, IV, ii, 11-13. 1947.

Kluckhohn, C. and Morgan, W. Some Notes on Navaho Dreams. PAC, 120-31. 1951.

Kluckhohn, C. and Rosenzweig, J.C. Two Navaho Children over a Five-Year Period. American Journal of Orthopsychiatry, XIX, 266-78. 1949.

Kluckhohn, C., and Spencer, K. A Bibliography of the Navaho Indians. 93 pp. New York, 1940.

Kluckhohn, C., and Wyman, L. An Introduction to Navaho Chant Practice. MAAA, LIII, 1-204. 1940.

Kroeber, A.L. Recent Ethnic Spreads. UCP, XLVII, 259-81. 1959.

Kroeber, A.L. A Southwestern Personality Type. SJA, III, 108-13. 1947.

Krug, J.A. Report on the Navaho. 49 pp. Washington, 1948.

Kutnewsky, F. and Holbrook, C. Navajo Rugs. Compressed Air Magazine, XLVII, 6658-62. 1942.

La Farge, O. Laughing Boy. 302 pp. Boston, 1929.

--- The Navajos. NH, LVII, 360-67. 1948.

Landar, H.J. Four Navaho Summer Tales. JAFL, LXXII, 161-4, 248-51, 298-309. 1959.

--- The Navaho Intonational System. Anthropological Linguistics, I, ix, 11-19. 1959.

Landgraf, J.L. Land Use in the Ramah Navaho Area, New Mexico. TNYAS, Series II, XIII, 77-84. 1950.

Langley, D. Land of Beginning Again. AH, XXX, vi, 26-29, 34-39. 1954.

Left-Handed Mexican Clansman. The Trouble at Round Rock. U.S. Indian Service. Navajo Historical Series, II, 88 pp. 1952.

Leighton, A.H. and D.C. Elements of Psychotherapy in Navaho Religion. Psychiatry, IV, 515-23. 1941.

--- A Navaho builds a House. NH, XLVII, 172-3. 1941.

--- The Navaho Door. 149 pp. Cambridge, 1944.

--- A Navaho makes a Blanket. NH, XLVII, 274. 1941.

--- A Navaho makes Soap. NH, XLVIII, 19. 1941.

--- A Navaho takes a "Turkish Bath." NH, XLVIII, 20-1. 1941.

--- Some Types of Uneasiness and Fear in a Navaho Indian Community. AA, n.s., XLIV, 194-209. 1942.

Letherman, J. Sketch of the Navajo Tribe of Indians. ARSI, 1855, 283-97.

Lincoln, J.S. The Dream in Primitive Cultures. 359 pp. London, 1935.

Link, M.S. The Pollen Path. 211 pp. Stanford, 1956.

Lockett, C. Hogans vs. Houses. FTD, 137-42. 1952.

--- Midwives and Childbirth among the Navajo. P, XII, 15-17. 1939.

Loeb, E.M. A Note on Two Far-Travelled Kachinas. JAFL, LVI, 192-9. 1943.

Luebben, R.A. The Navajo Dilemma. AmI, VIII, ii, 6-16. 1958-1959.

Luomala, K. Navaho Life of Yesterday and Today. 115 pp. Berkeley, 1938.

McAllester, D.P. Enemy Way Music. PMP, XLI, iii, 106 pp. 1954.

McAllester, D.P. (ed.) The Myth and Prayers of the Great Star Chant and the Myth of the Coyote Chant. NRS, IV, 190 pp. 1956.

McCombe, L., et al. Navaho Means People. 159 pp. Cambridge, 1951.

McCullough, C.W. Modiste to Miss Navajo. AH, XXXI, vii, 8-17. 1955.

McDermott, W., et al. Introducing Modern Medicine in a Navajo Community. Science, CXXXI, 197-205, 280-7. 1960.

McGregor, J.C. Zwei gegensätzliche Indianer-Stämme in Arizona. Natur und Volk, LXVIII, 535-44. 1938.

McKibbin, D.B. Revolt of the Navaho, 1913. NMHR, XXIX, 259-89. 1954.

McPhee, J.C. Indians in Non-Indian Communities. 68 pp. Window Rock, 1953.

Malcolm, R. Archaeological Remains, supposedly Navaho. AAn, V, 4-20. 1939.

Malouf, C. and A.A. The Effects of Spanish Slavery on the Indians of the Intermountain West. SJA, I, 378-91. 1945.

Marino, C.C. The Seboyetanos and the Navahos. NMHR, XXIX, 8-27. 1954.

Mason, O.T. Aboriginal Skin-Dressing. RUSNM, 1889, 574-80.

Matthews, W. The Basket Drum. AA, VII, 202-8. 1894.

--- The Gentile System of the Navajo Indians. JAFL, III, 89-110. 1890.

--- Ichthyophobia. JAFL, XI, 105-12. 1898.

--- Marriage Prohibitions on the Father's Side among Navajos. JAFL, IV, 78-9. 1891.

--- The Mountain Chant. ARBAE, V, 379-467. 1887.

--- Mythic Dry-Paintings of the Navajos. AN, XIX, 931-9. 1885.

--- Myths of Gestation and Parturition. AA, n.s., IV, 737-42. 1902.

--- Navaho. BBAE, XXX, ii, 41-5. 1910.

--- Navaho Legends. MAFLS, V, 1-300. 1897.

--- Navaho Myths, Prayers and Songs, ed. P.E. Goddard. UCP, V, 21-63. 1907.

--- Navaho Night Chant. JAFL, XIV, 12-19. 1901.

--- Navajo Dye Stuffs. ARSI, 1891, 613-15.

--- Navajo Gambling Songs. AA, II, 1-19. 1889.

--- A Navajo Initiation. LS, XV, 353-6. 1901.

--- Navajo Names for Plants. AN, XX, 767-77. 1886.

--- Navajo Silversmiths. ARBAE, II, 167-79. 1883.

--- Navajo Weavers. ARBAE, III, 371-91. 1884.

--- The Night Chant. MAMNH, VI, 1-332. 1902.

--- Noqoilpi, the Gambler: A Navajo Myth. JAFL, II, 89-94. 1889.

--- The Origin of the Utes, a Navajo Myth. AAOJ, VII, 271-4. 1885.

Matthews, W. A Part of the Navajos' Mythology. AAOJ, V, 207-24. 1883.

--- The Prayer of a Navajo Shaman. AA, I, 149-70. 1888.

--- Serpent Worship among the Navajos. LS, IX, 228-35. 1898.

--- Some Deities and Demons of the Navajos. AN, XX, 841-50. 1886.

--- Some Illustrations of the Connection between Myth and Ceremony. MICA, 1893, 246-51.

--- Some Sacred Objects of the Navajo Rites. Archives of the International Folk-Lore Association, I, 227-47. 1893.

--- Songs of Sequence of the Navajos. JAFL, VII, 185-94. 1894.

--- Songs of the Navajos. LS, V, 197-201. 1896.

--- A Study in Butts and Tips. AA, V, 345-50. 1892.

--- The Study of Ceremony. JAFL, X, 259-63. 1897.

--- The Study of Ethics among the Lower Races. JAFL, XII, 1-9. 1899.

--- The Treatment of Ailing Gods. JAFL, XIV, 20-3. 1901.

--- A Two-faced Navaho Blanket. AA, n.s., II, 638-42. 1900.

--- A Vigil of the Gods. AA, IX, 50-7. 1896.

Mera, H.P. Banded-background Blankets. BLA, VII, 1-13. 1939.

--- The Chinlee Rug. BLA, XIII, 1-15. 1942.

--- Cloth-strip Blankets of the Navaho. BLA, XVI, 1-14. 1945.

--- Navaho Textile Arts. 102 pp. Santa Fe, 1947.

--- Navaho Twilled Weaving. BLA, XIV, 1-12. 1943.

--- Navaho Woven Dresses. BLA, XV, 1-13. 1944.

--- Navajo Blankets of the "Classic" Period. BLA, III, 1-4. 1938.

--- The Serrate Designs of Navajo Blanketry. BLA, XI, 1-15. 1940.

--- Wedge-weave Blankets. BLA, IX, 1-13. 1939.

--- The Zoning Treatment in Navajo Blanket Design. BLA, XII, 1-13. 1940.

Mills, G. Navaho Art and Culture. 273 pp. Colorado Springs, 1959.

Mindeleff, C. Navaho Houses. ARBAE, XVII, ii, 475-517. 1898.

Mirkowich, N. A Note on Navajo Place-Names. AA, n.s., XLIII, 313-14. 1941.

Mitchell, F.G. Dine bizad: a Handbook for Beginners in the Study of the Navaho Language. 127 pp. Los Angeles, 1910.

--- Dineh Bizan: Navajo, His Language. 128 pp. New York, 1944.

Mollhausen, B. Reisen in die Felsengebirge Nord-Amerikas, II, 227-49. Leipzig, 1861.

Morgan, W. Human-Wolves among the Navaho. YUPA, XI, 1-43. 1936.

--- Navaho Dreams. AA, n.s., XXXIV, 390-405. 1932.

--- Navaho Treatment of Sickness. AA, n.s., XXXIII, 390-402. 1931.

--- The Organization of a Story and a Tale. JAFL, LVIII, 169-94. 1945.

Morgan, W., and Young, R.W. Coyote Tales. 53 pp. Washington, 1949.

Moskowitz, I., and Collier, J. Patterns and Ceremonials of the Indians of the Southwest, pp. 31-49, 163-92. New York, 1949.

Munk, J.A. Navajo Surgery. Journal of Eclectic Medicine, January, 1906, 10.

Murbarger, N. Sacred Sheep of the Navajos. AH, XXVI, 11-15. August 1950.

Neumann, D.L. The Future of Navaho Silversmithing. EP, LIII, 6-8. 1946.

--- Modern Developments in Indian Jewelry. EP, LVII, 173-80. 1950.

--- Navaho "Channel" Turquoise and Silver. EP, LXI, 410-12. 1954.

--- Navaho Silversmithing Survives. EP, L, 6-8. 1943.

--- Navajo Silver Dies. EP, XXXV, 71-5. 1933.

--- Navajo Silverwork. EP, XXXII, 102-8. 1932.

Newcomb, F.J. How the Navajo adopt Rites. EP, XLVI, 25-7. 1939.

--- The Navajo Listening Rite. EP, XLV, 46-9. 1938.

--- Navajo Omens and Taboos. 79 pp. Santa Fe, 1940.

--- Navajo Symbols of the Sun. New Mexico Quarterly, VI, 305-7. 1936.

--- Origin Legend of the Navajo Eagle Chant. JAFL, LIII, 50-77. 1940.

Newcomb, F.J., and Reichard, G.A. Sandpaintings of the Navajo Shooting Chant. 87 pp. New York, 1937.

Newcomb, F.J., et al. A Study of Navajo Symbolism. PMP, XXXII, iii, 108 pp. 1956.

Newell, W.W. Navaho Legends. JAFL, IX, 211-18. 1896.

Nigg, C. A Study of the Blood Groups among the American Indians. Journal of Immunology, XI, 319-22. 1926.

Nölle, W. Die Navajo und Tewa Heute. Tribus, VI, 102-08. 1957.

Norman, R.D., and Midkiff, K.L. Navaho Children on Raven Progressive Matrices and Goodenough Draw-a-Man Tests. SJA, XI, 129-36. 1955.

Oakes, M. Where the Two Came to Their Father.
New York, 1943.

Opler, M.E. Examples of Ceremonial Interchanges
among Southwestern Tribes. M, XVI, 77-80. 1942.

--- The Kinship Systems of the Southern Athabaskan-
speaking Tribes. AA, n.s., XXXVIII, 620-33.
1936.

--- Navaho Shamanistic Practice among the Jicarilla
Apache. NMA, VI-VII, 13-18. 1943.

Ostermann, L. The Navajo Indian Blanket. FMSW,
VI, 1-11. 1918.

--- Navajo Houses. FMSW, V, 20-30. 1917.

--- The Navajo Indians. A, III, 857-69. 1908.

--- Navajo Names. FMSW, VI, 11-15. 1918.

--- The Navajo Noun. ICA, XV, ii, 243-54. 1907.

--- Origin, Characteristics, and Costume of the
Navajo Indians. FMSW, V, 1-11. 1917.

--- Silversmithing among the Navajos. FMSW, VII,
18-24. 1919.

Overholt, M.E. Pictures in Sand. AAA, XXXIV,
262-5. 1933.

Page, G.B. Navaho House Types. MNMNA, IX,
47-9. 1937.

--- The Navajo Sweat House. NMA, II, 19-21. 1937.

Palmer, F.L. The Configuration Pattern of Navajo
Culture. EP, XLI, 19-24. 1936.

Parsons, E.C. Navaho Folk Tales. JAFL, XXXVI,
368-75. 1923.

--- Note on a Navajo War Dance. AA, n.s., XXI,
465-7. 1919.

--- Note on the Night Chant at Tuwelchedu. AA, n.
s., XXIII, 240-3. 1921.

Peet, S.D. The Suastika and Fire-Worship in America. AAOJ, XXVI, 185-92. 1904.

Pepper, G.H. Ah-jih-lee-hah-neh, a Navaho Legend.
JAFL, XXI, 178-83. 1908.

--- Die Deckenweberei der Navajo-Indianer. Globus,
LXXXII, 133-40. 1902.

--- The Making of a Navajo Blanket. Everybody's
Magazine, VI, 33-43. 1902.

--- Native Navajo Dyes. Papoose, I, iii, 1-11. 1903.

--- The Navaho Indians. SW, XXIX, 639-44. 1900.

--- An Unusual Navajo Medicine Ceremony. SW,
1905, 3-10.

Pfister, O. Instinktive Psychoanalyse unter den
Navajo Indianern. Imago, XVIII, 81-109. 1932.

--- Instinctive Psychoanalysis among the Navajos.
Journal of Nervous and Mental Disease, LXXVI,
234-54. 1932.

Phelps-Stokes Fund. The Navaho Indian Problem.
127 pp. New York, 1939.

Pillsbury, D. Tribal Meeting of the Navajo. Desert,
XV, 13-16. October 1952.

Pogue, J.E. The Aboriginal Use of Turquoise in
North America. AA, n.s., XIV, 437-66. 1912.

Pollock, F.A. Cultural Significance of the Navajo
Problem. TJS, II, 28-34. 1950.

Pospisil, F. Etnologické materiálie z jihozápadu U.
S.A. 256 pp. Brno, 1932.

Pousma, R.H. He-who-always-wins. 147 pp. Grand
Rapids, 1934.

--- Venereal Disease among the Navahos. Southwestern Medicine, XIII, 503-5. 1929.

Rapoport, R.N. Changing Navaho Religious Values.
PMP, XLI, ii, 152 pp. 1954.

Reagan, A.B. The Influenza and the Navajo. PIAS,
XXIX, 243-7. 1919.

--- A Navaho Fire Dance. AA, n.s., XXXVI, 434-
7. 1934.

--- Navaho Sports. PM, V, 68-71. 1932.

--- Utilization of the Navajo Country. Proceedings
of the Iowa Academy of Science, XLI, 215-37.
1934.

Reed, E.K. Information on the Navaho in 1706. AA,
n.s., XLIII, 485-7. 1941.

--- Navajo Independence and Acculturation. AA, n.
s., XLIII, 681-2. 1941.

--- Navajo Monolingualism. AA, n.s., XLVI, 147-
9. 1944.

Reeve, F.D. Early Navaho Geography. NMHR, XXXI,
290-309. 1956.

--- The Government and the Navaho. NMHR, XIV,
82-114. 1939.

--- The Government and the Navaho, 1883-1888.
NMHR, XVIII, 17-51. 1943.

--- The Navaho-Spanish Peace: 1720's-1770's.
NMHR, XXXIV, 9-40. 1959.

--- Navaho-Spanish Wars: 1680-1720. NMHR,
XXXIII, 205-31. 1958.

--- A Navaho Struggle for Land. NMHR, XXI, 1-
21. 1946.

--- Seventeenth Century Navaho-Spanish Relations.
NMHR, XXXII, 36-52. 1957.

Reichard, G.A. Attitudes toward Avoidance. Essays
in Anthropology presented to A.L. Kroeber, pp.
265-72. Berkeley, 1936.

--- The Character of the Navaho Verb Stem. Word,
V, 55-76. 1949.

--- Color in Navajo Weaving. Arizona Historical
Review, VII, 19-30. 1936.

--- Dezba, Woman of the Desert. 161 pp. New
York, 1939.

--- Distinctive Features of Navaho Religion. SJA,
I, 199-220. 1945.

--- A Few Instances of Cultural Resistance in Southwest North America. ICA, XXII, ii, 289-96. 1926.

Reichard, G.A. Good Characters in Myth. JAFL,
LVI, 141-3. 1943.

--- Human Nature as conceived by the Navajo Indians. Review of Religion, VI, 353-60. 1943.

--- Individualism and Mythological Style. JAFL,
LVII, 16-25. 1944.

--- Linguistic Diversity among the Navaho Indians.
IJAL, XI, 156-68. 1945.

--- The Navaho and Christianity. AA, n.s., LI,
66-71. 1949.

--- Navaho Grammar. PAES, XXI, 407 pp. 1951.

--- Navajo Classification of Natural Objects. P, XXI,
7-12. 1948.

--- Navajo Medicine Man. 83 pp. New York, 1939.

--- Navajo Shepherd and Weaver. 222 pp. New York,
1936.

--- Prayer: The Compulsive Word. MAES, VII, 1-
97. 1944.

--- Significance of Aspiration in Navaho. IJAL, XIV,
15-20. 1948.

--- Spider Woman. 287 pp. New York, 1934.

--- The Story of the Navajo Hail Chant. 155 pp.
New York, 1944.

--- The Translation of Two Navaho Chant Words. AA,
n.s., XLIV, 421-4. 1942.

Reichard, G.A., and Bittany, A.D. Agentive and
Causative Elements in Navajo. 22 pp. New York,
1940.

Richardson, C.C. Navajos are Witty People. AH,
XXVII, 26-29. August 1951.

--- Navajo Medicine Man. AH, XXVII, 26-29.
August 1951.

Riley, C.L. A Survey of Navajo Archaeology. UCSSA,
IV, 45-60. 1954.

Robinson, J.S. A Journal of the Santa Fe Expedition
under Col. Doniphan, ed. C.L. Cannon. 96 pp.
Princeton, 1932.

Rollins, W.E. Passing of the Spirit Dance. EP, VII,
187-91. 1919.

--- The Spirit of the Dead. EP, XII, 71-3. 1922.

Rush, E.M. Indian Legends. EP, XXXII, 137-54.
1932.

Salsbury, C.G. Disease Incidence among the Navajoes.
Southwestern Medicine, XXI, 230-33. 1937.

Sanchez, G.I. "The People." 90 pp. Lawrence,
1948.

Sapir, E. Glottalized Continuants in Navaho, Nootka,
and Kwakiutl. Lg, XIV, 248-74. 1938.

--- Internal Linguistic Evidence suggestive of the
Northern Origin of the Navaho. AA, n.s., XXXVIII,
224-35. 1936.

--- A Navaho Sand Painting Blanket. AA, n.s.,
XXXVII, 609-16. 1935.

Sapir, E. A Note on Navaho Pottery. AA, n.s.,
XXXII, 575-6. 1930.

--- Two Navaho Puns. Lg, VIII, 217-19. 1932.

Sapir, E., and Hoijer, H. Navaho Texts. 543 pp.
Iowa City, 1942.

Sasaki, T.T. Sociocultural Problems in Introducing
New Technology on a Navaho Irrigation Project.
Rural Sociology, XXI, 307-10. 1956.

Sasaki, T.T. and Adair, J. New Land to Farm.
HPTC, 97-112. 1952.

Schevill, M.E. Beautiful on the Earth. 155 pp. Tucson, 1947.

--- The Navajo Screen. K, XI, 3-5. 1945.

Sears, P.M. Tuberculosis and the Navahos. Colorado Quarterly, IV, 195-204. 1955.

Senter, D., and Hawley, F. Hopi and Navajo Child
Burials. AA, n.s., XXXIX, 131-4. 1937.

Service, E.R. The Navaho of the American Southwest. PPC, 157-81. 1958.

Shiya, T.S., ed. Navaho Saga. 56 pp. St. Michaels,
1949.

Shufeldt, R.W. Arrow-Release among the Navajos.
AN, XXI, 784-6. 1887.

--- The Drawings of a Navaho Artist. MAH, XXIII,
463-8. 1889.

--- The Evolution of House-Building among the Navajo Indians. PUSNM, XV, 279-82. 1892.

--- Head-flattening as seen among the Navajo Indians. PSM, XXXIX, 535-9. 1891.

--- Mortuary Customs of the Navajo Indians. AN,
XXV, 303-6. 1891.

--- A Navajo Artist and His Notions of Mechanical
Drawing. ARSI, 1886, 240-4.

--- The Navajo Belt-Weaver. PUSNM, XIV, 391-5.
1891.

--- A Navajo Skull. Journal of Anatomy and Physiology, XX, 426-9. 1886.

--- The Navajo Tanner. PUSNM, XI, 59-66. 1888.

--- A Skull of a Navajo Child. Journal of Anatomy
and Physiology, XXI, 66-71. 1886.

Sleight, F.W. The Navajo Sacred Mountain of the
East— A Controversy. EP, LVIII, 379-97. 1951.

Smith, D.M. Indian Tribes of the Southwest, pp.
56-79. Stanford, 1933.

Spencer, K. Mythology and Values. MAFLS, XLVIII,
248 pp. 1957.

--- Reflections of Social Life in the Navaho Origin
Myth. UNMPA, III, 1-140. 1947.

Spicer, E.H. and Collier, J. Sheepmen and Tech-
nicians. HPTC, 185-208. 1952.

Spiegelberg, A.F. The Navajo Blanket. Old Santa
Fe, II, 323-37. 1915.

Spiegelberg, A.F. Navajo Blankets. OW, XX, 447-9. 1904.

Spuhler, J.N. and Kluckhohn, C. Inbreeding Coefficients of the Ramah Navaho Population. HB,XXV, 295-317. 1953.

Steggerda, M. Form Discrimination Test as given to Navajo, Negro and White School Children. HB, XIII, 239-46. 1941.

--- The McAdory Art Test applied to Navaho Indian Children. Journal of Comparative Psychology,XXII, 283-5. 1936.

--- Physical Measurements on Negro, Navaho, and White Girls of College Age. AJPA, XXVI, 417-30. 1940.

Steggerda, M. and Eckardt, R.B. Navaho Foods and Their Preparation. American Dietetic Association, Journal, XVII, 217-25. 1941.

Steggerda, M., and Hill, T.J. Eruption Time of Teeth among White, Negro, and Indian. American Journal of Orthodontics and Oral Surgery, XXVIII, 361-70. 1942.

--- Incidence of Dental Caries among Maya and Navajo Indians. Journal of Dental Research, XV, 233-42. 1936.

Steggerda, M., and Macomber, E. Mental and Social Characteristics of Maya and Navajo Indians. JSP, X, 51-9. 1939.

Stephen, A.M. The Navajo. AA, VI, 345-62.1893.

--- Navajo Origin Legend. JAFL,XLIII, 88-104. 1932.

--- The Navajo Shoemaker. PUSNM, XI, 131-6. 1888.

--- When John the Jeweler was Sick. American Indian Life, ed. E.C.Parsons, pp. 153-6. New York, 1925.

Stevens, A. Once They were Nomads. Survey Graphic, XXX, 60-7. 1941.

Stevenson, J. Ceremonial of Hasjelti Dailjis and Mythical Sand Painting of the Navajo Indians. ARBAE, VIII, 235-85. 1891.

Stewart, O.C. The Navaho Wedding Basket. MNMNA, X, 25-8. 1938.

Stocker, J. Indian Country. AH, XXXI, vii, 18-29. 1955.

Streib, G.F. An Attempt to Unionize a Semi-Literate Navaho Group. HO, XI, i, 23-31. 1952.

Sullivan, B.S. The Unvanishing Navajos. 141 pp. Philadelphia, 1938.

Tanner, C.L. Navajo Silver Craft. AH, XXX, viii, 16-33. 1954.

Tanner, C.L. and Steen, C.R. A Navajo Burial of about 1850. PPHR, XXVIII, 110-18. 1955.

Thompson, L. Attitudes and Acculturation. AA, n. s., L, 200-15. 1948.

Tozzer, A.M. A Navajo Sand Picture of the Rain Gods and Its Attendant Ceremony. ICA, XIII, 147-56. 1902.

--- A Note on Star-Lore among the Navajos. JAFL, XXI, 28-32. 1908.

--- Notes on Religious Ceremonials of the Navaho. Putnam Anniversary Volume, pp. 299-343. New York, 1909.

Tremblay, M.A., et al. Navaho Housing in Transition. AI, XIV, 182-219. 1954.

Tschopik, H. Navaho Basketry. AA, n.s., XLII, 444-62. 1940.

--- Navaho Pottery Making. PMP, XVII, 1-85.1941.

--- Taboo as a Possible Factor involved in the Obsolescence of Navaho Pottery and Basketry. AA, n. s., XL, 257-62. 1938.

Underhill, R.M. Acculturation among the Navaho Indians. ICA, XXXI, i, 11-13. 1955.

--- Here Come the Navaho. ILC, VIII, 285 pp. 1953.

--- Men of the Mountain. Arizona Quarterly, VI, 147-57. 1950.

U.S. Bureau of Indian Affairs. You Asked about the Navajo. 42 pp. Lawrence, 1957.

U.S. Department of the Interior. Statistical Summary; Human Dependency Survey, Navajo Reservation and Grazing District. Window Rock, 1941.

United States Indian Service. You asked about the Navaho! 69 pp. Lawrence, 1949.

Valkenburgh, R.F. van. Christmas Legend of the Navajo. Desert Magazine, VI, 19-23. 1942.

--- Dinebikeyah. 175 pp. Window Rock, 1940.

--- Navajo Common Law. MNMNA, IX, 17-22, 51-4; X, 39-45. 1936-38.

--- Navajo Naat'a'ani. K, XIII, 14-23. 1948.

--- A Short History of the Navajo People. 56 pp. Window Rock, 1938.

--- A Striking Navaho Pictograph. M, XII, 153-7. 1938.

Valkenburgh, R.F. van, and Begay, S. Sacred Places and Shrines of the Navajo. MNMNA, XI, 29-34; XIII, 6-10. 1938-40.

Valkenburgh, R.F. van, and Walker, F.O. Old Placenames in the Navaho Country. M, XIX, 89-94. 1945.

Vann, D.V. Meals for Navajos. SS, III, ii, 5-6. 1951.

Vestal, P.A. Uncultivated Food Plants used by the Ramah Navaho. AJB, XXXI, viii, 65. 1944.

Vivian, G. Two Navaho Baskets. EP, LXIV, 145-55. 1957.

Vleet, T.S. van. Legendary Evolution of the Navajo Indians. AN, XXVII, 69-79. 1893.

Vogt, E.Z. The Automobile in Contemporary Navaho Culture. ACISA, V, 359-63. 1960.

--- Between Two Worlds. AmI, V, i, 13-21. 1949.

Wake, C.S. A Navaho Origin Legend. AAOJ, XXVI, 265-71. 1904.

Wall, L. and Morgan, W. Navaho-English Dictionary. 65 pp. Phoenix, 1958.

Walton, E.L. Dawn Boy; Blackfoot and Navaho Songs. 82 pp. New York, 1926.

--- Navaho Poetry. Texas Review, VII, 198-210. 1922.

--- Navaho Verse Rhythms. Poetry, XXIV, 40-4. 1924.

--- Navajo Song Patterning. JAFL, XLIII, 105-18. 1930.

Walton, E.L., and Waterman, T.T. American Indian Poetry. AA, n.s., XXVII, 25-52. 1925.

Waters, F. Masked Gods. 438 pp. Albuquerque, 1950.

--- The Navajo Missions. NMQR, XX, 5-20. 1950.

--- Navajo Yei-bet-chai. Yale Review, XXVIII, 558-71. 1939.

Watkins, F.E. The Navaho. SWML, XVI, 1-45. 1943.

--- Navaho Indians. M, XVI, 109-18, 149-56, 210-14; XVII, 20-24, 77-81, 136-40, 168-72. 1942-43.

--- Two Rare Navaho Masks. M, X, 188-9. 1936.

Weber, A. The Navajo Indians. Hearings before a Subcommittee of the Committee on Indian Affairs, United States Senate, 75th Congress, 1st Session, Part xxxiv, pp. 17553-75. 1937.

--- Navajos on the Warpath. FMSW, VII, 1-18. 1918.

--- On Navajo Myths and Superstitions. FMSW, IV, 38-46. 1916.

Wetherill, L.W. Navaho Stories. K, XII, 25-8, 36-9. 1947.

--- Some Navajo Recipes. K, XII, 5-6, 39-40. 1946.

Wetherill, L.W., and Cummings, B. A Navaho Folk Tale of Pueblo Bonito. AAA, XIV, 132-6. 1922.

Wheelwright, M.C. Atsah and Yohe. Museum of Navaho Ceremonial Art, Bulletin, III, 1-16. 1945.

--- Emergence Myth according to the Hanelth-nayhe or Upward-reaching Rite. NRS, III, 1-186. Santa Fe, 1949.

--- Hail Chant and Water Chant. NRS, II, 1-237. 1946.

--- The Myth and Prayers of the Great Star Chant. 198 pp. Santa Fe, 1956.

Wheelwright, M.C. Myth of Sontso (Big Star). Museum of Navaho Ceremonial Art, Bulletin, Vol. II. 1940.

--- Notes on Some Navajo Coyote Myths. NMFR, IV, 17-19. 1949/50.

--- Tleji or Yehbechai Myth. Bulletin of the House of Navajo Religion, I, 1-13. 1938.

Whitman, W. Navaho Tales. 217 pp. Boston, 1925.

Whittemore, M. Participation in Navajo Weaving. P, XIII, 49-52. 1941.

Wilson, E. Red, Black, Blond, and Olive, pp. 1-68. New York, 1956.

Wilson, E.F. The Navajo Indians. OFC, III, 115-17. 1890.

Woehlke, W.W. The Economic Rehabilitation of the Navajos. Proceedings of the National Conference of Social Work, 1934, 548-56.

Woerner, D. Education among the Navajo. 227 pp. New York, 1941.

Woodward, A. A Brief History of Navajo Silversmithing. BMNA, XIV, 1-78. 1938.

--- Navajo Silver Comes of Age. LACMQ, X, i, 9-14. 1953.

Worcester, D.E. The Navaho During the Spanish Regime in New Mexico. NMHR, XXVI, 101-18. 1951.

Wyman, L.C. The Female Shooting Life Chant. AA, n.s., XXXVIII, 634-53. 1936.

--- Navaho Diagnosticians. AA, n.s., XXXVIII, 236-46. 1936.

--- Navaho Indian Painting. 28 pp. Boston, 1959.

--- Notes on Obsolete Navaho Ceremonies. P, XXIII, 44-48. 1951.

--- Origin Legends of Navaho Divinatory Rites. JAFL, XLIX, 134-42. 1936.

--- Psychotherapy of the Navaho. Tomorrow, IV, iii, 77-84. 1956.

--- The Sandpaintings of the Kayenta Navaho. UNMPA, VII, 120 pp. 1952.

Wyman, L.C., and Amsden, C. A Patchwork Cloak. M, VIII, 133-7. 1934.

Wyman, L.C., and Bailey, F.L. Idea and Action Patterns in Navaho Flintway. SJA, I, 356-77. 1945.

--- Native Navaho Methods for the Control of Insect Pests. P, XXIV, 97-103. 1952.

--- Navaho Girl's Puberty Rite. NMA, VI-VII, 3-12. 1943.

--- Navaho Striped Windway, an Injury-Way Chant. SJA, II, 213-38. 1946.

--- Navaho Upward Reaching Way. UNMB, IV, ii, 1-47. 1943.

Wyman, L.C. and Bailey, F.L. Two Examples of Navaho Physiotherapy. AA, n.s., XLVI, 329-37. 1944.

Wyman, L.C., and Harris, S.K. Navajo Indian Medical Ethnobotany. UNMB, III, v, 1-76. 1941.

Wyman, L.C., Hill, W.W.,and Osinai, I. Navajo Eschatology. UNMB, IV, i. 1942.

Wyman, L.C., and Kluckhohn, C. Navaho Classification of Their Song Ceremonials. MAAA, L, 1-38. 1938.

Wyman, L.C., and Thorne, B. Notes on Navaho Suicide. AA, n.s., XLVII, 278-88. 1945.

Wyman, L.C., et al. Beautyway: A Navaho Ceremonial. 301 pp. New York, 1957.

Yealth, S. The Making of Navajo Blankets. EP,XL, 7-9, 43-4. 1936.

Yost, B.W. Bread Upon the Sands. 245 pp. Caldwell, 1958.

Young, R.W., ed. The Navajo Yearbook, Report No. VI, Fiscal Year 1957. 353 pp. Window Rock, 1957.

Young, R.W., and Harrington, J.P. Earliest Navaho and Quechua. AAm, II, 315-19. 1944.

Young, R.W., and Morgan, W. The A B C of Navaho. Phoenix, 1944.

--- The Navaho Language. 470 pp. Phoenix, 1943.

--- A Vocabulary of Colloquial Navaho. 461 pp. Phoenix, 1951.

Young, S. Navajo Dyes. Phoenix, 1939.

Young, S., and Bryan, N. Navaho Native Dyes.IH, II, 1-75. 1940.

Youngblood, B. Navajo Trading. Hearings before a Subcommittee of the Committee on Indian Affairs, United States Senate, 75th Congress, 1st Session, Part xxxiv, pp. 18036-115. 1937.

Zelditch, M. Statistical Marriage Preferences of the Ramah Navaho. AA, LXI, 470-91. 1959.

Zolotarevskaia, I.A. Navahi. Trudy Instituta Etnografii Imena N.N. Mikluho Maklaia, XXV, 135-46. 1955.

22. NEVOME

Including the Nevome or Pima Bajo, the Ure, and the Yecora.

Alegre, F.J. Historia de la Compania de Jesus en Nueva Espana. 3 vols. Mexico, 1841.

Anonymous. Rudo ensayo. RACHS, V, ii, 188-92. 1894.

Beals, R.L. The Comparative Ethnology of Northern Mexico. IA, II, 93-225. 1932.

Hodge, F.W. Nevome. BBAE, XXX, ii, 62-3. 1910.

Mason, J.A. and Brugge, D.M. Notes on the Lower Pima. MPR, i, 277-97. 1958.

Perez de Ribas, A. Historia de los triumphos de novestra santa fee en los missiones de la provincia de Nueva Espana. Madrid, 1645.

Sauer, C. The Distribution of Aboriginal Tribes and Languages in Northwestern Mexico. IA, V, 34-41. 1934.

Smith, B. Grammar of the Pima, or Nevome. New York, 1862.

23. OPATA

Including the Heve or Eudeve, the Jova, and the Opata.

Johnson, J.B. The Opata. UNMPA, VI, 50 pp. 1950.

Anonymous. Rudo ensayo. RACHS, V, ii, 166-88. 1894.

Beals, R.L. The Comparative Ethnology of Northern Mexico. IA, II, 93-225. 1932.

Featherman, A. Social History of the Races of Mankind, III, 42-9. Boston, 1890.

Forbes, J.D. Historical Survey of the Indians of Sonora, 1821-1910. E, IV, 335-68. 1957.

Hamy, E.T. Algunas observaciones sobre la distribucion geografica de los opatas, de los tarahumares y de los pimas. Anales del Museo de Arqueologia, Historia y Etnografia, epoca 4ª, V, 93-8. 1922.

Hodge, F.W. Opata. BBAE, XXX, ii, 138-9. 1910.

Hrdlicka, A. Notes on the Indians of Sonora. AA, n.s., VI, 71-84. 1904.

Kroeber, A.L. Uto-Aztecan Languages of Mexico. IA, VIII, 1-27. 1934.

Pimentel, D.F. Lenguas indigenas de México. Mexico, 1862.

Pimentel, F. Vocabulario manual de la lengua Opata. BSMGE, X, 288-313. 1863.

Radin, P. Mexican Kinship Terms. UCP, XXXI, 1-14. 1931.

Reyes, V. Terminaison du pluriel dans les langues Mexicano-opata. ICA, VIII, 548-49. 1892.

Sauer, C. The Distribution of Aboriginal Tribes and Languages in Northwestern Mexico. IA, V, 46-51. 1934.

Schroeder, A.H. The Cipias and Ypotlapiguas. Arizona Quarterly, XII, 101-10. 1956.

Smith, B. A Grammatical Sketch of the Heve Language. 26 pp. New York, 1861.

Whiting, A.F. The Tumacacori Census of 1796. K, XXIX, i, 1-12. 1953.

24. PAPAGO

Castetter, E.F., and Bell, W.H. Pima & Papago
Indian Agriculture. Inter-American Studies, I,
1-245. 1942.

Gabel, H.E. A Comparative Racial Study of the
Papago. UNMPA, IV, 1-96. 1949.

Joseph, A., Spicer, R., and Chesky, J. The Desert
People. 288 pp. Chicago, 1949.

Underhill, R.M. Papago Indian Religion. 359 pp.
New York, 1946.

--- Social Organization of the Papago Indians. CUCA,
XXX, 1-280. 1939.

Anonymous. The Fiesta of St. Francis Xavier. K,
XVI, i-ii, 32 pp. 1950.

--- History of the Papago Indians. EP, XIV, 96-9.
1923.

Beals, R.L. Material Culture of the Pima, Papago,
and Western Apache. 44 pp. Berkeley, 1934.

Becker, D.M. Music of the Papago. SS, VI, v, 2-4.
1954.

Bliss, W.L. In the Wake of the Wheel. HPTC, 23-
34. 1952.

Bowen, R. Saguaro Harvest in Papagoland. Desert
Magazine, II, viii, 3-5. 1939.

Castetter, E.F., and Underhill, R. The Ethnobiology
of the Papago Indians. UNMBB, IV, iii, 3-84. 1935.

Cazeneuve, L. Les Indiens de la Region de Tucson.
Ee, LI, 37-45. 1956.

Chesky, J. The Wiikita. K, VIII, 3-5. 1943.

Childs, T. Sketch of the "Sand Indians." K, XIX,
ii-iv, 27-39. 1954.

Curtis, E.S. The North American Indian, II, 27-43.
Cambridge, 1908.

Davis, E.H. The Papago Ceremony of Vikita. INM,
III, 155-77. 1920.

Densmore, F. Communication with the Dead as practised by the American Indians. Man, L, 40-1. 1950.

--- Papago Music. BBAE, XC, 1-230. 1929.

Dobyns, H.F. Blunders with Bolsas. HO, X, iii, 25-
32. 1951.

--- Experiment in Conservation. HPTC, 209-24. 1952.

--- Papagos in the Cotton Fields. 140 pp. Tucson,
1950.

--- Thirsty Indians. HO, XI, iv, 33-6. 1952.

Dolores, J. Papago Nicknames. Essays in Anthropology
presented to A.L. Kroeber, pp. 45-7. Berkeley,
1936.

--- Papago Nominal Stems. UCP, XX, 19-31. 1923.

--- Papago Verb Stems. UCP, X, 241-63. 1913.

Drucker, P. Yuman-Piman. AR, VI, 91-230. 1941.

Federal Writers' Project. The Papago. Arizona State
Teachers College Bulletin, XX, iii, 1-16. 1939.

Fontana, B.L., ed. Jose Lewis Brennan's Account of
Papago "Customs and other References." E, VI,
226-37. 1959.

Gabel, N.E. The Physical Status of the Papago.
FTD, 189-200. 1950.

Gaillard, U.S.A. The Papago of Arizona and Sonora.
AA, VII, 293-6. 1894.

Gifford, E.W. Apache-Pueblo. AR, IV, 1-207.
1940.

--- Clans and Moieties in Southern California. UCP,
XIV, 174-6. 1918.

Greene, R.A. The Composition and Uses of the Fruit
of the Giant Cactus. Journal of Chemical Education,
XIII, 309-12. 1936.

Hayden, J., and Steen, C.R. The Vikita Ceremony
of the Papago. SWMMR, April, 1937, 263-83.

Henderson, E. Well of Sacrifice. AH, XXIX, 2-3.
February, 1953.

Herbert, C.W. Saguaro Harvest in the Land of the
Papagos. Desert Magazine, XVIII, xi, 14-17. 1955.

Hill, G. Papago Legends from Santa Rosa. SWL, VI,
34-7. 1940.

Hodge, F.W. Papago. BBAE, XXX, ii, 200-1. 1910.

Hoover, J.W. Generic Descent of the Papago Villages. AA, n.s., XXXVII, 257-64. 1935.

--- The Indian Country of Southern Arizona. GR, XIX,
38-60. 1929.

Hrdlicka, A. Notes on the Indians of Sonora. AA, n.
s., VI, 51-89. 1904.

Ives, R.L. The Monster of Quitovac. M, XV, 195-
9. 1941.

--- Papago. IJAL, XI, 119. 1945.

--- Some Papago Migrations in the Sonoyta Valley.
M, X, 161-7. 1936.

Johnson, B. The Wind Ceremony. EP, LXVII, 28-31.
1960.

Jones, A.W. Additional Information about the Vikita.
SWMMR, May, 1937, 338-41.

Jones, C.F. Demographic Patterns in the Papago Indian Village of Chuichu, Arizona. HB, XXV, 191-
202. 1953.

Kate, H.F.C. ten. Indiens d'Amérique du Nord. Ane,
XXVIII, 369-401. 1917.

--- Somatological Observations on Indians of the
Southwest. JAEA, III, 117-44. 1892.

Kissell, M.L. Basketry of the Papago and Pima.
APAM, XVII, 115-264. 1916.

Kraus, B.S. Carabelli's Anomaly of the Maxillary
Molar Teeth. American Journal of Human Genetics,
III, 348-55. 1951.

Kraus, B.S. Occurrence of the Carabelli Trait in Southwest Ethnic Groups. AJPA, n.s., XVII, 117-23. 1959.

Kraus, B.S. and Jones, B.M. Indian Health in Arizona. RBER, II, 164 pp. 1954.

Kroeber, H.R. Papago Coyote Tales. JAFL, XXII, 339-42. 1909.

--- Traditions of the Papago Indians. JAFL, XXV, 95-105. 1912.

Kurath, W. A Brief Introduction to Papago. UASSB, XIII, 1-42. 1945.

Lloyd, E. The Papago Feast of St. Francis. SWMMR, 1940, 389-92.

Lumholtz, C. New Trails in Mexico. 411 pp. London, 1912.

McGee, W.J. The Beginning of Agriculture. AA, VIII, 350-75. 1895.

Mason, J.A. The Papago Harvest Festival. AA, n. s., XXII, 13-25. 1920.

--- The Papago Migration Legend. JAFL, XXXIV, 254-68. 1921.

Matson, D.S. Papago Recordings. Arizona Quarterly, IX, 45-54. 1953.

Neff, M.L. Pima and Papago Legends. JAFL, XXV, 51-65. 1912.

O'Neale, L.M., and Dolores, J. Notes on Papago Color Designations. AA, XLV, 387-97. 1943.

Phoenix Indian School. The New Trail: A Book of Creative Writing by Indian Students. 158 pp. Phoenix, 1941.

Ross, W. The Present-day Dietary Habits of the Papago Indians. University of Arizona Record, 1945, 1-25.

Sauer, C. The Distribution of Aboriginal Tribes and Languages in Northwestern Mexico. IA, V, 53-4. 1934.

Schweitzer, J. and Thomas, R.K. Fiesta of St. Francis at San Francis Quito, Sonora. K, XVIII, i-ii, 1-7. 1952.

Segundo, T.A. From the Tribe of the Papago Indians. Boletin Indigenista, XIV, 27-30. March, 1954.

Shreve, M. Modern Papago Basketry. K, VIII, 10-16. 1943.

Smith, W.N. The Papago Game of "Gince Goot." M, XIX, 194-7. 1945.

Spicer, E. The Papago Indians. K, VI, 21-4. 1941.

Spier, L. Cultural Relations of the Gila River and Lower Colorado Tribes. YUPA, III, 1-22. 1936.

Stocker, J. Tom Segundo. AmI, VI, ii, 18-24. 1951.

Stone, M. Bean People of the Cactus Forest. Desert Magazine, VI, xi, 5-10. 1943.

Stricklen, E.G. Notes on Eight Papago Songs. UCP, XX, 361-6. 1923.

Swadesh, M. Papago Stop Series. Word, XI, 191-3. 1955.

Thackeray, F.A. Sand Food of the Papagos. Desert Magazine, XVI, iv, 22-4. 1953.

Thackeray, F.A. and Gilman, M.F. A Rare Parasitic Food Plant of the Southwest. ARSI, 1930, 409-16. 1931.

Thackeray, F.A. and Leding, A.R. The Giant Cactus of Arizona. Journal of Heredity, XX, 401-14. 1929.

Underhill, R.M. The Autobiography of a Papago Woman. MAAA, XLVI, 1-64. 1936.

--- Hawk over Whirlpools. 255 pp. New York, 1940.

--- Note on Easter Devils at Kawori'k on the Papago Reservation. AA, n.s., XXXVI, 515-16. 1934.

--- A Papago Calendar Record. UNMB, II, v, 3-66. 1938.

--- The Papago Indians of Arizona and Their Relatives the Pima. ILC, III, 1-68. 1940.

--- People of the Crimson Evening. Lawrence, 1951.

--- Singing for Power: the Song Magic of the Papago Indians. 158 pp. Berkeley, 1938.

Vater, M. Ethnographische Gegendstände aus Arizona und Mexico. VBGA, 1892, 89-94.

Vavich, M.G., et al. Nutritional Status of Papago Indian Children. Journal of Nutrition, LIV, 375-83. 1956.

Whited, S. Pima Agency. RIT, 1890, 137-46.

Whiting, A.F. The Tumacacori Census of 1796. K, XXIX, i, 1-12. 1953.

Woodruff, J. Indian Oasis, pp. 223-320. Caldwell, 1939.

Wright, H.B. Long Ago Told: Legends of the Papago Indians. 290 pp. New York, 1929.

25. PIMA

Including the Qahatika, the Sobaipuri, and the Pima Alto.

Castetter E.F., and Bell, W.H. Pima & Papago Indian Agriculture. Inter-American Studies, I, 1-245. 1942.

DiPeso, C.C. The Sobaipuri Indians of the Upper San Pedro River Valley, Southeastern Arizona. PAF, XII, 285 pp. 1953.

--- The Upper Pima of San Cayetano del Tumacacori. PAF, VII, 613 pp. 1956.

Russell, F. The Pima Indians. ARBAE, XXVI, 3-390. 1908.

Bartlett, J.R. Personal Narrative of Explorations and Incidents in Texas, New Mexico, California, Sonora, and Chihuahua, II, 222-38. New York, 1854.

Beals, R.L. Material Culture of the Pima, Papago, and Western Apache. 44 pp. Berkeley, 1934.

Boas, F. Zur Anthropologie der nordamerikanischen Indianer. VBGA, 1895, 367-411.

Bolton, H.E., ed. Kino's Historical Memoir of Pimería Alta. 2 vols. Cleveland, 1919.

Breazeale, J.F. The Pima and His Basket. Tucson, 1925.

Brown, H. A Pima-Maricopa Ceremony. AA, n.s., VIII, 688-90. 1906.

Buschmann, J.C.E. Die Pima-Sprache und die Sprache der Koloschen. AKAWB, 1856, 321-432.

Castetter, E.F. Pima Ethnobotany. New Mexico Quarterly, XX, 373-5. 1950.

Curtin, L.S.M. By the Prophet of the Earth. 158 pp. Santa Fe, 1949.

Curtis, E.S. The North American Indian, II, 3-24, 39-45. Cambridge, 1908.

Curtis, N., ed. The Indians' Book, pp. 313-20. New York, 1907.

Dobyns, H.F., et al. Thematic Changes in Yuman Warfare. In V.F.Ray, ed., Cultural Stability and Cultural Change, 46-71. 1957.

Douglas, F.H. Pima Indian Close Coiled Basketry. DAMLS, V, 1-4. 1930.

--- A Pima Wood Bowl. MCN, XI, 43-6. 1939.

Douglas, F.H. et al. Five Pima Pots. MCN, XVIII, 8 pp. 1953.

Drucker, P. Yuman-Piman. AR, VI, 91-230. 1941.

Ewing, C.R. Investigations into the Causes of the Pima Uprising of 1751. Mid-America, XXIII, 139-51. 1941.

--- The Pima Uprising of 1751. In, Greater America: Essays in Honor of Herbert Eugene Bolton, 259-80. Berkeley, 1945.

Ezell, P.H. The Conditions of Hispanic-Piman Contacts on the Gila River. AI, XVII, 163-91. 1957.

--- The Hispanic Acculturation of the Gila River Pimas. E, III, 189-90. 1956.

Forbes, J.D. Historical Survey of the Indians of Sonora, 1821-1910. E, IV, 335-68. 1957.

Greene, R.A. The Composition and Uses of the Fruit of the Giant Cactus. Journal of Chemical Education, XIII, 309-12. 1936.

Grossmann, F.E. The Pima Indians of Arizona. ARSI, 1871, 407-19.

--- Three Pima Fables. K, XXIV, 24. 1958.

Hall, S.M. The Story of a Pima Record Rod. OW, XXVI, 413-23. 1907.

Hamy, E.T. Algunas observaciones sobre la distribucion geografica de los opatas, de los tarahumares y de los pimas. Anales del Museo de Arqueologia, Historia y Etnografia, epoca 4^a, V, 93-8. 1922.

Hanna, B.L., et al. A Preliminary Study of the Population History of the Pima Indians. American Journal of Human Genetics, V, 377-88. 1953.

Halseth, O.S. Archeology in the Making. M, VII, 37-41. 1933.

Hayden, J.D. Notes on Pima Pottery Making. K, XXIV, iii, 10-16. 1959.

Herzog, G. A Comparison of Pueblo and Pima Musical Styles. JAFL, XLIX, 283-417. 1936.

--- Culture Change and Language. Essays in Memory of Edward Sapir, pp. 66-74. Menasha, 1941.

--- Note on Pima Moieties. AA, n.s., XXXVIII, 520-1. 1936.

Hill, W.W. Note on the Pima Berdache. AA, n.s., XL, 338-40. 1938.

--- Notes on Pima Land Law and Tenure. AA, n.s., XXXVIII, 586-9. 1936.

Hodge, F.W. Pima. BBAE, XXX, ii, 251-3. 1910.

--- Sobaipuri. BBAE, XXX, ii, 608. 1910.

Hrdlicka, A. Notes on the Pima of Arizona. AA, n.s., VIII, 39-46. 1906.

Ives, R.L., ed. Sedelmayr's Relacion of 1746. BBAE, CXXIII, 97-117. 1939.

Kate, H.F.C.ten. Indiens d'Amérique du Nord. L'Anthropologie, XXVIII, 369-401. 1917.

--- Reizen en onderzoekingen in Noord-Amerika, pp. 152-60. Leiden, 1885.

--- Somatological Observations on Indians of the Southwest. JAEA, III, 117-44. 1892.

Kissell, M.L. Basketry of the Papago and Pima. APAM, XVII, 115-264. 1916.

Kraus, B.S. and Jones, B.M. Indian Health in Arizona. RBER, II, 164 pp. 1954.

Kroeber, A.L. Uto-Aztecan Languages of Mexico. IA, VIII, 1-27. 1934.

Kroeber, H.R. Pima Tales. AA, n.s., X, 231-5. 1910.

Lloyd, J.W. Aw-aw-tam Nights. Westfield, 1911.

Lumholtz, C. New Trails in Mexico. 411 pp. London, 1912.

Neff, M.L. Pima and Papago Legends. JAFL, XXV, 51-65. 1912.

Ocaranza, F. Parva crónica de la Sierra Madre y las Pimerías. Instituto Panamericano de Geografia e Historia, LXIV, 4-156. 1942.

Parsons, E.C. Notes on the Pima. AA, n.s., XXX, 445-64. 1928.

Phoenix Indian School. The New Trail: A Book of Creative Writing by Indian Students. 158 pp. Phoenix, 1941.

Robinson, B. Akimoel Awatam. AH, XXXI, vii, 30-
     39. 1955.
Russell, F. Pima Annals. AA, n.s., V, 76-80.1903.
--- A Pima Constitution. JAFL, XV, 222-8. 1903.
Sauer, C. Distribution of Aboriginal Tribes and Lan-
     guages in Northwestern Mexico. IA, V, 52-4.1934.
Schroeder, A.H. The Cipias and Ypotlapiguas. Ari-
     zona Quarterly, XII, 101-10. 1956.
Simpson, R.D. Those Who have gone still live. M,
     XX, 73-80. 1946.
Smith, D.M. Indian Tribes of the Southwest, pp.
     103-8. Stanford, 1933.
Spier, L. Cultural Relations of the Gila River and
     Lower Colorado Tribes. YUPA, III, 1-22. 1936.
Steen, C.R. Notes on Some 19th Century Pima Bur-
     ials. K, XII, 6-10. 1946.
--- Some Notes on the Use of Tobacco and Cane Pipes
     by the Pimas of the Gila Valley. AA, n.s., XLV,
     641-2. 1943.
Underhill, R.M. The Papago Indians of Arizona and
     Their Relatives the Pima. ILC, III, 1-68. 1940.
Velarde, L. Descripción de la Pimería. Documentos
     para la Historia de México, ser. 4, I, 343-90.
     Mexico, 1853-57.
Walton, E.L., and Waterman, T.T. American In-
     dian Poetry. AA, n.s., XXVII, 25-52. 1925.
Whited, S. Pima Agency. RIT, 1890, 137-46.
Whiting, A.F. The Tumacacori Census of 1796. K,
     XXIX, i, 1-12. 1953.
Whittemore, I.T. Among the Pimas. 136 pp. Al-
     bany, 1893.
Woodward, A. Historical Notes on the Pima. M,
     XXIII, 144-7. 1949.
Wyllys, R.K. Padre Luis Velarde's Relacion of
     Pimeria Alta. NMHR, VI, 111-57. 1931.

26. PIRO

Including the now extinct pueblos of Senecu and
Socorro del Sur.

Bandelier, A.F. Final Report of Investigations among
     the Indians of the Southwestern United States.
     PAIA, III, 1-323; IV, 1-591. 1890-92.
Bartlett, J.R. The Language of the Piro. AA, n.s.,
     XI, 426-33. 1909.
Fewkes, J.W. The Pueblo Settlements near El Paso.
     AA, n.s., IV, 72-5. 1902.
Hammond, G.P., and Rey, A., eds. Expedition into
     New Mexico made by Antonio de Espejo, pp. 74-7.
     Los Angeles, 1929.

Harrington, J.P. Notes on the Piro Language. AA,
     n.s., XI, 563-94. 1909.
Hodge, F.W. Piros. BBAE, XXX, ii, 261-2.1910.

27. QUERES

Including the eastern Keresan pueblos of Cochiti,
San Felipe, Santa Ana, Santo Domingo, and Sia.

Curtis, E.S. The North American Indian, XVI, 65-
     249. Norwood, 1926.
Dumarest, N. Notes on Cochiti. MAAA, VI, 137-
     237. 1919.
Goldfrank, E.S. The Social and Ceremonial Organi-
     zation of Cochiti. MAAA, XXXIII, 1-129. 1927.
Lange, C.H. Cochiti. 642 pp. Austin, 1959.
White, L.A. The Pueblo of San Felipe. MAAA,
     XXXVIII, 1-69. 1932.
--- The Pueblo of Santa Ana. MAAA, LX, 1-360.
     1942.
--- The Pueblo of Santo Domingo. MAAA, XLIII,
     1-210. 1935.

Aberle, S.B.D. Maternal Mortality among the Pueb-
     los. AJPA, XVIII, 431-57. 1934.
Anonymous. The Green Corn Ceremony. EP, XXVII,
     48-50. 1929.
--- Santo Domingo and San Felipe. EP, XXIV, 427-
     39. 1928.
Bandelier, A.F. The Delight Makers. 490 pp. New
     York, 1890.
Benedict, R. Tales of the Cochiti Indians. BBAE,
     XCVIII, 1-256. 1931.
Bloom, L.B., ed. Bourke on the Southwest. NMHR,
     XIII, 192-238. 1938.
Boas, F. Abstract Characteristics of Keresan Folk-
     tales. ICA, XX, i, 223-4. 1928.
Bourke, J.G. The Snake-Dance of the Moquis of
     Arizona, pp. 10-53. London, 1884.
Bunzel, R. The Emergence. JAFL, XLI, 288-90.1928.
Chapman, K.M. Pottery Decorations of Santo Do-
     mingo and Cochiti Pueblos. EP, XVI, 87-93. 1924.
--- The Pottery of Santo Domingo Pueblo. MLA, I,
     1-192. 1936.
DeHuff, E.W. More Pueblo Tales. EP, XI, 140-4.
     1921.
--- Taytay's Memories, pp. 3-5, 10-11, 129-30,
     135-8, 217-23. New York, 1924.
--- Taytay's Tales, pp. 92-4, 149-58, 172-82. New
     York, 1922.
Densmore, F. Music of Acoma, Isleta, Cochiti and
     Zuñi Pueblos. BBAE, CLXV, 129 pp. 1957.

Densmore, F. Music of Santo Domingo Pueblo. SWMP, XII, 1-186. 1938.

Douglas, F.H. Weaving of the Keres Pueblos. DAMLS, XCI, 162-4. 1939.

Dozier, E.P. A Comparison of Eastern Keresan and Tewa Kinship Systems. ACISA, V, 430-6. 1960.

Euler, R.C. Environmental Adaptation at Sia Pueblo. HO, XII, iv, 27-32. 1954.

Evans, B., and M.G. American Indian Dance Steps. 122 pp. New York, 1931.

Fergusson, E. Dancing Gods, pp. 40-9, 56-60. New York, 1931.

Fewkes, J.W. A Comparison of Sia and Tusayan Snake Ceremonials. AA, VIII, 118-41. 1895.

Gatschet, A.S. Classification into Seven Linguistic Stocks of Western Indian Dialects. RUSGS, VII, 403-85. 1879.

--- Zwölf Sprachen aus dem Sudwesten Nordamerikas. 150 pp. Weimar, 1876.

Gifford, E.W. Apache-Pueblo. AR, IV, 1-207. 1940.

Halseth, O.S. Report of Economic and Social Survey of the Keres Pueblo of Zia. EP, XVI, 67-75. 1924.

Hammond, G.P., and Rey, A., eds. Expedition into New Mexico made by Antonio de Espejo, pp. 82-5. Los Angeles, 1929.

Hartley, M. The Scientific Esthetic of the Redman. AAA, XIII, 113-19. 1922.

Hawley, F. An Examination of Problems Basic to Acculturation in the Rio Grande Pueblos. AA, n.s., L, 612-24. 1948.

--- Keresan Patterns of Kinship and Social Organization. AA, n.s., LII, 499-512. 1950.

Hawley, F., Pijoan, M., and Elkin, C.A. An Inquiry into Food Economy and Body Economy in Zia Pueblo. AA, n.s., XLV, 547-56. 1943.

Hawley, F., and Fenter, D. Group-designed Behavior Patterns in Two Acculturating Groups. SJA, II, 133-51. 1946.

Hewett, E.L. The Corn Ceremony at Santo Domingo. EP, V, 69-76. 1918.

--- From Barter to World Trade. EP, XLIX, 219-24. 1942.

Hodge, F.W. Cochiti. BBAE, XXX, i, 317-18. 1907.

--- Pueblo Snake Ceremonials. AA, IX, 133-6. 1896.

--- San Felipe. BBAE, XXX, ii, 432-3. 1910.

--- Santa Ana. BBAE, XXX, ii, 454. 1910.

--- Santo Domingo. BBAE, XXX, ii, 462. 1910.

--- Sia. BBAE, XXX, ii, 562-3. 1910.

Hoebel, E.A. Keresan Witchcraft. AA, LIV, 586-9. 1952.

--- Underground Kiva Passages. AAn, XIX, 76. 1953.

Huebener, G. The Green Corn Dance at Santo Domingo. EP, XLV, 1-17. 1938.

Humphrey, N.B. The Mock Battle Greeting. JAFL, LIV, 186-90. 1941.

Hurt, L.R. Notes on the Santa Ana Indians. EP, XLVIII, 131-42. 1941.

Keech, R.A. Green Corn Ceremony at the Pueblo of Zia. EP, XXXVI, 145-9. 1934.

Lange, C.H. An Animal Dance at Santo Domingo Pueblo, January 26, 1940. EP, LXI, 151-55. 1954.

--- Culture Change as Revealed in Cochiti Pueblo Hunting Customs. TJS, V, 178-84. 1953.

--- The Feast Day Dance at Zia Pueblo. TJS, IV, 19-26. 1952.

--- The Keresan Component of Southwestern Pueblo Culture. SJA, XIV, 34-50. 1958.

--- King's Day Ceremonies at a Rio Grande Pueblo, Jan. 6, 1940. EP, LVIII, 398-406. 1951.

--- The Role of Economics in Cochiti Pueblo Social Change. AA, LV, 674-94. 1953.

--- San Juan's Day at Cochiti Pueblo, New Mexico, 1894 and 1947. EP, LIX, 175-82. 1952.

Lange, C.H. and Bailey, W.C. Significant Factors in the Comparison of Explicitly Heterogeneous Cultures. TJS, VII, 256-274. 1955.

McHarg, J.B. The Lions of Cochiti. EP, XX, 99-104. 1926.

Orth, G.S. Report on the Pueblo of Santa Ana. 40th Congress, 2nd Session, House Report, LXX, Vol. 2, 1868.

Parsons, E.C. Early Relations between Hopi and Keres. AA, n.s., XXXVIII, 554-60. 1936.

--- Fiesta at Sant' Ana. SM, XVI, 178-83. 1923.

--- The Kinship Nomenclature of the Pueblo Indians. AA, n.s., XXXIV, 377-89. 1932.

--- Notes on Isleta, Santa Ana, and Acoma. AA, n.s., XXII, 56-69. 1920.

--- Notes on San Felipe and Santo Domingo. AA, n.s., XXV, 485-94. 1923.

--- Pueblo Indian Religion. 2 vols. Chicago, 1939.

Prince, L.B. The Stone Lions of Cochiti. RP, III, 151-60. 1904.

Reagan, A.B. Additional Notes on the Jemez-Zia Region. EP, XII, 120-1. 1922.

--- The Zia Indians. SW, XLV, 25-9. 1916.

--- The Zia Mesa and Ruins. Science, XXX, 713-14. 1909.

Smith, D.M. Indian Tribes of the Southwest, pp. 88-94. Stanford, 1933.

Spencer, R.F. The Phonemes of Keresan. IJAL, XII, 229-36. 1946.

--- Spanish Loanwords in Keresan. SJA, III, 130-46. 1947.

Starr, F. Shrines near Cochiti. AAOJ, XXII, 219-23. 1900.

Starr, F.   A Study of a Census of the Pueblo of
    Cochiti. PDAS, VII, 33-45. 1899.
Stevenson, J.   Illustrated Catalogue of the Collec-
    tions obtained from the Indians of New Mexico and
    Arizona. ARBAE, II, 405-9, 450-60. 1883.
Stevenson, M.C.   The Sia. ARBAE, XI, 9-157. 1894.
Underhill, R.M.   First Penthouse Dwellers of Ameri-
    ca, pp. 85-107. New York, 1938.
White, L.A.   A Comparative Study of Keresen Medi-
    cine Societies. ICA, XXIII, 604-19. 1928.
--- Keresan Indian Color Terms. PMA, XXVIII, 559-
    63. 1942.
--- Miscellaneous Notes on the Keresan Pueblos.
    PMA, XXXII, 365-76. 1946.
--- Notes on the Ethnobotany of the Keres. PMA,
    XXX, 557-68. 1944.
--- Notes on the Ethnozoology of the Keresan Pueblo
    Indians. PMA, XXXI, 223-46. 1945.
--- "Rohona" in Pueblo Culture. PMA, XXIX, 439-
    43. 1943.
Whitener, H.C., tr. Jesus Christo niya tawa-mani.
    72 pp. Albuquerque, 1935.
Wilson, E.H.   Enemy Bear, M, XXII, 80-5. 1948.

28. TANO

Harrington, J.P.   The Language of the Tano Indians.
    ICA, XVII, ii, 321-9. 1910.
Hodge, F.W.   Tano. BBAE, XXX, ii, 686-7. 1910.
Nelson, N.C.   Archeology of the Tano District. ICA,
    XIX, 114-19. 1915.
--- Chronology of the Tano Ruins. AA, n.s., XVIII,
    159-80. 1916.
Reed, E.K.   Test Excavations at San Marcos Pueblo.
    EP, LXI, 323-43. 1954.
Riley, C.L.   Early Spanish Reports of the Galisteo
    Basin. EP, LVIII, 237-43. 1951.
Whorf, B.L., and Trager, G.L.   The Relationship of
    Uto-Aztecan and Tanoan. AA, n.s., XXXIX, 609-
    24. 1937.

29. TAOS

Including the northern Tiwa pueblos of Picuris and
Taos.

Parsons, E.C.   Taos Pueblo. GSA, II, 1-120. 1936.

Aberle, S.B.D.   Maternal Mortality among the Pueb-
    los. AJPA, XVIII, 431-57. 1934.
Anderson, A.J.O.   Taos Uprising Legends. EP, LIII,
    331-7. 1946.

Angulo, J. de.   Taos Kinship Terminology. AA, n.
    s., XXVII, 482-3. 1925.
Austin, M., and Adams, A.E.   Taos Pueblo. 20 pp.
    San Francisco, 1931.
Bailey, F.M.   Some Plays and Dances of the Taos
    Indians. NH, XXIV, 85-95. 1924.
Bloom, L.B., ed.   Bourke on the Southwest. NMHR,
    XI, 217-82; XII, 41-77. 1936-37.
Boas, F.   Zur Anthropologie der nordamerikanischen
    Indianer. VBGA, 1895, 367-411.
Cassidy, I.S.   Taos. WF, VIII, 60-2. 1949.
--- New Mexico Place Names--Taos. EP, LXI, 296-
    99. 1954.
Clark, A.   Little Boy with Three Names. ILR, Pueb-
    lo Series. 55 pp. 1940.
--- Young Hunter of Picuris. ILR, Pueblo Series. 56
    pp. 1943.
Curtis, E.S.   The North American Indian, XVI, 27-
    63. Norwood, 1926.
DeHuff, E.W.   The Bear and the Deer. EP, XXXI,
    2-4. 1931.
--- The Fate of Yellow Corn and Blue Corn. EP, XVI,
    53-5. 1924.
--- The Greedy Fox. EP, XXXI, 20-2. 1931.
--- Infidelity. EP, XXXI, 200-1. 1931.
--- More Pueblo Tales. EP, XI, 140-4. 1921.
--- Myths told by the Pueblos. EP, XI, 86-92. 1921.
--- The Red Winged Hawk. EP, XVI, 51-3. 1924.
--- Taytay's Memories, pp. 34-9, 45-8, 91-122,
    147-57, 161-74, 207-12. New York, 1924.
--- Taytay's Tales, pp. 51-4, 61-4, 112-15, 159-
    61, 168-9, 183-90. New York, 1922.
--- The Witches' Feast is interrupted. EP, XLV, 69-
    73. 1938.
--- The Yellow House People. EP, XXX, 269-74.
    1931.
Douglas, F.H.   Weaving of the Tiwa Pueblos and
    Jemez. DAMLS, XCI, 162-4. 1939.
Fenton, W.N.   Factionalism at Taos Pueblo, New
    Mexico. BBAE, CLIV, 297-344.
Fergusson, E.   Dancing Gods, pp. 36-40. New York,
    1931.
Gatschet, A.S.   Classification into Seven Linguistic
    Stocks of Western Indian Dialects. RUSGS, VII, 403-
    85. 1879.
--- Migration of the Taos Indians. AA, V, 191-2.
    1892.
--- Zwölf Sprachen aus dem Südwesten Nordamerikas.
    150 pp. Weimar, 1876.
Grant, B.C.   Taos Indians. 127 pp. Taos, 1925.
--- Taos Today. 47 pp. Taos, 1925.
Hall, R.A.   A Note on Taos K'owena, "Horse." IJAL,
    XIII, 117-18. 1947.

Harrington, J.P. Ambiguity in the Taos Personal Pronoun. Holmes Anniversary Volume, pp. 142-56. Washington, 1916.

--- An Introductory Paper on the Tiwa Language. AA, n.s., XII, 11-46. 1910.

Harrington, J.P., and Roberts, H.H. Picuris Children's Stories. ARBAE, XLIII, 289-447. 1928.

Hodge, F.W. Ceremonial Shields of Taos. IN, III, 95-9. 1926.

--- Old Cradle from Taos. CMAI, V, 231-5. 1928.

--- Taos. BBAE, XXX, ii, 688-91. 1910.

--- Tigua. BBAE, XXX, ii, 747-9. 1910.

Hogue, A. Picturesque Games and Ceremonials of Indians. EP, XXVI, 177-83. 1929.

Jeançon, J.A. Archaeological Investigations in Taos Valley. SMC, LXXXI, xii, 1-29. 1930.

--- Taos Notes. EP, XXVIII, 3-11. 1930.

Jones, H. The Fiesta of San Geronimo at Taos. EP, XXXI, 300-2. 1931.

Jones, W.M. Origin of the Place-Name Taos. Anthropological Linguistics, II, iii, 2-4. 1960.

Lasswell, H.D. Collective Autism as a Consequence of Culture Contact: Notes on Religious Training and the Peyote Cult at Taos. Zeitschrift für Sozialforschung, IV, 232-47. 1935.

Luhan, M.D. Taos and Its Artists. 168 pp. New York, 1947.

Miller, M.L. Preliminary Study of the Pueblo of Taos. Chicago, 1898.

Pancoast, C.L. Last Dance of the Picuris. NH, XVIII, 308-11. 1918.

Parsons, E.C. The Kinship Nomenclature of the Pueblo Indians. AA, n.s., XXXIV, 377-89. 1932.

--- Picuris. AA, n.s., XLI, 206-22. 1939.

--- Pueblo Indian Religion. 2 vols. Chicago, 1939.

--- Taos Tales. MAFLS, XXXIV, 1-185. 1940.

Siegel, B.J. High Anxiety Levels and Cultural Integration. SF, XXXIV, 42-8. 1955.

--- Some Observations of the Pueblo Pattern at Taos. AA, n.s., LI, 562-77. 1949.

--- Suggested Factors of Culture Change at Taos Pueblo. ICA, XXIX, ii, 133-40. 1952.

Siegel, B.J. and Beals, A.R. Pervasive Factionalism. AA, LXII, 394-417. 1960.

Smith, D.M. Indian Tribes of the Southwest, pp. 112-24. Stanford, 1933.

Trager, G.L. Days of the Week in the Language of Taos Pueblo. Lg, XV, 51-5. 1939.

--- The Kinship and Status Terms of the Tiwa Languages. AA, n.s., XLV, 557-71. 1943.

--- The Name of Taos, New Mexico. Anthropological Linguistics, II, iii, 5-6. 1960.

Trager, G.L. An Outline of Taos Grammar. VFPA, VI, 184-221. 1946.

--- Spanish and English Loanwords in Taos. IJAL, X, 144-58. 1944.

--- A Status Symbol and Personality at Taos Pueblo. SJA, IV, 249-304. 1948.

--- Taos. IJAL, XIV, 155-60; XX, 173-80. 1948, 1954.

--- Taos III: Paralanguage. Anthropological Linguistics, II, ii, 24-30. 1960.

Underhill, R.M. First Penthouse Dwellers of America, pp. 131-54. New York, 1938.

Yarrow, H.C. The Pueblo of Taos. RUSGS, VII, 327-30. 1879.

30. TARAHUMARA

Including the Tarahumara and the Varohio.

Bennett, W.C., and Zingg, R.M. The Tarahumara. 412 pp. Chicago, 1935.

Lumholtz, C. Unknown Mexico. 2 vols. New York, 1902.

Almada, F.R. Apuntes Históricos Sobre la Región de Chinipas. Chihuahua, 1937.

--- La Rebelión de Tomochi. Chihuahua, 1938.

Anonymous. José Cañas pinta a los Indios Tarahumaras. YAN, II, 89-91. 1953.

--- La Raza Tarahumara. 195 pp. Mexico, Departamento del Trabajo, 1936.

Arpee, L.H. Los Indios Tarahumaras de Chihuahua. Anales del Museo Nacional de Mexico, II. 1937.

Artaud, A. Au pays des Tarahumaras. 40 pp. Paris, 1945.

Audobon, J.W. Western Journal: 1849-1850, p. 114. Cleveland, 1906.

Basauri, C. Creencias y practicas de los Tarahumaras. MF, III, 218-34. 1927.

--- Monografia de los Tarahumaras. 85 pp. Mexico, 1929.

--- La resistencia de los Tarahumaras. MF, II, 40-4. 1926.

Brambila, D. Gramatica Raramuri. Mexico, 1953.

Brandt, G.M. The Tarahumaras. NH, LVII, 392-99. 1948.

Buschmann, J.C. Grammatik der Sonorischen Sprache. AKAWB, XLVII, 369-454; LI, 23-216; LIII, i, 67-266. 1863, 1867, 1869.

Cabeza de Vaca, F. Apuntes sobre la Vida Tarahumaras. 49 pp. Mexico, 1943.

Carlson, P. and E. Primers I-III. Glendale, 1955-56.

Ceballos Novelo, R.J. Tarahumares, Coras y Huicholes. HDAC, 101-10. 1951.

Davila Garibi, J.I. Es el Coca un Idioma Tara-Cahita. HDAC, 143-52. 1951.

Dunne, P.M. Early Jesuit Missions in Tarahumara. 276 pp. Berkeley, 1948.

Ferrero, H.J. Pequena gramática y diccionario de la lengua Tarahumara. Mexico, 1920.

Fried, J. Picture Testing. AA, LVI, 95-97. 1954.

--- The Relation of Ideal Norms to Actual Behavior in Tarahumara Society. SJA, IX, 286-95. 1953.

Gajdusek, D.C. The Sierra Tarahumara. GR, XLIII, 15-38. 1953.

Gómez Gonzalez, F. Los Tarahumares. AI, XIII, 109-17. 1953.

Hamy, E.T. Algunas observaciones sobre la distribucion geografica de los opatas, de los tarahumares y de los pimas. Anales del Museo de Arqueologia, Historia y Etnografia, epoca 4^a, V, 93-8. 1922.

Hartman, C.V. Indianer i nordvestra Mexiko. Ymer, XV, 272-88. 1895.

--- The Indians of North-Western Mexico. ICA, X, 115-35. 1894.

Hilton, K. Cartilla Tarahumara. Mexico, 1946.

--- Cuentos Tarahumares. Mexico, 1948.

--- Palabras y frases de las lenguas tarahumara y guarijio. Anales del Instituto Nacional de Antropologia e Historia, II, 307-13. 1941-46.

Hilton, K. and M. Alphabet Book. Glendale, 1948.

--- Storybook. Glendale, 1948.

--- Tarahumara Stories. Glendale, 1950.

--- Tarahumara Text. Glendale, 1947.

Hodge, F.W. Tarahumare. BBAE, XXX, ii, 692-3. 1910.

Hrdlicka, A., and Lumholtz, C. A Trephined Skull. PAAAS, XLVI, 432-3. 1897.

Kroeber, A.L. Uto-Aztecan Languages of Mexico. IA, VIII, 1-27. 1934.

Leche, S. Dermatoglyphics and Functional Lateral Dominance in Mexican Indians. Middle American Research Series, V, ii, 27-42. 1933.

Lochon, H. En 2 CV chez les Primitifs. 224 pp. Lyon, 1956.

Lumholtz, C. The American Cave-Dwellers. JAGS, XXVI, 299-325. 1894.

--- Among the Tarahumaris. Scribner's Magazine, XVI, 31-48. 1894.

--- Cave-Dwellers of the Sierra Madre. MICA, 1893, 100-12.

--- Tarahumara Runners. AA, o.s., VIII, 92. 1895.

Lumholtz, C. Tarahumari Dances and Plant-Worship. Scribner's Magazine, XVI, 438-56. 1894.

--- Tarahumari Life and Customs. Scribner's Magazine, XVI, 296-311. 1894.

Nida, E.A. The Tarahumara Language. Investigaciones Lingüísticas, IV, 140-4. 1937.

Passin, H. The Place of Kinship in Tarahumara Social Organization. AAm, I, 344-59, 469-95. 1943.

--- Sorcery as a Phase of Tarahumara Economic Relations. Man, XLII, 11-15. 1942.

--- Tarahumara Prevarication: A Problem in Field Method. AA, n.s., XLIV, 235-47. 1942.

Peña, M.T. de la. Ensayo económico y social sobre el pueblo Tarahumar. Investigacíon Economica, IV, 363-400. 1944.

Plancarte, F.M. El Problema indigena Tarahumara. Memorias del Instituto Nacional Indigenista, V, 40 pp. 1954.

Radin, P. Mexican Kinship Terms. UCP, XXXI, 1-14. 1931.

Sauer, C. The Distribution of Aboriginal Tribes and Languages in Northwestern Mexico. IA, V, 58. 1934.

Spoehr, J. A Visit to the Tarahumaras. Cranbrook Institute of Science, News Letter, XXI, 2-8. 1951.

Thord-Gray, I. Tarahumara-English, English-Tarahumara Dictionary and an Introduction to Tarahumara Grammar. 170 pp. Coral Gables, 1955.

Zingg, R.M. Christmasing with the Tarahumaras. PTFLS, XIV, 207-24. 1939.

--- The Genuine and Spurious Values in Tarahumara Culture. AA, n.s., XLIV, 78-92. 1942.

--- Juguetes y juegos de los ninos Tarahumaras. MF, VII, 107-10. 1932.

--- The Southwestern Affiliation of Tarahumara Culture. SWL, IV, 6-9. 1938.

31. TEWA

Including the pueblos of Hano, Nambe, Pojoaque, San Ildefonso, San Juan, Santa Clara, and Tesuque.

Dozier, E.P. The Hopi-Tewa of Arizona. UCP, XLIV, 259-376. 1954.

Eggan, F. Social Organization of the Western Pueblos, pp. 139-75. Chicago, 1950.

Marriott, A. Maria the Potter of San Ildefonso. 294 pp. Norman, 1948.

Parsons, E.C. The Social Organization of the Tewa of New Mexico. MAAA, XXXVI, 1-309. 1929.

Whitman, W. The Pueblo Indians of San Ildefonso. CUCA, XXXIV, 1-164. 1947.

Aberle, S.B.D. Child Mortality among Pueblo Indians. AJPA, XVI, 339-51. 1932.

--- Maternal Mortality among the Pueblos. AJPA, XVIII, 431-57. 1934.

Aberle, S.B.D. et al. The Vital History of San Juan Pueblo. HB, XII, ii, 141-87. 1940.

Aitken, B. A Tewa Craftsman. EP, XVII, 91-7. 1924.

--- A Trance Experience. P, XXVIII, 67-70. 1956.

Alvarado Cata, R. Two Stories from San Juan Pueblo. WF, XV, 106-9. 1956.

Anonymous. The Animal Dance at San Ildefonso. EP, XXIV, 119-22. 1928.

Arnold, C. The Dance at Nambe. EP, XXIV, 26-8. 1928.

Bandelier, A.F. The Delight Makers. 490 pp. New York, 1890.

--- Po-sé. NMHR, I, 335-49. 1926.

Bayliss, C.K. A Tewa Sun Myth. JAFL, XXII, 333-5. 1909.

Bloom, L.B., ed. Bourke on the Southwest. NMHR, XI, 217-82; XII, 41-77. 1936-37.

Brant, C.S. Preliminary Data on Tesuque Pueblo. PMA, XXXIV, 253-9. 1948.

Bunzel, R.L. The Pueblo Potter. CUCA, VIII, 1-134. 1929.

Burton, H.K. The Re-Establishment of the Indians in Their Pueblo Life. Columbia University Teachers' College, Contributions to Education, DCLXXII, 102 pp. 1936.

Chapman, K.M. Sun Basket Dance at Santa Clara. EP, XVIII, 45-7. 1925.

Clark, A. In My Mother's House. ILR, Pueblo Series, 56 pp. 1941.

Curtis, N., ed. The Indians' Book, pp. 447-57. New York, 1907.

DeHuff, E.W. More Pueblo Tales. EP, XI, 140-4. 1921.

--- Myths told by the Pueblos. EP, XI, 86-92. 1921.

--- Pueblo Myths and Legends. EP, XI, 98-9. 1921.

--- Taytay's Memories, pp. 6-9, 12-19, 41-4, 49-54, 123-8, 139-46, 198-206. New York, 1924.

--- Taytay's Tales, pp. 3-17, 22-4, 55-60, 65-87, 122-4, 172-82. New York, 1922.

--- The Venomous Snake Girl. EP, XXXI, 73-4. 1931.

Douglas, F.H. Weaving in the Tewa Pueblos. DAMLS, XC, 158-60. 1939.

Douglass, W.B. Notes on the Shrines of the Tewa and Other Pueblo Indians. ICA, XIX, 344-78. 1915.

--- A World-Quarter Shrine of the Tewa Indians. RP, XI, 159-72. 1912.

Dozier, E.P. A Comparison of Eastern Keresan and Tewa Kinship Systems. ACISA, V, 430-6. 1960.

--- Kinship and Linguistic Change among the Arizona Tewa. IJAL, XXI, 242-51. 1955.

--- Tewa II. IJAL, XIX, 118-27. 1953.

--- Two Examples of Linguistic Acculturation. Lg, XXXII, 154. 1956.

Dunn, D. Awa Tsireh. EP, LXIII, 108-115, 1956.

Evans, B., and M.G. American Indian Dance Steps. 122 pp. New York, 1931.

Fay, G.E. Some Notes on the Cow Dance, Santa Clara Pueblo. EP, LIX, 186-88. 1952.

Fergusson, E. Dancing Gods, pp. 53-5, 60-1. New York, 1931.

Fewkes, J.W. The Kinship of a Tanoan-speaking Community in Tusayan. AA, VII, 162-7. 1894.

--- Tusayan Migration Traditions. ARBAE, XIX, ii, 573-633. 1900.

--- The Winter Solstice Altars at Hano Pueblo. AA, n.s., I, 251-76. 1899.

Freire-Marreco, B. Tewa Relationship Terms from the Pueblo of Hano. AA, n.s., XVI, 269-87. 1914.

Gatschet, A.S. Classification into Seven Linguistic Stocks of Western Indian Dialects. RUSGS, VII, 403-85. 1879.

--- Zwölf Sprachen aus dem Südwesten Nordamerikas. 150 pp. Weimar, 1876.

Gifford, E.W. Apache-Pueblo. AR, IV, 1-207. 1940.

Guthe, C.E. Pueblo Pottery Making. 88 pp. New Haven, 1925.

Harrington, J.P. A Brief Description of the Tewa Language. AA, n.s., XII, 497-504. 1910.

--- The Ethnogeography of the Tewa Indians. ARBAE, XXIX, 29-618. 1916.

--- Meanings of Old Tewa Indian Placenames. EP, VII, 78-83. 1919.

--- The Tewa Indian Game of "Canute." AA, n.s., XIV, 243-86. 1912.

--- Tewa Relationship Terms. AA, n.s., XIV, 472-98. 1912.

--- Three Tewa Texts. IJAL, XIII, 112-16. 1947.

Hawley, F. An Examination of Problems Basic to Acculturation in the Rio Grande Pueblos. AA, n.s., L, 612-24. 1948.

Henderson, J., and Harrington, J.P. Ethnozoology of the Tewa Indians. BBAE, LVI, 1-76. 1914.

Hodge, F.W. San Ildefonso. BBAE, XXX, ii, 440-1. 1910.

--- Santa Clara. BBAE, XXX, ii, 456-7. 1910.

--- Tesuque. BBAE, XXX, ii, 735. 1910.

--- Tewa. BBAE, XXX, ii, 737-8. 1910.

--- War God Idols of San Juan. EP, XXIII, 588-9. 1927.

Hoijer, H., and Dozier, E.P. The Phonemes of
   Tewa, Santa Clara Dialect. IJAL, XV, 139-44.
   1949.

Hough, W. Stone-working at Tewa. AA, X, 191.
   1897.

James, A. Tewa Firelight Tales. 248 pp. New York,
   1927.

Jeancon, J.A. A Rectangular Ceremonial Room.
   Colorado Magazine, III, 133-7. 1926.

--- Santa Clara and San Juan Pottery. DAMLS, XXXV,
   1-4. 1931.

Keech, R.A. The Blue Corn Dance. National Archaeological News, I, ix, 26-8. 1937.

Kurath, G.P. Plaza Circuits of Tewa Indian Dancers.
   EP, LXV, 16-26. 1958.

Laski, V.P. The Raingod Ceremony of the Tewa. M,
   XXXI, 76-84. 1957.

--- Seeking Life. MAFLS, L, 185 pp. 1958.

Lewis, O.L. Fiesta at Nambé Pueblo. EP, LX, 409-
   13. 1953.

Loeb, E.M. A Note on Two Far-Travelled Kachinas.
   JAFL, LVI, 192-9. 1943.

Lummis, C.F. Pueblo Indian Folk-Stories. 257 pp.
   New York, 1910.

Marriott, A. Greener Fields. 274 pp. New York,
   1953.

Morgan, L.H. Systems of Consanguinity and Affinity.
   SCK, XVII, 291-382. 1871.

Nölle, W. Die Navajo und Tewa Heute. Tribus, VI,
   102-8. 1957.

Parsons, E.C. The Ceremonial Calendar of the Tewa
   of Arizona. AA, n.s., XXVIII, 209-29, 1926.

--- Cérémonial Tewa au Nouveau Mexique et en Arizona. JSAP, n.s., XVIII, 9-15. 1926.

--- The Kinship Nomenclature of the Pueblo Indians.
   AA, n.s., XXXIV, 377-89. 1932.

--- Pueblo Indian Religion. 2 vols. Chicago, 1939.

--- Tewa Kin, Clan, and Moiety. AA, n.s., XXVI,
   333-9. 1924.

--- Tewa Mothers and Children. Man, XXIV, 148-
   51. 1924.

--- Tewa Tales. MAFLS, XIX, 1-304. 1926.

--- Witchcraft among the Pueblos. Man, XXVII, 106-
   12, 125-8. 1927.

Poley, H.S. An American Wedding. EP, VIII, 74-5.
   1920.

Reed, E.K. The Origins of Hano Pueblo. EP, L, 73-
   6. 1943.

--- The Southern Tewa Pueblos in the Historic Period.
   EP, L, 254-66, 276-88. 1943.

--- The Tewa Indians of the Hopi Country. P, XXV,
   11-18. 1952.

Renaud, E.B. Kokopelli. SWL, XIV, 25-40. 1948.

Robbins, W.W., Harrington, J.P., and Freire-
   Marreco, B. Ethnobotany of the Tewa Indians.
   BBAE, LV, 1-118. 1916.

Smith, D.M. Indian Tribes of the Southwest, pp.
   80-8. Stanford, 1933.

Spinden, H.J. Home Songs of the Tewa Indians. AMJ,
   XV, 73-8. 1915.

--- The Making of Pottery at San Ildefonso. AMJ, XI,
   192-6. 1911.

--- Songs of the Tewa. 125 pp. New York, 1933.

Stevenson, J. Illustrated Catalogue of the Collections obtained from the Indians of New Mexico and
   Arizona. ARBAE, II, 409-17, 429-64. 1883.

Stevenson, M.C. Strange Rites of the Tewa Indians.
   SMC, LXIII, viii, 73-83. 1914.

--- Studies of the Tewa Indians of the Rio Grande
   Valley. SMC, LX, xxx, 35-41. 1913.

--- The Sun and the Ice People among the Tewa Indians. SMC, LXV, vi, 73-8. 1916.

Underhill, R.M. First Penthouse Dwellers of America, pp. 109-30. New York, 1938.

Whitman, W. The San Ildefonso of New Mexico.
   ASAIT, 390-462, 1940.

Wilson, O. The Survival of an Ancient Art. AAA,
   IX, 24-31. 1920.

Yegerlehner, J. Arizona Tewa. IJAL, XXV, 1-7,
   75-80. 1959.

32. WALAPAI

Kroeber, A.L., ed. Walapai Ethnography. MAAA,
   XLII, 1-293. 1935.

Anonymous. Walapai. BBAE, XXX, ii, 899-900.
   1910.

--- Walapai Papers. Senate Documents, CCLXXIII,
   1-364. Washington, 1936.

Curtis, E.S. The North American Indian, II, 89-93.
   Cambridge, 1908.

Drucker, P. Yuman-Piman. AR, VI, 91-230. 1941.

Gatschet, A.S. Classification into Seven Linguistic
   Stocks of Western Indian Dialects. RUSGS, VII,
   403-85. 1879.

--- Der Yuma-Sprachstamm. ZE, IX, 377-8, 390-
   406. 1887.

Hoffman, W.J. Miscellaneous Ethnographic Observations. ARGGS, X, 461-78. 1876.

Iliff, F.G. People of the Blue Water. 271 pp. New
   York, 1954.

James, G.W. The Indians of the Painted Desert Region. 268 pp. Boston, 1903.

Kroeber, A.L. Ad hoc Reassurance Dreams. UCP,
XLVII, 205-8. 1957.
--- A Southwestern Personality Type. SJA,III, 108-
13. 1947.
Manners, R.A. Tribe and Tribal Boundaries: The
Walapai. E, IV, 1-26. 1957.
Writers' Program of Work Projects Administration. The
Havasupai and the Hualapar. Arizona State Teach-
ers College Bulletin, XXI, v, 1-36. 1940.

33. YAVAPAI

Including the Tulkepaia or Apache-Yuma and the
Yavapai or Mohave-Apache.

Gifford, E.W. Northeastern and Western Yavapai.
UCP, XXXIV, 247-354. 1936.
--- The Southeastern Yavapai. UCP, XXIX, 177-252.
1932.

Bloom, L.B., ed. Bourke on the Southwest. NMHR,
IX, 159-83. 1934.
Corbusier, W.F. The Apache-Yumas and Apache-
Mohaves. AAOJ, VIII, 276-84, 325-38. 1886.
Curtis, E.S. The North American Indian, II, 103-7.
Norwood, 1908.
Curtis, N., ed. The Indians' Book, pp. 329-38. New
York, 1907.
Dobyns, H.F., et al. Thematic Changes in Yuman
Warfare. In V.F.Ray, ed., Cultural Stability and
Cultural Change, 46-71. 1957.
Drucker, .P. Yuman-Piman. AR, VI, 91-230. 1941.
Gatschet, A.S. Classification into Seven Linguistic
Stocks of Western Indian Dialects. RUSGS, VII,403-
85. 1879.
--- Tulkepaia. BBAE, XXX, ii, 836. 1910.
--- Der Yuma-Sprachstamm. ZE, IX, 373-5, 390-
406, 408-12. 1887.
Gifford, E.W. Northeastern and Western Yavapai
Myths. JAFL, XLVI, 347-15. 1933.
Gould, M.K. Two Legends of the Mohave-Apache.
JAFL, XXXIV, 319-20. 1921.
Henshaw, H.W. Yavapai. BBAE, XXX, ii, 944-5.
1910.
Hoffman, W.J. Miscellaneous Ethnographic Observa-
tions. ARGGS, X, 461-77. 1876.
James, G.W. Palomas Apaches and Their Baskets.
Sunset, XI, 146-53. 1903.
Schroeder, A.H. A Brief History of the Yavapai of the
Middle Verde Valley. P, XXIV, 111-18. 1952.

34. YUMA

Castetter, E.F. and Bell, W.H. Yuman Indian Agri-
culture. 288 pp. Albuquerque, 1951.
Forde, C.D. Ethnography of the Yuma Indians. UCP,
XXVIII, 83-278. 1931.

Anonymous. Yuma. BBAE, XXX, ii, 1010-11. 1910.
Bartlett, J.H. Personal Narrative of Explorations and
Incidents in Texas, New Mexico, California,
Sonora, and Chihuahua, II, 177-81. New York,
1854.
Buschmann, J.C.E. Die Spuren der aztekischen
Sprache im nördlichen Mexico und höheren ameri-
kanischen Norden. AKAWB, 1854, Supplement-
Band, II, 267-76.
Curtis, E.S. The North American Indian, II, 63-79.
Cambridge, 1908.
Curtis, N. Creation Myth of the Cochans. Craftsman,
XV, 559.
--- The Indians' Book, pp. 339-41. New York, 1907.
Densmore, F. Communication with the Dead as prac-
tised by the American Indians. Man, L, 40-41. 1950.
--- Yuman and Yaqui Music. BBAE, CX, 1-216. 1932.
Dixon, R.B., and Kroeber, A.L. The Native Lan-
guages of California. AA, n.s., XV, 647-55. 1913.
Dobyns, H.F. et al. Thematic Changes in Yuman
Warfare. In Verne F.Ray, ed., Cultural Stability
and Cultural Change, 46-71. Seattle, 1957.
Douglas, F.H., et al. Ten Yuma Pots. MCN,XIX,
10 pp. 1953.
Driver, H.E. Estimation of Intensity of Land Use
from Ethnobiology. E, IV, 174-97. 1957.
Drucker, P. Southern California. AR, I, 1-52. 1937.
Ferrebee, W.E. Yuma Indians. RIT, 1890, 219-22.
Gatschet, A.S. Classification into Seven Linguistic
Stocks of Western Indian Dialects. RUSGS, VII, 403-
85. 1879.
--- The Waikuru, Seri and Yuma Languages. Science,
n.s., XII, 556-8. 1900.
--- Der Yuma-Sprachstamm. ZE, IX, 381-2, 391-
407. 1887.
Gifford, E.W. Californian Kinship Terminologies.
UCP, XVIII, 62-5. 1922.
--- Clans and Moieties in Southern California. UCP,
XIV, 156-67. 1918.
--- Yuma Dreams and Omens. JAFL, XXXIX, 58-69.
1926.
Halpern, A.M. Yuma. IJAL, XII, 25-33, 147-51,
204-12; XIII, 18-30, 92-107, 147-66. 1946-47.
--- Yuma. VFPA, VI, 249-88. 1946.

Halpern, A.M. Yuma Kinship Terms. AA, n.s.,
  XLIV, 425-41. 1942.
Harrington, J.P. A Yuma Account of Origins. JAFL,
  XXI, 324-48. 1908.
Heintzelman, S.P. Report. H.R.Ex.Doc.No. 76
  (Serial No. 906), 34th Congr., 3d Sess., pp. 34-
  53. 1857.
Herzog, G. The Yuman Musical Style. JAFL, XLI,
  183-231. 1928.
Ives, J.C. Report upon the Colorado River of the
  West. 131 pp. Washington, 1861.
Kate, H.F.C. ten. Reizen en onderzoekingen in
  Noord-Amerika, pp. 105-15. Leiden, 1885.
Kroeber, A.L. Handbook of the Indians of California.
  BBAE, LXXVIII, 781-95. 1925.
Lincoln, J.S. The Dream in Primitive Cultures. 359
  pp. London, 1935.
Mallery, G. Account of Yuma Ceremonies. SMC,
  XXXIV, ii, 143-4. 1885.
Nicholson, H.S. Four Songs from a Yuma Version of
  Los Pastores. University of Arizona General Bulletin,
  IX, 25-8. 1945.
North, A.W. The Native Tribes of Lower California.
  AA, n.s., X, 236-50. 1908.
Peet, S.D. The Worship of the Rain-God. AAOJ,
  XVI, 341-56. 1894.
Phoenix Indian School. The New Trail: A Book of
  Creative Writing by Indian Students. 158 pp.
  Phoenix, 1941.
Putnam, G.R. A Yuma Cremation. AA, VIII, 264-
  7. 1895.
Rogers, M.J. An Outline of Yuman Prehistory. SJA,
  I, 167-98. 1945.
--- Yuman Pottery Making. San Diego Museum
  Papers, II, vii, 1-44. 1936.
Roheim, G. Psycho-analysis of Primitive Cultural
  Types. International Journal of Psycho-analysis,
  XIII, 175-98. 1932.
Spier, L. Cultural Relations of the Gila River and
  Lower Colorado Tribes. YUPA, III, 1-22. 1936.
Trippel, E.J. The Yuma Indians. OM, ser. 2, XIII,
  561-84; XIV, 1-11. 1889.
Whiting, A.F. The Tumacacori Census of 1796. K,
  XXIX, i, 1-12. 1953.
Wood, C.W. Yuma Reservation. RIT, 1890, 216-
  19.

35. ZUNI

Eggan, F. Social Organization of the Western Pueblos,
  pp. 176-222. Chicago, 1950.
Roberts, J.M. Zuni Daily Life. NLAUN, III, ii, 143
  pp. 1956.

Smith, W., et al. Zuni Law. PMP, XLIII, i, 185
  pp. 1954.
Stevenson, M.C. The Zuni Indians. ARBAE, XXIII,
  13-608. 1904.

Aberle, S.B.D. Maternal Mortality among the Pueb-
  los. AJPA, XVIII, 431-57. 1934.
Adair, J., and Vogt, E. Navaho and Zuni Veterans:
  A Study of Contrasting Modes of Culture Change.
  AA, n.s., LI, 547-61. 1949.
Albert, E. and Cazeneuve, J. La Philosophie des In-
  diens Zunis. Revue de Psychologie des Peuples,
  XI, 112-23. 1956.
Anonymous. Turkeys at Hawikuh, New Mexico. M,
  XXVI, 13-14. 1952.
--- The Pueblo of Zuni. EP, XLVII, 162-3. 1940.
Bandelier, A.F. An Outline of the Documentary His-
  tory of the Zuni Tribe. JAEA, III, 1-115. 1892.
--- Po-sé. NMHR, I, 335-49. 1926.
Bartlett, F. The Creation of the Zunis. Old Santa
  Fe, II, 79-87. 1915.
Benedict, R. Patterns of Culture, pp. 57-129. Bos-
  ton, 1934.
--- They Dance for Rain in Zuni. In, M. Mead, An
  Anthropologist at Work, pp. 222-5. Boston, 1959.
--- Zuni Mythology. CUCA, XXI. 2 vols. 1934.
Bloom, L.B., ed. Bourke on the Southwest. NMHR,
  XI, 77-122, 188-207. 1936.
Boas, F. Tales of Spanish Provenience from Zuni.
  JAFL, XXXV, 62-98. 1922.
--- Zur Anthropologie der nordamerikanischen In-
  dianer. VBGA, 1895, 367-411.
Bohrer, V.L. Chinchweed (Pectes Papposa), a Zuñi
  Herb. EP, LXIV, 365. 1957.
Bourke, J.G. Sacred Hunts of the American Indians.
  ICA, VIII, 357-68. 1890.
--- The Urine Dance of the Zunis. PAAAS, XXXIV,
  400-4. 1885.
Bunzel, R.L. Introduction to Zuni Ceremonialism.
  ARBAE, XLVII, 467-544. 1930.
--- The Pueblo Potter. CUCA, VIII, 1-134. 1929.
--- Zuni. HAIL, IV, 389-415. 1935.
--- Zuni Katcinas. ARBAE, XLVII, 837-1086. 1930.
--- Zuni Origin Myths. ARBAE, XLVII, 545-609. 1930.
--- Zuni Ritual Poetry. ARBAE, XLVII, 611-835. 1930.
--- Zuni Texts. PAES, XV, 1-285. 1933.
Cabrero, L. Las Sociedades de Medicina de los
  Indios Zuñi. Noticiario Indigenista Español, XIX/
  XX, 1-2. 1957.
Cazeneuve, J. Les Dieux Dansent à Cibola. 273 pp.
  Paris, 1957.
--- Some Observations on the Zuñi Shalakho. EP,
  LXII, 347-56. 1955.

Cazeneuve, J. Les Zuñis dans l'Oevre de Levy-Bruhl. Revue Philosophique, CMLXVII, 530-8. 1957.

Chapman, K.M. Bird Forms in Zuni Pottery Decoration. EP, XXIV, 23-5. 1928.

--- Bird Forms in Zuñi Pottery Decoration. EP, LVIII, 316-24. 1951.

--- The Shalako Ceremony at Zuni. EP, XXIII, 622-7. 1927.

Chauvenet, B. A Zuni Shalako. EP, XXVII, 299-306. 1929.

Collins, G.N. Pueblo Indian Maize Breeding. Journal of Heredity, V, 255-68. 1914.

Coze, P. Twenty-four Hours of Magic. AH, XXX, xi, 10-27, 34-5. 1954.

Crimmins, M.L. The Rattlesnake in the Art and Life of the American Indian. BTAPS, XVII, 28-41. 1946.

Culin, S. Zuni Pictures. American Indian Life, ed. E.C. Parsons, pp. 175-8. New York, 1925.

Curtis, E.S. The North American Indian, XVII, 85-181. Norwood, 1926.

Curtis, N., ed. The Indians' Book, pp. 429-44. New York, 1907.

Curtis, W.E. Children of the Sun. 154 pp. Chicago, 1883.

Cushing, F.H. A Case of Primitive Surgery. Science, V, 977-81. 1897.

--- Katalog einer Sammlung von Idolen, Fetishen und priesterlichen Ausrüstungsgegenständen der Zuni- oder Ashiwi-Indianer. Veröffentlichungen aus dem Königlichen Museum für Völkerkunde, IV, 1-12. 1895.

--- Manual Concepts: A Study of the Influence of Hand-usage on Culture-growth. AA, V, 289-317. 1892.

--- My Adventures in Zuni. Century Magazine, XXV, 191-207, 500-11; XXVI, 28-47. 1882-83.

--- Outlines of Zuni Creation Myths. ARBAE, XIII, 321-447. 1896.

--- Preliminary Notes on the Origin, Working Hypothesis and Primary Researches of the Hemenway Southwestern Archaeological Expedition. ICA, VII, 151-94. 1888.

--- Primitive Copper Working – a Study. AA, VII, 93-117. 1894.

--- A Study of Pueblo Pottery as Illustrative of Zuni Culture-Growth. ARBAE, IV, 467-521. 1886.

--- Zuni Breadstuffs. INM, VIII, 7-642. 1920.

--- Zuni Fetishes. ARBAE, II, 9-45. 1883.

--- A Zuni Folk-Tale of the Underworld. JAFL, V, 49-56. 1892.

Cushing, F.H. Zuni Folk Tales. 474 pp. New York, 1901.

--- The Zuni Social, Mythic, and Religious Systems. PSM, XXI, 186-92. 1882.

DeHuff, E.W. Taytay's Memories, pp. 20-24. New York, 1924.

Denman, L.V.N. Pai Ya Tu Ma. 35 pp. San Francisco, 1955.

Densmore, F. Music of Acoma, Isleta, Cochiti and Zuñi Pueblos. BBAE, CLXV, 129 pp. 1957.

Donaldson, T. Moqui Indians of Arizona and Pueblo Indians of New Mexico. U.S. Census Office, Eleventh Census, Extra Bulletin, pp. 1-136. 1893.

Douglas, F.H. Main Types of Pueblo Cotton Textiles. DAMLS, XCII-XCIII, 166-72. 1940.

--- Main Types of Pueblo Woolen Textiles. DAMLS, XCIV-XCV, 174-80. 1940.

--- Weaving at Zuni Pueblo. DAMLS, XCVI-XCVII, 182-7. 1940.

Duggan, E.V. Health Work among the Zuni Indians. Public Health Nurse, XX, 20-2. 1928.

Espinosa, A.M. All-Souls' Day at Zuni, Acoma, and Laguna. JAFL, XXXI, 550-2. 1918.

Fergusson, E. Dancing Gods, pp. 67-113. New York, 1931.

Fewkes, J.W. Ancient Zuni Pottery. Putnam Anniversary Volume, pp. 43-83. New York, 1909.

--- A Few Summer Ceremonials at Zuni Pueblo. JAEA, I, 1-61. 1891.

--- Reconnaissance of Ruins in or near the Zuni Reservation. JAEA, I, 93-132. 1891.

--- A Study of Summer Ceremonials at Zuni and Moqui Pueblos. BEI, XXII, 89-113. 1890.

Fleming, H.C. Medical Observations on the Zuni Indians. CMAI, VII, ii, 39-48. 1924.

Gatschet, A.S. Zwölf Sprachen aus dem Südwesten Nordamerikas. 150 pp. Weimar, 1876.

Gifford, E.W. Apache-Pueblo. AR, IV, 1-207. 1940.

Gilman, B.I. Zuni Melodies. JAEA, I, 63-91. 1891.

Goldfrank, E. Socialization, Personality, and the Structure of Pueblo Society. AA, n.s., XLVII, 516-39. 1945.

--- Linguistic Note to Zuni Ethnography. Word, II, 191-6. 1946.

Goldman, I. The Zuni Indians of New Mexico. Cooperation and Competition among Primitive Peoples, ed. M. Mead, pp. 313-53. New York, 1937.

Gore, J.H. Regulative System of the Zuñis. SMC, XXV, 86-88. 1882.

Graham, S. The Shalaco Dance. EP, XV, 139-40. 1923.

Hammond, G.P., and Rey, A., eds. Expedition into New Mexico made by Antonio de Espejo, pp. 89-93. Los Angeles, 1929.

Handy, E.L. Zuni Tales. JAFL, XXXI, 451-71. 1918.

Helander, M. and Schramm, C.H. Range Management Plan for Zuni Pueblo Lands. 1942.

Hill, G. Turquoise and the Zuni Indian. K, XII, 42-51. 1947.

Hodge, F.W. The Age of the Zuni Pueblo of Kechipauan. INM, III, 43-60. 1920.

--- Circular Kivas near Hawikuh. CMAI, VII, i, 1-37. 1923.

--- Excavations at the Zuni Pueblo of Havikuh. AAA, VII, 367-79. 1918.

--- Excavations at Hawikuh. EFWSI, 1918, 61-72.

--- The First Discovered City of Cibola. AA, VIII, 142-52. 1895.

--- Hawikuh Bonework. INM, III, iii, 65-151. 1920.

--- History of Hawikuh. PHAPF, I, 1-155. 1937.

--- Pottery of Hawikuh. IN, I, 8-15. 1924.

--- Recent Excavations at Hawikuh. EP, XII, 3-11. 1922.

--- Snake Pens at Hawikuh. IN, I, 111-20. 1924.

--- A Square Kiva at Hawikuh. So Live the Works of men, ed. D.D.Brand and F.E.Harvey, pp. 195-214. Albuquerque, 1939.

--- Zuni. BBAE, XXX, ii, 1015-20. 1910.

--- A Zuni Foot Race. AA, III, 227-31. 1890.

Hodge, G.M. The Kachinas are coming. 129 pp. Los Angeles, 1937.

Hough, W. Sacred Springs in the Southwest. RP, V, 163-70. 1906.

Humphrey, N.B. The Mock Battle Greeting. JAFL, LIV, 186-90. 1941.

Jones, H. Mythology comes to Life at Zuni. EP, XXXII, 57-66. 1932.

--- Zuni Shalako Ceremony. EP, XXX, 1-10. 1931.

Judd, N.M. When Jemez Medicine Men came to Zuni. JAFL, LX, 182-4. 1947.

Kaplan, B. A Study of Rorschach Responses in Four Cultures. PMP, XLII, ii, 54 pp. 1954.

Kate, H.F.C.ten. Reizen en onderzoekingen in Noord-Amerika, pp. 273-306. Leiden, 1885.

--- Somatological Observations on Indians of the Southwest. JAEA, III, 117-44. 1892.

--- Zuni Fetishes. IAE, III, 118-36. 1890.

--- A Zuni Folk-Tale. JAFL, XXX, 496-9. 1917.

Keech, R.A. The Kick-stick Race at Zuni. EP, XXXVII, 61-4. 1934.

--- Pagans Praying. 94 pp. Clarendon, 1940.

--- A Zuni Indian Vocabulary. National Archaeological News, I, iv, 2-3; v, 2-3; vi, 2-3; vii, 12-13; viii, 11-12. 1937.

Kirk, R.F. Buffalo Hunting Fetish Jar. EP, LVII, 131-42. 1950.

Kirk, R.F. Introduction to Zuni Fetishism. EP, L, 117-29, 146-59, 183-98, 206-19, 235-45. 1943.

--- Southwestern Indian Jewelry. EP, LII, 21-32, 41-50. 1945.

--- Southwestern Indian Jewelry. Papers of the School of American Research, ser. 2, XXXVIII, 1-24. 1945.

--- War Rituals at Zuni. New Mexico, XXIII, viii, 14-15, 46-47. 1945.

Klett, F. The Cachina: a Dance at the Pueblo of Zuni. RUSGS, VII, 332-6. 1879.

--- The Zuni Indians of New Mexico. PSM, V, 580-91. 1874.

Kroeber, A.L. The Oldest Town in America and Its People. AMJ, XVI, 81-5. 1916.

--- The Speech of a Zuni Child. AA, n.s., XVIII, 529-34. 1916.

--- Thoughts on Zuni Religion. Holmes Anniversary Volume, pp. 269-77. Washington, 1916.

--- Zuni. ERE, X, 868-73. 1919.

--- Zuni Culture Sequences. PNAS, II, 42-5. 1916.

--- Zuni Kin and Clan. APAM, XVIII, 39-206.1917.

--- Zuni Potsherds. APAM, XVIII, 1-37. 1916.

Lawrence, D.D. Sleep and Dawn Ritual of the Zuñi Indians. ICA, XXX, 149-50. 1955.

Leigh, R.W. Dental Pathology of Indian Tribes. AJPA, VIII, 179-99. 1925.

Lemos, P.J. Zuni, the Strangest Art Center in America. School Arts Magazine, XXVII, 489-500.1928.

Lenneberg, E.H. and J.M.Roberts. The Language of Experience. MIJAL, XIII, 33 pp. 1956.

Li, A.C.Zuni. AA, n.s., XXXIX, 62-76. 1937.

Loeb, E.M. A Note on Two Far-Travelled Kachinas. JAFL, LVI, 192-9. 1943.

McFeat, T.F.S. Some Social and Spacial Aspects of Innovation at Zuni. An, n.s., II, i, 18-47. 1960.

Neumann, D.L. Modern Developments in Indian Jewelry. EP, LVII, 173-80. 1950.

--- Recent Lapidary Development at Zuñi. EP, LVIII, 215-17. 1951.

Newman, S. A Practical Zuni Orthography. PMP, XLIII, i, 163-70. 1954.

--- Vocabulary Levels: Zuñi Sacred and Slang Use. SJA, XI, 345-54. 1955.

--- Zuni Dictionary. MIJL, VI, 122 pp. 1958.

Nusbaum, A. The Seven Cities of Cibola. 167 pp. New York, 1926.

Owens, J. Some Games of the Zuñi. PSM, XXXIX, 39-50. 1891.

Parsons, E.C. All-Souls' Day at Zuni, Acoma, and Laguna. JAFL, XXX, 495-6. 1917.

--- Census of the Shi'wannakwe Society of Zuni. AA, n.s., XXI, 333-4. 1919.

Parsons, E.C. Ceremonial Dances at Zuni. EP, XIII, 119-22. 1922.

--- Ceremonial Friendship at Zuni. AA, n.s., XIX, 1-8. 1917.

--- The Favorite Number of the Zuni. SM, III, 596-601. 1916.

--- A Few Zuni Death Beliefs and Practices. AA, n.s., XVIII, 245-56. 1916.

--- Hopi and Zuni Ceremonialism. MAAA, XXXIX, 1-108. 1933.

--- Increase by Magic: a Zuni Pattern. AA, n.s., XXI, 279-86. 1919.

--- The Kinship Nomenclature of the Pueblo Indians. AA, n.s., XXXIV, 377-89. 1932.

--- The Last Zuni Transvestite. AA, n.s., XLI, 338-40. 1939.

--- Mothers and Children at Zuni. Man, XIX, 168-73. 1919.

--- Nativity Myth at Laguna and Zuni. JAFL, XXXI, 256-63. 1918.

--- A Note on Zuñi Deer Hunting. SJA, XII, 325-6. 1956.

--- Notes on Zuni. MAAA, IV, 151-327. 1917.

--- The Origin Myth of Zuni. JAFL, XXXVI, 135-62. 1923.

--- Pueblo-Indian Folk-Tales, probably of Spanish Provenience. JAFL, XXXI, 216-55. 1918.

--- Pueblo Indian Religion. 2 vols. Chicago, 1939.

--- Reasoning from Analogy at Zuni. SM, IV, 365-9. 1917.

--- The Scalp Ceremonial of Zuni. MAAA, XXXI, 1-42. 1924.

--- Spring Days in Zuni. SM, XXXVI, 49-54. 1933.

--- Teshlatiwa at Zuni. Journal of Philosophy, Psychology and Scientific Method, XVI, 272-3. 1919.

--- Waiyautitsa of Zuni. SM, IX, 443-57. 1933.

--- Waiyautitsa of Zuni. American Indian Life, ed. E.C. Parsons, pp. 157-73. New York, 1925.

--- War God Shrines of Laguna and Zuni. AA, n.s., XX, 381-405. 1918.

--- Winter and Summer Dance Series in Zuni. UCP, XVII, 171-216. 1922.

--- Witchcraft among the Pueblos. Man, XXVII, 106-12, 125-8. 1927.

--- The Zuni Adoshle and Suuke. AA, n.s., XVIII, 338-47. 1916.

--- Zuni Conception and Pregnancy Beliefs. ICA, XIX, 378-83. 1915.

--- Zuni Death Beliefs and Practices. AA, n.s., XVIII, 246. 1916.

--- A Zuni Detective. Man, XVI, 168-70. 1916.

--- Zuni Inoculative Magic. Science, n.s., XLIV, 469-70. 1916.

Parsons, E.C. The Zuni Lamana. AA, n.s., XVIII, 521-8. 1916.

--- The Zuni Mo'lawia. JAFL, XXIX, 392-9. 1916.

--- Zuni Names and Naming Practices. JAFL, XXXVI, 171-6. 1923.

--- Zuni Tales. JAFL, XLIII, 1-58. 1930.

Parsons, E.C., and Boas, F. Spanish Tales from Laguna and Zuni. JAFL, XXXIII, 47-72. 1920.

Peet, S.D. The Cross in America. AAOJ, X, 292-315. 1888.

--- The Worship of the Rain God. AAOJ, XVI, 341-56. 1894.

Reed, E.K. Painted Pottery and Zuñi History. SJA, XI, 178-93. 1955.

Reeve, F.D. Albert Franklin Banta. NMHR, XXVII, 200-55. 1952.

Renaud, E.B. Kokopelli. SWL, XIV, 25-40. 1948.

Risser, A. Seven Zuni Folk Tales. EP, XLVIII, 215-26. 1941.

Roberts, F.H.H. The Village of the Great Kivas on the Zuni Reservation. BBAE, CXI, 1-197. 1932.

Roberts, H.H. Chakwena Songs of Zuni and Laguna. JAFL, XXXVI, 177-84. 1923.

Robinson, E.L. Troubles at Zuni in 1702-03. M, XVIII, 110-16. 1944.

Schlater, K. An Easterner visits the Shalako. EP, LIV, 35-42. 1947.

Schmiedehaus, W. Las 7 Cindades Doradas de Cibola. Boletin de la Sociedad Chihuahuense de Estudios Historicos, VII, 571-85. 1952.

Schneider, D.M. and Roberts, J.M. Zuni Kin Terms. NLAUN, III, i, 29 pp. 1956.

Seltzer, C.C. Racial Prehistory in the Southwest and the Hawikuh Zunis. PMP, XXIII, 1-37. 1944.

Shufeldt, R.W. Examples of Unusual Zunian Pottery. RP, IX, 208-13. 1910.

Simpson, R. de E. An Ancient Custom in Modern Zuni. M, XXII, 102-4. 1948.

Smith, D.M. Indian Tribes of the Southwest, pp. 125-44. Stanford, 1933.

Smith, W. and Roberts, J.M. Some Aspects of Zuni Law and Legal Procedure. P, XXVII, 1-5. 1954.

Spier, L. An Outline for a Chronology of Zuni Ruins. APAM, XVIII, 207-331. 1917.

--- Zuni Chronology. PNAS, III, 280-3. 1917.

--- Zuni Weaving Technique. AA, n.s., XXVI, 64-85. 1924.

Stacey, R. Some Zuni Ceremonies and Melodies. Music-Lovers' Calendar, II, 54-61. 1907.

Stevenson, J. Illustrated Catalogue of the Collections obtained from the Indians of New Mexico and Arizona. ARBAE, II, 307-74. 1883.

Stevenson, J. Illustrated Catalogue of the Collections obtained from the Pueblos of Zuni, New Mexico, and Wolpi, Arizona. ARBAE, III, 511-86. 1884.

Stevenson, M.C. Ethnobotany of the Zuni Indians. ARBAE, XXX, 31-102. 1915.

--- The Religious Life of the Zuni Child. ARBAE, V, 533-55. 1887.

--- Zuni Ancestral Gods and Masks. AA, XI, 33-40. 1898.

--- Zuni Games. AA, n.s., V, 468-93. 1903.

Swadesh, M. Terminos de parentesco communes entre Tarasco y Zuñi. Cuadernos del Instituto de Historia, Serie Antropologica, III, 39 pp. 1957.

Trowbridge, L.J. Zuni. EP, XXII, 8-16. 1927.

Troyer, C. The Zuni Indians and Their Music. 44 pp. Philadelphia, 1913.

Underhill, R.M. First Penthouse Dwellers of America, pp. 57-84. New York, 1938.

Wilson, E. Red, Black, Blond, and Olive, pp. 1-68. New York, 1956.

Woodbury, R.B. The Antecedents of Zuni Culture. TNYAS, Ser. 2, XVII, 557-63. 1956.

Woodbury, R.B. and N.F.S. Zuni Prehistory and El Morro National Monument. SWL, XXI, 56-60. 1956.

Woodward, A. A Modern Zuni Pilgrimage. M, VI, 44-51. 1932.

Yarrow, H.C. Medical Facts relating to the Zuni Indians of New Mexico. Rocky Mountain Medical Review, I, 193-4. 1880-81.

Works on the North American Indians in general, or on a number of culture areas, are included below, especially when they contain no original ethnographic material and when they are topical rather than regional in scope. This list is admittedly incomplete, since the references were obtained only incidentally and without special research.

Abel, A.H. The American Indian as a Participant in the Civil War. 403 pp. Cleveland, 1919.

Ackerknecht, E.H. Head Trophies in America. Ciba Symposia, V, 1670-2. 1944.

--- Primitive Surgery. AA, n.s., XLIX, 25-45. 1947.

Adams, E.C. American Indian Education. 122 pp. New York, 1946.

Adams, G.S. and Kanner, L. General Paralysis among North American Indians. American Journal of Psychiatry, VI, 125-33. 1926.

Adams, W.R. Aboriginal American Medicine and Surgery. PIAS, LXI, 49-53. 1952.

Aginsky, B.W. The Evolution of American Indian Culture. ICA, XXXII, 79-87. 1958.

Aginsky, B.W. and E.G. Lateralization among American Indians. ICA, XXXII, 141-47. 1958.

Aitken, B. Temperament in Native American Religion. JAI, LX, 363-87. 1930.

Alexander, H.B. L'art et la philosophie des Indiens de l'Amerique du Nord. 118 pp. Paris, 1926.

--- North American. Mythology of All Races, ed. L.H.Gray, X, 1-325. Boston, 1916.

--- The Pictorial and Pictographic Art of the Indians of North America. Denver, 1927.

--- The World's Rim. 279 pp. Lincoln, 1953.

Allen, G.M. Dogs of the American Aborigines. Bulletin of the Museum of Comparative Zoology, LXIII, 431-517. 1920.

Altshuler, N. Linguistic Forms as Symbols of People. IJAL, XXII, 106-12. 1956.

Anderson, E. Basswood Bark and its Use by the Indians. Bulletin of Popular Information, Arnold Arboretum, Ser. 4, I, vii, 33-7. 1933.

Anderson, R.B. A Preliminary Check List of the Laws of the Indian Tribes. Law Library Journal, XXXIV, 126-48. 1941.

Anonymous. The Canadian Indian. Information Division, Department of External Affairs, Ottawa, Reference Papers, LXVIII, 14 pp. 1957.

--- Documents on Peyote...against U.S. Senate Bill 1399 (Feb. 8), Seventy-fifth Congress, First Session. Mimeographed, 137817. Washington, 1937.

--- Indian Captivities and Massacres. 70 pp. New York, 1943.

Anonymous. Indians. Bulletin of the Riverside Public Library, CXXXVI, 1-24. 1916.

--- Juvenile Delinquency (Indians). 461 pp. Washington, 1954.

--- Ninth Census of Canada, 1951. Dominion Bureau of Statistics, Bulletin 1-17. Ottawa, 1953.

Antevs, E. The Spread of Aboriginal Man to North America. GR, XXV, 302-9. 1935.

Appleton, L.H. Indian Art of the Americas. 279 pp. New York, 1950.

Appy, E.P. Ancient Mining in America. AAOJ, XI, 92-9. 1889.

Armillas, P. Pre-Columbian America. SSM, II, 74 pp. 1958.

Arnaud, G. Indiens Pas Morts. 172 pp. Paris, 1956.

Arpee, L.H. A Geographical List of American Indian Tribes. Chicago Y.M.C.A. College, Department of Anthropology, Bulletin I. 1936.

Ashton, D. Abstract Art Before Columbus. New York, 1957.

Astrov, M. The Winged Serpent, an Anthology of American Indian Prose and Poetry. 366 pp. New York, 1946.

Austin, M. Non-English Writings, II: Aboriginal. Cambridge History of American Literature, IV, 610-34, 826-7. 1921.

Baerreis, D.A., ed. The Indian in Modern America. 70 pp. Madison, 1956.

Baker, T. Über die Musik der nordamerikanischen Wilden. 86 pp. Leipzig, 1882.

Ball, S.H. The Mining of Gems and Ornamental Stones by American Indians. BBAE, CXXVIII, 1-77. 1941.

Barbeau, M. Indian Captivities. PAPS, XCIV, 522-48. 1950.

--- Indian-trade Silver. B, CCLXXIII, iii, 10-14. 1942.

--- Indian Tribes of Canada. Man, XIII, 122-7. 1913.

--- Les Indiens du Canada depuis la découverte. Memoirs of the Royal Society of Canada, ser. 3, VIII, i, 381-97. 1914.

--- Migrations Sibériennes en Amérique. MPR, i, 17-48. 1958.

--- The Native Races of Canada. PTRSC, ser. 3, XXI, ii, 41-53. 1927.

--- The Origin of Floral and Other Designs among the Canadian and Neighboring Indians. ICA, XXIII, 512. 1930.

--- Tobacco, a Peace-Maker. CGJ, XLVII, 106-15. 1953.

Barber, B. Acculturation and Messianic Movements. ASR, VI, 663-9. 1941.

Barkley, F.A. and Sweet, H.R. The Use of Sumacs
by the American Indian. Bulletin of the Missouri
Botanical Garden, XXV, 154-8. 1937.

Barnes, N. American Indian Love Lyrics and Other
Verse. 190 pp. New York, 1925.

--- American Indian Verse. Bulletin of the University of Kansas, Humanistic Studies, II, iv, 1-63.
1921.

Barnett, H.G. Indian Shakers. 378 pp. Carbondale,
1957.

Barton, B.S. New Views of the Origin of the Tribes
and Nations of America. 2d edit. Philadelphia,
1798.

Baulig, H. Sur la distribution des moyens de trans-
port et de circulation chez les indigènes de l'Amérique du Nord. Annales de Géographie, XVII, 433-
56. 1908.

Bayliss, C.K. A Treasury of Indian Tales. 120 pp.
New York, 1921.

Beale, C.L. Caracteristicas demográficas de los
indigenas des los Estados Unidos de América. AI,
XV, 127-37. 1955.

Beals, R.L. The Emergence of an American Culture.
The Civilization of the Americas, pp. 27-58.
Berkeley, 1939.

Beals, R.L. and Hester, J.A. A New Ecological
Typology of the California Indians. ACISA, V, 411-
19. 1960.

Beatty, W.W. La educación de los Indios en los
Estados Unidos. 33 pp. Washington, 1942.

Beatty, W.W., and Young, R.W. La educación
bilingüe en la escuelas para indígenas de los
Estados Unidos. AI, II, iv, 39-42. 1942.

Beauchamp, W.M. Indian Corn Stories and Customs.
JAFL, XI, 195-202. 1898.

Beck, H.P. The Acculturation of Old World Tales by
the American Indian. MWF, VIII, 205-16. 1958.

Beers, H.P. The French in North America. Baton
Rouge, 1957.

Benedict, R.F. The Concept of the Guardian Spirit
in North America. MAAA, XXIX, 1-97. 1923.

--- Configurations of Culture in North America. AA,
n.s., XXXIV, 1-27. 1932.

Berlin, A.F. Early Smoking Pipes of the North American Aborigines. PWHGS, IX, 107-36. 1905.

Biasutti, R. Le Razzi e i Popoli della Terra, 2nd
ed., IV, 271-733. Torino, 1957.

Birket-Smith, K. The Composite Comb in North
America. Ethnos, II, 33-7. 1937.

--- Drinking Tube and Tobacco Pipe in North
America. Ethnologische Studien, I, 29-39. 1931.

--- Folk Wanderings and Culture Drifts in Northern
North America. JSAP, n.s., XXII, 1-32. 1930.

Birket-Smith, K. A Geographic Study of the Early
History of the Algonquian Indians. IAE, XXIV, 174-
222. 1918.

--- Indianerliv i Nordens Skove. Menneskets Mangfoldighed, 40-59. København, 1957.

Bischoff, R. The Peyote Cult. WA, n.s., XXIX, 28-
37. 1948.

Blomkvist, E.E. and Shprincin, N.G. Lingvistiches-
kaia Klassifikaciia Korennogo Nasheleniia Ameriki.
Trudy Instita Etnografii imena N.N. Mikluho-
Maklaia, XXV, 11-24. 1955.

Blomkvist, E.E., and Zolotarevskaia, I.A. Istoriia
Kolonizacii Severnoj Ameriki. Trudy Instituta
Etnografii imena N.N. Mikluho-Maklaia, XXV,
27-67. 1955.

Blumensohn, J. The Fast among North American
Indians. AA, n.s., XXXV, 451-69. 1933.

Boas, F. America and the Old World. ICA, XXI,
21-8. 1925.

--- Classification of American Indian Languages.
Lg, V, 1-7. 1929.

--- The Classification of American Languages. AA,
n.s., XXII, 367-76. 1920.

--- The Decorative Art of the North American Indians. PSM, LXIII, 481-98. 1903.

--- Dissemination of Tales among the Natives of
North America. JAFL, IV, 13-20. 1891.

--- Ethnological Problems in Canada. JAI, XL, 529-
39. 1910.

--- The Half-Blood Indian. PSM, XLV, 761-70.
1894.

--- The History of the American Race. ANYAS,
XXI, 177-83. 1912.

--- The Indian Languages of Canada. AAR, 1905,
88-106.

--- The Mythologies of the Indians. International
Quarterly, XI, 327-42; XII, 127-73. 1905.

--- Mythology and Folk-Tales of the North American Indians. JAFL, XXVII, 374-410. 1914.

--- The Origin of Death. JAFL, XXX, 486-91. 1917.

--- Physical Types of the Indians of Canada. AAR,
1905, 84-8.

--- Relationships between North-West America and
North-East Asia. The American Aborigines, ed.
D. Jenness, pp. 355-70. Toronto, 1933.

--- Stylistic Aspects of Primitive Literature. JAFL,
XXXVIII, 329-39. 1925.

Bonin, G. von, and Morant, G.M. Indian Races in
the United States. Biometrika, XXX, 94-129.
1938.

Bonnerjea, B. Fish-Hooks in North America. Journal of the Indian Anthropological Institute, I,
69-147. Calcutta, 1938.

Bonnerjea, B. Hunting Superstitions of the American Aborigines. IAE, XXXII, 167-84. 1934.

Bosch Gimpera, P. Posibles Conexiones entre las Culturas de Norteamerica y las del Viejo Mundo. In, El Norte de Mexico y el Sur de Estados Unidos, 339-44. Mexico, 1943.

Bourke, J.G. Scatalogic Rites of all Nations. 496 pp. Washington, 1891.

Bouteiller, M. Le Défunt dans les Sociétés Indiennes de l'Amérique du Nord. Ee, XLVIII, 23-40. 1953.

--- Don Chamanistique et Adaptation à la Vie. JSAP, n.s., XXXIX, 1-14. 1950.

Boyd, W.C. The Blood Groups and Types. PPAAI, 127-37. 1951.

--- Blood Groups of American Indians. AJPA, XXV, 215-35. 1939.

--- Rh and the Races of Man. Scientific American, CLXXXV, v, 22-5. 1951.

Branch, E.D. The Hunting of the Buffalo. 245 pp. New York, 1929.

Brand, D.D., ed. Symposium on Prehistoric Agriculture. UNMB, I, v, 72 pp. 1936.

Bright, W. Glottochronologic Counts of Holcaltecan Material. Lg, XXXII, 42-8. 1956.

Brinton, D.G. Aboriginal American Authors and Their Productions. 63 pp. Philadelphia, 1883.

--- Aboriginal American Literature. ICA, V, 56-64. 1884.

--- American Hero-Myths. 251 pp. Philadelphia, 1882.

--- The American Race. 392 pp. New York, 1891.

--- The Myths of the New World. 307 pp. New York, 1868.

--- Native American Stringed Musical Instruments. AAOJ, XIX, 19-20. 1897.

Brooks, H. The Medicine of the American Indian. Journal of Laboratory and Clinical Medicine, XIX, 1-23. 1929.

--- The Medicine of the American Indian. Bulletin of the New York Academy of Medicine, V, 509-37. 1929.

Brown, W.L. and Anderson, E. The Northern Flint Corns. AMBG, XXXIV, 1-30. 1947.

Browne, C.A. The Chemical Industries of the American Aborigines. Isis, XXIII, 406-24. 1935.

Burlin, N.C. The Indians' Book. 573 pp. New York, 1907.

Burton, F.R. American Primitive Music. 281 pp. New York, 1909.

Bushnell, D.I. The Origin of Wampum. JAI, XXXVI, 172-7. 1906.

--- The Various Uses of Buffalo Hair by the North American Indians. AA, n.s., XI, 401-25. 1909.

Butler, R.L. A Bibliographical Checklist of North and Middle American Indian Linguistics in the Edward E. Ayer Collection. 2 vols. Chicago, 1941.

Buttree-Seton, J.M. The Rhythm of the Red Man. New York, 1930.

Campbell, M.W. Her Ladyship, My Squaw. B, CCLXXXV, ii, 14-17. 1954.

Canada. Department of Citizenship and Immigration. The Indians of Canada. Canada Year Book, 1951, 1125-33. 1951.

Canada, Government of. Census of Indians in Canada, 1954. Ottawa, 1956.

Candolle, A. de. Origin of Cultivated Plants. 468 pp. New York, 1902.

Carr, L. Dress and Ornaments of Certain American Indians. PAAS, n.s., XI, 381-454. 1897.

--- The Food of Certain American Indians and Their Methods of Preparing It. PAAS, n.s., X, 155-90. 1895.

--- The Food of the North American Indians. Lend a Hand, XV, 347-54. 1895.

Carr, L.G. Survival Foods of the American Aborigene. Journal of the American Dietetic Association, XIX, 845-7. 1943.

Carter, G.F. Sweet Corn among the Indians. GR, XXXVIII, 200-21. 1948.

--- Sweet Corn an Important Indian Food Plant in the Pre-Columbian Period. Journal of the American Society of Agronomy, XXXIX, 831-3. 1947.

Cartwright, W.D. American Indian Beadwork Designs. ICA, XXX, 127-35. 1955.

Casanowicz, I.M. Parallels in the Cosmogonies of the Old World and the New. Holmes Anniversary Volume, pp. 44-52. Washington, 1916.

Cass, L. Indians of North America. North American Review, XXII, 53-119. 1826.

Castetter, E.F. The Domain of Ethnobiology, AN, LXXVIII, 158-70. 1954.

Castiglioni, A. The Use of Tobacco among the American Indians. Ciba Symposia, IV, 1426-56. 1943.

Center, A.L. The Redman's Garden of Eden. NH, LX, 424-9. 1951.

Chamberlain, A.F. The Contributions of the American Indian to Civilization. PAAS, n.s., XVI, 91-126. 1903.

--- Note on Left-Handedness among the North American Indians. AA, n.s., X, 498-500. 1908.

--- Wisdom of the North American Indians in Speech and Legend. PAAS, n.s., XXIII, 63-96. 1913.

Chamberlain, L.S. Plants Used by the Indians of Eastern North America. AN, XXXV, 1-10. 1901.

Chard, C.S. Pre-Columbian Trade between North and South America. PKAS, I, 1-16. 1950.

--- Northwest Coast—Northeast Asiatic Similarities: A New Hypothesis. ACISA, V, 235-40. 1960.

Charency, de. Noms des points de l'espace dans divers dialectes américains. JSAP, II, 109-78. 1898.

Chown, B. and Lewis, M. The Kell Antigen in American Indians. AJPA, n.s., XV, 149-56. 1957.

Christiansen, E.O. Primitive Art. 384 pp. New York, 1955.

Clark, W.P. The Indian Sign Language. 443 pp. Philadelphia, 1884.

Clements, F.E. Primitive Concepts of Disease. UCP, XXXII, 185-252. 1932.

Clinton, D.W. An Introductory Discourse Delivered before Literary and Philosophical Society of New York on 4th May 1814. 143 pp. New York, 1815.

Cohen, F.S. Handbook of Federal Indian Law. 662 pp. Washington, 1941.

Collier, D. Indian Art of the Americas. 64 pp. Chicago, 1959.

Collier, J. The Indian in a Wartime Nation. APSS, CCXXIII, 29-35. 1942.

--- The Indians of the Americas. 326 pp. New York, 1947.

--- A Perspective on the United States Indian Situation of 1952 in its Hemispheric and World-Wide Bearing. AI, XIII, 7-13. 1953.

Comas, J. Principales Contribuciones Indigenas Pre-colombinas a la Cultura Universal. AI, XVII, 39-85. 1957.

Conard, E.L.M. Les idées des Indiens Algonquins relatives à la vie d'outre-tombe. Revue de l'His-toire des Religions, XLII, 1-95. 1900.

Connelley, W.E. Indian Myths. Chicago, 1928.

Cooke, D.C. Fighting Indians of the West. 208 pp. New York, 1954.

Cooke, O.F. Food Plants of Ancient America. ARSI, 1903, 481-97.

Cooper, J.M. Scapulimancy. Essays in Anthropology presented to A.L. Kroeber, pp. 29-43. Berkeley, 1936.

Cope, L. Calendars of the Indians North of Mexico. UCP, XVI, 119-76. 1919.

Corlett, W.T. The Medicine-Man of the American Indian. 335 pp. Springfield, 1935.

Count, E.W. The Earth-Diver and the Rival Twins. ICA, XXIX, iii, 55-62. 1952.

--- Red and Black: A Survey and a Query. A, XXXV, 68-77. 1940.

Covarrubias, M. The Eagle, the Jaguar, and the Ser-pent. 332 pp. New York, 1954.

Crawford, M.D.C. Design and Color in Ancient Fabrics. AMJ, XVI, 417-31. 1916.

--- The Loom in the New World. AMJ, XVI, 381-7. 1916.

Croft, K. A Guide to Source Materials on Extinct North American Indian Languages. IJAL, XIV, 260-8. 1948.

Cross, H.H. The T.B. Walker Collection of Indian Portraits. 164 pp. State Historical Society of Wisconsin, 1948.

Cuadra Downing, O. The Adventures of Don Coyote. 100 pp. New York, 1955.

Culin, S. American Indian Games. JAFL, XI, 245-52. 1898.

--- American Indian Games (1902). AA, n.s., V, 58-64. 1903.

--- Chess and Playing-Cards. RUSNM, 1896, 665-803. 1898.

--- Games of the North American Indians. ARBAE, XXIV, 29-809. 1903.

Curtin, L.S.M. By the Prophet of the Earth. 158 pp. Santa Fe, 1949.

Curtis, N. American Indian Cradle-Songs. Musical Quarterly, VII, 549-58. 1921.

--- The Indians' Book. 572 pp. New York, 1907.

Dadisman, A.J. The Canadian Indians. PWVAS, XXI, 105-09. 1949.

Dahlberg, A.A. The Dentition of the American In-dian. PPAAI, 138-76. 1951.

Dall, W.H. On Masks, Labrets, and Certain Aborigi-nal Customs. ARBAE, III, 67-202. 1884.

Dangel, R. Gibt es normannische Einflüsse auf den Mythos nordamerikanischer Indianer? MAGW, LVII, 44-50. 1927.

--- Die Kampf der Kraniche mit den Pygmaën bei den Indianern Nordamerikas. ICA, XXIV, 219. 1934.

--- Kice-Manito, der "grosse Geist." BA, XVII, 155-71. 1934.

Daniels, W.M. American Indians. 219 pp. New York, 1957.

Darling, D. Indian Diseases and Remedies. Boston Medical and Surgical Journal, XXXIV, 9-10. 1846.

Davidson, D.S. Knotless Netting in America and Oceania. AA, n.s., XXXVII, 117-34. 1935.

--- Snowshoes. MAPS, VI, 1-207. 1937.

Davis, A.M. Indian Games. BEI, XVII, 89-144. 1885.

Davis, E.C. Ancient Americans. New York, 1931.

Day, A.G. The Sky Clears. 220 pp. New York, 1951.

Day, G.M. The Indian as an Ecological Factor in the Northeastern Forest. Ecology, XXXIV, 329-46. 1953.

De Lien, H. and Dahlstrom, A.W. Tuberculosis Control among American Indians. Journal-Lancet, LXX, 131-4. 1950.

Dellenbaugh, F.S. The North Americans of Yesterday. 478 pp. New York, 1901.

Denman, L.V.N. The Peyote Ritual. San Francisco, 1957.

Densmore, F. The American Indians and Their Music. 143 pp. New York, 1926.

--- The Belief of the Indian in a Connection between Song and Supernatural. BBAE, CLI, 217-24. 1953.

--- Communication with the Dead as Practised by the American Indians. Man, L, 40-41. 1950.

--- Imitative Dances among the American Indians. JAFL, LX, 73-8. 1947.

--- The Importance of Recordings of Indian Songs. AA, n.s., XLVII, 637-9. 1945.

--- Indian Action Songs. Boston, 1921.

--- Music of the Indians in our Western States. JAFL, LXX, 176-78. 1957.

--- Notes on the Indians' Belief in the Friendliness of Nature. SJA, IV, 94-7. 1948.

--- Peculiarities in the Singing of the American Indians. AA, n.s., XXXII, 651-60. 1930.

--- The Poetry of Indian Songs. So Live the Works of Men, ed. D.D.Brand and F.E.Harvey, pp. 121-30. Albuquerque, 1939.

--- Rhythm in the Music of the American Indian. ICA, XX, i, 85-89. 1924.

--- The Songs of the Indians. American Mercury,VII, 65-8. 1926.

--- The Study of Indian Music. Musical Quarterly, I, 187-97. 1915.

--- Technique in the Music of the American Indian. BBAE, CLI, 211-16. 1953.

--- Traces of Foreign Influence in the Music of the American Indians. AA, n.s., XLVI, 106-12. 1944.

--- The Use of Meaningless Syllables in Indian Songs. AA, n.s., XLV, 160-2. 1943.

--- The Use of Music in the Treatment of the Sick by American Indians. ARSI, 1952, 439-54. 1953.

De Puy, H.F. A Bibliography of the English Colonial Treaties with the American Indians. New York,1917.

Deuel, T. American Indian Ways of Life. 76 pp. Springfield, 1958.

De Voto, B. Across the Wide Missouri. 511 pp. Boston, 1947.

--- The Course of Empire. 664 pp. Boston, 1952.

--- The Year of Decision, 1846. 555 pp. Boston, 1943.

Diebold, A.R. Determining the Centers of Dispersal of Language Groups. IJAL,XXVI, 1-10. 1960.

Dietschy, H. Die amerikanischen Keulen und Holzschwerter. 196 pp. Leiden, 1939.

Diskalkar, D.B. Materials on Which Indian Epigraphical Records Were Incised. Journal of Indiana History, XXXV, 289-309. 1957.

Dixon, R.B. The Color-Symbolism of the Cardinal Points. JAFL, XII, 10-16. 1899.

--- The Independence of the Culture of the American Indian. Science, n.s., XXXV, 46-55. 1912.

--- Some Aspects of North American Archeology. AA, n.s., XV, 549-77. 1913.

--- Some Aspects of the American Shaman. JAFL, XXI, 1-12. 1908.

--- Words for Tobacco in American Indian Languages. AA, n.s., XXIII, 19-49. 1921.

Dockstader, F.J. The American Indian in Graduate Studies; a Bibliography of Theses and Dissertations. CMAI, XV, 399 pp. 1957.

Dolch, E.W. and M.P. Tepee Stories, in Basic Vocabulary. 165 pp. Champaign, 1956.

Domenech, E. Seven Years Residence in the Great Deserts of North America. 2 vols., 469, 477 pp. London, 1860.

Dorman, R.M. The Origin of Primitive Superstitions. 398 pp. Philadelphia, 1881.

Dorson, R.M. Bloodstoppers and Bearwalkers. 305 pp. Cambridge, 1952.

Douglas, F.H. Basketry Construction Technics. DAMLS, LXVII, 66-8. 1935.

--- Basketry Decoration Technics. DAMLS, LXVIII, 70-2. 1935.

--- Birchbark and the Indians. DAMLS, LII, 5-8. 1941.

--- Colors in Indian Arts. DAMLS, LVI, 22-4.1933.

--- Copper and the Indian. DAMLS, LXXV-LXXVI, 98-104. 1936.

--- Design Areas in Indian Art. DAMLS, LXII, 46-8. 1934.

--- Indian Basketry. DAMLS, LVIII, 30-2. 1933.

--- Indian Basketry East of the Rockies. DAMLS, LXXXVII, 146-8. 1939.

--- Indian Cloth-making. DAMLS, LIX-LX, 34-40. 1933.

--- Indian Linguistic Stocks or Families. DAMLS, LI-LII, 2-8. 1933.

--- Indian Vegetable Dyes. DAMLS, LXIII, 50-2; LXXI, 82-4. 1934-36.

--- Main Types of Indian Cradles. DAMLS, CXV, 4 pp. 1952.

--- Main Types of Indian Metal Jewelry. DAMLS, CIV, 13-16. 1941.

--- Porcupine Quillwork. DAMLS, CIII, 9-12. 1941.

Douglas, F.H. Types of Indian Masks. DAMLS, LXV-LXVI, 58-64. 1935.

Douglas, F.H., and Harnoncourt, R.d'. Indian Art of the United States. 220 pp. New York, 1941.

Downey, J.E. Types of Dextrality among North American Indians. JEP, X, 478-88. 1927.

Dozier, E.P., et al. The Integration of Americans of Indian Descent. APSS, CCCXI, 158-65. 1957.

Drake, S.G. Book of the Indians of North America. Boston, 1833.

Driver, H.E. The Acorn in North American Diet. PIAS, LXII, 56-62. 1953.

Driver, H.E. and Massey, W.C. Comparative Studies of North American Indians. TAPS, XLVII, 165-456. 1957.

Driver, H.E., et al. Indian Tribes of North America. MIJL, IX, 30 pp. 1953.

Drummond, T. The Canadian Snowshoe. PTRSC, ser. 3, X, ii, 305-20. 1916.

Dubiez, P. Les Indiens Peaux-Rouges. Geographia, XXXVI, 10-16; XXXVII, 10-16; XXXVIII, 7-14; XXXIX, 12-17. 1954.

Duflot de Mofras, E. Exploration de l'Orégon, des Californies, et de la Mer Vermeille. 2 vols. Paris, 1844.

Dunn, D. America's First Painters. NGM, CVII, 349-77. 1955.

--- Massacres of the Mountains. 677 pp. New York, 1958.

Eastman, E.G. Indian Legends retold. Boston, 1929.

Easton, P.S. Food Resources of Alaska. 21 pp. Juneau, 1950.

Edmonson, M.S. Status Terminology and the Social Structure of North American Indians. MAES, 91 pp. 1958.

Edwards, E.E. Agriculture of the American Indians. U.S. Department of Agriculture, Bibliographical Contributions, XXIII, xii, 1-106. 1933.

Edwards, E.E. and Rasmussen, W.D. A Bibliography on the Agriculture of the American Indians. U.S. Department of Agriculture, Miscellaneous Publications, CCCCXLVII, 107pp. 1942.

Efimov, A.V. and Tokarev, S.A., eds. Narody Ameriki. 670 pp. Moscow, 1959.

Eggan, F.R. The Ethnological Cultures and their Archeological Backgrounds. AEUS, 35-45. 1952.

Eggan, F. Glottochronology. ICA, XXXII, 645-53. 1958.

Eiseley, L.C. Indian Mythology and Extinct Fossil Vertebrates. AA, n.s., XLVII, 318-20. 1945.

Ellis, E.S. The Indian Wars of the United States. 516 pp. New York, 1892.

Ellis, G.E. The Red Man and the White Man. 630 pp. Boston, 1882.

Ellis, H.H. Flint-working Techniques of the American Indians. 78 pp. Columbus, 1940.

Elmendorf, W.W. Soul Loss Illness in Western North America. ICA, XXIX, iii, 104-14. 1952.

Embree, E.R. Indians of the Americas. 260 pp. Boston, 1939.

Emerson, E.R. Indian Myths. 677 pp. Boston, 1884.

Erwin, A.T. Sweet Corn not an Important Indian Food Plant in the Pre-Columbian Period. Journal of the American Society of Agronomy, XXXIX, 117-21. 1947.

Evans, B., and M.G. American Indian Dance Steps. 122 pp. New York, 1931.

Evans, G.L. and Campbell, T.N. Indian Baskets. 70 pp. Austin, 1952.

Farabee, W.C. Indian Cradles. MJ, XI, 183-211. 1920.

--- The Use of Metals in Prehistoric America. MJ, XII, 35-42. 1921.

Farrand, L. The Basis of American History. 303 pp. New York, 1904.

Farwell, A. American Indian Melodies. New York, 1901.

Fenton, W.N., et al. American Indian and White Relations to 1830. 149 pp. Chapel Hill, 1957.

Fenton, W.N. Cultural Stability and Change in American Indian Societies. JAI, LXXXIII, 169-74. 1953.

--- Factionalism in American Indian Society. ACISA, IV, ii, 330-40. 1955.

Fewkes, J.W., ed. The Problems of the Unity or Plurality and the Probable Place of Origin of the American Aborigines. AA, n.s., XIV, 1-50. 1912.

Fey, H.E. and McNickle, D. Indians and Other Americans. 220 pp. New York, 1959.

Field, T.W. An Essay towards an Indian Bibliography. 430 pp. New York, 1873.

Fillmore, J.C. The Harmonic Structure of Indian Music. AA, n.s., I, 297-318. 1899.

Findeisen, H. Die Herkunft der Urbevölkerung Nordamerikas. Abhandlungen und Aufsätze aus dem Institut für Menschen- und Menschheitskunde, X, 40 pp. 1955.

Fisher, O.M. and Tyner, C.L. Totem, Tipi and Tumpline. 264 pp. Toronto, 1956.

Fiske, W.A.A. Indian Legends. Ithaca, 1930.

Fletcher, A.C. Indian Games and Dances with Native Songs. 137 pp. Boston, 1915.

--- Indian Story and Song from North America. Boston, 1907.

Fletcher, S.E. The American Indian. 152 pp. New York, 1954.

Foreman, G. Indian Removal. 415 pp. Norman, 1953.

Forsyth, T. The French, British and Spanish Methods of Treating Indians. E, IV, 210-217. 1957.

Foster, A.J. Jeffersonian America. 356 pp. San Marino, Cal., 1954.

Frazer, J.G. The Native Races of America, ed. R. A. Downie. 350 pp. London, 1939.

Frazier, B. American Indian Painting. Tulsa, 1947.

Freeman, L. Surgery of the Ancient Inhabitants of America. AAA, XVIII, 21-36. 1924.

Friederici, G. Die Behandlung weiblicher Gefangener durch die Indianer von Nordamerika. Globus, LXXV, xvi, 256-61. 1899.

--- Die Ethnographie in den 'Documentos Ineditos del Archivo de Indias.' Globus, XC, 287-9, 302-6. 1906.

--- Die Frage der vorkulumbischen Einwanderung nach Amerika. ZVS, V, 348-52. 1929.

--- Die geographische Verbreitung des Blasrohrs in Amerika. PMJP, LVII, 71-3. 1911.

--- Scalping in America. ARSI, 1906, 423-38. 1907.

--- Die Schiffahrt der Indianer. 130 pp. Stuttgart, 1907.

--- Skalpieren und ähnliche Kriegsgebräuche in Amerika. 170 pp. Braunschweig, 1906.

--- Über die Behandlung der Kriegsgefangenen durch die Indianer Amerikas. Festschrift Eduard Seler, pp. 59-128. Stuttgart, 1922.

--- Die Wirkung des Indianerbogens. Globus, XCI, 325-30. 1907.

Fry, M.C. The Witch Deer. 2nd ed. 40 pp. New York, 1955.

Fuhrmann, E. Der Grabbau. 166 pp. Munich, 1923.

Gaines, R.L. Books on Indian Arts North of Mexico. LEITA, 15 pp. 1931.

Gallatin, A., ed. Hale's Indians of North-West America and Vocabularies of North America. TAES, II, 1-130. 1848.

Gallatin, A. A Synopsis of the Indian Tribes in North America. Transactions of the American Antiquarian Society, II, 9-422. 1836.

Gatschet, A.S. "Real," "True," or "Genuine," in Indian Languages. AA, n.s., I, 155-61. 1899.

--- Water-Monsters of American Aborigines. JAFL, XII, 255-60. 1899.

Gayton, A.H. The Orpheus Myth in North America. JAFL, XLVIII, 263-93. 1935.

Gebhard, D. Nineteen Centuries of American Abstraction. Art News, LVI, x, 20-23. 1958.

Gessain, R. Le Motif Vagina Dentata. ICA, XXXII, 583-6. 1958.

Gibson, A.M. Sources for Research on the American Indian. E, VII, 121-36. 1960.

Gibson, G.D. A Bibliography of Anthropological Bibliographies: The Americas. Current Anthropology, I, 61-75. 1960.

Gifford, E.W. Pottery-making in the Southwest. UCP, XXIII, 253-73. 1928.

Gilbert, W.H. Synoptic Data on the Survival of Indian and Part-Indian Blood in the Eastern United States. 43 pp. Washington, 1947.

Gilmore, M.R. Indian Food Products from Native Wild Plants. Good Health, LXI, ix, 18-9, 46; x, 12-13, 28. 1926.

--- Indian Lore and Indian Gardens. 39 pp. Ithaca, 1930.

Gladwin, H.S. Men out of Asia. 390 pp. New York, 1947.

Goddard, P.E. The Present Condition of Our Knowledge of North American Languages. AA, n.s., XVI, 555-601. 1914.

Golden, G. The American Indian Then and Now. 76 pp. San Antonio, 1957.

--- Red Moon Called Me. 211 pp. San Antonio, 1954.

Goldenweiser, A.A. The Social Organization of the Indians of North America. JAFL, XXVII, 411-36. 1914.

Gray, G.W. New World Picture. 402 pp. Boston, 1936.

Gridley, M.E. Indians of Today. 111 pp. Chicago, 1947.

--- Indians of Yesterday. 63 pp. Chicago, 1940.

Griffin, J.B. United States and Canada, Indigenous Period. PIPGH, CLIV, 104 pp. Mexico, 1953.

Griffin, J.B., ed. Archeology of Eastern United States. 392 pp. Chicago, 1952.

Grinnell, G.B. The Indians of To-day. 175 pp. Chicago, 1900.

--- The Story of the Indian. 268 pp. New York, 1895.

Groewel, M. Haltung und Erziehung des Kindes bei den nordamerikanischen Indianern. 82 pp. Hamburg, 1937.

Gusinde, M. Der Peyote-Kult. Festschrift zum 50 jährigen Bestandsjubiläum des Missionhaus St. Gabriel, pp. 401-98. Wien, 1939.

Haas, M.R. Algonkian-Ritwan. IJAL, XXIV, 159-73. 1958.

--- Tonkawa and Algonquian. Anthropological Linguistics, I, ii, 1-6. 1959.

Haddon, A.C. A Few American String Figures and Tricks. AA, n.s., V, 213-23. 1903.

Hadley, J.N. Demography of the American Indian. APSS, CCCXI, 23-30. 1957.

Hadley, L.F. Indian Sign Talk. 262 pp. Chicago, 1893.

Hadlock, W.S. The Concept of Tribal Separation as rationalized in Indian Folklore. PA, XVI, 84-90. 1946.

Haekel, J. Zum Problem des Individualtotemismus in Nordamerika. IAE, XXXV, 14-22. 1938.

--- Zum Problem des Mutterrechtes. Paideuma, V, 298-323. 1953.

--- Zur Frage alter Kulturbeziehungen zwischen Alaska, Kalifornien und den Pueblo-Gebiet. ICA, XXXII, 88-96. 1958.

Hale, H. The Origin of Primitive Money. PSM, XXVIII, 296-307. 1886.

Hale, K. Internal Diversity in Uto-Aztecan. IJAL, XXIV, 101-7; XXV, 114-21. 1958-59.

Hallett, L.F. Indian Games. BMAS, XVI, 25-8. 1955.

Hallowell, A.I. The Backwash of the Frontier. ARSI, 1958, 447-72. 1959.

--- Bear Ceremonialism in the Northern Hemisphere. AA, n.s., XXVIII, 1-175. 1926.

--- The Impact of the American Indian on American Culture. AA, LIX, 201-17. 1957.

Hamilton, C.E., ed. Cry of the Thunderbird. 283 pp. New York, 1950.

Hamilton, S.S. Indian Treaties. 661 pp. Washington, 1830.

Hamperl, H. and Laughlin, W.S. Osteological Consequences of Scalping. HB, XXXI, 81-9. 1959.

Harding, A.D. and Bolling, P. Bibliography of Articles and Papers on North American Indian Art. 365 pp. Washington, [1937].

Hargrett, L. A Bibliography of the Constitutions and Laws of the American Indians. 124 pp. Cambridge, 1947.

Harmon, G.D. Sixty Years of Indian Affairs. 428 pp. Chapel Hill, 1941.

Harnoncourt, R. d'. El arte del Indio en los Estados Unidos. 22 pp. Washington, 1943.

Harper, A.G. Las tierras de los Indios en los Estudos Unidos. 54 pp. Washington, 1943.

Harper, A.G., Collier, J., and McCaskill, J.C. Los Indios de los Estados Unidos. 33 pp. Washington, 1942.

Harrington, J.P. Mollusca among the American Indians. AAm, III, 293-7. 1945.

Harshberger, J.W. Phytogeographic Influences in the Arts and Industries of American Aborigines. BGSP, IV, iii, 25-41. 1906.

Hartman, R.B. Costumes of the North American Indians. WA, n.s., XVIII, 1-9. 1937.

Hartweg, R. Les Variations Cuspidaires de la Première Molaire Inférieure. ICA, XXVIII, 1-18. 1948.

Hatt, G. Asiatic Influences in American Folklore. Kongelige Danske Videnskabernes Selskab, Hist.-Filol. Meddelelser, XXXI, 1-122. 1949.

--- The Corn Mother in America and in Indonesia. A, XLVI, 853-914. 1951.

--- Moccasins and Their Relation to Arctic Footwear. MAAA, III, 149-250. 1916.

--- North American and Eurasian Culture Connections. PPSC, V, iv, 2755-65. 1933.

Harvard, V. Drink Plants of the North American Indians. Bulletin of the Torrey Botanical Club, XXIII, ii, 33-46. 1896.

--- Food Plants of the North American Indians. Bulletin of the Torrey Botanical Club, XXII, iii, 98-123. 1895.

--- The Mezquit. AN, XVIII, 451-9. 1884.

Havighurst, R.I. Education among American Indians. APSS, CCCXI, 105-15. 1957.

Havighurst, R.J., and Neugarten, B.L. American Indian and White Children. 349 pp. Chicago, 1955.

Hayner, N.S. Variability in the Criminal Behavior of American Indians. AJS, XLVII, 602-13. 1942.

Haywood, C. A Bibliography of North American Folklore and Folksongs. II, 749-1159. New York, 1951.

Hazeltine, A.I. Red Man, White Man. 309 pp. New York, 1957.

Heath, V.S. Dramatic Elements in American Indian Ceremonials. Nebraska University Studies, XIV, iv, 377-415. 1914.

Heberer, G., et al. Rassengeschichte, Amerika. Das Fischer Lexicon, XV: Anthropologie, 274-9. Frankfurt, 1959.

Hedrick, U.P. Sturtevant's Notes on Edible Plants. New York Department of Agriculture, Annual Report, XXVII, ii, no. 2, 1-686. 1919.

Heiser, C.B. The Sunflower among the North American Indians. PAPS, XCV, 432-48. 1951.

Heizer, R.F. Aboriginal Fish Poisons. BBAE, CLI, 225-84. 1953.

--- The Use of the Enema by the Aboriginal American Indians. Ciba Symposia, V, 1686-93. 1944.

Henderson, A.C. Modern Indian Painting. LEITA. 11 pp. 1931.

Henshaw, H.W. Indian Origin of Maple Sugar. AA, III, 341-51. 1890.

--- Who are the American Indians? AA, II, 193-214. 1889.

Heriot, G. Travels through the Canadas. 602 pp. London, 1807.

Herold, L. The Origin and Diffusion of Maize in the New World. SWL, XX, 15-26. 1954.

Herrick, J. La agricultura de los Indios en los Estados Unidos. 32 pp. Washington, 1942.

Herzog, G. The Collections of Phonograph Records in North America and Hawaii. Zeitschrift für Vergleichende Musikwissenschaft, I, 58-62. 1933.

--- Musical Styles in North America. ICA, XXIII, 455-8. 1928.

--- Research in Primitive and Folk Music in the United States. Bulletin of the American Council of Learned Societies, XXIV, 561-657. 1936.

--- Special Song Types in North American Indian Music. Zeitschrift für Vergleichende Musikwissenschaft, III, 23-33. 1935.

Hewett, E. L. Native American Artists. Washington, 1922.

Hewitt, J. N. B. Polysynthesis in the Languages of the American Indian. AA, VI, 381-407. 1893.

Heyerdahl, T. American Indians in the Pacific. 835 pp. New York, 1953.

Higginson, J. V. Hymnody in the American Indian Missions. Papers of the Hymn Society, XVIII, New York, 1954.

Hodge, F. W., ed. Handbook of American Indians North of Mexico. BBAE, XXX. 2 vols. 1907-10.

Hoebel, E. A. The Wonderful Herb. Western Humanities Review, III, 126-30. 1949.

Hoffman, W. J. Remarks on Indian Tribal Names. PAPS, XXIII, 294-303. 1886.

Hofsinde, R. Indian Games and Crafts. 126 pp. New York, 1957.

--- Indian Sign Language. 96 pp. New York, 1956.

--- Talk-without-talk. NH, XLVII, 32-9. 1941.

Hoijer, H. Athapaskan Kinship Systems. AA, LVIII, 309-33. 1956.

--- The Chronology of the Athapaskan Languages. IJAL, XXII, 219-32. 1956.

--- Linguistic Structures of Native America, Introduction. VFPA, VI, 9-29. 1946.

Hollander, A. N. J. den. De peyote-cultus der noordamerikaansche Indianen. Mensch en Maatschaapij, XI, 17-29, 123-31. 1935.

Holmer, N. M. Amerindian Color Semantics. International Anthropological and Linguistic Review, II, 158-66. 1955-56.

--- Los Colores en la Semantica de las Lenguas Indigenas de America. Arsbok utgiven av Seminarierna i slaviska sprak, jämförande sprakforskning, finskugriska sprak och ostasiatiska sprak vid Lunds Universitet, 1951-52, 5-18. 1957.

--- Indian Place-Names in North America. Essays and Studies in American Language and Literature, VIII, 44 pp. 1948.

Holmer, N. M. Lexical and Morphological Contacts between Siouan and Algonquian. Lunds Universitet Arsskrift, N.F., I, 45, iv, 39 pp. 1949.

Holmes, G. K. Aboriginal Agriculture — the American Indians. In L. H. Bailey, ed., Cyclopedia of American Agriculture, 2nd ed., IV, 24-39. 1909-1910.

Holmes, W. H. Areas of American Culture Characterization. AA, n.s., XVI, 413-46. 1914.

--- Art in Shell of the Ancient Americans. ARBAE, II, 176-305. 1881.

--- Decorative Art of the Aborigines of America. Boas Anniversary Volume, pp. 179-88. 1906.

--- Some Problems of the American Race. AA, n.s., XII, 149-82. 1910.

--- A Study of the Textile Art in Its Relation to the Development of Form and Ornament. ARBAE, VI, 195-252. 1888.

--- The Tomahawk. AA, n.s., X, 264-76. 1908.

--- Use of Textiles in Pottery Making and Embellishment. AA, n.s., III, 397-403. 1901.

Honigmann, J. J. Circumpolar Forest North America as a Modern Culture Area. ACISA, V, 447-51. 1960.

Hooton, E. A. Racial Types in America and Their Relations to Old World Types. The American Aborigines, ed. D. Jenness, pp. 131-63. Toronto, 1933.

Hopkins, M. Wild Plants Used in Cookery. Journal of the New York Botanical Garden, XLIII, 71-6. 1942.

Hornborg, E. Indianer, en Folkstams Kanip och Undergang. 507 pp. Helsinki, 1936.

Hough, W. The Bison as a Factor in Ancient American Culture History. SM, XXX, 315-19. 1930.

--- Fire Origin Myths of the New World. ICA, XX, i, 179-84. 1924.

--- Primitive American Armor. RUSNM, 1893, 625-53.

Howard, E. B. Evidence of Early Man in North America. MJ, XXIV, 61-158. 1935.

--- An Outline of the Problem of Man's Antiquity in North America. AA, n.s., XXXVIII, 394-413. 1936.

Howard, O. O. My Life and Experiences among our Hostile Indians. 570 pp. Hartford, 1907.

Howells, W. W. The Origins of American Indian Race Types. The Maya and Their Neighbors, pp. 3-9. New York, 1940.

Hrdlicka, A. Catalogue of Human Crania in the U.S. National Museum Collections. PUSNM, LXIII, 1-51; LXXVIII, 1-95. 1924-31.

--- The Coming of Man from Asia in the Light of Recent Discoveries. ARSI, 1935, 463-70.

Hrdlicka, A. Disease, Medicine and Surgery among
the American Aborigines. Journal of the American
Medical Association, XCIX, 1661-6. 1932.

--- The Painting of Human Bones among the Indians.
ARSI, 1904, 607-18.

--- The People of the Main American Cultures. PAPS,
LXV, 157-60. 1926.

--- Skeletal Remains suggesting or attributed to
Early Man in North America. BBAE, XXXIII, 1-
113. 1907.

Hulbert, W. Indian Americans. 161 pp. New York,
1932.

Hultkrantz, A. Conceptions of the Soul among
North American Indians. 545 pp. Stockholm, 1953.

--- The North American Indian Orpheus Tradition.
PSMS, II, 340 pp. 1957.

Hunter, H.V. The Ethnography of Salt in Aboriginal
North America. 63 pp. Philadelphia, 1940.

Huntington, E. The Red Man's Continent. Chronicles
of America, ed. A. Johnson, I, 1-175. New Haven,
1919.

Hymes, D.H. Lexicostatistics So Far. Current Anthropology, I, 3-44. 1960.

--- More on Lexicostatistics. Current Anthropology,
I, 338-45. 1960.

--- Na-Déné and Positional Analysis of Categories.
AA, LVIII, 624-38. 1956.

--- A Note on Athapaskan Glottochronology. IJAL,
XXIII, 291-7. 1957.

--- Positional Analysis of Categories: a Frame for
Reconstruction. Word, XI, 10-23. 1955.

Hymes, D.H. and Driver, H.E. Concerning the
Proto-Athapaskan Kinship System. AA, LX, 152-
55. 1958.

Hymes, V.D. Athapaskan Numeral Systems. IJAL,
XXI, 26-45. 1955.

Imbelloni, J. Nouveaux Apports à la Classification
de l'Homme Américain. MPR, i, 107-36. 1958.

Ingersoll, E. Wampum and Its History. AN, XVII,
467-79. 1883.

Jacobs, W.R. Diplomacy and Indian Gifts. 208 pp.
Stanford, 1950.

Jacobson, D.B. and d'Ulcel, J. Les Peintres Indiens
d'Amérique. Nice, 1950.

James, E.O. Cremation and Preservation of the Dead
in North America. AA, n.s., XXX, 214-42. 1928.

James, G.W. Indian Basketry. 3d edit. New York,
1903.

Jamieson, K.B. Siouan and Uralian Numerals. New
World Antiquity, X, 3-6. 1954.

Jarcho, S. Origin of the American Indian as Suggested by Fray Joseph de Acosta (1589). Isis, L,
430-8. 1959.

Jarvis, S.F. A Discourse on the Religion of the Indian Tribes of North America. CNYHS, III, 181-
268. 1821.

Jayne, C.F. String Figures. 407 pp. New York, 1906.

Jeançon, J.A. Indian Musical and Noise-making Instruments. DAMLS, XXIX, 1-4. 1931.

--- Indian Song Book. Denver, 1924.

Jenness, D. Canada's Indian Problems. AI, II, i,
29-38. 1942.

--- Canadian Indian Religion. An, I, 1-17. 1955.

--- The Corn Goddess and Other Tales from Indian
Canada. BNMC, CXLI, 111 pp. 1956.

--- The Indian Background of Canadian History.
BCDM, LXXXVI, 1-46. 1937.

--- Indians of Canada. BCDM, LXV, 1-446. 1932.

--- The Prehistory of the Canadian Indians. Custom
is King, ed. L.H.D. Buxton, pp. 61-84. London,
1936.

Jenness, D., ed. The American Aborigines. 396 pp.
Toronto, 1933.

Jochelson, W. The Ethnological Problems of Bering
Sea. NH, XXVI, 90-5. 1926.

Johnson, E.B. Animal Stories the Indians told. 155
pp. New York, 1927.

Johnson, I.W. Twine-Plaiting in the New World.
ICA, XXXII, 198-213. 1958.

Johnson, N.B. The American Indian as Conservationist. CO, XXX, 333-40. 1952.

Johnson, W. The Indians have no Word for It. Quarterly Journal of Speech, XXX, 330-37, 456-65.
1944.

Jones, J.A. List of Unpublished Doctoral Dissertations and Masters Theses in the Field of Anthropology Bearing on North American Indians North of
Mexico. 19 pp. Washington, 1953.

Jones, J.E. Traditions of the North American Indians.
3 vols. London, 1830.

Jones, V.H. Notes on Indian Maize. PA, XVIII, 23-
4. 1948.

Judge, H.C. The Eagle of the American Indian and
its Origin. MPR, i, 77-82. 1958.

Kallay, U. von. Die zweierlei Farbenortungen
einiger Indianerstämme Nordamerikas. MAGW,
LXIX, 11-23. 1939.

Kappler, C.J. Indian Affairs: Laws and Treaties. 4
vols. Washington, 1903-29.

Kate, H.F.C. ten. On Paintings of North American
Indians and Their Ethnographical Value. A, VI,
521-45. 1911.

Keiter, F. Das indianische Gesicht. Zeitschrift für
Morphologie und Anthropologie, XXXV, 394-411.
1936.

Kelemen, P. Medieval American Art. 2 vols., New York, 1943; 1 vol., New York, 1956.

Kellar, J.H. The Atlatl in North America. PRS, III, 281-352. 1955.

Kelley, W.H. Economic Basis of Indian Life. APSS, CCCXI, 71-9. 1957.

Kelsay, L.E. List of Cartographic Records of the Bureau of Indian Affairs (Record Group 75). U.S. National Archives, Publication, 55-1; Special Lists, XIII. Washington, 1954.

Kelsey, F.E. The Pharmacology of Peyote. South Dakota Journal of Medicine and Pharmacy, XII, 213-33. 1959.

Kenny, H. The Founders of Amerindian Linguistics. American Speech, XXXII, 204-5. 1957.

Kidd, K.E. Canadians of Long Ago. 174 pp. Toronto, 1951.

Kiddle, L.B. Spanish Loan-Words in American Indian Languages. Hispania, XXXV, 179-84. 1952.

Kinietz, V. Notes on the Roached Headdress of Animal Hair among the North America Indians. PMA, XXIV, 463-7. 1941.

Kirchhoff, P. Relaciones entre el Area de los Recolectores-Cazadores del Norte de Mexico y las Areas Circunvecinas. In, El Norte de Mexico y el Sur de Estados Unidos, 255-7. Mexico, 1943.

Klauber, L.M. Rattlesnakes. 2 vols. 1530 pp. Berkeley, 1956.

Knortz, K. Die Märchen und Sagen der nordamerikanischen Indianer. 285 pp. Jena, 1871.

Kohler, J. Die Rechte der Urvölker Nordamerikas. ZVR, XII, 354-426. 1897.

Köngäs, E.K. The Earth-Diver (Th.A812). E, VII, 151-80. 1960.

Koppers, W. Der Hund in der Mythologie der zirkumpazifischen Völker. Wiener Beiträge zur Kulturgeschichte und Linguistik, I, 359-99. 1930.

Krickeberg, W. Ältere Ethnographica aus Nordamerika im Berliner Museum für Völkerkunde. BA, n.f., II, 280 pp. 1954.

--- Amerika. Die grosse Völkerkunde, ed. H.A. Bernatzik, III, 18-94. Leipzig, 1939.

--- Beiträge zur Frage der alten kulturgeschichtlichen Beziehungen zwischen Nord- und Südamerika. ZE, LXXVI, 287-373. 1935.

--- The Indian Sweat Bath. Ciba Symposia, I, 19-35. 1939.

--- Indianermärchen aus Nordamerika. 419 pp. Jena, 1924.

--- Die Völker Nord- und Mittel-Amerikas. Illustrierte Völkerkunde, ed. G. Buschan, I, 64-217. Stuttgart, 1922.

Krieger, H.W. American Indian Costumes in the United States National Museum. ARSI, 1928, 623-61.

--- Aspects of Aboriginal Decorative Art in America. ARSI, 1930, 519-56.

Krochmal, A., et al. Economic Botany. New York Botanical Garden, VIII, i, 3-20. 1954.

Kroeber, A.L. Arrow Release Distributions. UCP, XXIII, 283-96. 1927.

--- Cultural and Natural Areas of Native North America. UCP, XXXVIII, 1-242. 1939.

--- Cultural Relations between North and South America. ICA, XXIII, 5-22. 1928.

--- The Languages of the American Indians. SM, 1911, 500-15. 1911.

--- Native American Population. AA, n.s., XXXVI, 1-25. 1934.

--- The Nature of Culture. 448 pp. Chicago, 1952.

--- Noun Composition in American Languages. A, V, 204-18. 1910.

--- Recent Ethnic Spreads. UCP, XLVII, 259-81. 1959.

--- Reflections and Tests on Athabascan Glottochronology. UCP, XLVII, 241-58. 1959.

--- Salt, Dogs, Tobacco. AR, VI, 1-20. 1941.

--- Sign Language Inquiry. IJAL, XXIV, 1-19. 1958.

Krogman, W.M. Medical Practices and Diseases of the Aboriginal American Indians. Ciba Symposia, I, 11-18. 1939.

Kunike, H. Nordamerikanische Mondsagen. IAE, XXV, 27-54. 1920.

--- Zur Astralmythologie der nordamerikanischen Indianer. IAE, XXVII, 1-29, 55-78, 107-34. 1926.

Kurath, G.P. Basic Techniques of Amerindian Dance. Dance Notation Record, VIII, iv, 2-8. 1957.

--- Masked Clowns. Tomorrow, IV, iii, 108-12. 1956.

--- Pan-Indian Dances and Songs of the Midwest. Journal of Health, Physical Education and Recreation, XXVII, ix, 44-5, 51-2. 1956.

--- Songs of the Wigwam. 24 pp. Delaware, O., 1955.

La Barre, W. Mescalism and Peyotism. AA, LIX, 708-11. 1957.

--- Native American Beers. AA, n.s., XL, 224-34. 1938.

--- The Peyote Cult. YUPA, XIX, 1-188. 1938.

--- Primitive Psychotherapy in Native American Cultures. Journal of Abnormal and Social Psychology, XXIV, 294-309. 1947.

--- Twenty Years of Peyote Studies. Current Anthropology, I, 45-60. 1960.

La Farge, O. As Long as the Grass shall grow. 140 pp. New York, 1940.

La Farge, O. A Pictorial History of the American Indian. 272 pp. New York, 1956.

La Farge, O. ed. The Changing Indian. 184 pp. Norman, 1942.

Lamb, S.M. Some Proposals for Linguistic Taxonomy. Anthropological Linguistics, I, ii, 33-49. 1959.

Lambert, R.S. Exploring the Supernatural. 198 pp. Toronto, 1955.

Landogna Cassone, F. Sul Problema della Paleo-amerindiana. ACISA, IV, i, 304-8. 1954.

Landsteiner, K., Wiener, A.S., and Matson, G.A. Distribution of the Rh Factor in American Indians. Journal of Experimental Medicine, LXXVI, 73-8. 1942.

Lane, R. and B. On the Development of the Dakota-Iroquois and Crow-Omaha Kinship Terminologies. SJA, XV, 254-65. 1959.

Lasch, R. Die Verstümmlung der Zähne in Amerika. MAGW, XXXI, 12-33. 1901.

Latham, R.G. The Ethnology of the British Colonies and Dependencies, pp. 224-52. London, 1851.

--- On the Languages of Northern, Western, and Central America. Transactions of the Philological Society, 1856, 57-115.

Laubin, R. and G. The Indian Tipi. 226 pp. Norman, 1957.

Laufer, B. The American Plant Migration. SM, XXVIII, 239-51. 1929.

Lee, D.D. Freedom and Culture. 187 pp. Englewood Cliffs, 1959.

Leechman, D. Native Tribes of Canada. 358 pp. Toronto, 1956.

Leechman, D. and Hall, R.A. American Indian Pidgin English. American Speech, XXX, 163-71. 1955.

Leh, L.L. The Shaman in Aboriginal American Society. University of Colorado Studies, XX, 199-263. 1934.

Lehmann, W. Die Frage völkerkundlicher Beziehungen zwischen der Südsee und Amerika. Orientalistische Literaturzeitung, XXXIII, 321-40. 1930.

Le Moine, J.M. Les aborigènes d'Amérique--leurs rites mortuaires. PTRSC, II, i, 85-96. 1884.

Lemos, P.J. Indian Decorative Design. Worcester, 1926.

Lesser, A. Bibliography of American Folklore, 1915-1928. JAFL, XLI, 1-60. 1928.

Lewis, M., et al. The Blood Group Antigen Diego in North American Indians and in Japanese. Nature, CLXXVII, 1084. 1956.

Lincoln, J.S. The Dream in Primitive Cultures. London, 1935.

Lindquist, G.E.E. The Red Man in the United States. 461 pp. New York, 1923.

Lindquist, G.E.E., et al. The Indian in American Life. 180 pp. New York, 1944.

Linton, R. Crops, Soils, and Culture in America. The Maya and Their Neighbors, pp. 32-40. New York, 1940.

--- Land Tenure in Aboriginal America. The Changing Indian, ed. O. La Farge, pp. 42-54. Norman, 1942.

--- North American Cooking Pots. AAn, IX, 369-80. 1944.

--- The Significance of Certain Traits in North American Maize Culture. AA, n.s., XXVI, 345-9. 1924.

Lips, E. Das Indianerbuch. 443 pp. Leipzig, 1956.

Loeb, E.M. The Twin Cult in the Old and the New World. MPR, i, 151-74. 1958.

Loram, C.T., and McIlwraith, T.F., eds. The North American Indian Today. 361 pp. Toronto, 1943.

Lorimer, F. Observations on the Trend of Indian Population in the United States. The Changing Indian, ed. O. La Farge, pp. 11-18. Norman, 1942.

Lowie, R.H. American Culture History. AA, n.s., XLII, 409-28. 1940.

--- American Indian Dances. AMJ, XV, iii, 95-102. 1915.

--- Beiträge zur Völkerkunde Nordamerikas. MMVH, XXIII, 7-27, 1951.

--- Ceremonialism in North America. AA, n.s., XVI, 602-31. 1914.

--- Supernormal Experiences of American Indians. Tomorrow, IV, iii, 9-16. 1956.

--- The Test-Theme in North American Mythology. JAFL, XXI, 97-148. 1908.

Lucas, J.M. Indian Harvest. 118 pp. Philadelphia, 1945.

Ludewig, H.E. The Literature of American Aboriginal Languages. 258 pp. London, 1858.

Luomala, K. Oceanic, American Indian, and African Myths of Snaring the Sun. Bulletin of the Bernice P. Bishop Museum, CLXVIII, 5-24. 1940.

Lyback, J.R.M. Indian Legends. 355 pp. Chicago, 1925.

McAllester, D. Peyote Music. VFPA, XIII, 1-104. 1949.

McCaskill, J.C., and McNickle, D.A. La politica de los gobiernos tribales y las empresas comunales de los Indios. 26 pp. Washington, 1942.

McCown, T.D. The Antiquity of Man in the New World. AAn, VI, 203-13. 1941.

McGee, W J., and Thomas, C. Prehistoric North America. The History of North America, ed. F. N. Thorpe, XIX, 1-482. Philadelphia, 1905.

Macgregor, F.C. Twentieth Century Indians. 127 pp. New York, 1941.

McGuire, J.D. Pipes and Smoking Customs of the American Aborigines. RUSNM, 1897, 351-645.

McIntosh, J. Origin of the North American Indians. 345 pp. New York, 1843.

Mackay, J.E. Indian Nights. Toronto, 1930.

McKenney, T.L. Memoirs, Official and Personal. 2 vols. New York, 1846.

McKenney, T.L., and Hall, J. History of the Indian Tribes of North America. 2 vols. Philadelphia, 1848.

MacLachlan, B.B. Communities of Societal Indians in Canada. An, VI, 69-82. 1958.

MacLeod, W.C. The American Indian Frontier. 598 pp. New York, 1928.

--- Child Sacrifice in North America. JSAP, n.s., XXIII, 127-37. 1931.

--- Economic Aspects of Indigenous American Slavery. AA, n.s., XXX, 632-50. 1928.

--- The Nature, Origin, and Linkages of the Rite of Hook-swinging. A, XXIX, 1-38. 1934.

--- Self-Sacrifice in Mortuary and Non-Mortuary Ritual in North America. A, XXXIII, 349-400. 1938.

MacMillan, C. Glooskap's Country. 273 pp. Toronto, 1956.

McNickle, D. American Indian Affairs–1953. AI, XIII, 263-73. 1953.

--- The Healing Vision. Tomorrow, IV, iii, 25-31. 1956.

--- Indian and European. APSS, CCCXI, 1-11. 1957.

--- The Indians of the United States. AI, XVIII, 99-118. 1958.

--- Peyote and the Indian. SM, LVII, 220-9. 1943.

--- Process or Compulsion. AI, XVII, 261-70. 1957.

--- Runner in the Sun. 234 pp. Philadelphia, 1954.

--- They Came Here First. 325 pp. Philadelphia, 1949.

McNicol, D.M. The Amerindians. 360 pp. New York, 1937.

Madison, H.L. Indian Homes. Cleveland, 1925.

Mair, L.P. Independent Religious Movements in Three Continents. Studies in Science of Society, I, 113-36. 1958-59.

Major, R.C. Aboriginal American Medicine. Annals of Medical History, X, 534-49. 1938.

Mallery, G. Pictographs of the North American Indians. ARBAE, IV, 3-256. 1886.

Mallery, G. Picture-Writing of the American Indians. ARBAE, X, 1-822. 1893.

--- Sign Language among North American Indians. ARBAE, I, 263-552. 1880.

Mangelsdorf, P.C., and Reeves, R.G. The Origin of Indian Corn and Its Relatives. Texas Agricultural Experiment Station Bulletin, DLXXIV, 1-315. 1939.

Marriott, A.L. Greener Fields. 274 pp. New York, 1953.

--- The Opened Door. New Yorker, 80-82, 85-9. Sept. 25, 1954.

Martin, P.S. The Bow-Drill in North America. AA, n.s., XXXVI, 94-7. 1934.

Martin, P.S., Quimby, G.I., and Collier, D. Indians Before Columbus. 582 pp. Chicago, 1949.

Martin, W.B. Religious Ideas of the American Indians. Catholic University Bulletin, X, 35-68, 225-45. 1904.

Mason, B.S. The Book of Indian Crafts and Costumes. 118 pp. New York, 1946.

--- Dances and Stories of the American Indian. 279 pp. New York, 1944.

Mason, O.T. Aboriginal American Basketry. RUSNM, 1902, 171-548.

--- Aboriginal American Harpoons. RUSNM, 1900, ii, 193-304.

--- Aboriginal American Zoötechny. AA, n.s., I, 45-81. 1899.

--- Aboriginal Skin-Dressing. RUSNM, 1889, 553-89.

--- Amerindian Arrow Feathering. AA, n.s., I, 583-5. 1899.

--- Basket-Work of the North American Aborigines. RUSNM, 1884, ii, 291-306.

--- Cradles of the American Aborigines. RUSNM, 1887, 161-212.

--- The Human Beast of Burden. RUSNM, 1887, 237-95.

--- Influence of Environment upon Human Industries or Arts. ARSI, 1895, 639-65.

--- Introduction of the Iron Age into America. AA, IX, 191-215. 1896.

--- North American Bows, Arrows, and Quivers. ARSI, 1893, 631-79.

--- Overlaying with Copper by the American Aborigines. PUSNM, XVII, 475-7. 1894.

--- Primitive Travel and Transportation. RUSNM, 1894, 237-593.

--- The Technic of Aboriginal American Basketry. AA, n.s., III, 109-28. 1901.

--- Traps of the American Indians. ARSI, 1901, 461-73.

Mason, O.T. Traps of the Amerinds. AA, n.s., II, 657-75. 1900.

Mathews, W. and Pearce, R.H. American Diaries. 383 pp. Berkeley, 1945.

Matson, G.A. Anthropological Application of the Blood Groups. Proceedings of the Utah Academy of Science, Arts, and Letters, XXIII, 19-27. 1946.

Matson, J., and Hanks, M. Indian Vegetable Dyes. DAMLS, LXIII, 1-4; LXXI, 1-4. 1936.

Mead, M. An Anthropologist at Work. 607 pp. Boston, 1959.

Meeussen, A. Algonquian Clusters with Glottal Stop. IJAL, XXV, 189-90. 1959.

Meggers, B.J., ed. New Interpretations of Aboriginal American Culture History. 143 pp. Washington, 1955.

Meltzer, H., et al. Echinococcosis in North American Indians and Eskimos. Canadian Medical Association Journal, LXXV, 121-8. 1956.

Meriam, L., et al. The Problem of Indian Administration. 872 pp. Baltimore, 1928.

Merrill, E.D. Observations on Cultivated Plants with Reference to Certain American Problems. Ceiba, I, 1-36. 1950.

Michelson, T. Phonetic Shifts in Algonquian Languages. IJAL, VIII, 131-71. 1935.

--- Remarks on American Indian Languages. JWAS, VII, 222-34. 1917.

Miles, N.A. Personal Recollections and Observations. 590 pp. New York, 1896.

Miles, S.W. A Revaluation of the Old Copper Industry. AAn, XVI, 240-7. 1951.

Milewski, T. The Conception of the Word in the Languages of North American Natives. Lingua Posnaniensis, III, 248-68. 1951.

--- La Structure de la Phrase dans les Langues Indigènes de l'Amérique du Nord. Lingua Posnaniensis, II, 162-207. 1950.

Milke, W. Athapaskische Chronologie. IJAL,XXV, 182-8. 1959.

Miller, D.C. Flutes of the American Indian. Flutist, II, 509-12. 1921.

Miller, M.T. An Author, Title and Subject Check List of Smithsonian Institution Publications relating to Anthropology. 218 pp. Albuquerque, 1946.

Miner, W.H. The American Indians North of Mexico. 169 pp. Cambridge, 1917.

Mogensen, A.K. Hvor Tidligt Kom Mennesket til Amerika? Kulturgeografi, V, xxix, 172-5. 1953.

Møller, F.A. The Origin of the Indians and America's First Inhabitants Discovered. 70 pp. Pasco, Wash., 1956.

Mooney, J. The Aboriginal Population of America North of Mexico. SMC, LXXX, vii, 1-40. 1928.

Moore, P.E. Health for Indians and Eskimos. CGJ, XLVIII, 216-21. 1954.

Moorehead, W.K. The American Indian in the United States. 434 pp. Andover, 1914.

--- Stone Ornaments used by Indians in the United States and Canada. Andover, 1917.

Morgan, L.H. Houses and House-Life of the American Aborigines. CNAE, IV, 1-281. 1881.

--- The Indian Journals, 1859-62. 245 pp. Ann Arbor, 1959.

--- The Indian Mode of bestowing and changing Names. PAAS, XIII, 340-3. 1859.

--- A Study of the Houses of the American Aborigines. Annual Report of the Archaeological Institute of America, I, 29-80. 1880.

Morice, J.H. Romantic Lore of American Indian Origins. GM, XLVI, 170-86. 1944.

Morse, E.S. Ancient and Modern Methods of Arrow Release. BEI, XVII, 145-98. 1885.

Mourant, A.E. The Distribution of the Human Blood Groups. 438 pp. Springfield, Ill., 1954.

Mourant, A.E., et al. The A B O Blood Groups. 284 pp. Oxford, 1958.

Müller, J.G. Geschichte der amerikanischen Urreligionen. Basel, 1855.

Müller, W. Die Religionen der Waldlandindianer Nordamerikas. 392 pp. Berlin, 1956.

Murdock, G.P. North American Social Organization. DJA, I, 85-97. 1955.

Murphey, E.V.A. Indian Uses of Native Plants. 72 pp. Covello, Cal., 1959.

Myron, R. L'Art Précolumbien de l'Est des Etats-Unis. JSAP, XLIV, 55-66. 1956.

Nadeau, G. Indian Scalping. Bulletin of the History of Medicine, X, 178-94. 1941.

--- Indian Scalping Techniques in Different Tribes. Ciba Symposia, V, 1677-84. 1944.

National Geographic Society. National Geographic on Indians of the Americas. 432 pp. Washington, 1955.

National Resources Board. Indian Land Tenure, Economic Status, and Population Trends. Supplementary Report of the Land Planning Committee, Vol. X. 1935.

Nettl, B. North American Indian Musical Styles. JAFL, LXVII, 45-56, 297-308, 351-68. 1954.

--- North American Indian Musical Styles. MAFLS, XLV, 61 pp. 1954.

--- Observations on Meaningless Peyote Song Texts. JAFL, LXVI, 161-4. 1953.

Nettl, B. Stylistic Variety in North American Indian Music. Journal of the American Musicological Society, VI, 160-8. 1953.

Neumann, G.K. American Indian Crania with Low Vaults. HB, XIV, 178-91. 1942.

--- Archeology and Race in the American Indian. AEUS, 13-34. 1952.

--- The Varieties of Prehistoric Indians of the Eastern United States. In, El Norte de Mexico y el Sur de Estados Unidos, 171-80. Mexico, 1943.

Newberne, R.E.L., and Burke, C.H. Peyote. 38 pp. Washington, 1922.

Newberry, J.S. Food and Fiber Plants of the North American Indians. PSM, XXXII, 31-46. 1887.

Newberry Library. A Bibliographical Check List of North and Middle American Indian Linguistics in the Edward E. Ayer Collection. 2 vols. Chicago, 1941.

Newman, M.T. The Application of Ecological Rules to the Racial Anthropology of the New World. AA, LV, 311-27. 1953.

Nichols, C.A. Moral Education among the North American Indians. Columbia University Teachers' College, Contributions to Education, CCCCXXVII, 104 pp. 1930.

Nichols, F.S. Index to Schoolcraft's "Indian Tribes of the United States." BBAE, CLII, 263 pp. 1954.

Nieuwenhuis, A.W. Die dualistische Kultur in Amerika. IAE, XXXII, Supplement, 1-147. 1933.

--- Principles of Indian Medicine in American Ethnology and their Psychological Significance. Janus, XXVIII, 305-56.

Nordenskiöld, E. The American Indian as an Inventor. JAI, LIX, 273-311. 1929.

--- En jämforelse mellan indiankulturen i södra Sydamerika och i Nordamerika. Ymer, XXVI, 298-315. 1926.

Norona, D. Maps Drawn by North American Indians. BESAF, X, 6. 1951.

Northey, S. The American Indian. 216 pp. San Antonio, 1954.

Nuttall, Z. The Fundamental Principles of Old and New World Civilizations. PMP, II, 1-575. 1901.

Nykl, A.R. The Quinary-Vigesimal System of Counting in Europe, Asia, and America. Lg, II, 165-73. 1926.

Oetteking, B. Primitive Traits in the American Aboriginal Population. Institut Internationale d'Anthropologie, III, 20-29. 1927.

--- Über die geschichtliche Entwickelung der indianischen Volksdichte. Zeitschrift fur Rassenkunde, III, 171-6. 1936.

Ohlmarks, A. Studien zum Problem des Shamanismus. 395 pp. Lund, 1939.

Olson, R.L. Clan and Moiety in Native America. UCP, XXXIII, 351-422. 1933.

Orchard, W.C. Beads and Beadwork of the American Indians. CMAI, XI, 3-140. 1929.

--- The Technique of Porcupine-Quill Decoration among the North American Indians. CMAI, IV, i, 1-53. 1916.

Ortega y Medina, J.A. Ideas de la evangelización anglosajona entre los indigenas de los Estados Unidos de Norteamérica. AI, XVIII, 129-44. 1958.

Paccino, D. Arrivano i Nostri. 323 pp. Milan and Rome, 1956.

Palmer, E. The Berries of Rhamnus croceus as Indian Food. AN, VIII, 247. 1874.

--- Food Products of the North American Indians. Report of the Secretary of Agriculture, 1871, 404-28.

--- Plants used by the Indians of the United States. AN, XII, 593-606, 646-55. 1878.

Palmer, R.A. The North American Indians. Smithsonian Scientific Series, IV, 1-309. 1929.

Pardal, R. Medicina aborigen americana. Humanior, Bibliotheca del Americanista Moderno, III, 1-373. 1937.

Parker, A.C. The Indian How Book. 335 pp. New York, 1927.

--- Indian Medicine and Medicine Men. AAR, 1928, 9-17.

Parsons, E.C. Die Flucht auf den Baum. ZE, LIV, 1-29. 1922.

--- Riddles and Metaphors among Indian Peoples. JAFL, XLIX, 171-4. 1936.

Paullin, C.O. Atlas of the Historical Geography of the United States. 162 pp. Washington, 1932.

Payne, E.J. History of the New World called America. 2 vols. Oxford, 1892.

Peake, O.B. A History of the United States Indian Factory System, 1795-1822. 340 pp. Denver, 1954.

Pearce, R.H. The Savages of America. 267 pp. Baltimore, 1953.

Peet, S.D. Aboriginal Basketry. AAOJ, XXIX, 169-76. 1907.

--- The Cross in America. AAOJ, X, 292-315. 1888.

--- The Ethnography of Art in America. AAOJ, XXVI, 201-24. 1904.

--- Myths and Symbols, or Aboriginal Religions in America. 444 pp. Chicago, 1905.

--- Prehistoric America. 5 vols. Chicago, 1890-1905.

--- The Suastika and Fire-Worship in America. AAOJ, XXVI, 185-92. 1904.

Peet, S.D. The Symbolism of Basketry. AAOJ, XXIX, 251-8. 1907.

Pericot y Garcia, L. La América indígena. Historia de América y de los pueblos americanos, I, 1-727. Barcelona, 1936.

Peterson, H.L. American Indian Political Participation. APSS, CCCXI, 116-26. 1957.

--- American Knives. 178 pp. New York, 1958.

Peterson, S. How Well Are Indian Children Educated? 182 pp. Lawrence, 1948.

Petri, H.H. Der Schild der Indianer. 288 pp. Hamburg, 1938.

Pettazoni, R. Miti e Leggende III: America Settentrionale. 594 pp. Torino, 1953.

Pettitt, G.A. Primitive Education in North America. UCP, XLIII, 1-182. 1946.

Pierz, F. Die Indianer in Nord-Amerika. 132 pp. St. Louis, 1855.

Popham, R.E. A Bibliography and Historical Review of Physical Anthropology in Canada. Revue Canadienne de Biologie, IX, 175-98. 1950.

Pospisil, F. The Present Condition of Choreographic Research in Northern, Central and Southern America. ICA, XXIV, 212-3. 1934.

Powell, J.W. Indian Linguistic Families of America North of Mexico. ARBAE, VII, 1-142. 1891.

--- Introduction to the Study of Indian Languages. 228 pp. Washington, 1880.

--- The North American Indians. United States of America, ed. N.S. Shaler, I, 190-272. New York, 1894.

--- Outlines of the Philosophy of the North American Indian. 19 pp. New York, 1877.

--- Sketch of the Mythology of the North American Indians. ARBAE, I, 19-56. 1881.

--- Stone Art in America. AA, VIII, 1-7. 1895.

Priest, L.B. Uncle Sam's Stepchildren. 320 pp. New Brunswick, 1942.

Putnam, F.W. Conventionalism in American Art. BEI, XVIII, 155-67. 1887.

Quimby, G.I. Silver Ornaments and the Indians. MPR, i, 317-37. 1958.

Radin, P. The Basic Myth of the North American Indians. Eranos-Jahrbuch, XVII, 359-419. 1950.

--- The Genetic Relationship of the North American Indian Languages. UCP, XIV, 489-502. 1919.

--- Literary Aspects of North American Mythology. MBCDM, XVI, 1-51. 1915.

--- Religion of the North American Indians. JAFL, XXVII, 335-73. 1914.

--- The Story of the American Indian. 371 pp. New York, 1927.

Raphael, R.B. The Book of American Indians. Greenwich, 1953.

Ratzel, F. The History of Mankind, Vol. II. London, 1897.

Rau, C. Ancient Aboriginal Trade in North America. ARSI, 1872, 348-94.

--- Observations on Cup-shaped and Other Lapidarian Sculptures. CNAE, V, 1-104. 1881.

--- Prehistoric Fishing in Europe and North America. SCK, XXV, i, 113-319. 1884.

--- Die Tauschverhältnisse der Eingeborenen Nordamerikas. AFA, V, 1-43. 1872.

Raudot, A.D. Memoir concerning the Different Indian Nations of North America, ed. V. Kinietz. OCMA, X, 339-410. 1940.

Ray, V.F. The Contrary Behavior Pattern in American Indian Ceremonialism. SJA, I, 75-113. 1945.

Ray, V.F. and Lurie, N.O. The Contributions of Lewis and Clark to Ethnography. JWAS, XLIV, 358-70. 1954.

Reichard, G.A. Literary Types and Dissemination of Myths. JAFL, XXXIV, 269-307. 1921.

Reichel, L.T. Our Indian Mission, 1740-1850. MCM, V, 338-48, 366-9. 1854.

Renaud, A. Indian Education Today. An, VI, 1-49. 1958.

Renaud, E.B. L'antiquité de l'homme dans l'Amérique du Nord. Ane, XXXVIII, 23-50. 1928.

--- Influence of Food on Indian Culture. SF, X, 97-101. 1934.

--- The Tempering of Indian Pottery from the United States. EP, XXII, 378-89. 1927.

Rhodes, W. Acculturation in North American Indian Music. ICA, XXIX, ii, 127-32. 1952.

--- American Indian Music. Tomorrow, IV, iii, 97-102. 1956.

--- The Christian Hymnology of the North American Indians. ACISA, V, 324-31. 1960.

--- A Study of Musical Diffusion Based on the Wandering of the Opening Peyote Song. Journal of the International Folk Music Council, X, 42-9. 1958.

Rich, E.E. Trade Habits and Economic Motivation among the Indians of North America. CJEPS, XXVI, 35-53. 1960.

Rickard, T.A. The Use of Native Copper by the Indigenes of North America. JAI, LXIV, 265-87. 1934.

Riley, C.L. The Blowgun in the New World. SJA, VIII, 297-319. 1952.

Rivet, P. Langues de l'Amérique du Nord. Les langues du monde, ed. A. Meillet and M. Cohen, pp. 607-28. Paris, 1924.

Rivet, P., Stresser-Péan, G., and Loukotka, C. Langues de l'Amérique du Nord. In A. Meillet et Marcel Cohen, Les Langues du Monde, Nouvelle Edition, 959-1065. Paris, 1952.

Robert, F. Chaussures Indiennes d'Amérique du Nord. JSAP, n.s., XLVII, 67-110. 1958.

Roberts, F.H.H. Developments in the Problem of the North American Paleo-Indian. SMC, C, 51-116. 1940.

Roberts, H.H. Musical Areas in Aboriginal North America. YUPA, XII, 1-41. 1936.

Roe, F.G. The Indian and the Horse. 450 pp. Norman, 1955.

--- The North American Buffalo. 965 pp. Toronto, 1951.

Rogers, S.L. The Aboriginal Bow and Arrow of North America and Eastern Asia. AA, n.s., XLII, 255-69. 1940.

--- Disease Concepts in North America. AA, n.s., XLVI, 558-64. 1944.

Rôheim, G. Culture Hero and Trickster in North American Mythology. ICA, XXIX, iii, 190-4. 1952.

Rooth, A.B. The Creation Myths of the North American Indians. A, LII, 497-508. 1957.

Rosenblat, A. La Poblacion Indigena y el Mestizaje en America. 2 vols. 514 pp. Buenos Aires, 1954.

Ross, M.C., ed. George Catlin: Episodes from "Life Among the Indians" and "Last Rambles." Norman, 1959.

Rostlund, E. Freshwater Fish and Fishing in Native North America. UCPG, IX, 323 pp. 1952.

Roth, H.L. American Quillwork: a Possible Clue to Its Origin. Man, XXIII, 113-16. 1923.

--- Moccasins and Their Quill Work. JAI, XXXVIII, 47-57. 1908.

Rouse, I. and Goggin, J.M. An Anthropological Bibliography of the Eastern Seaboard. Eastern States Archeological Federation, Research Publication, I, 174 pp. 1947.

Rousseau, J.J. Astam Michoun! CD, XXII, 193-211. 1957.

--- Le Couteau Croche des Indiens de la Foret Boréale. Technique, XXI, 447. 1946.

Royce, C.C. Indian Land Cessions in the United States. ARBAE, XVIII, ii, 521-997. 1899.

Rusby, H.H. Beverages of Vegetable Origin. New York Botanical Garden Journal, V, 79-86. 1904.

Russell, C.P. Guns on the American Frontiers. 395 pp. Berkeley, 1957.

Russell, V.Y. Indian Artifacts. 170 pp. Boulder, 1957.

Rydberg, P.A. Plants Used by Ancient American Indians. New York Botanical Garden Journal, XXV, 204-5. 1924.

Safford, W.E. An Economic Amaranthus of Ancient America. Science, XLIV, 870. 1916.

--- Food Plants and Textiles of Ancient America. Proceedings of the 2nd Pan American Scientific Congress, Washington, 1915, Section I, 146-59. 1917.

--- Food Plants and Textiles of Ancient America. ICA, XIX, 12-30. 1915.

--- Foods Discovered with America. SM, XXI, 181-6. 1925.

--- Narcotic Plants and Stimulants of the Ancient Americans. ARSI, 1916, 387-424.

--- Our Heritage from American Indians. ARSI, 1926, 405-10.

--- Use of Nuts by the Aboriginal Americans. Northern Nut Growers' Association Report, XIV, 54-60. 1923.

Sapir, E. Central and North American Languages. Encyclopaedia Britannica, 14th edit., V, 138-41. 1929.

--- The Problem of Noun Incorporation in American Languages. AA, n.s., XIII, 250-82. 1911.

--- The Relation of American Indian Linguistics to General Linguistics. SJA, III, 1-4. 1947.

--- Time Perspective in Aboriginal American Culture. MCDM, XC, 1-87. 1916.

Sapir, E., and Swadesh, M. American Indian Grammatical Categories. Word, II, 103-12. 1946.

Sapper, K. Geographie der altindianischen Landwirtschaft. PMJP, LXXX, 41-4, 118-21. 1934.

--- Die Kulturzustand der Indianer vor der Beruhrung mit den Europäern und in der Gegenwart. ICA, XXIV, 73-96. 1930.

--- Die Zahl und Volksdichte der indianischen Bevölkerung in Amerika. ICA, XXI, 95-104. 1924.

Sarfert, E. Haus und Dorf bei den Eingeborenen Nordamerikas. 97 pp. Braunschweig, 1908.

Satchell, W.A. Aboriginal Tobaccos. AA, n.s., XXIII, 397-413. 1921.

Sauer, C.O. Agricultural Origins and Dispersals. 110 pp. New York, 1952.

--- American Agricultural Origins. Essays in Anthropology presented to A.L.Kroeber, pp. 279-97. Berkeley, 1936.

Saunders, C.F. The Yucca and the Indian. American Botanist, XVII, 1-3. 1911.

Schaeffer, C.E. and Roland, L.J. A Partial Bibliography of the Archaeology of Pennsylvania and Adjacent States. 46 pp. Harrisburg, 1941.

Schmeckbeier, L.F. The Office of Indian Affairs.
Institute for Government Research Service Monographs of the United States Government, XLVIII,
591 pp. 1927.

Schmidt, W. Die Altstämme Nordamerikas. Festschrift Eduard Seler, pp. 471-502. Stuttgart, 1922.

--- High Gods in North America. 148 pp. Oxford,
1933.

--- Die Ursprung der Gottesidee. II, 1-872, 1008-
33; V, 1-773, 857-95; VII, 705-89. Münster i.
W., 1929, 1934, 1940.

Schmitt, M.F. and Brown, D. Fighting Indians of the
West. 362 pp. New York, 1948.

Schoolcraft, H.R. The Indian in His Wigwam. 416
pp. New York, 1848.

Schuessler, K.F. and Driver, H. A Factor Analysis
of Sixteen Primitive Societies. ASR, XXI, 493-9.
1956.

Schultes, R.E. The Appeal of Peyote (Lophophora
Williamsii) as a Medicine. AA, n.s., XL, 698-
715. 1938.

--- Peyote--an American Indian Heritage from Mexico. Mexico Antiguo, IV, 199-208. 1938.

--- Peyote and Plants used in the Peyote Ceremony.
Harvard University Botanical Museum Leaflets, IV,
129-52. 1937.

Schusky, F. Pan-Indianism in the Eastern United
States. Anthropology Tomorrow, VI, i, 116-123.
1957.

Scull, G.D., ed. Voyages of Peter Esprit Radisson.
New York, 1943.

Sears, P.B. The Archeology of Environment in Eastern North America. AA, n.s., XXXIV, 610-22.
1932.

Seidel, H. Der Schneeschuh und seine geographische
Verbreitung. Globus, LXXIII, 155-61. 1898.

Seton, J.M. Rhythm of the Redman. 280 pp. Santa
Fe, 1947.

Shea, A. Conservation of Food among the Indians.
OM, series 2, LXXII, 441-2. 1918.

Shufeldt, R.W. Comparative Data from 200 Indian
Crania. Journal of Anatomy and Physiology, XXII,
191-214. 1888.

Siebert, F.T. Review of Lowie's the Crow Language.
IJAL, X, 212-3. 1944.

Siiger, H. Indianerne og Bisonen. GT, XLVII, 155-
74. 1945.

Sinclair, A.T. Tattooing of the North American Indians. AA, n.s., XI, 362-400. 1909.

Sloan, J., and La Farge, O. Introduction to American Indian Art. LEITA. 55 pp. New York, 1931.

Slotkin, J.S. The Peyote Religion. 195 pp. Glencoe,
1956.

Slotkin, J.S. The Peyote Way. Tomorrow, IV, iii,
64-70. 1956.

--- Peyotism, 1521-1891. AA, LVII, 202-30; LVIII,
184. 1955-56.

Smith, J. A Treatise on the Mode and Manner of Indian War. 59 pp. Paris, Ky., 1812 (Reprinted 1948,
Chicago).

Smith, M.G. Notes on the Depopulation of Aboriginal
America. AA, n.s., XXX, 669-74. 1928.

Smith, M.W. American Indian Warfare. TNYAS, ser.
2, XIII, 348-64. 1951.

--- Continuity in Culture Contact. Man, LV, 100-
105. 1955.

--- Toward a Classification of Cult Movements. Man,
LIX, 8-12. 1959.

Spaulding, K.A. On the Oregon Trail. 205 pp. Norman, 1953.

Spence, L. Calendar (American). ERE, III, 65-70.
1911.

--- The Myths of the North American Indians. 393
pp. New York, 1914.

Spier, L. The Distribution of Kinship Systems in
North America. UWPA, I, 69-88. 1925.

Spinden, H.J. Fine Art and the First Americans.
LEITA. 8 pp. New York, 1931.

--- Indian Symbolism. LEITA. 18 pp. New York,
1931.

--- The Population of Ancient America. GR, XVIII,
641-60. 1928.

--- Power Animals in American Indian Art. ICA,
XXIX, iii, 195-9. 1952.

--- Songs of the Tewa. 125 pp. New York, 1933.

Spindler, G.D. and L.S. American Indian Personality
Types and their Sociocultural Roots. APSS, CCCXI,
147-57. 1957.

Spranz, B. Die Speerschleuder in Amerika. Veröffentlichungen aus dem Übersee-Museum in Bremen,
Reihe B, I, ii, 148-62. 1956.

Spuhler, J.N. Some Genetic Variations in American
Indians. PPAAI, 177-202. 1951.

Stanford, E. Compendium of Geography and Travel.
6 vols. London, 1878-85.

Stanley, J.M. Portraits of North American Indians.
SMC, II, iii, 1-76. 1852.

Starr, F. American Indians. 227 pp. Boston, 1899.

Stearn, E.W. and A.E. The Effect of Smallpox on
the Destiny of the Amerindian. 153 pp. Boston,
1945.

Stearns, R.E.C. Ethno-Conchology. RUSNM, 1887,
297-334.

Stevens, C. The Rediscovery of the Indian Languages.
American Speech, XXXII, 43-8. 1957.

Steward, J.H. The Ceremonial Buffoon of the American Indian. PMA, XIV, 187-207. 1931.

--- The Changing American Indian. The Science of Man in the World Crisis, ed. R. Linton, pp. 282-305. New York, 1945.

--- Petroglyphs of the United States. ARSI, 1936, 405-25. 1936.

Stewart, K.M. Spirit Possession. Tomorrow, IV, iii, 41-9. 1956.

--- Spirit Possession in Native America. SJA, II, 323-9. 1946.

Stewart, O.C. The Victuals of Our Red Men. SWL, XXII, 49-54. 1957.

Stewart, T.D. Some Historical Implications of Physical Anthropology in North America. SMC, C, 15-50. 1940.

Stirling, M.W. Concepts of the Sun among American Indians. ARSI, 1945, 387-400.

Stolpe, H. Studier i Amerikansk Ornamentik. Stockholm, 1896.

Stone, E. Medicine among the American Indians. 139 pp. New York, 1932.

Stout, A.B. Vegetable Foods of the American Indians. Journal of the New York Botanical Garden, XV, 50-60. 1914.

Stow, E. Boys' Games among the North American Indians. New York, 1924.

Sullivan, L.R. The Fossa Pharyngea in American Indian Crania. AA, n.s., XXII, 237-43. 1920.

--- The Frequency and Distribution of Some Anatomical Variations in American Crania. APAM, XXIII, 207-58. 1922.

Swadesh, M. Perspectives and Problems in Amerindian Comparative Linguistics. Word, X, 306-32. 1954.

--- Some New Glottochronologic Dates for Amerindian Linguistic Groups. ICA, XXXII, 671-4. 1958.

--- Towards a Satisfactory Genetic Classification of Amerindian Languages. ICA, XXXI, ii, 1001-12. 1958.

Swanton, J.R. The Indian Tribes of North America. BBAE, CXLV, 732 pp. 1952.

--- The Social Organization of American Tribes. AA, n.s., VII, 663-73. 1905.

Tanner, D. Legends from the Red Man's Forest. Chicago, 1931.

Taube, E. Tribal Names Related with Algonkin. Names, III, 65-81. 1955.

Tax, S. Acculturation. ACISA, V, 192-6. 1960.

Taylor, A. American Indian Riddles. JAFL, LVII, 2-15. 1944.

Temple, W.C. The Piasa Bird: Fact or Fiction? 22 pp. Springfield, Ill., 1956.

Tentori, T. Gli indigeni attuali degli Stati Uniti e del Canada. In R. Biasutti, ed., Le Razzi e i Popoli della Terra, 2nd ed., IV, 727-33. 1957.

--- Rudimenti di Arte Drammática Fia Gli Indigeni Americani. MPR, i, 188-96. 1958.

Termer, F. Der Hund bei den Kulturvölkern Altamerikas. ZE, LXXXII, 1-57. 1957.

Thomas, C. Catalogue of Prehistoric Works East of the Rocky Mountains. BBAE, XII, 1-246. 1891.

--- Historical Account. AAR, 1905, 71-83.

--- The Indians of North America in Historic Times. The History of North America, ed. G.C. Lee, II, 3-461. Philadelphia, 1903.

--- Introduction to the Study of North American Archaeology. 391 pp. Cincinnati, 1898.

--- Some Suggestions in Regard to Primary Indian Migration in North America. ICA, XV, 189-204. 1906.

Thompson, H. Education among American Indians. APSS, CCCXI, 95-104. 1957.

Thompson, S. European Tales among the North American Indians. Colorado College Publications, Language Series, II, 319-471. 1919.

--- The Indian Legend of Hiawatha. Publications of the Modern Language Association, XXXVII, 128-40. 1922.

--- The Star Husband Tale. Studia Septentrionalia, IV, 93-163. 1953.

--- Tales of the North American Indians. 386 pp. Cambridge, 1929.

Thornthwaite, C.W. The Climates of North America according to a New Classification. GR, XXI, 633-55. 1931.

Tijm, J. Die Stellung der Frau bei den Indianern der Vereinigten Staaten und Canada's. 158 pp. Amsterdam, 1933.

Tischner, H. Völkerkunde, pp. 19-21, 41-56, 118-48. Das Fischer Lexicon, XIII. Frankfurt, 1959.

Titus, M.E. A Treatise on American Indian Music. Indianapolis, 1920.

Tompkins, W. Universal Indian Sign Language. 112 pp. San Diego, 1956.

Toomey, T.N. Bibliographies of Lesser North American Linguistic Families. BHLAL, I, 20 pp. 1917.

Townsend, J.G. Indian Health. The Changing Indian, ed. O. La Farge, pp. 28-41. Norman, 1942.

--- Tuberculosis in the North American Indian. Proceedings of the Eighth American Scientific Congress, VI, 261-72. 1942.

Townsend, J.G., et al. Tuberculosis Control among the North American Indians. Transactions of the National Tuberculosis Association, XXXVII, 66-76. 1941.

Trager, G. L. and Harben, F. E. North American Indian Languages. SLOP, V, 36 pp. 1958.

Trimble, H. Some Indian Food Plants. American Journal of Pharmacy, LX, 593-5; LXI, 4-6, 556-8; LXII, 281-2, 598-600; LXIII, 525-7. 1888-91.

Trobriand, P. R. Military Life in Dakota. 420 pp. St. Paul, 1951.

Tschopik, H. Indians of North America. 64 pp. New York, 1952.

Turner, G. Hair Embroidery in Siberia and North America. PRMOPT, VII, 83 pp. 1955.

--- Traits of Indian Character. 2 vols. Philadelphia, 1836.

Uhlenbeck, C. C. Present General Trends in the Grouping of American Aboriginal Languages. Lingua, I, 219-24. 1948.

--- Zu den einheimischen Sprachen Nord-Amerikas. A, V, 779-86. 1910.

Underhill, R. A Classification of Religious Practices among North American Indians. ACISA, IV, ii, 320-4. 1955.

--- Peyote. ICA, XXX, 143-48. 1955.

--- Red Man's America. 410 pp. Chicago, 1953.

--- Religion among American Indians. APSS, CCCXI, 127-36. 1957.

U. S. Bureau of Indian Affairs. Treaties between the United States of America and the Several Indian Tribes, from 1778-1837. 699 pp. Washington, 1837.

U. S. Bureau of the Census. Census of population: 1950. Vol. II, Characteristics of the population. 51 vols. Washington, 1953.

--- Nonwhite Population by Race. U. S. Census of Population: 1950, Special Reports, IV, iii, B, 88 pp. 1953.

--- ...Fifteenth Census of the United States, 1930. The Indian Population of the United States and Alaska. 238 pp. Washington, 1937.

--- Indian Population in the United States and Alaska, 1910. 285 pp. Washington, 1915.

U. S. Congress. House. Present Relations of the Federal Government to the American Indian. 85th Congress, 2d Session, House of Representatives Committee on Interior and Insular Affairs, Committee Print, XXXVIII, 346 pp. 1959.

--- Report with Respect to the House Resolution Authorizing the Committee on Interior and Insular Affairs to Conduct an Investigation of the Bureau of Indian Affairs. 1594 pp. 82d Congress, 2d Session, House Report No. 2503, Washington, 1953.

U. S. Congress. House. Report with Respect to the House Resolution Authorizing the Committee on Interior and Insular Affairs to Conduct an Investigation of the Bureau of Indian Affairs. 576 pp. 83d Congress, 2d Session, House Report, 2680, Washington, 1954.

--- Committee on Public Lands. Compilation of Material Relating to the Indians of the United States and the Territory of Alaska. 1119 pp. Washington, 1950.

U. S. Congress. Senate. Survey of Conditions of the Indians of the United States. 36 parts. 20,445 pp. Washington, 1929-39.

--- Committee on Interior and Insular Affairs. Alaska Indian Reservations. 53 pp. Washington, 1950.

U. S. Department of the Interior. Office of the Solicitor. Federal Indian Law. 1106 pp. Washington, 1958.

U. S. Government. A Compilation of All the Treaties between the United States and the Indian Tribes, Now in Force as Laws. 1075 pp. Washington, 1873.

U. S. National Resources Board. Indian Land Tenure, Economic Status, and Population Trends. Supplementary Report of the Land Planning Committee, X, 73 pp. 1935.

U. S. Public Health Service. Health Services for American Indians. 344 pp. Washington, 1957.

Utzinger, R. Indianer-Kunst. München, 1921.

Vail, R. W. G. A Bibliography of North American Frontier Literature, 1542-1800. The Voice of the Old Frontier, 84-492. Philadelphia, 1949.

Vaillant, G. C. Indian Arts in North America. 63 pp. New York, 1939.

Verrill, A. H. Foods America gave the World. 289 pp. Boston, 1937.

--- The Real Americans. 379 pp. New York, 1954.

Vinay, J. P. Classification de la Famille Algonquin-Ritwan. An, I, 103-18. 1955.

Virchow, R. Crania ethnica americana. Berlin, 1892.

Voegelin, C. F. The Dispersal Factor in Migrations and Immigrations of American Indians [with comment by H. Hoijer]. UASSB, XXVII, 47-62. 1958.

--- North American Indian Languages still spoken and Their Genetic Relationships. Essays in Memory of Edward Sapir, pp. 15-40. Menasha, 1941.

--- A Query on the Nominal Origin of Verb Stems in Athapaskan. IJAL, XVII, 80-83. 1951.

--- Relative Chronology of North American Linguistic Types. AA, n. s., XLVII, 232-4. 1945.

--- Sign Language Analysis. IJAL, XXIV, 71-7. 1958.

Voegelin, C. F. and E. W. Map of North American Indian Languages. PAES, vol. 20. 1945.

Voeglin, C.F., and Harris, Z.S. Index to the Franz Boas Collection of Materials for American Linguistics. Language Monographs, XXII, 1-43. 1945.

Voegelin, C.F. and Hymes, D.H. A Sample of North American Indian Dictionaries with Reference to Acculturation. PAPS, XCVII, 634-44. 1953.

Voget, F. The American Indian in Transition. AA, LVIII, 249-63. 1956.

--- The American Indian in Transition. AJS, LXII, 369-78. 1956-57.

Vogt, E.Z. The Acculturation of American Indians. APSS, CCCXI, 137-46. 1957.

Waitz, T. Die Indianer Nordamerica's. 180 pp. Leipzig, 1865.

Wake, C.S. The Distribution of American Totems. AAOJ, XI, 354-8. 1889.

Walker, E.F. America's Indian Background. M, XIX, 7-13, 83-8, 119-25. 1945.

Walton, E.L., and Waterman, T.T. American Indian Poetry. AA, n.s., XXVII, 25-52. 1925.

Wardle, H.N. The Scope of the Rite of Adoption in Aboriginal North America. PPAS, I, 211-19. 1937.

Washburn, W.E. The Moral and Legal Justifications for Dispossessing the Indians. In J.M.Smith, ed., Seventeenth-century America, 15-32. Chapel Hill, 1959.

Washburne, M.F. Indian Legends. Chicago, 1915.

Waterman, T.T. The Architecture of the American Indians. Source Book in Anthropology, ed. A.L. Kroeber and T.T.Waterman, pp. 512-24. Rev.edit. New York, 1931.

--- The Explanatory Element in the Folk-Tales of the North American Indians. JAFL, XXVII, 1-54. 1914.

--- North American Indian Dwellings. ARSI, 1924, 461-85.

Waugh, F.W. Canadian Aboriginal Canoes. CFN, XXXIII, 23-33. 1919.

Weatherwax, P. Indian Corn in Old America. 265 pp. New York, 1954.

Weltfish, G. Prehistoric North American Basketry Techniques and Modern Distributions. AA, n.'s., XXXII, 454-95. 1930.

--- Problems in the Study of Ancient and Modern Basket-Makers. AA, n.s., XXXIV, 108-17. 1932.

West, G.A. Tobacco, Pipes, and Smoking Customs of the American Indians. BPMCM, XVII. 2 vols. 1934.

Westlake, J.B. American Indian Designs. 2 vols. Philadelphia, 1925-30.

Wheeler-Voegelin, E., ed. Some Remarks Concerning the Traditions, Customs, Languages &c of the Indians in North America. E, VI, 42-69, 186. 1959.

Wheeler-Voegelin, E. and Moore, R.W. The Emergence Myth in Native North America. IUPFS, IX, 66-91. 1957.

Whipple, A.W., et al. Report upon the Indian Tribes. 127 pp. Washington, 1855.

White, C.B. Rejoinder [to "Concerning the Proto-Athapaskan Kinship System" by Hymes and Driver]. AA, LX, 155-6. 1958.

Whitford, A.C. Textile Fibers used in Eastern Aboriginal North America. APAM, XXXVIII, 1-22. 1941.

Whitney, C.F. Indian Designs and Symbols. Salem, 1925.

Willey, G., ed. Prehistoric Settlement Patterns in the New World. VFPA, XXIII, 210 pp. 1956.

Wilson, C.M. New Crops for the New World. 303 pp. New York, 1945.

Wilson, E.W. American Indian Concept of Saliva. MWF, I, 229-32. 1951.

--- The Owl and the American Indian. JAFL, LXIII, 336-44. 1950.

--- The Shell and the American Indian. SFQ, XVI, 192-200. 1952.

--- The Spider and the American Indian. WF, X, 290-7. 1951.

Wilson, T. The Use of Wild Plants as Food by Indians. Ottawa Naturalist, XXX, 17-21. 1916.

Winsor, J. Narrative and Critical History of America. 8 vols. Boston, 1884-89.

Wise, J.C. The Red Man in the New World Drama. 628 pp. Washington, 1931.

Wissler, C. The American Indian. 411 pp. New York, 1917.

--- Corn and Early American Civilization. NH, LIV, 56-65. 1945.

--- The Effect of Civilization upon the Length of Life of the American Indian. SM, XLIII, 5-13. 1936.

--- Ethnological Diversity in America and Its Significance. The American Aborigines, ed. D. Jenness, pp. 165-216. Toronto, 1933.

--- Indian Cavalcade. 351 pp. New York, 1938.

--- Indian Costumes in the United States. AMGLS, LXIII, 1-32. 1931.

--- Indians of the United States. 319 pp. New York, 1940.

--- The Lore of the Demon Mask. NH, XXVIII, 339-52. 1928.

--- The Material Culture of North American Indians. AA, n.s., XVI, 447-505. 1914.

--- Observations on the Face and Teeth of the North American Indians. APAM, XXXIII, 1-33. 1931.

--- The Relation of Nature to Man in Aboriginal America. 248 pp. New York, 1926.

Witthoft, J. The American Indian as Hunter. Pennsylvania Game News, XXIV, ii, 12-16, iii, 16-22, iv, 8-13. 1953.

Wittrock, M.A. and G.L. Food Plants of the Indians. Journal of the New York Botanical Garden, XLIII, 57-71. 1942.

Wolff, H. Bibliography of Bibliographies of North American Languages still spoken. IJAL, XIII, 268-73. 1947.

--- Comparative Siouan. IJAL, XVI, 61-6, 113-21, 168-78; XVII, 197-204. 1950-51.

Wolfgang, R.W. Indian and Eskimo Diphyllobothriasis. Canadian Medical Association Journal, LXX, 536-9. 1954.

Woods, C.A. A Criticism of Wissler's North American Culture Areas. AA, n.s., XXXVI, 517-23. 1934.

Woodward, A. The Metal Tomahawk. Fort Ticonderoga Museum Bulletin, VII, iii, 2-42. 1946.

Worcester, D.E. The Weapons of American Indians. NMHR, XX, 227-38. 1945.

Worcester, D.E. The Use of Saddles by American Indians. NMHR, XX, 136-43. 1945.

Wormington, H.M. Ancient Man in North America. 322 pp. Denver, 1957.

Yanovsky, E. Food Plants of the North American Indians. U.S.Department of Agriculture, Miscellaneous Publications, CCXXXVII, 1-83. 1936.

Yanovsky, E., and Kingsbury, R.M. Analyses of Some Indian Food Plants. Journal of the Association of Official Agricultural Chemists, XXI, 648-65. 1938.

Yarrow, H.C. A Further Contribution to the Study of the Mortuary Customs of the North American Indians. ARBAE, I, 89-203. 1881.

--- Introduction to the Study of Mortuary Customs among the North American Indians. 108 pp. Washington, 1880.

Youngken, H.W. Drugs of the North American Indians. American Journal of Pharmacy, XCVI, 489-502; XCVII, 158-85, 257-71. 1924-25.

ADDENDA

I. ARCTIC COAST

Allison, A.C., and Blumberg, B.S. Ability to taste Phenylthiocarbamide among Alaskan Eskimos and other Populations. HB, XXXI, 352-9. 1959.

Allison, A.C., et al. Urinary B-aminoisobutyric Acid Excretion in Eskimo and Indian Populations of Alaska. Nature, CLXXXIII, 118-9. 1959.

Andree, K.T. Die Skulpturen der Eskimos. Globus, LIX, 348. 1891.

Anonymous. The Eskimo and the Principle of Conserving Hot Air. Eskimo, XLII, 18-21. 1956.

--- On the Rights of the Eskimo. Eskimo, XXXIX, 3-5, 1956.

--- To Civilize the Eskimo. Eskimo, XLII, 3-9. 1956.

Belcher, E. On the Manufacture of Works of Art by the Esquimaux. TESL, n.s., I, 129-46. 1861.

Biasutti, R. Le Razzi e i Popoli della Terra, 2nd ed., IV, 352-73. Torino, 1957.

Birket-Smith, K. Eskimo Prehistory. Scientia, série 6, 1-4. Avril, 1959.

--- The Eskimos. 262 pp. London, 1959.

Bogoraz, V.G. O tak nazyvaemom iazykie dukhov (shamanskom). Akademiia Nauk SSSR, Izvestiia, ser. 6, VIII-XI, 489-95. 1919.

Breuil, H. L'art des populations arctiques américaines. Paris, College de France, Annuaire, XXXIX, 138-44. 1939.

Brun de Neergaard, H. Grønlaenderindernes Klaededrägt. Grønlandske Selskab, Arsskrift, 1951, 61-6.

Bugge, A. Grønlandsk Religiøsitet. Grønland, 1954, ii, 59-64.

Calder, R. The Changing Arctic. 4 pp. Montreal, 1956.

Chart, I.E. Sentinels in Mukluks. Flying Safety, XI, x, 20-1. 1955.

Chipman, P. The Living Stone. B, CCLXXXVI, 12-9. Spring, 1956.

Coffey, M.F. A Comparative Study of Young Eskimo and Indian Males with Acclimatized White Males. Conference on Cold Injury, III, 100-16. 1955.

Dannevig, K. Ingeniør i Polarstrøkene. Polarboken, 1956, 39-55.

Donaghue, L. and Lucier, C. The University of Alaska Eskimo Music and Folklore Project. ASC, 1952, 121-5. 1954.

Emerson, W.C. The Land of the Midnight Sun. 179 pp. Philadelphia, 1956.

Fainberg, L.A. K Voprosu o Rodovom Stroe u Eskimosov. SE, 1955, ii, 82-99.

Forbin, V. Industrie et commerce chez les Eskimaux. Nature (Paris), LIV, 97-100. 1926.

Gad, F. The Language Situation in Greenland. American-Scandinavian Review, XLV, 377-83. 1957.

Garber, C.M. Eskimo Infanticide. SM, LXIV, 98-102. 1947.

Goldschmidt, V. Samfundsforskning: Grønland. Grønland, 1959, iii, 112-20.

Gravesen, P.B. Tuberkulosen i Grønland. Ugeskrift for Laeger, CXIV, 801-5. 1952.

Halpern, J.M. Arctic Jade. Rocks and Minerals, XXVIII, 237-42. 1953.

Hansen, H.H. Eskimo Clothing. American-Scandinavian Review, XLVI, 342-51. 1958.

Harrington, R. Northern Exposures. 119 pp. New York, 1953.

Hughes, C.C. Reference Group Concepts in the Study of a Changing Eskimo Culture. Cultural Stability and Cultural Change, ed. by V.F.Ray, pp. 7-14. Seattle, 1957.

Jansen, J.V. The Life of the Eskimos. Antiquity and Survival, I, 83-92. 1955.

Jensen, L.A. Grønlandsk husflid. Grønlandske Selskab, Arsskrift, 1950, 81-93.

König, H. Präanimistische Vorstellungen im Weltbilde der Eskimos. ACISA, I, 232-3. 1934.

--- Waren die Eskimos die ersten Besiedler des hohen Nordens? Forschungen und Fortschritte, X, 426-7. 1934.

Lehmann-Filhés, M. Die letzten Isländer in Grønland. Verein für Volkskunde, Zeitschrift, XIX, 170-3. 1909.

Leroi-Gourhan, A. Le mammouth dans la zoologie des Eskimos. La Terre et la Vie, V, ii, 3-12. July, 1935.

Linnik, E. Eskimosy. Vokrug Sveta, viii, 22-3. 1956.

Malvesin-Fabre, G. Un redresseur de flèches orné en ivoire. Ane, LIII, 74-80. 1949.

Marcussen, P.V. and Rendal, J. Udryddelse af gonorrhoe i et grønlandsk laegedistrikt. Ugeskrift for Laeger, CXIV, 819-21. 1952.

Marriott, R.S. Canada's Eastern Arctic Patrol. CGJ, XX, 156-61. 1940.

Meldgaard, J. Eskimo Skulptur. 87 pp. København, 1959.

Menovshchikov, G.A. Ob ustoichivosti grammaticheskogo stroia. Akademiia Nauk SSSR, Institut Iazykoznaniia, Voprosy Teorii i Istorii Iazyka v Svete Taudov I.V. Stalina po Iazykoznaniiu, 1952, 430-60. 1952.

Michéa, J.P. La Baie d'Hudson. Géographia, VIII, 21-6; IX, 27-34. 1952.

Michie, G.H. and Neil, E.M. Cultural Conflict in
the Canadian Arctic. Canadian Geographer, V,
33-41. 1955.

Moore, P.E. Health for Indians and Eskimos. CGJ,
XLVIII, 216-21. 1954.

--- Medical Care of Canada's Indians and Eskimos.
Canadian Journal of Public Health, XLVII, 227-33.
1956.

Morant, G.M. A Contribution to Eskimo Craniology.
Biometrika, XXIX, 1-20. 1937.

Newman, M.T. Adaptation of Man to Cold Climates.
Evolution, X, 101-5. 1956.

Noyes, J.R. The Alaska National Guard. Military
Engineer, XLVIII, 96-8. 1956.

Oschinsky, L. and Smithurst, R. On Certain Dental
Characters of the Eskimo of the Canadian Arctic.
An, n.s., II, i, 105-12. 1960.

Parran, T., et al. Alaska's Health. Pittsburgh, 1954.

Peck, E.J. Revised Eskimo Grammar Book. 79 pp.
Toronto, 1954.

Rainey, F. The Vanishing Art of the Arctic. Expedition, I, ii, 3-13. 1959.

Ristvedt, P. Minner fra "Gjoa"-ferden. Polarboken,
1956, 137-46.

Rodahl, K. Eskimo Metabolism. Norsk Polarinstitutt,
Skrifter, XCIX, 83 pp. 1954.

Rosing, J. Renjakt i det gamle Grønland. Polarboken,
1956, 99-112.

Scott, E.M. Nutrition of Alaskan Eskimos. Nutrition
Reviews, XIV, 1-3. 1956.

Scott, E.M., et al. Anemia in Alaskan Eskimos.
Journal of Nutrition, LV, 137-49. 1955.

Shepard, B. Current Study of Six Alaskan Edible
Plants. Alaska's Health, IX, 4-5. June, 1952.

Soper, J.D. Eskimo Dogs of the Canadian Arctic.
CGJ, XX, 96-108. 1940.

Stefansson, V. Causes of Eskimo Birthrate Increase.
Nature, CLXXVIII, 1132. 1956.

--- The Fat of the Land. 381 pp. New York, 1956.

--- A Word Common to the Natives of Alaska, Canada,
Greenland and Brazil. Nature, CLXXVIII, 1008.
1956.

Tolboom, W.N. · People of the Snow. 96 pp. New
York, 1956.

Volkov, T. and Rudenko, S.I. Etnograficheskaia
kollektsii iz byvshikh rossiisko-amerikanskikh
vladienii. 47 pp. St. Petersburg, 1910.

Wachtmeister, A. Naming and Reincarnation among
the Eskimos. Ethnos, XXI, 130-42. 1956.

Willmott, W.E. The Flexibility of Eskimo Social
Organization. An, n.s., II, i, 48-59. 1960.

Winters, R.H. The Eskimos. Canadian Weekly Bulletin, VIII, xii, 6. 1953.

Young, H.A. Care of Indians, Eskimos. Canadian
Weekly Bulletin, VIII, vi, 5-6. 1952.

Zagoskin, L.A. Puteshestviia i Issledovaniia
Leitenanta Lavrentiia Zagoskina v Russkoi Amerike
v 1842-1844 gg. 453 pp. Moscow, 1956.

I-1. ALEUT

Babikov, S.S. Komandorskie Ostrova. Sovetskaia
Aziia, II, ii, 66-74. 1926.

Fainberg, L.A. K Voprosu o Rodovom Stroe Aleutov.
Akademiia Nauk SSSR, Institut Etnografii, Kratkie
Soobshcheniia, XXIII, 68-77. 1955.

Garn, S.M. and Gertler, M.M. Age and Sex Differences in Serum Cholesterol of Aleut. Canadian
Medical Association Journal, LXIV, 338-40. 1951.

Garn, S.M. and Moorrees, C.F.A. Stature, Body-
build, and Tooth Emergence in Aleutian Aleut
Children. Child Development, XXII, 261-70.
1951.

Georgi, J.G. Beschreibung aller Nationen des Russischen Reichs, pp. 357-74. St. Petersburg, 1776-
80.

Henry, V. Esquisse d'une grammaire raisonneé de
la langue aléoute. 73 pp. Paris, 1879.

Jacobi, A. Carl Heinrich Mercks ethnographische
Beobachtungen über die Völker des Beringsmeers
in 1791. BA, XX, 113-37. 1937.

Moorrees, C.F.A. Dentition as a Criterion of Race
with Special Reference to the Aleut. Journal of
Dental Research, XXX, 815-21. 1951.

Pfizmaier, A. Die Sprache der Aleuten und Fuchsin-
seln. Sitzungsberichte der Akademie der Wissenschaften der Wien, Phil.-hist. Classe, CV, 801-
80; CVI, 237-316. 1883-84.

Volkov, T. and Rudenko, S.I. Etnograficheskaia
kollektsii iz byvshikh rossiisko-amerikanskikh
vladienii. 47 pp. St. Petersburg, 1910.

Wilde, E. Health and Growth of Aleut Children.
Journal of Pediatrics, XXXVI, 149-58. 1950.

I-2. BAFFINLAND ESKIMO

Anonymous. Sailors in Eskimoland. Crowsnest,
VII, viii, 14-6. 1955.

Clark, E.M. and Rhodes, A.J. Poliomyelitis in
Canadian Eskimos. Canadian Journal of Medical
Sciences, XXIX, 216-35; XXX, 390-402. 1951-
52.

Corrigan, C. and Hanson, S. Brucellosis and Miliary
Tuberculosis in an Eskimo Woman. Canadian Medical Association Journal, LXXII, 217-8. 1955.

Danielo, E. Baptism by Misery. Eskimo, XLII, 13-7. 1956.

Fryer, A.C. Eskimo Rehabilitation Program at Craig Harbour. Royal Canadian Mounted Police Quarterly, XX, 139-42. 1954.

Gillis, E.M. North Pole Boarding House. 214 pp. Toronto, 1951.

Nielsen, F. Besøg hos Eskimoiske Stammefraender pa Baffinland. Grønland, 1956, xii, 441-50.

Mary-Rousselière, G. Issingut. Eskimo, XXXIV, 9-13. 1954.

Tweedsmuir, J.N.S.B. Men and Beasts in the Canadian Arctic Islands. Geographical Magazine, XXVI, 182-91. 1953.

Van Norman, R.D. Life at an Eastern Arctic Detachment. Royal Canadian Mounted Police Quarterly, XVII, 110-17. 1952.

I-3. CARIBOU ESKIMO

Estreichèr, Z. La musique des Esquimaux-Caribous. Société Neuchateloise de Géographie, Bulletin, LIV, 1-53. 1948.

--- Polyrhythmik in der Musik der Eskimos. Schweizerische Musikzeitung, LXXXVII, 411-5. 1947.

Gabus, J. Vie et Coutumes des Esquimaux Caribous. 224 pp. Paris, 1944.

--- Touctou. 205 pp. Neuchatel, 1943.

Gottschalk, C.W. and Riggs, D.W. Protein-bound Iodine in the Serum of Soldiers and of Eskimos in the Arctic. Journal of Clinical Endocrinology, XII, 235-43. 1952.

Leden, C. Eine Schlittenfahrt mit den kanadischen Eskimos. Erdball, I, 183-7. 1926.

--- Über Kiwatins Eisfelder. 285 pp. Leipzig, 1927.

Michéa, J.P. La Civilization du Caribou. Géographia, XVII, 31-5. 1953.

--- Uomini e Caribou. Vie del Mondo, XV, 847-56. 1953.

Philippe, J. Eskimo Psychology. Eskimo, V, 5-7; VIII, 8-15; IX, 2-7; X, 2-7; XI, 5-7; XII, 7-10. 1947-49.

Steenhoven, G. van den. Legal Concepts among the Caribou Eskimo. Arctic Circular, IX, i, 7-9. 1956.

--- Report to the Department of Northern Affairs on a Field-Research Journey for the Study of Legal Concepts among the Eskimos in Some Parts of the Keewatin District. 74 pp. Den Haag, 1956.

Troels-Smith, J. Nulevende Rensdyrjaegere. Fra Nationalmuseets Arbejdsmark, 1956, 23-40.

I-4. COPPER ESKIMO

Breynat, G.J.E. Bishop of the Winds. 266 pp. New York, 1955.

Leichner, G. Petulak, der Eskimo. 193 pp. Leipzig, 1933.

Matas, M. and Corrigan, C. Brucellosis in an Eskimo Boy. Canadian Medical Association Journal, LXIX, 531. 1953.

I-5. EAST GREENLAND ESKIMO

Barfod, H.P. Dansk-grønlandsk ordliste til skolebrug. 2nd ed. 34 pp. Godthaab, 1952.

Digby, P.S.B. and V. Beyond the Pack Ice. 186 pp. London, 1954.

Gessain, R. L'art squelettique des Eskimo. JSAP, n. s., XLVIII, 237-44. 1959.

Høygaard, A. Im Treibeisgürtel. 127 pp. Braunschweig, 1940.

Knudsen, E.H. Konebadsrejser i Angmagssalikdistriktet. Grønland, 1956, 341-50.

Krabbe, T.N. Greenland. 145 pp. Copenhagen, 1930.

Nielsen, F. Grønlands Kultur. Turistforeningen for Danmark, Arbog 1952-53, 65-88. 1952.

Nippgen, J. Le folklore des Eskimos. Revue d'Ethnographie et des Traditions Populaires, IV, 118-92. 1923.

Pedersen, A. Auf Jagd in Grönland. 158 pp. Wien, 1953.

Pedersen, P.O. Dental Investigations of Greenland Eskimos. Proceedings of the Royal Society of Medicine, London, XL, 726-32. 1947.

Sølver, C.V. Eskimoisk Kartografi. Grønland, 1954, v, 187-92.

I-6. IGLULIK ESKIMO

Bird, J.B. Southampton Island. Canada, Geographical Branch, Memoir, V, 84 pp. 1953.

Brown, M. The Occurrence of Cancer in an Eskimo. Cancer, V, 142-3. 1952.

--- Progress Report on Clinical and Biochemical Studies of the Eskimo. 20 pp. Ottawa, 1951.

Brown, M., et al. Blood Volume and Basal Metabolic Rate of Eskimos. Metabolism, III, 246-54. 1954.

--- Cold Acclimatization. Canadian Medical Association Journal, LXX, 258-61. 1954.

--- Some Remarks on Premature Ageing in the Eskimos. Proceedings of the Canadian Physiological Society, XI, 5. 1947.

Brown, M., et al. Temperature and Blood Flow in the Forearm of the Eskimo. Journal of Applied Physiology, V, 410-20. 1953.

Brown, M. and Page, J. The Effect of Chronic Exposure to Cold on Temperature and Blood Flow of the Hand. Journal of Applied Physiology, V, 221-7. 1952.

Carpenter, E.S. Witch-fear among the Aivilik Eskimos. American Journal of Psychiatry, CX, 194-9. 1953.

Mary-Rousselière, G. Mythical and Prehistoric Animals in Arviligjuarmiut Folklore. Eskimo, XLII, 10-12. 1956.

Mitchell, E.H. Stones of Mystery. B, CCLXXXIV, 26-7. Dec., 1953.

Rawson, N.R. Medical Practice in the Eastern Arctic. Manitoba Medical Association Review, XXXI, 587-95. 1951.

I-7. LABRADOR ESKIMO

Coffey, J.E. and Wiglesworth, F.W. Trichinosis in Canadian Eskimos. Canadian Medical Association Journal, LXXV, 295-9. 1956.

Kleivan, H. Labrador i Støpeskjeen. Polarboken, 1956, 65-98.

König, H. Die Eskimos von Labrador. Erdball, V, 465-9. 1931.

Lefebvre, G.R. A Comparative and Annotated Glossary of the East Hudson Bay Eskimo Dialect. 100 pp. Ottawa, 1955.

Lindow, H. Labrador och dess Eskimaer. Terra, XXXV, 4-19. 1923.

Murdock, P. Seeguapik. B, CCLXXXVII, 24-31. Winter, 1956.

Packard, A.S. Notes on the Labrador Eskimo. AN, XIX, 471-81, 553-60. 1885.

Payne, F.F. Some Customs and Habits of the Eskimo at Stupart Bay. Proceedings of the Royal Canadian Institute, ser. 3, VI, 10. 1887-88.

Peacock, F.W. Some Eskimo Remedies. Canadian Medical Association Journal, LVI, 328-30. 1947.

Rousseau, J.J. On Human and Animal Adaptation. Canadian Geographer, VI, 17-20. 1955.

Sapper, K.T. Nachrichten über Zukunfts-aussichten der Eskimobevölkerung von Grönland und Labrador. PMJP, LXIV, 210-18. 1918.

Tolboom, W.N. Arctic Bride. 256 pp. Toronto, 1956.

Waldmann, S. Les Esquimaux du Nord du Labrador. Société Neuchateloise de Géographie, Bulletin, XIX, 430-41. 1908.

I-9. NETSILIK ESKIMO

Danielo, E. The Story of a Medicine Man. Eskimo, XXXVI, 3-6. 1955.

Hyenaes, T. Noen Glimt fra Primitive Eskimostammer. Polarboken, 1954, 44-52.

Mary-Rousselière, G. Christmas Igloo. B, CCLXXXVII, 4-5. Winter, 1956.

Velde, F. van de. Infanticide among the Eskimo. Eskimo, XXXIV, 6-8. 1954.

--- Religion and Morals among the Pelly Bay Eskimos. Eskimo, XXXIX, 6-16. 1956.

--- Rules Governing the Sharing of Seal after the "aglus" Hunt. Eskimo, XLI, 3-7. 1956.

I-10. NORTH ALASKA ESKIMO

Harmeling, P.C. Therapeutic Theater of Alaska Eskimos. Group Psychotherapy, III, 74-6. 1950.

Pedersen, P.O. and Scott, D.B. Replica Studies of the Surfaces of Teeth from Alaskan Eskimo, West Greenland Natives, and American Whites. Acta Odontologica Scandinavica, IX, 261-92. 1951.

Shade, C.I. and Cain, H.T. An Anthropology Survey of the Pt. Barrow, Alaska, Region. ASC, 1951, 248-51. 1953.

Spencer, R.F. The Hunted and the Hunters. Pacific Discovery, VI, iii, 22-7. 1953.

I-11. POLAR ESKIMO

Freuchen, P. Ice Floes and Flaming Water. 242 pp. New York, 1954.

--- Vagrant Viking. 422 pp. New York, 1953.

Krabbe, T.N. Greenland. 145 pp. Copenhagen, 1930.

Nielsen, F. Grønlands Kultur. Turistforeningen for Danmark, Arbog, 1952-53, 65-88. 1952.

Steinhoff, I. Dreizehn Monate bei den Polareskimos von Thule. Atlantis, XXV, ii, 75-80. 1953.

Taubert, H. Die Eskimo-Siedlungsinsel Thule in Grönland. PMJP, XCVII, 295-6. 1953.

I-12. SOUTH ALASKA ESKIMO

Jacobi, A. Carl Heinrich Mercks ethnographische Beobachtungen über die Völker des Beringsmeers in 1791. BA, XX, 113-37. 1937.

Pinart, A.L. Eskimaux et Koloches. RA, II, 673-80. 1873.

I-13. SOUTHAMPTON ESKIMO

Bird, J.B. Southampton Island. Canada, Geographical Branch, Memoir, V, 84 pp. 1953.

I-14. WEST ALASKA ESKIMO

Eide, A.H. Drums of Diomede. 242 pp. Hollywood, 1952.

Lantis, M. Nunivak Eskimo Personality as Revealed in the Mythology. UAAP, II, i, 109-74. 1953.

Minner, J.L. Old Man of the Ice Floes. Alaska Sportsman, XIX, iii, 18-21, 38-9. 1953.

Thompson, D.J. The Eskimo Woman of Nome, Alaska. ASC, 1951, 251-5. 1953.

I-15. WEST GREENLAND ESKIMO

Borreby, K., et al. [Nutrition Studies.] Denmark, Grønlands Styrelse, Beretninger Ve drørende Grønland, 1955, 3-I, 24-117.

Brun, E. Vor Opgave i Grønland. Grønland, 1952, i, 8-12.

Bugge, A. Mødet mellem gammelt og nyt i grønlandsk tankegang. Grønlandske Selskab, Arsskrift, 1950, 136-44.

Ehström, M.C. Inre Medicinska Undersökningar pa Nord-Grönland 1948-1949. Finska Läkaresallskapet, Handlingar, XCIII, 3-24. 1950.

--- Internmedicenska Undersokningar pa Nord-Grönland 1948-1949. Nordisk Medicin, XLIV, 1668-73, 1707-10, 1750, 1787-9, 1823-5. 1950.

Findlay, M.C. Impressions in Greenland. Contemporary Review, MLI, 32-6. 1953.

--- Miss M.C.Findlay's Investigations of Sheep Farming in West Greenland, 1951. Polar Record, VI, 528-9. 1952.

--- Sheep Farming in Greenland. Arctic, VI, 166-7. 1952.

Gad, F. Samisk og Grønlandsk. Grønland, XI, 401-13. 1956.

Jensen, B. Lilleputsamfundet. Grønland, 1959, v, 181-92.

--- Lilleputsamfundet og de Fremmede. Grønland, 1959, viii, 281-90.

Krabbe, T.N. Greenland. 145 pp. Copenhagen, 1930.

Kreutzmann, J. De to Venner. Grønlanske Selskab, Arsskrift, 1951, 132-6.

--- En Fortaelling om Blodhaevn. Grønlandske Selskab, Arsskrift, 1950, 145-7.

Larsen, H. Paleo-Eskimo in Disko Bay, West Greenland. ACISA, V, 574-9. 1960.

Meldgaard, J. Fra en Grønlandsk Mumiehule. Fra Nationalmuseets Arbejdsmark, 1953, 14-21. København, 1953.

Nellemann, G. Mitarneq. Folk, II, 99-113. 1960.

Nielson, F. Grønlands Kultur. Turistforeningen for Danmark, Arbog 1952-53, 65-88. 1952.

Parbøl, I. Qivitut. Grønland, 1955, xii, 452-63.

Pedersen, A. Auf Jagd in Grönland. 158 pp. Wien, 1953.

Pedersen, P.O. Dental Investigations of Greenland Eskimos. Proceedings of the Royal Society of Medicine, London, XL, 726-32. 1947.

Pedersen, P.O. and Scott, D.B. Replica Studies of the Surfaces of Teeth from Alaskan Eskimo, West Greenland Natives, and American Whites. Acta Odontologica Scandinavica, IX, 261-92. 1951.

Thorborg, N.B., et al. Trikinose paa Grønland. Ugeskrift for Laeger, CX, 595-602. 1948.

Vebaek, M. De sma bopladser. Gronland, 1959, v, 193-9.

--- Sagnet om Kagssagssuk. Grønland, 1959, xi, 425-35.

--- Tuneq-en indlandsbo. Gronland, 1959, vi, 230-2.

I-16. YUIT

Ackerman, R. Siberians of the New World. Expedition, I, iv, 24-35. 1959.

Antropova, V.V. Sovremennaia Chukotskaia i Eskimosskaia Reznaia Kost'. ANMAE, XV, 5-96. 1953.

Bogdanovich, K.I. Ocherki Chukotskogo Poluostrova. 254 pp. St. Petersburg, 1901.

Bogoraz, V.G. Einshtein i Religiia. 120 pp. Moscow, 1923.

Buturlin, S.A. Polozhenie tuzemtsev Chukotsko-Anadyrskogo Kraia. Sovetskaia Aziia, II, ii, 90-2. 1926.

Christensen, L.A. Besøg pa Diomede-øen. Grønlandske Selskab, Arsskrift, 1951, 124-31.

Ivanov, S.V. Materialy po Izobrazitel'nomu Iskusstvu Narodov Sibiri. ANIET, n.s., XXII, 838 pp. 1954.

Levin, M.G. Antropologicheskie tipy Sibiri. Narody Sibiri, 1956, 108-14. Moscow, 1956.

--- Antropologicheskie tipy Sibiri i ikh genezis. 27 pp. Moscow, 1956.

--- Drevnie pereseleniia cheloveka v severnoi Azii po dannym antropologii. ANIET, n.s., XVI, 469-96. 1951.

Levin, M.G. Materialy po Kraniologii severovostochnoi Azii. Moskva Universitet, Nauchno-issledo-
vatel'skii Institut i Muzei Antropologii, Kratkie
soobshcheniia o Nauchnykh Rabotakh, 1938-39.
1941.

Malygin, V.M. Dalekie berega. 76 pp. Moscow,
1940.

Menovshchikov, G.A. Aggliutinatsiia i osnovye
Konstruktsii prostogo predlozheniia v eskimosskom
iazyke. Akademiia Nauk SSSR, Izvestiia, otdel
Literatury i Iazyka, VIII, iv, 355-68. 1949.

--- Un'-ipag'atyt. 83 pp. Leningrad, 1939.

Nechiporenko, G.P. Morzhovyi Promysel na Chokotke.
Ekonomicheskaia Zhizn' Dal'nego Vostoka, V,
vi-vii, 169-77. 1927.

Rubtsova, E.S. Materialy po Iazyku i Fol'kloru
Eskimosov. 556 pp. Moscow, 1954.

Rudenko, S.I., ed. Ob''iasnitel'naia zapiska k etno-
graficheskoi karte Sibiri. Akademiia Nauk SSSR,
kommissiia po izucheniiu plemennogo sostava
naseleniia SSSR i sopredel'nykh stran, Trudy, XVII,
104 pp. 1929.

Sergeev, M.A. Literatura Narodov Severa. Sibirskie
Ogni, XXXI, 155-66. 1952.

II. MACKENZIE-YUKON

Biasutti, R. Le Razzi e i Popoli della Terra, 2nd ed.,
IV, 402-24. Torino,1957.

Emerson, W.C. The Land of the Midnight Sun. 179
pp. Philadelphia, 1956.

Irving, L. Naming of Birds as Part of the Intellectual
Culture of Indians at Old Crow, Yukon Territory.
Arctic, XI, 117-22. 1958.

Sherwood, A. Some Remarks about the Athapascan
Indians. An, VI, 51-6. 1958.

II-11. KASKA

Honigmann, J.J. Cultural Dynamics of Sex. Psychiatry, X, 37-47. 1947.

II-12. KUTCHIN

Coffey, M.F. A Comparative Study of Young Eskimo
and Indian Males with Acclimatized White Males.
Conference on Cold Injury, III, 100-16. 1955.

Slobodin, R. Eastern Kutchin Warfare. An, n.s.,II,
i, 76-94. 1960.

II-13. MOUNTAIN

Michéa, J. Les Chittra-Gottinéké: groupe Athapascan des Montagnes Rocheuses. JSAP, n.s., XLVIII,
197-235. 1959.

II-15. SARSI

Schmidt, W. Die Sarsi (Sarcee)-Indianer. UG,
VII, 764-89. 1940.

II-20. TANAINA

Landar, H.J. Tanaina Subgroups. IJAL, XXVI, 121-
2. 1960.

Volkov, T. and Rudenko, S.I. Etnograficheskaia
kollektsii iz byvshikh rossiisko-amerikanskikh
vladienii. 47 pp. St. Petersburg, 1910.

III. NORTHWEST COAST

Biasutti, R. Le Razzi e i Popoli della Terra, 2nd
ed., IV, 374-401. Torino, 1957.

Brown, R. On the Vegetable Products Used by the
Northwest American Indians. Edinburgh Botanical
Society Transactions, IX, 378-96. 1868.

Chard, C.S. Northwest Coast-Northeast Asiatic
Similarities. ACISA, V, 235-40. 1960.

Douglas, D. Journal Kept by David Douglas during
his Travels in North America. London, 1914.

--- Sketch of a Journey to the Northwestern Parts of
the Continent of North America during the Years
1824-5-6-7. OHQ, V, 230-71, 325-69; VI,
76-97, 206-27, 288-309. 1904-05.

Rüstow, A. Die Objekte der Malaspina-Expedition
zu Madrid. BA, XXII, 173-204. 1939.

Schott, R. Erbrecht und Familiengüterrecht bei den
Nordwestküsten-Indianern. ZVR, LIX, 35-82.1957.

III-8. NOOTKA

Gunther, E. A Re-Evaluation of the Cultural Position
of the Nootka. ACISA, V, 270-6. 1960.

III-11. SNUQUALMIE

Reichard, G.A. A Comparison of Five Salish Languages. IJAL, XXIV, 293-300; XXV, 8-15, 90-
6, 154-67, 239-53; XXVI, 50-61. 1958-60.

III-12. TLINGIT

Mason, J.A. Louis Shotridge. Expedition, II, ii, 10-16. 1960.

Pinart, A.L. Eskimaux et Koloches. RA, II, 673-80. 1873.

Volkov, T. and Rudenko, S.I. Etnograficheskaia kollektsii iz byvshikh rossiisko-amerikanskikh vladienii. 47 pp. St. Petersburg, 1910.

IV. OREGON SEABOARD

Beals, R.L. and Hester, J.A. A New Ecological Typology of the California Indians. ACISA, V, 411-9. 1960.

Biasutti, R. Le Razzi e i Popoli della Terra, 2nd ed., IV, 374-401. Torino, 1957.

Dickson, E.E.M. Food Plants of the Western Oregon Indians. 218 pp. Palo Alto, 1946.

Elsasser, A.B. The History of Culture Classification in California. RUCAS, XLIX, 1-10. 1960.

Strong, E. Stone Age on the Columbia River. 254 pp. Portland, 1959.

IV-3. CHEHALIS

Reichard, G.A. A Comparison of Five Salish Languages. IJAL, XXIV, 293-300; XXV, 8-15, 90-6, 154-67, 239-53; XXVI, 50-61. 1958-60.

IV-4. CHINOOK

Jacobs, M. Clackamas Chinook Texts II. PRCA, XI, 377 pp. 1959.

--- Thoughts on Methodology for Comprehension of an Oral Literature. ACISA, V, 123-9. 1960.

IV-6. HUPA

Kroeber, A.L. and Barrett, S.A. Fishing among the Indians of Northwestern California. AR, XXI, i, 1-210. 1960.

IV-8. KAROK

Kroeber, A.L. and Barrett, S.A. Fishing among the Indians of Northwestern California. AR, XXI, i, 1-210. 1960.

IV-12. TILLAMOOK

Reichard, G.A. A Comparison of Five Salish Languages. IJAL, XXIV, 293-300; XXV, 8-15, 90-6, 154-67, 239-53; XXVI, 50-61. 1958-60.

IV-15. WIYOT

Kroeber, A.L. and Barrett, S.A. Fishing among the Indians of Northwestern California. AR, XXI, i, 1-210. 1960.

Teeter, K.V. Consonant Harmony in Wiyot. IJAL, XXV, 41-3. 1959.

IV-16. YUROK

Kroeber, A.L. Yurok National Character. UCP, XLVII, 236-40. 1959.

V. CALIFORNIA

Beals, R.L. and Hester, J.A. A New Ecological Typology of the California Indians. ACISA, V, 411-9. 1960.

Biasutti, R. Le Razzi e i Popoli della Terra, 2nd ed., IV, 374-401. Torino, 1957.

Elsasser, A.B. The History of Culture Classification in California. RUCAS, XLIX, 1-10. 1960.

Lea, F.J. Indian Bread-makers in Yosemite. OM, LXIV, 24-6. 1914.

Powers, S. Aboriginal Botany. PCAS, V, 373-9. 1873-4.

V-4. KLAMATH

Haskin, L.L. Frontier Food. Nature Magazine, XIV, 171-2. 1929.

V-6. MIWOK

Beeler, M.S. Saclan Once More. IJAL, XXV, 67-8. 1959.

Godfrey, E.H. Yosemite Indians Yesterday and Today. Yosemite Nature Notes, XX, viii. 1953.

Merriam, C.H. The Hang-e or Ceremonial House of the Northern Miwok near Railroad Flat, Calaveras County, California. RUCAS, XXXVIII, 34-5. 1957.

V-8. POMO

Worth, D.S. Russian Kniga, Southwestern Pomo
Kalikak. IJAL, XXVI, 62-6. 1960.

V-11. WAILAKI

Kroeber, A.L. Possible Athabascan Influence on
Yuki. IJAL, XXV, 59. 1959.

V-13. WINTUN

Lee, D.D. Noun Categories in Wintu. Kölner Zeitschrift, LXVII, 197-210. 1942.
Lohmann, J. Einige Bemerkungen zu den Genus-
Kategorien des Wintu. Kölner Zeitschrift, LXVIII,
99-121. 1943.
Merriam, J.C. The Cave of the Magic Pool. Scribner's Magazine, LXXXII, 264-72. 1927.
Merriam, C.H. Wintoon Houses. RUCAS, XXXVIII,
40-43. 1957.

V-16. YUKI

Kroeber, A.L. Possible Athabascan Influence on
Yuki. IJAL, XXV, 59. 1959.

VI. PENINSULA

Beals, R.L., and Hester, J.A. A New Ecological
Typology of the California Indians. ACISA, V,
411-9. 1960.
Biasutti, R. Le Razzi e i Popoli della Terra, 2nd
ed., IV, 374-401. Torino, 1957.
Elsasser, A.B. The History of Culture Classification.
RUCAS, XLIX, 1-10. 1960.
Kirchhoff, P. Las Tribus de la Baja California y el
Libro del P. Baegert. In, J.J. Baegert, Noticias de
la Peninsula Americana de California, pp. xiii-
xxxviii. Mexico, 1942.

VI-1. CAHUILLA

James, H.C. The Cahuilla Indians. Los Angeles,
1960.
Seiler, H. Zur Aufstellung der Wortklassen des
Cahuilla. Münchener Sprachwissenschaftlichen
Studienkreise, XII, 61-79. 1958.

VI-3. COCHIMI

Baegert, J.J. Noticias de la Peninsula Americana de
California. 305 pp. Mexico, 1942.

VI-5. GABRIELINO

Temple, T.W. Toypurina the Witch. M, XXXII,
136-52. 1958.
Wissler, M. A Cañalino Site near Deer Canyon, Ven-
tura County, California. M, XXXII, 73-87. 1958.

VI-7. KAWAIISU

Klein, S. Comparative Mono-Kawaiisu. IJAL, XXV,
233-8. 1959.

VI-8. LUISENO

Kroeber, A.L. Problems on Boscana. UCP, XLVII,
282-93. 1959.

VI-9. SERI

Eckhart, G.B. The Seri Indian Missions. K, XXV,
iii, 37-43. 1960.
Moser, E. and M. Alphabet Book. Glendale, 1956.
--- Number Book. Glendale, 1956.
--- Primers I-III. Glendale, 1959.
Smith, W.N. Origin of Seri Indian Legends. M,
XXXII, 193-6. 1958.

VI-11. TUBATULABAL

Voegelin, C.F. The Notion of Arbitrariness in
Structural Statement and Restatement. IJAL, XXV,
207-20. 1959.

VI-12. WAICURI

Baegert, J.J. Noticias de la Peninsula Americana de
California. 305 pp. Mexico, 1942.

VII-3. MONO

Klein, S. Comparative Mono-Kawaiisu. IJAL, XXV, 233-8. 1959.

VII-4. PAIUTE

Kroeber, A.L. Desert Mohave: Fact or Fancy. UCP, XLVII, 282-93. 1959.
Safford, W.E. A Forgotten Cereal of Ancient America. ICA, XIX, 286-97. 1915.

VII-7. SHOSHONI

Haines, F.D. Nez Percé and Shoshoni Influence on Northwest History. In, Greater America: Essays in Honor of Herbert Eugene Bolton, pp. 379-93. Berkeley, 1945.

VIII-2. COEUR D'ALENE

Reichard, G.A. A Comparison of Five Salish Languages. IJAL, XXIV, 293-300; XXV, 8-15, 90-6, 154-67, 239-53; XXVI, 50-61. 1958-60.

VIII-5. KALISPEL

Reichard, G.A. A Comparison of Five Salish Languages. IJAL, XXIV, 293-300; XXV, 8-15, 90-6, 154-67, 239-53; XXVI, 50-61. 1958-60.

VIII-11. NEZ PERCE

Haines, F.D. Nez Percé and Shoshoni Influence on Northwest History. In, Greater America: Essays in Honor of Herbert Eugene Bolton, pp. 379-93. Berkeley, 1945.

IX. PLAINS

Kehoe, T.F. Stone Tipi Rings in North-Central Montana and the Adjacent Portion of Alberta, Canada. BBAE, CLXXIII, 417-73. 1960.

IX-4. BLACKFOOT

Forbis, R.G. Some Late Sites in the Oldman River Region, Alberta. BNMC, CLXII, 119-64. 1960.
Kehoe, T.F. Stone Tipi Rings in North-Central Montana and the Adjacent Portion of Alberta, Canada. BBAE, CLXXIII, 417-74. 1960.

IX-6. CHEYENNE

Anderson, R. Notes on Northern Cheyenne Corn Ceremonialism. M, XXXII, 57-63. 1958.
Powell, P.J. Issiwun: Sacred Buffalo Hat of the Northern Cheyenne. Montana, X, i, 24-40. 1960.

IX-8. CROW

Matthews, G.H. On Tone in Crow. IJAL, XXV, 135-6. 1959.

IX-23. SANTEE

Hurt, W.R. The Urbanization of the Yankton Indians. MNUSD, XXI, iii, 1-6. 1960.

IX-24. TETON

Cohen, L.K. Big Missouri's Winter Count — A Sioux Calendar 1796-1926. Indians at Work, VI, vi, 16-20. 1939.
--- Even in Those Days Pictures were Important. Indians at Work, IX, v, 19-21. 1942.
--- Swift Bear's Winter Count. Indians at Work, IX, vi, 30-31, vii, 29-30. 1942.

IX-26. YANKTON

Hurt, W.R. The Urbanization of the Yankton Indians. MNUSD, XXI, iii, 1-6. 1960.

X. MIDWEST

Brown, L.A. Early Maps of the Ohio Valley. Pittsburgh, 1960.
Deuel, T. American Indian Ways of Life. Illinois State Museum, Story of Illinois Series, IX, 76 pp. 1958.

X-7. SAUK

Anonymous. Indian Yarn. M, XXXII, 34. 1958.

XII-5. IROQUOIS

Harrington, M.R. Some Iroquois Wampum. M, XXXII, 31-2. 1958.
Landy, D. Child Training in a Contemporary Iroquois Tribe. Boston University Graduate Journal, IV, 59-64. 1955.

XIII-1. ACOLAPISSA

Quimby, G.I. The Bayou Goula Site. FMAS, XLVII, ii. 1957.

XIII-20. PAMLICO

Quinn, D.B., ed. The Roanoke Voyages, 1584-1590. HSS, CIV-CV, 1040 pp. 1955.

XV. SOUTHWEST

Simpson, R.D. The Coyote in Southwestern Indian Tradition. M, XXXII, 43-54. 1958.

XV-11. HOPI

Lundahl, W.D. About Hopi Kachinas. M, XXXII, 122-6. 1958.
Nequatewa, E. The Morning-Echo Days. P, XIII, 15-16. 1940.

XV-21. NAVAHO

Chelf, C.R. Good Luck for Gray Head. M, XXXII, 21-8. 1958.

XV-35. ZUNI

Kirk, R.F. Zuni Fetish Worship. M, XVII, 129-35. 1943.

INDEX OF TRIBAL NAMES

Abihka XIII-12
Abitibi XI-2
Abnaki XI-1
Achomawi V-1
Acolapissa XIII-1
Acoma XV-1
Adai IX-5
Adshusheer XIII-6
Agua Caliente VI-8
Aht III-8
Ahtena II-1
Ahtna-khotana II-1
Ais XIII-5
Aivilingmiut I-6
Akakisa XIV-1
Akwa'ala VI-4
Alabama XIII-2
Alasapa XIV-2
Aleut I-1
Algonkin XI-2
Alibamu XIII-2
Alliklik VI-10
Alsea IV-1
Andaste XII-1
Angmagsalik I-5
Ankomenum III-4
Apache IX-13, XV-4, XV-7, XV-14, XV-16, XV-19
Apache-Yuma XV-33
Apalachee XIII-3
Apalachicola XIII-14
Apsaroke IX-8
Arapaho IX-1
Arctic Highlanders I-11
Arikara IX-2
Arivaipa XV-7
Arkansa IX-22
Arosaguntacook XI-1
Ashipoo XIII-13
Asinai IX-5
Assiniboin IX-3
Atakapa XIV-1
Ataronchronon XII-4
Atnah II-1
Atnatana II-1
Atsina IX-9
Atsugewi V-1
Attiwandaron XII-11
Attu III-12
Avoyel XIII-19
Babine II-3
Backhook XIII-6
Baffinland Eskimo I-2
Bannock VII-1
Bayogoula XIII-1
Bear River V-11
Beaver II-2
Belhoola III-2
Bellabella III-1
Bellacoola III-2
Beothuk XI-3
Bidai IX-5
Bilhoola III-2
Biloxi XIII-4
Bilqula III-2
Blackfoot IX-4
Blood IX-4
Borrado XIV-2
Brule IX-24

Bungi XI-8
Caddo IX-5
Cahita XV-2
Cahokia X-2
Cahuilla VI-1
Cajuenche XV-5
Calapooya IV-7
Calusa XIII-5
Cape Fear XIII-6
Cape Fox III-12
Cape York Eskimo I-11
Caribou Eskimo I-3
Carrier II-3
Carrizo XV-7
Catawba XIII-6
Cathlamet IV-4
Cava XIV-5
Cayuga XII-5
Cayuse VIII-1
Ceni IX-5
Chackta XIII-11
Chakchiuma XIII-7
Chastacosta IV-2
Chatot XIII-14
Chawasha XIII-1
Chehalis IV-3
Chelan VIII-3
Chemakum III-14
Chemehuevi VII-4
Cheraw XIII-6
Cherokee XIII-8
Chetco IV-14
Cheyenne IX-6
Chiaha XIII-14
Chickahominy XIII-21
Chickasaw XIII-9
Chilcotin II-4
Chilkat III-12
Chilliwack IV-3
Chilula IV-6
Chimariko V-2
Chimmesyan III-13
China Hat III-1
Chinarra XV-6
Chinipa XV-3
Chinook IV-4
Chinook Jargon IV
Chipewyan II-5
Chippewa XI-8
Chiricahua XV-4
Chitimacha XIII-10
Chizo XV-6
Choctaw XIII-11
Chonque XIII-18
Chugach I-14
Chumash VI-2
Chumeto V-3
Cibecue XV-7
Clackamas IV-4
Clallam III-6
Clatsop IV-4
Clayoquot III-8
Coahuila VI-1
Coahuilteco XIV-2
Coaque XIV-3
Coast Miwok V-7
Cochimi VI-3
Cochiti V-27
Cocopa XV-5
Coeur d'Alene VIII-2

Columbia VIII-3
Colville VIII-14
Comanche IX-7
Combahee XIII-13
Comecrudo XIV-2
Comox III-3
Concho XV-6
Conestoga XII-1
Congaree III-6
Conoy XII-10
Coos IV-5
Coosa XIII-12
Copalis IV-3
Coquille IV-2
Coree XIII-20
Costano V-3
Cosumne V-5
Coushatta XIII-2
Coweta XIII-12
Cowichan III-4
Cowlitz IV-3
Coyotero XV-7
Coyukon II-6
Cree XI-4
Creek XIII-12
Croatan XIII-20
Crow IX-8
Cumberland Sound Eskimo I-2
Cupeno VI-1
Cusabo XIII-13
Dakota IX-23, IX-24, IX-26
Delaware XII-2
Deschutes VIII-17
Diegueno VI-4
Digger V-5
Dogrib II-7
Duwamish III-11
East Greenland Eskimo I-5
Edisto XIII-13
Emet XIV-5
Eno XIII-6
Erie XII-3
Ervipiame XIV-5
Eskimo I
Esselen V-9
Etchareottine II-18
Etchimin XI-5
Etiwaw XIII-13
Eudeve XV-23
Eyak II-1
Faraon Apache XV-19
Fernandeno VI-5
Flathead VIII-4
Fox X-1
Gabrielino VI-5
Galice IV-2
Gila Apache XV-4
Gilutsa III-13
Gitksan III-13
Goshute VII-2
Grand Lake Victoria XI-2
Great Bear Lake II-16
Gros Ventre IX-9
Guacara XIII-5
Guale XIII-26
Guasave XV-8
Gyitamat III-7
Haida III-5
Hailtzuk III-1

Haisla III-1
Halchidhoma XV-9
Halkomelem III-4
Halyikwanai XV-5
Han II-8
Hankutchin II-8
Hano XV-31
Hare II-9
Harrison IV-3
Hasinai IX-5
Hassinunga XIII-17
Havasupai XV-10
Hawikuh XV-35
Heiltsuk III-1
Hekandika VII-7
Heye XV-23
Hidatsa IX-10
Hidery III-5
Hinai IX-5
Hitchiti XIII-14
Hochelaga XII-5
Hoh III-9
Homalco III-3
Hook XIII-6
Hopi XV-11
Hualapai XV-32
Huchnom V-16
Huida III-5
Huite XV-3
Huma XIII-15
Humptulip IV-3
Hunkpapa IX-24
Hupa IV-6
Hupachisat III-8
Huron XII-4
Hydah III-5
Ibitoupa XIII-7
Iglulik I-6
Iglulingmiut I-6
Illinois X-2
Ingalik II-10
Innuit I
Iowa IX-11
Inyo VII-3
Iroquois XII-5
Isleta XV-12
Isleta del Sur XV-12
Issa XIII-6
Itanese I-11
Jemez XV-13
Jicarilla XV-14
John Day VIII-17
Jova XV-23
Juaneno VI-8
Jumano XV-15
Kadohadacho IX-6
Kaibab VII-4
Kalapuya IV-7
Kalekau V-8
Kalispel VIII-5
Kalwan XV-5
Kamia VI-6
Kaniagmut I-12
Kansa IX-12
Karankawa XIV-3
Karok IV-8
Kasihta XIII-12
Kaska II-11
Kaskaskia X-2
Kaskinampo XIII-2

Katahdin XI-1
Kathlumet IV-4
Kato V-11
Kaw IX-12
Kuwaiisu VI-7
Kawchodinne II-9
Kayowe IX-13
Kenai II-20
Kenisteno XI-4
Kennebec XI-1
Keres XV-27
Keyauwee XIII-6
Klawaw XIII-13
Kichai IX-25
Kickapoo X-3
Kiliwa VI-4
Kiowa IX-13
Kiowa Apache IX-14
Kispiyox III-13
Kitanemuk VI-10
Kitelsagi XI-2
Kitimut III-1
Kilksan III-13
Kitonaqa VIII-7
Kityata III-13
Kitsela III-13
Kitunaha VIII-7
Klahuse III-3
Klallam III-6
Klamath V-4
Klikitat VIII-6
Knaiakhotana II-20
Koasati XIII-2
Kodiak Island Eskimo I-12
Kohuana XV-5
Kolosh III-12
Komookhs III-3
Koniag I-12
Kootenay VIII-7
Koroa XIII-24
Koskimo III-7
Koso VII-5
Koyukukhotana II-6
Kuitsh IV-10
Kullespelm VIII-5
Kuluwitcatca IX-24
Kusa IV-5
Kutchin II-12
Kutenai VIII-7
Kutonaqa VIII-7
Kwakiutl III-7
Kwalhiokwa IV-9
Kwapa IX-22
Kwexa III-7
Labrador Eskimo I-7
Laguna XV-1
Lake VIII-6
Lake Miwok V-7
Lassik V-11
Lemhi VII-7
Lenape XII-2
Lillooet VIII-6
Lilowat VIII-6
Lipan XV-16
Lkungen III-6
Long Island XII-8
Louchoux II-12
Luiseno VI-8
Lummi III-6
Lutuami V-4
Machapunga XIII-20
Mackenzie Eskimo I-6

Mahican XII-6
Maidu V-5
Makah III-8
Malecite XI-5
Manahoac XIII-17
Mandan IX-15
Manitunik Eskimo I-7
Maniwaki XI-2
Manso XV-17
Maricopa XV-18
Mariposa V-15
Mascouten X-2
Mashpi XII-7
Maskegon XI-4
Massachuset XII-7
Massett III-5
Matinecoc XII-8
Mattole V-11
Mayaye XIV-5
Mayo XV-2
Mdewakanton IX-23
Meearmeear X-5
Meherrin XIII-25
Menomini X-4
Mescale XIV-2
Mescalero XV-19
Meskwaki X-1
Methow VIII-3
Metoac XII-8
Mewan V-6
Miami X-5
Mical VIII-6
Michigamea X-2
Micmac XI-6
Midnoosky II-1
Mikasuke XIII-14
Mimbreno XV-4
Minitari IX-10
Minneconjou IX-24
Mishongnovi XV-11
Mission VI-4, VI-5, VI-8
Missisauga XI-8
Missouri IX-16
Mistassini XI-7
Miwok V-6, V-7
Mobile XIII-16
Modoc V-4
Mohave XV-20
Mohave-Apache XV-33
Mohawk XII-5
Mohegan XII-9
Moingwena X-2
Moki XV-11
Molala VIII-10
Monacan XIII-17
Mono VII-3
Montagnais XI-7
Montauk XII-8
Moqui XV-11
Moratoc XIII-20
Mosopelea XIII-18
Mountain II-13
Mugulasha XIII-1
Muklasa XIII-2
Munsee XII-2
Muskogee XIII-12
Muskwium III-4
Musquaki X-1
Mutsun V-3
Nabednche IX-5
Nabesna II-14

Nacogdoche IX-5
Nahane II-11, II-19
Nambe XV-31
Nanaimo III-4
Naniba XIII-16
Nanticoke XII-10
Narraganset XII-9
Naskapi XI-7
Nass River III-13
Natchez XIII-19
Natick XII-7
Nauset XII-7
Navaho XV-31
Neche IX-5
Nehalem IV-12
Nespelem VIII-14
Nestucca IV-12
Netsilik I-9
Neutral XII-11
Nevome XV-23
Nez Perce VIII-11
Niantic XII-9
Nicola VIII-12
Nicoleno VI-5
Nio XV-2
Nipigon XI-4
Nipissing XI-3
Nipmuc XII-7
Nisenan V-5
Niska III-13
Nisqualli III-11
Nitinat III-8
Nitkutemukh VIII-18
Nitlakapamuk VIII-18
Nongatl V-11
Nootka III-8
Nootsak III-6
Norridgewock XI-1
North Alaska Eskimo I-10
Northern Paiute VII-6
Northern Shoshoni VII-7
Nottoway XIII-25
Ntlakyapamuq VIII-18
Numipu VIII-11
Nusqually III-11'
Ocaneechi XIII-17
Oconee XIII-14
Ofo XIII-18
Oglala IX-24
Ojibwa XI-6
Okanagon VIII-13
Okelousa XIII-1
Okinaken VIII-13
Okmulgee XIII-14
Olamentke V-7
Omaha IX-17
Oneida XII-5
Onondaga XII-5
Ontponea XIII-17
Opata XV-23
Opelousa XIV-1
Oraibi XV-11
Orejone XIV-2
Osage IX-18
Oto IX-19
Ottawa XI-9
Outagami X-1
Owens Valley Paiute VII-3
Oyhut IV-5
Padlimiut I-2
Padouca IX-7

Paiute VII-3, VII-4, VII-6
Pakawa XIV-2
Palaihnihan V-1
Palomas Apache XV-33
Palus VIII-20
Pamlico XIII-20
Pampopa XIV-2
Pamunkey XIII-21
Panamint VII-5
Papago XV-24
Pascagoula XIII-16
Passamaquoddy XI-5
Patwin V-13
Pausane XIV-2
Paviotso VII-6
Pawnee IX-20
Pawokti XIII-2
Pecos XV-13
Peedee XIII-6
Pend d'Oreille VIII-5
Pennacook XII-12
Penobscot XI-1
Pensacola XIII-16
Pentlatch III-3
Peoria X-2
Pequot XII-9
Pericu VI-12
Piankashaw X-5
Picuris XV-29
Piegan IX-4
Pihuique XIV-2
Pima XV-25
Pima Bajo XV-23
Pinaleno XV-7
Pine Ridge Sioux IX-24
Pipai VI-4
Piro XV-28
Piscataway XII-10
Piskwau VIII-3
Pisqow VIII-3
Pitch V-11
Pocumtuc XII-12
Point Barrow Eskimo I-10
Pojoaque XV-31
Pokagon X-6
Polar Eskimo I-11
Pomo V-8
Ponca IX-21
Potawatomi X-6
Powhatan XIII-21
Pujuna V-5
Puyallup III-11
Qahatika XV-25
Quapaw IX-22
Queets III-10
Queres XV-27
Quileute III-9
Quillayute III-9
Quinault III-10
Quinipissa XIII-1
Quinnipiac XII-6
Rappahannock XIII-21
River Desert XI-2
Saboba VI-8
Sagdlirmiut I-13
Saquachee VII-8
Sahaptin VIII-11
St. Lawrence Island
  Eskimo I-16
Salina V-6
Salish VIII-4
Samamish III-11

Samish III-6
San Carlos XV-7
San Felipe XV-27
San Ildefonso XV-31
San Juan XV-31
Sandia XV-12
Sanetch III-4
Sanipao XIV-2
Sanpoil VIII-14
Sans Arc IX-24
Santa Ana XV-27
Santa Barbara VI-2, VI-5
Santa Catalina Island VI-6
Santa Clara XV-31
Santee IX-23
Santee Catawba XIII-6
Santo Domingo XV-27
Sanyakwan III-12
Saponi XIII-17
Sara XIII-6
Sarsi II-15
Satsop IV-3
Satudene II-16
Sauk X-7
Saulteaux XI-8
Sawokli XIII-14
Schitzui VIII-2
Secolan XIII-20
Sekani II-17
Semiamo III-6
Seminole XIII-22
Semteuse VIII-5
Seneca XII-5
Senecu XV-26
Senecu del Sur XV-12
Senijextee VIII-8
Seri VI-9
Serrano VI-10
Seshelt III-3
Sewee XIII-6
Shackaconia XIII-17
Shanel V-8
Shasta V-10
Shawnee X-8
Shetinasha XIII-10
Shihwapmukh VIII-15
Shinnecock XII-8
Shipaulovi XV-11
Shivwits VII-4
Shoalwater Salish IV-3
Shoccoree XIII-6
Shongopovi XV-11
Shoshoni VII-5, VII-7, VII-1
Shuswap VIII-15
Shwoyelpi VIII-14
Sia XV-27
Siberian Eskimo I-16
Sichomovi XV-11
Siciatl III-3
Siksika IX-4
Siletz IV-12
Sinkaietk VIII-13
Sinkaqualius VIII-3
Sinkiuse VIII-3
Sinkyone V-11
Sioux IX-23, IX-24, IX-26
Sisseton IX-23
Sissipahaw XIII-6
Siuslaw IV-10
Skagit III-11
Skedans III-5
Skidegate III-5

Skidi IX-20
Skitswish VIII-2
Skokomish III-14
Skoylpeli VIII-14
Sialamun III-3
Slave II-18
Smith Sound Eskimo I-11
Snanaimuq III-4
Snare VIII-18
Snohomish III-11
Snuqualmi III-11
Sobaipuri XV-25
Socorro del Sur XV-26
Sokoki XI-1
Songish III-6
Sooke III-6
South Alaska Eskimo I-12
Southampton Eskimo I-13
Southern Paiute VII-4
Spokan VIII-16
Squamish III-3
Squaxon III-11
Stegaraki XIII-17
Stockbridge XII-6
Stoney IX-3
Stono XIII-13
Sugaree XIII-6
Suhinimuit I-7
Suma XV-15
Susquehannock XII-1
Tacame XIV-2
Taensa XIII-19
Tahltan II-19
Taidnapam VIII-6
Takelma IV-11
Takulli II-3
Tamali XIII-14
Tamaroa X-2
Tamaulipeco XIV-4
Tanaina II-20
Tanana II-21
Tangipahoa XIII-1
Tano XV-28
Taos XV-29
Tapehanek XIII-21
Taposa XIII-7
Tarahumara XV-30
Tatsanottine II-24
Tauxitania XIII-17
Tawakani IX-25
Tawasa III-2
Tawehash IX-25
Tchiglit Eskimo I-6
Tegninateo XIII-17
Tehueco XV-2
Teja IX-5
Temiscaming XI-2
Ten'a II-6
Tenankutchin II-21
Tenino VIII-17
Tepahue XV-2
Tequesta XIII-5
Tesuque XV-31
Tete de Boule XI-4
Teton IX-24
Tewa XV-31
Texas IX-5
Thilanottine II-5
Thlingchadinne II-7
Thompson VIII-18
Tigua XV-12, XV-29
Tilijayo XIV-2

Tillamook IV-12
Timucua XIII-23
Tionontati XII-4
Tioux XIII-24
Tiwa XV-12, XV-29
Tlatskanai IV-13
Tlelding IV-6
Tlingit III-12
Tobacco XII-4
Tolowa IV-14
Tomome XIII-16
Tonaxa VIII-7
Tonkawa XIV-5
Tonto XV-7
Towa XV-13
Trochutin II-8
Tsattine II-2
Tsetsaut II-22
Tsimshian III-13
Tsishaat III-8
Tubar XV-3
Tubatulabal VI-11
Tulkepaia XV-33
Tunica XIII-24
Tununermiut I-6
Tusayan XV-11
Tuscarora XIII-25
Tutchone II-23
Tutelo XIII-17
Tututni IV-2
Twana III-14
Two Kettle IX-24
Tygh VIII-17
Uchi XIII-27
Uintah VII-8
Umatilla VIII-19
Umpqua IV-2, IV-10
Unalachtigo XII-3
Unami XII-2
Ungava Eskimo I-7
Upper Chinook VIII-21
Ure XV-22
Ushpee XIII-18
Ute VII-8
Vanyume VI-10
Varohio XV-30
Venado XIV-2
Vuntakutchin II-8
Wabanaki XI-1
Waccamaw XIII-6
Waco IX-25
Wahkiakum IV-4
Wahpekute IX-23
Wahpeton IX-23
Waicuri VI-12
Wailaki V-11
Walapai XV-32
Wallawaila VIII-20
Walpi XV-11
Wampanoag XII-7
Wapoo XIII-13
Wappinger XII-6
Wappo V-12
Warmsprings Sahaptin VIII-17
Warrennuncock XIII-6
Wasco VIII-21
Washa XIII-1
Washo VII-9
Waswanipi XI-7
Wateree XIII-6
Wauyukma VIII-20
Wawenock XI-1

Waxhaw XIII-6
Wayam VIII-17
Wea X-5
Weapemeoc XIII-20
Wenatchi VIII-3
Wenrohonronon XII-4
West Alaska Eskimo I-14
West Greenland Eskimo I-15
Western Shoshoni VII-5
Westo XIII-27
Whilkut IV-6
White Knife Shoshoni VII-7
White Mountain XV-7
Whonkenti XIII-17
Wiccomiss XII-10
Wikeno III-7
Wimbee XIII-13
Wichita IX-25
Wind River VII-10
Winnebago X-9
Wintu V-13
Wintun V-13
Winyaw XIII-6
Wishosk IV-15
Wishram VIII-21
Wiyot IV-15
Woccon XIII-6
Wunnashowetuckog XII-7
Wyandot XII-4
Xaihai III-7
Xaisla III-7
Xinesi IX-5
Yahi V-14
Yakima VIII-22
Yakutat III-12
Yamacraw XIII-26
Yamasee XIII-26
Yana V-14
Yankton IX-26
Yanktonnai IX-26
Yaqui XV-2
Yaquina IV-1
Yavapai XV-33
Yawelmani V-15
Yazoo XIII-24
Yecora XV-22
Yellowknife II-24
Yguase XIV-5
Yojuane XIV-5
Yokuts V-15
Yscani IX-25
Yuchi XIII-27
Yuit I-16
Yuki V-16
Yuma XV-34
Yurok IV-16
Zia XV-27
Zuaque XV-2
Zuni XV-35

1 TSETSAUT
2 BELLABELLA
3 BELLACOOLA
4 CHILCOTIN
5 LILLOOET
6 COWICHAN
7 KLALLAM
8 QUILEUTE
9 QUINAULT
10 TWANA
11 SNUQUALMI
12 THOMPSON
13 NICOLA
14 SANPOIL
15 SPOKAN
16 KALISPEL
17 COEUR D'ALENE
18 WALLAWALLA
19 CAYUSE
20 UMATILLA
21 TENINO
22 MOLALA
23 WISHRAM
24 KLIKITAT
25 CHEHALIS
26 KWALHIOQUA
27 CHINOOK
28 TLATSKANAI
29 TILLAMOOK
30 ALSEA
31 SIUSLAW
32 COOS
33 CHASTACOSTA
34 TOLOWA
35 TAKELMA
36 KLAMATH
37 ACHOMAWI
38 YANA
39 SHASTA
40 KAROK
41 CHIMARIKO
42 HUPA
43 YUROK
44 WIYOT
45 WAILAKI
46 YUKI
47 WINTUN
48 POMO
49 WAPPO
50 OLAMENTKE
51 COSTANO
52 SALINA
53 TUBATULABAL
54 KAWAIISU
55 CHUMASH
56 GABRIELINO
57 LUISENO
58 CAHUILLA
59 KAMIA
60 COCOPA
61 YUMA
62 MARICOPA
63 HALCHIDHOMA
64 MOHAVE
65 HAVASUPAI
66 HOPI
67 ZUNI
68 MANSO
69 ACOMA
70 ISLETA

71 QUERES
72 TANO
73 TEWA
74 JEMEZ
75 TAOS
76 KIOWA APACHE
77 HIDATSA
78 MISSOURI
79 WINNEBAGO
80 SOUTHAMPTON ESKIMO
81 PENNACOOK
82 MASSACHUSET
83 MOHEGAN
84 METOAC
85 NANTICOKE
86 POWHATAN
87 TUSCARORA
88 PAMLICO
89 CUSABO
90 APALACHEE
91 ALABAMA
92 CHAKCHIUMA
93 TUNICA
94 BILOXI
95 ACOLAPISSA
96 HUMA
97 CHITIMACHA
98 KARANKAWA
99 TARAHUMARA
100 CHINIPA
101 GUASAVE
102 HUICHOL
103 TAMAULIPECO
104 JANAMBRE
105 HUAXTEC
106 TOTONAC
107 CHINANTEC
108 ZAPOTEC
109 TEQUISTLATECO
110 HUAVE
111 CHIAPANEC